CREATING A VIEWING RECTANGLE

Each of the viewing rectangles shows portions of the graph of $y = 0.1x^4 - x^3 +$
The first viewing rectangle shows the most complete graph of the equation.

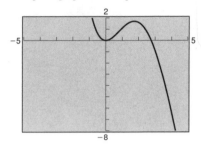

PARAMETRIC EQUATIONS OF A GRAPH

Circle	*Ellipse*	*Hyperbola*
$x = h + r \cos \theta$	$x = h + a \cos \theta$	$x = h + a \sec \theta$
$y = k + r \sin \theta$	$y = k + b \sin \theta$	$y = k + b \tan \theta$

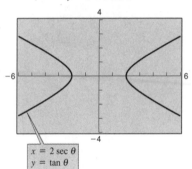

$x = 3 \sin \theta$
$y = 3 \cos \theta$

$x = 4 \cos \theta$
$y = 2 \sin \theta$

$x = 2 \sec \theta$
$y = \tan \theta$

GRAPHING POLAR EQUATIONS WITH A GRAPHING UTILITY

To graph the polar function $f(\theta)$, write the function in the parametric form $x = f(t) \cos t$ and $y = f(t) \sin t$.

Limaçon	*Rose Curve*	*Lemniscate*

$r = 1 - 2\cos\theta$

$r = 3\cos 2\theta$

$r^2 = 9 \sin 2\theta$

$x = (1 - 2\cos t)\cos t$

$x = (3\cos 2t)\cos t$

$x = \left(\pm 3\sqrt{\sin(2t)}\right)\cos t$

$y = (1 - 2\cos t)\sin t$

$y = (3\cos 2t)\sin t$

$y = \left(\pm 3\sqrt{\sin(2t)}\right)\sin t$

$0 \le t \le 2\pi$

$0 \le t \le 2\pi$

$0 \le t \le 2\pi$

PRECALCULUS

A GRAPHING APPROACH

PRECALCULUS

A GRAPHING APPROACH

Roland E. Larson
Robert P. Hostetler
THE PENNSYLVANIA STATE UNIVERSITY
THE BEHREND COLLEGE

Bruce H. Edwards
UNIVERSITY OF FLORIDA

WITH THE ASSISTANCE OF
David E. Heyd
THE PENNSYLVANIA STATE UNIVERSITY
THE BEHREND COLLEGE

D. C. Heath and Company
Lexington, Massachusetts   Toronto

Address editorial correspondence to:

D. C. Heath and Company
125 Spring Street
Lexington, MA 02173

Acquisitions Editor: Ann Marie Jones

Developmental Editor: Cathy Cantin

Production Editor: Jennifer Brett

Designer and Art Editor: Sally Steele

Production Coordinator: Lisa Merrill

Technical Art: Folium

Cover Designer: Linda Wade

Cover Photographer: Gabrielle Keller

Trademark Acknowledgments: TI is a registered trademark of Texas Instruments Incorporated. Casio is a registered trademark of Casio, Inc. Sharp is a registered trademark of Sharp Electronics Corporation.

Art and Photo Credits: p. 266 (top), from *The Fractal Geometry of Nature* by Benoit B. Mandelbrot, by permission; p. 266 (bottom), from *Chaos and Fractals: The Mathematics Behind the Computer Graphics,* edited by Robert L. Devaney and Linda Keen. Copyright © 1989 by the American Mathematical Society. All rights reserved. Used by permission of the publisher; p. 267, from *Technology in the Classroom: Fractal Programs for the TI-81 Graphing Calculator* by L. Charles Biehl, Leadership Program in Discrete Mathematics, Rutgers University, New Brunswick, N.J. Copyright © 1991 END Products/Publications.

We have included examples and exercises that use real-life data. This would not have been possible without the help of many people and organizations. Our wholehearted thanks goes to all for their time and effort.

Published simultaneously in Canada.

Printed in the United States of America.

International Standard Book Number: 0-669-28500-5

Library of Congress Catalog Card Number: 92-73088

10 9 8 7 6 5

PREFACE

Success in college-level mathematics courses begins with a good understanding of algebra and trigonometry, and one goal of this text is to help students develop this understanding. Another goal is to show students how algebra can be used as a modeling language for real-life problems. Although we review some of the basic concepts of algebra, we assume that most students in this course have completed two years of high school algebra.

FEATURES

The text has several key features designed to help students develop their problem-solving skills, as well as acquire an understanding of mathematical concepts.

GRAPHICS

The ability to visualize a problem is a critical part of a student's ability to solve the problem. To encourage the development of this skill, the text has many figures in examples and exercise sets and in answers to odd-numbered exercises in the back of the text. Various types of graphics show geometric representations, including graphs of functions, geometric figures, symmetry, displays of statistical information, and numerous screen outputs from graphing technology. All graphs of functions, computer- or calculator-generated for accuracy, are designed to resemble students' actual screen outputs as closely as possible.

APPLICATIONS

Numerous pertinent applications are integrated throughout every section of the text, both as solved examples and as exercises. This encourages students to use and review their problem-solving skills. The text applications are current and often involve multiple parts. Students learn to apply the process of mathematical modeling to real-world situations in many areas, such as business, economics, biology, engineering, chemistry, and physics. Many applications in the text use real-world data, and source lines are included to help motivate student interest. We tried to use the data accurately—to give honest and unbiased portrayals of real-life situations. In the cases in which models were fit to data, we used the least-squares method. In all cases the square of the correlation coefficient r^2 was at least 0.95. In most cases it was 0.99 or greater.

EXAMPLES

Each example was carefully chosen to illustrate a particular concept or problem-solving technique. Examples are titled for quick reference, and many include color side comments to justify or explain the solution. We have included problems solved graphically, analytically, numerically, or by a combination of these strategies, and the text helps students choose appropriate approaches to the problems. Several examples also preview ideas from calculus, building an intuitive foundation for future study.

DISCOVERY

Discovery notes encourage students to strengthen their intuition and understanding by exploring the relationships between functions and the behaviors of functions. The powerful features of graphing utilities enhance the study of functions because a graph as a step in a solution can be generated quickly and easily for use in the problem-solving process.

INTUITIVE FOUNDATION FOR CALCULUS

Throughout the text, many examples discuss algebraic techniques or graphically illustrate concepts that are used in calculus. These help students develop a natural and intuitive foundation for later work.

EXERCISE SETS

Exercise sets, including warm-up exercises, appear at the end of each text section. Many sets include a group of exercises that provide the graphs of functions involved. Review exercises are included at the end of each chapter, and cumulative tests are included to review what students have learned from the preceding chapters. The opportunity to use calculators is provided with topics that allow students to see patterns, experiment, calculate, or create graphic models.

DISCUSSION PROBLEMS

The discussion problems offer students the opportunity to think, reason, and communicate about mathematics in different ways. Individually or in teams, for in-class discussion, writing assignments, or class presentations, students are encouraged to draw new conclusions about the concepts presented. The problem might ask for further explanation, synthesis, experimentation, or extension of the section concepts. Discussion problems appear at the end of each text section.

TECHNOLOGY NOTES

Technology notes to students appear in the margins throughout the text. These notes offer additional insights, help students avoid common errors, and provide opportunities for problem solving using technology.

WARM-UP EXERCISES AND CUMULATIVE TESTS

We have found that students can benefit greatly from reinforcement of previously learned concepts. Most sections in the text contain a set of ten warm-up exercises that efficiently give students practice using techniques studied earlier in the course that are necessary to master the new ideas presented in the section.

Cumulative tests are included after Chapters 2, 5, 8, and 11. These tests help students assess their level of success and help them maintain the knowledge base they have been building throughout the text—preparing them for other exams and future courses.

These and other features of the text are described in greater detail on the following pages.

FEATURES OF THE TEXT

CHAPTER OPENER

Each chapter begins with a list of the topics to be covered. Each section begins with a list of important topics covered in that section.

CHAPTER 2

SOLVING EQUATIONS AND INEQUALITIES

2.1   LINEAR EQUATIONS

Equations and Solutions of Equations / Linear Equations in One Variable / Equations Involving Fractional Expressions / Applications

Equations and Solutions of Equations

An **equation** is a statement that two algebraic expressions are equal. Some examples of equations in x are

$$3x - 5 = 7, \quad x^2 - x - 6 = 0, \quad \text{and} \quad \sqrt{2x} = 4.$$

To **solve** an equation in x means to find all values of x for which the equation is true. Such values are **solutions.** For instance, $x = 4$ is a solution of the equation $3x - 5 = 7$, because $3(4) - 5 = 7$ is a true statement.

The solutions of an equation depend upon the kinds of numbers being considered. For instance, in the set of rational numbers, the equation $x^2 = 10$ has no solution because there is no rational number whose square is 10.

INTUITIVE FOUNDATION FOR CALCULUS

Special emphasis has been given to skills that are needed in calculus. Many examples include algebraic techniques or graphically show concepts that are used in calculus, providing an intuitive foundation for future work.

Technology Note

When you use a graphing utility to estimate the x- and y-values of a relative minimum or relative maximum, the automatic zoom feature will often produce graphs that are nearly flat. To overcome this problem, you can manually change the vertical setting of the viewing rectangle. You can stretch the graph vertically by making the values of Y_{min} and Y_{max} closer together.

EXAMPLE 4   Approximating a Relative Minimum

Use a graphing utility to approximate the relative minimum of the function $f(x) = 3x^2 - 4x - 2$.

SOLUTION

The graph of f is shown in Figure 1.35. By using the zoom and trace features of a graphing utility, you can estimate that the function has a relative minimum at the point

$$(0.67, -3.33). \qquad \textit{Relative minimum}$$

Later, in Section 3.1, you will be able to determine that the exact point at which the relative minimum occurs is $(\frac{2}{3}, -\frac{10}{3})$.

$f(x) = 3x^2 - 4x - 2$

FIGURE 1.35

EXAMPLE 5   Approximating Relative Minimums and Maximums

Use a graphing utility to approximate the relative minimum and relative maximum of the function $f(x) = -x^3 + x$.

SOLUTION

A sketch of the graph of f is shown in Figure 1.36. By using the zoom and trace features of the graphing utility, you can estimate that the function has a relative minimum at the point

$$(-0.58, -0.38) \qquad \textit{Relative minimum}$$

and a relative maximum at the point

$$(0.58, 0.38). \qquad \textit{Relative maximum}$$

If you go on to take a course in calculus, you will learn a technique for finding the exact points at which this function has a relative minimum and a relative maximum.

$f(x) = -x^3 + x$

FIGURE 1.36

CALCULATORS AND COMPUTER GRAPHING UTILITIES

To broaden the range of teaching and learning options, notes for working with calculators occur in many places. Students with access to graphics calculators or graphing utilities can solve exercises both graphically and analytically beginning with Chapter 1. Additionally, many exercises require a graphing utility.

REMARKS

These notes about definitions, theorems, rules, and examples anticipate students' needs by giving additional insight, identifying common errors, and describing generalizations.

---

152   CHAPTER 2   SOLVING EQUATIONS AND INEQUALITIES

Finding Solutions Graphically

Polynomial equations of degree one or two can be solved in relatively straightforward ways. Polynomial equations of higher degrees can, however, be quite difficult, especially if you rely only on algebraic techniques. For such equations, a graphing utility can be very helpful.

REMARK   In Chapter 3 you will learn techniques for determining the number of solutions of a polynomial equation. For now, you should know that a polynomial equation of degree n cannot have more than n different solutions.

GRAPHICAL APPROXIMATIONS OF SOLUTIONS OF AN EQUATION

To use a graphing utility to approximate the solutions of an equation in the variable x, use the following steps.

1. Write the equation in *standard form*, $f(x) = 0$, with all of the nonzero terms on one side of the equation and zero on the other side.
2. Use a graphing utility to graph the function $y = f(x)$. Be sure the viewing rectangle shows all the relevant features of the graph.
3. Use the zoom and trace features of the graphing utility to approximate each of the x-intercepts of the graph of f. Remember that a graph can have more than one x-intercept, so you may need to change the viewing rectangle a few times.

EXAMPLE 3   Finding Solutions of an Equation Graphically

Use a graphing utility to approximate the solutions of $2x^3 - 3x + 2 = 0$.

SOLUTION

Begin by graphing the function $y = 2x^3 - 3x + 2$, as shown in Figure 2.9(a). You can see from the graph that there is only one x-intercept that lies between -1 and -2 and is approximately -1.5. By using the zoom feature of a graphing utility you can improve the approximation as shown in the graph in Figure 2.9(b). To three decimal place accuracy, the solution is $x \approx -1.476$. Check this approximation on your calculator. You will find that the value of y is $y = 2(-1.476)^3 - 3(-1.476) + 2 \approx -0.003$.

DISCOVERY

Use a graphing utility to sketch the graph of $y = 24x^3 - 36x + 17$. Describe a viewing rectangle that allows you to determine the number of real solutions of the equation

$$24x^3 - 36x + 17 = 0.$$

Use the same technique to determine the number of real solutions of

$$97x^3 - 102x^2 - 200x - 63 = 0.$$

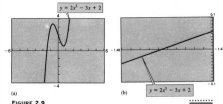

(a)   (b)

FIGURE 2.9

SECTION 1.4   GRAPHS OF FU

Because of the jumps in its graph, the greatest integer funct of a **step function**. Some values of the greatest integer funct

$$[[-1]] = -1 \qquad [[-0.5]] = -1$$
$$[[0]] = 0 \qquad [[0.5]] = 0$$
$$[[1]] = 1 \qquad [[1.5]] = 1$$

The range of the greatest integer function is the set of all integer

---

Technology Note

Most graphing utilities display graphs in what is called a *connected mode*, which means that the graph has no breaks. Thus, when you are sketching graphs that do have breaks, it is better to change the graphing utility to *dot mode*. Try sketching the graph of the greatest integer function [often called Int(x)] on a graphing utility in connected and dot modes, and compare the two results.

EXAMPLE 8   The Cost of a Telephone Call

Suppose the cost of a telephone call between Los Angeles and San Francisco is \$0.50 for the first minute and \$0.36 for each additional minute. The greatest integer function can be used to create a model for the cost of this call.

$$C = 0.50 + 0.36[[t]], \qquad 0 < t,$$

where C is the total cost of the call in dollars and t is the length of the call in minutes. Sketch the graph of this function.

SOLUTION

For calls up to 1 minute, the cost is \$0.50. For calls between 1 and 2 minutes, the cost is \$0.86, and so on.

Length of call: $0 < t < 1$ $1 \le t < 2$ $2 \le t < 3$ $3 \le t < 4$ $4 \le t < 5$
Cost of call: \$0.50   \$0.86   \$1.22   \$1.58   \$1.94

Using these values, you can sketch the graph shown in Figure 1.39.

FIGURE 1.39

DISCOVERY

Throughout the text, the discovery notes take advantage of the power of graphing utilities to explore and examine the behavior of complicated functions.

TECHNOLOGY NOTES

These notes appear in the margins. They provide additional insight and help students avoid common errors.

PROBLEM SOLVING

A consistent strategy for solving problems is emphasized throughout: analyze the problem, create a verbal model, construct an algebraic model, solve the problem, and check the answer in the statement of the original problem. This problem-solving process has wide applicability and can be used with analytical, graphical, and numerical approaches to problem solving.

---

138 CHAPTER 2 SOLVING EQUATIONS AND INEQUALITIES

EXAMPLE 1 Using a Verbal Model to Construct an Algebraic Equation

You have accepted a job for which your annual salary will be $24,740. This salary includes a year-end bonus of $500. If you are paid twice a month, what will be your gross pay for each paycheck?

SOLUTION

Because there are 12 months in a year and you will be paid twice a month, it follows that you will receive 24 paychecks during the year. You can construct an algebraic equation for this problem as follows. Begin with a verbal model, then assign labels, and finally form an algebraic equation.

VERBAL MODEL: Income for year = 24 · Amount of paycheck + Bonus

LABELS:
Income for year = 24,740   *(dollars)*
Amount of paycheck = x *(dollars)*
Bonus = 500   *(dollars)*

EQUATION: $24,740 = 24x + 500$

The equation for this problem is a *linear equation* in the variable x. Using the techniques discussed in Section 2.1, you can solve this equation for x. If you do that, you will find that the solution is $x = \$1010$.

TRANSLATING KEY WORDS AND PHRASES

Key Words and Phrases	Verbal Description	Algebraic Statement
Equality		
Equals, equal to, is, are, was, will be, represents	Sale price S is $10 less than the list price L	$S = L - 10$
Addition		
Sum, plus, greater, increased by, more than, exceeds, total of	The sum of 5 and x	$5 + x$
	7 more than y	$y + 7$
Subtraction		
Difference, minus, less, decreased by, subtracted from, reduced by, the remainder	4 decreased by b	$4 - b$
	3 less than z	$z - 3$
Multiplication		
Product, multiplied by, twice, times, percent of	2 times x	$2x$
Division		
Quotient, divided by, ratio, per	The ratio of x to 8	$\dfrac{x}{8}$

DEFINITIONS

All of the important formulas and definitions are boxed for emphasis. Each is also titled for easy reference.

---

430 CHAPTER 6 TRIGONOMETRY

EXAMPLE 4 Horizontal Stretching and Shrinking

Sketch the graph of $y = \sin 3x$.

SOLUTION

The amplitude is 1, and because $b = 3$, the period is

$$\frac{2\pi}{b} = \frac{2\pi}{3}.$$

Dividing the period-interval $[0, 2\pi/3]$ into four equal parts, you obtain the following key points on the graph.

$$(0, 0), \quad \left(\frac{\pi}{6}, 1\right), \quad \left(\frac{\pi}{3}, 0\right), \quad \left(\frac{\pi}{2}, -1\right), \quad \text{and} \quad \left(\frac{2\pi}{3}, 0\right)$$

The graph is shown in Figure 6.44. Use a graphing utility to check this result.

FIGURE 6.44

EXAMPLE 5 Using a Graphing Utility

Use a graphing utility to graph $y = 2 \cos 0.4x$ and $y = 2 \cos 4x$ on the same screen. Determine the period of each function from its graph.

SOLUTION

The standard viewing rectangle is not appropriate for graphing most sine and cosine functions. You should choose a viewing rectangle that accommodates the amplitudes of the functions as well as any stretching or shrinking that may occur. For these graphs, a y-scale ranging between -3 and 3 will accommodate the amplitudes of 2. Figure 6.45 shows the two graphs and an appropriate viewing rectangle. From the graph, you can estimate the period of $y = 2 \cos 0.4x$ to be about 16 and the period of $y = 2 \cos 4x$ to be about 1.5. Algebraically, the period of $y = 2 \cos 0.4x$ is

$$\frac{2\pi}{0.4} = 5\pi \approx 15.71,$$

and the period of $y = 2 \cos 4x$ is

$$\frac{2\pi}{4} = \frac{\pi}{2} \approx 1.57.$$

FIGURE 6.45

EXAMPLES

The text contains more than 800 text examples. They are titled for easy reference, and many include side comments that explain or justify steps in the solution. Students are encouraged to check their solutions.

DISCUSSION PROBLEMS

A discussion problem appears at the end of each section. Each one encourages students to think, reason, and write about mathematics, individually or in groups. Presenting the mathematics in a different way from in the section, these problems emphasize synthesis and experimentation.

EXAMPLE 7   Sequences of Transformations

Use a graphing utility to graph the two functions $g(x) = 5(x^2 - 2)$ and $h(x) = 5x^2 - 2$ on the same screen. Describe how each function was obtained from $f(x) = x^2$ as a sequence of shifts and stretches.

SOLUTION

Notice that the two graphs in Figure 1.52 are different. The graph of g is a downward shift of two units followed by a vertical stretch, whereas h is a vertical stretch followed by a downward shift of two units. Hence, the order of applying the transformations is important.

$g(x) = 5(x^2 - 2)$ $h(x) = 5x^2 - 2$

FIGURE 1.52

DISCUSSION PROBLEM

COMPARING MATHEMATICAL MODELS

The following two second-degree polynomial functions are models of the United States population from 1800 to 1990. In the first model, $f(t)$ represents the population and t represents the year.

Model 1

$$f(t) = 6722.5t^2 - 24,201,000t + 21,787,790,000, \qquad 1800 \le t \le 1990$$

In the second model, $g(t)$ represents the population in millions and t represents the year, with $t = 0$ corresponding to 1800, $t = 1$ corresponding to 1810, and so on. (See figure.)

United States Population

Model 2

$$g(t) = 0.67225t^2 + 6.89, \qquad 0 \le t \le 19$$

These two models are related as follows.

$$f(t) = 1,000,000g\left(\frac{t - 1800}{10}\right)$$

Which model do you think is better? Write a short paragraph explaining your reasons.

AN APPLICATION OF SLOPE

In 1982, a college had an enrollment of 5000 students. By 19[ ] had increased to 7000 students.

(a) What is the average annual change in enrollment from 19[ ]
(b) Use the average annual change in enrollment to estimate t[ ] 1986, 1990, and 1994.

Year	1982	1986	1990	1992	1994
Enrollment	5000			7000	

(c) Graph the line represented by the data given in the table in part (b). What is the slope of this line?
(d) Write a short paragraph that compares the concepts of *slope* and *average rate of change*.

WARM-UPS

Each section (except those in Prerequisites) contains a set of 10 warm-up exercises for students to review and practice the previously learned skills that are necessary to master the new skills and concepts presented in the section. All warm-up exercises are answered in the back of the text.

WARM-UP

The following warm-up exercises involve skills that were covered in earlier sections. You will use these skills in the exercise set for this section.

In Exercises 1 and 2, simplify the expression.

1. $\dfrac{4 - (-5)}{-3 - (-1)}$ 2. $\dfrac{-5 - 8}{0 - (-3)}$

3. Find $-1/m$ for $m = 4/5$.   4. Find $-1/m$ for $m = -2$.

In Exercises 5–10, solve for y in terms of x.

5. $2x - 3y = 5$ 6. $4x + 2y = 0$
7. $y - (-4) = 3[x - (-1)]$ 8. $y - 7 = \frac{2}{3}(x - 3)$
9. $y - (-1) = \dfrac{3 - (-1)}{2 - 4}(x - 4)$ 10. $y - 5 = \dfrac{3 - 5}{0 - 2}(x - 2)$

450 CHAPTER 6 Trigonometry

In Exercises 33–38, use a graphing utility to graph the function. Describe the behavior of the function as x approaches zero.

33. $y = \dfrac{6}{x} + \cos x, \quad x > 0$

34. $y = \dfrac{4}{x} + \sin 2x, \quad x > 0$

35. $g(x) = \dfrac{\sin x}{x}$

36. $f(x) = \dfrac{1 - \cos x}{x}$

37. $f(x) = \sin \dfrac{1}{x}$

38. $h(x) = x \sin \dfrac{1}{x}$

In Exercises 39–42, use a graphing utility to graph the functions f and g in the same viewing rectangle. Use the graphs to determine the relationship between the functions.

39. $f(x) = \sin x + \cos\left(x + \dfrac{\pi}{2}\right), \quad g(x) = 0$

40. $f(x) = \sin x - \cos\left(x + \dfrac{\pi}{2}\right), \quad g(x) = 2 \sin x$

41. $f(x) = \sin^2 x, \quad g(x) = \frac{1}{2}(1 - \cos 2x)$

42. $f(x) = \cos^2 \dfrac{\pi x}{2}, \quad g(x) = \frac{1}{2}(1 + \cos \pi x)$

In Exercises 43–46, use a graphing utility to graph the function over the specified interval.

Function	Interval
43. $f(t) = t^2 \sin t$	$[0, 2\pi]$
44. $f(x) = \sqrt{2x} \sin x$	$[0, 4\pi]$
45. $f(x) = \sin x - \frac{1}{3} \sin 3x + \frac{1}{5} \sin 5x$	$[0, \pi]$
46. $f(x) = \dfrac{1}{2} - \dfrac{4}{\pi^2}\left(\cos \pi x + \frac{1}{9} \cos 3\pi x\right)$	$[0, 2]$

47. *Sales* The projected monthly sales S (in thousands of units) of a seasonal product is modeled by

$$S = 74 + 3t + 40 \sin \dfrac{\pi t}{6},$$

where t is the time in months, with $t = 1$ corresponding to January. Graph this sales function over 1 year.

48. *Sales* The projected monthly sales S (in thousands of units) of a seasonal product is modeled by

$$S = 25 + 2t + 20 \sin \dfrac{\pi t}{6},$$

where t is the time in months, with $t = 1$ corresponding to January. Graph this sales function over 1 year.

49. *Predator-Prey Problem* Suppose the population of a certain predator at time t (in months) in a given region is estimated to be

$$P = 10,000 + 3000 \sin \dfrac{2\pi t}{24},$$

and the population of its primary food source (its prey) is estimated to be

$$p = 15,000 + 5000 \cos \dfrac{2\pi t}{24}.$$

Graph both of these functions in the same viewing rectangle, and explain the oscillations in the size of each population.

50. *Normal Temperatures* The normal monthly high temperature for Erie, Pennsylvania, is approximated by

$$H(t) = 54.33 - 20.38 \cos \dfrac{\pi t}{6} - 15.69 \sin \dfrac{\pi t}{6},$$

and the normal monthly low temperature is approximated by

$$L(t) = 39.36 - 15.70 \cos \dfrac{\pi t}{6} - 14.16 \sin \dfrac{\pi t}{6},$$

where t is the time in months, with $t = 1$ corresponding to January. (*Source:* NOAA) Use a graphing utility to graph the functions over a period of 1 year, and use the graphs to answer the following questions.

(a) During what part of the year is the difference between the normal high and low temperatures greatest? When is it smallest?

(b) The sun is farthest north in the sky around June 21, but the graph shows the warmest temperatures at a later date. Approximate the lag time of the temperatures relative to the position of the sun.

EXERCISES

The approximately 6100 exercises—computational, conceptual, exploratory, and applied problems—are designed to build competence, skill, and understanding. Each exercise set is graded in difficulty to allow students to gain confidence as they progress. Many exercises require the use of a graphing utility. All odd-numbered exercises are solved in detail in the *Study and Solutions Guide,* with answers appearing in the back of the text.

GEOMETRY

Geometric formulas and concepts are reviewed throughout the text. For easy reference, common formulas are given inside the back cover.

APPLICATIONS

Real-world applications are integrated throughout the text in examples and exercises. This offers students insight about the usefulness of algebra and trigonometry, develops strategies for solving problems, and emphasizes the relevance of the mathematics. Titled for reference, many of the applications involve multiple parts, use current real data, and include source lines.

GRAPHICS

Students must be able to visualize problems in order to solve them. To develop this skill and reinforce concepts, the text has over 2100 figures.

SECTION 8.2 Law of Cosines 545

a certain map, Minneapolis is 6.5 inches [from] Albany, Phoenix is 8.5 inches from Min[neapolis] [P]hoenix is 14.5 inches from Albany (see [figure].)

[bea]ring of Minneapolis from Phoenix.
[bea]ring of Albany from Phoenix.

FIGURE FOR 40

41. *Baseball* In a (square) baseball diamond with 90-foot sides, the pitcher's mound is 60 feet from home plate.
(a) How far is it from the pitcher's mound to third base?
(b) When a runner is halfway from second to third, how far is the runner from the pitcher's mound?

42. *Baseball* The baseball player in center field is playing approximately 330 feet from the television camera that is behind home plate. A batter hits a fly ball that goes to the wall 420 feet from the camera (see figure). Approximate the number of feet that the center fielder had to run to make the catch if the camera turned 9° in following the play.

FIGURE FOR 42

43. *Awning Design* A retractable awning lowers at an angle of 50° from the top of a patio door that is 7 feet high (see figure). Find the length x of the awning if no direct sunlight is to enter the door when the angle of elevation of the sun is greater than 65°.

44. *Circumscribed and Inscribed Circles* Let R and r be the radii of the circumscribed and inscribed circles of a triangle ABC, respectively, and let $s = (a + b + c)/2$ (see figure). Prove the following.

(a) $2R = \dfrac{a}{\sin A} = \dfrac{b}{\sin B} = \dfrac{c}{\sin C}$

(b) $r = \sqrt{\dfrac{(s - a)(s - b)(s - c)}{s}}$

FIGURE FOR 43   FIGURE FOR 44

Circumscribed and Inscribed Circles In Exercises 45 and 46, use the results of Exercise 44.

45. Given the triangle with $a = 25$, $b = 55$, and $c = 72$, find the areas of (a) the triangle, (b) the circumscribed circle, and (c) the inscribed circle.

46. Find the length of the largest circular track that can be built on a triangular piece of property whose sides measure 200 feet, 250 feet, and 325 feet.

47. Use the Law of Cosines to prove that

$$\frac{1}{2}bc(1 + \cos A) = \frac{a + b + c}{2} \cdot \frac{-a + b + c}{2}.$$

48. Use the Law of Cosines to prove that

$$\frac{1}{2}bc(1 - \cos A) = \frac{a - b + c}{2} \cdot \frac{a + b - c}{2}.$$

CHAPTER 8   REVIEW EXERCISES   575

35. *Resultant Force*   Find the direction and magnitude of the resultant of the three forces shown in the figure.

FIGURE FOR 35

$\tan \beta = \frac{1}{4}$ $\tan \alpha = \frac{12}{5}$

36. *Resultant Force*   Forces with magnitudes of 85 pounds and 50 pounds act on a single point. Find the magnitude of the resultant if the angle between the forces is 15°.

37. *Rope Tension*   A 100-pound weight is supported by two ropes, as shown in the figure. Find the tension in each rope.

FIGURE FOR 37

38. *Braking Force*   A 500-pound motorcycle is headed up a hill inclined at 12°. What force is required to keep the motorcycle from rolling back down the hill when stopped at a red light?

39. *Navigation*   An airplane has an air speed of 450 miles per hour at a bearing of N 30° E. If the wind velocity is 20 miles per hour from the west, find the ground speed and the direction of the plane.

40. *Angle Between Forces*   Forces of 60 pounds and 100 pounds have a resultant force of 125 pounds. Find the angle between the two forces.

In Exercises 41–44, find the trigonometric form of the complex number.

41. $5 - 5i$
42. $-3\sqrt{3} + 3i$
43. $5 + 12i$
44. -7

In Exercises 45–48, write the complex number in standard form.

45. $100(\cos 240° + i \sin 240°)$
46. $24(\cos 330° + i \sin 330°)$
47. $13(\cos 0 + i \sin 0)$
48. $8\left(\cos \frac{5\pi}{6} + i \sin \frac{5\pi}{6}\right)$

In Exercises 49–52, (a) express the two complex numbers in trigonometric form, and (b) use the trigonometric form to find $z_1 z_2$ and z_1/z_2.

49. $z_1 = -5$, $z_2 = 5i$
50. $z_1 = 2\sqrt{3} - 2i$, $z_2 = -10i$
51. $z_1 = -3(1 + i)$, $z_2 = (\sqrt{3} + i)$
52. $z_1 = 5i$, $z_2 = 2(1 - i)$

In Exercises 53–56, use DeMoivre's Theorem to find the indicated power of the complex number. Express the result in standard form.

53. $\left[5\left(\cos \frac{\pi}{12} + i \sin \frac{\pi}{12}\right)\right]^4$
54. $\left[2\left(\cos \frac{4\pi}{15} + i \sin \frac{4\pi}{15}\right)\right]^5$
55. $(2 + 3i)^6$
56. $(1 - i)^8$

In Exercises 57–60, use DeMoivre's Theorem to find the roots of the complex number.

57. Sixth roots of: $-729i$
58. Fourth roots of: 256
59. Cube roots of: -1
60. Fourth roots of: $-1 + i$

In Exercises 61–64, find all solutions of the equation and represent the solutions on a unit circle.

61. $x^4 + 81 = 0$
62. $x^3 - 32 = 0$
63. $(x^3 - 1)(x^2 + 1) = 0$
64. $x^3 + 8i = 0$

REVIEW EXERCISES

A set of review exercises at the end of each chapter gives students an opportunity for additional practice. The review exercises include computational, conceptual, and applied problems covering a wide range of topics.

CUMULATIVE TESTS

Cumulative tests appear after Chapters 2, 5, 8, and 11. These tests help students judge their mastery of previously covered concepts. They also help students maintain the knowledge base they have been building throughout the text, preparing them for other exams and future courses.

---

576   CHAPTER 8   ADDITIONAL TOPICS IN TRIGONOMETRY

CUMULATIVE TEST FOR CHAPTERS 6–8

Take this test as you would take a test in class. After you are done, check your work with the answers in the back of the book.

1. Express the angle $4\pi/9$ in degree measure and sketch the angle in standard position.

2. Express the angle $-120°$ in radian measure as a multiple of π and sketch the angle in standard position.

3. The terminal side of an angle θ in standard position passes through the point (12, 5). Evaluate the six trigonometric functions of the angle.

4. If $\cos t = -\frac{2}{3}$ where $\pi/2 < t < \pi$, find $\sin t$ and $\tan t$.

5. Use a calculator to approximate $\sin(-1.25)$. Round your answer to four decimal places.

6. Use a calculator to approximate two values of θ ($0° \le \theta < 360°$) such that $\sec \theta = 2.125$. Round your answers to two decimal places.

7. Sketch the graph of each of the following functions through two periods.

(a) $y = -3 \sin 2x$ (b) $f(x) = 2 \cos\left(x - \frac{\pi}{4}\right)$
(c) $g(x) = \tan\left(\frac{\pi x}{2}\right)$ (d) $h(t) = \sec t$

8. Write a sentence describing the relationship between the graph of the functions $f(x) = \sin x$ and g.

(a) $g(x) = 10 + \sin x$ (b) $g(x) = \sin \frac{\pi x}{2}$
(c) $g(x) = \sin\left(x + \frac{\pi}{4}\right)$ (d) $g(x) = -\sin x$

9. Find a, b, and c so that the graph of $f(x) = a \sin(bx + c)$ matches the given figure.

10. Consider the function $f(x) = \sin 3x - 2 \cos x$.

(a) Use a graphing utility to graph the function.
(b) Determine the period of the function.
(c) Approximate (accurate to one decimal place) the zero of the function in the interval [0, 3].
(d) Approximate (accurate to one decimal place) the maximum value of the function in the interval [0, 3].

FIGURE FOR 9

CUMULATIVE TEST FOR CHAPTERS 6–8   577

11. Consider the function

$$f(t) = 2^{-t/2} \cos\left(\frac{\pi t}{2}\right)$$

where t is the time in seconds.
(a) Use a graphing utility to graph the function.
(b) Is the function periodic?
(c) Beyond what time t is the maximum value of the function less than 0.3?

12. Evaluate the expression *without* the aid of a calculator.

(a) $\arcsin(\frac{1}{2})$ (b) $\arctan \sqrt{3}$

13. Write an algebraic expression that is equivalent to $\sin(\arccos 2x)$.

14. From a point on the ground 600 feet from the foot of a cliff, the angle of elevation of the top of the cliff is 32° 30'. How high is the cliff?

15. Add and simplify: $\dfrac{1 + \cos \beta}{\sin \beta} + \dfrac{\sin \beta}{1 + \cos \beta}$

16. Find all the solutions to the equation $2 \cos^2 x - \cos x = 0$ in the interval $[0, 2\pi)$.

17. Given $\sin x = \frac{3}{4}$, find the exact value of $\sin(2x)$ where x is a first quadrant angle.

18. Evaluate $\cos 105° = \cos(135° - 30°)$ *without* the aid of a calculator.

19. Find the remaining sides and angles of each triangle.

(a)   (b)

20. In a (square) baseball diamond with 90-foot sides, the pitcher's mound is 60 feet from home plate. How far is a runner from the pitcher's mound when the runner is halfway from third base to home?

21. Find the component form of $\mathbf{u} + \mathbf{v}$ if $\|\mathbf{u}\| = 3$, $\theta_u = 30°$, $\|\mathbf{v}\| = 5$, and $\theta_v = 120°$. (Assume the angles are measured counterclockwise from the x-axis to the vector.)

22. A projectile is fired with an initial velocity of 120 feet per second at an angle of 15° with the horizontal. Find the vertical and horizontal components of the velocity accurate to two decimal places.

23. Write the complex number $z = 2(1 - i)$ in trigonometric form and find z^3.

SUPPLEMENTS

This text is accompanied by a comprehensive supplements package for maximum teaching effectiveness and efficiency.

Instructor's Guide by Roland E. Larson, Robert P. Hostetler, Pennsylvania State University, Behrend College, and Bruce H. Edwards, University of Florida.

Study and Solutions Guide by Bruce H. Edwards, University of Florida, and Dianna L. Zook, Indiana University—Purdue University at Fort Wayne

Test Item File and Resource Guide by David C. Falvo, Pennsylvania State University, Behrend College

Graphing Technology Guide by William Martin, Pima County Community College

The Algebra of Calculus with Trigonometry and Analytic Geometry by Eric Braude

Test-Generating Software (IBM, Macintosh)

Transparency Package

BestGrapher Software (IBM, Macintosh) by George Best

Derive* **Software** by Soft Warehouse

This complete supplements package offers ancillary materials for students, for instructors, and for classroom resources. Most items are keyed directly to the textbook for easy use. For the convenience of software users, a technical support telephone number is available with all D. C. Heath software products: (617) 860-1218. The components of this comprehensive teaching and learning package are outlined on the following pages.

* *Derive* is available to adopters at a discounted price.

	PRINTED ANCILLARIES	SOFTWARE
INSTRUCTORS	**Instructor's Guide** • Solutions to all even-numbered text exercises and cumulative tests **Test Item File and Resource Guide** • Printed test bank • Over 2000 test items • Open-ended and multiple-choice test items • Available as test-generating software • Sample tests	**BestGrapher** • Function grapher • Screen simultaneously displays equation, graph, and table of values • Some features anticipate calculus • Includes zoom and print features for use on assignments **Computerized Testing Software** • Test-generating software • Over 2000 test items • Also available as a printed test item file **Derive** • Computer algebra system • Discount available to adopters
STUDENTS	**Study and Solutions Guide** • Solutions to all odd-numbered text exercises • Solutions match methods of text • Study strategies **Graphing Technology Guide** • Keystroke instructions for graphics calculators • Examples **The Algebra of Calculus** • Reviews the algebra, trigonometry, and analytic geometry that students will encounter in calculus • Over 200 examples • Pretests and exercise sets	**BestGrapher** • Function grapher • Screen simultaneously displays equation, graph, and table of values • Some features anticipate calculus • Includes zoom and print features for use on assignments
CLASSROOM RESOURCES	**Transparency Package** • 50 color transparencies • Color-coded by text topic	**BestGrapher** • Function grapher • Screen simultaneously displays equation, graph, and table of values • Some features anticipate calculus • Includes zoom and print features for use on assignments **Derive** • Computer algebra system • Discount available to adopters

Instructor's Guide

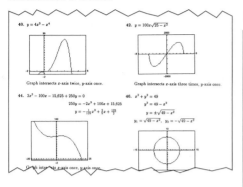

40. $y = 4x^3 - x^4$

42. $y = 100x\sqrt{25 - x^2}$

Graph intersects x-axis twice, y-axis once.

Graph intersects x-axis three times, y-axis once.

44. $2x^3 - 100x - 15,625 + 250y = 0$

$$250y = -2x^3 + 100x + 15,625$$
$$y = -\frac{1}{125}x^3 + \frac{2}{5}x + \frac{125}{2}$$

46. $x^2 + y^2 = 49$

$$y^2 = 49 - x^2$$
$$y = \pm\sqrt{49 - x^2}$$
$$y_1 = \sqrt{49 - x^2}, \quad y_2 = -\sqrt{49 - x^2}$$

Graph intersects x-axis once, y-axis once.

Study and Solutions Guide

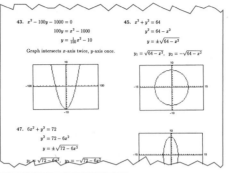

43. $x^2 - 100y - 1000 = 0$

$$100y = x^2 - 1000$$
$$y = \frac{1}{100}x^2 - 10$$

Graph intersects x-axis twice, y-axis once.

45. $x^2 + y^2 = 64$

$$y^2 = 64 - x^2$$
$$y = \pm\sqrt{64 - x^2}$$
$$y_1 = \sqrt{64 - x^2}, \quad y_2 = -\sqrt{64 - x^2}$$

47. $6x^2 + y^2 = 72$

$$y^2 = 72 - 6x^2$$
$$y = \pm\sqrt{72 - 6x^2}$$
$$y_1 = \sqrt{72 - 6x^2}, \quad y_2 = -\sqrt{72 - 6x^2}$$

BestGrapher

Test Item File and Resource Guide

18. Use a graphing utility to graph $y = 2x^3 + x^2 + x - 1$.

(a) (b) (c) (d)

(e) None of these

1—M—Answer: d

CHAPTER 1

FUNCTIONS AND GRAPHS

1.1 GRAPHS AND GRAPHING UTILITIES

The Graph of an Equation / Using a Graphing Utility / Determining a Viewing Rectangle / Applications

The Graph of an Equation

News magazines often show graphs comparing the rate of inflation, the federal deficit, wholesale prices, or the unemployment rate to the time of year. Industrial firms and businesses use graphs to report their monthly production and sales statistics. Such graphs provide geometric pictures of the way one quantity changes with respect to another.

Frequently, the relationship between two quantities is expressed as an equation. This section introduces the basic procedure for determining the geometric picture associated with an equation.

For an equation in variables x and y, a point (a, b) is a **solution point** if the substitution of $x = a$ and $y = b$ satisfies the equation. Most equations have *infinitely* many solution points. For example, the equation $3x + y = 5$ has solution points $(0, 5)$, $(1, 2)$, $(2, -1)$, $(3, -4)$, and so on. The set of all solution points of an equation is the **graph** of the equation.

THE POINT-PLOTTING METHOD OF GRAPHING

To sketch the graph of an equation by point plotting, use the following.

1. If possible, rewrite the equation so that one of the variables is isolated on the left side of the equation.
2. Make up a table of several solution points.
3. Plot these points in the coordinate plane.
4. Connect the points with a smooth curve.

51

Transparency Package

$y = \log_a x$

$(1, 0)$

Graph of $y = \log_a x$, $a > 1$
- Domain: $(0, \infty)$
- Range: $(-\infty, \infty)$
- Intercept: $(1, 0)$
- Increasing
- y-axis is a vertical asymptote ($\log_a x \to -\infty$ as $x \to 0^+$)
- Continuous
- Reflection of graph of $y = a^x$ about the line $y = x$

$y = \ln x$

$(1, 0)$

Graph of $y = \ln x$
- Domain: $(0, \infty)$
- Range: $(-\infty, \infty)$
- Intercept: $(1, 0)$
- Increasing
- y-axis is a vertical asymptote ($\ln x \to -\infty$ as $x \to 0^+$)
- Continuous
- Reflection of graph of $y = e^x$ about the line $y = x$

The Algebra of Calculus with Trigonometry and Analytic Geometry

8 Functions II: Combinations of Functions, Difficult Graphs

REVIEW OF FUNDAMENTALS

- The sum, product, and quotient of functions f and g are defined by the following statements.
  (a) $(f + g)(x) = f(x) + g(x)$
  (b) $[fg](x) = f(x) \cdot g(x)$
  (c) $\left(\frac{f}{g}\right)(x) = \frac{f(x)}{g(x)}$, $g(x) \neq 0$
- The composition of functions f and g is defined by $(f \circ g)(x) = f(g(x))$. Note that the domain of $f \circ g$ is $\{x : x \in \text{domain of } g \text{ and } g(x) \in \text{domain of } f\}$.
- The inverse of a function f, denoted by f^{-1}, has the following properties.
  (a) The inverse of f exists if no horizontal line intersects the graph of f in two or more places. Functions of this kind are called one-to-one. Formally, a function is one-to-one if $f(x_1) = f(x_2)$ implies $x_1 = x_2$.
  (b) The inverse of f is expressed in terms of x and y by solving the original equation $y = f(x)$ for x in terms of y, and then interchanging the symbols x and y.
  (c) The inverse of f has as its domain the range of f, and has as its range the domain of f.
  (d) The inverse of f is graphed by reflecting the graph of the original function about the line $y = x$.

EXAMPLE 1 Sums, Products, and Quotients of Functions

Let $f(x) = x^2 + 3$, $g(x) = 1/x$, and $h(x) = 3$. Find $(f + g)(x)$, $(fg)(x)$, and $(f/g)(x)$.

SOLUTION

(a) $(f + g)(x) = f(x) + g(x) = (x^2 + 3) + \frac{1}{x} = x^2 + \frac{1}{x} + 3$

(b) $(fgh)(x) = [f(x)g(x)h(x)] = (x^2 + 3) \cdot h\left[\frac{1}{x}\right] = x + \frac{9}{x}$

(c) $\left(\frac{f}{g}\right)(x) = \frac{h(x)}{f(x)} = \frac{1}{x^2 + 3}$

Computerized Testing Software

Open Select Edit View Print Quit | F1=HELP

Select Questions by Review
Chapter 002 - Question 20 of 27
Find the x-intercept of the function: $f(x) = \ln(x + 1)$

(a) (0, 0)   (b) (-1, 0)   (c) (0, -1)

(d) (1, 0)   (e) None of these

Answer

F5 Chap   F3 Prev   F4 Next   F2 Attr   F8 Select   (Esc)

Scroll - PgUp/PgDn for Question - <Ctrl>PgUp/PgDn for Answer   <Esc> - Done

Derive

ACKNOWLEDGMENTS

We would like to thank the many people who have helped us prepare the text and supplements package. Their encouragement, criticisms, and suggestions have been invaluable to us.

REVIEWERS

Marilyn Carlson, University of Kansas
John Dersh, Grand Rapids Community College
Patricia J. Ernst, St. Cloud State University
Eunice F. Everett, Seminole Community College
James R. Fryxell, College of Lake County
Bernard Greenspan, University of Akron
Lynda Hollingsworth, Northwest Missouri State University
Spencer Hurd, The Citadel
Luella Johnson, State University of New York, College at Buffalo
Peter A. Lappan, Michigan State University
Marilyn McCollum, North Carolina State University
David R. Peterson, University of Central Arkansas
Antonio Quesada, University of Akron
Stephen Slack, Kenyon College
Judith Smalling, St. Petersburg Junior College
Howard L. Wilson, Oregon State University

FOCUS GROUP

John Dersh, Grand Rapids Community College
Donald Shriner, Frostburg State University

TELEPHONE FOCUS GROUP

John Dersh, Grand Rapids Community College
Ruth Pruitt, Fort Hays State University
Sharon Sledge, San Jacinto College
Fredric W. Tufte, University of Wisconsin—Platteville
Darlene Whitkanack, Northern Illinois University

SURVEY RESPONDENTS

William C. Allgyer, Mountain Empire Community College
Gloria Child, Rollins College
Allan C. Cochran, University of Arkansas at Fayetteville
Ronald Dalla, Eastern Washington University
Ann Dinkheller, Xavier University
Gloria Dion, Pennsylvania State University—Ogontz Campus
Iris B. Fetta, Clemson University
Spencer P. Hurd, The Citadel
Marvin L. Johnson, College of Lake County
Donald A. Josephson, Wheaton College (Ill.)
Thomas J. Kearns, Northern Kentucky University
N. J. Kuenzi, University of Wisconsin—Oshkosh
Edward Laughbaum, Columbus State Community College
M. S. McCollum, North Carolina State University
Carolyn Meitler, Concordia University
Harold M. Ness, University of Wisconsin Centers—Fond du Lac
Michele Olson, College of the Redwoods
John Savige, St. Petersburg Junior College—Clearwater
Stephen Slack, Kenyon College
Marjie Vittum-Jones, South Seattle Community College
Charles Vander Embse, Central Michigan University

Our thanks to the staffs of Texas Instruments Incorporated; Casio, Inc.; and Sharp Electronics Corporation for their help and cooperation with the programs.

A special thanks to all the people at D. C. Heath and Company who worked with us in the development and production of the text, especially Ann Marie Jones, Mathematics Acquisitions Editor; Cathy Cantin, Senior Developmental Editor; Jennifer Brett, Senior Production Editor; Elizabeth Gale, Editorial Assistant; Sally Steele, Designer and Art Editor; Carolyn Johnson, Editorial Associate; Mike O'Dea, Production Manager; and Lisa Merrill, Production Supervisor.

Several other people worked on this project. David E. Heyd assisted us in writing the text and solved the exercises; David C. Falvo wrote the *Test Item File and Resource Guide;* Cathy Gardner and Linda McDonald checked the manuscript for accuracy. The following people also worked on the project: Richard J. Bambauer, Lisa K. Bickel, Linda M. Bollinger, Laurie A. Brooks, Patti Jo Campbell, Darin P. Johnson, Linda L. Kifer, Deanna G. Larson, Timothy R. Larson, Amy L. Marshall, John R. Musser, R. Scott O'Neil, Louis R. Rieger, Evelyn A. Wedzikowski, and Nancy L. Zawadski.

On a personal level, we are grateful to our wives, Deanna Gilbert Larson, Eloise Hostetler, and Consuelo Edwards, for their love, patience, and support. Also, a special thanks goes to R. Scott O'Neil.

If you have suggestions for improving the text, please feel free to write to us. Over the past two decades, we have received many useful comments from both instructors and students, and we value these very much.

Roland E. Larson
Robert P. Hostetler
Bruce H. Edwards

CONTENTS

Chapter 4   RATIONAL FUNCTIONS AND CONIC SECTIONS   279

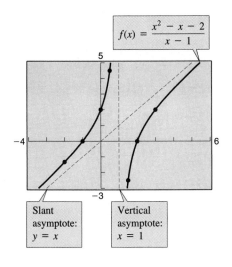

$$f(x) = \frac{x^2 - x - 2}{x - 1}$$

Slant asymptote: $y = x$

Vertical asymptote: $x = 1$

Chapter 5   EXPONENTIAL AND LOGARITHMIC FUNCTIONS   331

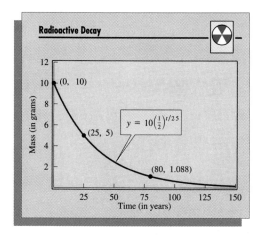

Radioactive Decay

$$y = 10\left(\tfrac{1}{2}\right)^{t/25}$$

(0, 10)

(25, 5)

(80, 1.088)

Mass (in grams)

Time (in years)

Chapter 6   TRIGONOMETRY   387

Chapter 7   ANALYTIC TRIGONOMETRY   477

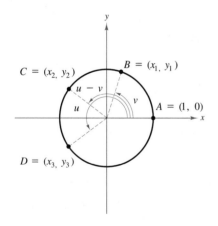

Chapter 8   ADDITIONAL TOPICS IN TRIGONOMETRY   527

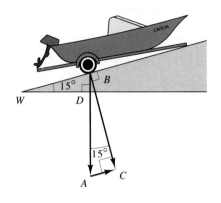

Chapter 9   LINEAR MODELS AND SYSTEMS OF EQUATIONS   579

Exactly One Solution

Chapter 10   SEQUENCES, MATHEMATICAL INDUCTION, AND PROBABILITY   675

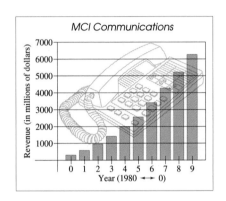

Chapter 11   PARAMETRIC EQUATIONS AND POLAR COORDINATES   757

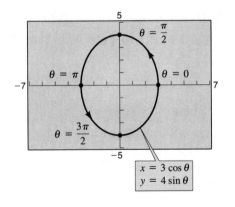

$$x = 3\cos\theta$$
$$y = 4\sin\theta$$

APPENDIXES

ANSWERS

INDEXES

INTRODUCTION TO CALCULATORS

Many examples and exercises in the text require the use of a calculator. Using this tool allows you to examine math in the context of real-life applications.

GRAPHING CALCULATORS

One of the basic differences in calculators is their order of operations. You should practice entering and evaluating expressions on your calculator to make sure you understand its order of operations. Some calculators use an order of operations called RPN (for Reverse Polish Notation). In this text, however, all calculator steps are given using algebraic order of operations. For example, the calculation

$$4.69[5 + 2(6.87 - 3.042)]$$

can be performed with the following steps using an algebraic order of operations.

4.69 $\boxed{\times}$ $\boxed{(}$ 5 $\boxed{+}$ 2 $\boxed{\times}$ $\boxed{(}$ 6.87 $\boxed{-}$ 3.042 $\boxed{)}$ $\boxed{)}$ $\boxed{\text{ENTER}}$

This yields the value of 59.35664. Without parentheses, you could enter the expression from the inside out with the sequence

6.87 $\boxed{-}$ 3.042 $\boxed{\text{ENTER}}$ $\boxed{\times}$ 2 $\boxed{+}$ 5 $\boxed{\text{ENTER}}$ $\boxed{\times}$ 4.69 $\boxed{\text{ENTER}}$

to obtain the same result.

Using a calculator with RPN, the calculation can be performed with the following steps.

6.87 $\boxed{\text{ENTER}}$ 3.042 $\boxed{-}$ 2 $\boxed{\times}$ 5 $\boxed{+}$ 4.69 $\boxed{\times}$

You should also practice using your calculator's graphing features. To help you become familiar with the graphing features, we have included Appendix

A, Graphing Utilities. Be sure to read the examples in Appendix A and work the exercises. Answers to odd-numbered exercises in Appendix A are given in the back of the book.

You can program your calculator to perform various procedures. Try entering and using the selection of optional programs included in this text. For convenience, Appendix B, Programs, contains translations of the text programs for several types of graphing calculators.

ROUNDING NUMBERS

For all their usefulness, calculators do have a problem representing numbers because they are limited to a finite number of digits. For instance, what does your calculator display when you compute $2 \div 3$? Some calculators simply truncate (drop) the digits that exceed their display range and display .66666666. Others will round the number and display .66666667. Although the second display is more accurate, both of these decimal representations of 2/3 contain a rounding error.

When rounding decimals, we suggest the following guidelines.

1. Determine the number of digits of accuracy you want to keep. The digit in the last position you keep is the **rounding digit,** and the digit in the first position you discard is the **decision digit.**

2. If the decision digit is 5 or greater, round up by adding 1 to the rounding digit.

3. If the decision digit is 4 or less, round down by leaving the rounding digit unchanged.

Here are some examples. Note that you round down in the first example because the decision digit is 4 or less, and you round up in the other two examples because the decision digit is 5 or greater.

Number	*Rounded to Three Decimal Places*	
a. $\sqrt{2} = 1.4142136$	1.414	*Round down*
b. $\pi = 3.1415927$	3.142	*Round up*
c. $\frac{7}{9} = 0.7777777$	0.778	*Round up*

One of the best ways to minimize error due to rounding is to leave numbers in your calculator until your calculations are complete. If you want to save a number for future use, store it in your calculator's memory.

Remember that once you (or your calculator) have rounded a number, a round-off error has been introduced. For instance, if a number is rounded to

$x = 27.3$, then the actual value of x can lie anywhere between 27.25 and 27.35, or at 27.25 exactly. That is, $27.25 \leq x < 27.35$.

PROBLEM SOLVING USING A CALCULATOR

Here are some guidelines to consider when using any type of calculator in problem solving.

1. Be sure you understand the operation of your own calculator. You need to be skilled at entering expressions in a way that will guarantee that your calculator is performing the operations correctly.

2. Focus first on analyzing the problem. After you have developed a strategy, you may be able to use your calculator to help implement the strategy. Write down your steps in an organized way to clearly outline the strategy used and the results.

3. Most problems can be solved in a variety of ways. If you choose to solve a problem using a table, try checking the solution with an analytic (or algebraic) approach. If you choose to solve a problem using algebra, try checking the solution with a graphing approach. Or, if you choose to solve a problem using a graphing approach, try checking the solution with an algebraic approach.

4. After obtaining a solution with a calculator, be sure to ask yourself if the solution is reasonable (within the context of the problem).

5. To lessen the chance of errors, clear the calculator display (and check the settings) before beginning a new problem.

PREREQUISITES: REVIEW OF BASIC ALGEBRA

1   THE REAL NUMBER SYSTEM

The Real Number System / The Real Number Line / Ordering the Real Numbers / The Absolute Value of a Real Number / The Distance Between Two Real Numbers

The Real Number System

Real numbers are used in everyday life to describe quantities such as age, miles per gallon, container size, population, and so on. To represent real numbers we use symbols such as

$$9, \ -5, \ 0, \ \frac{4}{3}, \ 0.6666\ldots, \ 28.21, \ \sqrt{2}, \ \pi, \ \text{and} \ \sqrt[3]{-32}.$$

The set of real numbers contains some important subsets with which you should be familiar:

$\{1, 2, 3, 4, \ldots\}$	*Set of **natural** numbers*
$\{0, 1, 2, 3, 4, \ldots\}$	*Set of **whole** numbers*
$\{\ldots, -3, -2, -1, 0, 1, 2, 3, \ldots\}$	*Set of **integers***

A real number is **rational** if it can be written as the ratio p/q of two integers, where $q \neq 0$. For instance, the numbers

$$\frac{1}{3} = 0.3333\ldots, \quad \frac{1}{8} = 0.125, \quad \text{and} \quad \frac{125}{111} = 1.126126\ldots$$

are rational. The decimal representation of a rational number either repeats (as in 3.1454545 . . .) or terminates (as in $\frac{1}{2}$ = 0.5). A real number that cannot be written as the ratio of two integers is called **irrational.** Irrational numbers have infinite *nonrepeating* decimal representations. For instance, the numbers

$$\sqrt{2} \approx 1.4142135 \ldots \quad \text{and} \quad \pi \approx 3.1415926 \ldots$$

are irrational. (The symbol $\approx$ means "is approximately equal to.")

EXAMPLE 1   Identifying Real Numbers

Consider the following subset of real numbers:

$$\left\{ -8, -\sqrt{5}, 1, \frac{2}{3}, 0, -\frac{1}{7}, \sqrt{3}, \pi, 9 \right\}.$$

List the numbers in this set that are

A. Natural numbers   **B.** Integers
C. Rational numbers   **D.** Irrational numbers

SOLUTION

A. Natural numbers: 1, 9
B. Integers: −8, 1, 0, 9
C. Rational numbers: $-8, 1, \frac{2}{3}, 0, -\frac{1}{7}, 9$

D. Irrational numbers: $-\sqrt{5}, \sqrt{3}, \pi$

The Real Number Line

The model used to represent the real number system is called the **real number line.** It consists of a horizontal line with a point (the **origin**) labeled 0. Numbers to the right of 0 are positive, and numbers to the left of 0 are negative, as shown in Figure 1. We use the term **nonnegative** to describe a number that is either positive or zero.

The Real Number Line

FIGURE 1

One-to-One Correspondence

(a) Every real number corresponds to exactly one point on the real number line.

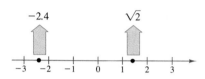

(b) Every point on the real number line corresponds to exactly one real number.

FIGURE 2

Each point on the real number line corresponds to one and only one real number and each real number corresponds to one and only one point on the real number line. This type of relationship is called a **one-to-one correspondence**, as shown in Figure 2.

The number associated with a point on the real number line is called the **coordinate** of the point. For example, in Figure 2(a), $-\frac{5}{3}$ is the coordinate of the leftmost point and π is the coordinate of the rightmost point.

Ordering the Real Numbers

One important property of real numbers is that they are **ordered.**

> ### DEFINITION OF ORDER ON THE REAL NUMBER LINE
>
> If a and b are real numbers, then a is **less than** b if $b - a$ is positive. We denote this order by the **inequality**
>
> $$a < b.$$
>
> This relationship can also be described by saying that b is **greater than** a and writing $b > a$. The inequality $a \le b$ means that a is **less than or equal to** b and the inequality $b \ge a$ means that b is **greater than or equal to** a. The symbols $<, >, \le,$ and $\ge$ are called **inequality symbols.**

$a < b$ if and only if a lies to the left of b.

FIGURE 3

Geometrically, this definition implies that $a < b$ if and only if a lies to the *left* of b on the real number line, as shown in Figure 3. For example, $1 < 2$ because 1 lies to the left of 2 on the real number line.

Inequalities are useful in denoting subsets of real numbers, as shown in Examples 2 and 3.

$x \le 2$

(a)

$-2 \le x < 3$

(b)

$x > -5$

(c)

FIGURE 4

EXAMPLE 2   Interpreting Inequalities

A. The inequality $x \le 2$ denotes all real numbers less than or equal to 2.

B. The inequality $-2 \le x < 3$ means that $x \ge -2$ *and* $x < 3$. This "double" inequality denotes all real numbers between -2 and 3, including -2 but *not* including 3.

C. The inequality $x > -5$ denotes all real numbers greater than -5.

The graphs of all three inequalities are shown in Figure 4. In the graphs, note that the brackets correspond to $\ge$ and $\le$ and the parentheses correspond to $>$ and $<$.

Each of the subsets of real numbers in Example 2 is an **interval.**

BOUNDED INTERVALS ON THE REAL NUMBER LINE

Let a and b be real numbers such that $a < b$. The following intervals on the real number line are **bounded intervals.** The numbers a and b are the **endpoints** of each interval.

Notation	Interval Type	Inequality	Graph
$[a, b]$	Closed	$a \leq x \leq b$	
(a, b)	Open	$a < x < b$	
$[a, b)$	Half-open	$a \leq x < b$	
$(a, b]$	Half-open	$a < x \leq b$	

UNBOUNDED INTERVALS ON THE REAL NUMBER LINE

Let a and b be real numbers. The following intervals on the real number line are **unbounded intervals.**

Notation	Interval Type	Inequality	Graph
$[a, \infty)$	Half-open	$x \geq a$	
(a, ∞)	Open	$x > a$	
$(-\infty, b]$	Half-open	$x \leq b$	
$(-\infty, b)$	Open	$x < b$	
$(-\infty, \infty)$	Entire real line		

The symbols ∞ (**positive infinity**) and $-\infty$ (**negative infinity**) do not represent real numbers. They are simply convenient symbols used to describe the unboundedness of an interval such as $(1, \infty)$.

EXAMPLE 3   Intervals and Inequalities

Write an inequality to represent each of the intervals and state whether the interval is bounded or unbounded.

A. $(-3, 5]$ **B.** $(-3, \infty)$ **C.** $[0, 2]$

SOLUTION

A. $(-3, 5]$ corresponds to $-3 < x \leq 5$.   *Bounded*
B. $(-3, \infty)$ corresponds to $-3 < x$.   *Unbounded*
C. $[0, 2]$ corresponds to $0 \leq x \leq 2$.   *Bounded*

EXAMPLE 4   Using Inequalities to Represent Sets of Real Numbers

Use inequality and interval notation to describe each of the following.

A. c is nonnegative.   **B.** b is at most 5.
C. d is negative and greater than -3.
D. x is positive or x is less than -6.

SOLUTION

A. "c is nonnegative" means that c is greater than or equal to zero. This can be written as $c \geq 0$. The interval notation is $[0, \infty)$.
B. "b is at most 5" can be written as $b \leq 5$. The interval notation is $(-\infty, 5]$.
C. "d is negative" can be written as $d < 0$, and "d is greater than -3" can be written as $-3 < d$. Combining these two inequalities produces the double inequality $-3 < d < 0$. The interval notation is $(-3, 0)$.
D. "x is positive" can be written as $0 < x$, and "x is less than -6" can be written as $x < -6$. Combining these two inequalities produces $0 < x$ or $x < -6$. This yields *two* intervals: $(-\infty, -6), (0, \infty)$.

The Absolute Value of a Real Number

The **absolute value** of a real number is its *magnitude*.

DEFINITION OF ABSOLUTE VALUE

If a is a real number, then the **absolute value** of a is given by

$$|a| = \begin{cases} a, & \text{if } a \geq 0 \\ -a, & \text{if } a < 0. \end{cases}$$

Notice from this definition that the absolute value of a real number is never negative. For instance, if $a = -5$, then $|-5| = -(-5) = 5$. Zero is the only real number whose absolute value is zero. That is, $|0| = 0$.

The following list gives four useful properties of absolute value.

PROPERTIES OF ABSOLUTE VALUES

Let a and b be real numbers.

1. $|a| \geq 0$

2. $|-a| = |a|$

3. $|ab| = |a||b|$

4. $\left|\dfrac{a}{b}\right| = \dfrac{|a|}{|b|}, \quad b \neq 0$

The Distance Between Two Real Numbers

Absolute value is used to define the distance between two numbers on the real number line.

DISTANCE BETWEEN TWO POINTS ON THE REAL NUMBER LINE

Let a and b be real numbers. The **distance between a and b** is

$$d(a, b) = |b - a| = |a - b|.$$

EXAMPLE 5   Distance and Absolute Value

A. The distance between $\sqrt{7}$ and 4 is given by

$$d\left(\sqrt{7}, 4\right) = \left|4 - \sqrt{7}\right| = 4 - \sqrt{7}.$$

B. ne statement "the distance between c and -2 is at least 7" is written as

$$d(c, -2) = |c - (-2)| = |c + 2| \geq 7.$$

C. The distance between -4 and the origin is given by

$$d(-4, 0) = |-4 - 0| = |-4| = 4.$$

See Figure 5.

FIGURE 5

SECTION 1 · EXERCISES

In Exercises 1–6, determine which numbers in the set are (a) natural numbers, (b) integers, (c) rational numbers, and (d) irrational numbers.

*1. $-9, -\frac{7}{2}, 5, \frac{2}{3}, \sqrt{2}, 0, 1$

2. $\sqrt{5}, -7, -\frac{7}{3}, 0, 3.12, \frac{5}{4}$

3. $12, -13, 1, \sqrt{4}, \sqrt{6}, \frac{3}{2}$

4. $\frac{8}{2}, -\frac{8}{3}, \sqrt{10}, -4, 9, 14.2$

5. $-\pi, -\frac{1}{3}, \frac{6}{3}, \frac{1}{2}\sqrt{2}, -7.5$

6. $25, -17, -\frac{12}{5}, \sqrt{9}, 3.12, \frac{1}{2}\pi$

In Exercises 7–12, plot the two real numbers on the real number line, and then write them with the appropriate inequality sign (< or >) between them.

7. $\frac{3}{2}, 7$

8. $-3.5, 1$

9. $-4, -8$

10. $1, \frac{16}{3}$

11. $\frac{5}{6}, \frac{2}{3}$

12. $-\frac{8}{7}, -\frac{3}{7}$

In Exercises 13–16, write an inequality to represent the given interval and state whether the interval is bounded or unbounded.

13. $[-1, 3]$

14. $(4, 10]$

15. $(10, \infty)$

16. $(-6, \infty)$

In Exercises 17–26, use interval notation to describe the subset of real numbers that is represented by the inequality. Then sketch the subset on the real number line.

17. $x \leq 5$

18. $x \geq -2$

19. $x < 0$

20. $x > 3$

21. $x \geq 4$

22. $x < 2$

23. $-2 < x < 2$

24. $0 \leq x \leq 5$

25. $-1 \leq x < 0$

26. $0 < x \leq 6$

In Exercises 27–34, use inequality and interval notation to describe the set of real numbers.

27. x is negative.

28. z is at least 10.

29. y is no more than 25.

30. y is greater than 5 and less than or equal to 12.

31. The person's age A is at least 30.

32. The yield Y is no more than 45 bushels per acre.

33. The annual rate of inflation r is expected to be at least 3.5%, but no more than 6%.

34. The price p of unleaded gasoline is not expected to go above $1.35 per gallon during the coming year.

In Exercises 35–40, write the expression without using absolute value signs.

35. $\dfrac{-5}{|-5|}$

36. $|4 - \pi|$

37. $-3|-3|$

38. $|-1| - |-2|$

39. $-|16.25| + 20$

40. $2|33|$

In Exercises 41–46, fill in the blank with <, >, or =.

41. $|-3| \quad - |-3|$

42. $|-4| \quad |4|$

43. $-5 \quad - |5|$

44. $-|-6| \quad |-6|$

45. $-|-2| \quad - |2|$

46. $-(-2) \quad -2$

In Exercises 47–52, find the distance between a and b.

47.

$a = -\frac{5}{2}$ $b = 0$

48.

$a = \frac{1}{4}$ $b = \frac{11}{4}$

49. $a = 126, b = 75$

50. $a = -126, b = -75$

51. $a = 9.34, b = -5.65$

52. $a = \frac{16}{5}, b = \frac{112}{75}$

In Exercises 53–58, use absolute value notation to describe the expression.

53. The distance between x and 5 is no more than 3.

54. The distance between x and -10 is at least 6.

55. The distance between z and $\frac{3}{2}$ is greater than 1.

56. The distance between z and 0 is less than 8.

57. y is at least 6 units from 0.

58. y is at most 2 units from a.

* Detailed solutions to all odd-numbered exercises can be found in the *Study and Solutions Guide.*

In Exercises 59 and 60, use a calculator to order the numbers from smallest to largest.

59. $\frac{7071}{5000}$, $\frac{584}{413}$, $\sqrt{2}$, $\frac{47}{33}$, $\frac{127}{90}$

60. $\frac{26}{15}$, $\sqrt{3}$, 1.7320, $\frac{381}{220}$, $\sqrt{10} - \sqrt{2}$

In Exercises 61–64, use a calculator to find the decimal form of the rational number. If it is a nonterminating decimal, write the repeating pattern.

61. $\frac{5}{8}$

62. $\frac{1}{3}$

63. $\frac{41}{333}$

64. $\frac{6}{11}$

In Exercises 65–68, determine whether the statement is true or false. Explain your reasoning.

65. The reciprocal of every nonzero integer is an integer.

66. Every integer is a rational number.

67. Every real number is either rational or irrational.

68. The absolute value of every real number is positive.

2   PROPERTIES OF REAL NUMBERS AND THE BASIC RULES OF ALGEBRA

Algebraic Expressions / Basic Rules of Algebra / Equations / Exponents / Scientific Notation

Algebraic Expressions

One characteristic of algebra is the use of letters or combinations of letters to represent numbers. The letters are called **variables** and combinations of letters and numbers are called **algebraic expressions.** Here are a few examples of algebraic expressions:

$$5x, \qquad 2x - 3, \qquad \frac{4}{x^2 + 2}, \qquad 7x + y.$$

DEFINITION OF AN ALGEBRAIC EXPRESSION

An **algebraic expression** is a collection of letters (**variables**) and real numbers (**constants**) combined using the operations of addition, subtraction, multiplication, division, and exponentiation.

The **terms** of an algebraic expression are those parts that are separated by *addition.* For example,

$$x^2 - 5x + 8 = x^2 + (-5x) + 8$$

has three terms: x^2 and $-5x$ are the **variable terms** and 8 is the **constant term.** The numerical factor of a variable term is the **coefficient** of the variable term. For instance, the coefficient of $-5x$ is -5, and the coefficient of x^2 is 1.

To **evaluate** an algebraic expression, substitute numerical values for each of the variables in the expression. Here are two examples.

Expression	Value of Variable	Substitute	Value of Expression
$-3x + 5$	$x = 3$	$-3(3) + 5$	$-9 + 5 = -4$
$3x^2 + 2x - 1$	$x = -1$	$3(-1)^2 + 2(-1) - 1$	$3 - 2 - 1 = 0$

Basic Rules of Algebra

There are four arithmetic operations with real numbers: **addition, multiplication, subtraction,** and **division,** denoted by the symbols $+$, $\times$ or $\cdot$, $-$, and $\div$. Of these, addition and multiplication are the two primary operations. Subtraction and division are defined as the inverse operations of addition and multiplication.

Subtraction	Division
$a - b = a + (-b)$	If $b \neq 0$, then $\dfrac{a}{b} = a\left(\dfrac{1}{b}\right)$.

In these definitions, $-b$ is the **additive inverse** (or opposite) of b, and $1/b$ is the **multiplicative inverse** (or reciprocal) of b. In the fractional form a/b, a is the **numerator** of the fraction and b is the **denominator.**

Be sure you see that the following **basic rules of algebra** are true for variables and algebraic expressions as well as for real numbers.

BASIC RULES OF ALGEBRA

Let a, b, and c be real numbers, variables, or algebraic expressions.

Property		Example
Commutative Property of Addition:	$a + b = b + a$	$4x + x^2 = x^2 + 4x$
Commutative Property of Multiplication:	$ab = ba$	$(4 - x)x^2 = x^2(4 - x)$
Associative Property of Addition:	$(a + b) + c = a + (b + c)$	$(-x + 5) + 2x^2 = -x + (5 + 2x^2)$
Associative Property of Multiplication:	$(ab)c = a(bc)$	$(2x \cdot 3y)(8) = (2x)(3y \cdot 8)$
Distributive Property:	$a(b + c) = ab + ac$	$x(5 + 2x) = x \cdot 5 + x \cdot 2x$
	$(a + b)c = ac + bc$	$(y + 8)y = y \cdot y + 8 \cdot y$
Additive Identity Property:	$a + 0 = a$	$5y^2 + 0 = 5y^2$
Multiplicative Identity Property:	$a \cdot 1 = 1 \cdot a = a$	$(4x^2)(1) = (1)(4x^2) = 4x^2$
Additive Inverse Property:	$a + (-a) = 0$	$5x^3 + (-5x^3) = 0$
Multiplicative Inverse Property:	$a \cdot \dfrac{1}{a} = 1, \quad a \neq 0$	$(x^2 + 4)\left(\dfrac{1}{x^2 + 4}\right) = 1$

REMARK The Distributive Properties are also true for subtraction. For instance, the "subtraction form" of $a(b + c) = ab + ac$ is

$$a(b - c) = a[b + (-c)] = ab + a(-c) = ab - ac.$$

·····

PROPERTIES OF NEGATION

Let a and b be real numbers, variables, or algebraic expressions.

Property	Example
1. $(-1)a = -a$	$(-1)7 = -7$
2. $-(-a) = a$	$-(-6) = 6$
3. $(-a)b = -(ab) = a(-b)$	$(-5)3 = -(5 \cdot 3) = 5(-3) = -15$
4. $(-a)(-b) = ab$	$(-2)(-6) = 2 \cdot 6 = 12$
5. $-(a + b) = (-a) + (-b)$	$-(3 + 8) = (-3) + (-8) = -11$

Be sure you see the difference between the *additive inverse of a number* and a *negative number.* If a is already negative, then its additive inverse, $-a$, is positive. For instance, if $a = -5$, then $-a = -(-5) = 5$.

PROPERTIES OF ZERO

Let a and b be real numbers, variables, or algebraic expressions.

1. $a + 0 = a$ and $a - 0 = a$
2. $a \cdot 0 = 0$
3. $\dfrac{0}{a} = 0, \quad a \neq 0$
4. $\dfrac{a}{0}$ is undefined.
5. Zero-Factor Property: If $ab = 0$, then $a = 0$ or $b = 0$.

The "or" in the Zero-Factor Property includes the possibility that both factors may be zero. This is an **inclusive or,** and it is the way the word "or" is always used in mathematics.

PROPERTIES OF FRACTIONS

Let a, b, c, and d be real numbers, variables, or algebraic expressions such that $b \neq 0$ and $d \neq 0$.

1. Equivalent Fractions: $\dfrac{a}{b} = \dfrac{c}{d}$ if and only if $ad = bc$.

2. Rules of Signs: $-\dfrac{a}{b} = \dfrac{-a}{b} = \dfrac{a}{-b}$ and $\dfrac{-a}{-b} = \dfrac{a}{b}$

3. Generate Equivalent Fractions: $\dfrac{a}{b} = \dfrac{ac}{bc}$, $c \neq 0$

4. Add or Subtract with Like Denominators: $\dfrac{a}{b} \pm \dfrac{c}{b} = \dfrac{a \pm c}{b}$

5. Add or Subtract with Unlike Denominators: $\dfrac{a}{b} \pm \dfrac{c}{d} = \dfrac{ad \pm bc}{bd}$

6. Multiply Fractions: $\dfrac{a}{b} \cdot \dfrac{c}{d} = \dfrac{ac}{bd}$

7. Divide Fractions: $\dfrac{a}{b} \div \dfrac{c}{d} = \dfrac{a}{b} \cdot \dfrac{d}{c} = \dfrac{ad}{bc}$, $c \neq 0$

In Property 1 (equivalent fractions) the phrase "if and only if" implies two statements. One statement is: If $a/b = c/d$, then $ad = bc$. The other statement is: If $ad = bc$, where $b \neq 0$ and $d \neq 0$, then $a/b = c/d$.

EXAMPLE 1   Properties of Zero and Properties of Fractions

A. $x - \dfrac{0}{5} = x - 0 = x$ *Properties 3 and 1 of zero*

B. $\dfrac{x}{5} = \dfrac{3 \cdot x}{3 \cdot 5} = \dfrac{3x}{15}$ *Generate equivalent fractions*

C. $\dfrac{x}{3} + \dfrac{2x}{5} = \dfrac{5 \cdot x + 3 \cdot 2x}{15}$ *Add fractions with unlike denominators*

D. $\dfrac{7}{x} \div \dfrac{3}{2} = \dfrac{7}{x} \cdot \dfrac{2}{3} = \dfrac{14}{3x}$ *Divide fractions*

If a, b, and c are integers such that $ab = c$, then a and b are **factors** or **divisors** of c. For example, 2 and 3 are factors of 6. A **prime number** is a positive integer that has exactly two factors: itself and 1. For example, 2, 3, 5, 7, and 11 are prime numbers. The numbers 4, 6, 8, 9, and 10 are **composite** because they can be written as the product of two or more prime numbers. The number 1 is neither prime nor composite. The **Fundamental Theorem of Arithmetic** states that every positive integer greater than 1 can be written as the product of prime numbers in precisely one way (disregarding order). For instance, the prime factorization of 24 is $24 = 2 \cdot 2 \cdot 2 \cdot 3$.

When adding or subtracting fractions with unlike denominators, you have two options. You can use Property 5 of fractions as in Example 1(C). Or you can use the **least common denominator** (LCD) method—rewrite both fractions so that they have the same denominator. For adding or subtracting *two* fractions, Property 5 is often more convenient. For *three or more* fractions, the LCD method is usually preferred.

EXAMPLE 2   The LCD Method of Adding or Subtracting Fractions

Evaluate the following as a single fraction.

$$\frac{2}{15} - \frac{5}{9} + \frac{4}{5}$$

SOLUTION

By factoring the denominators ($15 = 3 \cdot 5$, $9 = 3 \cdot 3$, and $5 = 5$), you can see that the least common denominator is $3 \cdot 3 \cdot 5 = 45$. Therefore, it follows that

$$\frac{2}{15} - \frac{5}{9} + \frac{4}{5} = \frac{2(3)}{15(3)} - \frac{5(5)}{9(5)} + \frac{4(9)}{5(9)} = \frac{6 - 25 + 36}{45} = \frac{17}{45}.$$

Equations

An **equation** is a statement of equality between two expressions. Thus, the statement $a + b = c + d$ means that the expressions $a + b$ and $c + d$ represent the same number.

PROPERTIES OF EQUALITY

Let a, b, and c be real numbers, variables, or algebraic expressions.

1. Reflexive: $a = a$
2. Symmetric: If $a = b$, then $b = a$.
3. Transitive: If $a = b$ and $b = c$, then $a = c$.
4. Substitution Principle: If $a = b$, then a can be replaced by b in any expression involving a.

Two important consequences of the Substitution Principle are as follows.

1. If $a = b$, then $a + c = b + c$.   *Add c to both sides*
2. If $a = b$, then $ac = bc$.   *Multiply both sides by c*

The first rule allows you to add the same number to both sides of an equation. The second allows you to multiply both sides of an equation by the same number. The converses of these two rules are the **Cancellation Laws** for addition and multiplication. Note that $c \neq 0$ in the second rule.

1. If $a + c = b + c$, then $a = b$.   *Subtract c from both sides*
2. If $ac = bc$ and $c \neq 0$, then $a = b$.   *Divide both sides by nonzero c*

Exponents

Repeated factors can be written in **exponential form.**

Repeated Factors	Exponential Form
$7 \cdot 7$	7^2
$(-4)(-4)(-4)$	$(-4)^3$
$(2x)(2x)(2x)(2x)$	$(2x)^4$

EXPONENTIAL NOTATION

Let a be a real number, a variable, or an algebraic expression, and let n be a positive integer. Then

$$a^n = \underbrace{a \cdot a \cdot a \cdots a}_{n \text{ factors}},$$

where n is the **exponent** and a is the **base.** The expression a^n is read as "a to the nth **power.**"

It is important to recognize the difference between expressions such as $(-2)^4$ and -2^4. In $(-2)^4$, the parentheses indicate that the exponent applies to the negative sign as well as to the 2, but in $-2^4 = -(2^4)$, the exponent applies only to the 2. Hence, $(-2)^4 = 16$, whereas $-2^4 = -16$.

When multiplying exponential expressions with the same base, you *add* exponents, $a^m \cdot a^n = a^{m+n}$. When dividing exponential expressions with the same base, you *subtract* exponents,

$$\frac{a^m}{a^n} = a^{m-n}, \qquad a \neq 0.$$

PROPERTIES OF EXPONENTS

Let a and b be real numbers, variables, or algebraic expressions, and let m and n be integers. (Assume all denominators and bases are nonzero.)

Property	*Example*
1. $a^m a^n = a^{m+n}$	$3^2 \cdot 3^4 = 3^{2+4} = 3^6$
2. $\dfrac{a^m}{a^n} = a^{m-n}$	$\dfrac{x^7}{x^4} = x^{7-4} = x^3$
3. $a^{-n} = \dfrac{1}{a^n} = \left(\dfrac{1}{a}\right)^n$	$y^{-4} = \dfrac{1}{y^4} = \left(\dfrac{1}{y}\right)^4$
4. $a^0 = 1, \quad a \neq 0$	$(x^2 + 1)^0 = 1$
5. $(ab)^m = a^m b^m$	$(5x)^3 = 5^3 x^3 = 125x^3$
6. $(a^m)^n = a^{mn}$	$(y^3)^{-4} = y^{3(-4)} = y^{-12} = \dfrac{1}{y^{12}}$
7. $\left(\dfrac{a}{b}\right)^m = \dfrac{a^m}{b^m}$	$\left(\dfrac{2}{x}\right)^3 = \dfrac{2^3}{x^3} = \dfrac{8}{x^3}$
8. $|a^2| = |a|^2 = a^2$	$|(-2)^2| = |-2|^2 = (-2)^2 = 4$

EXAMPLE 3   Using Properties of Exponents to Simplify

A. $(-3ab^4)(4ab^{-3}) = -12(a)(a)(b^4)(b^{-3}) = -12a^2 b$

B. $(2xy^2)^3 = 2^3(x)^3(y^2)^3 = 8x^3 y^6$

C. $3a(-4a^2)^0 = 3a(1) = 3a, \quad a \neq 0$

D. $\left(\dfrac{5x^3}{y}\right)^2 = \dfrac{5^2(x^3)^2}{y^2} = \dfrac{25x^6}{y^2}$

EXAMPLE 4   Rewriting with Positive Exponents

A. $x^{-1} = \dfrac{1}{x}$ *Property 3: $a^{-n} = \dfrac{1}{a^n}$*

B. $\dfrac{1}{3x^{-2}} = \dfrac{1(x^2)}{3} = \dfrac{x^2}{3}$ *-2 exponent does not apply to 3*

C. $\dfrac{12a^3 b^{-4}}{4a^{-2}b} = \dfrac{12a^3 \cdot a^2}{4b \cdot b^4} = \dfrac{3a^5}{b^5}$

D. $\left(\dfrac{3x^2}{y}\right)^{-2} = \dfrac{3^{-2}(x^2)^{-2}}{y^{-2}} = \dfrac{3^{-2}x^{-4}}{y^{-2}} = \dfrac{y^2}{3^2 x^4} = \dfrac{y^2}{9x^4}$

Rarely in algebra is there only one way to solve a problem. Don't be concerned if the steps you use to solve a problem are not exactly the same as the steps presented in this text. The important thing is to use steps that you understand *and*, of course, that are justified by the rules of algebra. For instance, you might prefer the following solution to Example 4(D).

$$\left(\frac{3x^2}{y}\right)^{-2} = \left(\frac{y}{3x^2}\right)^2 = \frac{y^2}{9x^4}$$

EXAMPLE 5   Using a Calculator to Raise a Number to a Power

Use a calculator to evaluate the following expressions. Round your answers to two decimal places.

	Expression	*Display*	*Rounded Answer*
A.	$13^4 + 5$	28566	28,566.00
B.	$3^{-2} + 4^{-1}$	.3611111111	0.36
C.	$\dfrac{3^5 + 1}{3^5 - 1}$	1.008264463	1.01

REMARK   In Example 5, note that the number of displayed digits depends on the particular type of calculator being used.

Scientific Notation

Exponents provide an efficient way of writing and computing with very large (or very small) numbers. For instance, a drop of water contains more than 33 billion billion molecules—that is, 33 followed by 18 zeros:

33,000,000,000,000,000,000.

It is convenient to write such numbers in **scientific notation.** This notation has the form $c \times 10^n$, where $1 \le c < 10$ and n is an integer. Thus, the number of molecules in a drop of water can be written in scientific notation as

$$3.3 \times 10,000,000,000,000,000,000 = 3.3 \times 10^{19}.$$

The *positive* exponent 19 indicates that the number is large (10 or more) and that the decimal point has been moved 19 places. A *negative* exponent in scientific notation indicates that the number is *small* (less than 1). For instance, the mass (in grams) of one electron is approximately

$$9.0 \times 10^{-28} = 0.0000000000000000000000000009 .$$

28 decimal places

EXAMPLE 6   Scientific Notation

A. $1.345 \times 10^2 = 134.5$ **B.** $9.36 \times 10^{-6} = 0.00000936$
C. $0.0000782 = 7.82 \times 10^{-5}$ **D.** $836,100,000.0 = 8.361 \times 10^8$

Most calculators automatically switch to scientific notation when they are showing large (or small) numbers that exceed the display range. Try multiplying $86,500,000 \times 6000$. If your calculator follows standard conventions, its display should be $\boxed{5.19 \quad 11}$ or $\boxed{5.19 \quad \text{E} \quad 11}$. This means that $c = 5.19$ and the exponent of 10 is $n = 11$, which implies that the number is 5.19×10^{11}.

EXAMPLE 7   Using Scientific Notation with a Calculator

Use a calculator to evaluate $65,000 \times 3,400,000,000$.

SOLUTION

Because $65,000 = 6.5 \times 10^4$ and $3,400,000,000 = 3.4 \times 10^9$, you can multiply the two numbers as follows:

$$65,000 \times 3,400,000,000 = (6.5 \times 10^4)(3.4 \times 10^9).$$

Display: $\boxed{2.21 \quad \text{E} \quad 14}$

The product of the two numbers is

$$(6.5 \times 10^4)(3.4 \times 10^9) = 2.21 \times 10^{14} = 221,000,000,000,000.$$

SECTION 2 · EXERCISES

In Exercises 1–6, identify the terms of the expression.

1. $7x + 4$

2. $-5 + 3x$

3. $x^2 - 4x + 8$

4. $3x^2 - 8x - 11$

5. $4x^3 + x - 5$

6. $3x^4 + 3x^3$

In Exercises 7–12, evaluate the expression for the given values of x. If not possible, state the reason.

Expression	Values	
7. $4x - 6$	(a) $x = -1$	(b) $x = 0$
8. $9 - 7x$	(a) $x = -3$	(b) $x = 3$
9. $x^2 - 3x + 4$	(a) $x = -2$	(b) $x = 2$
10. $-x^2 + 5x - 4$	(a) $x = -1$	(b) $x = 1$
11. $\dfrac{x + 1}{x - 1}$	(a) $x = 1$	(b) $x = -1$
12. $\dfrac{x}{x + 2}$	(a) $x = 2$	(b) $x = -2$

In Exercises 13–22, identify the rule(s) of algebra illustrated by the equation.

13. $x + 9 = 9 + x$

14. $(x + 3) - (x + 3) = 0$

15. $\dfrac{1}{h + 6}(h + 6) = 1, \quad h \neq -6$

16. $2(\tfrac{1}{2}) = 1$

17. $2(x + 3) = 2x + 6$

18. $(z - 2) + 0 = z - 2$

19. $1 \cdot (1 + x) = 1 + x$

20. $x + (y + 10) = (x + y) + 10$

21. $x(3y) = (x \cdot 3)y = (3x)y$

22. $\tfrac{1}{7}(7 \cdot 12) = (\tfrac{1}{7} \cdot 7)12 = 1 \cdot 12 = 12$

In Exercises 23–26, evaluate the expression. If not possible, state the reason.

23. $\dfrac{81 - (90 - 9)}{5}$

24. $10(23 - 30 + 7)$

25. $\dfrac{8 - 8}{-9 + (6 + 3)}$

26. $15 - \dfrac{3 - 3}{5}$

In Exercises 27–40, perform the indicated operations. (Write fractional answers in reduced form.)

27. $10 - 6 - 2$

28. $-3(5 - 2)$

29. $(4 - 7)(-2)$

30. $\dfrac{27 - 35}{4}$

31. $\frac{3}{16} + \frac{5}{16}$

32. $\frac{6}{7} - \frac{4}{7}$

33. $\frac{5}{8} - \frac{5}{12} + \frac{1}{6}$

34. $\frac{10}{11} + \frac{6}{33} - \frac{13}{66}$

35. $\frac{4}{5} \cdot \frac{1}{2} \cdot \frac{3}{4}$

36. $\frac{1}{3} \cdot \frac{5}{8} \cdot \frac{5}{16} \cdot \frac{3}{4}$

37. $\frac{2}{3} \div 8$

38. $\frac{11}{16} \div \frac{3}{4}$

39. $12 \div \frac{1}{4}$

40. $(\frac{3}{5} \div 3) - (6 \cdot \frac{4}{8})$

In Exercises 41–48, use a calculator to evaluate the expression. (Round the result to two decimal places.)

41. $-3 + \frac{3}{7}$

42. $3(-\frac{5}{12} + \frac{3}{8})$

43. $\dfrac{11.46 - 5.37}{3.91}$

44. $\dfrac{\frac{1}{5}(-8 - 9)}{-\frac{1}{3}}$

45. $5^{-1} + 2^{-3}$

46. $(\frac{3}{2})^{-2} - (\frac{3}{4})^3$

47. $\dfrac{7^4 + 32}{7^4 - 200}$

48. $\dfrac{1 - 3^{-5}}{0.5 + (0.3)^4}$

In Exercises 49–56, evaluate the expression.

49. $\dfrac{5^5}{5^2}$

50. $3 \cdot 3^3$

51. $(3^3)^2$

52. -3^2

53. $(2^3 \cdot 3^2)^2$

54. $(-\frac{3}{5})^3(\frac{5}{3})^2$

55. $\dfrac{4 \cdot 3^{-2}}{2^{-2} \cdot 3^{-1}}$

56. $(-2)^0$

In Exercises 57–60, evaluate the expression for the given value of x.

Expression	Value
57. $-3x^3$	2
58. $7x^{-2}$	4
59. $6x^0 - (6x)^0$	10
60. $5(-x)^3$	3

In Exercises 61–78, simplify the expression. (Use only positive exponents.)

61. $(-5z)^3$

62. $(3x)^2$

63. $6y^2(2y^4)^2$

64. $(-z)^3(3z^4)$

65. $\dfrac{3x^5}{x^3}$

66. $\dfrac{25y^8}{10y^4}$

67. $\dfrac{7x^2}{x^3}$

68. $\dfrac{r^4}{r^6}$

69. $\dfrac{12(x + y)^3}{9(x + y)}$

70. $\left(\dfrac{4}{y}\right)^3\left(\dfrac{3}{y}\right)^4$

71. $(x + 5)^0, \quad x \neq -5$

72. $(2x^5)^0, \quad x \neq 0$

73. $(-2x^2)^3(4x^3)^{-1}$

74. $(4y^{-2})(8y^4)$

75. $\left(\dfrac{x}{10}\right)^{-1}$

76. $\left(\dfrac{x^{-3}y^4}{5}\right)^{-3}$

77. $3^n \cdot 3^{2n}$

78. $\dfrac{x^2 \cdot x^n}{x^3 \cdot x^n}$

In Exercises 79–82, write the number in scientific notation.

79. Land area of earth: 57,500,000 square miles

80. Light year: 9,461,000,000,000,000 kilometers

81. Relative density of hydrogen: 0.0000899 gram per cm^3

82. One micron (millionth of a meter): 0.00003937 inch

In Exercises 83–86, write the number in decimal form.

83. U.S. daily Coca-Cola consumption: 5.24×10^8 servings

84. Interior temperature of the sun: 1.3×10^7 degrees Celsius

85. Charge of electron: 4.8×10^{-10} electrostatic units

86. Width of human hair: 9.0×10^{-4} meters

In Exercises 87 and 88, use a calculator to evaluate the expression. (Round the result to three decimal places.)

87. (a) $750\left(1 + \dfrac{0.11}{365}\right)^{800}$

(b) $\dfrac{67,000,000 + 93,000,000}{0.0052}$

88. (a) $(9.3 \times 10^6)^3(6.1 \times 10^{-4})$

(b) $\dfrac{(2.414 \times 10^4)^6}{(1.68 \times 10^5)^5}$

3   RADICALS AND RATIONAL EXPONENTS
....
Radicals and Properties of Radicals / Simplifying Radicals / Rationalizing
Denominators and Numerators / Rational Exponents / Radicals and
Calculators

Radicals and Properties of Radicals

You already know how to square a number—raise it to the second power by
using the number *twice* as a factor. For instance, 5 squared is $5^2 = 5 \cdot 5 = 25$.
Conversely, the **square root of a number** is one of its two equal factors. For
example, 5 is a square root of 25 because 5 is one of the two equal factors of
25. In a similar way, the **cube root** of a number is one of its three equal factors.
Consider the following examples.

Number	Equal Factors	Root
$16 = 4^2$	$4 \cdot 4$	4 (square root)
$-64 = (-4)^3$	$(-4)(-4)(-4)$	-4 (cube root)
$81 = 3^4$	$3 \cdot 3 \cdot 3 \cdot 3$	3 (fourth root)

DEFINITION OF *N*TH ROOT OF A NUMBER

Let a and b be real numbers, and let $n \geq 2$ be a positive integer. If

$$a = b^n,$$

then b is the **nth root of a.** If $n = 2$, then the root is a **square root.** If
$n = 3$, then the root is a **cube root.**

Some numbers have more than one *n*th root. For example, both 5 and -5
are square roots of 25. The **principal *n*th root** of a number is defined as
follows.

PRINCIPAL *N*TH ROOT OF A NUMBER

Let a be a real number that has at least one *n*th root. The **principal *n*th
root of a** is the *n*th root that has the same sign as a. It is denoted by a
radical symbol:

$$\sqrt[n]{a}. \qquad \text{\textit{Principal nth root}}$$

The positive integer n is the **index** of the radical, and the number a is the
radicand. If $n = 2$, we omit the index and write $\sqrt{a}$ rather than $\sqrt[2]{a}$.

EXAMPLE 1   Evaluating Expressions Involving Radicals

A. $\sqrt{49} = 7$ because $7^2 = 49$.

B. $-\sqrt{49} = -7$ because $-(\sqrt{49}) = -(7) = -7$.

C. $\sqrt[3]{\dfrac{125}{64}} = \dfrac{5}{4}$ because $\left(\dfrac{5}{4}\right)^3 = \dfrac{5^3}{4^3} = \dfrac{125}{64}$.

D. $\sqrt[5]{-32} = -2$ because $(-2)^5 = -32$.

E. $\sqrt[4]{-81}$ is not a real number because there is no real number that can be raised to the fourth power to produce -81.

Here are some generalizations about the nth roots of a real number.

1. If a is a positive real number and n is a positive *even* integer, then a has exactly two (real) nth roots. We denote these roots by $\sqrt[n]{a}$ and $-\sqrt[n]{a}$. See Example 1(A) and (B).
2. If a is any real number and n is an *odd* integer, then a has only one (real) nth root, which is denoted by $\sqrt[n]{a}$. See Example 1(C) and (D).
3. If a is a negative real number and n is an *even* integer, then a has no (real) nth root. See Example 1(E).
4. $\sqrt[n]{0} = 0$.

Integers such as 1, 4, 9, 16, 25, and 49 are called **perfect squares** because they have integer square roots. Similarly, integers such as 1, 8, 27, 64, and 125 are called **perfect cubes** because they have integer cube roots.

PROPERTIES OF RADICALS

Let a and b be real numbers, variables, or algebraic expressions such that the indicated roots are real numbers, and let m and n be positive integers.

Property	*Example*
1. $\sqrt[n]{a^m} = \left(\sqrt[n]{a}\right)^m$	$\sqrt[3]{8^2} = \left(\sqrt[3]{8}\right)^2 = (2)^2 = 4$
2. $\sqrt[n]{a} \cdot \sqrt[n]{b} = \sqrt[n]{ab}$	$\sqrt{3} \cdot \sqrt{12} = \sqrt{3 \cdot 12} = \sqrt{36} = 6$
3. $\dfrac{\sqrt[n]{a}}{\sqrt[n]{b}} = \sqrt[n]{\dfrac{a}{b}}, \ b \neq 0$	$\dfrac{\sqrt[4]{27}}{\sqrt[4]{9}} = \sqrt[4]{\dfrac{27}{9}} = \sqrt[4]{3}$
4. $\sqrt[m]{\sqrt[n]{a}} = \sqrt[mn]{a}$	$\sqrt[3]{\sqrt{10}} = \sqrt[6]{10}$
5. $\left(\sqrt[n]{a}\right)^n = a$	$\left(\sqrt{3}\right)^2 = 3$
6. For n even, $\sqrt[n]{a^n} = \lvert a \rvert$.	$\sqrt{(-12)^2} = \lvert -12 \rvert = 12$
For n odd, $\sqrt[n]{a^n} = a$.	$\sqrt[3]{(-12)^3} = -12$

REMARK   A common special case of Property 6 is $\sqrt{a^2} = \lvert a \rvert$. For instance, $\sqrt{(-2)^2} = \lvert -2 \rvert = 2$.

Simplifying Radicals

An expression involving radicals is in **simplest form** when the following conditions are satisfied.

1. All possible factors have been removed from the radical.
2. All fractions have radical-free denominators (accomplished by a process called *rationalizing the denominator*).
3. The index of the radical is reduced.

To simplify a radical, we factor the radicand into factors whose exponents are multiples of the index. The roots of these factors are written outside the radical, and the "leftover" factors make up the new radicand.

EXAMPLE 2   **Simplifying Even Roots**

A. $\sqrt[4]{48} = \sqrt[4]{16 \cdot 3} = \sqrt[4]{2^4 \cdot 3} = \sqrt[4]{2^4} \cdot \sqrt[4]{3} = 2\sqrt[4]{3}$

B. $\sqrt{75x^3} = \sqrt{25x^2 \cdot 3x}$ *Find largest square factor*

$= \sqrt{(5x)^2 \cdot 3x}$

$= 5|x|\sqrt{3x}, \quad x \geq 0$ *Find root of perfect square*

C. $\sqrt[4]{(5x)^4} = |5x| = 5|x|$

EXAMPLE 3   **Simplifying Odd Roots**

A. $\sqrt[3]{24} = \sqrt[3]{8 \cdot 3} = \sqrt[3]{2^3 \cdot 3} = 2\sqrt[3]{3}$

B. $\sqrt[3]{24a^4} = \sqrt[3]{8a^3 \cdot 3a}$ *Find largest cube factor*

$= \sqrt[3]{(2a)^3 \cdot 3a}$

$= 2a\sqrt[3]{3a}$ *Find root of perfect cube*

C. $\sqrt[3]{-40x^6} = \sqrt[3]{(-8x^6) \cdot 5} = \sqrt[3]{(-2x^2)^3 \cdot 5} = -2x^2\sqrt[3]{5}$

Rationalizing Denominators and Numerators

To rationalize a denominator or numerator of the form $a - b\sqrt{m}$, or $a + b\sqrt{m}$, multiply both numerator and denominator by a **conjugate** factor: $a + b\sqrt{m}$ and $a - b\sqrt{m}$ are conjugates of each other. If $a = 0$, then the rationalizing factor for $\sqrt{m}$ is itself, $\sqrt{m}$.

EXAMPLE 4   **Rationalizing Single-Term Denominators**

A. $\dfrac{5}{2\sqrt{3}} = \dfrac{5}{2\sqrt{3}} \cdot \dfrac{\sqrt{3}}{\sqrt{3}} = \dfrac{5\sqrt{3}}{2(3)} = \dfrac{5\sqrt{3}}{6}$

B. $\dfrac{2}{\sqrt[3]{5}} = \dfrac{2}{\sqrt[3]{5}} \cdot \dfrac{\sqrt[3]{5^2}}{\sqrt[3]{5^2}}$ *Multiply numerator and*
denominator by $\sqrt[3]{5^2}$ to produce
a perfect cube radicand.

$\phantom{\dfrac{2}{\sqrt[3]{5}}} = \dfrac{2\sqrt[3]{(5)^2}}{\sqrt[3]{5^3}} = \dfrac{2\sqrt[3]{25}}{5}$

EXAMPLE 5   **Rationalizing a Denominator with Two Terms**

$\dfrac{2}{3 + \sqrt{7}} = \dfrac{2}{3 + \sqrt{7}} \cdot \dfrac{3 - \sqrt{7}}{3 - \sqrt{7}}$ *Multiply numerator and*
denominator by conjugate.

$ = \dfrac{2(3 - \sqrt{7})}{(3)^2 - (\sqrt{7})^2}$

$ = \dfrac{2(3 - \sqrt{7})}{9 - 7}$

$ = \dfrac{2(3 - \sqrt{7})}{2}$ *Cancel like factors.*

$ = 3 - \sqrt{7}$

In some applications, it helps to rationalize the numerator of a fraction.

EXAMPLE 6   **Rationalizing the Numerator**

$\dfrac{\sqrt{5} - \sqrt{7}}{2} = \dfrac{\sqrt{5} - \sqrt{7}}{2} \cdot \dfrac{\sqrt{5} + \sqrt{7}}{\sqrt{5} + \sqrt{7}}$ *Multiply numerator and*
denominator by conjugate.

$ = \dfrac{5 - 7}{2(\sqrt{5} + \sqrt{7})}$

$ = \dfrac{-2}{2(\sqrt{5} + \sqrt{7})}$

$ = \dfrac{-1}{\sqrt{5} + \sqrt{7}}$

Do not confuse an expression such as $\sqrt{5} + \sqrt{7}$ with the expression $\sqrt{5 + 7}$. In general, $\sqrt{x + y}$ does not equal $\sqrt{x} + \sqrt{y}$. Similarly, $\sqrt{x^2 + y^2}$ does not equal $x + y$. For instance, $\sqrt{3^2 + 4^2} \neq 3 + 4$.

Rational Exponents

In the following definition, radicals are used to define **rational exponents.**

DEFINITION OF RATIONAL EXPONENTS

If a is a real number and n is a positive integer such that the principal nth root of a exists, then we define $a^{1/n}$ to be

$$a^{1/n} = \sqrt[n]{a}.$$

Moreover, if m is a positive integer that has no common factor with n, then

$$a^{m/n} = (a^{1/n})^m = (\sqrt[n]{a})^m \quad \text{and} \quad a^{m/n} = (a^m)^{1/n} = \sqrt[n]{a^m}.$$

The numerator of a rational exponent denotes the *power* to which the base is raised, and the denominator denotes the *index* or the *root* to be taken, as shown below.

$$\overset{\displaystyle \text{Power}}{\underset{\displaystyle \text{Index}}{b^{m/n}}} = (\sqrt[n]{b})^m = \sqrt[n]{b^m}$$

EXAMPLE 7   Changing from Radical to Exponential Form

A. $\sqrt{3} = 3^{1/2}$

B. $\sqrt{(3xy)^5} = \sqrt[2]{(3xy)^5} = (3xy)^{(5/2)}$

C. $2x\sqrt[4]{x^3} = (2x)(x^{3/4}) = 2x^{1+(3/4)} = 2x^{7/4}$

EXAMPLE 8   Changing from Exponential to Radical Form

A. $(x^2 + y^2)^{3/2} = (\sqrt{x^2 + y^2})^3 = \sqrt{(x^2 + y^2)^3}$

B. $2y^{3/4}z^{1/4} = 2(y^3z)^{1/4} = 2\sqrt[4]{y^3z}$

C. $a^{-3/2} = \dfrac{1}{a^{3/2}} = \dfrac{1}{\sqrt{a^3}}$

D. $x^{0.2} = x^{1/5} = \sqrt[5]{x}$

REMARK Rational exponents can be tricky, and you must remember that the expression $b^{m/n}$ is not defined unless $\sqrt[n]{b}$ is a real number. For instance, $(-8)^{1/2}$ is not defined because $\sqrt{-8}$ is not a real number, whereas $(-8)^{1/3}$ is defined because $\sqrt[3]{-8} = -2$.

Rational exponents are particularly useful for evaluating roots of numbers on a calculator, for reducing the index of a radical, and for simplifying expressions encountered in calculus.

EXAMPLE 9   **Simplifying with Rational Exponents**

A. $(27)^{2/6} = (27)^{1/3} = \sqrt[3]{27} = 3$

B. $(-32)^{-4/5} = \left(\sqrt[5]{(-32)}\right)^{-4} = (-2)^{-4} = \dfrac{1}{(-2)^4} = \dfrac{1}{16}$

C. $(-5x^{5/3})(3x^{-3/4}) = -15x^{(5/3)-(3/4)} = -15x^{11/12}, \quad x \neq 0$

EXAMPLE 10   **Reducing the Index of a Radical**

A. $\sqrt[9]{a^3} = a^{3/9}$ *Rewrite with rational exponents*

$\qquad\quad = a^{1/3}$ *Reduce exponent*

$\qquad\quad = \sqrt[3]{a}$ *Rewrite in radical form*

B. $\sqrt[3]{\sqrt{125}} = \sqrt[6]{125} = \sqrt[6]{(5)^3} = 5^{3/6} = 5^{1/2} = \sqrt{5}$

EXAMPLE 11   **Simplifying Algebraic Expressions Involving Exponents**

A. $(2x - 1)^{4/3}(2x - 1)^{-1/3} = (2x - 1)^{(4/3)-(1/3)}$ *Add exponents*

$\qquad\qquad\qquad\qquad\quad = (2x - 1)^1$

$\qquad\qquad\qquad\qquad\quad = 2x - 1, \quad x \neq \dfrac{1}{2}$

B. $\dfrac{x - 1}{(x - 1)^{-1/2}} = (x - 1)^{1+(1/2)}$ *Subtract exponents*

$\qquad\qquad\quad = (x - 1)^{3/2}$

Radical expressions can be combined (added or subtracted) if they are **like radicals**—that is, if they have the same index and radicand. For instance, $2\sqrt{3x}$, $-\sqrt{3x}$, and $\sqrt{3x}/2$ are like radicals but $\sqrt[3]{3x}$ and $2\sqrt{3x}$ are not like radicals. To determine whether two radicals are like radicals, you should first simplify each radical.

EXAMPLE 12   Combining Radicals

A. $2\sqrt{48} - 3\sqrt{27} = 2\sqrt{16 \cdot 3} - 3\sqrt{9 \cdot 3}$ *Find square factors*

$\qquad\qquad\qquad\quad = 8\sqrt{3} - 9\sqrt{3}$ *Find square roots*

$\qquad\qquad\qquad\quad = (8 - 9)\sqrt{3}$ *Distributive Property*

$\qquad\qquad\qquad\quad = -\sqrt{3}$

B. $\sqrt[3]{16x} - \sqrt[3]{54x^4} = \sqrt[3]{8 \cdot 2x} - \sqrt[3]{27 \cdot x^3 \cdot 2x}$

$\qquad\qquad\qquad\quad = 2\sqrt[3]{2x} - 3x\sqrt[3]{2x}$

$\qquad\qquad\qquad\quad = (2 - 3x)\sqrt[3]{2x}$

Radicals and Calculators

There are two basic methods of evaluating radicals on most calculators. For square roots, use the *square root key*. For other roots, first convert the radical to exponential form and then use the *exponential key*.

EXAMPLE 13   Evaluating Radicals with a Calculator

A. $\dfrac{1 + \sqrt{5}}{2} = 1.618033989 \approx 1.618$

B. $\sqrt[3]{56} = 56^{1/3} = 3.825862366 \approx 3.826$

C. $\sqrt[3]{-4} = \sqrt[3]{(-1)(4)} = \sqrt[3]{-1}\sqrt[3]{4} = -\sqrt[3]{4} \approx -1.587$

D. $(1.2)^{-1/6} \approx 0.970$

SECTION 3 · EXERCISES

In Exercises 1–10, fill in the missing description.

In Exercises 11–30, evaluate the expression. (Do each exercise with and without a calculator.)

Radical Form	*Rational Exponent Form*
1. $\sqrt{9} = 3$	
2. $\sqrt[3]{64} = 4$	
3.	$196^{1/2} = 14$
4.	$-(144^{1/2}) = -12$
5. $\sqrt[3]{-216} = -6$	
6. $\sqrt[3]{614.125} = 8.5$	
7.	$27^{2/3} = 9$
8.	$(-243)^{1/5} = -3$
9. $\sqrt[4]{81^3} = 27$	
10. $\left(\sqrt[4]{81}\right)^3 = 27$	

11. $\sqrt{9}$ **12.** $\sqrt{49}$

13. $\sqrt[3]{8}$ **14.** $\sqrt[3]{64}$

15. $\sqrt{36}$ **16.** $\sqrt[3]{\frac{27}{8}}$

17. $-\sqrt[3]{-27}$ **18.** $\sqrt[3]{0}$

19. $\dfrac{4}{\sqrt{64}}$ **20.** $\dfrac{\sqrt[4]{81}}{3}$

21. $\left(\sqrt[3]{-125}\right)^3$ **22.** $\sqrt[4]{562^4}$

23. $16^{1/2}$ **24.** $27^{1/3}$

25. $32^{-3/5}$ **26.** $100^{-3/2}$

27. $\left(\frac{16}{81}\right)^{-3/4}$ **28.** $\left(\frac{9}{4}\right)^{-1/2}$

29. $\left(-\frac{1}{64}\right)^{-1/3}$ **30.** $\left(-\frac{125}{27}\right)^{-1/3}$

In Exercises 31–40, simplify by removing all possible factors from the radical.

31. $\sqrt{8}$

32. $\sqrt[3]{\frac{16}{27}}$

33. $\sqrt{9 \times 10^{-4}}$

34. $\sqrt{4.5 \times 10^9}$

35. $\sqrt{72x^3}$

36. $\sqrt{54xy^4}$

37. $\sqrt[3]{16x^5}$

38. $\sqrt[4]{(3x^2)^4}$

39. $\sqrt{75x^2y^{-4}}$

40. $\sqrt[5]{96x^5}$

In Exercises 41–48, rationalize the denominator. Then, simplify the result.

41. $\dfrac{1}{\sqrt{3}}$

42. $\dfrac{5}{\sqrt{10}}$

43. $\dfrac{8}{\sqrt[3]{2}}$

44. $\dfrac{5}{\sqrt[3]{(5x)^2}}$

45. $\dfrac{2x}{5 - \sqrt{3}}$

46. $\dfrac{5}{\sqrt{14} - 2}$

47. $\dfrac{3}{\sqrt{5} + \sqrt{6}}$

48. $\dfrac{5}{2\sqrt{10} - 5}$

In Exercises 49–54, rationalize the numerator. Then, simplify the result.

49. $\dfrac{\sqrt{8}}{2}$

50. $\dfrac{\sqrt{2}}{3}$

51. $\dfrac{\sqrt{5} + \sqrt{3}}{3}$

52. $\dfrac{\sqrt{3} - \sqrt{2}}{2}$

53. $\dfrac{\sqrt{7} - 3}{4}$

54. $\dfrac{2\sqrt{3} + \sqrt{3}}{3}$

In Exercises 55–58, reduce the index of the radical.

55. $\sqrt[4]{3^2}$

56. $\sqrt[6]{x^3}$

57. $\sqrt[6]{(x + 1)^4}$

58. $\sqrt[4]{(3x^2)^4}$

In Exercises 59–62, write as a single radical. Then, simplify the result.

59. $\sqrt{\sqrt{32}}$

60. $\sqrt{\sqrt{243(x + 1)}}$

61. $\sqrt{\sqrt[4]{2x}}$

62. $\sqrt{\sqrt[3]{10a^7b}}$

In Exercises 63–68, simplify the expression.

63. $5\sqrt{x} - 3\sqrt{x}$

64. $3\sqrt{x + 1} + 10\sqrt{x + 1}$

65. $2\sqrt{50} + 12\sqrt{8}$

66. $4\sqrt{27} - \sqrt{75}$

67. $-2\sqrt{9y} + 10\sqrt{y}$

68. $7\sqrt{80x} - 2\sqrt{125x}$

In Exercises 69–78, perform the indicated operations and simplify. Assume that all variables are positive real numbers.

69. $\dfrac{x^{-3} \cdot x^{1/2}}{x^{3/2} \cdot x^{-1}}$

70. $\dfrac{5^{-1/2} \cdot 5x^{5/2}}{(5x)^{3/2}}$

71. $(3x^{-1/3}y^{3/4})^2$

72. $(-2u^{3/5}v^{-1/5})^3$

73. $\dfrac{18y^{4/3}z^{-1/3}}{24y^{-2/3}z}$

74. $\dfrac{a^{3/4} \cdot a^{1/2}}{a^{5/2}}$

75. $\left(\dfrac{x^{1/4}}{x^{1/6}}\right)^3$

76. $\left(\dfrac{3m^{1/6}n^{1/3}}{4n^{-2/3}}\right)^2$

77. $(c^{3/2})^{1/3}$

78. $(k^{-1/3})^{3/2}$

In Exercises 79–84, use a calculator to approximate the number. (Round the result to three decimal places.)

79. $\sqrt{57}$

80. $\sqrt[3]{45^2}$

81. $\sqrt[6]{125}$

82. $(15.25)^{-1.4}$

83. $\sqrt{75 + 3\sqrt{8}}$

84. $(2.65 \times 10^{-4})^{1/3}$

In Exercises 85–90, fill in the blank with $<$, $=$, or $>$.

85. $\sqrt{5} + \sqrt{3}$ ___ $\sqrt{5 + 3}$

86. $\sqrt{3} - \sqrt{2}$ ___ $\sqrt{3 - 2}$

87. 5 ___ $\sqrt{3^2 + 2^2}$

88. 5 ___ $\sqrt{3^2 + 4^2}$

89. $\sqrt{3} \cdot \sqrt[4]{3}$ ___ $\sqrt[8]{3}$

90. $\sqrt{\dfrac{3}{11}}$ ___ $\dfrac{\sqrt{3}}{\sqrt{11}}$

91. *Calculator Experiment*   Enter any positive real number in your calculator and repeatedly take the square root. What real number does the display appear to be approaching?

92. Square the real number $2/\sqrt{5}$ and note that the radical is eliminated from the denominator. Is this equivalent to rationalizing the denominator? Why or why not?

4   POLYNOMIALS AND SPECIAL PRODUCTS

Polynomials / Operations with Polynomials / Special Products

Polynomials

The most common kind of algebraic expression is the **polynomial.** Some examples are

$$2x + 5, \quad 3x^4 - 7x^2 + 2x + 4, \quad \text{and} \quad 5x^2y^2 - xy + 3.$$

The first two are *polynomials in x* and the third one is a *polynomial in x and y*. The terms of a polynomial in x have the form ax^k, where a is called the **coefficient** and k the **degree** of the term. For instance, the third-degree polynomial

$$2x^3 - 5x^2 + 1 = 2x^3 + (-5)x^2 + (0)x + 1$$

has coefficients 2, -5, 0, and 1.

DEFINITION OF A POLYNOMIAL IN X

REMARK Polynomials with one, two, and three terms are called **monomials, binomials,** and **trinomials,** respectively.

Let $a_0, a_1, a_2, \ldots, a_n$ be *real numbers*, and let n be a *nonnegative integer*. A **polynomial in x** is an expression of the form

$$a_n x^n + a_{n-1} x^{n-1} + \cdots + a_1 x + a_0$$

where $a_n \neq 0$. The polynomial is of **degree n**, a_n is the **leading coefficient,** and a_0 is the **constant term.**

In **standard form,** a polynomial is written with descending powers of x.

EXAMPLE 1   Writing Polynomials in Standard Form

Polynomial	Standard Form	Degree
A. $4x^2 - 5x^7 - 2 + 3x$	$-5x^7 + 4x^2 + 3x - 2$	7
B. $4 - 9x^2$	$-9x^2 + 4$	2
C. 8	$8 \quad (8 = 8x^0)$	0

A polynomial that has all zero coefficients is called the **zero polynomial,** denoted by 0. We do not assign a degree to the zero polynomial. Expressions such as $\sqrt{x^2 - 3x}$ and $x^2 + 5x^{-1}$ are not polynomials.

For polynomials in more than one variable, the degree of a *term* is the sum of the exponents of the variables in the term. The degree of the *polynomial* is the highest degree of its terms. For instance, the polynomial $5x^3y - x^2y^2 + 2xy - 5$ has two terms of degree 4, one term of degree 2, and one term of degree 0. The degree of the polynomial is 4.

Operations with Polynomials

You can **add** and **subtract** polynomials in much the same way you add and subtract real numbers. Simply add or subtract the *like terms* (terms having the same variables to the same powers) by adding their coefficients. For instance, $-3xy^2$ and $5xy^2$ are like terms and their sum is

$$-3xy^2 + 5xy^2 = (-3 + 5)xy^2 = 2xy^2.$$

EXAMPLE 2 **Sums and Differences of Polynomials**

A. $(5x^3 - 7x^2 - 3) + (x^3 + 2x^2 - x + 8)$

$\qquad = (5x^3 + x^3) + (2x^2 - 7x^2) - x + (8 - 3)$ *Group like terms*

$\qquad = 6x^3 - 5x^2 - x + 5$ *Combine like terms*

B. $(7x^4 - x^2 - 4x + 2) - (3x^4 - 4x^2 + 3x)$

$\qquad = 7x^4 - x^2 - 4x + 2 - 3x^4 + 4x^2 - 3x$

$\qquad = (7x^4 - 3x^4) + (4x^2 - x^2) + (-3x - 4x) + 2$ *Group like terms*

$\qquad = 4x^4 + 3x^2 - 7x + 2$ *Combine like terms*

REMARK A common mistake is to fail to change the sign of *each* term inside parentheses preceded by a negative sign. For instance, note that

$$-(3x^4 - 4x^2 + 3x) = -3x^4 + 4x^2 - 3x \quad \text{and}$$
$$-(3x^4 - 4x^2 + 3x) \quad \text{does not equal} \quad -3x^4 - 4x^2 + 3x.$$

To find the **product** of two polynomials, use the left and right Distributive Properties. For example, if you treat $(5x + 7)$ as a single quantity, you can multiply $(3x - 2)$ by $(5x + 7)$ as follows.

$$(3x - 2)(5x + 7) = 3x(5x + 7) - 2(5x + 7)$$
$$= (3x)(5x) + (3x)(7) - (2)(5x) - (2)(7)$$
$$= 15x^2 + 21x - 10x - 14$$

Product of Product of Product of Product of
First terms Outer terms Inner terms Last terms

$$= 15x^2 + 11x - 14$$

Note in this **FOIL method** that for binomials the outer (O) and inner (I) terms are alike and can be combined into one term.

When multiplying two polynomials, be sure to multiply *each* term of one polynomial by *each* term of the other. The vertical pattern shown in Example 3 is a convenient way to multiply two polynomials.

EXAMPLE 3 Using a Vertical Arrangement to Multiply
Polynomials

Multiply $(x^2 - 2x + 2)$ by $(x^2 + 2x + 2)$.

SOLUTION

$$
\begin{array}{ll}
x^2 - 2x + 2 & \textit{Standard form} \\
x^2 + 2x + 2 & \textit{Standard form} \\
\hline
x^4 - 2x^3 + 2x^2 & \longleftarrow x^2(x^2 - 2x + 2) \\
\quad\quad 2x^3 - 4x^2 + 4x & \longleftarrow 2x(x^2 - 2x + 2) \\
\quad\quad\quad\quad 2x^2 - 4x + 4 & \longleftarrow 2(x^2 - 2x + 2) \\
\hline
x^4 + 0x^3 + 0x^2 - 0x + 4 = x^4 + 4 &
\end{array}
$$

Thus,

$$(x^2 - 2x + 2)(x^2 + 2x + 2) = x^4 + 4.$$

Special Products

SPECIAL PRODUCTS

Let u and v be real numbers, variables, or algebraic expressions.

Special Product	*Example*
Sum and Difference of Two Terms $(u + v)(u - v) = u^2 - v^2$	$(x + 4)(x - 4) = x^2 - 4^2$ $ = x^2 - 16$
Square of Binomial $(u + v)^2 = u^2 + 2uv + v^2$	$(x + 3)^2 = x^2 + 2(x)(3) + 3^2$ $ = x^2 + 6x + 9$
$(u - v)^2 = u^2 - 2uv + v^2$	$(3x - 2)^2$ $ = (3x)^2 - 2(3x)(2) + 2^2$ $ = 9x^2 - 12x + 4$
Cube of a Binomial $(u + v)^3 = u^3 + 3u^2v + 3uv^2 + v^3$	$(x + 2)^3$ $ = x^3 + 3x^2(2) + 3x(2^2) + 2^3$ $ = x^3 + 6x^2 + 12x + 8$
$(u - v)^3 = u^3 - 3u^2v + 3uv^2 - v^3$	$(x - 1)^3$ $ = x^3 - 3x^2(1) + 3x(1^2) - 1^3$ $ = x^3 - 3x^2 + 3x - 1$

EXAMPLE 4 Sum and Difference of Two Terms

Find the product of $(5x + 9)$ and $(5x - 9)$.

SOLUTION

The product of a sum and a difference of the *same* two terms has no middle term and it takes the form $(u + v)(u - v) = u^2 - v^2$.

$$(5x + 9)(5x - 9) = (5x)^2 - 9^2 = 25x^2 - 81$$

EXAMPLE 5 Square and Cube of a Binomial

A. $(6x - 5)^2 = (6x)^2 - 2(6x)(5) + 5^2$ *Square of a binomial*
$$= 36x^2 - 60x + 25$$

B. $(3x + 2)^3 = (3x)^3 + 3(3x)^2(2) + 3(3x)(2)^2 + 2^3$ *Cube of a binomial*
$$= 27x^3 + 54x^2 + 36x + 8$$

Occasionally the formulas for special products can be extended to cover products of two trinomials, as demonstrated in the following example.

EXAMPLE 6 The Product of Two Trinomials

$$(x + y - 2)(x + y + 2)$$
$$= [(x + y) - 2][(x + y) + 2] \quad \textit{Group } (x + y)$$
$$= (x + y)^2 - 2^2 \quad \textit{Sum and difference of terms}$$
$$= x^2 + 2xy + y^2 - 4$$

SECTION 4 · EXERCISES

In Exercises 1–6, find the degree and leading coefficient of the polynomial.

1. $2x^2 - x + 1$ **2.** $-3x^4 + 2x^2 - 5$

3. $x^5 - 1$ **4.** 3

5. $4x^5 + 6x^4 - x - 1$ **6.** $2x$

In Exercises 7–12, determine whether the expression is a polynomial. If it is, write the polynomial in standard form.

7. $2x - 3x^3 + 8$ **8.** $2x^3 + x - 3x^{-1}$

9. $\dfrac{3x + 4}{x}$ **10.** $\dfrac{x^2 + 2x - 3}{2}$

11. $y^2 - y^4 + y^3$ **12.** $\sqrt{y^2 - y^4}$

In Exercises 13–26, perform the indicated operations. Write the resulting polynomial in standard form.

13. $(6x + 5) - (8x + 15)$

14. $(2x^2 + 1) - (x^2 - 2x + 1)$

15. $-(x^3 - 2) + (4x^3 - 2x)$

16. $-(5x^2 - 1) - (-3x^2 + 5)$

17. $(15x^2 - 6) - (-8x^3 - 14x^2 - 17)$

18. $(15x^4 - 18x - 19) - (13x^4 - 5x + 15)$

19. $5z - [3z - (10z + 8)]$

20. $(y^3 + 1) - [(y^2 + 1) + (3y - 7)]$

21. $3x(x^2 - 2x + 1)$ **22.** $y^2(4y^2 + 2y - 3)$

23. $-5z(3z - 1)$ **24.** $-4x(3 - x^3)$

25. $(-2x)(-3x)(5x + 2)$ **26.** $(1 - x^3)(4x)$

In Exercises 27–60, find the product. Write the resulting polynomial in standard form.

27. $(x + 3)(x + 4)$ **28.** $(x - 5)(x + 10)$

29. $(3x - 5)(2x + 1)$ **30.** $(7x - 2)(4x - 3)$

31. $(x + 6)^2$ **32.** $(3x - 2)^2$

33. $(2x - 5y)^2$ **34.** $(5 - 8x)^2$

35. $[(x - 3) + y]^2$ **36.** $[(x + 1) - y]^2$

37. $(x + 10)(x - 10)$ **38.** $(2x + 3)(2x - 3)$

39. $(x + 2y)(x - 2y)$ **40.** $(2x + 3y)(2x - 3y)$

41. $(m - 3 + n)(m - 3 - n)$

42. $(x + y + 1)(x + y - 1)$

43. $(2r^2 - 5)(2r^2 + 5)$ **44.** $(3a^3 - 4b^2)(3a^3 + 4b^2)$

45. $(x + 1)^3$ **46.** $(x - 2)^3$

47. $(2x - y)^3$ **48.** $(3x + 2y)^3$

49. $\left(\sqrt{x} + \sqrt{y}\right)\left(\sqrt{x} - \sqrt{y}\right)$

50. $\left(5 + \sqrt{x}\right)\left(5 - \sqrt{x}\right)$

51. $(4x^3 - 3)^2$

52. $(8x + 3)^2$

53. $(x^2 + 9)(x^2 - x - 4)$

54. $(x - 2)(x^2 + 2x + 4)$

55. $(x^2 - x + 1)(x^2 + x + 1)$

56. $(x^2 + 3x - 2)(x^2 - 3x - 2)$

57. $5x(x + 1) - 3x(x + 1)$

58. $(2x - 1)(x + 3) + 3(x + 3)$

59. $\left(x + \sqrt{5}\right)\left(x - \sqrt{5}\right)(x + 4)$

60. $(x + y)(x - y)(x^2 + y^2)$

61. Determine the degree of the product of two polynomials of degrees m and n.

62. Determine the degree of the sum of two polynomials of degrees m and n if $m < n$.

5   FACTORING

Introduction / Factoring Special Polynomial Forms / Trinomials with Binomial Factors / Factoring by Grouping

Introduction

The process of writing a polynomial as a product is called **factoring.** It is an important tool for solving equations and for reducing fractional expressions.

   Unless noted otherwise, we will limit our discussion of factoring to polynomials whose factors have integer coefficients. If a polynomial cannot be factored using integer coefficients, then it is called **prime** or **irreducible over the integers.** For instance, the polynomial $x^2 - 3$ is irreducible over the integers. [Over the *real numbers,* this polynomial can be factored as $x^2 - 3 = (x + \sqrt{3})(x - \sqrt{3})$.]

   A polynomial is said to be **completely factored** when each of its factors is prime. For instance,

$$x^3 - x^2 + 4x - 4 = (x - 1)(x^2 + 4)$$

is completely factored, but

$$x^3 - x^2 - 4x + 4 = (x - 1)(x^2 - 4)$$

is not completely factored. Its complete factorization is

$$(x - 1)(x + 2)(x - 2).$$

Some polynomials can be written as the product of a monomial and another polynomial. The technique used is the Distributive Property, $a(b + c) = ab + ac$, in the *reverse* direction:

$$ab + ac = a(b + c).$$ *a is common factor*

EXAMPLE 1 **Removing Common Factors**

A. $6x^3 - 4x = 2x(3x^2) - 2x(2)$ *2x is common factor*
$= 2x(3x^2 - 2)$

B. $(x - 2)(2x) + (x - 2)(3) = (x - 2)(2x + 3)$ *x − 2 is common factor*

Factoring Special Polynomial Forms

FACTORING SPECIAL POLYNOMIAL FORMS

Factored Form	*Example*
Difference of Two Squares	
$u^2 - v^2 = (u + v)(u - v)$	$9x^2 - 4 = (3x)^2 - 2^2$
	$= (3x + 2)(3x - 2)$
Perfect Square Trinomial	
$u^2 + 2uv + v^2 = (u + v)^2$	$x^2 + 6x + 9$
	$= x^2 + 2(x)(3) + 3^2$
	$= (x + 3)^2$
$u^2 - 2uv + v^2 = (u - v)^2$	$x^2 - 6x + 9$
	$= x^2 - 2(x)(3) + 3^2$
	$= (x - 3)^2$
Sum or Difference of Two Cubes	
$u^3 + v^3 = (u + v)(u^2 - uv + v^2)$	$x^3 + 8 = x^3 + 2^3$
	$= (x + 2)(x^2 - 2x + 4)$
$u^3 - v^3 = (u - v)(u^2 + uv + v^2)$	$27x^3 - 1$
	$= (3x)^3 - 1^3$
	$= (3x - 1)(9x^2 + 3x + 1)$

One of the easiest special polynomial forms to factor is the difference of two squares. Think of the form as follows:

$$u^2 - v^2 = (u + v)(u - v).$$

Difference   Opposite signs

To recognize perfect square terms, look for coefficients that are squares of integers and variables raised to *even powers*.

REMARK In Example 2, note that the first step in factoring a polynomial is to check for common factors. Once the common factor has been removed, it is often possible to recognize patterns that were not immediately obvious.

EXAMPLE 2   **Removing a Common Factor First**

$$3 - 12x^2 = 3(1 - 4x^2) \qquad \text{\textit{Common factor}}$$
$$= 3[1^2 - (2x)^2] \qquad \text{\textit{Difference of squares}}$$
$$= 3(1 + 2x)(1 - 2x)$$

EXAMPLE 3   **Factoring the Difference of Two Squares**

A. $(x + 2)^2 - y^2 = [(x + 2) + y][(x + 2) - y] \qquad \text{\textit{Difference of two squares}}$
$$= (x + 2 + y)(x + 2 - y)$$
$$= (x + y + 2)(x - y + 2)$$
B. $16x^4 - 81 = (4x^2)^2 - 9^2$
$$= (4x^2 + 9)(4x^2 - 9) \qquad \text{\textit{Difference of two squares}}$$
$$= (4x^2 + 9)[(2x)^2 - 3^2]$$
$$= (4x^2 + 9)(2x + 3)(2x - 3) \qquad \text{\textit{Difference of two squares}}$$

A perfect square trinomial is the square of a binomial, and it has the following form:

$$u^2 + 2uv + v^2 = (u + v)^2 \quad \text{or} \quad u^2 - 2uv + v^2 = (u - v)^2.$$

Same sign   Same sign

Note that the first and last terms are squares and the middle term is twice the product of u and v.

EXAMPLE 4   **Factoring Perfect Square Trinomials**

A. $16x^2 + 8x + 1 = (4x)^2 + 2(4x)(1) + 1^2$
$$= (4x + 1)^2$$
B. $x^2 - 10x + 25 = x^2 - 2(x)(5) + 5^2$
$$= (x - 5)^2$$

The next two formulas show sums and differences of cubes. Pay special attention to the signs of the terms.

Like signs   Like signs

$$u^3 + v^3 = (u + v)(u^2 - uv + v^2) \qquad u^3 - v^3 = (u - v)(u^2 + uv + v^2)$$

Unlike signs   Unlike signs

EXAMPLE 5   Factoring the Difference of Cubes

$$x^3 - 27 = x^3 - 3^3 = (x - 3)(x^2 + 3x + 9)$$

Notice that the last factor is prime.

EXAMPLE 6   Factoring the Sum of Cubes

$$
\begin{aligned}
3x^3 + 192 &= 3(x^3 + 64) && \textit{Common factor} \\
&= 3(x^3 + 4^3) \\
&= 3(x + 4)(x^2 - 4x + 16) && \textit{Sum of two cubes}
\end{aligned}
$$

Trinomials with Binomial Factors

To factor a trinomial of the form $ax^2 + bx + c$, use the following pattern:

Factors of a

$$ax^2 + bx + c = (\blacksquare x + \blacksquare)(\blacksquare x + \blacksquare).$$

Factors of c

The goal is to find a combination of factors of a and c so that the outer and inner products add up to the middle term bx. For instance, in the trinomial $6x^2 + 17x + 5$, you can write

$$
\begin{matrix}
\text{F} & \text{O} & \text{I} & \text{L} \\
\downarrow & \downarrow & \downarrow & \downarrow
\end{matrix}
$$

$$(2x + 5)(3x + 1) = 6x^2 + 2x + 15x + 5 = 6x^2 + 17x + 5.$$

Note that the outer (**O**) and inner (**I**) products add up to $17x$.

EXAMPLE 7   Factoring a Trinomial: Leading Coefficient is 1

Factor the trinomial $x^2 - 7x + 12$.

SOLUTION

The possible factorizations are

$$(x - 2)(x - 6), \quad (x - 1)(x - 12), \quad \text{and} \quad (x - 3)(x - 4).$$

Testing the middle term in each, you will find the correct factorization to be

$$x^2 - 7x + 12 = (x - 3)(x - 4).$$

EXAMPLE 8   Factoring a Trinomial: Leading Coefficient is Not 1

Factor the trinomial $2x^2 + x - 15$.

SOLUTION

The eight possible factorizations are as follows:

$$(2x - 1)(x + 15) \qquad (2x + 1)(x - 15)$$
$$(2x - 3)(x + 5) \qquad (2x + 3)(x - 5)$$
$$(2x - 5)(x + 3) \qquad (2x + 5)(x - 3)$$
$$(2x - 15)(x + 1) \qquad (2x + 15)(x - 1).$$

Testing the middle term in each, you will find the correct factorization to be

$$2x^2 + x - 15 = (2x - 5)(x + 3).$$

Factoring by Grouping

Sometimes polynomials with more than three terms can be factored by a method called **factoring by grouping.** It is not always obvious which terms to group, and sometimes several different groupings will work.

EXAMPLE 9   Factoring by Grouping

$$\begin{aligned}
x^3 - 2x^2 - 3x + 6 &= (x^3 - 2x^2) - (3x - 6) && \textit{Group terms} \\
&= x^2(x - 2) - 3(x - 2) && \textit{Factor groups} \\
&= (x - 2)(x^2 - 3) && \textit{Common factor}
\end{aligned}$$

As general guidelines for completely factoring polynomials, consider the following factorizations, in order.

GUIDELINES FOR FACTORING POLYNOMIALS

1. Factor out any common factors.
2. Factor according to one of the special polynomial forms.
3. Factor $ax^2 + bx + c$ using the FOIL method.
4. Factor by grouping.

SECTION 5 · EXERCISES

In Exercises 1–6, factor out the common factor.

1. $3x + 6$

2. $5y - 30$

3. $2x^3 - 6x$

4. $4x^3 - 6x^2 + 12x$

5. $(x - 1)^2 + 6(x - 1)$

6. $3x(x + 2) - 4(x + 2)$

In Exercises 7–12, factor the difference of two squares.

7. $x^2 - 36$

8. $x^2 - \frac{1}{4}$

9. $16y^2 - 9$

10. $49 - 9y^2$

11. $(x - 1)^2 - 4$

12. $25 - (z + 5)^2$

In Exercises 13–18, factor the perfect square trinomial.

13. $x^2 - 4x + 4$

14. $x^2 + 10x + 25$

15. $4t^2 + 4t + 1$

16. $9x^2 - 12x + 4$

17. $25y^2 - 10y + 1$

18. $z^2 + z + \frac{1}{4}$

In Exercises 19–32, factor the trinomial.

19. $x^2 + x - 2$

20. $x^2 + 5x + 6$

21. $s^2 - 5s + 6$

22. $t^2 - t - 6$

23. $y^2 + y - 20$

24. $z^2 - 5z - 24$

25. $x^2 - 30x + 200$

26. $x^2 - 13x + 42$

27. $3x^2 - 5x + 2$

28. $2x^2 - x - 1$

29. $9z^2 - 3z - 2$

30. $12x^2 + 7x + 1$

31. $5x^2 + 26x + 5$

32. $5u^2 + 13u - 6$

In Exercises 33–38, factor the sum or difference of cubes.

33. $x^3 - 8$

34. $x^3 - 27$

35. $y^3 + 64$

36. $z^3 + 125$

37. $8t^3 - 1$

38. $27x^3 + 8$

In Exercises 39–44, factor by grouping.

39. $x^3 - x^2 + 2x - 2$

40. $x^3 + 5x^2 - 5x - 25$

41. $2x^3 - x^2 - 6x + 3$

42. $5x^3 - 10x^2 + 3x - 6$

43. $6 + 2x - 3x^3 - x^4$

44. $x^5 + 2x^3 + x^2 + 2$

In Exercises 45–50, factor the trinomial by grouping. For instance, to factor the polynomial in Exercise 45, you can group its terms as $(3x^2 + 6x) + (4x + 8)$.

45. $3x^2 + 10x + 8$

46. $2x^2 + 9x + 9$

47. $6x^2 + x - 2$

48. $6x^2 - x - 15$

49. $15x^2 - 11x + 2$

50. $12x^2 - 13x + 1$

In Exercises 51–54, make a "geometric factoring model" to represent the given factorization. For instance, a factoring model for $2x^2 + 5x + 2 = (2x + 1)(x + 2)$ is shown in the accompanying figure.

FIGURE FOR 51–54

51. $3x^2 + 7x + 2 = (3x + 1)(x + 2)$

52. $x^2 + 4x + 3 = (x + 3)(x + 1)$

53. $2x^2 + 7x + 3 = (2x + 1)(x + 3)$

54. $x^2 + 3x + 2 = (x + 2)(x + 1)$

In Exercises 55–80, completely factor the expression.

55. $x^3 - 9x$

56. $12x^2 - 48$

57. $x^3 - 4x^2$

58. $6x^2 - 54$

59. $x^2 - 2x + 1$

60. $16 + 6x - x^2$

61. $1 - 4x + 4x^2$

62. $9x^2 - 6x + 1$

63. $-2x^2 - 4x + 2x^3$

64. $2y^3 - 7y^2 - 15y$

65. $9x^2 + 10x + 1$

66. $13x + 6 + 5x^2$

67. $3x^3 + x^2 + 15x + 5$

68. $5 - x + 5x^2 - x^3$

69. $x^4 - 4x^3 + x^2 - 4x$

70. $3u - 2u^2 + 6 - u^3$

71. $25 - (x + 5)^2$

72. $(t - 1)^2 - 49$

73. $(x^2 + 1)^2 - 4x^2$

74. $(x^2 + 8)^2 - 36x^2$

75. $2t^3 - 16$

76. $5x^3 + 40$

77. $4x(2x - 1) + (2x - 1)^2$

78. $5(3 - 4x)^2 - 8(3 - 4x)(5x - 1)$

79. $2(x + 1)(x - 3)^2 - 3(x + 1)^2(x - 3)$

80. $7(3x + 2)^2(1 - x)^2 + (3x + 2)(1 - x)^3$

6   FRACTIONAL EXPRESSIONS

Domain of an Algebraic Expression   /   Simplifying Rational Expressions   /
Operations with Rational Expressions   /   Compound Fractions

Domain of an Algebraic Expression

The set of real numbers for which an expression is defined is the **domain** of the expression. Two algebraic expressions are said to be **equivalent** if they yield the same value for all numbers in their domain. For instance, the expressions $[(x + 1) + (x + 2)]$ and $2x + 3$ are equivalent.

EXAMPLE 1   Finding the Domain of an Algebraic Expression

A. The domain of the polynomial $2x^3 + 3x + 4$ is the set of all real numbers. In fact, the domain of any polynomial is the set of all real numbers (unless the domain is specifically restricted).

B. The domain of the polynomial $x^2 + 5x + 2$, $x > 0$, is the set of positive real numbers, because the polynomial is specifically restricted to that set.

C. The domain of the radical expression $\sqrt{x}$ is the set of nonnegative real numbers, because the square root of a negative number is not a real number.

D. The domain of the expression $(x + 2)/(x - 3)$ is the set of all real numbers except $x = 3$, which would produce an undefined division by zero.

The quotient of two algebraic expressions is a **fractional expression.** Moreover, the quotient of two *polynomials* such as

$$\frac{1}{x}, \quad \frac{2x - 1}{x + 1}, \quad \text{or} \quad \frac{x^2 - 1}{x^2 + 1}$$

is a **rational expression.** Recall that a fraction is in reduced form if its numerator and denominator have no factors in common aside from ± 1. To write a fraction in reduced form, apply the following rule.

$$\frac{a \cdot \cancel{c}}{b \cdot \cancel{c}} = \frac{a}{b}, \qquad b \neq 0 \quad \text{and} \quad c \neq 0$$

The key to success in simplifying rational expressions lies in your ability to *factor* polynomials.

EXAMPLE 2   Reducing a Rational Expression

Write the following rational expression in reduced form.

$$\frac{x^2 + 4x - 12}{3x - 6}$$

SOLUTION

Factoring both numerator and denominator, and then reducing, produces the following:

$$\frac{x^2 + 4x - 12}{3x - 6} = \frac{(x + 6)(x - 2)}{3(x - 2)} \qquad \textit{Factor completely}$$

$$= \frac{x + 6}{3}, \quad x \neq -2. \qquad \textit{Reduce}$$

Note that the original expression is undefined when $x = 2$ (because division by zero is undefined). To make sure that the reduced expression is *equivalent* to the original expression, you must restrict the domain of the reduced expression by excluding the value $x = 2$.

Simplifying Rational Expressions

When simplifying rational expressions, be sure to factor each polynomial completely before concluding that the numerator and denominator have no factors in common. Moreover, changing the sign of a factor may allow further reduction, as seen in part (B) of the next example.

EXAMPLE 3   Reducing Rational Expressions

A. $\dfrac{x^3 - 4x}{x^2 + x - 2} = \dfrac{x(x^2 - 4)}{(x + 2)(x - 1)}$

$$= \frac{x(x + 2)(x - 2)}{(x + 2)(x - 1)} \qquad \textit{Factor completely}$$

$$= \frac{x(x - 2)}{x - 1}, \quad x \neq -2 \qquad \textit{Reduce}$$

B. $\dfrac{12 + x - x^2}{2x^2 - 9x + 4} = \dfrac{(4 - x)(3 + x)}{(2x - 1)(x - 4)}$ *Factor completely*

$= \dfrac{-(x - 4)(3 + x)}{(2x - 1)(x - 4)}$ *$(4 - x) = -(x - 4)$*

$= -\dfrac{3 + x}{2x - 1}, \quad x \neq 4$ *Reduce*

Operations with Rational Expressions

To multiply or divide rational expressions, use the properties of fractions discussed in Section 2.

EXAMPLE 4   Multiplying and Dividing Rational Expressions

A. $\dfrac{2x^2 + x - 6}{x^2 + 4x - 5} \cdot \dfrac{x^3 - 3x^2 + 2x}{4x^2 - 6x}$

$= \dfrac{(2x - 3)(x + 2)}{(x + 5)(x - 1)} \cdot \dfrac{x(x - 2)(x - 1)}{2x(2x - 3)}$ *Factor and reduce*

$= \dfrac{(x + 2)(x - 2)}{2(x + 5)}, \quad x \neq 0, x \neq 1, x \neq \dfrac{3}{2}$

B. $\dfrac{x^3 - 8}{x^2 - 4} \div \dfrac{x^2 + 2x + 4}{x^3 + 8} = \dfrac{x^3 - 8}{x^2 - 4} \cdot \dfrac{x^3 + 8}{x^2 + 2x + 4}$ *Invert and multiply*

$= \dfrac{(x - 2)(x^2 + 2x + 4)}{(x + 2)(x - 2)} \cdot \dfrac{(x + 2)(x^2 - 2x + 4)}{x^2 + 2x + 4}$

$= x^2 - 2x + 4, \quad x \neq \pm 2$

To add or subtract rational expressions, use the least common denominator (LCD) method or the basic definition

$$\frac{a}{b} \pm \frac{c}{d} = \frac{ad \pm bc}{bd}, \quad b \neq 0 \quad \text{and} \quad d \neq 0.$$

This definition provides an efficient way of adding or subtracting *two* fractional expressions that have no common factors in their denominators.

EXAMPLE 5   Subtracting Rational Expressions Using the Basic Definition

$\dfrac{x}{x - 3} - \dfrac{2}{3x + 4} = \dfrac{x(3x + 4) - 2(x - 3)}{(x - 3)(3x + 4)}$ *Definition of subtraction*

$= \dfrac{3x^2 + 4x - 2x + 6}{(x - 3)(3x + 4)}$ *Remove parentheses*

$= \dfrac{3x^2 + 2x + 6}{(x - 3)(3x + 4)}$ *Combine like terms*

For three or more fractions, or for fractions with a repeated factor in the denominator, the LCD method works well. Recall that the LCD of several fractions consists of the product of all prime factors in the denominators, with each factor given the highest power of its occurrence in any denominator.

EXAMPLE 6   **The LCD Method for Combining Rational Expressions**

Perform the given operations and simplify.

$$\frac{3}{x-1} - \frac{2}{x} + \frac{x+3}{x^2-1}$$

SOLUTION

Using the factored denominators $(x-1)$, x, and $(x+1)(x-1)$, you can see that the LCD is $x(x+1)(x-1)$.

$$\frac{3}{x-1} - \frac{2}{x} + \frac{x+3}{(x+1)(x-1)}$$

$$= \frac{3(x)(x+1)}{x(x+1)(x-1)} - \frac{2(x+1)(x-1)}{x(x+1)(x-1)} + \frac{(x+3)(x)}{x(x+1)(x-1)}$$

$$= \frac{3(x)(x+1) - 2(x+1)(x-1) + (x+3)(x)}{x(x+1)(x-1)}$$

$$= \frac{3x^2 + 3x - 2x^2 + 2 + x^2 + 3x}{x(x+1)(x-1)}$$

$$= \frac{2x^2 + 6x + 2}{x(x+1)(x-1)}$$

$$= \frac{2(x^2 + 3x + 1)}{x(x+1)(x-1)}$$

Compound Fractions

Fractional expressions with fractions in the numerator or denominator, or both, are called **compound fractions** (or complex fractions).

A compound fraction can be simplified by first simplifying both its numerator and its denominator into single fractions, then inverting the denominator and multiplying.

EXAMPLE 7   Simplifying a Compound Fraction

$$\frac{\left(\dfrac{2}{x} - 3\right)}{\left(1 - \dfrac{1}{x-1}\right)} = \frac{\left(\dfrac{2 - 3(x)}{x}\right)}{\left(\dfrac{1(x-1) - 1}{x-1}\right)} \qquad \textit{Combine fractions}$$

$$= \frac{\left(\dfrac{2 - 3x}{x}\right)}{\left(\dfrac{x-2}{x-1}\right)} \qquad \textit{Simplify}$$

$$= \frac{2 - 3x}{x} \cdot \frac{x-1}{x-2} \qquad \textit{Invert and multiply}$$

$$= \frac{(2 - 3x)(x-1)}{x(x-2)}, \quad x \neq 1$$

Another way to simplify a compound fraction is to multiply each term in its numerator and denominator by the LCD of all fractions in both its numerator and denominator. Each product is then reduced to obtain a single fraction.

EXAMPLE 8   Simplifying a Compound Fraction by Multiplying by the LCD

Use the LCD to simplify the following compound fraction.

$$\frac{\left(\dfrac{1}{x^2} - \dfrac{1}{y^2}\right)}{\left(\dfrac{1}{x} + \dfrac{1}{y}\right)}$$

SOLUTION

For the four fractions in the numerator and denominator, the LCD is x^2y^2. Multiplying each term of the numerator and denominator by this LCD yields the following.

$$\frac{\left(\dfrac{1}{x^2} - \dfrac{1}{y^2}\right)x^2y^2}{\left(\dfrac{1}{x} + \dfrac{1}{y}\right)x^2y^2} = \frac{\left(\dfrac{1}{x^2}\right)x^2y^2 - \left(\dfrac{1}{y^2}\right)x^2y^2}{\left(\dfrac{1}{x}\right)x^2y^2 + \left(\dfrac{1}{y}\right)x^2y^2}$$

$$= \frac{y^2 - x^2}{xy^2 + x^2y}$$

$$= \frac{(y - x)\cancel{(y + x)}}{xy\cancel{(y + x)}}$$

$$= \frac{y - x}{xy}, \quad x \neq -y$$

The next two examples illustrate some methods for simplifying expressions involving radicals and negative exponents. (These types of expressions occur frequently in calculus.)

EXAMPLE 9   **Simplifying an Expression with Negative Exponents**

Simplify the expression $x(1 - 2x)^{-3/2} + (1 - 2x)^{-1/2}$.

SOLUTION

By rewriting the given expression with positive exponents, we obtain

$$\frac{x}{(1 - 2x)^{3/2}} + \frac{1}{(1 - 2x)^{1/2}},$$

which could then be combined by the LCD method. However, if we first remove the common factor with the *smaller exponent,* the process is simpler.

$$x(1 - 2x)^{-3/2} + (1 - 2x)^{-1/2} = (1 - 2x)^{-3/2}\left[x + (1 - 2x)^{(-1/2)-(-3/2)}\right]$$
$$= (1 - 2x)^{-3/2}\left[x + (1 - 2x)^{1}\right]$$
$$= \frac{1 - x}{(1 - 2x)^{3/2}}$$

Note that when factoring, you subtract exponents.

EXAMPLE 10   **Simplifying a Compound Fraction: LCD Method**

$$\frac{\sqrt{4 - x^2} + \dfrac{x^2}{\sqrt{4 - x^2}}}{4 - x^2} = \frac{\sqrt{4 - x^2} + \dfrac{x^2}{\sqrt{4 - x^2}}}{4 - x^2} \cdot \frac{\sqrt{4 - x^2}}{\sqrt{4 - x^2}}$$
$$= \frac{(4 - x^2) + x^2}{(4 - x^2)^{3/2}}$$
$$= \frac{4}{\sqrt{(4 - x^2)^3}}$$

SECTION 6 · EXERCISES

In Exercises 1–10, find the domain of the expression.

1. $3x^2 - 4x + 7$ **2.** $2x^2 + 5x - 2$

3. $4x^3 + 5x + 3,\quad x \geq 0$

4. $6x^2 + 7x - 9,\quad x > 0$

5. $\dfrac{1}{x - 2}$ **6.** $\dfrac{x + 1}{2x + 1}$

7. $\dfrac{x - 1}{x^2 - 4x}$

8. $\dfrac{2x + 1}{x^2 - 9}$

9. $\sqrt{x + 1}$

10. $\dfrac{1}{\sqrt{x + 1}}$

In Exercises 11–16, find the factor that makes the two fractions equivalent.

11. $\dfrac{5}{2x} = \dfrac{5(\quad)}{6x^2}$

12. $\dfrac{3}{4} = \dfrac{3(\quad)}{4(x+1)}$

13. $\dfrac{x+1}{x} = \dfrac{(x+1)(\quad)}{x(x-2)}$

14. $\dfrac{3y-4}{y+1} = \dfrac{(3y-4)(\quad)}{y^2-1}$

15. $\dfrac{3x}{x-3} = \dfrac{3x(\quad)}{x^2-x-6}$

16. $\dfrac{1-z}{z^2} = \dfrac{(1-z)(\quad)}{z^3+z^2}$

In Exercises 17–30, write the expression in reduced form.

17. $\dfrac{15x^2}{10x}$

18. $\dfrac{18y^2}{60y^5}$

19. $\dfrac{3xy}{xy+x}$

20. $\dfrac{9x^2+9x}{2x+2}$

21. $\dfrac{x-5}{10-2x}$

22. $\dfrac{x^2-25}{5-x}$

23. $\dfrac{x^3+5x^2+6x}{x^2-4}$

24. $\dfrac{x^2+8x-20}{x^2+11x+10}$

25. $\dfrac{y^2-7y+12}{y^2+3y-18}$

26. $\dfrac{10+x}{x^2+11x+10}$

27. $\dfrac{2-x+2x^2-x^3}{x-2}$

28. $\dfrac{x^2-9}{x^3+x^2-9x-9}$

29. $\dfrac{z^3-8}{z^2+2z+4}$

30. $\dfrac{y^3-2y^2-3y}{y^3+1}$

In Exercises 31–54, perform the indicated operations and simplify.

31. $\dfrac{5}{x-1} \cdot \dfrac{x-1}{25(x-2)}$

32. $\dfrac{(x+5)(x-3)}{x+2} \cdot \dfrac{1}{(x+5)(x+2)}$

33. $\dfrac{r}{r-1} \cdot \dfrac{r^2-1}{r^2}$

34. $\dfrac{4y-16}{5y+15} \cdot \dfrac{2y+6}{4-y}$

35. $\dfrac{y^3-8}{2y^3} \cdot \dfrac{4y}{y^2-5y+6}$

36. $\dfrac{x^3-1}{x+1} \cdot \dfrac{x^2+1}{x^2-1}$

37. $\dfrac{3(x+y)}{4} \div \dfrac{x+y}{2}$

38. $\dfrac{x+2}{5(x-3)} \div \dfrac{x-2}{5(x-3)}$

39. $\dfrac{\left(\dfrac{x^2}{(x+1)^2}\right)}{\left(\dfrac{x}{(x+1)^3}\right)}$

40. $\dfrac{\left(\dfrac{x^2-1}{x}\right)}{\left(\dfrac{(x-1)^2}{x}\right)}$

41. $\dfrac{5}{x-1} + \dfrac{x}{x-1}$

42. $\dfrac{2x-1}{x+3} + \dfrac{1-x}{x+3}$

43. $6 - \dfrac{5}{x+3}$

44. $\dfrac{3}{x-1} - 5$

45. $\dfrac{3}{x-2} + \dfrac{5}{2-x}$

46. $\dfrac{2x}{x-5} - \dfrac{5}{5-x}$

47. $\dfrac{2}{x^2-4} - \dfrac{1}{x^2-3x+2}$

48. $\dfrac{x}{x^2+x-2} - \dfrac{1}{x+2}$

49. $-\dfrac{1}{x} + \dfrac{2}{x^2+1} + \dfrac{1}{x^3+x}$

50. $\dfrac{2}{x+1} + \dfrac{2}{x-1} + \dfrac{1}{x^2-1}$

51. $x^2(x^2-1)^{-1/2} + (x^2-1)^{1/2}$

52. $(1-x^3)^{1/3} - x^3(1-x^3)^{-2/3}$

53. $3(x-2)^{-1/3} - x(x-2)^{-4/3}$

54. $2(2+x)^{-1/2} + (1-x)(2+x)^{-3/2}$

In Exercises 55–66, simplify the compound fraction.

55. $\dfrac{\left(\dfrac{x}{2}-1\right)}{x-2}$

56. $\dfrac{x-4}{\left(\dfrac{x}{4}-\dfrac{4}{x}\right)}$

57. $\dfrac{\left(\dfrac{1}{x}-\dfrac{1}{x+1}\right)}{\left(\dfrac{1}{x+1}\right)}$

58. $\dfrac{\left(\dfrac{5}{y}-\dfrac{6}{2y+1}\right)}{\left(\dfrac{5}{y}+4\right)}$

59. $\dfrac{\left(\dfrac{1}{(x+h)^2}-\dfrac{1}{x^2}\right)}{h}$

60. $\dfrac{\left(\dfrac{x+h}{x+h+1}-\dfrac{x}{x+1}\right)}{h}$

61. $\dfrac{2a^{-1}+b^{-1}}{ab}$

62. $\dfrac{z^{-1}-2(z+2)^{-1}}{z^{-2}}$

63. $\dfrac{\left(\sqrt{x}-\dfrac{1}{2\sqrt{x}}\right)}{\sqrt{x}}$

64. $\dfrac{3x^{1/3}-x^{-2/3}}{3x^{-2/3}}$

65. $\dfrac{\left(\dfrac{t^2}{\sqrt{t^2+1}}-\sqrt{t^2+1}\right)}{t^2}$

66. $\dfrac{-x^3(1-x^2)^{-1/2}-2x(1-x^2)^{1/2}}{x^4}$

In Exercises 67 and 68, rationalize the numerator of the expression.

67. $\dfrac{\sqrt{x+2}-\sqrt{x}}{2}$

68. $\dfrac{\sqrt{z-3}-\sqrt{z}}{3}$

7   THE CARTESIAN PLANE

The Cartesian Plane   /   The Distance Between Two Points in the Plane   /
The Midpoint Formula   /   The Equation of a Circle

The Cartesian Plane

Just as real numbers are represented by points on the real number line, ordered pairs of real numbers are represented by points in a plane. This plane is called a **rectangular coordinate system** or the **Cartesian plane,** after the French mathematician René Descartes (1596–1650).

The Cartesian plane is formed by two real number lines intersecting at right angles, as shown in Figure 6(a). The horizontal number line is usually called the **x-axis** and the vertical number line is usually called the **y-axis.** (The plural of axis is *axes.*) The point of intersection of the two axes is the **origin.** The axes separate the plane into four regions called **quadrants.**

REMARK   It is customary to use the notation (x, y) to denote both a point in the plane and an open interval on the real number line. The nature of a specific problem will show which of the two we are talking about.

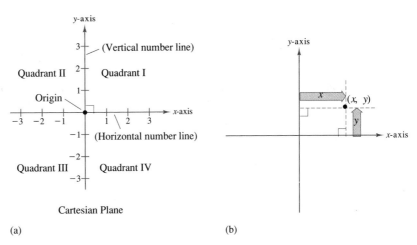

(a)   (b)

FIGURE 6

Each point in the plane corresponds to an **ordered pair** (x, y) of real numbers x and y, called **coordinates** of the point. The first number (**x-coordinate**) tells how far to the left or right the point is from the vertical axis, and the second number (**y-coordinate**) tells how far up or down the point is from the horizontal axis, as shown in Figure 6(b). Figure 7 shows several points that have been plotted in the plane.

The rectangular coordinate system allows you to visualize relationships between variables x and y. Today, Descartes's ideas are commonly used in every scientific and business-related field.

FIGURE 7

FIGURE 8

EXAMPLE 1   **Number of Doctorates in Mathematics**
....

The numbers of doctorates in mathematics granted to United States citizens by universities in the United States in the years 1974 to 1989 are given in Table 1. Plot these points in a rectangular coordinate system. (*Source*: American Mathematical Society)

TABLE 1

Year	1974	1975	1976	1977	1978	1979	1980	1981
Degrees	677	741	722	689	634	596	578	567
Year	1982	1983	1984	1985	1986	1987	1988	1989
Degrees	519	455	433	396	386	362	363	419

SOLUTION

The points are shown in Figure 8. Note that the break in the x-axis indicates that the numbers for years prior to 1974 have been omitted.   ·········

The Distance Between Two Points in the Plane

Let (x_1, y_1) and (x_2, y_2) represent two points in the plane that do not lie on the same horizontal or vertical line. With these two points, a right triangle can be formed, as shown in Figure 9. Note that the third vertex of the triangle is (x_1, y_2). Because (x_1, y_1) and (x_1, y_2) lie on the same vertical line, the length of the vertical side of the triangle is $|y_2 - y_1|$. Similarly, the length of the horizontal side is $|x_2 - x_1|$. Thus, by the Pythagorean Theorem, the distance d between (x_1, y_1) and (x_2, y_2) is

$$d^2 = |x_2 - x_1|^2 + |y_2 - y_1|^2.$$

Because the distance d must be positive, choose the positive square root and write

$$d = \sqrt{|x_2 - x_1|^2 + |y_2 - y_1|^2}.$$

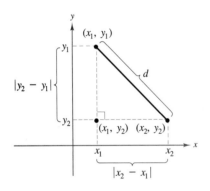

Distance Between Two Points

FIGURE 9

Finally, replacing $|x_2 - x_1|^2$ and $|y_2 - y_1|^2$ by the equivalent expressions $(x_2 - x_1)^2$ and $(y_2 - y_1)^2$ gives the following formula for the distance between two points in a rectangular coordinate plane.

THE DISTANCE FORMULA

The distance d between the two points (x_1, y_1) and (x_2, y_2) in the coordinate plane is

$$d = \sqrt{(x_2 - x_1)^2 + (y_2 - y_1)^2}.$$

EXAMPLE 2   Finding the Distance Between Two Points

Find the distance between the points $(-2, 1)$ and $(3, 4)$.

SOLUTION

Letting $(x_1, y_1) = (-2, 1)$ and $(x_2, y_2) = (3, 4)$, apply the Distance Formula to obtain

$$d = \sqrt{[3 - (-2)]^2 + (4 - 1)^2}$$
$$= \sqrt{5^2 + 3^2}$$
$$= \sqrt{25 + 9}$$
$$= \sqrt{34}$$
$$\approx 5.83.$$

See Figure 10.

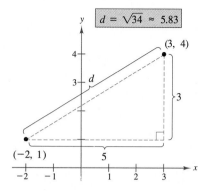

$d = \sqrt{34} \approx 5.83$

FIGURE 10

EXAMPLE 3   An Application of the Distance Formula

Show that the points $(2, 1)$, $(4, 0)$, and $(5, 7)$ are vertices of a right triangle.

SOLUTION

The three points are plotted in Figure 11. Using the Distance Formula, you can find the lengths of the three sides of the triangle:

$$d_1 = \sqrt{(5 - 2)^2 + (7 - 1)^2} = \sqrt{9 + 36} = \sqrt{45}$$
$$d_2 = \sqrt{(4 - 2)^2 + (0 - 1)^2} = \sqrt{4 + 1} = \sqrt{5}$$
$$d_3 = \sqrt{(5 - 4)^2 + (7 - 0)^2} = \sqrt{1 + 49} = \sqrt{50}.$$

Because $d_1^2 + d_2^2 = 45 + 5 = 50 = d_3^2$, you can conclude from the Pythagorean Theorem that the triangle is a right triangle.

FIGURE 11

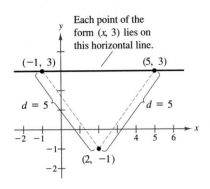

Each point of the form $(x, 3)$ lies on this horizontal line.

$(-1, 3)$ $(5, 3)$

$d = 5$ $d = 5$

$(2, -1)$

FIGURE 12

EXAMPLE 4   **Finding Points at a Specified Distance from a Given Point**

Find x so that the distance between $(x, 3)$ and $(2, -1)$ is 5.

SOLUTION

$$\sqrt{(x - 2)^2 + (3 + 1)^2} = 5 \qquad \textit{Distance Formula}$$

$$(x^2 - 4x + 4) + 16 = 25 \qquad \textit{Square both sides}$$

$$x^2 - 4x - 5 = 0 \qquad \textit{Standard form}$$

$$(x - 5)(x + 1) = 0 \qquad \textit{Factor}$$

$$x - 5 = 0 \ \longrightarrow \ x = 5 \qquad \textit{Set 1st factor equal to 0}$$

$$x + 1 = 0 \ \longrightarrow \ x = -1 \qquad \textit{Set 2nd factor equal to 0}$$

There are two solutions: $(5, 3)$ and $(-1, 3)$. Note that each of the points $(5, 3)$ and $(-1, 3)$ lies five units from the point $(2, -1)$, as shown in Figure 12.

The Midpoint Formula

The coordinates of the midpoint of a line segment are the average values of the corresponding coordinates of the two endpoints.

> **THE MIDPOINT FORMULA**
>
> The **midpoint** of the line segment joining the points (x_1, y_1) and (x_2, y_2) in the coordinate plane is
>
> $$\left(\frac{x_1 + x_2}{2}, \frac{y_1 + y_2}{2} \right).$$

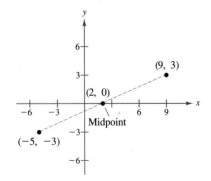

$(9, 3)$

$(2, 0)$

Midpoint

$(-5, -3)$

FIGURE 13

EXAMPLE 5   **Finding the Midpoint of a Line Segment**

Find the midpoint of the line segment joining the points $(-5, -3)$ and $(9, 3)$.

SOLUTION

Figure 13 shows the two given points and their midpoint. Using the Midpoint Formula, you can write

$$\text{Midpoint} = \left(\frac{-5 + 9}{2}, \frac{-3 + 3}{2} \right)$$

$$= (2, 0).$$

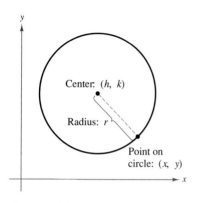

FIGURE 14

The Equation of a Circle

The Distance Formula provides a convenient way to define circles. A **circle of radius r** with **center** at the point (h, k) is shown in Figure 14. The point (x, y) is on this circle if and only if its distance from the center (h, k) is r. This means that a **circle** in the plane consists of all points (x, y) that are a given positive distance r from a fixed point (h, k). Using the Distance Formula, you can express this relationship by saying that the point (x, y) lies on the circle if and only if

$$\sqrt{(x - h)^2 + (y - k)^2} = r.$$

By squaring both sides of this equation, you can obtain the **standard form of the equation of a circle.**

STANDARD FORM OF THE EQUATION OF A CIRCLE

The **standard form of the equation of a circle** is

$$(x - h)^2 + (y - k)^2 = r^2.$$

The point (h, k) is the **center** of the circle, and the positive number r is the **radius** of the circle. The standard form of the equation of a circle whose center is the *origin* is $x^2 + y^2 = r^2$.

EXAMPLE 6   Finding an Equation of a Circle

The point $(3, 4)$ lies on a circle whose center is at $(-1, 2)$, as shown in Figure 15. Find an equation for the circle.

SOLUTION

The radius r of the circle is the distance between $(-1, 2)$ and $(3, 4)$.

$$r = \sqrt{[3 - (-1)]^2 + (4 - 2)^2}$$
$$= \sqrt{16 + 4}$$
$$= \sqrt{20}$$

Thus, the center of the circle is $(h, k) = (-1, 2)$ and the radius is $r = \sqrt{20}$, and you can write the standard form of the equation of the circle as follows.

$$(x - h)^2 + (y - k)^2 = r^2 \qquad \textit{Standard form}$$
$$[x - (-1)]^2 + (y - 2)^2 = (\sqrt{20})^2 \qquad \textit{Let } h = -1, k = 2, \text{ and } r = \sqrt{20}$$
$$(x + 1)^2 + (y - 2)^2 = 20 \qquad \textit{Equation of circle}$$

FIGURE 15

SECTION 7 · EXERCISES

In Exercises 1–4, sketch the polygon with the indicated vertices.

1. Triangle: $(-1, 1)$, $(2, -1)$, $(3, 4)$
2. Triangle: $(0, 3)$, $(-1, -2)$, $(4, 8)$
3. Square: $(2, 4)$, $(5, 1)$, $(2, -2)$, $(-1, 1)$
4. Parallelogram: $(5, 2)$, $(7, 0)$, $(1, -2)$, $(-1, 0)$

In Exercises 5–8, find the distance between the points. (Note: In each case, the two points lie on the same horizontal or vertical line.)

5. $(6, -3)$, $(6, 5)$ **6.** $(1, 4)$, $(8, 4)$
7. $(-3, -1)$, $(2, -1)$ **8.** $(-3, -4)$, $(-3, 6)$

In Exercises 9–12, (a) find the lengths of the two perpendicular sides of the right triangle and use the Pythagorean Theorem to find the length of the hypotenuse, and (b) use the Distance Formula to find the length of the hypotenuse of the triangle.

9.

10.

11.

12.

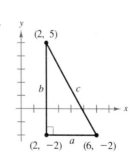

In Exercises 13–24, (a) plot the points, (b) find the distance between the points, and (c) find the midpoint of the line segment joining the points.

13. $(1, 1)$, $(9, 7)$ **14.** $(1, 12)$, $(6, 0)$
15. $(-4, 10)$, $(4, -5)$ **16.** $(-7, -4)$, $(2, 8)$
17. $(-1, 2)$, $(5, 4)$ **18.** $(2, 10)$, $(10, 2)$
19. $(\frac{1}{2}, 1)$, $(-\frac{5}{2}, \frac{4}{3})$ **20.** $(-\frac{1}{3}, -\frac{1}{3})$, $(-\frac{1}{6}, -\frac{1}{2})$
21. $(6.2, 5.4)$, $(-3.7, 1.8)$ **22.** $(-16.8, 12.3)$, $(5.6, 4.9)$
23. $(-36, -18)$, $(48, -72)$
24. $(1.451, 3.051)$, $(5.906, 11.360)$

In Exercises 25 and 26, use the Midpoint Formula to estimate the sales of a company for 1991, given the sales in 1989 and 1993. Assume the sales followed a linear pattern.

25.

Year	1989	1993
Sales	$520,000	$740,000

26.

Year	1989	1993
Sales	$4,200,000	$5,650,000

In Exercises 27–30, show that the points form the vertices of the indicated polygon. (A rhombus is a parallelogram whose sides are all of the same length.)

27. Right triangle: $(4, 0)$, $(2, 1)$, $(-1, -5)$
28. Isosceles triangle: $(1, -3)$, $(3, 2)$, $(-2, 4)$
29. Rhombus: $(0, 0)$, $(1, 2)$, $(2, 1)$, $(3, 3)$
30. Parallelogram: $(0, 1)$, $(3, 7)$, $(4, 4)$, $(1, -2)$

In Exercises 31 and 32, find x so that the distance between the points is 13.

31. $(1, 2)$, $(x, -10)$ **32.** $(-8, 0)$, $(x, 5)$

In Exercises 33 and 34, find y so that the distance between the points is 17.

33. $(0, 0)$, $(8, y)$ **34.** $(-8, 4)$, $(7, y)$

In Exercises 35 and 36, find an equation that relates x and y so that (x, y) is equidistant from the two given points.

35. $(4, -1)$, $(-2, 3)$ **36.** $(3, \frac{5}{2})$, $(-7, 1)$

In Exercises 37–48, determine the quadrant(s) in which (x, y) is located so that the given conditions are satisfied.

37. $x > 0$ and $y < 0$ **38.** $x < 0$ and $y < 0$

39. $x > 0$ and $y > 0$ **40.** $x < 0$ and $y > 0$

41. $x = -4$ and $y > 0$ **42.** $x > 2$ and $y = 3$

43. $y < -5$ **44.** $x > 4$

45. $xy > 0$ **46.** $xy < 0$

47. $(x, -y)$ is in the second quadrant.

48. $(-x, y)$ is in the fourth quadrant.

49. Plot the points $(2, 1)$, $(-3, 5)$, and $(7, -3)$ on the rectangular coordinate system. Now plot the corresponding points when the sign of the x-coordinate is negated. What inference can you make about the result of the location of a point when the sign of the x-coordinate is changed?

50. Plot the points $(2, 1)$, $(-3, 5)$, and $(7, -3)$ on the rectangular coordinate system. Now plot the corresponding points when the sign of the y-coordinate is negated. What inference can you make about the result of the location of a point when the sign of the y-coordinate is changed?

In Exercises 51–58, find the standard form of the equation of the specified circle.

51. Center: $(0, 0)$; radius: 3   **52.** Center: $(0, 0)$; radius: 5

53. Center: $(2, -1)$; radius: 4   **54.** Center: $(0, \frac{1}{3})$; radius: $\frac{1}{3}$

55. Center: $(-1, 2)$; solution point: $(0, 0)$

56. Center: $(3, -2)$; solution point: $(-1, 1)$

57. Endpoints of a diameter: $(0, 0)$, $(6, 8)$

58. Endpoints of a diameter: $(-4, -1)$, $(4, 1)$

FUNCTIONS AND GRAPHS

1.1   GRAPHS AND GRAPHING UTILITIES

The Graph of an Equation / **Using a Graphing Utility** / **Determining a Viewing Rectangle** / **Applications**

The Graph of an Equation

News magazines often show graphs comparing the rate of inflation, the federal deficit, wholesale prices, or the unemployment rate to the time of year. Industrial firms and businesses use graphs to report their monthly production and sales statistics. Such graphs provide geometric pictures of the way one quantity changes with respect to another.

Frequently, the relationship between two quantities is expressed as an equation. This section introduces the basic procedure for determining the geometric picture associated with an equation.

For an equation in variables x and y, a point (a, b) is a **solution point** if the substitution of $x = a$ and $y = b$ satisfies the equation. Most equations have *infinitely* many solution points. For example, the equation $3x + y = 5$ has solution points $(0, 5)$, $(1, 2)$, $(2, -1)$, $(3, -4)$, and so on. The set of all solution points of an equation is the **graph** of the equation.

THE POINT-PLOTTING METHOD OF GRAPHING

To sketch the graph of an equation by point plotting, use the following.

1. If possible, rewrite the equation so that one of the variables is isolated on the left side of the equation.
2. Make up a table of several solution points.
3. Plot these points in the coordinate plane.
4. Connect the points with a smooth curve.

FIGURE 1.1

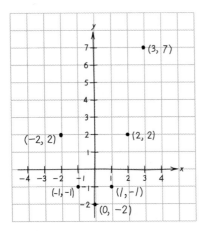

Plot several points.

FIGURE 1.2

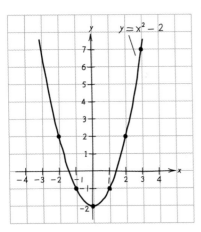

Connect points with a smooth curve.

FIGURE 1.3

EXAMPLE 1   Sketching the Graph of an Equation by Point Plotting
· · · · · · · · · · · · · · · ·

Use point plotting and graph paper to sketch the graph of $3x + y = 6$.

SOLUTION

In this case you can isolate the variable y to obtain

$$y = 6 - 3x.$$

Using negative, zero, and positive values for x, you can obtain the following table of values (solution points).

x	-1	0	1	2	3
$y = 6 - 3x$	9	6	3	0	-3

Next, plot these points and connect them as shown in Figure 1.1. It appears that the graph is a straight line. (We will discuss lines extensively in Section 1.2.)
· · · · · · · · · ·

The points at which a graph touches or crosses an axis are the **intercepts** of the graph. For instance, in Example 1 the point $(0, 6)$ is the y-intercept of the graph because the graph crosses the y-axis at that point. The point $(2, 0)$ is the x-intercept of the graph because the graph crosses the x-axis at that point.

EXAMPLE 2   Sketching the Graph of an Equation by Point Plotting
· · · · · · · · · · · · · · · ·

Use point plotting and graph paper to sketch the graph of $y = x^2 - 2$.

SOLUTION

First, make a table of values by choosing several convenient values of x and calculating the corresponding values of y.

x	-2	-1	0	1	2	3
$y = x^2 - 2$	2	-1	-2	-1	2	7

Next, plot the corresponding solution points, as shown in Figure 1.2. Finally, connect the points with a smooth curve, as shown in Figure 1.3. This graph is called a **parabola.**
· · · · · · · · · ·

Using a Graphing Utility

One of the disadvantages of the point-plotting method is that to get a good idea about the shape of a graph you need to plot *many* points. With only a few points, you could badly misrepresent the graph. For instance, consider the equation

$$y = \frac{1}{30}x(x^4 - 10x^2 + 39).$$

Suppose you plotted only five points: $(-3, -3)$, $(-1, -1)$, $(0, 0)$, $(1, 1)$ and $(3, 3)$, as shown in Figure 1.4. From these five points, a person might assume that the graph of the equation is a straight line. That, however, is not correct. By plotting several more points, you can see that the actual graph is not straight at all! (See Figure 1.5.)

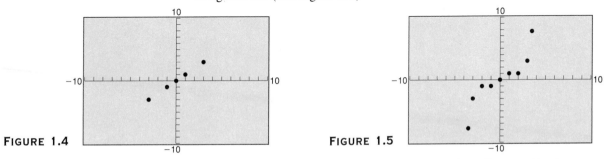

FIGURE 1.4

FIGURE 1.5

Thus, the point-plotting method leaves us with a dilemma. On the one hand, the method can be very inaccurate if only a few points are plotted. But on the other hand, it is very time consuming to plot a dozen (or more) points. Technology can help solve this dilemma. Plotting several (even several hundred) points in a rectangular coordinate system is something that a computer or calculator can do easily.

The point-plotting method is the method used by *all* graphing utilities. Each computer or calculator screen is made up of a grid of hundreds or thousands of small areas called **pixels.** Screens that have many pixels per inch are said to have a higher **resolution** than screens that don't have as many. Screens on most graphing calculators have 48 pixels per inch, whereas screens on computer monitors typically have between 32 and 100 pixels per inch.

With most graphing utilities, you can graph an equation by using the following steps.

USING A GRAPHING UTILITY TO GRAPH AN EQUATION

To graph an equation involving x and y on a graphing utility, use the following.

1. Rewrite the equation so that y is isolated on the left side of the equation.
2. Enter the equation into a graphing utility.
3. Determine a **viewing window** for the graph. For some graphing utilities, the standard viewing window ranges between -10 and 10 for both the x and y values.
4. Activate the graphing utility.

EXAMPLE 3   Using a Graphing Utility

Use a graphing utility to graph $2y + x^3 = 4x$.

SOLUTION

To begin, solve the equation for y in terms of x.

$$2y + x^3 = 4x \qquad \textit{Given equation}$$

$$2y = -x^3 + 4x \qquad \textit{Subtract } x^3 \textit{ from both sides}$$

$$y = -\frac{1}{2}x^3 + 2x \qquad \textit{Divide both sides by 2}$$

Now, by entering this equation into a graphing utility (using a standard viewing rectangle), you can obtain the graph shown in Figure 1.6.

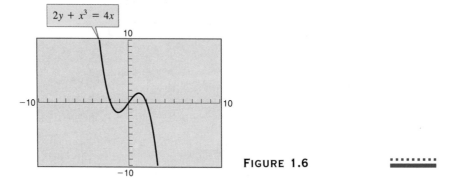

FIGURE 1.6

Determining a Viewing Rectangle

A **viewing rectangle** for a graph is a rectangular portion of the Cartesian plane. A viewing rectangle is determined by six values: the minimum x-value, the maximum x-value, the x-scale, the minimum y-value, the maximum y-value, and the y-scale. When you enter these six values into the graphing utility, you are setting the **range** of the viewing rectangle. The **standard** viewing rectangle for some graphing utilities is shown in Figure 1.7.

FIGURE 1.7

By choosing different viewing rectangles for a graph, it is possible to obtain very different impressions of the graph's shape. For instance, Figure 1.8 shows four different viewing rectangles for the graph of

$$y = 0.1x^4 - x^3 + 2x^2.$$

Of these, the view shown in Figure 1.8(a) is the most complete because it shows more of the distinguishing portions of the graph.

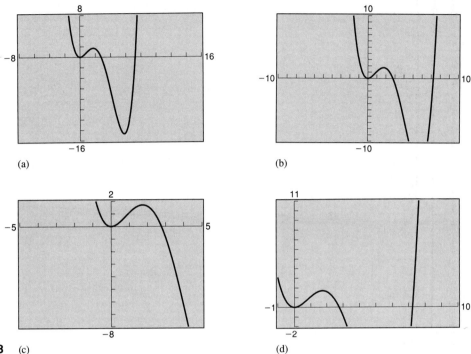

(a)

(b)

FIGURE 1.8   (c)

(d)

EXAMPLE 4   **Sketching a Circle with a Graphing Utility**

Use a graphing utility to graph $x^2 + y^2 = 9$.

SOLUTION

The graph of $x^2 + y^2 = 9$ is a circle whose center is the origin and whose radius is 3. (See Section 7 in preceding chapter on prerequisites.) To graph the equation, begin by solving the equation for y.

$$x^2 + y^2 = 9$$
$$y^2 = 9 - x^2$$
$$y = \pm\sqrt{9 - x^2}$$

The graph of $y = \sqrt{9 - x^2}$ is the upper semicircle. The graph of $y = -\sqrt{9 - x^2}$ is the lower semicircle. Enter *both* the equations in your

Technology Note _____

The standard viewing rectangle on many graphing utilities does not give a true geometric perspective. That is, perpendicular lines will not appear to be perpendicular and circles will not appear to be circular. To overcome this, you can use a square setting, as demonstrated in Example 4.

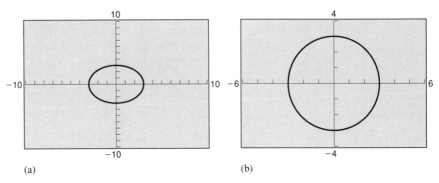

(a)   (b)

FIGURE 1.9

graphing utility and generate the resulting graphs. In Figure 1.9(a), note that if you use a standard viewing rectangle, the two graphs do not appear to form a circle. You can overcome this problem by using a **square setting,** in which the horizontal and vertical tick marks have equal spacing, as shown in Figure 1.9(b). On many graphing utilities, a square setting can be obtained by using the ratio $(Y_{max} - Y_{min})/(X_{max} - X_{min}) = 2/3$.

Applications

The following two applications show how to develop mathematical models to represent real-world situations. You will see that both a graphing utility and algebra can be used to understand and resolve the problems posed.

Once an appropriate viewing rectangle is chosen for a particular graph, the *zoom* and *trace* features of a graphing utility are useful for approximating specific values from the graph.

*Technology Note*_____

In applications, it is convenient to use variable names that suggest real-life quantities; d for distance, t for time, and so on. Most graphing utilities, however, require the variable names to be x and y.

EXAMPLE 5   **Using the Zoom and Trace Features of a Graphing Utility**

A runner runs at a constant rate of 4.8 miles per hour. The verbal model and algebraic equation relating distance run in terms of time are given by

VERBAL MODEL   Distance = Rate · Time

EQUATION $d = 4.8t$

A. Use a graphing utility and an appropriate viewing rectangle to graph the equation $d = 4.8t$. (Represent d by y and t by x.)

B. Use the zoom and trace features to estimate how far the runner can run in 3.2 hours.

C. Use the zoom and trace features to estimate how long it will take to run a 26-mile marathon.

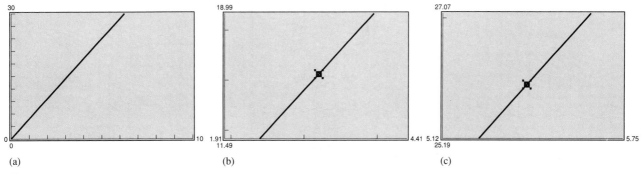

30

0
0   10

(a)

18.99

1.91
11.49   4.41

(b)

27.07

5.12
25.19   5.75

(c)

FIGURE 1.10

SOLUTION

A. An appropriate viewing rectangle and the associated graph are shown in Figure 1.10(a).

REMARK   The viewing rectangle on your graphing utility may differ from those shown in parts (b) and (c) of Figure 1.10.

B. Figure 1.10(b) shows the viewing rectangle after zooming in (near $x = 3.2$) once by a factor of 4. Using the trace feature, you can determine that for $x = 3.2$, the distance is $y \approx 15.36$ miles.

C. Figure 1.10(c) shows the viewing rectangle after zooming in (near $y = 26$) twice by a factor of 4. Using the trace feature, you can determine that for $y = 26$, the time is $x \approx 5.42$ hours.

EXAMPLE 6   An Application: Monthly Wages

You receive a monthly salary of $2000 plus a commission of 10% of sales.

A. Find an equation expressing the monthly wages y in terms of sales x.

B. If sales are $x = 1480$ in August, what are your wages for that month?

C. If you receive $2225 in wages for September, what were your sales for that month?

SOLUTION

A. The monthly wages are the sum of the fixed $2000 salary and the 10% commission on sales x.

VERBAL
MODEL   Wages = Salary + Commission on sales

EQUATION $y = 2000 + 0.1x$

B. If $x = 1480$, then the corresponding wages would be

$$y = 2000 + 0.1(1480) = 2000 + 148 = \$2148.$$

You can confirm this result using a graphing utility. Because $x \geq 0$ and the monthly wages are at least $2000, a reasonable viewing rectangle is shown below. [See Figure 1.11(a).] Using the zoom and trace features near $x = 1480$ shows that the wages are about $2148.

```
RANGE
Xmin=0
Xmax=3000
Xsc1=300
Ymin=2000
Ymax=2300
Ysc1=30
```

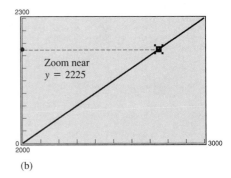

FIGURE 1.11   (a)   (b)

c. To answer the third question, you can use the graphing utility to find the value along the x-axis (sales) that corresponds to a y-value of 2225 (wages). Beginning with Figure 1.11(b) and using the zoom and trace features, you can estimate x to be $x \approx 2250$. You can verify this answer by observing that

$$
\begin{aligned}
\text{Wages} &= 2000 + 0.1(2250) \\
&= 2000 + 225 \\
&= 2225.
\end{aligned}
$$

DISCUSSION PROBLEM

COMPARISON OF WAGES

Michael receives a monthly salary of $3100 plus commission of 7% of sales, whereas Janet receives a salary of $3400 plus a 6% commission. Discuss their relative wages depending on sales. Can there be a month in which they receive exactly the same amount of wages? Be sure to take advantage of your graphing utility.

WARM-UP

The following warm-up exercises involve skills that were covered in earlier sections. You will use these skills in the exercise set for this section.

In Exercises 1–6, simplify the expression.

1. $4(x - 3) - 5(6 - 2x)$ **2.** $-s(5s + 2) + 5(s^2 - 3s)$

3. $3y(-2y^2)^3$ **4.** $\dfrac{18a^2b^{-3}}{27ab^2}$

5. $\sqrt{150x^4}$ **6.** $8^{-1/3}$

In Exercises 7–10, completely factor the expression.

7. $2x^3 - 6x^2$ **8.** $2t(t + 3)^2 - 4(t + 3)$

9. $6z^2 + 5z - 50$ **10.** $4s^2 - 25$

SECTION 1.1 · EXERCISES

In Exercises 1–6, determine whether the points lie on the graph of the equation.

Equation	Points	
*1. $y = \sqrt{x} + 4$	(a) (0, 2)	(b) (5, 3)
2. $y = x^2 - 3x + 2$	(a) (2, 0)	(b) (-2, 8)
3. $2x - y - 3 = 0$	(a) (1, 2)	(b) (1, -1)
4. $x^2 + y^2 = 20$	(a) (3, -2)	(b) (-4, 2)
5. $x^2 y - x^2 + 4y = 0$	(a) $(1, \frac{1}{5})$	(b) $(2, \frac{1}{2})$
6. $y = \dfrac{1}{x^2 + 1}$	(a) (0, 0)	(b) (3, 0.1)

In Exercises 7–10, find the constant C such that the ordered pair is a solution point of the equation.

7. $y = x^2 + C$, (2, 6)   8. $y = Cx^3$, (-4, 8)

9. $y = C\sqrt{x + 1}$, (3, 8)   10. $x + C(y + 2) = 0$, (4, 3)

In Exercises 11 and 12, complete the table and use the resulting solution points to graph the equation.

11. $2x + y = 3$

x	-4			2	4
y			7	3	
(x, y)					

12. $y = 4 - x^2$

x		-1		2	
y	0		4		-5
(x, y)					

In Exercises 13–18, match the equation with its graph and describe the given viewing rectangle. [The graphs are labeled (a), (b), (c), (d), (e), and (f).]

13. $y = 4 - x$ 14. $y = x^2 + 2x$

15. $y = \sqrt{4 - x^2}$ 16. $y = \sqrt{x}$

17. $y = x^3 - x$ 18. $y = |x| - 2$

*Detailed solutions to all odd-numbered exercises can be found in the *Study and Solutions Guide.*

(a)

(b)

(c)

(d)

(e)

(f)

In Exercises 19–30, use the point-plotting method to graph the equation. Use a graphing utility to verify your graph. (Use the standard viewing rectangle.)

19. $y = -3x + 2$ 20. $y = 2x - 3$

21. $y = 1 - x^2$ 22. $y = x^2 - 1$

23. $y = x^3 + 2$ 24. $y = x^3 - 1$

25. $y = (x - 3)(x + 2)$ 26. $y = x(x - 5)$

27. $y = \sqrt{x - 3}$ 28. $y = \sqrt{1 - x}$

29. $y = |x - 2|$ 30. $y = 4 - |x|$

In Exercises 31–38, use a graphing utility to graph the equation. (Use the standard viewing rectangle.) Determine the number of times (if any) the graph intersects each coordinate axis.

31. $y = x^2 - 4x + 3$ 32. $y = 4 - 4x - x^2$

33. $y = 3x^4 - 6x^2$ 34. $y = \frac{1}{27}(x^4 + 4x^3)$

35. $y = x\sqrt{4 - x}$ 36. $y = x\sqrt{4 - x^2}$

37. $y = \dfrac{10x}{x^2 + 1}$ 38. $y = \dfrac{10}{x^2 + 1}$

In Exercises 39–44, use a graphing utility to graph the equation. Use the specified viewing rectangle. Determine the number of times the graph intersects each coordinate axis.

39. $y = x^4 - 4x^3 + 16x$ **40.** $y = 4x^3 - x^4$

```
RANGE
Xmin=-5
Xmax=5
Xscl=1
Ymin=-15
Ymax=30
Yscl=5
```
```
RANGE
Xmin=-2
Xmax=6
Xscl=1
Ymin=-2
Ymax=30
Yscl=2
```

41. $y = 100x\sqrt{25 - x}$ **42.** $y = 100x\sqrt{25 - x^2}$

```
RANGE
Xmin=-30
Xmax=30
Xscl=5
Ymin=-5000
Ymax=5000
Yscl=1000
```
```
RANGE
Xmin=-8
Xmax=8
Xscl=1
Ymin=-2000
Ymax=2000
Yscl=500
```

43. $x^2 - 100y - 1000 = 0$

```
RANGE
Xmin=-100
Xmax=100
Xscl=10
Ymin=-10
Ymax=10
Yscl=1
```

44. $2x^3 - 100x - 15,625 + 250y = 0$

```
RANGE
Xmin=-20
Xmax=25
Xscl=2
Ymin=-2
Ymax=100
Yscl=5
```

In Exercises 45–48, solve for y and use a graphing utility to graph each of the resulting equations on the same viewing rectangle. Adjust the viewing rectangle so a circle really does appear circular. (Your graphing utility may have a *square* setting that does this automatically.)

45. Circle: $x^2 + y^2 = 64$ **46.** Circle: $x^2 + y^2 = 49$
47. Ellipse: $6x^2 + y^2 = 72$ **48.** Ellipse: $x^2 + 9y^2 = 81$

In Exercises 49–52, describe the given viewing rectangle.

49. $9x + 27y - 1000 = 0$ **50.** $0.75x - 3y + 200 = 0$

51. $y = -(x - 5)^2(x - 15)$ **52.** $y = \sqrt{x^3 + 8}$

In Exercises 53 and 54, use a graphing utility to graph the equation using each of the suggested viewing rectangles. Assume that the equation gives the profit y when x units of a product are sold. Note that a graph can distort the information presented simply by changing the viewing rectangle. Which viewing rectangle would be selected by a person who wishes to argue that profits will increase dramatically with increased sales?

53. $y = 0.25x - 50$

```
RANGE
Xmin=-3
Xmax=800
Xscl=50
Ymin=-20
Ymax=100
Yscl=10
```
```
RANGE
Xmin=-3
Xmax=1000
Xscl=100
Ymin=-100
Ymax=500
Yscl=40
```

54. $y = 2.44x - \dfrac{x^2}{20,000} - 5000$

```
RANGE
Xmin=-5000
Xmax=22000
Xscl=5000
Ymin=-20000
Ymax=60000
Yscl=10000
```
```
RANGE
Xmin=-5000
Xmax=22000
Xscl=5000
Ymin=-5000
Ymax=24000
Yscl=5000
```

In Exercises 55 and 56, use the equation to complete each table. Note the importance of increasing the number of solution points to increase the accuracy of the graph.

(a) Use the table to sketch a graph of the equation.

x	-1	0	1
y			

(b) Use the table to sketch a graph of the equation.

x	-1	$-\frac{3}{4}$	$-\frac{1}{2}$	$-\frac{1}{4}$	0	$\frac{1}{4}$	$\frac{1}{2}$	$\frac{3}{4}$	1
y									

(c) Use a graphing utility to graph the equation for $-1 \le x \le 1$.

55. $y = \sqrt[3]{x}$

56. $y = x^3(3x + 4)$

In Exercises 57–60, use a graphing utility to graph the equation. Move the cursor along the curve to approximate the unknown coordinate(s) of the given solution point accurate to two decimal places. (*Hint:* You may need to use the zoom feature of the calculator to obtain the required accuracy.)

57. $y = \sqrt{5 - x}$
  (a) $(2, y)$
  (b) $(x, 3)$
58. $y = x^3(x - 3)$
  (a) $(2.25, y)$
  (b) $(x, 20)$
59. $y = x^5 - 5x$
  (a) $(-0.5, y)$
  (b) $(x, -4)$
60. $y = |x^2 - 6x + 5|$
  (a) $(2, y)$
  (b) $(x, 1.5)$

61. *Depreciation*   A manufacturing plant purchases a new molding machine for $225,000. The depreciated value y after x years is given by $y = 225,000 - 20,000x$, $0 \le x \le 8$.
  (a) Use the constraints of the model to determine an appropriate viewing rectangle.
  (b) Graph the equation.

62. *Dimensions of a Rectangle*   A rectangle of length x and width w has a perimeter of 12 meters.
  (a) Show that the area of the rectangle is $y = x(6 - x)$.
  (b) Use the physical constraints of the problem to determine the horizontal component of the viewing rectangle.
  (c) Use a graphing utility to graph the equation for the area. (*Note:* You may have to sketch the graph more than once in order to determine an appropriate vertical component of the viewing rectangle.)
  (d) From the graph in part (c), estimate the dimensions of the rectangle that yields a maximum area.

In Exercises 63 and 64, (a) graph the model and compare it with the data, and (b) use the model to predict y for the year 1994.

63. *Federal Debt*   The table gives the per capita federal debt for the United States for selected years from 1950 to 1990. (*Source:* U.S. Treasury Department)

Year	1950	1960	1970	1980	1985	1990
Per capita debt	$1688	$1572	$1807	$3981	$7614	$12,848

A model for the per capita debt during this period is

$$y = 0.40x^3 - 9.42x^2 + 1053.24,$$

where y represents the per capita debt and x is the year, with $x = 0$ corresponding to 1950.

64. *Life Expectancy*   The table gives the life expectancy of a child (at birth) for selected years from 1920 to 1989. (*Source:* Department of Health and Human Services)

Year	1920	1930	1940	1950
Life expectancy	54.1	59.7	62.9	68.2

Year	1960	1970	1980	1989
Life expectancy	69.7	70.8	73.7	75.2

A model for the life expectancy during this period is

$$y = \frac{x + 66.94}{0.01x + 1},$$

where y represents the life expectancy and x represents the year, with $x = 0$ corresponding to 1950.

65. *Earnings Per Share*   The earnings per share for Eli Lilly Corporation from 1980 to 1986 can be approximated by the model

$$y = 1.097x + 0.15, \qquad 0 \le x \le 6,$$

where y is the earnings and x represents the year, with $x = 0$ corresponding to 1980. Graph this equation. (*Source:* NYSE Stock Reports)

66. *Copper Wire*   The resistance y in ohms of 1000 feet of solid copper wire at 77 degrees Fahrenheit can be approximated by the model

$$y = \frac{10,770}{x^2} - 0.37, \qquad 5 \le x \le 100,$$

where x is the diameter of the wire in mils (0.001 in.). Use the model to estimate the resistance when $x = 50$.

67. Find a and b if the x-intercept of the graph of $y = \sqrt{ax + b}$ is $(5, 0)$. (There is more than one correct answer.)

1.2   LINES IN THE PLANE

The Slope of a Line   /   The Point-Slope Form of the Equation of a Line   /
Sketching Graphs of Lines   /   Changing the Viewing Rectangle   /
Parallel and Perpendicular Lines

The Slope of a Line

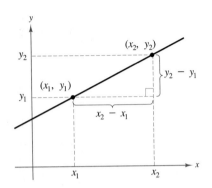

FIGURE 1.12

In this section, you will study lines and their equations. Throughout this text, the term **line** always means a *straight* line.

The **slope** of a nonvertical line represents the number of units a line rises or falls vertically for each unit of horizontal change from left to right. For instance, consider the two points (x_1, y_1) and (x_2, y_2) on the line shown in Figure 1.12. As you move from left to right along this line, a change of $(y_2 - y_1)$ units in the vertical direction corresponds to a change of $(x_2 - x_1)$ units in the horizontal direction. That is,

$$y_2 - y_1 = \text{the change in } y$$

and

$$x_2 - x_1 = \text{the change in } x.$$

The slope of the line is given by the ratio of these two changes.

DEFINITION OF THE SLOPE OF A LINE

The **slope** m of the nonvertical line passing through the points (x_1, y_1) and (x_2, y_2) is

$$m = \frac{y_2 - y_1}{x_2 - x_1} = \frac{\text{change in } y}{\text{change in } x},$$

where $x_1 \ne x_2$.

When this formula is used, the *order of subtraction* is important. Given two points on a line, you are free to label either one of them as (x_1, y_1), and the other as (x_2, y_2). However, once this is done, you must form the numerator and denominator using the same order of subtraction.

$$m = \frac{y_2 - y_1}{x_2 - x_1} \qquad m = \frac{y_1 - y_2}{x_1 - x_2} \qquad m = \frac{y_2 - y_1}{x_1 - x_2}$$

   Correct   Correct   Incorrect

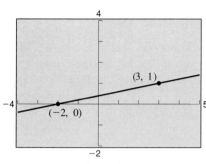

(a) The slope is $\frac{1}{5}$.

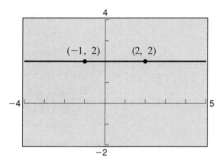

(b) The slope is zero.

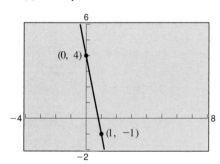

(c) The slope is -5.

FIGURE 1.13

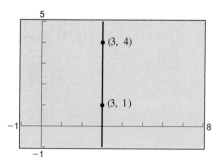

The slope is undefined.

FIGURE 1.14

EXAMPLE 1   **Finding the Slope of a Line Passing Through**
Two Points

Find the slopes of the lines passing through the following pairs of points.

A. $(-2, 0)$ and $(3, 1)$
B. $(-1, 2)$ and $(2, 2)$
C. $(0, 4)$ and $(1, -1)$

SOLUTION

Difference in y-values

A. $m = \dfrac{\overbrace{y_2 - y_1}}{\underbrace{x_2 - x_1}} = \dfrac{1 - 0}{3 - (-2)} = \dfrac{1}{3 + 2} = \dfrac{1}{5}$

Difference in x-values

B. $m = \dfrac{2 - 2}{2 - (-1)} = \dfrac{0}{3} = 0$

C. $m = \dfrac{-1 - 4}{1 - 0} = \dfrac{-5}{1} = -5$

The graphs of the three lines are shown in Figure 1.13. In parts (a) and (c), note that the "square" setting gives the correct "steepness" of the line.

The definition of slope does not apply to vertical lines. For instance, consider the points $(3, 4)$ and $(3, 1)$ on the vertical line shown in Figure 1.14. Applying the formula for slope, you obtain

$$m = \frac{4 - 1}{3 - 3}. \qquad \textit{Undefined division by zero}$$

Because division by zero is undefined, the slope of a vertical line is undefined.
From the slopes of the lines shown in Figures 1.13 and 1.14, you can make the following generalizations about the slope of a line.

1. A line with positive slope $(m > 0)$ *rises* from left to right.
2. A line with negative slope $(m < 0)$ *falls* from left to right.
3. A line with zero slope $(m = 0)$ is *horizontal*.
4. A line with undefined slope is *vertical*.

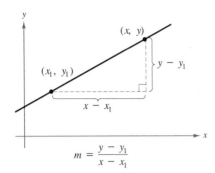

$$m = \frac{y - y_1}{x - x_1}$$

FIGURE 1.15

The Point-Slope Form of the Equation of a Line

If you know the slope of a line *and* you also know the coordinates of one point on the line, then you can find an equation for the line. For instance, in Figure 1.15, let (x_1, y_1) be a given point on the line whose slope is m. If (x, y) is any *other* point on the line, then it follows that

$$\frac{y - y_1}{x - x_1} = m.$$

This equation in the variables x and y can be rewritten in the form

$$y - y_1 = m(x - x_1),$$

which is the **point-slope form** of the equation of a line.

POINT-SLOPE FORM OF THE EQUATION OF A LINE

The **point-slope** form of the equation of the line that passes through the point (x_1, y_1) and has a slope of m is

$$y - y_1 = m(x - x_1).$$

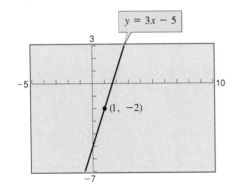

FIGURE 1.16

EXAMPLE 2 The Point-Slope Form of the Equation of a Line

Find an equation of the line that passes through the point $(1, -2)$ and has a slope of 3.

SOLUTION

$$y - y_1 = m(x - x_1)$$ *Point-slope form*
$$y - (-2) = 3(x - 1)$$ *Substitute $y_1 = -2$, $x_1 = 1$, and $m = 3$*
$$y + 2 = 3x - 3$$
$$y = 3x - 5$$ *Equation of line*

This line is shown in Figure 1.16.

The point-slope form can be used to find the equation of a nonvertical line passing through two points (x_1, y_1) and (x_2, y_2). First, use the formula for the slope of the line passing through two points.

$$m = \frac{y_2 - y_1}{x_2 - x_1}$$

Then, once you know the slope, use the point-slope form to obtain the equation

$$y - y_1 = \frac{y_2 - y_1}{x_2 - x_1}(x - x_1).$$

This is sometimes called the **two-point form** of the equation of a line.

EXAMPLE 3 A Linear Model for Sales Prediction
....

During the first two quarters of the year, a company had total sales of $3.4 million and $3.7 million, respectively.

A. Write a linear equation giving the total sales y in terms of the quarter x.
B. Use the equation to predict the total sales during the fourth quarter.

SOLUTION

A. In Figure 1.17, let (1, 3.4) and (2, 3.7) be two points on the line representing the total sales. The slope of the line passing through these two points is

$$m = \frac{3.7 - 3.4}{2 - 1} = 0.3.$$

FIGURE 1.17

By the point-slope form, the equation of the line is as follows.

$$y - y_1 = m(x - x_1)$$
$$y - 3.4 = 0.3(x - 1)$$
$$y = 0.3x - 0.3 + 3.4$$
$$y = 0.3x + 3.1$$

B. Using the equation from part (A), estimate the fourth-quarter sales ($x = 4$) to be $y = 0.3(4) + 3.1 = 1.2 + 3.1 = 4.3 million. ....

Linear Extrapolation

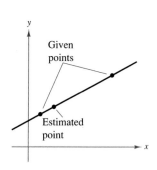

Linear Interpolation

FIGURE 1.18

The approximation method illustrated in Example 3 is **linear extrapolation.** Note in Figure 1.18 that for linear extrapolation, the estimated point lies outside of the given points. When the estimated point lies *between* two given points, the procedure is called **linear interpolation.**

Sketching Graphs of Lines

Many problems in coordinate (or analytic) geometry can be classified in two basic categories.

1. Given a graph (or parts of it), find its equation.
2. Given an equation, find its graph.

For lines, the first problem is solved easily by using the point-slope form. This formula, however, is not particularly useful for solving the second type of problem. The form that is better suited to graphing linear equations is the **slope-intercept form** $y = mx + b$ of the equation of a line.

FIGURE 1.19

FIGURE 1.20

EXAMPLE 4   Determining the Slope and y-Intercepts

A. By graphing the equations $y = 2x + 1$, $y = \frac{1}{2}x + 1$, and $y = -2x + 1$ on the same coordinate axes, you can see that they each have the same y-intercept $(0, 1)$, but slopes of 2, $\frac{1}{2}$, and -2, respectively (see Figure 1.19).

B. By graphing the equations $y = 2x + 1$, $y = 2x$, and $y = 2x - 1$ on the same coordinate axes, you can see that they each have the same slope of 2, but y-intercepts of $(0, 1)$, $(0, 0)$, and $(0, -1)$, respectively (see Figure 1.20).

SLOPE-INTERCEPT FORM OF THE EQUATION OF A LINE

The graph of the equation

$$y = mx + b$$

is a line whose slope is m and whose y-intercept is $(0, b)$.

To derive algebraically the slope-intercept form, write the following.

$$y - y_1 = m(x - x_1) \qquad \textit{Point-slope form}$$
$$y = mx - mx_1 + y_1$$
$$y = mx + b \qquad\qquad \textit{Slope-intercept form}$$

(a)

(b)

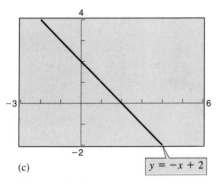

(c)

FIGURE 1.21

EXAMPLE 5   Using the Slope-Intercept Form

Describe the graphs of the linear equations.

A. $y = \dfrac{3}{2}x$

B. $y = 2$

C. $x + y = 2$

SOLUTION

A. Because $b = 0$, the y-intercept is $(0, 0)$. Moreover, because the slope is $m = \frac{3}{2}$, this line *rises* three units for every two units the line moves to the right, as shown in Figure 1.21(a).

B. By writing the equation $y = 2$ in the form $y = (0)x + 2$, you can see that the y-intercept is $(0, 2)$ and the slope is zero. A zero slope implies that the line is horizontal, as shown in Figure 1.21(b).

C. By writing the equation $x + y = 2$ in slope-intercept form, $y = -x + 2$, you can see that the y-intercept is $(0, 2)$. Moreover, because the slope is $m = -1$, this line *falls* one unit for each unit the line moves to the right, as shown in Figure 1.21(c).

From the slope-intercept form of the equation of a line, you can see that a horizontal line ($m = 0$) has an equation of the form $y = b$. This is consistent with the fact that each point on a horizontal line through $(0, b)$ has a y-coordinate of b.

Similarly, each point on a vertical line through $(a, 0)$ has an x-coordinate of a. Hence, a vertical line has an equation of the form $x = a$. This equation cannot be written in the slope-intercept form, because the slope of a vertical line is undefined. However, *every* line has an equation that can be written in the **general form** $Ax + By + C = 0$, where A and B are not *both* zero.

SUMMARY OF EQUATIONS OF LINES

1. General form: $Ax + By + C = 0$
2. Vertical line: $x = a$
3. Horizontal line: $y = b$
4. Slope-intercept form: $y = mx + b$
5. Point-slope form: $y - y_1 = m(x - x_1)$

Changing the Viewing Rectangle

When using a graphing utility to sketch a straight line, it is important to realize that the graph of the line may not visually appear to have the slope indicated by its equation. This occurs because of the viewing rectangle used for the graph. For instance, Figure 1.22 shows a graph of $y = 2x + 1$ using a graphing utility with three different viewing rectangles.

Notice that the slopes of the first two lines do not visually appear to be equal to 2. If you use the "square" viewing rectangle (right), then the slope will visually appear to be 2. In general, two graphs of the same equation can appear to be quite different depending upon the viewing rectangle selected.

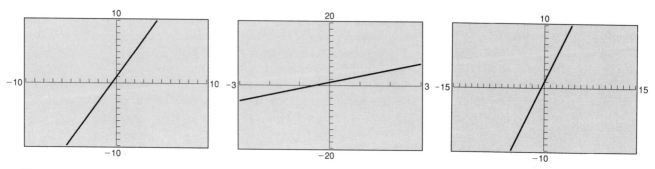

FIGURE 1.22

Effects of Different Viewing Rectangles
on Graph of $y = 2x + 1$

EXAMPLE 6   Different Viewing Rectangles

The graphs of the two lines $y = -x - 1$ and $y = -10x - 1$ are shown in Figure 1.23. Even though the slopes of these lines are different (-1 and -10, respectively), the graphs seem similar because the viewing rectangles are different.

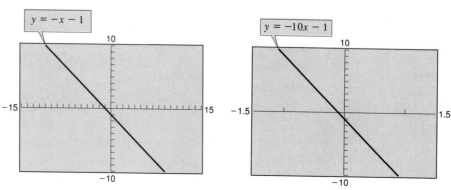

FIGURE 1.23

Parallel and Perpendicular Lines

The slope of a line is a convenient tool for determining whether two lines are parallel or perpendicular. Example 4(B) suggests the following property of parallel lines.

PARALLEL LINES

Two distinct nonvertical lines are **parallel** if and only if their slopes are equal.

EXAMPLE 7   **Equations of Parallel Lines**

Find an equation of the line that passes through the point $(2, -1)$ and is parallel to the line $2x - 3y = 5$, as shown in Figure 1.24.

SOLUTION

Write the given equation in slope-intercept form.

$$2x - 3y = 5 \qquad \text{\textit{Given equation}}$$
$$3y = 2x - 5$$
$$y = \frac{2}{3}x - \frac{5}{3} \qquad \text{\textit{Slope-intercept form}}$$

Therefore, the given line has a slope of $m = \frac{2}{3}$. Because any line parallel to the given line must also have a slope of $\frac{2}{3}$, the required line through $(2, -1)$ has the following equation.

$$y - (-1) = \frac{2}{3}(x - 2) \qquad \text{\textit{Point-slope form}}$$
$$y = \frac{2}{3}x - \frac{4}{3} - 1$$
$$y = \frac{2}{3}x - \frac{7}{3} \qquad \text{\textit{Slope-intercept form}}$$

Notice the similarity between the slope-intercept form of the original equation and the slope-intercept form of the parallel equation.   ·········

Two nonvertical lines are *perpendicular* if and only if their slopes are negative reciprocals of each other. For instance, the lines $y = 2x$ and $y = -\frac{1}{2}x$ are perpendicular because one has a slope of 2 and the other has a slope of $-\frac{1}{2}$.

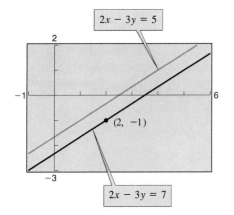

$2x - 3y = 5$

$(2, -1)$

$2x - 3y = 7$

FIGURE 1.24

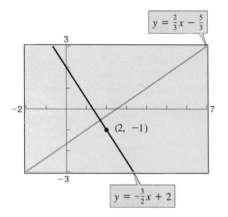

$y = \frac{2}{3}x - \frac{5}{3}$

$(2, -1)$

$y = -\frac{3}{2}x + 2$

FIGURE 1.25

(a)

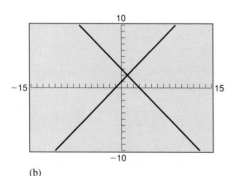

(b)

FIGURE 1.26

PERPENDICULAR LINES

Two nonvertical lines are **perpendicular** if and only if their slopes are negative reciprocals of each other. That is,

$$m_1 = -\frac{1}{m_2}.$$

EXAMPLE 8   Equations of Perpendicular Lines

Find an equation of the line that passes through the point $(2, -1)$ and is perpendicular to the line $2x - 3y = 5$.

SOLUTION

By writing the given line in the form $y = \frac{2}{3}x - \frac{5}{3}$ you can see that the line has a slope of $\frac{2}{3}$. Hence, any line that is perpendicular to this line must have a slope of $-\frac{3}{2}$ (because $-\frac{3}{2}$ is the negative reciprocal of $\frac{2}{3}$). Therefore, the required line through the point $(2, -1)$ has the following equation.

$$y - (-1) = -\frac{3}{2}(x - 2) \qquad \textit{Point-slope form}$$

$$y = -\frac{3}{2}x + 3 - 1$$

$$y = -\frac{3}{2}x + 2 \qquad \textit{Slope-intercept form}$$

The graphs of both equations are shown in Figure 1.25.

EXAMPLE 9   Graphs of Perpendicular Lines

Use a graphing utility to graph the lines given by $y = x + 1$ and $y = -x + 3$. Display *both* graphs on the same screen. The lines are supposed to be perpendicular (they have slopes of $m_1 = 1$ and $m_2 = -1$). Do they appear to be perpendicular on the display?

SOLUTION

If the viewing window has the *standard* range settings, then the tick marks on both the x-axis and the y-axis will vary between -10 and 10, as in Figure 1.26(a). However, because most display screens are not square, the lines might *not* appear to be perpendicular. That is, the graphs of two perpendicular lines will appear to be perpendicular only if the tick marks on the x-axis have the same spacing as the tick marks on the y-axis, as in Figure 1.26(b). This can be done by using a "square" setting for the viewing rectangle.

In 1982, a college had an enrollment of 5000 students. By 1992, the enrollment had increased to 7000 students.

(a) What is the average annual change in enrollment from 1982 to 1992?
(b) Use the average annual change in enrollment to estimate the enrollment in 1986, 1990, and 1994.

Year	1982	1986	1990	1992	1994
Enrollment	5000			7000	

(c) Graph the line represented by the data given in the table in part (b). What is the slope of this line?
(d) Write a short paragraph that compares the concepts of *slope* and *average rate of change*.

The following warm-up exercises involve skills that were covered in earlier sections. You will use these skills in the exercise set for this section.

In Exercises 1 and 2, simplify the expression.

1. $\dfrac{4 - (-5)}{-3 - (-1)}$

2. $\dfrac{-5 - 8}{0 - (-3)}$

3. Find $-1/m$ for $m = 4/5$.

4. Find $-1/m$ for $m = -2$.

In Exercises 5–10, solve for y in terms of x.

5. $2x - 3y = 5$

6. $4x + 2y = 0$

7. $y - (-4) = 3[x - (-1)]$

8. $y - 7 = \frac{2}{3}(x - 3)$

9. $y - (-1) = \dfrac{3 - (-1)}{2 - 4}(x - 4)$

10. $y - 5 = \dfrac{3 - 5}{0 - 2}(x - 2)$

SECTION 1.2 · EXERCISES

In Exercises 1–6, estimate the slope of the line.

1.

2.

3.

4.

5.

6.
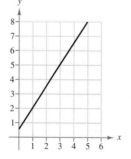

In Exercises 7 and 8, graph the lines through the given point with the indicated slopes. Graph the lines on the same set of coordinate axes.

Point	Slopes
7. (2, 3)	(a) 0 (b) 1 (c) 2 (d) −3
8. (−4, 1)	(a) 3 (b) −3 (c) $\frac{1}{2}$ (d) Undefined

In Exercises 9–14, plot the points and find the slope of the line passing through the points.

9. (−3, −2), (1, 6)   **10.** (2, 4), (4, −4)
11. (−6, −1), (−6, 4)   **12.** (0, −10), (−4, 0)
13. (1, 2), (−2, −2)   **14.** $\left(\frac{7}{8}, \frac{3}{4}\right)$, $\left(\frac{5}{4}, -\frac{1}{4}\right)$

In Exercises 15–18, use the given point on the line and the slope of the line to find three additional points through which the line passes. (There are many correct answers.)

	Point	Slope		Point	Slope
15.	(2, 1)	$m = 0$	**16.**	(−4, 1)	m is undefined
17.	(5, −6)	$m = 1$	**18.**	(10, −6)	$m = -1$

In Exercises 19–22, determine whether the lines L_1 and L_2 passing through the given pairs of points are parallel, perpendicular, or neither.

19. L_1: (0, −1), (5, 9)   **20.** L_1: (−2, −1), (1, 5)
     L_2: (0, 3), (4, 1) L_2: (1, 3), (5, −5)
21. L_1: (3, 6), (−6, 0)   **22.** L_1: (4, 8), (−4, 2)
     L_2: (0, −1), $\left(5, \frac{7}{3}\right)$ L_2: (3, −5), $\left(-1, \frac{1}{3}\right)$

In Exercises 23 and 24, use the concept of slope to determine whether the three points are collinear.

23. (0, −4), (2, 0), (3, 2)   **24.** (−2, 1), (−1, 0), (2, −2)

25. *Mountain Driving*   While driving down a mountain road, you notice a "12% grade" warning sign. This means that the slope of the road is $-\frac{12}{100}$. Determine the amount of horizontal change in your position if you note from elevation markers that you have descended 2000 feet vertically.

26. *Attic Height*   The "rise to run" in determining the steepness of the roof on the house in the figure is 3 to 4. Determine the maximum height in the attic of the house if the house is 30 feet wide.

FIGURE FOR 26

In Exercises 27–30, find the slope and y-intercept (if possible) of the line specified by the equation. Graph the line.

27. $5x - y + 3 = 0$ **28.** $2x + 3y - 9 = 0$
29. $5x - 2 = 0$ **30.** $3y + 5 = 0$

In Exercises 31–36, find an equation for the line passing through the points.

31. $(5, -1), (-5, 5)$ **32.** $(4, 3), (-4, -4)$

33. $(2, \frac{1}{2}), (\frac{1}{2}, \frac{5}{4})$ **34.** $(-1, 4), (6, 4)$

35. $(-8, 1), (-8, 7)$ **36.** $(-8, 0.6), (2, -2.4)$

In Exercises 37–42, find an equation of the line that passes through the point and has the indicated slope.

Point	Slope		Point	Slope
37. $(0, -2)$	$m = 3$		**38.** $(0, 0)$	$m = 4$
39. $(4, \frac{5}{2})$	$m = -\frac{4}{3}$		**40.** $(-2, -5)$	$m = \frac{3}{4}$
41. $(6, -1)$	m is undefined		**42.** $(-10, 4)$	$m = 0$

In Exercises 43 and 44, use a graphing utility to graph the equation using each of the suggested viewing rectangles. Note that the viewing rectangle selected will alter the appearance of the slope.

43. $y = 0.5x - 3$

```
RANGE
Xmin=-5
Xmax=10
Xscl=1
Ymin=-10
Ymax=5
Yscl=1
```
```
RANGE
Xmin=-2
Xmax=10
Xscl=1
Ymin=-4
Ymax=1
Yscl=1
```

44. $y = -8x + 5$

```
RANGE
Xmin=-5
Xmax=5
Xscl=1
Ymin=-10
Ymax=10
Yscl=1
```
```
RANGE
Xmin=-5
Xmax=10
Xscl=1
Ymin=-80
Ymax=80
Yscl=20
```

In Exercises 45–48, use a graphing utility to graph the three equations on the same viewing rectangle. Adjust the viewing rectangle so the slope appears visually correct. (Your calculator may have a *square* setting that does this automatically.)

45. $y = 2x$ $y = -2x$ $y = \frac{1}{2}x$

46. $y = \frac{2}{3}x$ $y = -\frac{3}{2}x$ $y = \frac{2}{3}x + 2$

47. $y = -\frac{1}{2}x$ $y = -\frac{1}{2}x + 3$ $y = 2x - 4$

48. $y = x - 8$ $y = x + 1$ $y = -x + 3$

In Exercises 49 and 50, use the given values of a and b and a graphing utility to graph the equation of the line given by

$$\frac{x}{a} + \frac{y}{b} = 1, \qquad a \neq 0, b \neq 0.$$

Use the graphs to determine the meaning of the constants a and b.

49. $a = 5, \quad b = -3$ **50.** $a = -6, \quad b = 2$

In Exercises 51 and 52, use the results of Exercises 49 and 50 to write an equation of the line that passes through the given points.

51. x-intercept: $(2, 0)$ **52.** x-intercept: $(-\frac{1}{6}, 0)$
y-intercept: $(0, 3)$ y-intercept: $(0, -\frac{2}{3})$

In Exercises 53–56, write an equation of the line through the point (a) parallel to the given line and (b) perpendicular to the given line.

Point	Line		Point	Line
53. $(2, 1)$	$4x - 2y = 3$		**54.** $(\frac{7}{8}, \frac{3}{4})$	$5x + 3y = 0$
55. $(-1, 0)$	$y = -3$		**56.** $(2, 5)$	$x = 4$

In Exercises 57–60, you are given the dollar value of a product in 1990 *and* the rate at which the value of the item is expected to increase during the next five years. Use this information to write a linear equation that gives the dollar value V of the product in terms of the year t. (Let $t = 0$ represent 1990.)

	1990 Value	Rate
57.	$2540	$125 per year
58.	$156	$4.50 per year
59.	$20,400	$2000 per year
60.	$245,000	$5600 per year

In Exercises 61–64, match the description with a graph. Determine the slope and how it is interpreted in the situation. [The graphs are labeled (a), (b), (c), and (d).]

61. A person is paying $10 per week to a friend to repay a $100 loan.

62. An employee is paid $12.50 per hour plus $1.50 for each unit produced per hour.

63. A sales representative receives $20 per day for food plus $0.25 for each mile traveled.

64. A typewriter purchased for $600 depreciates $100 per year.

(a)

(b)

(c)

(d)

65. *Temperature* Find an equation of the line giving the relationship between the temperature in degrees Celsius, C, and degrees Fahrenheit, F. Remember that water freezes at 0° Celsius (32° Fahrenheit) and boils at 100° Celsius (212° Fahrenheit).

66. *Temperature* Use the result of Exercise 65 to complete the table.

C		−10°	10°			177°
F	0°			68°	90°	

67. *Annual Salary* Suppose your salary was $28,500 in 1990 and $32,900 in 1992. Assume your salary follows a linear growth pattern.
(a) Write a linear equation giving the salary S in terms of the year t where $t = 0$ corresponds to the year 1990.
(b) Use the linear equation to predict your salary in 1995.

68. *College Enrollment* A small college had 2546 students in 1990 and 2702 students in 1992. Assume the enrollment follows a linear growth pattern.
(a) Write a linear equation giving the enrollment E in terms of the year t where $t = 0$ corresponds to the year 1990.
(b) Use the linear equation to predict the enrollment in 1997.

69. *Straight-Line Depreciation* A small business purchases a piece of equipment for $875. After 5 years the equipment will be outdated and have no value.
(a) Write a linear equation giving the value y of the equipment in terms of the time x, $0 \leq x \leq 5$.
(b) Use a graphing utility to graph the equation.
(c) Move the cursor along the graph and estimate (to two decimal place accuracy) the value of the equipment when $x = 2$.
(d) Move the cursor along the graph and estimate (to two decimal place accuracy) the time when the value of the equipment is $200.

70. *Hourly Wages* A manufacturer pays its assembly line workers $11.50 per hour plus $0.75 per unit produced.
(a) Write the linear equation for the hourly wages y in terms of the number of units x produced per hour.
(b) Use a graphing utility to graph the equation.
(c) Move the cursor along the graph and estimate (to two decimal place accuracy) the hourly wage when a worker produces $x = 6$ units per hour.
(d) Move the cursor along the graph and determine the number of units that must be produced per hour to have an hourly wage of $18.25.

71. *Sales Commission* A salesperson receives a monthly salary of $2500 plus a commission of 7% of sales. Write a linear equation for the salesperson's monthly wage W in terms of monthly sales S.

72. *Daily Cost* A sales representative of a company receives $120 per day for lodging and meals plus $0.26 per mile driven. Write a linear equation giving the daily cost C to the company in terms of x, the number of miles driven.

73. *Contracting Purchase* A contractor purchases a piece of equipment for $36,500. The equipment has an average expense of $5.25 per hour for fuel and maintenance, and the operator is paid $11.50 per hour.
(a) Write a linear equation for the total cost C of operating the equipment for t hours. (Include the purchase cost.)
(b) Customers are charged $37 per hour of machine use. Write an equation for the revenue R derived from t hours of use.
(c) *Break-Even Point* Use a graphing utility to graph the cost and revenue equations on the same viewing rectangle. Move the cursor to the point of intersection of the graphs to estimate (to the nearest hour) the number of hours the equipment must be used to break even.

74. *Real Estate*   A real estate office handles an apartment complex with 50 units. When the rent per unit is $380 per month, all 50 units are occupied. However, when the rent is $425 per month, the average number of occupied units drops to 47. Assume that the relationship between the monthly rent *p* and the demand *x* is linear.

  (a) Write an equation of the line giving the demand *x* in terms of the rent *p*.

  (b) Use a graphing utility to graph the demand equation.

  (c) Move the cursor along the graph to predict the number of units occupied if the rent is raised to $455.

  (d) Move the cursor along the graph to predict the number of units occupied if the rent is lowered to $395.

75.

76.

In Exercises 75 and 76, create a realistic problem that is modeled by the graph.

77. Use the theorem that the ratios of corresponding sides of similar triangles are equal to verify that any two points on a line can be used to calculate its slope.

1.3   FUNCTIONS
....
Introduction to Functions   /   Function Notation   /   The Domain of a Function   /   Function Keys on a Graphing Utility   /   Applications
▬▬▬▬▬

Introduction to Functions

Many everyday phenomena involve two quantities that are related to each other by some rule of correspondence. Such a rule of correspondence is called a **function.** Here are two examples.

1. The simple interest *I* earned on $1000 for one year is related to the annual percentage rate *r* by the formula $I = 1000r$.
2. The area *A* of a circle is related to its radius *r* by the formula $A = \pi r^2$.

REMARK   Note that this use of the word *range* is not the same as the use of *range* relating to the viewing window for a graph.

DEFINITION OF A FUNCTION

A **function** *f* from a set *A* to a set *B* is a rule of correspondence that assigns to each element *x* in the set *A* exactly one element *y* in the set *B*. The set *A* is the **domain** (or set of inputs) of the function *f*, and the set *B* contains the **range** (or set of outputs).

To help understand this definition, look at the function illustrated in Figure 1.27. This function can be represented by the following set of ordered pairs.

$$\{(1, 9°), (2, 13°), (3, 15°), (4, 15°), (5, 12°), (6, 4°)\}$$

In each ordered pair, the first coordinate is the input and the second coordinate is the output.

The following characteristics are true of a function from a set A to a set B.

1. Each element in A must be matched with an element in B.
2. Some elements in B may not be matched with any element in A.
3. Two or more elements of A may be matched with the same element of B.

The converse of the third statement is not true. That is, an element of A (the domain) cannot be matched with two different elements of B.

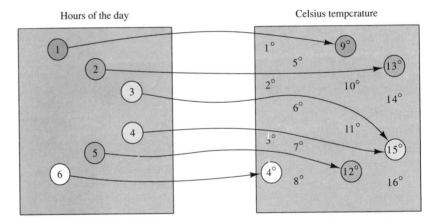

Hours of the day   Celsius temperature

Set A is the domain.
Input: 1, 2, 3, 4, 5, 6

Set B contains the range.
Output: $4°, 9°, 12°, 13°, 15°$

FIGURE 1.27   Function from Set A to Set B

EXAMPLE 1   **Testing for Functions**

Let $A = \{a, b, c\}$ and $B = \{1, 2, 3, 4, 5\}$. Does the set of ordered pairs or figures represent a function from set A to set B?

A. $\{(a, 2), (b, 3), (c, 4)\}$ **B.** $\{(a, 4), (b, 5)\}$

C.

D.

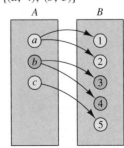

SOLUTION

  A. Yes, because each element of A is matched with exactly one element of B.
  B. No, because not all elements of A are matched with an element of B.
  C. Yes. It does not matter that each element of A is matched with the same element of B.
  D. No, because the element a in A is matched with *two* elements, 1 and 2, in B. This is also true of the element b.

  Representing functions by sets of ordered pairs is a common practice in *discrete mathematics*. In algebra, however, it is more common to represent functions by equations or formulas involving two variables. For instance, the equation

$$y = x^2$$

represents the variable y as a function of the variable x. Here, x is the **independent variable** and y is the **dependent variable.** The domain of the function is the set of all values (inputs) taken on by the independent variable x, and the range of the function is the set of all values (outputs) taken on by the dependent variable y.

EXAMPLE 2   **Testing for Functions Represented by Equations**

Determine whether the equations represent y as a function of x.

  A. $x^2 + y = 1$ **B.** $-x + y^2 = 1$

SOLUTION

In each case, to determine whether y is a function of x, it is helpful to solve for y in terms of x.

  A. $x^2 + y = 1$ *Given equation*
  $\qquad y = 1 - x^2$ *Solve for y*
  To each value of x there corresponds one value of y. Therefore, y is a function of x.

  B. $-x + y^2 = 1$ *Given equation*
  $\qquad y^2 = 1 + x$ *Add x to both sides*
  $\qquad y = \pm\sqrt{1 + x}$ *Solve for y*
  The $\pm$ indicates that to a given value of x there correspond two values of y. Therefore, y is *not* a function of x. For instance, if $x = 3$, then y could be either 2 or -2.

DISCOVERY

Use a graphing utility to graph $x^2 + y = 1$. Then use the graph to write a convincing argument that each x-value has at most one y-value.

  Use a graphing utility to graph $-x + y^2 = 1$. (*Hint:* You will need to use two equations.) Then use the graph to find an x-value that corresponds to two y-values. Why does the graph not represent y as a function of x?

Function Notation

When using an equation to represent a function, it is convenient to name the function so that it can be referenced easily. For example, the equation $y = 1 - x^2$, Example 2(A), describes y as a function of x. Suppose you give this function the name "f." Then you can use the following **function notation.**

Input	Output	Equation
x	$f(x)$	$f(x) = 1 - x^2$

The symbol $f(x)$ is read as the **value of f at x** or simply "f of x." This corresponds to the y-value for a given x. Thus, you can write $y = f(x)$.

Keep in mind that f is the *name* of the function, whereas $f(x)$ is the *value* of the function at x. For instance, the function

$$f(x) = 3 - 2x$$

has *function values* denoted by $f(-1)$, $f(0)$, $f(2)$, and so on. To find these values, substitute the specified input values into the equation.

For $x = -1$, $f(-1) = 3 - 2(-1) = 3 + 2 = 5.$
For $x = 0$, $f(0) = 3 - 2(0) = 3 + 0 = 3.$
For $x = 2$, $f(2) = 3 - 2(2) = 3 - 4 = -1.$

Although it is convenient to use f as a function name and x as the independent variable, you can use other letters. For instance, $f(x) = x^2 - 4x + 7$, $f(t) = t^2 - 4t + 7$, and $g(s) = s^2 - 4s + 7$ all define the same function. In fact, the role of the independent variable in a function is simply that of a "placeholder." Consequently, the above function could be described by the form

$$f(\ ) = (\ )^2 - 4(\ ) + 7,$$

where the parentheses are used in place of a letter. To evaluate $f(-2)$, simply place -2 in each set of parentheses.

$f(\ ) = (\ )^2 - 4(\ ) + 7$
$f(-2) = (-2)^2 - 4(-2) + 7$ *Place -2 in each set of parentheses*
$= 4 + 8 + 7$ *Evaluate each term*
$= 19$ *Simplify*

Similarly, the value of $f(3x)$ is obtained as follows.

$f(\ ) = (\ )^2 - 4(\ ) + 7$
$f(3x) = (3x)^2 - 4(3x) + 7$ *Place $3x$ in each set of parentheses*
$= 9x^2 - 12x + 7$ *Simplify*

EXAMPLE 3   Evaluating a Function

Let $g(x) = -x^2 + 4x + 1$ and find the following.

A. $g(2)$ **B.** $g(t)$ **C.** $g(x + 2)$

Technology Note _____

Most graphing utilities can be used to evaluate a function at a real value of x.

The technique depends on the graphing utility, but here is a sample program.

```
Prgml: EVALUATE
Lbl 1
:Disp "ENTER X"
:Input X
:Disp Y₁
:Goto 1
```

To use this program, enter a function in y_1. Then run the program—it will allow you to evaluate the function at several values of x.

REMARK Example 3 shows that
$g(x + 2) \neq g(x) + g(2)$ because
$-x^2 + 5 \neq (-x^2 + 4x + 1) + 5$. In
general, $g(u + v) \neq g(u) + g(v)$.

SOLUTION

A. Replacing x with 2 in $g(x) = -x^2 + 4x + 1$ yields

$$g(2) = -(2)^2 + 4(2) + 1 = -4 + 8 + 1 = 5.$$

B. Replacing x with t yields

$$g(t) = -(t)^2 + 4(t) + 1 = -t^2 + 4t + 1.$$

C. Replacing x with $x + 2$ yields

$$
\begin{aligned}
g(x + 2) &= -(x + 2)^2 + 4(x + 2) + 1 \\
&= -(x^2 + 4x + 4) + 4x + 8 + 1 \\
&= -x^2 - 4x - 4 + 4x + 8 + 1 \\
&= -x^2 + 5.
\end{aligned}
$$

Sometimes a function is defined using more than one equation.

EXAMPLE 4   A Function Defined by Two Equations

Evaluate the function

$$f(x) = \begin{cases} x^2 + 1, & x < 0 \\ x - 1, & x \geq 0 \end{cases}$$

at $x = -1, 0$, and 1.

SOLUTION

Because $x = -1$ is less than 0, use $f(x) = x^2 + 1$ to obtain

$$f(-1) = (-1)^2 + 1 = 2.$$

For $x = 0$, use $f(x) = x - 1$ to obtain

$$f(0) = (0) - 1 = -1.$$

For $x = 1$, use $f(x) = x - 1$ to obtain

$$f(1) = (1) - 1 = 0.$$

The Domain of a Function

The domain of a function may be explicitly described along with the function, or it may be *implied* by the expression used to define the function. The **implied domain** is the set of all real numbers for which the expression is defined. For instance, the function

$$f(x) = \frac{1}{x^2 - 4}$$

has an implied domain that consists of all real x other than $x = \pm 2$. These two values are excluded from the domain because division by zero is undefined. Another common type of implied domain is used to avoid even roots of negative numbers. For example, the function

$$f(x) = \sqrt{x}$$

is defined only for $x \geq 0$. Hence, its implied domain is the interval $[0, \infty)$. In general, the domain of a function *excludes* values that would cause division by zero *or* result in the even root of a negative number.

    The *range* of a function is more difficult to find, and can best be obtained from the graph of the function (see Section 1.4).

EXAMPLE 5   **Finding the Domain of a Function**

Find the domain of each of the following functions.

A. f: $\{(-3, 0), (-1, 4), (0, 2), (2, 2), (4, -1)\}$

B. Volume of a sphere: $V = \dfrac{4}{3}\pi r^3$

C. $g(x) = \dfrac{1}{x + 5}$

D. $h(x) = \sqrt{4 - x}$

SOLUTION

A. The domain of f consists of all first coordinates in the set of ordered pairs, and is therefore the set

    Domain $= \{-3, -1, 0, 2, 4\}$.

B. For the volume of a sphere you must choose nonnegative values for the radius r. Thus, the domain is the set of all real numbers r such that $r \geq 0$.

C. Excluding x-values that yield zero in the denominator, the domain of g is the set of all real numbers $x \neq -5$.

D. Choose x-values for which $4 - x \geq 0$. The domain is all real numbers that are less than or equal to 4.

REMARK In Example 5(B), note that the domain of a function may be implied by the physical context. For instance, from the equation $V = \frac{4}{3}\pi r^3$, you would have no reason to restrict r to nonnegative values, but the physical context tells you that a sphere cannot have a negative radius.

Function Keys on a Graphing Utility

Calculators and computers have many built-in functions that can be evaluated with a simple keystroke. For instance, you can use the square root key to calculate square roots of nonnegative numbers. If you attempt to take the square root of a negative number, you will get an error message. Here are some more examples of built-in functions that you can verify on your calculator or computer.

EXAMPLE 6   Function Keys

A. $\sqrt{10} = 3.16227766$
B. $64^{1/3} = 4$
C. $|-3| = \text{abs}(-3) = 3$
D. $10^3 = 1000$
E. $\log 2 = .3010299957$ (You will study logarithms in Chapter 5.)

Applications

EXAMPLE 7   The Dimensions of a Container

A standard soft-drink can has a height of about 4.75 inches and a radius of about 1.3 inches. For this standard can, the ratio of the height to the radius is about 3.65. Suppose you work in the marketing department of a soft-drink company, and are experimenting with a new soft-drink can that is slightly narrower and taller. For your experimental can, the ratio of the height to the radius is 4, as shown in Figure 1.28.

A. Express the volume of the can as a function of the radius r.
B. Express the volume of the can as a function of the height h.

$\dfrac{h}{r} = 4$

FIGURE 1.28

SOLUTION

The volume of a right circular cylinder is given by the formula

$$V = \pi(\text{radius})^2(\text{height}) = \pi r^2 h.$$

Because the ratio of the height to the radius is 4, you can write $h = 4r$.

A. To write the volume as a function of the radius, use the fact that $h = 4r$.

$$V = \pi r^2 h = \pi r^2 (4r) = 4\pi r^3$$

B. To write the volume as a function of the height, use the fact that $r = h/4$.

$$V = \pi\left(\frac{h}{4}\right)^2 h = \frac{\pi h^3}{16}$$

EXAMPLE 8   The Path of a Baseball

A baseball is hit three feet above the ground at a velocity of 100 feet per second and at an angle of 45° with respect to the ground. The path of the baseball is given by the function

$$y = -0.0032x^2 + x + 3,$$

where the height y and the horizontal distance x are measured in feet, as shown in Figure 1.29. (From this equation, note that the height of the baseball is a function of the horizontal distance from home plate.) Will the baseball clear a 10-foot fence located 300 feet from home plate?

FIGURE 1.29

DISCOVERY

Use a graphing utility to graph $y = -0.0032x^2 + x + 3$ and $y = 10$ on the same viewing rectangle. (Use a viewing rectangle in which $0 \le x \le 300$ and $0 \le y \le 90$.) Explain how the graphs can be used to answer the question asked in Example 8.

Suppose the fence in Example 8 is raised to 20 feet and the distance from home plate is 295 feet. Will the ball clear this fence?

SOLUTION

When $x = 300$, the height of the baseball is

$$y = -0.0032(300^2) + 300 + 3 = 15 \text{ feet}.$$

Thus, the ball will clear the fence.

One of the basic definitions in calculus employs a ratio called a **difference quotient.**

$$\frac{f(x + h) - f(x)}{h}, \qquad h \neq 0$$

EXAMPLE 9   Evaluating a Difference Quotient

For the function given by $f(x) = x^2 - 4x + 7$, find

$$\frac{f(x + h) - f(x)}{h}.$$

SOLUTION

$$\begin{aligned}
\frac{f(x + h) - f(x)}{h} &= \frac{[(x + h)^2 - 4(x + h) + 7] - [x^2 - 4x + 7]}{h} \\
&= \frac{x^2 + 2xh + h^2 - 4x - 4h + 7 - x^2 + 4x - 7}{h} \\
&= \frac{2xh + h^2 - 4h}{h} \\
&= \frac{h(2x + h - 4)}{h} \\
&= 2x + h - 4, \quad (h \neq 0)
\end{aligned}$$

SUMMARY OF FUNCTION TERMINOLOGY

Function
A **function** is a relationship between two variables such that to each value of the independent variable there corresponds exactly one value of the dependent variable.

Function Notation: $y = f(x)$

  f is the **name** of the function.
  y is the **dependent variable.**
  x is the **independent variable.**
  $f(x)$ is the **value of the function at x.**

Domain
The **domain** of a function is the set of all values (inputs) of the independent variable for which the function is defined. If x is in the domain of f, then f is **defined** at x. If x is not in the domain of f, then f is **undefined** at x.

Range
The **range** of a function is the set of all values (outputs) assumed by the dependent variable (that is, the set of all function values).

Implied Domain
If f is defined by an algebraic expression and the domain is not specified, then the **implied domain** consists of all real numbers for which the expression is defined.

Write two statements describing relationships in everyday life that *are* functions and two that are *not* functions. Here are two examples.

(a) The statement "The sale price of an item is a function of the amount of sales tax on the item" is *not* a correct mathematical use of the word "function." The problem is that the sales tax does not determine the sale price. For instance, suppose the sales tax is 6%. Knowing that the sales tax on a particular item is $0.12 is not sufficient information to determine the sale price. (It could be any price between $1.92 and $2.08.)

(b) The statement "Your federal income tax is a function of your adjusted gross income" *is* a correct mathematical use of the word "function." Once you have determined your adjusted gross income, then your income tax can be determined.

WARM-UP
....

The following warm-up exercises involve skills that were covered in earlier sections. You will use these skills in the exercise set for this section.

In Exercises 1–4, simplify the expression.

1. $2(-3)^3 + 4(-3) - 7$

2. $4(-1)^2 - 5(-1) + 4$

3. $(x + 1)^2 + 3(x + 1) - (x^2 + 3x)$

4. $(x - 2)^2 - 4(x - 2) - (x^2 - 4)$

In Exercises 5 and 6, solve for y in terms of x.

5. $2x + 5y - 7 = 0$

6. $y^2 = x^2$

In Exercises 7–10, simplify the expression. Assume the variables are positive.

7. $\sqrt{50x^3y^2}$

8. $\sqrt{18z^4 - 9z^2}$

9. $\dfrac{(x - y)^2}{x^2 - y^2}$

10. $\dfrac{x^2}{x + 2} \cdot \dfrac{x^2 - x - 6}{2x}$

SECTION 1.3 · EXERCISES
....

In Exercises 1 and 2, determine which of the sets of ordered pairs represents a function from A to B. Give reasons for your answers.

1. $A = \{0, 1, 2, 3\}$ and $B = \{-2, -1, 0, 1, 2\}$
   (a) $\{(0, 1), (1, -2), (2, 0), (3, 2)\}$
   (b) $\{(2, 2), (1, -2), (3, 0), (1, 1)\}$
   (c) $\{(0, 0), (1, 0), (2, 0), (3, 0)\}$
   (d) $\{(0, 2), (3, 0), (1, 1)\}$

2. $A = \{a, b, c\}$ and $B = \{0, 1, 2, 3\}$
   (a) $\{(a, 1), (c, 2), (c, 3), (b, 3)\}$
   (b) $\{(a, 1), (b, 2), (c, 3)\}$
   (c) $\{(1, a), (0, a), (2, c), (3, b)\}$
   (d) $\{(c, 0), (b, 0), (a, 3)\}$

In Exercises 3–10, state whether the equation determines y as a function of x.

3. $x^2 + y^2 = 4$ **4.** $x = y^2$

5. $x^2 + y = 4$ **6.** $x + y^2 = 4$

7. $x^2 y - x^2 + 4y = 0$ **8.** $x^2 + y^2 - 2x - 4y + 1 = 0$

9. $y^2 = x^2 - 1$ **10.** $y = \sqrt{x + 5}$

In Exercises 11–14, fill in the blanks and simplify the result.

11. $f(x) = 6 - 4x$
(a) $f(3) = 6 - 4(\quad)$
(b) $f(-7) = 6 - 4(\quad)$
(c) $f(t) = 6 - 4(\quad)$
(d) $f(c + 1) = 6 - 4(\quad)$

12. $g(x) = x^2 - 2x$
(a) $g(2) = (\quad)^2 - 2(\quad)$
(b) $g(-3) = (\quad)^2 - 2(\quad)$
(c) $g(t + 1) = (\quad)^2 - 2(\quad)$
(d) $g(x + h) = (\quad)^2 - 2(\quad)$

13. $f(s) = \dfrac{1}{s + 1}$
(a) $f(4) = \dfrac{1}{(\quad) + 1}$
(b) $f(0) = \dfrac{1}{(\quad) + 1}$
(c) $f(4x) = \dfrac{1}{(\quad) + 1}$
(d) $f(x + h) = \dfrac{1}{(\quad) + 1}$

14. $f(t) = \sqrt{25 - t^2}$
(a) $f(3) = \sqrt{25 - (\quad)^2}$
(b) $f(5) = \sqrt{25 - (\quad)^2}$
(c) $f(x + 5) = \sqrt{25 - (\quad)^2}$
(d) $f(2 + h) = \sqrt{25 - (\quad)^2}$

In Exercises 15–22, evaluate (if possible) the function at the specified value of the independent variable and simplify the result.

15. $f(x) = 2x - 3$ **16.** $V(r) = \frac{4}{3}\pi r^3$
(a) $f(1)$ (a) $V(3)$
(b) $f(-3)$ (b) $V(0)$
(c) $f(x - 1)$ (c) $V(\frac{3}{2})$
(d) $f(\frac{1}{4})$ (d) $V(2r)$

17. $h(t) = t^2 - 2t$ **18.** $f(x) = \sqrt{x + 8} + 2$
(a) $h(2)$ (a) $f(-8)$
(b) $h(-1)$ (b) $f(1)$
(c) $h(x + 2)$ (c) $f(x - 8)$
(d) $h(1.5)$ (d) $f(h + 8)$

19. $f(x) = \dfrac{|x|}{x}$ **20.** $q(t) = \dfrac{2t^2 + 3}{t^2}$
(a) $f(2)$ (a) $q(2)$
(b) $f(-2)$ (b) $q(0)$
(c) $f(x^2)$ (c) $q(x)$
(d) $f(x - 1)$ (d) $q(-x)$

21. $f(x) = \begin{cases} 2x + 1, & x < 0 \\ 2x + 2, & x \geq 0 \end{cases}$ **22.** $f(x) = \begin{cases} x^2 + 2, & x \leq 1 \\ 2x^2 + 2, & x > 1 \end{cases}$
(a) $f(-1)$ (a) $f(-2)$
(b) $f(0)$ (b) $f(0)$
(c) $f(1)$ (c) $f(1)$
(d) $f(2)$ (d) $f(2)$

In Exercises 23–30, find the domain of the function.

23. $f(x) = 5x^2 + 2x - 1$ **24.** $f(t) = \sqrt[3]{t + 4}$

25. $g(y) = \sqrt{y - 10}$ **26.** $f(x) = \sqrt[4]{1 - x^2}$

27. $h(t) = \dfrac{4}{t}$ **28.** $h(x) = \dfrac{10}{x^2 - 2x}$

29. $g(x) = \dfrac{1}{x} - \dfrac{3}{x + 2}$ **30.** $f(s) = \dfrac{\sqrt{s - 1}}{s - 4}$

In Exercises 31–34, assume that the domain of f is the set $A = \{-2, -1, 0, 1, 2\}$. Determine the set of ordered pairs representing the function f.

31. $f(x) = x^2$ **32.** $f(x) = \dfrac{2x}{x^2 + 1}$

33. $f(x) = \sqrt{x + 2}$ **34.** $f(x) = |x + 1|$

In Exercises 35–38, use a function key on a calculator to evaluate each expression. (Round the result to three decimal places.)

35. (a) 32.5^2 (b) 4.3^5 **36.** (a) $\sqrt{232}$ (b) $\sqrt[3]{2500}$

37. (a) $\dfrac{1}{8.5}$ (b) $\dfrac{1}{0.047}$ **38.** (a) $|-326.8|$ (b) $10^{3.8}$

In Exercises 39–42, select a function from (a) $f(x) = cx$, (b) $g(x) = cx^2$, (c) $h(x) = c\sqrt{|x|}$, or (d) $r(x) = c/x$ and determine the value of the constant c so that the function fits the data given in the table.

39.

x	-4	-1	0	1	4
y	-32	-2	0	-2	-32

40.

x	-4	-1	0	1	4
y	-1	$-\frac{1}{4}$	0	$\frac{1}{4}$	1

41.

x	-4	-1	0	1	4
y	-8	-32	undef.	32	8

42.

x	-4	-1	0	1	4
y	6	3	0	3	6

In Exercises 43–46, evaluate the difference quotient. Then simplify the result.

43. $f(x) = 2x$

$$\frac{f(x + h) - f(x)}{h}$$

44. $f(x) = 5x - x^2$

$$\frac{f(5 + h) - f(5)}{h}$$

45. $f(x) = x^3$

$$\frac{f(x + h) - f(x)}{h}$$

46. $f(t) = \dfrac{1}{t}$

$$\frac{f(t) - f(1)}{t - 1}$$

47. *Area of a Circle* Express the area A of a circle as a function of its circumference C.

48. *Area of a Triangle* Express the area A of an equilateral triangle as a function of the length s of its sides.

49. *Area of a Triangle* A right triangle is formed in the first quadrant by the x- and y-axes and a line through the point $(1, 2)$ (see figure). Express the area of the triangle as a function of x, and determine the domain of the function.

50. *Area of a Rectangle* A rectangle is bounded by the x-axis and the semicircle $y = \sqrt{25 - x^2}$ (see figure). Express the area of the rectangle as a function of x, and determine the domain of the function.

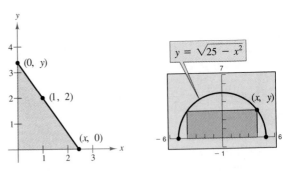

FIGURE FOR 49   **FIGURE FOR 50**

51. *Volume of a Package* A rectangular package to be sent by a postal service can have a maximum combined length and girth (perimeter of a cross section) of 108 inches (see figure). Express the volume of the package as a function of x. What is the domain of the function?

FIGURE FOR 51

52. *Volume of a Box* An open box is to be made from a square piece of material 12 inches on a side by cutting equal squares from each corner and turning up the sides (see figure). Express the volume V of the box as a function of x. What is the domain of this function?

FIGURE FOR 52

53. *Height of a Balloon*   A transmitting balloon ascends vertically from a point 2000 feet from the receiving station (see figure). Let d be the distance between the balloon and the receiving station. Express the height of the balloon as a function of d. What is the domain of the function?

2000 ft   **FIGURE FOR 53**

54. *Price of Mobile Homes*   The average price p of a new mobile home in the United States from 1974 to 1988 can be modeled by the function

$$p(t) = \begin{cases} 19{,}503.6 + 1753.6t, & -6 \le t \le -1 \\ 19{,}838.8 + 81.11t^2, & 0 \le t \le 8 \end{cases}$$

where t is the year with $t = 0$ corresponding to 1980. Use this model to find the average price of a mobile home in 1978 and in 1988. (*Source:* U.S. Bureau of Census, Construction Reports)

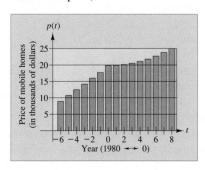

FIGURE FOR 54

55. *Cost, Revenue, and Profit*   A company invests \$98,000 for equipment to produce a product. Each unit of the product costs \$12.30 and is sold for \$17.98. Let x be the number of units produced and sold.
(a) Write the total cost C as a function of x.
(b) Write the revenue R as a function of x.
(c) Write the profit P as a function of x.
   (*Note:* $P = R - C$)

56. *Charter Bus Fares*   For groups of 80 or more people, a charter bus company determines the rate per person according to the formula

Rate $= 8 - 0.05(n - 80)$, $n \ge 80$,

where the rate is given in dollars and n is the number of people.
(a) Express the revenue R for the bus company as a function of n.
(b) Use the function from part (a) to complete the following table.

n	90	100	110	120	130	140	150
$R(n)$							

(c) Graph R and determine the number of people that will produce a maximum revenue.

1.4   GRAPHS OF FUNCTIONS

The Graph of a Function   /   Increasing and Decreasing Functions   /
Relative Minimum and Maximum Values   /   Step Functions   /
Even and Odd Functions

The Graph of a Function

In Section 1.3 you studied functions from an algebraic point of view. In this section, you will study functions from a geometric perspective. The **graph of a function** f is the collection of ordered pairs $(x, f(x))$ such that x is in the domain of f. As you study this section, remember the following geometrical interpretation of x and $f(x)$.

$$x = \text{the directed distance from the } y\text{-axis}$$
$$f(x) = \text{the directed distance from the } x\text{-axis}$$

EXAMPLE 1   Finding Domain and Range from the Graph of a Function

Use the graph of the function f, shown in Figure 1.30.

A. Find the domain of f.
B. Find the function values $f(-1)$ and $f(2)$.
C. Find the range of f.

SOLUTION

A. The closed dot (on the left) indicates that $x = -1$ is in the domain of f, whereas the open dot (on the right) indicates $x = 4$ is not in the domain. Thus, the domain of f is all x in the interval $[-1, 4)$.
B. Because $(-1, -5)$ is a point on the graph of f, it follows that $f(-1) = -5$. Similarly, because $(2, 4)$ is a point on the graph of f, it follows that $f(2) = 4$.
C. Because the graph does not extend below $f(-1) = -5$ nor above $f(2) = 4$, the range of f is the interval $[-5, 4]$.

By the definition of a function, at most one y-value corresponds to a given x-value. It follows, then, that a vertical line can intersect the graph of a function at most once. This observation provides a convenient visual test for functions.

FIGURE 1.30

REMARK   In Figure 1.30, the solid dot representing the point $(-1, -5)$ indicates that $(-1, -5)$ is a point on the graph. The open dot indicates that $(4, 0)$ is not a point on the graph.

VERTICAL LINE TEST FOR FUNCTIONS

A set of points in a coordinate plane is the graph of y as a function of x if and only if no vertical line intersects the graph at more than one point.

(a)

(b)

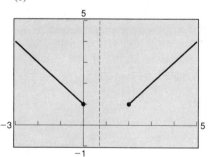

(c)

FIGURE 1.31

EXAMPLE 2   Vertical Line Test for Functions
··············

Which of the graphs in Figure 1.31 represent y as a function of x?

SOLUTION

A. This is *not* a graph of y as a function of x because you can find a vertical line that intersects the graph twice.

B. This *is* a graph of y as a function of x because every vertical line intersects the graph at most once.

C. This *is* a graph of y as a function of x. (Note that if a vertical line does not intersect the graph, it simply means that the function is undefined for this particular value of x.)
·········

Increasing and Decreasing Functions

The more you know about the graph of a function, the more you know about the function itself. Consider the graph shown in Figure 1.32. Moving from *left to right,* this graph falls from $x = -2$ to $x = 0$, is constant from $x = 0$ to $x = 2$, and rises from $x = 2$ to $x = 4$. These observations indicate that the function has the following characteristics.

1. The function is **decreasing** on the interval $(-2, 0)$.
2. The function is **constant** on the interval $(0, 2)$.
3. The function is **increasing** on the interval $(2, 4)$.

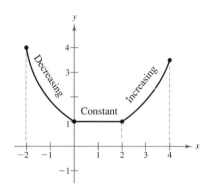

FIGURE 1.32

INCREASING, DECREASING, AND CONSTANT FUNCTIONS

A function f is **increasing** on an interval if, for any x_1 and x_2 in the interval, $x_1 < x_2$ implies $f(x_1) < f(x_2)$.

A function f is **decreasing** on an interval if, for any x_1 and x_2 in the interval, $x_1 < x_2$ implies $f(x_1) > f(x_2)$.

A function f is **constant** on an interval if, for any x_1 and x_2 in the interval, $f(x_1) = f(x_2)$.

(a)

(b)

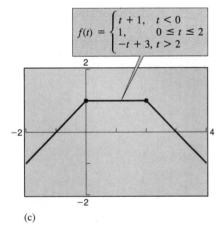

(c)

FIGURE 1.33

EXAMPLE 3   **Increasing and Decreasing Functions**

In Figure 1.33, determine the open intervals on which each function is increasing, decreasing, or constant.

SOLUTION

A. Although it might appear that there is an interval about zero over which this function is constant, you can see that if $x_1 < x_2$, then $f(x_1) = x_1^3 < x_2^3 = f(x_2)$. Thus, you can conclude that the function is increasing over the entire real line.

B. This function is increasing on the interval $(-\infty, -1)$, decreasing on the interval $(-1, 1)$, and increasing on the interval $(1, \infty)$.

C. This function is increasing on the interval $(-\infty, 0)$, constant on the interval $(0, 2)$, and decreasing on the interval $(2, \infty)$.

Relative Minimum and Maximum Values

The points at which a function changes its increasing, decreasing, or constant behavior are helpful in determining the relative maximum or relative minimum values of the function.

DEFINITION OF RELATIVE MINIMUM AND RELATIVE MAXIMUM

A function value $f(a)$ is called a **relative minimum** of f if there exists an interval (x_1, x_2) that contains a such that

$$x_1 < x < x_2 \quad \text{implies} \quad f(a) \leq f(x).$$

A function $f(a)$ is called a **relative maximum** of f if there exists an interval (x_1, x_2) that contains a such that

$$x_1 < x < x_2 \quad \text{implies} \quad f(a) \geq f(x).$$

Figure 1.34 shows several different examples of relative minimums and relative maximums.

FIGURE 1.34

In Section 3.1, you will study a technique for finding the *exact points* at which a second-degree polynomial function has a relative minimum or relative maximum. For the time being, however, you can use a graphing utility to find reasonable approximations for these points.

Technology Note

When you use a graphing utility to estimate the x- and y-values of a relative minimum or relative maximum, the automatic zoom feature will often produce graphs that are nearly flat. To overcome this problem, you can manually change the vertical setting of the viewing rectangle. You can stretch the graph vertically by making the values of Y_{min} and Y_{max} closer together.

EXAMPLE 4 Approximating a Relative Minimum

Use a graphing utility to approximate the relative minimum of the function $f(x) = 3x^2 - 4x - 2$.

SOLUTION

The graph of f is shown in Figure 1.35. By using the zoom and trace features of a graphing utility, you can estimate that the function has a relative minimum at the point

$(0.67, -3.33)$. *Relative minimum*

Later, in Section 3.1, you will be able to determine that the exact point at which the relative minimum occurs is $\left(\frac{2}{3}, -\frac{10}{3}\right)$.

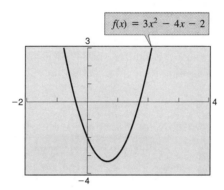

FIGURE 1.35

EXAMPLE 5 Approximating Relative Minimums and Maximums

Use a graphing utility to approximate the relative minimum and relative maximum of the function $f(x) = -x^3 + x$.

SOLUTION

A sketch of the graph of f is shown in Figure 1.36. By using the zoom and trace features of the graphing utility, you can estimate that the function has a relative minimum at the point

$(-0.58, -0.38)$ *Relative minimum*

and a relative maximum at the point

$(0.58, 0.38)$. *Relative maximum*

If you go on to take a course in calculus, you will learn a technique for finding the exact points at which this function has a relative minimum and a relative maximum.

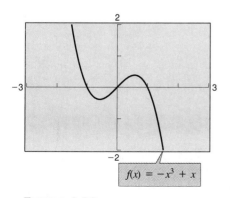

FIGURE 1.36

EXAMPLE 6 The Price of Diamonds

During the 1980s the average price of a 1-carat polished diamond decreased and then increased according to the model

$$C = -0.7t^3 + 16.25t^2 - 106t + 388, \qquad 2 \le t \le 10,$$

where C is the average price in dollars (on the Antwerp Index) and t represents the calendar year with $t = 2$ corresponding to January 1, 1982. (*Source: Diamond High Council*) According to this model, during which years was the price of diamonds decreasing? During which years was the price of diamonds increasing? Approximate the minimum price of a 1-carat diamond between 1982 and 1990.

SOLUTION

To solve this problem, sketch an accurate graph of the function, as shown in Figure 1.37. From the graph, you can see that the price of diamonds decreased from 1982 until late 1984. Then from late 1984 to 1990 the price increased. The minimum price during the eight-year period was approximately $175.

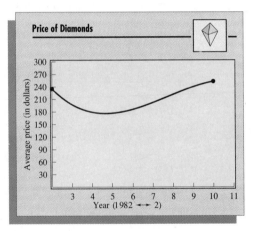

FIGURE 1.37

$f(x) = [[x]]$

Greatest Integer Function

FIGURE 1.38

Step Functions

EXAMPLE 7 The Greatest Integer Function

The **greatest integer function** is denoted by $[[x]]$ and is defined by

$$f(x) = [[x]] = \text{the greatest integer less than or equal to } x.$$

The graph of this function is shown in Figure 1.38. Note that the graph of the greatest integer function jumps vertically one unit at each integer and is constant (a horizontal line segment) between each pair of consecutive integers.

Because of the jumps in its graph, the greatest integer function is an example of a **step function.** Some values of the greatest integer function are as follows.

$$[[-1]] = -1 \qquad [[-0.5]] = -1$$
$$[[0]] = 0 \qquad [[0.5]] = 0$$
$$[[1]] = 1 \qquad [[1.5]] = 1$$

The range of the greatest integer function is the set of all integers.

Technology Note _____

Most graphing utilities display graphs in what is called a *connected mode,* which means that the graph has no breaks. Thus, when you are sketching graphs that do have breaks, it is better to change the graphing utility to *dot mode.* Try sketching the graph of the greatest integer function [often called Int(x)] on a graphing utility in connected and dot modes, and compare the two results.

EXAMPLE 8 The Cost of a Telephone Call

Suppose the cost of a telephone call between Los Angeles and San Francisco is $0.50 for the first minute and $0.36 for each additional minute. The greatest integer function can be used to create a model for the cost of this call.

$$C = 0.50 + 0.36[[t]], \qquad 0 < t,$$

where C is the total cost of the call in dollars and t is the length of the call in minutes. Sketch the graph of this function.

SOLUTION

For calls up to 1 minute, the cost is $0.50. For calls between 1 and 2 minutes, the cost is $0.86, and so on.

Length of call: $0 < t < 1$ $1 \le t < 2$ $2 \le t < 3$ $3 \le t < 4$ $4 \le t < 5$
Cost of call: $0.50 $0.86 $1.22 $1.58 $1.94

Using these values, you can sketch the graph shown in Figure 1.39.

FIGURE 1.39

Even and Odd Functions

A graph has symmetry with respect to the y-axis if, whenever (x, y) is on the graph, so is the point $(-x, y)$. A function whose graph is symmetric with respect to the y-axis is an **even** function.

A graph has symmetry with respect to the origin if, whenever (x, y) is on the graph, so is the point $(-x, -y)$. A function whose graph is symmetric with respect to the origin is an **odd** function.

A graph has symmetry with respect to the x-axis if, whenever (x, y) is on the graph, so is the point $(x, -y)$. The graph of a (nonzero) function cannot be symmetric with respect to the x-axis.

(a)

(b)

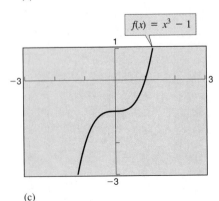

(c)

FIGURE 1.40

TEST FOR EVEN AND ODD FUNCTIONS

A function f is **even** if, for each x in the domain of f, $f(-x) = f(x)$.
A function f is **odd** if, for each x in the domain of f, $f(-x) = -f(x)$.

EXAMPLE 9   Even and Odd Functions

Determine whether the following functions are even, odd, or neither.

A. $g(x) = x^3 - x$
B. $h(x) = x^2 + 1$
C. $f(x) = x^3 - 1$

SOLUTION

A. This function is odd because

$$g(-x) = (-x)^3 - (-x) = -x^3 + x = -(x^3 - x) = -g(x).$$

B. This function is even because

$$h(-x) = (-x)^2 + 1 = x^2 + 1 = h(x).$$

C. Substituting $-x$ for x produces

$$f(-x) = (-x)^3 - 1 = -x^3 - 1.$$

Because $f(x) = x^3 - 1$ and $-f(x) = -x^3 + 1$, you can conclude that $f(-x) \neq f(x)$ and $f(-x) \neq -f(x)$. Hence, the function is neither even nor odd.

The graphs of the three functions are shown in Figure 1.40.

FIGURE 1.41

EXAMPLE 10   The Absolute Value Function

Figure 1.41 shows the V-shape of the absolute value function, $f(x) = |x|$. This was produced using the "abs" key and the standard viewing rectangle. Because the graph is symmetric about the y-axis, you can see that it is an even function. You can verify this by observing that $f(-x) = |-x| = |x| = f(x)$.

DISCUSSION PROBLEM

INCREASING AND DECREASING FUNCTIONS

Use your school's library or some other reference source to find examples of three different functions that represent quantities between 1980 and 1990. Find one that decreased during the decade, one that increased, and one that was constant. For instance, the value of the dollar decreased, the population of the United States increased, and the land size of the United States remained constant. Can you find three other examples? Present your results graphically.

WARM-UP

The following warm-up exercises involve skills that were covered in earlier sections. You will use these skills in the exercise set for this section.

1. Find $f(2)$ for $f(x) = -x^3 + 5x$.

2. Find $f(6)$ for $f(x) = x^2 - 6x$.

3. Find $f(-x)$ for $f(x) = \dfrac{3}{x}$.

4. Find $f(-x)$ for $f(x) = x^2 + 3$.

In Exercises 5 and 6, find the x- and y-intercepts of the graph of the line.

5. $5x - 2y + 12 = 0$

6. $-0.3x - 0.5y + 1.5 = 0$

In Exercises 7–10, find the domain of the function.

7. $g(x) = \dfrac{4}{x - 4}$

8. $f(x) = \dfrac{2x}{x^2 - 9x + 20}$

9. $h(t) = \sqrt[4]{5 - 3t}$

10. $f(t) = t^3 + 3t - 5$

SECTION 1.4 · EXERCISES

In Exercises 1–6, use a graphing utility to graph the function and find its domain and range.

1. $f(x) = \sqrt{x - 1}$ **2.** $f(x) = 4 - x^2$

3. $f(x) = \sqrt{x^2 - 4}$ **4.** $f(x) = |x - 2|$

5. $f(x) = \sqrt{25 - x^2}$ **6.** $f(x) = \dfrac{|x - 2|}{x - 2}$

In Exercises 7–12, use the vertical line test to determine whether y is a function of x. Describe how your graphing utility can be used to produce the given graph.

7. $y = x^2$ **8.** $y = x^3 - 1$

9. $x - y^2 = 0$ **10.** $x^2 + y^2 = 9$

11. $x^2 = xy - 1$ **12.** $x = |y|$

In Exercises 13–16, select the viewing rectangle on a graphing utility that shows the most complete graph of the function.

13. $f(x) = -0.2x^2 + 3x + 32$

(a)
```
RANGE
Xmin=-2
Xmax=20
Xscl=1
Ymin=-10
Ymax=30
Yscl=4
```
(b)
```
RANGE
Xmin=-10
Xmax=30
Xscl=5
Ymin=-5
Ymax=50
Yscl=5
```
(c)
```
RANGE
Xmin=0
Xmax=10
Xscl=0.5
Ymin=0
Ymax=200
Yscl=25
```

14. $f(x) = 6[x - (0.1x)^5]$

(a)
```
RANGE
Xmin=-500
Xmax=500
Xscl=50
Ymin=-500
Ymax=500
Yscl=50
```
(b)
```
RANGE
Xmin=-25
Xmax=25
Xscl=5
Ymin=-25
Ymax=25
Yscl=5
```
(c)
```
RANGE
Xmin=-20
Xmax=20
Xscl=5
Ymin=-100
Ymax=100
Yscl=20
```

15. $f(x) = 4x^3 - x^4$

(a)
```
RANGE
Xmin=-2
Xmax=6
Xscl=1
Ymin=-10
Ymax=30
Yscl=4
```
(b)
```
RANGE
Xmin=-50
Xmax=50
Xscl=5
Ymin=-50
Ymax=50
Yscl=5
```
(c)
```
RANGE
Xmin=0
Xmax=2
Xscl=0.2
Ymin=-2
Ymax=2
Yscl=0.5
```

16. $f(x) = 10x\sqrt{400 - x^2}$

(a)
```
RANGE
Xmin=-5
Xmax=50
Xscl=5
Ymin=-5000
Ymax=5000
Yscl=500
```
(b)
```
RANGE
Xmin=-20
Xmax=20
Xscl=2
Ymin=-500
Ymax=500
Yscl=50
```
(c)
```
RANGE
Xmin=-25
Xmax=25
Xscl=5
Ymin=-2000
Ymax=2000
Yscl=200
```

In Exercises 17–24, use a graphing utility to graph the function. Approximate the intervals over which the function is increasing, decreasing, or constant.

17. $f(x) = 2x$ **18.** $f(x) = x^2 - 2x$

19. $f(x) = x^3 - 3x^2$ **20.** $f(x) = \sqrt{x^2 - 4}$

21. $f(x) = 3x^4 - 6x^2$ **22.** $f(x) = x^{2/3} = (x^2)^{1/3}$

23. $f(x) = x\sqrt{x + 3}$ **24.** $f(x) = |x + 1| + |x - 1|$

In Exercises 25–30, use a graphing utility to approximate (to two decimal place accuracy) any relative minimum or maximum values of the function.

25. $f(x) = x^2 - 6x$ **26.** $f(x) = (x - 1)^2(x + 2)$

27. $g(x) = 2x^3 + 3x^2 - 12x$ **28.** $g(x) = x^3 - 6x^2 + 15$

29. $h(x) = (x - 1)\sqrt{x}$ **30.** $h(x) = x\sqrt{4 - x}$

31. *Maximum Area* The perimeter of a rectangle is 100 feet (see figure).

(a) Show that the area of the rectangle is given by $A = x(50 - x)$, where x is its length.

(b) Use a graphing utility to graph the area function.

(c) Move the cursor along the graph to approximate (to two decimal place accuracy) the maximum of the area function. Approximate the dimensions of the rectangle that yields the maximum area.

FIGURE FOR 31

32. *Minimum Cost* A power station is on one side of a river that is $\frac{1}{2}$ mile wide, and a factory is 6 miles downstream on the other side (see figure). It costs $6 per foot to run power lines overland and $8 per foot to run them underwater.

(a) Show that the total cost for the power line is given by

$$T = 8(5280)\sqrt{x^2 + \tfrac{1}{4}} + 6(5280)(6 - x).$$

(b) Use a graphing utility to graph the cost function.

(c) To determine the most economical path for the power line, approximate (to two decimal place accuracy) the value of x that minimizes the cost function.

Factory

Power station

FIGURE FOR 32

33. *Maximum Profit* The marketing department of a company estimates that the demand for a product is given by $p = 100 - 0.0001x$, where p is the price per unit and x is the number of units. The cost of producing x units is given by $C = 350,000 + 30x$, and the profit for producing and selling x units is given by

$$P = R - C = xp - C.$$

Graph the profit function and estimate the number of units that would produce a maximum profit.

34. *Maximum Revenue* When a wholesaler sold a certain product at $25 per unit, sales were 800 units per week. After a price increase of $5, the average number of units sold dropped to 775 per week. Assume that the price p is a linear function of the demand x. Graph the revenue function $R = xp$ and estimate (to two decimal place accuracy) the price that will maximize total revenue.

In Exercises 35–38, use a graphing utility to obtain the graph of the compound function.

35. $f(x) = \begin{cases} 2x + 3, & x < 0 \\ 3 - x, & x \geq 0 \end{cases}$

36. $f(x) = \begin{cases} \sqrt{4 + x}, & x < 0 \\ \sqrt{4 - x}, & x \geq 0 \end{cases}$

37. $f(x) = \begin{cases} x^2 + 5, & x \leq 1 \\ -x^2 + 4x + 3, & x > 1 \end{cases}$

38. $f(x) = \begin{cases} 1 - (x - 1)^3, & x \leq 2 \\ \sqrt{x - 2}, & x > 2 \end{cases}$

In Exercises 39 and 40, use a graphing utility to graph the step function. State the domain and range of the function.

39. $s(x) = 2[[x - 1]]$ **40.** $g(x) = 6 - [[x]]$

41. *Price of a Telephone Call* The cost of a telephone call between two cities is $0.65 for the first minute and $0.42 for each additional minute (or portion thereof).

(a) Use the greatest integer function to create a model for the cost C of a telephone call between the two cities lasting t minutes.

(b) Use a graphing utility to graph the cost model.

(c) Move the cursor along the graph to determine the maximum length of a call that cannot cost more than $6.

42. *Cost of Overnight Delivery* Suppose the cost of sending an overnight package from New York to Atlanta is $9.80 for the first pound and $2.50 for each additional pound (or portion thereof).

(a) Use the greatest integer function to create a model for the cost C of overnight delivery of a package weighing x pounds.

(b) Use a graphing utility to graph the cost function.

(c) Move the cursor along the graph to determine the cost of overnight delivery of a package weighing 12 pounds.

In Exercises 43–46, find the coordinates of a second point on the graph of a function f if the given point is on the graph and the function is (a) even and (b) odd.

43. $(5, 6)$ **44.** $(-3, 7)$

45. $\left(-\tfrac{3}{2}, -2\right)$ **46.** $\left(\tfrac{3}{4}, -\tfrac{7}{8}\right)$

In Exercises 47–56, use a graphing utility to graph the function and determine whether the function is even, odd, or neither.

47. $f(x) = 3$ **48.** $g(x) = x$

49. $f(x) = 5 - 3x$ **50.** $h(x) = x^2 - 4$

51. $g(s) = \dfrac{s^3}{4}$

52. $f(t) = -t^4$

53. $f(x) = \sqrt{1 - x}$

54. $f(x) = x^2\sqrt[3]{x}$

55. $g(x) = \dfrac{5x}{x^2 + 1}$

56. $f(x) = |x + 2|$

In Exercises 57–62, use an algebraic test to determine whether the function is even, odd, or neither. Verify your result graphically.

57. $f(x) = \frac{1}{3}x^6 - 2x^2$

58. $h(x) = x^3 - 5$

59. $g(x) = x^3 - 5x$

60. $f(x) = x\sqrt{1 - x^2}$

61. $f(t) = t^2 + 2t - 3$

62. $g(s) = 4s^{2/3}$

In Exercises 63–68, graph the function and determine the interval(s) (if any) on the real axis for which $f(x) \geq 0$.

63. $f(x) = 4 - x$

64. $f(x) = x^2 - 4x$

65. $f(x) = 1 - x^4$

66. $f(x) = \sqrt{x + 2}$

67. $f(x) = 5$

68. $f(x) = -(1 + |x|)$

In Exercises 69–72, express the height h of the rectangle as a function of x.

69.

70.

71.

72.

In Exercises 73 and 74, express the length L of the rectangle as a function of y.

73.

74.

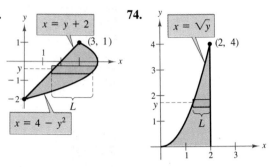

75. *Water Intake* When the intake pipe of a 100-gallon tank is turned on, water flows into the tank at the rate of 10 gallons per minute. When either of the two drain pipes is turned on, water flows out of the tank at the rate of 5 gallons per minute. The graph below shows the volume of water in the tank over a 60-minute period. Which pipes are turned on during the various periods of time indicated by the graph? (There is more than one correct answer.)

FIGURE FOR 75

76. Prove that the following function is odd.
$$f(x) = a_{2n+1}x^{2n+1} + a_{2n-1}x^{2n-1} + \cdots + a_3x^3 + a_1x$$

77. Prove that the following function is even.
$$f(x) = a_{2n}x^{2n} + a_{2n-2}x^{2n-2} + \cdots + a_2x^2 + a_0$$

1.5   SHIFTING, REFLECTING, AND STRETCHING GRAPHS

Summary of Graphs of Common Functions / Vertical and Horizontal
Shifts / Reflections / Nonrigid Transformations

Summary of Graphs of Common Functions

One of the goals of this text is to enable you to build your intuition for the basic
shapes of the graphs of different types of functions. For instance, from your
study of lines in Section 1.2, you can determine the basic shape of the graph
of the linear function

$$f(x) = ax + b.$$

Specifically, you know that the graph of this function is a line whose slope is
a and whose y-intercept is b.

The six graphs shown in Figure 1.42 represent the most commonly used
functions in algebra. Familiarity with the basic characteristics of these simple
graphs will help you analyze the shapes of more complicated graphs. Try using
a graphing utility to verify these graphs.

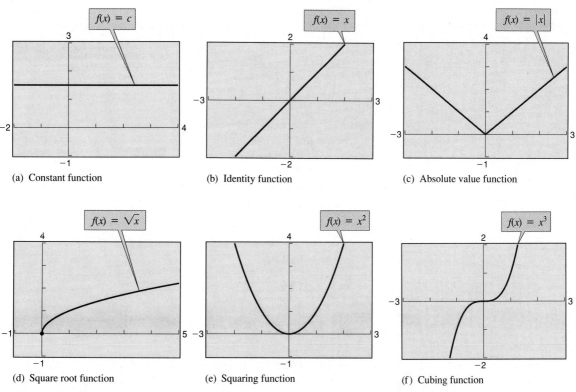

(a) Constant function   (b) Identity function   (c) Absolute value function

(d) Square root function   (e) Squaring function   (f) Cubing function

FIGURE 1.42

Vertical and Horizontal Shifts

Many functions have graphs that are simple transformations of the common graphs summarized in Figure 1.42. For example, you can obtain the graph of $h(x) = x^2 + 2$ by shifting the graph of $f(x) = x^2$ *up* two units, as shown in Figure 1.43. In function notation, h and f are related as follows.

$$h(x) = x^2 + 2 = f(x) + 2 \qquad \textit{Upward shift of 2}$$

Similarly, you can obtain the graph of $g(x) = (x - 2)^2$ by shifting the graph of $f(x) = x^2$ to the *right* two units, as shown in Figure 1.44. In this case, the functions g and f have the following relationship.

$$g(x) = (x - 2)^2 = f(x - 2) \qquad \textit{Right shift of 2}$$

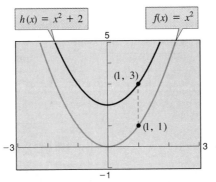

Vertical shift upward: 2 units

FIGURE 1.43

Horizontal shift to the right: 2 units

FIGURE 1.44

VERTICAL AND HORIZONTAL SHIFTS

Let c be a positive real number. **Vertical** and **horizontal shifts** in the graph of $y = f(x)$ are represented as follows.

1. Vertical shift c units **upward:** $h(x) = f(x) + c$
2. Vertical shift c units **downward:** $h(x) = f(x) - c$
3. Horizontal shift c units to the **right:** $h(x) = f(x - c)$
4. Horizontal shift c units to the **left:** $h(x) = f(x + c)$

EXAMPLE 1   **Shifts in the Graph of a Function**

Compare the graph of each function with the graph of $f(x) = x^3$.

A. $g(x) = x^3 + 1$ **B.** $h(x) = (x - 1)^3$ **C.** $k(x) = (x + 2)^3 + 1$

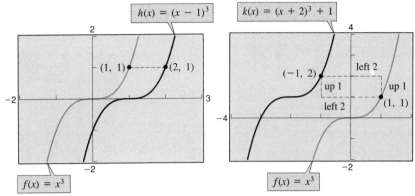

(a) Vertical shift: 1 unit up

(b) Horizontal shift: 1 unit right

(c) Horizontal shift: 2 units left
    Vertical shift: 1 unit up

FIGURE 1.45

SOLUTION

Relative to the graph of $f(x) = x^3$, the graph of $g(x) = x^3 + 1$ is an upward shift of one unit. The graph of $h(x) = (x - 1)^3$ is a right shift of one unit. The graph of $k(x) = (x + 2)^3 + 1$ involves a left shift of two units *followed* by an upward shift of one unit. (See Figure 1.45.)

EXAMPLE 2   Finding Equations from Graphs

Each of the graphs shown in Figure 1.46 is a vertical or horizontal shift of the graph of $f(x) = x^2$. Find an equation for each function.

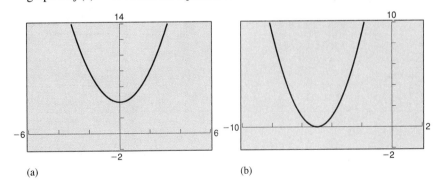

FIGURE 1.46   (a)   (b)

SOLUTION

A. The graph of g is a vertical shift of four units upward of the graph of $f(x) = x^2$. Thus, the equation for g is $g(x) = x^2 + 4$.

B. The graph of h is a horizontal shift of five units to the left of the graph of $f(x) = x^2$. Thus, the equation for h is $h(x) = (x + 5)^2$.

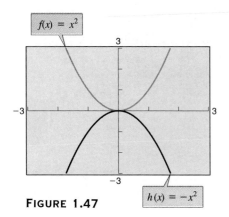

FIGURE 1.47

Reflections

The second common type of transformation is called a **reflection.** For instance, if you consider the x-axis to be a mirror, the graph of

$$h(x) = -x^2$$

is the mirror image (or reflection) of the graph of

$$f(x) = x^2,$$

as shown in Figure 1.47.

REFLECTIONS IN THE COORDINATE AXES

Reflections in the coordinate axes of the graph of $y = f(x)$ are represented as follows.

1. Reflection in the x-axis: $h(x) = -f(x)$
2. Reflection in the y-axis: $h(x) = f(-x)$

EXAMPLE 3 Finding Equations from Graphs

Each of the graphs shown in Figure 1.48(a) and 1.48(b) is a transformation of the graph of $f(x) = x^4$ (shown at left in Figure 1.48). Find an equation for each function.

FIGURE 1.48

(a) $y = g(x)$

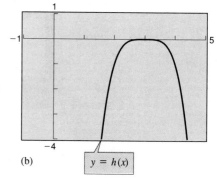

(b) $y = h(x)$

SOLUTION

A. The graph of g is a reflection in the x-axis *followed* by an upward shift of two units of the graph of $f(x) = x^4$. Thus, the equation for g is $g(x) = -x^4 + 2$.

B. The graph of h is a horizontal shift of three units to the right followed by a reflection in the x-axis of the graph of $f(x) = x^4$. Thus, the equation for h is $h(x) = -(x - 3)^4$.

(a)

$g(x) = -\sqrt{x}$

$h(x) = \sqrt{-x}$

(b)

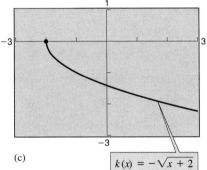

(c)

FIGURE 1.49

$k(x) = -\sqrt{x+2}$

EXAMPLE 4   **Reflections and Shifts**
....

Compare the graph of each function with the graph of $f(x) = \sqrt{x}$.

A. $g(x) = -\sqrt{x}$

B. $h(x) = \sqrt{-x}$

C. $k(x) = -\sqrt{x+2}$

SOLUTION

A. Relative to the graph of $f(x) = \sqrt{x}$, the graph of g is a reflection in the x-axis because

$$g(x) = -\sqrt{x} = -f(x).$$

B. The graph of h is a reflection of the graph of $f(x) = \sqrt{x}$ in the y-axis because

$$h(x) = \sqrt{-x} = f(-x).$$

C. From the equation

$$k(x) = -\sqrt{x+2} = -f(x+2)$$

you can conclude that the graph of k is a left shift of two units, followed by a reflection in the x-axis.

The graphs of all three functions are shown in Figure 1.49.   ....

EXAMPLE 5   **A Program for Practice**
....

If you have a programmable calculator, try entering the following program. (These program steps are for a Texas Instruments TI-81. Programs for other calculators are listed in the appendix.)

```
:Rand→H                      :-6→Ymin
:-6+Int (12H)→H              :6→Ymax
:Rand→V                      :1→Yscl
:-3+ Int (6V)→V              :DispGraph
:Rand→R                      :Pause
:If R<.5                     :Disp "Y=R(X+H)²+V"
:-1→R                        :Disp "R="
:If R>.49                    :Disp R
:1→R                         :Disp "H="
:"R(X+H)²+V"→Y₁              :Disp H
:-9→Xmin                     :Disp "V="
:9→Xmax                      :Disp V
:1→Xscl                      :End
```

This program will sketch a graph of the function

$$y = R(x + H)^2 + V,$$

where $R = \pm 1$, H is an integer between -6 and 6, and V is an integer between -3 and 3. (Each time you run the program, different values of R, H, and V are possible.) From the graph, you should be able to determine the values of R, H, and V. After you have determined the values, press ENTER to see the answer. (To look at the graph again, press GRAPH.)

For example, in the graph shown in Figure 1.50, you can make the following conclusions. Because the graph of $f(x) = x^2$ has been reflected about the x-axis, you know that $R = -1$. Because the graph of $f(x) = x^2$ has been shifted four units to the left, you know that $H = 4$. Because the graph of $f(x) = x^2$ has been shifted three units up, you know that $V = 3$. Thus, the equation of the graph shown in Figure 1.50 must be

$$y = -(x + 4)^2 + 3.$$

Try running this program several times. It will give you practice in working with reflections, horizontal shifts, and vertical shifts.   ·········

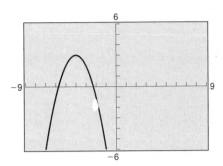

FIGURE 1.50

Nonrigid Transformations

Horizontal shifts, vertical shifts, and reflections are called **rigid** transformations because the basic shape of the graph is unchanged. These transformations change only the *position* of the graph in the xy-plane. **Nonrigid** transformations are those that cause a *distortion*—a change in the shape of the original graph. For instance, a nonrigid transformation of the graph of $y = f(x)$ is represented by $y = cf(x)$, where the transformation is a **vertical stretch** if $c > 1$ and a **vertical shrink** if $0 < c < 1$.

EXAMPLE 6   Nonrigid Transformations
·················

Compare the graph of each function with the graph of $f(x) = |x|$.

A. $h(x) = 3|x|$ **B.** $g(x) = \dfrac{1}{3}|x|$

SOLUTION

A. Relative to the graph of $f(x) = |x|$, the graph of

$$h(x) = 3|x| = 3f(x)$$

is a vertical stretch (multiply each y-value by 3) of the graph of f.
B. Similarly, the equation

$$g(x) = \frac{1}{3}|x| = \frac{1}{3}f(x)$$

indicates that the graph of g is a vertical shrink of the graph of f.

The graphs of all three functions are shown in Figure 1.51.   ·········

(a)

(b)

FIGURE 1.51

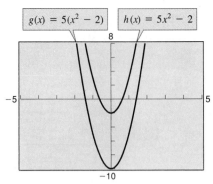

$g(x) = 5(x^2 - 2)$ $h(x) = 5x^2 - 2$

FIGURE 1.52

EXAMPLE 7   Sequences of Transformations

Use a graphing utility to graph the two functions $g(x) = 5(x^2 - 2)$ and $h(x) = 5x^2 - 2$ on the same screen. Describe how each function was obtained from $f(x) = x^2$ as a sequence of shifts and stretches.

SOLUTION

Notice that the two graphs in Figure 1.52 are different. The graph of g is a downward shift of two units followed by a vertical stretch, whereas h is a vertical stretch followed by a downward shift of two units. Hence, the order of applying the transformations is important.

DISCUSSION PROBLEM

COMPARING MATHEMATICAL MODELS

The following two second-degree polynomial functions are models of the United States population from 1800 to 1990. In the first model, $f(t)$ represents the population and t represents the year.

Model 1

$$f(t) = 6722.5t^2 - 24,201,000t + 21,787,790,000, \qquad 1800 \le t \le 1990$$

In the second model, $g(t)$ represents the population in millions and t represents the year, with $t = 0$ corresponding to 1800, $t = 1$ corresponding to 1810, and so on. (See figure.)

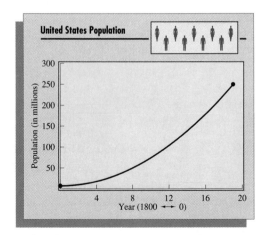

United States Population

Population (in millions)

Year (1800 ←→ 0)

Model 2

$$g(t) = 0.67225t^2 + 6.89, \qquad 0 \le t \le 19$$

These two models are related as follows.

$$f(t) = 1,000,000 g\left(\frac{t - 1800}{10}\right)$$

Which model do you think is better? Write a short paragraph explaining your reasons.

WARM-UP

The following warm-up exercises involve skills that were covered in earlier sections. You will use these skills in the exercise set for this section.

In Exercises 1–6, graph the function. Determine its domain and range.

1. $f(x) = \sqrt{16 - x^2}$ **2.** $h(x) = \frac{1}{2}|x - 3|$

3. $g(x) = \frac{1}{4}x^2 - 1$ **4.** $f(x) = 1 - \frac{1}{3}x^3$

5. $f(s) = \dfrac{|s - 2|}{s - 2}$ **6.** $g(t) = \sqrt{t - 2}$

In Exercises 7–10, determine whether the function is even, odd, or neither.

7. $p(x) = -0.25x$ **8.** $h(x) = x^2 - 3$

9. $g(t) = \frac{3}{8}t^4 - t^2$ **10.** $f(s) = s^{4/3} + 3$

SECTION 1.5 · EXERCISES

In Exercises 1–8, sketch the graphs of the three functions *by hand* on the same coordinate plane. Verify your result with a graphing utility.

1. $f(x) = x$
 $g(x) = x - 4$
 $h(x) = 3x$

2. $f(x) = \frac{1}{2}x$
 $g(x) = \frac{1}{2}x + 2$
 $h(x) = \frac{1}{2}(x - 2)$

3. $f(x) = x^2$
 $g(x) = x^2 + 2$
 $h(x) = (x - 2)^2$

4. $f(x) = x^2$
 $g(x) = x^2 - 4$
 $h(x) = (x + 2)^2 + 1$

5. $f(x) = -x^2$
 $g(x) = -x^2 + 1$
 $h(x) = -(x - 2)^2$

6. $f(x) = (x - 2)^2$
 $g(x) = (x - 2)^2 + 2$
 $h(x) = -(x - 2)^2 + 4$

7. $f(x) = x^2$
 $g(x) = (\frac{1}{2}x)^2$
 $h(x) = (2x)^2$

8. $f(x) = x^2$
 $g(x) = (\frac{1}{4}x)^2 + 2$
 $h(x) = -(\frac{1}{4}x)^2$

11.

12.

In Exercises 13–16, use a graphing utility to graph the three functions on the same set of coordinate axes. Describe the graphs of g and h relative to the graph of f.

13. $f(x) = x^3 - 3x^2$
 $g(x) = f(x + 2)$
 $h(x) = f(\frac{1}{2}x)$

14. $f(x) = x^3 - 3x^2 + 2$
 $g(x) = f(x - 1)$
 $h(x) = f(2x)$

15. $f(x) = x^3 - 3x^2$
 $g(x) = -\frac{1}{3}f(x)$
 $h(x) = f(-x)$

16. $f(x) = x^3 - 3x^2 + 2$
 $g(x) = -f(x)$
 $h(x) = f(-x)$

In Exercises 17 and 18, use the graph of $f(x) = x^3 - 3x^2$ (see Exercise 13) to write a formula for the function g shown in the given graph.

In Exercises 9–12, use the graph of $f(x) = x^2$ to write formulas for the functions g and h shown in the given graphs.

9.

10.

17.

18.

In Exercises 19–24, compare the graph of the given function with the graph of $f(x) = \sqrt{x}$.

19. $y = \sqrt{x} + 2$ **20.** $y = -\sqrt{x}$

21. $y = \sqrt{x} - 2$ **22.** $y = \sqrt{x + 3}$

23. $y = \sqrt{2x}$ **24.** $y = \sqrt{-x}$

In Exercises 25–30, compare the graph of the given function with the graph of $f(x) = \sqrt[3]{x}$.

25. $y = \sqrt[3]{x} - 1$ **26.** $y = \sqrt[3]{x + 1}$

27. $y = \sqrt[3]{x - 1}$ **28.** $y = -\sqrt[3]{x} - 2$

29. $y = \sqrt[3]{-x}$ **30.** $y = \frac{1}{2}\sqrt[3]{x}$

In Exercises 31–36, use the graph of $f(x)$ (see figure) to sketch the graph of the specified function.

31. $f(x - 4)$

32. $f(x + 2)$

33. $f(x) + 4$

34. $f(x) - 1$

35. $2f(x)$

36. $\frac{1}{2}f(x)$

FIGURES FOR 31–36

In Exercises 37–42, specify a sequence of transformations that will yield the graph of the given function from the graph of the function $f(x) = x^3$.

37. $g(x) = 4 - x^3$ **38.** $g(x) = (x - 4)^3$

39. $h(x) = \frac{1}{4}(x + 2)^3$ **40.** $h(x) = -2(x - 1)^3 + 3$

41. $p(x) = (\frac{1}{3}x)^3 + 2$ **42.** $p(x) = [3(x - 2)]^3$

43. *Profit* The profit P per week on a certain product is given by the model
$$P(x) = 80 + 20x - 0.5x^2, \qquad 0 \le x \le 20,$$
where x is the amount spent on advertising. In this model, x and P are both measured in hundreds of dollars.
(a) Use a graphing utility to graph the profit function.
(b) The business estimates that taxes and operating costs will increase by an average of $2500 per week during the next year. Rewrite the profit equation to reflect this expected decrease in profits. Identify the type of transformation made to the graph of the equation.
(c) Rewrite the original profit equation so that x measures advertising expenditures in dollars. [Find $P(x/100)$.] Describe the transformation made to the graph of the profit function.

44. *Automobile Aerodynamics* The number of horsepower H required to overcome wind drag on a certain automobile is approximated by
$$H(x) = 0.002x^2 + 0.005x - 0.029, \qquad 10 \le x \le 100,$$
where x is the speed of the car in miles per hour.
(a) Use the graphing utility to graph the power function.
(b) Rewrite the power function so that x represents the speed in kilometers per hour. [Find $H(1.6x)$.] Describe the transformation made to the graph of the power function.

45. Use a graphing utility to graph $f(x) = x^2$, $g(x) = x^4$, and $h(x) = x^6$ in the same viewing rectangle. Describe any similarities and differences you observe among the graphs.

46. Use a graphing utility to graph $f(x) = x$, $g(x) = x^3$, and $h(x) = x^5$ in the same viewing rectangle. Describe any similarities and differences you observe among the graphs.

47. Use the results of Exercises 45 and 46 to sketch the graphs of $f(x) = x^{10}$ and $g(x) = x^{11}$, without the aid of a graphing utility.

48. Use the results of Exercises 45 and 46 to sketch the graphs of $f(x) = (x - 3)^3$, $g(x) = (x + 1)^2$, and $h(x) = (x - 4)^5$, without the aid of a graphing utility.

In Exercises 49–52, use the results of Exercises 45–48 and your imagination to guess the shape of the graph of the function. Then use a graphing utility to graph the function, and compare the result with the graph drawn by hand.

49. $f(x) = x^2(x - 6)^2$ **50.** $f(x) = x^3(x - 6)^2$

51. $f(x) = x^2(x - 6)^3$ **52.** $f(x) = x^3(x - 6)^3$

1.6   COMBINATIONS OF FUNCTIONS

Arithmetic Combinations of Functions / Compositions of Functions /
Applications

Arithmetic Combinations of Functions

Just as two real numbers can be combined by the operations of addition, subtraction, multiplication, and division to form other real numbers, two *functions* can be combined to create new functions. For example, if

$$f(x) = 2x - 3 \quad \text{and} \quad g(x) = x^2 - 1,$$

you can form the sum, difference, product, and quotient of f and g as follows.

$$f(x) + g(x) = (2x - 3) + (x^2 - 1) = x^2 + 2x - 4 \qquad \textit{Sum}$$
$$f(x) - g(x) = (2x - 3) - (x^2 - 1) = -x^2 + 2x - 2 \qquad \textit{Difference}$$
$$f(x)g(x) = (2x - 3)(x^2 - 1) = 2x^3 - 3x^2 - 2x + 3 \quad \textit{Product}$$
$$\frac{f(x)}{g(x)} = \frac{2x - 3}{x^2 - 1}, \qquad x \neq \pm 1 \qquad\qquad\qquad \textit{Quotient}$$

The domain of an arithmetic combination of functions f and g consists of all real numbers that are common to the domains of f and g. In the case of the quotient $f(x)/g(x)$, there is the further restriction that $g(x) \neq 0$.

DEFINITIONS OF SUM, DIFFERENCE, PRODUCT, AND QUOTIENT OF FUNCTIONS

Let f and g be two functions with overlapping domains. Then, for all x common to both domains, the **sum, difference, product,** and **quotient** of f and g are defined as follows.

1. Sum: $(f + g)(x) = f(x) + g(x)$
2. Difference: $(f - g)(x) = f(x) - g(x)$
3. Product: $(fg)(x) = f(x) \cdot g(x)$
4. Quotient: $\left(\dfrac{f}{g}\right)(x) = \dfrac{f(x)}{g(x)}, \quad g(x) \neq 0$

EXAMPLE 1   Finding the Sum of Two Functions

Given $f(x) = 2x + 1$ and $g(x) = x^2 + 2x - 1$, find $(f + g)(x)$. Then evaluate this sum when $x = 2$.

SOLUTION

The sum of the functions f and g is given by

$$(f + g)(x) = f(x) + g(x)$$
$$= (2x + 1) + (x^2 + 2x - 1)$$
$$= x^2 + 4x.$$

When $x = 2$, the value of this sum is

$$(f + g)(2) = 2^2 + 4(2) = 12.$$

EXAMPLE 2   Finding the Difference of Two Functions

Given $f(x) = 2x + 1$ and $g(x) = x^2 + 2x - 1$, find $(f - g)(x)$. Then evaluate this difference when $x = 2$.

SOLUTION

The difference of the functions f and g is given by

$$(f - g)(x) = f(x) - g(x)$$
$$= (2x + 1) - (x^2 + 2x - 1)$$
$$= -x^2 + 2.$$

When $x = 2$, the value of this difference is

$$(f - g)(2) = -(2)^2 + 2 = -2.$$

In Examples 1 and 2, both f and g have domains that consist of all real numbers. Thus, the domain of both $(f + g)$ and $(f - g)$ is also the set of all real numbers. Remember that any restrictions on the domains of f or g must be taken into account when forming the sum, difference, product, or quotient of f and g. For instance, the domain of $f(x) = 1/x$ is all $x \neq 0$, and the domain of $g(x) = \sqrt{x}$ is $[0, \infty)$. This implies that the domain of $f + g$ is $(0, \infty)$.

EXAMPLE 3   The Quotient of Two Functions

Find $(f/g)(x)$ and $(g/f)(x)$ for the functions $f(x) = \sqrt{x}$ and $g(x) = \sqrt{4 - x^2}$. Then find the domains of f/g and g/f.

SOLUTION

The quotient of f and g is given by

$$\left(\frac{f}{g}\right)(x) = \frac{f(x)}{g(x)} = \frac{\sqrt{x}}{\sqrt{4 - x^2}},$$

and the quotient of g and f is given by

$$\left(\frac{g}{f}\right)(x) = \frac{g(x)}{f(x)} = \frac{\sqrt{4 - x^2}}{\sqrt{x}}.$$

The domain of f is $[0, \infty)$ and the domain of g is $[-2, 2]$. The intersection of these two domains is $[0, 2]$. Thus, the domains for f/g and g/f are as follows.

$$\text{Domain of } \frac{f}{g}: [0, 2) \qquad \text{Domain of } \frac{g}{f}: (0, 2]$$

Can you see why these two domains differ slightly?

Compositions of Functions

Another way of combining two functions is to form the **composition** of one with the other. For instance, if $f(x) = x^2$ and $g(x) = x + 1$, then the composition of f with g is

$$f(g(x)) = f(x + 1) = (x + 1)^2.$$

This composition is denoted as $f \circ g$.

DEFINITION OF COMPOSITION OF TWO FUNCTIONS

The **composition** of the functions f and g is

$$(f \circ g)(x) = f(g(x)).$$

The domain of $f \circ g$ is the set of all x in the domain of g such that $g(x)$ is in the domain of f. (See figure.)

EXAMPLE 4   Forming the Composition of f with g

Find $(f \circ g)(x)$ for $f(x) = \sqrt{x}$, $x \geq 0$, and $g(x) = x - 1$, $x \geq 1$. If possible, find $(f \circ g)(2)$ and $(f \circ g)(0)$.

SOLUTION

$$
\begin{aligned}
(f \circ g)(x) &= f(g(x)) && \textit{Definition of } f \circ g \\
&= f(x - 1) && \textit{Definition of } g(x) \\
&= \sqrt{x - 1}, \quad x \geq 1 && \textit{Definition of } f(x)
\end{aligned}
$$

The domain of $f \circ g$ is $[1, \infty)$. Thus,

$$(f \circ g)(2) = \sqrt{2 - 1} = 1$$

is defined, but $(f \circ g)(0)$ is not defined because 0 is not in the domain of $f \circ g$.

The composition of f with g is generally *not* the same as the composition of g with f. This is illustrated in Example 5.

EXAMPLE 5   Compositions of Functions

Given $f(x) = x + 2$ and $g(x) = 4 - x^2$, find the following.

A. $(f \circ g)(x)$
B. $(g \circ f)(x)$

SOLUTION

A. $(f \circ g)(x) = f(g(x))$ *Definition of $f \circ g$*

           $= f(4 - x^2)$ *Definition of $g(x)$*

           $= (4 - x^2) + 2$ *Definition of $f(x)$*

           $= -x^2 + 6$

B. $(g \circ f)(x) = g(f(x))$ *Definition of $g \circ f$*

           $= g(x + 2)$ *Definition of $f(x)$*

           $= 4 - (x + 2)^2$ *Definition of $g(x)$*

           $= 4 - (x^2 + 4x + 4)$

           $= -x^2 - 4x$

Note in this case that $(f \circ g)(x) \neq (g \circ f)(x)$.

EXAMPLE 6   Finding the Domain of a Composite Function

Given $f(x) = x^2 - 9$ and $g(x) = \sqrt{9 - x^2}$, find $(f \circ g)(x)$. Then find the domain of $f \circ g$.

SOLUTION

To begin, notice that the domain of g is $-3 \leq x \leq 3$.

$$(f \circ g)(x) = f(g(x)), \qquad\qquad -3 \leq x \leq 3$$

$$= f\left(\sqrt{9 - x^2}\right), \qquad\qquad -3 \leq x \leq 3$$

$$= \left(\sqrt{9 - x^2}\right)^2 - 9, \qquad -3 \leq x \leq 3$$

$$= 9 - x^2 - 9, \qquad\qquad -3 \leq x \leq 3$$

$$= -x^2, \qquad\qquad\qquad -3 \leq x \leq 3$$

Thus, the domain of $f \circ g$ is $-3 \leq x \leq 3$. To convince yourself of this, use a graphing utility to graph

$$y = \left(\sqrt{9 - x^2}\right)^2 - 9,$$

as shown in Figure 1.53. Notice that the graphing utility does not extend the graph to the left of $x = -3$ or to the right of $x = 3$.

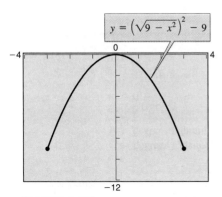

$y = \left(\sqrt{9 - x^2}\right)^2 - 9$

FIGURE 1.53

EXAMPLE 7 A Case in Which $f \circ g = g \circ f$

Given $f(x) = 2x + 3$ and $g(x) = \frac{1}{2}(x - 3)$, find the following.

A. $(f \circ g)(x)$
B. $(g \circ f)(x)$

SOLUTION

REMARK In Example 7, note that the two composite functions $f \circ g$ and $g \circ f$ are equal, and both represent the identity function. That is, $(f \circ g)(x) = (g \circ f)(x) = x$. We will discuss this special case in the next section.

A. $(f \circ g)(x) = f(g(x)) = f\left(\frac{1}{2}(x - 3)\right) = 2\left[\frac{1}{2}(x - 3)\right] + 3$
$$= x - 3 + 3 = x$$

B. $(g \circ f)(x) = g(f(x)) = g(2x + 3) = \frac{1}{2}[(2x + 3) - 3] = \frac{1}{2}(2x) = x$

In Examples 5, 6, and 7 we formed the composition of two given functions. In calculus, it is also important to be able to identify two functions that *make up a given* composite function. For instance, the function h given by $h(x) = (3x - 5)^3$ is the composition of f with g, where $f(x) = x^3$ and $g(x) = 3x - 5$. That is,

$$h(x) = (3x - 5)^3 = [g(x)]^3 = f(g(x)).$$

Basically, to "decompose" a composite function, look for an "inner" and an "outer" function. In the function h above, $g(x) = 3x - 5$ is the inner function and $f(x) = x^3$ is the outer function.

EXAMPLE 8 Identifying a Composite Function

Express the function

$$h(x) = \frac{1}{(x - 2)^2}$$

as a composition of two functions.

SOLUTION

One way to write h as a composite of two functions is to take the inner function to be $g(x) = x - 2$ and the outer function to be

$$f(x) = \frac{1}{x^2} = x^{-2}.$$

Then you can write

$$h(x) = \frac{1}{(x - 2)^2} = (x - 2)^{-2} = f(x - 2) = f(g(x)).$$

This function can be decomposed in other ways. For instance, let $g(x) = 1/(x - 2)$ and $f(x) = x^2$. Then $h(x) = f(g(x))$.

Applications

EXAMPLE 9   Bacteria Count
....

The number of bacteria in a refrigerated food is given by

$$N(T) = 20T^2 - 80T + 500, \qquad 2 \leq T \leq 14,$$

where T is the Celsius temperature of the food. When the food is removed from refrigeration, the temperature is given by

$$T(t) = 4t + 2, \qquad 0 \leq t \leq 3,$$

where t is the time in hours. Find the following.

A. The composite function $N(T(t))$. What does this function represent?

B. The number of bacteria in the food when $t = 2$ hours

C. The time when the bacteria count reaches 2000

SOLUTION

A.
$$\begin{aligned}
N(T(t)) &= 20(4t + 2)^2 - 80(4t + 2) + 500 \\
&= 20(16t^2 + 16t + 4) - 320t - 160 + 500 \\
&= 320t^2 + 320t + 80 - 320t - 160 + 500 \\
&= 320t^2 + 420
\end{aligned}$$

This composite function represents the number of bacteria as a function of the amount of time the food has been out of refrigeration.

B. When $t = 2$, the number of bacteria is

$$N = 320(2)^2 + 420 = 1280 + 420 = 1700.$$

C. The bacteria count will reach $N = 2000$ when $320t^2 + 420 = 2000$. You can solve this equation for t algebraically as follows.

$$\begin{aligned}
320t^2 + 420 &= 2000 \\
320t^2 &= 1580 \\
t^2 &= \frac{1580}{320} = \frac{79}{16} \\
t &= \frac{\sqrt{79}}{4} \approx 2.2 \text{ hours}
\end{aligned}$$

Or you can use a graphing utility to approximate the solution, as shown in Figure 1.54.
....

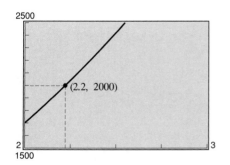

FIGURE 1.54

You are considering buying a new car for which the regular price is $15,800. The dealership has advertised a factory rebate of $1500 *and* a 12% discount. Using function notation, the rebate and the discount can be represented as

$$f(x) = x - 1500 \qquad \textit{Rebate of \$1500}$$

and

$$g(x) = 0.88x, \qquad \textit{Discount of 12\%}$$

where x is the price of the car, $f(x)$ is the price after subtracting the rebate, and $g(x)$ is the price after taking the 12% discount. Compare the sale price obtained by subtracting the rebate first and then taking the discount with the sale price obtained by taking the discount first and then subtracting the rebate.

WARM-UP
· · · · · · · · · · · · · · · ·

The following warm-up exercises involve skills that were covered in earlier sections. You will use these skills in the exercise set for this section.

In Exercises 1–10, perform the indicated operations and simplify the result.

1. $\dfrac{1}{x} + \dfrac{1}{1 - x}$

2. $\dfrac{2}{x + 3} - \dfrac{2}{x - 3}$

3. $\dfrac{3}{x - 2} - \dfrac{2}{x(x - 2)}$

4. $\dfrac{x}{x - 5} + \dfrac{1}{3}$

5. $(x - 1)\left(\dfrac{1}{\sqrt{x^2 - 1}}\right)$

6. $\left(\dfrac{x}{x^2 - 4}\right)\left(\dfrac{x^2 - x - 2}{x^2}\right)$

7. $(x^2 - 4) \div \left(\dfrac{x + 2}{5}\right)$

8. $\left(\dfrac{x}{x^2 + 3x - 10}\right) \div \left(\dfrac{x^2 + 3x}{x^2 + 6x + 5}\right)$

9. $\dfrac{(1/x) + 5}{3 - (1/x)}$

10. $\dfrac{(x/4) - (4/x)}{x - 4}$

SECTION 1.6 · EXERCISES
· ·

In Exercises 1–6, find (a) $(f + g)(x)$, (b) $(f - g)(x)$, (c) $(fg)(x)$, and (d) $(f/g)(x)$. What is the domain of f/g?

1. $f(x) = x + 1, \quad g(x) = x - 1$

2. $f(x) = 2x - 5, \quad g(x) = 5$

3. $f(x) = x^2 + 5, \quad g(x) = \sqrt{1 - x}$

4. $f(x) = \sqrt{x^2 - 4}, \quad g(x) = \dfrac{x^2}{x^2 + 1}$

5. $f(x) = \dfrac{1}{x}, \quad g(x) = \dfrac{1}{x^2}$

6. $f(x) = \dfrac{x}{x + 1}, \quad g(x) = x^3$

In Exercises 7–16, evaluate the indicated function for $f(x) = x^2 + 1$ and $g(x) = x - 4$.

7. $(f + g)(3)$ **8.** $(f - g)(-2)$

9. $(f - g)(2t)$ **10.** $(f + g)(t - 1)$

11. $(fg)(4)$ **12.** $(fg)(-6)$

13. $\left(\dfrac{f}{g}\right)(5)$ **14.** $\left(\dfrac{f}{g}\right)(0)$

15. $\left(\dfrac{f}{g}\right)(-1) - g(3)$ **16.** $(2f)(5)$

In Exercises 17–20, graph the functions f, g, and $f + g$ on the same set of coordinate axes.

17. $f(x) = \frac{1}{2}x$, $g(x) = x - 1$

18. $f(x) = \frac{1}{3}x$, $g(x) = -x + 4$

19. $f(x) = x^2$, $g(x) = -2x$

20. $f(x) = 4 - x^2$, $g(x) = x$

In Exercises 21 and 22, use a graphing utility to graph f, g, and $f + g$ in the same viewing rectangle. Which function contributes most to the magnitude of the sum when $0 \le x \le 2$? Which function contributes most to the sum when $x > 5$?

21. $f(x) = 3x$, $g(x) = -\dfrac{x^3}{10}$

22. $f(x) = \dfrac{x}{2}$, $g(x) = \sqrt{x}$

23. *Stopping Distance*   While traveling in a car at x miles per hour, you are required to stop quickly to avoid an accident. The distance the car travels during your reaction time is given by $R(x) = \frac{3}{4}x$. The distance traveled while braking is given by $B(x) = \frac{1}{15}x^2$. Find the function giving total stopping distance T. Graph the functions R, B, and T on the same set of coordinate axes for $0 \le x \le 60$.

24. *Comparing Sales*   Suppose you own two fast-food restaurants in town. From 1985 to 1990, the sales for one restaurant have been decreasing according to the function

$$R_1 = 500 - 0.8t^2, \qquad t = 5, 6, 7, 8, 9, 10,$$

where R_1 represents the sales for the first restaurant (in thousands of dollars) and t represents the calendar year with $t = 5$ corresponding to 1985. During the same 6-year period, the sales for the second restaurant have been increasing according to the function

$$R_2 = 250 + 0.78t, \qquad t = 5, 6, 7, 8, 9, 10.$$

Write a function that represents the total sales for the two restaurants. Use the *stacked bar graph* in the figure, which represents the total sales during the 6-year period, to determine whether the total sales have been increasing or decreasing.

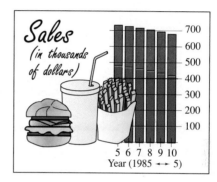

FIGURE FOR 24

In Exercises 25–28, find (a) $f \circ g$, (b) $g \circ f$, and (c) $f \circ f$.

25. $f(x) = x^2$, $g(x) = x - 1$

26. $f(x) = \sqrt[3]{x - 1}$, $g(x) = x^3 + 1$

27. $f(x) = 3x + 5$, $g(x) = 5 - x$

28. $f(x) = x^3$, $g(x) = \dfrac{1}{x}$

In Exercises 29–34, find (a) $f \circ g$ and (b) $g \circ f$.

29. $f(x) = \sqrt{x + 4}$, $g(x) = x^2$

30. $f(x) = \sqrt[5]{x + 1}$, $g(x) = x^5 - 2$

31. $f(x) = \frac{1}{3}x - 3$, $g(x) = 3x + 1$

32. $f(x) = \sqrt{x}$, $g(x) = \sqrt{x}$

33. $f(x) = |x|$, $g(x) = x + 6$

34. $f(x) = x^{2/3}$, $g(x) = x^6$

In Exercises 35–38, use the graphs of f and g to evaluate the indicated functions.

35. (a) $(f + g)(3)$ (b) $\left(\dfrac{f}{g}\right)(2)$

36. (a) $(f - g)(1)$ (b) $(fg)(4)$

37. (a) $(f \circ g)(2)$ (b) $(g \circ f)(2)$

38. (a) $(f \circ g)(1)$ (b) $(g \circ f)(3)$

$y = f(x)$

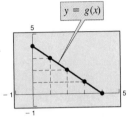

$y = g(x)$

FIGURES FOR 35–38

In Exercises 39–46, find two functions f and g such that $(f \circ g)(x) = h(x)$. (There are many correct answers to these exercises.)

39. $h(x) = (2x + 1)^2$

40. $h(x) = (1 - x)^3$

41. $h(x) = \sqrt[3]{x^2 - 4}$

42. $h(x) = \sqrt{9 - x}$

43. $h(x) = \dfrac{1}{x + 2}$

44. $h(x) = \dfrac{4}{(5x + 2)^2}$

45. $h(x) = (x + 4)^2 + 2(x + 4)$

46. $h(x) = (x + 3)^{3/2}$

In Exercises 47–50, determine the domain of (a) f, (b) g, and (c) $f \circ g$.

47. $f(x) = \sqrt{x}$, $g(x) = x^2 + 1$

48. $f(x) = \dfrac{1}{x}$, $g(x) = x + 3$

49. $f(x) = \dfrac{3}{x^2 - 1}$, $g(x) = x + 1$

50. $f(x) = 2x + 3$, $g(x) = \dfrac{x}{2}$

51. *Ripples* A pebble is dropped into a calm pond, causing ripples in the form of concentric circles (see figure). The radius (in feet) of the outer ripple is given by $r(t) = 0.6t$, where t is the time in seconds after the pebble strikes the water. The area of the circle is given by the function $A(r) = \pi r^2$.
(a) Find and interpret $(A \circ r)(t)$.

(b) Use a graphing utility to graph the area as a function of t. Move the cursor along the graph to estimate (to two decimal place accuracy) the time required for the area enclosed by a ripple to increase to 20 square feet.

FIGURE FOR 51

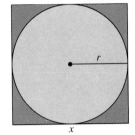

FIGURE FOR 52

52. *Area* A square concrete foundation was prepared as a base for a large cylindrical gasoline tank (see figure).
(a) Express the radius r of the tank as a function of the length x of the sides of the square.
(b) Express the area A of the circular base of the tank as a function of the radius r.
(c) Find and interpret $(A \circ r)(x)$.

53. *Cost* The weekly cost (in dollars) of producing x units in a manufacturing process is given by the function $C(x) = 60x + 750$. The number of units produced in t hours is given by $x(t) = 50t$.
(a) Find and interpret $(C \circ x)(t)$.
(b) Use a graphing utility to graph the cost as a function of time. Move the cursor along the curve to estimate (to two decimal place accuracy) the time that must elapse until the cost increases to \$15,000.

54. *Air Traffic Control* An air traffic controller spots two planes at the same altitude flying toward the same point (see figure). Their flight paths form a right angle at point P. One plane is 150 miles from point P and is moving at 450 miles per hour. The second plane is 200 miles from point P and is moving at 450 miles per hour. Write the distance s between the planes as a function of time t.

FIGURE FOR 54

Distance (in miles)

55. *Rebate and Discount*   A car dealership is offering a rebate of $1200 *and* a discount of 15% on a car for which the regular price is $18,400. Write a function that represents each type of discount. Then use composition of functions to compare the sale price obtained by subtracting the rebate first with the sale price obtained by taking the discount first.

56. Prove that the product of two odd functions is an even function, and that the product of two even functions is an even function.

57. Use examples to hypothesize whether the product of an odd function and an even function is even or odd. Then prove your hypothesis.

58. Given a function *f*, prove that $g(x)$ is even and $h(x)$ is odd where

$$g(x) = \tfrac{1}{2}[f(x) + f(-x)] \quad \text{and} \quad h(x) = \tfrac{1}{2}[f(x) - f(-x)].$$

59. Use the result of Exercise 58 to prove that any function can be written as a sum of even and odd functions. (*Hint:* Add the two equations in Exercise 58.)

60. Use the result of Exercise 59 to write each of the following functions as a sum of even and odd functions.

(a) $f(x) = x^2 - 2x + 1$ (b) $f(x) = \dfrac{1}{x + 1}$

1.7   INVERSE FUNCTIONS

The Inverse of a Function   /   The Graph of the Inverse of a Function   /
The Existence of an Inverse Function   /   Finding the Inverse of a Function

The Inverse of a Function

In Section 1.3 you saw that a function can be represented by a set of ordered pairs. For instance, the function $f(x) = x + 4$ from the set $A = \{1, 2, 3, 4\}$ to the set $B = \{5, 6, 7, 8\}$ can be written as follows.

$$f(x) = x + 4: \{(1, 5), (2, 6), (3, 7), (4, 8)\}$$

By interchanging the first and second coordinates of each of these ordered pairs, you can form the **inverse function** of *f*, denoted by f^{-1}. This is a function from the set *B* to the set *A*, and can be written as follows.

$$f^{-1}(x) = x - 4: \{(5, 1), (6, 2), (7, 3), (8, 4)\}$$

Note that the domain of *f* is equal to the range of f^{-1}, and vice versa, as shown in Figure 1.55. Also note that the functions *f* and f^{-1} have the effect of "undoing" each other. In other words, when you form the composition of *f* with f^{-1} or the composition of f^{-1} with *f*, you obtain the identity function.

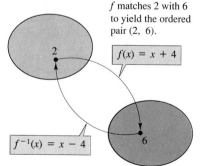

f matches 2 with 6 to yield the ordered pair (2, 6).

$f(x) = x + 4$

$f^{-1}(x) = x - 4$

f^{-1} matches 6 with 2 to yield the ordered pair (6, 2).

FIGURE 1.55

REMARK   Don't be confused by the use of -1 to denote the inverse function f^{-1}. In this book f^{-1} will *always* refer to the inverse of the function *f* and *not* to the reciprocal of $f(x)$.

EXAMPLE 1   Finding Inverse Functions Informally

Find the inverse of the following.

A. $f(x) = 4x$
B. $f(x) = x - 6$

SOLUTION

A. The given function is a function that *multiplies* each input by 4. To "undo" this function, you need to *divide* each input by 4. Thus, the inverse function of $f(x) = 4x$ is

$$f^{-1}(x) = \frac{x}{4}.$$

B. The given function is a function that *subtracts* 6 from each input. To "undo" this function, you need to *add* 6 to each input. Thus, the inverse function of $f(x) = x - 6$ is

$$f^{-1}(x) = x + 6.$$

DEFINITION OF THE INVERSE OF A FUNCTION

Let f and g be two functions such that $f(g(x)) = x$ for every x in the domain of g and $g(f(x)) = x$ for every x in the domain of f. Then the function g is the **inverse** of the function f. The inverse function is denoted by f^{-1} (read "f-inverse"). Thus,

$$f(f^{-1}(x)) = x \quad \text{and} \quad f^{-1}(f(x)) = x.$$

The domain of f must be equal to the range of f^{-1}, and the range of f must be equal to the domain of f^{-1}.

Note from this definition that if the function g is the inverse of the function f, then it must also be true that the function f is the inverse of the function g.

EXAMPLE 2   Verifying Inverse Functions

Show that $f(x) = x^3 - 1$ and $g(x) = \sqrt[3]{x + 1}$ are inverses of each other.

SOLUTION

Begin by noting that the domain (and the range) of both functions is the entire set of real numbers. To show that f and g are inverses of each other, you need to show that $f(g(x)) = x$ and $g(f(x)) = x$.

$$f(g(x)) = f\left(\sqrt[3]{x + 1}\right) = \left(\sqrt[3]{x + 1}\right)^3 - 1 = (x + 1) - 1 = x$$
$$g(f(x)) = g(x^3 - 1) = \sqrt[3]{(x^3 - 1) + 1} = \sqrt[3]{x^3} = x$$

You can see that the two functions f and g "undo" each other: the function f first cubes the input x and then subtracts 1, whereas the function g first adds 1 and then takes the cube root of the result. ·········

EXAMPLE 3 Verifying Inverse Functions
·················

Which of the functions

$$g(x) = \frac{x - 2}{5} \quad \text{and} \quad h(x) = \frac{5}{x} + 2$$

is the inverse of the function $f(x) = \dfrac{5}{x - 2}$?

SOLUTION

$$f(g(x)) = f\left(\frac{x - 2}{5}\right) = \frac{5}{[(x - 2)/5] - 2} = \frac{25}{(x - 2) - 10} = \frac{25}{x - 12} \neq x$$

Because this composition is not equal to the identity function x, you can conclude that g is *not* the inverse of f.

$$f(h(x)) = f\left(\frac{5}{x} + 2\right) = \frac{5}{(5/x) + 2 - 2} = \frac{5}{5/x} = x$$

Thus, it appears that h is the inverse of f. You can confirm this by showing that the composition of h with f is also equal to the identity function. ·········

The Graph of the Inverse of a Function

The graphs of f and f^{-1} are related to each other in the following way. If the point (a, b) lies on the graph of f, then the point (b, a) lies on the graph of f^{-1} and vice versa. This means that the graph of f^{-1} is a reflection of the graph of f in the line $y = x$, as shown in Figure 1.56.

In Examples 2 and 3, inverse functions were verified algebraically. A graphing utility can also be helpful in checking to see whether one function is the inverse of another function.

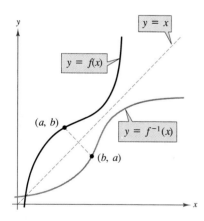

The graph of f^{-1} is a reflection of the graph of f in the line $y = x$.

FIGURE 1.56

FIGURE 1.57

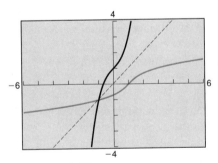

FIGURE 1.58

EXAMPLE 4   Graphical Check for Inverse Functions

Sketch the graphs of

$$f(x) = 2x^3 - 1 \quad \text{and} \quad g(x) = \sqrt[3]{\frac{x+1}{2}}$$

on the same coordinate plane and show that the graph of g is the reflection of the graph of f in the line $y = x$.

SOLUTION

Using a graphing utility, you can obtain the graphs shown in Figure 1.57. From this figure you can see that the graph of g is the reflection of the graph of f in the line $y = x$, which graphically confirms that g is the inverse of f.

EXAMPLE 5   A Graph Reflecting Program

The following program will graph a function f *and* its reflection in the line $y = x$. (The program steps listed are for a Texas Instruments TI-81. Program steps for other programmable calculators are given in the appendix.)

```
:2Xmin/3→Ymin               :Lbl 1
:2Xmax/3→Ymax               :PT-On(Y₁,X)
:Xscl→Yscl                  :X+I→X
:"X"→Y₂                     :If X>Xmax
:DispGraph                  :End
:(Xmax-Xmin)/95→I           :Goto 1
:Xmin→X
```

Use this program to graph the inverse of $f(x) = x^3 + x + 1$.

SOLUTION

To run the program, enter the function f into the calculator. Then set a viewing rectangle. (For the program to run, the viewing rectangle must not contain x-values outside the domain of f.) The resulting display is shown in Figure 1.58.

The Existence of an Inverse Function

A function need not have an inverse function. For instance, the function $f(x) = x^2$ has no inverse [assuming a domain of $(-\infty, \infty)$]. To have an inverse, a function must be **one-to-one,** which means that no two elements in the domain of f correspond to the same element in the range of f.

DEFINITION OF A ONE-TO-ONE FUNCTION

A function f is **one-to-one** if, for a and b in its domain,

$f(a) = f(b)$ implies that $a = b$.

The function $f(x) = x + 1$ *is* one-to-one because $a + 1 = b + 1$ implies that a and b must be equal. However, the function $f(x) = x^2$ is *not* one-to-one because $a^2 = b^2$ does not imply that $a = b$. For instance, $(-1)^2 = 1^2$ and yet $-1 \neq 1$.

EXISTENCE OF AN INVERSE FUNCTION

A function f has an inverse function f^{-1} if and only if f is one-to-one.

EXAMPLE 6   Testing for One-to-One Functions

Which functions are one-to-one and have inverse functions?

A. $f(x) = x^3 + 1$ **B.** $g(x) = x^2 - x$ **C.** $h(x) = \sqrt{x}$

SOLUTION

A. Let a and b be real numbers with $f(a) = f(b)$.

$$a^3 + 1 = b^3 + 1 \qquad \textit{Set } f(a) = f(b)$$
$$a^3 = b^3$$
$$a = b$$

Therefore, $f(a) = f(b)$ implies that $a = b$. From this, it follows that f *is* one-to-one and has an inverse function.

B. Because $g(-1) = (-1)^2 - (-1) = 2$ and $g(2) = 2^2 - 2 = 2$, you have two distinct inputs matched with the same output. Thus, g *is not* a one-to-one function and has no inverse.

C. Let a and b be nonnegative real numbers with $h(a) = h(b)$.

$$\sqrt{a} = \sqrt{b} \qquad \textit{Set } h(a) = h(b)$$
$$a = b$$

Therefore, $h(a) = h(b)$ implies that $a = b$. Thus, h *is* one-to-one and has an inverse.

From its graph, it is easy to tell whether a function of x is one-to-one. Simply check to see that every *horizontal* line intersects the graph of the function at most once. For instance, Figure 1.59 shows the graphs of the three functions given in Example 6. On the graph of $g(x) = x^2 - x$, you can find a horizontal line that intersects the graph twice.

Two special types of functions that pass the **horizontal line test** are those that are increasing or decreasing on their entire domains.

1. If f is *increasing* on its entire domain, then f is one-to-one.
2. If f is *decreasing* on its entire domain, then f is one-to-one.

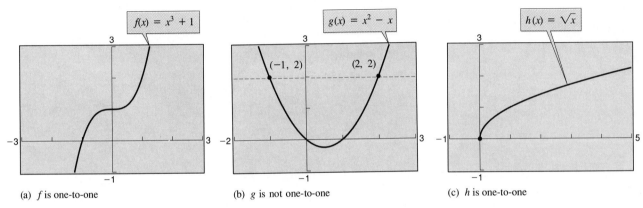

(a) f is one-to-one   (b) g is not one-to-one   (c) h is one-to-one

FIGURE 1.59

Finding the Inverse of a Function

For simple functions (such as the ones in Example 1) you can find inverse functions by inspection. For instance, the inverse of $f(x) = 8x$ is equal to $f^{-1}(x) = x/8$. For more complicated functions, however, it is best to use the following procedure for finding the inverse of a function.

FINDING THE INVERSE OF A FUNCTION

To find the inverse of f, use the following steps.

1. In the equation for $f(x)$, replace $f(x)$ by y.
2. Interchange the roles of x and y.
3. If the new equation does not represent y as a function of x, then the function f does not have an inverse function. If the new equation does represent y as a function of x, then solve the new equation for y.
4. Replace y by $f^{-1}(x)$.
5. Verify that f and f^{-1} are inverses of each other by showing that $f(f^{-1}(x)) = x$ and $f^{-1}(f(x)) = x$.

EXAMPLE 7   Finding the Inverse of a Function

Find the inverse (if it exists) of

$$f(x) = \frac{5 - 3x}{2}.$$

SOLUTION

From Figure 1.60, you can see that f is one-to-one, and therefore has an inverse.

$$y = \frac{5 - 3x}{2} \qquad \text{Write in form } y = f(x)$$

$$x = \frac{5 - 3y}{2} \qquad \text{Interchange } x \text{ and } y$$

$$2x = 5 - 3y$$

$$3y = 5 - 2x$$

$$y = \frac{5 - 2x}{3} \qquad \text{Solve for } y$$

$$f^{-1}(x) = \frac{5 - 2x}{3} \qquad \text{Replace } y \text{ by } f^{-1}(x)$$

The domain and range of both f and f^{-1} consist of all real numbers.

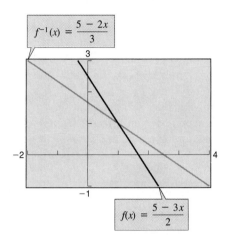

$$f^{-1}(x) = \frac{5 - 2x}{3}$$

$$f(x) = \frac{5 - 3x}{2}$$

FIGURE 1.60

EXAMPLE 8   Finding the Inverse of a Function

Find the inverse of the function $f(x) = \sqrt{2x - 3}$ and sketch the graphs of f and f^{-1}

SOLUTION

$$y = \sqrt{2x - 3}$$

$$x = \sqrt{2y - 3} \qquad \text{Interchange } x \text{ and } y$$

$$x^2 = 2y - 3$$

$$2y = x^2 + 3 \qquad \text{Solve for } y$$

$$y = \frac{x^2 + 3}{2} \qquad x \geq 0$$

$$f^{-1}(x) = \frac{x^2 + 3}{2}, \quad x \geq 0 \qquad \text{Replace } y \text{ by } f^{-1}(x)$$

The graph of f^{-1} is the reflection of the graph of f in the line $y = x$, as shown in Figure 1.61. Note that the domain of f is the interval $[\frac{3}{2}, \infty)$ and the range of f is the interval $[0, \infty)$. Moreover, the domain of f^{-1} is the interval $[0, \infty)$ and the range of f^{-1} is the interval $[\frac{3}{2}, \infty)$.

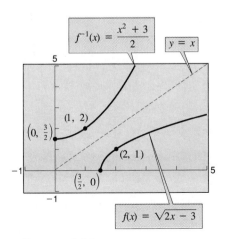

$$f^{-1}(x) = \frac{x^2 + 3}{2}$$

$$y = x$$

$(1, 2)$

$\left(0, \frac{3}{2}\right)$

$(2, 1)$

$\left(\frac{3}{2}, 0\right)$

$$f(x) = \sqrt{2x - 3}$$

FIGURE 1.61

The problem of finding the inverse of a function can be difficult (or even impossible) for two reasons. First, given $y = f(x)$, it may be algebraically difficult to solve for x in terms of y. Second, if f is not one-to-one, then f^{-1} does not exist.

DISCUSSION PROBLEM

· ·

THE EXISTENCE OF AN INVERSE FUNCTION

Write a short paragraph describing why the following functions do or do not have inverse functions.

(a) Let x represent the retail price of an item (in dollars), and let $f(x)$ represent the sales tax on the item. Assume that the sales tax is 7% of the retail price *and* that the sales tax is rounded to the nearest cent. Does this function have an inverse? (*Hint:* Can you undo this function? For instance, if you know that the sales tax is $0.14, can you determine *exactly* what the retail price is?)

(b) Let x represent the temperature in degrees Celsius, and let $f(x)$ represent the temperature in degrees Fahrenheit. Does this function have an inverse? (*Hint:* The formula for converting from degrees Celsius to degrees Fahrenheit is $F = \frac{9}{5}C + 32$.)

WARM-UP

· · · · · · · · · · · · · · · · ·

The following warm-up exercises involve skills that were covered in earlier sections. You will use these skills in the exercise set for this section.

In Exercises 1–4, find the domain of the function.

1. $f(x) = \sqrt[3]{x + 1}$ **2.** $f(x) = \sqrt{x + 1}$

3. $g(x) = \dfrac{2}{x^2 - 2x}$ **4.** $h(x) = \dfrac{x}{3x + 5}$

In Exercises 5–8, simplify the expression.

5. $2\left(\dfrac{x + 5}{2}\right) - 5$ **6.** $7 - 10\left(\dfrac{7 - x}{10}\right)$

7. $\sqrt[3]{2\left(\dfrac{x^3}{2} - 2\right) + 4}$ **8.** $\left(\sqrt[5]{x + 2}\right)^5 - 2$

In Exercises 9 and 10, solve for x in terms of y.

9. $y = \dfrac{2x - 6}{3}$ **10.** $y = \sqrt[3]{2x - 4}$

SECTION 1.7 · EXERCISES

In Exercises 1–6, find the inverse f^{-1} of the function f informally. Verify that $f(f^{-1}(x))$ and $f^{-1}(f(x))$ are equal to the identity function.

1. $f(x) = 8x$

2. $f(x) = \frac{1}{5}x$

3. $f(x) = x + 10$

4. $f(x) = x - 5$

5. $f(x) = \sqrt[3]{x}$

6. $f(x) = x^5$

In Exercises 7–16, show that f and g are inverse functions (a) algebraically and (b) graphically.

7. $f(x) = 2x, \quad g(x) = \dfrac{x}{2}$

8. $f(x) = x - 5, \quad g(x) = x + 5$

9. $f(x) = 5x + 1, \quad g(x) = \dfrac{x - 1}{5}$

10. $f(x) = 3 - 4x, \quad g(x) = \dfrac{3 - x}{4}$

11. $f(x) = x^3, \quad g(x) = \sqrt[3]{x}$

12. $f(x) = \dfrac{1}{x}, \quad g(x) = \dfrac{1}{x}$

13. $f(x) = \sqrt{x - 4}$
$g(x) = x^2 + 4, \quad x \geq 0$

14. $f(x) = 1 - x^3$
$g(x) = \sqrt[3]{1 - x}$

15. $f(x) = 9 - x^2, \quad x \geq 0$
$g(x) = \sqrt{9 - x}, \quad x \leq 9$

16. $f(x) = \dfrac{1}{1 + x}, \quad x \geq 0$
$g(x) = \dfrac{1 - x}{x}, \quad 0 < x \leq 1$

In Exercises 17–22, use a graphing utility to graph the function and use the graph to determine whether the function is one-to-one.

17. $g(x) = \dfrac{4 - x}{6}$

18. $f(x) = 10$

19. $h(x) = |x + 4| - |x - 4|$

20. $g(x) = (x + 5)^3$

21. $f(x) = -2x\sqrt{16 - x^2}$

22. $f(x) = \frac{1}{8}(x + 2)^2 - 1$

In Exercises 23–32, find the inverse of the one-to-one function f. Then use a graphing utility to graph both f and f^{-1} in the same viewing rectangle.

23. $f(x) = 2x - 3$

24. $f(x) = 3x$

25. $f(x) = x^5$

26. $f(x) = x^3 + 1$

27. $f(x) = \sqrt{x}$

28. $f(x) = x^2, \quad x \geq 0$

29. $f(x) = \sqrt{4 - x^2}, \quad 0 \leq x \leq 2$

30. $f(x) = \dfrac{4}{x}$

31. $f(x) = \sqrt[3]{x - 1}$

32. $f(x) = x^{3/5}$

In Exercises 33–46, determine whether the given function is one-to-one. If it is, find its inverse.

33. $f(x) = x^4$

34. $f(x) = \dfrac{1}{x^2}$

35. $g(x) = \dfrac{x}{8}$

36. $f(x) = -3$

37. $f(x) = (x + 3)^2, \quad x \geq -3$

38. $q(x) = (x - 5)^2$

39. $h(x) = \dfrac{1}{x}$

40. $f(x) = |x - 2|, \quad x \leq 2$

41. $f(x) = \sqrt{2x + 3}$

42. $f(x) = \sqrt{x - 2}$

43. $g(x) = x^2 - x^4$

44. $f(x) = \dfrac{x^2}{x^2 + 1}$

45. $f(x) = 25 - x^2, \quad x \leq 0$

46. $f(x) = ax + b, \quad a \neq 0$

In Exercises 47–50, delete part of the graph of the function so that the part that remains is one-to-one. Find the inverse of the remaining part and give the domain of the inverse. (There is more than one correct answer.)

47. $f(x) = (x - 3)^2$

48. $f(x) = 16 - x^4$

49. $f(x) = |x + 3|$

50. $f(x) = |x - 3|$

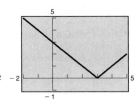

In Exercises 51 and 52, use the graph of the function f to complete the table and to graph f^{-1}.

51.

x	0	1	2	3	4
$f^{-1}(x)$					

52.

x	0	2	4	6
$f^{-1}(x)$				

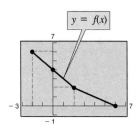

In Exercises 53–56, use the functions $f(x) = \frac{1}{8}x - 3$ and $g(x) = x^3$ to find the indicated value.

53. $(f^{-1} \circ g^{-1})(1)$ **54.** $(g^{-1} \circ f^{-1})(-3)$

55. $(f^{-1} \circ f^{-1})(6)$ **56.** $(g^{-1} \circ g^{-1})(-4)$

CHAPTER 1 · REVIEW EXERCISES

In Exercises 1–10, sketch the graph of the equation *by hand.* Verify your result with a graphing utility.

1. $y - 2x - 3 = 0$ **2.** $3x + 2y + 6 = 0$

3. $x - 5 = 0$ **4.** $y = 8 - |x|$

5. $y = \sqrt{5 - x}$ **6.** $y = \sqrt{x + 2}$

7. $y + 2x^2 = 0$ **8.** $y = x^2 - 4x$

9. $y = \sqrt{25 - x^2}$ **10.** $x^2 + y^2 = 10$

In Exercises 57–60, use the functions $f(x) = x + 4$ and $g(x) = 2x - 5$ to find the specified functions.

57. $g^{-1} \circ f^{-1}$ **58.** $f^{-1} \circ g^{-1}$

59. $(f \circ g)^{-1}$ **60.** $(g \circ f)^{-1}$

Diesel Engine   In Exercises 61 and 62, use the following function, which approximates the exhaust temperature y in degrees Fahrenheit

$$y = 0.03x^2 + 254.50, \quad 0 < x < 100,$$

where x is the percentage load for a diesel engine (see figure).

FIGURE

FOR 61 AND 62

61. (a) Find the inverse of the function and state what the variables x and y represent in the inverse function.
   (b) Graph the inverse function.

62. Determine the percentage load interval if the exhaust temperature of the engine must not exceed 500 degrees Fahrenheit.

In Exercises 63–66, determine whether the statement is true or false. Explain your reasoning.

63. If f is an even function, then f^{-1} exists.

64. If the inverse of f exists, then the y-intercept of f is an x-intercept of f^{-1}.

65. If $f(x) = x^n$ where n is odd, then f^{-1} exists.

66. There exists no function f such that $f = f^{-1}$.

In Exercises 11–18, use a graphing utility to graph the equation. Determine the number of times (if any) the graph intersects the coordinate axes.

11. $y = \frac{1}{4}(x + 1)^3$ **12.** $y = 4 - (x - 4)^2$

13. $y = \frac{1}{4}x^4 - 2x^2$ **14.** $y = \frac{1}{4}x^3 - 3x$

15. $y = x\sqrt{9 - x^2}$ **16.** $y = x\sqrt{x + 3}$

17. $y = |x - 4| - 4$ **18.** $y = |x + 2| + |3 - x|$

In Exercises 19 and 20, solve for y and use a graphing utility to graph each of the resulting equations on the same viewing rectangle.

19. $2y^2 = x^3$ **20.** $(x + 2)^2 + y^2 = 16$

In Exercises 21–24, use the concept of slope to find t so that the three points are collinear.

21. $(-2, 5), (0, t), (1, 1)$ **22.** $(-6, 1), (1, t), (10, 5)$
23. $(1, -4), (t, 3), (5, 10)$ **24.** $(-3, 3), (t, -1), (8, 6)$

In Exercises 25–30, find an equation of the line through the two points.

25. $(0, 0), (0, 10)$ **26.** $(-1, 4), (2, 0)$
27. $(2, 1), (14, 6)$ **28.** $(-2, 2), (3, -10)$
29. $(-1, 0), (6, 2)$ **30.** $(1, 6), (4, 2)$

In Exercises 31–34, find an equation of the line that passes through the given point and has the specified slope. Sketch the graph of the line *by hand*.

Point	Slope	Point	Slope
31. $(0, -5)$	$m = \frac{3}{2}$	**32.** $(-2, 6)$	$m = 0$
33. $(3, 0)$	$m = -\frac{2}{3}$	**34.** $(5, 4)$	m is undefined

In Exercises 35 and 36, write an equation of the line through the point (a) parallel to the given line and (b) perpendicular to the given line. Verify your result with a graphing utility.

Point	Line	Point	Line
35. $(3, -2)$	$5x - 4y = 8$	**36.** $(-8, 3)$	$2x + 3y = 5$

37. *Fourth Quarter Sales*   During the second and third quarters of the year, a business had sales of $160,000 and $185,000. If the growth of sales follows a linear pattern, estimate sales during the fourth quarter.

38. *Dollar Value*   The dollar value of a product in 1990 is $85, and the item will increase in value at an expected rate of $3.75 per year.
(a) Write a linear equation that gives the dollar value V of the product in terms of the year t. (Let $t = 0$ represent 1990.)
(b) Use a graphing utility to graph the sales equation.
(c) Move the cursor along the graph of the sales model to estimate the dollar value of the product in 1995.

In Exercises 39–42, evaluate the function at the specified values of the independent variable. Simplify your results.

39. $f(x) = x^2 + 1$
(a) $f(2)$ (b) $f(-4)$
(c) $f(t^2)$ (d) $-f(x)$

40. $g(x) = x^{4/3}$
(a) $g(8)$ (b) $g(t + 1)$
(c) $\dfrac{g(8) - g(1)}{8 - 1}$ (d) $g(-x)$

41. $h(x) = 6 - 5x^2$
(a) $h(2)$
(b) $h(x + 3)$
(c) $\dfrac{h(4) - h(2)}{4 - 2}$
(d) $\dfrac{h(x + t) - h(x)}{t}$

42. $f(t) = \sqrt[4]{t}$
(a) $f(16)$
(b) $f(t + 5)$
(c) $\dfrac{f(16) - f(0)}{16}$
(d) $f(t + h)$

43. Sketch (on the same set of coordinate axes) a graph of f for $c = -2, 0,$ and 2.
(a) $f(x) = \frac{1}{2}x + c$ (b) $f(x) = \frac{1}{2}(x - c)$
(c) $f(x) = \frac{1}{2}(cx)$

44. Sketch (on the same set of coordinate axes) a graph of f for $c = -2, 0,$ and 2.
(a) $f(x) = x^3 + c$ (b) $f(x) = (x - c)^3$
(c) $f(x) = (x - 2)^3 + c$

In Exercises 45–50, determine the domain of the function. Verify your result with a graphing utility.

45. $f(x) = \sqrt{25 - x^2}$ **46.** $f(x) = 3x + 4$

47. $g(s) = \dfrac{5}{3s - 9}$ **48.** $f(x) = \sqrt{x^2 + 8x}$

49. $h(x) = \dfrac{x}{x^2 - x - 6}$ **50.** $h(t) = |t + 1|$

51. *Vertical Motion*   The velocity of a ball thrown vertically upward from ground level is given by $v(t) = -32t + 48$, where t is the time in seconds and v is the velocity in feet per second.
(a) Find the velocity when $t = 1$.
(b) Find the time when the ball reaches its maximum height. (*Hint:* Find the time when $v(t) = 0$.)
(c) Find the velocity when $t = 2$.

52. *Cost and Profit*   A company produces a product for which the variable cost is $5.35 per unit and the fixed costs are $16,000. The company sells the product for $8.20, and can sell all that it produces.
(a) Find the total cost as a function of x, the number of units produced.
(b) Find the profit as a function of x.

53. *Dimensions of a Rectangle*   A wire 24 inches long is to be cut into four pieces to form a rectangle whose shortest side has a length of x. Express the area A of the rectangle as a function of x. Determine the domain of the function and use a graphing utility to graph the function over that domain.

54. *Cost of a Phone Call*   Suppose the cost of a telephone call between Dallas and Philadelphia is $0.70 for the first minute and $0.38 for each additional minute (or portion thereof). A model for the total cost of the phone call is

$$C = 0.70 + 0.38[[x]],$$

where C is the total cost of the call in dollars and x is the length of the call in minutes. Sketch the graph of this function.

In Exercises 55–58, use a graphing utility to graph the function and use the graph to (a) approximate the intervals in which the function is increasing, decreasing, or constant; (b) approximate (to two decimal place accuracy) any relative maximum or minimum values of the function; and (c) determine if the function is even, odd, or neither.

55. $g(x) = |x + 2| - |x - 2|$

56. $f(x) = (x^2 - 4)^2$

57. $h(x) = 4x^3 - x^4$

58. $g(x) = \sqrt[3]{x(x + 3)^2}$

59. *Navigation*   At noon, ship A was 100 miles due east of ship B. Ship A is sailing west at 12 miles per hour, and ship B is sailing south at 10 miles per hour (see figure).

(a) Verify that the distance between the ships is given by

$$d = \sqrt{(100 - 12t)^2 + (10t)^2}$$

where t is the time in hours with $t = 0$ corresponding to noon.

(b) Use a graphing utility to graph the distance function. Move the cursor along the function to estimate (to two decimal place accuracy) the minimum distance between the ships. At what time will this occur?

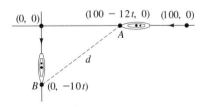

FIGURE FOR 59

60. *Maximum Revenue*   For groups of 80 or more, a charter bus company determines the rate per person according to the formula

$$\text{Rate} = \$8.00 - \$0.05(n - 80), \qquad n \geq 80.$$

(a) Determine the revenue as a function of n.

(b) Use a graphing utility to graph the revenue function. Move the cursor along the function to estimate the number of passengers that will maximize the revenue.

In Exercises 61–66, (a) find f^{-1}, (b) use a graphing utility to graph both f and f^{-1} in the same viewing rectangle, and (c) verify that $f^{-1}(f(x)) = x$ and $f(f^{-1}(x)) = x$.

61. $f(x) = \frac{1}{2}x - 3$

62. $f(x) = 5x - 7$

63. $f(x) = \sqrt{x + 1}$

64. $f(x) = x^3 + 2$

65. $f(x) = x^2 - 5, \quad x \geq 0$

66. $f(x) = \sqrt[3]{x + 1}$

In Exercises 67–70, restrict the domain of the function f to an interval where the function is increasing and determine f^{-1} over that interval. Then use a graphing utility to graph both f and f^{-1} in the same viewing rectangle.

67. $f(x) = 2(x - 4)^2$

68. $f(x) = |x - 2|$

69. $f(x) = \sqrt{x^2 - 4}$

70. $f(x) = x^{4/3}$

In Exercise 71–78, let

$$f(x) = 3 - 2x, \quad g(x) = \sqrt{x}, \quad \text{and} \quad h(x) = 3x^2 + 2$$

and find the indicated value.

71. $(f - g)(4)$

72. $(f + h)(5)$

73. $(fh)(1)$

74. $\left(\dfrac{g}{h}\right)(1)$

75. $(h \circ g)(7)$

76. $(g \circ f)(-2)$

77. $g^{-1}(3)$

78. $(h \circ f^{-1})(1)$

CHAPTER 2

SOLVING EQUATIONS AND INEQUALITIES

2.1 LINEAR EQUATIONS

Equations and Solutions of Equations / Linear Equations in One Variable /
Equations Involving Fractional Expressions / Applications

Equations and Solutions of Equations

An **equation** is a statement that two algebraic expressions are equal. Some examples of equations in x are

$$3x - 5 = 7, \quad x^2 - x - 6 = 0, \quad \text{and} \quad \sqrt{2x} = 4.$$

To **solve** an equation in x means to find all values of x for which the equation is true. Such values are **solutions.** For instance, $x = 4$ is a solution of the equation $3x - 5 = 7$, because $3(4) - 5 = 7$ is a true statement.

The solutions of an equation depend upon the kinds of numbers being considered. For instance, in the set of rational numbers, the equation $x^2 = 10$ has no solution because there is no rational number whose square is 10. However, in the set of real numbers this equation has two solutions, $\sqrt{10}$ and $-\sqrt{10}$, because $\left(\sqrt{10}\right)^2 = 10$ and $\left(-\sqrt{10}\right)^2 = 10$.

An equation that is true for *every* real number in the domain of the variable is an **identity.** For instance, $x^2 - 9 = (x + 3)(x - 3)$ is an identity because it is a true statement for any real value of x. Similarly, $x/(3x^2) = 1/(3x)$, where $x \neq 0$, is an identity because it is true for any nonzero real value of x.

An equation that is true for just *some* (or even none) of the real numbers in the domain of the variable is a **conditional equation.** For example, the equation $x^2 - 9 = 0$ is conditional because $x = 3$ and $x = -3$ are the only values in the domain that satisfy the equation. Learning to solve conditional equations is the primary focus of this chapter. As you study the chapter, you will see that some equations are best solved algebraically, whereas others are best solved with a graphing utility.

Linear Equations in One Variable

The most common type of conditional equation is a **linear equation.**

DEFINITION OF LINEAR EQUATION

A **linear equation** in one variable x is an equation that can be written in the standard form

$$ax + b = 0,$$

where a and b are real numbers with $a \neq 0$.

A linear equation has exactly one solution. To see this, consider the following steps. (Remember that $a \neq 0$.)

$ax + b = 0$	*Original equation*
$ax = -b$	*Subtract b from both sides*
$x = -\dfrac{b}{a}$	*Divide both sides by a, a $\neq$ 0*

To solve a conditional equation in x, isolate x on one side of the equation by a sequence of **equivalent** (and usually simpler) equations, each having the same solution(s) as the original equation. The operations that yield equivalent equations come from the Substitution Principle and the simplification techniques reviewed in the chapter on prerequisites.

GENERATING EQUIVALENT EQUATIONS

An equation can be transformed into an *equivalent equation* by one or more of the following steps.

	Original Equation	*Equivalent Equation*
1. Remove symbols of grouping, combine like terms, or reduce fractions on one or both sides of the equation.	$2x - x = 4$	$x = 4$
2. Add (or subtract) the same quantity to *both* sides of the equation.	$x + 1 = 6$	$x = 5$
3. Multiply (or divide) *both* sides of the equation by the same *nonzero* quantity.	$2x = 6$	$x = 3$
4. Interchange the two sides of the equation.	$2 = x$	$x = 2$

EXAMPLE 1   Solving a Linear Equation

$$3x - 6 = 0 \qquad \textit{Original equation}$$
$$3x = 6 \qquad \textit{Add 6 to both sides}$$
$$x = 2 \qquad \textit{Divide both sides by 3}$$

After solving an equation, you should **check each solution** in the *original* equation. In Example 1, you can check that 2 is a solution by substituting 2 for x in the original equation $3x - 6 = 0$ to obtain

$$3(2) - 6 = 6 - 6 = 0. \qquad \textit{Check solution}$$

EXAMPLE 2   Solving a Linear Equation

$$6(x - 1) + 4 = 3(7x + 1) \qquad \textit{Original equation}$$
$$6x - 6 + 4 = 21x + 3 \qquad \textit{Remove parentheses}$$
$$6x - 2 = 21x + 3 \qquad \textit{Simplify}$$
$$-15x = 5 \qquad \textit{Add 2 and subtract 21x}$$
$$x = -\frac{1}{3} \qquad \textit{Divide by } -15$$

The solution is $x = -\frac{1}{3}$. Check this solution by substituting in the original equation.

DISCOVERY

Use a graphing utility to graph $y = 6(x - 1) + 4$ and $y = 3(7x + 1)$ on the same viewing rectangle. Explain how the result can be used to approximate the solution of $6(x - 1) + 4 = 3(7x + 1)$ or to perform a graphic check for a solution that was obtained algebraically.

Students sometimes tell us that a solution looks easy when we work it out in class, but that they don't see where to begin when trying it alone. Keep in mind that no one—not even great mathematicians—can expect to look at every mathematical problem and immediately know where to begin. Many problems involve some trial and error before a solution is found. To make algebra work for you, you must put in a lot of time, you must expect to try solution methods that end up not working, and you must learn from both your successes and your failures.

Equations Involving Fractional Expressions

To solve an equation involving fractional expressions, find the least common denominator of all terms in the equation and multiply every term by this LCD. This procedure clears the equation of fractions.

EXAMPLE 3   Solving an Equation Involving Fractional Expressions

Solve the equation for x.

$$\frac{x}{3} + \frac{3x}{4} = 2$$

SOLUTION

The least common denominator is 12.

$$\frac{x}{3} + \frac{3x}{4} = 2 \qquad \text{\textit{Original equation}}$$

$$(12)\frac{x}{3} + (12)\frac{3x}{4} = (12)2 \qquad \text{\textit{Multiply by the LCD}}$$

$$4x + 9x = 24 \qquad \text{\textit{Reduce and multiply}}$$

$$13x = 24 \qquad \text{\textit{Combine like terms}}$$

$$x = \frac{24}{13} \qquad \text{\textit{Divide by 13}}$$

The equation has one solution: $\frac{24}{13}$. Check this in the original equation.

■■■■■■■■■

When multiplying or dividing an equation by a *variable* quantity, it is possible to lose solutions *or* to introduce an **extraneous** solution that does not satisfy the original equation.

EXAMPLE 4   An Equation with an Extraneous Solution

Solve the equation for x.

$$\frac{1}{x-2} = \frac{3}{x+2} - \frac{6x}{x^2 - 4}$$

SOLUTION

The LCD is $x^2 - 4$ or $(x+2)(x-2)$. Multiplying every term by this LCD and reducing produces the following.

$$\frac{1}{x-2}(x+2)(x-2) = \frac{3}{x+2}(x+2)(x-2) - \frac{6x}{x^2-4}(x+2)(x-2)$$

$$x + 2 = 3(x-2) - 6x, \quad x \neq \pm 2$$

$$x + 2 = 3x - 6 - 6x$$

$$4x = -8$$

$$x = -2$$

Substituting $x = -2$ in the original equation yields a denominator of zero. Therefore, $x = -2$ is an extraneous solution, and the equation has *no solution*.

■■■■■■■■■

An equation with a *single fraction* on each side can be cleared of denominators by **cross multiplying,** which is equivalent to multiplying by the least common denominator and then reducing.

EXAMPLE 5 Cross Multiplying to Solve an Equation

Solve the equation for y.

$$\frac{3y - 2}{2y + 1} = \frac{6y - 9}{4y + 3}$$

SOLUTION

Because the equation has a single fraction on each side, you can cross multiply.

$$\frac{3y - 2}{2y + 1} = \frac{6y - 9}{4y + 3}$$
Original equation

$$(3y - 2)(4y + 3) = (6y - 9)(2y + 1), \quad y \neq -\frac{1}{2}, \ -\frac{3}{4}$$
Cross multiply

$$12y^2 + y - 6 = 12y^2 - 12y - 9$$
Combine like terms

$$13y = -3$$
Divide by 13

$$y = -\frac{3}{13}$$

Check that $y = -\frac{3}{13}$ is a solution of the original equation.

Real-world problems frequently involve numbers that are not simple integers or fractions. In such cases a calculator is useful to do the number crunching.

EXAMPLE 6 Using a Calculator to Solve an Equation

Solve the equation for x.

$$\frac{1}{9.38} - \frac{3}{x} = \frac{5}{0.3714}$$

SOLUTION

$$\frac{1}{9.38} - \frac{3}{x} = \frac{5}{0.3714}$$
Original equation

$$-\frac{3}{x} = \frac{5}{0.3714} - \frac{1}{9.38}$$

$$-\frac{3}{x} \approx 13.3560$$
Use a calculator

$$-\frac{3}{13.3560} \approx x$$
Cross multiply

$$-0.225 \approx x$$
Use a calculator

Applications

Of all the different mathematical models you will be studying, linear models are the most commonly used.

EXAMPLE 7   An Application: Weekly Earnings

The average weekly earnings for workers in the United States between 1980 and 1990 can be approximated by the linear equation

$$y = 14.5t + 270,$$

where y represents the average weekly earnings in dollars and t represents the year (with $t = 0$ corresponding to 1980). From Figure 2.1, you can see that the average weekly earnings increased in a linear pattern during the 1980s. Assuming that this pattern continues, find the year when the average weekly earnings will reach $500. (*Source:* U.S. Bureau of Labor Statistics)

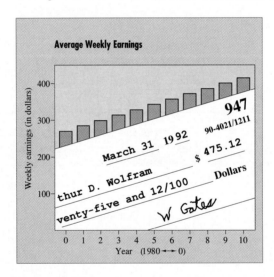

FIGURE 2.1

SOLUTION

Let $y = 500$ and solve the resulting equation for t.

$y = 14.5t + 270$	*Original equation*
$500 = 14.5t + 270$	*Let y = 500*
$230 = 14.5t$	*Subtract 270 from both sides*
$t = \dfrac{230}{14.5}$	*Divide both sides by 14.5*
$t \approx 16$	*Solution*

Because $t = 0$ corresponds to 1980, $t = 16$ must correspond to 1996. Thus, from this model you can expect the average weekly earnings will reach $500 by 1996.

DISCUSSION PROBLEM
....
A MATHEMATICAL FALLACY

A mathematical **fallacy** is an argument that appears to prove something that you know is incorrect. For instance, the following argument appears to prove that $1 = 0$. Can you find the error in this argument?

$$x = 1 \qquad\qquad\qquad \textit{Original equation}$$

$$x - 1 = 0 \qquad\qquad\qquad \textit{Subtract 1 from both sides}$$

$$x(x - 1) = 0 \qquad\qquad\qquad \textit{Multiply both sides by x}$$

$$\frac{x(x - 1)}{x - 1} = \frac{0}{x - 1} \qquad\qquad \textit{Divide both sides by } x - 1$$

$$\frac{x(x - 1)}{x - 1} = 0 \qquad\qquad\qquad \textit{Reduce}$$

$$x = 0 \qquad\qquad\qquad \textit{Solution}$$

WARM-UP
....

The following warm-up exercises involve skills that were covered in earlier sections. You will use these skills in the exercise set for this section.

In Exercises 1–10, perform the indicated operations and simplify your result.

1. $(2x - 4) - (5x + 6)$ **2.** $(3x - 5) + (2x - 7)$

3. $2(x + 1) - (x + 2)$ **4.** $-3(2x - 4) + 7(x + 2)$

5. $\dfrac{x}{3} + \dfrac{x}{5}$ **6.** $x - \dfrac{x}{4}$

7. $\dfrac{1}{x + 1} - \dfrac{1}{x}$ **8.** $\dfrac{2}{x} + \dfrac{3}{x}$

9. $\dfrac{4}{x} + \dfrac{3}{x - 2}$ **10.** $\dfrac{1}{x + 1} - \dfrac{1}{x - 1}$

SECTION 2.1 · EXERCISES
....

In Exercises 1–10, determine whether the equation is an identity or a conditional equation.

1. $2(x - 1) = 2x - 2$

2. $3(x + 2) = 3x + 4$

3. $-2(x - 3) + 5 = -2x + 10$

4. $3(x + 2) - 5 = 3x + 1$

5. $4(x + 1) - 2x = 2(x + 2)$

6. $-7(x - 3) + 4x = 3(7 - x)$

7. $x^2 - 8x + 5 = (x - 4)^2 - 11$

8. $x^2 + 2(3x - 2) = x^2 + 6x - 4$

9. $3 + \dfrac{1}{x + 1} = \dfrac{4x}{x + 1}$

10. $\dfrac{5}{x} + \dfrac{3}{x} = 24$

In Exercises 11–18, determine whether the value of x is a solution of the equation.

Equation	Values
11. $5x - 3 = 3x + 5$	(a) $x = 0$ (b) $x = -5$ (c) $x = 4$ (d) $x = 10$
12. $7 - 3x = 5x - 17$	(a) $x = -3$ (b) $x = 0$ (c) $x = 8$ (d) $x = 3$
13. $3x^2 + 2x - 5 = 2x^2 - 2$	(a) $x = -3$ (b) $x = 1$ (c) $x = 4$ (d) $x = -5$
14. $5x^3 + 2x - 3$ $\quad = 4x^3 + 2x - 11$	(a) $x = 2$ (b) $x = -2$ (c) $x = 0$ (d) $x = 10$
15. $\dfrac{5}{2x} - \dfrac{4}{x} = 3$	(a) $x = -\frac{1}{2}$ (b) $x = 4$ (c) $x = 0$ (d) $x = \frac{1}{4}$
16. $3 + \dfrac{1}{x + 2} = 4$	(a) $x = -1$ (b) $x = -2$ (c) $x = 0$ (d) $x = 5$
17. $(x + 5)(x - 3) = 20$	(a) $x = 3$ (b) $x = -5$ (c) $x = 5$ (d) $x = -7$
18. $\sqrt[3]{x - 8} = 3$	(a) $x = 2$ (b) $x = -2$ (c) $x = 35$ (d) $x = 8$

In Exercises 19–56, solve the equation (if possible). Check your result algebraically or graphically.

19. $x + 10 = 15$ **20.** $7 - x = 18$

21. $7 - 2x = 15$ **22.** $7x + 2 = 16$

23. $8x - 5 = 3x + 10$ **24.** $7x + 3 = 3x - 13$

25. $2(x + 5) - 7 = 3(x - 2)$

26. $2(13t - 15) + 3(t - 19) = 0$

27. $6[x - (2x + 3)] = 8 - 5x$

28. $8(x + 2) - 3(2x + 1) = 2(x + 5)$

29. $\dfrac{5x}{4} + \dfrac{1}{2} = x - \dfrac{1}{2}$ **30.** $\dfrac{x}{5} - \dfrac{x}{2} = 3$

31. $\frac{3}{2}(z + 5) - \frac{1}{4}(z + 24) = 0$

32. $0.25x + 0.75(10 - x) = 3$

33. $x + 8 = 2(x - 2) - x$

34. $3(x + 3) = 5(1 - x) - 1$

35. $\dfrac{100 - 4u}{3} = \dfrac{5u + 6}{4} + 6$

36. $\dfrac{17 + y}{y} + \dfrac{32 + y}{y} = 100$

37. $\dfrac{5x - 4}{5x + 4} = \dfrac{2}{3}$ **38.** $\dfrac{10x + 3}{5x + 6} = \dfrac{1}{2}$

39. $10 - \dfrac{13}{x} = 4 + \dfrac{5}{x}$ **40.** $\dfrac{15}{x} - 4 = \dfrac{6}{x} + 3$

41. $\dfrac{1}{x - 3} + \dfrac{1}{x + 3} = \dfrac{10}{x^2 - 9}$

42. $\dfrac{1}{x - 2} + \dfrac{3}{x + 3} = \dfrac{4}{x^2 + x - 6}$

43. $\dfrac{x}{x + 4} + \dfrac{4}{x + 4} + 2 = 0$

44. $\dfrac{2}{(x - 4)(x - 2)} = \dfrac{1}{x - 4} + \dfrac{2}{x - 2}$

45. $\dfrac{7}{2x + 1} - \dfrac{8x}{2x - 1} = -4$

46. $\dfrac{4}{u - 1} + \dfrac{6}{3u + 1} = \dfrac{15}{3u + 1}$

47. $\dfrac{1}{x} + \dfrac{2}{x - 5} = 0$

48. $\dfrac{6}{x} - \dfrac{2}{x + 3} = \dfrac{3(x + 5)}{x(x + 3)}$

49. $\dfrac{3}{x(x - 3)} + \dfrac{4}{x} = \dfrac{1}{x - 3}$

50. $3 = 2 + \dfrac{2}{z + 2}$

51. $(x + 2)^2 - x^2 = 4(x + 1)$

52. $(2x + 1)^2 = 4(x^2 + x + 1)$

53. $4(x + 1) - ax = x + 5$

54. $6x + ax = 2x + 5$

55. $4 - 2(x - 2b) = ax + 3$

56. $5 + ax = 12 - bx$

In Exercises 57–62, solve the equation. (Round the result to three decimal places.)

57. $0.275x + 0.725(500 - x) = 300$

58. $2.763 - 4.5(2.1x - 5.1432) = 6.32x + 5$

59. $\dfrac{x}{0.6321} + \dfrac{x}{0.0692} = 1000$

60. $\dfrac{2}{7.398} - \dfrac{4.405}{x} = \dfrac{1}{x}$

61. $(x + 5.62)^2 + 10.83 = (x + 7)^2$

62. $\dfrac{x}{2.625} + \dfrac{x}{4.875} = 1$

In Exercises 63 and 64, find an equation of the form $ax + b = cx$ that has the specified solution. (There are many correct answers.)

63. $x = 2$ **64.** $x = \frac{1}{3}$

65. *Surface Area*   The surface area S of the rectangular solid in the figure is given by

$$S = 2(24) + 2(4x) + 2(6x).$$

Find the length of the box x if the surface area is 248 square inches.

FIGURE FOR 65

66. *Operating Cost*   A delivery company has a fleet of vans. The annual operating cost per van is

$$C = 0.32m + 2500,$$

where m is the number of miles traveled by a van in a year. What number of miles will yield an annual operating cost of $10,000?

Human Height   In Exercises 67 and 68, use the following information. The relationship between the length of an adult's thigh bone and the height of the adult can be approximated by the linear equations

$$y = 0.432x - 10.44 \qquad \text{Female}$$
$$y = 0.449x - 12.15 \qquad \text{Male}$$

where y is the length of the thigh bone in inches and x is the height in inches (see figure).

FIGURE FOR 67 AND 68

67. An anthropologist discovers a thigh bone belonging to an adult human female. The bone is 16 inches long. Estimate the height of the female.

68. From the foot bones of an adult human male, an anthropologist estimates that the height of the male was 69 inches. A few feet from the site where the foot bone was discovered, the anthropologist finds a male adult thigh bone 19 inches long. Is it possible that both bones came from the same person? Explain your reasoning.

2.2   LINEAR EQUATIONS AND MODELING

Introduction to Problem Solving / Using Mathematical Models to Solve Problems / Common Formulas

Introduction to Problem Solving

In this section you will learn how algebra can be used to solve problems that occur in real-life situations. This procedure is called **mathematical modeling.**

A good approach to mathematical modeling is to use two stages. Begin by using the verbal description of the problem to form a *verbal model*. Then, after assigning labels to the unknown quantities in the verbal model, form a *mathematical model* or *algebraic equation*.

Verbal description → Verbal model → Algebraic equation

When you are trying to construct a verbal model, it is helpful to look for a *hidden equality*—a statement that two algebraic expressions are equal. These two expressions might be explicitly stated as being equal, or they might be known to be equal (based on prior knowledge or experience).

EXAMPLE 1 Using a Verbal Model to Construct an Algebraic
················ Equation

You have accepted a job for which your annual salary will be $24,740. This salary includes a year-end bonus of $500. If you are paid twice a month, what will be your gross pay for each paycheck?

SOLUTION

Because there are 12 months in a year and you will be paid twice a month, it follows that you will receive 24 paychecks during the year. You can construct an algebraic equation for this problem as follows. Begin with a verbal model, then assign labels, and finally form an algebraic equation.

VERBAL
MODEL   Income for year = 24 · Amount of paycheck + Bonus

LABELS   Income for year = 24,740   *(dollars)*
             Amount of paycheck = x *(dollars)*
             Bonus = 500   *(dollars)*

EQUATION $24{,}740 = 24x + 500$

The equation for this problem is a *linear equation* in the variable x. Using the techniques discussed in Section 2.1, you can solve this equation for x. If you do that, you will find that the solution is $x = \$1010$. ·········

TRANSLATING KEY WORDS AND PHRASES

Key Words and Phrases	*Verbal Description*	*Algebraic Statement*
Equality		
Equals, equal to, is, are, was, will be, represents	Sale price S is $10 less than the list price L	$S = L - 10$
Addition		
Sum, plus, greater, increased by, more than,	The sum of 5 and x	$5 + x$
exceeds, total of	7 more than y	$y + 7$
Subtraction		
Difference, minus, less, decreased by,	4 decreased by b	$4 - b$
subtracted from, reduced by, the remainder	3 less than z	$z - 3$
Multiplication		
Product, multiplied by, twice, times, percent of	2 times x	$2x$
Division		
Quotient, divided by, ratio, per	The ratio of x to 8	$\dfrac{x}{8}$

Using Mathematical Models to Solve Problems

Study the next several examples carefully. Your goal should be to develop a *general problem-solving strategy*.

EXAMPLE 2   Finding the Percentage of a Raise

Suppose you accept a job that pays $8 an hour. You are told that after a 2-month probationary period, your hourly wage will be increased to $9 an hour. What percent raise will you receive after the 2-month period?

SOLUTION

VERBAL
MODEL

$$\text{Raise} = \text{Percent} \cdot \text{Old wage}$$

LABELS

Old wage $= 8$ *(dollars per hour)*
New wage $= 9$ *(dollars per hour)*
Raise $= 9 - 8 = 1$ *(dollars per hour)*
Percent $= r$ *(in decimal form)*

EQUATION

$$1 = r \cdot 8$$

$$\frac{1}{8} = r$$

$$0.125 = r$$

You will receive a raise of $0.125 = 12.5\%$.

EXAMPLE 3   Finding the Percentage of a Benefits Package

Suppose your annual salary is $22,000. In addition to your salary, your employer provides the following benefits.

Social Security (employer's portion):	7.65% of salary	$1683
Workman's compensation:	0.5% of salary	110
Unemployment compensation:	0.75% of salary	165
Medical insurance:	$2240 per year	2240
Retirement contribution:	6.5% of salary	1430

The total benefits package represents what percent of your annual salary?

SOLUTION

To begin, add the dollar amount of the benefits package and obtain a total of $5628. Then set up the following model.

VERBAL
MODEL   Benefits package = Percent · Salary

LABELS   Benefits package = 5628   *(dollars)*
                   Percent = r   *(in decimal form)*
                   Salary = 22,000   *(dollars)*

EQUATION

$$5628 = r \cdot 22{,}000$$

$$\frac{5628}{22{,}000} = r$$

$$0.256 \approx r$$

Your benefits package is approximately $0.256 = 25.6\%$ of your annual salary.

EXAMPLE 4   Finding the Dimensions of a Room

A rectangular family room is twice as long as it is wide, and its perimeter is 84 feet. Find the dimensions and area of the family room.

SOLUTION

For this problem, it helps to sketch a picture as shown in Figure 2.2.

FIGURE 2.2

VERBAL
MODEL   2 · Width + 2 · Length = Perimeter

LABELS   Width = w   *(feet)*
                   Length = l = 2w   *(feet)*
                   Perimeter = 84   *(feet)*

EQUATION

$$2w + 2(2w) = 84$$
$$6w = 84$$
$$w = 14 \text{ feet}$$
$$l = 2w = 28 \text{ feet}$$

The dimensions of the room are 14 feet by 28 feet. The area is 392 square feet.

EXAMPLE 5   A Distance Problem

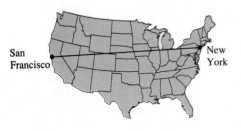

FIGURE 2.3

A plane is flying nonstop from New York to San Francisco (see Figure 2.3), a distance of about 2700 miles. After $1\frac{1}{2}$ hours in the air, the plane flies over Chicago (a distance of 800 miles from New York). How long will it take the plane to fly from New York to San Francisco? (Assume that the plane flies at a constant speed during the entire flight.)

SOLUTION

To solve this problem, use the formula that relates distance, rate, and time.

VERBAL
MODEL

Distance = Rate · Time

LABELS

Distance = 2700   *(miles)*

Time = t *(hours)*

Rate = $\dfrac{800}{1.5}$ ≈ 533.33   *(miles per hour)*

EQUATION

$2700 = 533.33t$

$\dfrac{2700}{533.33} = t$

$t ≈ 5.06$ hours

Because 0.06 hours represents about 4 minutes, you can conclude that the trip will take about 5 hours and 4 minutes.

EXAMPLE 6   **An Application Involving Similar Triangles**

In order to measure the height of the twin towers of the World Trade Center (in New York City), suppose you use the following scheme. You measure the shadow cast by the building to be 170.25 feet long, as shown in Figure 2.4. Then you measure the shadow cast by a 4-foot post and find that its shadow is 6 inches long. Use this information to determine the height of the building.

SOLUTION

To solve this problem, use a theorem from geometry that states that the ratios of corresponding sides of similar triangles are equal.

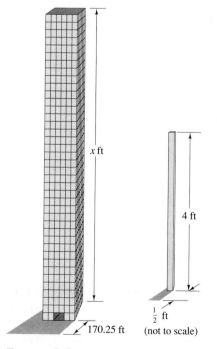

x ft

4 ft

$\frac{1}{2}$ ft

(not to scale)

170.25 ft

FIGURE 2.4

VERBAL
MODEL

$$\frac{\text{Height of building}}{\text{Length of shadow}} = \frac{\text{Height of post}}{\text{Length of shadow}}$$

LABELS

Height of building = x *(feet)*
Length of building's shadow = 170.25   *(feet)*
Height of post = 4   *(feet)*

Length of post's shadow = $\dfrac{1}{2}$ *(feet)*

EQUATION

$$\frac{x}{170.25} = \frac{4}{1/2}$$

$x = 8 \cdot 170.25$
$x = 1362$ feet

The World Trade Center is about 1362 feet high.

EXAMPLE 7   A Simple Interest Problem

You received $10,000 from an inheritance and invested it in two ways. Part of the money was invested at $9\frac{1}{2}\%$ simple interest and the remainder was invested at 11% simple interest. After one year, the two investments returned a combined interest of $1038.50. How much did you invest in each type of account?

SOLUTION

This problem uses the formula $I = Prt$, where I is the interest, P is the principal, r is the annual interest rate (in decimal form), and t is the time in years.

VERBAL
MODEL
$$\frac{\text{Interest}}{\text{from } 9\frac{1}{2}\%} + \frac{\text{Interest}}{\text{from } 11\%} = \frac{\text{Total}}{\text{interest}}$$

LABELS

Amount invested at $9\frac{1}{2}\%$ = x	*(dollars)*
Amount invested at 11% = $10,000 - x$	*(dollars)*
Interest from $9\frac{1}{2}\%$ = Prt = $(x)(0.095)(1)$	*(dollars)*
Interest from 11% = Prt = $(10,000 - x)(0.11)(1)$	*(dollars)*
Total interest = 1038.50	*(dollars)*

EQUATION
$$0.095(x) + 0.11(10,000 - x) = 1038.5$$
$$0.095x + 1100 - 0.11x = 1038.5$$
$$-0.015x = -61.5$$
$$x = \$4100 \text{ at } 9\frac{1}{2}\%$$
$$10,000 - x = \$5900 \text{ at } 11\%$$

The amount invested at $9\frac{1}{2}\%$ was $4100. The amount invested at 11% was $5900.

EXAMPLE 8   An Inventory Problem

A store has $30,000 of inventory in 12-inch and 19-inch television sets. The profit on a 12-inch set is 22%. The profit on a 19-inch set is 40%. If the profit for the entire stock is 35%, how much was invested in each type of television set?

SOLUTION

VERBAL
MODEL
$$\frac{\text{Profit from}}{\text{12-inch sets}} + \frac{\text{Profit from}}{\text{19-inch sets}} = \frac{\text{Total}}{\text{profit}}$$

LABELS

Inventory of 12-inch sets = x	*(dollars)*
Inventory of 19-inch sets = $30,000 - x$	*(dollars)*
Profit from 12-inch sets = $0.22x$	*(dollars)*
Profit from 19-inch sets = $0.40(30,000 - x)$	*(dollars)*
Total profit = $0.35(30,000)$ = $10,500$	*(dollars)*

EQUATION $0.22(x) + 0.40(30{,}000 - x) = 0.35(30{,}000)$
$0.22x + 12{,}000 - 0.4x = 10{,}500$
$-0.18x = -1500$
$x \approx \$8333.33$ 12-inch sets
$30{,}000 - x \approx \$21{,}666.67$ 19-inch sets

Thus, the total inventory for 12-inch sets is approximately \$8333.33 and the total inventory for 19-inch sets is approximately \$21,666.67.   ·········

Common Formulas

Many common types of geometric, scientific, and investment problems use ready-made equations, called **formulas.** Knowing these formulas will help you translate and solve a wide variety of real-life problems.

COMMON FORMULAS

These formulas give the area A, perimeter P (or circumference C), and volume V.

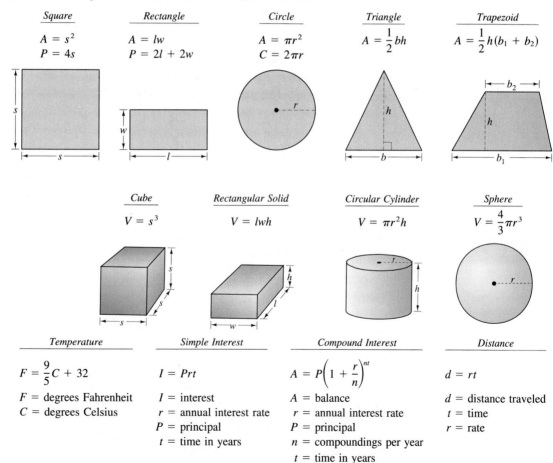

Square	Rectangle	Circle	Triangle	Trapezoid
$A = s^2$	$A = lw$	$A = \pi r^2$	$A = \dfrac{1}{2}bh$	$A = \dfrac{1}{2}h(b_1 + b_2)$
$P = 4s$	$P = 2l + 2w$	$C = 2\pi r$		

Cube	Rectangular Solid	Circular Cylinder	Sphere
$V = s^3$	$V = lwh$	$V = \pi r^2 h$	$V = \dfrac{4}{3}\pi r^3$

Temperature	Simple Interest	Compound Interest	Distance
$F = \dfrac{9}{5}C + 32$	$I = Prt$	$A = P\left(1 + \dfrac{r}{n}\right)^{nt}$	$d = rt$
F = degrees Fahrenheit	I = interest	A = balance	d = distance traveled
C = degrees Celsius	r = annual interest rate	r = annual interest rate	t = time
	P = principal	P = principal	r = rate
	t = time in years	n = compoundings per year	
		t = time in years	

When working with applied problems you often need to rewrite one of the common formulas. For instance, the formula $P = 2l + 2w$, for the perimeter of a rectangle, can be rewritten or solved for W in the following manner.

$$P = 2l + 2w \qquad \text{\textit{Given formula}}$$

$$P - 2l = 2w$$

$$\frac{P - 2l}{2} = w \qquad \text{\textit{Solve for w}}$$

–3 cm–

h

FIGURE 2.5

EXAMPLE 9   Using a Formula

A cylindrical can (see Figure 2.5) has a volume of 300 cubic centimeters (cm^3) and a radius of 3 centimeters (cm). Find the height of the can.

SOLUTION

The formula for the *volume of a cylinder* is $V = \pi r^2 h$. To find the height of the can, solve for h.

$$h = \frac{V}{\pi r^2}$$

Then, using $V = 300 \text{ cm}^3$ and $r = 3$ cm, find the height.

$$h = \frac{300 \text{ cm}^3}{\pi (3 \text{ cm})^2}$$

$$= \frac{300 \text{ cm}^3}{9\pi \text{ cm}^2} \qquad \text{\textit{$\pi \approx 3.14159$}}$$

$$\approx 10.61 \text{ cm} \qquad \text{\textit{Round to two decimal places}}$$

DISCUSSION PROBLEM

RED HERRINGS

Applied problems in textbooks often give precisely the right amount of information that is necessary to solve a given problem. In real life, however, you often must sort through the given information and discard information that is irrelevant to the problem. Such irrelevant information is called a **red herring.** Find the red herrings in the following problems.

(a) You have accepted a job for which your annual salary will be $18,600. You will be paid once a month, which implies that your monthly salary will be $1550. How much of your annual salary will be deducted for Social Security tax? (Assume that the Social Security tax rate is 7.65%.)

(b) You are driving 240 miles to attend a concert. After traveling for 1 hour, you stop for a snack, which takes 20 minutes. You then continue driving for 4 more hours until you reach the theater where the concert is being held. At this point you notice that you have used $10\frac{1}{2}$ gallons of gasoline (for the entire trip). How many miles per gallon did your car average on the trip?

WARM-UP

WARM-UP

The following warm-up exercises involve skills that were covered in earlier sections. You will use these skills in the exercise set for this section.

In Exercises 1–10, solve the equation (if possible). Check your result.

1. $3x - 42 = 0$

2. $64 - 16x = 0$

3. $2 - 3x = 14 + x$

4. $7 + 5x = 7x - 1$

5. $5[1 + 2(x + 3)] = 6 - 3(x - 1)$

6. $2 - 5(x - 1) = 2[x + 10(x - 1)]$

7. $\dfrac{x}{3} + \dfrac{x}{2} = \dfrac{1}{3}$

8. $\dfrac{2}{x} + \dfrac{2}{5} = 1$

9. $1 - \dfrac{2}{z} = \dfrac{z}{z + 3}$

10. $\dfrac{x}{x + 1} - \dfrac{1}{2} = \dfrac{4}{3}$

SECTION 2.2 · EXERCISES

In Exercises 1–10, write an algebraic expression for the verbal phrase.

1. The sum of two consecutive natural numbers

2. The product of two consecutive natural numbers

3. *Distance Traveled* The distance traveled in t hours by a car traveling at 50 miles per hour

4. *Travel Time* The travel time for a plane traveling at a rate of r miles per hour for 200 miles

5. *Acid Solution* The amount of acid in x gallons of a 20% acid solution

6. *Discount* The sale price for an item that is discounted 20% off its list price L

7. *Perimeter of a Rectangle* The perimeter of a rectangle whose width is x and whose length is twice the width

8. *Area of a Triangle* The area of a triangle whose base is 20 inches and whose height is h inches

9. *Total Cost* The total cost of producing x units for which the fixed costs are $1200 and the cost per unit is $25

10. *Total Revenue* The total revenue obtained by selling x units at $3.59 per unit

Number Problems In Exercises 11–24, write a mathematical model for the problem and solve the problem.

11. The sum of two consecutive natural numbers is 525. Find the two numbers.

12. Find three consecutive natural numbers whose sum is 804.

13. One positive number is 5 times another positive number. The difference between the two numbers is 148. Find the numbers.

14. One number is one-fifth of another number. The difference between the two numbers is 76. Find the numbers.

15. Find two consecutive integers whose product is 5 less than the square of the smaller number.

16. Find two consecutive natural numbers such that the difference of their reciprocals is one-fourth the reciprocal of the smaller number.

17. What is 30% of 45?   **18.** What is 175% of 360?

19. What is 0.045% of 2,650,000?

20. 432 is what percent of 1600?

21. 459 is what percent of 340?

22. 12 is $\frac{1}{2}$% of what number?

23. 70 is 40% of what number?

24. 825 is 250% of what number?

25. *Federal Government Income*   The pie chart shows the sources of income for the federal government in 1989. The total income was $990,800,000,000. Find the income for each of the indicated categories. (Round the result to the nearest billion dollars.) (*Source:* Office of Management and Budget)

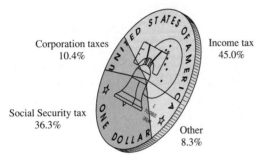

Corporation taxes
10.4%

Income tax
45.0%

Social Security tax
36.3%

Other
8.3%

FIGURE FOR 25

26. *Federal Government Expenses*   The pie chart shows the types of expenses for the federal government in 1989. The total expenses were $1,142,869,000,000. Find the expense for each of the indicated categories. (Round the result to the nearest billion dollars.) (*Source:* Office of Management and Budget)

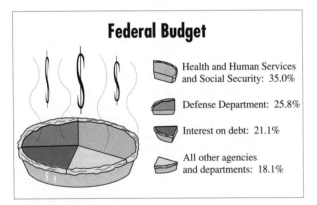

Federal Budget

Health and Human Services and Social Security: 35.0%

Defense Department: 25.8%

Interest on debt: 21.1%

All other agencies and departments: 18.1%

FIGURE FOR 26

27. *Private Debt*   A family has annual loan payments equaling 58.6% of their annual income. During the year, their loan payments total $13,077.75. What is their income?

28. *Discount*   The price of a swimming pool has been discounted 16.5%. The sale price is $1210.75. Find the original list price of the pool.

29. *Monthly Profit*   The total profit for a company in February was 20% higher than it was in January. The total profit for the two months was $157,498. Find the profit for each month.

30. *Weekly Paycheck*   Your weekly paycheck is 15% *less* than your co-worker's. The total of your paycheck and your co-worker's paycheck is $645. Find the amount of each paycheck.

Then and Now   In Exercises 31–34, the prices of different items are given for 1940 and 1990. Find the percentage increase for each item. (*Source: USA Today*)

Item	1940	1990
31. Worker's annual earnings	$1500.00	$27,000.00
32. A new car	$800.00	$16,400.00
33. A pound of ground beef	$0.15	$1.44
34. $2\frac{1}{2}$ acres on the Potomac	$7500.00	$2,500,000.00

35. *Dimensions of a Room*   A room is 1.5 times as long as it is wide, and its perimeter is 75 feet (see figure). Find the dimensions of the room.

36. *Dimensions of a Picture*   A picture frame has a total perimeter of 3 feet (see figure). The width of the frame is 0.62 times its height. Find the dimensions of the frame.

w

l

FIGURE FOR 35

h

w

FIGURE FOR 36

37. *Course Grade*   To get an A in a course you must have an average of at least 90 on four tests of 100 points each. Your scores on the first three tests were 87, 92, and 84. What must you score on the fourth test to get an A in the course?

38. *Course Grade*   Suppose you are taking a course that has four tests. The first three tests have 100 points each and the fourth test has 200 points. To get an A in the course, you must have an average of at least 90% on the four tests. Your scores on the first three tests were 87, 92, and 84. What must you score on the fourth test to get an A in the course?

39. *Travel Time*   Suppose you are driving on a freeway to a town 150 miles from your home. After 30 minutes you pass a freeway exit that you know is 25 miles from your home. Assuming that you continue at the same constant speed, how long will the entire trip take?

40. *Travel Time*   On the first part of a 317-mile trip, a salesman averaged 58 miles per hour. He averaged only 52 miles per hour on the last part of the trip because of the increased volume of traffic. Find the amount of time at each of the speeds if the total time was 5 hours and 45 minutes.

41. *Travel Time*   Two cars start at one point and travel in the same direction at average speeds of 40 and 55 miles per hour. How much time must elapse before the two cars are 5 miles apart?

42. *Catch-Up Time*   Students are traveling in two cars to a football game 135 miles away. The first car travels at an average speed of 45 miles per hour. The second car starts one-half hour after the first and travels at an average speed of 55 miles per hour. How long will it take the second car to catch up to the first car? Will the second car catch up to the first car before the first car arrives at the game?

43. *Travel Time*   Two families meet at a park for a picnic. At the end of the day one family travels east at an average speed of 42 miles per hour and the other family travels west at an average speed of 50 miles per hour. Both families have approximately 160 miles to travel.
(a) Find the time it takes each family to get home.
(b) Find the time that will have elapsed when they are 100 miles apart.
(c) Find the distance the eastbound family has to travel after the westbound family has arrived home.

44. *Average Speed*   A truck driver traveled at an average speed of 55 miles per hour on a 200-mile trip to pick up a load of freight. On the return trip (with the truck fully loaded), the average speed was 40 miles per hour. Find the average speed for the round trip.

45. *Wind Speed*   An executive flew in the corporate jet to a meeting in a city 1500 miles away (see figure). After traveling the same amount of time on the return flight, the pilot mentioned that they still had 300 miles to go. If the air speed of the plane was 600 miles per hour, how fast was the wind blowing? (Assume that the wind direction was parallel to the flight path and constant all day.)

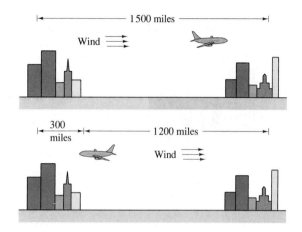

FIGURE FOR 45

46. *Speed of Light*   Light travels at the speed of 3.0×10^8 meters per second. Find the time in minutes required for light to travel from the sun to the earth (a distance of 1.5×10^{11} meters).

47. *Radio Waves*   Radio waves travel at the speed of light, 3.0×10^8 meters per second. Find the time required for a radio wave to travel from mission control in Houston to NASA astronauts on the surface of the moon 3.86×10^8 meters away.

48. *Height of a Tree*   Suppose you want to measure the height of a tree. To do this, you measure the tree's shadow and find that it is 25 feet long. You also measure the shadow of a 5-foot lamp post and find that its shadow is 2 feet long (see figure). How tall is the tree?

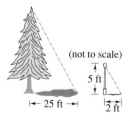

FIGURE FOR 48

49. *Height of a Building*   Suppose you want to measure the height of a building. To do this, you measure the building's shadow and find that it is 50 feet long. You also measure the shadow of a 4-foot stake and find that its shadow is $3\frac{1}{2}$ feet long. How tall is the building?

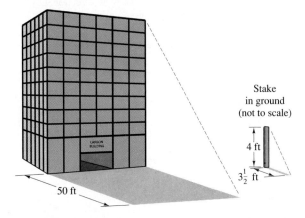

FIGURE FOR 49

50. *Height of a Flagpole*   A person who is 6 feet tall walks away from a flagpole toward the tip of the shadow of the pole. When the person is 30 feet from the pole, the tip of the person's shadow and the shadow cast by the pole coincide at a point 5 feet in front of the person. Find the height of the pole.

51. *Walking Distance*   A person who is 6 feet tall walks away from a 50-foot silo toward the tip of the silo's shadow. At a distance of 32 feet from the silo, the person's shadow begins to emerge beyond the silo's shadow. How much farther must the person walk to be completely out of the silo's shadow?

52. *Investment Mix*   Suppose you invest $12,000 in two funds paying $10\frac{1}{2}\%$ and 13% simple interest. The total annual interest is $1447.50. How much is invested in each fund?

53. *Investment Mix*   Suppose you invest $25,000 in two funds paying 11% and $12\frac{1}{2}\%$ simple interest. The total annual interest is $2975. How much is invested in each fund?

54. *Comparing Investment Returns*   A person invested $12,000 in a fund paying $9\frac{1}{2}\%$ simple interest and $8000 in a fund with a variable interest rate. At the end of the year, the person received notification that the total interest for both funds was $2054.40. Find the equivalent simple interest rate on the variable rate fund.

55. *Comparing Investment Returns*   A person has $10,000 on deposit earning simple interest with the interest rate linked to the *prime rate*. Because of a drop in the prime rate, the rate on the person's investment dropped by $1\frac{1}{2}\%$ for the last quarter of the year. The annual earnings on the fund are $1112.50. Find the interest rate for the first three quarters of the year and for the last quarter.

56. *Mixture Problem*   Using the values from the table, determine the amounts of solutions 1 and 2, respectively, needed to obtain the desired amount and concentration of the final mixture.

	Concentration			
	Solution 1	Solution 2	Final solution	Amount of final solution
(a)	10%	30%	25%	100 gal
(b)	25%	50%	30%	5 L
(c)	15%	45%	30%	10 qt
(d)	70%	90%	75%	25 gal

57. *Mixture Problem*   A 55-gallon barrel contains a mixture with a concentration of 40% (see figure). How much of this mixture must be withdrawn and replaced by 100% concentrate to bring the mixture up to 75% concentration?

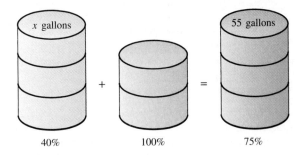

FIGURE FOR 57

58. *Mixture Problem*   A farmer mixed gasoline and oil in order to have 2 gallons of mixture for his two-cycle chain saw engine. This mixture was 32 parts gasoline and 1 part two-cycle oil. How much gasoline must be added to bring the mixture to 40 parts gasoline and 1 part oil?

59. *Mixture Problem*   A grocer mixed two kinds of nuts, costing $2.49 per pound and $3.89 per pound, respectively, to make 100 pounds of a mixture costing $3.19 per pound. How much of each kind of nut was put into the mixture?

60. *Production Limit*   A company has fixed costs of $10,000 per month and variable costs of $8.50 per unit manufactured. The company has $85,000 available to cover the monthly costs. How many units can the company manufacture? (*Fixed costs* occur regardless of the level of production. *Variable costs* depend on the level of production.)

61. *Production Limit*   A company has fixed costs of $10,000 per month and variable costs of $9.30 per unit manufactured. The company has $85,000 available to cover the monthly costs. How many units can the company manufacture?

62. *Water Depth*   A trough is 12 feet long, 3 feet deep, and 3 feet wide (see figure). Find the depth of the water when the trough contains 70 gallons (1 gallon ≈ 0.13368 cubic feet).

FIGURE FOR 62

Static Problems   In Exercises 63 and 64, suppose you have a uniform beam of length L with a fulcrum x feet from the one end (see figure). If there are objects with weights W_1 and W_2 placed at opposite ends of the beam, then the beam will balance if

$$W_1 x = W_2 (L - x).$$

Find x so the beam will balance.

FIGURE FOR 63 AND 64

63. Two children weighing 50 and 75 pounds are going to play on a seesaw that is 10 feet long.

64. A person weighing 200 pounds is attempting to move a 550-pound rock with a bar that is 5 feet long.

In Exercises 65–76, solve for the indicated variable.

65. *Area of a Triangle*
Solve for h: $A = \frac{1}{2}bh$

66. *Volume of a Right Circular Cylinder*
Solve for h: $V = \pi r^2 h$

67. *Investment at Simple Interest*
Solve for r: $I = Prt$

68. *Investment at Compound Interest*
Solve for P: $A = P\left(1 + \dfrac{r}{n}\right)^{nt}$

69. *Area of a Trapezoid*
Solve for b: $A = \frac{1}{2}(a + b)h$

70. *Area of a Sector of a Circle*
Solve for θ: $A = \dfrac{\pi r^2 \theta}{360}$

71. *Volume of a Spherical Segment*
Solve for r: $V = \frac{1}{3}\pi h^2 (3r - h)$

72. *Free-Falling Body*
Solve for a: $h = v_0 t + \frac{1}{2}at^2$

73. *Newton's Law of Universal Gravitation*
Solve for m_2: $F = \alpha\dfrac{m_1 m_2}{r^2}$

74. *Capacitance in Series Circuits*
Solve for C_1: $C = \dfrac{1}{\dfrac{1}{C_1} + \dfrac{1}{C_2}}$

75. *Geometric Progression*
Solve for r: $S = \dfrac{rL - a}{r - 1}$

76. *Prismoidal Formula*
Solve for S_1: $V = \frac{1}{6}H(S_0 + 4S_1 + S_2)$

2.3   SOLVING EQUATIONS GRAPHICALLY

Intercepts, Zeros, and Solutions / Finding Solutions Graphically / Viewing Rectangles, Scale, and Accuracy / Points of Intersection of Two Graphs

Intercepts, Zeros, and Solutions

In Section 1.1, you learned that the **intercepts** of a graph are the points at which the graph intersects the x- or y-axis.

DEFINITION OF INTERCEPTS

1. The point $(a, 0)$ is called an **x-intercept** of the graph of an equation if it is a solution point of the equation. To find the x-intercepts, let y be zero and solve the equation for x.
2. The point $(0, b)$ is called a **y-intercept** of the graph of an equation if it is a solution point of the equation. To find the y-intercepts, let x be zero and solve the equation for y.

REMARK   Sometimes it is convenient to denote the x-intercept as simply the x-coordinate of the point $(a, 0)$ rather than the point itself. Unless it is necessary to make a distinction, we will use "intercept" to mean either the point or the coordinate.

It is possible that a particular graph will have no intercepts or several intercepts. For instance, consider the three graphs in Figure 2.6.

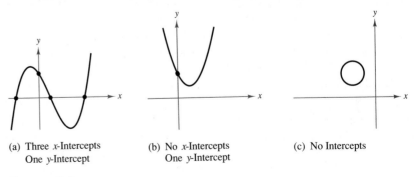

(a) Three x-Intercepts   (b) No x-Intercepts   (c) No Intercepts
    One y-Intercept   One y-Intercept

FIGURE 2.6

EXAMPLE 1   Finding x- and y-Intercepts

Find the x- and y-intercepts of the graph of $2x + 3y = 5$.

SOLUTION

To find the x-intercept, let $y = 0$. This produces

$$2x = 5$$

$$x = \frac{5}{2},$$

which implies that the graph has one x-intercept: $(\frac{5}{2}, 0)$. To find the y-intercept, let $x = 0$. This produces

$$3y = 5$$

$$y = \frac{5}{3},$$

which implies that the graph has one y-intercept: $(0, \frac{5}{3})$. See Figure 2.7.

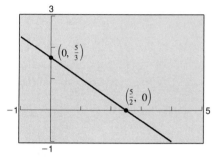

FIGURE 2.7

A **zero** of a function $y = f(x)$ is a number a such that $f(a) = 0$. Thus, to find the zeros of a function, you must solve the equation $f(x) = 0$.

EXAMPLE 2   Verifying Zeros of Functions

A. The real number 3 is a zero of the function $f(x) = 4x - 12$. Check that $f(3) = 0$.
B. The real numbers -2 and 1 are zeros of the function $f(x) = x^2 + x - 2$. Check that $f(-2) = 0$ and $f(1) = 0$.

The concepts of x-intercepts, zeros of functions, and solutions of equations are closely related. In fact, the following statements are equivalent.

1. The point $(a, 0)$ is an x-*intercept* of the graph of $y = f(x)$.
2. The number a is a *zero* of the function f.
3. The number a is a *solution* of the equation $f(x) = 0$.

Figure 2.8 shows the graph of the function $y = f(x) = x^2 - x - 6$. Notice that the graph has x-*intercepts* of $(3, 0)$ and $(-2, 0)$ because the equation

$$0 = x^2 - x - 6$$

has the *solutions* $x = 3$ and $x = -2$.

This close connection between x-intercepts, zeros, and solutions is crucial to our study of algebra, and you can take advantage of this connection in two basic ways. You can use your algebraic "equation solving skills" to find the x-intercepts of a graph, and you can use your "graphing skills" to approximate the solutions of an equation.

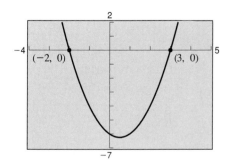

FIGURE 2.8

Finding Solutions Graphically

Polynomial equations of degree one or two can be solved in relatively straightforward ways. Polynomial equations of higher degrees can, however, be quite difficult, especially if you rely only on algebraic techniques. For such equations, a graphing utility can be very helpful.

REMARK In Chapter 3 you will learn techniques for determining the number of solutions of a polynomial equation. For now, you should know that a polynomial equation of degree n cannot have more than n different solutions.

GRAPHICAL APPROXIMATIONS OF SOLUTIONS OF AN EQUATION

To use a graphing utility to approximate the solutions of an equation in the variable x, use the following steps.

1. Write the equation in *standard form*, $f(x) = 0$, with all of the nonzero terms on one side of the equation and zero on the other side.
2. Use a graphing utility to graph the function $y = f(x)$. Be sure the viewing rectangle shows all the relevant features of the graph.
3. Use the zoom and trace features of the graphing utility to approximate each of the x-intercepts of the graph of f. Remember that a graph can have more than one x-intercept, so you may need to change the viewing rectangle a few times.

EXAMPLE 3   Finding Solutions of an Equation Graphically

Use a graphing utility to approximate the solutions of $2x^3 - 3x + 2 = 0$.

SOLUTION

Begin by graphing the function $y = 2x^3 - 3x + 2$, as shown in Figure 2.9(a). You can see from the graph that there is only one x-intercept that lies between -1 and -2 and is approximately -1.5. By using the zoom feature of a graphing utility you can improve the approximation as shown in the graph in Figure 2.9(b). To three decimal place accuracy, the solution is $x \approx -1.476$. Check this approximation on your calculator. You will find that the value of y is $y = 2(-1.476)^3 - 3(-1.476) + 2 \approx -0.003$.

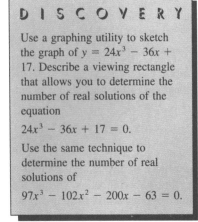

DISCOVERY

Use a graphing utility to sketch the graph of $y = 24x^3 - 36x + 17$. Describe a viewing rectangle that allows you to determine the number of real solutions of the equation

$$24x^3 - 36x + 17 = 0.$$

Use the same technique to determine the number of real solutions of

$$97x^3 - 102x^2 - 200x - 63 = 0.$$

(a)   (b)

FIGURE 2.9

(a)

(b)

(c)

FIGURE 2.10

Viewing Rectangles, Scale, and Accuracy

Here are some suggestions for using the *zoom-in* feature of a graphing utility.

1. With each successive zoom-in, adjust the x-scale (if necessary) so that the resulting viewing rectangle shows at least the two scale marks between which the solution lies.
2. The accuracy of the approximation will always be such that the error is less than the distance between two scale marks.
3. If you have a *trace* feature on your graphing utility, you can generally add one more decimal place of accuracy without changing the viewing rectangle.

Unless stated otherwise, this book will approximate all real solutions with an error of *at most* 0.01.

EXAMPLE 4   Rewriting in Standard Form First

Use a graphing utility to approximate the solutions of $x^2 + 3 = 5x$.

SOLUTION

In standard form, this equation is $x^2 - 5x + 3 = 0$. Thus, you can begin by graphing $y = x^2 - 5x + 3$, as shown in Figure 2.10(a). This graph has two x-intercepts, and by using the zoom and trace features you can approximate the corresponding solutions to be $x \approx 0.697$ and $x \approx 4.303$, as shown in Figure 2.10(b) and (c).

EXAMPLE 5   An Equation with Three Solutions

Use a graphing utility to approximate the solutions of $2x^3 - 3x - 0.75 = 0$.

SOLUTION

Begin by graphing the function $y = 2x^3 - 3x - 0.75$, as shown in Figure 2.11. From the viewing rectangle shown, you can see that the graph has three x-intercepts. Using the zoom and trace features, approximate the corresponding solutions to be

$$x \approx -1.07, \quad x \approx -0.26, \quad \text{and} \quad x \approx 1.33,$$

using an x-scale of 0.01.

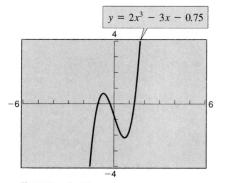

$y = 2x^3 - 3x - 0.75$

FIGURE 2.11

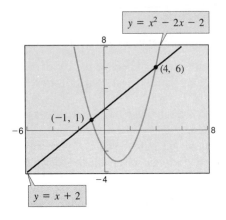

FIGURE 2.12

Points of Intersection of Two Graphs

An ordered pair that is a solution of two different equations is called a **point of intersection** of the graphs of the two equations. For instance, from Figure 2.12, you can see that the graphs of the equations

$$y = x + 2 \quad \text{and} \quad y = x^2 - 2x - 2$$

have two points of intersection. The point $(-1, 1)$ is a solution of both equations, and the point $(4, 6)$ is a solution of both equations.

To find the points of intersection of the graphs of two equations, solve each equation for y (or x) and set the two results equal to each other. The resulting equation will be an equation in one variable, which can be solved using standard procedures, as shown in Example 6.

EXAMPLE 6   Finding Points of Intersection

Find the points of intersection of the graphs of $2x - 3y = -2$ and $4x - y = 6$.

SOLUTION

To begin, solve each equation for y.

$$y = \frac{2}{3}x + \frac{2}{3} \quad \text{and} \quad y = 4x - 6$$

Next, set the two expressions for y equal to each other and solve the resulting equation for x, as follows.

$$\frac{2}{3}x + \frac{2}{3} = 4x - 6$$
$$2x + 2 = 12x - 18$$
$$-10x = -20$$
$$x = 2$$

When $x = 2$, the y-value of each of the given equations is 2. Thus, the graphs of the given equations have one point of intersection, $(2, 2)$, as shown in Figure 2.13.

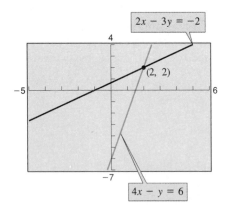

FIGURE 2.13

Another way to approximate points of intersection of two graphs is to graph both equations and use the zoom and trace features to find the point or points at which the two graphs intersect.

EXAMPLE 7   Approximating Points of Intersection

Approximate the point(s) of intersection of the graphs of

$$y = x^2 - 3x - 4 \quad \text{and} \quad y = x^3 + 3x^2 - 2x - 1.$$

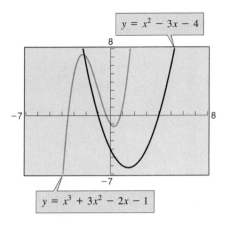

$y = x^2 - 3x - 4$

$y = x^3 + 3x^2 - 2x - 1$

FIGURE 2.14

SOLUTION

Begin by using a graphing utility to graph both functions, as shown in Figure 2.14. From the display, you can see that the two graphs have only one point of intersection. Then, using the zoom and trace features, approximate the point of intersection to be $(-2.17, 7.25)$. To test the reasonableness of this approximation, you can evaluate both functions when $x = -2.17$.

Quadratic function: $y = (-2.17)^2 - 3(-2.17) - 4 \approx 7.22$

Cubic function: $y = (-2.17)^3 + 3(-2.17)^2 - 2(-2.17) - 1$
$$\approx 7.25$$

Because both functions yield approximately the same y-value, you can conclude that the approximate coordinates of the point of intersection are $x \approx -2.17$ and $y \approx 7.25$.

The method shown in Example 7 gives a nice graphical picture of points of intersection of two graphs. However, for actual approximation purposes, it is better to use the procedure described in Example 6. That is, the point of intersection of $y = x^2 - 3x - 4$ and $y = x^3 + 3x^2 - 2x - 1$ coincides with the solution of the equation

$$x^3 + 3x^2 - 2x - 1 = x^2 - 3x - 4$$
$$x^3 + 2x^2 + x + 3 = 0.$$

By graphing $y = x^3 + 2x^2 + x + 3$ on a graphing utility and using the zoom feature, you can approximate the solution of this equation to be $x \approx -2.175$. The corresponding y-value for *both* of the functions given in Example 7 is $y \approx 7.25$.

EXAMPLE 8   Compact Disc Players and Turntables

Between 1983 and 1987 the number of compact disc players sold each year in the United States was *increasing* and the number of turntables was *decreasing*. Two models that approximate the sales are

$$S = -1700 + 496t \qquad \qquad \textit{Compact disc players}$$

and

$$S = 1972 - 82t, \qquad \qquad \textit{Turntables}$$

where S represents the annual sales in thousands of units and t represents the year, with $t = 3$ corresponding to 1983. According to these two models, when would you expect the sales of compact disc players to have exceeded the sales of turntables? (*Source:* Dealerscope Merchandising)

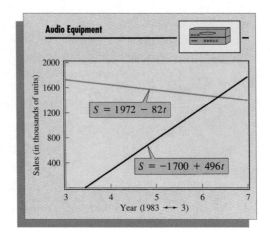

FIGURE 2.15

SOLUTION

Because the first equation has already been solved for S in terms of t, substitute this value into the second equation and solve for t, as follows.

$$-1700 + 496t = 1972 - 82t$$
$$496t + 82t = 1972 + 1700$$
$$578t = 3672$$
$$t \approx 6.35$$

Thus, from the given models, you would expect that the sales of compact disc players exceeded the sales of turntables sometime during 1986. The graphs of $y_1 = -1700 + 496t$ and $y_2 = 1972 - 82t$ are shown in Figure 2.15, confirming that they intersect at approximately $t = 6.35$.   ■■■■■■■■■

DISCUSSION PROBLEM
••••••••••••••••••••
JUDGING THE ACCURACY OF AN APPROXIMATE SOLUTION

Suppose you are solving the equation

$$\frac{x}{x-1} - \frac{99}{100} = 0$$

for x, and you obtain $x = -99.1$ as your solution. Substituting this value back into the equation produces

$$\frac{-99.1}{-99.1 - 1} - \frac{99}{100} = 0.00000999 = 9.99 \times 10^{-6} \approx 0.$$

Does this mean that -99.1 is a good approximation to the solution? Explain your reasoning.

WARM-UP
· · · · · · · · · · · · · · · · ·

The following warm-up exercises involve skills that were covered in earlier sections. You will use these skills in the exercise set for this section.

In Exercises 1–6, solve the equation.

1. $9 - 2(x - 3) = 12$

2. $5(t + 5) - 2(t - 1) = 0$

3. $\dfrac{z}{4} - \dfrac{z}{10} = 2$

4. $\dfrac{y + 2}{3} + \dfrac{y - 6}{4} = 20$

5. $\dfrac{8}{x} - \dfrac{6}{x} = 1$

6. $\dfrac{3}{x - 2} + \dfrac{3}{2} = 1$

In Exercises 7–10, use a graphing utility to graph the equation.

7. $y = 0.5x^2 - 2x - 1.2$

8. $y = 5 - 0.3(x - 4)^2$

9. $y = \frac{1}{9}x^3 - 6x + 3$

10. $y = \sqrt{225 - x^2}$

SECTION 2.3 · EXERCISES
· ·

In Exercises 1–8, find the x- and y-intercepts of the graph of the equation.

1. $y = x - 5$

2. $y = (x - 1)(x - 3)$

3. $y = x^2 + x - 2$

4. $y = 4 - x^2$

5. $y = x\sqrt{x + 2}$

6. $xy = 4$

7. $xy - 2y - x + 1 = 0$

8. $x^2y - x^2 + 4y = 0$

In Exercises 9–14, use a graphing utility to graph the function and verify its zero(s).

Function	Zeros
9. $f(x) = 12 - 4x$	$x = 3$
10. $f(x) = 3(x - 5) + 9$	$x = 2$
11. $f(x) = x^2 - 2.5x - 6$	$x = -1.5, \quad x = 4$
12. $f(x) = x^3 - 9x^2 + 18x$	$x = 0, \quad x = 3, \quad x = 6$
13. $f(x) = \dfrac{x + 2}{3} - \dfrac{x - 1}{5} - 1$	$x = 1$
14. $f(x) = x - 3 - \dfrac{10}{x}$	$x = -2, \quad x = 5$

In Exercises 15–20, write the equation in the form $f(x) = 0$. There are many correct answers.

15. $25(x - 3) = 12(x + 2) - 10$

16. $1200 = 300 + 2(x - 500)$

17. $\dfrac{2x}{3} = 10 - \dfrac{1}{x}$

18. $\dfrac{x - 3}{25} = \dfrac{x - 5}{12}$

19. $\dfrac{3}{x + 2} - \dfrac{4}{x - 2} = 5$

20. $\dfrac{6}{x} + \dfrac{8}{x + 5} = 10$

In Exercises 21–26, solve the equation algebraically. Then write the equation in the form $f(x) = 0$ and use a graphing utility to verify the algebraic solution.

21. $27 - 4x = 12$

22. $3.5x - 8 = 0.5x$

23. $\dfrac{3x}{2} + \dfrac{1}{4}(x - 2) = 10$

24. $0.60x + 0.40(100 - x) = 50$

25. $3(x + 3) = 5(1 - x) - 1$

26. $(x + 1)^2 + 2(x - 2) = (x + 1)(x - 2)$

In Exercises 27–36, use a graphing utility to approximate any solutions (accurate to three decimal places) of the equation. [Remember to write the equation in the form $f(x) = 0$.]

27. $\frac{1}{4}(x^2 - 10x + 17) = 0$

28. $-2(x^2 - 6x + 6) = 0$

29. $x^3 + x + 4 = 0$

30. $\frac{1}{9}x^3 + x + 4 = 0$

31. $2x^3 - x^2 - 18x + 9 = 0$

32. $4x^3 + 12x^2 - 26x - 24 = 0$

33. $x^4 = 2x^3 + 1$

34. $x^5 = 3 + 2x^3$

35. $\dfrac{2}{z + 2} = 3$

36. $\dfrac{5}{x} = 1 + \dfrac{3}{x + 2}$

In Exercises 37–46, use a graphing utility to approximate any points of intersection (accurate to three decimal places) of the graphs of the equations.

37. $y = 2 - x$
$y = 2x - 1$

38. $y = 7 - x$
$y = \frac{3}{2} - \frac{11}{2}x$

39. $y = 4 - x^2$
$y = 2x - 1$

40. $y = x^3 - 3$
$y = 5 - 2x$

41. $y = 8$
$y = 3x^2 + 2x$

42. $y = 32$
$y = x^5 - x^2$

43. $y = 3(x + 1)$
$y = x^2 + 2x + 1$

44. $y = x + 2$
$y = -x^2 + 4x + 2$

45. $y = 2x^2$
$y = x^4 - 2x^2$

46. $y = -x$
$y = 2x - x^2$

In Exercises 47–50, evaluate the expression in two ways.
(a) Calculate entirely on your calculator by storing intermediate results, and then round the answer to two decimal places.
(b) Round both the numerator and the denominator to two decimal places before dividing, and then round the final answer to two decimal places. Does the second method decrease the accuracy?

47. $\dfrac{1 + 0.73205}{1 - 0.73205}$

48. $\dfrac{1 + 0.86603}{1 - 0.86603}$

49. $\dfrac{3.33 + \dfrac{1.98}{0.74}}{4 + \dfrac{6.25}{3.15}}$

50. $\dfrac{1.73205 - 1.19195}{3 - (1.73205)(1.19195)}$

51. *Travel Time*   On the first part of a 280-mile trip, a salesman averaged 63 miles per hour. He averaged only 54 miles per hour on the last part of the trip because of the increased volume of traffic.
(a) Express the total time for the trip as a function of the distance x traveled at an average speed of 63 miles per hour.
(b) Use a graphing utility to graph the time function. What is the domain of the function?
(c) Approximate the number of miles traveled at 63 miles per hour if the total time was 4 hours and 45 minutes.

52. *Production Limit*   A company has fixed costs of $25,000 per month and a variable cost of $18.65 per unit manufactured. (*Fixed costs* are those that occur regardless of the level of production.)
(a) Write the total monthly costs C as a function of the number of units x produced.

(b) Approximate the number of units that can be produced per month if total costs cannot exceed $200,000. Is this problem better solved algebraically or graphically? Explain your reasoning.

53. *Mixture Problem*   A 55-gallon barrel contains a mixture with a concentration of 33%. You are instructed to remove x gallons of this mixture and replace it with 100% concentrate.
(a) Write the amount of concentrate in the final mixture as a function of x.
(b) Use a graphing utility to graph the concentration function. What is the domain of the function?
(c) Approximate (accurate to one decimal place) the value of x if the final mixture is 60% concentrate.

54. *Dimensions of a Region*   A rectangular region with perimeter 230 feet has length x.
(a) Express the area of the rectangle as a function of x.
(b) Use a graphing utility to graph the area function. Because area is nonnegative, what is the domain of the function?
(c) Approximate (accurate to one decimal place) the dimensions of the region if its area is 2000 square feet. (Note that there are two values of x such that the area of the region is 2000 square feet.) Which x-value is appropriate in this problem? Explain.

Negative Income Tax   In Exercises 55–58, use the following information about a possible negative income tax for a family consisting of two adults and two children. The plan would guarantee the poor a minimum income while encouraging the family to increase their private income.

Family's earned income: $I = x$

Government payment: $G = 8000 - \frac{1}{2}x, \quad 0 \le x \le 16{,}000$

Spendable income: $S = I + G$

55. Express the spendable income S in terms of x. Use a graphing utility to graph the functions I, G, and S. What effect does an increase in the family's earned income have on (a) the size of the government payment and (b) the family's spendable income?

56. Find the earned income x if the government payment is $4600.

57. Find the earned income x if the spendable income is $11,800.

58. Find the government payment G if the spendable income is $10,500.

2.4   QUADRATIC EQUATIONS

Solving Quadratic Equations by Factoring / Solving Quadratic Equations by Extracting Square Roots / Solving Quadratic Equations by Completing the Square / Applications

Solving Quadratic Equations by Factoring

> **DEFINITION OF A QUADRATIC EQUATION**
>
> A **quadratic equation** in x is an equation that can be written in the standard form
>
> $$ax^2 + bx + c = 0,$$
>
> where a, b, and c are real numbers with $a \neq 0$. A quadratic equation in x is also known as a **second-degree polynomial equation in x.**

D I S C O V E R Y

On a graphing utility, store the value 5 in A, -2 in B, and 1 in C. Then use a graphing utility to sketch the graph of $y = C(x - A)(x - B)$. Explain how the values of A and B can be determined from the graph. Now store any other nonzero value in C. Does the value of C affect the x-intercepts of the graph? Find values of A, B, and C so that the graph opens downward and has x-intercepts at $(-5, 0)$ and $(0, 0)$.

You will study four algebraic methods for *solving* quadratic equations: factoring, extracting square roots, completing the square, and the Quadratic Formula. (The Quadratic Formula is discussed in the next section.) You can also use the graphical approximation technique discussed in Section 2.3 either before or after you solve the equation algebraically. The first technique is based on the Zero-Factor Property given in the prerequisite chapter, Section 2.

If $ab = 0$, then $a = 0$ or $b = 0$.   *Zero-Factor Property*

To use this principle, write the left side of the standard form of a quadratic equation as the product of two linear factors. Then find the solutions of the quadratic equation by setting each linear factor equal to zero. For instance, the solutions of the equation $x^2 - 3x - 10 = 0$ are found as follows.

$$x^2 - 3x - 10 = 0 \qquad \text{\textit{Standard form}}$$
$$(x - 5)(x + 2) = 0 \qquad \text{\textit{Factored form}}$$
$$x - 5 = 0 \;\longrightarrow\; x = 5 \qquad \text{\textit{Set 1st factor equal to 0}}$$
$$x + 2 = 0 \;\longrightarrow\; x = -2 \qquad \text{\textit{Set 2nd factor equal to 0}}$$

Be sure you see that the Zero-Factor Property works *only* for equations written in standard form (in which the right side of the equation is zero). Therefore, all terms must be collected on one side *before* factoring. For instance, in the equation $(x - 5)(x + 2) = 8$, it is *incorrect* to set each factor equal to 8. Can you solve this equation correctly?

EXAMPLE 1 Solving a Quadratic Equation by Factoring

$$2x^2 + 9x + 7 = 3 \qquad \textit{Original equation}$$

$$2x^2 + 9x + 4 = 0 \qquad \textit{Standard form}$$

$$(2x + 1)(x + 4) = 0 \qquad \textit{Factored form}$$

$$2x + 1 = 0 \quad \longrightarrow \quad x = -\frac{1}{2} \qquad \textit{Set 1st factor equal to 0}$$

$$x + 4 = 0 \quad \longrightarrow \quad x = -4 \qquad \textit{Set 2nd factor equal to 0}$$

CHECK: You can check each solution in the original equation as follows.

$$2\left(-\frac{1}{2}\right)^2 + 9\left(-\frac{1}{2}\right) + 7 = \frac{1}{2} - \frac{9}{2} + 7 = 3 \qquad x = -\frac{1}{2} \ \textit{checks}$$

$$2(-4)^2 + 9(-4) + 7 = 32 - 36 + 7 = 3 \qquad x = -4 \ \textit{checks}$$

The equation has two solutions: $-\frac{1}{2}$ and -4. The graph of $y = 2x^2 + 9x + 4$, shown in Figure 2.16, visually reinforces these two solution values.

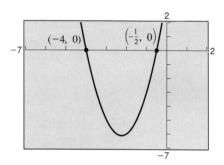

FIGURE 2.16

EXAMPLE 2 Solving a Quadratic Equation by Factoring

$$6x^2 - 3x = 0 \qquad \textit{Original equation}$$

$$3x(2x - 1) = 0 \qquad \textit{Factored form}$$

$$3x = 0 \quad \longrightarrow \quad x = 0 \qquad \textit{Set 1st factor equal to 0}$$

$$2x - 1 = 0 \quad \longrightarrow \quad x = \frac{1}{2} \qquad \textit{Set 2nd factor equal to 0}$$

The equation has two solutions: 0 and $\frac{1}{2}$. Check these solutions in the original equation. The graph of $y = 6x^2 - 3x$, shown in Figure 2.17, reinforces these two solution values.

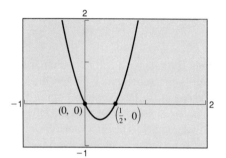

FIGURE 2.17

If the two factors of a quadratic expression are the same, then the corresponding solution is called a **double** or **repeated** solution.

EXAMPLE 3 A Quadratic Equation with a Repeated Solution

$$9x^2 - 6x + 1 = 0 \qquad \textit{Standard form}$$

$$(3x - 1)^2 = 0 \qquad \textit{Factored form}$$

$$3x - 1 = 0 \qquad \textit{Set repeated factor equal to 0}$$

$$x = \frac{1}{3} \qquad \textit{Solution}$$

The equation has only one solution: $\frac{1}{3}$. Check this solution in the original equation. The graph of $y = 9x^2 - 6x + 1$, shown in Figure 2.18, reinforces this solution value. Note that the graph of a quadratic function with one repeated zero *touches,* rather than crosses, the x-axis.

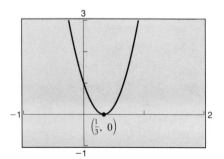

FIGURE 2.18

Solving Quadratic Equations by Extracting Square Roots

There is a nice shortcut for solving quadratic equations of the form $u^2 = d$, where $d > 0$ and u is an algebraic expression. By factoring, you can see that this equation has two solutions.

$$u^2 = d \qquad \text{\textit{Original equation}}$$
$$u^2 - d = 0 \qquad \text{\textit{Standard form}}$$
$$\left(u + \sqrt{d}\right)\left(u - \sqrt{d}\right) = 0 \qquad \text{\textit{Factor}}$$
$$u + \sqrt{d} = 0 \;\longrightarrow\; u = -\sqrt{d} \quad \text{\textit{Set 1st factor equal to 0}}$$
$$u - \sqrt{d} = 0 \;\longrightarrow\; u = \sqrt{d} \quad \text{\textit{Set 2nd factor equal to 0}}$$

Because the solutions differ only in sign, you can write both of the solutions together, using a "plus or minus" sign, as $u = \pm\sqrt{d}$. This form of the solution is read as "u is equal to plus or minus the square root of d." Solving an equation of the form $u^2 = d$ without going through the steps of factoring is called **extracting square roots.**

EXTRACTING SQUARE ROOTS

The equation $u^2 = d$, where $d > 0$, has exactly two solutions:

$$u = \sqrt{d} \quad \text{and} \quad u = -\sqrt{d}.$$

These solutions can also be written as $u = \pm\sqrt{d}$.

EXAMPLE 4   **Solving a Quadratic Equation by Extracting Square Roots**

$$4x^2 = 12 \qquad\qquad \text{\textit{Original equation}}$$
$$x^2 = 3 \qquad\qquad \text{\textit{Divide both sides by 4}}$$
$$x = \pm\sqrt{3} \qquad\qquad \text{\textit{Extract square roots}}$$

The equation has two solutions: $\sqrt{3}$ and $-\sqrt{3}$. Note that $x^2 - 3 = 0$ factors as $\left(x + \sqrt{3}\right)\left(x - \sqrt{3}\right) = 0$, which gives the same two solutions. Check these two solutions in the original equation. The graph of $y = 4x^2 - 12$, shown in Figure 2.19, reinforces these two solution values.

FIGURE 2.19

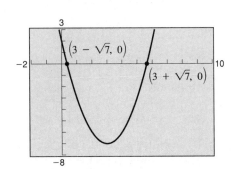

FIGURE 2.20

EXAMPLE 5   Solving a Quadratic Equation by Extracting Square Roots

Solve $(x - 3)^2 = 7$.

SOLUTION

In this case, an extra step is needed *after* extracting square roots.

$$(x - 3)^2 = 7 \qquad \text{\textit{Original equation}}$$
$$x - 3 = \pm\sqrt{7} \qquad \text{\textit{Extract square roots}}$$
$$x = 3 \pm \sqrt{7} \qquad \text{\textit{Add 3 to both sides}}$$

Thus, the equation has two solutions: $3 + \sqrt{7}$ and $3 - \sqrt{7}$. Check these two solutions in the original equation. The graph of $y = (x - 3)^2 - 7$, shown in Figure 2.20, reinforces these two solution values.

Solving Quadratic Equations by Completing the Square

The equation in Example 5 was given in the form $(x - 3)^2 = 7$ so that you could find the solution by extracting square roots. Suppose, however, that the equation $(x - 3)^2 = 7$ had been given in the standard form

$$x^2 - 6x + 2 = 0. \qquad \text{\textit{Standard form}}$$

This equation is equivalent to the original and thus has the same two solutions, $x = 3 \pm \sqrt{7}$. The left side of the equation is not factorable, and you cannot find its solutions unless you can *reverse* the steps followed in Example 5.

COMPLETING THE SQUARE

To **complete the square** for the expression $x^2 + bx$, add $(b/2)^2$, which is the square of half the coefficient of x. Consequently,

$$x^2 + bx + \left(\frac{b}{2}\right)^2 = \left(x + \frac{b}{2}\right)^2.$$

When solving quadratic equations by completing the square, you must add $(b/2)^2$ to *both sides* to maintain equality.

EXAMPLE 6   Completing the Square: Leading Coefficient is 1

Solve the equation $x^2 - 6x + 2 = 0$ by completing the square. Compare the solutions to those obtained in Example 5.

SOLUTION

$$x^2 - 6x + 2 = 0 \qquad \text{\textit{Original equation}}$$

$$x^2 - 6x = -2 \qquad \text{\textit{Subtract 2 from both sides}}$$

$$x^2 - 6x + 3^2 = -2 + 3^2 \qquad \text{\textit{Add 3^2 to both sides}}$$

$$\underbrace{}_{(b/2)^2}$$

$$x^2 - 6x + 9 = 7 \qquad \text{\textit{Simplify}}$$

$$(x - 3)^2 = 7 \qquad \text{\textit{Perfect square trinomial}}$$

$$x - 3 = \pm\sqrt{7} \qquad \text{\textit{Extract square roots}}$$

$$x = 3 \pm \sqrt{7} \qquad \text{\textit{Solutions}}$$

If the leading coefficient of a quadratic equation is not 1, you should divide both sides of the equation by this coefficient *before* completing the square.

EXAMPLE 7   **Completing the Square: Leading Coefficient Is Not 1**

Solve $3x^2 - 4x - 5 = 0$.

SOLUTION

$$3x^2 - 4x - 5 = 0 \qquad \text{\textit{Original equation}}$$

$$3x^2 - 4x = 5 \qquad \text{\textit{Add 5 to both sides}}$$

$$x^2 - \frac{4}{3}x = \frac{5}{3} \qquad \text{\textit{Divide both sides by 3}}$$

$$x^2 - \frac{4}{3}x + \left(\frac{2}{3}\right)^2 = \frac{5}{3} + \left(\frac{2}{3}\right)^2 \qquad \text{\textit{Add $(\frac{2}{3})^2$ to both sides}}$$

$$\underbrace{\phantom{x^2 - \frac{4}{3}x + \left(\frac{2}{3}\right)^2}}_{(\text{half})^2}$$

$$\left(x - \frac{2}{3}\right)^2 = \frac{19}{9}$$

$$x - \frac{2}{3} = \pm\frac{\sqrt{19}}{3} \qquad \text{\textit{Extract square roots}}$$

$$x = \frac{2}{3} \pm \frac{\sqrt{19}}{3} \qquad \text{\textit{Solutions}}$$

FIGURE 2.21

Using a calculator, you can see that the two solutions are approximately 2.11963 and -0.78630, which agree with the graphical solution shown in Figure 2.21.

When rewriting algebraic expressions by completing the square, you must add *and subtract* the quantity $(b/2)^2$.

EXAMPLE 8   **Completing the Square within an Algebraic Expression**

Rewrite $x^2 - 2x - 3$ as the sum or difference of two squares.

SOLUTION

$$
\begin{aligned}
x^2 - 2x - 3 &= x^2 - 2x + 1^2 - 3 - 1^2 &&\textit{Add and subtract } 1^2 \\
&= (x^2 - 2x + 1) - 4 &&\textit{Group terms} \\
&= (x - 1)^2 - 2^2 &&\textit{Difference of two squares}
\end{aligned}
$$

Applications

Quadratic equations often occur in problems dealing with area. Here is a simple example. "A square room has an area of 144 square feet. Find the dimensions of the room." To solve this problem, let x represent the length of each side of the room. Then, by solving the equation

$$x^2 = 144,$$

you can conclude that each side of the room is 12 feet long. Note that although the equation $x^2 = 144$ has two solutions, -12 and 12, the negative solution makes no sense (for this problem), so you should choose the positive solution.

EXAMPLE 9   **Finding the Dimensions of a Room**

A bedroom is 3 feet longer than it is wide (see Figure 2.22) and has an area of 154 square feet. Find the dimensions of the room.

FIGURE 2.22

SOLUTION

VERBAL
MODEL   Width of room · Length of room = Area of room

LABELS   Width of room = w (*feet*)
               Length of room = $w + 3$ (*feet*)
               Area of room = 154   (*square feet*)

EQUATION $w(w + 3) = 154$

$$
\begin{aligned}
w^2 + 3w - 154 &= 0 \\
(w - 11)(w + 14) &= 0 \\
w - 11 = 0 &\longrightarrow w = 11 \\
w + 14 = 0 &\longrightarrow w = -14
\end{aligned}
$$

Choosing the positive value, you find that the width is 11 feet and the length is $w + 3 = 14$ feet. You can check this solution by observing that the length is 3 feet longer than the width *and* that the product of the length and width is 154 square feet.

Another common application of quadratic equations involves an object that is falling (or projected vertically into the air). The general equation that gives the height of such an object is a **position equation,** and (on the earth's surface) it has the form

$$s = -16t^2 + v_0 t + s_0.$$

In this equation, s represents the height of the object (in feet), v_0 represents the original velocity of the object (in feet per second), s_0 represents the original height of the object (in feet), and t represents the time (in seconds).

EXAMPLE 10   Falling Time

A construction worker on the 24th floor of a building project (see Figure 2.23) accidentally drops a wrench and immediately yells "Look out below!" Could a person at ground level hear this warning in time to get out of the way of the falling wrench?

SOLUTION

Let's assume that each floor of the building is 10 feet high, so that the wrench is dropped from a height of 240 feet. Because sound travels at about 1100 feet per second, you can estimate that a person at ground level hears the warning within 1 second of the time the wrench is dropped. To set up a mathematical model for the height of the wrench, use the position equation

$$s = -16t^2 + v_0 t + s_0.$$

Because the object is dropped (rather than thrown), you can conclude that the initial velocity is $v_0 = 0$. Moreover, because the initial height is $s_0 = 240$ feet, you have the following model.

$$s = -16t^2 + 240, \qquad t \geq 0$$

Note that after falling for 1 second, the wrench is at a height of $-16(1^2) + 240 = 214$. After 2 seconds, the height of the wrench is $-16(2^2) + 240 = 176$. To find the number of seconds it takes the wrench to hit the ground, let the height s be zero and solve the resulting equation for t.

240 ft

FIGURE 2.23

$s = -16t^2 + 240$	*Position equation*
$0 = -16t^2 + 240$	*Set height equal to 0*
$16t^2 = 240$	*Add $16t^2$ to both sides*
$t^2 = 15$	*Divide both sides by 16*
$t = \sqrt{15} \approx 3.87$	*Extract positive square root*

Thus, the wrench will take about 3.87 seconds to hit the ground. If the person hears the warning 1 second after the wrench is dropped, the person still has almost 3 seconds to get out of the way.

$$a^2 + b^2 = c^2$$

a c

b

Pythagorean Theorem

FIGURE 2.24

A third type of application that often involves a quadratic equation is one dealing with the hypotenuse of a right triangle. Recall from geometry that the sides of a right triangle are related by the **Pythagorean Theorem,** as indicated in Figure 2.24. This theorem states that if a and b are the lengths of the sides of the triangle and c is the length of the hypotenuse, then $a^2 + b^2 = c^2$.

EXAMPLE 11   **Cutting Across the Lawn**

Suppose your house is on a large corner lot. Several of the children in the neighborhood cut across your lawn, as shown in Figure 2.25. The distance across the lawn is 32 feet. Assuming that the picture in Figure 2.25 is drawn to scale, how many feet does a person save by walking across the lawn instead of walking on the sidewalk?

SOLUTION

In Figure 2.25, let x represent the length of the shorter part of the sidewalk. When a ruler is used, it appears that the length of the longer part of the sidewalk is twice the shorter, so you can represent its length by $2x$. Now, the Pythagorean Theorem produces

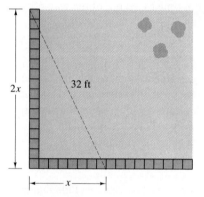

2x   32 ft

|← x →|

FIGURE 2.25

$x^2 + (2x)^2 = 32^2$	*Pythagorean Theorem*
$5x^2 = 1024$	*Add like terms*
$x^2 = 204.8$	*Divide both sides by 5*
$x = \sqrt{204.8}.$	*Extract positive square root*

Thus, the total distance on the sidewalk is

$$x + 2x = 3x = 3\sqrt{204.8} \approx 42.9 \text{ feet.}$$

Therefore, cutting across the lawn saves a person about 10.9 feet of walking distance.

A fourth type of common application of a quadratic equation is one in which a quantity y is changing over time t according to the quadratic model

$$y = at^2 + bt + c.$$

Note how this type of model is used in Example 12.

EXAMPLE 12   **The Cost of a New Car**

Between 1970 and 1990, the average cost of a new car increased according to the model

$$C = 30.5t^2 + 4192, \qquad 0 \le t \le 20.$$

In this model, the cost is measured in dollars and the time t represents the year, with $t = 0$ corresponding to 1970. If the average cost of a new car continued to increase according to this model, when would the average cost reach $20,000? (See Figure 2.26.) (*Source:* Commerce Department, American Auto-datum)

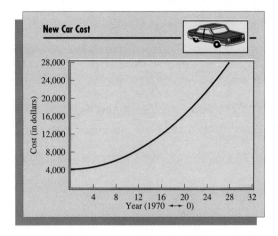

FIGURE 2.26

SOLUTION

To solve this problem, let the cost be $20,000 and solve the equation $20,000 = 30.5t^2 + 4192$ for t.

$30.5t^2 + 4192 = 20,000$	*Set cost equal to 20,000*
$30.5t^2 = 15,808$	*Subtract 4192 from both sides*
$t^2 \approx 518.295$	*Divide both sides by 30.5*
$t \approx \sqrt{518.295}$	*Extract positive square root*

Thus, the solution is $t \approx 23$. Because $t = 0$ represents 1970, you can conclude that the average cost of a new car will reach $20,000 in 1993. You could use a graphing utility to solve this problem. By finding the positive zero of $30.5t^2 + 4192 - 20,000 = 0$, you will find that $t \approx 23$. ·········

DISCUSSION PROBLEM
·····················

COMPARING ALGEBRAIC METHODS

In this section you studied three algebraic methods for solving a quadratic equation. Which of the three methods do you think works best for each of the following quadratic equations? Write a short paragraph explaining your choices.

(a) $x^2 - 2x - 3 = 0$ (b) $x^2 - 4x - 3 = 0$ (c) $x^2 - 3 = 0$

WARM-UP

The following warm-up exercises involve skills that were covered in earlier sections. You will use these skills in the exercise set for this section.

In Exercises 1–4, simplify the expression.

1. $\sqrt{\frac{7}{50}}$ **2.** $\sqrt{32}$

3. $\sqrt{7^2 + 3 \cdot 7^2}$ **4.** $\sqrt{\frac{1}{4} + \frac{3}{8}}$

In Exercises 5–10, factor the algebraic expression.

5. $3x^2 + 7x$ **6.** $4x^2 - 25$

7. $16 - (x - 11)^2$ **8.** $x^2 + 7x - 18$

9. $10x^2 + 13x - 3$ **10.** $6x^2 - 73x + 12$

SECTION 2.4 · EXERCISES

In Exercises 1–6, write the quadratic equation in standard quadratic form.

1. $2x^2 = 3 - 5x$ **2.** $10x^2 = 90$

3. $(x - 3)^2 = 2$ **4.** $12 - 3(x + 7)^2 = 0$

5. $\dfrac{3x^2 - 10}{5} = 12x$ **6.** $x(x + 5) = 2(x + 5)$

In Exercises 7–18, solve the quadratic equation by factoring. (In Exercises 7–16, check your solution graphically.)

7. $6x^2 + 3x = 0$ **8.** $9x^2 - 1 = 0$

9. $x^2 - 2x - 8 = 0$ **10.** $x^2 - 10x + 9 = 0$

11. $x^2 + 10x + 25 = 0$ **12.** $16x^2 + 56x + 49 = 0$

13. $3 + 5x - 2x^2 = 0$ **14.** $2x^2 = 19x + 33$

15. $2x^2 + 8x - 6 = x^2 + 4x + 6$

16. $x(8 - x) = 12$

17. $x^2 + 2ax + a^2 = 0$ **18.** $(x + a)^2 - b^2 = 0$

In Exercises 19–30, solve the equation by extracting square roots. List both the exact answer *and* the decimal answer rounded to two decimal places.

19. $x^2 = 16$ **20.** $x^2 = 144$

21. $x^2 = 7$ **22.** $x^2 = 27$

23. $3x^2 = 36$ **24.** $9x^2 = 25$

25. $(x - 12)^2 = 18$ **26.** $(x + 13)^2 = 21$

27. $(x + 2)^2 = 12$ **28.** $(x - 5)^2 = 20$

29. $(x - 7)^2 = (x + 3)^2$ **30.** $(x + 5)^2 = (x + 4)^2$

In Exercises 31–40, solve the quadratic equation by completing the square.

31. $x^2 - 2x = 0$ **32.** $x^2 + 4x = 0$

33. $x^2 + 4x - 32 = 0$ **34.** $x^2 - 2x - 3 = 0$

35. $x^2 + 6x + 2 = 0$ **36.** $x^2 + 8x + 14 = 0$

37. $x(9x - 18) = -3$

38. $10x^2 - 5x + 1 = x^2 + 7x + 15$

39. $8 + 4x - x^2 = 0$ **40.** $4x^2 - 4x - 99 = 0$

In Exercises 41–44, use a graphing utility to solve the equation.

41. $0.23x^2 - 0.78x - 1.15 = 0$

42. $-17.5x^2 + 5x + 7.5 = 0$

43. $\frac{1}{50}x(41 - x) + 55 = 0$ **44.** $x(x - 14) = 10$

In Exercises 45–64, solve the equation by any convenient method (including using a graphing utility).

45. $x^2 - 2x - 1 = 0$ **46.** $x^2 - 6x + 4 = 0$

47. $16x^2 - 9 = 0$ **48.** $11x^2 + 33x = 0$

49. $4x^2 - 12x + 9 = 0$ **50.** $x^2 - 14x + 49 = 0$

51. $(x + 3)^2 = 81$ **52.** $(x - 5)^2 = 8$

53. $50 + 5x = 3x^2$ **54.** $144 - 73x + 4x^2 = 0$

55. $12x = x^2 + 27$ **56.** $26x = 8x^2 + 15$

57. $x^2 - x - \frac{11}{4} = 0$ **58.** $x^2 + 3x - \frac{3}{4} = 0$

59. $50x^2 - 60x - 7 = 0$ **60.** $9x^2 + 12x + 3 = 0$

61. $(x + 3)^2 - 4 = 0$ **62.** $a^2x^2 - b^2 = 0$

63. $(x + 1)^2 = x^2$ **64.** $(x + 1)^2 = 4x^2$

In Exercises 65–70, complete the square for the quadratic portion of the algebraic expression.

65. $\dfrac{1}{x^2 + 2x + 5}$ **66.** $\dfrac{1}{x^2 - 4x + 13}$

67. $\dfrac{1}{x^2 - 4x - 12}$ **68.** $\dfrac{4}{4x^2 + 4x - 3}$

69. $\dfrac{1}{\sqrt{6x - x^2}}$ **70.** $\dfrac{1}{\sqrt{16 - 6x - x^2}}$

71. *Dimensions of a Building*   A one-story building is 14 feet longer than it is wide (see figure). It has 1632 square feet of floor space. Find the length and width of the building.

72. *Dimensions of a Triangular Sign*   The height of a triangular sign is equal to its base. The area of the sign is 10 square feet. Find the base and height of the sign.

In Exercises 73 and 74, use the position equation in Example 10 as the model for the problem.

73. *CN Tower*   The CN Tower in Toronto, Ontario is the world's tallest self-supporting structure. It is 1821 feet tall. An object is dropped from the top of the tower. How long will it take for it to hit the ground?

74. *Warfare*   A bomber flying at 32,000 feet over level terrain drops a 500-pound bomb.
(a) How long will it take for the bomb to strike the ground?
(b) If the plane is flying at 600 miles per hour, how far will the bomb travel horizontally during its descent?

75. *An Isosceles Right Triangle*   The hypotenuse of an isosceles right triangle is 5 centimeters long. How long are its sides? (An isosceles triangle has two sides of equal length.)

76. *An Equilateral Triangle*   An equilateral triangle has a height of 10 inches. How long are its sides? (*Hint:* Use the height of the triangle to partition the triangle into two congruent right triangles.)

77. *Depth of a Submarine*   The sonar of a Navy cruiser detects a submarine that is 3000 feet from the cruiser. The angle between the water level and the submarine is 45° (see figure). How deep is the submarine?

78. *Height of a Kite*   You have a spool of 100 feet of string that is attached to a kite. When the kite has pulled all the string from the spool you estimate that the angle of elevation to the kite is 45°. Approximate the height of the kite.

79. *Total Revenue*   The demand equation for a certain product is $p = 20 - 0.0002x$, where p is the price per unit and x is the number of units sold. The total revenue is given by

$$\text{Revenue} = xp = x(20 - 0.0002x).$$

(a) Use a graphing utility to graph the revenue function.
(b) Move the cursor along the graph to approximate the number of units that will yield the maximum revenue. What is the price per unit when the revenue is maximum?
(c) Determine the number of units and the corresponding prices that yield a revenue of $400,000. If you were the one setting the price of the product, which price would you select and why?

80. *Population of the U.S.* The population of the United States from 1800 to 1890 can be approximated by the model

Population $= 0.6942t^2 + 6.183,$

where the population is given in millions of people and the time t represents the year, with $t = 0$ corresponding to 1800, $t = 1$ corresponding to 1810, and so on. If this model had continued to be valid up through the present time, when would the population of the United States have reached 250,000,000? Judging from the given figure, would you say this model was a good representation of the population through 1890? Through 1990? (*Source:* U.S. Bureau of Census)

FIGURE FOR 80

81. If a and b are nonzero real numbers, determine the solutions of the equation $ax^2 + bx = 0$.

82. If a is a nonzero real number, determine the solutions of the equation $ax^2 - ax = 0$.

83. Find a quadratic equation with solutions $x = -4$ and $x = 6$. (There are many correct answers.)

2.5   THE QUADRATIC FORMULA

Development of the Quadratic Formula   /   The Discriminant   /   Solving a Quadratic Equation by the Quadratic Formula   /   Applications

Development of the Quadratic Formula

In Section 2.4 you learned to solve a nonfactorable quadratic equation by completing the square. This can be thought of as a "long way" of solving a quadratic equation. When you use completing the square to solve a quadratic equation, you must complete the square for *each* equation separately. The following development completes the square *once* in a general setting to obtain the **Quadratic Formula**—a shortcut for solving a quadratic equation.

$$ax^2 + bx + c = 0 \qquad \textit{Standard form, } a \neq 0$$

$$ax^2 + bx = -c \qquad \textit{Subtract c from both sides}$$

$$x^2 + \frac{b}{a}x = -\frac{c}{a} \qquad \textit{Divide both sides by a}$$

$$x^2 + \frac{b}{a}x + \left(\frac{b}{2a}\right)^2 = -\frac{c}{a} + \left(\frac{b}{2a}\right)^2 \qquad \textit{Complete the square}$$

$$\left(x + \frac{b}{2a}\right)^2 = \frac{b^2 - 4ac}{4a^2} \qquad \textit{Simplify}$$

$$x + \frac{b}{2a} = \pm\sqrt{\frac{b^2 - 4ac}{4a^2}} \qquad \textit{Extract square roots}$$

$$x = -\frac{b}{2a} \pm \frac{\sqrt{b^2 - 4ac}}{2|a|} \qquad \textit{Solutions}$$

Note that because $\pm 2|a|$ represents the same numbers as $\pm 2a$, you can omit the absolute value sign.

THE QUADRATIC FORMULA

The solutions of a quadratic equation in the standard form $ax^2 + bx + c = 0$, where $a \neq 0$, are given by the **Quadratic Formula**

$$x = \frac{-b \pm \sqrt{b^2 - 4ac}}{2a}.$$

The Quadratic Formula is one of the most important formulas in algebra, and you should learn the verbal statement of the rule: "Negative b plus or minus the square root of b squared minus $4ac$, *all* divided by $2a$."

The Discriminant

In the Quadratic Formula, the quantity under the radical sign, $b^2 - 4ac$, is the **discriminant** of the quadratic expression $ax^2 + bx + c$. It can be used to determine the nature of the solutions of a quadratic equation.

REMARK   If the discriminant of a quadratic equation is negative, as in case 3, then its square root is imaginary (not a real number) and the quadratic formula yields two complex solutions. You will study this case in Section 3.6.

1. If the discriminant $b^2 - 4ac$ is positive, then the quadratic equation has *two* different real solutions.
2. If the discriminant $b^2 - 4ac$ is zero, then the quadratic equation has *one* repeated real solution.
3. If the discriminant $b^2 - 4ac$ is negative, then the quadratic equation has *no* real solution.

EXAMPLE 1   Using the Discriminant

A. For the equation $5x^2 - 8x = 0$, you have $a = 5$, $b = -8$, and $c = 0$. Because the discriminant, $b^2 - 4ac = 64 - 4(5)(0) = 64$, is positive, you can conclude that the equation has two different real solutions.

B. For the equation $4x^2 - 20x + 25 = 0$, you have $a = 4$, $b = -20$, and $c = 25$. Because the discriminant, $b^2 - 4ac = 400 - 4(4)(25) = 0$, is zero, you can conclude that there is *one* repeated real solution.

C. For the equation $13x^2 + 7x + 1 = 0$, you have $a = 13$, $b = 7$, and $c = 1$. Because the discriminant, $b^2 - 4ac = 49 - 4(13)(1) = -3$, is negative, you can conclude that the equation has no real solution.

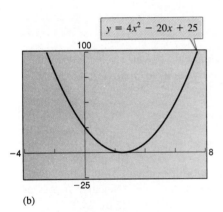

(a)

The graphs of the functions corresponding to the equations given in Example 1 are shown in Figure 2.27. From these three graphs, you can make the following graphical interpretations of the discriminant.

1. If the discriminant is positive, then the graph of $y = ax^2 + bx + c$ crosses the x-axis twice, and the graph has two x-intercepts.
2. If the discriminant is zero, then the graph of $y = ax^2 + bx + c$ touches the x-axis once, and the graph has one x-intercept.
3. If the discriminant is negative, then the graph of $y = ax^2 + bx + c$ lies entirely above or entirely below the x-axis, and the graph has no x-intercept.

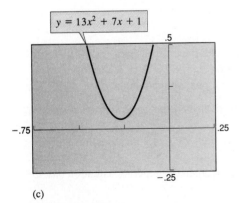

(b)

Solving a Quadratic Equation by the Quadratic Formula

When using the Quadratic Formula, remember that *before* the formula can be applied, you must first write the quadratic equation in standard form.

EXAMPLE 2   Using the Quadratic Formula: Two Distinct Solutions

$x^2 + 3x = 9$	*Original equation*
$x^2 + 3x - 9 = 0$	*Standard form with $a = 1$, $b = 3$, $c = -9$*
$x = \dfrac{-b \pm \sqrt{b^2 - 4ac}}{2a}$	*Quadratic Formula*
$x = \dfrac{-3 \pm \sqrt{(3)^2 - 4(1)(-9)}}{2(1)}$	*Substitute*
$x = \dfrac{-3 \pm \sqrt{45}}{2}$	
$x = \dfrac{-3 \pm 3\sqrt{5}}{2}$	
$x \approx 1.85$ or -4.85	*Solutions*

(c)

FIGURE 2.27

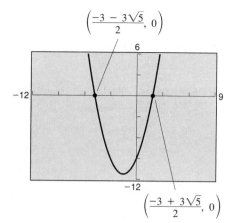

$$\left(\frac{-3 - 3\sqrt{5}}{2}, 0\right)$$

$$\left(\frac{-3 + 3\sqrt{5}}{2}, 0\right)$$

FIGURE 2.28

Therefore, the equation has two solutions: $x \approx 1.85$ and $x \approx -4.85$. Check these two solutions in the original equation. The graph of $y = x^2 + 3x - 9$, as shown in Figure 2.28, reinforces the solutions graphically.   ·········

EXAMPLE 3   **Using the Quadratic Formula: One Repeated Solution**
·············

Solve $8x^2 - 24x + 18 = 0$.

SOLUTION

Note that this equation has a common factor of 2. To simplify things, first divide both sides of the equation by 2.

$8x^2 - 24x + 18 = 0$	*Common factor of 2*
$4x^2 - 12x + 9 = 0$	*Standard form with $a = 4$, $b = -12$, $c = 9$*
$x = \dfrac{-b \pm \sqrt{b^2 - 4ac}}{2a}$	*Quadratic Formula*
$x = \dfrac{-(-12) \pm \sqrt{(-12)^2 - 4(4)(9)}}{2(4)}$	*Substitute*
$x = \dfrac{12 \pm \sqrt{0}}{8} = \dfrac{3}{2}$	*Repeated solution*

This quadratic equation has only one solution: $\frac{3}{2}$. Check this solution in the original equation. The graph of $y = 8x^2 - 24x + 18$ is shown in Figure 2.29.   ·········

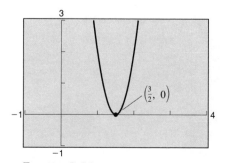

$\left(\frac{3}{2}, 0\right)$

FIGURE 2.29

Technology Note _____

Try programming the Quadratic Formula into a programmable calculator. For instance, the following program is for the TI-81.

```
:Disp "ENTER,A"
:Input A
:Disp "ENTER,B"
:Input B
:Disp "ENTER,C"
:Input C
:B²-4AC→D
:If D<0
:Goto 1
:((-B-√D)/(2A))→S
:Disp S
:((-B-√D)/(2A))→S
:Disp S
:End
:Lbl 1
:Disp "NO REAL SOLUTION"
:End
```

To use this program, you must first write the equation in standard form. Then, enter the values of *a*, *b*, and *c*. After the final value has been entered, the program will display either two solutions *or* the words "No Real Solution."

The discriminant in Example 3 is a perfect square (zero in this case), and you could have factored to conclude that the solution is $x = \frac{3}{2}$. Because factoring is quicker than applying the Quadratic Formula, try factoring first.

EXAMPLE 4 **Using a Calculator to Evaluate the Quadratic Formula**

$$16.3x^2 - 197.6x + 7.042 = 0 \qquad \textit{Original equation}$$

$$x = \frac{-b \pm \sqrt{b^2 - 4ac}}{2a}$$

$$x = \frac{-(-197.6) \pm \sqrt{(-197.6)^2 - 4(16.3)(7.042)}}{2(16.3)}$$

By evaluating this expression or by using the programmable calculator program listed in the Technology Note, you can find the two solutions to be $x \approx 12.087$ and $x \approx 0.036$.

Applications

EXAMPLE 5 **School Expenditures**

From 1975 to 1989, the total school expenditures (elementary through university) in the United States closely followed the quadratic model

$$\text{Expenditures} = 459.5t^2 + 9170.3t + 107,298, \qquad 0 \le t \le 14,$$

where the expenditures are measured in millions of dollars and the time *t* represents the year, with $t = 0$ corresponding to 1975. These expenses are shown graphically in Figure 2.30. Assuming that this model continues to be valid, when will the total school expenditures reach $400,000,000,000 per year? (*Source:* U.S. National Center for Education Statistics)

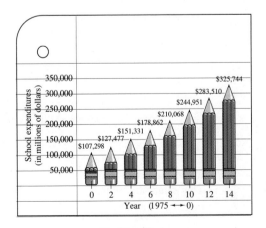

School Expenditures

FIGURE 2.30

SOLUTION

$$459.5t^2 + 9170.3t + 107,298 = 400,000$$

$$459.5t^2 + 9170.3t - 292,702 = 0$$

$$t = \frac{-9170.3 \pm \sqrt{9170.3^2 - 4(459.5)(-292,702)}}{2(459.5)}$$

$$t \approx 17 \quad \text{or} \quad -37$$

Choosing the positive solution, you find that $t \approx 17$. Because $t = 0$ corresponds to 1975, it follows that $t = 17$ must correspond to 1992. Thus, from the model you can conclude that the total school expenditures will have reached $400,000,000,000 by 1992.

The position equation given in Section 2.4, $s = -16t^2 + v_0t + s_0$, gives the height of a free-falling object on the surface of the earth. Because of the difference in gravitational force, this equation is different on other planets (and their moons). For instance, on the surface of the moon, the position equation is

$$s = -2.7t^2 + v_0t + s_0.$$

In this equation, s represents the height of the object (in feet), v_0 represents the original velocity of the object (in feet per second), s_0 represents the original height of the object (in feet), and t represents the time (in seconds).

EXAMPLE 6 Throwing an Object on the Moon

An astronaut standing on the surface of the moon throws a rock upward, as shown in Figure 2.31. The height of the rock is given by

$$s = -2.7t^2 + 27t + 6, \qquad 0 \le t.$$

How long will it take for the rock to hit the surface of the moon? If the rock were thrown with the same initial velocity on the surface of the earth, how long would it remain in the air?

SOLUTION

Because s gives the height of the rock at any time t, you can find the time that the rock hits the surface of the moon by setting s equal to zero and solving for t.

$$-2.7t^2 + 27t + 6 = 0$$

$$t = \frac{-27 \pm \sqrt{27^2 - 4(-2.7)(6)}}{2(-2.7)}$$

$$\approx -0.2 \quad \text{or} \quad 10.2 \text{ seconds}$$

FIGURE 2.31

In this problem it makes no sense to choose a negative value for t. Thus, you choose the positive solution. To find the time the rock would have remained in the air on the earth, use the position equation

$$s = -16t^2 + 27t + 6.$$

After setting s equal to zero and solving for t, you can find that the rock would have remained in the air for only 1.9 seconds. The reason that the rock remains in the air so much longer on the moon is that the moon's gravitational force is much weaker than the earth's.

DISCUSSION PROBLEM

A REVENUE FUNCTION

From your experience as a consumer, you know that the demand for a product tends to decrease as the price increases. This relationship can be represented by a **demand equation** such as

$$p = 50 - 0.0001x,$$

where p is the price of the item and x is the total demand in number of units. For instance, if the price of an item is $50, then $x = 0$, which means that no one is willing to pay that much for the item. On the other hand, if the price is $25, then $x = 250{,}000$, which means that a quarter of a million units of the product could be sold. The total revenue obtained by selling x units of this product is given by the following **revenue equation.**

$$R = (\text{number of units})(\text{price per unit})$$
$$= xp$$
$$= x(50 - 0.0001x)$$

From this model, would it be possible to obtain a revenue of $50,000,000? Would it be possible to obtain a revenue of $70,000,000? Are these questions better answered algebraically or graphically? Explain your reasoning.

WARM-UP

The following warm-up exercises involve skills that were covered in earlier sections. You will use these skills in the exercise set for this section.

In Exercises 1–4, simplify the expression.

1. $\sqrt{9 - 4(3)(-12)}$ **2.** $\sqrt{36 - 4(2)(3)}$

3. $\sqrt{12^2 - 4(3)(4)}$ **4.** $\sqrt{15^2 + 4(9)(12)}$

In Exercises 5–10, solve the quadratic equation by factoring.

5. $x^2 - x - 2 = 0$ **6.** $2x^2 + 3x - 9 = 0$

7. $x^2 - 4x = 5$ **8.** $2x^2 + 13x = 7$

9. $x^2 = 5x - 6$ **10.** $x(x - 3) = 4$

SECTION 2.5 · EXERCISES

In Exercises 1–6, use the discriminant to determine the number of real solutions of the quadratic equation.

1. $4x^2 - 4x + 1 = 0$ **2.** $2x^2 - x - 1 = 0$

3. $2x^2 - 5x + 5 = 0$ **4.** $3x^2 - 6x + 3 = 0$

5. $\frac{1}{5}x^2 + \frac{6}{5}x - 8 = 0$ **6.** $\frac{1}{3}x^2 - 5x + 25 = 0$

In Exercises 7–28, use the Quadratic Formula to solve the equation.

7. $2x^2 + x - 1 = 0$ **8.** $2x^2 - x - 1 = 0$

9. $16x^2 + 8x - 3 = 0$ **10.** $25x^2 - 20x + 3 = 0$

11. $2 + 2x - x^2 = 0$ **12.** $x^2 - 10x + 22 = 0$

13. $x^2 + 14x + 44 = 0$ **14.** $6x = 4 - x^2$

15. $x^2 + 8x - 4 = 0$ **16.** $4x^2 - 4x - 4 = 0$

17. $12x - 9x^2 = -3$ **18.** $16x^2 + 22 = 40x$

19. $36x^2 + 24x - 7 = 0$ **20.** $3x + x^2 - 1 = 0$

21. $4x^2 + 4x = 7$ **22.** $16x^2 - 40x + 5 = 0$

23. $28x - 49x^2 = 4$ **24.** $9x^2 + 24x + 16 = 0$

25. $25h^2 + 80h + 61 = 0$ **26.** $8t = 5 + 2t^2$

27. $(y - 5)^2 = 2y$ **28.** $(z + 6)^2 = -2z$

In Exercises 29–32, use a graphing utility to approximate (accurate to three decimal places) the solutions of the equation.

29. $5.1x^2 - 1.7x - 3.2 = 0$

30. $-0.005x^2 + 0.101x - 0.193 = 0$

31. $422x^2 - 506x - 347 = 0$

32. $2x^2 - 2.50x - 0.42 = 0$

In Exercises 33–42, solve the equation by any convenient method (including a graphing utility).

33. $3x + 4 = 2x - 7$ **34.** $x^2 - 2x + 5 = x^2 - 5$

35. $4x^2 - 15 = 25$ **36.** $4x^2 + 2x + 4 = 2x + 8$

37. $x^2 + 3x + 1 = 0$ **38.** $x^2 + 3x - 4 = 0$

39. $(x - 1)^2 = 9$ **40.** $2x^2 - 4x - 6 = 0$

41. $100x^2 - 400 = 0$ **42.** $2x^2 + 4x - 9 = 2(x - 1)^2$

Number Problems In Exercises 43–46, solve the number problem *and* make up an applied problem that could be represented by this verbal model. (For example, an applied problem that could be represented by Exercise 43 is "The perimeter of a one-story house is 200 feet and that house has 2500 square feet of floor space. What are the length and width of the house?")

43. Find two numbers whose sum is 100 and whose product is 2500.

44. Find two consecutive positive integers whose product is 72.

45. Find two consecutive positive integers such that the sum of their squares is 113.

46. Find two consecutive even integers whose product is 440.

In Exercises 47–50, use the cost equation to find the number of units x that a manufacturer can produce for the given cost C. (Round your answer to the nearest positive integer.)

47. $C = 0.125x^2 + 20x + 500$ $C = \$14,000$

48. $C = 0.5x^2 + 15x + 5000$ $C = \$11,500$

49. $C = 800 + 0.04x + 0.002x^2$ $C = \$1680$

50. $C = 800 - 10x + \dfrac{x^2}{4}$ $C = \$896$

51. *Seating Capacity* A rectangular classroom seats 72 students. If the seats were rearranged with three more seats in each row, the classroom would have two fewer rows. Find the original number of seats in each row.

52. *Lawn Mowing* Two people must mow a rectangular lawn 100 feet by 200 feet. Each wants to mow no more than half of the lawn. The first starts by mowing around the outside of the lawn. How wide a strip must the person mow on each of the four sides? If the mower has a 24-inch cut, approximate the required number of trips around the lawn.

53. *Lawn Mowing* Two people must mow a rectangular lawn 100 feet by 200 feet. The first person agrees to mow three-fourths of the lawn and starts by mowing around the outside. How wide a strip must the person mow on each of the four sides? If the mower has a 24-inch cut, approximate the required number of trips around the lawn.

54. *Dimensions of a Corral* A rancher has 200 feet of fencing to enclose two adjacent rectangular corrals (see figure). Find the dimensions such that the enclosed area will be 1400 square feet.

$$4x + 3y = 200$$

FIGURE FOR 54

55. *Dimensions of a Box*   An open box with a square base is to be constructed from 108 square inches of material (see figure). What should be the dimensions of the base if the height of the box is to be 3 inches? (*Hint:* The surface area is given by $S = x^2 + 4xh$.)

Open Box   **FIGURE FOR 55**

56. *Dimensions of a Box*   An open box is to be made from a square piece of material by cutting 2-inch squares from each corner and turning up the sides (see figure). The volume of the finished box is to be 200 cubic inches. Find the size of the original piece of material.

FIGURE FOR 56

57. *Recreation Spending*   The total number of dollars spent on recreation in the United States from 1980 to 1988 can be approximated by the model

$$S = 116{,}289 + 9506.7t + 841.45t^2,$$

where the spending is measured in millions of dollars and the time t represents the year, with $t = 0$ corresponding to 1980.

(a) Use a graphing utility to graph the recreational spending function.

(b) Move the cursor along the graph to predict the year when total recreational spending will reach $300,000,000,000. (*Source:* U.S. Bureau of Economic Analysis)

58. *Oxygen Consumption*   The metabolic rate of ectothermic organisms increases with increasing temperature within a certain range. The figure shows experimental data for oxygen consumption (microliters per gram per hour) of a beetle

for certain temperatures. This data can be approximated by the model

$$C = 0.45x^2 - 1.65x + 50.75, \qquad 10 \le x \le 25,$$

where x is the air temperature in degrees Celsius.

(a) Use a graphing utility to graph the consumption function over the specified domain.

(b) Move the cursor along the graph to approximate the air temperature if the oxygen consumption is 150 microliters per gram per hour.

(c) If the temperature is increased from 10 to 20 degrees, the oxygen consumption is increased by approximately what factor?

FIGURE FOR 58

59. *Flying Speed*   Two planes leave simultaneously from the same airport, one flying due east and the other due south (see figure). The eastbound plane is flying 50 miles per hour faster than the southbound plane. After 3 hours the planes are 2440 miles apart. Find the speed of each plane.

FIGURE FOR 59

60. *Flying Distance*   A small commuter airline flies to three cities whose locations form the vertices of a right triangle (see figure). The total flight distance (from City A to City B to City C and back to City A) is 1400 miles. It is 600 miles between the two cities that are farthest apart. Find the other two distances between cities.

City B

600 miles

City C   City A

FIGURE FOR 60

61. *Distance from the Dock*   A windlass is used to tow a boat to the dock. The rope is attached to the boat at a point 15 feet below the level of the windlass (see figure). Find the distance from the boat to the dock when 75 feet of rope have been let out.

x

75 ft   15 ft

FIGURE FOR 61

62. *Total Revenue*   The demand equation for a certain product is $p = 60 - 0.0004x$, where p is the price per unit and x is the number of units sold. The total revenue for selling x units is given by

$$\text{Revenue} = xp = x(60 - 0.0004x).$$

(a) Use a graphing utility to graph the revenue function.

(b) Move the cursor along the graph to approximate the number of units that will yield the maximum revenue. What is the price per unit when the revenue is maximum?

(c) Determine the number of units and the corresponding prices that yield a revenue of $1,500,000. If you were the one setting the price of the product, which price would you select and why?

63. *Fuel Efficiency*   The distance a car can travel on one tank of fuel is approximated by the model

$$\text{Distance} = -0.024s^2 + 1.455s + 431.5, \quad 0 < s \le 75,$$

where s is the average speed of the car.

(a) Use a graphing utility to graph the distance function over the specified domain.

(b) Move the cursor along the graph to determine the greatest distance that can be traveled on a tank of fuel. How long will the trip take?

(c) Determine the greatest distance that can be traveled in this car in 8 hours with no refueling. How fast should the car be driven? (*Hint:* The distance traveled in 8 hours is $8s$. Graph this expression on the same viewing rectangle as the graph of part (a) and approximate the point of intersection.)

2.6   OTHER TYPES OF EQUATIONS
Solving Polynomial Equations   /   Solving Equations Involving Radicals   /
Solving Equations Involving Fractions or Absolute Values   /   Applications

Solving Polynomial Equations

This section extends the techniques for solving equations to include special types of nonlinear and nonquadratic equations. This illustrates a basic strategy of algebra—to rewrite complex problems into simpler forms that lend themselves to previously learned methods of solution.

Up to now, you have only two basic *algebraic* methods for solving nonlinear equations—factoring and the Quadratic Formula. One goal of this section is to teach you to rewrite nonlinear equations in factorable or quadratic form. Another is to show you how to extend the use of a *graphing utility* to solve more complex equations. In this section, we list only real solutions. Complex solutions will be discussed in detail in Section 3.5.

EXAMPLE 1   Solving a Polynomial Equation by Factoring

Solve $3x^4 = 48x^2$.

SOLUTION

The basic approach is to write the equation in standard form (with zero on the right side), factor the left side, and then set each factor equal to zero.

$$3x^4 = 48x^2 \qquad \textit{Original equation}$$
$$3x^4 - 48x^2 = 0 \qquad \textit{Collect terms on left side}$$
$$(3x^2)(x^2 - 16) = 0 \qquad \textit{Common monomial factor}$$
$$3(x^2)(x + 4)(x - 4) = 0 \qquad \textit{Difference of two squares}$$
$$x^2 = 0 \;\longrightarrow\; x = 0 \qquad \textit{Set 1st factor equal to 0}$$
$$x + 4 = 0 \;\longrightarrow\; x = -4 \qquad \textit{Set 2nd factor equal to 0}$$
$$x - 4 = 0 \;\longrightarrow\; x = 4 \qquad \textit{Set 3rd factor equal to 0}$$

The equation has three solutions: 0, -4, and 4. Check these solutions in the original equation. The graph of $y = 3x^4 - 48x^2$ is shown in Figure 2.32.

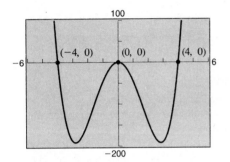

FIGURE 2.32

REMARK   A mistake that is made in factoring equations such as that given in Example 1 is dividing both sides of the equation by the variable factor x^2. This loses the solution $x = 0$. When using factoring to solve an equation, be sure to set *each* factor equal to zero.

EXAMPLE 2   Solving a Polynomial Equation by Factoring

Solve $x^3 - 3x^2 - 3x + 9 = 0$.

SOLUTION

Use factoring by grouping to solve this equation.

$$x^3 - 3x^2 - 3x + 9 = 0 \qquad \textit{Original equation}$$
$$x^2(x - 3) - 3(x - 3) = 0 \qquad \textit{Group terms}$$
$$(x - 3)(x^2 - 3) = 0 \qquad \textit{Factor by grouping}$$
$$x - 3 = 0 \;\longrightarrow\; x = 3 \qquad \textit{Set 1st factor equal to 0}$$
$$x^2 - 3 = 0 \;\longrightarrow\; x = \pm\sqrt{3} \qquad \textit{Set 2nd factor equal to 0}$$

Thus, the equation has three solutions: 3, $\sqrt{3}$, and $-\sqrt{3}$. Check these solutions in the original equation. The graph of $y = x^3 - 3x^2 - 3x + 9$, shown in Figure 2.33, verifies the algebraic solution.

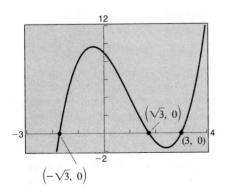

FIGURE 2.33

Occasionally, mathematical models involve equations that are of **quadratic type.** In general, an equation is of quadratic type if it can be written in the form $au^2 + bu + c = 0$, where $a \neq 0$ and u is an algebraic expression. For instance, the equation

$$x^4 - 3x^2 + 2 = 0 \quad \longrightarrow \quad \overset{u^2}{\overbrace{(x^2)^2}} - 3\overset{u}{\overbrace{(x^2)}} + 2 = 0$$

is of quadratic type with $u = x^2$. Once an equation is in quadratic form, you can solve it by factoring or by the Quadratic Formula.

EXAMPLE 3   **Solving an Equation of Quadratic Type**

$$x^4 - 3x^2 + 2 = 0 \qquad \textit{Original equation}$$

$$\overset{u^2}{\overbrace{(x^2)^2}} - 3\overset{u}{\overbrace{x^2}} + 2 = 0 \qquad \textit{Quadratic form}$$

$$(x^2 - 1)(x^2 - 2) = 0 \qquad \textit{Partially factor}$$

$$(x + 1)(x - 1)(x^2 - 2) = 0 \qquad \textit{Completely factor}$$

$$x + 1 = 0 \quad \longrightarrow \quad x = -1 \qquad \textit{Set 1st factor equal to 0}$$

$$x - 1 = 0 \quad \longrightarrow \quad x = 1 \qquad \textit{Set 2nd factor equal to 0}$$

$$x^2 - 2 = 0 \quad \longrightarrow \quad x = \pm\sqrt{2} \qquad \textit{Set 3rd factor equal to 0}$$

The equation has four solutions: -1, 1, $\sqrt{2}$, and $-\sqrt{2}$. Check these solutions in the original equation. The graph of $y = x^4 - 3x^2 + 2$, shown in Figure 2.34, verifies the algebraic solution. Note that the function is even and that its graph is symmetrical about the y-axis.

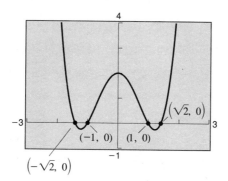

FIGURE 2.34

Solving Equations Involving Radicals

The steps involved in solving the remaining equations in this section will often introduce *extraneous solutions,* as discussed in Section 2.1. Operations such as squaring both sides of an equation, raising both sides of an equation to a rational power, and multiplying both sides by a variable quantity all have this potential danger. Thus, when you use any of these operations, a check of *each tentative solution* is crucial. A graphing utility can often aid in this verification process.

EXAMPLE 4   An Equation Involving a Rational Exponent

Solve $4x^{3/2} - 8 = 0$. Round your answer to three decimal places.

SOLUTION

The essential technique used to solve this equation is to raise both sides to the $\frac{2}{3}$ power (because $\frac{2}{3}$ is the *reciprocal* of $\frac{3}{2}$). Before doing this, however, you must isolate the expression $x^{3/2}$.

$4x^{3/2} - 8 = 0$	*Original equation*
$4x^{3/2} = 8$	*Add 8 to both sides*
$x^{3/2} = 2$	*Divide both sides by 4*
$x = 2^{2/3}$	*Raise both sides to $\frac{2}{3}$ power*
$x \approx 1.587$	*Round to three decimal places*

CHECK

$4x^{3/2} - 8 = 0$	*Original equation*
$4(2^{2/3})^{3/2} \stackrel{?}{=} 8$	*Replace x by $2^{2/3}$*
$4(2) \stackrel{?}{=} 8$	*Property of exponents*
$8 = 8$	*Solution checks*

Thus, the equation has one solution: $2^{2/3} \approx 1.587$. The graph of $y = 4x^{3/2} - 8$, shown in Figure 2.35, verifies our algebraic solution. Note that the domain of the function is all nonnegative real numbers ($x^{3/2}$ is defined only for $x \geq 0$) and the range is all reals greater than or equal to -8.

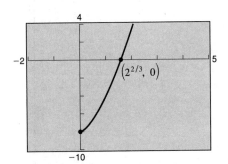

FIGURE 2.35

EXAMPLE 5   An Equation Involving a Radical

Solve $\sqrt{2x + 7} - x = 2$.

SOLUTION

The graph of $y = \sqrt{2x + 7} - x - 2$ is shown in Figure 2.36(a). Notice that the domain is $x \geq -\frac{7}{2}$, because the expression under the radical cannot be negative. Furthermore, there seems to be one solution near $x = 1$. Using the zoom and trace features shown in Figure 2.36(b), you can verify that $x = 1$ is

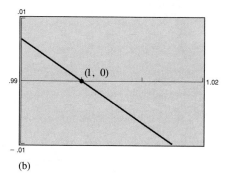

(a)

$y = \sqrt{2x + 7} - x - 2$

(b)

FIGURE 2.36

the only solution. The equation can also be solved algebraically. To do this, first isolate the radical. Then, eliminate the square root by squaring both sides of the equation.

$\sqrt{2x + 7} - x = 2$	*Original equation*
$\sqrt{2x + 7} = x + 2$	*Add x to both sides*
$2x + 7 = x^2 + 4x + 4$	*Square both sides*
$0 = x^2 + 2x - 3$	*Standard form*
$0 = (x + 3)(x - 1)$	*Factor*
$x + 3 = 0 \longrightarrow x = -3$	*Set 1st factor equal to 0*
$x - 1 = 0 \longrightarrow x = 1$	*Set 2nd factor equal to 0*

CHECK

$\sqrt{2(-3) + 7} + 3 = \sqrt{1} + 3 \neq 2$	*−3 does not check*
$\sqrt{2(1) + 7} - 1 = \sqrt{9} - 1 = 2$	*1 checks*

To algebraically solve equations with two or more radicals, it may be necessary to repeat the "isolate a radical and square both sides" routine demonstrated in the preceding example. The benefits of a graphing utility are obvious in such cases.

EXAMPLE 6 An Equation Involving Two Radicals

$\sqrt{2x + 6} - \sqrt{x + 4} = 1$	*Original equation*
$\sqrt{2x + 6} = 1 + \sqrt{x + 4}$	*Isolate radical*
$2x + 6 = 1 + 2\sqrt{x + 4} + (x + 4)$	*Square both sides*
$x + 1 = 2\sqrt{x + 4}$	*Isolate radical*
$x^2 + 2x + 1 = 4(x + 4)$	*Square both sides*
$x^2 - 2x - 15 = 0$	*Standard form*
$(x - 5)(x + 3) = 0$	*Factor*
$x - 5 = 0 \longrightarrow x = 5$	*Set 1st factor equal to 0*
$x + 3 = 0 \longrightarrow x = -3$	*Set 2nd factor equal to 0*

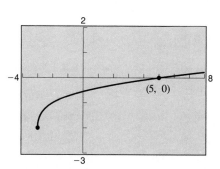

FIGURE 2.37

From Figure 2.37, you can conclude that $x = 5$ is the only solution.

EXAMPLE 7   An Equation Involving a Rational Exponent

Solve $(x^2 - x - 4)^{3/4} = 8$.

SOLUTION

Because the left side of the equation is raised to the $\frac{3}{4}$ power, you should begin by raising both sides to the *reciprocal* power, $\frac{4}{3}$. Note that $8^{4/3} = (\sqrt[3]{8})^4 = 2^4 = 16$.

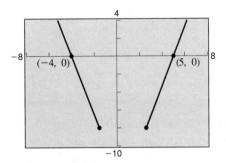

$$(x^2 - x - 4)^{3/4} = 8 \qquad \text{\textit{Original equation}}$$
$$(x^2 - x - 4) = (8)^{4/3} \qquad \text{\textit{Raise both sides to} } \tfrac{4}{3} \text{ \textit{power}}$$
$$x^2 - x - 4 = 16 \qquad \text{\textit{Simplify}}$$
$$x^2 - x - 20 = 0 \qquad \text{\textit{Standard form}}$$
$$(x - 5)(x + 4) = 0 \qquad \text{\textit{Factor}}$$
$$x - 5 = 0 \longrightarrow x = 5 \qquad \text{\textit{Set 1st factor equal to 0}}$$
$$x + 4 = 0 \longrightarrow x = -4 \qquad \text{\textit{Set 2nd factor equal to 0}}$$

The equation has two solutions: 5 and -4. Check these solutions in the original equation. The graph of $y = (x^2 - x - 4)^{3/4} - 8$ is shown in Figure 2.38.

FIGURE 2.38

Solving Equations Involving Fractions or Absolute Values

To algebraically solve an equation involving fractions, multiply both sides of the equation by the least common denominator of each term in the equation. This procedure will "clear an equation of fractions." For instance, in the equation

$$\frac{2}{x^2 + 1} + \frac{1}{x} = \frac{2}{x},$$

you can multiply both sides of the equation by $x(x^2 + 1)$ to obtain

$$(2x) + (x^2 + 1) = 2(x^2 + 1).$$

Try solving this equation. You should obtain one solution: $x = 1$.

EXAMPLE 8   An Equation Involving Fractions

Solve $\dfrac{2}{x} = \dfrac{3}{x - 2} - 1$.

SOLUTION

For this equation, the least common denominator of the three terms is $x(x - 2)$, so you can begin by multiplying each term in the equation by this expression.

$$\frac{2}{x} = \frac{3}{x - 2} - 1$$

$$x(x - 2)\frac{2}{x} = x(x - 2)\frac{3}{x - 2} - x(x - 2)(1)$$

$$2(x - 2) = 3x - x(x - 2), \quad x \neq 0, 2$$

$$2x - 4 = -x^2 + 5x$$

$$x^2 - 3x - 4 = 0$$

$$(x - 4)(x + 1) = 0$$

$$x - 4 = 0 \longrightarrow x = 4$$

$$x + 1 = 0 \longrightarrow x = -1$$

The equation has two solutions: 4 and -1. Check these solutions in the original equation. Use a graphing utility to graph

$$y = \frac{2}{x} - \frac{3}{x - 2} + 1$$

to verify these solutions.

REMARK   Graphs of functions involving variable denominators can be tricky because of the way graphing utilities skip over points where the denominator is zero. You will study graphs of this type of function in Sections 4.1 and 4.2.

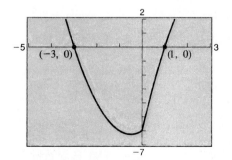

FIGURE 2.39

EXAMPLE 9   An Equation Involving Absolute Value

Solve $|x^2 - 3x| = -4x + 6$.

SOLUTION

From Figure 2.39, you can estimate the solutions to be -3 and 1. These can be verified by substitution into the equation. To *algebraically* solve an equation involving an absolute value, you must consider the fact that the expression inside the absolute value can be positive or negative. This consideration results in *two* separate equations, each of which must be solved.

First Equation

$$x^2 - 3x = -4x + 6 \qquad \text{\textit{Use positive expression}}$$
$$x^2 + x - 6 = 0 \qquad \text{\textit{Standard form}}$$
$$(x + 3)(x - 2) = 0 \qquad \text{\textit{Factor}}$$
$$x + 3 = 0 \;\longrightarrow\; x = -3 \qquad \text{\textit{Set 1st factor equal to 0}}$$
$$x - 2 = 0 \;\longrightarrow\; x = 2 \qquad \text{\textit{Set 2nd factor equal to 0}}$$

Second Equation

$$-(x^2 - 3x) = -4x + 6 \qquad \text{\textit{Use negative expression}}$$
$$x^2 - 7x + 6 = 0 \qquad \text{\textit{Standard form}}$$
$$(x - 1)(x - 6) = 0 \qquad \text{\textit{Factor}}$$
$$x - 1 = 0 \;\longrightarrow\; x = 1 \qquad \text{\textit{Set 1st factor equal to 0}}$$
$$x - 6 = 0 \;\longrightarrow\; x = 6 \qquad \text{\textit{Set 2nd factor equal to 0}}$$

CHECK

$$\left|(-3)^2 - 3(-3)\right| = -4(-3) + 6 \qquad \text{\textit{-3 checks}}$$
$$\left|2^2 - 3(2)\right| \neq -4(2) + 6 \qquad \text{\textit{2 does not check}}$$
$$\left|1^2 - 3(1)\right| = -4(1) + 6 \qquad \text{\textit{1 checks}}$$
$$\left|6^2 - 3(6)\right| \neq -4(6) + 6 \qquad \text{\textit{6 does not check}}$$

The equation has only two solutions: -3 and 1, just as you obtained by graphing.

Applications

It would be impossible to categorize the many different types of applications that involve nonlinear and nonquadratic models. However, from the few examples and exercises given, we hope that you will gain some appreciation for the variety of applications that can occur.

EXAMPLE 10   Reduced Rates

A ski club chartered a bus for a ski trip at a cost of $480. In an attempt to lower the bus fare per skier, the club invited nonmembers to go along. After five nonmembers joined the trip, the fare per skier decreased by $4.80. How many club members are going on the trip?

SOLUTION

VERBAL
MODEL   Cost per skier · Number of skiers = Cost of trip

LABELS   Cost of trip = 480   *(dollars per person)*

               Number of members = x   *(people)*

               Number of skiers = x + 5   *(people)*

               Original cost per member = $\dfrac{480}{x}$ *(dollars)*

               Cost per skier = $\dfrac{480}{x}$ − 4.80   *(dollars)*

EQUATION $\left(\dfrac{480}{x} - 4.80 \right)(x + 5) = 480$

Using a graphing utility, and the *zoom-out* feature, you can find that, to the nearest positive integer, $x = 20$. Check this result in the original statement of the problem.

EXAMPLE 11   Market Research

The marketing department at a publishing firm is asked to determine the price of a book. The department determines that the demand for the book depends upon the price of the book according to the formula

$$p = 40 - \sqrt{0.0001x + 1},$$

where p is the price per book in dollars and x is the number of books sold at the given price. For instance, in Figure 2.40 note that if the price is $39, then (according to the model) no one would be willing to buy the book. On the other hand, if the price were $17.60, then 5 million copies could be sold. If the publisher sets the price at $12.95, how many copies could be sold?

SOLUTION

$$p = 40 - \sqrt{0.0001x + 1} \qquad \text{\textit{Original model}}$$
$$12.95 = 40 - \sqrt{0.0001x + 1} \qquad \text{\textit{Set price at 12.95}}$$
$$\sqrt{0.0001x + 1} = 27.05 \qquad \text{\textit{Isolate radical}}$$
$$0.0001x + 1 = 731.7025 \qquad \text{\textit{Square both sides}}$$
$$0.0001x = 730.7025 \qquad \text{\textit{Subtract 1 from both sides}}$$
$$x = 7,307,025 \qquad \text{\textit{Divide both sides by 0.0001}}$$

With a price of $12.95, the publisher could expect to sell about 7.3 million copies.

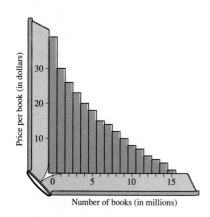

FIGURE 2.40

DISCUSSION PROBLEM

MARKET ANALYSIS REVISITED

In Example 11, suppose the cost of producing the book was $450,000 plus $9.50 per book. Then the **cost equation** for the book is

$$C = 9.5x + 450,000,$$

where C is measured in dollars and x represents the number of books produced. From Example 11, the total revenue is

$$R = xp.$$

How much profit (Profit $= R - C$) would the company make if the price of the book were set at $12.95?

WARM-UP

The following warm-up exercises involve skills that were covered in earlier sections. You will use these skills in the exercise set for this section.

In Exercises 1–10, find the real solution(s) of the equation.

1. $x^2 - 22x + 121 = 0$
2. $x(x - 20) + 3(x - 20) = 0$
3. $(x + 20)^2 = 625$
4. $5x^2 + x = 0$
5. $3x^2 + 4x - 4 = 0$
6. $12x^2 + 8x - 55 = 0$
7. $x^2 + 4x - 5 = 0$
8. $4x^2 + 4x - 15 = 0$
9. $x^2 - 3x + 1 = 0$
10. $x^2 - 4x + 2 = 0$

SECTION 2.6 · EXERCISES

In Exercises 1–36, find all real solutions of the equation. Check your answers in the original equation or use a graphic check.

1. $x^3 - 2x^2 - 3x = 0$
2. $2x^4 - 15x^3 + 18x^2 = 0$
3. $5x^3 + 30x^2 + 45x = 0$
4. $20y^3 - 125y = 0$
5. $x^3 - 3x^2 - x + 3 = 0$
6. $x^3 + 2x^2 + 3x + 6 = 0$
7. $x^4 - 10x^2 + 9 = 0$
8. $36t^4 + 29t^2 - 7 = 0$
9. $\dfrac{1}{t^2} + \dfrac{8}{t} + 15 = 0$
10. $6\left(\dfrac{s}{s + 1}\right)^2 + 5\left(\dfrac{s}{s + 1}\right) - 6 = 0$
11. $5 - 3x^{1/3} - 2x^{2/3} = 0$
12. $9t^{2/3} + 24t^{1/3} + 16 = 0$

13. $\sqrt{2x} - 10 = 0$
14. $\sqrt{5 - x} - 3 = 0$
15. $\sqrt[3]{2x + 5} + 3 = 0$
16. $\sqrt[3]{3x + 1} - 5 = 0$
17. $\sqrt{x + 1} - 3x = 1$
18. $\sqrt{x + 5} = \sqrt{x - 5}$
19. $\sqrt{x} + \sqrt{x - 20} = 10$
20. $\sqrt{x} - \sqrt{x - 5} = 1$
21. $\sqrt{x + 5} + \sqrt{x - 5} = 10$
22. $2\sqrt{x + 1} - \sqrt{2x + 3} = 1$
23. $(x - 5)^{2/3} = 16$
24. $(x + 3)^{2/3} = 8$
25. $3x(x - 1)^{1/2} + 2(x - 1)^{3/2} = 0$
26. $4x^2(x - 1)^{1/3} + 6x(x - 1)^{4/3} = 0$
27. $\dfrac{20 - x}{x} = x$
28. $\dfrac{4}{x} - \dfrac{5}{3} = \dfrac{x}{6}$
29. $\dfrac{1}{x} - \dfrac{1}{x + 1} = 3$
30. $\dfrac{x}{x^2 - 4} + \dfrac{1}{x + 2} = 3$
31. $\dfrac{4}{x + 1} - \dfrac{3}{x + 2} = 1$
32. $\dfrac{x + 1}{3} - \dfrac{x + 1}{x + 2} = 0$

33. $|2x - 1| = 5$

34. $|3x + 2| = 7$

35. $|x| = x^2 + x - 3$

36. $|x^2 + 6x| = 3x + 18$

In Exercises 37–56, use a graphing utility to approximate the real solutions of the equation accurate to two decimal places.

37. $x^4 - x^3 + x - 1 = 0$

38. $x^4 + 2x^3 - 8x - 16 = 0$

39. $x^4 + 5x^2 - 36 = 0$

40. $x^4 - 4x^2 + 3 = 0$

41. $2x + 9\sqrt{x} - 5 = 0$

42. $6x - 7\sqrt{x} - 3 = 0$

43. $-\sqrt{26 - 11x} + 4 = x$

44. $x + \sqrt{31 - 9x} = 5$

45. $\sqrt{7x + 36} - \sqrt{5x + 16} = 2$

46. $3\sqrt{x} - \dfrac{4}{\sqrt{x}} = 4$

47. $x = \dfrac{3}{x} + \dfrac{1}{2}$

48. $4x + 1 = \dfrac{3}{x}$

49. $\dfrac{1}{x} = \dfrac{4}{x - 1} + 1$

50. $x + \dfrac{9}{x + 1} = 5$

51. $|x - 10| = x^2 - 10x$

52. $|x + 1| = x^2 - 5$

53. $3.2x^4 - 1.5x^2 - 2.1 = 0$

54. $7.08x^6 + 4.15x^3 - 9.6 = 0$

55. $1.8x - 6\sqrt{x} - 5.6 = 0$

56. $4x^{2/3} + 8x^{1/3} + 3.6 = 0$

57. *Sharing the Cost*   A college charters a bus for $1700 to take a group of students to a museum. When six more students join the trip, the cost per student drops by $7.50. How many students were in the original group?

58. *Sharing the Cost*   Three students are planning to rent an apartment for a year and share equally in the monthly rent. By adding a fourth person to the group, each person could save $75 a month. How much is the monthly rent?

59. *Airspeed*   An airline runs a commuter flight between two cities that are 720 miles apart. If the average speed of the planes is increased by 40 miles per hour, the travel time is decreased by 12 minutes. What airspeed is required to obtain this decrease in travel time?

60. *Average Speed*   A family drove 1080 miles to their vacation lodge. Because of increased traffic density, their average speed on the return trip was decreased by 6 miles per hour and the trip took $2\frac{1}{2}$ hours longer. Determine their average speed on the way to the lodge.

61. *Compound Interest*   A deposit of $2500 reaches a balance of $3544.06 after 5 years. The interest in the account is compounded monthly. What is the annual percentage rate for this investment?

62. *Compound Interest*   A sales representative for a mutual fund company describes a "guaranteed investment fund" that the company is offering new investors. You are told that if you deposit $10,000 in the fund you will be guaranteed a return of at least $25,000 after 20 years. (a) What is the annual percentage rate if the investment only meets the minimum guaranteed amount? (b) If after 20 years you received $35,000, what annual percentage rate did you receive? (Assume the interest is compounded quarterly.)

63. *Saturated Steam*   The temperature (in degrees Fahrenheit) of saturated steam increases as pressure increases. This relationship is approximated by the model

Temperature $= 75.82 - 2.11x + 43.51\sqrt{x}$, $\quad 5 \le x \le 40$,

where x is the absolute pressure in pounds per square inch.
(a) Use a graphing utility to graph the temperature function over the specified domain.
(b) The temperature of steam at sea level ($x = 14.696$) is 212°. Evaluate the model at this pressure.
(c) Use the model to approximate the pressure if the temperature of the steam is 240°.

64. *Airline Passengers*   An airline offers daily flights between Chicago and Denver. The total monthly cost of these flights is given by

$$C = \sqrt{0.2x + 1},$$

where C is measured in millions of dollars and x is measured in thousands of passengers.
(a) Use a graphing utility to graph the cost function.
(b) Approximate the number of passengers that flew during a month when the total cost of the flights was 2.5 million dollars.

65. *Market Research*   The demand equation for a product is

$$p = 40 - \sqrt{0.01x + 1},$$

where x is the number of units demanded per day and p is the price per unit. Find the demand if the price is set at $37.55.

66. *Market Research*   The demand equation for a product is

$$p = 30 - \sqrt{0.0001x + 1},$$

where x is the number of units demanded per day and p is the price per unit. Find the demand if the price is set at $13.95.

67. *Power Line*   A power station is on one side of a river that is $\frac{1}{2}$ mile wide. A factory is 6 miles downstream on the other side of the river (see figure). It costs $18 per foot to run power lines over land and $24 per foot to run them under water.

(a) Show that the total cost of running the power lines is given by

$$C = 24(5280)\sqrt{x^2 + \tfrac{1}{4}} + 18(5280)(6 - x).$$

(b) Determine the domain of the cost function.

(c) Use a graphing utility to graph the cost function.

(d) Approximate x (accurate to two decimal places) if the total cost of the project is $625,000.

68. *Baseball Diamond*   A baseball diamond has the shape of a square where the distance from home plate to second base is approximately $127\frac{1}{2}$ feet. Approximate the distance between each of the bases.

69. *Surface Area*   The surface area of a cone is $S = \pi r \sqrt{r^2 + h^2}$. Solve this equation for h.

70. *Inductance*   An equation describing a circuit containing inductance i and capacitance C is

$$i = \pm \sqrt{\frac{1}{LC}} \sqrt{Q^2 - q}.$$

Solve this equation for Q.

FIGURE FOR 67

2.7   LINEAR INEQUALITIES AND GRAPHING UTILITIES

Inequalities and Intervals on the Real Number Line / Properties of Inequalities / Solving a Linear Inequality / Inequalities Involving Absolute Value / Applications

Inequalities and Intervals on the Real Number Line

Simple inequalities were reviewed in Section 1 of the prerequisite chapter. There, inequality symbols $<, \leq, >$, and $\geq$ were used to compare two numbers and to denote subsets of real numbers. For instance, the simple inequality $x \geq 3$ denotes all real numbers x that are greater than or equal to 3. In this section you will study inequalities that contain more involved statements such as

$$5x - 7 < 3x + 9 \quad \text{and} \quad -3 \leq 6x - 1 < 3.$$

As with an equation, you **solve an inequality** in the variable x by finding all values of x for which the inequality is true. These values are **solutions** and are said to **satisfy** the inequality. The set of all real numbers that are solutions of an inequality is the **solution set** of the inequality.

The set of all points on the real number line that represent the solution set is the **graph** of the inequality.

Properties of Inequalities

The procedures for solving linear inequalities in one variable are much like those for solving linear equations. To isolate the variable you can use **properties of inequalities.** These properties are similar to the properties of equality, but there are two important exceptions. When both sides of an inequality are multiplied or divided by a negative number, *the direction of the inequality symbol must be reversed.* Here is an example.

$$-2 < 5 \qquad \text{\textit{Original inequality}}$$
$$(-3)(-2) > (-3)(5) \qquad \text{\textit{Multiply both sides by }} -3$$
$$6 > -15 \qquad \text{\textit{and reverse the inequality}}$$

Two inequalities that have the same solution set are **equivalent.** The following list describes operations that can be used to create equivalent inequalities.

PROPERTIES OF INEQUALITIES

Let a, b, c, and d be real numbers.

REMARK   Each of the properties is true if the symbol $<$ is replaced by $\leq$.

Property	*Example*
1. Transitive Property: $a < b$ and $b < c \longrightarrow a < c$	Because $-2 < 5$ and $5 < 7$, it follows that $-2 < 7$.
2. Addition of Inequalities: $a < b$ and $c < d \longrightarrow a + c < b + d$	Because $2 < 4$ and $3 < 5$, it follows that $2 + 3 < 4 + 5$.
3. Addition of a Constant: $a < b \longrightarrow a + c < b + c$	Because $-3 < 7$, it follows that $-3 + 2 < 7 + 2$.
4. Multiplying by a Constant: (a) For $c > 0$, $\qquad a < b \longrightarrow ac < bc$	Because $5 > 0$ and $3 < 9$, it follows that $3(5) < 9(5)$.
(b) For $c < 0$, $\qquad a < b \longrightarrow ac > bc$	Because $-5 < 0$ and $3 < 9$, it follows that $3(-5) > 9(-5)$.

Solving a Linear Inequality

The simplest type of inequality to solve is a **linear inequality** in a single variable. Each of the inequalities

$$2x + 3 > 4, \quad 3x - 4 \leq 2x + 5, \quad \text{and} \quad 3 \geq -5x + 4$$

is a linear inequality in the variable x.

As you read through the examples, pay special attention to the steps in which the inequality symbol is reversed. Remember that when you multiply or divide an inequality by a negative number, you must reverse the inequality symbol.

EXAMPLE 1   Solving a Linear Inequality

$5x - 7 > 3x + 9$	*Original inequality*
$5x > 3x + 16$	*Add 7 to both sides*
$5x - 3x > 16$	*Subtract 3x from both sides*
$2x > 16$	*Combine terms*
$x > 8$	*Divide both sides by 2*

Thus, the solution set consists of all real numbers that are greater than 8. The interval notation for this solution set is $(8, \infty)$. The number line graph of this solution set is shown in Figure 2.41.

Checking the solution set of an inequality is not as simple as checking the solution of an equation. (There are usually too many x-values to substitute back into the original inequality.) You can, however, get an indication of the validity of a solution set by substituting a few convenient values of x. For instance, in Example 1 the solution of $5x - 7 > 3x + 9$ was found to be $x > 8$. Check that $x = 9$ satisfies the original inequality, whereas $x = 7$ does not.

EXAMPLE 2   Solving a Linear Inequality Algebraically and Graphically

$1 - \dfrac{3x}{2} \geq x - 4$	*Original inequality*
$2 - 3x \geq 2x - 8$	*Multiply both sides by LCD*
$-3x \geq 2x - 10$	*Subtract 2 from both sides*
$-5x \geq -10$	*Subtract 2x from both sides*
$x \leq 2$	*Divide both sides by -5 and reverse inequality*

The solution set consists of all real numbers that are less than or equal to 2. The interval notation for this solution set is $(-\infty, 2]$. The number line graph of this solution set is shown in Figure 2.42. Graphically, you can solve the given inequality by sketching the graphs of the left and right sides

$$f(x) = 1 - \frac{3x}{2} \quad \text{and} \quad g(x) = x - 4.$$

From Figure 2.43 the graphs appear to intersect at the point $(2, -2)$. This is confirmed by the fact that $f(2) = -2 = g(2)$. Moreover, the graph of f lies above the graph of g to the left of their point of intersection, which implies that $f(x) \geq g(x)$ for $x \leq 2$.

Solution interval: $(8, \infty)$

FIGURE 2.41

REMARK The five inequalities forming the solution steps of Example 1 are all **equivalent** in the sense that each has the same solution set.

Solution interval: $(-\infty, 2]$

FIGURE 2.42

FIGURE 2.43

Solution interval: $[-\frac{1}{3}, \frac{2}{3})$

FIGURE 2.44

Sometimes it is convenient to write two inequalities as a **double inequality.** For instance, you can write the two inequalities $-4 \le 5x - 2$ and $5x - 2 < 7$ more simply as $-4 \le 5x - 2 < 7$. This form allows you to solve the two given inequalities together.

EXAMPLE 3 **Solving a Double Inequality**

Solve $-3 \le 6x - 1 < 3$.

SOLUTION

To solve this double inequality, isolate x as the middle term.

$$-3 \le 6x - 1 < 3 \qquad \textit{Original inequality}$$

$$-2 \le 6x < 4 \qquad \textit{Add 1 to all three parts}$$

$$-\frac{1}{3} \le x < \frac{2}{3} \qquad \textit{Divide by 6 and reduce}$$

The solution set consists of all real numbers that are greater than or equal to $-\frac{1}{3}$ and less than $\frac{2}{3}$. The interval notation for this solution set is $[-\frac{1}{3}, \frac{2}{3})$. The number line graph of this solution set is shown in Figure 2.44.

When combining two inequalities to form a double inequality, be sure that the inequalities satisfy the Transitive Property. For instance, it is *incorrect* to combine the inequalities $3 < x$ and $x \le -1$ as $3 < x \le -1$. This "inequality" is obviously wrong because 3 is not less than -1.

Inequalities Involving Absolute Value

To see how to solve inequalities involving absolute values, consider the following comparisons.

Equation or Inequality	Solution	Verbal Description	Graph
$\lvert x \rvert = 2$	$x = -2$ and $x = 2$	Values of x that lie 2 units from 0	$x = -2$ and $x = 2$
$\lvert x \rvert < 2$	$-2 < x < 2$	Values of x that lie *less than* 2 units from 0	$-2 < x < 2$
$\lvert x \rvert > 2$	$x < -2$ or $x > 2$	Values of x that lie *more than* 2 units from 0	$x < -2$ or $x > 2$

SOLVING AN ABSOLUTE VALUE INEQUALITY

Let x be a variable or an algebraic expression and let a be a real number such that $a \geq 0$.

1. The solutions of $|x| < a$ are all values of x that lie between $-a$ and a. That is,

$$|x| < a \quad \text{if and only if} \quad -a < x < a.$$

2. The solutions of $|x| > a$ are all values of x that are less than $-a$ or greater than a. That is,

$$|x| > a \quad \text{if and only if} \quad x < -a \quad \text{or} \quad x > a.$$

These two rules are also valid if $<$ is replaced by $\leq$ and $>$ is replaced by $\geq$.

EXAMPLE 4 Solving an Absolute Value Inequality

$$|x - 5| < 2 \qquad \textit{Original inequality}$$
$$-2 < x - 5 < 2 \qquad \textit{Equivalent inequalities}$$
$$-2 + 5 < x - 5 + 5 < 2 + 5 \qquad \textit{Add 5 to all three parts}$$
$$3 < x < 7 \qquad \textit{Solution set}$$

$|x - 5| < 2$

FIGURE 2.45

The solution set consists of all real numbers that are greater than 3 and less than 7. The interval notation for this solution set is $(3, 7)$. The graph of this solution set is shown in Figure 2.45.

EXAMPLE 5 Solving an Absolute Value Inequality

$$|x + 3| \geq 7 \qquad \textit{Original inequality}$$
$$x + 3 \leq -7 \qquad \text{or} \qquad x + 3 \geq 7 \qquad \textit{Equivalent inequalities}$$
$$x + 3 - 3 \leq -7 - 3 \qquad x + 3 - 3 \geq 7 - 3 \qquad \textit{Subtract 3 from both sides}$$
$$x \leq -10 \qquad\qquad\qquad x \geq 4 \qquad \textit{Solution set}$$

$|x + 3| \geq 7$

FIGURE 2.46

The solution set consists of all real numbers that are less than or equal to -10 or greater than or equal to 4. The interval notation for this solution set is $(-\infty, -10] \cup [4, \infty)$. The symbol $\cup$ is a **union** symbol, and is used to denote the combining of two sets. The graph of this solution set is shown in Figure 2.46.

EXAMPLE 6   Solving An Absolute Value Inequality Graphically

Use a graphing utility to solve the following inequality.

$$\left| 2 - \frac{x}{3} \right| < 0.01$$

SOLUTION

You can solve the given absolute value inequality graphically by graphing the function

$$f(x) = \left| 2 - \frac{x}{3} \right| - 0.01$$

and determining the values of x for which the graph lies *below* the x-axis, as shown in Figure 2.47. Using the zoom and trace feature, you can determine the x-intercepts occur at $x \approx 5.97$ and $x \approx 6.03$. Because the graph of f lies below the x-axis between these two values, the solution interval is $(5.97, 6.03)$. Try solving this inequality algebraically to verify the solution interval.

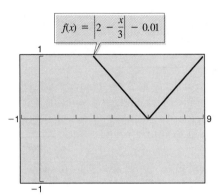

FIGURE 2.47

Applications

Linear inequalities in real-life problems arise from statements that involve phrases such as "at least," "no more than," "minimum value," and so on.

EXAMPLE 7   Comparative Shopping

A subcompact car can be rented from Company A for $180 per week with no extra charge for mileage. A similar car can be rented from Company B for $100 per week, plus 20 cents for each mile driven. How many miles must a person drive in a week to make the rental fee for Company A less than that for Company B?

SOLUTION

VERBAL
MODEL   Weekly cost for Company B > Weekly cost for Company A

LABELS   Miles driven in a week = m *(miles)*

             Weekly cost for Company A = 180   *(dollars)*

             Weekly cost for Company B = $100 + 0.2m$ *(dollars)*

INEQUALITY $100 + 0.2m > 180$

             $0.2m > 80$

             $m > 400$ miles

The car from Company A is cheaper if the person plans to drive more than 400 miles in a week.

EXAMPLE 8   Accuracy of a Measurement

Suppose you go to a candy store to buy chocolates that cost $9.89 per pound. The scale that is used in the store has a state seal of approval that indicates the scale is accurate to within half an ounce. According to the scale, your purchase weighs one-half pound and costs $4.95. How much might you have been undercharged or overcharged due to an error in the scale?

SOLUTION

To solve this problem, let x represent the *true* weight of the candy. Because the state seal indicates that the scale is accurate to within half an ounce (or $\frac{1}{32}$ of a pound), you can conclude that the difference between the exact weight (x) and the scale weight ($\frac{1}{2}$) is less than or equal to $\frac{1}{32}$ of a pound. That is,

$$\left| x - \frac{1}{2} \right| \leq \frac{1}{32}.$$

You can solve this inequality as follows.

$$-\frac{1}{32} \leq x - \frac{1}{2} \leq \frac{1}{32}$$

$$\frac{15}{32} \leq x \leq \frac{17}{32}$$

$$0.46875 \leq x \leq 0.53125$$

In other words, your "one-half" pound of candy could have weighed as little 0.46875 pounds (which would have cost $4.64) or as much as 0.53125 pounds (which would have cost $5.25). Thus, you could have been undercharged by as much as

$$5.25 - 4.95 = \$0.30$$

or overcharged by as much as

$$4.95 - 4.64 = \$0.31.$$

DISCUSSION PROBLEM

VERBAL STATEMENTS OF PROPERTIES

It is sometimes easier to memorize a verbal statement than to memorize a mathematical formula. For instance, you can remember the Pythagorean Theorem, $a^2 + b^2 = c^2$, as "the sum of the squares of the two sides is equal to the square of the hypotenuse."

Early in this section we stated four different properties of inequalities. Translate these mathematical statements into *verbal statements*.

WARM-UP
....

The following warm-up exercises involve skills that were covered in earlier sections. You will use these skills in the exercise set for this section.

In Exercises 1–4, determine which of the two numbers is larger.

1. $-\frac{1}{2}, -7$ **2.** $-\frac{1}{3}, -\frac{1}{6}$

3. $-\pi, -3$ **4.** $-6, -\frac{13}{2}$

In Exercises 5–8, use inequality notation to describe the statement.

5. x is nonnegative.   **6.** z is strictly between -3 and 10.

7. P is no more than 2.   **8.** W is at least 200.

In Exercises 9 and 10, evaluate the expression for the given values of x.

9. $|x - 10|$, $x = 12, x = 3$ **10.** $|2x - 3|$, $x = \frac{3}{2}, x = 1$

SECTION 2.7 · EXERCISES
....

In Exercises 1–4, determine whether the given values of x are solutions of the inequality.

Inequality	*Values*	
1. $5x - 12 > 0$	(a) $x = 3$	(b) $x = -3$
	(c) $x = \frac{5}{2}$	(d) $x = \frac{3}{2}$
2. $x + 1 < \dfrac{2x}{3}$	(a) $x = 0$	(b) $x = 4$
	(c) $x = -4$	(d) $x = -3$
3. $0 < \dfrac{x - 2}{4} < 2$	(a) $x = 4$	(b) $x = 10$
	(c) $x = 0$	(d) $x = \frac{7}{2}$
4. $-1 < \dfrac{3 - x}{2} \le 1$	(a) $x = 0$	(b) $x = \sqrt{5}$
	(c) $x = 1$	(d) $x = 5$

In Exercises 5–12, match the inequality with its graph. [The graphs are labeled (a), (b), (c), (d), (e), (f), (g), and (h).]

5. $x < 4$ **6.** $x \ge 6$

7. $-2 < x \le 5$ **8.** $0 \le x \le \frac{7}{2}$

9. $|x| < 4$ **10.** $|x| > 3$

11. $|x - 5| > 2$ **12.** $|x + 6| < 3$

(a)

(b)

(c)

(d)

(e)

(f)

(g)

(h)

In Exercises 13–38, solve the inequality algebraically and sketch the solution on the real number line.

13. $4x < 12$

14. $2x > 3$

15. $-10x < 40$

16. $-6x > 15$

17. $x - 5 \geq 7$

18. $x + 7 \leq 12$

19. $4(x + 1) < 2x + 3$

20. $3x + 1 \geq 2$

21. $1 < 2x + 3 < 9$

22. $-8 \leq 1 - 3(x - 2) < 13$

23. $-4 < \dfrac{2x - 3}{3} < 4$

24. $0 \leq \dfrac{x + 3}{2} < 5$

25. $\dfrac{3}{4} > x + 1 > \dfrac{1}{4}$

26. $-1 < -\dfrac{x}{3} < 1$

27. $|x| < 5$

28. $|2x| < 6$

29. $\left|\dfrac{x}{2}\right| > 3$

30. $|5x| > 10$

31. $|x - 20| \leq 4$

32. $|x - 7| < 6$

33. $|x - 20| \geq 4$

34. $|x + 14| + 3 > 17$

35. $|9 - 2x| - 2 < -1$

36. $\left|1 - \dfrac{2x}{3}\right| < 1$

37. $|x - 5| < 0$

38. $|x - 5| \geq 0$

In Exercises 39–48, use a graphing utility to solve the inequality.

39. $4 - 2x < 3$

40. $2x + 7 < 3$

41. $\dfrac{-4x + 25}{5} \geq \dfrac{3x - 10}{10}$

42. $2x - 9 < \dfrac{-4x + 3}{3}$

43. $-\dfrac{5}{2} < 0.75x + 2 < 4$

44. $-1 \leq 13 - 2x \leq 9$

45. $\left|\dfrac{x - 3}{2}\right| \geq 5$

46. $|1 - 2x| < 5$

47. $2|x + 10| \geq 9$

48. $3|4 - 5x| \leq 9$

In Exercises 49–52, find the interval(s) on the real number line for which the radicand is nonnegative (greater than or equal to zero).

49. $\sqrt{3 - x}$

50. $\sqrt{x - 10}$

51. $\sqrt[4]{7 - 2x}$

52. $\sqrt[4]{6x + 15}$

In Exercises 53–60, use absolute value notation to define each interval (or pair of intervals) on the real line.

53.

54.

55.

56.

57. All real numbers within 10 units of 12

58. All real numbers at least 5 units from 8

59. All real numbers whose distances from -3 are more than 5

60. All real numbers whose distances from -6 are no more than 7

61. *Comparative Shopping* Suppose you can rent a midsize car from Company A for $250 per week with no extra charge for mileage. A similar car can be rented from Company B for $150 per week, plus $0.25 cents for each mile driven. How many miles must you drive in a week to make the rental fee for Company B *greater than* that for Company A?

62. *Comparative Shopping* Suppose your department sends its copying to the photocopy center of your company. The center bills your department $0.10 per page. You have investigated the possibility of buying a departmental copier for $3000. With your own copier the cost per page would be $0.03. The expected life of the copier is 4 years. How many copies must you make in the 4-year period to justify purchasing the copier?

63. *Simple Interest* For an investment of $1000 to grow to *more than* $1250 in 2 years, what must the interest rate be? $[A = P(1 + rt)]$

64. *Simple Interest* For an investment of $750 to grow to *more than* $1050 in 2 years, what must the interest rate be?

Break Even Analysis In Exercises 65 and 66, the functions giving the cost of producing x units of a product and the revenue for selling x units are given. In order to obtain a profit, the revenue must be *greater than* the cost. Use a graphing utility to graph the cost and revenue functions and determine the values of x for which the product will return a profit.

Cost Function	Revenue Function
65. $C = 95x + 750$	$R = 115.95x$
66. $C = 15.40x + 150,000$	$R = 24.55x$

67. *Daily Sales* A doughnut shop at a shopping mall sells a dozen doughnuts for $2.95. Beyond the fixed costs (for rent, utilities, and insurance) of $150 per day it costs $1.45 for enough materials (flour, sugar, and so on) and labor to produce a dozen doughnuts.
(a) Write the daily cost C as a function of the number of dozens x of doughnuts produced.
(b) Write the daily revenue R as a function of the number of dozens x of doughnuts sold.
(c) Write the daily profit as a function of x.
(d) Use a graphing utility to graph the profit function. If the daily profit varies between $50 and $200, between what levels (in dozens) do the daily sales vary?
(e) Rework parts (c) and (d) if on average there are 10 dozen unsold doughnuts at the end of each day.

68. *Annual Operating Cost* A utility company has a fleet of vans. The annual operating cost per van is

$$C = 0.32m + 2300,$$

where m is the number of miles traveled by a van in a year. What number of miles will yield an annual operating cost that is less than $10,000?

69. *Cable Television Subscribers* The number of cable television subscribers in the United States between 1980 and 1989 is approximated by the model

Subscribers $= 3.657t + 14.784$,

where the number of subscribers is given in millions and the time t represents the year, with $t = 0$ corresponding to 1980 (see figure). Assuming this model is correct, when will the number of subscribers *exceed* 55 million? (*Source:* Television and Cable Fact Book)

FIGURE FOR 69

70. *Teachers' Salaries* The average salary for elementary and secondary teachers in the United States from 1980 to 1989 is approximated by the model

Salary $= 16,116 + 1496t$,

where the salary is given in dollars and the time t represents the year, with $t = 0$ corresponding to 1980 (see figure). Use a graphing utility to graph the salary function. Assuming the model is correct, move the cursor along the graph to determine when the average salary will *exceed* $35,000. (*Source:* National Education Association)

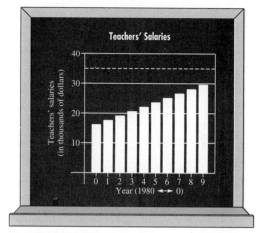

FIGURE FOR 70

71. *Accuracy of Measurement* The side of a square is measured as 10.4 inches with a possible error of $\frac{1}{16}$ inch. Using these measurements, determine the interval containing the area of the square.

72. *Accuracy of Measurement* Suppose you buy a bag of oranges that cost $0.95 per pound. The weight that is listed on the bag is 4.65 pounds. If the scale that weighed the bag is only accurate to within 1 ounce, how much money might you have been undercharged or overcharged?

73. *Heights* The heights, h, of two-thirds of the members of a certain population satisfy the inequality

$$\left| \frac{h - 68.5}{2.7} \right| \leq 1,$$

where h is measured in inches. Determine the interval on the real line in which these heights lie.

74. *Relative Humidity* A certain electronic device is to be operated in an environment with relative humidity h in the interval defined by

$$|h - 50| \leq 30.$$

What are the minimum and maximum relative humidities for the operation of this device?

75. Given two real numbers a and b, such that $a > b > 0$, prove that

$$\frac{1}{a} < \frac{1}{b}.$$

2.8   OTHER TYPES OF INEQUALITIES AND GRAPHING UTILITIES

Polynomial Inequalities / Rational Inequalities / Applications

Polynomial Inequalities

To solve a polynomial inequality such as

$$x^2 - 2x - 3 < 0,$$

use the fact that a polynomial can change signs only at its zeros (the x-values that make the polynomial zero). Between two consecutive zeros a polynomial must be entirely positive or entirely negative. This means that when the real zeros of a polynomial are put in order, they divide the real line into intervals in which the polynomial has no sign changes. These zeros are the **critical numbers** of the inequality, and the resulting intervals are the **test intervals** for the inequality. For example, the polynomial

$$x^2 - 2x - 3 = (x + 1)(x - 3)$$

has two zeros, $x = -1$ and $x = 3$, and these zeros divide the real line into three test intervals,

$$(-\infty, -1), \quad (-1, 3), \quad \text{and} \quad (3, \infty).$$

To solve the inequality $x^2 - 3x - 3 < 0$, you need only to test one value from each of these test intervals.

FINDING TEST INTERVALS FOR A POLYNOMIAL

To determine the intervals on which the values of a polynomial are entirely negative or entirely positive, use the following steps.

1. Find all real zeros of the polynomial, and arrange the zeros in increasing order (from smallest to largest). The zeros of a polynomial are its **critical numbers.**
2. Use the critical numbers of the polynomial to determine its **test intervals.**
3. Choose one representative x-value in each test interval and evaluate the polynomial at that value. If the value of the polynomial is negative, then the polynomial will have negative values for *every* x-value in the interval. If the value of the polynomial is positive, then the polynomial will have positive values for *every* x-value in the interval.

EXAMPLE 1   Solving a Polynomial Inequality

Determine the intervals on which $x^2 - x - 6$ is entirely negative and those on which it is entirely positive.

TABLE 2.1

Test interval	Representative x-value	Value of polynomial	Conclusion
$(-\infty, -2)$	$x = -3$	$(-3)^2 - (-3) - 6 = 6$	Polynomial is positive
$(-2, 3)$	$x = 0$	$(0)^2 - (0) - 6 = -6$	Polynomial is negative
$(3, \infty)$	$x = 4$	$(4)^2 - (4) - 6 = 6$	Polynomial is positive

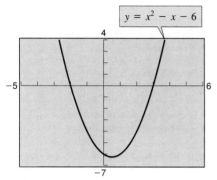

FIGURE 2.48

SOLUTION

By factoring the quadratic as

$$x^2 - x - 6 = (x + 2)(x - 3),$$

you can see that the critical numbers occur at $x = -2$ and $x = 3$. Therefore, the test intervals for the quadratic are $(-\infty, -2)$, $(-2, 3)$, and $(3, \infty)$. In each test interval, choose a representative x-value and evaluate the polynomial, as shown in Table 2.1.

The polynomial has positive values for every x in the intervals $(-\infty, -2)$ and $(3, \infty)$, and negative values for every x in the interval $(-2, 3)$. This result is shown graphically in Figure 2.48.

To determine the test intervals for a polynomial inequality, the inequality must first be written in standard form (with the polynomial on the left and zero on the right).

EXAMPLE 2   Solving a Polynomial Inequality

$$\begin{aligned}
2x^2 + 5x &> 12 && \textit{Original inequality} \\
2x^2 + 5x - 12 &> 0 && \textit{Write in standard form} \\
(x + 4)(2x - 3) &> 0 && \textit{Factor}
\end{aligned}$$

Critical numbers: $x = -4, x = \dfrac{3}{2}$

Test intervals: $(-\infty, -4), \left(-4, \dfrac{3}{2}\right), \left(\dfrac{3}{2}, \infty\right)$

Test: Is $(x + 4)(2x - 3) > 0$?

After testing these intervals, you can see that the polynomial $2x^2 + 5x - 12$ is positive in the open intervals $(-\infty, -4)$ and $(\frac{3}{2}, \infty)$. Therefore, the solution set of the inequality is $(-\infty, -4) \cup (\frac{3}{2}, \infty)$. You could have solved this example with a graphing utility by graphing the polynomial function $y = 2x^2 + 5x - 12$ and noting where the graph is *above* the x-axis. You can see in Figure 2.49 that the polynomial lies above the x-axis for $x < -4$ or $x > \frac{3}{2}$.

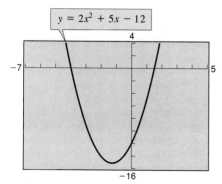

FIGURE 2.49

EXAMPLE 3   Using the Quadratic Formula

Solve $x^2 + 4x + 1 \leq 0$.

SOLUTION

By the Quadratic Formula, the zeros of $x^2 + 4x + 1$ are

$$x = \frac{-4 \pm \sqrt{16 - 4}}{2} = \frac{-4 \pm 2\sqrt{3}}{2} = -2 \pm \sqrt{3}.$$

Now, having found the zeros of the polynomial $x^2 + 4x + 1$, proceed as usual.

Critical numbers: $x = -2 - \sqrt{3}, x = -2 + \sqrt{3}$

Test intervals: $\left(-\infty, -2 - \sqrt{3}\right), \left(-2 - \sqrt{3}, -2 + \sqrt{3}\right),$
$\left(-2 + \sqrt{3}, \infty\right)$

Test: Is $x^2 + 4x + 1 \leq 0$?

After testing these intervals, you can see that the polynomial $x^2 + 4x + 1$ is less than or equal to zero in the *closed* interval $\left[-2 - \sqrt{3}, -2 + \sqrt{3}\right]$. Therefore, the solution set of the inequality is $\left[-2 - \sqrt{3}, -2 + \sqrt{3}\right]$. You can see in Figure 2.50 that the polynomial lies below the x-axis in the interval $\left[-2 - \sqrt{3}, -2 + \sqrt{3}\right]$.

FIGURE 2.50

When solving a polynomial inequality, be sure you have accounted for the particular type of inequality symbol given in the inequality. For instance, in Example 3, note that the solution is a closed interval because the original inequality contained a "less than or equal to" symbol. Do this even if the endpoints are only approximations. For instance, if the original inequality had been $x^2 + 4x + 1 < 0$, the solution would have been the *open* interval $\left(-2 - \sqrt{3}, -2 + \sqrt{3}\right)$.

EXAMPLE 4   Unusual Solution Sets

A. The solution set of $x^2 + 2x + 4 > 0$ consists of the entire set of real numbers, $(-\infty, \infty)$. In other words, the quadratic $x^2 + 2x + 4$ is positive for every real value of x, as indicated in Figure 2.51(a). (Note that this quadratic inequality has *no* critical numbers. In such a case, there is only one test interval—the entire real line.)

B. The solution set of $x^2 + 2x + 1 \leq 0$ consists of the single real number, -1, because the graph touches the x-axis just at -1, as shown in Figure 2.51(b).

C. The solution set of $x^2 + 3x + 5 < 0$ is empty. In other words, the quadratic $x^2 + 3x + 5$ is not less than zero for any value of x, as indicated in Figure 2.51(c).

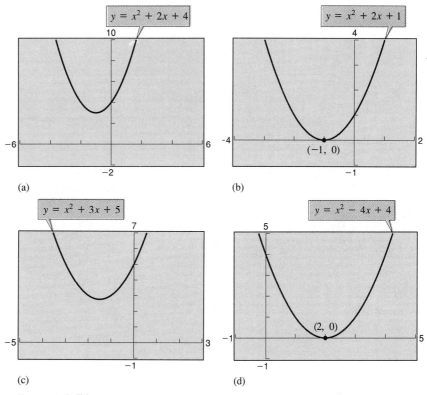

FIGURE 2.51

D. The solution set of $x^2 - 4x + 4 > 0$ consists of all real numbers *except* the number 2. In interval notation, this solution set can be written as $(-\infty, 2) \cup (2, \infty)$. The graph of $x^2 - 4x + 4$ is above the x-axis except at $x = 2$, where it touches, as indicated in Figure 2.51(d). ⬛⬛⬛⬛⬛⬛⬛⬛⬛

Rational Inequalities

The concepts of critical numbers and test intervals can be extended to inequalities involving rational expressions. To do this, use the fact that the value of a rational expression can change sign only at its *zeros* (the x-values for which its numerator is zero) and its *undefined values* (the x-values for which its denominator is zero). These two types of numbers make up the **critical numbers** of a rational inequality. For instance, the critical numbers of the inequality

$$\frac{x - 1}{(x - 2)(x + 3)} < 0$$

are $x = 1$ (the numerator is zero), and $x = 2$ and $x = -3$ (the denominator is zero). From these three critical numbers you can see that the inequality has *four* test intervals: $(-\infty, -3)$, $(-3, 1)$, $(1, 2)$, and $(2, \infty)$.

EXAMPLE 5   Solving a Rational Inequality

Solve $\dfrac{2x - 7}{x - 5} \leq 3$.

SOLUTION

From Figure 2.52, you can see that the graph of

$$y = \frac{2x - 7}{x - 5} - 3$$

is negative on the intervals $(-\infty, 5)$ and $(8, \infty)$. To solve the inequality algebraically, use the following steps.

$$\frac{2x - 7}{x - 5} \leq 3 \qquad\qquad \textit{Original inequality}$$

$$\frac{2x - 7}{x - 5} - 3 \leq 0 \qquad\qquad \textit{Standard form}$$

$$\frac{2x - 7 - 3x + 15}{x - 5} \leq 0 \qquad\qquad \textit{Add fractions}$$

$$\frac{-x + 8}{x - 5} \leq 0 \qquad\qquad \textit{Simplify}$$

Now, in standard form you can see that the critical numbers are 5 and 8, and proceed as follows.

Critical numbers: $x = 5, x = 8$

Test intervals: $(-\infty, 5), (5, 8), (8, \infty)$

Test: Is $\dfrac{-x + 8}{x - 5} \leq 0$?

By testing these intervals, you can determine that the rational expression $(-x + 8)/(x - 5)$ is negative in the open intervals $(-\infty, 5)$ and $(8, \infty)$. Moreover, because $(-x + 8)/(x - 5) = 0$ when $x = 8$, you can conclude that the solution set of the inequality is $(-\infty, 5) \cup [8, \infty)$.

$$y = \frac{2x - 7}{x - 5} - 3$$

FIGURE 2.52

EXAMPLE 6   Solving a Rational Inequality

Solve $\dfrac{x}{x - 2} > \dfrac{1}{x + 3}$.

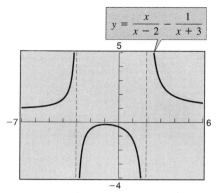

FIGURE 2.53

SOLUTION

Using a graphing utility, you can determine that the graph of the function

$$y = \frac{x}{x - 2} - \frac{1}{x + 3}$$

is positive (lies above the x-axis) for $x < -3$ or $x > 2$, as shown in Figure 2.53. Hence, the solution set is $(-\infty, -3) \cup (2, \infty)$. The algebraic solution is shown as follows.

$$\frac{x}{x - 2} > \frac{1}{x + 3} \qquad\qquad \textit{Original inequality}$$

$$\frac{x}{x - 2} - \frac{1}{x + 3} > 0 \qquad\qquad \textit{Standard form}$$

$$\frac{x^2 + 3x - x + 2}{(x - 2)(x + 3)} > 0 \qquad\qquad \textit{Combine fractions}$$

$$\frac{x^2 + 2x + 2}{(x - 2)(x + 3)} > 0 \qquad\qquad \textit{Simplify}$$

The discriminant $b^2 - 4ac = 4 - 8 = -4 < 0$ indicates that the numerator has no zeros. Therefore, $x = 2$ and $x = -3$ are the only critical numbers.

Critical numbers: $x = -3, x = 2$

Test intervals: $(-\infty, -3), (-3, 2), (2, \infty)$

Test: Is $\dfrac{x^2 + 2x + 2}{(x - 2)(x + 3)} > 0$?

By testing these intervals, you can determine that the rational expression $(x^2 + 2x + 2)/[(x - 2)(x + 3)]$ is positive in the open intervals $(-\infty, -3)$ and $(2, \infty)$. Therefore, the solution set of the inequality is $(-\infty, -3) \cup (2, \infty)$, as was determined graphically.   ∎

Applications

EXAMPLE 7   **Finding the Domain of an Expression**

Find the domain of the expression $\sqrt{64 - 4x^2}$.

SOLUTION

Remember that the domain of an expression is the set of all x-values for which the expression is defined (has real values). Because $\sqrt{64 - 4x^2}$ is defined only if $64 - 4x^2$ is nonnegative, the domain is given by $64 - 4x^2 \geq 0$.

$$64 - 4x^2 \geq 0 \qquad\qquad \textit{Standard form}$$

$$16 - x^2 \geq 0 \qquad\qquad \textit{Divide both sides by 4}$$

$$(4 - x)(4 + x) \geq 0 \qquad\qquad \textit{Factor}$$

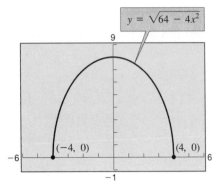

FIGURE 2.54

The inequality has two critical numbers: -4 and 4. You can use these two numbers to test the inequality as follows.

Critical numbers:	$x = -4, x = 4$
Test intervals:	$(-\infty, -4), (-4, 4), (4, \infty)$
Test:	Is $(4 - x)(4 + x) \geq 0$?

A test shows that $64 - 4x^2 \geq 0$ in the *closed interval* $[-4, 4]$. The graph of $y = \sqrt{64 - 4x^2}$, shown in Figure 2.54, confirms that the domain is $[-4, 4]$.

EXAMPLE 8   The Height of a Projectile

A projectile is fired straight upward from ground level with an initial velocity of 384 feet per second. During what time period will its height exceed 2000 feet?

SOLUTION

The position of an object moving in a vertical path is given by $s = -16t^2 + v_0 t + s_0$, where s is the height in feet and t is the time in seconds. In this case, $s_0 = 0$ and $v_0 = 384$. Thus, you need to solve the inequality $-16t^2 + 384t > 2000$. Using a graphing utility, graph $s = -16t^2 + 384t$ and $s = 2000$, as shown in Figure 2.55. From the graph, you can determine that $-16t^2 + 384t > 2000$ for t between 7.64 and 16.36. You can verify this result algebraically as follows.

$-16t^2 + 384t > 2000$	*Original inequality*
$t^2 - 24t < -125$	*Divide by -16 and reverse inequality*
$t^2 - 24t + 125 < 0$	*Standard form*

By the Quadratic Formula, the critical numbers are 7.64 and 16.36. A test will verify that the height of the projectile will exceed 2000 feet during the time interval 7.64 sec $< t <$ 16.36 sec.

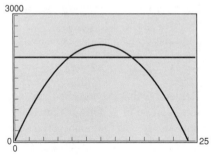

FIGURE 2.55

DISCUSSION PROBLEM

. . . .

A COMPUTER EXPERIMENT

If you have access to a computer that has the BASIC language, try running the following program.

```
 10 DEF FNY(X)=X^2-9
 20 FOR I=1 TO 80
 30 X=(I-38)/6
 40 IF FNY(X)<0 THEN PRINT "-";
 50 IF FNY(X)=0 THEN PRINT "0";
 60 IF FNY(X)>0 THEN PRINT "+";
 70 NEXT
 80 PRINT: FOR I=-6 TO 6: PRINT "-|----";: NEXT: PRINT: "-|";
 90 FOR I=-6 TO 6: PRINT USING "##";I;:PRINT " ";: NEXT: PRINT "7"
100 END
```

```
++++++++++++++++++0----------------------------------0++++++++++++++++++++++++
-|-----|-----|-----|-----|-----|-----|-----|-----|-----|-----|-----|-----|-----|
-6    -5    -4    -3    -2    -1     0     1     2     3     4     5     6     7
```

The printout from this program is shown in the figure. Notice that the program evaluates the expression $x^2 - 9$ at several values between -6 and 7. If the value of $x^2 - 9$ is negative, a minus sign is printed above the number line; if the value of $x^2 - 9$ is zero, a zero is printed; and if the value of $x^2 - 9$ is positive, a plus sign is printed. Solve Example 3 by appropriately changing the program.

WARM-UP

. . . .

The following warm-up exercises involve skills that were covered in earlier sections. You will use these skills in the exercise set for this section.

In Exercises 1–10, solve the inequality.

1. $-\dfrac{y}{3} > 2$

2. $-6z < 27$

3. $-3 \le 2x + 3 < 5$

4. $-3x + 5 \ge 20$

5. $10 > 4 - 3(x + 1)$

6. $3 < 1 + 2(x - 4) < 7$

7. $2|x| \le 7$

8. $|x - 3| > 1$

9. $|x + 4| > 2$

10. $|2 - x| \le 4$

SECTION 2.8 · EXERCISES

In Exercises 1–24, solve the inequality algebraically or graphically.

1. $x^2 \leq 9$

2. $(x - 3)^2 \geq 1$

3. $x^2 + 4x + 4 \geq 9$

4. $x^2 - 6x + 9 < 16$

5. $x^2 + x < 6$

6. $x^2 + 2x > 3$

7. $3(x - 1)(x + 1) > 0$

8. $6(x + 2)(x - 1) < 0$

9. $x^2 + 2x - 3 < 0$

10. $x^2 - 4x - 1 > 0$

11. $4x^3 - 6x^2 < 0$

12. $4x^3 - 12x^2 > 0$

13. $x^3 - 4x \geq 0$

14. $2x^3 - x^4 \leq 0$

15. $\dfrac{1}{x} > x$

16. $\dfrac{1}{x} < 4$

17. $\dfrac{x + 6}{x + 1} < 2$

18. $\dfrac{x + 12}{x + 2} \geq 3$

19. $\dfrac{3x - 5}{x - 5} > 4$

20. $\dfrac{5 + 7x}{1 + 2x} < 4$

21. $\dfrac{4}{x + 5} > \dfrac{1}{2x + 3}$

22. $\dfrac{1}{x - 3} \leq \dfrac{9}{4x + 3}$

23. $|x^2 - 4x + 5| < 2x^{-1}$

24. $|x^3 + 6x - 1| \geq 2x + 4$

In Exercises 25–32, use a graphing utility to solve the inequality.

25. $(x - 1)^2(x + 2)^3 \geq 0$

26. $x^4(x - 3) \leq 0$

27. $-0.5x^2 + 12.5x + 1.6 > 0$

28. $1.2x^2 + 4.8x + 3.1 < 5.3$

29. $\dfrac{5}{x - 6} > \dfrac{3}{x + 2}$

30. $\dfrac{1}{x} \geq \dfrac{1}{x + 3}$

31. $\dfrac{3}{x - 1} - \dfrac{2}{x + 1} < 1$

32. $\dfrac{x^2 + x - 6}{x} \geq 0$

In Exercises 33–40, find the domain of x in the expression.

33. $\sqrt[4]{4 - x^2}$

34. $\sqrt{x^2 - 4}$

35. $\sqrt{x^2 - 7x + 12}$

36. $\sqrt{144 - 9x^2}$

37. $\sqrt{12 - x - x^2}$

38. $\sqrt{x^2 + 4}$

39. $\sqrt{\dfrac{x}{x^2 - 9}}$

40. $\sqrt{\dfrac{x}{x + 4} - \dfrac{3x}{x - 1}}$

41. *Height of a Projectile*   A projectile is fired straight upward from ground level with an initial velocity of 160 feet per second.
(a) At what instant will it be back at ground level?
(b) During what time period will its height exceed 384 feet?

42. *Height of a Projectile*   A projectile is fired straight upward from ground level with an initial velocity of 128 feet per second.
(a) At what instant will it be back at ground level?
(b) During what time period will its height be less than 128 feet?

43. *Dimensions of a Field*   A rectangular playing field with a perimeter of 100 meters is to have an area of at least 500 square meters. Within what bounds must the length of the rectangle lie?

44. *Compound Interest* P dollars, invested at interest rate r compounded annually, increases to an amount

$$A = P(1 + r)^2$$

in 2 years. If an investment of $1000 is to increase to an amount greater than $1200 in 2 years, then the interest rate must be greater than what percentage?

45. *Resistors*   When two resistors of resistance R_1 and R_2 are connected in parallel, the total resistance R satisfies the equation

$$\frac{1}{R} = \frac{1}{R_1} + \frac{1}{R_2}.$$

(a) Solve the equation for R.
(b) If $R_2 = 2$ ohms in a given parallel circuit, use the result of part (a) to write R as a function of R_1. Use a graphing utility to graph the function.
(c) If the R must be at least 1 ohm, find R_1 which is a solution to the resulting inequality.

46. *Company Profits*   The revenue and cost equations for a product are given by

$$R = x(50 - 0.0002x) \quad \text{and} \quad C = 12x + 150,000,$$

where R and C are measured in dollars and x represents the numbers of units sold.
(a) Write the profit P as a function of x.
(b) Use a graphing utility to graph the profit function.
(c) How many units must be sold to obtain a profit of at least $1,650,000?

47. *Percent of College Graduates* The percentage of the American population that graduated from college between 1940 and 1987 is approximated by the model

Percent of graduates $= 5.136 + 0.0069t^2$,

where the time t represents the year, with $t = 0$ corresponding to 1940. Use a graphing utility to graph this model and determine the year when the percentage of college graduates exceeds 25% of the population. (*Source:* U.S. Bureau of Census)

48. *Safe Beam Loads* The maximum safe load uniformly distributed over a 1-foot section of a 2-inch wide wooden beam is approximated by the model

Load $= 168.5d^2 - 472.1$,

where d is the depth of the beam in inches. Use a graphing utility to graph this model and determine the minimum depth of the beam that will safely support a load of 2000 pounds.

CHAPTER 2 · REVIEW EXERCISES

In Exercises 1 and 2, determine whether the equation is an identity or a conditional equation.

1. $6 - (x - 2)^2 = 2 + 4x - x^2$
2. $3(x - 2) + 2x = 2(x + 3)$

In Exercises 3 and 4, determine whether the values of x are solutions of the equation.

Equation	Values

3. $3x^2 + 7x + 5 = x^2 + 9$ (a) $x = 0$ (b) $x = -4$
                   (c) $x = \frac{1}{2}$ (d) $x = -1$

4. $6 + \dfrac{3}{x - 4} = 5$ (a) $x = 4$ (b) $x = 0$
                   (c) $x = -2$ (d) $x = 1$

In Exercises 5–28, solve the equation (if possible) and check your answer either algebraically or graphically.

5. $3x - 2(x + 5) = 10$
6. $4(x + 3) - 3 = 2(4 - 3x) - 4$
7. $3\left(1 - \dfrac{1}{5t}\right) = 0$
8. $\dfrac{1}{x - 2} = 3$
9. $6x^2 = 5x + 4$
10. $15 + x - 2x^2 = 0$
11. $(x + 4)^2 = 18$
12. $16x^2 = 25$
13. $x^2 - 12x + 30 = 0$
14. $5x^4 - 12x^3 = 0$
15. $4t^3 - 12t^2 + 8t = 0$
16. $2 - x^{-2} = 0$
17. $\dfrac{4}{(x - 4)^2} = 1$
18. $\dfrac{4}{x - 3} - \dfrac{4}{x} = 1$
19. $\sqrt{x + 4} = 3$
20. $\sqrt{x - 2} - 8 = 0$
21. $2\sqrt{x} - 5 = 0$
22. $\sqrt{2x + 3} + \sqrt{x - 2} = 2$
23. $(x - 1)^{2/3} - 25 = 0$
24. $(x + 2)^{3/4} = 27$
25. $(x + 4)^{1/2} + 5x(x + 4)^{3/2} = 0$
26. $8x^2(x^2 - 4)^{1/3} + (x^2 - 4)^{4/3} = 0$
27. $|x - 5| = 10$
28. $|x^2 - 6| = x$

In Exercises 29–36, use a graphing utility to solve the equation (if possible).

29. $x^2 + 6x - 3 = 0$
30. $12t^3 - 84t^2 + 120t = 0$
31. $5\sqrt{x} - \sqrt{x - 1} = 6$
32. $\sqrt{3x - 2} = 4 - x$
33. $\dfrac{1}{x} + \dfrac{1}{x + 1} = 2$
34. $\dfrac{1}{(t + 1)^2} = 1$
35. $|x^2 - 3| = 2x$
36. $|2x + 3| = 7$

In Exercises 37–40, solve the equation for the indicated variable.

37. Solve for r: $V = \frac{1}{3}\pi r^2 h$
38. Solve for X: $Z = \sqrt{R^2 - X^2}$
39. Solve for p: $L = \dfrac{k}{3\pi r^2 p}$
40. Solve for v: $E = 2kw\left(\dfrac{v}{2}\right)^2$

In Exercises 41–48, solve the inequality.

41. $\frac{1}{2}(3 - x) > \frac{1}{3}(2 - 3x)$
42. $x^2 - 2x \geq 3$
43. $\dfrac{x - 5}{3 - x} < 0$
44. $\dfrac{2}{x + 1} \leq \dfrac{3}{x - 1}$
45. $|x - 2| < 1$
46. $|x| \leq 4$
47. $|x - \frac{3}{2}| \geq \frac{3}{2}$
48. $|x + 3| > 4$

In Exercises 49–52, use a graphing utility to solve the inequality.

49. $\dfrac{x}{5} - 6 \le -\dfrac{x}{2} + 6$

50. $2x^2 + x \ge 15$

51. $(x - 4)|x| > 0$

52. $|x(x - 6)| < 5$

In Exercises 53 and 54, find the domain of the expression by finding the interval(s) on the real number line for which the radicand is nonnegative.

53. $\sqrt{2x - 10}$

54. $\sqrt{x(x - 4)}$

55. *Monthly Profit* In October, a company's total profit was 12% more than it was in September. The total profit for the two months was $689,000. Find the profit for each month.

56. *Discount Rate* The price of a television set has been discounted $85. The sale price is $340. What percent is the discount?

57. *Mixture Problem* A car radiator contains 10 quarts of a 30% antifreeze solution. How many quarts will have to be replaced with pure antifreeze if the resulting solution is to be 50% antifreeze?

58. *Starting Position* A fitness center has two running tracks around a rectangular playing floor. The tracks are 3 feet wide and form semicircles at the narrow end of the rectangular floor (see figure). Determine the distance between the starting positions if two runners must run the same distance to the finish line in one lap around the track.

59. *Depth of an Underwater Cable* The sonar of a ship locates a cable 2000 feet from the ship (see figure). The angle between the water level and the cable is 45 degrees. How deep is the cable?

FIGURE FOR 58   FIGURE FOR 59

60. *Average Speed* You drove 56 miles on a service call for your company and it took 10 minutes longer than the return trip when you drove an average of 8 miles per hour faster. What was your average speed on the return trip?

61. *Cost Sharing* A group of farmers agree to share equally in the cost of a $48,000 piece of machinery. If they could find two more farmers to join the group, each person's share of the cost would decrease by $4000. How many farmers are presently in the group?

62. *Venture Capital* An individual is planning to start a small business that will require $90,000 before any income can be generated. Because it is difficult to borrow for new ventures, the individual wants a group of friends to divide the cost equally for a future share of the profit. Some are willing, but three more are needed so the price per person will be $2500 less. How many investors are needed?

63. *Market Research* The demand equation for a product is

$$p = 42 - \sqrt{0.001x + 2},$$

where x is the number of units demanded per day and p is the price per unit. Find the demand if the price is set at $29.95.

64. *Compound Interest* P dollars invested at interest rate r compounded annually for 5 years increases to an amount $A = P(1 + r)^5$. If an investment of $1000 is to increase to an amount greater than $1400 in 5 years, then the interest rate must be greater than what percentage?

65. *Break Even Analysis* The revenue for selling x units of a product is $R = 125.95x$. The cost of producing x units is $C = 92x + 1200$. In order to obtain a profit, the revenue must be greater than the cost. For what values of x will this product return a profit?

66. *Simply Supported Beam* A simply supported beam of length 20 feet supports a uniformly distributed load of 1000 pounds per foot (see figure). The bending moment M in foot-pounds x feet from one end of the beam is given by

$$M = 500x(20 - x).$$

Load (1000 lb/ft)

20 ft

FIGURE FOR 66

(a) Use a graphing utility to graph the function. Because of the physical constraints of the problem, give the domain of the function.

(b) Determine any points on the beam where the bending moment is zero.

(c) Use the graph to determine the point on the beam where the bending moment is greatest. What is the moment at that point?

(d) Determine the positions on the beam where the bending moment is less than 40,000 foot-pounds.

67. *Pendulum* The period of a pendulum is

$$T = 2\pi\sqrt{\dfrac{L}{32}},$$

where T is the time in seconds and L is the length of the pendulum in feet. If the period is to be at least 2 seconds, determine the minimum length of the pendulum.

CUMULATIVE TEST FOR PREREQUISITES, CHAPTERS 1 AND 2

Take this test as you would take a test in class. After you are done, check your work with the answers in the back of the book.

1. Evaluate: $(\frac{12}{5} \div 9) - (10 - \frac{1}{45})$

2. Simplify: $\dfrac{8x^2y^{-3}}{30x^{-1}y^2}$

3. Simplify: $\sqrt{24x^4y^3}$

4. Expand and simplify: $(x - 2)(x^2 + x - 3)$

5. Factor completely: $x - 5x^2 - 6x^3$

6. Subtract and simplify: $\dfrac{2}{s + 3} - \dfrac{1}{s + 1}$

7. Simplify: $\dfrac{\frac{2x + 1}{2\sqrt{x}} - \sqrt{x}}{2x + 1}$

8. Sketch a graph of the following equations without the aid of a graphing utility.

(a) $x - 3y + 12 = 0$ (b) $y = x^2 - 4x + 1$

(c) $y = \sqrt{4 - x}$ (d) $y = 3 - |x - 2|$

9. Find the constant C such that $(2, -3)$ is a solution point of the equation $2x - C(y + 1) = 10$.

10. Use the given point $(4, 9)$ on a line and the slope $m = -\frac{2}{3}$ of the line to find the coordinates of three additional points on the line. (The answers are not unique.)

11. Find an equation for the line passing through the points $(-\frac{1}{2}, 1)$ and $(3, 8)$.

12. Evaluate (if possible) the function

$$f(x) = \frac{x}{x - 2}$$

at the specified values of the independent variable.

(a) $f(6)$ (b) $f(2)$

(c) $f(2t)$ (d) $f(s + 2)$

13. Determine the domain and range of the function $g(x) = \dfrac{4}{\sqrt{3 - x}}$.

14. Express the area A of an equilateral triangle as a function of the length s of its sides.

15. Explain why the following graph does not represent y as a function of x.

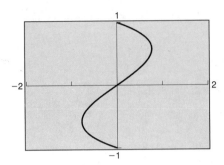

16. Describe how the graphs of each of the following functions would differ from the graph of $y = \sqrt[3]{x}$. It is not necessary to sketch the graphs.

(a) $f(x) = \sqrt[3]{\dfrac{x}{2}}$

(b) $r(x) = \dfrac{1}{2}\sqrt[3]{x}$

(c) $h(x) = \sqrt[3]{x} + 2$

(d) $g(x) = \sqrt[3]{x + 2}$

17. Find $f \circ g$ if $f(x) = \sqrt{x}$ and $g(x) = x^2 + 3$.

18. Determine whether the function $h(x) = 5x - 2$ is one-to-one. If it is, find its inverse.

19. Solve (if possible) the following equations.

(a) $2x - 3(x - 4) = 5$

(b) $\dfrac{2}{t - 3} + \dfrac{2}{t - 2} = \dfrac{10}{t^2 - 5t + 6}$

(c) $3y^2 + 6y + 2 = 0$

(d) $\sqrt{x + 10} = x - 2$

20. Use a graphing utility to approximate (accurate to one decimal place) any solutions of the equation $\sqrt{x + 4} + \sqrt{x} = 6$. (Remember to write the equation in the form $f(x) = 0$.)

21. Solve and sketch the solution on the real number line: $\left| \dfrac{x - 2}{3} \right| < 1$

22. Solve and sketch the solution on the real number line: $x^2 - x < 6$

23. An inheritance of $12,000 is divided between two investments earning 7.5% and 9% simple interest. How much is in each investment if the total interest for one year is $960?

24. Three gallons of a mixture is 60% water by volume. Determine the number of gallons of water that must be added to bring the mixture to 75% water.

25. A group of n people decide to buy a $36,000 minibus for a charitable organization. Each person will pay an equal share of the cost. If three additional people were to join the group, the cost per person would decrease by $1000. Find n.

POLYNOMIAL FUNCTIONS: GRAPHS AND ZEROS

3.1 QUADRATIC FUNCTIONS

The Graph of a Quadratic Function / The Standard Form of a Quadratic Function / Applications

The Graph of a Quadratic Function

Polynomial functions are the most commonly used functions in algebra. Let n be a nonnegative integer and let $a_n, a_{n-1}, \ldots, a_2, a_1, a_0$ be real numbers with $a_n \neq 0$. The function given by

$$f(x) = a_n x^n + a_{n-1} x^{n-1} + \cdots + a_2 x^2 + a_1 x + a_0$$

is called a **polynomial function of x with degree n.**

The function $f(x) = a$, where $a \neq 0$, has degree 0 and is a **constant function.** The polynomial function $f(x) = ax + b$, where $a \neq 0$, has degree 1 and is a **linear function.** In this section you will study second-degree polynomial functions, called **quadratic functions.**

DEFINITION OF A QUADRATIC FUNCTION

Let a, b, and c be real numbers with $a \neq 0$. The function

$$f(x) = ax^2 + bx + c$$

is a **quadratic function.** The graph of a quadratic function is called a **parabola.**

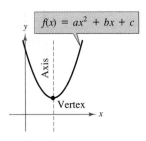

$a > 0$: Parabola opens upward.

$a < 0$: Parabola opens downward.

FIGURE 3.1

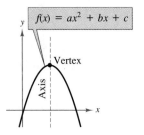

$a > 0$: Parabola opens upward.

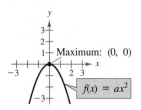

$a < 0$: Parabola opens downward.

FIGURE 3.2

All parabolas are symmetric with respect to a line called the **axis of symmetry,** or simply the **axis** of the parabola. The point where the axis intersects the parabola is the **vertex** of the parabola, as shown in Figure 3.1. If the leading coefficient is positive, then the graph of $f(x) = ax^2 + bx + c$ is a parabola that opens upward, and if the leading coefficient is negative, then the graph is a parabola that opens downward.

The simplest type of quadratic function is $f(x) = ax^2$. Its graph is a parabola whose vertex is $(0, 0)$. If $a > 0$, then the vertex is the *minimum* point on the graph, and if $a < 0$, then the vertex is the *maximum* point on the graph, as shown in Figure 3.2. When sketching the graph of $f(x) = ax^2$, it is helpful to use the graph of $y = x^2$ as a reference, as discussed in Section 1.5.

EXAMPLE 1   **Sketching the Graphs of Simple Quadratic Functions**

Describe how the graphs of the following functions are related to the graph of $y = x^2$.

A. $f(x) = \dfrac{1}{3}x^2$ **B.** $g(x) = 2x^2$

SOLUTION

A. Compared with $y = x^2$, each output of f "shrinks" by a factor of $\frac{1}{3}$. The result is a parabola that opens upward and is broader than the parabola represented by $y = x^2$, as shown in Figure 3.3.

B. Compared with $y = x^2$, each output of g "stretches" by a factor of 2, creating the more narrow parabola shown in Figure 3.4.

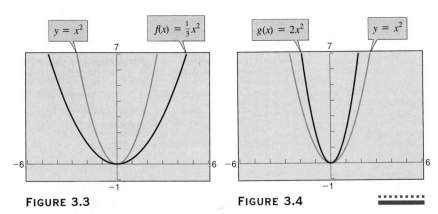

FIGURE 3.3   **FIGURE 3.4**

Recall from Section 1.5 that the graphs of $y = f(x \pm c)$, $y = f(x) \pm c$, and $y = -f(x)$ are rigid transformations of the graph of $y = f(x)$.

$$y = f(x \pm c)$$ *Horizontal shift*
$$y = f(x) \pm c$$ *Vertical shift*
$$y = -f(x)$$ *Reflection*

REMARK   In Example 1, note that the coefficient a determines how widely the parabola given by $f(x) = ax^2$ opens. If $|a|$ is small, the parabola opens more widely than if $|a|$ is large.

EXAMPLE 2   Sketching a Parabola

Describe how the graphs of the following quadratic functions are related to the graph of $y = x^2$.

A. $f(x) = -x^2 + 1$ **B.** $g(x) = (x + 2)^2 - 3$

SOLUTION

A. With respect to the graph of $y = x^2$, the negative coefficient in $f(x) = -x^2 + 1$ reflects the graph *downward* and the positive constant term shifts the vertex *up one unit*. The graph of f is shown in Figure 3.5. Note that the axis of the parabola is the y-axis and the vertex is $(0, 1)$.

B. With respect to the graph of $y = x^2$, the graph of $g(x) = (x + 2)^2 - 3$ is obtained by a horizontal shift two units *to the left* and a vertical shift three units *down*, as shown in Figure 3.6. Note that the axis of the parabola is the vertical line $x = -2$ and the vertex is $(-2, -3)$.

FIGURE 3.5

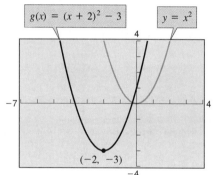

FIGURE 3.6

The Standard Form of a Quadratic Function

The equation in Example 2(B) is written in **standard form**

$$f(x) = a(x - h)^2 + k.$$

This form is especially convenient for sketching a parabola because it identifies the vertex of the parabola as (h, k).

STANDARD FORM OF A QUADRATIC FUNCTION

The quadratic function

$$f(x) = a(x - h)^2 + k, \qquad a \neq 0$$

is said to be in **standard form.** The graph of f is a parabola whose axis is the vertical line $x = h$ and whose vertex is the point (h, k). If $a > 0$, the parabola opens upward, and if $a < 0$, the parabola opens downward.

EXAMPLE 3   Writing a Quadratic Function in Standard Form

Describe the graph of $f(x) = 2x^2 + 8x + 7$.

SOLUTION

Write the quadratic function in standard form by completing the square. Notice that the first step is to factor out any coefficient of x^2 that is different from 1.

$$f(x) = 2x^2 + 8x + 7 \qquad \textit{Original form}$$
$$= 2(x^2 + 4x) + 7 \qquad \textit{Factor 2 out of x terms}$$
$$= 2(x^2 + 4x + 4 - 4) + 7 \qquad \textit{Add and subtract 4 within parentheses}$$
$$\underbrace{}_{(b/2)^2}$$
$$= 2(x^2 + 4x + 4) - 2(4) + 7 \qquad \textit{Regroup terms}$$
$$= 2(x + 2)^2 - 1 \qquad \textit{Standard form}$$

From the standard form, you can see that the graph of f is a parabola that opens upward with vertex $(-2, -1)$, as shown in Figure 3.7.

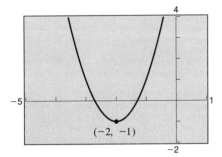

FIGURE 3.7

EXAMPLE 4   Writing a Quadratic Function in Standard Form

Describe the graph of $f(x) = -x^2 + 6x - 8$.

SOLUTION

$$f(x) = -x^2 + 6x - 8 \qquad \textit{Original form}$$
$$= -(x^2 - 6x) - 8 \qquad \textit{Factor} -1 \textit{ out of x terms}$$
$$= -(x^2 - 6x + 9 - 9) - 8 \qquad \textit{Add and subtract 9 within parentheses}$$
$$\underbrace{}_{b/2^2}$$
$$= -(x^2 - 6x + 9) - (-9) - 8 \qquad \textit{Regroup terms}$$
$$= -(x - 3)^2 + 1 \qquad \textit{Standard form } a < 0$$

The graph of f is a parabola that opens downward with vertex at $(3, 1)$, as shown in Figure 3.8.

FIGURE 3.8

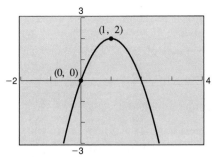

FIGURE 3.9

EXAMPLE 5   Finding the Equation of a Parabola

Find an equation for the parabola that has its vertex at $(1, 2)$ and that passes through the point $(0, 0)$, as shown in Figure 3.9.

SOLUTION

Because the parabola has a vertex at $(h, k) = (1, 2)$, the equation has the form

$$\overset{\overset{h}{\downarrow}\quad\overset{k}{\downarrow}}{f(x) = a(x - 1)^2 + 2.}\qquad\qquad \textit{Standard form}$$

Because the parabola passes through the point $(0, 0)$, it follows that $f(0) = 0$. Thus, you obtain

$$0 = a(0 - 1)^2 + 2,$$

which implies that $a = -2$. The equation is

$$f(x) = -2(x - 1)^2 + 2 = -2x^2 + 4x.$$

Try graphing $f(x) = -2x^2 + 4x$ with a graphing utility to confirm that its vertex is $(1, 2)$ and that it passes through the point $(0, 0)$.

To find the x-intercepts of the graph of $f(x) = ax^2 + bx + c$, solve the equation $ax^2 + bx + c = 0$. For example, from the equation

$$-2x^2 + 4x = -2x(x - 2) = 0$$

you can see that the parabola shown in Figure 3.9 has x-intercepts at $(0, 0)$ and $(2, 0)$. If $ax^2 + bx + c$ does not factor, you can use the Quadratic Formula or a graphing utility to find the x-intercepts. Remember, however, that a parabola may have no x-intercept.

Applications

Many applications involve finding the maximum or minimum value of a quadratic function. By writing the quadratic function $f(x) = ax^2 + bx + c$ in standard form,

$$f(x) = a\left(x + \frac{b}{2a}\right)^2 + \left(c - \frac{b^2}{4a}\right),$$

you can see that the vertex occurs as $x = -b/2a$, which implies the following.

1. If $a > 0$ then the quadratic function $f(x) = ax^2 + bx + c$ has a *minimum* that occurs at $x = -b/2a$.
2. If $a < 0$ then the quadratic function $f(x) = ax^2 + bx + c$ has a *maximum* that occurs at $x = -b/2a$.

In either case, you can find the minimum or maximum value of f by evaluating the function at $x = -b/2a$ or by graphing the function.

EXAMPLE 6 **The Maximum Height of a Baseball**

A baseball is hit 3 feet above ground at a velocity of 100 feet per second and at an angle of 45 degrees with respect to level ground. The path of the baseball is given by the function

$$f(x) = -0.0032x^2 + x + 3,$$

where $f(x)$ is the height of the baseball (in feet) and x is the distance from home plate (in feet). What is the maximum height reached by the baseball?

SOLUTION

For this quadratic function, you have

$$f(x) = ax^2 + bx + c = -0.0032x^2 + x + 3,$$

which implies that $a = -0.0032$ and $b = 1$. Because the function has a maximum when $x = -b/2a$, you can conclude that the baseball reaches its maximum height when x is

$$x = -\frac{b}{2a} = \frac{1}{2(-0.0032)} = 156.25$$

from home plate. At this distance, the maximum height is

$$f(156.25) = -0.0032(156.25)^2 + 156.25 + 3 = 81.125.$$

The path of the baseball is shown in Figure 3.10. You can also solve this problem by using a graphing utility. By using the zoom and trace feature, you can determine that the maximum height on the graph occurs when $x \approx 156.25$. Note that you might have to change the y-scale in order to avoid a graph that is "too flat."

FIGURE 3.10

EXAMPLE 7   Charitable Contributions

According to a survey conducted in 1990 by *Independent Sector,* the percentage of their income that Americans give to charities is related to their household income. For families with an annual income of $100,000 or less, the percentage is approximately given by

$$P = 0.0014x^2 - 0.1529x + 5.855, \qquad 5 \le x \le 100,$$

where P is the percentage of annual income given and x is the annual income in thousands of dollars. According to this model, what income level corresponds to the least percentage of charitable contributions?

SOLUTION

There are two ways to answer this question. One is to use a graphing utility to graph the quadratic function, as shown in Figure 3.11. From this graph, it appears that the minimum percentage corresponds to an income level of about $55,000. By using the zoom feature, you can improve the approximation to $x \approx 54,600$. The other way to answer the question is to use the fact that the minimum point of the parabola occurs when $x = -b/2a$. For this function, you have $a = 0.0014$ and $b = -0.1529$. Thus,

$$x = -\frac{b}{2a} = -\frac{-0.1529}{2(0.0014)} \approx 54.6.$$

From this x-value, you can conclude that the minimum percentage corresponds to an income level of about $54,600.

FIGURE 3.11

DISCUSSION PROBLEM

....

FINDING AN EQUATION FOR A CURVE

The parabola in the figure has an equation of the form $y = x^2 + bx + c$. Find the equation for this parabola, and write a short paragraph describing the method you used.

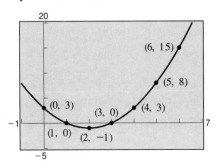

WARM-UP

....

The following warm-up exercises involve skills that were covered in earlier sections. You will use these skills in the exercise set for this section.

In Exercises 1–4, solve the quadratic equation by factoring.

1. $2x^2 + 11x - 6 = 0$ **2.** $5x^2 - 12x - 9 = 0$
3. $3 + x - 2x^2 = 0$ **4.** $x^2 + 20x + 100 = 0$

In Exercises 5–8, solve the quadratic equation by completing the square.

5. $x^2 - 6x + 4 = 0$ **6.** $x^2 + 4x + 1 = 0$
7. $2x^2 - 16x + 25 = 0$ **8.** $3x^2 + 30x + 74 = 0$

In Exercises 9 and 10, use the Quadratic Formula to solve the quadratic equation.

9. $x^2 + 3x + 1 = 0$ **10.** $x^2 + 3x - 3 = 0$

SECTION 3.1 · EXERCISES

In Exercises 1–6, match the quadratic function with its graph, and describe the viewing rectangle. [The graphs are labeled (a), (b), (c), (d), (e), and (f).]

1. $f(x) = (x - 3)^2$

2. $f(x) = (x + 5)^2$

3. $f(x) = x^2 - 4$

4. $f(x) = 5 - x^2$

5. $f(x) = 4 - (x - 1)^2$

6. $f(x) = (x + 2)^2 - 2$

(a)

(b)

(c)

(d)

(e)

(f)

In Exercises 7–10, use a graphing utility to compare the graph of each function with the graph of $y = x^2$.

7. (a) $f(x) = \frac{1}{6}x^2$
   (b) $g(x) = -3x^2$

8. (a) $f(x) = -\frac{1}{2}x^2 + 4$
   (b) $g(x) = 2x^2 - 5$

9. (a) $f(x) = -(x + 3)^2 + 3$
   (b) $g(x) = \frac{4}{3}(x - 4)^2 - 3$

10. (a) $f(x) = 0.75(x - 4.5)^2 + 5.2$
   (b) $g(x) = -0.2(x + 1.4)^2 + 3.8$

In Exercises 11–16, find an equation for the given parabola.

11.

12.

13.

14.

15.

16.

In Exercises 17–26, sketch the graph of the given quadratic function without the aid of a graphing utility. Identify the vertex and intercepts. Then use a graphing utility to check your result.

17. $f(x) = x^2 - 5$

18. $h(x) = 25 - x^2$

19. $f(x) = (x + 5)^2 - 6$

20. $f(x) = (x - 6)^2 + 3$

21. $h(x) = x^2 - 8x + 16$

22. $f(x) = x^2 + 3x + \frac{1}{4}$

23. $f(x) = -x^2 + 2x + 5$

24. $f(x) = -x^2 - 4x + 1$

25. $h(x) = 4x^2 - 4x + 21$

26. $f(x) = 2x^2 - x + 1$

In Exercises 27–30, use a graphing utility to graph the quadratic function. Identify the vertex and intercepts. Then check your result algebraically by completing the square.

27. $f(x) = -(x^2 + 2x - 3)$

28. $g(x) = x^2 + 8x + 11$

29. $f(x) = 2x^2 - 16x + 31$

30. $g(x) = \frac{1}{2}(x^2 + 4x - 2)$

In Exercises 31–34, find the quadratic function that has the indicated vertex and whose graph passes through the given point. Confirm your result with a graphing utility.

31. Vertex: (3, 4); point: (1, 2)

32. Vertex: (2, 3); point: (0, 2)

33. Vertex: (5, 12); point: (7, 15)

34. Vertex: (−2, −2); point: (−1, 0)

In Exercises 35–40, find two quadratic functions whose graphs have the given x-intercepts. (Find one function that has a graph that opens upward and another that has a graph that opens downward.)

35. (−1, 0), (3, 0)

36. $(-\frac{5}{2}, 0)$, (2, 0)

37. (0, 0), (10, 0)

38. (4, 0), (8, 0)

39. (−3, 0), $(-\frac{1}{2}, 0)$

40. (−5, 0), (5, 0)

In Exercises 41 and 42, find two positive real numbers that satisfy the given requirements.

41. The sum is 110 and the product is a maximum.

42. The sum is S and the product is a maximum.

Maximum Area   In Exercises 43 and 44, consider a rectangle of length x and perimeter P (see figure). (a) Express the area A as a function of x and determine the domain of the function. (b) Graph the area function. (c) Find the length and width of the rectangle of maximum area.

43. P = 100 feet

44. P = 36 meters

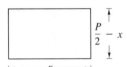

FIGURE FOR 43 AND 44

45. *Maximum Area*   A rancher has 200 feet of fencing to enclose two adjacent rectangular corrals (see figure). What dimensions will produce a maximum enclosed area?

FIGURE FOR 45

46. *Maximum Area*   An indoor physical fitness room consists of a rectangular region with a semicircle on each end (see figure). The perimeter of the room is to be a 200-meter running track. What dimensions will produce a maximum area of the rectangle?

FIGURE FOR 46

47. *Maximum Revenue*   Find the number of units that produce a maximum revenue,

$R = 900x - 0.1x^2,$

where R is the total revenue in dollars and x is the number of units sold.

48. *Maximum Revenue*   Find the number of units that produce a maximum revenue,

$R = 100x - 0.0002x^2,$

where R is the total revenue in dollars and x is the number of units sold.

49. From 1950 to 1990, the average annual per capita consumption C of cigarettes by Americans (18 and older) can be modeled by

$C = 4024.5 + 51.4t - 3.1t^2,$

where t is the year, with t = 0 corresponding to 1960. The graph of the model is shown in the figure. (*Source:* U.S. Center for Disease Control)

(a) Beginning in 1966, all cigarette packages were required by law to carry a health warning. Do you think the warnings had any effect? Explain.

(b) In 1960, the U.S. had a population (18 and over) of 116,530,000. Of those, about 48,500,000 were smokers. What was the average annual cigarette consumption *per smoker* in 1960? What was the average daily cigarette consumption *per smoker*?

FIGURE FOR 49

50. *Maximum Profit*   Let x be the amount (in hundreds of dollars) a company spends on advertising, and let P be the profit, where

$$P = 230 + 20x - 0.5x^2.$$

What expenditure for advertising gives the maximum profit?

51. *Trajectory of a Ball*   The height y (in feet) of a ball thrown by a child is

$$y = -\tfrac{1}{12}x^2 + 2x + 4,$$

where x is the horizontal distance (in feet) from where the ball is thrown (see figure).
(a) Use a graphing utility to sketch the path of the ball.
(b) How high is the ball when it leaves the child's hand? (*Note:* Find y when $x = 0$.)
(c) How high is the ball when it reaches its maximum height?
(d) How far from the child does the ball strike the ground?

FIGURE FOR 51

52. *Maximum Height of a Dive*   The path of a dive is given by

$$y = -\tfrac{4}{9}x^2 + \tfrac{24}{9}x + 10,$$

where y is the height in feet and x is the horizontal distance from the end of the diving board in feet (see figure). What is the maximum height of the dive?

(0, 10)

FIGURE FOR 52

53. *Forestry*   The number of board feet in a 16-foot log is approximated by the model

$$V = 0.77x^2 - 1.32x - 9.31, \qquad 0 \le x \le 40,$$

where V is the number of board feet and x is the diameter of the log at the small end in inches. (One board foot is a measure of volume equivalent to a board that is 12 inches wide, 12 inches long, and 1 inch thick.)
(a) Use a graphing utility to graph the function.
(b) Estimate the number of board feet in a 16-foot log with a diameter of 16 inches.
(c) Estimate the diameter of a 16-foot log that yielded 500 board feet when the lumber was sold.

54. *Automobile Aerodynamics*   The amount of horsepower y required to overcome wind drag on a certain automobile is approximated by

$$y = 0.002x^2 + 0.005x - 0.0029, \qquad 0 \le x \le 100,$$

where x is the speed of the car in miles per hour.
(a) Use a graphing utility to graph the function.
(b) Estimate the maximum speed of the car if the power required to overcome wind drag is not to exceed 10 horsepower.

55. Complete the square for the quadratic function $f(x) = ax^2 + bx + c \ (a \ne 0)$ and show that the vertex is at

$$\left(-\frac{b}{2a}, \ -\frac{b^2 - 4ac}{4a} \right).$$

56. Use Exercise 55 to verify the vertices found in Exercises 21 and 22.

57. Assume that the function $f(x) = ax^2 + bx + c \ (a \ne 0)$ has two real zeros. Show that the x-coordinate of the vertex of the graph is the average of the zeros of f. (*Hint:* Use the Quadratic Formula.)

58. Use a graphing utility to demonstrate the result of Exercise 57 for each of the following equations.
(a) $f(x) = \tfrac{1}{2}(x - 3)^2 - 2$ (b) $f(x) = 6 - \tfrac{2}{3}(x + 1)^2$

3.2   POLYNOMIAL FUNCTIONS OF HIGHER DEGREE
....

**Graphs of Polynomial Functions   /   The Leading Coefficient Test   /
Zeros of Polynomial Functions   /   The Intermediate Value Theorem**

Graphs of Polynomial Functions

DISCOVERY

Use a graphing utility to graph
$y = x^n$ with $n = 2$, 4, and 8.
(Use $-1.5 \le x \le 1.5$ and
$-1 \le y \le 6$.) Compare the
graphs. In the interval $(-1, 1)$,
which graph is on the bottom?
Outside the interval $(-1, 1)$,
which graph is on the bottom?
    Use a graphing utility to graph
$y = x^n$ with $n = 3$, 5, and 7.
(Use $-1.5 \le x \le 1.5$ and
$-4 \le y \le 4$.) Compare the
graphs. In the interval $(-1, 1)$,
which graph is on the bottom?
Outside the interval $(-1, 1)$,
which graph is on the bottom?

At this point you should be able to sketch an accurate graph of polynomial functions of degrees 0, 1, and 2.

Function	*Graph*
$f(x) = a$	Horizontal line
$f(x) = ax + b$	Line of slope a
$f(x) = ax^2 + bx + c$	Parabola

The graphs of polynomial functions of degree greater than 2 are more difficult to sketch by hand. However, in this section you will learn how to recognize some of the basic features of the graphs of polynomial functions.

The graph of a polynomial function is **continuous.** Essentially, this means that the graph of a polynomial function has no breaks, as shown in Figure 3.12.

Another feature of the graph of a polynomial function is that it has only smooth, rounded turns, as shown in Figure 3.13(a); it cannot have a sharp, pointed turn such as the one shown in Figure 3.13(b). A specific example of a nonpolynomial function is $f(x) = |x|$, the graph of which has a sharp turn at the point $(0, 0)$.

FIGURE 3.12   Continuous

Discontinuous

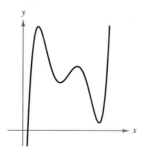

(a) Polynomial functions have
     smooth, rounded graphs.

FIGURE 3.13

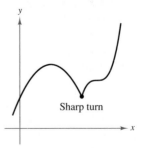

(b) The graph of a polynomial function
     cannot have a sharp pointed turn.

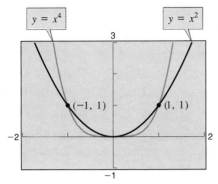

If n is even, the graph of $y = x^n$ *touches* axis at x-intercept.

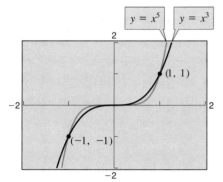

If n is odd, the graph of $y = x^n$ *crosses* axis at x-intercept.

FIGURE 3.14

The polynomial functions that have the simplest graphs are monomials of the form

$$f(x) = x^n,$$

where n is an integer greater than zero. From Figure 3.14, you can see that when n is *even* the graph is similar to the graph of $f(x) = x^2$, and when n is *odd* the graph is similar to the graph of $f(x) = x^3$. Moreover, the greater the value of n, the flatter the graph is on the interval $[-1, 1]$.

EXAMPLE 1   **Sketching Transformations of Monomial Functions**

Sketch the graphs of the following polynomial functions.

A. $f(x) = -x^5$ **B.** $g(x) = x^4 + 1$ **C.** $h(x) = (x + 1)^4$

SOLUTION

A. Because the degree of f is odd, the graph is similar to the graph of $y = x^3$. Moreover, the negative coefficient reflects the graph in the x-axis. Plotting the intercept $(0, 0)$ and the points $(1, -1)$ and $(-1, 1)$, you can obtain the graph shown in Figure 3.15.

B. In this case, the graph of g is an upward shift, by one unit, of the graph of $y = x^4$ (see Figure 3.14). Thus, you can obtain the graph shown in Figure 3.16.

C. The graph of h is a left shift, by one unit, of the graph of $y = x^4$ and it is shown in Figure 3.17.

FIGURE 3.15

FIGURE 3.16

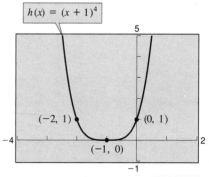

FIGURE 3.17

DISCOVERY

Use a graphing utility to investigate the behavior of the graph of

$y = x^3 - 105x^2 + 21.$

First use a viewing rectangle in which $-2 \le x \le 2$ and $-10 \le y \le 30$. How complete a view of the graph does this viewing rectangle show? Does the graph move down as x increases indefinitely? Find a viewing rectangle that gives a good view of the basic characteristics of the graph.

The Leading Coefficient Test

In Example 1, note that the three graphs eventually rise or fall without bound as x moves to the right or left. Symbolically, this is written as

$$f(x) \longrightarrow \infty \quad \text{as} \quad x \longrightarrow \infty,$$

which means that $f(x)$ increases without bound as x moves to the right without bound. (The infinity symbol ∞ is used to indicate unboundedness.) Whether the graph of a polynomial eventually rises or falls can be determined by the function's degree (even or odd) and by its leading coefficient, as indicated by the **Leading Coefficient Test.**

LEADING COEFFICIENT TEST

As x increases or decreases without bound, the graph of the polynomial function $f(x) = a_n x^n + \cdots + a_1 x + a_0$ eventually rises or falls in the following manner. (*Note:* The dashed portions of the graphs indicate that the test determines *only* the right and left behavior of the graph.

1. When n is *odd:*

If the leading coefficient is positive ($a_n > 0$), then the graph falls to the left and rises to the right.

If the leading coefficient is negative ($a_n < 0$), then the graph rises to the left and falls to the right.

2. When n is *even:*

If the leading coefficient is positive ($a_n > 0$), then the graph rises to the left and right.

If the leading coefficient is negative ($a_n < 0$), then the graph falls to the left and right.

FIGURE 3.18

FIGURE 3.19

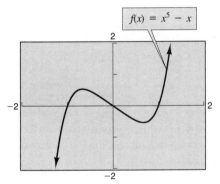

FIGURE 3.20

EXAMPLE 2   Applying the Leading Coefficient Test

Use the Leading Coefficient Test to determine the right and left behavior of the graphs of the following polynomial functions.

A. $f(x) = -x^3 + 4x$ **B.** $f(x) = x^4 - 5x^2 + 4$
C. $f(x) = x^5 - x$

SOLUTION

A. Because the degree is odd and the leading coefficient is negative, the graph rises to the left and falls to the right, as shown in Figure 3.18.
B. Because the degree is even and the leading coefficient is positive, the graph rises to the left and right, as shown in Figure 3.19.
C. Because the degree is odd and the leading coefficient is positive, the graph falls to the left and rises to the right, as shown in Figure 3.20.

Zeros of Polynomial Functions

It can be shown that for a polynomial function f of degree n, the following statements are true.

1. The function f has at most n real zeros. (This result is discussed in detail in Section 3.6.)
2. The graph of f has at most $n - 1$ relative extrema (local minimums or maximums).

Recall that a **zero** of a function f is a number x for which $f(x) = 0$. For instance, 0 and -3 are zeros of the function $f(x) = x^2 + 3x$ because $f(0) = 0^2 + 3(0) = 0$ and $f(-3) = (-3)^3 + 3(-3) = 0$.

Finding the zeros of polynomial functions is one of the most important problems in algebra. You have already seen that there is a strong interplay between graphical and algebraic approaches to this problem. Sometimes you can use information about the graph of a function to help find its zeros, and in other cases you can use information about the zeros of a function to help find a good viewing rectangle.

REAL ZEROS OF POLYNOMIAL FUNCTIONS

If f is a polynomial function and a is a real number, then the following statements are equivalent.

1. $x = a$ is a *zero* of the function f.
2. $x = a$ is a *solution* of the polynomial equation $f(x) = 0$.
3. $(x - a)$ is a *factor* of the polynomial $f(x)$.
4. $(a, 0)$ is an *x-intercept* of the graph of f.

Finding zeros of polynomial functions is closely related to factoring and finding x-intercepts, as demonstrated in Examples 3, 4, and 5.

EXAMPLE 3   Finding Zeros of a Third-Degree Polynomial Function

Find all real zeros of $f(x) = x^3 - x^2 - 2x$.

SOLUTION

$$f(x) = x^3 - x^2 - 2x \qquad \textit{Original function}$$
$$= x(x^2 - x - 2) \qquad \textit{Remove common monomial factor}$$
$$= x(x - 2)(x + 1) \qquad \textit{Factor completely}$$

Thus, the real zeros are $x = 0$, $x = 2$, and $x = -1$, and the corresponding x-intercepts are $(0, 0)$, $(2, 0)$, and $(-1, 0)$, as shown in Figure 3.21. In the figure, note that the graph has two relative (local) extrema. This is consistent with the fact that a third-degree polynomial can have *at most* two relative extrema.

FIGURE 3.21

EXAMPLE 4   Finding Zeros of a Fourth-Degree Polynomial Function

Find all real zeros of $f(x) = -2x^4 + 2x^2$.

SOLUTION

$$f(x) = -2x^4 + 2x^2 \qquad \textit{Original function}$$
$$= -2x^2(x^2 - 1) \qquad \textit{Remove common monomial factor}$$
$$= -2x^2(x - 1)(x + 1) \qquad \textit{Factor completely}$$

Thus, the real zeros are $x = 0$, $x = 1$, and $x = -1$, and the corresponding x-intercepts are $(0, 0)$, $(1, 0)$, and $(-1, 0)$, as shown in Figure 3.22. Note in the figure that the graph has three relative extrema, which is consistent with the fact that a fourth-degree polynomial can have at most three relative extrema.

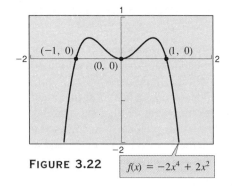

FIGURE 3.22

In Example 4, the real zero arising from $-2x^2 = 0$ is a **repeated zero.** In general, a factor of $(x - a)^k$ yields a repeated zero $x = a$ of **multiplicity** k. If k is odd, then the graph *crosses* the x-axis at $x = a$. If k is even, then the graph *touches* (but does not cross) the x-axis at $x = a$, as shown in Figure 3.22.

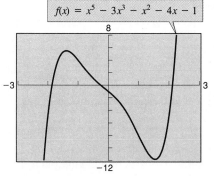

$f(x) = x^5 - 3x^3 - x^2 - 4x - 1$

8

−3

3

−12

FIGURE 3.23

EXAMPLE 5   Finding Zeros of a Fifth-Degree Polynomial Function

Find all zeros of $f(x) = x^5 - 3x^3 - x^2 - 4x - 1$.

SOLUTION

Use a graphing utility to obtain the graph shown in Figure 3.23. From the graph, you can see that there are three zeros. Using the zoom and trace features, you can determine that the zeros are approximately $x = -1.861$, $x = -0.254$, and $x = 2.115$. It should be noted that this fifth-degree polynomial factors as

$$f(x) = x^5 - 3x^3 - x^2 - 4x - 1$$
$$= (x^2 + 1)(x^3 - 4x - 1).$$

The three zeros obtained above are the zeros to the cubic on the right (the quadratic $x^2 + 1$ has no real zeros).

To find mathematical models, you may need to create a polynomial function that has a particular set of zeros.

EXAMPLE 6   Finding a Polynomial Function with Given Zeros

Find polynomial functions with the following zeros. (There are many correct solutions.)

A. $-2, -1, 1, 2$ **B.** $-\dfrac{1}{2}, 3, 3$

SOLUTION

A. For each of the given zeros, form a corresponding factor. For instance, the zero given by $x = -2$ corresponds to the factor $(x + 2)$. Thus, you can write the function as

$$f(x) = (x + 2)(x + 1)(x - 1)(x - 2)$$
$$= (x^2 - 4)(x^2 - 1)$$
$$= x^4 - 5x^2 + 4.$$

B. Note that the zero $x = -\frac{1}{2}$ corresponds to either $(x + \frac{1}{2})$ or $(2x + 1)$. To avoid fractions, choose the second factor and write

$$f(x) = (2x + 1)(x - 3)^2$$
$$= (2x + 1)(x^2 - 6x + 9)$$
$$= 2x^3 - 11x^2 + 12x + 9.$$

FIGURE 3.24

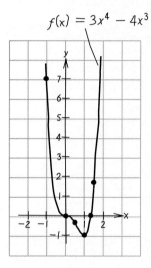

$$f(x) = 3x^4 - 4x^3$$

FIGURE 3.25

EXAMPLE 7   **Sketching the Graph of a Polynomial Function**

Sketch the graph of $f(x) = 3x^4 - 4x^3$ by hand.

SOLUTION

Because the leading coefficient is positive and the degree is even, you know that the graph eventually rises to the left and to the right, as shown in Figure 3.24. By factoring to obtain

$$f(x) = 3x^4 - 4x^3 = x^3(3x - 4),$$

you can see that the zeros of f are $x = 0$ and $x = \frac{4}{3}$ (both of odd multiplicity). Thus, the x-intercepts occur at $(0, 0)$ and $(\frac{4}{3}, 0)$. Finally, plot a few additional points as indicated in the accompanying table and obtain the graph shown in Figure 3.25.

x	-1	0.5	1	1.5
$f(x)$	7	-0.3125	-1	1.6875

The Intermediate Value Theorem

The **Intermediate Value Theorem** concerns the existence of real zeros of polynomial functions. The theorem states that if $(a, f(a))$ and $(b, f(b))$ are two points on the graph of a polynomial such that $f(a) \neq f(b)$, then for any number d between $f(a)$ and $f(b)$ there must be a number c between a and b such that $f(c) = d$. (See Figure 3.26.)

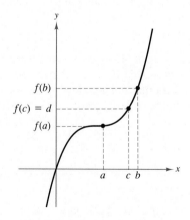

If d lies between $f(a)$ and $f(b)$, then there exists c between a and b such that $f(c) = d$.

FIGURE 3.26

INTERMEDIATE VALUE THEOREM

Let a and b be real numbers such that $a < b$. If f is a polynomial function such that $f(a) \neq f(b)$, then in the interval $[a, b]$, f takes on every value between $f(a)$ and $f(b)$.

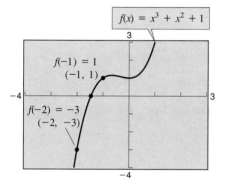

$f(x) = x^3 + x^2 + 1$

$f(-1) = 1$
$(-1, 1)$

$f(-2) = -3$
$(-2, -3)$

f has a zero between -2 and -1.

FIGURE 3.27

This theorem helps locate the real zeros of a polynomial function in the following way. If you can find a value $x = a$ where a polynomial function is positive, and another value $x = b$ where it is negative, then you can conclude that the function has at least one real zero between these two values. For example, the function $f(x) = x^3 + x^2 + 1$ is negative when $x = -2$ and positive when $x = -1$. Therefore, it follows from the Intermediate Value Theorem that f must have a real zero somewhere between -2 and -1, as shown in Figure 3.27.

EXAMPLE 8   Locating Zeros with the Intermediate Value Theorem

Use the Intermediate Value Theorem to find three intervals of length 1 in which the polynomial $f(x) = 12x^3 - 32x^2 + 3x + 5$ is guaranteed to have a zero.

SOLUTION

With a graphing utility, you can see that there are three zeros, as shown in Figure 3.28. The following table shows several function values.

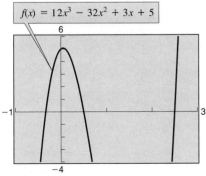

$f(x) = 12x^3 - 32x^2 + 3x + 5$

FIGURE 3.28

x	-1	0	1	2	3
$f(x)$	-42	5	-12	-21	50

Because $f(-1)$ is negative and $f(0)$ is positive, you can conclude from the Intermediate Value Theorem that the function has a zero between -1 and 0, as indicated in the figure. Similarly, the function has a zero between 0 and 1, and another between 2 and 3. You could obtain more accurate approximations to these zeros using the zoom and trace features.

DISCUSSION PROBLEM

THE GRAPHS OF CUBIC POLYNOMIALS

The graphs of cubic polynomials can be categorized according to the four basic shapes shown in the figure.

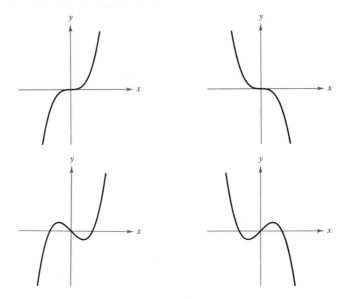

Match the graph of each of the following four functions with one of the basic shapes and write a short paragraph describing how you reached your conclusions.

(a) $f(x) = -x^3$ (b) $f(x) = -x^3 + x$
(c) $f(x) = x^3$ (d) $f(x) = x^3 - x$

WARM-UP

The following warm-up exercises involve skills that were covered in earlier sections. You will use these skills in the exercise set for this section.

In Exercises 1–6, factor the expression completely.

1. $12x^2 + 7x - 10$ 2. $25x^3 - 60x^2 + 36x$ 3. $12z^4 + 17z^3 + 5z^2$
4. $y^3 + 125$ 5. $x^3 + 3x^2 - 4x - 12$ 6. $x^3 + 2x^2 + 3x + 6$

In Exercises 7–10, find all real solutions to the equation.

7. $5x^2 + 8 = 0$ 8. $x^2 - 6x + 4 = 0$
9. $4x^2 + 4x - 11 = 0$ 10. $x^4 - 18x^2 + 81 = 0$

SECTION 3.2 · EXERCISES

1. Compare the graph of f with the graph of $y = x^3$.
  (a) $f(x) = (x - 2)^3$
  (b) $f(x) = x^3 - 2$
  (c) $f(x) = (x - 2)^3 - 2$
  (d) $f(x) = -\frac{1}{2}x^3$

2. Compare the graph of f with the graph of $y = x^4$.
  (a) $f(x) = (x + 3)^4$
  (b) $f(x) = x^4 - 3$
  (c) $f(x) = 4 - x^4$
  (d) $f(x) = \frac{1}{2}(x - 1)^4$

In Exercises 3–10, match the polynomial function with its graph and describe the viewing rectangle. [The graphs are labeled (a), (b), (c), (d), (e), (f), (g), and (h).]

3. $f(x) = -3x + 5$
4. $f(x) = x^2 - 2x$
5. $f(x) = -2x^2 - 8x - 9$
6. $f(x) = 3x^3 - 9x + 1$
7. $f(x) = -\frac{1}{3}x^3 + x - \frac{2}{3}$
8. $f(x) = -\frac{1}{4}x^4 + 2x^2$
9. $f(x) = 3x^4 + 4x^3$
10. $f(x) = x^5 - 5x^3 + 4x$

(a)

(b)

(c)

(d)

(e)

(f)

(g)

(h)

In Exercises 11–14, use a graphing utility to graph the functions f and g in the same viewing rectangle. Zoom out sufficiently far to show that the right-hand and left-hand behavior of f and g are identical.

11. $f(x) = x^3 - 9x + 1$ $g(x) = x^3$
12. $f(x) = -\frac{1}{3}(x^3 - 3x + 2)$ $g(x) = -\frac{1}{3}x^3$
13. $f(x) = -(x^4 - 4x^3 + 16x)$ $g(x) = -x^4$
14. $f(x) = 3x^4 - 6x^2$ $g(x) = 3x^4$

In Exercises 15–20, determine the right-hand and left-hand behavior of the graph of the polynomial function based on the Leading Coefficient Test. Use a graphing utility to verify your result.

15. $f(x) = 2x^2 - 3x + 1$
16. $g(x) = 5 - \frac{7}{2}x - 3x^2$
17. $h(t) = -\frac{2}{3}(t^2 - 5t + 3)$
18. $f(s) = -\frac{7}{8}(s^3 + 5s^2 - 7s + 1)$
19. $f(x) = 6 - 2x + 4x^2 - 5x^3$
20. $f(x) = \dfrac{3x^4 - 2x + 5}{4}$

In Exercises 21–36, find all the real zeros of the polynomial function. In each case, state whether you solved the problem algebraically or graphically and give reasons for your choice.

21. $f(x) = x^2 - 25$
22. $f(x) = 49 - x^2$
23. $h(t) = t^2 - 6t + 9$
24. $f(x) = x^2 + 10x + 25$
25. $f(x) = x^2 + x - 2$
26. $f(x) = \frac{1}{2}x^2 + \frac{5}{2}x - \frac{3}{2}$
27. $f(x) = 3x^2 - 12x + 3$
28. $g(x) = 5(x^2 - 2x - 1)$
29. $f(t) = t^3 - 4t^2 + 4t$
30. $f(x) = x^4 - x^3 - 20x^2$
31. $g(t) = \frac{1}{2}t^4 - \frac{1}{2}$
32. $f(x) = x^5 + x^3 - 6x$
33. $f(x) = 2x^4 - 2x^2 - 40$
34. $g(t) = t^5 - 6t^3 + 9t$
35. $f(x) = 5x^4 + 15x^2 + 10$
36. $f(x) = x^3 - 4x^2 - 25x + 100$

In Exercises 37–46, find a polynomial function that has the given zeros. (There are many correct answers.)

37. 0, 10

38. 0, −3

39. 2, −6

40. −4, 5

41. 0, −2, −3

42. 0, 2, 5

43. 4, −3, 3, 0

44. −2, −1, 0, 1, 2

45. $1 + \sqrt{3}, 1 - \sqrt{3}$

46. $2, 4 + \sqrt{5}, 4 - \sqrt{5}$

In Exercises 47–62, sketch the graph of the function. Describe a viewing rectangle that gives a good view of the basic characteristics of the graph.

47. $f(x) = -\frac{3}{2}$

48. $h(x) = \frac{1}{3}x - 3$

49. $f(t) = \frac{1}{4}(t^2 - 2t + 15)$

50. $g(x) = -x^2 + 10x - 16$

51. $f(x) = x^3 - 3x^2$

52. $f(x) = 1 - x^3$

53. $f(x) = x^3 - 4x$

54. $f(x) = \frac{1}{4}x^4 - 2x^2$

55. $g(t) = -\frac{1}{4}(t - 2)^2(t + 2)^2$

56. $f(x) = x^2(x - 4)$

57. $f(x) = \frac{1}{5}(x + 2)^2(x - 3)(2x - 9)$

58. $f(x) = \frac{1}{5}(x + 2)^2(3x - 5)^2$

59. $h(x) = \frac{1}{3}x^3(x - 4)^2$

60. $g(x) = \frac{1}{10}(x + 1)^2(x - 3)^3$

61. $f(x) = 1 - x^6$

62. $g(x) = 1 - (x + 1)^6$

In Exercises 63–66, use the Intermediate Value Theorem and a graphing utility to find the intervals of length 1 in which the polynomial function is guaranteed to have a zero. (See Example 8.)

63. $f(x) = x^3 - 3x^2 + 3$

64. $f(x) = 0.11x^3 - 2.07x^2 + 9.81x - 6.88$

65. $g(x) = 3x^4 + 4x^3 - 3$

66. $h(x) = x^4 - 10x^2 + 2$

67. *Volume of a Box* An open box is made from a 12-inch square piece of material by cutting equal squares from all corners and turning up the sides (see figure).
(a) Verify that the volume of the box is $V(x) = 4x(6 - x)^2$.
(b) Determine the domain of the function V.
(c) Sketch a graph of the function and use the graph to estimate the value of x for which $V(x)$ is maximum.

FIGURE FOR 67

68. *Volume of a Box* An open box with locking tabs is made from a 12-inch square piece of material. This is done by cutting equal squares from all corners and folding along the dashed lines shown in the figure.
(a) Verify that the volume of the box is $V(x) = 8x(3 - x)(6 - x)$.
(b) Determine the domain of the function V.
(c) Sketch the graph of the function and use the graph to estimate the value of x for which $V(x)$ is maximum.

FIGURE FOR 68

69. *Advertising Expenses* The total revenue for a soft-drink company is related to its advertising expense by the function

$$R = \frac{1}{50,000}(-x^3 + 600x^2), \qquad 0 \le x \le 400,$$

where R is the total revenue in millions of dollars and x is the amount spent on advertising (in 10,000s of dollars). Use a graphing utility to obtain a graph of this function. Estimate the point on the graph where the function is increasing most rapidly. This point is called the **point of diminishing returns** because any expense above this amount will yield less return per dollar invested in advertising. (*Hint:* Use a viewing rectangle in which $-200 \le x \le 600$ and $0 \le y \le 650$.)

70. *Tree Growth* The growth of a red oak tree is approximated by the function

$$G = -0.003t^3 + 0.137t^2 + 0.458t - 0.839,$$
$$2 \le t \le 34,$$

where G is the height of the tree in feet and t is its age in years. Use a graphing utility to obtain a graph of this function. Estimate the age of the tree when it is growing most rapidly. This point is called the **point of diminishing returns** because the increase in yield will be less with each additional year. (*Hint:* Use a viewing rectangle in which $-10 \le x \le 45$ and $-5 \le y \le 60$.)

3.3 POLYNOMIAL DIVISION AND SYNTHETIC DIVISION

Long Division of Polynomials / Synthetic Division /
The Remainder and Factor Theorems

Long Division of Polynomials

Up to this point in the text you have added, subtracted, and multiplied polynomials. In this section, you will study a procedure for *dividing* polynomials. This procedure has many important applications and is especially valuable in factoring and finding the zeros of polynomial functions algebraically. To begin, consider the graph of

$$f(x) = 6x^3 - 19x^2 + 16x - 4.$$

Notice that a zero of f occurs at $x = 2$, as shown in Figure 3.29. Because $x = 2$ is a zero of the polynomial function f, you know that $(x - 2)$ is a factor of $f(x)$. This means that there exists a second-degree polynomial $q(x)$ such that

$$f(x) = (x - 2) \cdot q(x).$$

To find $q(x)$, you can use **long division of polynomials.**

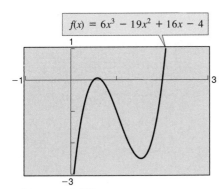

$f(x) = 6x^3 - 19x^2 + 16x - 4$

FIGURE 3.29

EXAMPLE 1 Long Division of Polynomials

Divide $f(x) = 6x^3 - 19x^2 + 16x - 4$ by $x - 2$, and use the result to factor $f(x)$ completely.

SOLUTION

Partial quotients

$$
\begin{array}{r}
6x^2 - 7x + 2 \\
x - 2 \overline{)6x^3 - 19x^2 + 16x - 4} \\
\underline{6x^3 - 12x^2} \\
-7x^2 + 16x \\
\underline{-7x^2 + 14x} \\
2x - 4 \\
\underline{2x - 4} \\
0
\end{array}
$$

Multiply: $6x^2(x - 2)$
Subtract
Multiply: $-7x(x - 2)$
Subtract
Multiply: $2(x - 2)$
Subtract

You can see that

$$
\begin{aligned}
6x^3 - 19x^2 + 16x - 4 &= (x - 2)(6x^2 - 7x + 2) \\
&= (x - 2)(2x - 1)(3x - 2).
\end{aligned}
$$

Note that this factorization agrees with the graph of f (Figure 3.29) in that the three x-intercepts occur at $x = 2$, $x = \frac{1}{2}$, and $x = \frac{2}{3}$.

In Example 1, $x - 2$ is a factor of the polynomial $6x^3 - 19x^2 + 16x - 4$, and the long division process produced a remainder of zero. Often, long division will produce a nonzero remainder. For instance, if you divide $x^2 + 3x + 5$ by $x + 1$, you obtain the following.

$$
\begin{array}{r}
x + 2 \quad \longleftarrow \text{Quotient} \\
x + 1 \overline{)x^2 + 3x + 5} \quad \longleftarrow \text{Dividend} \\
\underline{x^2 + x} \\
2x + 5 \\
\underline{2x + 2} \\
3 \quad \longleftarrow \text{Remainder}
\end{array}
$$

Divisor $\longrightarrow$

You can write this result as

$$
\underbrace{\frac{\overbrace{x^2 + 3x + 5}^{\text{Dividend}}}{\underbrace{x + 1}_{\text{Divisor}}}} = \overbrace{x + 2}^{\text{Quotient}} + \frac{\overbrace{3}^{\text{Remainder}}}{\underbrace{x + 1}_{\text{Divisor}}}
$$

or

$$
x^2 + 3x + 5 = (x + 2)(x + 1) + 3.
$$

This example illustrates the following **Division Algorithm.**

REMARK   The Division Algorithm can also be written as

$$\frac{f(x)}{d(x)} = q(x) + \frac{r(x)}{d(x)}.$$

THE DIVISION ALGORITHM

If $f(x)$ and $d(x)$ are polynomials such that $d(x) \neq 0$, and the degree of $d(x)$ is less than or equal to the degree of $f(x)$, then there exist unique polynomials $q(x)$ and $r(x)$ such that

$$f(x) = d(x)q(x) + r(x),$$

Dividend   Divisor   Quotient   Remainder

where $r(x) = 0$ or the degree of $r(x)$ is less than the degree of $d(x)$. If the remainder $r(x)$ is zero, then $d(x)$ **divides evenly** into $f(x)$.

In the Division Algorithm the rational expression $f(x)/d(x)$ is **improper** because the degree of $f(x)$ is greater than or equal to the degree of $d(x)$. On the other hand, the rational expression $r(x)/d(x)$ is **proper** because the degree of $r(x)$ is less than the degree of $d(x)$.

EXAMPLE 2   Long Division of Polynomials

Divide $x^3 - 1$ by $x - 1$.

SOLUTION

Because there is no x^2-term or x-term in the dividend, line up the subtraction by using zero coefficients (or leaving spaces) for the missing terms.

$$
\begin{array}{r}
x^2 + x + 1 \\
x - 1 \overline{\smash{)}\, x^3 + 0x^2 + 0x - 1} \\
\underline{x^3 - x^2} \\
x^2 \\
\underline{x^2 - x} \\
x - 1 \\
\underline{x - 1} \\
0
\end{array}
$$

Thus, $x - 1$ divides evenly into $x^3 - 1$ and you can write

$$\frac{x^3 - 1}{x - 1} = x^2 + x + 1.$$

EXAMPLE 3 Long Division of Polynomials

Divide $2x^4 + 4x^3 - 5x^2 + 3x - 2$ by $x^2 + 2x - 3$.

SOLUTION

$$
\begin{array}{r}
2x^2 + 1 \\
x^2 + 2x - 3 \overline{\smash{\big)}\, 2x^4 + 4x^3 - 5x^2 + 3x - 2} \\
\underline{2x^4 + 4x^3 - 6x^2 } \\
x^2 + 3x - 2 \\
\underline{x^2 + 2x - 3} \\
x + 1
\end{array}
$$

Note that the first subtraction eliminates two terms from the dividend. When this happens, the quotient skips a term. Thus, you can write

$$
\frac{2x^4 + 4x^3 - 5x^2 + 3x - 2}{x^2 + 2x - 3} = 2x^2 + 1 + \frac{x + 1}{x^2 + 2x - 3}.
$$

Synthetic Division

Synthetic division is a shortcut for long division of polynomials of the form $x - k$. To see how it works, let's take another look at Example 1.

$$
\begin{array}{r}
6x^2 - 7x + 2 \\
x - 2 \overline{\smash{\big)}\, 6x^3 - 19x^2 + 16x - 4} \\
\underline{6x^3 - 12x^2 } \\
-7x^2 + 16x \\
\underline{-7x^2 + 14x } \\
2x - 4 \\
\underline{2x - 4} \\
0
\end{array}
$$

You can retain the essential steps of this division tableau by using only the coefficients, as follows.

$$
\begin{array}{r}
6 -7 2 \\
-2 \overline{\smash{\big)}\, 6 -19 16 -4} \\
\underline{6 -12 } \\
-7 16 \\
\underline{-7 14 } \\
2 -4 \\
\underline{2 -4} \\
0
\end{array}
$$

Because the coefficients shown in color are duplicates of those in the quotient or the dividend, you can omit them and condense vertically.

$$\begin{array}{r} 6 \quad -7 \quad 2 \\ \hline -2\overline{)6 \quad -19 \quad 16 \quad -4} \\ -12 \quad 14 \quad -4 \\ \hline 0 \end{array}$$

Now, move the quotient to the bottom row.

$$\begin{array}{r} -2\overline{)6 \quad -19 \quad 16 \quad -4} \\ -12 \quad 14 \quad -4 \\ \hline 6 \quad -7 \quad 2 \quad 0 \end{array}$$

Finally, change from subtraction to addition (and reduce the likelihood of errors) by changing the sign of the divisor and of row 2. This produces the following synthetic division array.

$$\begin{array}{r|rrrr} 2 & 6 & -19 & 16 & -4 \\ & & 12 & -14 & 4 \\ \hline & 6 & -7 & 2 & 0 \end{array}$$

The pattern for synthetic division of a cubic polynomial is summarized as follows. (The pattern for higher-degree polynomials is similar.)

REMARK Synthetic division works *only* for divisors of the form $x - k$. You cannot use synthetic division to divide a polynomial by a quadratic such as $x^2 - 3$.

SYNTHETIC DIVISION (FOR A CUBIC POLYNOMIAL)

To divide $ax^3 + bx^2 + cx + d$ by $x - k$, use the following pattern.

Coefficients of quotient

Vertical pattern: Add terms.
Diagonal pattern: Multiply by k.

EXAMPLE 4   Using Synthetic Division

Use synthetic division to divide $x^4 - 10x^2 - 2x + 4$ by $x + 3$.

SOLUTION

You can set up the array as follows. (Note that a zero is included for each missing term in the dividend.)

Divisor: $x - (-3)$ Dividend: $x^4 - 10x^2 - 2x + 4$

$$
\begin{array}{r|rrrrr}
-3 & 1 & 0 & -10 & -2 & 4 \\
   &   & -3 & 9 & 3 & -3 \\
\hline
   & 1 & -3 & -1 & 1 & \boxed{1} \leftarrow \text{Remainder: } 1
\end{array}
$$

Quotient: $x^3 - 3x^2 - x + 1$

Thus, you have

$$\frac{x^4 - 10x^2 - 2x + 4}{x + 3} = x^3 - 3x^2 - x + 1 + \frac{1}{x + 3}.$$

The Remainder and Factor Theorems

Notice that in the previous example, if $f(x) = x^4 - 10x^2 - 2x + 4$, then

$$f(-3) = (-3)^4 - 10(-3)^2 - 2(-3) + 4 = 1,$$

which is the remainder $r = 1$. This observation leads to the following **Remainder Theorem.**

THE REMAINDER THEOREM

If a polynomial $f(x)$ is divided by $x - k$, then the remainder is $r = f(k)$.

EXAMPLE 5   Evaluating a Polynomial by the Remainder Theorem

Use the Remainder Theorem to evaluate the following function at $x = -2$.

$$f(x) = 3x^3 + 8x^2 + 5x - 7$$

SOLUTION

Using synthetic division, you obtain the following.

$$
\begin{array}{r|rrrr}
-2 & 3 & 8 & 5 & -7 \\
   &   & -6 & -4 & -2 \\
\hline
   & 3 & 2 & 1 & -9
\end{array}
$$

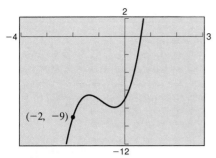

FIGURE 3.30

Because the remainder is $r = -9$, you can conclude that

$$f(-2) = -9.$$

This means that $(-2, -9)$ is a point on the graph of f, as shown in Figure 3.30. Check this by substituting $x = -2$ in the original function.

The Remainder Theorem can be used to prove the following important result.

FACTOR THEOREM

A polynomial $f(x)$ has a factor $(x - k)$ if and only if $f(k) = 0$.

EXAMPLE 6   **Using Synthetic Division to Find Factors of a Polynomial**

Show that $(x - 2)$ and $(x + 3)$ are factors of the polynomial

$$f(x) = 2x^4 + 7x^3 - 4x^2 - 27x - 18.$$

Then find the remaining factors of $f(x)$.

SOLUTION

Using synthetic division with 2 and -3 successively produces the following.

$$
\begin{array}{r|rrrrr}
2 & 2 & 7 & -4 & -27 & -18 \\
  &   & 4 & 22 & 36 & 18 \\
\hline
  & 2 & 11 & 18 & 9 & 0
\end{array}
$$

$$
\begin{array}{r|rrrr}
-3 & 2 & 11 & 18 & 9 \\
   &   & -6 & -15 & -9 \\
\hline
   & 2 & 5 & 3 & 0
\end{array}
$$

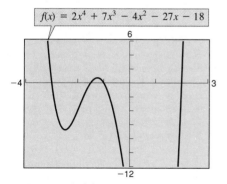

FIGURE 3.31

Because the resulting quadratic $2x^2 + 5x + 3$ factors as

$$2x^2 + 5x + 3 = (2x + 3)(x + 1),$$

the complete factorization of $f(x)$ is

$$f(x) = (x - 2)(x + 3)(2x + 3)(x + 1).$$

This factorization implies that f has four real zeros: 2, -3, $-\frac{3}{2}$, and -1. This can be verified by a graph, as shown in Figure 3.31.

In summary, the remainder r, obtained in the synthetic division of $f(x)$ by $x - k$, provides the following information.

1. The remainder r gives the value of f at $x = k$. That is, $r = f(k)$.
2. If $r = 0$, then $(x - k)$ is a factor of $f(x)$.
3. If $r = 0$, then $(k, 0)$ is an x-intercept of the graph of f.

DISCUSSION PROBLEM

FINDING PATTERNS IN POLYNOMIAL DIVISION

Compete the following polynomial divisions.

(a) $\dfrac{x^2 - 1}{x - 1} = $ ▢

(b) $\dfrac{x^3 - 1}{x - 1} = $ ▢

(c) $\dfrac{x^4 - 1}{x - 1} = $ ▢

Describe the pattern that you obtain and use your result to find a formula for the polynomial division

$$\dfrac{x^n - 1}{x - 1}.$$

WARM-UP

The following warm-up exercises involve skills that were covered in earlier sections. You will use these skills in the exercise set for this section.

In Exercises 1–4, write the expression in standard polynomial form.

1. $(x - 1)(x^2 + 2) + 5$

2. $(x^2 - 3)(2x + 4) + 8$

3. $(x^2 + 1)(x^2 - 2x + 3) - 10$

4. $(x + 6)(2x^3 - 3x) - 5$

In Exercises 5 and 6, factor the polynomial.

5. $x^2 - 4x + 3$

6. $4x^3 - 10x^2 + 6x$

In Exercises 7–10, find a polynomial function that has the given zeros.

7. $0, 3, 4$

8. $-6, 1$

9. $-3, 1 + \sqrt{2}, 1 - \sqrt{2}$

10. $1, -2, 2 + \sqrt{3}, 2 - \sqrt{3}$

SECTION 3.3 · EXERCISES

In Exercises 1–14, divide by long division.

1. $\dfrac{2x^2 + 10x + 12}{x + 3}$

2. $\dfrac{5x^2 - 17x - 12}{x - 4}$

3. $\dfrac{4x^3 - 7x^2 - 11x + 5}{4x + 5}$

4. $\dfrac{6x^3 - 16x^2 + 17x - 6}{3x - 2}$

5. $\dfrac{x^4 + 5x^3 + 6x^2 - x - 2}{x + 2}$

6. $\dfrac{x^3 + 4x^2 - 3x - 12}{x^2 - 3}$

7. $\dfrac{7x + 3}{x + 2}$

8. $\dfrac{8x - 5}{2x + 1}$

9. $\dfrac{6x^3 + 10x^2 + x + 8}{2x^2 + 1}$

10. $\dfrac{x^3 - 9}{x^2 + 1}$

11. $\dfrac{x^4 + 3x^2 + 1}{x^2 - 2x + 3}$

12. $\dfrac{x^5 + 7}{x^3 - 1}$

13. $\dfrac{2x^3 - 4x^2 - 15x + 5}{(x - 1)^2}$

14. $\dfrac{x^4}{(x - 1)^3}$

In Exercises 15–32, divide by synthetic division.

15. $\dfrac{3x^3 - 17x^2 + 15x - 25}{x - 5}$

16. $\dfrac{5x^3 + 18x^2 + 7x - 6}{x + 3}$

17. $\dfrac{4x^3 - 9x + 8x^2 - 18}{x + 2}$

18. $\dfrac{9x^3 - 16x - 18x^2 + 32}{x - 2}$

19. $\dfrac{-x^3 + 75x - 250}{x + 10}$

20. $\dfrac{3x^3 - 16x^2 - 72}{x - 6}$

21. $\dfrac{5x^3 - 6x^2 + 8}{x - 4}$

22. $\dfrac{5x^3 + 6x + 8}{x + 2}$

23. $\dfrac{10x^4 - 50x^3 - 800}{x - 6}$

24. $\dfrac{x^5 - 13x^4 - 120x + 80}{x + 3}$

25. $\dfrac{x^3 + 512}{x + 8}$

26. $\dfrac{5x^3}{x + 3}$

27. $\dfrac{-3x^4}{x - 2}$

28. $\dfrac{-3x^4}{x + 2}$

29. $\dfrac{5 - 3x + 2x^2 - x^3}{x + 1}$

30. $\dfrac{180x - x^4}{x - 6}$

31. $\dfrac{4x^3 + 16x^2 - 23x - 15}{x + \frac{1}{2}}$

32. $\dfrac{3x^3 - 4x^2 + 5}{x - \frac{3}{2}}$

In Exercises 33–40, use synthetic division to show that x is a zero of the third-degree polynomial function, and use the result to factor the polynomial completely. List all the real zeros of the function, and use a graphing utility to verify your result.

Polynomial Function	Value of x
33. $f(x) = x^3 - 7x + 6$	$x = 2$
34. $g(x) = x^3 - 28x - 48$	$x = -4$
35. $g(x) = 2x^3 - 15x^2 + 27x - 10$	$x = \frac{1}{2}$
36. $h(x) = 48x^3 - 80x^2 + 41x - 6$	$x = \frac{2}{3}$
37. $h(x) = x^3 + 2x^2 - 3x - 6$	$x = \sqrt{3}$
38. $f(x) = x^3 + 2x^2 - 2x - 4$	$x = \sqrt{2}$
39. $f(x) = x^3 - 3x^2 + 2$	$x = 1 + \sqrt{3}$
40. $f(x) = x^3 - x^2 - 13x - 3$	$x = 2 - \sqrt{5}$

In Exercises 41–44, express the function in the form $f(x) = (x - k)q(x) + r$ for the given value of k, and demonstrate that $f(k) = r$.

Function	Value of k
41. $f(x) = x^3 - x^2 - 14x + 11$	$k = 4$
42. $f(x) = \frac{1}{3}(15x^4 + 10x^3 - 6x^2 + 17x + 14)$	$k = -\frac{2}{3}$
43. $f(x) = x^3 + 3x^2 - 2x - 14$	$k = \sqrt{2}$
44. $f(x) = 4x^3 - 6x^2 - 12x - 4$	$k = 1 - \sqrt{3}$

In Exercises 45–50, use synthetic division and the Remainder Theorem to find the function values.

45. $f(x) = 4x^3 - 13x + 10$
   (a) $f(1)$ (b) $f(-2)$
   (c) $f(\frac{1}{2})$ (d) $f(8)$

46. $g(x) = x^6 - 4x^4 + 3x^2 + 2$
   (a) $g(2)$ (b) $g(-4)$
   (c) $g(3)$ (d) $g(-1)$

47. $h(x) = 3x^3 + 5x^2 - 10x + 1$
   (a) $h(3)$ (b) $h(\frac{1}{3})$
   (c) $h(-2)$ (d) $h(-5)$

48. $f(x) = 0.4x^4 - 1.6x^3 + 0.7x^2 - 2$
   (a) $f(1)$ (b) $f(-2)$
   (c) $f(5)$ (d) $f(-10)$

49. $f(x) = x^3 - 2x^2 - 11x + 52$
   (a) $f(5)$ (b) $f(-4)$
   (c) $f(1.2)$ (d) $f(2)$

50. $g(x) = x^3 - x^2 + 25x - 25$
   (a) $g(5)$ (b) $g(\frac{1}{5})$
   (c) $g(-1.5)$ (d) $g(-1)$

In Exercises 51–56, simplify the rational expression.

51. $\dfrac{4x^3 - 8x^2 + x + 3}{2x - 3}$

52. $\dfrac{x^3 + x^2 - 64x - 64}{x + 8}$

53. $\dfrac{x^3 + 3x^2 - x - 3}{x + 1}$

54. $\dfrac{2x^3 + 3x^2 - 3x - 2}{x - 1}$

55. $\dfrac{x^4 + 6x^3 + 11x^2 + 6x}{x^2 + 3x + 2}$

56. $\dfrac{x^4 + 9x^3 - 5x^2 - 36x + 4}{x^2 - 4}$

57. *Power of an Engine* The horsepower y developed by a compact car engine is approximated by the model

$$y = -1.42x^3 + 5.04x^2 + 32.45x - 0.75, \quad 1 \le x \le 5,$$

where x is the engine speed in thousands of revolutions per minute.

(a) Use a graphing utility to graph the power function.

(b) It is observed from the graph that two engine speeds develop 110 horsepower with one of the speeds being 5000 rpm. Use the graph to approximate the second engine speed.

(c) Algebraically approximate the second engine speed that yields 110 horsepower. (*Hint:* Because you know the engine develops 110 horsepower at 5000 rpm, you can use synthetic division.)

58. *Automobile Emissions* The number of parts per million of nitric oxide emissions y from a certain car engine is approximated by the model

$$y = -5.05x^3 + 3857x - 38{,}411.25, \quad 13 \le x \le 18,$$

where x is the air-fuel ratio.

(a) Use a graphing utility to graph the emissions function.

(b) It is observed from the graph that two air-fuel ratios produce 2400 parts per million of nitric oxide with one being 15. Use the graph to approximate the second air-fuel ratio.

(c) Algebraically approximate the second air-fuel ratio that produces 2400 parts per million of nitric oxide. (*Hint:* Because you know an air-fuel ratio of 15 produces the specified nitric oxide emission, you can use synthetic division.)

59. Use the form $f(x) = (x - k)q(x) + r$ to create a cubic function that passes through the specified point. (There is more than one correct answer.)

(a) $(2, 5)$ (b) $(-3, 1)$

3.4   REAL ZEROS OF POLYNOMIAL FUNCTIONS

Descartes's Rule of Signs / The Rational Zero Test / Bounds for Real Zeros of Polynomial Functions / Applications / Bisection Method

Descartes's Rule of Signs

In Section 3.2, we noted that an nth degree polynomial function can have *at most n* real zeros. Of course, many nth degree polynomials do not have that many real zeros. For instance, $f(x) = x^2 + 1$ has no real zeros, and $f(x) = x^3 + 1$ has only one real zero. **Descartes's Rule of Signs** sheds more light on the number of real zeros that a polynomial can have.

REMARK When there is only one variation in sign, Descartes's Rule of Signs guarantees the existence of exactly one positive (or negative) real zero.

DESCARTES'S RULE OF SIGNS

Let $f(x) = a_n x^n + a_{n-1} x^{n-1} + \cdots + a_2 x^2 + a_1 x + a_0$ be a polynomial with real coefficients and $a_0 \ne 0$.

1. The number of *positive real zeros* of f is either equal to the number of variations in signs of $f(x)$ or is less than that number by an even integer.

2. The number of *negative real zeros* of f is either equal to the number of variations in sign of $f(-x)$ or is less than that number by an even integer.

A **variation in sign** means that two consecutive coefficients have opposite signs. For example, the polynomial

$$f(x) = 3x^3 - 5x^2 + 6x - 4$$

has *three* variations in sign, whereas

$$f(-x) = 3(-x)^3 - 5(-x)^2 + 6(-x) - 4$$
$$= -3x^3 - 5x^2 - 6x - 4$$

has no variations in sign. Thus, from Descartes's Rule of Signs, the polynomial $f(x) = 3x^3 - 5x^2 + 6x - 4$ has either three positive real zeros or one positive real zero, and has no negative real zeros. From the graph of f shown in Figure 3.32, you can see that the function has only one positive real zero.

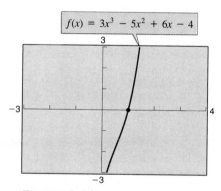

$$f(x) = 3x^3 - 5x^2 + 6x - 4$$

FIGURE 3.32

EXAMPLE 1   Using Descartes's Rule of Signs

Apply Descartes's Rule of Signs to the following polynomial function to determine the possible numbers of positive and negative zeros.

$$f(x) = 2x^4 + 7x^3 - 4x^2 - 27x - 18$$

SOLUTION

Because $f(x)$ has only *one* variation in sign, f must have *exactly one* positive real zero. Moreover, because

$$f(-x) = 2(-x)^4 + 7(-x)^3 - 4(-x)^2 - 27(-x) - 18$$
$$= 2x^4 - 7x^3 - 4x^2 + 27x - 18$$

has *three* variations in sign, f has either three negative zeros or one negative zero. This result agrees with Example 6 in Section 3.3, where the zeros of f were determined to be 2, -3, $-\frac{3}{2}$, and -1.

$f(x) = x^3 - x + 1$

FIGURE 3.33

EXAMPLE 2   Using Descartes's Rule of Signs

Apply Descartes's Rule of Signs to the polynomial function

$$f(x) = x^3 - x + 1.$$

SOLUTION

Because $f(x)$ has two variations in sign, it follows that f can have either two or no positive real zeros. Moreover, because

$$f(-x) = -x^3 + x + 1$$

has one variation in sign, f has exactly one negative real zero. The graph of f in Figure 3.33 shows that f actually has only one real zero (it is a negative number between -2 and -1).

The Rational Zero Test

The **Rational Zero Test** relates the possible rational zeros of a polynomial (having integer coefficients) to the leading coefficient and to the constant term of the polynomial.

THE RATIONAL ZERO TEST

If the polynomial $f(x) = a_n x^n + a_{n-1} x^{n-1} + \cdots + a_2 x^2 + a_1 x + a_0$ has *integer* coefficients, then every rational zero of f has the form

$$\text{Rational zero} = \frac{p}{q},$$

where p and q have no common factors other than 1, p is a factor of the constant term a_0, and q is a factor of the leading coefficient a_n.

To use the Rational Zero Test, first list all rational numbers whose numerators are factors of the constant term and whose denominators are factors of the leading coefficient.

$$\text{Possible rational zeros} = \frac{\text{factors of constant term}}{\text{factors of leading coefficient}}$$

Having formed this list of *possible rational zeros,* use a trial and error method to determine which, if any, are actual zeros of the polynomial. Note that when the leading coefficient is 1, the possible rational zeros are simply the factors of the constant term. This case is illustrated in Examples 3 and 4.

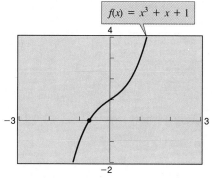

$f(x) = x^3 + x + 1$

FIGURE 3.34

EXAMPLE 3 Rational Zero Test with Leading Coefficient of 1

Find the rational zeros of $f(x) = x^3 + x + 1$.

SOLUTION

Because the leading coefficient is 1, the possible rational zeros are simply the factors of the constant term.

Possible rational zeros: ± 1

By testing these possible zeros, you can see that neither works.

$$f(1) = (1)^3 + 1 + 1 = 3$$
$$f(-1) = (-1)^3 + (-1) + 1 = -1$$

Thus, the polynomial has *no* rational zeros. Note from the graph of f in Figure 3.34 that f does have one real zero (between -1 and 0). However, by the Rational Zero Test, you know that this real zero is *not* a rational number.

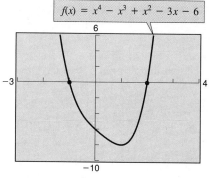

$f(x) = x^4 - x^3 + x^2 - 3x - 6$

FIGURE 3.35

EXAMPLE 4 Rational Zero Test with Leading Coefficient of 1

Find the rational zeros of $f(x) = x^4 - x^3 + x^2 - 3x - 6$.

SOLUTION

For $f(x) = x^4 - x^3 + x^2 - 3x - 6$, the leading coefficient is 1. Hence, the possible rational zeros are the factors of the constant term.

Possible rational zeros: $\pm 1, \pm 2, \pm 3, \pm 6$

A test of these possible zeros would show that $x = -1$ and $x = 2$ are the only two that work. Check the others to be sure. The graph shown in Figure 3.35 confirms that the function has only two real zeros.

If the leading coefficient of a polynomial is not 1, the list of possible rational zeros can increase dramatically. In such cases the search can be shortened in several ways. (1) A programmable calculator can be used to speed up the calculations. (2) A graphing utility can give a good estimate of the location of the zeros. (3) Synthetic division can be used to test the possible rational zeros.

To see how to use synthetic division to test the possible rational zeros, let's take another look at the function

$$f(x) = x^4 - x^3 + x^2 - 3x - 6$$

given in Example 4. To test that $x = -1$ and $x = 2$ are zeros of f, you can apply synthetic division.

$$
\begin{array}{r|rrrrr}
-1 & 1 & -1 & 1 & -3 & -6 \\
& & -1 & 2 & -3 & 6 \\
\hline
& 1 & -2 & 3 & -6 & 0
\end{array}
$$

$$
\begin{array}{r|rrrr}
2 & 1 & -2 & 3 & -6 \\
& & 2 & 0 & 6 \\
\hline
& 1 & 0 & 3 & 0
\end{array}
$$

Thus, $f(x) = (x + 1)(x - 2)(x^2 + 3)$. Because the factor $(x^2 + 3)$ produces no real zeros, you can conclude that $x = -1$ and $x = 2$ are the *only* real zeros of f.

Finding the first zero is often the most difficult part. After that, the search is simplified by working with the lower-degree polynomial obtained in synthetic division.

EXAMPLE 5   Using the Rational Zero Test

Find the rational zeros of $f(x) = 2x^3 + 3x^2 - 8x + 3$.

SOLUTION

Because the leading coefficient is 2 and the constant term is 3, you have the following.

$$\textit{Possible rational zeros:} \quad \frac{\text{Factors of 3}}{\text{Factors of 2}} = \frac{\pm 1, \pm 3}{\pm 1, \pm 2} = \pm 1, \pm 3, \pm \frac{1}{2}, \pm \frac{3}{2}$$

By synthetic division, you can determine that $x = 1$ is a zero.

$$
\begin{array}{r|rrrr}
1 & 2 & 3 & -8 & 3 \\
& & 2 & 5 & -3 \\
\hline
& 2 & 5 & -3 & 0
\end{array}
$$

Thus, $f(x)$ factors as

$$
\begin{aligned}
f(x) &= (x - 1)(2x^2 + 5x - 3) \\
&= (x - 1)(2x - 1)(x + 3),
\end{aligned}
$$

and you can conclude that the zeros of f are $x = 1$, $x = \frac{1}{2}$, and $x = -3$.

A graphing utility can help you determine which possible rational zeros to test, as demonstrated in Example 6.

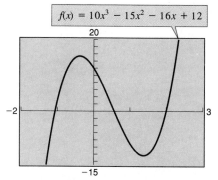

$f(x) = 10x^3 - 15x^2 - 16x + 12$

FIGURE 3.36

EXAMPLE 6   Using the Rational Zero Test

Find all the real zeros of $f(x) = 10x^3 - 15x^2 - 16x + 12$.

SOLUTION

Because the leading coefficient is 10 and the constant term is 12, there is a long list of possible rational zeros.

$$\text{Possible rational zeros:} \quad \frac{\text{Factors of 12}}{\text{Factors of 10}} = \frac{\pm 1, \pm 2, \pm 3, \pm 4, \pm 6, \pm 12}{\pm 1, \pm 2, \pm 5, \pm 10}$$

With so many possibilities (32, in fact), it is worth your time to use a graphing utility to focus on just a few. From Figure 3.36, it looks like three reasonable choices would be $x = -\frac{6}{5}$, $x = \frac{1}{2}$, and $x = 2$. Testing these by synthetic division shows that only $x = 2$ works. Thus, you have

$$f(x) = (x - 2)(10x^2 + 5x - 6).$$

Using the Quadratic Formula, you can find that the two additional zeros are irrational numbers.

$$x = \frac{-5 + \sqrt{265}}{20} \approx 0.5639 \quad \text{and} \quad x = \frac{-5 - \sqrt{265}}{20} \approx -1.0639$$

Bounds for Real Zeros of Polynomial Functions

The final test for zeros of a polynomial function is related to the sign pattern in the last row of the synthetic division tableau. This test can give you an upper or a lower bound of the real zeros of f. A real number b is an **upper bound** for the real zeros of f if no real zero is greater than b. Similarly, b is a **lower bound** if no real zero of f is less than b.

LOWER AND UPPER BOUND RULE

Let $f(x)$ be a polynomial with real coefficients and a positive leading coefficient. Suppose $f(x)$ is divided by $x - c$, using synthetic division.

1. If $c > 0$ and each number in the last row is either positive or zero, then c is an *upper bound* for the real zeros of f.
2. If $c < 0$ and the numbers in the last row are alternately positive and negative (zero entries count as positive or negative), then c is a *lower bound* for the real zeros of f.

EXAMPLE 7   **Finding the Real Zeros of a Polynomial**

Find the real zeros of $f(x) = x^3 - 53x^2 + 103x - 51$.

SOLUTION

A preliminary graph (see Figure 3.37) indicates that there is a zero between 0 and 2. You can apply the lower and upper bond rule with $c = -1$ and $c = 2$, as follows.

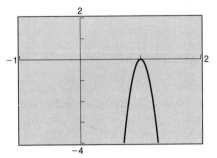

FIGURE 3.37

$c = -1$:

$$\begin{array}{r|rrrr} -1 & 1 & -53 & 103 & -51 \\ & & -1 & 54 & -157 \\ \hline & 1 & -54 & 157 & -208 \end{array}$$

Signs alternate

$c = 2$:

$$\begin{array}{r|rrrr} 2 & 1 & -53 & 103 & -51 \\ & & 2 & -102 & 2 \\ \hline & 1 & -51 & 1 & -49 \end{array}$$

Not all positive or zero

Because $c = -1 < 0$ and the numbers in the last row alternate in sign, -1 is a lower bound for the real zeros of f. That is, you can be sure that there are no zeros less than -1. For $c = 2$, because the numbers in the last row are not all positive, you cannot be sure that there are no zeros to the right of 2. In fact, if you zoom-out a couple of times, you can observe that there is a zero at $x = 51$ (see Figure 3.38). This example illustrates one of the limitations of a graphing utility: you may miss important features of a graph the first time you graph it. From Figure 3.37, you might have concluded that $x = 1$ was the only zero of f, but a more complete graph of this cubic brings to light its essential feature, as indicated in Figure 3.38.

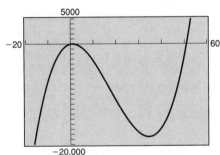

FIGURE 3.38

Example 8 uses all three tests presented in this section to search for the real zeros of a polynomial function. In addition, the example shows how to handle rational coefficients by factoring out the reciprocal of their least common denominator.

EXAMPLE 8   A Polynomial Function with Rational Coefficients

Find the real zeros of

$$f(x) = x^3 - \frac{2}{3}x^2 + \frac{1}{2}x - \frac{1}{3}.$$

SOLUTION

To find the rational zeros, rewrite $f(x)$ by factoring out the reciprocal of the least common denominator of the coefficients.

$$f(x) = \frac{6}{6}x^3 - \frac{4}{6}x^2 + \frac{3}{6}x - \frac{2}{6} = \frac{1}{6}(6x^3 - 4x^2 + 3x - 2)$$

Now, for the purpose of finding the zeros of f, you can drop the factor $\frac{1}{6}$. This is legitimate because the zeros of f are the same as the zeros of

$$g(x) = 6x^3 - 4x^2 + 3x - 2,$$

which has the following possible rational zeros.

$$\frac{\text{Factors of 2}}{\text{Factors of 6}} = \frac{\pm 1, \pm 2}{\pm 1, \pm 2, \pm 3, \pm 6} = \pm 1, \pm \frac{1}{2}, \pm \frac{1}{3}, \pm \frac{1}{6}, \pm \frac{2}{3}, \pm 2$$

Because $g(x)$ has three variations in sign and $g(-x)$ has none, you can conclude by Descartes's Rule of Signs that there are three positive real zeros or one positive real zero, and no negative zeros. Trying $x = 1$, you can obtain the following.

$$\begin{array}{r|rrrr}
1 & 6 & -4 & 3 & -2 \\
  &   & 6 & 2 & 5 \\
\hline
  & 6 & 2 & 5 & 3 \\
\end{array} \leftarrow \text{All positive entries}$$

Thus, $x = 1$ is not a zero, but because the last row has all positive entries, you know that $x = 1$ is an upper bound for the real zeros. Thus, you can restrict your search to zeros between 0 and 1. Choosing $x = \frac{2}{3}$, you can obtain the following.

$$\begin{array}{r|rrrr}
\frac{2}{3} & 6 & -4 & 3 & -2 \\
  &   & 4 & 0 & 2 \\
\hline
  & 6 & 0 & 3 & 0 \\
\end{array}$$

Thus, $f(x)$ factors as

$$f(x) = \frac{1}{6}\left(x - \frac{2}{3}\right)(6x^2 + 3) = \frac{1}{6}(3x - 2)(2x^2 + 1).$$

Because $2x^2 + 1$ has no real zeros, you can conclude that $x = \frac{2}{3}$ is the only real zero of f. A graph of f is shown in Figure 3.39.

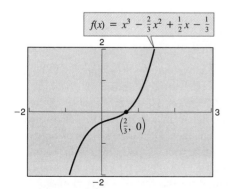

$$f(x) = x^3 - \frac{2}{3}x^2 + \frac{1}{2}x - \frac{1}{3}$$

$\left(\frac{2}{3}, 0\right)$

FIGURE 3.39

Here are two additional hints that should be helpful.

1. If the terms of $f(x)$ have a common monomial factor, it should be factored out before applying the tests in this section. For instance, by writing

$$f(x) = x^4 - 5x^3 + 3x^2 + x$$
$$= x(x^3 - 5x^2 + 3x + 1)$$

you can see that $x = 0$ is a zero of f and the remaining zeros can be obtained by analyzing the cubic factor.

2. If you are able to find all but two zeros of $f(x)$, then you are home free because you can always use the Quadratic Formula on the remaining quadratic factor. For instance, if you succeeded in writing

$$f(x) = x^4 - 5x^3 + 3x^2 + x$$
$$= x(x - 1)(x^2 - 4x - 1),$$

then you can apply the Quadratic Formula to $x^2 - 4x - 1$ to find the two remaining zeros.

Applications

EXAMPLE 9   Profit and Advertising Expenses

A company that produces sports clothes estimates that the profit for selling a particular line of sports wear is given by

$$P = -140x^3 + 7520x^2 - 400,000, \qquad 0 \le x \le 50,$$

where P is the profit in dollars and x is the advertising expense (in 10,000s of dollars). According to this model, how much money should the company spend to obtain a profit of $2,750,000?

SOLUTION

$$-140x^3 + 7520x^2 - 400,000 = 2,750,000$$
$$-140x^3 + 7520x^2 - 3,150,000 = 0$$
$$7x^3 - 376x^2 + 157,500 = 0$$

From Figure 3.40, it appears that there are two different values of x between 0 and 50 that will produce a profit of $2,750,000. However, because of the context of the problem, it is clear that the better answer is the smaller of the two numbers. Because there are two sign changes, Descartes's Rule of Signs guarantees that these are the only two positive roots. Finally, using the zoom and trace feature, you can determine that $x \approx 32.8$. Thus, the company should plan to spend about $328,000 in advertising for the line of sports clothes.

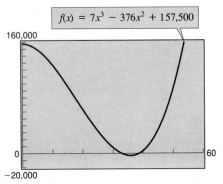

$f(x) = 7x^3 - 376x^2 + 157,500$

160,000

0

60

−20,000

FIGURE 3.40

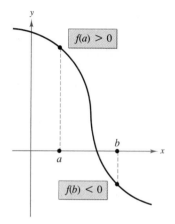

FIGURE 3.41

Bisection Method

One of the simplest methods for approximating the zeros of a polynomial is the **Bisection Method.** To apply this method, we must find two x-values—one at which the function is positive and one at which it is negative. Because the function is a polynomial, we know that it has at least one zero between the two x-values, as shown in Figure 3.41.

In Figure 3.41, we can see that a zero must occur somewhere in the interval (a, b). To apply the Bisection Method, we cut this interval in half and consider the two intervals

$$\left(a, \frac{a + b}{2}\right) \quad \text{and} \quad \left(\frac{a + b}{2}, b\right).$$

Depending upon the value of $f(x)$ at the midpoint $(a + b)/2$, we apply the Bisection Method again to one of these intervals. The process is illustrated in Example 10.

EXAMPLE 10   Using the Bisection Method

Use the Bisection Method to approximate the real zero of

$$f(x) = x^3 - x^2 + 1$$

to within 0.001 unit.

SOLUTION

We begin by graphing f, as shown in Figure 3.42. Note that

$$f(-0.8) = -0.152 < 0 \quad \text{and} \quad f(-0.7) = 0.167 > 0,$$

which implies that f has a zero between -0.8 and -0.7. Using the midpoint of this interval, we approximate the zero to be

$$c = \frac{-0.8 + (-0.7)}{2} = -0.75.$$

The maximum error of this approximation is one-half the length of the interval. That is,

$$\text{Maximum error} \leq \frac{-0.7 - (-0.8)}{2} = 0.05.$$

Now, we calculate the value of $f(-0.75)$ and make one of the following deductions.

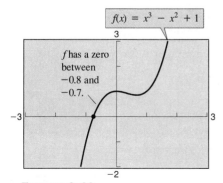

FIGURE 3.42

1. If $f(-0.75) = 0$, then -0.75 is a zero of f.
2. If $f(-0.75) > 0$, then a zero occurs between -0.8 and -0.75.
3. If $f(-0.75) < 0$, then a zero occurs between -0.75 and -0.7.

Because $f(-0.75) = 0.015625$ is positive, we choose $(-0.8, -0.75)$ as our new interval. The results of several iterations are shown in Table 3.1. After the seventh iteration, the maximum error is less than 0.001, and we approximate the zero of f to be

$$c = -0.75546875 \approx -0.755. \qquad \textit{To three-place accuracy}$$

TABLE 3.1

	a	c	b	$f(a)$	$f(c)$	$f(b)$	Maximum error
1	-0.8	-0.75	-0.7	-0.1520	0.0156	0.1670	0.05
2	-0.8	-0.775	-0.75	-0.1520	-0.0661	0.0156	0.025
3	-0.775	-0.7625	-0.75	-0.0661	-0.0247	0.0156	0.0125
4	-0.7625	-0.7563	-0.75	-0.0247	-0.0044	0.0156	0.0063
5	-0.7563	-0.7531	-0.75	-0.0044	0.0056	0.0156	0.0031
6	-0.7563	-0.7547	-0.7531	-0.0044	0.0006	0.0056	0.0016
7	-0.7563	-0.7555	-0.7547	-0.0044	-0.0019	0.0006	0.0008

By continuing the process in Table 3.1, we could approximate the zero to *any* desired accuracy, and we say that the sequence of successively better approximations *converges* to the zero of the function. The convergence of the Bisection Method is relatively slow and several iterations are usually necessary to obtain a very fine accuracy.

In Example 10, the function had only one real zero. However, the Bisection Method can be applied just as well to functions that have several real zeros.

DISCUSSION PROBLEM

COMPARING REAL ZEROS AND RATIONAL ZEROS

Compare the *real* zeros of a polynomial function with the *rational* zeros of a polynomial function. Then answer the following questions.

(a) Is it possible for a polynomial function to have no rational zeros but to have real zeros? If so, give an example.
(b) If a polynomial function has three real zeros, and only one of them is a rational number, then must the other two zeros be irrational numbers?
(c) Consider a cubic polynomial function $f(x) = ax^3 + bx^2 + cx + d$, where $a \neq 0$. Is it possible that f has no real zeros? If so, give an example. Is it possible that f has no rational zeros? If so, give an example.

WARM-UP
....

The following warm-up exercises involve skills that were covered in earlier sections. You will use these skills in the exercise set for this section.

In Exercises 1 and 2, find a polynomial function with integer coefficients having the given zeros.

1. $-1, \frac{2}{3}, 3$

2. $-2, 0, \frac{3}{4}, 2$

In Exercises 3 and 4, divide by synthetic division.

3. $\dfrac{x^5 - 9x^3 + 5x + 18}{x + 3}$

4. $\dfrac{3x^4 + 17x^3 + 10x^2 - 9x - 8}{x + (2/3)}$

In Exercises 5–8, use the given zero to find all the real zeros of f.

Polynomial Function	Value of x
5. $f(x) = 2x^3 + 11x^2 + 2x - 4$	$x = \frac{1}{2}$
6. $f(x) = 6x^3 - 47x^2 - 124x - 60$	$x = 10$
7. $f(x) = 4x^3 - 13x^2 - 4x + 6$	$x = -\frac{3}{4}$
8. $f(x) = 10x^3 + 51x^2 + 48x - 28$	$x = \frac{2}{5}$

In Exercises 9 and 10, find all real solutions of the polynomial equation.

9. $x^4 - 3x^2 + 2 = 0$

10. $x^4 - 7x^2 + 12 = 0$

SECTION 3.4 · EXERCISES
....

In Exercises 1–10, use Descartes's Rule of Signs to determine the possible number of positive and negative zeros of the function.

1. $f(x) = x^3 + 3$

2. $g(x) = x^3 + 3x^2$

3. $h(x) = 3x^4 + 2x^2 + 1$

4. $h(x) = 2x^4 - 3x + 2$

5. $g(x) = 2x^3 - 3x^2 - 3$

6. $f(x) = 4x^3 - 3x^2 + 2x - 1$

7. $f(x) = -5x^3 + x^2 - x + 5$

8. $g(x) = 5x^5 + 10x$

9. $h(x) = 4x^2 - 8x + 3$

10. $f(x) = 3x^3 + 2x^2 + x + 3$

In Exercises 11–14, use the Rational Zero Test to list all possible rational zeros of f. Verify that the zeros of f on the graph are contained in the list.

11. $f(x) = x^3 + x^2 - 4x - 4$

12. $f(x) = -3x^3 + 20x^2 - 36x + 16$

13. $f(x) = -4x^3 + 15x^2 - 8x - 3$

14. $f(x) = 4x^3 - 12x^2 - x + 15$

In Exercises 15–20, (a) list the possible rational zeros of f, (b) use a graphing utility to obtain the graph of f so that some of the possible zeros in part (a) can be disregarded, and then (c) determine all real zeros of f.

15. $f(x) = -2x^4 + 13x^3 - 21x^2 + 2x + 8$

16. $f(x) = 4x^4 - 17x^2 + 4$

17. $f(x) = 32x^3 - 52x^2 + 17x + 3$

18. $f(x) = 6x^3 - x^2 - 13x + 8$

19. $f(x) = 4x^3 + 7x^2 - 11x - 18$

20. $f(x) = 2x^3 + 5x^2 - 21x - 10$

In Exercises 21–24, use synthetic division to determine if each given x-value is an upper bound of the zeros of f, a lower bound of the zeros of f, or neither.

21. $f(x) = x^4 - 4x^3 + 15$
   (a) $x = 4$
   (b) $x = -1$
   (c) $x = 3$

22. $f(x) = 2x^3 - 3x^2 - 12x + 8$
   (a) $x = 2$
   (b) $x = 4$
   (c) $x = -1$

23. $f(x) = x^4 - 4x^3 + 16x - 16$
   (a) $x = -1$
   (b) $x = -3$
   (c) $x = 5$

24. $f(x) = 2x^4 - 8x + 3$
   (a) $x = 1$
   (b) $x = 3$
   (c) $x = -4$

In Exercises 25–40, find the real zeros of the function.

25. $f(x) = x^3 - 6x^2 + 11x - 6$

26. $f(x) = x^3 - 7x - 6$

27. $g(x) = x^3 - 4x^2 - x + 4$

28. $h(x) = x^3 - 9x^2 + 20x - 12$

29. $h(t) = t^3 + 12t^2 + 21t + 10$

30. $f(x) = x^3 + 6x^2 + 12x + 8$

31. $f(x) = x^3 - 4x^2 + 5x - 2$

32. $p(x) = x^3 - 9x^2 + 27x - 27$

33. $C(x) = 2x^3 + 3x^2 - 1$

34. $f(x) = 3x^3 - 19x^2 + 33x - 9$

35. $f(x) = 4x^3 - 3x - 1$

36. $f(z) = 12z^3 - 4z^2 - 27z + 9$

37. $f(y) = 4y^3 + 3y^2 + 8y + 6$

38. $g(x) = 3x^3 - 2x^2 + 15x - 10$

39. $f(x) = x^4 - 3x^2 + 2$

40. $P(t) = t^4 - 7t^2 + 12$

In Exercises 41–44, find all real solutions of the polynomial equation.

41. $x^4 - 13x^2 - 12x = 0$

42. $2y^4 + 7y^3 - 26y^2 + 23y - 6 = 0$

43. $2x^4 - 11x^3 - 6x^2 + 64x + 32 = 0$

44. $6x^4 - 11x^3 - 51x^2 + 99x - 27 = 0$

In Exercises 45–48, find the rational zeros of the polynomial function.

45. $P(x) = x^4 - \frac{25}{4}x^2 + 9$

46. $f(x) = x^3 - \frac{3}{2}x^2 - \frac{23}{2}x + 6$

47. $f(x) = x^3 - \frac{1}{4}x^2 - x + \frac{1}{4}$

48. $f(z) = z^3 + \frac{11}{6}z^2 - \frac{1}{2}z - \frac{1}{3}$

In Exercises 49–52, match the cubic equation with the number of rational and irrational zeros (a), (b), (c), or (d).

49. $f(x) = x^3 - 1$ **50.** $f(x) = x^3 - 2$

51. $f(x) = x^3 - x$ **52.** $f(x) = x^3 - 2x$

    (a) Rational zeros: 0   (b) Rational zeros: 3

       Irrational zeros: 1   Irrational zeros: 0

    (c) Rational zeros: 1   (d) Rational zeros: 1

       Irrational zeros: 2   Irrational zeros: 0

In Exercises 53–56, find all real zeros of the function and classify them as rational or irrational.

53. $f(x) = 3x^3 - 2x^2 - 15x + 10$

54. $f(x) = 2x^3 - 9x^2 - 4x + 21$

55. $g(x) = x^3 + 3x^2 - 34x - 42$

56. $h(x) = x^4 + 2x^3 - 37x^2 - 8x + 42$

In Exercises 57–60, (a) list the possible rational zeros of f and show that none are zeros, (b) use a graphing utility to verify that there are real zeros of f, and (c) move the cursor along the graph to approximate the irrational zero(s) of the function accurate to two decimal places.

57. $f(x) = x^3 + x - 1$ **58.** $f(x) = x^3 - 3x - 1$

59. $f(x) = x^4 - x - 3$ **60.** $f(x) = x^5 + x - 1$

61. *Dimensions of a Box*   An open box is made from a rectangular piece of material, 9 inches by 5 inches, by cutting equal squares from all corners and turning up the sides (see figure). Find the dimensions of the box, given that the volume is to be 18 cubic inches.

FIGURE FOR 61

62. *Dimensions of a Package*   A rectangular package to be sent by a postal service can have a maximum combined length and girth (perimeter of a cross section) of 108 inches (see figure). Find the dimensions of the package, given that the volume is 11,664 cubic inches.

FIGURE FOR 62

63. *Advertising Costs*   A company that produces portable cassette players estimates that the profit for selling a particular model is given by

$$P = -76x^3 + 4830x^2 - 320,000, \qquad 0 \le x \le 60,$$

where P is the profit in dollars and x is the advertising expense (in 10,000s of dollars). According to this model, find the smaller of two advertising amounts that yields a profit of $2,500,000.

64. *Advertising Costs*   A company that manufactures bicycles estimates that the profit for selling a particular model is given by

$$P = -45x^3 + 2500x^2 - 275,000, \qquad 0 \le x \le 50,$$

where P is the profit in dollars and x is the advertising expense (in 10,000s of dollars). According to this model, find the smaller of two advertising amounts that yields a profit of $800,000.

65. *Transportation Cost*   The ordering and transportation cost C of the components used in manufacturing a certain product is given by

$$C = 100\left(\frac{200}{x^2} + \frac{x}{x + 30}\right), \qquad 1 \leq x,$$

where C is measured in thousands of dollars and x is the order size in hundreds. In calculus, it can be shown that the cost is a minimum when $3x^3 - 40x^2 - 2400x - 36{,}000 = 0$. Approximate the optimal order size to the nearest hundred units.

66. *Imports into the United States*   The value of goods imported to the United States between 1984 and 1992 follows the model

$$I = -0.467t^3 + 11.457t^2 - 53.319t + 397.783,$$

where I is the annual value of goods imported (in billions of dollars) and t represents the year, with $t = 4$ corresponding to 1984 (see figure). According to this model, when did the annual value of goods imported reach 525 billion dollars? (*Source:* U.S. General Imports and Imports for Consumption)

FIGURE FOR 66

In Exercises 67–70, use the bisection method to find the zero of the function (in the given interval) to the nearest hundredth.

67. $f(x) = 4x^3 + 14x - 8$, $[0, 1]$

68. $f(x) = 4x^3 - 14x^2 - 2$, $[3, 4]$

69. $f(x) = 7x^4 - 42x^3 + 43x^2 + 216x - 324$, $[1, 2]$

70. $f(x) = 3x^4 - 12x^3 + 27x^2 + 4x - 4$, $[0, 1]$

3.5   COMPLEX NUMBERS
· ·

The Imaginary Unit i /   Operations with Complex Numbers   /
Complex Conjugates and Division   /   Complex Solutions of Quadratic
Equations   /   Applications

The Imaginary Unit i

In Section 2.5 you learned that some quadratic equations have no real solutions. For instance, the quadratic equation $x^2 + 1 = 0$ has no real solution because there is no real number x that can be squared to produce -1. To overcome this deficiency, mathematicians created an expanded system of numbers using the **imaginary unit i,** defined as

$$i = \sqrt{-1},$$

where $i^2 = -1$. Adding real numbers to real multiples of this imaginary unit produces the set of **complex numbers.** Each complex number can be written in the **standard form,** $a + bi$.

DEFINITION OF A COMPLEX NUMBER

For real numbers a and b, the number

$\quad a + bi$

is a **complex number.** If $a = 0$ and $b \neq 0$, then the complex number bi is an **imaginary number.**

The set of real numbers is a subset of the set of complex numbers because every real number a can be written as a complex number using $b = 0$. That is, for every real number a, you can write $a = a + 0i$.

Two complex numbers $a + bi$ and $c + di$, written in standard from, are **equal** to each other

$\quad a + bi = c + di$ *Equality of two complex numbers*

if and only if $a = c$ and $b = d$.

Operations with Complex Numbers

To add (or subtract) two complex numbers, you add (or subtract) the real and imaginary parts of the numbers separately.

ADDITION AND SUBTRACTION OF COMPLEX NUMBERS

If $a + bi$ and $c + di$ are two complex numbers written in standard form, then their sum and difference are defined as follows.

Sum: $(a + bi) + (c + di) = (a + c) + (b + d)i$
Difference: $(a + bi) - (c + d) = (a - c) + (b - d)i$

The **additive identity** in the complex number system is zero (the same as in the real number system). Furthermore, the **additive inverse** of the complex number $a + bi$ is

$\quad -(a + bi) = -a - bi.$ *Additive inverse*

Thus, $(a + bi) + (-a - bi) = 0 + 0i = 0$.

Technology Note _____

Some graphing utilities can perform
operations with complex numbers.
Check your user's manual to see if
your graphing utility has this
capability.

REMARK Note in Example 1(B) that
the sum of two complex numbers can
be a real number.

EXAMPLE 1   Adding and Subtracting Complex Numbers

Write the sums and differences in standard form.

A. $(3 - i) + (2 + 3i)$
B. $2i + (-4 - 2i)$
C. $3 - (-2 + 3i) + (-5 + i)$

SOLUTION

A.
$$
\begin{aligned}
(3 - i) + (2 + 3i) &= 3 - i + 2 + 3i && \text{Remove parentheses} \\
&= 3 + 2 - i + 3i && \text{Group real and} \\
& && \text{imaginary terms} \\
&= (3 + 2) + (-1 + 3)i \\
&= 5 + 2i && \text{Standard form}
\end{aligned}
$$

B.
$$
\begin{aligned}
2i + (-4 - 2i) &= 2i - 4 - 2i && \text{Remove parentheses} \\
&= -4 + 2i - 2i && \text{Group real and} \\
& && \text{imaginary terms} \\
&= -4 && \text{Standard form}
\end{aligned}
$$

C.
$$
\begin{aligned}
3 - (-2 + 3i) + (-5 + i) &= 3 + 2 - 3i - 5 + i \\
&= 3 + 2 - 5 - 3i + i \\
&= 0 - 2i \\
&= -2i
\end{aligned}
$$

Many of the properties of real numbers are valid for complex numbers as
well. Here are some.

Associative Property of Addition and Multiplication
Commutative Property of Addition and Multiplication
Distributive Property of Multiplication over Addition

Notice how these properties are used when two complex numbers are multiplied.

$$
\begin{aligned}
(a + bi)(c + di) &= a(c + di) + bi(c + di) && \text{Distributive} \\
&= ac + (ad)i + (bc)i + (bd)i^2 && \text{Distributive} \\
&= ac + (ad)i + (bc)i + (bd)(-1) && i^2 = -1 \\
&= ac - bd + (ad)i + (bc)i && \text{Commutative} \\
&= (ac - bd) + (ad + bc)i && \text{Distributive}
\end{aligned}
$$

Rather than trying to memorize this multiplication rule, just remember how the
distributive property is used to multiply two complex numbers. The procedure
is similar to multiplying two polynomials and combining like terms (as in the
FOIL method).

EXAMPLE 2   Multiplying Complex Numbers

Find the following products.

A. $(i)(-3i)$
B. $(2 - i)(4 + 3i)$
C. $(3 + 2i)(3 - 2i)$

SOLUTION

A. $(i)(-3i) = -3i^2 = -3(-1) = 3$
B. $(2 - i)(4 + 3i) = 8 + 6i - 4i - 3i^2$ *Binomial product*

$\qquad\qquad\qquad\quad = 8 + 6i - 4i - 3(-1)$ $i^2 = -1$

$\qquad\qquad\qquad\quad = 8 + 3 + 6i - 4i$ *Collect terms*

$\qquad\qquad\qquad\quad = 11 + 2i$ *Standard form*

C. $(3 + 2i)(3 - 2i) = 9 - 6i + 6i - 4i^2$

$\qquad\qquad\qquad\quad = 9 - 4(-1)$

$\qquad\qquad\qquad\quad = 9 + 4$

$\qquad\qquad\qquad\quad = 13$

Complex Conjugates and Division

Notice in Example 2(C) that the product of two complex numbers can be a real number. This occurs with pairs of complex numbers of the form $a + bi$ and $a - bi$, called **complex conjugates.** In general, the product of two complex conjugates can be written as follows.

$$(a + bi)(a - bi) = a^2 - abi + abi - b^2i^2$$
$$= a^2 - b^2(-1)$$
$$= a^2 + b^2$$

Complex conjugates can be used to divide one complex number by another. That is, to find the quotient

$$\frac{a + bi}{c + di}, \qquad c \text{ and } d \text{ not both zero,}$$

multiply the numerator and denominator by the conjugate of the denominator to obtain

$$\frac{a + bi}{c + di} = \frac{a + bi}{c + di}\left(\frac{c - di}{c - di}\right) = \frac{(ac + bd) + (bc - ad)i}{c^2 + d^2}.$$

This procedure is demonstrated in Examples 3 and 4.

EXAMPLE 3   Dividing Complex Numbers

Write the complex number $\dfrac{1}{1 + i}$ in standard form.

SOLUTION

$$\frac{1}{1 + i} = \frac{1}{1 + i}\left(\frac{1 - i}{1 - i}\right) = \frac{1 - i}{1^2 - i^2} = \frac{1 - i}{1 - (-1)} = \frac{1 - i}{2} = \frac{1}{2} - \frac{1}{2}i$$

EXAMPLE 4   Dividing Complex Numbers

Write the complex number $\dfrac{2 + 3i}{4 - 2i}$ in standard form.

SOLUTION

$$\frac{2 + 3i}{4 - 2i} = \frac{2 + 3i}{4 - 2i}\left(\frac{4 + 2i}{4 + 2i}\right)$$

$$= \frac{8 + 4i + 12i + 6i^2}{16 - 4i^2}$$

$$= \frac{8 - 6 + 16i}{16 + 4}$$

$$= \frac{1}{20}(2 + 16i) = \frac{1}{10} + \frac{4}{5}i$$

Complex Solutions of Quadratic Equations

Using the Quadratic Formula to solve a quadratic equation can produce a result such as $\sqrt{-3}$, which is not a real number. By factoring out $i = \sqrt{-1}$, you can write this number in standard form.

$$\sqrt{-3} = \sqrt{3(-1)} = \sqrt{3}\sqrt{-1} = \sqrt{3}i$$

The number $\sqrt{3}i$ is the principal square root of -3.

PRINCIPAL SQUARE ROOT OF A NEGATIVE NUMBER

If a is a positive number, then the **principal square root** of the negative number $-a$ is defined as

$$\sqrt{-a} = \sqrt{a}i.$$

REMARK When working with square roots of negative numbers, be sure to convert to standard form *before* multiplying.

In this definition you are using the rule $\sqrt{ab} = \sqrt{a}\sqrt{b}$, for $a > 0$ and $b < 0$. This rule is not valid if *both* a and b are negative. For example,

$$\sqrt{-5}\sqrt{-5} = \left(\sqrt{5}i\right)\left(\sqrt{5}i\right) = 5i^2 = -5$$

whereas

$$\sqrt{(-5)(-5)} = \sqrt{25} = 5.$$

Consequently, $\sqrt{(-5)(-5)} \neq \sqrt{-5}\sqrt{-5}$.

EXAMPLE 5   Writing Complex Numbers in Standard Form

A. $\sqrt{-3}\sqrt{-12} = \sqrt{3}i\sqrt{12}i = \sqrt{36}i^2 = 6(-1) = -6$

B. $\sqrt{-48} - \sqrt{-27} = \sqrt{48}i - \sqrt{27}i = 4\sqrt{3}i - 3\sqrt{3}i = \sqrt{3}i$

C. $\left(-1 + \sqrt{-3}\right)^2 = \left(-1 + \sqrt{3}i\right)^2$

$$= (-1)^2 - 2\sqrt{3}i + \left(\sqrt{3}\right)^2(i^2)$$

$$= 1 - 2\sqrt{3}i + 3(-1)$$

$$= -2 - 2\sqrt{3}i$$

Example 6 shows how the principal square root of a negative number is used to represent complex solutions of a quadratic equation.

EXAMPLE 6   Complex Solutions of a Quadratic Equation

Solve the equation $3x^2 - 2x + 5 = 0$.

SOLUTION

By the Quadratic Formula, you can write the solutions as follows.

$$x = \frac{-(-2) \pm \sqrt{(-2)^2 - 4(3)(5)}}{2(3)}$$

$$= \frac{2 \pm \sqrt{-56}}{6}$$

$$= \frac{2 \pm 2\sqrt{14}i}{6}$$

$$= \frac{1}{3} \pm \frac{\sqrt{14}}{3}i$$

The equation has two solutions:

$$\frac{1}{3} + \frac{\sqrt{14}}{3}i \quad \text{and} \quad \frac{1}{3} - \frac{\sqrt{14}}{3}i.$$

In Figure 3.43, notice that the graph of $y = 3x^2 - 2x + 5$ has no x-intercept.

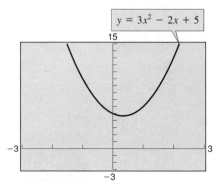

$y = 3x^2 - 2x + 5$

FIGURE 3.43

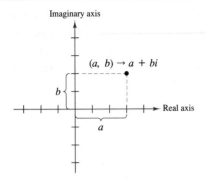

FIGURE 3.44

Applications

Most applications involving complex numbers are either theoretical (as seen in Section 3.6) or very technical, and are therefore not appropriate for inclusion in this text. However, to give you some idea of how complex numbers can be used in applications, we will give a general description of their use in **fractal geometry.**

To begin, we consider a coordinate system called the **complex plane.** Just as every real number corresponds to a point on the real number line, every complex number corresponds to a point in the complex plane, as shown in Figure 3.44. In this figure, note that the vertical axis is called the **imaginary axis** and the horizontal axis is called the **real axis.**

EXAMPLE 7   **Plotting Complex Numbers in the Complex Plane**

Plot the following complex numbers in the complex plane.

A. $2 + 3i$ **B.** $-1 + 2i$ **C.** 4

SOLUTION

A. To plot the complex number $2 + 3i$, we move (from the origin) two units to the right on the real axis and then three units up, as shown in Figure 3.45. In other words, plotting the complex number $2 + 3i$ in the complex plane is comparable to plotting the point $(2, 3)$ in the Cartesian plane.
B. The complex number $-1 + 2i$ corresponds to the point $(-1, 2)$, as shown in Figure 3.45.
C. The complex number 4 corresponds to the point $(4, 0)$, as shown in Figure 3.45.

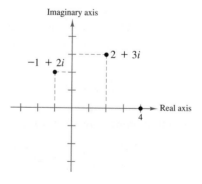

FIGURE 3.45

In the hands of a person who understands "fractal geometry," the complex plane can become an easel on which stunning pictures, called **fractals,** can be drawn. The most famous such picture is called the **Mandelbrot Set,** named after the Polish-born mathematician Benoit Mandelbrot. To draw the Mandelbrot Set, we consider the sequence of numbers

$$c, \quad c^2 + c, \quad (c^2 + c)^2 + c, \quad [(c^2 + c)^2 + c]^2 + c, \quad \ldots.$$

The behavior of this sequence depends on the value of the complex number c. For some values of c this sequence is **bounded,** and for other values it is **unbounded.** If the sequence is bounded, then the complex number c is in the Mandelbrot Set, and if the sequence is unbounded, then the complex number c is not in the Mandelbrot Set.

EXAMPLE 8   **Members of the Mandelbrot Set**

A. The complex number -2 is in the Mandelbrot Set because for $c = -2$, the corresponding Mandelbrot sequence is

$$-2, \quad 2, \quad 2, \quad 2, \quad 2, \quad 2, \quad \ldots,$$

which is bounded.

B. The complex number i is also in the Mandelbrot Set because for $c = i$, the corresponding Mandelbrot sequence is

$$i, \quad -1 + i, \quad -i, \quad -1 + i, \quad -i, \quad -1 + i, \quad \ldots,$$

which is bounded.

C. The complex number $1 + i$ is *not* in the Mandelbrot Set because for $c = 1 + i$, the corresponding Mandelbrot sequence is

$$1 + i, \quad 1 + 3i, \quad -7 + 7i, \quad 1 - 97i, \quad -9407 - 193i,$$
$$88454401 + 3631103i, \quad \ldots,$$

which is unbounded.

With this definition, a picture of the Mandelbrot Set would have only two colors—one color for points that are in the set (the sequence is bounded) and one color for points that are outside the set (the sequence is not bounded). Figure 3.46 shows a black and blue picture of the Mandelbrot Set. The points that are colored black are in the Mandelbrot Set and the points that are colored blue are not.

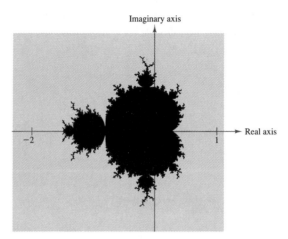

FIGURE 3.46

To add more interest to the picture, computer scientists discovered that the points that are not in the Mandelbrot Set can be assigned a variety of colors, depending on "how quickly" their sequences diverge. Figure 3.47 shows three different appendages of the Mandelbrot Set. (The black portions of the picture represent points that are in the Mandelbrot Set.)

FIGURE 3.47

In Figures 3.48–3.50, we show other types of fractal sets. From these pictures, you can see why fractals have fascinated people since their discovery (around 1980). The fractals shown were produced on a graphing calculator, using programs written by Chuck Biehl. Listings of the programs are in the Appendix.

The Sierpinski Gasket

The Fractal "Dragon"

A Fractal Fern

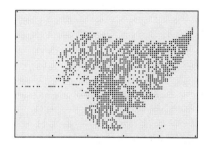

FIGURE 3.48

FIGURE 3.49

FIGURE 3.50

DISCUSSION PROBLEM

. . . .

CUBE ROOTS OF UNITY

In the real number system, the equation $x^3 = 1$ has 1 as its only solution. However, in the complex number system, this equation has three solutions,

$$1, \quad \frac{-1 + \sqrt{3}i}{2}, \quad \text{and} \quad \frac{-1 - \sqrt{3}i}{2}.$$

Try cubing each of these numbers to show that each number has the property that $x^3 = 1$. Then show how you can use the Quadratic Formula to *find* each number from the equation $x^3 = 1$.

WARM-UP

. . . .

The following warm-up exercises involve skills that were covered in earlier sections. You will use these skills in the exercise set for this section.

In Exercises 1–8, simplify the expression.

1. $\sqrt{12}$

2. $\sqrt{500}$

3. $\sqrt{20} - \sqrt{5}$

4. $\sqrt{27} - \sqrt{243}$

5. $\sqrt{24}\sqrt{6}$

6. $2\sqrt{18}\sqrt{32}$

7. $\dfrac{1}{\sqrt{3}}$

8. $\dfrac{2}{\sqrt{2}}$

In Exercise 9 and 10, solve the quadratic equation.

9. $x^2 + x - 1 = 0$

10. $x^2 + 2x - 1 = 0$

SECTION 3.5 · EXERCISES

1. Write the first 16 positive integer powers of i (that is, i, i^2, i^3, ..., i^{16}), and express each as i, $-i$, 1, or -1.

2. Express each of the following powers of i as i, -1, 1, or -1.
   (a) i^{40} (b) i^{25}
   (c) i^{50} (d) i^{67}

In Exercises 3–6, find real numbers a and b so that the equation is true.

3. $a + bi = -10 + 6i$ 4. $a + bi = 13 + 4i$
5. $(a - 1) + (b + 3)i = 5 + 8i$
6. $(a + 6) + 2bi = 6 - 5i$

In Exercises 7–18, write the complex number in standard form.

7. $4 + \sqrt{-9}$ 8. $3 + \sqrt{-16}$
9. $2 - \sqrt{-27}$ 10. $1 + \sqrt{-8}$
11. $\sqrt{-75}$ 12. 45
13. $-6i + i^2$ 14. $-4i^2 + 2i$
15. $-5i^5$ 16. $(-i)^3$
17. 8   18. $\left(\sqrt{-4}\right)^2 - 5$

In Exercises 19–26, perform the indicated addition or subtraction and write the result in standard form.

19. $(5 + i) + (6 - 2i)$ 20. $(13 - 2i) + (-5 + 6i)$
21. $(8 - i) - (4 - i)$ 22. $(3 + 2i) - (6 + 13i)$
23. $\left(-2 + \sqrt{-8}\right) + \left(5 - \sqrt{-50}\right)$
24. $\left(8 + \sqrt{-18}\right) - \left(4 + 3\sqrt{2}i\right)$
25. $-\left(\frac{3}{2} + \frac{5}{2}i\right) + \left(\frac{5}{3} + \frac{11}{3}i\right)$
26. $(1.6 + 3.2i) + (-5.8 + 4.3i)$

In Exercises 27–30, write the conjugate of the complex number, and find the product of the number and its conjugate.

27. $5 + 3i$ 28. $9 - 12i$
29. $-2 - \sqrt{5}i$ 30. $20i$

In Exercises 31–54, perform the specified operation and write the result in standard form.

31. $\sqrt{-6} \cdot \sqrt{-2}$ 32. $\sqrt{-5} \cdot \sqrt{-10}$
33. $\left(\sqrt{-10}\right)^2$ 34. $\left(\sqrt{-75}\right)^2$
35. $(1 + i)(3 - 2i)$ 36. $(6 - 2i)(2 - 3i)$
37. $6i(5 - 2i)$ 38. $-8i(9 + 4i)$
39. $\left(\sqrt{14} + \sqrt{10}i\right)\left(\sqrt{14} - \sqrt{10}i\right)$
40. $\left(3 + \sqrt{-5}\right)\left(7 - \sqrt{-10}\right)$
41. $(4 + 5i)^2$ 42. $(2 - 3i)^2$
43. $(2 + 3i)^2 + (2 - 3i)^2$ 44. $(1 - 2i)^2 - (1 + 2i)^2$
45. $\dfrac{4}{4 - 5i}$ 46. $\dfrac{3}{1 - i}$
47. $\dfrac{2 + i}{2 - i}$ 48. $\dfrac{8 - 7i}{1 - 2i}$
49. $\dfrac{6 - 7i}{i}$ 50. $\dfrac{8 + 20i}{2i}$
51. $\dfrac{5}{(1 + i)^3}$ 52. $\dfrac{1}{i^3}$
53. $\dfrac{(21 - 7i)(4 + 3i)}{2 - 5i}$ 54. $\dfrac{(2 - 3i)(5i)}{2 + 3i}$

In Exercises 55–62, use the Quadratic Formula to solve the quadratic equation.

55. $x^2 - 2x + 2 = 0$ 56. $x^2 + 6x + 10 = 0$
57. $4x^2 + 16x + 17 = 0$ 58. $9x^2 - 6x + 37 = 0$
59. $4x^2 + 16x + 15 = 0$ 60. $9x^2 - 6x - 35 = 0$
61. $16t^2 - 4t + 3 = 0$ 62. $5s^2 + 6s + 3 = 0$

In Exercises 63–68, plot the given complex number in the complex plane.

63. $-2 + i$ 64. i
65. 3   66. $-2 - 3i$
67. $1 - 2i$ 68. $-2i$

In Exercises 69–74, find the first six terms in the following sequence.

$$c, \quad c^2 + c, \quad (c^2 + c)^2 + c, \quad [(c^2 + c)^2 + c]^2 + c, \quad \ldots$$

From these terms, do you think the given complex number is in the Mandelbrot Set?

69. $c = 0$ **70.** $c = 2$
71. $c = \frac{1}{2}i$ **72.** $c = -i$
73. $c = 1$ **74.** $c = -1$

75. Cube the complex numbers 2, $-1 + \sqrt{3}i$, and $-1 - \sqrt{3}i$. What do you notice?

76. Raise the complex numbers 2, -2, $2i$, and $-2i$ to the fourth power. What do you notice?

77. Prove that the sum of a complex number $a + bi$ and its conjugate is a real number.

78. Prove that the difference of a complex number $a + bi$ and its conjugate is an imaginary number.

79. Prove that the product of a complex number $a + bi$ and its conjugate is a real number.

80. Prove that the conjugate of the product of two complex numbers $a_1 + b_1i$ and $a_2 + b_2i$ is the product of their conjugates.

3.6   COMPLEX ZEROS AND THE FUNDAMENTAL THEOREM OF ALGEBRA

The Fundamental Theorem of Algebra / Conjugate Pairs / Factoring a Polynomial

The Fundamental Theorem of Algebra

You already know that an nth degree polynomial can have at most n real zeros. In this section you will learn that, in the complex number system, every nth degree polynomial function has *precisely* n zeros. This important result is derived from the **Fundamental Theorem of Algebra,** first proved by the famous German mathematician Carl Friedrich Gauss (1777–1855).

> **THE FUNDAMENTAL THEOREM OF ALGEBRA**
>
> If $f(x)$ is a polynomial of degree n, where $n > 0$, then f has at least one zero in the complex number system.

Using the Fundamental Theorem of Algebra and the equivalence of zeros and factors, you can prove the following theorem.

LINEAR FACTORIZATION THEOREM

If $f(x)$ is a polynomial of degree n, where $n > 0$, then f has precisely n linear factors,

$$f(x) = a(x - c_1)(x - c_2) \cdots (x - c_n),$$

where $c_1, c_2, \ldots, c_n$ are complex numbers and a is the leading coefficient of $f(x)$.

Note that neither the Fundamental Theorem of Algebra nor the Linear Factorization Theorem explains *how* to find the zeros or factors of a polynomial. Such theorems are called **existence theorems.** To find the zeros of a polynomial function, you must still rely on the techniques developed in the earlier parts of the text.

The Linear Factorization Theorem states that an nth degree polynomial has precisely n linear factors. Therefore, it follows that an nth degree polynomial *function* has precisely n zeros. Remember, however, that these n zeros can be real or complex, and that they may be repeated.

EXAMPLE 1   Zeros of Polynomial Functions

A. The first-degree polynomial function

$$f(x) = x - 2$$

has exactly *one* zero: $x = 2$.

B. Counting multiplicity, the second-degree polynomial function

$$f(x) = x^2 - 6x + 9 = (x - 3)(x - 3)$$

has exactly *two* zeros: $x = 3$ and $x = 3$.

C. The third-degree polynomial function

$$f(x) = x^3 + 4x = x(x - 2i)(x + 2i)$$

has exactly *three* zeros: $x = 0$, $x = 2i$, and $x = -2i$.

D. The fourth-degree polynomial function

$$f(x) = x^4 - 1 = (x - 1)(x + 1)(x - i)(x + i)$$

has exactly *four* zeros: $x = 1$, $x = -1$, $x = i$, and $x = -i$. ....

Technology Note _____

Some graphing utilities have an "equation-solving" feature that will list decimal approximations of the real *and* complex solutions of an equation. Check your user's manual to see if your graphing utility has this capability.

Example 2 shows how you can use the methods described in previous sections—Descartes's Rule of Signs, Rational Zero Test, synthetic division, and factoring—to find all the zeros of a polynomial function, including the complex zeros.

EXAMPLE 2   Finding the Zeros of a Polynomial Function

Write the polynomial function $f(x) = x^5 + x^3 + 2x^2 - 12x + 8$ as the product of linear factors and list all of its zeros.

SOLUTION

Descartes's Rule of Signs indicates two or no positive real zeros and one negative real zero. The graph of f shown in Figure 3.51 indicates that the negative real zero is near -2, and a positive real zero is perhaps $x = 1$. Choose these values from the possible rational zeros of ± 1, ± 2, ± 4, and ± 8. Synthetic division can be used to show that -2 is a zero and 1 is a repeated zero. Thus, you can write

$$\begin{aligned} f(x) &= x^5 + x^3 + 2x^2 - 12x + 8 \\ &= (x - 1)(x - 1)(x + 2)(x^2 + 4) \\ &= (x - 1)(x - 1)(x + 2)(x - 2i)(x + 2i), \end{aligned}$$

which tells you that the five zeros of f are 1, 1, -2, $2i$, and $-2i$. Note from the graph of f shown in Figure 3.51 that the *real* zeros are the only ones that appear as x-intercepts.

$x^5 + x^3 + 2x^2 - 12x + 8$

FIGURE 3.51

Conjugate Pairs

In Example 2, note that the two complex zeros are **conjugates.** That is, they are of the form $a + bi$ and $a - bi$.

REMARK Be sure you see that this result is true only if the polynomial function has *real coefficients*. For instance, the result applies to the function $f(x) = x^2 + 1$, but not to the function $g(x) = x - i$.

COMPLEX ZEROS OCCUR IN CONJUGATE PAIRS

Let $f(x)$ be a polynomial function that has real coefficients. If $a + bi$, where $b \neq 0$, is a zero of the function, then the conjugate $a - bi$ is also a zero of the function.

EXAMPLE 3   **Finding a Polynomial with Given Zeros**

Find a *fourth-degree* polynomial function, with real coefficients, that has -1, -1, and $3i$ as zeros.

SOLUTION

Because $3i$ is a zero *and* the polynomial is stated to have real coefficients, the conjugate $-3i$ must also be a zero. Thus, from the Linear Factorization theorem, $f(x)$ can be written as

$$f(x) = a(x + 1)(x + 1)(x - 3i)(x + 3i).$$

For simplicity, let $a = 1$, and obtain

$$f(x) = (x^2 + 2x + 1)(x^2 + 9) = x^4 + 2x^3 + 10x^2 + 18x + 9.$$

EXAMPLE 4   **Finding a Polynomial with Given Zeros**

Find a *cubic* polynomial function f, with real coefficients, that has 2 and $1 - i$ as zeros, and such that $f(1) = 3$.

SOLUTION

Because $1 - i$ is a zero of f, so is $1 + i$.

$$
\begin{aligned}
f(x) &= a(x - 2)[x - (1 - i)][x - (1 + i)] \\
&= a(x - 2)[x^2 - x(1 + i) - x(1 - i) + 1 - i^2] \\
&= a(x - 2)(x^2 - 2x + 2) \\
&= a(x^3 - 4x^2 + 6x - 4)
\end{aligned}
$$

To find the value of a, use the fact that $f(1) = 3$ and obtain $f(1) = a(1 - 4 + 6 - 4) = 3$. Thus, $a = -3$ and you can conclude that

$$f(x) = -3(x^3 - 4x^2 + 6x - 4) = -3x^3 + 12x^2 - 18x + 12.$$

Factoring a Polynomial

The Linear Factorization Theorem states that any nth degree polynomial can be written as the product of n linear factors,

$$f(x) = a(x - c_1)(x - c_2)(x - c_3) \cdots (x - c_n).$$

However, this result includes the possibility that some of the values of c_i are complex. The following result tells you that even if you do not want to get involved with "complex factors," you can still write $f(x)$ as the product of linear and/or quadratic factors.

FACTORS OF A POLYNOMIAL

Every polynomial of degree $n > 0$ with real coefficients can be written as the product of linear and quadratic factors with real coefficients, where the quadratic factors have no real zeros.

A quadratic factor with no real zeros is **irreducible over the reals.** Be sure you see that this is not the same as being *irreducible over the rationals.* For example, the quadratic

$$x^2 + 1 = (x - i)(x + i)$$

is irreducible over the reals (and therefore over the rationals). On the other hand, the quadratic

$$x^2 - 2 = \left(x - \sqrt{2}\right)\left(x + \sqrt{2}\right)$$

is irreducible over the rationals, but *reducible* over the reals.

EXAMPLE 5   Factoring a Polynomial

Write the polynomial $f(x) = x^4 - x^2 - 20$ in the following forms.

A. As the product of factors that are irreducible over the *rationals*
B. As the product of linear factors and quadratic factors that are irreducible over the *reals*
C. In completely factored form

SOLUTION

A. Begin by factoring the polynomial into the product of two quadratic polynomials.

$$x^4 - x^2 - 20 = (x^2 - 5)(x^2 + 4)$$

Both of these factors are irreducible over the rationals.

B. By factoring over the reals, you have

$$x^4 - x^2 - 20 = \left(x + \sqrt{5}\right)\left(x - \sqrt{5}\right)(x^2 + 4),$$

where the quadratic factor is irreducible over the reals.

C. In completely factored form, you have

$$x^4 - x^2 - 20 = \left(x + \sqrt{5}\right)\left(x - \sqrt{5}\right)(x - 2i)(x + 2i).$$

EXAMPLE 6   Finding the Zeros of a Polynomial Function

Find all the zeros of $f(x) = x^4 - 3x^3 + 6x^2 + 2x - 60$ given that $1 + 3i$ is a zero of f.

SOLUTION

Because complex zeros occur in conjugate pairs, you know that $1 - 3i$ is also a zero of f. This means that both

$$[x - (1 + 3i)] \quad \text{and} \quad [x - (1 - 3i)]$$

are factors of $f(x)$. Multiplying these two factors produces

$$
\begin{aligned}
[x - (1 + 3i)][x - (1 - 3i)] &= [(x - 1) - 3i][(x - 1) + 3i] \\
&= (x - 1)^2 - 9i^2 \\
&= x^2 - 2x + 10.
\end{aligned}
$$

Using long division, you can divide $x^2 - 2x + 10$ into $f(x)$ to obtain the following.

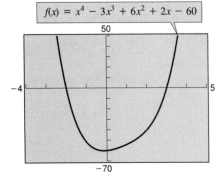

Therefore, you have

$$
\begin{aligned}
f(x) &= (x^2 - 2x + 10)(x^2 - x - 6) \\
&= (x^2 - 2x + 10)(x - 3)(x + 2),
\end{aligned}
$$

and you conclude that the zeros of f are $1 + 3i$, $1 - 3i$, 3, and -2. The graph in Figure 3.52 confirms these results.

FIGURE 3.52

Throughout this chapter, we have basically stated the results and examples in terms of *zeros of polynomial functions*. Be sure you see that the same results could have been stated in terms of *solutions of polynomial equations*. This is true because the zeros of the polynomial function

$$f(x) = a_n x^n + a_{n-1} x^{n-1} + \cdots + a_2 x^2 + a_1 x + a_0$$

are precisely the solutions of the polynomial equation

$$a_n x^n + a_{n-1} x^{n-1} + \cdots + a_2 x^2 + a_1 x + a_0 = 0.$$

DISCUSSION PROBLEM
....

FACTORING A POLYNOMIAL

Write a short paper summarizing the various techniques used to factor a polynomial. Include all of the techniques covered up to this point in the text. In what ways does a graphing utility help in factoring?

WARM-UP
....

The following warm-up exercises involve skills that were covered in earlier sections. You will use these skills in the exercise set for this section.

In Exercises 1–4, write each complex number in standard form and give its complex conjugate.

1. $4 - \sqrt{-29}$

2. $-5 - \sqrt{-144}$

3. $-1 + \sqrt{-32}$

4. $6 + \sqrt{-\frac{1}{4}}$

In Exercises 5–10, perform the indicated operations and write the result in standard form.

5. $(-3 + 6i) - (10 - 3i)$

6. $(12 - 4i) + 20i$

7. $(4 - 2i)(3 + 7i)$

8. $(2 - 5i)(2 + 5i)$

9. $\dfrac{1 + i}{1 - i}$

10. $(3 + 2i)^3$

SECTION 3.6 · EXERCISES
....

In Exercises 1–20, find all the zeros of the function and write the polynomial as a product of linear factors. When there is an extended list of possible rational zeros, use a graphing utility to graph the function in order to discard any rational number that is obviously not a zero of the function.

1. $f(x) = x^2 + 25$

2. $f(x) = x^2 - x + 56$

3. $h(x) = x^2 - 4x + 1$

4. $g(x) = x^2 + 10x + 23$

5. $f(x) = x^4 - 81$

6. $f(y) = y^4 - 625$

7. $f(z) = z^2 - 2z + 2$

8. $h(x) = x^3 - 3x^2 + 4x - 2$

9. $f(t) = t^3 - 3t^2 - 15t + 125$

10. $f(x) = x^3 + 11x^2 + 39x + 29$

11. $f(x) = 16x^3 - 20x^2 - 4x + 15$

12. $f(s) = 2s^3 - 5s^2 + 12s - 5$

13. $f(x) = 5x^3 - 9x^2 + 28x + 6$

14. $g(x) = 3x^3 - 4x^2 + 8x + 8$

15. $f(x) = x^4 + 10x^2 + 9$

16. $f(x) = x^4 + 29x^2 + 100$

17. $g(x) = x^4 - 4x^3 + 8x^2 - 16x + 16$

18. $h(x) = x^4 + 6x^3 + 10x^2 + 6x + 9$

19. $f(x) = 2x^4 + 5x^3 + 4x^2 + 5x + 2$

20. $g(x) = x^5 - 8x^4 + 28x^3 - 56x^2 + 64x - 32$

In Exercises 21–30, find a polynomial with integer coefficients that has the given zeros. (There are many correct answers.)

21. $1, 5i, -5i$

22. $4, 3i, -3i$

23. $2, 4 + i, 4 - i$

24. $6, -5 + 2i, -5 - 2i$

25. $i, -i, 6i, -6i$

26. $2, 2, 2, 4i, -4i$

27. $-5, -5, 1 + \sqrt{3}i$

28. $\frac{2}{3}, -1, 3 + \sqrt{2}i$

29. $\frac{3}{4}, -2, -\frac{1}{2} + i$

30. $0, 0, 4, 1 + i$

In Exercises 31–34, write the polynomial function (a) as the product of factors that are irreducible over the *rationals,* (b) as the product of linear and quadratic factors that are irreducible over the *reals,* and (c) in completely factored form.

31. $f(x) = x^4 + 6x^2 - 27$

32. $f(x) = x^4 - 2x^3 - 3x^2 + 12x - 18$
   (*Hint:* One factor is $x^2 - 6$.)

33. $f(x) = x^4 - 4x^3 + 5x^2 - 2x - 6$
   (*Hint:* One factor is $x^2 - 2x - 2$.)

34. $f(x) = x^4 - 3x^3 - x^2 - 12x - 20$
   (*Hint:* One factor is $x^2 + 4$.)

In Exercises 35–44, use the given zero of f to find all the zeros of f.

Function	Zero of the Function
35. $f(x) = 2x^3 + 3x^2 + 50x + 75$	$r = 5i$
36. $f(x) = x^3 + x^2 + 9x + 9$	$r = 3i$
37. $f(x) = 2x^4 - x^3 + 7x^2 - 4x - 4$	$r = 2i$
38. $g(x) = x^3 - 7x^2 - x + 87$	$r = 5 + 2i$
39. $g(x) = 4x^3 + 23x^2 + 34x - 10$	$r = -3 + i$
40. $h(x) = 3x^3 - 4x^2 + 8x + 8$	$r = 1 - \sqrt{3}i$
41. $f(x) = x^4 + 2x^3 - 9x^2 - 20x + 44$	$r = -3 + \sqrt{2}i$
42. $f(x) = x^3 + 4x^2 + 14x + 20$	$r = -1 - 3i$
43. $h(x) = 8x^3 - 14x^2 + 18x - 9$	$r = \dfrac{1 - \sqrt{5}i}{2}$
44. $f(x) = 25x^3 - 55x^2 - 54x - 18$	$r = \dfrac{-2 + \sqrt{2}i}{5}$

45. *Maximum Height*   A baseball is thrown upward from ground level with an initial velocity of 48 feet per second and its height h in feet is given by

$$h = -16t^2 + 48t, \qquad 0 \le t \le 3,$$

where t is the time in seconds. Suppose you are told the ball reaches a height of 64 feet. Is this possible? Explain.

46. *Profit*   The demand equation for a certain product is given by $p = 140 - 0.0001x$, where p is the unit price (in dollars) of the product and x is the number of units produced and sold. The cost equation for the product is $C = 80x + 150{,}000$, where C is the total cost (in dollars) and x is the number of units produced. The total profit obtained by producing and selling x units is given by

$$P = R - C = xp - C.$$

Suppose you are working in the marketing department of the company that produces this product, and you are asked to determine a price p that would yield a profit of 9 million dollars. Is this possible? Explain.

47. Find a quadratic function f (with integer coefficients) that has $\pm \sqrt{b}\, i$ as zeros. Assume that b is a positive integer.

48. Find a quadratic function f (with integer coefficients) that has $a \pm bi$ as zeros. Assume that b is a positive integer.

CHAPTER 3 · REVIEW EXERCISES

In Exercises 1–4, sketch the graph of the quadratic function. Identify the vertex and the intercepts.

1. $f(x) = (x + \frac{3}{2})^2 + 1$ **2.** $f(x) = (x - 4)^2 - 4$

3. $f(x) = \frac{1}{3}(x^2 + 5x - 4)$ **4.** $f(x) = 3x^2 - 12x + 11$

In Exercises 5 and 6, find the quadratic function that has the indicated vertex and whose graph passes through the given point.

5. Vertex: $(1, -4)$;   point: $(2, -3)$

6. Vertex: $(2, 3)$;   point: $(-1, 6)$

In Exercises 7–14, find the maximum or minimum value of the quadratic function.

7. $g(x) = x^2 - 2x$

8. $f(x) = x^2 + 8x + 10$

9. $f(x) = 6x - x^2$

10. $h(x) = 3 + 4x - x^2$

11. $f(t) = -2t^2 + 4t + 1$

12. $h(x) = 4x^2 + 4x + 13$

13. $h(x) = x^2 + 5x - 4$

14. $f(x) = 4x^2 + 4x + 5$

15. *Maximum Area* A rectangle is inscribed in the region bounded by the x-axis, the y-axis, and the graph of $x + 2y - 6 = 0$ (see figure). Find the coordinates (x, y) that yield a maximum area for the rectangle.

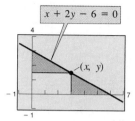

FIGURE FOR 15

16. *Maximum Area* The perimeter of a rectangle is 200 feet. Let x represent the width of the rectangle and write a quadratic function that expresses the area of the rectangle in terms of x. Of all possible rectangles with a perimeter of 200 feet, find the dimensions of the one that has the greatest area.

17. *Maximum Revenue* Find the number of units x that produce a maximum revenue R, where

$$R = 900x - 0.1x^2.$$

18. *Maximum Profit* Let x be the amount (in hundreds of dollars) that a company spends on advertising, and let P be the profit, where

$$P = 230 + 20x - \tfrac{1}{2}x^2.$$

What amount of advertising will yield a maximum profit?

19. *Maximum Profit* A real estate office handles 50 apartment units. When the rent is $540 per month, all units are occupied. However, for each $30 increase in rent, one unit becomes vacant. Each occupied unit requires an average of $18 per month for service and repairs. What rent should be charged to realize the most profit?

20. *Minimum Cost* A manufacturer has daily production costs of

$$C = 20,000 - 120x + 0.055x^2,$$

where C is the total cost in dollars and x is the number of units produced. How many units should be produced each day to yield a minimum cost?

In Exercises 21–24, determine the right-hand and left-hand behavior of the graph of the polynomial function. Use a graphing utility to verify your answer.

21. $f(x) = -x^2 + 6x + 9$ **22.** $f(x) = \frac{1}{2}x^3 + 2x$

23. $g(x) = \frac{3}{4}(x^4 + 3x^2 + 2)$

24. $h(x) = -x^5 - 7x^2 + 10x$

In Exercises 25–32, sketch a graph of the function.

25. $f(x) = -(x - 2)^3$ **26.** $f(x) = (x + 1)^3$

27. $g(x) = x^4 - x^3 - 2x^2$ **28.** $h(x) = -2x^3 - x^2 + x$

29. $f(t) = t^3 - 3t$ **30.** $f(x) = -x^3 + 3x - 2$

31. $f(x) = x(x + 3)^2$ **32.** $f(t) = t^4 - 4t^2$

In Exercises 33–38, divide by long division.

33. $\dfrac{24x^2 - x - 8}{3x - 2}$ **34.** $\dfrac{5x^3 - 13x^2 - x + 2}{x^2 - 3x + 1}$

35. $\dfrac{x^4 - 3x^2 + 2}{x^2 - 1}$ **36.** $\dfrac{3x^4}{x^2 - 1}$

37. $\dfrac{x^4 - 3x^3 + 4x^2 - 6x + 3}{x^2 + 2}$

38. $\dfrac{6x^4 + 10x^3 + 13x^2 - 5x + 2}{2x^2 - 1}$

In Exercises 39–42, use synthetic division to perform the division.

39. $\dfrac{0.25x^4 - 4x^3}{x - 2}$ **40.** $\dfrac{2x^3 + 2x^2 - x + 2}{x - (1/2)}$

41. $\dfrac{2x^3 - 5x^2 + 12x - 5}{x - (1 + 2i)}$ **42.** $\dfrac{9x^3 - 15x^2 - 11x - 5}{x - [(1/3) + (2/3)i]}$

In Exercises 43–46, use synthetic division to determine whether the values of x are zeros of the function.

43. $f(x) = 2x^3 + 3x^2 - 20x - 21$
  (a) $x = 4$ (b) $x = -1$
  (c) $x = -\frac{7}{2}$ (d) $x = 0$

44. $f(x) = 20x^4 + 9x^3 - 14x^2 - 3x$
  (a) $x = -1$ (b) $x = \frac{3}{4}$
  (c) $x = 0$ (d) $x = 1$

45. $f(x) = 2x^3 + 7x^2 - 18x - 30$
  (a) $x = 1$ (b) $x = \frac{5}{2}$
  (c) $x = -3 + \sqrt{3}$ (d) $x = 0$

46. $f(x) = 3x^3 - 26x^2 + 364x - 232$
  (a) $x = 4 - 10i$ (b) $x = 4$
  (c) $x = \frac{2}{3}$ (d) $x = -1$

In Exercises 47–50, use synthetic division and the Remainder Theorem to find the specified value of the function.

47. $g(x) = 2x^4 - 17x^3 + 58x^2 - 77x + 26$
   (a) $g(-2)$ (b) $g(\frac{1}{2})$

48. $h(x) = 5x^5 - 2x^4 - 45x + 18$
   (a) $h(2)$ (b) $h(\sqrt{3})$

49. $f(x) = x^4 + 10x^3 - 24x^2 + 20x + 44$
   (a) $f(-3)$ (b) $f(\sqrt{2}i)$

50. $g(t) = 2t^5 - 5t^4 - 8t + 20$
   (a) $g(-4)$ (b) $g(\sqrt{2})$

In Exercises 51–56, perform the indicated operations and write the result in standard form.

51. $-(6 - 2i) + (-8 + 3i)$

52. $\left(\dfrac{\sqrt{2}}{2} - \dfrac{\sqrt{2}}{2}i\right) - \left(\dfrac{\sqrt{2}}{2} + \dfrac{\sqrt{2}}{2}i\right)$

53. $5i(13 - 8i)$ **54.** $i(6 + i)(3 - 2i)$

55. $\dfrac{6 + i}{i}$ **56.** $\dfrac{3 + 2i}{5 + i}$

In Exercises 57–60, find a polynomial with integer coefficients that has the given zeros.

57. $-1, -1, \frac{1}{3}, -\frac{1}{2}$ **58.** $5, 1 - \sqrt{2}, 1 + \sqrt{2}$

59. $\frac{2}{3}, 4, \sqrt{3}i, -\sqrt{3}i$ **60.** $2, -3, 1 - 2i, 1 + 2i$

In Exercises 61 and 62, use Descartes's Rule of Signs to determine the possible number of positive and negative zeros of the function.

61. $g(x) = 5x^3 + 3x^2 - 6x + 9$
62. $h(x) = -2x^5 + 4x^3 - 2x^2 + 5$

In Exercises 63 and 64, use the Rational Zero Test to list all possible rational zeros of f.

63. $f(x) = -4x^3 + 8x^2 - 3x + 15$
64. $f(x) = 3x^4 + 4x^3 - 5x^2 - 8$

In Exercises 65–70, find all the zeros of the function. When there is an extended list of possible rational zeros, use a graphing utility to graph the function in order to discard any rational number that is obviously not a zero of the function.

65. $f(x) = 4x^3 - 11x^2 + 10x - 3$
66. $f(x) = 10x^3 + 21x^2 - x - 6$
67. $f(x) = 6x^3 - 5x^2 + 24x - 20$
68. $f(x) = x^3 - 1.3x^2 - 1.7x + 0.6$
69. $f(x) = 6x^4 - 25x^3 + 14x^2 + 27x - 18$
70. $f(x) = 5x^4 + 126x^2 + 25$

In Exercises 71–74, (a) list the possible rational zeros of f and show that none are zeros, (b) use a graphing utility to verify that there are real zeros of f, and (c) move the cursor along the graph to approximate the irrational zero(s) of the function accurate to two decimal places.

71. $f(x) = x^4 + 2x - 1$ **72.** $g(x) = x^3 - 3x^2 + 3x + 2$
73. $h(x) = x^3 - 6x^2 + 12x - 10$
74. $f(x) = x^5 + 2x^3 - 3x - 20$

75. *Volume Marker*   A spherical tank of radius 50 feet (see figure) will be two-thirds full when the depth of the fluid is $x + 50$ feet, where

$$3x^3 - 22{,}500x + 250{,}000 = 0.$$

Use a graphing utility to approximate x to within 0.01 unit.

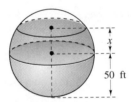

50 ft

FIGURE FOR 75

76. *Age of the Groom*   The average age of the groom in a marriage for the given age of the bride can be approximated by the model

$$y = -0.00428x^2 + 1.442x - 3.136, \qquad 20 \le x \le 55,$$

where y is the age of the groom and x is the age of the bride. For what age of the bride is the average age of the groom 30? (*Source:* U.S. National Center for Health Statistics)

RATIONAL FUNCTIONS AND CONIC SECTIONS

4.1 RATIONAL FUNCTIONS AND ASYMPTOTES

Introduction to Rational Functions / Horizontal and Vertical Asymptotes / Applications

Introduction to Rational Functions

A **rational function** is one that can be written in the form

$$f(x) = \frac{p(x)}{q(x)},$$

where $p(x)$ and $q(x)$ are polynomials and $q(x)$ is not the zero polynomial. In this section we assume $p(x)$ and $q(x)$ have no common factors. Some examples of rational functions are

$$f(x) = \frac{1}{x + 2}, \quad g(x) = \frac{x - 1}{(x + 1)(x - 2)}, \quad \text{and} \quad h(x) = \frac{x}{x^2 + 1}.$$

The domain of f excludes $x = -2$, and the domain of g excludes $x = 2$ and $x = -1$. The domain of h is all real numbers because there are no real values of x that make the denominator $x^2 + 1$ equal to zero.

In general, the *domain* of a rational function of x includes all real numbers except x-values that make the denominator zero.

Technology Note _____

The standard mode on most graphing utilities is the "connected mode" in which the plotted points are connected by line segments. When graphing rational functions, it can be better to use the "dot" or "plot" mode. Try graphing $y = 1/(x - 3)$ in both modes to see which you prefer.

EXAMPLE 1   Finding the Domain of a Rational Function

Find the domain of $f(x) = 1/x$. Discuss the behavior of f near any excluded x-values.

SOLUTION

Because the denominator is zero when $x = 0$, the domain of f is all real numbers except $x = 0$. To determine the behavior of f near this excluded value, evaluate $f(x)$ to the left and right of $x = 0$, as indicated in the tables.

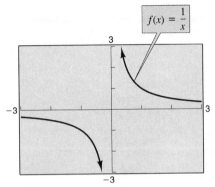

$f(x) = \dfrac{1}{x}$

FIGURE 4.1

x Approaches 0 from the Left			*x* Approaches 0 from the Right	
x	$f(x)$		x	$f(x)$
-1	-1		1	1
-0.5	-2		0.5	2
-0.1	-10		0.1	10
-0.01	-100		0.01	100
-0.001	-1000		0.001	1000

Note that as x approaches 0 *from the left*, $f(x)$ appears to decrease without bound, whereas as x approaches 0 *from the right*, $f(x)$ appears to increase without bound. This behavior is confirmed by the graph of f that is shown in Figure 4.1.

Horizontal and Vertical Asymptotes

In Example 1, the behavior of $f(x) = 1/x$ near $x = 0$ is denoted as follows.

$$f(x) \to -\infty \text{ as } x \to 0^- \qquad\qquad f(x) \to \infty \text{ as } x \to 0^+$$

$f(x)$ decreases without bound as x approaches 0 from the left. $\qquad$ $f(x)$ increases without bound as x approaches 0 from the right.

The line $x = 0$ is a **vertical asymptote** of the graph of f, as shown in Figure 4.2. The graph of f also has a **horizontal asymptote**—the line $y = 0$. This means that the values of $f(x) = 1/x$ approach zero as x increases or decreases without bound.

$$f(x) \to 0 \text{ as } x \to -\infty \qquad\qquad f(x) \to 0 \text{ as } x \to \infty$$

$f(x)$ approaches 0 as x decreases without bound. $\qquad$ $f(x)$ approaches 0 as x increases without bound.

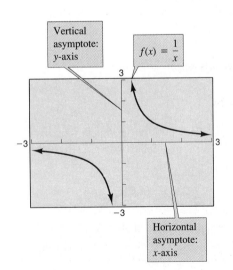

Vertical asymptote: y-axis

$f(x) = \dfrac{1}{x}$

Horizontal asymptote: x-axis

FIGURE 4.2

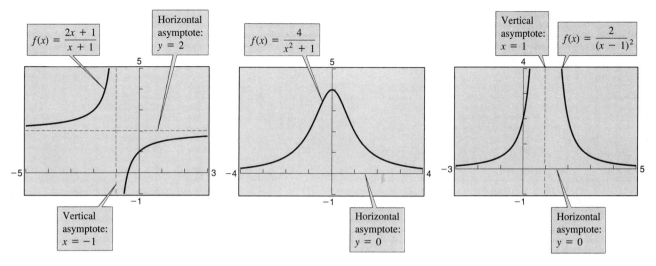

FIGURE 4.3

In general, the line $x = a$ is a **vertical asymptote** of the graph of f if $f(x) \to \infty$ or $f(x) \to -\infty$ as x approaches a either from the right or from the left. The line $y = b$ is a **horizontal asymptote** of the graph of f if $f(x)$ approaches b as $x \to \infty$ or $x \to -\infty$.

Though the graph of a rational function never intersects its vertical asymptote(s), it may intersect its horizontal asymptote. Eventually, however, the distance between the horizontal asymptote and the points on the graph must approach zero (as $x \to \infty$ or $x \to -\infty$). Figure 4.3 shows the horizontal and vertical asymptotes of the graphs of three rational functions.

A rational function can have several vertical asymptotes, but it can have at most one horizontal asymptote.

ASYMPTOTES OF A RATIONAL FUNCTION

Let f be the rational function given by

$$f(x) = \frac{p(x)}{q(x)} = \frac{a_n x^n + a_{n-1} x^{n-1} + \cdots + a_1 x + a_0}{b_m x^m + b_{m-1} x^{m-1} + \cdots + b_1 x + b_0},$$

where $p(x)$ and $q(x)$ have no common factors.

1. The graph of f has vertical asymptotes at the zeros of $q(x)$.
2. The graph of f has at most one horizontal asymptote, as follows.
   (a) If $n < m$, then the x-axis ($y = 0$) is a horizontal asymptote.
   (b) If $n = m$, then the line $y = a_n / b_m$ is a horizontal asymptote.
   (c) If $n > m$, then the graph of f has no horizontal asymptote.

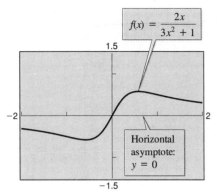

Vertical asymptote: None
Horizontal asymptote: $y = 0$

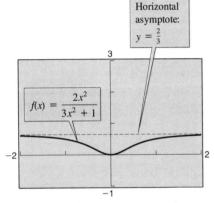

Vertical asymptote: None
Horizontal asymptote: $y = \frac{2}{3}$

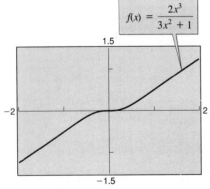

Vertical asymptote: None
Horizontal asymptote: None

FIGURE 4.4

You can apply this theorem by comparing the degrees of the numerator and denominator, as illustrated in Figure 4.4.

EXAMPLE 2   A Calculator Experiment

Find the horizontal asymptote of the graph of

$$f(x) = \frac{3x^3 + 7x^2 + 2}{-4x^3 + 5}.$$

SOLUTION

Because the degree of the numerator and denominator are the same, the horizontal asymptote is given by the ratio of the leading coefficients,

$$y = \frac{\text{leading coefficient of numerator}}{\text{leading coefficient of denominator}} = \frac{3}{-4} = -\frac{3}{4}.$$

The following table shows how the values of $f(x)$ become closer and closer to $-\frac{3}{4}$ as x becomes increasingly large or small.

x Decreases Without Bound		*x* Increases Without Bound	
x	$f(x)$	x	$f(x)$
-1	0.6667	1	12
-10	-0.5738	10	-0.9267
-100	-0.7325	100	-0.7675
-1000	-0.7482	1000	-0.7518
$-10,000$	-0.7498	10,000	-0.7502

Graphs of rational functions that are produced by a graphing utility can be misleading. Try using a graphing utility to confirm the graph shown in Figure 4.5.

FIGURE 4.5

A function that is not rational can have two horizontal asymptotes—one to the left and one to the right.

EXAMPLE 3   **A (Nonrational) Graph with Two Horizontal Asymptotes**

Use a graphing utility to find the horizontal asymptotes of

$$f(x) = \frac{x + 10}{|x| + 2}.$$

SOLUTION

The graph of f is shown in Figure 4.6. Note that the graph appears to have two different horizontal asymptotes. You can confirm this by rewriting the function as follows.

$$f(x) = \begin{cases} \dfrac{x + 10}{-x + 2}, & x \leq 0 \\ \dfrac{x + 10}{x + 2}, & x > 0 \end{cases}$$

In this form, you can see that the line $y = -1$ is a horizontal asymptote to the left and the line $y = 1$ is a horizontal asymptote to the right.

$$f(x) = \frac{x + 10}{|x| + 2}$$

FIGURE 4.6

Applications

EXAMPLE 4   Cost-Benefit Model for Smokestack Emission

A utility company burns coal to generate electricity. The cost C of removing $p\%$ of the smokestack pollutants is given by

$$C = \frac{80{,}000p}{100 - p}.$$

Sketch the graph of this function. The state legislature is considering a law that will require utility companies to remove 90% of the pollutants from their smokestack emissions. The current law requires 85% removal. How much additional expense is the new law imposing on the utility company?

SOLUTION

The graph of this function is shown in Figure 4.7. Note that the graph has a vertical asymptote at $p = 100$. Because the current law requires 85% removal, the current cost to the utility company is

$$C = \frac{80{,}000(85)}{100 - 85} \approx \$453{,}333.$$

At 90% removal, the cost to the utility company will be

$$C = \frac{80{,}000(90)}{100 - 90} = \$720{,}000.$$

Therefore, the new law requires the utility company to spend an additional

$$720{,}000 - 453{,}333 = \$266{,}667.$$

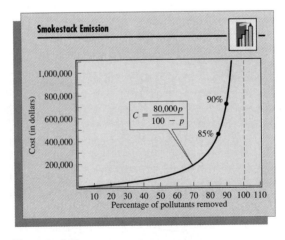

The cost of removing a certain percentage of the pollutants from the stack emission is typically not a linear function. As the percentage of removed pollutants approaches 100%, the cost tends to become prohibitive.

FIGURE 4.7

EXAMPLE 5 Average Cost of Producing a Product

A business has a cost function of $C = 0.5\,x + 5000$, where C is measured in dollars and x is the number of units produced. The *average cost per unit* is given by

$$\overline{C} = \frac{C}{x} = \frac{0.5x + 5000}{x}.$$

Find the average cost per unit when $x = 1000$, 10,000, and 100,000. What is the horizontal asymptote for this function, and what does it represent?

SOLUTION

When $x = 1000$, $\overline{C} = \dfrac{0.5(1000) + 5000}{1000} = \$5.50.$

When $x = 10,000$, $\overline{C} = \dfrac{0.5(10,000) + 5000}{10,000} = \$1.00.$

When $x = 100,000$, $\overline{C} = \dfrac{0.5(100,000) + 5000}{100,000} = \$0.55.$

As shown in Figure 4.8, the horizontal asymptote is given by the line $C = 0.50$. This line represents the least possible unit cost for the product. Note that this example points out one of the major problems of a small business—that it is difficult to have competitively low prices when the production level is low.

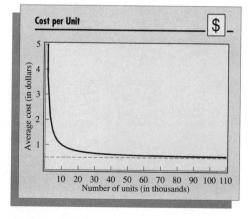

FIGURE 4.8

DISCUSSION PROBLEM

COMMON FACTORS IN THE NUMERATOR AND DENOMINATOR

In the guidelines for graphing a rational function, we noted that the rational function should have no factor that is common to its numerator and denominator. To see why we required this, consider the function given by

$$f(x) = \frac{x(x-1)}{x},$$

which has a common factor of x in the numerator and denominator. Graph this function. Does it have a vertical asymptote at $x = 0$? Does your graphing utility indicate the domain of the function f?

WARM-UP

The following warm-up exercises involve skills that were covered in earlier sections. You will use these skills in the exercise set for this section.

In Exercises 1–4, factor the polynomials.

1. $x^2 - 3x - 10$
2. $x^2 - 7x + 10$
3. $x^3 + 4x^2 + 3x$
4. $x^3 - 4x^2 - 2x + 8$

In Exercises 5–8, graph the equation.

5. $y = 2$
6. $x = -1$
7. $y = x - 2$
8. $y = -x + 1$

In Exercises 9 and 10, use long division to write the rational expression as the sum of a polynomial and a rational expression.

9. $\dfrac{x^2 + 5x + 6}{x - 4}$
10. $\dfrac{x^2 + 5x + 6}{x + 4}$

SECTION 4.1 · EXERCISES

In Exercises 1–6, (a) complete each table, (b) determine the vertical and horizontal asymptotes of the graph, and (c) find the domain of the function.

x	$f(x)$
1	
1.5	
1.9	
1.99	
1.999	

x	$f(x)$
3	
2.5	
2.1	
2.01	
2.001	

x	$f(x)$
3	
5	
10	
100	
1000	

1. $f(x) = \dfrac{1}{x - 2}$

2. $f(x) = \dfrac{5x}{x - 2}$

3. $f(x) = \dfrac{3x}{|x - 2|}$

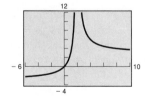

4. $f(x) = \dfrac{3}{|x - 2|}$

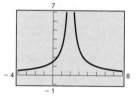

5. $f(x) = \dfrac{3x^2}{x^2 - 4}$

6. $f(x) = \dfrac{4x}{x^2 - 4}$

In Exercises 7–14, find the domain of the function and identify any horizontal and vertical asymptotes.

7. $f(x) = \dfrac{1}{x^2}$

8. $f(x) = \dfrac{4}{(x - 2)^3}$

9. $f(x) = \dfrac{2 + x}{2 - x}$

10. $f(x) = \dfrac{1 - 5x}{1 + 2x}$

11. $f(x) = \dfrac{x^3}{x^2 - 1}$

12. $f(x) = \dfrac{2x^2}{x + 1}$

13. $f(x) = \dfrac{3x^2 + 1}{x^2 + 9}$

14. $f(x) = \dfrac{3x^2 + x - 5}{x^2 + 1}$

In Exercises 15–20, match the rational function with its graph, and describe the given viewing rectangle. [The graphs are labeled (a), (b), (c), (d), (e), and (f).]

15. $f(x) = \dfrac{2}{x + 1}$

16. $f(x) = \dfrac{1}{x - 4}$

17. $f(x) = \dfrac{x + 1}{x}$

18. $f(x) = \dfrac{1 - 2x}{x}$

19. $f(x) = \dfrac{x - 2}{x - 1}$

20. $f(x) = -\dfrac{x + 2}{x + 1}$

(a)

(b)

(c)

(d)

(e)

(f)

In Exercises 21–24, (a) determine the domain of f and g, (b) find any vertical asymptotes of f, (c) use a graphing utility to obtain the graphs of f and g in the same viewing rectangle, and (d) explain why the graphing utility does or does not show the difference in the domains of f and g.

21. $f(x) = \dfrac{x^2 - 4}{x + 2}$

   $g(x) = x - 2$

22. $f(x) = \dfrac{x^2(x - 3)}{x^2 - 3x}$

   $g(x) = x$

23. $f(x) = \dfrac{x - 3}{x^2 - 3x}$

   $g(x) = \dfrac{1}{x}$

24. $f(x) = \dfrac{2x - 8}{x^2 - 9x + 20}$

   $g(x) = \dfrac{2}{x - 5}$

25. *Cost of Clean Water*   The cost in millions of dollars for removing $p\%$ of the industrial and municipal pollutants discharged into a river is given by

$$C = \dfrac{255p}{100 - p}, \qquad 0 \le p < 100.$$

(a) Find the cost of removing 10% of the pollutants.
(b) Find the cost of removing 40%.
(c) Find the cost of removing 75%.
(d) According to this model, would it be possible to remove 100% of the pollutants?

26. *Recycling Costs*   In a pilot project, a rural township was given recycling bins for separating and storing recyclable products. The cost in dollars for giving bins to $p\%$ of the population is given by

$$C = \dfrac{25{,}000p}{100 - p}, \qquad 0 \le p < 100.$$

(a) Find the cost of giving bins to 15% of the population.
(b) Find the cost of giving bins to 50% of the population.
(c) Find the cost of giving bins to 90% of the population.
(d) According to this model, would it be possible to give bins to 100% of the residents?

27. *Population of Deer*   The game commission introduces 50 deer into newly acquired state game lands. The population of the herd is given by

$$N = \dfrac{10(5 + 3t)}{1 + 0.04t}, \qquad 0 \le t,$$

where t is the time in years (see figure).
(a) Find the population when t is 5, 10, and 25.
(b) What is the limiting size of the herd as time increases?

FIGURE FOR 27

28. *Food Consumption*   A biology class performs an experiment comparing the quantity of food consumed by a certain kind of moth with the quantity supplied (see figure). The model for their experimental data is given by

$$y = \dfrac{1.568x - 0.001}{6.360x + 1},$$

where x is the quantity (in milligrams) of food supplied and y is the quantity (in milligrams) eaten. At what level of consumption will the moth become filled?

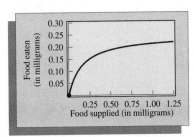

FIGURE FOR 28

29. *Human Memory Model* Psychologists have developed mathematical models to predict performance as a function of the number of trials n for a certain task. Consider the learning curve given by

$$P = \frac{0.5 + 0.9(n-1)}{1 + 0.9(n-1)}, \qquad 0 < n,$$

where P is the percentage of correct responses after n trials.

(a) Complete the following table for this model.

n	1	2	3	4	5	6	7	8	9	10
P										

(b) According to this model, what is the limiting percentage of correct responses as n increases?

30. As the magnitude of x increases, what value does the function f approach in each of the following? Is $f(x)$ greater than or less than this functional value when (i) x is positive and large in magnitude, and (ii) x is negative and large in magnitude?

(a) $f(x) = 4 - \dfrac{1}{x}$

(b) $f(x) = 2 + \dfrac{1}{x-3}$

(c) $f(x) = \dfrac{2x-1}{x-3}$

(d) $f(x) = \dfrac{2x-1}{x^2+1}$

4.2   GRAPHS OF RATIONAL FUNCTIONS
• •
The Graph of a Rational Function / Slant Asymptotes / Applications

The Graph of a Rational Function

In this section you will study techniques for analyzing the graph of a rational function.

ANALYZING THE GRAPHS OF RATIONAL FUNCTIONS

Let $f(x) = p(x)/q(x)$, when $p(x)$ and $q(x)$ are polynomials with no common factors.

1. The y-intercept (if any) is the value $f(0)$.
2. The x-intercepts (if any) are the zeros of the numerator—that is, the solutions to the equation $p(x) = 0$.
3. The vertical asymptotes (if any) are the zeros of the denominator—that is, the solutions to the equation $q(x) = 0$.
4. The horizontal asymptote (if any) is the value that $f(x)$ approaches as x increases or decreases without bound.
5. Determining the behavior of the graph *between* and *beyond* each x-intercept and vertical asymptote is crucial for describing the complete graph of a rational function.

REMARK Testing for symmetry can be useful, especially for simple rational functions. For example, the graph of $f(x) = 1/x$ is symmetrical with respect to the origin, and the graph of $g(x) = 1/x^2$ is symmetrical with respect to the y-axis.

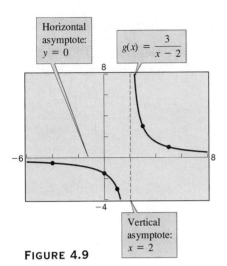

FIGURE 4.9

REMARK   The graph of g is a vertical stretch and a right shift of the graph of $f(x) = 1/x$ because

$$g(x) = \frac{3}{x-2} = 3\left(\frac{1}{x-2}\right)$$

$$= 3f(x-2).$$

EXAMPLE 1   Graphing a Rational Function

Graph the function

$$g(x) = \frac{3}{x-2}.$$

SOLUTION

Begin by noting that the numerator and denominator have no common factors.

$$y\text{-}intercept: \quad \left(0, -\frac{3}{2}\right), \quad \text{from } g(0) = -\frac{3}{2}$$

$x\text{-}intercept:$ None, because $3 \neq 0$

$Vertical\ asymptote:$ $x = 2$,   zero of denominator

$Horizontal\ asymptote:$ $y = 0$,   degree of $p(x) <$ degree of $q(x)$

Additional points:

x	-4	1	3	5
$g(x)$	-0.5	-3	3	1

By plotting the intercepts, asymptotes, and a few additional points, we obtain the graph shown in Figure 4.9. Use a graphing utility to confirm these results.

EXAMPLE 2   Graphing a Rational Function

Graph the function

$$f(x) = \frac{2x-1}{x}.$$

SOLUTION

Begin by noting that the numerator and denominator have no common factors.

$y\text{-}intercept:$ None, because $x = 0$ is not in the domain

$$x\text{-}intercept: \quad \left(\frac{1}{2}, 0\right), \quad \text{from } 2x - 1 = 0$$

$Vertical\ asymptote:$ $x = 0$,   zero of denominator

$Horizontal\ asymptote:$ $y = 2$,   degree of $p(x) =$ degree of $q(x)$

Additional points:

x	-4	-1	$\frac{1}{4}$	4
$f(x)$	2.25	3	-2	1.75

By plotting the intercepts, asymptotes, and a few additional points, we obtain the graph shown in Figure 4.10. Use a graphing utility to confirm these results.

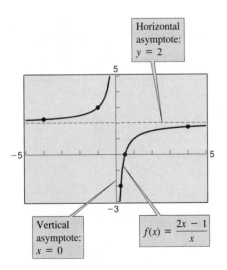

FIGURE 4.10

EXAMPLE 3   Graphing a Rational Function

Graph the function

$$f(x) = \frac{x}{x^2 - x - 2}.$$

SOLUTION

Factoring the denominator produces

$$f(x) = \frac{x}{x^2 - x - 2} = \frac{x}{(x + 1)(x - 2)}.$$

Thus, the numerator and denominator have no common factors.

y-intercept:	$(0, 0)$, because $f(0) = 0$
x-intercept:	$(0, 0)$
Vertical asymptotes:	$x = -1$, $x = 2$, zeros of denominator
Horizontal asymptote:	$y = 0$, degree of $p(x) <$ degree of $q(x)$

Additional points:

x	-3	-0.5	1	3
$f(x)$	-0.3	0.4	-0.5	0.75

By plotting the intercept, asymptotes, and a few additional points, we obtain the graph shown in Figure 4.11. Use a graphing utility to confirm these results.

FIGURE 4.11

EXAMPLE 4   Graphing a Rational Function

Graph the function

$$f(x) = \frac{2(x^2 - 9)}{x^2 - 4}.$$

SOLUTION

Factoring the numerator and denominator produces

$$f(x) = \frac{2(x^2 - 9)}{x^2 - 4} = \frac{2(x - 3)(x + 3)}{(x - 2)(x + 2)}.$$

Thus, the numerator and denominator have no common factors.

y-intercept: $\left(0, \frac{9}{2}\right)$, from $f(0) = \frac{9}{2}$

x-intercepts: $(-3, 0)$ and $(3, 0)$

Vertical asymptotes: $x = -2$, $x = 2$,   zeros of denominator

Horizontal asymptote: $y = 2$,   degree of $p(x) =$ degree of $q(x)$

Symmetry: With respect to y-axis, because $f(-x) = f(x)$

Additional points:

x	0.5	2.5	6
$f(x)$	4.67	−2.44	1.69

By plotting the intercepts, asymptotes, and a few additional points, we obtain the graph shown in Figure 4.12. Use a graphing utility to confirm these results.

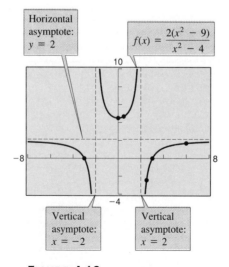

FIGURE 4.12

D I S C O V E R Y

Use a graphing utility to graph
$y = (x^2 - x)/(x + 1)$ and
$y = x - 2$ on the same viewing
rectangle. What do you observe
as x increases or decreases
without bound? Write a
convincing argument that the
line $y = x - 2$ is an asymptote
of the graph of the rational
function. (*Hint:* Use the long
division shown at the right as
part of your argument.)

Slant Asymptotes

If the degree of the numerator of a rational function is exactly *one more* than
the degree of its denominator, then the graph of the function has a **slant
asymptote.** For example, the graphs of

$$f(x) = \frac{x^2 - x}{x + 1} \quad \text{and} \quad g(x) = \frac{-x^3 + x^2 + 4}{x^2}$$

have slant asymptotes, as shown in Figure 4.13. You can use long division to
find the equation of a slant asymptote. For instance, dividing $x + 1$ into
$x^2 - x$ produces

$$f(x) = \frac{x^2 - x}{x + 1} = \underbrace{x - 2}_{\substack{\text{Slant asymptote} \\ (y = x - 2)}} + \frac{2}{x + 1}.$$

FIGURE 4.13

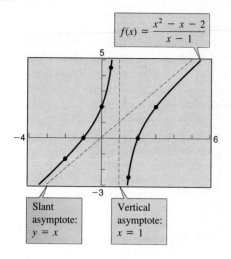

$$f(x) = \frac{x^2 - x - 2}{x - 1}$$

Slant
asymptote:
$y = x$

Vertical
asymptote:
$x = 1$

FIGURE 4.14

EXAMPLE 5   A Rational Function with a Slant Asymptote

Graph the function

$$f(x) = \frac{x^2 - x - 2}{x - 1}.$$

SOLUTION

As a preliminary step, write $f(x)$ in two different ways. Factoring the numerator

$$f(x) = \frac{x^2 - x - 2}{x - 1} = \frac{(x - 2)(x + 1)}{x - 1}$$

allows you to recognize the x-intercepts, and long division

$$f(x) = \frac{x^2 - x - 2}{x - 1} = x - \frac{2}{x - 1}$$

allows you to recognize that the line $y = x$ is a slant asymptote of the graph.

y-intercept:	$(0, 2)$, because $f(0) = 2$
x-intercepts:	$(-1, 0)$ and $(2, 0)$
Vertical asymptote:	$x = 1$
Slant asymptote:	$y = x$

Additional points:

x	-2	0.5	1.5	3
$f(x)$	-1.33	4.5	-2.5	2

The graph of f is shown in Figure 4.14. Use a graphing utility to graph f and its slant asymptote $y = x$ on the same screen and confirm the above results.

Note that it is possible for the graph of a rational function to cross its horizontal asymptote or its slant asymptote, as shown in Figure 4.15.

Horizontal
asymptote:
$y = 0$

$$f(x) = \frac{x}{x^2 + 1}$$

FIGURE 4.15

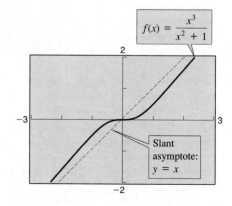

$$f(x) = \frac{x^3}{x^2 + 1}$$

Slant
asymptote:
$y = x$

Applications

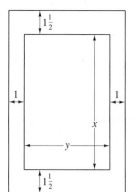

FIGURE 4.16

EXAMPLE 6   Finding the Minimum Area
....

A rectangular page is to contain 48 square inches of print. The margins at the top and bottom of the page are each $1\frac{1}{2}$ inches. The margins on each side are 1 inch. What should the dimensions of the page be so that the least amount of paper is used?

SOLUTION

Let A be the area to be minimized. From Figure 4.16, you can write

$$A = (x + 3)(y + 2).$$

The printed area inside the margins is given by

$$48 = xy \quad \text{or} \quad y = \frac{48}{x}.$$

To find the minimum area, rewrite the equation for A in terms of just one variable by substituting $y = 48/x$.

$$A = (x + 3)\left(\frac{48}{x} + 2\right) = \frac{(x + 3)(48 + 2x)}{x}, \qquad x > 0$$

The graph of this rational function is shown in Figure 4.17. Because x represents the height of the printed area, you need consider only the portion of the graph for which x is positive. Using the zoom and trace features of a graphing utility, you can approximate the minimum value of A to occur when $x \approx 8.5$ inches. The corresponding value of y is $y \approx 48/(8.5) \approx 5.6$ inches. Thus, the dimensions of the page should be

$$x + 3 \approx 11.5 \text{ inches} \quad \text{by} \quad y + 2 \approx 7.6 \text{ inches.}$$

If you go on to take a course in calculus, you will learn a technique for finding the exact value of x that produces a minimum area. In this case, that value is $x = 6\sqrt{2} \approx 8.485$.

FIGURE 4.17

The technique used to find slant asymptotes works for rational functions in which the degree of the numerator is one more than the degree of the denominator. If the degree of the numerator is two more than the degree of the denominator, then the graph of the rational function has a *parabolic asymptote*. For instance, consider the rational function given by

$$f(x) = \frac{x^3 + 1}{x} = x^2 + \frac{1}{x}.$$

The graphs of f and $y = x^2$ are both shown in the figure. Note that as x approaches positive or negative infinity, the two graphs nearly coincide. Write a short paragraph describing how you can use a parabolic asymptote as an aid to analyzing the graph of a rational function.

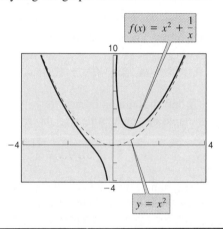

$f(x) = x^2 + \dfrac{1}{x}$

$y = x^2$

The following warm-up exercises involve skills that were covered in earlier sections. You will use these skills in the exercise set for this section.

In Exercises 1 and 2, find any intercepts of the graph of the equation.

1. $2x - xy - y + 6 = 0$ **2.** $4x - 5y + 12 = 0$

In Exercises 3 and 4, determine whether the function is even, odd, or neither.

3. $g(x) = x(x^2 - 5)$ **4.** $h(x) = \frac{1}{8}x^4 - 3x^2 - 4$

In Exercises 5–8, find the domain of the function and identify any horizontal or vertical asymptotes.

5. $f(x) = \dfrac{6}{x - 8}$ **6.** $f(x) = \dfrac{3x - 1}{4x + 1}$ **7.** $h(x) = \dfrac{2x^2 + 5}{x^2 - 9}$ **8.** $g(x) = 4 - \dfrac{1}{x}$

In Exercises 9 and 10, perform the specified division.

9. $\dfrac{4x^2 + 5x + 8}{2x - 1}$ **10.** $\dfrac{x^3 + 1}{x^2}$

SECTION 4.2 · EXERCISES

In Exercises 1–4, use the graph of $f(x) = 1/x$ to sketch the graph of g.

1. $g(x) = \dfrac{1}{x} + 1$

2. $g(x) = \dfrac{1}{x - 1}$

3. $g(x) = -\dfrac{1}{x}$

4. $g(x) = \dfrac{1}{x + 2}$

In Exercises 5–8, use the graph of $f(x) = 4/x^2$ to sketch the graph of g.

5. $g(x) = \dfrac{4}{x^2} - 2$

6. $g(x) = -\dfrac{4}{x^2}$

7. $g(x) = \dfrac{4}{(x - 2)^2}$

8. $g(x) = \dfrac{1}{x^2}$

In Exercises 9–12, use the graph of $f(x) = 8/x^3$ to sketch the graph of g.

9. $g(x) = \dfrac{8}{(x + 2)^3}$

10. $g(x) = \dfrac{8}{x^3} + 1$

11. $g(x) = -\dfrac{8}{x^3}$

12. $g(x) = \dfrac{1}{x^3}$

In Exercises 13–28, sketch the graph of the rational function without the aid of a graphing utility. As sketching aids, check for intercepts, symmetry, vertical asymptotes, and horizontal asymptotes. Use a graphing utility to verify your graph.

13. $f(x) = \dfrac{1}{x + 2}$

14. $f(x) = \dfrac{1}{x - 3}$

15. $h(x) = \dfrac{-1}{x + 2}$

16. $g(x) = \dfrac{1}{3 - x}$

17. $C(x) = \dfrac{5 + 2x}{1 + x}$

18. $P(x) = \dfrac{1 - 3x}{1 - x}$

19. $g(x) = \dfrac{1}{x + 2} + 2$

20. $f(t) = \dfrac{1 - 2t}{t}$

21. $f(x) = \dfrac{x^2}{x^2 + 9}$

22. $f(x) = 2 - \dfrac{3}{x^2}$

23. $h(x) = \dfrac{x^2}{x^2 - 9}$

24. $g(x) = \dfrac{x}{x^2 - 9}$

25. $g(x) = -\dfrac{1}{(x - 2)^2} + 3$

26. $f(x) = -\dfrac{1}{(x - 2)^2}$

27. $f(x) = \dfrac{3x}{x^2 - x - 2}$

28. $f(x) = \dfrac{2x}{x^2 + x - 2}$

In Exercises 29–36, use a graphing utility to graph the function, and give its domain and range.

29. $f(x) = \dfrac{2 + x}{1 - x}$

30. $f(x) = \dfrac{3 - x}{2 - x}$

31. $f(t) = \dfrac{3t + 1}{t}$

32. $h(x) = \dfrac{1}{x - 3} + 1$

33. $h(t) = \dfrac{4}{t^2 + 1}$

34. $g(x) = -\dfrac{x}{(x - 2)^2}$

35. $f(x) = \dfrac{20x}{x^2 + 1} - \dfrac{1}{x}$

36. $f(x) = 5\left(\dfrac{1}{x - 4} - \dfrac{1}{x + 2}\right)$

In Exercises 37–46, sketch the graph of the rational function. As sketching aids, check for intercepts, symmetry, vertical asymptotes, and slant asymptotes. Use a graphing utility to verify your graph.

37. $f(x) = \dfrac{2x^2 + 1}{x}$

38. $f(x) = \dfrac{1 - x^2}{x}$

39. $g(x) = \dfrac{x^2 + 1}{x}$

40. $h(x) = \dfrac{x^2}{x - 1}$

41. $f(x) = \dfrac{x^3}{x^2 - 1}$

42. $g(x) = \dfrac{x^3}{2x^2 - 8}$

43. $f(x) = \dfrac{x^2 - x + 1}{x - 1}$

44. $f(x) = \dfrac{2x^2 - 5x + 5}{x - 2}$

45. $f(x) = \dfrac{x^2 + 5x + 8}{x + 3}$

46. $f(x) = \dfrac{2x^2 + x}{x + 1}$

In Exercises 47 and 48, use a graphing utility to graph the function and note that a graph may have two horizontal asymptotes.

47. $h(x) = \dfrac{6x}{\sqrt{x^2 + 1}}$

48. $g(x) = \dfrac{4|x - 2|}{x + 1}$

In Exercises 49 and 50, use a graphing utility to graph the function and note that a graph may cross its horizontal asymptote.

49. $f(x) = \dfrac{4(x - 1)^2}{x^2 - 4x + 5}$

50. $g(x) = \dfrac{3x^4 - 5x + 3}{x^4 + 1}$

In Exercises 51 and 52, use a graphing utility to graph the function. Explain why there is no vertical asymptote when a superficial examination of the function may indicate that there should be one.

51. $h(x) = \dfrac{6 - 2x}{3 - x}$

52. $g(x) = \dfrac{x^2 + x - 2}{x - 1}$

In Exercises 53 and 54, use a graphing utility to graph the function and locate any relative maximum or minimum points on the graph.

53. $f(x) = \dfrac{3(x + 1)}{x^2 + x + 1}$

54. $C(x) = x + \dfrac{16}{x}$

55. *Concentration of a Mixture*   A 250-gallon storage tank contains 10 gallons of a 25% brine solution. A person adds x gallons of a 75% brine solution to the tank.
(a) Show that the concentration C of the final mixture is given by
$$C = \frac{3x + 10}{4(x + 10)}.$$
(b) Determine the domain of the function based on the physical constraints of the problem.
(c) Use a graphing utility to graph the function. As the tank is filled, what happens to the rate at which the concentration of brine is increasing? What does the concentration of brine appear to approach?

56. *Dimensions of a Rectangle*   A rectangular region of length x and width y has an area of 500 square meters.
(a) Express the width y as a function of x.
(b) Determine the domain of the function based on the physical constraints of the problem.
(c) Sketch a graph of the function and determine the width of the rectangle if $x = 30$ meters.

57. *Page Design*   A page that is x inches wide and y inches high contains 30 square inches of print. The margins at the top and bottom are 2 inches, and the margins on each side are 1 inch (see figure).
(a) Show that the total area A of the page is given by
$$A = \frac{2x(2x + 11)}{x - 2}.$$
(b) Determine the domain of the function based on the physical constraints of the problem.
(c) Use a graphing utility to graph the area function and approximate the page size so the least amount of paper will be used.

FIGURE FOR 57

58. *Minimum Area*   A right triangle is formed in the first quadrant by the x-axis, the y-axis, and a line segment through the point $(2, 3)$ (see figure).
(a) Show that an equation of the line segment is
$$y = \frac{3(x - a)}{2 - a}, \qquad 0 \le x \le a.$$
(b) Show that the area of the triangle is
$$A = \frac{-3a^2}{2(2 - a)}.$$
(c) Use a graphing utility to graph the area function, and, from the graph, estimate the value of a that yields a minimum area.

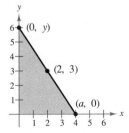

FIGURE FOR 58

59. *Ordering and Transportation Cost*   The ordering and transportation cost C of the components used in manufacturing a certain product is given by

$$C = 100\left(\frac{200}{x^2} + \frac{x}{x + 30}\right), \qquad 1 \le x,$$

where C is measured in thousands of dollars and x is the order size in hundreds. Use a graphing utility to graph the cost function and, from the graph, estimate the order size that minimizes cost.

60. *Average Cost*   The cost of producing x units is $C = 0.2x^2 + 10x + 5$, and therefore the average cost per unit is

$$\overline{C} = \frac{C}{x} = \frac{0.2x^2 + 10x + 5}{x}, \qquad 0 < x.$$

Sketch the graph of the average cost function, and estimate the number of units that should be produced to minimize the average cost per unit.

61. *Medicine*   The concentration of a certain chemical in the bloodstream t hours after injection into muscle tissue is given by

$$C = \frac{3t^2 + t}{t^3 + 50}, \qquad 0 \le t.$$

(a) Determine the horizontal asymptote of the function and interpret its meaning in the context of the problem.

(b) Use a graphing utility to graph the function, and approximate the time when the bloodstream concentration is greatest.

4.3   PARTIAL FRACTIONS

Introduction to Partial Fractions   /   Partial Fraction Decomposition

Introduction to Partial Fractions

In this section, you will study a procedure for writing a rational expression as the sum of two or more simpler rational expressions. (This procedure is useful in calculus.) For example, the rational expression $(x + 7)/(x^2 - x - 6)$ can be written as the sum of two fractions with first-degree denominators.

$$\frac{x + 7}{x^2 - x - 6} = \frac{2}{x - 3} + \frac{-1}{x + 2}$$

Each fraction on the right side of the equation is a **partial fraction,** and together they make up the **partial fraction decomposition** of the left side.

In Chapter 3, you learned that it is theoretically possible to write any polynomial as the product of linear and irreducible quadratic factors. For instance,

$$x^5 + x^4 - x - 1 = (x - 1)(x + 1)^2(x^2 + 1),$$

where $(x - 1)$ is a linear factor, $(x + 1)$ is a repeated linear factor, and $(x^2 + 1)$ is an irreducible quadratic factor.

You can use this factorization to find the partial fraction decomposition of any rational expression having $x^5 + x^4 - x - 1$ as its denominator. Specifically, if $N(x)$ is a polynomial of degree 4 or less, then the partial fraction decomposition of $N(x)/(x^5 + x^4 - x - 1)$ has the form

$$\frac{N(x)}{x^5 + x^4 - x - 1} = \frac{N(x)}{(x - 1)(x + 1)^2(x^2 + 1)}$$

$$= \frac{A}{x - 1} + \frac{B}{x + 1} + \frac{C}{(x + 1)^2} + \frac{Dx + F}{x^2 + 1}.$$

Note that the factor $(x + 1)^2$ results in *two* fractions: one for $(x + 1)$ and one for $(x + 1)^2$. If $(x + 1)^3$ were a factor, then you would use three fractions: one for $(x + 1)$, one for $(x + 1)^2$, and one for $(x + 1)^3$. In general, the number of fractions resulting from a repeated factor is equal to the exponent of the factor.

The following guidelines summarize the steps used to find the partial fraction decomposition of a rational expression.

DECOMPOSITION OF $N(x)/D(x)$ INTO PARTIAL FRACTIONS

1. *Divide if improper:* If $N(x)/D(x)$ is an improper fraction, then divide the denominator into the numerator to obtain

$$\frac{N(x)}{D(x)} = \text{(polynomial)} + \frac{N_1(x)}{D(x)}$$

and apply Steps 2, 3, and 4 to the proper rational expression $N_1(x)/D(x)$.

2. *Factor denominator:* Completely factor the denominator into factors of the form

$$(px + q)^m \quad \text{and} \quad (ax^2 + bx + c)^n,$$

where $(ax^2 + bx + c)$ is irreducible.

3. *Linear factors:* For *each* factor of the form $(px + q)^m$, the partial fraction decomposition must include the following sum of m fractions.

$$\frac{A_1}{(px + q)} + \frac{A_2}{(px + q)^2} + \cdots + \frac{A_m}{(px + q)^m}$$

4. *Quadratic factors:* For *each* factor of the form $(ax^2 + bx + c)^n$, the partial fraction decomposition must include the following sum of n fractions.

$$\frac{B_1x + C_1}{ax^2 + bx + c} + \frac{B_2x + C_2}{(ax^2 + bx + c)^2} + \cdots + \frac{B_nx + C_n}{(ax^2 + bx + c)^n}$$

Partial Fraction Decomposition

Algebraic techniques for determining the constants in the numerators of the partial fractions are demonstrated in the examples that follow. Note that the techniques vary slightly depending on the type of factors of the denominator—linear or quadratic, distinct or repeated.

EXAMPLE 1   **Distinct Linear Factors**

Write the partial fraction decomposition for

$$\frac{x + 7}{x^2 - x - 6}.$$

SOLUTION

Because $x^2 - x - 6 = (x - 3)(x + 2)$, you include one partial fraction with a constant numerator for each linear factor of the denominator and write

$$\frac{x + 7}{x^2 - x - 6} = \frac{A}{x - 3} + \frac{B}{x + 2}.$$

Multiplying both sides of this equation by the least common denominator, $(x - 3)(x + 2)$, leads to the **basic equation**

$$x + 7 = A(x + 2) + B(x - 3). \qquad \textit{Basic equation}$$

Because this equation is true for all x, you can substitute any *convenient* values of x that will help determine the constants A and B. Values of x that are especially convenient are ones that make the factors $(x + 2)$ and $(x - 3)$ equal to zero. For instance, if you let $x = -2$, then

$$
\begin{aligned}
-2 + 7 &= A(0) + B(-5) \qquad \textit{Substitute convenient value of x} \\
5 &= -5B \\
-1 &= B.
\end{aligned}
$$

To solve for A, let $x = 3$ to obtain

$$
\begin{aligned}
3 + 7 &= A(5) + B(0) \qquad \textit{Substitute convenient value of x} \\
10 &= 5A \\
2 &= A.
\end{aligned}
$$

Therefore, the decomposition is

$$\frac{x + 7}{x^2 - x - 6} = \frac{2}{x - 3} - \frac{1}{x + 2},$$

as indicated at the beginning of this section. Check this result by combining the two partial fractions on the right side of the equation. You can check the decomposition graphically by graphing

$$y = \frac{x + 7}{x^2 - x - 6} \quad \text{and} \quad y = \frac{2}{x - 3} - \frac{1}{x + 2}$$

on the same screen. If the decomposition is correct, then the two graphs will be identical, as shown in Figure 4.18.

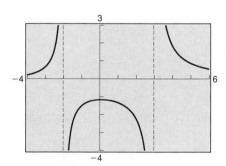

FIGURE 4.18

EXAMPLE 2   Repeated Linear Factors

Write the partial fraction decomposition for

$$\frac{5x^2 + 20x + 6}{x^3 + 2x^2 + x}.$$

SOLUTION

Because the denominator factors as

$$x^3 + 2x^2 + x = x(x^2 + 2x + 1) = x(x + 1)^2,$$

include one fraction with a constant numerator for each power of x and $(x + 1)$, and write

$$\frac{5x^2 + 20x + 6}{x(x + 1)^2} = \frac{A}{x} + \frac{B}{x + 1} + \frac{C}{(x + 1)^2}.$$

Multiplying by the least common denominator, $x(x + 1)^2$, leads to the basic equation

$$5x^2 + 20x + 6 = A(x + 1)^2 + Bx(x + 1) + Cx. \quad \text{\textit{Basic equation}}$$

Letting $x = -1$ eliminates the A and B terms and yields

$$5 - 20 + 6 = 0 + 0 - C \qquad \text{\textit{Substitute convenient value of x}}$$
$$C = 9.$$

Letting $x = 0$ eliminates the B and C terms and yields

$$6 = A(1) + 0 + 0 \qquad \text{\textit{Substitute convenient value of x}}$$
$$6 = A.$$

At this point, the most convenient choices for x have been used. To find the value of B, you can use *any other value* for x along with the known values of A and C. For instance, using $x = 1$, $A = 6$, and $C = 9$ produces

$$5 + 20 + 6 = A(4) + B(2) + C$$
$$31 = 6(4) + 2B + 9$$
$$-2 = 2B$$
$$-1 = B.$$

Therefore, the partial fraction decomposition is

$$\frac{5x^2 + 20x + 6}{x(x + 1)^2} = \frac{6}{x} - \frac{1}{x + 1} + \frac{9}{(x + 1)^2}.$$

Use a graphing utility to confirm this result.

The procedure used to solve for the constants A, B in Example 1 and A, B, C in Example 2 works well when the factors of the denominator are linear.

However, when the denominator contains irreducible quadratic factors, you should use a different procedure, which involves writing the right side of the basic equation in polynomial form and *equating the coefficients* of like terms.

EXAMPLE 3   Distinct Linear and Quadratic Factors

Write the partial fraction decomposition for

$$\frac{3x^2 + 4x + 4}{x^3 + 4x}.$$

SOLUTION

Because the denominator factors as $x^3 + 4x = x(x^2 + 4)$, include one partial fraction with a constant numerator and one partial fraction with a linear numerator and write

$$\frac{3x^2 + 4x + 4}{x^3 + 4x} = \frac{A}{x} + \frac{Bx + C}{x^2 + 4}.$$

Multiplying by the least common denominator, $x(x^2 + 4)$, yields the basic equation

$$3x^2 + 4x + 4 = A(x^2 + 4) + (Bx + C)x. \quad \textit{Basic equation}$$

Expanding this basic equation and collecting like terms produces

$$3x^2 + 4x + 4 = Ax^2 + 4A + Bx^2 + Cx$$
$$= (A + B)x^2 + Cx + 4A. \quad \textit{Polynomial form}$$

Finally, two polynomials are equal if and only if the coefficients of like terms are equal. Therefore, from

$$3x^2 + 4x + 4 = (A + B)x^2 + Cx + 4A, \quad \textit{Equate coefficients of like terms}$$

you can obtain the following equations.

$$3 = A + B, \quad 4 = C, \quad \text{and} \quad 4 = 4A$$

Thus, $A = 1$ and $C = 4$. Substituting $A = 1$ in the equation $3 = A + B$ produces

$$3 = 1 + B$$
$$2 = B.$$

Therefore, the partial fraction decomposition is

$$\frac{3x^2 + 4x + 4}{x^3 + 4x} = \frac{1}{x} + \frac{2x + 4}{x^2 + 4}.$$

Use a graphing utility to confirm this result.

EXAMPLE 4   **Repeated Quadratic Factors**

Write the partial fraction decomposition for

$$\frac{8x^3 + 13x}{(x^2 + 2)^2}.$$

SOLUTION

Include one partial fraction with a linear numerator for each power of $(x^2 + 2)$, and write

$$\frac{8x^3 + 13x}{(x^2 + 2)^2} = \frac{Ax + B}{x^2 + 2} + \frac{Cx + D}{(x^2 + 2)^2}.$$

Multiplying by the least common denominator, $(x^2 + 2)^2$, yields the basic equation

$$
\begin{aligned}
8x^3 + 13x &= (Ax + B)(x^2 + 2) + Cx + D && \textit{Basic equation} \\
&= Ax^3 + 2Ax + Bx^2 + 2B + Cx + D \\
&= Ax^3 + Bx^2 + (2A + C)x + (2B + D). && \textit{Polynomial form}
\end{aligned}
$$

Equating coefficients of like terms,

REMARK   By equating coefficients of like terms in Examples 3 and 4, you obtained several equations involving A, B, C, and D, which were solved by *substitution*. You will study a more general method for solving systems of equations later in this text.

$$8x^3 + 0x^2 + 13x + 0 = Ax^3 + Bx^2 + (2A + C)x + (2B + D),$$

produces

$$8 = A, \quad 0 = B, \quad 13 = 2A + C, \quad \text{and} \quad 0 = 2B + D. \quad \textit{Equate coefficients}$$

Finally, use the values $A = 8$ and $B = 0$ to obtain the following.

$$
\begin{aligned}
13 = 2A + C &= 2(8) + C && 0 = 2B + D = 2(0) + D \\
-3 &= C && 0 = D
\end{aligned}
$$

Therefore, the partial fraction decomposition is

$$\frac{8x^3 + 13x}{(x^2 + 2)^2} = \frac{8x}{x^2 + 2} + \frac{-3x}{(x^2 + 2)^2}.$$

Use a graphing utility to confirm this result.

GUIDELINES FOR SOLVING THE BASIC EQUATION

Linear Factors
1. Substitute the *zeros* of the distinct linear factors into the basic equation.
2. For repeated linear factors, use the coefficients determined in Step 1 to rewrite the basic equation. Then substitute *other* convenient values for x and solve for the remaining coefficients.

Quadratic Factors
1. Expand the basic equation.
2. Collect terms according to powers of x.
3. Equate the coefficients of like terms to obtain equations involving A, B, C, and so on.
4. Use substitution to solve for A, B, C, etc.

Keep in mind that for *improper* rational expressions such as

$$\frac{N(x)}{D(x)} = \frac{2x^3 + x^2 - 7x + 7}{x^2 + x - 2},$$

you must first divide to obtain the form

$$\frac{N(x)}{D(x)} = (\text{polynomial}) + \frac{N_1(x)}{D(x)}.$$

The proper rational expression $N_1(x)/D(x)$ is then decomposed into its partial fractions by the usual methods.

DISCUSSION PROBLEM

YOU BE THE INSTRUCTOR

Suppose you are tutoring a student in algebra. In trying to find a partial fraction decomposition, your student writes the following.

$$\frac{x^2 + 1}{x(x - 1)} = \frac{A}{x} + \frac{B}{x - 1}$$

$$\frac{x^2 + 1}{x(x - 1)} = \frac{A(x - 1)}{x(x - 1)} + \frac{Bx}{x(x - 1)}$$

$$x^2 + 1 = A(x - 1) + Bx \qquad \textit{Basic equation}$$

By substituting $x = 0$ and $x = 1$ into the basic equation, your student concludes that $A = -1$ and $B = 2$. However, in checking this solution your student obtains

$$\frac{-1}{x} + \frac{2}{x - 1} = \frac{(-1)(x - 1) + 2(x)}{x(x - 1)} = \frac{x + 1}{x(x - 1)} \neq \frac{x^2 + 1}{x(x - 1)}.$$

What has gone wrong?

WARM-UP
....

The following warm-up exercises involve skills that were covered in earlier sections. You will use these skills in the exercise set for this section.

In Exercises 1–10, find the sum and simplify.

1. $\dfrac{2}{x} + \dfrac{3}{x+1}$

2. $\dfrac{5}{x+2} + \dfrac{3}{x}$

3. $\dfrac{7}{x-2} - \dfrac{3}{2x-1}$

4. $\dfrac{2}{x+5} - \dfrac{5}{x+12}$

5. $\dfrac{1}{x-3} + \dfrac{3}{(x-3)^2} - \dfrac{5}{(x-3)^3}$

6. $\dfrac{-5}{x+2} + \dfrac{4}{(x+2)^2}$

7. $\dfrac{-3}{x} + \dfrac{3x-1}{x^2+3}$

8. $\dfrac{5}{x+1} - \dfrac{x-6}{x^2+5}$

9. $\dfrac{3}{x^2+1} + \dfrac{x-3}{(x^2+1)^2}$

10. $\dfrac{x}{x^2+x+1} - \dfrac{x-1}{(x^2+x+1)^2}$

SECTION 4.3 · EXERCISES
....

In Exercises 1–32, write the partial fraction decomposition for the rational expression. Check your result algebraically *and* graphically.

1. $\dfrac{1}{x^2-1}$

2. $\dfrac{1}{4x^2-9}$

3. $\dfrac{1}{x^2+x}$

4. $\dfrac{3}{x^2-3x}$

5. $\dfrac{1}{2x^2+x}$

6. $\dfrac{5}{x^2+x-6}$

7. $\dfrac{3}{x^2+x-2}$

8. $\dfrac{x+1}{x^2+4x+3}$

9. $\dfrac{5-x}{2x^2+x-1}$

10. $\dfrac{3x^2-7x-2}{x^3-x}$

11. $\dfrac{x^2+12x+12}{x^3-4x}$

12. $\dfrac{x+2}{x(x-4)}$

13. $\dfrac{4x^2+2x-1}{x^2(x+1)}$

14. $\dfrac{2x-3}{(x-1)^2}$

15. $\dfrac{x-1}{x^3+x^2}$

16. $\dfrac{4x^2-1}{2x(x+1)^2}$

17. $\dfrac{3x}{(x-3)^2}$

18. $\dfrac{6x^2+1}{x^2(x-1)^3}$

19. $\dfrac{x^2-1}{x(x^2+1)}$

20. $\dfrac{x}{(x-1)(x^2+x+1)}$

21. $\dfrac{x^2}{x^4-2x^2-8}$

22. $\dfrac{2x^2+x+8}{(x^2+4)^2}$

23. $\dfrac{x}{16x^4-1}$

24. $\dfrac{x^2-4x+7}{(x+1)(x^2-2x+3)}$

25. $\dfrac{x^2+x+2}{(x^2+2)^2}$

26. $\dfrac{x^3}{(x+2)^2(x-2)^2}$

27. $\dfrac{x^2+5}{(x+1)(x^2-2x+3)}$

28. $\dfrac{x+1}{x^3+x}$

29. $\dfrac{2x^3-4x^2-15x+5}{x^2-2x-8}$

30. $\dfrac{x^3-x+3}{x^2+x-2}$

31. $\dfrac{x^4}{(x-1)^3}$

32. $\dfrac{x^2-x}{x^2+x+1}$

In Exercises 33–36, write the partial fraction decomposition for the rational expression. Check your result algebraically. Then assign a value to the constant a to check the result graphically.

33. $\dfrac{1}{a^2-x^2}$

34. $\dfrac{1}{x(x+a)}$

35. $\dfrac{1}{x(a-x)}$

36. $\dfrac{1}{(x+1)(a-x)}$

4.4   CONIC SECTIONS AND GRAPHS

Introduction to Conic Sections / Parabolas / Ellipses / Hyperbolas

Introduction to Conic Sections

Conic sections were discovered during the classical Greek period, 600 to 300 B.C. This early Greek study was largely concerned with the geometric properties of conics. It was not until the early 17th century that the broad applicability of conics became apparent and played a prominent role in the early development of calculus.

A **conic section** (or simply **conic**) is the intersection of a plane and a double-napped cone. Notice in Figure 4.19 that in the formation of the four basic conics, the intersecting plane does not pass through the vertex of the cone. When the plane does pass through the vertex, the resulting figure is a **degenerate conic,** as shown in Figure 4.20.

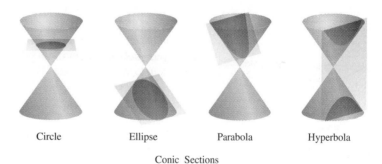

| Circle | Ellipse | Parabola | Hyperbola |

Conic Sections

FIGURE 4.19

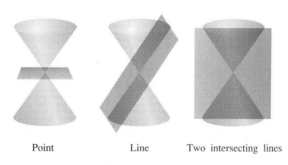

| Point | Line | Two intersecting lines |

Degenerate Conics

FIGURE 4.20

There are several ways to begin a study of conics. You could define conics as the intersections of planes and cones, as the Greeks did, or you could define them algebraically, in terms of the general second-degree equation $Ax^2 + Bxy + Cy^2 + Dx + Ey + F = 0$. However, we will use a third approach, in which each of the conics is defined as a collection of points satisfying a certain geometric property. For example, in Section 7 of the prerequisite chapter, you saw how the definition of a circle as *the collection of all points (x, y) that are equidistant from a fixed point (h, k)* led easily to the standard equation of a circle, $(x - h)^2 + (y - k)^2 = r^2$.

In this section you will study parabolas with vertices at the origin and ellipses and hyperbolas with centers at the origin. In the following section, you will study the more general cases.

Parabolas

FIGURE 4.21

In Section 3.1, you learned that the graph of the quadratic function $f(x) = ax^2 + bx + c$ is a parabola that opens upward or downward. The following definition of a parabola is more general in the sense that it is independent of the orientation of the parabola.

A **parabola** is the set of all points (x, y) that are equidistant from a fixed line called the **directrix** and a fixed point called the **focus** (not on the line). See Figure 4.21. The midpoint between the focus and the directrix is called the **vertex,** and the line passing through the focus and the vertex is called the **axis** of the parabola.

Using this definition, you can derive the following standard form of the equation of a parabola.

REMARK Be sure you understand that the term *parabola* is a technical term used in mathematics and does not simply refer to *any* U-shaped curve.

STANDARD EQUATION OF A PARABOLA (VERTEX AT ORIGIN)

The **standard form of the equation of a parabola** with vertex at $(0, 0)$ and directrix $y = -p$ is

$$x^2 = 4py, \qquad p \neq 0. \qquad\qquad \textit{Vertical axis}$$

For directrix $x = -p$, the equation is

$$y^2 = 4px, \qquad p \neq 0. \qquad\qquad \textit{Horizontal axis}$$

The focus is on the axis p units from the vertex.

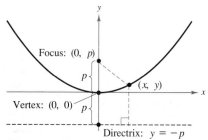

FIGURE 4.22

PROOF

Because the two cases are similar, we give a proof for the first case only. Suppose the directrix ($y = -p$) is parallel to the x-axis. In Figure 4.22 we assume $p > 0$, and because p is the distance from the vertex to the focus, the focus must lie above the vertex. Because the point (x, y) is equidistant from $(0, p)$ and $y = -p$, you can apply the distance formula to obtain

$$\sqrt{(x - 0)^2 + (y - p)^2} = y + p$$
$$x^2 + (y - p)^2 = (y + p)^2$$
$$x^2 + y^2 - 2py + p^2 = y^2 + 2py + p^2$$
$$x^2 = 4py.$$

EXAMPLE 1 Finding the Focus of a Parabola

Find the focus of the parabola whose equation is $y = -2x^2$.

SOLUTION

Because the squared term in the equation involves x, the axis is vertical, which implies the standard form

$$x^2 = 4py.$$

Writing the given equation in this form produces

$$x^2 = -\frac{1}{2}y$$

$$x^2 = 4\left(-\frac{1}{8}\right)y. \qquad \textit{Standard form}$$

Thus, $p = -\frac{1}{8}$. Because p is negative, the parabola opens downward (see Figure 4.23), and the focus of the parabola is $(0, p) = (0, -\frac{1}{8})$.

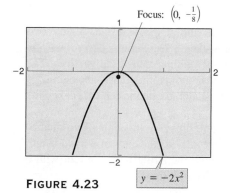

FIGURE 4.23

EXAMPLE 2 A Parabola with a Horizontal Axis

Write the standard form of the equation of the parabola with vertex at the origin and focus at (2, 0).

SOLUTION

The axis of the parabola is horizontal, passing through (0, 0) and (2, 0), as shown in Figure 4.24. Thus, you should consider the standard form

$$y^2 = 4px.$$

FIGURE 4.24

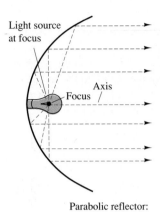

Light source
at focus

Axis

Focus

Parabolic reflector:
Light is reflected
in parallel rays.

FIGURE 4.25

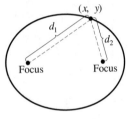

(x, y)

d_1

d_2

Focus

Focus

$d_1 + d_2$ is constant.

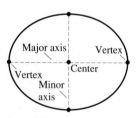

Major axis

Vertex

Center

Vertex

Minor
axis

FIGURE 4.26

Because the focus is $p = 2$ units from the vertex, the equation is

$$y^2 = 4(2)x$$
$$y^2 = 8x.$$

The equation $y^2 = 8x$ does not define y as a function of x. Thus, to use a graphing utility to graph $y^2 = 8x$, you need to break the graph into two equations, $y = 2\sqrt{2x}$ and $y = -2\sqrt{2x}$, each of which is a function of x.

Parabolas occur in a wide variety of applications. For instance, a parabolic reflector can be formed by revolving a parabola about its axis. The resulting surface has the property that all incoming rays parallel to the axis are reflected through the focus of the parabola—this is the principle behind the construction of the parabolic mirrors used in reflecting telescopes and satellite dishes. Conversely, the light rays emanating from the focus of a parabolic reflector used in a flashlight are all parallel to one another, as shown in Figure 4.25.

Ellipses

An **ellipse** is the set of all points (x, y) the sum of whose distances from two distinct fixed points, called **foci,** is constant. (See Figure 4.26.) The line through the foci intersects the ellipse at two points, called the **vertices.** The chord joining the vertices is the **major axis,** and its midpoint is the **center** of the ellipse. The chord perpendicular to the major axis at the center is called the **minor axis** of the ellipse.

You can visualize the definition of an ellipse by imagining two thumbtacks placed at the foci, as shown in Figure 4.27. If the ends of a fixed length of string are fastened to the thumbtacks and the string is drawn taut with a pencil, the path traced by the pencil will be an ellipse.

The standard form of the equation of an ellipse takes one of two forms, depending upon whether the major axis is horizontal or vertical.

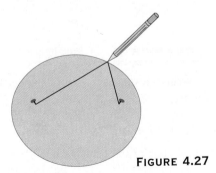

FIGURE 4.27

STANDARD EQUATION OF AN ELLIPSE (CENTER AT ORIGIN)

The **standard form of the equation of an ellipse** with center at the origin and major and minor axes of lengths $2a$ and $2b$ (where $0 < b < a$), is

$$\frac{x^2}{a^2} + \frac{y^2}{b^2} = 1 \quad \text{or} \quad \frac{x^2}{b^2} + \frac{y^2}{a^2} = 1, \qquad 0 < b < a.$$

The vertices and foci lie on the major axis, a and c units, respectively, from the center. Moreover, a, b, and c are related by the equation $c^2 = a^2 - b^2$. (See figure.)

Major axis is horizontal.
Minor axis is vertical.

Major axis is vertical.
Minor axis is horizontal.

EXAMPLE 3 Finding the Standard Equation of an Ellipse

Find the standard form of the equation of the ellipse that has a major axis of length 6 and foci at $(-2, 0)$ and $(2, 0)$, as shown in Figure 4.28.

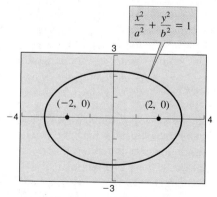

FIGURE 4.28

SOLUTION

Because the foci occur at $(-2, 0)$ and $(2, 0)$, the center of the ellipse is $(0, 0)$, and the major axis is horizontal. Thus, the ellipse has an equation of the form

$$\frac{x^2}{a^2} + \frac{y^2}{b^2} = 1. \qquad\qquad \textit{Standard form}$$

Because the length of the major axis is 6, you have

$$2a = 6, \qquad\qquad \textit{Length of major axis}$$

which implies that $a = 3$. Moreover, the distance from the center to either focus is $c = 2$. Finally,

$$b^2 = a^2 - c^2 = 3^2 - 2^2 = 9 - 4 = 5,$$

which yields the equation

$$\frac{x^2}{9} + \frac{y^2}{5} = 1.$$

EXAMPLE 4   **Graphing an Ellipse**

Graph the ellipse given by $4x^2 + y^2 = 36$, and identify the vertices.

SOLUTION

$$4x^2 + y^2 = 36 \qquad\qquad \textit{Original equation}$$

$$\frac{4x^2}{36} + \frac{y^2}{36} = \frac{36}{36}$$

$$\frac{x^2}{3^2} + \frac{y^2}{6^2} = 1 \qquad\qquad \textit{Standard form}$$

Because the denominator of the y^2 term is larger than the denominator of the x^2 term, you can conclude that the major axis is vertical. Moreover, because $a = 6$, the vertices are $(0, -6)$ and $(0, 6)$. Finally, because $b = 3$, the endpoints of the minor axis are $(-3, 0)$ and $(3, 0)$, as shown in Figure 4.29. Verify the graph using a graphing utility with $y = \sqrt{36 - 4x^2}$ and $y = -\sqrt{36 - 4x^2}$ and a "square" viewing rectangle.

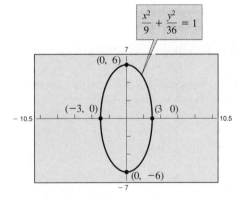

FIGURE 4.29

In Example 4, note that from the standard form of the equation you can graph the ellipse by locating the endpoints of the two axes. Because 3^2 is the denominator of the x^2 term, move three units to the *right and left* of the center to locate the endpoints of the horizontal axis. Similarly, because 6^2 is the denominator of the y^2 term, move six units *up and down* from the center to locate the endpoints of the vertical axis.

Technology Note

Most graphing utilities have a "parametric mode." To use this mode to sketch the graph of the ellipse in Example 4, however, you need to use two trigonometric function keys labeled "sin" and "cos" (for sine and cosine). Try using the parametric mode to graph the ellipse given by $x = 3 \cos t$ and $y = 6 \sin t$. How does the result compare to the graph given in Figure 4.29? (*Hint:* Set your graphing utility to radian mode before graphing the ellipse.)

Hyperbolas

The definition of a **hyperbola** is similar to that of an ellipse. The distinction is that, for an ellipse, the *sum* of the distances between the foci and a point on the ellipse is constant, whereas for a hyperbola the *difference* of these distances is constant.

A **hyperbola** is the set of all points (x, y) the difference of whose distances from two distinct fixed points, called **foci,** is constant. (See Figure 4.30.) The graph of a hyperbola has two disconnected parts, called **branches.** The line through the two foci intersects the hyperbola at two points, called **vertices.** The line segment connecting the vertices is the **transverse axis,** and the midpoint of the transverse axis is the **center** of the hyperbola.

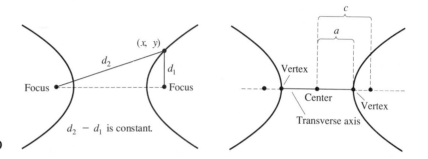

FIGURE 4.30

STANDARD EQUATION OF A HYPERBOLA (CENTER AT ORIGIN)

The **standard form of the equation of a hyperbola** with center at $(0, 0)$ is

$$\frac{x^2}{a^2} - \frac{y^2}{b^2} = 1 \quad \text{or} \quad \frac{y^2}{a^2} - \frac{x^2}{b^2} = 1.$$

The vertices and foci are, respectively, a and c units from the center, and $b^2 = c^2 - a^2$. (See figure.)

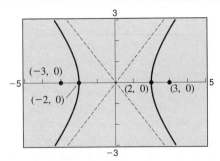

FIGURE 4.31

EXAMPLE 5   **Finding the Standard Equation of a Hyperbola**
....

Find the standard form of the equation of the hyperbola with foci at $(-3, 0)$ and $(3, 0)$ and vertices at $(-2, 0)$ and $(2, 0)$, as shown in Figure 4.31.

SOLUTION

It can be seen that $c = 3$, because the foci are three units from the center. Moreover, $a = 2$, because the vertices are two units from the center. Thus, it follows that

$$b^2 = c^2 - a^2 = 3^2 - 2^2 = 9 - 4 = 5.$$

Because the transverse axis is horizontal, the standard form of the equation is

$$\frac{x^2}{a^2} - \frac{y^2}{b^2} = 1.$$

Finally, substitute $a^2 = 4$ and $b^2 = 5$ to obtain

$$\frac{x^2}{4} - \frac{y^2}{5} = 1. \qquad \textit{Standard form}$$

....

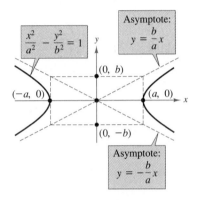

Transverse axis is horizontal.

An important aid in graphing a hyperbola is the determination of its **asymptotes,** as shown in Figure 4.32. Each hyperbola has two asymptotes that intersect at the center of the hyperbola. Furthermore, the asymptotes pass through the corners of a rectangle of dimensions $2a$ by $2b$. The line segment of length $2b$, joining $(0, b)$ and $(0, -b)$ [or $(-b, 0)$ and $(b, 0)$], is referred to as the **conjugate axis** of the hyperbola.

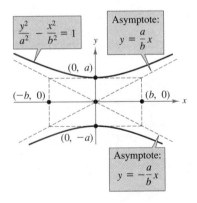

Transverse axis is vertical.

FIGURE 4.32

ASYMPTOTES OF A HYPERBOLA (CENTER AT ORIGIN)

The asymptotes of a hyperbola with center at $(0, 0)$ are

$$y = \frac{b}{a}x \quad \text{and} \quad y = -\frac{b}{a}x \qquad \textit{Transverse axis is horizontal}$$

or

$$y = \frac{a}{b}x \quad \text{and} \quad y = -\frac{a}{b}x. \qquad \textit{Transverse axis is vertical}$$

FIGURE 4.33

FIGURE 4.34

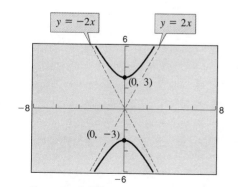

FIGURE 4.35

EXAMPLE 6 Graphing a Hyperbola

Graph the hyperbola whose equation is $4x^2 - y^2 = 16$.

SOLUTION

$$4x^2 - y^2 = 16 \qquad \textit{Original equation}$$

$$\frac{4x^2}{16} - \frac{y^2}{16} = \frac{16}{16}$$

$$\frac{x^2}{2^2} - \frac{y^2}{4^2} = 1 \qquad \textit{Standard form}$$

Because the x^2 term is positive, you can conclude that the transverse axis is horizontal and the vertices occur at $(-2, 0)$ and $(2, 0)$. Moreover, the endpoints of the conjugate axis occur at $(0, -4)$ and $(0, 4)$, and you are able to sketch the rectangle shown in Figure 4.33. Finally, by drawing the asymptotes through the corners of this rectangle, you can complete the sketch shown in Figure 4.34. Check this result with a graphing utility by displaying the hyperbola and both asymptotes on the same screen.

EXAMPLE 7 Finding the Standard Equation of a Hyperbola

Find the standard form of the equation of the hyperbola having vertices at $(0, -3)$ and $(0, 3)$ and asymptotes $y = -2x$ and $y = 2x$, as shown in Figure 4.35.

SOLUTION

Because the transverse axis is vertical, the asymptotes are of the form

$$y = \frac{a}{b}x \quad \text{and} \quad y = -\frac{a}{b}x.$$

Thus, $a/b = 2$, and because $a = 3$, it follows that $b = \frac{3}{2}$. Finally, you can see that the hyperbola has the equation

$$\frac{y^2}{3^2} - \frac{x^2}{(3/2)^2} = 1. \qquad \textit{Standard form}$$

DISCUSSION PROBLEM

······················

CONICS AND GRAPHING UTILITIES

To graph an equation on most graphing utilities, you must first write the equation as one or more functions. For instance, to graph the circle given by $x^2 + y^2 = 9$, you can write the upper part of the circle as

$$y = \sqrt{9 - x^2}$$ *Upper semicircle*

and the lower part of the circle as

$$y = -\sqrt{9 - x^2}.$$ *Lower semicircle*

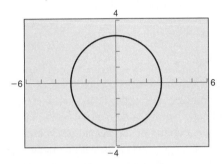

When using a graphing utility to graph conics (especially circles), you should use a "square setting" that has the same space between the tic marks on the x-axis and y-axis, as shown in the figure. Use a graphing utility to graph the following conics.

(a) $y^2 = x$ (b) $\dfrac{x^2}{4} + \dfrac{y^2}{9} = 1$ (c) $\dfrac{x^2}{4} - \dfrac{y^2}{9} = 1$

WARM-UP

··················

The following warm-up exercises involve skills that were covered in earlier sections. You will use these skills in the exercise set for this section.

In Exercises 1–4, rewrite the equation so that it has no fractions.

1. $\dfrac{x^2}{16} + \dfrac{y^2}{9} = 1$ **2.** $\dfrac{x^2}{32} + \dfrac{4y^2}{32} = \dfrac{32}{32}$

3. $\dfrac{x^2}{1/4} - \dfrac{y^2}{4} = 1$ **4.** $\dfrac{3x^2}{1/9} + \dfrac{4y^2}{9} = 1$

In Exercises 5–8, solve for c. (Assume $c > 0$.)

5. $c^2 = 3^2 - 1^2$ **6.** $c^2 = 2^2 + 3^2$
7. $c^2 + 2^2 = 4^2$ **8.** $c^2 - 1^2 = 2^2$

In Exercises 9 and 10, find the distance between the point and the origin.

9. $(0, -4)$ **10.** $(-2, 0)$

SECTION 4.4 · EXERCISES

In Exercises 1–8, match the equation with its graph, and describe the given viewing rectangle. [The graphs are labeled (a), (b), (c), (d), (e), (f), (g), and (h).]

1. $x^2 = 4y$

2. $x^2 = -4y$

3. $y^2 = 4x$

4. $y^2 = -4x$

5. $\dfrac{x^2}{1} + \dfrac{y^2}{4} = 1$

6. $\dfrac{x^2}{4} + \dfrac{y^2}{1} = 1$

7. $\dfrac{x^2}{1} - \dfrac{y^2}{4} = 1$

8. $\dfrac{y^2}{4} - \dfrac{x^2}{1} = 1$

(a)

(b)

(c)

(d)

(e)

(f)

(g)

(h)

In Exercises 9–14, find the vertex and focus of the parabola and graph the parabola.

9. $y = 4x^2$

10. $y = 2x^2$

11. $y^2 = -6x$

12. $y^2 = 3x$

13. $x^2 + 8y = 0$

14. $x + y^2 = 0$

In Exercises 15 and 16, the equations of a parabola and a tangent line to the parabola are given. Use a graphing utility to graph the parabola and the tangent line in the same viewing rectangle.

Parabola	*Tangent Line*
15. $y^2 - 8x = 0$	$x - y + 2 = 0$
16. $x^2 + 12y = 0$	$x + y - 3 = 0$

In Exercises 17–26, find an equation of the specified parabola with vertex at the origin.

17. Focus: $(0, -\frac{3}{2})$

18. Focus: $(2, 0)$

19. Focus: $(-2, 0)$

20. Focus: $(0, -2)$

21. Directrix: $y = -1$

22. Directrix: $x = 3$

23. Directrix: $y = 2$

24. Directrix: $x = -2$

25. Horizontal axis; passes through the point $(4, 6)$

26. Vertical axis; passes through the point $(-2, -2)$

27. *Satellite Antenna*   The receiver in a parabolic television dish antenna is 3 feet from the vertex and is located at the focus (see figure). Find an equation of a cross section of the reflector. (Assume that the dish is directed upward and the vertex is at the origin.)

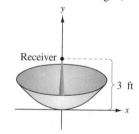

FIGURE FOR 27

28. *Suspension Bridge*   Each cable of a suspension bridge is suspended (in the shape of a parabola) between two towers that are 400 feet apart and 50 feet above the roadway (see figure). The cables touch the roadway midway between the towers. Find an equation for the parabolic shape of each cable.

FIGURE FOR 28

In Exercises 29–34, find the center and vertices of the ellipse and graph the ellipse.

29. $\dfrac{x^2}{25} + \dfrac{y^2}{16} = 1$ **30.** $\dfrac{x^2}{144} + \dfrac{y^2}{169} = 1$

31. $\dfrac{x^2}{16} + \dfrac{y^2}{25} = 1$ **32.** $\dfrac{x^2}{169} + \dfrac{y^2}{144} = 1$

33. $\dfrac{x^2}{9} + \dfrac{y^2}{5} = 1$ **34.** $\dfrac{x^2}{28} + \dfrac{y^2}{64} = 1$

In Exercises 35 and 36, use a graphing utility to graph the ellipse. (Recall that it is first necessary to solve the equation for y and obtain two functions.)

35. $5x^2 + 3y^2 = 15$ **36.** $x^2 + 4y^2 = 4$

In Exercises 37–44, find an equation of the specified ellipse with center at the origin.

37. Vertices: $(0, \pm 2)$
    Minor axis of length 2

38. Vertices: $(\pm 2, 0)$
    Minor axis of length 3

39. Vertices: $(\pm 5, 0)$
    Foci: $(\pm 2, 0)$

40. Vertices: $(0, \pm 8)$
    Foci: $(0, \pm 4)$

41. Foci: $(\pm 5, 0)$
    Major axis of length 12

42. Foci: $(\pm 2, 0)$
    Major axis of length 8

43. Vertices: $(0, \pm 5)$
    Passes through $(4, 2)$

44. Major axis vertical
    Passes through $(0, 4)$
    and $(2, 0)$

45. *Fireplace Arch*   A fireplace arch is to be constructed in the shape of a semi-ellipse. The opening is to have a height of 2 feet at the center and a width of 5 feet along the base (see figure). The contractor draws the outline of the ellipse by the method shown in Figure 4.27. Where should the tacks be placed and what should be the length of the piece of string?

FIGURE FOR 45

46. *Mountain Tunnel*   A semi-elliptical arch over a tunnel for a road through a mountain has a major axis of 100 feet, and its height at the center is 30 feet (see figure). Determine the height of the arch 5 feet from the edge of the tunnel.

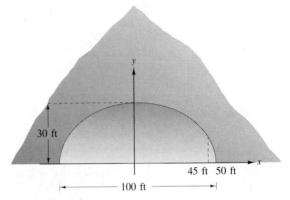

FIGURE FOR 46

47. Graph the ellipse that consists of all points (x, y) such that the sum of the distances between (x, y) and two fixed points is 16 units and the foci are located at the centers of the two sets of concentric circles in the figure.

48. A line segment through a focus with endpoints on the ellipse and perpendicular to the major axis is a **latus rectum** of the ellipse. Therefore, an ellipse has two latus recta. Knowing the length of the latus recta is helpful in graphing an ellipse because it yields other points on the curve (see figure). Show that the length of each latus rectum is $2b^2/a$.

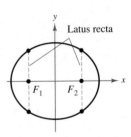

FIGURE FOR 47   **FIGURE FOR 48**

In Exercises 49–52, graph the ellipse, making use of the latus recta (see Exercise 48).

49. $\dfrac{x^2}{4} + \dfrac{y^2}{1} = 1$ **50.** $\dfrac{x^2}{9} + \dfrac{y^2}{16} = 1$

51. $9x^2 + 4y^2 = 36$ **52.** $5x^2 + 3y^2 = 15$

In Exercises 53–58, find the center and vertices of the hyperbola and graph the hyperbola, using asymptotes as an aid.

53. $x^2 - y^2 = 1$

54. $\dfrac{x^2}{9} - \dfrac{y^2}{16} = 1$

55. $\dfrac{y^2}{1} - \dfrac{x^2}{4} = 1$

56. $\dfrac{y^2}{9} - \dfrac{x^2}{1} = 1$

57. $\dfrac{y^2}{25} - \dfrac{x^2}{144} = 1$

58. $\dfrac{x^2}{36} - \dfrac{y^2}{4} = 1$

In Exercises 59 and 60, use a graphing utility to graph the hyperbola and its asymptotes.

59. $2x^2 - 3y^2 = 6$

60. $3y^2 - 5x^2 = 15$

In Exercises 61–68, find an equation of the specified hyperbola with center at the origin.

61. Vertices: $(0, \pm 2)$
Foci: $(0, \pm 4)$

62. Vertices: $(\pm 3, 0)$
Foci: $(\pm 5, 0)$

63. Vertices: $(\pm 1, 0)$
Asymptotes: $y = \pm 3x$

64. Vertices: $(0, \pm 3)$
Asymptotes: $y = \pm 3x$

65. Foci: $(0, \pm 8)$
Asymptotes: $y = \pm 4x$

66. Foci: $(\pm 10, 0)$
Asymptotes: $y = \pm \frac{3}{4}x$

67. Vertices: $(0, \pm 3)$
Passes through $(-2, 5)$

68. Vertices: $(\pm 2, 0)$
Passes through $(3, \sqrt{3})$

69. *LORAN* Long-distance radio navigation for aircraft and ships uses synchronized pulses transmitted by widely separated transmitting stations. These pulses travel at the speed of light (186,000 miles per second). The difference in the times of arrival of these pulses at an aircraft or ship is constant on a hyperbola having the transmitting stations as foci. Assume that two stations, 300 miles apart, are positioned on the rectangular coordinate system at points with coordinates $(-150, 0)$ and $(150, 0)$ and that a ship is traveling on a path with coordinates $(x, 75)$ (see figure). Find the x-coordinate of the position of the ship if the time difference between the pulses from the transmitting stations is 1000 microseconds (0.001 second).

FIGURE FOR 69

70. *Hyperbolic Mirror* A hyperbolic mirror (used in some telescopes) has the property that a light ray directed at the first focus will be reflected to the second focus (see figure). The first focus of a hyperbolic mirror has coordinates $(12, 0)$. Find the vertex of the mirror if its mount has coordinates $(12, 12)$.

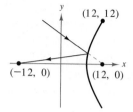

FIGURE FOR 70

71. Use the definition of an ellipse to derive the standard form of the equation of an ellipse.

72. Use the definition of a hyperbola to derive the standard form of the equation of a hyperbola.

73. Discuss the change in shape and orientation of the graph of the ellipse

$$\frac{x^2}{a^2} + \frac{y^2}{16} = 1$$

as a increases continuously from 1 to 8.

4.5   CONIC SECTIONS AND TRANSLATIONS

Vertical and Horizontal Shifts of Conics   /   Writing Equations of Conics in Standard Form   /   Applications

Vertical and Horizontal Shifts of Conics

In Section 4.4, you studied conic sections whose graphs were in *standard position*. In this section, you will study the equations of conic sections that have been shifted vertically or horizontally in the plane.

STANDARD FORMS OF EQUATIONS OF CONICS

Circle (r = radius)

$$(x - h)^2 + (y - k)^2 = r^2$$

Ellipse ($2a$ = major axis length, $2b$ = minor axis length)
Center: (h, k)

$$\frac{(x - h)^2}{a^2} + \frac{(y - k)^2}{b^2} = 1$$

$$\frac{(x - h)^2}{b^2} + \frac{(y - k)^2}{a^2} = 1$$

Hyperbola ($2a$ = transverse axis length, $2b$ = conjugate axis length)
Center: (h, k)

$$\frac{(x - h)^2}{a^2} - \frac{(y - k)^2}{b^2} = 1$$

$$\frac{(y - k)^2}{a^2} - \frac{(x - h)^2}{b^2} = 1$$

Parabola (p = directed distance from vertex to focus)
Vertex: (h, k)

$$(x - h)^2 = 4p(y - k)$$

Focus: $(h, k + p)$
Vertex: (h, k)

$$(y - k)^2 = 4p(x - h)$$

$p > 0$
Vertex: (h, k) Focus: $(h + p, k)$

(a)

(b)

(c)

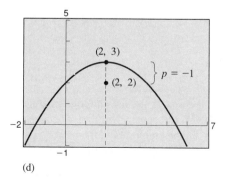

(d)

FIGURE 4.36

EXAMPLE 1   Equations of Conic Sections

A. The graph of

$$(x - 1)^2 + (y + 2)^2 = 3^2$$

is a circle whose center is the point $(1, -2)$ and whose radius is 3, as shown in Figure 4.36(a).

B. The graph of

$$\frac{(x - 2)^2}{3^2} + \frac{(y - 1)^2}{2^2} = 1$$

is an ellipse whose center is the point $(2, 1)$. The major axis of the ellipse is horizontal and of length $2(3) = 6$, and the minor axis of the ellipse is vertical and of length $2(2) = 4$, as shown in Figure 4.36(b).

C. The graph of

$$\frac{(x - 3)^2}{1^2} - \frac{(y - 2)^2}{3^2} = 1$$

is a hyperbola whose center is the point $(3, 2)$. The transverse axis is horizontal and of length $2(1) = 2$, and the conjugate axis is vertical and of length $2(3) = 6$, as shown in Figure 4.36(c).

D. The graph of

$$(x - 2)^2 = 4(-1)(y - 3)$$

is a parabola whose vertex is the point $(2, 3)$. The axis of the parabola is vertical. The focus of the parabola is one unit above or below the vertex. Moreover, because $p = -1$, it follows that the focus lies *below* the vertex, as shown in Figure 4.36(d).

Writing Equations of Conics in Standard Form

To write the equation of a conic in standard form, complete the square as demonstrated in Examples 2, 3, and 4.

EXAMPLE 2   Finding the Standard Form of a Parabola

Find the vertex and focus of the parabola given by $x^2 - 2x + 4y - 3 = 0$.

SOLUTION

$$x^2 - 2x + 4y - 3 = 0 \qquad \text{\textit{Original equation}}$$
$$x^2 - 2x = -4y + 3 \qquad \text{\textit{Group terms}}$$
$$x^2 - 2x + 1 = -4y + 3 + 1 \qquad \text{\textit{Add 1 to both sides}}$$
$$(x - 1)^2 = -4y + 4 \qquad \text{\textit{Completed square form}}$$
$$(x - 1)^2 = 4(-1)(y - 1) \qquad \text{\textit{Standard form}}$$
$$(x - h)^2 = 4p(y - k)$$

From this standard form, you can see that $h = 1$, $k = 1$, and $p = -1$. Because the axis is vertical and p is negative, the parabola opens downward. The vertex and focus are

$$\text{\textit{Vertex:}} \quad (h, k) = (1, 1)$$
$$\text{\textit{Focus:}} \quad (h, k + p) = (1, 0).$$

The graph of this parabola is shown in Figure 4.37. Check this with a graphing utility by sketching the graph of $y = \frac{1}{4}(-x^2 + 2x + 3)$. ••••••••

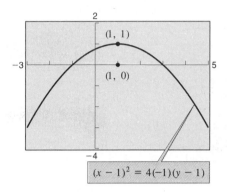

$$(x - 1)^2 = 4(-1)(y - 1)$$

FIGURE 4.37

REMARK Note in Example 2 that p is the directed distance *from* the vertex *to* the focus. Because the axis of the parabola is vertical and $p = -1$, the focus is one unit *below* the vertex, and the parabola opens downward.

EXAMPLE 3   Graphing an Ellipse
•••••••••••••••

Graph the ellipse whose equation is

$$x^2 + 4y^2 + 6x - 8y + 9 = 0.$$

SOLUTION

$$x^2 + 4y^2 + 6x - 8y + 9 = 0 \qquad \text{\textit{Original equation}}$$
$$(x^2 + 6x + \quad) + (4y^2 - 8y + \quad) = -9 \qquad \text{\textit{Group terms}}$$
$$(x^2 + 6x + \quad) + 4(y^2 - 2y + \quad) = -9 \qquad \text{\textit{Factor 4 out of y-terms}}$$
$$(x^2 + 6x + 9) + 4(y^2 - 2y + 1) = -9 + 9 + 4(1) \qquad \text{\textit{Add 9 and 4 to both sides}}$$
$$(x + 3)^2 + 4(y - 1)^2 = 4 \qquad \text{\textit{Completed square form}}$$
$$\frac{(x + 3)^2}{4} + \frac{(y - 1)^2}{1} = 1 \qquad \text{\textit{Standard form}}$$
$$\frac{(x - h)^2}{a^2} + \frac{(y - k)^2}{b^2} = 1$$

From this standard form, you can see that the center is $(h, k) = (-3, 1)$. Because the denominator of the x-term is $4 = a^2 = 2^2$, the endpoints of the major axis lie two units to the right and left of the center. Similarly, because the denominator of the y-term is $1 = b^2 = 1^2$, the endpoints of the minor axis lie one unit up and down from the center. The graph of this ellipse is shown in Figure 4.38. ••••••••

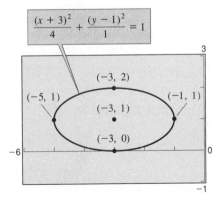

$$\frac{(x + 3)^2}{4} + \frac{(y - 1)^2}{1} = 1$$

FIGURE 4.38

To use a graphing utility to graph the ellipse in Example 3, you should first solve the equation for y.

$$(y - 1)^2 = 1 - \frac{1}{4}(x + 3)^2$$

$$y - 1 = \pm \sqrt{1 - \frac{1}{4}(x + 3)^2}$$

$$y = 1 \pm \sqrt{1 - \frac{1}{4}(x + 3)^2}$$

You can obtain the entire ellipse by graphing its upper part,

$$y = 1 + \sqrt{1 - \frac{1}{4}(x + 3)^2},$$

and lower part,

$$y = 1 - \sqrt{1 - \frac{1}{4}(x + 3)^2},$$

on the same screen.

EXAMPLE 4 Graphing a Hyperbola

Graph the hyperbola given by the equation

$$y^2 - 4x^2 + 4y + 24x - 41 = 0.$$

SOLUTION

$y^2 - 4x^2 + 4y + 24x - 41 = 0$	*Original equation*
$(y^2 + 4y + \quad) - (4x^2 - 24x + \quad) = 41$	*Group terms*
$(y^2 + 4y + \quad) - 4(x^2 - 6x + \quad) = 41$	*Factor 4 out of x-terms*
$(y^2 + 4y + 4) - 4(x^2 - 6x + 9) = 41 + 4 - 4(9)$	*Add 4, subtract 36*
$(y + 2)^2 - 4(x - 3)^2 = 9$	*Completed square form*
$\dfrac{(y + 2)^2}{9} - \dfrac{4(x - 3)^2}{9} = 1$	*Divide both sides by 9*
$\dfrac{(y + 2)^2}{9} - \dfrac{(x - 3)^2}{9/4} = 1$	*Change 4 to $\dfrac{1}{1/4}$*
$\dfrac{(y + 2)^2}{3^2} - \dfrac{(x - 3)^2}{(3/2)^2} = 1$	*Standard form*
$\dfrac{(y - k)^2}{a^2} - \dfrac{(x - h)^2}{b^2} = 1$	

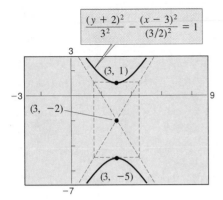

$$\frac{(y + 2)^2}{3^2} - \frac{(x - 3)^2}{(3/2)^2} = 1$$

FIGURE 4.39

From the standard form, you can see that the transverse axis is vertical and the center lies at $(h, k) = (3, -2)$. Because the denominator of the y-term is $a^2 = 3^2$, you know that the vertices occur three units above and below the center.

Vertices: $(3, -5)$ and $(3, 1)$

To graph the hyperbola, draw a rectangle whose top and bottom pass through the vertices. Because the denominator of the x-term is $b^2 = (\frac{3}{2})^2$, you should locate the sides of the rectangle $\frac{3}{2}$ units to the right and left of center, as shown in Figure 4.39. Finally, sketch the asymptotes by drawing lines through the opposite corners of the rectangle. Using these asymptotes, complete the graph of the hyperbola, as shown in Figure 4.39. ■■■■■■■■■

To find the foci in Example 4, first find c. Using

$$c^2 = a^2 + b^2 = 9 + \frac{9}{4} = \frac{45}{4},$$

you can conclude that $c = 3\sqrt{5}/2$. Because the transverse axis is vertical, the foci lie c units above and below the center.

Foci: $\left(3, -2 + \frac{3\sqrt{5}}{2}\right)$ and $\left(3, -2 - \frac{3\sqrt{5}}{2}\right)$

EXAMPLE 5 **Writing the Equation of an Ellipse**

Write the standard form of the equation of the ellipse whose vertices are $(2, -2)$ and $(2, 4)$. The length of the minor axis of the ellipse is 4, as shown in Figure 4.40.

SOLUTION

The center of the ellipse lies at the midpoint of its vertices. Thus, the center is

$(h, k) = (2, 1)$.   *Center*

Because the vertices lie on a vertical line and are six units apart, it follows that the major axis is vertical and has a length of $2a = 6$. Thus, $a = 3$. Moreover, because the minor axis has a length of 4, it follows that $2b = 4$ and thus $b = 2$. Therefore, the standard form of the equation of the ellipse is as follows.

$$\frac{(x - h)^2}{b^2} + \frac{(y - k)^2}{a^2} = 1 \qquad \textit{Major axis is vertical}$$

$$\frac{(x - 2)^2}{2^2} + \frac{(y - 1)^2}{3^2} = 1 \qquad \textit{Standard form}$$

FIGURE 4.40

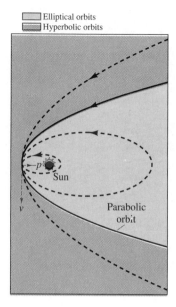

□ Elliptical orbits
▨ Hyperbolic orbits

Parabolic orbit

Sun

p

v

FIGURE 4.41

Applications

An interesting application of conic sections involves the orbits of comets in our solar system. Of the 610 comets identified prior to 1970, 245 have elliptical orbits, 295 have parabolic orbits, and 70 have hyperbolic orbits. For example, Halley's Comet has an elliptical orbit, and you can predict the reappearance of this comet every 75 years. The center of the sun is a focus of each of these orbits, and each orbit has a vertex at the point where the comet is closest to the sun, as shown in Figure 4.41.

If p is the distance between the vertex and the focus, and v is the speed of the comet at the vertex, then the orbit is

$$\text{an } ellipse \text{ if } \quad v < \sqrt{\frac{2GM}{p}},$$

$$\text{a } parabola \text{ if } \quad v = \sqrt{\frac{2GM}{p}},$$

$$\text{a } hyperbola \text{ if } \quad v > \sqrt{\frac{2GM}{p}},$$

where M is the mass of the sun and $G \approx 6.67(10^{-8})$ cm^3/(gm · sec^2).

**DISCUSSION
PROBLEM**

··················

**ASYMPTOTES
OF A
HYPERBOLA**

In Section 4.4, you learned how to find equations for the asymptotes of a hyperbola whose center is the origin. Write a paragraph describing how to find equations for the asymptotes of a hyperbola whose center is the point (h, k). Then use your procedure to find the asymptotes of the hyperbola given by

$$\frac{(x - 1)^2}{3^2} - \frac{(y - 2)^2}{2^2} = 1.$$

Find equations for the asymptotes and use a graphing utility to graph them in the same viewing rectangle as the hyperbola.

WARM-UP

The following warm-up exercises involve skills that were covered in earlier sections. You will use these skills in the exercise set for this section.

In Exercises 1–10, identify the conic represented by each equation.

1. $\dfrac{x^2}{4} - \dfrac{y^2}{4} = 1$ **2.** $\dfrac{x^2}{9} + \dfrac{y^2}{1} = 1$

3. $2x + y^2 = 0$ **4.** $\dfrac{x^2}{9} - \dfrac{y^2}{4} = 1$

5. $\dfrac{x^2}{4} + \dfrac{y^2}{16} = 1$ **6.** $4x^2 + 4y^2 = 25$

7. $\dfrac{y^2}{4} - \dfrac{x^2}{2} = 1$ **8.** $x^2 - 6y = 0$

9. $3x - y^2 = 0$ **10.** $\dfrac{x^2}{9/4} + \dfrac{y^2}{4} = 1$

SECTION 4.5 · EXERCISES

In Exercises 1–8, find the vertex, focus, and directrix of the parabola, and sketch its graph without the aid of a graphing utility.

1. $(x - 1)^2 + 8(y + 2) = 0$ **2.** $(x + 3) + (y - 2)^2 = 0$
3. $(y + \tfrac{1}{2})^2 = 2(x - 5)$ **4.** $(x + \tfrac{1}{2})^2 = 4(y - 3)$
5. $y = \tfrac{1}{4}(x^2 - 2x + 5)$ **6.** $4x - y^2 - 2y - 33 = 0$
7. $y^2 + 6y + 8x + 25 = 0$ **8.** $y^2 - 4y - 4x = 0$

In Exercises 9–12, find the vertex, focus, and directrix of the parabola, and use a graphing utility to obtain its graph.

9. $y = -\tfrac{1}{6}(x^2 + 4x - 2)$ **10.** $x^2 - 2x + 8y + 9 = 0$
11. $y^2 + x + y = 0$ **12.** $y^2 - 4x - 4 = 0$

In Exercises 13–20, find an equation of the specified parabola.

13. Vertex: $(3, 2)$ **14.** Vertex: $(-1, 2)$
     Focus: $(1, 2)$ Focus: $(-1, 0)$
15. Vertex: $(0, 4)$ **16.** Vertex: $(-2, 1)$
     Directrix: $y = 2$ Directrix: $x = 1$
17. Focus: $(2, 2)$ **18.** Focus: $(0, 0)$
     Directrix: $x = -2$ Directrix: $y = 4$

19.

20.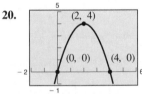

21. *Satellite Orbit*   A satellite in a 100-mile-high circular orbit around the earth has a velocity of approximately 17,500 miles per hour. If this velocity is multiplied by $\sqrt{2}$, then the satellite will have the minimum velocity necessary to escape the earth's gravity and it will follow a parabolic path with the center of the earth as the focus (see figure).
(a) Find the escape velocity of the satellite.
(b) Find an equation of its path (assume the radius of the earth is 4000 miles).

FIGURE FOR 21

22. *Fluid Flow*   Water is flowing from a horizontal pipe 48 feet above the ground. The falling stream of water has the shape of a parabola whose vertex (0, 48) is at the end of the pipe (see figure). The stream of water strikes the ground at the point $(10\sqrt{3}, 0)$. Find the equation of the path taken by the water.

FIGURE FOR 22

23. *Path of a Projectile*   The path of a softball thrown by a child is given by the equation

$$y = -0.08x^2 + x + 4.$$

The coordinates x and y are measured in feet, with $x = 0$ corresponding to the position where the child is standing.
(a) Use a graphing utility to graph the trajectory of the softball.
(b) Move the cursor along the path to approximate the highest point and the range of the trajectory.

24. *Revenue*   The revenue R generated by the sale of x units is given by

$$R = 375x - \tfrac{3}{2}x^2.$$

Use a graphing utility to graph the function and approximate the number of sales that will maximize revenue.

In Exercises 25–30, find the center, foci, and vertices of the ellipse, and sketch its graph without the aid of a graphing utility.

25. $\dfrac{(x-1)^2}{9} + \dfrac{(y-5)^2}{25} = 1$

26. $(x+2)^2 + \dfrac{(y+4)^2}{1/4} = 1$

27. $9x^2 + 4y^2 + 36x - 24y + 36 = 0$

28. $9x^2 + 4y^2 - 36x + 8y + 31 = 0$

29. $16x^2 + 25y^2 - 32x + 50y + 16 = 0$

30. $9x^2 + 25y^2 - 36x - 50y + 61 = 0$

In Exercises 31 and 32, find the center, foci, and vertices of the ellipse, and graph the ellipse with the aid of a graphing utility.

31. $12x^2 + 20y^2 - 12x + 40y - 37 = 0$

32. $36x^2 + 9y^2 + 48x - 36y + 43 = 0$

In Exercises 33–40, find an equation for the specified ellipse.

33. Vertices: (0, 2), (4, 2)
Minor axis of length 2

34. Foci: (0, 0), (4, 0)
Major axis of length 8

35. Foci: (0, 0), (0, 8)
Major axis of length 16

36. Center: (2, −1)
Vertex: $(2, \tfrac{1}{2})$
Minor axis of length 2

37. Vertices: (3, 1), (3, 9)
Minor axis of length 6

38. Center: (3, 2)
$a = 3c$
Foci: (1, 2), (5, 2)

39. Center: (0, 4)
$a = 2c$
Vertices: (−4, 4), (4, 4)

40. Vertices: (5, 0), (5, 12)
Co-vertices: (0, 6), (10, 6)

In Exercises 41–46, e is called the **eccentricity** of the ellipse and is defined by $e = c/a$. It measures the flatness of the ellipse.

41. Find an equation of the ellipse with vertices $(\pm 5, 0)$ and eccentricity $e = \tfrac{3}{5}$.

42. Find an equation of the ellipse with vertices $(0, \pm 8)$ and eccentricity $e = \tfrac{1}{2}$.

43. *Orbit of Pluto*   The planet Pluto moves in an elliptical orbit with the sun at one of the foci (see figure). The length of half of the major axis is 3.666×10^9 miles, and the eccentricity is 0.248. Find the smallest distance (*perihelion*) and the greatest distance (*aphelion*) of Pluto from the sun.

44. *Orbit of Saturn*   The planet Saturn moves in an elliptical orbit with the sun at one of the foci (see figure). The smallest distance and the greatest distance of the planet from the sun are 1.3495×10^9 and 1.5045×10^9 kilometers, respectively. Find the eccentricity of the orbit.

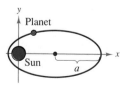

FIGURE FOR 43 AND 44

45. *Satellite Orbit*   The first artificial satellite to orbit the earth was Sputnik I (launched by the USSR in 1957). Its highest point above the earth's surface was 583 miles, and its lowest point was 132 miles (see figure). Assume that the center of the earth is the focus of the elliptical orbit and the radius of the earth is 4000 miles. Find the eccentricity of the orbit.

132 miles   583 miles

FIGURE FOR 45

46. Show that the equation of an ellipse can be written as

$$\frac{(x - h)^2}{a^2} + \frac{(y - k)^2}{a^2(1 - e^2)} = 1.$$

True or False: As e approaches zero, the ellipse approaches a circle of radius a. Explain.

In Exercises 47–54, find the center, vertices, and foci of the hyperbola and sketch its graph without the aid of a graphing utility. Sketch the asymptotes as an aid in obtaining the graph of the hyperbola.

47. $\dfrac{(x - 1)^2}{4} - \dfrac{(y + 2)^2}{1} = 1$

48. $\dfrac{(x + 1)^2}{144} - \dfrac{(y - 4)^2}{25} = 1$

49. $(y + 6)^2 - (x - 2)^2 = 1$

50. $\dfrac{(y - 1)^2}{1/4} - \dfrac{(x + 3)^2}{1/9} = 1$

51. $9x^2 - y^2 - 36x - 6y + 18 = 0$

52. $x^2 - 9y^2 + 36y - 72 = 0$

53. $x^2 - 9y^2 + 2x - 54y - 80 = 0$

54. $16y^2 - x^2 + 2x + 64y + 63 = 0$

In Exercises 55 and 56, find the center, vertices, and foci of the hyperbola and graph the hyperbola and its asymptotes with the aid of a graphing utility.

55. $9y^2 - x^2 + 2x + 54y + 62 = 0$

56. $9x^2 - y^2 + 54x + 10y + 55 = 0$

In Exercises 57–64, find an equation for the specified hyperbola.

57. Vertices: (2, 0), (6, 0)
     Foci: (0, 0), (8, 0)

58. Vertices: (2, 3), (2, −3)
     Foci: (2, 5), (2, −5)

59. Vertices: (4, 1), (4, 9)
     Foci: (4, 0), (4, 10)

60. Vertices: (−2, 1), (2, 1)
     Foci: (−3, 1), (3, 1)

61. Vertices: (2, 3), (2, −3)
     Passes through (0, 5)

62. Vertices: (−2, 1), (2, 1)
     Passes through (4, 3)

63. Vertices: (0, 2), (6, 2)
     Asymptotes: $y = \frac{2}{3}x$,
     $y = 4 - \frac{2}{3}x$

64. Vertices: (3, 0), (3, 4)
     Asymptotes: $y = \frac{2}{3}x$,
     $y = 4 - \frac{2}{3}x$

In Exercises 65–72, classify the graph of the equation as a circle, a parabola, an ellipse, or a hyperbola.

65. $x^2 + y^2 - 6x + 4y + 9 = 0$

66. $x^2 + 4y^2 - 6x + 16y + 21 = 0$

67. $4x^2 - y^2 - 4x - 3 = 0$

68. $y^2 - 4y - 4x = 0$

69. $4x^2 + 3y^2 + 8x - 24y + 51 = 0$

70. $4y^2 - 2x^2 - 4y - 8x - 15 = 0$

71. $25x^2 - 10x - 200y - 119 = 0$

72. $4x^2 + 4y^2 - 16y + 15 = 0$

CHAPTER 4 · REVIEW EXERCISES

In Exercises 1–4, find the domain of the function and identify any horizontal or vertical asymptotes.

1. $f(x) = \dfrac{4}{x + 3}$

2. $f(x) = \dfrac{2x^2 + 5x - 3}{x^2 + 2}$

3. $g(x) = \dfrac{x^2}{x^2 - 4}$

4. $g(x) = \dfrac{1}{(x - 3)^2}$

In Exercises 5–14, sketch the graph of the rational function. As sketching aids, check for intercepts, symmetry, vertical asymptotes, horizontal asymptotes, and slant asymptotes.

5. $f(x) = \dfrac{-5}{x^2}$

6. $f(x) = \dfrac{4}{x}$

7. $g(x) = \dfrac{2 + x}{1 - x}$

8. $g(x) = \dfrac{-2}{(x + 3)^2}$

9. $P(x) = \dfrac{x^2}{x^2 + 1}$

10. $f(x) = \dfrac{2x}{x^2 + 4}$

11. $y = \dfrac{x}{x^2 - 1}$

12. $h(x) = \dfrac{4}{(x - 1)^2}$

13. $f(x) = \dfrac{2x^3}{x^2 + 1}$

14. $y = \dfrac{2x^2}{x^2 - 4}$

In Exercises 15–18, use a graphing utility to graph the function.

15. $s(x) = \dfrac{8x^2}{x^2 + 4}$

16. $y = \dfrac{5x}{x^2 - 4}$

17. $g(x) = \dfrac{x^2 + 1}{x + 1}$

18. $y = \dfrac{1}{x + 3} + 2$

19. *Average Cost*   A business has a cost of $C = 0.5x + 500$ for producing x units. The average cost per unit is

$$\bar{C} = \frac{C}{x} = \frac{0.5x + 500}{x}, \qquad 0 < x.$$

Determine the average cost per unit as x increases without bound. (Find the horizontal asymptote.)

20. *Average Cost*   The cost of producing x units of a product is C, and therefore the average cost per unit is

$$\bar{C} = \frac{C}{x} = \frac{100,000 + 0.9x}{x}, \qquad 0 < x.$$

Use a graphing utility to graph the average cost function and find the average cost of producing $x = 1000$, $x = 10,000$, and $x = 100,000$ units.

21. *Seizure of Illegal Drugs*   The cost, in millions of dollars, for the federal government to seize $p\%$ of an illegal drug as it enters the country is given by

$$C = \frac{528p}{100 - p}, \qquad 0 \le p < 100.$$

(a) Find the cost of seizing 25% of an illegal drug.
(b) Find the cost of seizing 50%.
(c) Find the cost of seizing 75%.
(d) According to this model, would it be possible to seize 100% of the drug?

22. *Population of Fish*   The Parks and Wildlife Commission introduces 80,000 fish into a large man-made lake. The population of the fish, in thousands, is given by

$$N = \frac{20(4 + 3t)}{1 + 0.05t}, \qquad 0 \le t,$$

where t is the time in years.
(a) Find the population when t is 5, 10, and 25.
(b) What is the limiting number of fish in the lake as time increases?

23. *Capillary Attraction*   The rise of distilled water in tubes x inches in diameter is approximated by the model

$$y = \left(\frac{0.80 - 0.54x}{1 + 2.72x}\right)^2, \qquad 0 < x,$$

where y is measured in inches. Use a graphing utility to graph the model and approximate the diameter of the tube that will cause the water to rise 0.1 inch.

24. *Photosynthesis*   The amount y of CO_2 uptake in milligrams per square decimeter per hour at optimal temperatures and with the natural supply of CO_2 is approximated by the model

$$y = \frac{18.47x - 2.96}{0.23x + 1}, \qquad 0 < x,$$

where x is the light intensity in watts per square meter. Use a graphing utility to graph the function and determine the limiting amount of CO_2 uptake.

In Exercise 25–32, write the partial fraction decomposition for the rational expression.

25. $\dfrac{4 - x}{x^2 + 6x + 8}$ **26.** $\dfrac{-x}{x^2 + 3x + 2}$

27. $\dfrac{x^2}{x^2 + 2x - 15}$ **28.** $\dfrac{9}{x^2 - 9}$

29. $\dfrac{x^2 + 2x}{x^3 - x^2 + x - 1}$ **30.** $\dfrac{4x - 2}{3(x - 1)^2}$

31. $\dfrac{3x^3 + 4x}{(x^2 + 1)^2}$ **32.** $\dfrac{4x^2}{(x - 1)(x^2 + 1)}$

In Exercises 33–44, identify the conic and sketch its graph.

33. $4x - y^2 = 0$ **34.** $8y + x^2 = 0$

35. $x^2 - 6x + 2y + 9 = 0$

36. $y^2 - 12y - 8x + 20 = 0$

37. $x^2 + y^2 - 2x - 4y + 5 = 0$

38. $16x^2 + 16y^2 - 16x + 24y - 3 = 0$

39. $4x^2 + y^2 = 16$ **40.** $2x^2 + 6y^2 = 18$

41. $x^2 + 9y^2 + 10x - 18y + 25 = 0$

42. $4x^2 + y^2 - 16x + 15 = 0$

43. $5y^2 - 4x^2 = 20$

44. $x^2 - 9y^2 + 10x + 18y + 7 = 0$

In Exercises 45 and 46, consider the general form of a conic where its axes are not parallel to either the x-axis or the y-axis (note the xy term). Use the quadratic formula to solve for y, and use a graphing utility to graph the equation. Identify the conic.

45. $x^2 - 10xy + y^2 + 1 = 0$

46. $40x^2 + 36xy + 25y^2 - 52 = 0$

In Exercises 47–50, find an equation of the specified parabola.

47. Vertex: $(4, 2)$ **48.** Vertex: $(2, 0)$
     Focus: $(4, 0)$ Focus: $(0, 0)$

49. Vertex: $(0, 2)$ **50.** Vertex: $(2, 2)$
     Passes through $(-1, 0)$ Directrix: $y = 0$
     Horizontal axis

In Exercises 51–54, find an equation of the specified ellipse.

51. Vertices: $(-3, 0)$, $(7, 0)$ **52.** Vertices: $(2, 0)$, $(2, 4)$
     Foci: $(0, 0)$, $(4, 0)$ Foci: $(2, 1)$, $(2, 3)$

53. Vertices: $(0, \pm 6)$ **54.** Vertices: $(0, 1)$, $(4, 1)$
     Passes through $(2, 2)$ Co-vertices: $(2, 0)$, $(2, 2)$

In Exercises 55–58, find an equation of the specified hyperbola.

55. Vertices: $(0, \pm 1)$
     Foci: $(0, \pm 3)$

56. Vertices: $(2, 2)$, $(-2, 2)$
     Foci: $(4, 2)$, $(-4, 2)$

57. Foci: $(0, 0)$, $(8, 0)$
     Asymptotes: $y = \pm 2(x - 4)$

58. Foci: $(3, \pm 2)$
     Asymptotes: $y = \pm 2(x - 3)$

59. *Satellite Antenna*   A cross section of a large parabolic antenna (see figure) is given by

$$y = \dfrac{x^2}{200}, \qquad 0 \le x \le 100.$$

The receiving and transmitting equipment is positioned at the focus. Find the coordinates of the focus.

FIGURE FOR 59

60. *Semi-elliptical Archway*   A semi-elliptical archway is to be formed over the entrance to an estate. The arch is to be set on pillars that are 10 feet apart and is to have a height (atop the pillars) of 4 feet (see figure). Where should the foci be placed in order to sketch the semi-elliptical arch?

FIGURE FOR 60

EXPONENTIAL AND LOGARITHMIC FUNCTIONS

5.1 EXPONENTIAL FUNCTIONS AND THEIR GRAPHS

Exponential Functions / Graphs of Exponential Functions / The Natural Base e / Compound Interest / Other Applications

Exponential Functions

So far in the text, you have been studying **algebraic functions,** which include polynomial functions and rational functions. In this chapter you will study two types of nonalgebraic functions—*exponential* functions and *logarithmic* functions. These functions are **transcendental functions.**

Exponential functions are used in describing economic and physical phenomena such as compound interest, population growth, memory retention, and decay of radioactive material. Exponential functions involve a *constant base* and a *variable exponent* such as $f(x) = 2^x$ or $g(x) = 3^{-x}$.

DEFINITION OF EXPONENTIAL FUNCTION

The **exponential function f with base a** is denoted by

$$f(x) = a^x,$$

where $a > 0$, $a \neq 1$, and x is any real number.

REMARK The base $a = 1$ is not used because it yields $f(x) = 1^x = 1$, which is a constant function, not an exponential function.

You already know how to evaluate a^x for integer and rational values of x. For example, $8^3 = 512$ and $8^{2/3} = 4$. However, to evaluate a^x for any real number x, you need to interpret forms with *irrational* exponents, such as $a^{\sqrt{2}}$

and 8^{π}. A technical definition of such forms is beyond the scope of this text. For now, it is sufficient to think of $a^{\sqrt{2}}$ as that value that has the successively closer approximations

$$a^{1.4}, a^{1.41}, a^{1.414}, a^{1.4142}, a^{1.41421}, a^{1.414214}, \ldots$$

The properties of exponents (reviewed in Section 2 in the prerequisite chapter) can be extended to cover exponential functions.

EXAMPLE 1   Using a Calculator to Evaluate Exponential Expressions

	Number	Display	Rounded to 3 Decimal Places
A.	$(1.085)^3$	1.277289125	1.277
B.	$12^{5/7}$	5.899887726	5.900
C.	$2^{-\pi}$	0.1133147323	0.113

Graphs of Exponential Functions

EXAMPLE 2   Graphs of $y = a^x$

On the same coordinate plane, graph the following functions.

A. $f(x) = 2^x$ **B.** $g(x) = 4^x$

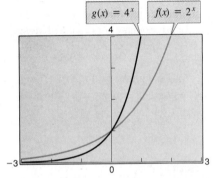

FIGURE 5.1

SOLUTION

Table 5.1 lists some values for each function, and Figure 5.1 shows their graphs. Note that both graphs are increasing. Moreover, the graph of $g(x) = 4^x$ is increasing more rapidly than the graph of $f(x) = 2^x$.

TABLE 5.1

x	-2	-1	0	1	2	3
A. $f(x) = 2^x$	$\frac{1}{4}$	$\frac{1}{2}$	1	2	4	8
B. $g(x) = 4^x$	$\frac{1}{16}$	$\frac{1}{4}$	1	4	16	64

EXAMPLE 3   Graphs of $y = a^{-x}$

On the same coordinate plane, graph the following functions.

A. $F(x) = 2^{-x} = \left(\dfrac{1}{2}\right)^x$ **B.** $G(x) = 4^{-x} = \left(\dfrac{1}{4}\right)^x$

REMARK   Examples 2 and 3 illustrate that the function $f(x) = a^x$ *increases* if $a > 1$ and *decreases* if $0 < a < 1$.

SOLUTION

Table 5.2 lists some values for each function, and Figure 5.2 shows their graphs. Note that both graphs are decreasing. Moreover, the graph of $G(x) = 4^{-x}$ is decreasing more rapidly than the graph of $F(x) = 2^{-x}$.

TABLE 5.2

x	-3	-2	-1	0	1	2
A. $F(x) = 2^{-x}$	8	4	2	1	$\frac{1}{2}$	$\frac{1}{4}$
B. $G(x) = 4^{-x}$	64	16	4	1	$\frac{1}{4}$	$\frac{1}{16}$

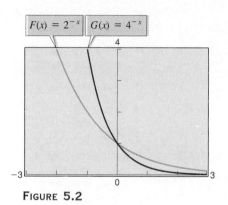

FIGURE 5.2

D I S C O V E R Y

Use a graphing utility to graph $y = a^x$ with $a = 2, 3,$ and 5 on the same viewing rectangle. (Use a viewing rectangle in which $-2 \le x \le 1$ and $0 \le y \le 2$.) How do the graphs compare with each other? Which graph is on the top in the interval $(-\infty, 0)$? Which is on the bottom? Which graph is on the top in the interval $(0, \infty)$? Which is on the bottom?

Repeat this experiment with the graphs of $y = a^{-x}$ with $a = 2, 3,$ and 5.

The graphs in Figures 5.1 and 5.2 are typical of the exponential functions a^x and a^{-x}. They have $(0, 1)$ as their y-intercept, they have the x-axis as a horizontal asymptote, and they are continuous. The basic characteristics of these exponential functions are summarized in Figure 5.3. Try using a graphing utility to verify the characteristics listed in this summary.

Graph of $y = a^x$
- Domain: $(-\infty, \infty)$
- Range: $(0, \infty)$
- Intercept: $(0, 1)$
- Increasing
- x-axis is a horizontal asymptote
  ($a^x \to 0$ as $x \to -\infty$)
- Continuous

Graph of $y = a^{-x}$
- Domain: $(-\infty, \infty)$
- Range: $(0, \infty)$
- Intercept: $(0, 1)$
- Decreasing
- x-axis is a horizontal asymptote
  ($a^{-x} \to 0$ as $x \to \infty$)
- Continuous
- Reflection of graph of $y = a^x$ about y-axis

Characteristics of the Exponential Functions a^x and $a^{-x}(a > 1)$

FIGURE 5.3

(a)

(b)

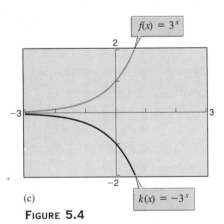

(c)

FIGURE 5.4

EXAMPLE 4   Graphing Exponential Functions

Compare the graph of each of the following with the graph of $f(x) = 3^x$. Identify the domain and range of each function.

A. $g(x) = 3^{x+1}$
B. $h(x) = 3^x - 2$
C. $k(x) = -3^x$

SOLUTION

A. Because $g(x) = 3^{x+1} = f(x + 1)$, the graph of g can be obtained by shifting the graph of f one unit to the left, as shown in Figure 5.4(a). The domain is $(-\infty, \infty)$ and the range is $(0, \infty)$.
B. Because $h(x) = 3^x - 2 = f(x) - 2$, the graph of h can be obtained by shifting the graph of f down two units, as shown in Figure 5.4(b). The domain is $(-\infty, \infty)$ and the range is $(-2, \infty)$.
C. Because $k(x) = -3^x = -f(x)$, the graph of k can be obtained by reflecting the graph of f in the x-axis, as shown in Figure 5.4(c). The domain is $(-\infty, \infty)$ and the range is $(-\infty, 0)$.

The Natural Base e

For many applications, the convenient choice for a base is the irrational number

$$e \approx 2.71828 \ldots ,$$

called the **natural base.** The function $f(x) = e^x$ is the **natural exponential function.** Its graph is shown in Figure 5.5. Be sure you see that for the exponential function $f(x) = e^x$, e is the constant $2.71828 \ldots$, whereas x is the variable.

FIGURE 5.5

(a)

(b)

FIGURE 5.6

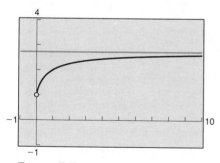

FIGURE 5.7

EXAMPLE 5   **Evaluating the Natural Exponential Function**

Number	Display	Rounded to 3 Decimal Places
A. e^2	7.389056099	7.389
B. e^{-1}	0.3678794412	0.368
C. $e^{0.48}$	1.616074402	1.616

EXAMPLE 6   **Graphing a Natural Exponential Function**

Graph the following natural exponential functions.

A. $f(x) = 2e^{0.24x}$ **B.** $g(x) = \dfrac{1}{2}e^{-0.58x}$

SOLUTION

In Figure 5.6, note that each graph has the x-axis as a horizontal asymptote.

EXAMPLE 7   **Approximation of the Number e**

Evaluate the expression

$$\left(1 + \frac{1}{x}\right)^x$$

for several large values of x to see that the values approach $e \approx 2.71828$ as x increases without bound.

SOLUTION

Using a calculator, you can complete Table 5.3. From this table, it seems reasonable to conclude that

$$\left(1 + \frac{1}{x}\right)^x \to e \quad \text{as} \quad x \to \infty.$$

You can further confirm this conclusion by using a graphing utility to graph $f(x) = [1 + (1/x)]^x$ and $y = e$ on the same display, as shown in Figure 5.7. Note that as x increases, the graph of f gets closer and closer to the line given by $y = e$.

TABLE 5.3

x	10	100	1000	10,000	100,000	1,000,000
$\left(1 + \dfrac{1}{x}\right)^x$	2.59374	2.70481	2.71692	2.71815	2.71827	2.71828

Compound Interest

One of the most familiar examples of exponential growth is that of an investment earning *continuously compounded interest.* Suppose a principal P is invested at an annual percentage rate r, compounded once a year. If the interest is added to the principal at the end of the year, then the balance is

$$P_1 = P + Pr = P(1 + r).$$

This pattern of multiplying the previous principal by $1 + r$ is then repeated each successive year, as shown in Table 5.4.

TABLE 5.4

Time in years	Balance after each compounding
0	$P = P$
1	$P_1 = P(1 + r)$
2	$P_2 = P_1(1 + r) = P(1 + r)(1 + r) = P(1 + r)^2$
3	$P_3 = P_2(1 + r) = P(1 + r)^2(1 + r) = P(1 + r)^3$
.	.
.	.
.	.
n	$P_n = P(1 + r)^n$

To accommodate more frequent (quarterly, monthly, or daily) compounding of interest, let n be the number of compoundings per year and let t be the number of years. Then the rate per compounding is r/n, and the account balance after t years is

$$A = P\left(1 + \frac{r}{n}\right)^{nt}.$$ *Amount with n compoundings per year*

If you let the number of compoundings, n, increase without bound, you approach **continuous compounding.** In the formula for n compoundings per year, let $m = n/r$. This produces

$$A = P\left(1 + \frac{r}{n}\right)^{nt} = P\left(1 + \frac{1}{m}\right)^{mrt} = P\left[\left(1 + \frac{1}{m}\right)^m\right]^{rt}.$$

As m increases without bound, you know from Example 7 that $[1 + (1/m)]^m$ approaches e. Hence, for continuous compounding, it follows that

$$P\left[\left(1 + \frac{1}{m}\right)^m\right]^{rt} \to P[e]^{rt},$$

and you can write $A = Pe^{rt}$. This result is part of the reason that e is the "natural" choice for a base of an exponential function.

FORMULAS FOR COMPOUND INTEREST

After t years, the balance A in an account with principal P and annual percentage rate r (expressed as a decimal) is given by the following formulas.

1. For n compoundings per year: $A = P\left(1 + \dfrac{r}{n}\right)^{nt}$

2. For continuous compounding: $A = Pe^{rt}$

EXAMPLE 8   Finding the Balance for Compound Interest

A sum of \$9000 is invested at an annual percentage rate of 8.5%, compounded annually. Find the balance in the account after 3 years.

SOLUTION

In this case, $P = 9000$, $r = 8.5\% = 0.085$, $n = 1$, and $t = 3$. Using the formula

$$A = P\left(1 + \frac{r}{n}\right)^{nt},$$

you have

$$A = 9000(1 + 0.085)^3 = 9000(1.085)^3 \approx \$11{,}495.60.$$

The graph of $f(t) = 9000(1 + 0.085)^t$ is shown in Figure 5.8.

FIGURE 5.8

EXAMPLE 9   Compounding n Times and Compounding Continuously

A total of $12,000 is invested at an annual percentage rate of 9%. Find the balance after 5 years if it is compounded

A. quarterly.
B. continuously.

SOLUTION

A. For quarterly compoundings, you have $n = 4$. Thus, in 5 years at 9%, the balance is

$$A = P\left(1 + \frac{r}{n}\right)^{nt}$$

$$= 12,000\left(1 + \frac{0.09}{4}\right)^{4(5)}$$

$$= \$18,726.11.$$

B. Compounding continuously, the balance is

$$A = Pe^{rt} = 12,000e^{0.09(5)} = \$18,819.75.$$

Note that continuous compounding yields

$$\$18,819.75 - \$18,726.11 = \$93.64$$

more than quarterly compounding.

Other Applications

EXAMPLE 10   An Application Involving Radioactive Decay

Let y represent the mass of a particular radioactive element whose half-life is 25 years. After t years, the mass (in grams) is given by

$$y = 10\left(\frac{1}{2}\right)^{t/25}.$$

A. What is the initial mass (when $t = 0$)?
B. How much of the initial mass is present after 80 years?

FIGURE **5.9**

SOLUTION

A. When $t = 0$, the mass is

$$y = 10\left(\frac{1}{2}\right)^{0} = 10(1) = 10 \text{ grams.}$$

B. When $t = 80$, the mass is

$$y = 10\left(\frac{1}{2}\right)^{80/25} = 10(0.5)^{3.2} \approx 1.088 \text{ grams.}$$

The graph of this function is shown in Figure 5.9.

EXAMPLE 11   Population Growth

The approximate number of fruit flies in an experimental population after t hours is given by

$$Q(t) = 20e^{0.03t}, \qquad t \geq 0.$$

A. Find the initial number of fruit flies in the population.
B. How large is the population of fruit flies after 72 hours?
C. Sketch the graph of Q.

FIGURE 5.10

SOLUTION

A. To find the initial population, evaluate $Q(t)$ at $t = 0$.

$$Q(0) = 20e^{0.03(0)} = 20e^0 = 20(1) = 20 \text{ flies}$$

B. After 72 hours, the population size is

$$Q(72) = 20e^{(0.03)(72)} = 20e^{2.16} \approx 173 \text{ flies.}$$

C. The graph of Q is shown in Figure 5.10.

DISCUSSION PROBLEM

EXPONENTIAL GROWTH

Consider the following sequences of numbers.

Sequence 1:   2, 4, 6, 8, 10, 12, . . . , $2n$

Sequence 2:   2, 4, 8, 16, 32, 64, . . . , 2^n

The first sequence, $f(n) = 2n$, is an example of **linear growth.** The second sequence, $f(n) = 2^n$, is an example of **exponential growth.** Which of the following sequences represents linear growth and which represents exponential growth? Can you find a linear function and an exponential function that represent the two sequences?

(a) 3, 6, 9, 12, 15, . . .
(b) 3, 9, 27, 81, 243, . . .

Later you will see that sequences that represent linear growth are *arithmetic sequences* and sequences that represent exponential growth are *geometric sequences.*

WARM-UP

The following warm-up exercises involve skills that were covered in earlier sections. You will use these skills in the exercise set for this section.

In Exercises 1–10, use the properties of exponents to simplify the expression.

1. $5^{2x}(5^{-x})$

2. $3^{-x}(3^{3x})$

3. $\dfrac{4^{5x}}{4^{2x}}$

4. $\dfrac{10^{2x}}{10^{x}}$

5. $(4^{x})^{2}$

6. $(4^{2x})^{5}$

7. $\left(\dfrac{2^{x}}{3^{x}}\right)^{-1}$

8. $(4^{6x})^{1/2}$

9. $(2^{3x})^{-1/3}$

10. $(16^{x})^{1/4}$

SECTION 5.1 · EXERCISES

In Exercises 1–10, use a calculator to evaluate the expression. Round your result to three decimal places.

1. $(3.4)^{5.6}$

2. $5000(2^{-1.5})$

3. $1000(1.06)^{-5}$

4. $(1.005)^{400}$

5. $5^{-\pi}$

6. $\sqrt[3]{4395}$

7. $100^{\sqrt{2}}$

8. $e^{1/2}$

9. $e^{-3/4}$

10. $e^{3.2}$

In Exercises 11–18, match the exponential function with its graph, and describe the given viewing rectangle. [The graphs are labeled (a), (b), (c), (d), (e), (f), (g), and (h).]

11. $f(x) = 3^{x}$

12. $f(x) = -3^{x}$

13. $f(x) = 3^{-x}$

14. $f(x) = -3^{-x}$

15. $f(x) = 3^{x} - 4$

16. $f(x) = 3^{x} + 1$

17. $f(x) = -3^{x-2}$

18. $f(x) = 3^{x-2}$

(a)

(b)

(c)

(d)

(e)

(f)

(g)

(h)

19. Use a graphing utility to graph $y = 3^{x}$ and $y = 4^{x}$ in the same viewing rectangle. Use the graphs to solve the inequality

$$4^{x} < 3^{x}.$$

20. Use a graphing utility to graph $y = (\tfrac{1}{2})^{x}$ and $y = (\tfrac{1}{4})^{x}$ in the same viewing rectangle. Use the graphs to solve the inequality

$$(\tfrac{1}{4})^{x} < (\tfrac{1}{2})^{x}.$$

In Exercises 21–30, sketch the graph of the exponential function *by hand.* Then use a graphing utility to confirm your graph.

21. $g(x) = 5^x$

22. $f(x) = (\frac{3}{2})^x$

23. $f(x) = (\frac{1}{5})^x = 5^{-x}$

24. $h(x) = (\frac{3}{2})^{-x}$

25. $h(x) = 5^{x-2}$

26. $g(x) = (\frac{3}{2})^{x+2}$

27. $g(x) = 5^{-x} - 3$

28. $f(x) = (\frac{3}{2})^{-x} + 2$

29. $y = 3^{x-2} + 1$

30. $y = 4^{x+1} - 2$

In Exercises 31–36, use a graphing utility to graph the exponential function.

31. $y = 1.08^{-5x}$

32. $y = 1.08^{5x}$

33. $s(t) = 2e^{0.12t}$

34. $s(t) = 3e^{-0.2t}$

35. $g(x) = 1 + e^{-x}$

36. $h(x) = e^{x-2}$

37. Graph the following functions in the same viewing rectangle of a graphing utility.
(a) $f(x) = 3^x$
(b) $g(x) = f(x - 2) = 3^{x-2}$
(c) $h(x) = -\frac{1}{2}f(x) = -\frac{1}{2}3^x$
(d) $q(x) = f(-x) + 3 = 3^{-x} + 3$

38. Use a graphing utility to graph each of the following functions. Use the graphs to determine any asymptotes of the functions.
(a) $f(x) = \dfrac{8}{1 + e^{-0.5x}}$ (b) $g(x) = \dfrac{8}{1 + e^{-0.5/x}}$

39. Use a graphing utility to graph each of the following functions. Use the graphs to determine where each function is increasing and decreasing, and approximate any relative maximum or minimum values of each function.
(a) $f(x) = x^2 e^{-x}$ (b) $g(x) = x2^{3-x}$

40. Use a graphing utility to demonstrate that
$$\left(1 + \frac{0.5}{x}\right)^x \rightarrow e^{0.5}$$
as x increases without bound.

In Exercises 41–44, complete the table to determine the balance A for P dollars invested at rate r for t years and compounded n times per year.

n	1	2	4	12	365	Continuous compounding
A						

41. $P = \$2500$, $r = 12\%$, $t = 10$ years

42. $P = \$1000$, $r = 10\%$, $t = 10$ years

43. $P = \$2500$, $r = 12\%$, $t = 20$ years

44. $P = \$1000$, $r = 10\%$, $t = 40$ years

In Exericses 45–48, complete the table to determine the amount of money P that should be invested at rate r to produce a final balance of \$100,000 in t years.

t	1	10	20	30	40	50
P						

45. $r = 9\%$, compounded continuously

46. $r = 12\%$, compounded continuously

47. $r = 10\%$, compounded monthly

48. $r = 7\%$, compounded daily

49. *Trust Fund* On the day of your grandchild's birth, you deposited \$25,000 in a trust fund that pays 8.75% interest, compounded continuously. Determine the balance in this account on your grandchild's 25th birthday.

50. *Trust Fund* Suppose you deposit \$5000 in a trust fund that pays 7.5% interest, compounded continuously. In the trust fund, you specify that the balance will be given to the college from which you graduated after the money has earned interest for 50 years. How much will your college receive after 50 years?

51. *Demand Function* The demand equation for a certain product is
$$p = 500 - 0.5e^{0.004x}.$$
Find the price p for a demand of (a) $x = 1000$ units and (b) $x = 1500$ units. Describe the graph of p. What is the domain? What is the range?

52. *Demand Function* The demand equation for a certain product is
$$p = 5000\left(1 - \frac{4}{4 + e^{-0.002x}}\right).$$
Find the price p for a demand of (a) $x = 100$ units and (b) $x = 500$ units. Describe the graph of p. What is the domain? What is the range?

53. *Bacteria Growth* A certain type of bacteria increases according to the model
$$P(t) = 100e^{0.2197t},$$
where t is the time in hours. Find (a) $P(0)$, (b) $P(5)$, and (c) $P(10)$.

54. *Population Growth* The population of a town increases according to the model
$$P(t) = 2500e^{0.0293t},$$
where t is the time in years, with $t = 0$ corresponding to 1990. Use the model to approximate the population in (a) 1995, (b) 2000, and (c) 2010.

55. *Radioactive Decay* Let Q represent the mass of radium (^{226}Ra) whose half-life is 1620 years. The quantity of radium present after t years is given by

$$Q = 25 \left(\tfrac{1}{2}\right)^{t/1620}.$$

(a) Determine the initial quantity (when $t = 0$).

(b) Determine the quantity present after 1000 years.

(c) Use a graphing utility to graph this function over the interval $t = 0$ to $t = 5000$.

56. *Radioactive Decay* Let Q represent the mass of carbon-14 (^{14}C) whose half-life is 5730 years. The quantity of carbon-14 present after t years is given by

$$Q = 10\left(\tfrac{1}{2}\right)^{t/5730}.$$

(a) Determine the initial quantity (when $t = 0$).

(b) Determine the quantity present after 2000 years.

(c) Sketch the graph of this function over the interval $t = 0$ to $t = 10,000$.

57. *Forest Defoliation* To estimate the amount of defoliation caused by the gypsy moth during a given year, a forester counts the number of egg masses on $\tfrac{1}{40}$ of an acre the preceding fall. The percentage of defoliation y is approximated by

$$y = \frac{300}{3 + 17e^{-1.57x}},$$

where x is the number of egg masses in thousands.

(a) Use a graphing utility to graph the function.

(b) Estimate the percentage of defoliation if 2000 egg masses are counted.

(c) Estimate the number of egg masses that existed if you observe that approximately $\tfrac{2}{3}$ of a forest is defoliated. (*Source:* Department of Environmental Resources)

58. *Inflation* If the annual rate of inflation averages 5% over the next 10 years, then the approximate cost C of goods or services during any year in that decade will be given by

$$C(t) = P(1.05)^t,$$

where t is the time in years and P is the present cost. If the price of an oil change for your car is presently $19.95, estimate the price 10 years from now.

59. *Depreciation* After t years, the value of a car that cost $20,000 is given by

$$V(t) = 20,000 \left(\tfrac{3}{4}\right)^t.$$

Graph the function and determine the value of the car 2 years after it was purchased.

60. Given the exponential function $f(x) = a^x$, show that

(a) $f(u + v) = f(u) \cdot f(v)$ (b) $f(2x) = [f(x)]^2$.

5.2 LOGARITHMIC FUNCTIONS AND THEIR GRAPHS

Logarithmic Functions / Graphs of Logarithmic Functions / The Natural Logarithmic Function / Applications

Logarithmic Functions

In Section 1.7, you learned that if a function has the property that no horizontal line intersects its graph more than once, then the function must have an inverse. By looking back at the graphs of the exponential functions introduced in Section 5.1, you will see that every function of the form $f(x) = a^x$ passes the "horizontal line test," and therefore must have an inverse. This inverse function is the **logarithmic function with base a.**

REMARK The equations $y = \log_a x$ and $a^y = x$ are equivalent. The first equation is in logarithmic form and the second is in exponential form.

> **DEFINITION OF LOGARITHMIC FUNCTION**
>
> For $x > 0$ and $0 < a \neq 1$,
>
> $\qquad y = \log_a x$ if and only if $a^y = x$.
>
> The function $f(x) = \log_a x$ is the **logarithmic function with base a.**

When evaluating logarithms, remember that *a logarithm is an exponent.* This means that $\log_a x$ is the exponent to which a must be raised to obtain x. For instance, $\log_2 8 = 3$ because 2 must be raised to the third power to obtain 8.

EXAMPLE 1   Evaluating Logarithms

A. $\log_2 32 = 5$ $\qquad$ because $\quad 2^5 = 32$.
B. $\log_3 27 = 3$ $\qquad$ because $\quad 3^3 = 27$.

C. $\log_4 2 = \dfrac{1}{2}$ $\qquad$ because $\quad 4^{1/2} = \sqrt{4} = 2$.

D. $\log_{10} \dfrac{1}{100} = -2$ because $\quad 10^{-2} = \dfrac{1}{10^2} = \dfrac{1}{100}$.

E. $\log_3 1 = 0$ $\qquad$ because $\quad 3^0 = 1$.
F. $\log_2 2 = 1$ $\qquad$ because $\quad 2^1 = 2$.

The logarithmic function with base 10 is the **common logarithmic function.** On most calculators, this function is denoted by *log*. You can tell whether this key denotes base 10 by evaluating log 10. The display should be 1.

EXAMPLE 2   Evaluating Logarithms on a Calculator

Number	Display	Rounded to 3 Decimal Places
A. $\log_{10} 54$	1.73239376	1.732
B. $2 \log_{10} 2.5$	0.7958800173	0.796
C. $\log_{10}(-2)$	ERROR	

Note that most calculators display an error message when you try to evaluate $\log_{10}(-2)$. The reason for this is that the domain of every logarithmic function is the set of *positive real numbers.*

PROPERTIES OF LOGARITHMS

1. $\log_a 1 = 0$ because 0 is the power to which a must be raised to obtain 1.
2. $\log_a a = 1$ because 1 is the power to which a must be raised to obtain a.
3. $\log_a a^x = x$ because x is the power to which a must be raised to obtain a^x.

Graphs of Logarithmic Functions

To sketch the graph of $y = \log_a x$, you can use the fact that the graphs of inverse functions are reflections of each other in the line $y = x$.

EXAMPLE 3   Graphs of Exponential and Logarithmic Functions

On the same coordinate plane, sketch graphs of the following functions by hand.

A. $f(x) = 2^x$
B. $g(x) = \log_2 x$

SOLUTION

A. For $f(x) = 2^x$, construct a table of values.

x	-2	-1	0	1	2	3
$f(x) = 2^x$	$\frac{1}{4}$	$\frac{1}{2}$	1	2	4	8

By plotting these points and connecting them with a smooth curve, you obtain the graph shown in Figure 5.11.

B. Because $g(x) = \log_2 x$ is the inverse of $f(x) = 2^x$, the graph of g is obtained by reflecting the graph of f in the line $y = x$, as shown in Figure 5.11. This reflection is formed by interchanging the x- and y-coordinates of the points in the above table of values.

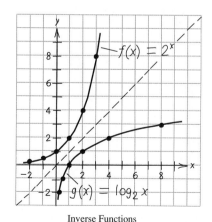

Inverse Functions

FIGURE 5.11

EXAMPLE 4   Sketching the Graph of a Logarithmic Function
··················

Sketch the graph of $f(x) = \log_{10} x$ by hand. Then verify your result with a graphing utility.

SOLUTION

Begin by making a table of values. Note that some of the values can be obtained without a calculator, whereas others require a calculator. Plot the corresponding points and sketch the graph in Figure 5.12.

FIGURE 5.12

	Without a calculator				With a calculator		
x	$\frac{1}{100}$	$\frac{1}{10}$	1	10	2	5	8
$\log_{10} x$	-2	-1	0	1	0.301	0.699	0.903

Compare this graph with that obtained with a graphing utility, and note that the domain and range are $(0, \infty)$ and $(-\infty, \infty)$, respectively.   ·········

The graph in Figure 5.12 is typical of functions of the form $f(x) = \log_a x$, where $a > 1$. They have one x-intercept, $(1, 0)$, and one vertical asymptote, $x = 0$. Notice how slowly the graph rises for $x > 1$. In Figure 5.12 you would need to move out to $x = 1000$ before the graph would rise to $y = 3$. The basic characteristics of logarithmic graphs are summarized in Figure 5.13.

In Example 5, the graph of $\log_a x$ is used to sketch the graphs of functions of the form $y = b \pm \log_a(x + c)$. The function $f(x) = \log_a(bx + c)$ has a domain that consists of all x such that $bx + c > 0$. The vertical asymptote occurs when $bx + c = 0$, and the x-intercept occurs when $bx + c = 1$.

REMARK In Figure 5.13, note that the vertical asymptote occurs at $x = 0$, where $\log_a x$ is *undefined*. As x gets close to 0, the value of $\log_a x$ approaches negative infinity.

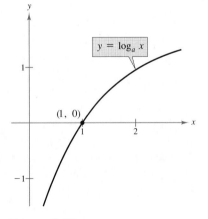

Graph of $y = \log_a x,\ a > 1$
- Domain: $(0, \infty)$
- Range: $(-\infty, \infty)$
- Intercept: $(1, 0)$
- Increasing
- y-axis is a vertical asymptote
  ($\log_a x \to -\infty$ as $x \to 0^+$)
- Continuous
- Reflection of graph of $y = a^x$ about the line $y = x$

FIGURE 5.13

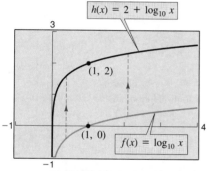

(a) Right shift of 1 unit
Vertical asymptote is $x = 1$.

(b) Upward shift of 2 units
Vertical asymptote remains $x = 0$.

FIGURE 5.14

EXAMPLE 5   Sketching the Graphs of Logarithmic Functions

Compare the graphs of the following functions with the graph of $f(x) = \log_{10} x$.

A. $g(x) = \log_{10}(x - 1)$ **B.** $h(x) = 2 + \log_{10} x$

SOLUTION

The graph of each of these functions is similar to the graph of $f(x) = \log_{10} x$, as shown in Figure 5.14.

A. Because $g(x) = \log_{10}(x - 1) = f(x - 1)$, the graph of g can be obtained by shifting the graph of f one unit to the right.

B. Because $h(x) = 2 + \log_{10} x = 2 + f(x)$, the graph of h can be obtained by shifting the graph of f two units up.

The Natural Logarithmic Function

As with exponential functions, the most widely used base for logarithmic functions is the number e. The logarithmic function with base e is called the **natural logarithmic function.** It is denoted by the symbol $\ln x$, read as "el en of x."

THE NATURAL LOGARITHMIC FUNCTION

The function defined by

$$f(x) = \log_e x = \ln x, \qquad x > 0$$

is called the **natural logarithmic function.**

The three properties of logarithms listed earlier in this section are also valid for natural logarithms.

PROPERTIES OF NATURAL LOGARITHMS

1. $\ln 1 = 0$ because 0 is the power to which e must be raised to obtain 1.
2. $\ln e = 1$ because 1 is the power to which e must be raised to obtain e.
3. $\ln e^x = x$ because x is the power to which e must be raised to obtain e^x.

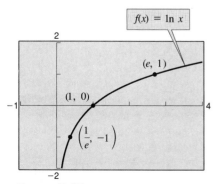

FIGURE 5.15

The graph of the natural logarithmic function is shown in Figure 5.15.

EXAMPLE 6 Evaluating the Natural Logarithmic Function

A. $\ln \dfrac{1}{e} = \ln e^{-1} = -1$ *Property 3*

B. $\ln e^2 = 2$ *Property 3*

On most calculators, the natural logarithm is denoted by *ln*. Try using your calculator to evaluate the natural logarithmic expressions shown in the next example.

EXAMPLE 7 Evaluating the Natural Logarithmic Function

Number	Display	Rounded to 3 Decimal Places
A. $\ln 2$	0.6931471806	0.693
B. $\ln 0.3$	−1.203972804	−1.204
C. $\ln e$	1	1.000
D. $\ln(-1)$	ERROR	

Be sure you see that $\ln(-1)$ gives an error. This occurs because the domain of $\ln x$ is the set of positive real numbers. (See Figure 5.15.) Hence, $\ln(-1)$ is undefined.

EXAMPLE 8 Finding the Domains of Logarithmic Functions

Find the domains and ranges of the following functions.

A. $f(x) = \ln(x - 2)$
B. $g(x) = \ln(2 - x)$
C. $h(x) = \ln x^2$

Then use a graphing utility to graph each function.

SOLUTION

A. Because $\ln(x - 2)$ is defined only if $x - 2 > 0$, it follows that the domain of f is $(2, \infty)$.
B. Because $\ln(2 - x)$ is defined only if $2 - x > 0$, it follows that the domain of g is $(-\infty, 2)$. The graph of g is shown in Figure 5.16.
C. Because $\ln x^2$ is defined only if $x^2 > 0$, it follows that the domain of h is all real numbers except $x = 0$. Note that $\ln x^2$ means $\ln(x^2)$.

REMARK Note how the graphing utility confirms that the domains are correct.

(a)

(b)

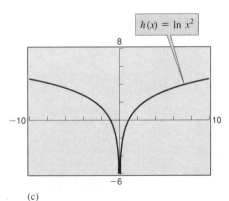

(c)

FIGURE 5.16

Applications

EXAMPLE 9   Human Memory Model

Students participating in a psychological experiment attended several lectures on a subject. Every month for a year after that, the students were tested to see how much of the material they remembered. The average scores for the group were given by the *human memory model*

$$f(t) = 75 - 6 \ln(t + 1), \qquad 0 \le t \le 12,$$

where t is the time in months.

A. What was the average score on the original ($t = 0$) exam?
B. What was the average score at the end of $t = 2$ months?
C. What was the average score at the end of $t = 6$ months?
D. Choose an appropriate viewing rectangle and sketch the graph of f.

SOLUTION

A. The original average score was

$$f(0) = 75 - 6 \ln(0 + 1) = 75 - 6(0) = 75.$$

B. After 2 months, the average score was

$$f(2) = 75 - 6 \ln 3 \approx 75 - 6(1.0986) \approx 68.4.$$

C. After 6 months, the average score was

$$f(6) = 75 - 6 \ln 7 \approx 75 - 6(1.9459) \approx 63.3.$$

D. The graph of f is shown in Figure 5.17.

FIGURE 5.17

DISCUSSION PROBLEM

....

THE GRAPH OF A LOGARITHMIC FUNCTION

Because the range of the logarithmic function $f(x) = \log_a x$ is $(-\infty, \infty)$, you can make the value of $\log_a x$ as large as you want. Can you find values of x that satisfy the following equations?

(a) $\log_{10} x = 10$ (b) $\log_{10} x = 1000$ (c) $\log_{10} x = 10,000,000$

WARM-UP

....

The following warm-up exercises involve skills that were covered in earlier sections. You will use these skills in the exercise set for this section.

In Exercises 1–4, solve for x.

1. $2^x = 8$ **2.** $4^x = 1$
3. $10^x = 0.1$ **4.** $e^x = e$

In Exercises 5 and 6, evaluate the expression. (Round your result to three decimal places.)

5. e^2 **6.** e^{-1}

In Exercises 7–10, describe how the graph of g is related to the graph of f.

7. $g(x) = f(x + 2)$ **8.** $g(x) = -f(x)$
9. $g(x) = -1 + f(x)$ **10.** $g(x) = f(-x)$

SECTION 5.2 · EXERCISES
....

In Exercises 1–12, evaluate the expression without using a calculator.

1. $\log_2 16$ **2.** $\log_2 \frac{1}{8}$
3. $\log_{16} 4$ **4.** $\log_{27} 9$
5. $\log_7 1$ **6.** $\log_{10} 1000$
7. $\log_{10} 0.01$ **8.** $\log_{10} 10$
9. $\ln e^3$ **10.** $\ln 1$
11. $\log_a a^2$ **12.** $\log_a \frac{1}{a}$

In Exercises 13–20, use the definition of a logarithm to rewrite the exponential equation as a logarithmic equation. For instance, the logarithmic form of $2^3 = 8$ is $\log_2 8 = 3$.

13. $5^3 = 125$ **14.** $8^2 = 64$
15. $81^{1/4} = 3$ **16.** $9^{3/2} = 27$
17. $6^{-2} = \frac{1}{36}$ **18.** $10^{-3} = 0.001$
19. $e^3 = 20.0855 \ldots$ **20.** $e^0 = 1$

In Exercises 21–26, use a calculator to evaluate the logarithm. (Round your result to three decimal places.)

21. $\log_{10} 345$

22. $\log_{10}(\frac{4}{5})$

23. $\log_{10} 0.48$

24. $\log_{10} 12.5$

25. $\ln 18.42$

26. $\ln\left(\sqrt{5} - 2\right)$

In Exercises 27–30, graph f and g on the same coordinate plane to demonstrate that one is the inverse of the other.

27. $f(x) = 3^x$, $g(x) = \log_3 x$

28. $f(x) = 5^x$, $g(x) = \log_5 x$

29. $f(x) = e^x$, $g(x) = \ln x$

30. $f(x) = 10^x$, $g(x) = \log_{10} x$

In Exercises 31–36, use the graph of $y = \ln x$ to match the function with its graph, and describe the given viewing rectangle. [The graphs are labeled, (a), (b), (c), (d), (e), and (f).]

31. $f(x) = \ln x + 2$

32. $f(x) = -\ln x$

33. $f(x) = -\ln(x + 2)$

34. $f(x) = \ln(x - 1)$

35. $f(x) = \ln(1 - x)$

36. $f(x) = -\ln(-x)$

(a)

(b)

(c)

(d)

(e)

(f)

In Exercises 37–42, find the domain, vertical asymptote, and x-intercept of the logarithmic function, and sketch its graph.

37. $f(x) = \log_4 x$

38. $f(x) = -\log_6(x + 2)$

39. $y = -\log_3(x + 2)$

40. $y = \log_{10}\left(\dfrac{x}{5}\right)$

41. $f(x) = \ln(x - 2)$

42. $g(x) = \ln(-x)$

In Exercises 43 and 44, use a graphing utility to graph the function. Use the graph to determine the intervals in which the function is increasing and decreasing and approximate any relative maximum or minimum values of the function.

43. $f(x) = \dfrac{x}{2} - \ln\dfrac{x}{4}$

44. $g(x) = \dfrac{12 \ln x}{x}$

45. Use a graphing utility to graph f and g on the same screen. Then determine which is increasing at the greater rate for "large" values of x. What can you conclude about the rate of growth of the natural logarithmic function?

(a) $f(x) = \ln x$, $g(x) = \sqrt{x}$

(b) $f(x) = \ln x$, $g(x) = \sqrt[4]{x}$

46. The table of values was obtained by evaluating a function. Determine which of the statements may be true and which must be false.

x	1	2	8
y	0	1	3

(a) y is an exponential function of x.

(b) y is a logarithmic function of x.

(c) x is an exponential function of y.

(d) y is linear function of x.

47. *Human Memory Model*   Students in a mathematics class were given an exam and then tested monthly with an equivalent exam. The average score for the class was given by the human memory model

$$f(t) = 80 - 17 \log_{10}(t + 1), \qquad 0 \le t \le 12,$$

where t is the time in months.

(a) What was the average score on the original exam ($t = 0$)?

(b) What was the average score after 4 months?

(c) What was the average score after 10 months?

48. *Population Growth* The population of a town will double in

$$t = \frac{10 \ln 2}{\ln 67 - \ln 50} \text{ years.}$$

Find t.

49. *World Population Growth* The time in years required for the world population to double if it is increasing at a continuous rate of r is given by

$$t = \frac{\ln 2}{r}.$$

Complete the table.

r	0.005	0.010	0.015	0.020	0.025	0.030
t						

50. *Investment Time* A principal P, invested at $9\frac{1}{2}\%$ and compounded continuously, increases to an amount K times the original principal after t years, where t is given by

$$t = \frac{\ln K}{0.095}.$$

(a) Complete the table.

K	1	2	4	6	8	10	12
t							

(b) Use a graphing utility to graph this function.

Ventilation Rates In Exercises 51 and 52, use the model

$$y = 80.4 - 11 \ln x, \qquad 100 \le x \le 1500,$$

which approximates the minimum required ventilation rate in terms of the air space per child in a public school classroom. In the model, x is the air space per child in cubic feet and y is the ventilation rate in cubic feet per minute.

51. Use a graphing utility to graph the function and approximate the required ventilation rate if there are 300 cubic feet of air space per child.

52. A classroom is designed for 30 students. The air-conditioning system in the room has the capacity of moving 450 cubic feet of air per minute.
(a) Determine the ventilation rate per child assuming the room is filled to capacity.
(b) Use the graph from Exercise 51 to estimate the air space required per child.
(c) Determine the minimum number of square feet of floor space required for the room if the ceiling height is 30 feet.

Monthly Payment In Exercises 53–56, use the model

$$t = \frac{5.315}{-6.7968 + \ln x}, \qquad 1000 < x,$$

which approximates the length of a home mortgage of $120,000 at 10% in terms of the monthly payment. In the model, t is the length of the mortgage in years and x is the monthly payment in dollars (see figure).

FIGURE FOR 53–56

53. Use the model to approximate the length of a home mortgage (for $120,000 at 10%) that has a monthly payment of $1167.41.

54. Use the model to approximate the length of a home mortgage (for $120,000 at 10%) that has a monthly payment of $1068.45.

55. Approximate the total amount paid over the term of a mortgage with a monthly payment of $1167.41.

56. Approximate the total amount paid over the term of a mortgage with a monthly payment of $1068.45.

57. *Work* The work (in foot-pounds) done in compressing an initial volume of 9 cubic feet at a pressure of 15 pounds per square inch to a volume of 3 cubic feet is

$$W = 19{,}440(\ln 9 - \ln 3).$$

Find W.

58. *Sound Intensity*   The relationship between the number of decibels β and the intensity of a sound I in watts per square meter is given by

$$\beta = 10 \log_{10}\left(\frac{I}{10^{-16}}\right).$$

Determine the number of decibels of a sound with an intensity of 10^{-4} watts per square meter.

59. (a) Use a calculator to complete the table for the function

$$f(x) = \frac{\ln x}{x}.$$

x	1	5	10	10^2	10^4	10^6
$f(x)$						

(b) Use the table in part (a) to determine what $f(x)$ approaches as x increases without bound.

(c) Use a graphing utility to confirm the result of part (b).

60. Answer the following for the function $f(x) = \log_{10} x$. Do not use a calculator.
   (a) What is the domain of f?
   (b) Find f^{-1}.
   (c) If x is a real number between 1000 and 10,000, determine the interval in which $f(x)$ will be found.
   (d) Determine the interval in which x will be found if $f(x)$ is negative.
   (e) If $f(x)$ is increased by one unit, then x must have been increased by what factor?
   (f) If $f(x_1) = 3n$ and $f(x_2) = n$, find the ratio of x_1 to x_2.

61. Use a graphing utility to determine whether $y = 2 \ln x$ and $y = \ln x^2$ are identical. Explain your reasoning.

5.3   PROPERTIES OF LOGARITHMS
....

**Change of Base / Properties of Logarithms /
Rewriting Logarithmic Expressions**

▬▬▬

Change of Base

Most calculators have only two types of "log keys," one for common logarithms (base 10) and one for natural logarithms (base e). Although common logs and natural logs are the most frequently used, you may occasionally need to evaluate logarithms to other bases. To do this, the following *change of base formula* is useful. (This formula is derived in Example 9 in Section 5.4.)

REMARK   One way to look at the change of base formula is that logarithms to base a are simply *constant multiples* of logarithms to base b. The constant multiplier is $1/(\log_b a)$.

CHANGE OF BASE FORMULA

Let a, b, and x be positive real numbers such that $a \neq 1$ and $b \neq 1$. Then $\log_a x$ is given by

$$\log_a x = \frac{\log_b x}{\log_b a}.$$

EXAMPLE 1 Changing Bases
....

Use *common logarithms* to evaluate the following.

A. $\log_4 30$ **B.** $\log_2 14$

SOLUTION

A. Using the change of base formula with $a = 4$, $b = 10$, and $x = 30$, convert to common logarithms and obtain

$$\log_4 30 = \frac{\log_{10} 30}{\log_{10} 4} \approx \frac{1.47712}{0.60206} \approx 2.4534.$$

B. Using the change of base formula with $a = 2$, $b = 10$, and $x = 14$, convert to common logarithms and obtain

$$\log_2 14 = \frac{\log_{10} 14}{\log_{10} 2} \approx \frac{1.14613}{0.30103} \approx 3.8074.$$

EXAMPLE 2 Changing Bases
....

Use *natural logarithms* to evaluate the following.

A. $\log_4 30$ **B.** $\log_2 14$

SOLUTION

A. Using the change of base formula with $a = 4$, $b = e$, and $x = 30$, convert to natural logarithms and obtain

$$\log_4 30 = \frac{\ln 30}{\ln 4} \approx \frac{3.40120}{1.38629} \approx 2.4534.$$

B. Using the change of base formula with $a = 2$, $b = e$, and $x = 14$, convert to natural logarithms and obtain

$$\log_2 14 = \frac{\ln 14}{\ln 2} \approx \frac{2.63906}{0.693147} \approx 3.8074.$$

Note that the results agree with those obtained in Example 1, using common logarithms.

DISCOVERY

Use a graphing utility to graph $y = \log_a x$ and $y = (\ln x)/(\ln a)$ with $a = 2, 3,$ and 5 on the same viewing rectangle. (Use a viewing rectangle in which $0 \le x \le 10$ and $-4 \le y \le 4$.) On the interval $(0, 1)$, which graph is on top? Which is on the bottom? On the interval $(1, \infty)$, which graph is on top? Which is on the bottom?

Properties of Logarithms

You know from the previous section that the logarithmic function with base a is the *inverse* of the exponential function with base a. Thus, it makes sense that the properties of exponents should have corresponding properties involving logarithms. For instance, the exponential property $a^0 = 1$ corresponds to the logarithmic property $\log_a 1 = 0$.

In this section you will learn how to use the logarithmic properties that correspond to the following three exponential properties.

1. $a^n a^m = a^{n+m}$

2. $\dfrac{a^n}{a^m} = a^{n-m}$

3. $(a^n)^m = a^{nm}$

PROPERTIES OF LOGARITHMS

Let a be a positive number such that $a \neq 1$, and let n be a real number. If u and v are positive real numbers, then the following properties are true.

Base a Logarithm	*Natural Logarithm*
1. $\log_a(uv) = \log_a u + \log_a v$	1. $\ln(uv) = \ln u + \ln v$
2. $\log_a \dfrac{u}{v} = \log_a u - \log_a v$	2. $\ln \dfrac{u}{v} = \ln u - \ln v$
3. $\log_a u^n = n \log_a u$	3. $\ln u^n = n \ln u$

PROOF

We give a proof of Property 1 and leave the other two proofs for you. To prove Property 1, let

$$x = \log_a u \quad \text{and} \quad y = \log_a v.$$

The corresponding exponential forms of these two equations are

$$a^x = u \quad \text{and} \quad a^y = v.$$

Multiplying u and v produces $uv = a^x a^y = a^{x+y}$. The corresponding logarithmic form of $uv = a^{x+y}$ is

$$\log_a(uv) = x + y.$$

Hence, $\log_a(uv) = \log_a u + \log_a v.$

REMARK   There is no general property that can be used to rewrite $\log_a(u \pm v)$. Specifically,

$$\log_a(x + y) \quad \text{DOES NOT EQUAL} \quad \log_a x + \log_a y.$$

EXAMPLE 3   Using Properties of Logarithms

Given $\ln 2 \approx 0.693$, $\ln 3 \approx 1.099$, and $\ln 7 \approx 1.946$, use the properties of logarithms to approximate the following. Then use a calculator to verify the result.

A. $\ln 6$

B. $\ln \dfrac{7}{27}$

SOLUTION

A. $\ln 6 = \ln(2 \cdot 3)$

$\qquad = \ln 2 + \ln 3$ *Property 1*

$\qquad \approx 0.693 + 1.099$

$\qquad = 1.792$

B. $\ln \dfrac{7}{27} = \ln 7 - \ln 27$ *Property 2*

$\qquad = \ln 7 - \ln 3^3$

$\qquad = \ln 7 - 3 \ln 3$ *Property 3*

$\qquad \approx 1.946 - 3(1.099)$

$\qquad = -1.351$

EXAMPLE 4   Using Properties of Logarithms

Use the properties of logarithms to verify that

$$-\ln \frac{1}{2} = \ln 2.$$

SOLUTION

$$-\ln \frac{1}{2} = -\ln(2^{-1}) = -(-1)\ln 2 = \ln 2$$

Try verifying this result on your calculator.

Rewriting Logarithmic Expressions

The properties of logarithms are useful for rewriting logarithmic expressions in forms that simplify the operations of algebra. This is true because they convert complicated products, quotients, and exponential forms into simpler sums, differences, and products, respectively.

EXAMPLE 5   Rewriting the Logarithm of a Product

Use the properties of logarithms to rewrite

$$\log_{10} 5x^3 y$$

as the sum of logarithms.

SOLUTION

$$
\begin{aligned}
\log_{10} 5x^3 y &= \log_{10} 5 + \log_{10} x^3 y && \textit{Property 1}\\
&= \log_{10} 5 + \log_{10} x^3 + \log_{10} y && \textit{Property 1}\\
&= \log_{10} 5 + 3 \log_{10} x + \log_{10} y && \textit{Property 3}
\end{aligned}
$$

EXAMPLE 6   Rewriting the Logarithm of a Quotient

Use the properties of logarithms to rewrite

$$\ln \frac{\sqrt{3x - 5}}{7}$$

as the sum and/or difference of logarithms.

SOLUTION

$$
\ln \frac{\sqrt{3x - 5}}{7} = \ln(3x - 5)^{1/2} - \ln 7 \qquad \textit{Property 2}
$$

$$
= \frac{1}{2} \ln(3x - 5) - \ln 7 \qquad \textit{Property 3}
$$

Examples 5 and 6 use the properties of logarithms to *expand* logarithmic expressions. Examples 7 and 8 reverse the procedure by using properties of logarithms to *condense* logarithmic expressions.

EXAMPLE 7   Condensing a Logarithmic Expression

Rewrite the following expression as the logarithm of a single quantity.

$$\frac{1}{2} \log_{10} x - 3 \log_{10}(x + 1)$$

SOLUTION

$$
\frac{1}{2} \log_{10} x - 3 \log_{10}(x + 1) = \log_{10} x^{1/2} - \log_{10}(x + 1)^3
$$

$$
= \log_{10} \frac{\sqrt{x}}{(x + 1)^3}
$$

EXAMPLE 8   Condensing a Logarithmic Expression

Rewrite the following expression as the logarithm of a single quantity.

$$2 \ln(x + 2) - \ln x$$

SOLUTION

$$2 \ln(x + 2) - \ln x = \ln(x + 2)^2 - \ln x$$

$$= \ln \frac{(x + 2)^2}{x}$$

When expanding or condensing logarithmic expressions, you should compare the domain of the original expression with the domain of the expanded or condensed expression. For instance, the domain of $\ln x^2$ is all nonzero real numbers, whereas the domain of $2 \ln x$ is all positive real numbers.

DISCUSSION PROBLEM

DEMONSTRATING PROPERTIES OF LOGARITHMS

Use a calculator to demonstrate that

$$\frac{\ln x}{\ln y} \neq \ln \frac{x}{y} = \ln x - \ln y$$

by completing the table.

x	y	$\dfrac{\ln x}{\ln y}$	$\ln \dfrac{x}{y}$	$\ln x - \ln y$
1	2			
3	4			
10	5			
4	0.5			

WARM-UP

The following warm-up exercises involve skills that were covered in earlier sections. You will use these skills in the exercise set for this section.

In Exercises 1–4, evaluate the expression without using a calculator.

1. $\log_7 49$ **2.** $\log_2(\frac{1}{32})$ **3.** $\ln \dfrac{1}{e^2}$ **4.** $\log_{10} 0.001$

In Exercises 5–8, simplify the expression.

5. $e^2 e^3$ **6.** $\dfrac{e^2}{e^3}$ **7.** $(e^2)^3$ **8.** $(e^2)^0$

In Exercises 9 and 10, rewrite the expression in exponential form.

9. $\dfrac{1}{x^2}$ **10.** $\sqrt{x}$

SECTION 5.3 · EXERCISES

In Exercises 1–4, use the change of base formula to write the logarithm as a quotient of common logarithms. For instance, $\log_2 3 = (\log_{10} 3)/(\log_{10} 2)$.

1. $\log_3 5$ **2.** $\log_4 10$ **3.** $\log_2 x$ **4.** $\ln 5$

In Exercises 5–8, use the change of base formula to write the logarithm as a quotient of natural logarithms. For instance, $\log_2 3 = (\ln 3)/(\ln 2)$.

5. $\log_3 5$ **6.** $\log_4 10$ **7.** $\log_2 x$ **8.** $\log_{10} 5$

In Exercises 9–16, evaluate the logarithm using the change of base formula. Do the problem twice, once with common logarithms and once with natural logarithms. Round your result to three decimal places.

9. $\log_3 7$ **10.** $\log_7 4$

11. $\log_{1/2} 4$ **12.** $\log_4 0.55$

13. $\log_9 0.4$ **14.** $\log_{20} 125$

15. $\log_{15} 1250$ **16.** $\log_{1/3} 0.015$

In Exercises 17–36, use the properties of logarithms to write the expression as a sum, difference, and/or constant multiple of logarithms.

17. $\log_{10} 5x$ **18.** $\log_{10} 10z$

19. $\log_{10} \dfrac{5}{x}$ **20.** $\log_{10} \dfrac{y}{2}$

21. $\log_8 x^4$ **22.** $\log_6 z^{-3}$

23. $\ln \sqrt{z}$ **24.** $\ln \sqrt[3]{t}$

25. $\ln xyz$ **26.** $\ln \dfrac{xy}{z}$

27. $\ln \sqrt{a-1}$ **28.** $\ln\left(\dfrac{x^2-1}{x^3}\right)$

29. $\ln z(z-1)^2$ **30.** $\ln \sqrt{\dfrac{x^2}{y^3}}$

31. $\ln \sqrt[3]{\dfrac{x}{y}}$ **32.** $\ln \dfrac{x}{\sqrt{x^2+1}}$

33. $\ln \dfrac{x^4 \sqrt{y}}{z^5}$ **34.** $\ln \sqrt{x^2(x+2)}$

35. $\log_b \dfrac{x^2}{y^2 z^3}$ **36.** $\log_b \dfrac{\sqrt{xy^4}}{z^4}$

In Exercises 37–56, write the expression as the logarithm of a single quantity.

37. $\ln x + \ln 2$

38. $\ln y + \ln z$

39. $\log_4 z - \log_4 y$

40. $\log_5 8 - \log_5 t$

41. $2 \log_2(x + 4)$

42. $-4 \log_6 2x$

43. $\frac{1}{3} \log_3 5x$

44. $\frac{3}{2} \log_7(z - 2)$

45. $\ln x - 3 \ln(x + 1)$

46. $2 \ln 8 + 5 \ln z$

47. $\ln(x - 2) - \ln(x + 2)$

48. $3 \ln x + 2 \ln y - 4 \ln z$

49. $\ln x - 2[\ln(x + 2) + \ln(x - 2)]$

50. $4[\ln z + \ln(z + 5)] - 2 \ln(z - 5)$

51. $\frac{1}{3}[2 \ln(x + 3) + \ln x - \ln(x^2 - 1)]$

52. $2[\ln x - \ln(x + 1) - \ln(x - 1)]$

53. $\frac{1}{3}[\ln y + 2 \ln(y + 4)] - \ln(y - 1)$

54. $\frac{1}{2}[\ln(x + 1) + 2 \ln(x - 1)] + 3 \ln x$

55. $2 \ln 3 - \frac{1}{2} \ln(x^2 + 1)$

56. $\frac{3}{2} \ln 5t^6 - \frac{3}{4} \ln t^4$

In Exercises 57–66, approximate the logarithm using the properties of logarithms, given $\log_b 2 \approx 0.3562$, $\log_b 3 \approx 0.5646$, and $\log_b 5 \approx 0.8271$.

57. $\log_b 6$

58. $\log_b\left(\frac{5}{3}\right)$

59. $\log_b 40$ $(40 = 2^3 \cdot 5)$

60. $\log_b 18$

61. $\log_b \dfrac{\sqrt{2}}{2}$

62. $\log_b \sqrt[3]{75}$

63. $\log_b \sqrt{5b}$

64. $\log_b (3b^2)$

65. $\log_b \dfrac{(4.5)^3}{\sqrt{3}}$

66. $\log_b 1$

In Exercises 67–72, find the exact value of the logarithm.

67. $\log_3 9$

68. $\log_6 \sqrt[3]{6}$

69. $\log_4 16^{1.2}$

70. $\log_5\left(\frac{1}{125}\right)$

71. $\ln e^{4.5}$

72. $\ln \sqrt[4]{e^3}$

In Exercises 73–80, use the properties of logarithms to simplify the logarithmic expression.

73. $\log_4 8$

74. $\log_5\left(\frac{1}{15}\right)$

75. $\log_7 \sqrt{70}$

76. $\log_2(4^2 \cdot 3^4)$

77. $\log_5\left(\frac{1}{250}\right)$

78. $\log_{10}\left(\frac{9}{300}\right)$

79. $\ln(5e^6)$

80. $\ln \dfrac{6}{e^2}$

81. *Sound Intensity* The relationship between the number of decibels β and the intensity of a sound I in watts per square meter is given by

$$\beta = 10 \log_{10}\left(\frac{I}{10^{-16}}\right).$$

Use properties of logarithms to write the formula in simpler form, and determine the number of decibels of a sound with an intensity of 10^{-10} watts per square meter.

82. Approximate the natural logarithms of as many integers as possible between 1 and 20 given that $\ln 2 \approx 0.6931$, $\ln 3 \approx 1.0986$, and $\ln 5 \approx 1.6094$.

83. Use a graphing utility to graph

$$f(x) = \ln \frac{x}{2}, \qquad g(x) = \frac{\ln x}{\ln 2}, \qquad h(x) = \ln x - \ln 2$$

in the same viewing rectangle. Which two functions have identical graphs?

84. Prove that $\log_b \dfrac{u}{v} = \log_b u - \log_b v$.

85. Prove that $\log_b u^n = n \log_b u$.

5.4   SOLVING EXPONENTIAL AND LOGARITHMIC EQUATIONS

Introduction / Solving Exponential Equations / Solving Logarithmic Equations / Approximating Solutions / Applications

Introduction

So far in this chapter, you have studied the definitions, graphs, and properties of exponential and logarithmic functions. In this section, you will study procedures for *solving equations* involving these exponential and logarithmic functions. As a simple example, consider the exponential equation $2^x = 32$. You can solve this equation by rewriting it as $2^x = 2^5$, which implies that $x = 5$. Although this method works in some cases, it does not work for an equation as simple as $e^x = 7$. To solve for x in this case, you can take the natural logarithm of both sides to obtain

$e^x = 7$	*Original equation*
$\ln e^x = \ln 7$	*Take ln of both sides*
$x = \ln 7.$	*Solution*

GUIDELINES FOR SOLVING EXPONENTIAL AND LOGARITHMIC EQUATIONS

1. *To solve an exponential equation,* first isolate the exponential expression, then take the logarithm of both sides and solve for the variable.
2. *To solve a logarithmic equation,* rewrite the equation in exponential form and solve for the variable.

Note that these two guidelines are based on the **inverse properties** of exponential and logarithmic functions.

Base a	Base e
1. $\log_a a^x = x$	$\ln e^x = x$
2. $a^{\log_a x} = x$	$e^{\ln x} = x$

Solving Exponential Equations

EXAMPLE 1   Solving an Exponential Equation

$e^x = 72$	*Original equation*
$\ln e^x = \ln 72$	*Take ln of both sides*
$x = \ln 72$	*Inverse property of logs and exponents*
$x \approx 4.277$	

The solution is $x = \ln 72$. Check this solution in the original equation.

EXAMPLE 2   Solving an Exponential Equation

Solve $e^x + 5 = 60$.

SOLUTION

$e^x + 5 = 60$	*Original equation*
$e^x = 55$	*Subtract 5 from both sides*
$\ln e^x = \ln 55$	*Take ln of both sides*
$x = \ln 55$	*Inverse property of logs and exponents*
$x \approx 4.007$	

The solution is $x = \ln 55$. Check this solution in the original equation. The graph of $y = e^x - 55$ is shown in Figure 5.18. Use the zoom feature of your graphing utility to find the x-intercept and thus confirm the solution.

FIGURE 5.18

EXAMPLE 3   Solving an Exponential Equation

$4e^{2x} = 5$	*Original equation*
$e^{2x} = \dfrac{5}{4}$	*Divide both sides by 4*
$\ln e^{2x} = \ln \dfrac{5}{4}$	*Take ln of both sides*
$2x = \ln \dfrac{5}{4}$	*Inverse property of logs and exponents*
$x = \dfrac{1}{2} \ln \dfrac{5}{4}$	*Divide both sides by 2*
$x \approx 0.112$	

The solution is $x = \frac{1}{2} \ln \frac{5}{4}$. Check this solution in the original equation. The graph of $y = 4e^{2x} - 5$, shown in Figure 5.19, helps to confirm this solution.

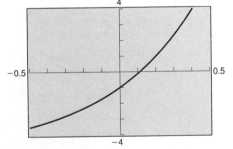

FIGURE 5.19

When an equation involves two or more exponential expressions, you can still use a procedure similar to that demonstrated in the first three examples. However, the algebra is a bit more complicated and a graphical approach is often easier. Study the next example carefully.

EXAMPLE 4   Solving an Exponential Equation

Solve for x in the equation $e^{2x} - 3e^x + 2 = 0$.

SOLUTION

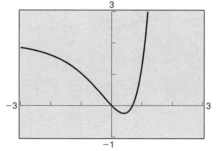

FIGURE 5.20

The graph of the function $f(x) = e^{2x} - 3e^x + 2$ in Figure 5.20 indicates that there are two solutions: one near $x = 0$ and one near $x = 0.7$. You can verify that $x = 0$ is indeed a solution by noting that $f(0) = e^{2(0)} - 3e^0 + 2 = 1 - 3 + 2 = 0$. Similarly, you can use the zoom and trace features to determine that $x \approx 0.693$. You can also solve this problem algebraically.

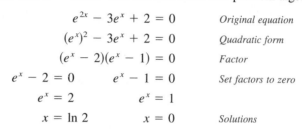

$e^{2x} - 3e^x + 2 = 0$	*Original equation*
$(e^x)^2 - 3e^x + 2 = 0$	*Quadratic form*
$(e^x - 2)(e^x - 1) = 0$	*Factor*
$e^x - 2 = 0 \qquad e^x - 1 = 0$	*Set factors to zero*
$e^x = 2 \qquad\qquad e^x = 1$	
$x = \ln 2 \qquad\quad x = 0$	*Solutions*

The equation has two solutions: $x = \ln 2 \approx 0.693$ and $x = 0$, which confirms the graphical analysis.

Examples 1 through 4 all deal with exponential equations in which the base is e. The same approach can be used to solve exponential equations involving other bases, as shown in Example 5.

EXAMPLE 5   A Base Other Than e

Solve $2^x = 10$.

SOLUTION

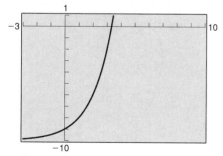

FIGURE 5.21

$2^x = 10$	*Original equation*
$\ln 2^x = \ln 10$	*Take log of both sides*
$x \ln 2 = \ln 10$	*Property of logarithms*
$x = \dfrac{\ln 10}{\ln 2}$	*Divide both sides by ln 2*

The equation has one solution: $x = \ln 10 / \ln 2 \approx 3.32$. Check this solution in the original equation. The graph of $y = 2^x - 10$, shown in Figure 5.21, helps to confirm this solution. (*Note:* Using the change of base formula, the solution could be written as $x = \log_2 10$.)

Solving Logarithmic Equations

To solve a logarithmic equation such as $\ln x = 3$, you can write the equation in exponential form as follows.

$\ln x = 3$	*Logarithmic form*
$e^{\ln x} = e^3$	*Exponentiate both sides*
$x = e^3$	*Exponential form*

This procedure is called *exponentiating* both sides of an equation. It is applied after isolating the logarithmic expression.

EXAMPLE 6   Solving a Logarithmic Equation

Solve $5 + 2 \ln x = 4$.

SOLUTION

$5 + 2 \ln x = 4$	*Original equation*
$2 \ln x = -1$	*Subtract 5 from both sides*
$\ln x = -\dfrac{1}{2}$	*Divide both sides by 2*
$e^{\ln x} = e^{-1/2}$	*Exponentiate both sides*
$x = e^{-1/2}$	*Inverse property of exponents and logs*
$x \approx 0.607$	

The equation has one solution: $x = e^{-1/2}$. Check this solution in the original equation. The graph of $y = 1 + 2 \ln x$, shown in Figure 5.22, helps to confirm this solution.

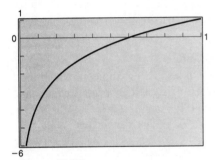

FIGURE 5.22

EXAMPLE 7   Solving a Logarithmic Equation

Solve $2 \ln 3x = 4$.

SOLUTION

$2 \ln 3x = 4$	*Original equation*
$\ln 3x = 2$	*Divide both sides by 2*
$e^{\ln 3x} = e^2$	*Exponentiate both sides*
$3x = e^2$	*Inverse property of exponents and logs*
$x = \dfrac{1}{3}e^2$	*Divide both sides by 3*
$x \approx 2.463$	

The equation has one solution: $x = \frac{1}{3}e^2$. Check this solution in the original equation. The graph of $y = -4 + 2 \ln 3x$, shown in Figure 5.23, helps to confirm this solution.

FIGURE 5.23

Complicated equations involving logarithmic expressions can be solved using a graphing utility, as demonstrated in Example 8.

EXAMPLE 8   Solving a Logarithmic Equation

Solve for x in the equation $\ln(x - 2) + \ln(2x - 3) = 2 \ln x$.

SOLUTION

The graph of the function $f(x) = \ln(x - 2) + \ln(2x - 3) - 2 \ln x$, shown in Figure 5.24, indicates that the only zero is $x = 6$. This can be verified by substituting $x = 6$ into the original equation. You could also solve this equation algebraically. Notice that in this case the technique produces an extraneous solution.

$$\ln(x - 2) + \ln(2x - 3) = 2 \ln x \qquad \text{\textit{Original equation}}$$

$$\ln(x - 2)(2x - 3) = \ln x^2 \qquad \text{\textit{Properties of logarithms}}$$

$$\ln(2x^2 - 7x + 6) = \ln x^2$$

$$e^{\ln(2x^2 - 7x + 6)} = e^{\ln x^2} \qquad \text{\textit{Exponentiate both sides}}$$

$$2x^2 - 7x + 6 = x^2 \qquad \text{\textit{Inverse property of exponents and logs}}$$

$$x^2 - 7x + 6 = 0 \qquad \text{\textit{Quadratic form}}$$

$$(x - 6)(x - 1) = 0 \qquad \text{\textit{Factor}}$$

$$x - 6 = 0 \ \longrightarrow \ x = 6 \qquad \text{\textit{Set 1st factor equal to 0}}$$

$$x - 1 = 0 \ \longrightarrow \ x = 1 \qquad \text{\textit{Set 2nd factor equal to 0}}$$

Finally, by checking these two "solutions" in the original equation, you can conclude that $x = 1$ is not valid. Can you see why? Thus, the only solution is $x = 6$.

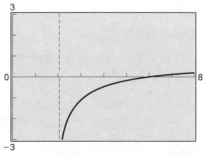

FIGURE 5.24

EXAMPLE 9   The Change of Base Formula
. . . .

Prove the change of base formula given in Section 5.3.

$$\log_a x = \frac{\log_b x}{\log_b a}$$

SOLUTION

Begin by letting $y = \log_a x$ and writing the equivalent exponential form $a^y = x$. Now, taking the logarithm *with base b* of both sides, produces the following.

$$\log_b a^y = \log_b x$$
$$y \log_b a = \log_b x$$
$$y = \frac{\log_b x}{\log_b a}$$
$$\log_a x = \frac{\log_b x}{\log_b a}$$

▬▬▬▬▬

When solving exponential or logarithmic equations, the following properties are useful.

1. $x = y$ if and only if $\log_a x = \log_a y$.
2. $x = y$ if and only if $a^x = a^y$, $a > 0$, $a \neq 1$.

Can you see where these properties were used in the examples in this section?

Approximating Solutions

Equations that involve combinations of algebraic functions, exponential functions, and/or logarithmic functions can be very difficult to solve by algebraic procedures. Here again you can take advantage of a graphing utility.

EXAMPLE 10   Approximating the Solution of an Equation
. . . .

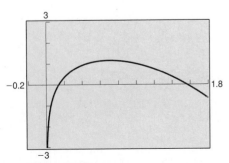

FIGURE 5.25

Approximate the solutions of $\ln x = x^2 - 2$.

SOLUTION

To begin, use a graphing utility to graph

$$y = -x^2 + 2 + \ln x,$$

as shown in Figure 5.25. From this graph, you can see that the equation has two solutions. Next, using the zoom and trace features, you can approximate the two solutions to be $x \approx 0.138$ and $x \approx 1.564$.

▬▬▬▬▬

FIGURE 5.26

Applications

EXAMPLE 11 Waste Processed for Energy Recovery

From 1960 to 1986, the amount of municipal waste processed for energy recovery in the United States can be approximated by the equation

$$y = 0.00643e^{0.00533t^2},$$

where y is the amount of waste (in pounds per person) that was processed for energy recovery and t represents the year, with $t = 0$ corresponding to 1960. According to this model, during which year did the amount of waste reach 0.2 pound? (*Source:* Franklin Associates *Characterization of Municipal Solid Waste in U.S.*)

SOLUTION

To solve for t in the equation $0.00643e^{0.00533t^2} = 0.2$, use a graphing utility to graph

$$y = 0.00643e^{0.00533t^2} - 0.2$$

on the domain $0 \le t \le 28$. From the graph (Figure 5.26), you can see that there is a zero between $t = 25$ and $t = 26$. Using the zoom and trace features, you can determine that $t \approx 25.4$ years. Because $t = 0$ represents 1960, it follows that the amount of waste would have reached 0.2 pound per person in 1985.

> **DISCOVERY**
>
> Use a graphing utility to graph $y = \ln x$ and $y = x^2 - 2$ on the same viewing rectangle. (Use a viewing rectangle in which $0 \le x \le 3$ and $-5 \le y \le 5$.) Then zoom in to approximate the two points of intersection. Compare your results with those given in Example 10. Which solution technique do you prefer? Explain your reasons.

DISCUSSION PROBLEM

VERIFYING INVERSE RELATIONSHIPS

Use a graphing utility to verify the following inverse relationships between logarithmic and exponential functions.

Base 10	*Base e*
1. $\log_{10} 10^x = x$	$\ln e^x = x$
2. $10^{\log_{10} x} = x$	$e^{\ln x} = x$

You can do this by sketching the graph of each relationship. For instance, to verify that $\ln e^x = x$, try sketching the graphs of $y = \ln e^x$ and $y = x$. The two graphs should be identical. Be sure to determine the domain of each function.

WARM-UP
....

The following warm-up exercises involve skills that were covered in earlier sections. You will use these skills in the exercise set for this section.

In Exercises 1–6, solve for x.

1. $x \ln 2 = \ln 3$ **2.** $(x - 1)\ln 4 = 2$ **3.** $2xe^2 = e^3$
4. $4xe^{-1} = 8$ **5.** $x^2 - 4x + 5 = 0$ **6.** $2x^2 - 3x + 1 = 0$

In Exercises 7–10, simplify the expression.

7. $\log_{10} 100^x$ **8.** $\log_4 64^x$ **9.** $\ln e^{2x}$ **10.** $\ln e^{-x^2}$

SECTION 5.4 · EXERCISES
....

In Exercises 1–10, solve for x.

1. $4^x = 16$ **2.** $3^x = 243$
3. $7^x = \frac{1}{49}$ **4.** $8^x = 4$
5. $(\frac{3}{4})^x = \frac{27}{64}$ **6.** $3^{x-1} = 27$
7. $\log_4 x = 3$ **8.** $\log_5 5x = 2$
9. $\log_{10} x = -1$ **10.** $\ln(2x - 1) = 0$

In Exercises 11–16, apply the inverse properties of $\ln x$ and e^x to simplify the expression.

11. $\ln e^{x^2}$ **12.** $\ln e^{2x-1}$
13. $e^{\ln(5x+2)}$ **14.** $-1 + \ln e^{2x}$
15. $e^{\ln x^2}$ **16.** $-8 + e^{\ln x^3}$

In Exercises 17–36, solve the exponential equation algebraically. (Round your result to three decimal places.)

17. $e^x = 10$ **18.** $4e^x = 91$
19. $7 - 2e^x = 5$ **20.** $-14 + 3e^x = 11$
21. $e^{3x} = 12$ **22.** $e^{2x} = 50$
23. $500e^{-x} = 300$ **24.** $1000e^{-4x} = 75$
25. $e^{2x} - 4e^x - 5 = 0$ **26.** $e^{2x} - 5e^x + 6 = 0$
27. $20(100 - e^{x/2}) = 500$ **28.** $\dfrac{400}{1 + e^{-x}} = 200$
29. $10^x = 42$ **30.** $10^x = 570$
31. $3^{2x} = 80$ **32.** $6^{5x} = 3000$
33. $5^{-t/2} = 0.20$ **34.** $4^{-3t} = 0.10$
35. $\left(1 + \dfrac{0.10}{12}\right)^{12t} = 2$ **36.** $2^{3-x} = 565$

In Exercises 37–44, use a graphing utility to solve the exponential equation. (Round your result to three decimal places.)

37. $3e^{3x/2} = 962$ **38.** $6e^{1-x} = 25$
39. $e^{0.09t} = 3$ **40.** $e^{0.125t} = 8$
41. $8(10^{3x}) = 12$ **42.** $3(5^{x-1}) = 21$
43. $\left(1 + \dfrac{0.065}{365}\right)^{365t} = 4$ **44.** $\dfrac{3000}{2 + e^{2x}} = 2$

In Exercises 45–60, solve the logarithmic equation algebraically. (Round your result to three decimal places.)

45. $\ln x = -3$ **46.** $\ln x = 2$
47. $\ln 2x = 2.4$ **48.** $3 \ln 5x = 10$
49. $\ln \sqrt{x + 2} = 1$ **50.** $\ln(x + 1)^2 = 2$
51. $\ln x + \ln(x - 2) = 1$ **52.** $\ln x + \ln(x + 3) = 1$
53. $\log_{10}(z - 3) = 2$ **54.** $\log_{10} x^2 = 6$
55. $\log_{10}(x + 4) - \log_{10} x = \log_{10}(x + 2)$
56. $\log_4 x - \log_4(x - 1) = \frac{1}{2}$
57. $\log_3 x + \log_3(x^2 - 8) = \log_3 8x$
58. $\log_2 x + \log_2(x + 2) = \log_2(x + 6)$
59. $\ln(x + 5) = \ln(x - 1) - \ln(x + 1)$
60. $\ln(x + 1) - \ln(x - 2) = \ln x^2$

In Exercises 61–64, use a graphing utility to solve the logarithmic equation. (Round your result to three decimal places.)

61. $2 \ln x = 7$ **62.** $\ln 4x = 1$
63. $\ln x + \ln(x^2 + 1) = 8$
64. $\log_{10} 8x - \log_{10}\left(1 + \sqrt{x}\right) = 2$

Compound Interest In Exercises 65 and 66, find the time required for a $1000 investment to double at interest rate r, compounded continuously.

65. $r = 0.085$ **66.** $r = 0.12$

Compound Interest In Exercises 67 and 68, find the time required for a $1000 investment to triple at interest rate r, compounded continuously.

67. $r = 0.085$ **68.** $r = 0.12$

69. *Demand Function* The demand equation for a product is

$$p = 500 - 0.5(e^{0.004x}).$$

Find the demand x for a price of (a) $p = \$350$ and (b) $p = \$300$.

70. *Demand Function* The demand equation for a product is

$$p = 5000\left(1 - \frac{4}{4 + e^{-0.002x}}\right).$$

Find the demand x for a price of (a) $p = \$600$ and (b) $p = \$400$.

71. *Forest Yield* The yield V (in millions of cubic feet per acre) for a forest at age t years is given by

$$V = 6.7e^{-48.1/t}.$$

(a) Use a graphing utility to graph the function.

(b) Determine the horizontal asymptote of the function. Interpret its meaning in the context of the problem.

(c) Find the time necessary to have a yield of 1.3 million cubic feet.

72. *Trees per Acre* The number of trees per acre N of a certain species is approximated by the model

$$N = 68 \cdot 10^{-0.04x}, \qquad 5 \le x \le 40,$$

where x is the average diameter of the trees 3 feet above the ground. Use the model to approximate the average diameter of the trees in a test plot when $N = 21$.

73. *Average Heights* The percentage of American males between the ages of 18 and 24 who are no more than x inches tall is given by

$$m(x) = \frac{100}{1 + e^{-0.6114(x-69.71)}}, \qquad 60 \le x \le 80,$$

where m is the percentage and x is the height in inches. (*Source:* U.S. National Center for Health Statistics) The function giving the percentages f for females for the same ages is given by

$$f(x) = \frac{100}{1 + e^{-0.66607(x-64.51)}}, \qquad 55 \le x \le 75.$$

(a) Use a graphing utility to graph each function in the same viewing rectangle.

(b) Determine the horizontal asymptotes of the functions.

(c) What is the median height of each sex?

74. *Human Memory Model* In a group project in learning theory, a mathematical model for the proportion P of correct responses after n trials was found to be

$$P = \frac{0.83}{1 + e^{-0.2n}}.$$

(a) Use a graphing utility to graph the function.

(b) Determine the horizontal asymptotes of the function. Interpret the meaning of the upper asymptote in the context of this problem.

(c) After how many trials will 60% of the responses be correct?

5.5   APPLICATIONS OF EXPONENTIAL AND LOGARITHMIC FUNCTIONS

Compound Interest   /   Growth and Decay   /
Logistics Growth Models   /   Logarithmic Models

Compound Interest

In this section, you will study four basic types of applications: (1) Compound Interest, (2) Growth and Decay, (3) Logistics Models, and (4) Intensity Models. The problems presented in this section involve the full range of solution techniques studied in this chapter.

EXAMPLE 1   Doubling Time for an Investment

An investment is made in a trust fund at an annual percentage rate of 9.5%, compounded quarterly. How long will it take for the investment to double in value?

SOLUTION

For quarterly compounding, use the formula

$$A = P\left(1 + \frac{r}{4}\right)^{4t}.$$

Using $r = 0.095$, the time required for the investment to double is given by solving for t in the equation $2P = A$.

$$2P = P\left(1 + \frac{0.095}{4}\right)^{4t} \qquad 2P = A$$

$$2 = (1.02375)^{4t} \qquad\qquad \textit{Divide both sides by P}$$

$$\ln 2 = \ln(1.02375)^{4t} \qquad\qquad \textit{Take ln of both sides}$$

$$\ln 2 = 4t \ln(1.02375)$$

$$t = \frac{\ln 2}{4 \ln(1.02375)} \approx 7.4$$

Therefore, it will take approximately 7.4 years for the investment to double in value with quarterly compounding.

Try reworking Example 1 using continuous compounding. To do this you will need to solve the equation

$$2P = Pe^{0.095t}.$$

The solution is $t \approx 7.3$ years, which makes sense because the principal should double more quickly with continuous compounding than with quarterly compounding.

DISCOVERY

A person deposits $1000 in an account that pays 9.5% per year, compounded quarterly. The balance after t years is

$$A = 1000\left(1 + \frac{0.095}{4}\right)^{4t}.$$

Another person deposits $1000 in an account that pays 9.5% per year, compounded continuously. The balance after t years is $A = 1000e^{0.095t}$. Use a graphing utility to graph both equations on the same viewing rectangle. (Use a viewing rectangle in which $0 \le x \le 8$ and $1000 \le y \le 2200$.) What do you conclude? Which of the two accounts will reach a balance of $2000 first? Justify your answer by zooming in near $x = 7$.

EXAMPLE 2   Finding an Annual Percentage Rate

An investment of $10,000 is compounded continuously. What annual percentage rate will produce a balance of $25,000 in 10 years?

SOLUTION

Use the formula $A = Pe^{rt}$ with $P = 10{,}000$, $A = 25{,}000$, and $t = 10$, and solve the equation for r.

$$10{,}000e^{10r} = 25{,}000$$
$$e^{10r} = 2.5$$
$$10r = \ln 2.5$$
$$r = \frac{1}{10}\ln 2.5 \approx 0.0916$$

Thus, the annual percentage rate must be approximately 9.16%. You can verify this result using the zoom and trace features of a graphing utility. By graphing $y = 10{,}000e^{10x}$ and $y = 25{,}000$ in the same viewing rectangle with an x scale of 0.1, you can confirm that $r \approx 0.0916$, as shown in Figure 5.27.

FIGURE 5.27

EXAMPLE 3   The Effective Yield for an Investment

A deposit is compounded continuously at an annual percentage rate of 7.5%. Find the **effective yield.** That is, find the simple interest rate that would yield the same balance at the end of 1 year.

SOLUTION

Using the formula $A = Pe^{rt}$ with $r = 0.075$ and $t = 1$, the balance at the end of 1 year is

$$A = Pe^{0.075(1)}$$
$$\approx P(1.0779)$$
$$= P(1 + 0.0779). \qquad\qquad A = P(1 + r)$$

Because the formula for simple interest after 1 year is $A = P(1 + r)$, it follows that the effective yield is approximately 7.79%.

Growth and Decay

The balance in an account earning *continuously compounded* interest is one example of a quantity that increases over time according to the **exponential growth model**

$$Q(t) = Ce^{kt}.$$

In general, $Q(t)$ is the size of the "population" at any time t, C is the original population (when $t = 0$), and k is a constant determined by the rate of growth. If $k > 0$, the population *grows* (increases) over time, and if $k < 0$ it *decays* (decreases) over time. Example 11 in Section 5.1 is an example of population growth. It may help to remember this growth model as *(Then)* = *(Now)* (e^{kt}).

EXAMPLE 4   Exponential Decay

Radioactive iodine is a by-product of some types of nuclear reactors. Its **half-life** is 60 days. That is, after 60 days, a given amount of radioactive iodine will have decayed to half the original amount. Suppose a contained nuclear accident occurs and gives off an initial amount C of radioactive iodine.

A. Write an equation for the amount of radioactive iodine present at any time t following the accident.

B. How long will it take for the radioactive iodine to decay to a level of 20% of the original amount?

SOLUTION

A. We first need to find the rate k in the exponential model $Q(t) = Ce^{kt}$. Knowing that half the original amount remains after $t = 60$ days, you obtain

$$Q(60) = Ce^{k(60)} = \frac{1}{2}C$$

$$e^{60k} = \frac{1}{2}$$

$$60k = -\ln 2$$

$$k = \frac{-\ln 2}{60} \approx -0.0116.$$

Thus, the exponential model is

$$Q(t) = Ce^{-0.0116t}.$$

B. The time required to decay to 20% of the original amount is given by

$$Q(t) = Ce^{-0.0116t} = (0.2)C$$
$$e^{-0.0116t} = 0.2$$
$$-0.0116t = \ln 0.2$$
$$t = \frac{\ln 0.2}{-0.0116} \approx 139 \text{ days.}$$

In living organic material, the ratio of radioactive carbon isotopes (carbon-14) to the number of nonradioactive carbon isotopes (carbon-12) is about 1 to 10^{12}. When organic material dies, its carbon-12 content remains fixed, whereas its radioactive carbon-14 begins to decay with a half-life of about 5700 years. To estimate the age of dead organic material, scientists use the following formula, which denotes the ratio of carbon-14 to carbon-12 present at any time t (in years).

$$R = \frac{1}{10^{12}} e^{-t/8223}$$

The graph of R is shown in Figure 5.28. Note that R decreases as the time t increases.

FIGURE 5.28

EXAMPLE 5   Carbon Dating

Suppose the carbon-14/carbon-12 ratio of a newly discovered fossil is

$$R = \frac{1}{10^{13}}.$$

Estimate the age of the fossil.

SOLUTION

In the carbon dating model, substitute the given value of R to obtain the following.

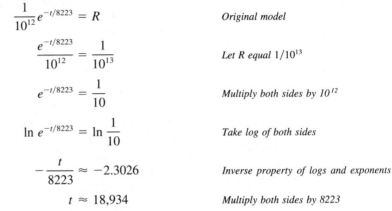

$$\frac{1}{10^{12}}e^{-t/8223} = R \qquad\qquad\text{Original model}$$

$$\frac{e^{-t/8223}}{10^{12}} = \frac{1}{10^{13}} \qquad\qquad\text{Let R equal } 1/10^{13}$$

$$e^{-t/8223} = \frac{1}{10} \qquad\qquad\text{Multiply both sides by } 10^{12}$$

$$\ln e^{-t/8223} = \ln\frac{1}{10} \qquad\qquad\text{Take log of both sides}$$

$$-\frac{t}{8223} \approx -2.3026 \qquad\qquad\text{Inverse property of logs and exponents}$$

$$t \approx 18{,}934 \qquad\qquad\text{Multiply both sides by 8223}$$

Thus, to the nearest thousand years, you can estimate the age of the fossil to be 19,000 years. You could obtain this solution graphically by graphing the equation $y = e^{-t/8223} - \frac{1}{10}$, as indicated in Figure 5.29.

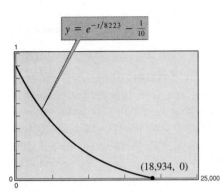

FIGURE 5.29

REMARK The carbon dating model in Example 5 assumes that the carbon-14/carbon-12 ratio was one part in 10,000,000,000,000. Suppose an error in measurement occurred and the actual ratio was only one part in 8,000,000,000,000. The fossil age corresponding to the actual ratio would then be approximately 17,000 years. Try checking this result.

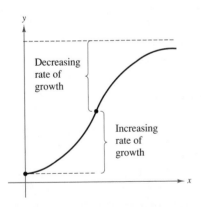

Logistics Curve

FIGURE 5.30

Logistics Growth Models

Some populations initially have rapid growth, followed by a declining rate of growth, as indicated by the graph in Figure 5.30. One model for describing this type of growth pattern is the **logistics curve** given by the function

$$y = \frac{a}{1 + be^{-(t-c)/d}},$$

where y is the population size and t is the time. An example would be a bacteria culture allowed to grow initially under ideal conditions, followed by less favorable conditions that inhibit growth, such as overcrowding. A logistics growth curve is also called a **sigmoidal curve.**

EXAMPLE 6   Spread of a Virus
················

On a college campus of 5000 students, one student returned from vacation with a contagious flu virus. The spread of the virus through the student body is given by

$$y = \frac{5000}{1 + 4999e^{-0.8t}},$$

where y is the total number infected after t days. The college will cancel classes when 40% or more of the students are ill.

A. How many are infected after 5 days?
B. After how many days will the college cancel classes?

SOLUTION

A. After 5 days, the number of students infected is

$$y = \frac{5000}{1 + 4999e^{-0.8(5)}} = \frac{5000}{1 + 4999e^{-4}} \approx 54.$$

B. In this case, the number of students infected is $(0.40)(5000) = 2000$. Therefore, you can solve for t in the following equation.

$$2000 = \frac{5000}{1 + 4999e^{-0.8t}}$$

Using a graphing utility, graph $y = 2000$ and $y = 5000/(1 + 4999e^{-0.8t})$ and find the point of intersection. In Figure 5.31, you can see that the point of intersection occurs near $t \approx 10.1$. Hence, after 10 days, at least 40% of the students will be infected, and the college will cancel classes.

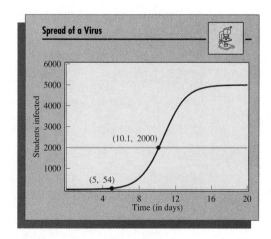

FIGURE **5.31**

Logarithmic Models

Sound and shock waves can be measured by the **intensity model**

$$S = K \log_{10} \frac{I}{I_0},$$

where I is the intensity of the stimulus wave, I_0 is the **threshold intensity** (the smallest value of I that can be detected by the listening device), and K determines the units in which S is measured. Sound heard by the human ear is measured in decibels. One **decibel** is considered to be the smallest detectable difference in the loudness of two sounds.

EXAMPLE 7   **Magnitude of Earthquakes**

On the Richter Scale, the magnitude R of an earthquake of intensity I is given by

$$R = \log_{10} \frac{I}{I_0},$$

where $I_0 = 1$ is the minimum intensity used for comparison. Find the intensity per unit of area for the following earthquakes. (Intensity is a measure of the wave energy of an earthquake.)

A. San Francisco in 1906, $R = 8.6$
B. Mexico City in 1978, $R = 7.85$
C. San Francisco Bay Area in 1989, $R = 7.1$

SOLUTION

A. Because $I_0 = 1$ and $R = 8.6$, you have

$$8.6 = \log_{10} I$$
$$I = 10^{8.6} \approx 398,107,171.$$

B. For Mexico City, you have $7.85 = \log_{10} I$, and

$$I = 10^{7.85} \approx 70,795,000.$$

C. For $R = 7.1$, you have $7.1 = \log_{10} I$, and

$$I = 10^{7.1} \approx 12,589,254.$$

Note that an increase of 1.5 units on the Richter Scale (from 7.1 to 8.6) represents an intensity change by a factor of

$$\frac{398,107,171}{12,589,254} \approx 31.6.$$

In other words, the "great San Francisco earthquake" in 1906 had a magnitude that was about 32 times greater than the one in 1989.

DISCUSSION PROBLEM

COMPARING POPULATION MODELS

The population (in millions) of the United States from 1800 to 1990 is given in the accompanying table.

t	0	1	2	3	4	5	6	7	8	9
Year	1800	1810	1820	1830	1840	1850	1860	1870	1880	1890
Population	5.31	7.23	9.64	12.87	17.07	23.19	31.44	39.82	50.16	62.95

t	10	11	12	13	14	15	16	17	18	19
Year	1900	1910	1920	1930	1940	1950	1960	1970	1980	1990
Population	75.99	91.97	105.71	122.78	131.67	151.33	179.32	203.30	226.55	250.00

Using a statistical procedure called *least squares regression analysis,* we found the best quadratic and exponential models for this data. Which of the following two equations is a better model for the population of the United States between 1800 and 1990? Write a short paragraph describing the method you used to reach your conclusion.

Quadratic Model

$$P = 0.662t^2 + 0.211t + 6.165$$

Exponential Model

$$P = 7.7899e^{0.2013t}$$

WARM-UP

The following warm-up exercises involve skills that were covered in earlier sections. You will use these skills in the exercise set for this section.

In Exercises 1–6, sketch the graph of the equation.

1. $y = 2^{0.25x}$

2. $y = 2^{-0.25x}$

3. $y = 4 \log_2 x$

4. $y = \ln(x - 3)$

5. $y = e^{-x^2/5}$

6. $y = \dfrac{2}{1 + e^{-x}}$

In Exercises 7–10, solve the given equation for x. (Round your result to three decimal places.)

7. $3e^{2x} = 7$

8. $2e^{-0.2x} = 0.002$

9. $4 \ln 5x = 14$

10. $6 \ln 2x = 12$

SECTION 5.5 · EXERCISES

Compound Interest   In Exercises 1–10, complete the table for a savings account in which interest is compounded continuously.

	Initial Investment	Annual % Rate	Effective Yield	Time to Double	Amount After 10 Years
1.	$1000	12%			
2.	$20,000	$10\frac{1}{2}$%			
3.	$750			$7\frac{3}{4}$ yr	
4.	$10,000			5 yr	
5.	$500				$1292.85
6.	$2000		4.5%		
7.		11%			$19,205.00
8.		8%			$20,000.00
9.	$5000		8.33%		
10.	$250		12.19%		

Compound Interest   In Exercises 11 and 12, determine the principal P that must be invested at rate r, compounded monthly, so that $500,000 will be available for retirement in t years.

11. $r = 7\frac{1}{2}$%, $t = 20$ **12.** $r = 12$%, $t = 40$

Compound Interest   In Exercises 13 and 14, determine the time necessary for $1000 to double if it is invested at interest rate r compounded (a) annually, (b) monthly, (c) daily, and (d) continuously.

13. $r = 11$%   **14.** $r = 10\frac{1}{2}$%

15. *Compound Interest*   Complete the table for the time t necessary for P dollars to triple if interest is compounded continuously at rate r.

r	2%	4%	6%	8%	10%	12%
t						

16. *Compound Interest*   Complete the table for the time t necessary for P dollars to triple if interest is compounded annually at rate r.

r	2%	4%	6%	8%	10%	12%
t						

17. *Comparing Investments*   If $1 is invested in an account over a 10-year period, the amount in the account is given by

$$A = 1 + 0.075t \quad \text{or} \quad A = e^{0.07t}$$

depending on whether it is simple interest at $7\frac{1}{2}$% or continuous compound interest at 7%. Use a graphing utility to graph each function in the same viewing rectangle, and determine which grows at the higher rate.

18. *Comparing Investments*   If $1 is invested in an account over a 10-year period, the amount in the account is given by

$$A = 1 + 0.06t \quad \text{or} \quad A = \left(1 + \frac{0.055}{365}\right)^{365t}$$

depending on whether it is simple interest at 6% or compound interest at $5\frac{1}{2}$% compounded daily. Use a graphing utility to graph each function in the same viewing rectangle, and determine which grows at the higher rate.

Radioactive Decay   In Exercises 19–24, complete the table for the given radioactive isotope.

	Isotope	Half-life (Years)	Initial Quantity	Amount After 1000 Years	Amount After 10,000 Years
19.	^{226}Ra	1620	10 g		
20.	^{226}Ra	1620		1.5 g	
21.	^{14}C	5730			2 g
22.	^{14}C	5730	3 g		
23.	^{230}Pu	24,360		2.1 g	
24.	^{230}Pu	24,360			0.4 g

In Exercises 25–28, find the constant k such that the exponential function $y = Ce^{kt}$ passes through the given points on the graph.

25.   **26.**

27.

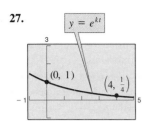

$y = e^{kt}$

$(0, 1)$

$\left(4, \frac{1}{4}\right)$

28.

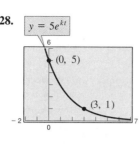

$y = 5e^{kt}$

$(0, 5)$

$(3, 1)$

29. *Population*   The population P of a city is given by

$$P = 105{,}300e^{0.015t},$$

where t is the time in years, with $t = 0$ corresponding to 1990. What was the population in 1990? According to this model, in what year will the city have a population of 150,000?

30. *Population*   The population P of a city is given by

$$P = 240{,}360e^{0.012t},$$

where t is the time in years, with $t = 0$ corresponding to 1990. What was the population in 1990? According to this model, in what year will the city have a population of 250,000?

31. *Population*   The population P of a city is given by

$$P = 2500e^{kt},$$

where t is the time in years, with $t = 0$ corresponding to the year 1990. In 1945, the population was 1350. Find the value of k and use this result to predict the population in the year 2010.

32. *Population*   The population P of a city is given by

$$P = 140{,}500e^{kt},$$

where t is the time in years, with $t = 0$ corresponding to the year 1990. In 1960, the population was 100,250. Find the value of k and use this result to predict the population in the year 2000.

33. *Population*   The population of Dhaka, Bangladesh was 4.22 million in 1990 and its projected population for the year 2000 is 6.49 million. Find the exponential growth model $y = Ce^{kt}$ for the population growth of Dhaka by letting $t = 0$ correspond to 1990. Use the model to predict the population of the city in 2010. (*Source:* United Nations)

34. *Population*   The population of Houston, Texas was 2.30 million in 1990 and its projected population for the year 2000 is 2.65 million. Find the exponential growth model $y = Ce^{kt}$ for the population growth of Houston by letting $t = 0$ correspond to 1990. Use the model to predict the population of the city in 2010. (*Source:* U. S. Bureau of the Census)

35. *Bacteria Growth*   The number of bacteria N in a culture is given by the model

$$N = 100e^{kt},$$

where t is the time in hours, with $t = 0$ corresponding to the time when $N = 100$. If $N = 300$ when $t = 5$, estimate the time required for the population to double in size.

36. *Bacteria Growth*   The number of bacteria N in a culture is given by the model

$$N = 250e^{kt},$$

where t is the time in hours, with $t = 0$ corresponding to the time when $N = 250$. If $N = 280$ when $t = 10$, estimate the time required for the population to double in size.

37. *Radioactive Decay*   The half-life of radioactive radium (^{226}Ra) is 1620 years. What percentage of a present amount of radioactive radium will remain after 100 years?

38. *Radioactive Decay* ^{14}C dating assumes that the carbon dioxide on earth today has the same radioactive content as it did centuries ago. If this is true, then the amount of ^{14}C absorbed by a tree that grew several centuries ago should be the same as the amount of ^{14}C absorbed by a tree growing today. A piece of ancient charcoal contains only 15% as much of the radioactive carbon as a piece of modern charcoal. How long ago was the tree burned to make the ancient charcoal if the half-life of ^{14}C is 5730 years?

39. *Depreciation*   A certain car that cost $22,000 new has a depreciated value of $16,500 after 1 year. Find the value of the car when it is 3 years old by using the exponential model $y = Ce^{kt}$.

40. *Depreciation*   A computer that cost $4600 new has a depreciated value of $3000 after 2 years. Find the value of the computer after 3 years by using the exponential model $y = Ce^{kt}$.

41. *Sales*   The sales S (in thousands of units) of a new product after it has been on the market t years are given by

$$S(t) = 100(1 - e^{kt}).$$

(a) Find S as a function of t if 15,000 units have been sold after 1 year.

(b) How many units will be sold after 5 years?

42. *Learning Curve*   The management at a factory has found that the maximum number of units a worker can produce in a day is 30. The learning curve for the number of units N produced per day after a new employee has worked t days is given by $N = 30(1 - e^{kt})$. After 20 days on the job, a particular worker produced 19 units.

(a) Find the learning curve for this worker (that is, find the value of k).

(b) How many days should pass before this worker is producing 25 units per day?

43. *Women's Heights*   The distribution of the heights of American women between the ages of 25 and 34 can be approximated by the function

$$p = 0.166e^{-(x-64.5)^2/11.5},$$

where x is the height in inches. Use a graphing utility to graph this function. What is the average height of women in this age bracket? (*Source:* U.S. National Center for Health Statistics)

44. *Men's Heights*   The distribution of the heights of American men between the ages of 25 and 34 can be approximated by the function

$$p = 0.193e^{-(x-70)^2/14.32},$$

where x is the height in inches. Use a graphing utility to graph this function. What is the average height of men in this age bracket? (*Source:* U.S. National Center for Health Statistics)

45. *Stocking a Lake with Fish*   A certain lake was stocked with 500 fish and the fish population increased according to the logistics curve

$$p(t) = \frac{10,000}{1 + 19e^{-t/5}},$$

where t is the time in months.
  (a) Use a graphing utility to graph the function. Determine the larger of the two horizontal asymptotes and interpret its meaning in the context of the problem.
  (b) Estimate the fish population after 5 months.
  (c) After how many months will the fish population be 2000?

46. *Endangered Species*   A conservation organization releases 100 animals of an endangered species into a game preserve. The organization believes that the preserve has a carrying capacity of 1000 animals and that the growth of the herd will be modeled by the logistics curve

$$p(t) = \frac{1000}{1 + 9e^{-0.1656t}},$$

where t is the time in months.
  (a) Use a graphing utility to graph the function. Determine the larger of the two horizontal asymptotes and interpret its meaning in the context of the problem.
  (b) Estimate the population after 5 months.
  (c) After how many months will the population be 500?

47. *Sales and Advertising*   The sales S (in thousands of units) of a product after x hundred dollars is spent on advertising is given by

$$S = 10(1 - e^{kx}).$$

  (a) Find S as a function of x if 2500 units are sold when $500 is spent on advertising.
  (b) Estimate the number of units that will be sold if advertising expenditures are raised to $700.

48. *Sales and Advertising*   After discontinuing all advertising for a certain product in 1988, the manufacturer noted that sales began to drop according to the model

$$S = \frac{500,000}{1 + 0.6e^{kt}},$$

where S represents the number of units sold and t represents the year, with $t = 0$ corresponding to 1988.
  (a) Find k if the company sold 300,000 units in 1990.
  (b) According to this model, what will sales be in 1993?

Earthquake Magnitudes   In Exercises 49 and 50, use the Richter Scale (see Example 7) for measuring the magnitude of earthquakes.

49. Find the magnitude R of an earthquake of intensity I (let $I_0 = 1$).
  (a) $I = 80,500,000$
  (b) $I = 48,275,000$

50. Find the intensity I of an earthquake measuring R on the Richter Scale (let $I_0 = I$).
  (a) Mexico City in 1985, $R = 8.1$
  (b) Los Angeles in 1971, $R = 6.7$

Intensity of Sound   In Exercises 51–54, use the following information to determine the level of sound (in decibels) for the given sound intensity. The level of sound β, in decibels, with an intensity of I is given by

$$\beta(I) = 10 \log_{10} \frac{I}{I_0},$$

where I_0 is an intensity of 10^{-16} watts per square centimeter, corresponding roughly to the faintest sound that can be heard by the human ear.

51. (a) $I = 10^{-14}$ watts per square centimeter (faint whisper)
  (b) $I = 10^{-9}$ watts per square centimeter (busy street corner)
  (c) $I = 10^{-6.5}$ watts per square centimeter (air hammer)
  (d) $I = 10^{-4}$ watts per square centimeter (threshold of pain)

52. (a) $I = 10^{-13}$ watts per square centimeter (whisper)
    (b) $I = 10^{-7.5}$ watts per square centimeter (DC-8 4 miles from takeoff)
    (c) $I = 10^{-7}$ watts per square centimeter (diesel truck at 25 feet)
    (d) $I = 10^{-4.5}$ watts per square centimeter (auto horn at 3 feet)

53. *Noise Level* Due to the installation of noise suppression materials, the noise level in an auditorium was reduced from 93 to 80 decibels. Find the percentage decrease in the intensity level of the noise because of the installation of these materials.

54. *Noise Level* Due to the installation of a muffler, the noise level in an engine was reduced from 88 to 72 decibels. Find the percentage decrease in the intensity level of the noise because of the installation of the muffler.

Acidity In Exercises 55–60, use the acidity model given by
$$pH = -\log_{10}[H^+],$$
where acidity (pH) is a measure of the hydrogen ion concentration $[H^+]$ (measured in moles of hydrogen per liter) of a solution.

55. Find the pH if $[H^+] = 2.3 \times 10^{-5}$.
56. Find the pH if $[H^+] = 11.3 \times 10^{-6}$.
57. Compute $[H^+]$ for a solution in which pH $= 5.8$.
58. Compute $[H^+]$ for a solution in which pH $= 3.2$.
59. A certain fruit has a pH of 2.5 and an antacid tablet has a pH of 9.5. The hydrogen ion concentration of the fruit is how many times the concentration of the tablet?
60. If the pH of a solution is decreased by one unit, the hydrogen ion concentration is increased by what factor?

61. *Home Mortgage* An $80,000 home mortgage for 35 years at $9\frac{1}{2}\%$ has a monthly payment of $657.28. Part of the monthly payment goes for the interest charge on the unpaid balance and the remainder of the payment is used to reduce the principal. The amount that goes for interest is given by
$$u = M - \left(M - \frac{Pr}{12}\right)\left(1 + \frac{r}{12}\right)^{12t},$$
and the amount that goes toward reduction of the principal is given by
$$v = \left(M - \frac{Pr}{12}\right)\left(1 + \frac{r}{12}\right)^{12t}.$$
In these formulas, P is the size of the mortgage, r is the interest rate, M is the monthly payment, and t is the time in years.

(a) Use a graphing utility to graph each function in the same viewing rectangle. (The viewing rectangle should show all 35 years of mortgage payments.)
(b) In the early years of the mortgage, the larger part of the monthly payment goes for what purpose? Approximate the time when the monthly payment is evenly divided between interest and principal reduction.

62. *Home Mortgage* The total interest paid on a home mortgage of P dollars, at interest rate r for t years, is given by
$$u = P\left[\frac{rt}{1 - \left(\dfrac{1}{1 + r/12}\right)^{12t}} - 1\right].$$
Consider an $80,000 home mortgage at $9\frac{1}{2}\%$.
(a) Use a graphing utility to graph the total interest function.
(b) Approximate the length of the mortgage when the total interest paid is the same as the size of the mortgage. Is it possible that some people are paying twice as much in interest charges as the size of the mortgage?

63. *Estimating the Time of Death* At 8:30 A.M., a coroner was called to the home of a person who had died during the night. In order to estimate the time of death, the coroner took the person's temperature twice. At 9:00 A. M., the temperature was 85.7°, and at 9:30 A. M., the temperature was 82.8°. From these two temperatures, the coroner was able to determine that
$$t = -2.5 \ln \frac{T - 70}{98.6 - 70},$$
where t is the time in hours that has elapsed since the person died and T is the temperature (in degrees Fahrenheit) of the person's body at 9:00 A. M. (The person had a normal body temperature of 98.6° at death, and the room temperature was a constant 70°. This formula is derived from a general cooling principle called Newton's Law of Cooling.) Use this formula to estimate the time of death of the person.

64. *Population Growth* In Exercises 33 and 34, you can see that the populations of Dhaka and Houston are growing at different rates. What constant in the equation $y = Ce^{kt}$ is affected by these different growth rates? Discuss the relationship between the different growth rates and the magnitude of the constant.

CHAPTER 5 · REVIEW EXERCISES

In Exercises 1–6, match the function with its graph and describe the given viewing rectangle. [The graphs are labeled (a), (b), (c), (d), (e), and (f).]

1. $f(x) = 2^x$ **2.** $f(x) = 2^{-x}$

3. $f(x) = -2^x$ **4.** $f(x) = 2^x + 1$

5. $f(x) = \log_2 x$ **6.** $f(x) = \log_2(x - 1)$

(a)

(b)

(c)

(d)

(e)

(f)

In Exercises 7–14, sketch the graph of the function.

7. $f(x) = 6^x$ **8.** $f(x) = 0.3^x$

9. $g(x) = 6^{-x}$ **10.** $g(x) = 0.3^{-x}$

11. $h(x) = e^{-x/2}$ **12.** $h(x) = 2 - e^{-x/2}$

13. $f(x) = e^{x+2}$ **14.** $s(t) = 4e^{-2/t},\ t > 0$

In Exercises 15 and 16, complete the table to determine the balance A for P dollars invested at rate r for t years and compounded n times per year.

n	1	2	4	12	365	Continuous compounding
A						

15. $P = \$3500,\ r = 10.5\%,\ t = 10$ years

16. $P = \$2000,\ r = 12\%,\ t = 30$ years

In Exercises 17 and 18, complete the following table to determine the amount of money P that should be invested at rate r to produce a final balance of \$200,000 in t years.

t	1	10	20	30	40	50
P						

17. $r = 8\%$, compounded continuously

18. $r = 10\%$, compounded monthly

19. *Trust Fund* On the day your child was born you deposited \$50,000 in a trust fund that pays 8.75% interest, compounded continuously. Determine the balance in the account at the time of your child's 35th birthday.

20. *Depreciation* After t years, the value of a car that cost \$14,000 is given by

$$V(t) = 14{,}000\left(\tfrac{3}{4}\right)^t.$$

Use a graphing utility to graph the function and determine the value of the car 2 years after it was purchased.

21. *Drug Decomposition* A solution of a certain drug contained 500 units per milliliter when prepared. It was analyzed after 40 days and found to contain 300 units per milliliter. Assuming that the rate of decomposition is proportional to the amount present, the equation giving the amount A after t days is

$$A = 500e^{-0.013t}.$$

Use this model to find A when $t = 60$. Solve this problem algebraically and graphically. Which method do you prefer?

22. *Waiting Times* The average time between incoming calls at a switchboard is 3 minutes. The probability of waiting less than t minutes until the next incoming call is approximated by the model

$$P(t) = 1 - e^{-t/3}.$$

If a call has just come in, find the probability that the next call will be within

(a) $\tfrac{1}{2}$ minute.   (b) 2 minutes.   (c) 5 minutes.

Solve the problem algebraically and graphically. Which method do you prefer?

23. *Fuel Efficiency*   A certain automobile gets 28 miles per gallon of gasoline for speeds up to 50 miles per hour. Over 50 miles per hour, the number of miles per gallon drops at the rate of 12% for each 10 miles per hour. If s is the speed and y is the number of miles per gallon, then

$$y = 28e^{0.6 - 0.012s}, \quad s \geq 50.$$

Use this function to complete the table. Write a short paragraph describing the results.

Speed	50	55	60	65	70
Miles per gallon					

24. *Inflation*   If the annual rate of inflation averages 4.5% over the next 10 years, then the approximate cost C of goods or services during any year in that decade will be given by

$$C(t) = P(1.05)^t,$$

where t is the time in years and P is the present cost. If the price of a tire for your car is presently $69.95, estimate the price 10 years from now.

In Exercises 25–30, sketch the graph of the function.

25. $g(x) = \log_3 x$

26. $g(x) = \log_5 x$

27. $f(x) = \ln x + 3$

28. $f(x) = \ln(x - 3)$

29. $h(x) = \ln(e^{x-1})$

30. $f(x) = \frac{1}{4} \ln x$

In Exercises 31 and 32, use the definition of a logarithm to write the given equation in logarithmic form.

31. $4^3 = 64$

32. $25^{3/2} = 125$

In Exercises 33–40, evaluate the expression.

33. $\log_{10} 1000$

34. $\log_9 3$

35. $\log_3 \frac{1}{9}$

36. $\log_4 \frac{1}{16}$

37. $\ln e^7$

38. $\log_a \frac{1}{a}$

39. $\ln 1$

40. $\ln e^{-3}$

In Exercises 41–44, evaluate the logarithm using the change of base formula. Do each problem twice, once with common logarithms and once with natural logarithms. (Round your result to three decimal places.)

41. $\log_4 9$

42. $\log_{1/2} 5$

43. $\log_{12} 200$

44. $\log_3 0.28$

In Exercises 45–50, use the properties of logarithms to write the expression as a sum, difference, and/or multiple of logarithms.

45. $\log_5 5x^2$

46. $\log_7 \frac{\sqrt{x}}{4}$

47. $\log_{10} \frac{5\sqrt{y}}{x^2}$

48. $\ln \left| \frac{x-1}{x+1} \right|$

49. $\ln[(x^2 + 1)(x - 1)]$

50. $\ln \sqrt[5]{\frac{4x^2 - 1}{4x^2 + 1}}$

In Exercises 51–56, write the expression as the logarithm of a single quantity.

51. $\log_2 5 + \log_2 x$

52. $\log_6 y - 2 \log_6 z$

53. $\frac{1}{2} \ln |2x - 1| - 2 \ln |x + 1|$

54. $5 \ln |x - 2| - \ln |x + 2| - 3 \ln |x|$

55. $\ln 3 + \frac{1}{3} \ln(4 - x^2) - \ln x$

56. $3[\ln x - 2 \ln(x^2 + 1)] + 2 \ln 5$

In Exercises 57–60, determine whether the statement or equation is true or false. Explain how to use a graphing utility to support your conclusion.

57. The domain of $f(x) = \ln x$ is the set of all real numbers.

58. $\log_b b^{2x} = 2x$

59. $\ln(x + 2) = \ln x + \ln 2$

60. $e^{x-1} = \frac{e^x}{e}$

In Exercises 61–64, approximate the logarithm using the properties of logarithms given $\log_b 2 \approx 0.3562$, $\log_b 3 \approx 0.5646$, and $\log_b 5 \approx 0.8271$.

61. $\log_b 25$

62. $\log_b \left(\frac{25}{9} \right)$

63. $\log_b \sqrt{3}$

64. $\log_b 30$

65. *Snow Removal*   The number of miles s of roads cleared of snow is approximated by the model

$$s = 25 - \frac{13 \ln(h/12)}{\ln 3}, \quad 2 \leq h \leq 15,$$

where h is the depth of the snow in inches. Use this model to find s when $h = 10$ inches.

66. *Climb Rate* The time t, in minutes, required for a small plane to climb to an altitude of h feet is given by

$$t = 50 \log_{10} \frac{18{,}000}{18{,}000 - h},$$

where 18,000 feet is the plane's absolute ceiling. Find the time for the plane to climb to an altitude of 4000 feet.

In Exercises 67–72, solve the exponential equation. (Round your result to three decimal places.)

67. $e^x = 12$ **68.** $e^{3x} = 25$

69. $3e^{-5x} = 132$ **70.** $14e^{3x+2} = 560$

71. $e^{2x} - 7e^x + 10 = 0$ **72.** $e^{2x} - 6x + 8 = 0$

In Exercises 73–76, solve the logarithmic equation. (Round your result to three decimal places.)

73. $\ln 3x = 8.2$ **74.** $2 \ln 4x = 15$

75. $\ln x - \ln 3 = 2$ **76.** $\ln \sqrt{x+1} = 2$

In Exercises 77–80, find the exponential function $y = Ce^{kt}$ that passes through the two points.

77. $(0, 2)$, $(4, 3)$ **78.** $(0, \frac{1}{2})$, $(5, 5)$

79. $(0, 4)$, $(5, \frac{1}{2})$ **80.** $(0, 2)$, $(5, 1)$

81. *Demand Function* The demand equation for a certain product is given by

$$p = 500 - 0.5e^{0.004x}.$$

Find the demand x for a price of (a) $p = \$450$ and (b) $p = \$400$.

82. *Typing Speed* In a typing class, the average number of words per minute typed after t weeks of lessons was found to be

$$N = \frac{157}{1 + 5.4e^{-0.12t}}.$$

Find the time necessary to type (a) 50 words per minute and (b) 75 words per minute.

83. *Compound Interest* A deposit of $750 is made in a savings account for which the interest is compounded continuously. The balance will double in $7\frac{3}{4}$ years.
(a) What is the annual percentage rate for this account?
(b) Find the balance in the account after 10 years.
(c) Find the effective yield.

84. *Compound Interest* A deposit of $10,000 is made in a savings account for which the interest is compounded continuously. The balance will double in 5 years.
(a) What is the annual percentage rate for this account?
(b) Find the balance after 1 year.
(c) Find the effective yield.

85. *Sound Intensity* The relationship between the number of decibels β and the intensity of a sound I in watts per square centimeter is given by

$$\beta = 10 \log_{10}\left(\frac{I}{10^{-16}}\right).$$

Determine the intensity of a sound in watts per square centimeter if the decibel level is 125.

86. *Earthquake Magnitudes* On the Richter Scale, the magnitude R of an earthquake of intensity I is given by

$$R = \log_{10} \frac{I}{I_0},$$

where $I_0 = 1$ is the minimum intensity used for comparison. Find the intensity per unit of area for the following values of R.
(a) $R = 8.4$ (b) $R = 6.85$ (c) $R = 9.1$

CUMULATIVE TEST FOR CHAPTERS 3–5

Take this test as you would take a test in class. After you are done, check your work with the answers in the back of the book.

1. Use a graphing utility to graph the quadratic function
$$f(x) = \tfrac{1}{4}(4x^2 - 12x + 17).$$
Find the coordinates of the vertex of the parabola.

2. Find a quadratic function whose graph is a parabola with vertex at $(0, 6)$ and passes through the point $(2, 5)$.

3. Describe the right-hand and left-hand behavior of the polynomial function
$$f(x) = -\tfrac{2}{3}x^3 + 3x^2 - 2x + 1.$$

4. Find a polynomial function with integer coefficients whose zeros are $-4, \tfrac{1}{2}$, and 2.

5. Sketch a graph of the function $f(t) = \tfrac{1}{4}t(t - 2)^2$ without the aid of a graphing utility.

6. Perform the division: $\dfrac{6x^3 - 4x^2}{2x^2 + 1}$

7. Use synthetic division to perform the division: $\dfrac{3x^3 - 5x + 4}{x - 2}$

8. Multiply and simplify: $(3 - 2i)(5 + 4i)$

9. Find all the zeros of the function $f(x) = 2x^3 - 11x^2 + 38x - 39$.

10. Find the rational zeros of the function
$$f(x) = 6x^3 - 25x^2 - 8x + 48.$$
(*Hint:* Use a graphing utility to eliminate some of the possible rational zeros.)

11. Use a graphing utility to approximate (accurate to one decimal place) the zero of the function $g(t) = t^3 - 5t - 2$ in the interval $[2, 3]$.

12. Sketch a graph of each of the following.

(a) $g(s) = \dfrac{2s}{s - 3}$

(b) $g(s) = \dfrac{2s^2}{s - 3}$

(c) $6x - y^2 = 0$

(d) $\dfrac{(x - 2)^2}{4} + \dfrac{(y + 1)^2}{9} = 1$

13. Find an equation of the hyperbola with foci $(0, 0)$ and $(0, 4)$ and asymptotes $y = \pm\tfrac{1}{2}x + 2$.

14. Sketch a graph of each of the following.

(a) $f(x) = 6(2^{-x})$ (b) $g(x) = \log_3 x$

15. Evaluate without the aid of a calculator: $\log_5 125$

16. Use the properties of a logarithm to write the expression
$$2 \ln x - \tfrac{1}{2} \ln(x + 5)$$
as the logarithm of a single quantity.

17. Solve each of the following, giving your answers accurate to two decimal places.

(a) $6e^{2x} = 72$ (b) $\log_2 x + \log_2 5 = 6$

18. Let x be the amount (in hundreds of dollars) that a company spends on advertising, and let P be the profit, where
$$P = 230 + 20x - \tfrac{1}{2}x^2.$$
What amount of advertising will yield maximum profit?

19. On the day a grandchild is born, a grandparent deposits $2500 into a fund earning 7.5%, compounded continuously. Determine the balance in the account at the time of the grandchild's 25th birthday.

CHAPTER 6

TRIGONOMETRY

6.1 ANGLES AND THEIR MEASURE

Introduction / Angles / Degree Measure / Radian Measure / Conversion of Angle Measure / Applications

Introduction

As derived from the Greek language, the word **trigonometry** means "measurement of triangles." Initially, trigonometry dealt with relationships among the sides and angles of triangles, and was used in the development of astronomy, navigation, and surveying.

With the development of calculus and the physical sciences in the 17th century, a different perspective arose—one that viewed the classic trigonometric relationships as *functions* with the set of real numbers as their domains. Consequently, the applications of trigonometry expanded to include a vast number of physical phenomena involving rotations, or vibrations. These include sound waves, light rays, planetary orbits, vibrating strings, pendulums, and orbits of atomic particles.

The approach in this text incorporates *both* perspectives, starting with angles and their measure.

FIGURE 6.1

Standard position of an angle

FIGURE 6.2

Angles

An **angle** is determined by rotating a ray (half-line) about its endpoint. The starting position of the ray is the **initial side** of the angle, and the position after rotation is the **terminal side,** as shown in Figure 6.1. The endpoint of the ray is the **vertex** of the angle. This perception of an angle fits a coordinate system in which the origin is the vertex and the initial side coincides with the positive x-axis. Such an angle is in **standard position,** as shown in Figure 6.2. **Positive angles** are generated by counterclockwise rotation, and **negative angles** by clockwise rotation, as shown in Figure 6.3. To label angles in trigonometry, we use the Greek letters α (alpha), β (beta), and θ (theta), as well as uppercase letters A, B, and C. In Figure 6.4, note that the angles α and β have the same initial and terminal sides. Such angles are **coterminal.**

FIGURE 6.3

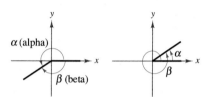

Coterminal Angles

FIGURE 6.4

Degree Measure

The **measure of an angle** is determined by the amount of rotation from the initial to the terminal side. The most common unit of angle measure is the **degree,** denoted by the symbol $°$. A measure of **one degree (1°)** is equivalent to a rotation of $\frac{1}{360}$ of a complete revolution about the vertex. To measure angles, it is convenient to mark degrees on the circumference of a circle, as shown in Figure 6.5. Thus, a full revolution (counterclockwise) corresponds to 360°, a half revolution to 180°, a quarter revolution to 90°, and so on.

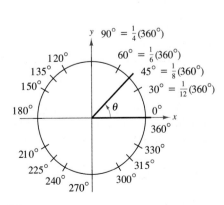

FIGURE 6.5   Degree Measure of an Angle

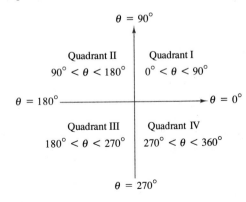

FIGURE 6.6   Quadrant Location of Terminal Sides of Angles

REMARK   The phrase "the terminal side of θ lies in a quadrant" can be abbreviated by simply saying that "θ lies in a quadrant." The terminal sides of the "quadrant angles" $0°$, $90°$, $180°$, and $270°$ do not lie within any of the four quadrants.

Recall that the four quadrants in a coordinate system are numbered counterclockwise as I, II, III, and IV. Figure 6.6 shows which angles between $0°$ and $360°$ lie in each of the four quadrants. Figure 6.7 shows several common angles with their degree measures. Angles between $0°$ and $90°$ are **acute** and angles between $90°$ and $180°$ are **obtuse.**

Two angles are coterminal if they have the same initial and terminal sides. For instance, the angles $0°$ and $360°$ are coterminal, as are the angles $30°$ and $390°$. You can find an angle that is coterminal to a given angle θ by adding or subtracting $360°$ (one revolution), as demonstrated in Example 1. A given angle θ has infinitely many coterminal angles. For instance, $\theta = 30°$ is coterminal with $30° \pm n(360°)$, where n is an integer.

FIGURE 6.7

(a)

(b)

(c)

FIGURE 6.8

EXAMPLE 1   **Sketching and Finding Coterminal Angles**

A. To find an angle that is coterminal to the positive angle $\theta = 390°$, you can subtract $360°$ to obtain

$$390° - 360° = 30°,$$

as shown in Figure 6.8(a).

B. To find an angle that is coterminal to the positive angle $\theta = 135°$, you can subtract $360°$ to obtain

$$135° - 360° = -225°,$$

as shown in Figure 6.8(b).

C. To find an angle that is coterminal to the negative angle $\theta = -120°$, you can add $360°$ to obtain

$$\theta = -120° + 360° = 240°,$$

as shown in Figure 6.8(c).

(a) Complementary angles

(b) Supplementary angles

FIGURE 6.9

Two *positive* angles α and β are **complementary** (complements of each other) if their sum is 90°, as shown in Figure 6.9(a). For example, 30° and 60° are complementary angles because 30° + 60° = 90°. Two positive angles are **supplementary** (supplements of each other) if their sum is 180°, as shown in Figure 6.9(b). For example, 50° and 130° are supplementary angles because 50° + 130° = 180°.

EXAMPLE 2   **Complementary and Supplementary Angles**

If possible, find the complement and the supplement of the following angles.

A. 72°   **B.** 148°

SOLUTION

A. The complement of $\theta = 72°$ is

$$90° - \theta = 90° - 72° = 18°.$$

The supplement of $\theta = 72°$ is

$$180° - \theta = 180° - 72° = 108°.$$

B. Because $\theta = 148°$ is greater than 90°, it has no complement. (Remember, only *positive* angles are used for complements.) The supplement of $\theta = 148°$ is

$$180° - \theta = 180° - 148° = 32°.$$

With calculators it is convenient to use *decimal* degrees to denote fractional parts of degrees. Historically, however, fractional parts of degrees were expressed in *minutes* and *seconds,* using the prime (′) and double prime (″) notations, respectively. That is,

$$1' = \text{one minute} = \frac{1}{60}(1°)$$

$$1'' = \text{one second} = \frac{1}{60}(1') = \frac{1}{3600}(1°).$$

Consequently, an angle of 64 degrees, 32 minutes, and 47 seconds is represented by $\theta = 64° \, 32' \, 47''$.

Many calculators have special keys for converting an angle in degrees, minutes, and seconds (D° M′ S″) into decimal degree form, and conversely. If your calculator does not have these special keys, you can use the techniques demonstrated in the next example to make the conversions.

EXAMPLE 3   Converting an Angle from D° M′ S″ to Decimal Form

Convert 152° 15′ 29″ to decimal degree form.

SOLUTION

$$152° \ 15′ \ 29″ = 152° + \left(\frac{15}{60}\right)° + \left(\frac{29}{3600}\right)°$$
$$\approx 152° + 0.25° + 0.00806°$$
$$= 152.25806°$$

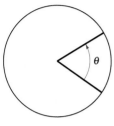

Central Angle θ

FIGURE 6.10

Radian Measure

Another way to measure angles is in terms of radians. This type of (real number) measure is especially useful in calculus. To define a radian we use a **central angle** of a circle, one whose vertex is the center of the circle, as shown in Figure 6.10.

DEFINITION OF A RADIAN

One **radian** is the measure of a central angle θ that intercepts (subtends) an arc s equal in length to the radius r of the circle (see figure).

arc length = radius when $\theta = 1$ radian

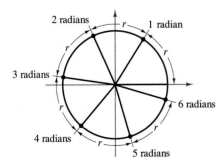

FIGURE 6.11

Because the circumference of a circle is $2\pi r$, it follows that a central angle of one full revolution (counterclockwise) corresponds to an arc length of $s = 2\pi r$. Moreover, because each radian intercepts an arc of length r, you can conclude that one full revolution corresponds to an angle of $(2\pi r)/r = 2\pi$ radians. Note that because $2\pi \approx 6.28$, there are just over six radius lengths in a full circle, as shown in Figure 6.11.

In general, the radian measure of a central angle θ is obtained by dividing the arc length s by r. That is,

$$\frac{s}{r} = \theta,$$ *Radian measure*

where θ *is measured in radians.* Because the units of measure for s and r are the same, this ratio has no units—*it is simply a real number.*

Figure 6.12 shows the radian measure of several common angles. All the previous ideas of coterminal, complementary, and supplementary angles can be used with radian measure.

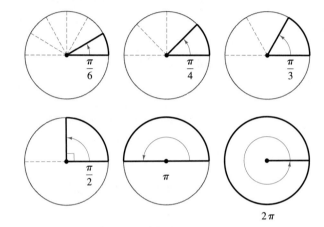

Radian Measure for Several Common Angles   **FIGURE 6.12**

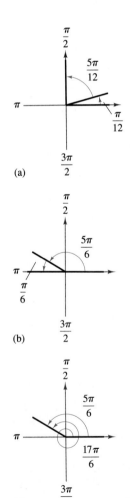

(a)

(b)

(c)   **FIGURE 6.13**

EXAMPLE 4   **Complementary, Supplementary, and Coterminal**
····················   **Angles**

A. Because $90°$ equals $\pi/2$ radians, the complement of $\theta = \pi/12$ is

$$\frac{\pi}{2} - \frac{\pi}{12} = \frac{6\pi}{12} - \frac{\pi}{12} = \frac{5\pi}{12},$$

as shown in Figure 6.13(a).

B. Because $180°$ equals π radians, the supplement of $\theta = 5\pi/6$ is

$$\pi - \frac{5\pi}{6} = \frac{6\pi}{6} - \frac{5\pi}{6} = \frac{\pi}{6},$$

as shown in Figure 6.13(b).

C. In radian measure, a coterminal angle is found by adding or subtracting 2π. For $\theta = 17\pi/6$, you subtract 2π to obtain

$$\frac{17\pi}{6} - 2\pi = \frac{17\pi}{6} - \frac{12\pi}{6} = \frac{5\pi}{6},$$

as shown in Figure 6.13(c). Thus, $17\pi/6$ and $5\pi/6$ are coterminal.

··········

REMARK Note that when no units of angle measure are specified, *radian measure is implied.* For instance, if we write $\theta = \pi$ or $\theta = 2$, we mean $\theta = \pi$ radians or $\theta = 2$ radians.

Conversion of Angle Measure

Because 2π radians corresponds to one complete revolution, degrees and radians are related by the equations

$$360° = 2\pi \text{ rad} \quad \text{and} \quad 180° = \pi \text{ rad}.$$

From the latter equation, you obtain

$$1° = \frac{\pi}{180} \text{ rad} \quad \text{and} \quad 1 \text{ rad} = \left(\frac{180}{\pi}\right)°,$$

which lead to the following conversion rules.

Technology Note _____

Calculators and graphing utilities have both degree and radian modes. When you are using a calculator or graphing utility, be sure you use the correct mode.

CONVERSIONS BETWEEN DEGREES AND RADIANS

1. To convert degrees to radians, multiply degrees by $\dfrac{\pi \text{ rad}}{180°}$.

2. To convert radians to degrees, multiply radians by $\dfrac{180°}{\pi \text{ rad}}$.

To apply these two conversion rules, use the basic relationship $\pi \text{ rad} = 180°$.

EXAMPLE 5   Converting from Degrees to Radians

A. $135° = (135 \text{ deg})\left(\dfrac{\pi \text{ rad}}{180 \text{ deg}}\right) = \dfrac{3\pi}{4} \text{ rad}$ *Multiply by $\pi/180$*

B. $540° = (540 \text{ deg})\left(\dfrac{\pi \text{ rad}}{180 \text{ deg}}\right) = 3\pi \text{ rad}$ *Multiply by $\pi/180$*

C. $-270° = (-270 \text{ deg})\left(\dfrac{\pi \text{ rad}}{180 \text{ deg}}\right) = -\dfrac{3\pi}{2} \text{ rad}$ *Multiply by $\pi/180$*

EXAMPLE 6   Converting from Radians to Degrees

A. $-\dfrac{\pi}{2} \text{ rad} = \left(-\dfrac{\pi}{2} \text{ rad}\right)\left(\dfrac{180 \text{ deg}}{\pi \text{ rad}}\right) = -90°$ *Multiply by $180/\pi$*

B. $\dfrac{9\pi}{2} \text{ rad} = \left(\dfrac{9\pi}{2} \text{ rad}\right)\left(\dfrac{180 \text{ deg}}{\pi \text{ rad}}\right) = 810°$ *Multiply by $180/\pi$*

C. $2 \text{ rad} = (2 \text{ rad})\left(\dfrac{180 \text{ deg}}{\pi \text{ rad}}\right) = \dfrac{360°}{\pi} \approx 114.59°$ *Multiply by $180/\pi$*

Applications

The *radian measure* formula, $\theta = s/r$, can be used to measure arc length along a circle. Specifically, for a circle of radius r, a central angle θ intercepts an arc of length s given by

$$s = r\theta, \qquad\qquad \textit{Length of circular arc}$$

where θ is measured in radians.

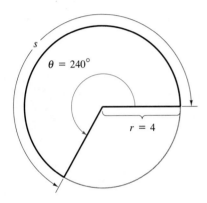

FIGURE 6.14

EXAMPLE 7   Finding Arc Length

A circle has a radius of 4 inches. Find the length of the arc intercepted by a central angle of 240°, as shown in Figure 6.14.

SOLUTION

To use the formula $s = r\theta$, you must first convert 240° to radian measure.

$$240° = (240 \text{ deg})\left(\frac{\pi \text{ rad}}{180 \text{ deg}}\right) = \frac{4\pi}{3} \text{ rad}$$

Then, using a radius of $r = 4$ inches, you can find the arc length to be

$$s = r\theta = 4\left(\frac{4\pi}{3}\right) = \frac{16\pi}{3} \approx 16.76 \text{ inches.}$$

Note that the units for $r\theta$ are determined by the units for r because θ is given in radian measure and therefore has no units.

The formula for the length of a circular arc can be used to analyze the motion of a particle moving at a *constant speed* along a circular path. Consider a circle of radius r. If s is the length of the arc traveled in time t, then the **speed** of the particle is

$$\text{Speed} = \frac{\text{distance}}{\text{time}} = \frac{s}{t}.$$

Moreover, if θ is the angle (in radian measure) corresponding to the arc length s, then the **angular speed** of the particle is

$$\text{Angular speed} = \frac{\theta}{t}.$$

FIGURE 6.15

EXAMPLE 8   Finding the Speed of an Object

The second hand of a clock is 4 inches long, as shown in Figure 6.15. Find the speed of the tip of this second hand.

SOLUTION

The time required for the second hand to make one full revolution is

$$t = 60 \text{ seconds} = 1 \text{ minute.}$$

Moreover, the distance traveled by the tip of the second hand in one revolution is

$$s = 2\pi(\text{radius}) = 2\pi(4) = 8\pi \text{ inches.}$$

Therefore, the speed of the tip of the second hand is

$$\text{Speed} = \frac{s}{t} = \frac{8\pi \text{ inches}}{60 \text{ seconds}} \approx 0.419 \text{ in./sec.}$$

FIGURE 6.16

EXAMPLE 9   Finding Angular Speed and Speed

A lawn roller that is 30 inches in diameter makes one revolution every $\frac{5}{6}$ second, as shown in Figure 6.16.

A. Find the angular speed of the roller in radians per second.
B. How fast is the roller moving across the lawn?

SOLUTION

A. Because there are 2π radians in one revolution, it follows that the angular speed is

$$\text{Angular speed} = \frac{\theta}{t} = \frac{2\pi \text{ rad}}{5/6 \text{ sec}} = 2.4\pi \text{ rad/sec.}$$

B. Because the diameter is 30 inches, $r = 15$ and $s = 2\pi r = 30\pi$ inches. Thus,

$$\text{Speed} = \frac{s}{t} = \frac{30\pi \text{ inches}}{5/6 \text{ sec}} = 36\pi \text{ in./sec} \approx 113.1 \text{ in./sec.}$$

DISCUSSION PROBLEM

AN ANGLE-DRAWING PROGRAM

If you have a programmable calculator, try entering an "angle-drawing program." Then use the program to draw several different angles. For instance, the following program is for the TI-81. (Other programs are presented in the appendix.)

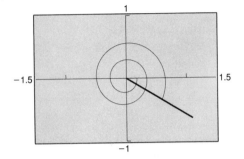

```
:Disp "ENTER,MODE"            :0→Tmin
:Disp "0,RADIAN"              :abs T→Tmax
:Disp "1,DEGREE"              :.15→Tstep
:Input M                      :cos T→A
:Disp "ENTER,ANGLE"           :sin T→B
:Input T                      :Param
:If M=1                       :1→S
:πT/180→T                     :If T<0
:Rad                          :-1→S
:ClrDraw                      :"(.25+.04T) cosT"→X₁ₜ
:All-Off                      :"S(.25+.04T)sinT"→Y₁ₜ
:-1.5→Xmin                    :DispGraph
:1.5→Xmax                     :Line(0,0,A,B)
:1→Xscl                       :Pause
:-1→Ymin                      :Function
:1→Ymax                       :End
:1→Yscl
```

To run this program, enter 0 for radian mode or 1 for degree mode. Then enter any angle (the angle can be negative or larger than 360°). After the angle is displayed, press ENTER to clear the display. The figure shows an angle of −750°, as drawn by this program.

WARM-UP

The following warm-up exercises involve skills that were covered in earlier sections. You will use these skills in the exercise set for this section.

In Exercises 1–10, solve for x.

1. $x + 135 = 180$

2. $790 = 720 + x$

3. $\pi = \dfrac{5\pi}{6} + x$

4. $2\pi - x = \dfrac{5\pi}{3}$

5. $\dfrac{45}{180} = \dfrac{x}{\pi}$

6. $\dfrac{240}{180} = \dfrac{x}{\pi}$

7. $\dfrac{\pi}{180} = \dfrac{x}{20}$

8. $\dfrac{180}{\pi} = \dfrac{330}{x}$

9. $\dfrac{x}{60} = \dfrac{3}{4}$

10. $\dfrac{x}{3600} = 0.0125$

SECTION 6.1 · EXERCISES

In Exercises 1–4, determine the quadrant in which the terminal side of the angle lies.

1. (a) 130°   (b) 285°

2. (a) 8.3°   (b) 257° 30′

3. (a) −132° 50′   (b) −336°

4. (a) −260°   (b) −3.4°

In Exercises 5–10, determine the quadrant in which the terminal side of the angle lies. (The angle measure is given in radians.)

5. (a) $\dfrac{\pi}{5}$ (b) $\dfrac{7\pi}{5}$ **6.** (a) $\dfrac{5\pi}{4}$ (b) $\dfrac{7\pi}{4}$

7. (a) $-\dfrac{\pi}{12}$ (b) $-\dfrac{11\pi}{9}$ **8.** (a) −1   (b) −2

9. (a) 3.5   (b) 2.25   **10.** (a) 5.63   (b) −2.25

In Exercises 11–16, sketch the angle in standard position.

11. (a) 30°   (b) 150°   **12.** (a) −270°   (b) −120°

13. (a) 405°   (b) −480°   **14.** (a) $\dfrac{5\pi}{4}$ (b) $\dfrac{2\pi}{3}$

15. (a) $-\dfrac{7\pi}{4}$ (b) $-\dfrac{5\pi}{2}$ **16.** (a) $\dfrac{11\pi}{6}$ (b) 7π

In Exercises 17–20, determine two coterminal angles (one positive and one negative) for the given angle. Give your results in degrees.

17. (a) $\theta = 36°$ (b) $\theta = -45°$

18. (a) $\theta = -120°$ (b) $\theta = 390°$

19. (a) $\theta = 300°$ (b) $\theta = 740°$

20. (a) $\theta = -420°$ (b) $\theta = 230°$

In Exercises 21–24, determine two coterminal angles (one positive and one negative) for the given angle. Give your results in radians.

21. (a) $\theta = \dfrac{\pi}{9}$ (b) $\theta = \dfrac{4\pi}{3}$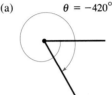

22. (a) $\theta = \dfrac{11\pi}{6}$ (b) $\theta = -\dfrac{7\pi}{6}$

23. (a) $\theta = -\dfrac{9\pi}{4}$ (b) $\theta = -\dfrac{2\pi}{15}$

24. (a) $\theta = \dfrac{8\pi}{9}$ (b) $\theta = \dfrac{8\pi}{45}$

In Exercises 25–28, find (if possible) the complement and the supplement of the angle.

25. (a) 18° (b) 115°   **26.** (a) 79° (b) 150°

27. (a) $\dfrac{\pi}{3}$ (b) $\dfrac{3\pi}{4}$ **28.** (a) 1 (b) 2

In Exercises 29–32, express the angle in radian measure as a multiple of π. Verify your result with a calculator.

29. (a) 30° (b) 150°   **30.** (a) 315° (b) 120°

31. (a) $-20°$ (b) $-240°$ **32.** (a) $-270°$ (b) 144°

In Exercises 33–36, express the angle in degree measure. Verify your result with a calculator.

33. (a) $\dfrac{3\pi}{2}$ (b) $\dfrac{7\pi}{6}$ **34.** (a) $-\dfrac{7\pi}{12}$ (b) $\dfrac{\pi}{9}$

35. (a) $\dfrac{7\pi}{3}$ (b) $-\dfrac{11\pi}{30}$ **36.** (a) $\dfrac{11\pi}{6}$ (b) $\dfrac{34\pi}{15}$

In Exercises 37–44, convert the angle from degrees to radian measure. (Round your result to three decimal places.)

37. 115°   **38.** 87.4°
39. $-216.35°$ **40.** $-48.27°$
41. 532°   **42.** 0.54°
43. $-0.83°$ **44.** 345°

In Exercises 45–52, convert the angle from radian to degree measure. (Round your result to three decimal places.)

45. $\dfrac{\pi}{7}$ **46.** $\dfrac{5\pi}{11}$

47. $\dfrac{15\pi}{8}$ **48.** 6.5π

49. -4.2π **50.** 4.8
51. -2 **52.** -0.57

In Exercises 53–56, convert the angle measurement to decimal form.

53. (a) 54° 45′ (b) $-128°$ 30′
54. (a) 245° 10′ (b) 2° 12′
55. (a) 85° 18′ 30″ (b) 330° 25″
56. (a) $-135°$ 36″ (b) $-408°$ 16′ 25″

In Exercises 57–60, convert the angle measurement to D° M′ S″ form.

57. (a) 240.6° (b) $-145.8°$ **58.** (a) $-345.12°$ (b) 0.45
59. (a) 2.5 (b) -3.58 **60.** (a) -0.355 (b) 0.7865

In Exercises 61–64, find the radian measure of the central angle of a circle of radius r that intercepts an arc of length s.

Radius	Arc Length
61. 15 inches	4 inches
62. 16 feet	10 feet
63. 14.5 centimeters	25 centimeters
64. 80 kilometers	160 kilometers

In Exercises 65–68, on a circle of radius r, find the length of the arc intercepted by the central angle θ.

Radius	Central Angle
65. 15 inches	180°
66. 9 feet	60°
67. 6 meters	2 radians
68. 40 centimeters	$\dfrac{3\pi}{4}$ radians

Distance Between Cities   In Exercises 69–72, find the distance between the two cities of given latitudes. Assume that the earth is a sphere of radius 4000 miles and that the cities are on the same meridian (one city is due north of the other).

City	Latitude
69. Dallas	32° 47′ 9″ N
Omaha	41° 15′ 42″ N
70. San Francisco	37° 46′ 39″ N
Seattle	47° 36′ 32″ N
71. Miami	25° 46′ 37″ N
Erie	42° 7′ 15″ N
72. Johannesburg, South Africa	26° 10′ S
Jerusalem, Israel	31° 47′ N

73. *Difference in Latitudes*   Assuming that the earth is a sphere of radius 4000 miles, what is the difference in latitude of two cities, one of which is 325 miles due north of the other?

74. *Difference in Latitudes*   Assuming that the earth is a sphere of radius 4000 miles, what is the difference in latitude of two cities, one of which is 500 miles due north of the other?

75. *Instrumentation*   The pointer on a voltmeter is 2 inches long (see figure). Find the angle through which the pointer rotates when it moves $\frac{1}{2}$ inch on the scale.

FIGURE FOR 75

76. *Electric Hoist*   An electric hoist is being used to lift a piece of equipment (see figure). The diameter of the drum on the hoist is 8 inches and the equipment must be raised 1 foot. Find the number of degrees through which the drum must rotate.

FIGURE FOR 76

77. *Angular Speed*   A car is moving at the rate of 50 miles per hour, and the diameter of its wheels is 2.5 feet.
   (a) Find the number of revolutions per minute of the rotating wheels.
   (b) Find the angular speed of the wheels in radians per minute.

78. *Angular Speed*   A 2-inch-diameter pulley on an electric motor that runs at 1700 revolutions per minute is connected by a belt to a 4-inch-diameter pulley on a saw arbor.
   (a) Find the angular speed (in radians per minute) of each pulley.
   (b) Find the rotational speed of the saw, in revolutions per minute.

79. *Circular Saw Speed*   The circular blade on a saw has a diameter of 7.5 inches and rotates at 2400 revolutions per minute (see figure).
   (a) Find the angular speed in radians per second.
   (b) Find the speed of the saw teeth (in feet per second) as they contact the wood being cut.

FIGURE FOR 79

80. *Speed of a Bicycle*   The radii of the sprocket assemblies and the wheel of the bicycle in the figure are 4 inches, 2 inches, and 13 inches, respectively. If the cyclist is pedaling at the rate of one revolution per second, find the speed of the bicycle in (a) feet per second and (b) miles per hour.

FIGURE FOR 80

6.2   RIGHT TRIANGLE TRIGONOMETRY
The Six Trigonometric Functions / Trigonometric Identities / Evaluating Trigonometric Functions with a Calculator / Applications Involving Right Triangles

FIGURE 6.17

The Six Trigonometric Functions

Our first look at the trigonometric functions is from a *right triangle* perspective. Consider a right triangle, one of whose acute angles is labeled θ, as shown in Figure 6.17. The three sides of the triangle are the **hypotenuse,** the **opposite side** (the side opposite the angle θ), and the **adjacent side** (the side adjacent to the angle θ). Using the lengths of these three sides, you can form six ratios that define the six trigonometric functions of the acute angle θ.

sine (sin)	**cosecant (csc)**
cosine (cos)	**secant (sec)**
tangent (tan)	**cotangent (cot)**

In the following definition it is important to see that $0° < \theta < 90°$ and that for such angles the value of each of the six trigonometric functions is *positive.*

REMARK   As a memorization aid, note that the functions in the second column are the *reciprocals* of the corresponding members of the first column.

> ### RIGHT TRIANGLE DEFINITION OF TRIGONOMETRIC FUNCTIONS
>
> Let θ be an *acute* angle of a right triangle. Then the six trigonometric functions *of the angle* θ are defined as follows (see Example 1).
>
> $$\sin \theta = \frac{\text{opp}}{\text{hyp}} \qquad \csc \theta = \frac{\text{hyp}}{\text{opp}}$$
>
> $$\cos \theta = \frac{\text{adj}}{\text{hyp}} \qquad \sec \theta = \frac{\text{hyp}}{\text{adj}}$$
>
> $$\tan \theta = \frac{\text{opp}}{\text{adj}} \qquad \cot \theta = \frac{\text{adj}}{\text{opp}}$$
>
> The abbreviations opp, adj, and hyp represent the lengths of the three sides of a right triangle.
>
> opp = the length of the side *opposite* θ
>
> adj = the length of the side *adjacent* to θ
>
> hyp = the length of the *hypotenuse*

FIGURE 6.18

EXAMPLE 1   Evaluating Trigonometric Functions

Find the values of the six trigonometric functions of θ in the right triangle shown in Figure 6.18.

SOLUTION

By the Pythagorean Theorem, $(\text{hyp})^2 = (\text{opp})^2 + (\text{adj})^2$, it follows that

$$\text{hyp} = \sqrt{3^2 + 4^2} = \sqrt{25} = 5.$$

Thus, adj $= 3$, opp $= 4$, and hyp $= 5$.

$$\sin \theta = \frac{\text{opp}}{\text{hyp}} = \frac{4}{5} \qquad \csc \theta = \frac{\text{hyp}}{\text{opp}} = \frac{5}{4}$$

$$\cos \theta = \frac{\text{adj}}{\text{hyp}} = \frac{3}{5} \qquad \sec \theta = \frac{\text{hyp}}{\text{adj}} = \frac{5}{3}$$

$$\tan \theta = \frac{\text{opp}}{\text{adj}} = \frac{4}{3} \qquad \cot \theta = \frac{\text{adj}}{\text{opp}} = \frac{3}{4}$$

In Example 1, you were given the lengths of the sides of the right triangle, but not the angle θ. A much more common problem in trigonometry is to be asked to find the trigonometric functions for a *given* acute angle θ. To do this, construct a right triangle having θ as one of its angles.

EXAMPLE 2   Evaluating Trigonometric Functions of 45°

Find the values of sin 45°, cos 45°, and tan 45°.

SOLUTION

Construct a right triangle having 45° as one of its acute angles, as shown in Figure 6.19. Choose the length of the adjacent side to be 1. From geometry, you know that the other acute angle is also 45°. Hence, the triangle is isosceles and the length of the opposite side is also 1. Using the Pythagorean Theorem, you can find the length of the hypotenuse to be

$$\text{hyp} = \sqrt{1^2 + 1^2} = \sqrt{2}.$$

Finally, you can write the following.

$$\sin 45° = \frac{\text{opp}}{\text{hyp}} = \frac{1}{\sqrt{2}} = \frac{\sqrt{2}}{2}$$

$$\cos 45° = \frac{\text{adj}}{\text{hyp}} = \frac{1}{\sqrt{2}} = \frac{\sqrt{2}}{2}$$

$$\tan 45° = \frac{\text{opp}}{\text{adj}} = \frac{1}{1} = 1$$

FIGURE 6.19

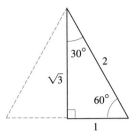

FIGURE 6.20

EXAMPLE 3   Evaluating Trigonometric Functions of 30° and 60°

Use the equilateral triangle shown in Figure 6.20 to find the values of sin 60°, cos 60°, sin 30°, and cos 30°.

SOLUTION

Try using the Pythagorean Theorem to verify the lengths of the sides given in Figure 6.20. For $\theta = 60°$, you have adj = 1, opp = $\sqrt{3}$, and hyp = 2, which implies that

$$\sin 60° = \frac{\text{opp}}{\text{hyp}} = \frac{\sqrt{3}}{2} \quad \text{and} \quad \cos 60° = \frac{\text{adj}}{\text{hyp}} = \frac{1}{2}.$$

For $\theta = 30°$, you have adj = $\sqrt{3}$, opp = 1, and hyp = 2, which implies that

$$\sin 30° = \frac{\text{opp}}{\text{hyp}} = \frac{1}{2} \quad \text{and} \quad \cos 30° = \frac{\text{adj}}{\text{hyp}} = \frac{\sqrt{3}}{2}.$$

Because the angles 30°, 45°, and 60° ($\pi/6$, $\pi/4$, and $\pi/3$) occur frequently in trigonometry, we suggest that you learn to construct the triangles shown in Figures 6.19 and 6.20.

SINE, COSINE, AND TANGENT OF SPECIAL ANGLES

$$\sin 30° = \sin \frac{\pi}{6} = \frac{1}{2}, \qquad \cos 30° = \cos \frac{\pi}{6} = \frac{\sqrt{3}}{2}, \qquad \tan 30° = \tan \frac{\pi}{6} = \frac{\sqrt{3}}{3}$$

$$\sin 45° = \sin \frac{\pi}{4} = \frac{\sqrt{2}}{2}, \qquad \cos 45° = \cos \frac{\pi}{4} = \frac{\sqrt{2}}{2}, \qquad \tan 45° = \tan \frac{\pi}{4} = 1$$

$$\sin 60° = \sin \frac{\pi}{3} = \frac{\sqrt{3}}{2}, \qquad \cos 60° = \cos \frac{\pi}{3} = \frac{1}{2}, \qquad \tan 60° = \tan \frac{\pi}{3} = \sqrt{3}$$

In the preceding box, note $\sin 30° = \frac{1}{2} = \cos 60°$. This occurs because 30° and 60° are complementary angles. In general, it can be shown from the right triangle definitions that *cofunctions of complementary angles are equal.* That is, if θ is an acute angle, then the following relationships are true.

$$\sin(90° - \theta) = \cos \theta \qquad \cos(90° - \theta) = \sin \theta$$
$$\tan(90° - \theta) = \cot \theta \qquad \cot(90° - \theta) = \tan \theta$$
$$\sec(90° - \theta) = \csc \theta \qquad \csc(90° - \theta) = \sec \theta$$

For instance, because 10° and 80° are complementary angles, it follows that $\sin 10° = \cos 80°$ and $\tan 10° = \cot 80°$.

Trigonometric Identities

In trigonometry, a great deal of time is spent studying trigonometric identities.

FUNDAMENTAL TRIGONOMETRIC IDENTITIES

Reciprocal Identities

$$\sin \theta = \frac{1}{\csc \theta} \qquad \sec \theta = \frac{1}{\cos \theta} \qquad \tan \theta = \frac{1}{\cot \theta}$$

$$\csc \theta = \frac{1}{\sin \theta} \qquad \cos \theta = \frac{1}{\sec \theta} \qquad \cot \theta = \frac{1}{\tan \theta}$$

Quotient Identities

$$\tan \theta = \frac{\sin \theta}{\cos \theta} \qquad \cot \theta = \frac{\cos \theta}{\sin \theta}$$

Pythagorean Identities

$$\sin^2 \theta + \cos^2 \theta = 1 \qquad 1 + \tan^2 \theta = \sec^2 \theta \qquad 1 + \cot^2 \theta = \csc^2 \theta$$

REMARK We use $\sin^2 \theta$ to represent $(\sin \theta)^2$, $\cos^2 \theta$ to represent $(\cos \theta)^2$, and so on.

EXAMPLE 4   Applying Trigonometric Identities

Let θ be an acute angle such that $\sin \theta = 0.6$. Use trigonometric identities to find the values of the following.

A. $\cos \theta$ **B.** $\tan \theta$

SOLUTION

A. $\sin^2 \theta + \cos^2 \theta = 1$ *Pythagorean Identity*

$$(0.6)^2 + \cos^2 \theta = 1$$

$$\cos^2 \theta = 1 - (0.6)^2 = 0.64$$

$$\cos \theta = \sqrt{0.64} = 0.8$$

B. Now, knowing the values of $\sin \theta$ and $\cos \theta$, you can find the value of $\tan \theta$.

$$\tan \theta = \frac{\sin \theta}{\cos \theta} = \frac{0.6}{0.8} = 0.75$$

Try using the definitions of $\cos \theta$ and $\tan \theta$, and the triangle shown in Figure 6.21 to check these results.

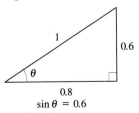

$$\sin \theta = 0.6$$

FIGURE 6.21

$\sqrt{10}$ 3

θ

1

$\tan \theta = 3$

FIGURE 6.22

EXAMPLE 5   Applying Trigonometric Identities

Let θ be an acute angle such that $\tan \theta = 3$. Use trigonometric identities to find the values of the following.

A. $\cot \theta$

B. $\sec \theta$

SOLUTION

A. $\cot \theta = \dfrac{1}{\tan \theta}$ *Reciprocal Identity*

$\quad\quad\quad = \dfrac{1}{3}$

B. $\sec^2 \theta = \tan^2 \theta + 1$ *Pythagorean Identity*

$\quad \sec^2 \theta = 3^3 + 1$

$\quad \sec^2 \theta = 10$

$\quad\ \sec \theta = \sqrt{10}$

Try using the definitions of $\cot \theta$ and $\sec \theta$, and the triangle shown in Figure 6.22 to check these results.

Evaluating Trigonometric Functions with a Calculator

A scientific calculator can be used to obtain decimal approximations of the values of trigonometric functions. Before doing this, however, you must be sure that the calculator is set to the correct mode: degrees or radians. Here are two examples.

Degree mode: $\cos 28$ *Display 0.8829475929*

Radian mode: $\tan \dfrac{\pi}{12}$ *Display 0.2679491924*

Most calculators do not have keys for the cosecant, secant, or cotangent functions. To evaluate these functions, use the reciprocal key with the functions sine, cosine, and tangent. Here is one example.

$$\csc \frac{\pi}{8} = \frac{1}{\sin(\pi/8)} \approx 2.613$$

EXAMPLE 6   Using a Calculator to Evaluate Trigonometric
Functions

Use a calculator to evaluate the following. (Round your result to three decimal places.)

A. $\sin(-76.4)°$

B. $\cot 1.5$

C. $\sec(5°\ 40'\ 12'')$

SOLUTION

Function	Mode	Display	Rounded to 3 Decimal Places
A. $\sin(-76.4)°$	Degree	-0.9719610006	-0.972
B. $\cot 1.5$	Radian	0.0709148443	0.071
C. $\sec 5°\ 40'\ 12''$	Degree	1.004916618	1.005

Note that $5°\ 40'\ 12'' = 5.67°$.

Applications Involving Right Triangles

Many applications of trigonometry involve a process called **solving right triangles.** In this type of application, you are usually given two sides of a right triangle and asked to find one of its acute angles, *or* you are given one side and one of the acute angles and asked to find one of the other sides.

EXAMPLE 7   Using Trigonometry to Solve a Right Triangle

A surveyor is standing 50 feet from the base of a large tree, as shown in Figure 6.23. The surveyor measures the angle of elevation to the top of the tree as 71.5°. How tall is the tree?

SOLUTION

From Figure 6.23, you can see that

$$\tan 71.5° = \frac{\text{opp}}{\text{adj}} = \frac{y}{x},$$

where $x = 50$ and y is the height of the tree. Thus, you can determine the height of the tree to be

$$y = x \tan 71.5° \approx 50(2.98868) \approx 149.4 \text{ feet.}$$

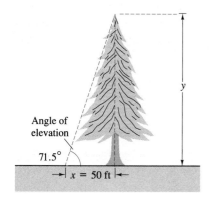

Angle of elevation

71.5°

$x = 50$ ft

y

FIGURE 6.23

FIGURE 6.24

EXAMPLE 8   Using Trigonometry to Solve a Right Triangle

A person is standing 200 yards from a river. Rather than walking directly to the river, the person walks 400 yards along a straight path to the river's edge. Find the acute angle θ between this path and the river's edge, as indicated in Figure 6.24.

SOLUTION

From Figure 6.24, you can see that the sine of the angle θ is

$$\sin \theta = \frac{\text{opp}}{\text{hyp}} = \frac{200}{400} = \frac{1}{2}.$$

Now, you can recognize that $\theta = 30°$.

In Example 8, you were able to recognize that the acute angle that satisfies the equation $\sin \theta = \frac{1}{2}$ is $\theta = 30°$. Suppose, however, that you were given the equation $\sin \theta = 0.6$ and asked to find the acute angle θ. Because

$$\sin 30° = \frac{1}{2} = 0.5000 \quad \text{and} \quad \sin 45° = \frac{1}{\sqrt{2}} \approx 0.7071,$$

you can figure that θ lies somewhere between $30°$ and $45°$. A more precise value of θ can be found using the inverse key on a calculator. (Consult your calculator manual to see how this key works on your own calculator.) For most calculators, one of the following keystroke sequences will work.

Degree mode: .6 [INV] [sin]   *Display 36.86989765*
Degree mode: [2nd] [sin] .6 [ENTER]   *Display 36.86989765*

Thus, you can conclude that if $\sin \theta = 0.6$, then $\theta \approx 36.87°$.

EXAMPLE 9   Using Trigonometry to Solve a Right Triangle

A 40-foot flagpole casts a 30-foot shadow, as shown in Figure 6.25. Find θ, the angle of elevation of the sun.

SOLUTION

Figure 6.25 shows that the *opposite* and *adjacent* sides are known. Thus,

$$\tan \theta = \frac{\text{opp}}{\text{adj}} = \frac{40}{30}.$$

With a calculator in degree mode, you can obtain $\theta \approx 53.13°$.

40 ft

Angle of
elevation

θ

30 ft

FIGURE 6.25

DISCUSSION PROBLEM

YOU BE THE INSTRUCTOR

Suppose you are tutoring a student in trigonometry. Your student is asked to evaluate the cosine of 30° and, using a calculator, obtains the following.

Function	Display
cos 30	0.1542514

Because you know that $\cos 30° = \sqrt{3}/2 \approx 0.866$, you realize that your student has not obtained the correct answer. What has your student done wrong?

WARM-UP

The following warm-up exercises involve skills that were covered in earlier sections. You will use these skills in the exercise set for this section.

In Exercises 1–4, find the distance between the points.

1. (3, 8), (1, 4)   **2.** (5, 2), (2, −7)

3. (−4, 0), (2, 8)   **4.** (−3, −3), (0, 0)

In Exercises 5–10, perform the indicated operation(s). (Round your result to two decimal places.)

5. 0.300×4.125 **6.** 7.30×43.50

7. $\dfrac{151.5}{2.40}$ **8.** $\dfrac{3740}{28.0}$

9. $\dfrac{19{,}500}{0.007}$ **10.** $\dfrac{(10.5)(3401)}{1240}$

SECTION 6.2 · EXERCISES

In Exercises 1–8, find the exact value of the six trigonometric functions of the angle θ. (Use the Pythagorean Theorem to find the third side of the triangle.)

In Exercises 9–16, sketch a right triangle corresponding to the trigonometric function of the acute angle θ. Use the Pythagorean Theorem to determine the third side and then find the other five trigonometric functions of θ.

9. $\sin \theta = \frac{2}{3}$ 10. $\cot \theta = 5$

11. $\sec \theta = 2$ 12. $\cos \theta = \frac{5}{7}$

13. $\tan \theta = 3$ 14. $\csc \theta = \frac{17}{4}$

15. $\cot \theta = \frac{3}{2}$ 16. $\sin \theta = \frac{3}{8}$

1.

2.

3.

4.

In Exercises 17–20, use the given values to evaluate the trigonometric functions as indicated.

17. $\sin 60° = \dfrac{\sqrt{3}}{2}$, $\cos 60° = \dfrac{1}{2}$

    (a) $\tan 60°$ (b) $\sin 30°$

    (c) $\cos 30°$ (d) $\cot 60°$

18. $\sin 30° = \dfrac{1}{2}$, $\tan 30° = \dfrac{\sqrt{3}}{3}$

    (a) $\csc 30°$ (b) $\cot 60°$

    (c) $\cos 30°$ (d) $\cot 30°$

19. $\csc \theta = 3$, $\sec \theta = \dfrac{3\sqrt{2}}{4}$

    (a) $\sin \theta$ (b) $\cos \theta$

    (c) $\tan \theta$ (d) $\sec(90° - \theta)$

20. $\sec \theta = 5$, $\tan \theta = 2\sqrt{6}$

    (a) $\cos \theta$ (b) $\cot \theta$

    (c) $\cot(90° - \theta)$ (d) $\sin \theta$

5.

6.

7.

8.
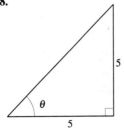

In Exercises 21–24, evaluate the trigonometric functions.

21. (a) $\cos 60°$ (b) $\tan \dfrac{\pi}{4}$

22. (a) $\csc 30°$ (b) $\sin \dfrac{\pi}{4}$

23. (a) $\cot 45°$ (b) $\cos 45°$

24. (a) $\sin \dfrac{\pi}{3}$ (b) $\csc 45°$

In Exercises 25–34, use a calculator to evaluate each function. Round your result to four decimal places. (Be sure the calculator is in the correct mode.)

25. (a) $\sin 10°$ (b) $\cos 80°$

26. (a) $\tan 23.5°$ (b) $\cot 66.5°$

27. (a) $\sin 16.35°$ (b) $\csc 16.35°$

28. (a) $\cos 16° \, 18'$ (b) $\sin 73° \, 56'$

29. (a) $\sec 42° \, 12'$ (b) $\csc 48° \, 7'$

30. (a) $\cos 4° \, 50' \, 15''$ (b) $\sec 4° \, 50' \, 15''$

31. (a) $\cot \dfrac{\pi}{16}$ (b) $\tan \dfrac{\pi}{16}$

32. (a) $\sec 0.75$ (b) $\cos 0.75$

33. (a) $\csc 1$ (b) $\sec\left(\dfrac{\pi}{2} - 1\right)$

34. (a) $\tan \dfrac{1}{2}$ (b) $\cot\left(\dfrac{\pi}{2} - \dfrac{1}{2}\right)$

In Exercises 35–40, find the value of θ in degrees $(0° < \theta < 90°)$ and radians $(0 < \theta < \pi/2)$ without using a calculator.

35. (a) $\sin \theta = \dfrac{1}{2}$ **36.** (a) $\cos \theta = \dfrac{\sqrt{2}}{2}$

    (b) $\csc \theta = 2$ (b) $\tan \theta = 1$

37. (a) $\sec \theta = 2$ **38.** (a) $\tan \theta = \sqrt{3}$

    (b) $\cot \theta = 1$ (b) $\cos \theta = \tfrac{1}{2}$

39. (a) $\csc \theta = \dfrac{2\sqrt{3}}{3}$ **40.** (a) $\cot \theta = \dfrac{\sqrt{3}}{3}$

    (b) $\sin \theta = \dfrac{\sqrt{2}}{2}$ (b) $\sec \theta = \sqrt{2}$

In Exercises 41–44, find the value of θ in degrees $(0° < \theta < 90°)$ and radians $(0 < \theta < \pi/2)$ by using the inverse key on a calculator.

41. (a) $\sin \theta = 0.8191$ **42.** (a) $\cos \theta = 0.9848$

    (b) $\cos \theta = 0.0175$ (b) $\cos \theta = 0.8746$

43. (a) $\tan \theta = 1.1920$ **44.** (a) $\sin \theta = 0.3746$

    (b) $\tan \theta = 0.4663$ (b) $\cos \theta = 0.3746$

45. Solve for y.

46. Solve for x.

47. Solve for x.

48. Solve for r.

49. Solve for r.

50. Solve for x.

51. Solve for y.

52. Solve for r.

53. *Height*   A 6-foot person standing 12 feet from a streetlight casts an 8-foot shadow (see figure). What is the height of the streetlight?

FIGURE FOR 53

54. *Height*   A 6-foot man walked from the base of a broadcasting tower directly toward the tip of the shadow cast by the tower. When he was 132 feet from the tower, his shadow started to appear beyond the tower's shadow. What is the height of the tower if the man's shadow is 3 feet long?

55. *Length*   A 20-foot ladder leaning against the side of a house makes a 75° angle with the ground (see figure). How far up the side of the house does the ladder reach?

FIGURE FOR 55

56. *Width of a River*   A biologist wants to know the width w of a river in order to properly set instruments for studying the pollutants in the water. From point A, the biologist walks downstream 100 feet and sights to point C. From this sighting, it is determined that $\theta = 50°$ (see figure). How wide is the river?

FIGURE FOR 56

57. *Distance*   From a 150-foot observation tower on the coast, a Coast Guard officer sights a boat in difficulty. The angle of depression of the boat is 4° (see figure). How far is the boat from the shoreline?

FIGURE FOR 57

58. *Angle of Elevation*   A ramp $17\frac{1}{2}$ feet in length rises to a loading platform that is $3\frac{1}{3}$ feet off the ground (see figure). Find the angle θ that the ramp makes with the ground.

FIGURE FOR 58

59. *Machine Shop Calculations*   A steel plate has the form of a quarter circle with a radius of 24 inches. Two $\frac{3}{8}$-inch holes are to be drilled in the plate positioned as shown in the figure. Find the coordinates of the center of each hole.

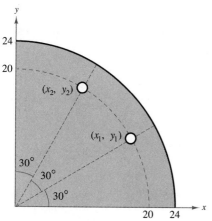

FIGURE FOR 59

60. *Machine Shop Calculations*   A tapered shaft has a diameter of 2 inches at the small end and is 6 inches long (see figure). If the taper is 3°, find the diameter d of the large end of the shaft.

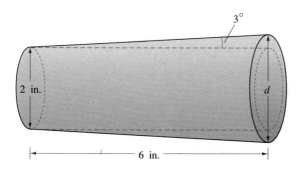

FIGURE FOR 60

61. *Trigonometric Functions by Actual Measurement*   Use a compass to sketch a quarter of a circle of radius 10 centimeters. Using a protractor, construct an angle of 25° in standard position (see figure). Drop a perpendicular line from the point of intersection of the terminal side of the angle and the arc of the circle. By actual measurement, calculate the coordinates (x, y) of the point of intersection and use these measurements to approximate the six trigonometric functions of a 25° angle.

FIGURE FOR 61

62. *Trigonometric Functions by Actual Measurement*   Repeat Exercise 61 using an angle of 75°.

In Exercises 63–68, determine whether the statement is true or false, and give a reason for your answer.

63. $\sin 60° \csc 60° = 1$

64. $\sec 30° = \csc 60°$

65. $\sin 45° + \cos 45° = 1$

66. $\cot^2 10° - \csc^2 10° = -1$

67. $\dfrac{\sin 60°}{\sin 30°} = \sin 2°$

68. $\tan[(0.8)^2] = \tan^2(0.8)$

6.3   TRIGONOMETRIC FUNCTIONS OF ANY ANGLE OR REAL NUMBER

Trigonometric Functions of Any Angle / Reference Angles /
Trigonometric Functions of Real Numbers

Trigonometric Functions of Any Angle

In Section 6.2, you learned to evaluate trigonometric functions of an acute angle. In this section, you will learn to evaluate trigonometric functions of any angle.

REMARK   Because $r = \sqrt{x^2 + y^2}$ *cannot* be zero, it follows that the sine and cosine functions are defined for any real value of θ. However, if $x = 0$, the tangent and secant of θ are undefined. For example, the tangent of 90° is undefined. Try calculating the tangent of 90° with your calculator. Similarly, if $y = 0$, the cotangent and cosecant of θ are undefined.

DEFINITION OF TRIGONOMETRIC FUNCTIONS OF ANY ANGLE

Let θ be an angle in standard position with any point (x, y) (except the origin) on the terminal side of θ and $r = \sqrt{x^2 + y^2}$ (see figure).

$$\sin \theta = \frac{y}{r} \qquad\qquad \csc \theta = \frac{r}{y}, \quad y \neq 0$$

$$\cos \theta = \frac{x}{r} \qquad\qquad \sec \theta = \frac{r}{x}, \quad x \neq 0$$

$$\tan \theta = \frac{y}{x}, \quad x \neq 0 \qquad\qquad \cot \theta = \frac{x}{y}, \quad y \neq 0$$

$$r = \sqrt{x^2 + y^2}$$

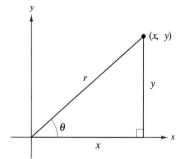

FIGURE 6.26

If θ is an *acute* angle, then these definitions coincide with those given in the previous section. To see this, note in Figure 6.26 that for an acute angle θ, $x = $ adj, $y = $ opp, and $r = $ hyp.

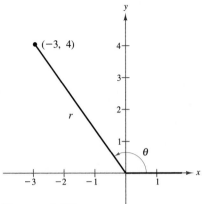

FIGURE 6.27

EXAMPLE 1   Evaluating Trigonometric Functions

Let $(-3, 4)$ be a point on the terminal side of θ. Find the sine, cosine, and tangent of θ.

SOLUTION

Referring to Figure 6.27, you can see that $x = -3$, $y = 4$, and

$$r = \sqrt{x^2 + y^2} = \sqrt{(-3)^2 + 4^2} = \sqrt{25} = 5.$$

Thus, you can write the following.

$$\sin \theta = \frac{y}{r} = \frac{4}{5}$$

$$\cos \theta = \frac{x}{r} = \frac{-3}{5} = -\frac{3}{5}$$

$$\tan \theta = \frac{y}{x} = \frac{4}{-3} = -\frac{4}{3}$$

The *signs* of trigonometric function values in the four quadrants can be determined easily from the definitions of the functions. For instance, because $\cos \theta = x/r$, it follows that $\cos \theta$ is positive wherever $x > 0$, which is in Quadrants I and IV. (Remember, r is always positive.) In a similar manner, you can verify the results shown in Figure 6.28.

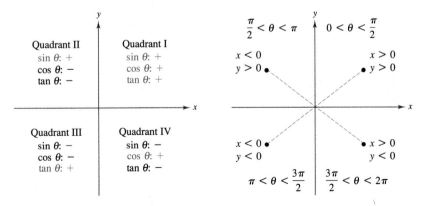

Signs of Trigonometric Functions

FIGURE 6.28

EXAMPLE 2   Evaluating Trigonometric Functions

Given $\tan \theta = -\frac{5}{4}$ and $\cos \theta > 0$, find $\sin \theta$ and $\sec \theta$.

SOLUTION

Note that θ lies in Quadrant IV because that is the only quadrant in which the tangent is negative and the cosine is positive. Moreover, using

$$\tan \theta = \frac{y}{x} = -\frac{5}{4}$$

and the fact that y is negative in Quadrant IV, you can let $y = -5$ and $x = 4$. Hence, $r = \sqrt{25 + 16} = \sqrt{41}$, and you have

$$\sin \theta = \frac{y}{r} = \frac{-5}{\sqrt{41}} \approx -0.7809$$

and

$$\sec \theta = \frac{r}{x} = \frac{\sqrt{41}}{4} \approx 1.6008.$$

EXAMPLE 3   Trigonometric Functions of Quadrant Angles

Evaluate the sine function at the four quadrant angles 0, $\pi/2$, π, and $3\pi/2$.

SOLUTION

To begin, choose a point on the terminal side of each angle, as shown in Figure 6.29. For each of the four given points, $r = 1$, and you have

$$\sin 0 = \frac{y}{r} = \frac{0}{1} = 0 \qquad\qquad (x, y) = (1, 0)$$

$$\sin \frac{\pi}{2} = \frac{y}{r} = \frac{1}{1} = 1 \qquad\qquad (x, y) = (0, 1)$$

$$\sin \pi = \frac{y}{r} = \frac{0}{1} = 0 \qquad\qquad (x, y) = (-1, 0)$$

$$\sin \frac{3\pi}{2} = \frac{y}{r} = \frac{-1}{1} = -1. \qquad\qquad (x, y) = (0, -1)$$

Try using Figure 6.29 to evaluate some of the other trigonometric functions at the four quadrant angles and check them on your calculator.

FIGURE 6.29

Quadrant II

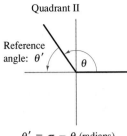

$\theta' = \pi - \theta$ (radians)
$\theta' = 180° - \theta$ (degrees)

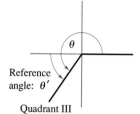

Reference
angle: θ'

Quadrant III
$\theta' = \theta - \pi$ (radians)
$\theta' = \theta - 180°$ (degrees)

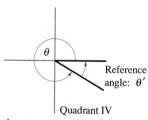

Reference
angle: θ'

Quadrant IV
$\theta' = 2\pi - \theta$ (radians)
$\theta' = 360° - \theta$ (degrees)

FIGURE 6.30

Reference Angles

The values of the trigonometric functions of angles greater than 90° (or less than 0°) can be determined from their values at corresponding acute angles called **reference angles.**

DEFINITION OF REFERENCE ANGLES

Let θ be an angle in standard position. Its **reference angle** is the acute angle θ' formed by the terminal side of θ and the horizontal axis.

Figure 6.30 shows the reference angle for θ in Quadrants II, III, and IV.

EXAMPLE 4   **Finding Reference Angles**
....

Find the reference angle θ' for each of the following.

A. $\theta = 300°$ **B.** $\theta = 2.3$ **C.** $\theta = -135°$

SOLUTION

A. Because $\theta = 300°$ lies in Quadrant IV, the angle it makes with the x-axis is

$$\theta' = 360° - 300° = 60° \qquad \textit{Degrees}$$

B. Because $\theta = 2.3$ lies between $\pi/2 \approx 1.5708$ and $\pi \approx 3.1416$, it follows that θ is in Quadrant II and its reference angle is

$$\theta' = \pi - 2.3 \approx 0.8416. \qquad \textit{Radians}$$

C. Because $\theta = -135°$ is coterminal with 225°, it lies in Quadrant III. Hence, the reference angle is

$$\theta' = 225° - 180° = 45°. \qquad \textit{Degrees}$$

Figure 6.31 shows each angle θ and its reference angle θ'.

(a) θ in Quadrant IV   (b) θ in Quadrant II   (c) θ in Quadrant III

FIGURE 6.31

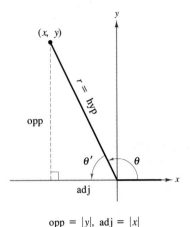

opp = $|y|$, adj = $|x|$

FIGURE 6.32

To see how a reference angle is used to evaluate a trigonometric function, consider the point (x, y) on the terminal side of θ, as shown in Figure 6.32. By definition, you know that

$$\sin \theta = \frac{y}{r} \quad \text{and} \quad \tan \theta = \frac{y}{x}.$$

For the right triangle with acute angle θ' and sides of lengths $|x|$ and $|y|$, you have

$$\sin \theta' = \frac{\text{opp}}{\text{hyp}} = \frac{|y|}{r} \quad \text{and} \quad \tan \theta' = \frac{\text{opp}}{\text{adj}} = \frac{|y|}{|x|}.$$

Thus, it follows that $\sin \theta$ and $\sin \theta'$ are equal, *except possibly in sign*. The same is true for $\tan \theta$ and $\tan \theta'$ *and* for the other four trigonometric functions. In all cases, the sign of the function value can be determined by the quadrant in which θ lies.

EVALUATING TRIGONOMETRIC FUNCTIONS OF ANY ANGLE

To find the value of a trigonometric function of any angle θ:

1. Determine the function value for the associated reference angle θ'.
2. Depending on the quadrant in which θ lies, prefix the appropriate sign to the function value.

By using reference angles and the special angles discussed in the previous section, you can greatly extend your scope of *exact* trigonometric values (see Table 6.1). For instance, knowing the function values of 30° means that you know the function values of all angles for which 30° is a reference angle.

TABLE 6.1

θ (degrees)	0°	30°	45°	60°	90°	180°	270°
θ (radians)	0	$\dfrac{\pi}{6}$	$\dfrac{\pi}{4}$	$\dfrac{\pi}{3}$	$\dfrac{\pi}{2}$	π	$\dfrac{3\pi}{2}$
$\sin \theta$	0	$\dfrac{1}{2}$	$\dfrac{\sqrt{2}}{2}$	$\dfrac{\sqrt{3}}{2}$	1	0	-1
$\cos \theta$	1	$\dfrac{\sqrt{3}}{2}$	$\dfrac{\sqrt{2}}{2}$	$\dfrac{1}{2}$	0	-1	0
$\tan \theta$	0	$\dfrac{\sqrt{3}}{3}$	1	$\sqrt{3}$	undef.	0	undef.

EXAMPLE 5   Trigonometric Functions of Nonacute Angles

Evaluate the following.

A. $\cos \dfrac{4\pi}{3}$ **B.** $\tan(-210°)$ **C.** $\csc \dfrac{11\pi}{4}$

SOLUTION

A. Because $\theta = 4\pi/3$ lies in Quadrant III, the reference angle is $\theta' = (4\pi/3) - \pi = \pi/3$, as shown in Figure 6.33(a). Moreover, the cosine is negative in Quadrant III, so that

$$\cos \frac{4\pi}{3} = (-) \cos \frac{\pi}{3} = -\frac{1}{2}.$$ *Reference angle,* $\dfrac{\pi}{3}$

B. Because $-210° + 360° = 150°$, it follows that $-210°$ is coterminal with the second-quadrant angle $150°$. Therefore, the reference angle is $\theta' = 180° - 150° = 30°$, as shown in Figure 6.33(b). Finally, because the tangent is negative in Quadrant II, you have

$$\tan(-210°) = (-) \tan 30° = -\frac{\sqrt{3}}{3}.$$ *Reference angle,* $30°$

C. Because $(11\pi/4) - 2\pi = 3\pi/4$, it follows that $11\pi/4$ is coterminal with the second-quadrant angle $3\pi/4$. Therefore, the reference angle is $\theta' = \pi - (3\pi/4) = \pi/4$, as shown in Figure 6.33(c). Because the cosecant is positive in Quadrant II, you have

$$\csc \frac{11\pi}{4} = (+) \csc \frac{\pi}{4} = \frac{1}{\sin(\pi/4)} = \sqrt{2}.$$ *Reference angle,* $\dfrac{\pi}{4}$

Check the above values with your calculator.

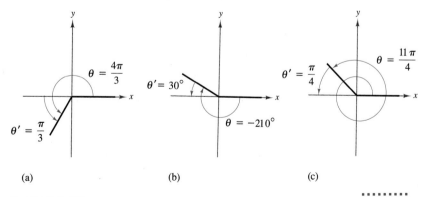

(a)   (b)   (c)

FIGURE 6.33

The fundamental trigonometric identities listed in the previous section (for an acute angle θ) are also valid when θ is any angle.

EXAMPLE 6   Using Identities to Evaluate Trigonometric Functions

Let θ be an angle in Quadrant II such that $\sin \theta = \frac{1}{3}$. Find the following.

A. $\cos \theta$ **B.** $\tan \theta$

SOLUTION

A. Because $\sin \theta = \frac{1}{3}$, use the Pythagorean Identity $\sin^2 \theta + \cos^2 \theta = 1$ to obtain

$$\left(\frac{1}{3}\right)^2 + \cos^2 \theta = 1$$

$$\cos^2 \theta = 1 - \frac{1}{9} = \frac{8}{9}.$$

Because $\cos \theta < 0$ in Quadrant II, use the negative root

$$\cos \theta = -\frac{\sqrt{8}}{\sqrt{9}} = -\frac{2\sqrt{2}}{3}.$$

B. Using the result from part (A) and the trigonometric identity $\tan \theta = \sin \theta / \cos \theta$, you obtain

$$\tan \theta = \frac{1/3}{-2\sqrt{2}/3} = -\frac{1}{2\sqrt{2}} = -\frac{\sqrt{2}}{4}.$$

Scientific calculators can be used to approximate the values of trigonometric functions of any angle, as demonstrated in Example 7.

EXAMPLE 7   Evaluating Trigonometric Functions with a Calculator

Use a calculator to approximate the following values. (Round your answers to three decimal places.)

A. $\cot 410°$ **B.** $\sin(-7)$ **C.** $\tan \dfrac{14\pi}{5}$

SOLUTION

Function	Mode	Display	Rounded to 3 Decimal Places
A. $\cot 410°$	Degree	0.8390996312	0.839
B. $\sin(-7)$	Radian	−0.6569865987	−0.657
C. $\tan \dfrac{14\pi}{5}$	Radian	−0.726542528	−0.727

Trigonometric Functions of Real Numbers

To define a trigonometric function of a real number (rather than an angle), let *t* represent any real number. Then imagine that the real number line is wrapped around a *unit circle,* as shown in Figure 6.34. Note that positive numbers correspond to a counterclockwise wrapping, and negative numbers correspond to a clockwise wrapping.

As the real number line is wrapped around the unit circle, each real number *t* will correspond with a central angle θ. Moreover, because the circle has a radius of 1, the arc *s* subtended by the angle θ will have a length of $s = r\theta = 1 \cdot \theta = \theta$. Thus, *if θ is measured in radians, then $t = \theta$.*

Positive numbers

Negative numbers

FIGURE 6.34

EXAMPLE 8   **Evaluating Trigonometric Functions of Real Numbers**

Evaluate $f(t) = \sin t$ for the following.

A. $t = 1$

B. $t = \dfrac{3\pi}{2}$

SOLUTION

A. $f(1) = \sin 1 \approx 0.8414709848$

B. $f\left(\dfrac{3\pi}{2}\right) = \sin \dfrac{3\pi}{2} = -1$

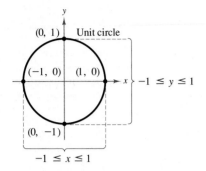

FIGURE 6.35

The *domain* of the sine and cosine functions is the set of all real numbers. To determine the *range* of these two functions, consider the unit circle shown in Figure 6.35. Because $r = 1$, it follows that $\sin t = y$ and $\cos t = x$. Moreover, because (x, y) is on the unit circle, you know that $-1 \leq y \leq 1$ and $-1 \leq x \leq 1$, and it follows that the values of the sine and cosine also range between -1 and 1.

$$-1 \leq \; y \; \leq 1 \qquad\qquad -1 \leq \; x \; \leq 1$$
$$-1 \leq \sin t \leq 1 \quad \text{and} \quad -1 \leq \cos t \leq 1$$

Suppose you add 2π to each value of t in the interval $[0, 2\pi]$, thus completing a second revolution around the unit circle, as shown in Figure 6.36. The values of $\sin(t + 2\pi)$ and $\cos(t + 2\pi)$ correspond to those of $\sin t$ and $\cos t$. Similar results can be obtained for repeated revolutions (positive or negative) on the unit circle. This leads to the general result

$$\sin(t + 2\pi n) = \sin t \quad \text{and} \quad \cos(t + 2\pi n) = \cos t$$

for any integer n and real number t. Functions that behave in such a repetitive (or cyclic) manner are **periodic.**

$$t = \frac{\pi}{2}, \frac{\pi}{2} + 2\pi, \frac{\pi}{2} + 4\pi, \cdots$$

$$t = \frac{3\pi}{4}, \frac{3\pi}{4} + 2\pi, \cdots \qquad\qquad t = \frac{\pi}{4}, \frac{\pi}{4} + 2\pi, \frac{\pi}{4} + 4\pi, \cdots$$

$$t = \pi, 3\pi, \cdots \qquad\qquad t = 0, 2\pi, 4\pi, \cdots$$

$$t = \frac{5\pi}{4}, \frac{5\pi}{4} + 2\pi, \cdots \qquad\qquad t = \frac{7\pi}{4}, \frac{7\pi}{4} + 2\pi, \frac{7\pi}{4} + 4\pi, \cdots$$

Repeated Revolutions on the Unit Circle

FIGURE 6.36

DEFINITION OF A PERIODIC FUNCTION

A function f is **periodic** if there exists a positive real number c such that

$$f(t + c) = f(t)$$

for all t in the domain of f. The least number c for which f is periodic is the **period** of f.

From this definition it follows that the sine and cosine functions are periodic and have a period of 2π. The other four trigonometric functions are also periodic (see Section 6.5).

Recall from Section 1.4 that a function f is *even* if $f(-t) = f(t)$, and is *odd* if $f(-t) = -f(t)$.

EVEN AND ODD TRIGONOMETRIC FUNCTIONS

The cosine and secant functions are *even*.

$$\cos(-t) = \cos t \qquad \sec(-t) = \sec t$$

The sine, cosecant, tangent, and cotangent functions are *odd*.

$$\sin(-t) = -\sin t \qquad \csc(-t) = -\csc t$$
$$\tan(-t) = -\tan t \qquad \cot(-t) = -\cot t$$

At this point, you have completed your introduction to basic trigonometry. You have measured angles in both degrees and radians. You have studied the definitions of the six trigonometric functions from a right triangle perspective and as functions of real numbers. In your remaining study of trigonometry, you will continue to rely on both perspectives.

For your convenience, we have included on the inside cover of this text a summary of basic trigonometry.

**DISCUSSION
PROBLEM**

················

**MEMORIZATION
AIDS**

There are many different techniques that people use to memorize (or reconstruct) trigonometric formulas. Here is one that we like to use for the sines and cosines of common angles.

θ	0°	30°	45°	60°	90°
$\sin \theta$	$\dfrac{\sqrt{0}}{2}$	$\dfrac{\sqrt{1}}{2}$	$\dfrac{\sqrt{2}}{2}$	$\dfrac{\sqrt{3}}{2}$	$\dfrac{\sqrt{4}}{2}$
$\cos \theta$	$\dfrac{\sqrt{4}}{2}$	$\dfrac{\sqrt{3}}{2}$	$\dfrac{\sqrt{2}}{2}$	$\dfrac{\sqrt{1}}{2}$	$\dfrac{\sqrt{0}}{2}$

Write a paragraph describing the pattern indicated by this table. Discuss other memory aids for trigonometric formulas.

WARM-UP

The following warm-up exercises involve skills that were covered in earlier sections. You will use these skills in the exercise set for this section.

In Exercises 1–6, evaluate the trigonometric function without using a calculator.

1. $\sin 30°$ **2.** $\tan 45°$ **3.** $\cos \dfrac{\pi}{4}$

4. $\cot \dfrac{\pi}{3}$ **5.** $\sec \dfrac{\pi}{6}$ **6.** $\csc \dfrac{\pi}{4}$

In Exercises 7–10, use the given trigonometric function of an acute angle θ to find the values of the remaining trigonometric functions.

7. $\tan \theta = \frac{3}{2}$ **8.** $\cos \theta = \frac{2}{3}$ **9.** $\sin \theta = \frac{1}{5}$ **10.** $\sec \theta = 3$

SECTION 6.3 · EXERCISES

In Exercises 1–4, determine the exact value of the six trigonometric functions of the angle θ.

1. (a)

(b)

3. (a)

(b)

2. (a)

(b)

4. (a)

(b)

In Exercises 5–8, the point is on the terminal side of an angle in standard position. Determine the exact values of the six trigonometric functions of the angle.

5. (a) $(7, 24)$ (b) $(7, -24)$

6. (a) $(8, 15)$ (b) $(-9, -40)$

7. (a) $(-4, 10)$ (b) $(3, -5)$

8. (a) $(-5, -2)$ (b) $(-\frac{3}{2}, 3)$

In Exercises 9–12, determine the quadrant in which θ lies.

9. (a) $\sin \theta < 0$ and $\cos \theta < 0$
   (b) $\sin \theta > 0$ and $\cos \theta < 0$

10. (a) $\sin \theta > 0$ and $\cos \theta > 0$
   (b) $\sin \theta < 0$ and $\cos \theta > 0$

11. (a) $\sin \theta > 0$ and $\tan \theta < 0$
   (b) $\cos \theta > 0$ and $\tan \theta < 0$

12. (a) $\sec \theta > 0$ and $\cot \theta < 0$
   (b) $\csc \theta < 0$ and $\tan \theta > 0$

In Exercises 13–22, find the values (if possible) of the six trigonometric functions of θ using the function value and constraint.

Function Value	Constraint
13. $\sin \theta = \frac{3}{5}$	θ lies in Quadrant II
14. $\cos \theta = -\frac{4}{5}$	θ lies in Quadrant III
15. $\tan \theta = -\frac{15}{8}$	$\sin \theta < 0$
16. $\cos \theta = \frac{8}{17}$	$\tan \theta < 0$
17. $\sec \theta = -2$	$\sin \theta > 0$
18. $\cot \theta$ is undefined	$\frac{\pi}{2} \leq \theta \leq \frac{3\pi}{2}$
19. $\sin \theta = 0$	$\sec \theta = -1$
20. $\tan \theta$ is undefined	$\pi \leq \theta \leq 2\pi$

21. The terminal side of θ is in Quadrant III and lies on the line $y = 2x$.

22. The terminal side of θ is in Quadrant IV and lies on the line $4x + 3y = 0$.

In Exercises 23–30, sketch θ in standard position and find the reference angle θ'.

23. (a) $\theta = 203°$ (b) $\theta = 127°$

24. (a) $\theta = 309°$ (b) $\theta = 226°$

25. (a) $\theta = -245°$ (b) $\theta = -72°$

26. (a) $\theta = -145°$ (b) $\theta = -239°$

27. (a) $\theta = \frac{2\pi}{3}$ (b) $\theta = \frac{7\pi}{6}$

28. (a) $\theta = \frac{7\pi}{4}$ (b) $\theta = \frac{8\pi}{9}$

29. (a) $\theta = 3.5$ (b) $\theta = 5.8$

30. (a) $\theta = \frac{11\pi}{3}$ (b) $\theta = -\frac{7\pi}{10}$

In Exercises 31–40, evaluate the sine, cosine, and tangent of the angles without using a calculator.

31. (a) $225°$ (b) $-225°$ **32.** (a) $300°$ (b) $330°$

33. (a) $750°$ (b) $510°$ **34.** (a) $-405°$ (b) $-120°$

35. (a) $\frac{4\pi}{3}$ (b) $\frac{2\pi}{3}$ **36.** (a) $\frac{\pi}{4}$ (b) $\frac{5\pi}{4}$

37. (a) $-\frac{\pi}{6}$ (b) $\frac{5\pi}{6}$ **38.** (a) $-\frac{\pi}{2}$ (b) $\frac{\pi}{2}$

39. (a) $\frac{11\pi}{4}$ (b) $-\frac{13\pi}{6}$ **40.** (a) $\frac{10\pi}{3}$ (b) $\frac{17\pi}{3}$

In Exercises 41–48, use a calculator to evaluate the trigonometric functions. (Round your results to four decimal places.)

41. (a) $\sin 10°$ (b) $\csc 10°$

42. (a) $\sec 225°$ (b) $\sec 135°$

43. (a) $\cos(-110°)$ (b) $\cos 250°$

44. (a) $\csc 330°$ (b) $\csc 150°$

45. (a) $\tan 240°$ (b) $\cot 210°$

46. (a) $\cot 1.35$ (b) $\tan 1.35$

47. (a) $\tan \frac{\pi}{9}$ (b) $\tan \frac{10\pi}{9}$

48. (a) $\sin(-0.65)$ (b) $\sin 5.63$

In Exercises 49–54, find two values of θ that satisfy the equation. List your results in degrees ($0° \leq \theta < 360°$) and radians ($0 \leq \theta < 2\pi$). Do not use a calculator.

49. (a) $\sin \theta = \frac{1}{2}$ (b) $\sin \theta = -\frac{1}{2}$

50. (a) $\cos \theta = \frac{\sqrt{2}}{2}$ (b) $\cos \theta = -\frac{\sqrt{2}}{2}$

51. (a) $\csc \theta = \frac{2\sqrt{3}}{3}$ (b) $\cot \theta = -1$

52. (a) $\sec \theta = 2$ (b) $\sec \theta = -2$

53. (a) $\tan \theta = 1$ (b) $\cot \theta = -\sqrt{3}$

54. (a) $\sin \theta = \frac{\sqrt{3}}{2}$ (b) $\sin \theta = -\frac{\sqrt{3}}{2}$

In Exercises 55 and 56, use a calculator to approximate two values of θ ($0° \le \theta < 360°$) that satisfy the equation. (Round your results to two decimal places.)

55. (a) $\sin \theta = 0.8191$ (b) $\sin \theta = -0.2589$
56. (a) $\cos \theta = 0.8746$ (b) $\cos \theta = -0.2419$

In Exercises 57–60, use a calculator to approximate two values of θ ($0 \le \theta < 2\pi$) that satisfy the equation. (Round your results to three decimal places.)

57. (a) $\cos \theta = 0.9848$ (b) $\cos \theta = -0.5890$
58. (a) $\sin \theta = 0.0175$ (b) $\sin \theta = -0.6691$
59. (a) $\tan \theta = 1.192$ (b) $\tan \theta = -8.144$
60. (a) $\cot \theta = 5.671$ (b) $\cot \theta = -1.280$

In Exercises 61–66, use the value of the trigonometric function to find the indicated trigonometric value in the specified quadrant.

Given Function	Quadrant	Find
61. $\sin \theta = -\frac{3}{5}$	IV	$\cos \theta$
62. $\cot \theta = -3$	II	$\sin \theta$
63. $\tan \theta = \frac{3}{2}$	III	$\sec \theta$
64. $\csc \theta = -2$	IV	$\cot \theta$
65. $\cos \theta = \frac{5}{8}$	I	$\sec \theta$
66. $\sec \theta = -\frac{9}{4}$	III	$\tan \theta$

67. *Average Temperature*   The average daily temperature T (in degrees Fahrenheit) for a certain city is given by

$$T = 45 - 23 \cos\left[\frac{2\pi}{365}(t - 32)\right],$$

where t is the time in days, with $t = 1$ corresponding to January 1. Find the average daily temperature on the following days.
(a) January 1
(b) July 4 ($t = 185$)
(c) October 18 ($t = 291$)

68. *Sales*   A company that produces a seasonal product forecasts monthly sales over the next 2 years to be

$$S = 23.1 + 0.442t + 4.3 \sin\frac{\pi t}{6},$$

where S is measured in thousands of units and t is the time in months, with $t = 1$ representing January 1991. Predict sales for the following months.
(a) February 1991   (b) February 1992
(c) September 1991   (d) September 1992

69. *Harmonic Motion*   The displacement from equilibrium of an oscillating weight suspended by a spring is given by

$$y(t) = \tfrac{1}{4} \cos 6t,$$

where y is the displacement in feet and t is the time in seconds. Find the displacement when (a) $t = 0$, (b) $t = \frac{1}{4}$, and (c) $t = \frac{1}{2}$.

70. *Harmonic Motion*   The displacement from equilibrium of an oscillating weight suspended by a spring and subject to the damping effect of friction is given by

$$y(t) = \tfrac{1}{4} e^{-t} \cos 6t,$$

where y is the displacement in feet and t is the time in seconds. Find the displacement when (a) $t = 0$, (b) $t = \frac{1}{4}$, and (c) $t = \frac{1}{2}$.

71. *Distance*   An airplane flying at an altitude of 5 miles is on a flight path that passes directly over an observer (see figure). If θ is the angle from the observer to the plane, find the distance d from the observer to the plane when (a) $\theta = 30°$, (b) $\theta = 90°$, and (c) $\theta = 120°$.

FIGURE FOR 71

72. Consider an angle in standard position with $r = 10$ centimeters, as shown in the figure. Write a short paragraph describing the changes in the magnitudes of x, y, $\sin \theta$, $\cos \theta$, and $\tan \theta$ as θ increases continuously from $0°$ to $90°$.

FIGURE FOR 72

6.4   GRAPHS OF SINE AND COSINE FUNCTIONS

Basic Sine and Cosine Curves / Key Points on Basic Sine and Cosine Curves / Amplitude and Period of Sine and Cosine Curves / Translations of Sine and Cosine Curves

Basic Sine and Cosine Curves

In this section you will study techniques for sketching the graphs of the sine and cosine functions. The graph of the sine function is called a **sine curve.** In Figure 6.37, the solid portion of the graph represents one period of the function and is called **one cycle** of the sine curve. The gray portion of the graph indicates that the basic sine wave repeats indefinitely to the right and left. The graph of the cosine function is shown in Figure 6.38. To produce these graphs with a graphing utility, make sure you have set the mode to *radians*.

Recall from Section 6.3 that the domain of the sine and cosine function is the set of all real numbers. Moreover, the range of each function is the interval $[-1, 1]$, and each function has a period of 2π. Do you see how this information is consistent with the basic graphs given in Figures 6.37 and 6.38?

Note from Figures 6.37 and 6.38 that the sine graph is symmetric with respect to the *origin*, whereas the cosine graph is symmetric with respect to the *y*-axis. These properties of symmetry follow from the fact that the sine function is odd whereas the cosine function is even.

x	0	$\dfrac{\pi}{6}$	$\dfrac{\pi}{3}$	$\dfrac{\pi}{2}$	$\dfrac{3\pi}{4}$	π	$\dfrac{3\pi}{2}$	2π
$\sin x$	0	$\dfrac{1}{2}$	$\dfrac{\sqrt{3}}{2}$	1	$\dfrac{\sqrt{2}}{2}$	0	-1	0

FIGURE 6.37

Range: $-1 \le y \le 1$

Period: 2π

x	0	$\dfrac{\pi}{6}$	$\dfrac{\pi}{3}$	$\dfrac{\pi}{2}$	$\dfrac{3\pi}{4}$	π	$\dfrac{3\pi}{2}$	2π
$\cos x$	1	$\dfrac{\sqrt{3}}{2}$	$\dfrac{1}{2}$	0	$-\dfrac{\sqrt{2}}{2}$	-1	0	1

FIGURE 6.38

Range: $-1 \le y \le 1$

Period: 2π

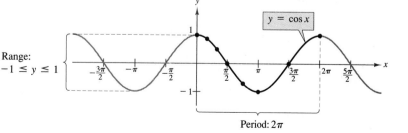

Key Points on Basic Sine and Cosine Curves

To construct the graphs of the basic sine and cosine functions *by hand,* it helps to note five **key points** in one period of each graph: the intercepts, maximum points, and minimum points. For the sine function, the key points are

Intercept   Maximum   Intercept   Minimum   Intercept

$$(0, 0), \quad \left(\frac{\pi}{2}, 1\right), \quad (\pi, 0), \quad \left(\frac{3\pi}{2}, -1\right), \quad (2\pi, 0).$$

For the cosine function, the key points are

Maximum   Intercept   Minimum   Intercept   Maximum

$$(0, 1), \quad \left(\frac{\pi}{2}, 0\right), \quad (\pi, -1), \quad \left(\frac{3\pi}{2}, 0\right), \quad (2\pi, 1).$$

Note how the *x*-coordinates of these points divide the period of sin *x* and cos *x* into *four* equal parts, as indicated in Figure 6.39.

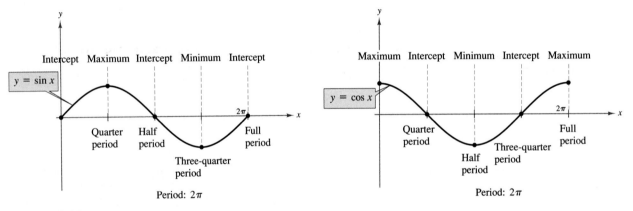

FIGURE 6.39

Technology Note

When using a graphing utility to graph trigonometric functions, pay special attention to the viewing rectangle you use. For instance, try graphing $y = [\sin(30x)]/30$ on the standard viewing rectangle. What do you observe? Use the zoom feature to find a viewing rectangle that displays a good view of the graph.

EXAMPLE 1   **Using Key Points to Sketch a Sine Curve**

Sketch the graph of $y = 2 \sin x$ on the interval $[-\pi, 4\pi]$.

SOLUTION

The *y*-values for the key points of $y = 2 \sin x$ have twice the magnitude of those of $y = \sin x$. Thus, the key points for $y = 2 \sin x$ are

$$(0, 0), \quad \left(\frac{\pi}{2}, 2\right), \quad (\pi, 0), \quad \left(\frac{3\pi}{2}, -2\right), \quad \text{and} \quad (2\pi, 0).$$

By connecting these key points with a smooth curve and extending the curve in both directions over the interval $[-\pi, 4\pi]$, you obtain the graph shown in Figure 6.40. Try using a graphing utility to check this result.

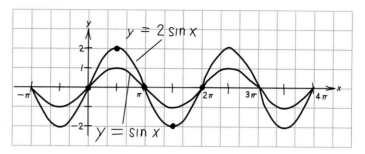

FIGURE 6.40

Amplitude and Period of Sine and Cosine Curves

In the rest of this section, you will study the graphic effect of each of the constants a, b, c, and d in equations of the forms

$$y = d + a \sin(bx - c) \quad \text{and} \quad y = d + a \cos(bx - c).$$

A quick review of the transformations studied in Section 1.5 should help in this investigation.

The constant factor a in $y = a \sin x$ acts as a *vertical stretch* or *vertical shrink* of the basic sine curve, as shown in Example 1. (If $|a| > 1$, the basic sine curve is stretched, and if $|a| < 1$, the basic sine curve is shrunk.) The result is that the graph of $y = a \sin x$ ranges between $-a$ and a instead of between -1 and 1. The absolute value of a is the **amplitude** of the function $y = a \sin x$.

DEFINITION OF AMPLITUDE OF SINE AND COSINE CURVES

The **amplitude** of $y = a \sin x$ and $y = a \cos x$ is the largest value of y, and is given by

$$\text{Amplitude} = |a|.$$

EXAMPLE 2 Vertical Shrinking and Stretching

Sketch the graphs of $y = \frac{1}{2} \cos x$ and $y = 3 \cos x$.

SOLUTION

Because the amplitude of $y = \frac{1}{2} \cos x$ is $\frac{1}{2}$, the maximum value is $\frac{1}{2}$ and the minimum value is $-\frac{1}{2}$. For one cycle, $0 \leq x \leq 2\pi$, the key points are

$$\left(0, \frac{1}{2}\right), \quad \left(\frac{\pi}{2}, 0\right), \quad \left(\pi, -\frac{1}{2}\right), \quad \left(\frac{3\pi}{2}, 0\right), \quad \text{and} \quad \left(2\pi, \frac{1}{2}\right).$$

The amplitude of $y = 3 \cos x$ is 3, and the key points are

$$(0, 3), \quad \left(\frac{\pi}{2}, 0\right), \quad (\pi, -3), \quad \left(\frac{3\pi}{2}, 0\right), \quad \text{and} \quad (2\pi, 3).$$

The graphs of these two functions are shown in Figure 6.41. Try using a graphing utility to check this result.

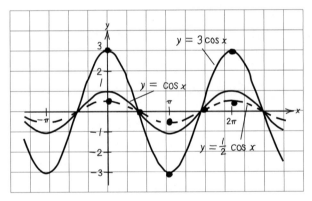

Amplitude Determines Vertical Stretch or Shrink

FIGURE 6.41

You know from Section 1.5 that the graph of $y = -f(x)$ is a **reflection** (in the x-axis) of the graph of $y = f(x)$. For instance, the graph of $y = -3 \cos x$ is a reflection of the graph of $y = 3 \cos x$, as shown in Figure 6.42.

Because $y = a \sin x$ completes one cycle from $x = 0$ to $x = 2\pi$, it follows that $y = a \sin bx$ completes one cycle from $bx = 0$ to $bx = 2\pi$. This implies that $y = a \sin bx$ completes one cycle from $x = 0$ to $x = 2\pi/b$.

$y = 3 \cos x$ $y = -3 \cos x$

4

−4.71   7.85

−4

Reflection in the x-Axis

FIGURE 6.42

D I S C O V E R Y

Use a graphing utility to draw the graph of $y = \sin bx$, where $b = 0.5$, 1, and 2. (Use a viewing rectangle in which $0 \le X \le 6.3$ and $-2 \le Y \le 2$.) How does the value of b affect the graph?

PERIOD OF SINE AND COSINE FUNCTIONS

Let b be a positive real number. The **period** of $y = a \sin bx$ and $y = a \cos bx$ is $2\pi/b$.

Note that if $0 < b < 1$, the period of $y = a \sin bx$ is greater than 2π and represents a *horizontal stretching* of the graph of $y = a \sin x$. Similarly, if $b > 1$, the period of $y = a \sin bx$ is less than 2π and represents a *horizontal shrinking* of the graph of $y = a \sin x$.

If b is negative, use the identities $\sin(-x) = -\sin x$ and $\cos(-x) = \cos x$ to rewrite the function.

EXAMPLE 3   Horizontal Stretching and Shrinking

Sketch the graph of

$$y = \sin \frac{x}{2}.$$

SOLUTION

The amplitude is 1. Moreover, because $b = \frac{1}{2}$, the period is $2\pi/(\frac{1}{2}) = 4\pi$. By dividing the period-interval $[0, 4\pi]$ into four equal parts with the values $\pi, 2\pi$, and 3π, you obtain the following key points on the graph.

$$(0, 0), \quad (\pi, 1), \quad (2\pi, 0), \quad (3\pi, -1), \quad \text{and} \quad (4\pi, 0)$$

The graph is shown in Figure 6.43. Use a graphing utility to check this result.

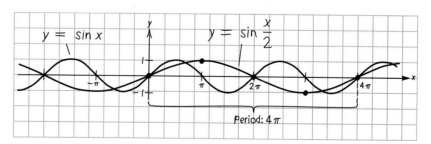

FIGURE 6.43

EXAMPLE 4   Horizontal Stretching and Shrinking

Sketch the graph of $y = \sin 3x$.

SOLUTION

The amplitude is 1, and because $b = 3$, the period is

$$\frac{2\pi}{b} = \frac{2\pi}{3}.$$

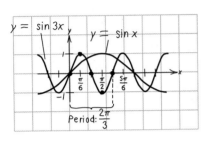

$y = \sin 3x$ $y = \sin x$

Period: $\dfrac{2\pi}{3}$

FIGURE 6.44

Dividing the period-interval $[0, 2\pi/3]$ into four equal parts, you obtain the following key points on the graph.

$$(0, 0), \quad \left(\frac{\pi}{6}, 1\right), \quad \left(\frac{\pi}{3}, 0\right), \quad \left(\frac{\pi}{2}, -1\right), \quad \text{and} \quad \left(\frac{2\pi}{3}, 0\right)$$

The graph is shown in Figure 6.44. Use a graphing utility to check this result.

EXAMPLE 5   Using a Graphing Utility

Use a graphing utility to graph $y = 2 \cos 0.4x$ and $y = 2 \cos 4x$ on the same screen. Determine the period of each function from its graph.

SOLUTION

The standard viewing rectangle is not appropriate for graphing most sine and cosine functions. You should choose a viewing rectangle that accommodates the amplitudes of the functions as well as any stretching or shrinking that may occur. For these graphs, a y-scale ranging between -3 and 3 will accommodate the amplitudes of 2. Figure 6.45 shows the two graphs and an appropriate viewing rectangle. From the graph, you can estimate the period of $y = 2 \cos 0.4x$ to be about 16 and the period of $y = 2 \cos 4x$ to be about 1.5. Algebraically, the period of $y = 2 \cos 0.4x$ is

$$\frac{2\pi}{0.4} = 5\pi \approx 15.71,$$

and the period of $y = 2 \cos 4x$ is

$$\frac{2\pi}{4} = \frac{\pi}{2} \approx 1.57.$$

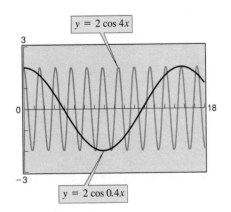

$y = 2 \cos 4x$

$y = 2 \cos 0.4x$

FIGURE 6.45

Translations of Sine and Cosine Curves

The constant c in the general equations

$$y = a \sin(bx - c) \quad \text{and} \quad y = a \cos(bx - c)$$

creates a horizontal shift of the basic sine and cosine curves. The graph of $y = a \sin(bx - c)$ completes one cycle from $bx - c = 0$ to $bx - c = 2\pi$. By solving for x in the inequality $0 \le bx - c \le 2\pi$, you can find the interval for one cycle to be

$$
\overbrace{\frac{c}{b}}^{\text{Left endpoint}} \le x \le \overbrace{\frac{c}{b} + \underbrace{\frac{2\pi}{b}}_{\text{Period}}}^{\text{Right endpoint}}.
$$

This implies that the period of $y = a \sin(bx - c)$ is $2\pi/b$, and the graph of $y = a \sin bx$ is shifted by an amount c/b. The number c/b is the **phase shift.**

DISCOVERY

Use a graphing utility to draw the graph of $y = \sin(x + c)$, where $c = -\pi/4$, 0, and $\pi/4$. (Use a viewing rectangle in which $0 \le X \le 6.3$ and $-2 \le Y \le 2$.) How does the value of c affect the graph?

GRAPHS OF THE SINE AND COSINE FUNCTIONS

The graphs of $y = a \sin(bx - c)$ and $y = a \cos(bx - c)$ have the following characteristics. (Assume $b > 0$.)

   Amplitude $= |a|$

   Period $= 2\pi/b$

The left and right endpoints corresponding to a one-cycle interval of the graphs can be determined by solving the equations $bx - c = 0$ and $bx - c = 2\pi$.

EXAMPLE 6 Horizontal Shift

Describe the graph of

$$y = \frac{1}{2} \sin\left(x - \frac{\pi}{3}\right).$$

SOLUTION

Because $a = \frac{1}{2}$ and $b = 1$, the amplitude is $\frac{1}{2}$ and the period is 2π. By solving the inequality

$$0 \le x - \frac{\pi}{3} \le 2\pi$$

$$\frac{\pi}{3} \le x \qquad \le \frac{7\pi}{3},$$

you can see that the interval $[\pi/3, 7\pi/3]$ corresponds to one cycle of the graph. Dividing this interval into four equal parts produces the following key points.

$$\left(\frac{\pi}{3}, 0\right), \quad \left(\frac{5\pi}{6}, \frac{1}{2}\right), \quad \left(\frac{4\pi}{3}, 0\right), \quad \left(\frac{11\pi}{6}, -\frac{1}{2}\right), \quad \text{and} \quad \left(\frac{7\pi}{3}, 0\right)$$

The graph is shown in Figure 6.46.

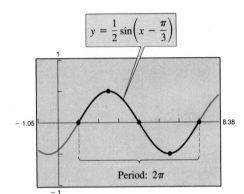

$y = \frac{1}{2} \sin\left(x - \frac{\pi}{3}\right)$

Period: 2π

FIGURE 6.46

The final type of transformation is the *vertical shift* caused by the constant d in the equations

$$y = d + a \sin(bx - c) \quad \text{and} \quad y = d + a \cos(bx - c).$$

The shift is d units upward for $d > 0$ and downward for $d < 0$. In other words, the graph oscillates about the horizontal line $y = d$ instead of the x-axis.

EXAMPLE 7 Vertical Shift

Describe the graph of $y = 2 + 3 \sin 2x$.

SOLUTION

The amplitude is 3 and the period is π. The key points over the interval $[0, \pi]$ are

$$(0, 2), \quad \left(\frac{\pi}{4}, 5\right), \quad \left(\frac{\pi}{2}, 2\right), \quad \left(\frac{3\pi}{4}, -1\right), \quad \text{and} \quad (\pi, 2).$$

The graph is shown in Figure 6.47.

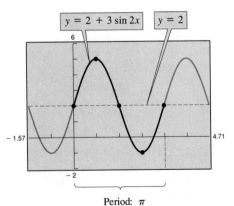

$y = 2 + 3 \sin 2x$ $y = 2$

Period: π

FIGURE 6.47

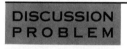

A Shifted Sine Curve

FIGURE 6.48

EXAMPLE 8   Finding an Equation for a Given Graph

Find the amplitude, period, and phase shift for the sine function whose graph is shown in Figure 6.48. Write an equation for this graph.

SOLUTION

The amplitude for this sine curve is 2. The period is 2π, and there is a right phase shift of $\pi/2$. Thus, you can write the following equation.

$$y = 2 \sin\left(x - \frac{\pi}{2}\right)$$

Try finding a cosine function with the same graph.

DISCUSSION PROBLEM

A SINE SHOW

If you have a programmable calculator, try running the following "sine-show program." This program simultaneously draws the unit circle and the corresponding points on the sine curve. After the circle and sine curve are drawn, you can connect points on the unit circle with their corresponding points on the sine curve by repeatedly pressing ENTER. After the program is complete, the screen should look like that shown in the figure. (This program is for the TI-81. Program steps for other calculators are given in Appendix B.)

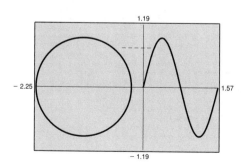

```
:Rad                            :Line(-1.25,1.19,-1.25,1.19)
:ClrDraw                        :DispGraph
:All-Off                        :0→N
:Param                          :Lbl 1
:Simul                          :N+1→N
:-2.25→Xmin                     :Nπ/6.5→T
:π/2→Xmax                       :-1.25+cos T→A
:3→Xscl                         :sin T→B
:-1.19→Ymin                     :T/4→C
:1.19→Ymax                      :Line(A,B,C,B)
:1→Yscl                         :Pause
:0→Tmin                         :If N=12
:6.3→Tmax                       :Goto 2
:.15→Tstep                      :Goto 1
:"-1.25+cos T"→X₁ₜ              :Lbl 2
:"sin T"→Y₁ₜ                    :Function
:"T/4"→X₂ₜ                      :Sequence
:"sin T"→Y₂ₜ                    :End
```

WARM-UP

· · · · · · · · · · · · · · · ·

The following warm-up exercises involve skills that were covered in earlier sections. You will use these skills in the exercise set for this section.

In Exercises 1 and 2, simplify the expression.

1. $\dfrac{2\pi}{1/3}$ **2.** $\dfrac{2\pi}{4\pi}$

In Exercises 3–6, solve for x.

3. $2x - \dfrac{\pi}{3} = 0$ **4.** $2x - \dfrac{\pi}{3} = 2\pi$

5. $3\pi x + 6\pi = 0$ **6.** $3\pi x + 6\pi = 2\pi$

In Exercises 7–10, evaluate the trigonometric function without using a calculator.

7. $\sin \dfrac{\pi}{2}$ **8.** $\sin \pi$ **9.** $\cos 0$ **10.** $\cos \dfrac{\pi}{2}$

SECTION 6.4 · EXERCISES

· ·

In Exercises 1–10, determine the period and amplitude of the function. Then describe the viewing rectangle for Exercises 1–6.

1. $y = 2 \sin 2x$ **2.** $y = 3 \cos 3x$

3. $y = \dfrac{3}{2} \cos \dfrac{x}{2}$ **4.** $y = -2 \sin \dfrac{x}{3}$

5. $y = \frac{1}{2} \sin \pi x$ **6.** $y = \dfrac{5}{2} \cos \dfrac{\pi x}{2}$

7. $y = -3 \sin 10x$

8. $u = -\dfrac{5}{2} \cos \dfrac{x}{4}$

9. $y = 3 \sin 4\pi x$

10. $y = \dfrac{2}{3} \cos \dfrac{\pi x}{10}$

In Exercises 11–16, describe the relationship between the graphs of f and g.

11. $f(x) = \sin x$
$g(x) = \sin(x - \pi)$

12. $f(x) = \cos x$
$g(x) = \cos(x + \pi)$

13. $f(x) = \cos 2x$
$g(x) = -\cos 2x$

14. $f(x) = \sin 3x$
$g(x) = \sin(-3x)$

15. $f(x) = \sin x$
$g(x) = 2 + \sin x$

16. $f(x) = \cos 4x$
$g(x) = -2 + \cos 4x$

In Exercises 17–24, sketch the graphs of the two functions on the same coordinate plane. (Include two full periods, and use a graphing utility to verify your result.)

17. $f(x) = -2 \sin x$
$g(x) = 4 \sin x$

18. $f(x) = \sin x$
$g(x) = \sin \dfrac{x}{3}$

19. $f(x) = \cos x$
$g(x) = 1 + \cos x$

20. $f(x) = 2 \cos 2x$
$g(x) = -\cos 4x$

21. $f(x) = -\dfrac{1}{2} \sin \dfrac{x}{2}$
$g(x) = 3 - \dfrac{1}{2} \sin \dfrac{x}{2}$

22. $f(x) = 4 \sin \pi x$
$g(x) = 4 \sin \pi x - 3$

23. $f(x) = 2 \cos x$
$g(x) = 2 \cos(x + \pi)$

24. $f(x) = -\cos x$
$g(x) = -\cos(x - \pi)$

In Exercises 25–28, sketch the graphs of f and g on the same coordinate axes and show that $f(x) = g(x)$ for all x. (Include two full periods, and use a graphing utility to verify your result.)

25. $f(x) = \sin x$
$g(x) = \cos\left(x - \dfrac{\pi}{2}\right)$

26. $f(x) = \sin x$
$g(x) = -\cos\left(x + \dfrac{\pi}{2}\right)$

27. $f(x) = \cos x$
$g(x) = -\sin\left(x - \dfrac{\pi}{2}\right)$

28. $f(x) = \cos x$
$g(x) = -\cos(x - \pi)$

In Exercises 29–42, sketch the graph of the function. (Include two full periods, and use a graphing utility to verify your result.)

29. $y = -2 \sin 6x$

30. $y = -3 \cos 4x$

31. $y = \cos 2\pi x$

32. $y = \dfrac{3}{2} \sin \dfrac{\pi x}{4}$

33. $y = -\sin \dfrac{2\pi x}{3}$

34. $y = 10 \cos \dfrac{\pi x}{6}$

35. $y = 2 - \sin \dfrac{2\pi x}{3}$

36. $y = 2 \cos x - 3$

37. $y = \sin\left(x - \dfrac{\pi}{4}\right)$

38. $y = \dfrac{1}{2} \sin(x - \pi)$

39. $y = 3 \cos (x + \pi)$

40. $y = 4 \cos\left(x + \dfrac{\pi}{4}\right)$

41. $y = \dfrac{1}{10} \cos 60\pi x$

42. $y = -3 + 5 \cos \dfrac{\pi t}{12}$

In Exercises 43–54, use a graphing utility to graph the function. (Include two full periods.)

43. $y = 3 \cos(x + \pi) - 3$

44. $y = 4 \cos\left(x + \dfrac{\pi}{4}\right) + 4$

45. $y = \dfrac{2}{3} \cos\left(\dfrac{x}{2} - \dfrac{\pi}{4}\right)$

46. $y = -3 \cos(6x + \pi)$

47. $y = -2 \sin(4x + \pi)$

48. $y = -4 \sin\left(\dfrac{2}{3}x - \dfrac{\pi}{3}\right)$

49. $y = \cos\left(2\pi x - \dfrac{\pi}{2}\right) + 1$

50. $y = 3 \cos\left(\dfrac{\pi x}{2} + \dfrac{\pi}{2}\right) - 2$

51. $y = -0.1 \sin\left(\dfrac{\pi x}{10} + \pi\right)$

52. $y = 5 \sin(\pi - 2x) + 10$

53. $y = 5 \cos(\pi - 2x) + 2$

54. $y = \tfrac{1}{100} \sin 120\pi t$

In Exercises 55–58, use the graph of the trigonometric function to find all real numbers x in the interval $[-2\pi, 2\pi]$ that give the specified function value.

Function	Function Value
55. $\sin x$	$-\dfrac{1}{2}$
56. $\cos x$	-1
57. $\cos x$	$\dfrac{\sqrt{2}}{2}$
58. $\sin x$	$\dfrac{\sqrt{3}}{2}$

In Exercises 59 and 60, find a and d for the function $f(x) = a \cos x + d$ so that the graph of f matches the figure.

59.

60.

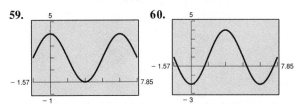

In Exercises 61–64, find a, b, and c so that the graph of the function matches the graph in the figure.

61. $y = a \sin(bx - c)$

62. $y = a \sin(bx - c)$

63. $y = a \cos(bx - c)$

64. $y = a \sin(bx - c)$

65. Use a graphing utility to graph the functions $f(x) = 2e^x$ and $g(x) = 5 \cos x$. Approximate any points of intersection of the graphs in the interval $[-\pi, \pi]$.

66. Use a graphing utility to determine the smallest *integer* value of a such that the graphs of $f(x) = 2 \ln x$ and $g(x) = a \cos x$ intersect more than once.

67. *Respiratory Cycle* For a person at rest, the velocity v (in liters per second) of air flow during a respiratory cycle is

$$v = 0.85 \sin \frac{\pi t}{3},$$

where t is the time in seconds. (Inhalation occurs when $v > 0$, and exhalation occurs when $v < 0$.)
(a) Find the time for one full respiratory cycle.
(b) Find the number of cycles per minute.
(c) Use a graphing utility to graph the velocity function.

68. *Respiratory Cycle* After exercising for a few minutes, a person has a respiratory cycle for which the velocity of air flow is approximated by

$$v = 1.75 \sin \frac{\pi t}{2}.$$

Use this model to repeat Exercise 67.

69. *Piano Tuning* When tuning a piano, a technician strikes a tuning fork for the A above middle C and sets up wave motion that can be approximated by

$$y = 0.001 \sin 880 \pi t,$$

where t is the time in seconds.
(a) What is the period p of this function?
(b) The frequency f is given by $f = 1/p$. What is the frequency of this note?
(c) Use a graphing utility to graph this function.

70. *Blood Pressure* The function

$$P = 100 - 20 \cos \frac{5 \pi t}{3}$$

approximates the blood pressure P in millimeters of mercury at time t in seconds for a person at rest.
(a) Find the period of the function.
(b) Find the number of heartbeats per minute.
(c) Use a graphing utility to graph the pressure function.

Sales In Exercises 71 and 72, use a graphing utility to graph the sales function over 1 year where S is sales in thousands of units and t is the time in months, with $t = 1$ corresponding to January. Use the graph to determine the month of maximum sales and the month of minimum sales.

71. $S = 22.3 - 3.4 \cos \dfrac{\pi t}{6}$

72. $S = 74.50 + 43.75 \sin \dfrac{\pi t}{6}$

In Exercises 73–76, describe the relationship between the graph of the functions f and g.

73.

74.

75.

76.

6.5   GRAPHS OF OTHER TRIGONOMETRIC FUNCTIONS
....
**Graph of the Tangent Function   /   Graph of the Cotangent Function   /
Graphs of the Reciprocal Functions**

Graph of the Tangent Function

Recall from Section 6.3 that the tangent function is odd. That is, $\tan(-x) = -\tan x$. Consequently, the graph of $y = \tan x$ is symmetric with respect to the origin. From the identity $\tan x = \sin x / \cos x$, you know that the tangent is undefined when $\cos x = 0$. Two such values are $x = \pm \pi/2 \approx \pm 1.5708$.

x	$-\dfrac{\pi}{2}$	-1.57	-1.5	-1	0	1	1.5	1.57	$\dfrac{\pi}{2}$
$\tan x$	undef.	-1255.8	-14.1	-1.56	0	1.56	14.1	1255.8	undef.

$\tan x$ approaches $-\infty$ as x approaches $-\pi/2$ from the right

$\tan x$ approaches ∞ as x approaches $\pi/2$ from the left

REMARK The period of the function $y = a \tan(bx - c)$ is the distance between two consecutive asymptotes. The amplitude of a tangent function is not defined.

As indicated in the table, $\tan x$ increases without bound as x approaches $\pi/2$ from the left, and decreases without bound as x approaches $-\pi/2$ from the right. Thus, the graph of $y = \tan x$ has *vertical asymptotes* at $x = \pi/2$ and $-\pi/2$, as shown in Figure 6.49. Moreover, because the period of the tangent function is π, vertical asymptotes also occur when $x = \pi/2 \pm n\pi$. The domain of the tangent function is the set of all real numbers other than $x = \pi/2 \pm n\pi$, and the range is the set of all real numbers.

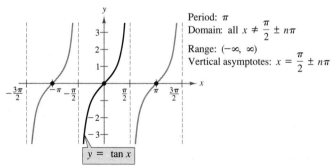

Period: π
Domain: all $x \neq \dfrac{\pi}{2} \pm n\pi$

Range: $(-\infty, \infty)$
Vertical asymptotes: $x = \dfrac{\pi}{2} \pm n\pi$

$y = \tan x$

FIGURE 6.49

Sketching the graph of a function with the form $y = a \tan(bx - c)$ is similar to sketching the graph of $y = a \sin(bx - c)$ in that you locate key points that identify the intercepts and asymptotes. Two consecutive asymptotes can be found by solving the equations

$$bx - c = -\frac{\pi}{2} \quad \text{and} \quad bx - c = \frac{\pi}{2}.$$

The midpoint between two consecutive asymptotes is an *x*-intercept of the graph. After plotting the asymptotes and the *x*-intercept, plot a few additional points between the two asymptotes and sketch one cycle. Finally, sketch one or two additional cycles to the left and right.

EXAMPLE 1   Sketching the Graph of a Tangent Function

Sketch the graph of

$$y = \tan \frac{x}{2}.$$

SOLUTION

By solving the inequality

$$-\frac{\pi}{2} < \frac{x}{2} < \frac{\pi}{2}$$

$$-\pi < x < \pi,$$

you can see that two consecutive asymptotes occur at $x = -\pi$ and $x = \pi$. Between these two asymptotes, plot a few points including the *x*-intercept, as shown in the table. Three cycles of the graph are shown in Figure 6.50. Use a graphing utility to confirm this result.

x	$-\dfrac{\pi}{2}$	0	$\dfrac{\pi}{2}$
$\tan \dfrac{x}{2}$	-1	0	1

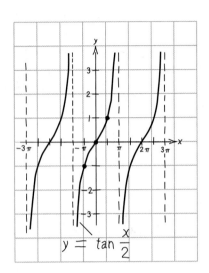

FIGURE 6.50

EXAMPLE 2   Sketching the Graph of a Tangent Function

Sketch the graph of $y = -3 \tan 2x$.

SOLUTION

By solving the inequality

$$-\frac{\pi}{2} < 2x < \frac{\pi}{2}$$

$$-\frac{\pi}{4} < x < \frac{\pi}{4},$$

you can see that two consecutive asymptotes occur at $x = -\pi/4$ and $x = \pi/4$. Between these two asymptotes, plot a few points as shown in the table, and complete one cycle. Four cycles of the graph are shown in Figure 6.51. Use a graphing utility to confirm this result.

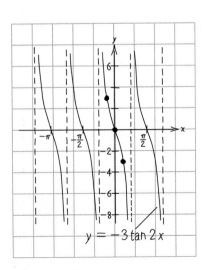

FIGURE 6.51

x	$-\dfrac{\pi}{8}$	0	$\dfrac{\pi}{8}$
$-3 \tan 2x$	3	0	-3

By comparing the graphs in Examples 1 and 2, you can see that the graph of $y = a \tan(bx + c)$ is increasing between consecutive vertical asymptotes if $a > 0$ and decreasing between consecutive vertical asymptotes if $a < 0$. In other words, the graph for $a < 0$ is a reflection of the graph for $a > 0$.

Graph of the Cotangent Function

The graph of the cotangent function is similar to the graph of the tangent function. It also has a period of π. However, from the identity

$$y = \cot x = \frac{\cos x}{\sin x},$$

you can see that the cotangent function has vertical asymptotes at $x = n\pi$ (because $\sin x$ is zero at these x-values). The graph of the cotangent function is shown in Figure 6.52.

Period: π
Domain: all $x \neq n\pi$
Range: $(-\infty, \infty)$
Vertical asymptotes: $x = n\pi$

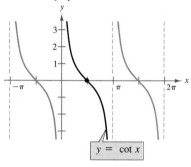

$y = \cot x$

FIGURE 6.52

EXAMPLE 3   **Sketching the Graph of a Cotangent Function**

Sketch the graph of

$$y = 2 \cot \frac{x}{3}.$$

SOLUTION

To locate two consecutive vertical asymptotes of the graph, you can solve the following inequality.

$$0 < \frac{x}{3} < \pi$$

$$0 < x < 3\pi$$

Then, between these two asymptotes, plot the points shown in the following table, and complete one cycle of the graph. (Note that the period is 3π, the distance between consecutive asymptotes.) Three cycles of the graph are shown in Figure 6.53. Use a graphing utility to confirm this result.

x	$\dfrac{3\pi}{4}$	$\dfrac{3\pi}{2}$	$\dfrac{9\pi}{4}$
$2 \cot \dfrac{x}{3}$	2	0	-2

$y = 2 \cot \dfrac{x}{3}$

FIGURE 6.53

Graphs of the Reciprocal Functions

The graphs of the two remaining trigonometric functions can be obtained from the graphs of the sine and cosine functions using the reciprocal identities

$$\csc x = \frac{1}{\sin x} \quad \text{and} \quad \sec x = \frac{1}{\cos x}.$$

For instance, at a given value of x, the y-coordinate for sec x is the reciprocal of the y-coordinate for cos x. Of course, when cos $x = 0$, the reciprocal does not exist. Near such values of x, the behavior of the secant function is similar to that of the tangent function. In other words, the graphs of

$$\tan x = \frac{\sin x}{\cos x} \quad \text{and} \quad \sec x = \frac{1}{\cos x}$$

have vertical asymptotes at $x = (\pi/2) + n\pi$, because the cosine is zero at these x-values. Similarly,

$$\cot x = \frac{\cos x}{\sin x} \quad \text{and} \quad \csc x = \frac{1}{\sin x}$$

have vertical asymptotes where $\sin x = 0$, that is, at $x = n\pi$.

   To sketch the graph of a secant or cosecant function, we suggest that you first make a sketch of its reciprocal function. For instance, to sketch the graph of $y = \csc x$, first sketch the graph of $y = \sin x$. Then take reciprocals of the y-coordinates to obtain points on the graph of $y = \csc x$. You can use this procedure to obtain the graphs shown in Figure 6.54. You can verify these graphs with a graphing utility for the functions $y = 1/\cos x$ and $y = 1/\sin x$.

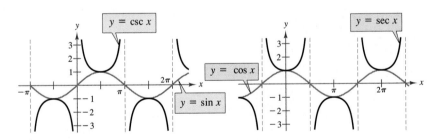

Period: 2π
Domain: all $x \ne n\pi$
Range: all y not in $(-1, 1)$
Vertical asymptotes: $x = n\pi$
Symmetry: origin

Period: 2π
Domain: all $x \ne \dfrac{\pi}{2} + n\pi$
Range: all y not in $(-1, 1)$
Vertical asymptotes: $x = \dfrac{\pi}{2} + n\pi$
Symmetry: y-axis

FIGURE 6.54

In comparing the graphs of the secant and cosecant functions with those of the sine and cosine functions, note that the "hills" and "valleys" are interchanged. For example, a hill (or maximum point) on the sine curve corresponds to a valley (a local minimum) on the cosecant curve. Similarly, a valley (or minimum point) on the sine curve corresponds to a hill (a local maximum) on the cosecant curve, as shown in Figure 6.55.

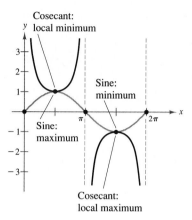

FIGURE 6.55

EXAMPLE 4   Graphing a Cosecant Function

Use a graphing utility to graph

$$y = 2 \sin\left(x + \frac{\pi}{4}\right) \quad \text{and} \quad y = 2 \csc\left(x + \frac{\pi}{4}\right).$$

SOLUTION

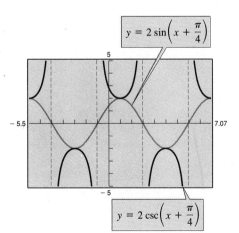

$y = 2 \sin\left(x + \dfrac{\pi}{4}\right)$

$y = 2 \csc\left(x + \dfrac{\pi}{4}\right)$

FIGURE 6.56

The two curves are shown in Figure 6.56. Note how the "hills" and "valleys" of each curve are related. For the function $y = 2 \sin[x + (\pi/4)]$, the amplitude is 2 and the period is 2π. By solving the inequalities

$$0 < x + \frac{\pi}{4} < 2\pi$$

and

$$-\frac{\pi}{4} < x < \frac{7\pi}{4},$$

you can see that one cycle of the sine function corresponds to the interval from $x = -\pi/4$ to $x = 7\pi/4$. Because the sine function is zero at the endpoints of this interval, the corresponding cosecant function

$$y = 2 \csc\left(x + \frac{\pi}{4}\right) = 2\left(\frac{1}{\sin[x + (\pi/4)]}\right)$$

has vertical asymptotes at $x = -\pi/4$, $x = 3\pi/4$, and $7\pi/4$.

In Figure 6.57, we summarize the graphs, domains, ranges, and periods of the six basic trigonometric functions.

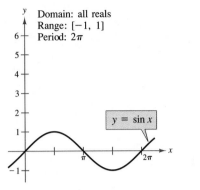

Domain: all reals
Range: [−1, 1]
Period: 2π

$y = \sin x$

Domain: all reals
Range: [−1, 1]
Period: 2π

$y = \cos x$

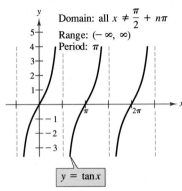

Domain: all $x \neq \dfrac{\pi}{2} + n\pi$
Range: $(-\infty, \infty)$
Period: π

$y = \tan x$

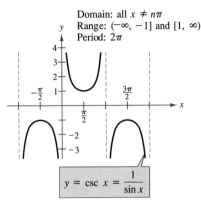

Domain: all $x \neq n\pi$
Range: $(-\infty, -1]$ and $[1, \infty)$
Period: 2π

$y = \csc x = \dfrac{1}{\sin x}$

Domain: all $x \neq \dfrac{\pi}{2} + n\pi$
Range: $(-\infty, -1]$ and $[1, \infty)$
Period: 2π

$y = \sec x = \dfrac{1}{\cos x}$

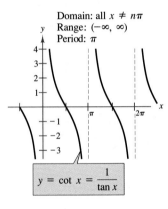

Domain: all $x \neq n\pi$
Range: $(-\infty, \infty)$
Period: π

$y = \cot x = \dfrac{1}{\tan x}$

Graphs of the Six Trigonometric Functions

FIGURE 6.57

**DISCUSSION
PROBLEM**

••••••••••••••••••••••

**GRAPHING
UTILITIES**

Use a graphing utility to graph the following functions for varying values of a, b, c, and d.

$$y = d + a\sin(bx + c) \qquad y = d + a\cos(bx + c)$$
$$y = d + a\tan(bx + c) \qquad y = d + a\cot(bx + c)$$
$$y = d + a\sec(bx + c) \qquad y = d + a\csc(bx + c)$$

In a paper or a discussion, summarize the effects of the constants a, b, c, and d in these graphs.

WARM-UP
....

The following warm-up exercises involve skills that were covered in earlier sections. You will use these skills in the exercise set for this section.

In Exercises 1–6, evaluate the trigonometric function without using a calculator.

1. $\tan 0$ **2.** $\cos \dfrac{\pi}{4}$ **3.** $\tan \dfrac{\pi}{4}$

4. $\cot \dfrac{\pi}{2}$ **5.** $\sin \pi$ **6.** $\cos \dfrac{\pi}{2}$

In Exercises 7–10, sketch the graph of the function. (Include two full periods.)

7. $y = -2 \cos 2x$ **8.** $y = 3 \sin \dfrac{x}{4}$

9. $y = \dfrac{3}{2} \sin 2\pi x$ **10.** $y = -2 \cos \dfrac{\pi x}{2}$

SECTION 6.5 · EXERCISES
....

In Exercises 1–8, match the trigonometric function with its graph and describe the viewing rectangle. [The graphs are labeled (a), (b), (c), (d), (e), (f), (g), and (h).]

1. $y = \sec 2x$

2. $y = \tan 3x$

3. $y = \tan \dfrac{x}{2}$

4. $y = 2 \csc \dfrac{x}{2}$

5. $y = \cot \pi x$

6. $y = \frac{1}{2} \sec \pi x$

7. $y = -\sec x$

8. $y = -2 \csc 2\pi x$

(c)

(d)

(e)

(f)

(a)

(b)

(g)

(h)

In Exercises 9–30, sketch the graph of the function. (Include two full periods, and use a graphing utility to verify your result.)

9. $y = \frac{1}{3} \tan x$

10. $y = \frac{1}{4} \tan x$

11. $y = \tan 2x$

12. $y = -3 \tan \pi x$

13. $y = -\frac{1}{2} \sec x$

14. $y = \frac{1}{4} \sec x$

15. $y = -\sec \pi x$

16. $y = 2 \sec 4x$

17. $y = \sec \pi x - 1$

18. $y = -2 \sec 4x + 2$

19. $y = \csc \frac{x}{2}$

20. $y = \csc \frac{x}{3}$

21. $y = \cot \frac{x}{2}$

22. $y = 3 \cot \frac{\pi x}{2}$

23. $y = \frac{1}{2} \sec 2x$

24. $y = -\frac{1}{2} \tan x$

25. $y = \tan \frac{\pi x}{4}$

26. $y = \sec(x + \pi)$

27. $y = \csc(\pi - x)$

28. $y = \sec(\pi - x)$

29. $y = \frac{1}{4} \csc\left(x + \frac{\pi}{4}\right)$

30. $y = 2 \cot\left(x + \frac{\pi}{2}\right)$

In Exercises 31–40, use a graphing utility to graph the function. (Include two full periods.)

31. $y = \tan \frac{x}{3}$

32. $y = -\tan 2x$

33. $y = -2 \sec 4x$

34. $y = \sec \pi x$

35. $y = \tan\left(x - \frac{\pi}{4}\right)$

36. $y = -\csc(4x - \pi)$

37. $y = \frac{1}{4} \cot\left(x - \frac{\pi}{2}\right)$

38. $y = \frac{1}{3} \sec\left(\frac{\pi x}{2} + \frac{\pi}{2}\right)$

39. $y = 2 \sec(2x - \pi)$

40. $y = 0.1 \tan\left(\frac{\pi x}{4} + \frac{\pi}{4}\right)$

In Exercises 41–44, use the graph of the trigonometric function to find all real numbers x in the interval $[-2\pi, 2\pi]$ that give the specified function value.

Function	Function Value
41. $\tan x$	1
42. $\cot x$	$-\sqrt{3}$
43. $\sec x$	-2
44. $\csc x$	$\sqrt{2}$

In Exercises 45 and 46, use the graph of the function to determine whether the function is even, odd, or neither.

45. $f(x) = \sec x$

46. $f(x) = \tan x$

47. Consider the functions $f(x) = 2 \sin x$ and $g(x) = \frac{1}{2} \csc x$ over the interval $(0, \pi)$.
   (a) Use a graphing utility to graph f and g in the same viewing rectangle.
   (b) Approximate the interval where $f > g$.
   (c) Describe the behavior of each of the functions as x approaches π. How is the behavior of g related to the behavior of f as x approaches π?

48. Consider the functions $f(x) = \tan(\pi x/2)$ and $g(x) = \frac{1}{2} \sec(\pi x/2)$ over the interval $(-1, 1)$.
   (a) Use a graphing utility to graph f and g in the same viewing rectangle.
   (b) Approximate the interval where $f < g$.

49. *Distance*   A plane flying at an altitude of 6 miles over level ground will pass directly over a radar antenna (see figure). Let d be the ground distance from the antenna to the point directly under the plane and let x be the angle of elevation to the plane from the antenna. Write d as a function of x, and graph the function over the interval $0 < x < \pi$.

50. *Television Coverage*   A television camera is on a reviewing platform 100 feet from the street on which a parade will be passing from left to right (see figure). Express the distance d from the camera to a particular unit in the parade as a function of the angle x, and graph the function over the interval $-\pi/2 < x < \pi/2$. (Consider x as negative when a unit in the parade approaches from the left.)

6 mi

FIGURE FOR 49

100 ft

Camera

FIGURE FOR 50

6.6 ADVANCED GRAPHING TECHNIQUES

Graphs of Combinations of Trigonometric Functions / Graphs of
Combinations of Algebraic and Trigonometric Functions / Damped
Trigonometric Graphs

Graphs of Combinations of Trigonometric Functions

Some physical phenomena are best modeled by combinations of trigonometric
functions or by combinations of algebraic and trigonometric functions. Graphing utilities are especially helpful for graphing complicated functions such as

$$y = \sin x - \cos 2x \quad \text{or} \quad y = x + \cos x.$$

Sums, differences, products, and quotients of periodic functions are often
periodic.

EXAMPLE 1 **Finding the Period and Relative Extrema of a Function**

Graph $y = \sin x - \cos 2x$, and find the period and the relative minimums and
maximums of this function.

SOLUTION

The period of $\sin x$ is 2π, and the period of $\cos 2x$ is π. Thus, the period of
the given function is 2π, because 2π is the least common multiple of 2π and
π. This conclusion is further reinforced by graphing the function, as shown in
Figure 6.58. From the graph, it appears that the function has two relative
maximums and two relative minimums in each complete cycle. For instance,
between 0 and 2π, the graph appears to have relative maximums when
$x = \pi/2 \approx 1.57$ and when $x = 3\pi/2 \approx 4.71$. Using the zoom and trace
features of the graphing utility, you can find that the relative minimums occur
when $x \approx 3.40$ and when $x \approx 6.03$.

Relative maximums: (1.57, 2.00)   (4.71, 0.00)

Relative minimums: (3.40, −1.13) (6.03, −1.13)

FIGURE 6.58

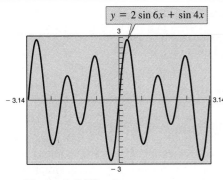

FIGURE 6.59

EXAMPLE 2   Finding the Period and Range of a Function

Graph $y = 2 \sin 6x + \sin 4x$, and find the period and range of this function.

SOLUTION

The period of $2 \sin 6x$ is $\pi/3$, and the period of $\sin 4x$ is $\pi/2$. Thus, the period of the given function is π, because π is the least common multiple of $\pi/3$ and $\pi/2$. This conclusion is further reinforced by graphing the function, as shown in Figure 6.59. In the interval from 0 to π, the maximum y-value occurs when $x \approx 0.29$ and $y \approx 2.89$. The minimum value in this interval occurs when $x \approx 2.86$ and $y \approx -2.89$. Thus, the range of the function is approximated by

$$-2.89 \le y \le 2.89. \qquad \textit{Range}$$

Graphs of Combinations of Algebraic and Trigonometric Functions

Functions that are combinations of algebraic and trigonometric functions are not, in general, periodic.

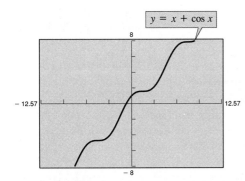

FIGURE 6.60

EXAMPLE 3   The Graph of a Nonperiodic Function

Graph $y = x + \cos x$, and find the domain and range of the function. Approximate any zeros of $y = x + \cos x$.

SOLUTION

The graph of the function is shown in Figure 6.60. Notice that, even though the function is not periodic, it does have a pattern that repeats. Notice that the graph of $y = x + \cos x$ oscillates about the line $y = x$. Both the domain and range of the function are the set of all real numbers. Using the zoom feature, you can find that the zero of $y = x + \cos x$ is approximately $x = -0.739$.

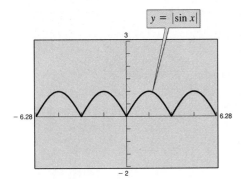

FIGURE 6.61

EXAMPLE 4   A Function Involving Absolute Value

Graph $y = |\sin x|$, and find the domain and range of the function.

SOLUTION

The domain of the function is the set of all real numbers. The graph of the function is shown in Figure 6.61. Notice that the minimum value of the function is 0 and the maximum value is 1. Thus, the range of the function is given by $0 \le y \le 1$.

Damped Trigonometric Graphs

A *product* of two functions can be graphed using properties of the individual functions involved. For instance, consider the function

$$f(x) = x \sin x$$

as the product of the functions $y = x$ and $y = \sin x$. Using properties of absolute value and the fact that $|\sin x| \le 1$, you obtain $0 \le |x||\sin x| \le |x|$. Consequently,

$$-|x| \le x \sin x \le |x|,$$

which means that the graph of $f(x) = x \sin x$ lies between the lines $y = -x$ and $y = x$. Furthermore, because

$$f(x) = x \sin x = \pm x \quad \text{at} \quad x = \frac{\pi}{2} + n\pi$$

and

$$f(x) = x \sin x = 0 \quad \text{at} \quad x = n\pi,$$

the graph of f touches the line $y = -x$ or the line $y = x$ at $x = (\pi/2) + n\pi$ and has x-intercepts at $x = n\pi$. A sketch of f, together with $y = x$ and $y = -x$, is shown in Figure 6.62.

In the function $f(x) = x \sin x$, the factor x is called the **damping factor.** By changing the damping factor, you can change the graph significantly. For example, look in Figure 6.63 at the graphs of

$$y = \frac{1}{x} \sin x \quad \text{and} \quad y = e^{-x} \sin 3x.$$

FIGURE 6.62

FIGURE 6.63

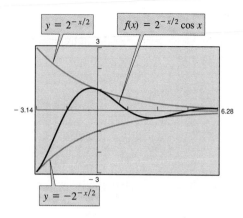

$y = 2^{-x/2}$

$f(x) = 2^{-x/2} \cos x$

$y = -2^{-x/2}$

FIGURE 6.64

EXAMPLE 5   Damped Cosine Wave

Graph $f(x) = 2^{-x/2} \cos x$.

SOLUTION

A graph of $f(x) = 2^{-x/2} \cos x$ is shown in Figure 6.64. To analyze this function further, consider $f(x)$ as the product of the two functions

$$y = 2^{-x/2} \quad \text{and} \quad y = \cos x,$$

each of which has the set of real numbers as its domain. For any real number x, you know that $2^{-x/2} \geq 0$ and $|\cos x| \leq 1$. Therefore, $|2^{-x/2}| |\cos x| \leq 2^{-x/2}$, which means that

$$-2^{-x/2} \leq 2^{-x/2} \cos x \leq 2^{-x/2}.$$

Furthermore, because

$$f(x) = 2^{-x/2} \cos x = \pm 2^{-x/2} \quad \text{at} \quad x = n\pi$$

and

$$f(x) = 2^{-x/2} \cos x = 0 \quad \text{at} \quad x = \frac{\pi}{2} + n\pi,$$

the graph of f touches the curve $y = -2^{-x/2}$ or the curve $y = 2^{-x/2}$ at $x = n\pi$ and has intercepts at $x = (\pi/2) + n\pi$.

DISCUSSION PROBLEM

••••••••••••••••••••

PERIODIC FUNCTIONS AS MODELS

Trigonometric functions can be used as models for real-life situations that are periodic. For example, at most locations on the earth, the average temperature is periodic (it cycles from lower temperatures in winter to higher temperatures in summer). Here is a model for the average temperature (in degrees Fahrenheit) in Washington, DC.

$$T = 57.44 + 21.88 \sin(0.522x + 4.110), \qquad \text{Jan.} = 1, \text{Feb.} = 2, \ldots$$

Compare the temperatures given by this model with the actual average temperatures in Washington, DC shown in the table. (*Source:* P.C. U.S.A.)

x	1	2	3	4	5	6	7	8	9	10	11	12
T	35.2	37.5	45.8	56.7	66.0	74.5	78.9	77.6	71.1	59.3	48.7	38.9

Describe several other examples of periodic behavior that occur in real-life situations.

The following warm-up exercises involve skills that were covered in earlier sections. You will use these skills in the exercise set for this section.

In Exercises 1–4, find the x-values in the interval $[0, 2\pi]$ for which $f(x)$ is -1, 0, or 1.

1. $f(x) = \sin x$ **2.** $f(x) = \cos x$ **3.** $f(x) = \sin 2x$ **4.** $f(x) = \cos \dfrac{x}{2}$

In Exercises 5–8, graph the function.

5. $y = |x|$ **6.** $y = e^{-x}$ **7.** $y = \sin \pi x$ **8.** $y = \cos 2x$

In Exercises 9 and 10, evaluate $f(x)$ when $x = 0$, $\pi/6$, $\pi/4$, $\pi/3$, and $\pi/2$.

9. $f(x) = x \cos x$ **10.** $f(x) = x + \sin x$

SECTION 6.6 · EXERCISES

In Exercises 1–6, sketch the graph of the function. (Use a graphing utility to verify your result.)

1. $y = 2 - 2 \sin \dfrac{x}{2}$ **2.** $y = -3 + \cos x$

3. $y = 4 - 2 \cos \pi x$ **4.** $y = 5 - \frac{1}{2} \sin 2\pi x$

5. $y = 1 + \csc x$ **6.** $y = 2 + \tan \pi x$

In Exercises 7–12, use a graphing utility to graph the function. Determine the period of the function and approximate any relative minimums and maximums of the function through one period.

7. $y = \sin x + \cos x$ **8.** $y = \cos x + \cos 2x$

9. $f(x) = 2 \sin x + \sin 2x$ **10.** $f(x) = 2 \sin x + \cos 2x$

11. $g(x) = \cos x - \cos \dfrac{x}{2}$ **12.** $g(x) = \sin x - \dfrac{1}{2} \sin \dfrac{x}{2}$

In Exercises 13–16, use a graphing utility to graph the function through three periods.

13. $h(x) = \sin x + \frac{1}{3} \sin 5x$ **14.** $h(x) = \cos x - \frac{1}{4} \cos 2x$

15. $y = -3 + \cos x + 2 \sin 2x$

16. $y = \sin \pi x + \sin \dfrac{\pi x}{2}$

In Exercises 17–24, use a graphing utility to graph the given function and the algebraic component of the function in the same viewing rectangle. Notice that the graph of the function oscillates about the graph of the algebraic component.

17. $y = x + \sin x$ **18.** $y = x + \cos x$

19. $f(x) = \frac{1}{2}x - 2 \cos x$ **20.** $f(x) = 2x - \sin x$

21. $g(t) = -t + \sin \dfrac{\pi t}{2}$ **22.** $h(s) = -\dfrac{s}{2} - \dfrac{1}{2} \sin \dfrac{\pi s}{4}$

23. $y = \dfrac{x^2}{8} + \sin \dfrac{\pi x}{2}$ **24.** $y = 4 - \dfrac{x^2}{16} + 4 \cos \pi x$

In Exercises 25–28, use a graphing utility to graph the function and the damping factor of the function in the same viewing rectangle. Describe the behavior of the function as x increases without bound.

25. $f(x) = 2^{-x/4} \cos \pi x$ **26.** $f(t) = e^{-t} \cos t$

27. $g(x) = e^{-x^2/2} \sin x$ **28.** $h(t) = 2^{-t^2/4} \sin t$

In Exercises 29–32, use a graphing utility to graph the function and the equations $y = x$ and $y = -x$ in the same viewing rectangle. Describe the behavior of the given function as x approaches zero.

29. $f(x) = x \cos x$ **30.** $f(x) = |x \sin x|$

31. $g(x) = |x| \sin x$ **32.** $g(x) = |x| \cos x$

In Exercises 33–38, use a graphing utility to graph the function. Describe the behavior of the function as x approaches zero.

33. $y = \dfrac{6}{x} + \cos x, \quad x > 0$

34. $y = \dfrac{4}{x} + \sin 2x, \quad x > 0$

35. $g(x) = \dfrac{\sin x}{x}$

36. $f(x) = \dfrac{1 - \cos x}{x}$

37. $f(x) = \sin \dfrac{1}{x}$

38. $h(x) = x \sin \dfrac{1}{x}$

In Exercises 39–42, use a graphing utility to graph the functions f and g in the same viewing rectangle. Use the graphs to determine the relationship between the functions.

39. $f(x) = \sin x + \cos\left(x + \dfrac{\pi}{2}\right), \quad g(x) = 0$

40. $f(x) = \sin x - \cos\left(x + \dfrac{\pi}{2}\right), \quad g(x) = 2 \sin x$

41. $f(x) = \sin^2 x, \quad g(x) = \frac{1}{2}(1 - \cos 2x)$

42. $f(x) = \cos^2 \dfrac{\pi x}{2}, \quad g(x) = \dfrac{1}{2}(1 + \cos \pi x)$

In Exercises 43–46, use a graphing utility to graph the function over the specified interval.

Function	Interval
43. $f(t) = t^2 \sin t$	$[0, 2\pi]$
44. $f(x) = \sqrt{2x} \sin x$	$[0, 4\pi]$
45. $f(x) = \sin x - \frac{1}{3} \sin 3x + \frac{1}{5} \sin 5x$	$[0, \pi]$
46. $f(x) = \dfrac{1}{2} - \dfrac{4}{\pi^2}\left(\cos \pi x + \dfrac{1}{9}\cos 3\pi x\right)$	$[0, 2]$

47. *Sales* The projected monthly sales S (in thousands of units) of a seasonal product is modeled by

$$S = 74 + 3t + 40 \sin \dfrac{\pi t}{6},$$

where t is the time in months, with $t = 1$ corresponding to January. Graph this sales function over 1 year.

48. *Sales* The projected monthly sales S (in thousands of units) of a seasonal product is modeled by

$$S = 25 + 2t + 20 \sin \dfrac{\pi t}{6},$$

where t is the time in months, with $t = 1$ corresponding to January. Graph this sales function over 1 year.

49. *Predator-Prey Problem* Suppose the population of a certain predator at time t (in months) in a given region is estimated to be

$$P = 10,000 + 3000 \sin \dfrac{2\pi t}{24},$$

and the population of its primary food source (its prey) is estimated to be

$$p = 15,000 + 5000 \cos \dfrac{2\pi t}{24}.$$

Graph both of these functions in the same viewing rectangle, and explain the oscillations in the size of each population.

50. *Normal Temperatures* The normal monthly high temperature for Erie, Pennsylvania, is approximated by

$$H(t) = 54.33 - 20.38 \cos \dfrac{\pi t}{6} - 15.69 \sin \dfrac{\pi t}{6},$$

and the normal monthly low temperature is approximated by

$$L(t) = 39.36 - 15.70 \cos \dfrac{\pi t}{6} - 14.16 \sin \dfrac{\pi t}{6},$$

where t is the time in months, with $t = 1$ corresponding to January. (*Source:* NOAA) Use a graphing utility to graph the functions over a period of 1 year, and use the graphs to answer the following questions.

(a) During what part of the year is the difference between the normal high and low temperatures greatest? When is it smallest?

(b) The sun is farthest north in the sky around June 21, but the graph shows the warmest temperatures at a later date. Approximate the lag time of the temperatures relative to the position of the sun.

51. *Harmonic Motion*   An object weighing W pounds is suspended from the ceiling by a steel spring (see figure). The weight is pulled downward (positive direction) from its equilibrium position and released. The resulting motion of the weight is described by the function

$$y = \tfrac{1}{2}e^{-t/4} \cos 4t, \qquad t > 0,$$

where y is distance in feet and t is the time in seconds. Graph the function.

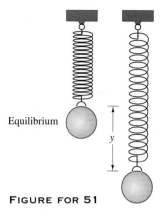

Equilibrium

FIGURE FOR 51

6.7   INVERSE TRIGONOMETRIC FUNCTIONS

Inverse Sine Function / Other Inverse Trigonometric Functions / Compositions of Trigonometric and Inverse Trigonometric Functions

Inverse Sine Function

Recall that for a function to have an inverse, it must be one-to-one. From Figure 6.65 it is clear that $y = \sin x$ is not one-to-one because different values of x yield the same y-value. If, however, you restrict the domain to the interval $-\pi/2 \le x \le \pi/2$ (corresponding to the solid portion of the graph in Figure 6.65), the following properties hold.

1. On the interval $[-\pi/2, \pi/2]$, the function $y = \sin x$ is increasing.
2. On the interval $[-\pi/2, \pi/2]$, $y = \sin x$ takes on its full range of values, $-1 \le \sin x \le 1$.
3. On the interval $[-\pi/2, \pi/2]$, $y = \sin x$ is a one-to-one function.

Thus, on the restricted domain $-\pi/2 \le x \le \pi/2$, $y = \sin x$ has a unique inverse called the **inverse sine function.** It is denoted by

$$y = \arcsin x \quad \text{or} \quad y = \sin^{-1} x.$$

$y = \sin x$

Sin x is one-to-one on this interval.

FIGURE 6.65

The notation $\sin^{-1} x$ is consistent with the inverse function notation $f^{-1}(x)$, which is used in Section 1.7. The arcsin x notation (read as "the arcsine of x") comes from the association of a central angle with its subtended *arc length* on a unit circle. Thus, arcsin x means the angle (or arc) whose sine is x. Both notations, arcsin x and $\sin^{-1} x$, are commonly used in mathematics, so remember that $\sin^{-1} x$ denotes the *inverse* sine function rather than $1/\sin x$.

The values of arcsin x lie in the interval $-\pi/2 \le$ arcsin $x \le \pi/2$. The graph of $y =$ arcsin x is shown in Example 2. Try producing this graph with a graphing utility. Note that the domain of $y =$ arcsin x is $-1 \le x \le 1$.

REMARK When evaluating the inverse sine function, it helps to remember the phrase "the arcsine of x is the angle (or number) whose sine is x."

DEFINITION OF INVERSE SINE FUNCTION

The **inverse sine function** is defined by

$$y = \arcsin x \quad \text{if and only if} \quad \sin y = x,$$

where $-1 \le x \le 1$ and $-\pi/2 \le y \le \pi/2$. The domain of $y =$ arcsin x is $[-1, 1]$, and the range is $[-\pi/2, \pi/2]$.

As with trigonometric functions, much of the work with inverse trigonometric functions can be done by *exact* calculations rather than by calculator approximations. Exact calculations help to increase your understanding of the inverse functions by relating them to the triangle definitions of the trigonometric functions.

EXAMPLE 1 Evaluating the Inverse Sine Function

Find the values of the following (if possible).

REMARK Try verifying the answers in Example 1 with your calculator. What happens when you try to calculate $\sin^{-1} 2$?

A. $\arcsin\left(-\dfrac{1}{2}\right)$ **B.** $\sin^{-1} \dfrac{\sqrt{3}}{2}$ **C.** $\sin^{-1} 2$

SOLUTION

A. By definition, $y = \arcsin(-\frac{1}{2})$ implies that

$$\sin y = -\frac{1}{2}, \quad \text{for} \quad -\frac{\pi}{2} \le y \le \frac{\pi}{2}.$$

Because $\sin(-\pi/6) = -\frac{1}{2}$, you can conclude that $y = -\pi/6$ and

$$\arcsin\left(-\frac{1}{2}\right) = -\frac{\pi}{6}.$$

B. By definition, $y = \sin^{-1}\left(\sqrt{3}/2\right)$ implies that

$$\sin y = \frac{\sqrt{3}}{2}, \quad \text{for} \quad -\frac{\pi}{2} \le y \le \frac{\pi}{2}.$$

Because $\sin(\pi/3) = \sqrt{3}/2$, you can conclude that $y = \pi/3$ and

$$\sin^{-1}\frac{\sqrt{3}}{2} = \frac{\pi}{3}.$$

C. It is not possible to evaluate $y = \sin^{-1} x$ when $x = 2$, because there is no angle whose sine is 2. Remember that the domain of the inverse sine function is $[-1, 1]$.

From Section 1.7, you know that graphs of inverse functions are reflections of each other in the line $y = x$.

EXAMPLE 2   Sketching the Graph of the Arcsine Function

Sketch a graph of $y = \arcsin x$ *by hand*.

SOLUTION

By definition, the equations

$$y = \arcsin x \quad \text{and} \quad \sin y = x$$

are equivalent for $-\pi/2 \le y \le \pi/2$. Hence, their graphs are the same. By assigning values to y in the second equation, you can construct the following table of values.

y	$-\frac{\pi}{2}$	$-\frac{\pi}{4}$	$-\frac{\pi}{6}$	0	$\frac{\pi}{6}$	$\frac{\pi}{4}$	$\frac{\pi}{2}$
$x = \sin y$	-1	$-\frac{\sqrt{2}}{2}$	$-\frac{1}{2}$	0	$\frac{1}{2}$	$\frac{\sqrt{2}}{2}$	1

The resulting graph of $y = \arcsin x$ is shown in Figure 6.66. Note that it is the reflection (in the line $y = x$) of the solid part of Figure 6.65. Be sure you see that Figure 6.66 shows the *entire* graph of the inverse sine function. Remember that the range of $y = \arcsin x$ is the closed interval $[-\pi/2, \pi/2]$.

FIGURE 6.66

Cos x is one-to-one on this interval.

FIGURE 6.67

Other Inverse Trigonometric Functions

The cosine function is decreasing on the interval $0 \leq x \leq \pi$, as shown in Figure 6.67. Consequently, on this interval the cosine has an inverse function, which is called the **inverse cosine function** and is denoted by

$$y = \arccos x \quad \text{or} \quad y = \cos^{-1} x.$$

Similarly, you can define an **inverse tangent function** by restricting the domain of $y = \tan x$ to the interval $(-\pi/2, \pi/2)$. The following list summarizes the definitions of the three most common inverse trigonometric functions. The remaining three are discussed in the exercise set.

DEFINITION OF THE INVERSE TRIGONOMETRIC FUNCTIONS

Function	Domain	Range
$y = \arcsin x$ if and only if $\sin y = x$	$-1 \leq x \leq 1$	$-\dfrac{\pi}{2} \leq y \leq \dfrac{\pi}{2}$
$y = \arccos x$ if and only if $\cos y = x$	$-1 \leq x \leq 1$	$0 \leq y \leq \pi$
$y = \arctan x$ if and only if $\tan y = x$	$-\infty < x < \infty$	$-\dfrac{\pi}{2} < y < \dfrac{\pi}{2}$

The graphs of these three inverse trigonometric functions are shown in Figure 6.68.

Domain: $[-1, 1]$
Range: $\left[-\dfrac{\pi}{2}, \dfrac{\pi}{2}\right]$

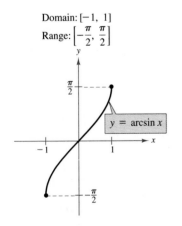

Domain: $[-1, 1]$
Range: $[0, \pi]$

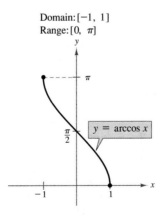

Domain: $(-\infty, \infty)$
Range: $\left(-\dfrac{\pi}{2}, \dfrac{\pi}{2}\right)$

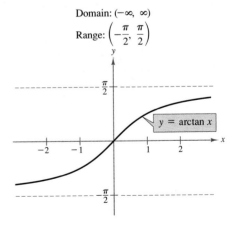

FIGURE 6.68

EXAMPLE 3   Evaluating Inverse Trigonometric Functions

Find the exact value of the following.

A. $\arccos \dfrac{\sqrt{2}}{2}$ **B.** $\arccos(-1)$ **C.** $\arctan 0$

SOLUTION

A. Because $\cos(\pi/4) = \sqrt{2}/2$ and $\pi/4$ lies in $[0, \pi]$, it follows that

$$\arccos \dfrac{\sqrt{2}}{2} = \dfrac{\pi}{4}.$$

B. Because $\cos \pi = -1$ and π lies in $[0, \pi]$, it follows that

$$\arccos(-1) = \pi.$$

C. Because $\tan 0 = 0$ and 0 lies in $(-\pi/2, \pi/2)$, it follows that

$$\arctan 0 = 0.$$

In Example 3, you were able to find the *exact* value of the given inverse trigonometric function without a calculator. In the next example, a calculator is necessary to approximate the function values.

REMARK   In Example 4, had you set the calculator to the degree mode, the display would have been in degrees rather than radians. This convention is peculiar to calculators. By definition, the values of inverse trigonometric functions are always *in radians*.

EXAMPLE 4   Using a Calculator to Evaluate Inverse Trigonometric Functions

Use a calculator to approximate the value (if possible).

A. $\arctan(-8.45)$ **B.** $\arcsin 0.2447$ **C.** $\arccos 2$

SOLUTION

Function	Mode	Display	Rounded to 3 Decimal Places
A. $\arctan(-8.45)$	Radian	-1.453001005	-1.453
B. $\arcsin 0.2447$	Radian	0.2472102741	0.247
C. $\arccos 2$	Radian	ERROR	

Note that the *error* in part (C) occurs because the domain of the inverse cosine function is $[-1, 1]$.

Compositions of Trigonometric and Inverse Trigonometric Functions

Recall from Section 1.7 that inverse functions possess the properties

$$f(f^{-1}(x)) = x \quad \text{and} \quad f^{-1}(f(x)) = x.$$

The inverse trigonometric versions of these properties are as follows.

REMARK Keep in mind that these inverse properties do not apply for arbitrary values of x and y. For instance,

$$\arcsin\left(\sin\frac{3\pi}{2}\right) = \arcsin(-1)$$

$$= -\frac{\pi}{2} \neq \frac{3\pi}{2}.$$

In other words, the property $\arcsin(\sin y) = y$ is not valid for values of y outside the interval $[-\pi/2, \pi/2]$.

INVERSE PROPERTIES

If $-1 \leq x \leq 1$ and $-\pi/2 \leq y \leq \pi/2$, then

$$\sin(\arcsin x) = x \quad \text{and} \quad \arcsin(\sin y) = y.$$

If $-1 \leq x \leq 1$ and $0 \leq y \leq \pi$, then

$$\cos(\arccos x) = x \quad \text{and} \quad \arccos(\cos y) = y.$$

If $-\pi/2 < y < \pi/2$, then

$$\tan(\arctan x) = x \quad \text{and} \quad \arctan(\tan y) = y.$$

DISCOVERY

(a) Use a graphing utility to graph $y = \arcsin(\sin x)$. What is the domain and range of the function? Explain why $\arcsin(\sin 4)$ does not equal 4.

(b) Use a graphing utility to graph $y = \sin(\arcsin x)$. What is the domain and range of the function? Explain why $\sin(\arcsin 4)$ is not defined.

EXAMPLE 5   Using Inverse Properties

If possible, find the exact value.

A. $\tan[\arctan(-5)]$ **B.** $\arcsin\left(\sin\frac{5\pi}{3}\right)$ **C.** $\cos(\cos^{-1}\pi)$

SOLUTION

A. Because -5 lies in the domain of $\arctan x$, the inverse property applies, and you have $\tan[\arctan(-5)] = -5$.

B. In this case, $5\pi/3$ does not lie within the range of the arcsine function, $-\pi/2 \leq x \leq \pi/2$. However, $5\pi/3$ is coterminal with

$$\frac{5\pi}{3} - 2\pi = -\frac{\pi}{3},$$

which does lie in the range of the arcsine function, and you have

$$\arcsin\left(\sin\frac{5\pi}{3}\right) = \arcsin\left[\sin\left(-\frac{\pi}{3}\right)\right] = -\frac{\pi}{3}.$$

C. The expression $\cos(\cos^{-1}\pi)$ is not defined, because $\cos^{-1}\pi$ is not defined. Remember that the domain of the inverse cosine function is $[-1, 1]$.

REMARK Try verifying these results with your calculator.

Example 6 shows how to use right triangles to find exact values of functions of inverse functions. Example 7 shows how to use triangles to convert a trigonometric expression into an algebraic one. This conversion technique is used frequently in calculus.

EXAMPLE 6   Evaluating Functions of Inverse Trigonometric Functions

Find the exact value of the following.

A. $\tan\left(\arccos\dfrac{2}{3}\right)$ **B.** $\cos\left[\arcsin\left(-\dfrac{3}{5}\right)\right]$

SOLUTION

A. If you let $u = \arccos\frac{2}{3}$, then $\cos u = \frac{2}{3}$. Because $\cos u$ is positive, u is a *first* quadrant angle. You can sketch and label angle u as shown in Figure 6.69. Consequently,

$$\tan\left(\arccos\frac{2}{3}\right) = \tan u = \frac{\text{opp}}{\text{adj}} = \frac{\sqrt{5}}{2}.$$

B. If you let $u = \arcsin(-\frac{3}{5})$, then $\sin u = -\frac{3}{5}$. Because $\sin u$ is negative, u is a *fourth* quadrant angle. You can sketch and label u as shown in Figure 6.70. Consequently,

$$\cos\left[\arcsin\left(-\frac{3}{5}\right)\right] = \cos u = \frac{\text{adj}}{\text{hyp}} = \frac{4}{5}.$$

FIGURE 6.69

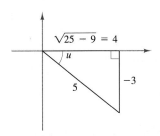

FIGURE 6.70

EXAMPLE 7   Some Problems from Calculus

Write each of the following as an algebraic expression in x.

A. $\sin(\arccos 3x), \quad 0 \le x \le \dfrac{1}{3}$ **B.** $\cot(\arccos 3x), \quad 0 \le x < \dfrac{1}{3}$

SOLUTION

If you let $u = \arccos 3x$, then $\cos u = 3x$. Because

$$\cos u = \frac{3x}{1} = \frac{\text{adj}}{\text{hyp}},$$

you can sketch a right triangle with acute angle u, as shown in Figure 6.71. From this triangle, you can convert each expression to algebraic form.

A. $\sin(\arccos 3x) = \sin u = \dfrac{\text{opp}}{\text{hyp}} = \sqrt{1 - 9x^2}, \quad 0 \le x \le \dfrac{1}{3}$

B. $\cot(\arccos 3x) = \cot u = \dfrac{\text{adj}}{\text{opp}} = \dfrac{3x}{\sqrt{1 - 9x^2}}, \quad 0 \le x < \dfrac{1}{3}$

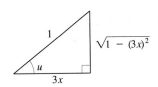

FIGURE 6.71

REMARK   In Example 7, a similar argument can be made for x-values lying in the interval $[-1/3, 0]$. Why do we restrict $x < \frac{1}{3}$ in part (B)?

You have studied inverses for several types of functions. Match each of the functions in the left column with its inverse function in the right column.

1. $f(x) = x$ (a) $f^{-1}(x) = \arcsin x$
2. $f(x) = x^2, \quad 0 \le x$ (b) $f^{-1}(x) = \ln x$
3. $f(x) = x^3$ (c) $f^{-1}(x) = \sqrt{x}$
4. $f(x) = e^x$ (d) $f^{-1}(x) = \arctan x$
5. $f(x) = \ln x$ (e) $f^{-1}(x) = \arccos x$

6. $f(x) = \sin x, \quad -\dfrac{\pi}{2} \le x \le \dfrac{\pi}{2}$ (f) $f^{-1}(x) = \sqrt[3]{x}$

7. $f(x) = \cos x, \quad 0 \le x \le \pi$ (g) $f^{-1}(x) = e^x$

8. $f(x) = \tan x, \quad -\dfrac{\pi}{2} < x < \dfrac{\pi}{2}$ (h) $f^{-1}(x) = x$

Provide reasons for your answers.

The following warm-up exercises involve skills that were covered in earlier sections. You will use these skills in the exercise set for this section.

In Exercises 1–4, evaluate the trigonometric function without using a calculator.

1. $\sin\left(-\dfrac{\pi}{2}\right)$ **2.** $\cos \pi$

3. $\tan\left(-\dfrac{\pi}{4}\right)$ **4.** $\sin \dfrac{\pi}{4}$

In Exercises 5 and 6, find a real number x in the interval $[-\pi/2, \pi/2]$ that has the same sine value as the given value.

5. $\sin 2\pi$ **6.** $\sin \dfrac{5\pi}{6}$

In Exercises 7 and 8, find a real number x in the interval $[0, \pi]$ that has the same cosine value as the given value.

7. $\cos 3\pi$ **8.** $\cos\left(-\dfrac{\pi}{4}\right)$

In Exercises 9 and 10, find a real number x in the interval $(-\pi/2, \pi/2)$ that has the same tangent value as the given value.

9. $\tan 4\pi$ **10.** $\tan \dfrac{3\pi}{4}$

SECTION 6.7 · EXERCISES

In Exercises 1–16, evaluate the expression without using a calculator.

1. $\arcsin \frac{1}{2}$

2. $\arcsin 0$

3. $\arccos \frac{1}{2}$

4. $\arccos 0$

5. $\arctan \dfrac{\sqrt{3}}{3}$

6. $\arctan(-1)$

7. $\arccos\left(-\dfrac{\sqrt{3}}{2}\right)$

8. $\arcsin\left(-\dfrac{\sqrt{2}}{2}\right)$

9. $\arctan\left(-\sqrt{3}\right)$

10. $\arctan\left(\sqrt{3}\right)$

11. $\arccos\left(-\dfrac{1}{2}\right)$

12. $\arcsin \dfrac{\sqrt{2}}{2}$

13. $\arcsin \dfrac{\sqrt{3}}{2}$

14. $\arctan\left(-\dfrac{\sqrt{3}}{3}\right)$

15. $\arctan 0$

16. $\arccos 1$

In Exercises 17–28, use a calculator to approximate the given value. (Round your result to two decimal places.)

17. $\arccos 0.28$

18. $\arcsin 0.45$

19. $\arcsin(-0.75)$

20. $\arccos(-0.8)$

21. $\arctan(-2)$

22. $\arctan 15$

23. $\arcsin 0.31$

24. $\arccos 0.26$

25. $\arccos(-0.41)$

26. $\arcsin(-0.125)$

27. $\arctan 0.92$

28. $\arctan 2.8$

In Exercises 29 and 30, use a graphing utility to graph f, g, and $y = x$ in the same viewing rectangle to verify geometrically that g is the inverse of f. (Be sure to properly restrict the domain of f.)

29. $f(x) = \tan x$, $\quad g(x) = \arctan x$

30. $f(x) = \sin x$, $\quad g(x) = \arcsin x$

In Exercises 31–36, use the properties of inverse trigonometric functions to evaluate the expression.

31. $\sin(\arcsin 0.3)$

32. $\tan(\arctan 25)$

33. $\cos[\arccos(-0.1)]$

34. $\sin[\arcsin(-0.2)]$

35. $\arcsin(\sin 3\pi)$

36. $\arccos\left(\cos \dfrac{7\pi}{2}\right)$

In Exercises 37–44, find the exact value of the expression without using a calculator. (*Hint:* Make a sketch of a right triangle, as illustrated in Example 6.)

37. $\sin(\arctan \frac{3}{4})$

38. $\sec(\arcsin \frac{4}{5})$

39. $\cos(\arctan 2)$

40. $\sin\left(\arccos \dfrac{\sqrt{5}}{5}\right)$

41. $\cos(\arcsin \frac{5}{13})$

42. $\csc[\arctan(-\frac{5}{12})]$

43. $\sec[\arctan(-\frac{3}{5})]$

44. $\tan[\arcsin(-\frac{3}{4})]$

In Exercises 45 and 46, use a graphing utility to graph f and g in the same viewing rectangle to verify that the two are equal. Identify any asymptotes of the graphs.

45. $f(x) = \sin(\arctan 2x)$, $\quad g(x) = \dfrac{2x}{\sqrt{1 + 4x^2}}$

46. $f(x) = \tan\left(\arccos \dfrac{x}{2}\right)$, $\quad g(x) = \dfrac{\sqrt{4 - x^2}}{x}$

In Exercises 47–56, write an algebraic expression that is equivalent to the given expression. (*Hint:* Sketch a right triangle, as demonstrated in Example 7.)

47. $\cot(\arctan x)$

48. $\sin(\arctan x)$

49. $\cos(\arcsin 2x)$

50. $\sec(\arctan 3x)$

51. $\sin(\arccos x)$

52. $\cot\left(\arctan \dfrac{1}{x}\right)$

53. $\tan\left(\arccos \dfrac{x}{3}\right)$

54. $\sec[\arcsin(x - 1)]$

55. $\csc\left(\arccos \dfrac{x}{\sqrt{2}}\right)$

56. $\cos\left(\arcsin \dfrac{x - h}{r}\right)$

In Exercises 57–60, fill in the blanks.

57. $\arctan \dfrac{9}{x} = \arcsin\left(\rule{1cm}{0.4pt}\right)$, $\quad x \ne 0$

58. $\arcsin \dfrac{\sqrt{36 - x^2}}{6} = \arccos\left(\rule{1cm}{0.4pt}\right)$, $\quad 0 \le x \le 6$

59. $\arccos \dfrac{3}{\sqrt{x^2 - 2x + 10}} = \arcsin\left(\rule{1cm}{0.4pt}\right)$

60. $\arccos \dfrac{x - 2}{2} = \arctan\left(\rule{1cm}{0.4pt}\right)$, $\quad |x - 2| \le 2$

In Exercises 61–64, graph the function.

61. $f(x) = \arcsin(x - 1)$

62. $f(x) = \dfrac{\pi}{2} + \arctan x$

63. $f(x) = \arctan 2x$

64. $f(x) = \arccos \dfrac{x}{4}$

In Exercises 65 and 66, write the given function in terms of the sine function by using the identity

$$A \cos \omega t + B \sin \omega t = \sqrt{A^2 + B^2} \sin\left(\omega t + \arctan \dfrac{B}{A}\right).$$

Verify your result by using a graphing utility to graph both forms of the function.

65. $f(t) = 3 \cos 2t + 3 \sin 2t$

66. $f(t) = 4 \cos \pi t + 3 \sin \pi t$

67. *Photography*   A photographer is taking a picture of a 4-foot-square painting hung in an art gallery. The camera lens is 1 foot below the lower edge of the painting (see figure). The angle β subtended by the camera lens x feet from the painting is given by

$$\beta = \arctan \dfrac{4x}{x^2 + 5}, \qquad x > 0.$$

(a) Use a graphing utility to graph β as a function of x.
(b) Move the cursor along the graph to approximate the distance from the picture when β is maximum.
(c) Identify any asymptote of the graph and discuss its meaning in the context of the problem.

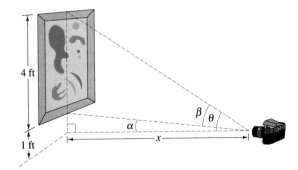

FIGURE FOR 67

68. *Photography*   A television camera at ground level is filming the lift-off of the space shuttle at a point 2000 feet from the launch pad (see figure). If θ is the angle of elevation to the shuttle and s is the height of the shuttle in feet, write θ as a function of s. Find θ when (a) $s = 1000$ and (b) $s = 4000$.

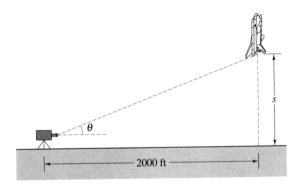

FIGURE FOR 68

69. *Docking a Boat*   A boat is pulled in by means of a winch located on a dock 12 feet above the deck of the boat (see figure). If θ is the angle of elevation from the boat to the winch and s is the length of the rope from the winch to the boat, write θ as a function of s. Find θ when (a) $s = 48$ feet and (b) $s = 24$ feet.

FIGURE FOR 69

70. *Area*   In calculus, it is shown that the area of the region bounded by the graphs of $y = 0$, $y = 1/(x^2 + 1)$, $x = a$, and $x = b$ is given by

Area $= \arctan b - \arctan a$

(see figure). Find the area for the following values of a and b.

(a) $a = 0$, $b = 1$ (b) $a = -1$, $b = 1$

(c) $a = 0$, $b = 3$ (d) $a = -1$, $b = 3$

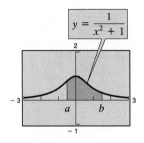

FIGURE FOR 70

71. Define the inverse cotangent function by restricting the domain of the cotangent to the interval $(0, \pi)$, and sketch its graph.

72. Define the inverse secant function by restricting the domain of the secant to the intervals $[0, \pi/2)$ and $(\pi/2, \pi]$, and sketch its graph.

73. Define the inverse cosecant function by restricting the domain of the cosecant to the intervals $[-\pi/2, 0)$ and $(0, \pi/2]$, and sketch its graph.

74. Use the results of Exercises 71–73 to evaluate the following without using a calculator.

(a) $\operatorname{arcsec} \sqrt{2}$ (b) $\operatorname{arcsec} 1$

(c) $\operatorname{arccot} -\sqrt{3}$ (d) $\operatorname{arccsc} 2$

In Exercises 75–80, prove the identity.

75. $\arcsin(-x) = -\arcsin x$

76. $\arctan(-x) = -\arctan x$

77. $\arccos(-x) = \pi - \arccos x$

78. $\arctan x + \arctan \dfrac{1}{x} = \dfrac{\pi}{2}, \quad x > 0$

79. $\arcsin x + \arccos x = \dfrac{\pi}{2}$

80. $\arcsin x = \arctan \dfrac{x}{\sqrt{1 - x^2}}$

6.8   APPLICATIONS OF TRIGONOMETRY
Applications Involving Right Triangles   /   Trigonometry and Bearings   /
Harmonic Motion

Applications Involving Right Triangles

In keeping with our twofold perspective of trigonometry, this section includes both right triangle applications and applications that emphasize the periodic nature of the trigonometric functions.

In this section, the three angles of a right triangle are denoted by the letters A, B, and C (where C is the right angle), and the lengths of the sides opposite these angles are denoted by the letters a, b, and c (where c is the hypotenuse).

FIGURE 6.72

EXAMPLE 1   **Solving a Right Triangle, Given One Acute Angle and One Side**

Solve the right triangle having $A = 34.2°$ and $b = 19.4$, as shown in Figure 6.72.

SOLUTION

Because $C = 90°$, it follows that $A + B = 90°$ and

$$B = 90° - 34.2° = 55.8°.$$

To solve for a, use the fact that

$$\tan A = \frac{\text{opp}}{\text{adj}} = \frac{a}{b} \longrightarrow a = b \tan A.$$

Thus,

$$a = 19.4 \tan 34.2° \approx 13.18.$$

Similarly, to solve for c, use the fact that

$$\cos A = \frac{\text{adj}}{\text{hyp}} = \frac{b}{c} \longrightarrow c = \frac{b}{\cos A}.$$

Thus,

$$c = \frac{19.4}{\cos 34.2°} \approx 23.46.$$

FIGURE 6.73

EXAMPLE 2   Finding a Side of a Right Triangle

A safety regulation states that the maximum angle of elevation for a rescue ladder is 72°. If a fire department's longest ladder is 110 feet, what is the maximum safe rescue height?

SOLUTION

A sketch is shown in Figure 6.73. From the equation

$$\sin A = \frac{a}{c},$$

it follows that

$$a = c \sin A = 110(\sin 72°) \approx 104.6 \text{ feet.}$$

EXAMPLE 3   Finding a Side of a Right Triangle

At a point 200 feet from the base of a building, the angle of elevation to the *bottom* of a smokestack is 35°, whereas the angle of elevation to the *top* is 53°, as shown in Figure 6.74. Find the height s of the smokestack alone.

SOLUTION

Note from Figure 6.74 that this problem involves two right triangles. In the smaller right triangle, use the fact that $\tan 35° = a/200$ to conclude that the height of the building is

$$a = 200 \tan 35°.$$

Now, from the larger right triangle, use the equation

$$\tan 53° = \frac{a + s}{200}$$

to conclude that $a + s = 200 \tan 53°$. Hence, the height of the smokestack is

$$s = 200 \tan 53° - a = 200 \tan 53° - 200 \tan 35° \approx 125.4 \text{ feet.}$$

FIGURE 6.74

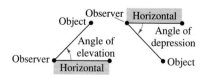

FIGURE 6.75

Examples 2 and 3 used the term **angle of elevation** to represent the angle from the horizontal upward to an object. For objects that lie below the horizontal, it is common to use the term **angle of depression,** as shown in Figure 6.75.

In Examples 1 through 3, you found the lengths of the sides of a right triangle, given an acute angle and the length of one of the sides. You can also find the angles of a right triangle given only the lengths of two sides, as demonstrated in Example 4.

EXAMPLE 4   **Finding an Acute Angle of a Right Triangle**

A swimming pool is 20 meters long and 12 meters wide. The bottom of the pool is slanted so that the water depth is 1.3 meters at the shallow end and 4 meters at the deep end, as shown in Figure 6.76. Find the angle of depression of the bottom of the pool.

FIGURE 6.76

REMARK   Note that the width of the pool, 12 meters, is irrelevant to the problem.

SOLUTION

Using the tangent function, you can see that

$$\tan A = \frac{\text{opp}}{\text{adj}} = \frac{2.7}{20} = 0.135.$$

Thus, the angle of depression is given by

$$A = \arctan 0.135 \approx 0.13419 \text{ radians} \approx 7.69°.$$

Trigonometry and Bearings

In surveying and navigation, directions are generally given in terms of **bearings.** A bearing measures the acute angle a path or line of sight makes with a fixed north-south line. For instance, in Figure 6.77(a), the bearing is S 35° E, meaning 35 *degrees east of south.* Similarly, the bearings in Figure 6.77(b) and (c) are N 80° W and N 45° E, respectively.

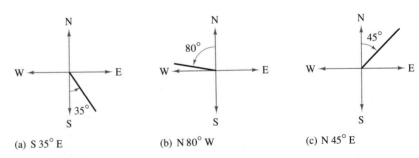

(a) S 35° E   (b) N 80° W   (c) N 45° E

FIGURE 6.77

EXAMPLE 5   Finding Directions in Terms of Bearings
....

A ship leaves port at noon and heads due west at 20 knots (nautical miles per hour). At 2 P.M., to avoid a storm, the ship changes course to N 54° W, as shown in Figure 6.78. Find the ship's bearing and distance from the port of departure at 3 P.M..

FIGURE 6.78

SOLUTION

Because the ship travels west at 20 knots for two hours, the length of AB is 40. Similarly, BD is 20. In triangle BCD, you have $B = 90° - 54° = 36°$. The two sides of this triangle are determined as follows.

$$\sin B = \frac{b}{20} \qquad \text{and} \quad \cos B = \frac{d}{20}$$

$$b = 20 \sin 36° \qquad\qquad d = 20 \cos 36°$$

Now, in triangle ACD, you can determine angle A as follows.

$$\tan A = \frac{b}{d + 40} = \frac{20 \sin 36°}{20 \cos 36° + 40} \approx 0.2092494$$

$$A \approx \arctan 0.2092494 \approx 0.2062732 \text{ radians} \approx 11.82°$$

The angle with the north-south line is $90° - 11.82° = 78.18°$. Therefore, the bearing of the ship is

N 78.18° W.   *Bearing*

Finally, from triangle ACD, you have $\sin A = b/c$, which yields

$$c = \frac{b}{\sin A} = \frac{20 \sin 36°}{\sin(11.82)}$$

$$c \approx 57.4 \text{ nautical miles.} \qquad \textit{Distance from port}$$

Harmonic Motion

The periodic nature of the trigonometric functions is useful for describing the motion of a point on an object that vibrates, oscillates, rotates, or is moved by wave motion.

For example, consider a ball that is bobbing up and down on the end of a spring, as shown in Figure 6.79. Suppose that 10 centimeters is the maximum distance the ball moves vertically upward or downward from its equilibrium (at rest) position. Suppose further that the time it takes for the ball to move from its maximum displacement above zero to its maximum displacement below zero and back again is $t = 4$ seconds. Assuming the ideal conditions of perfect elasticity and no friction or air resistance, the ball would continue to move up and down in a uniform and regular manner.

From this spring you can conclude that the period (time for one complete cycle) of the motion is

Period = 4 seconds

and that its amplitude (maximum displacement from equilibrium) is

Amplitude = 10 centimeters.

Motion of this nature can be described by a sine or cosine function, and is called **simple harmonic motion.**

Simple Harmonic Motion

FIGURE 6.79

DEFINITION OF SIMPLE HARMONIC MOTION

A point that moves on a coordinate line is in **simple harmonic motion** if its distance d from the origin at time t is given by either

$$d = a \sin \omega t \quad \text{or} \quad d = a \cos \omega t,$$

where a and ω are real numbers such that $\omega > 0$. The motion has **amplitude** $|a|$, **period** $2\pi/\omega$, and **frequency** $\omega/2\pi$.

EXAMPLE 6   Simple Harmonic Motion

Write the equation for the simple harmonic motion of the ball described in Figure 6.79, where the period is 4 seconds. What is the frequency of this motion?

SOLUTION

Because the spring is at equilibrium ($d = 0$) when $t = 0$, use the equation

$$d = a \sin \omega t.$$

Moreover, because the maximum displacement from zero is 10 and the period is 4, you have

$$\text{Amplitude} = |a| = 10$$

$$\text{Period} = \frac{2\pi}{\omega} = 4 \quad \longrightarrow \quad \omega = \frac{\pi}{2}.$$

Consequently, the equation of motion is

$$d = 10 \sin \frac{\pi}{2} t.$$

Note that the choice of $a = 10$ or $a = -10$ depends on whether the ball initially moves up or down. The frequency is given by

$$\text{Frequency} = \frac{\omega}{2\pi} = \frac{\pi/2}{2\pi} = \frac{1}{4} \text{ cycle per second.}$$

FIGURE 6.80

One illustration of the relation between sine waves and harmonic motion is seen in the wave motion resulting from dropping a stone into a calm pool of water. The waves move outward in roughly the shape of sine (or cosine) waves, as shown in Figure 6.80. As an example, suppose you are fishing and your fishing bob is attached so that it does not move horizontally. As the waves move outward from the dropped stone, your fishing bob will move up and down in simple harmonic motion, as shown in Figure 6.81.

A fishing bob moves in a vertical
direction as waves move to the right.

FIGURE 6.81

EXAMPLE 7   Simple Harmonic Motion

Given the equation for simple harmonic motion,

$$d = 6 \cos \frac{3\pi}{4} t,$$

find the following.

A. The maximum displacement
B. The frequency
C. The value of d when $t = 4$
D. The least positive value of t for which $d = 0$

SOLUTION

The given equation has the form $d = a \cos \omega t$, with $a = 6$ and $\omega = 3\pi/4$.

A. The maximum displacement (from the point of equilibrium) is given by the amplitude. Thus, the maximum displacement is 6.

B. Frequency $= \dfrac{\omega}{2\pi} = \dfrac{3\pi/4}{2\pi} = \dfrac{3}{8}$ cycle per unit of time

C. $d = 6 \cos \left[\dfrac{3\pi}{4}(4) \right] = 6 \cos 3\pi = 6(-1) = -6$

D. To find the least positive value of t for which $d = 0$, solve the equation

$$d = 6 \cos \frac{3\pi}{4} t = 0$$

to obtain

$$\frac{3\pi}{4} t = \frac{\pi}{2}, \frac{3\pi}{2}, \frac{5\pi}{2}, \cdots$$

$$t = \frac{2}{3}, 2, \frac{10}{3}, \ldots .$$

Thus, the least positive value of t is $t = \frac{2}{3}$.

Many other physical phenomena can be characterized by wave motion. These include electromagnetic waves such as radio waves, television waves, and microwaves. Radio waves transmit sound in two different ways. For an AM station, the *amplitude* of the wave is modified to carry sound (AM stands for **amplitude modulation**). See Figure 6.82(a). An FM radio signal has its *frequency* modified in order to carry sound, hence the term **frequency modulation.** See Figure 6.82(b).

(a) AM: Amplitude modulation

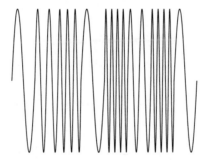

(b) FM: Frequency modulation

FIGURE 6.82

Radio Waves

DISCUSSION PROBLEM

· · · · · · · · · · · · · ·

YOU BE THE INSTRUCTOR

Suppose you are teaching a class in trigonometry. Write two "right triangle problems" that you think would be reasonable to ask your students to solve. (Assume that your students have 5 minutes to solve each problem.)

WARM-UP

The following warm-up exercises involve skills that were covered in earlier sections. You will use these skills in the exercise set for this section.

In Exercises 1–4, evaluate the expression and round to two decimal places.

1. $20 \sin 25°$ **2.** $42 \tan 62°$

3. $\arcsin 0.8723$ **4.** $\arctan 2.8703$

In Exercises 5 and 6, solve for x and round to two decimal places.

5. $\cos 22° = \dfrac{x + 13 \sin 22°}{13 \sin 54°}$ **6.** $\tan 36° = \dfrac{x + 85 \tan 18°}{85}$

In Exercises 7–10, find the amplitude and period of the function.

7. $f(x) = -4 \sin 2x$ **8.** $f(x) = \frac{1}{2} \sin \pi x$

9. $g(x) = 3 \cos 3\pi x$ **10.** $g(x) = 0.2 \cot \dfrac{x}{4}$

SECTION 6.8 · EXERCISES

In Exercises 1–10, solve the right triangle shown in the figure. (Round your result to two decimal places.)

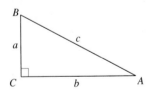

FIGURE FOR 1–10

1. $A = 20°, \quad b = 10$

3. $B = 71°, \quad b = 24$

5. $A = 12° 15', \quad c = 430.5$

7. $a = 6, \quad b = 10$

9. $b = 16, \quad c = 52$

2. $B = 54°, \quad c = 15$

4. $A = 8.4°, \quad a = 40.5$

6. $B = 65° 12', \quad a = 14.2$

8. $a = 25, \quad c = 35$

10. $b = 1.32, \quad c = 9.45$

In Exercises 11 and 12, find the altitude of the isosceles triangle shown in the figure. (Round your result to two decimal places.)

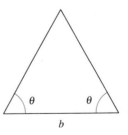

FIGURE FOR 11 AND 12

11. $\theta = 52°, \quad b = 4$ inches

12. $\theta = 18°, \quad b = 10$ meters

13. *Length of a Shadow*   If the sun is 30° above the horizon, find the length of a shadow cast by a silo that is 70 feet high (see figure).

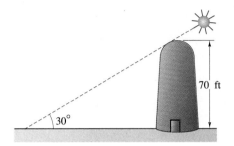

70 ft

30°

FIGURE FOR 13

14. *Length of a Shadow*   The sun is 20° above the horizon. Find the length of a shadow cast by a building that is 600 feet high (see figure).

600 ft

20°

FIGURE FOR 14

15. *Height*   A ladder of length 16 feet leans against the side of a house (see figure). Find the height h of the top of the ladder if the angle of elevation of the ladder is 74°.

16 ft h

74°

FIGURE FOR 15

16. *Height*   The length of a shadow of a tree is 125 feet when the angle of elevation of the sun is 33° (see figure). Approximate the height h of the tree.

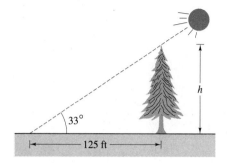

h

33°

125 ft

FIGURE FOR 16

17. *Angle of Elevation*   An amateur radio operator erects a 75-foot vertical tower for his antenna (see figure). Find the angle of elevation to the top of the tower at a point on level ground 50 feet from the base.

75 ft

θ

50 ft

FIGURE FOR 17

18. *Angle of Elevation*   The height of an outdoor basketball backboard is $12\frac{1}{2}$ feet, and the backboard casts a shadow $17\frac{1}{3}$ feet long (see figure). Find the angle of elevation of the sun.

$12\frac{1}{2}$ ft

θ

$17\frac{1}{3}$ ft

FIGURE FOR 18

19. *Angle of Depression*   A spacecraft is traveling in a circular orbit 100 miles above the surface of the earth (see figure). Find the angle of depression from the spacecraft to the horizon. Assume that the radius of the earth is 4000 miles.

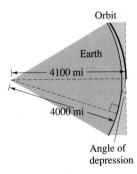

Orbit

Earth

|←—— 4100 mi ——→|

4000 mi

Angle of depression

FIGURE FOR 19

20. *Angle of Depression*   Find the angle of depression from the top of a lighthouse 250 feet above water level to the water line of a ship 2 miles offshore.

21. *Airplane Ascent*   When an airplane leaves the runway (see figure), its angle of climb is 18° and its speed is 275 feet per second. Find the altitude of the plane after 1 minute.

a

18°

FIGURE FOR 21

22. *Mountain Descent*   A sign on the roadway at the top of a mountain indicates that for the next 4 miles the grade is 12.5° (see figure). Find the change in elevation for a car descending the mountain.

4 mi

12.5°

FIGURE FOR 22

23. *Height*   From a point 50 feet in front of a church, the angles of elevation to the base of the steeple and to the top of the steeple are 35° and 47° 40′, respectively (see figure). Find the height of the steeple.

47° 40′

35°

|←—50 ft—→|

FIGURE FOR 23

24. *Height*   From a point 100 feet in front of a public library, the angles of elevation to the base of the flagpole and to the top of the pole are 28° and 39° 45′, respectively. The flagpole is mounted on the front of the library's roof (see figure). Find the height of the pole.

39° 45′

28°

|←———— 100 ft ————→|

FIGURE FOR 24

25. *Navigation*   An airplane flying at 550 miles per hour has a bearing of N 52° E. After flying for 1.5 hours, how far north and how far east has the plane traveled from its point of departure?

26. *Navigation*   A ship leaves port at noon and has a bearing of S 27° W. If the ship is sailing at 20 knots, how many nautical miles south and how many nautical miles west has the ship traveled by 6:00 P.M.?

27. *Navigation*   A ship is 45 miles east and 30 miles south of port. If the captain wants to sail directly to port, what bearing should be taken?

28. *Navigation*   A plane is 120 miles north and 85 miles east of an airport. If the pilot wants to fly directly to the airport, what bearing should be taken?

29. *Surveying*   A surveyor wishes to find the distance across a swamp (see figure). The bearing from *A* to *B* is N 32° W. The surveyor walks 50 yards from *A*, and at point *C* the bearing to *B* is N 68° W. (a) Find the bearing from *A* to *C*. (b) Find the distance from *A* to *B*.

FIGURE FOR 29

30. *Location of a Fire*   Two fire towers are 20 miles apart, tower *A* being due west of tower *B*. A fire is spotted from the towers, and the bearings from *A* and *B* are N 76° E and N 56° W (see figure). Find the distance *d* of the fire from the line segment *AB*. [*Hint:* Use the fact that *d* = 20/(cot 14° + cot 34°).]

FIGURE FOR 30

31. *Distance Between Ships*   An observer in a lighthouse 300 feet above sea level spots two ships directly offshore. The angles of depression to the ships are 4° and 6.5° (see figure). How far apart are the ships?

FIGURE FOR 31

32. *Distance Between Towns*   A passenger in an airplane flying at 30,000 feet sees two towns directly to the left of the airplane. The angles of depression to the towns are 28° and 55° (see figure). How far apart are the towns?

FIGURE FOR 32

33. *Altitude of a Plane*   A plane is observed approaching your home, and you assume it is traveling at 550 miles per hour. If the angle of elevation of the plane is 16° at one time, and 1 minute later the angle is 57°, approximate the altitude of the plane.

34. *Height of a Mountain*   In traveling across flat land, you notice a mountain directly in front of you. The angle of elevation (to the peak) is 3.5°. After you drive 13 miles closer to the mountain, the angle of elevation is 9°. Approximate the height of the mountain.

35. *Length*   A regular pentagon is inscribed in a circle of radius 25 inches. Find the length of the sides of the pentagon.

36. *Length*   A regular hexagon is inscribed in a circle of radius 25 inches. Find the length of the sides of the hexagon.

37. *Wrench Size*   Use the figure to find the distance *y* across the flat sides of the hexagonal nut as a function of *r*.

FIGURE FOR 37

38. *Bolt Circle*   The figure shows a circular sheet 25 cm in diameter containing 12 equally spaced bolt holes. Determine the straight-line distance between the centers of adjacent bolt holes.

FIGURE FOR 38

Trusses   In Exercises 39 and 40, find the lengths of all the pieces of the truss.

39.

40.

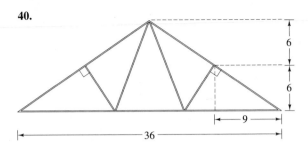

Harmonic Motion   In Exercises 41–44, for the simple harmonic motion described by the given trigonometric function, find (a) the maximum displacement, (b) the frequency, and (c) the least possible value of t for which $d = 0$.

41. $d = 4 \cos 8\pi t$

42. $d = \frac{1}{2} \cos 20\pi t$

43. $d = \frac{1}{16} \sin 120\pi t$

44. $d = \frac{1}{64} \sin 792\pi t$

45. *Tuning Fork*   A point on the end of a tuning fork moves in simple harmonic motion described by $d = a \sin \omega t$. Find ω given that the tuning fork for middle C has a frequency of 264 vibrations per second.

46. *Wave Motion*   A buoy oscillates in simple harmonic motion as waves go past. At a given time it is noted that the buoy moves a total of 3.5 feet from its low point to its high point, and that it returns to its high point every 10 seconds. Write an equation that describes the motion of the buoy if, at $t = 0$, it is at its high point.

CHAPTER 6 · REVIEW EXERCISES

In Exercises 1–4, sketch the angle in standard position, and list one positive and one negative coterminal angle.

1. $\dfrac{11\pi}{4}$ **2.** $\dfrac{2\pi}{9}$

3. $-110°$ **4.** $-405°$

In Exercises 5–8, convert the angle measurement to decimal form. (Round your result to two decimal places.)

5. $135° \ 16' \ 45''$ **6.** $-234° \ 50''$

7. $5° \ 22' \ 53''$ **8.** $280° \ 8' \ 50''$

In Exercises 9–12, convert the angle measurement to D° M′ S″ form.

9. $135.27°$ **10.** $25.1°$

11. $-85.15°$ **12.** $-327.85°$

In Exercises 13–16, convert the angle measurement from radians to degrees. (Round your result to two decimal places.)

13. $\dfrac{5\pi}{7}$ **14.** $-\dfrac{3\pi}{5}$

15. -3.5 **16.** 1.75

In Exercises 17–20, convert the angle measurement from degrees to radians. (Round your result to four decimal places.)

17. $480°$ **18.** $-16.5°$

19. $-33° \ 45'$ **20.** $84° \ 15'$

In Exercises 21–24, find the reference angle for the given angle.

21. $252°$ **22.** $640°$

23. $-\dfrac{6\pi}{5}$ **24.** $\dfrac{17\pi}{3}$

In Exercises 25–30, find the six trigonometric functions of the angle θ (in standard position) whose terminal side passes through the point.

25. $(12, 16)$ **26.** $(x, 4x)$

27. $(-7, 2)$ **28.** $(4, -8)$

29. $(-4, -6)$ **30.** $(\frac{2}{3}, \frac{5}{2})$

In Exercises 31–34, find the remaining five trigonometric functions of θ satisfying the given conditions. (*Hint:* Sketch a right triangle.)

31. $\sec \theta = \frac{6}{5}$, $\tan \theta < 0$

32. $\tan \theta = -\frac{12}{5}$, $\sin \theta > 0$

33. $\sin \theta = \frac{3}{8}$, $\cos \theta < 0$

34. $\cos \theta = -\frac{2}{5}$, $\sin \theta > 0$

In Exercises 35–40, evaluate the trigonometric function without using a calculator.

35. $\tan \dfrac{\pi}{3}$ **36.** $\sec \dfrac{\pi}{4}$

37. $\sin \dfrac{5\pi}{3}$ **38.** $\cot\left(\dfrac{5\pi}{6}\right)$

39. $\cos 495°$ **40.** $\csc 270°$

In Exercises 41–44, use a calculator to evaluate the trigonometric function. (Round your result to two decimal places.)

41. $\tan 33°$ **42.** $\csc 105°$

43. $\sec \dfrac{12\pi}{5}$ **44.** $\sin\left(-\dfrac{\pi}{9}\right)$

In Exercises 45–48, find two values of θ in degrees $(0° \le \theta < 360°)$ and in radians $(0 \le \theta < 2\pi)$ without using a calculator.

45. $\cos \theta = -\dfrac{\sqrt{2}}{2}$ **46.** $\sec \theta$ is undefined

47. $\csc \theta = -2$ **48.** $\tan \theta = \dfrac{\sqrt{3}}{3}$

In Exercises 49–52, find two values of θ in degrees $(0° \le \theta < 360°)$ and in radians $(0 \le \theta < 2\pi)$ by using a calculator.

49. $\sin \theta = 0.8387$ **50.** $\cot \theta = -1.5399$

51. $\sec \theta = -1.0353$ **52.** $\csc \theta = 11.4737$

In Exercises 53–56, write an algebraic expression for the given expression.

53. $\sec[\arcsin (x - 1)]$ **54.** $\tan\left(\arccos \dfrac{x}{2}\right)$

55. $\sin\left(\arccos \dfrac{x^2}{4 - x^2}\right)$ **56.** $\csc(\arcsin 10x)$

In Exercises 57–70, sketch a graph of the function through two full periods. (Use a graphing utility to verify your result.)

57. $y = 3 \cos 2\pi x$ **58.** $y = -2 \sin \pi x$

59. $f(x) = 5 \sin \dfrac{2x}{5}$ **60.** $f(x) = 8 \cos\left(-\dfrac{x}{4}\right)$

61. $f(x) = -\dfrac{1}{4} \cos \dfrac{\pi x}{4}$ **62.** $f(x) = -\tan \dfrac{\pi x}{4}$

63. $g(t) = \frac{5}{2} \sin(t - \pi)$ **64.** $g(t) = 3 \cos(t + \pi)$

65. $h(t) = \tan\left(t - \dfrac{\pi}{4}\right)$ **66.** $h(t) = \sec\left(t - \dfrac{\pi}{4}\right)$

67. $f(t) = \csc\left(3t - \dfrac{\pi}{2}\right)$ **68.** $f(t) = 3 \csc\left(2t + \dfrac{\pi}{4}\right)$

69. $f(\theta) = \cot \dfrac{\pi\theta}{8}$

70. $E(t) = 110 \cos\left(120\pi t - \dfrac{\pi}{3}\right)$

In Exercises 71–80, use a graphing utility to graph the function.

71. $f(x) = \dfrac{x}{4} - \sin x$ **72.** $g(x) = 3\left(\sin \dfrac{\pi x}{3} + 1\right)$

73. $y = \dfrac{x}{3} + \cos \pi x$ **74.** $y = 4 - \dfrac{x}{4} + \cos \pi x$

75. $h(\theta) = \theta \sin \pi\theta$ **76.** $f(t) = 2.5e^{-t/4} \sin 2\pi t$

77. $y = \arcsin \dfrac{x}{2}$ **78.** $y = 2 \arccos x$

79. $f(x) = \dfrac{\pi}{2} + \arctan x$ **80.** $f(x) = \arccos(x - \pi)$

In Exercises 81–84, use a graphing utility to graph the function. Use the graph to determine if the function is periodic. If the function is periodic, find any relative maximum or minimum points through one period.

81. $f(x) = e^{\sin x}$ **82.** $g(x) = \sin e^x$

83. $g(x) = 2 \sin x \cos^2 x$ **84.** $h(x) = 4 \sin^2 x \cos^2 x$

85. *Altitude of a Triangle*   Find the altitude of the triangle in the figure.

FIGURE FOR 85

86. *Angle of Elevation*   The height of a radio transmission tower is 225 feet, and it casts a shadow of length 105 feet (see figure). Find the angle of elevation of the sun.

FIGURE FOR 86

87. *Shuttle Height*   An observer 2.5 miles from the launch pad of a space shuttle measures the angle of elevation to the base of the vehicle to be 28° soon after lift-off (see figure). How high is the shuttle at that instant? (Assume the shuttle is still moving vertically.)

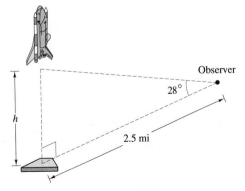

FIGURE FOR 87

88. *Distance*   From city A to city B, a plane flies 650 miles at a bearing of N 48° E. From city B to city C, the plane flies 810 miles at a bearing of S 65° E. Find the distance from A to C and the bearing from A to C.

89. *Railroad Grade*   A train travels 2.5 miles on a straight track with a grade of 1° 10′ (see figure). What is the vertical rise of the train in that distance?

FIGURE FOR 89

90. *Distance Between Towns*   A passenger in an airplane flying at 35,000 feet sees two towns directly to the left of the airplane. The angles of depression to the towns are 32° and 76° (see figure). How far apart are the towns?

FIGURE FOR 90

91. Using calculus, it can be shown that the sine and cosine functions can be approximated by the polynomials

$$\sin x \approx x - \frac{x^3}{3!} + \frac{x^5}{5!} - \frac{x^7}{7!}$$

and

$$\cos x \approx 1 - \frac{x^2}{2!} + \frac{x^4}{4!} - \frac{x^6}{6!},$$

where *x* is in radians.

(a) Use a graphing utility to graph the sine function and its polynomial approximation in the same viewing rectangle.

(b) Use a graphing utility to graph the cosine function and its polynomial approximation in the same viewing rectangle.

(c) Study the patterns in the polynomial approximations of the sine and cosine functions and guess the next term in each. Then repeat parts (a) and (b). Do you think your guesses were correct? How did the accuracy of the approximations change when additional terms were added?

ANALYTIC TRIGONOMETRY

7.1 APPLICATIONS OF FUNDAMENTAL IDENTITIES
....

Introduction / Some Uses of the Fundamental Identities

Introduction

In Chapter 6, you studied the basic definitions, properties, graphs, and applications of the individual trigonometric functions. In this chapter, you will learn how to use the fundamental identities to perform the following.

1. Evaluate trigonometric functions.
2. Simplify trigonometric expressions.
3. Develop additional trigonometric identities.
4. Solve trigonometric equations.

You will also make use of many algebraic skills, such as finding special products, factoring, performing operations with fractional expressions, rationalizing denominators, and solving equations.

As you study this chapter, remember that the best problem solvers are those that can solve problems by a variety of means. For instance, in this chapter many of the problems can be solved graphically, analytically, and numerically (using a table). Even after you have solved a problem one way, we encourage you to check your solution by solving the problem another way.

For convenience, we have summarized the fundamental trigonometric identities on the next page. Because these identities are used so frequently, it would be a good idea to commit them to memory.

477

FUNDAMENTAL TRIGONOMETRIC IDENTITIES

Reciprocal Identities

$$\sin u = \frac{1}{\csc u} \qquad \sec u = \frac{1}{\cos u} \qquad \tan u = \frac{1}{\cot u}$$

$$\csc u = \frac{1}{\sin u} \qquad \cos u = \frac{1}{\sec u} \qquad \cot u = \frac{1}{\tan u}$$

Quotient Identities

$$\tan u = \frac{\sin u}{\cos u} \qquad \cot u = \frac{\cos u}{\sin u}$$

Pythagorean Identities

$$\sin^2 u + \cos^2 u = 1 \qquad 1 + \tan^2 u = \sec^2 u \qquad 1 + \cot^2 u = \csc^2 u$$

Cofunction Identities

$$\sin\left(\frac{\pi}{2} - u\right) = \cos u \quad \sec\left(\frac{\pi}{2} - u\right) = \csc u \quad \tan\left(\frac{\pi}{2} - u\right) = \cot u$$

$$\cos\left(\frac{\pi}{2} - u\right) = \sin u \quad \csc\left(\frac{\pi}{2} - u\right) = \sec u \quad \cot\left(\frac{\pi}{2} - u\right) = \tan u$$

Even-Odd Identities

$$\sin(-u) = -\sin u \qquad \sec(-u) = \sec u \qquad \tan(-u) = -\tan u$$

$$\csc(-u) = -\csc u \qquad \cos(-u) = \cos u \qquad \cot(-u) = -\cot u$$

REMARK The Pythagorean identities are sometimes used in radical forms such as

$$\sin u = \pm\sqrt{1 - \cos^2 u} \quad \text{or}$$
$$\tan u = \pm\sqrt{\sec^2 u - 1},$$

where the sign depends on the choice of u.

Some Uses of the Fundamental Identities

One common use of trigonometric identities is to use given values of one or more trigonometric functions to find the values of the other trigonometric functions.

EXAMPLE 1   Using Identities to Evaluate a Function

Use the conditions $\sec u = -\frac{3}{2}$ and $\tan u > 0$ to find the values of all six trigonometric functions.

SOLUTION

Using a reciprocal identity, you can write

$$\cos u = \frac{1}{\sec u} = \frac{1}{-3/2} = -\frac{2}{3}.$$

By a Pythagorean identity, you obtain

$$\sin^2 u = 1 - \cos^2 u = 1 - \left(-\frac{2}{3}\right)^2 = 1 - \frac{4}{9} = \frac{5}{9}.$$

Because $\sec u < 0$ and $\tan u > 0$, it follows that u lies in Quadrant III. Moreover, because $\sin u$ is negative when u is in Quadrant III, choose the negative root to obtain

$$\sin u = -\frac{\sqrt{5}}{3}.$$

Now, knowing the values of the sine and cosine, you can find the values of all six trigonometric functions.

$$\sin u = -\frac{\sqrt{5}}{3} \qquad\qquad \csc u = \frac{1}{\sin u} = -\frac{3}{\sqrt{5}}$$

$$\cos u = -\frac{2}{3} \qquad\qquad \sec u = -\frac{3}{2}$$

$$\tan u = \frac{\sin u}{\cos u} = \frac{-\sqrt{5}/3}{-2/3} = \frac{\sqrt{5}}{2} \qquad \cot u = \frac{1}{\tan u} = \frac{2}{\sqrt{5}}$$

Compare this approach with the triangle approach in Example 2, Section 6.2.

The next four examples use algebra and the fundamental identities to simplify, factor, and/or combine trigonometric *expressions* such as

$$\cot x - \cos x \sin x, \quad \frac{1 - \sin x}{\cos^2 x}, \quad \text{and} \quad \frac{\tan x}{\sec x - 1}.$$

EXAMPLE 2   Simplifying a Trigonometric Expression

Simplify the expression $\sin x \cos^2 x - \sin x$.

SOLUTION

First factor out a common monomial factor and then use a fundamental identity.

$$\sin x \cos^2 x - \sin x = \sin x (\cos^2 x - 1) \qquad \textit{Monomial factor}$$
$$= -\sin x (1 - \cos^2 x)$$
$$= -\sin x (\sin^2 x) \qquad\qquad \textit{Pythagorean Identity}$$
$$= -\sin^3 x \qquad\qquad\qquad \textit{Multiply}$$

You can graphically confirm this result with a graphing utility. Graph $y = \sin x \cos^2 x - \sin x$ and $y = -\sin^3 x$ on the same display screen, and notice that the two graphs coincide, as shown in Figure 7.1.

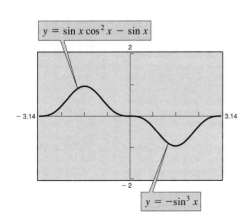

$y = \sin x \cos^2 x - \sin x$

$y = -\sin^3 x$

FIGURE 7.1

EXAMPLE 3   **Factoring Trigonometric Expressions**

Factor the following.

A. $\sec^2 \theta - 1$ **B.** $4 \tan^2 \theta + \tan \theta - 3$

SOLUTION

A. Using the difference of two squares pattern, you can factor the expression as

$$\sec^2 \theta - 1 = (\sec \theta - 1)(\sec \theta + 1).$$

B. This expression has the polynomial form, $ax^2 + bx + c$, where $x = \tan \theta$, and it factors as

$$4 \tan^2 \theta + \tan \theta - 3 = (4 \tan \theta - 3)(\tan \theta + 1).$$

On occasion, factoring or simplifying can best be done by first rewriting the expression in terms of just *one* trigonometric function or in terms of *sine and cosine alone.*

EXAMPLE 4   **Factoring a Trigonometric Expression**

Factor the expression $\csc^2 x - \cot x - 3$.

SOLUTION

As given, this expression cannot be factored. If, however, you use the identity $\csc^2 x = 1 + \cot^2 x$ to rewrite the expression in terms of the cotangent alone, you can factor to obtain

$$\csc^2 x - \cot x - 3 = (1 + \cot^2 x) - \cot x - 3 \qquad \textit{Pythagorean Identity}$$
$$= \cot^2 x - \cot x - 2 \qquad \textit{Combine terms}$$
$$= (\cot x - 2)(\cot x + 1). \qquad \textit{Factor}$$

EXAMPLE 5   **Combining Fractional Expressions**

Perform the indicated addition and simplify the result.

$$\frac{\sin \theta}{1 + \cos \theta} + \frac{\cos \theta}{\sin \theta}$$

SOLUTION

$$\frac{\sin \theta}{1 + \cos \theta} + \frac{\cos \theta}{\sin \theta} = \frac{(\sin \theta)(\sin \theta) + (\cos \theta)(1 + \cos \theta)}{(1 + \cos \theta)(\sin \theta)}$$

$$= \frac{\sin^2 \theta + \cos^2 \theta + \cos \theta}{(1 + \cos \theta)\sin \theta} \qquad \textit{Multiply}$$

$$= \frac{1 + \cos \theta}{(1 + \cos \theta)\sin \theta} \qquad \textit{Pythagorean Identity}$$

$$= \frac{1}{\sin \theta} \qquad \textit{Cancel common factor}$$

$$= \csc \theta \qquad \textit{Reciprocal Identity}$$

EXAMPLE 6   **Verifying Trigonometric Identities Graphically**

Use a graphing utility to determine which of the following is an identity.

A. $\cos 3x \overset{?}{=} 4 \cos^3 x - 3 \cos x$ **B.** $\cos 3x \overset{?}{=} \sin\left(3x - \frac{\pi}{2}\right)$

SOLUTION

A. Using a graphing utility, you can see that the graphs of $y = \cos 3x$ and $y = 4 \cos^3 x - 3 \cos x$ appear to coincide, as shown in Figure 7.2(a). Therefore, this appears to be an identity.

B. From the graphs shown in Figure 7.2(b), you can see that this is not an identity.

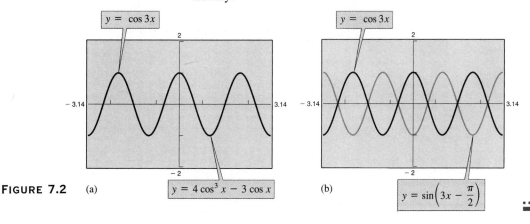

FIGURE 7.2   (a)   (b)

The last two examples of this section involve techniques for rewriting expressions into forms that are useful in calculus.

EXAMPLE 7   Rewriting a Trigonometric Expression

Rewrite

$$\frac{1}{1 + \sin x}$$

so that it is *not* in fractional form.

SOLUTION

$$\frac{1}{1 + \sin x} = \frac{1}{1 + \sin x} \cdot \frac{1 - \sin x}{1 - \sin x}$$

  Multiply numerator and denominator by $(1 - \sin x)$

$$= \frac{1 - \sin x}{1 - \sin^2 x}$$ *Multiply*

$$= \frac{1 - \sin x}{\cos^2 x}$$ *Pythagorean Identity*

$$= \frac{1}{\cos^2 x} - \frac{\sin x}{\cos^2 x}$$ *Separate fractions*

$$= \frac{1}{\cos^2 x} - \frac{\sin x}{\cos x} \cdot \frac{1}{\cos x}$$

$$= \sec^2 x - \tan x \sec x$$ *Identities*

EXAMPLE 8   Trigonometric Substitution

Use the substitution $x = 2 \tan \theta$ to express $\sqrt{4 + x^2}$ as a trigonometric function of θ where $0 < \theta < \pi/2$.

SOLUTION

Letting $x = 2 \tan \theta$ produces the following.

$$\sqrt{4 + x^2} = \sqrt{4 + (2 \tan \theta)^2}$$

$$= \sqrt{4(1 + \tan^2 \theta)}$$

$$= \sqrt{4 \sec^2 \theta}$$ *Pythagorean Identity*

$$= 2 \sec \theta$$ $\sec \theta > 0 \text{ for } 0 < \theta < \dfrac{\pi}{2}$

Figure 7.3 shows a right triangle illustration of the trigonometric substitution in Example 8. For $0 < \theta < \pi/2$, you obtain opp $= x$, adj $= 2$, and hyp $= \sqrt{4 + x^2}$. Thus, you can write

$$\sec \theta = \frac{\sqrt{4 + x^2}}{2} \quad \text{or} \quad \sqrt{4 + x^2} = 2 \sec \theta.$$

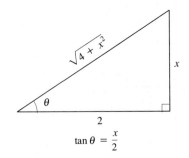

$$\tan \theta = \frac{x}{2}$$

FIGURE 7.3

DISCUSSION
PROBLEM
....
REMEMBERING
TRIGONOMETRIC
IDENTITIES

Most people find the Pythagorean Identity involving sine and cosine to be fairly easy to remember: $\sin^2 u + \cos^2 u = 1$. The one involving tangent and secant, however, tends to give some people trouble. They can't remember if the identity is

$$1 + \tan^2 u \overset{?}{=} \sec^2 u$$

or

$$1 + \sec^2 u \overset{?}{=} \tan^2 u.$$

Which of these two is the correct Pythagorean Identity involving tangent and secant? Write a short paragraph describing how a person can remember (or derive) this identity.

WARM-UP
....

The following warm-up exercises involve skills that were covered in earlier sections. You will use these skills in the exercise set for this section.

In Exercises 1 and 2, use a right triangle to evaluate the other five trigonometric functions of the acute angle θ.

1. $\tan \theta = \frac{3}{2}$ **2.** $\sec \theta = 3$

In Exercises 3 and 4, determine the exact value of the six trigonometric functions of θ. Assume the given point is on the terminal side of an angle θ in standard position.

3. $(7, -3)$ **4.** $(-10, 5)$

In Exercises 5–8, simplify the expression.

5. $\sqrt{1 - \left(\dfrac{\sqrt{3}}{2}\right)^2}$ **6.** $\sqrt{\left(\dfrac{3}{4}\right)^2 + 1}$

7. $\sqrt{1 + \left(\dfrac{3}{8}\right)^2}$ **8.** $\sqrt{1 - \left(\dfrac{\sqrt{5}}{3}\right)^2}$

In Exercises 9 and 10, perform the indicated operations and simplify the result.

9. $\dfrac{4}{1 + x} + \dfrac{x}{4}$ **10.** $\dfrac{3}{1 - x} - \dfrac{5}{1 + x}$

SECTION 7.1 · EXERCISES

In Exercises 1–10, use the fundamental identities to evaluate (if possible) the other trigonometric functions.

1. $\sin x = \dfrac{1}{2}, \quad \cos x = \dfrac{\sqrt{3}}{2}$

2. $\tan x = \dfrac{\sqrt{3}}{3}, \quad \cos x = -\dfrac{\sqrt{3}}{2}$

3. $\sec \theta = \sqrt{2}, \quad \sin \theta = -\dfrac{\sqrt{2}}{2}$

4. $\csc \theta = \dfrac{5}{3}, \quad \tan \theta = \dfrac{3}{4}$

5. $\sin(-x) = -\dfrac{2}{3}, \quad \tan x = -\dfrac{2\sqrt{5}}{5}$

6. $\cos\left(\dfrac{\pi}{2} - x\right) = \dfrac{3}{5}, \quad \cos x = \dfrac{4}{5}$

7. $\tan \theta = 2, \quad \sin \theta < 0$

8. $\sec \theta = -3, \quad \tan \theta < 0$

9. $\sin \theta = -1, \quad \cot \theta = 0$

10. $\tan \theta$ is undefined, $\quad \sin \theta > 0$

In Exercises 11–16, match the trigonometric expression with one of the following.
(a) -1 　　　(b) $\cos x$ 　　　(c) $\cot x$
(d) 1 　　　(e) $-\tan x$ 　　　(f) $\sin x$

11. $\sec x \cos x$

12. $\dfrac{\sin(-x)}{\cos(-x)}$

13. $\tan^2 x - \sec^2 x$

14. $\dfrac{1 - \cos^2 x}{\sin x}$

15. $\cot x \sin x$

16. $\dfrac{\sin[(\pi/2) - x]}{\cos[(\pi/2) - x]}$

In Exercises 17–22, match the trigonometric expression with one of the following.
(a) $\csc x$ 　　　(b) $\tan x$ 　　　(c) $\sin^2 x$
(d) $\sin x \tan x$ 　　　(e) $\sec^2 x$ 　　　(f) $\sec^2 x + \tan^2 x$

17. $\sin x \sec x$

18. $\cos^2 x(\sec^2 x - 1)$

19. $\dfrac{\sec^2 x - 1}{\sin^2 x}$

20. $\cot x \sec x$

21. $\sec^4 x - \tan^4 x$

22. $\dfrac{\cos^2[(\pi/2) - x]}{\cos x}$

In Exercises 23–36, use fundamental identities to simplify the expression. Use a graphing utility to verify your result. (See Example 2.)

23. $\tan \phi \csc \phi$

24. $\sin \phi(\csc \phi - \sin \phi)$

25. $\cos \beta \tan \beta$

26. $\sec \alpha \dfrac{\sin \alpha}{\tan \alpha}$

27. $\dfrac{\cot x}{\csc x}$

28. $\dfrac{\csc \theta}{\sec \theta}$

29. $\sec^2 x(1 - \sin^2 x)$

30. $\dfrac{1}{\tan^2 x + 1}$

31. $\dfrac{\sin(-x)}{\cos x}$

32. $\dfrac{\tan^2 \theta}{\sec^2 \theta}$

33. $\cos\left(\dfrac{\pi}{2} - x\right)\sec x$

34. $\cot\left(\dfrac{\pi}{2} - x\right)\cos x$

35. $\dfrac{\cos^2 y}{1 - \sin y}$

36. $\cos t(1 + \tan^2 t)$

In Exercises 37–44, factor the expression and use fundamental identities to simplify. Use a graphing utility to verify your result.

37. $\tan^2 x - \tan^2 x \sin^2 x$

38. $\sec^2 x \tan^2 x + \sec^2 x$

39. $\sin^2 x \sec^2 x - \sin^2 x$

40. $\dfrac{\sec^2 x - 1}{\sec x - 1}$

41. $\tan^4 x + 2 \tan^2 x + 1$

42. $1 - 2 \cos^2 x + \cos^4 x$

43. $\sin^4 x - \cos^4 x$

44. $\csc^3 x - \csc^2 x - \csc x + 1$

In Exercises 45–48, perform the multiplication and use fundamental identities to simplify.

45. $(\sin x + \cos x)^2$

46. $(\cot x + \csc x)(\cot x - \csc x)$

47. $(\sec x + 1)(\sec x - 1)$

48. $(3 - 3 \sin x)(3 + 3 \sin x)$

In Exercises 49–52, perform the addition or subtraction and use fundamental identities to simplify.

49. $\dfrac{1}{1 + \cos x} + \dfrac{1}{1 - \cos x}$

50. $\dfrac{1}{\sec x + 1} - \dfrac{1}{\sec x - 1}$

51. $\dfrac{\cos x}{1 + \sin x} + \dfrac{1 + \sin x}{\cos x}$

52. $\tan x - \dfrac{\sec^2 x}{\tan x}$

In Exercises 53–56, rewrite the expression so that it is *not* in fractional form.

53. $\dfrac{\sin^2 y}{1 - \cos y}$ **54.** $\dfrac{5}{\tan x + \sec x}$

55. $\dfrac{3}{\sec x - \tan x}$ **56.** $\dfrac{\tan^2 x}{\csc x + 1}$

In Exercises 57–60, use a graphing utility to determine whether or not the equation is an identity. (See Example 6.)

57. $\csc x = \cot \dfrac{x}{2} - \cot x$

58. $\sec^2 x \csc x = \sec^2 x + \csc x$

59. $\sin 2x = 2 \sin x$

60. $\sin x \tan x = \csc x - \cos x$

61. Use a graphing utility to determine the values of x in the interval $[0, 2\pi]$ for which (a) $\cos x = \sqrt{1 - \sin^2 x}$, and (b) $\cos x = -\sqrt{1 - \sin^2 x}$.

62. Use a graphing utility to determine which of the six trigonometric functions is equal to the expression

$$\sin x \tan x + \cos x.$$

In Exercises 63–72, use the specified trigonometric substitution to write the algebraic expression as a trigonometric function of θ, where $0 < \theta < \pi/2$.

63. $\sqrt{25 - x^2}$, $x = 5 \sin \theta$

64. $\sqrt{16 - 4x^2}$, $x = 2 \sin \theta$

65. $\sqrt{x^2 - 9}$, $x = 3 \sec \theta$

66. $\sqrt{x^2 - 4}$, $x = 2 \sec \theta$

67. $\sqrt{x^2 + 25}$, $x = 5 \tan \theta$

68. $\sqrt{x^2 + 100}$, $x = 10 \tan \theta$

69. $\sqrt{1 - (x - 1)^2}$, $x - 1 = \sin \theta$

70. $\sqrt{1 - e^{2x}}$, $e^x = \sin \theta$

71. $\sqrt{(9 + x^2)^3}$, $x = 3 \tan \theta$

72. $\sqrt{(x^2 - 16)^3}$, $x = 4 \sec \theta$

In Exercises 73 and 74, determine the values of $\theta, 0 \le \theta < 2\pi$, for which the equation is true.

73. $\sec \theta = \sqrt{1 + \tan^2 \theta}$

74. $\sin \theta = -\sqrt{1 - \cos^2 \theta}$

In Exercises 75 and 76, rewrite the expression as a single logarithm and simplify the result.

75. $\ln |\cos \theta| - \ln |\sin \theta|$

76. $\ln |\cot t| + \ln(1 + \tan^2 t)$

In Exercises 77–80, determine whether or not the equation is an identity, and give a reason for your answer.

77. $\dfrac{\sin k\theta}{\cos k\theta} = \tan \theta$, k is constant   **78.** $\dfrac{1}{5 \cos \theta} = 5 \sec \theta$

79. $\sin \theta \csc \theta = 1$ **80.** $\sin \theta \csc \phi = 1$

In Exercises 81–84, use a calculator to demonstrate the identity for the given values of θ.

81. $\csc^2 \theta - \cot^2 \theta = 1$
    (a) $\theta = 132°$ (b) $\theta = \dfrac{2\pi}{7}$

82. $\tan^2 \theta + 1 = \sec^2 \theta$
    (a) $\theta = 346°$ (b) $\theta = 3.1$

83. $\cos\left(\dfrac{\pi}{2} - \theta\right) = \sin \theta$
    (a) $\theta = 80°$ (b) $\theta = 0.8$

84. $\sin(-\theta) = -\sin \theta$
    (a) $\theta = 250°$ (b) $\theta = \frac{1}{2}$

85. Express each of the other trigonometric functions of θ in terms of $\sin \theta$.

86. Express each of the other trigonometric functions of θ in terms of $\cos \theta$.

7.2   VERIFYING TRIGONOMETRIC IDENTITIES

Introduction   /   Verifying Trigonometric Identities

Introduction

In the previous section, you learned how to rewrite trigonometric expressions in equivalent forms. In this section, you will learn to prove or verify trigonometric identities. (In the next section, you will learn to solve trigonometric equations.) The key to verifying identities and solving equations is the ability to use the fundamental identities and the rules of algebra to rewrite trigonometric expressions.

Before going on, let's review some distinctions among expressions, equations, and identities. An *expression* has no equal sign. It is merely a combination of terms. When simplifying expressions, you use an equal sign only to indicate the equivalence of the original expression and the new form. An *equation* is a statement containing an equal sign that is true for a specific set of values. In this sense, it is really a *conditional* equation. For example, the equation

$$\sin x = -1$$

is true only for $x = (3\pi/2) \pm 2n\pi$. Hence, it is a conditional equation. On the other hand, an equation that is true for all real values in the domain of the variable is an *identity*. For example, the familiar equation

$$\sin^2 x = 1 - \cos^2 x$$

is true for all real numbers x. Hence, it is an identity.

Although there are similarities, proving that a trigonometric equation is an identity is quite different from solving an equation. There is no well-defined set of rules to follow in verifying trigonometric identities, and the process is best learned by practice. However, the following guidelines should be helpful.

GUIDELINES FOR VERIFYING TRIGONOMETRIC IDENTITIES

1. Work with one side of the equation at a time. It is often better to work with the more complicated side first.
2. Look for opportunities to factor an expression, add fractions, square a binomial, or create a monomial denominator.
3. Look for opportunities to use the fundamental identities. Note which functions are in the final expression you want. Sines and cosines pair up well, as do secants and tangents, and cosecants and cotangents.
4. If the preceding guidelines do not help, try converting all terms to sines and cosines.
5. Do not just sit and stare at the problem. Try something! Even paths that lead to dead ends can give you insights.

Verifying Trigonometric Identities

EXAMPLE 1 Verifying a Trigonometric Identity

Verify the identity

$$\frac{\sec^2 \theta - 1}{\sec^2 \theta} = \sin^2 \theta.$$

SOLUTION

Technology Note

A graphing utility can be used to confirm trigonometric identities graphically. For instance, in Example 1 you can graph

$$y = \frac{\sec^2 \theta - 1}{\sec^2 \theta} \text{ and } y = \sin^2 \theta$$

on the same viewing rectangle and observe that the graphs are the same. You can also use this technique to confirm intermediate steps in your verification process.

Start with the left side, because it is more complicated.

$$\frac{\sec^2 \theta - 1}{\sec^2 \theta} = \frac{(\tan^2 \theta + 1) - 1}{\sec^2 \theta} \qquad \textit{Pythagorean Identity}$$

$$= \frac{\tan^2 \theta}{\sec^2 \theta} \qquad \textit{Simplify}$$

$$= \tan^2 \theta (\cos^2 \theta) \qquad \textit{Reciprocal Identity}$$

$$= \frac{\sin^2 \theta}{\cos^2 \theta}(\cos^2 \theta) \qquad \textit{Tangent Identity}$$

$$= \sin^2 \theta \qquad \textit{Reduce}$$

ALTERNATIVE SOLUTION

Sometimes it is helpful to separate a fraction into two parts.

$$\frac{\sec^2 \theta - 1}{\sec^2 \theta} = \frac{\sec^2 \theta}{\sec^2 \theta} - \frac{1}{\sec^2 \theta} \qquad \textit{Separate fractions}$$

$$= 1 - \cos^2 \theta \qquad \textit{Reciprocal Identity}$$

$$= \sin^2 \theta \qquad \textit{Pythagorean Identity}$$

As you can see in Example 1, there can be more than one way to verify an identity. Your method may differ from that used by your instructor or fellow students. Here is a good chance to be creative and establish your own style, but try to be as efficient as possible.

EXAMPLE 2 Combining Fractions Before Using Identities

Verify the identity

$$\frac{1}{1 - \sin \alpha} + \frac{1}{1 + \sin \alpha} = 2 \sec^2 \alpha.$$

SOLUTION

$$\frac{1}{1 - \sin \alpha} + \frac{1}{1 + \sin \alpha} = \frac{1 + \sin \alpha + 1 - \sin \alpha}{(1 - \sin \alpha)(1 + \sin \alpha)} \qquad \textit{Add fractions}$$

$$= \frac{2}{1 - \sin^2 \alpha} \qquad \textit{Simplify}$$

$$= \frac{2}{\cos^2 \alpha} \qquad \textit{Pythagorean Identity}$$

$$= 2 \sec^2 \alpha \qquad \textit{Reciprocal Identity}$$

EXAMPLE 3   **Verifying a Trigonometric Identity**

Verify the identity $(\tan^2 x + 1)(\cos^2 x - 1) = -\tan^2 x$.

SOLUTION

By applying identities before multiplying, you obtain the following.

$$(\tan^2 x + 1)(\cos^2 x - 1) = (\sec^2 x)(-\sin^2 x) \qquad \textit{Pythagorean identities}$$

$$= -\frac{\sin^2 x}{\cos^2 x} \qquad \textit{Reciprocal Identity}$$

$$= -\left(\frac{\sin x}{\cos x}\right)^2 \qquad \textit{Rule of exponents}$$

$$= -\tan^2 x \qquad \textit{Tangent Identity}$$

EXAMPLE 4   **Converting to Sines and Cosines**

Verify the identity $\tan x + \cot x = \sec x \csc x$.

SOLUTION

In this case, there appear to be no fractions to add, no products to find, and no opportunity to use one of the Pythagorean identities. Notice, however, what happens when you convert the left side to sines and cosines.

$$\tan x + \cot x = \frac{\sin x}{\cos x} + \frac{\cos x}{\sin x} \qquad \textit{Identities}$$

$$= \frac{\sin^2 x + \cos^2 x}{\cos x \sin x} \qquad \textit{Add fractions}$$

$$= \frac{1}{\cos x \sin x} \qquad \sin^2 x + \cos^2 x = 1$$

$$= \frac{1}{\cos x} \cdot \frac{1}{\sin x} \qquad \textit{Product of fractions}$$

$$= \sec x \csc x \qquad \textit{Reciprocal identities}$$

EXAMPLE 5   Verifying a Trigonometric Identity

Verify the identity $\sec y + \tan y = \dfrac{\cos y}{1 - \sin y}$.

SOLUTION

Work with the *right* side. Note that you can create a monomial denominator by multiplying the numerator and denominator by $(1 + \sin y)$.

$$\frac{\cos y}{1 - \sin y} = \frac{\cos y}{1 - \sin y}\left(\frac{1 + \sin y}{1 + \sin y}\right) \qquad \textit{Multiply numerator and}$$
$$\textit{denominator by } (1 + \sin y)$$

$$= \frac{\cos y + \cos y \sin y}{1 - \sin^2 y}$$

$$= \frac{\cos y + \cos y \sin y}{\cos^2 y} \qquad \textit{Pythagorean Identity}$$

$$= \frac{\cos y}{\cos^2 y} + \frac{\cos y \sin y}{\cos^2 y} \qquad \textit{Separate fractions}$$

$$= \frac{1}{\cos y} + \frac{\sin y}{\cos y} \qquad \textit{Reduce}$$

$$= \sec y + \tan y \qquad \textit{Identities}$$

So far in this section, you have been verifying trigonometric identities by working with one side of the equation and converting to the form given on the other side. On occasion, it is practical to work with each side *separately,* to obtain one common form equivalent to both sides.

EXAMPLE 6   Working with Each Side Separately

Verify the identity

$$\frac{\cot^2 \theta}{1 + \csc \theta} = \frac{1 - \sin \theta}{\sin \theta}.$$

SOLUTION

Working with the left side, you have

$$\frac{\cot^2 \theta}{1 + \csc \theta} = \frac{\csc^2 \theta - 1}{1 + \csc \theta} \qquad \cot^2 \theta = \csc^2 \theta - 1$$

$$= \frac{(\csc \theta - 1)(\csc \theta + 1)}{1 + \csc \theta} \qquad \textit{Factor}$$

$$= \csc \theta - 1. \qquad \textit{Reduce}$$

Now, simplifying the right side, you have

$$\frac{1 - \sin \theta}{\sin \theta} = \frac{1}{\sin \theta} - \frac{\sin \theta}{\sin \theta} = \csc \theta - 1.$$

The identity is verified, because both sides are equal to $\csc \theta - 1$.

In Example 7, powers of trigonometric functions are rewritten as more complicated sums or products of trigonometric functions. This is a common procedure in calculus.

EXAMPLE 7 Two Examples from Calculus

Verify the identities.

A. $\tan^4 x = \tan^2 x \sec^2 x - \tan^2 x$
B. $\sin^3 x \cos^4 x = (\cos^4 x - \cos^6 x)\sin x$

SOLUTION

Note the use of the Pythagorean identities in the verifications.

A. $\tan^4 x = (\tan^2 x)(\tan^2 x)$	*Separate factors*
$= \tan^2 x(\sec^2 x - 1)$	*Pythagorean Identity*
$= \tan^2 x \sec^2 x - \tan^2 x$	*Multiply*
B. $\sin^3 x \cos^4 x = \sin^2 x \cos^4 x \sin x$	*Separate factors*
$= (1 - \cos^2 x)\cos^4 x \sin x$	*Pythagorean Identity*
$= (\cos^4 x - \cos^6 x)\sin x$	*Multiply*

DISCUSSION PROBLEM

YOU BE THE INSTRUCTOR

Suppose you are tutoring a student in trigonometry. After working several home-work problems, your student becomes discouraged because of an inability to get answers that agree with those in the back of the textbook. Which of the following answers has your student actually gotten right? Which are wrong? Why?

Student's Answers	*Text's Answers*
(a) $\dfrac{1}{2 \csc x}$	$\dfrac{1}{2} \sin x$
(b) $(1 - \cos x)(1 + \cos x)$	$\sin^2 x$
(c) $\dfrac{\sin^2 x}{1 - \cos x}$	$1 + \cos x$
(d) $\cot^2 x + 2$	$1 + \csc^2 x$
(e) $(\sec x - \tan x)(\sec x + \tan x)$	1

WARM-UP

The following warm-up exercises involve skills that were covered in earlier sections. You will use these skills in the exercise set for this section.

In Exercises 1–6, factor each expression and, if possible, simplify the results.

1. (a) $x^2 - x^2 y^2$
   (b) $\sin^2 x - \sin^2 x \cos^2 x$

2. (a) $x^2 + x^2 y^2$
   (b) $\cos^2 x + \cos^2 x \tan^2 x$

3. (a) $x^4 - 1$
   (b) $\tan^4 x - 1$

4. (a) $z^3 + 1$
   (b) $\tan^3 x + 1$

5. (a) $x^3 - x^2 + x - 1$
   (b) $\cot^3 x - \cot^2 x + \cot x - 1$

6. (a) $x^4 - 2x^2 + 1$
   (b) $\sin^4 x - 2\sin^2 x + 1$

In Exercises 7–10, perform the additions or subtractions and, if possible, simplify the results.

7. (a) $\dfrac{y^2}{x} - x$

   (b) $\dfrac{\csc^2 x}{\cot x} - \cot x$

8. (a) $1 - \dfrac{1}{x^2}$

   (b) $1 - \dfrac{1}{\sec^2 x}$

9. (a) $\dfrac{y}{1+z} + \dfrac{1+z}{y}$

   (b) $\dfrac{\sin x}{1 + \cos x} + \dfrac{1 + \cos x}{\sin x}$

10. (a) $\dfrac{y}{z} - \dfrac{z}{1+y}$

   (b) $\dfrac{\tan x}{\sec x} - \dfrac{\sec x}{1 + \tan x}$

SECTION 7.2 · EXERCISES

In Exercises 1–50, verify the identity, and confirm it graphically.

1. $\sin t \csc t = 1$

2. $\tan y \cot y = 1$

3. $(1 + \sin \alpha)(1 - \sin \alpha) = \cos^2 \alpha$

4. $\cot^2 y(\sec^2 y - 1) = 1$

5. $\cos^2 \beta - \sin^2 \beta = 1 - 2\sin^2 \beta$

6. $\cos^2 \beta - \sin^2 \beta = 2\cos^2 \beta - 1$

7. $\tan^2 \theta + 4 = \sec^2 \theta + 3$

8. $2 - \sec^2 z = 1 - \tan^2 z$

9. $\sin^2 \alpha - \sin^4 \alpha = \cos^2 \alpha - \cos^4 \alpha$

10. $\cos x + \sin x \tan x = \sec x$

11. $\dfrac{\sec^2 x}{\tan x} = \sec x \csc x$

12. $\dfrac{\cot^3 t}{\csc t} = \cos t(\csc^2 t - 1)$

13. $\dfrac{\cot^2 t}{\csc t} = \csc t - \sin t$

14. $\dfrac{1}{\sin x} - \sin x = \dfrac{\cos^2 x}{\sin x}$

15. $\sin^{1/2} x \cos x - \sin^{5/2} x \cos x = \cos^3 x \sqrt{\sin x}$

16. $\sec^6 x(\sec x \tan x) - \sec^4 x(\sec x \tan x) = \sec^5 x \tan^3 x$

17. $\dfrac{1}{\sec x \tan x} = \csc x - \sin x$

18. $\dfrac{\sec \theta - 1}{1 - \cos \theta} = \sec \theta$

19. $\csc x - \sin x = \cos x \cot x$

20. $\dfrac{\sec x + \tan x}{\sec x - \tan x} = (\sec x + \tan x)^2$

21. $\dfrac{1}{\tan x} + \dfrac{1}{\cot x} = \tan x + \cot x$

22. $\dfrac{1}{\sin x} - \dfrac{1}{\csc x} = \csc x - \sin x$

23. $\dfrac{\cos \theta \cot \theta}{1 - \sin \theta} - 1 = \csc \theta$

24. $\cos x - \dfrac{\cos x}{1 - \tan x} = \dfrac{\sin x \cos x}{\sin x - \cos x}$

25. $2 \sec^2 x - 2 \sec^2 x \sin^2 x - \sin^2 x - \cos^2 x = 1$

26. $\csc x(\csc x - \sin x) + \dfrac{\sin x - \cos x}{\sin x} + \cot x = \csc^2 x$

27. $2 + \cos^2 x - 3 \cos^4 x = \sin^2 x(2 + 3 \cos^2 x)$

28. $4 \tan^4 x + \tan^2 x - 3 = \sec^2 x(4 \tan^2 x - 3)$

29. $\sec^4 \theta - \tan^4 \theta = 1 + 2 \tan^2 \theta$

30. $\csc^4 \theta - \cot^4 \theta = 2 \csc^2 \theta - 1$

31. $\dfrac{\sin \beta}{1 - \cos \beta} = \dfrac{1 + \cos \beta}{\sin \beta}$

32. $\dfrac{\cot \alpha}{\csc \alpha - 1} = \dfrac{\csc \alpha + 1}{\cot \alpha}$

33. $\cos\left(\dfrac{\pi}{2} - x\right)\csc x = 1$

34. $\dfrac{\cos[(\pi/2) - x]}{\sin[(\pi/2) - x]} = \tan x$

35. $\dfrac{\csc(-x)}{\sec(-x)} = -\cot x$

36. $(1 + \sin y)[1 + \sin(-y)] = \cos^2 y$

37. $\dfrac{\cos(-\theta)}{1 + \sin(-\theta)} = \sec \theta + \tan \theta$

38. $\dfrac{1 + \sec(-\theta)}{\sin(-\theta) + \tan(-\theta)} = -\csc \theta$

39. $\sin^2 x + \sin^2\left(\dfrac{\pi}{2} - x\right) = 1$

40. $\sec^2 y - \cot^2\left(\dfrac{\pi}{2} - y\right) = 1$

41. $\sqrt{\dfrac{1 + \sin \theta}{1 - \sin \theta}} = \dfrac{1 + \sin \theta}{|\cos \theta|}$

42. $\sqrt{\dfrac{1 - \cos \theta}{1 + \cos \theta}} = \dfrac{1 - \cos \theta}{|\sin \theta|}$

43. $\dfrac{\sin x \cos y + \cos x \sin y}{\cos x \cos y - \sin x \sin y} = \dfrac{\tan x + \tan y}{1 - \tan x \tan y}$

44. $\dfrac{\tan x + \tan y}{1 - \tan x \tan y} = \dfrac{\cot x + \cot y}{\cot x \cot y - 1}$

45. $\dfrac{\tan x + \cot y}{\tan x \cot y} = \tan y + \cot x$

46. $\dfrac{\cos x - \cos y}{\sin x + \sin y} + \dfrac{\sin x - \sin y}{\cos x + \cos y} = 0$

47. $\ln|\tan \theta| = \ln|\sin \theta| - \ln|\cos \theta|$

48. $\ln|\sec \theta| = -\ln|\cos \theta|$

49. $-\ln(1 + \cos \theta) = \ln(1 - \cos \theta) - 2 \ln|\sin \theta|$

50. $-\ln|\sec \theta + \tan \theta| = \ln|\sec \theta - \tan \theta|$

In Exercises 51–54, explain why the equation is *not* an identity, and find one value of the variable for which the equation is not true.

51. $\sin \theta = \sqrt{1 - \cos^2 \theta}$

52. $\tan \theta = \sqrt{\sec^2 \theta - 1}$

53. $\sqrt{\tan^2 x} = \tan x$

54. $\sqrt{\sin^2 x + \cos^2 x} = \sin x + \cos x$

55. *Friction*   The force acting on a stationary object weighing W units on an inclined plane positioned at an angle of θ with the horizontal is modeled by

$$\mu W \cos \theta = W \sin \theta,$$

where μ is the coefficient of friction (see figure). Solve the equation for μ and simplify the result.

FIGURE FOR 55

56. *Rate of Change*   The rate of change of the function $f(x) = \sin x + \csc x$ with respect to change in the variable x is given by the expression $\cos x - \csc x \cot x$. Show that the expression for the rate of change can also be given by $-\cos x \cot^2 x$.

7.3   SOLVING TRIGONOMETRIC EQUATIONS

Introduction / Equations of Quadratic Type / Functions Involving Multiple
Angles / Using Inverse Functions and a Calculator

Introduction

In this section, you will switch from *verifying* trigonemetric identities to
solving trigonometric equations. To see the difference, consider the two
equations

$$\sin^2 x + \cos^2 x = 1$$

and

$$\sin x = 1.$$

The first equation is an identity because it is true for *all* real values of x. The
second equation, however, is true only for *some* values of x. When you find
these values, you are solving the equation.

EXAMPLE 1   Solving a Trigonometric Equation

Solve $2 \sin x - 1 = 0$.

SOLUTION

$2 \sin x - 1 = 0$	*Original equation*
$2 \sin x = 1$	*Add 1 to both sides*
$\sin x = \dfrac{1}{2}$	*Divide both sides by 2*

To solve for x, note that the equation $\sin x = \frac{1}{2}$ has solutions $x = \pi/6$ and
$x = 5\pi/6$ in the interval $[0, 2\pi)$. Moreover, because $\sin x$ has a period of 2π,
there are infinitely many other solutions, which can be written as

$$x = \frac{\pi}{6} + 2n\pi \quad \text{and} \quad x = \frac{5\pi}{6} + 2n\pi, \quad \text{\textit{General solution}}$$

where n is an integer, as shown in Figure 7.4. This is called the **general form**
of the solution.

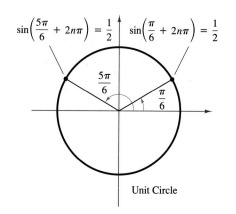

$$\sin\left(\frac{5\pi}{6} + 2n\pi\right) = \frac{1}{2} \qquad \sin\left(\frac{\pi}{6} + 2n\pi\right) = \frac{1}{2}$$

Unit Circle

FIGURE 7.4

Another way to see that the equation $\sin x = \frac{1}{2}$ has infinitely many solutions is indicated in Figure 7.5, which shows the graphs of $y_1 = \sin x$ and $y_2 = \frac{1}{2}$. For $0 \leq x < 2\pi$, the solutions are $x = \pi/6$ and $x = 5\pi/6$. Any angles that are coterminal with $\pi/6$ or $5\pi/6$ will also be solutions of the equation.

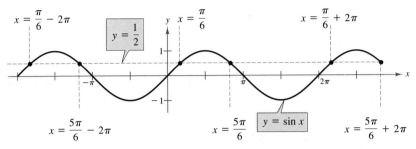

FIGURE 7.5

EXAMPLE 2 Collecting Like Terms

Solve $\sin x + \sqrt{2} = -\sin x$.

SOLUTION

$$\sin x + \sqrt{2} = -\sin x \qquad \textit{Original equation}$$

$$\sin x + \sin x = -\sqrt{2} \qquad \textit{Add $\sin x$ to both sides and subtract $\sqrt{2}$ from both sides}$$

$$2 \sin x = -\sqrt{2} \qquad \textit{Collect like terms}$$

$$\sin x = -\frac{\sqrt{2}}{2} \qquad \textit{Divide both sides by 2}$$

Because $\sin x$ has a period of 2π, you can begin by finding all solutions in the interval $[0, 2\pi)$. These are $x = 5\pi/4$ and $x = 7\pi/4$. Next, add $2n\pi$ to each of these solutions to obtain the general form

$$x = \frac{5\pi}{4} + 2n\pi \quad \text{and} \quad x = \frac{7\pi}{4} + 2n\pi, \quad \textit{General solution}$$

where n is an integer. The graph of $y = 2 \sin x + \sqrt{2}$, shown in Figure 7.6, confirms this result.

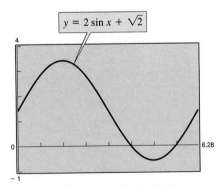

FIGURE 7.6

EXAMPLE 3 Extracting Square Roots

Solve $3 \tan^2 x - 1 = 0$.

SOLUTION

$$3 \tan^2 x - 1 = 0 \qquad \text{\textit{Original equation}}$$

$$3 \tan^2 x = 1 \qquad \text{\textit{Add 1 to both sides}}$$

$$\tan^2 x = \frac{1}{3} \qquad \text{\textit{Divide both sides by 3}}$$

$$\tan x = \pm \frac{1}{\sqrt{3}} \qquad \text{\textit{Extract square roots}}$$

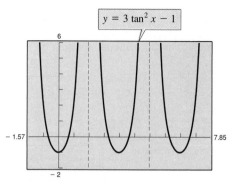

FIGURE 7.7

Because $\tan x$ has a period of π, you can begin by finding all solutions in the interval $[0, \pi)$. These are $x = \pi/6 \approx 0.52$ and $x = 5\pi/6 \approx 2.62$. Next, add $n\pi$ to each to obtain the general form

$$x = \frac{\pi}{6} + n\pi \quad \text{and} \quad x = \frac{5\pi}{6} + n\pi, \qquad \text{\textit{General solution}}$$

where n is an integer. The graph of $y = 3 \tan^2 x - 1$, shown in Figure 7.7, confirms these results.   ·········

When two or more functions occur in the same equation, collect all terms on one side and try to separate the functions by factoring.

EXAMPLE 4   Factoring
················

Solve $\cot x \cos^2 x = 2 \cot x$.

SOLUTION

$$\cot x \cos^2 x = 2 \cot x \qquad \text{\textit{Original equation}}$$

$$\cot x \cos^2 x - 2 \cot x = 0 \qquad \text{\textit{Subtract 2 cot x from both sides}}$$

$$\cot x (\cos^2 x - 2) = 0 \qquad \text{\textit{Factor left side}}$$

By setting each of these factors equal to zero, you obtain the following.

$$\cot x = 0 \qquad \text{and} \qquad \cos^2 x - 2 = 0$$
$$x = \frac{\pi}{2} \qquad\qquad\qquad \cos^2 x = 2$$
$$\cos x = \pm \sqrt{2}$$

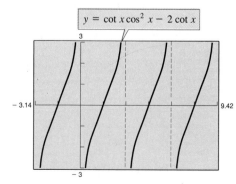

FIGURE 7.8

No solution is obtained from $\cos x = \pm\sqrt{2}$, because $\pm\sqrt{2}$ are outside the range of the cosine function. Therefore, the general form of the solution is obtained by adding multiples of π to $x = \pi/2$, to obtain

$$x = \frac{\pi}{2} + n\pi, \qquad \text{\textit{General solution}}$$

where n is an integer. The graph of $y = \cot x \cos^2 x - 2 \cot x$, shown in Figure 7.8, confirms these results.   ·········

Equations of Quadratic Type

Many trigonometric equations are of quadratic type. Here are two examples.

Quadratic in sin x

$$2 \sin^2 x - \sin x - 1 = 0$$
$$2(\sin x)^2 - (\sin x) - 1 = 0$$

Quadratic in sec x

$$\sec^2 x - 3 \sec x - 2 = 0$$
$$(\sec x)^2 - 3(\sec x) - 2 = 0$$

To solve equations of this type, factor the quadratic or, if this is not possible, use the Quadratic Formula.

$y = 2 \sin^2 x - \sin x - 1$

FIGURE 7.9

EXAMPLE 5   **Factoring an Equation of Quadratic Type**

Solve $2 \sin^2 x - \sin x - 1 = 0$.

SOLUTION

The graph of $y = 2 \sin^2 x - \sin x - 1$, shown in Figure 7.9, indicates that there are three solutions in the interval $[0, 2\pi)$. Treating the equation as a quadratic in $\sin x$ and factoring, you can obtain the following.

$$2 \sin^2 x - \sin x - 1 = 0 \qquad \textit{Original equation}$$
$$(2 \sin x + 1)(\sin x - 1) = 0 \qquad \textit{Factor}$$

Setting each factor equal to zero produces the following solutions.

$$2 \sin x + 1 = 0 \qquad \text{and} \qquad \sin x - 1 = 0$$

$$\sin x = -\frac{1}{2} \qquad\qquad\qquad \sin x = 1$$

$$x = \frac{7\pi}{6}, \frac{11\pi}{6} \qquad\qquad\qquad x = \frac{\pi}{2}$$

The general solution is

$$x = \frac{7\pi}{6} + 2n\pi, \qquad x = \frac{11\pi}{6} + 2n\pi, \qquad x = \frac{\pi}{2} + 2n\pi,$$

where n is an integer.

EXAMPLE 6   **Writing in Terms of a Single Trigonometric Function**

Solve $2 \sin^2 x + 3 \cos x - 3 = 0$.

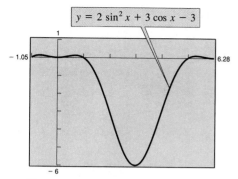

$y = 2 \sin^2 x + 3 \cos x - 3$

FIGURE 7.10

SOLUTION

The graph of $y = 2 \sin^2 x + 3 \cos x - 3$, shown in Figure 7.10, indicates that there are three solutions in the interval $[0, 2\pi)$. Proceeding algebraically, you can write the following.

$$2 \sin^2 x + 3 \cos x - 3 = 0 \qquad \textit{Original equation}$$
$$2(1 - \cos^2 x) + 3 \cos x - 3 = 0 \qquad \textit{Pythagorean Identity}$$
$$2 \cos^2 x - 3 \cos x + 1 = 0 \qquad \textit{Multiply both sides by} -1$$
$$(2 \cos x - 1)(\cos x - 1) = 0 \qquad \textit{Factor}$$

By setting each factor equal to zero, you can find the solutions in the interval $[0, 2\pi)$ to be $x = 0$, $x = \pi/3$, and $x = 5\pi/3$. The general solution is therefore

$$x = 2n\pi, \qquad x = \frac{\pi}{3} + 2n\pi, \qquad x = \frac{5\pi}{3} + 2n\pi, \qquad \textit{General solution}$$

where n is an integer.

Squaring both sides of an equation can introduce extraneous solutions, as indicated in Example 7.

EXAMPLE 7   Squaring and Converting to Quadratic Type

$$\cos x + 1 = \sin x \qquad \textit{Original equation}$$
$$\cos^2 x + 2 \cos x + 1 = \sin^2 x \qquad \textit{Square both sides}$$
$$\cos^2 x + 2 \cos x + 1 = 1 - \cos^2 x \qquad \textit{Identity}$$
$$2 \cos^2 x + 2 \cos x = 0 \qquad \textit{Collect terms}$$
$$2 \cos x(\cos x + 1) = 0 \qquad \textit{Factor}$$

Setting each factor equal to zero produces the following.

$$2 \cos x = 0 \qquad \text{and} \qquad \cos x + 1 = 0$$
$$\cos x = 0 \qquad\qquad\qquad \cos x = -1$$
$$x = \frac{\pi}{2}, \frac{3\pi}{2} \qquad\qquad\qquad x = \pi$$

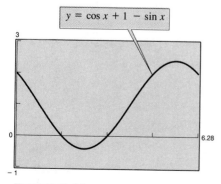

$y = \cos x + 1 - \sin x$

FIGURE 7.11

Because you squared both sides of the original equation, you must check for extraneous solutions. Of the three possible solutions, $x = 3\pi/2$ turns out to be extraneous. (Check this.) Thus, in the interval $[0, 2\pi)$, the only two solutions are $x = \pi/2$ and $x = \pi$. You can confirm this from the graph of $y = \cos x + 1 - \sin x$, shown in Figure 7.11. The general solution is $x = \pi/2 + 2n\pi$ and $x = \pi + 2n\pi$, where n is an integer.

Functions Involving Multiple Angles

EXAMPLE 8 **Functions of Multiple Angles**

Solve $2 \cos 3t - 1 = 0$.

SOLUTION

The graph of $y = 2 \cos 3t - 1$, shown in Figure 7.12, indicates that there are six solutions in the interval $[0, 2\pi)$. Proceeding algebraically, you can write the following.

$$2 \cos 3t - 1 = 0 \qquad \textit{Original equation}$$

$$2 \cos 3t = 1 \qquad \textit{Add 1 to both sides}$$

$$\cos 3t = \frac{1}{2} \qquad \textit{Divide both sides by 2}$$

In the interval $[0, 2\pi)$, you know that $3t = \pi/3$ and $3t = 5\pi/3$, so that

$$3t = \frac{\pi}{3} + 2n\pi \quad \text{and} \quad 3t = \frac{5\pi}{3} + 2n\pi$$

$$t = \frac{\pi}{9} + \frac{2n\pi}{3} \quad \text{and} \quad t = \frac{5\pi}{9} + \frac{2n\pi}{3}, \qquad \textit{General solution}$$

where n is an integer. The six solutions in the interval $[0, 2\pi)$ are as follows.

$$\frac{\pi}{9}, \quad \frac{7\pi}{9}, \quad \frac{13\pi}{9}, \quad \frac{5\pi}{9}, \quad \frac{11\pi}{9}, \quad \frac{17\pi}{9}$$

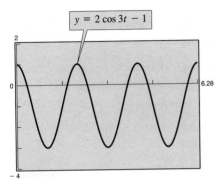

FIGURE 7.12

EXAMPLE 9 **Functions of Multiple Angles**

Solve $3 \tan(x/2) + 3 = 0$.

SOLUTION

The graph of $y = 3 \tan(x/2) + 3$, shown in Figure 7.13, indicates that there is only one solution in the interval $[0, 2\pi)$. Using the zoom and trace features, you can determine that the solution is $x \approx 4.712$. Algebraically, you can solve the equation as follows.

$$3 \tan \frac{x}{2} + 3 = 0 \qquad \textit{Original equation}$$

$$3 \tan \frac{x}{2} = -3 \qquad \textit{Subtract 3 from both sides}$$

$$\tan \frac{x}{2} = -1 \qquad \textit{Divide both sides by 3}$$

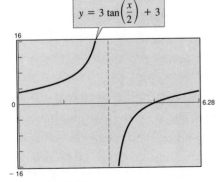

FIGURE 7.13

In the interval $[0, \pi)$, you know that $x/2 = 3\pi/4$, so that

$$\frac{x}{2} = \frac{3\pi}{4} + n\pi$$

$$x = \frac{3\pi}{2} + 2n\pi, \qquad\qquad \textit{General solution}$$

where n is an integer.

Using Inverse Functions and a Calculator

EXAMPLE 10   Using Inverse Functions

Solve $\sec^2 x - 2 \tan x = 4$.

SOLUTION

$$\sec^2 x - 2 \tan x = 4 \qquad\qquad \textit{Original equation}$$
$$1 + \tan^2 x - 2 \tan x - 4 = 0 \qquad\qquad \textit{Pythagorean Identity}$$
$$\tan^2 x - 2 \tan x - 3 = 0 \qquad\qquad \textit{Combine like terms}$$
$$(\tan x - 3)(\tan x + 1) = 0 \qquad\qquad \textit{Factor}$$

Setting each factor equal to zero produces two solutions in the interval $(-\pi/2, \pi/2)$.

$$\tan x = 3, \qquad\qquad \tan x = -1$$
$$x = \arctan 3 \qquad\qquad x = -\frac{\pi}{4}$$

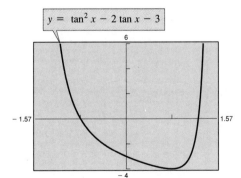

$y = \tan^2 x - 2 \tan x - 3$

FIGURE 7.14

Adding multiples of π (the period of the tangent) produces the general solution

$$x = \arctan 3 + n\pi \quad \text{and} \quad x = -\frac{\pi}{4} + n\pi, \qquad \textit{General solution}$$

where n is an integer. Note that the graph of $y = \tan^2 x - 2 \tan x - 3$, shown in Figure 7.14, has the two x-intercepts

$$x = \arctan 3 \ \approx\ 1.2490 \quad \text{and} \quad x = -\frac{\pi}{4} \approx -0.7854$$

in the interval $(-\pi/2, \pi/2)$.

When a calculator is used for $\arcsin x$, $\arccos x$, and $\arctan x$, the displayed solution may need to be adjusted to obtain solutions in the desired interval.

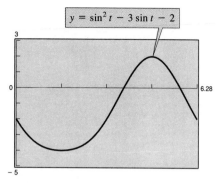

FIGURE 7.15

EXAMPLE 11   Using the Quadratic Formula

Solve $\sin^2 t - 3 \sin t - 2 = 0$ in the interval $[0, 2\pi)$.

SOLUTION

The graph of $y = \sin^2 t - 3 \sin t - 2$, shown in Figure 7.15, indicates that there are two solutions in the interval $[0, 2\pi)$. To find these solutions algebraically, you can use the Quadratic Formula as follows.

$$\sin^2 t - 3 \sin t - 2 = 0 \qquad \textit{Original equation}$$

$$\sin t = \frac{-(-3) \pm \sqrt{(-3)^2 - 4(1)(-2)}}{2(1)} \qquad \textit{Quadratic Formula}$$

$$= \frac{3 \pm \sqrt{17}}{2} \qquad \textit{Simplify}$$

$$\approx 3.561553 \quad \text{or} \quad -0.5615528$$

Because the range of the sine function is $[-1, 1]$, the equation $\sin t = 3.561553$ has no solution. To solve the equation $\sin t = -0.5615528$, use a calculator and the inverse sine function to obtain

$$t \approx \arcsin(-0.5615528) \approx -0.5962612.$$

Note that this solution is not in the interval $[0, 2\pi)$. In this interval, the two solutions are $t \approx \pi + 0.60 \approx 3.74$ and $t \approx 2\pi - 0.60 \approx 5.68$. ....

For the next example, there is no analytic way to solve the equation: we rely solely on a graphing utility to approximate the solutions.

FIGURE 7.16

EXAMPLE 12   Approximating Solutions

Approximate the solutions of $x = 2 \sin x$.

SOLUTION

The graph of $y = x - 2 \sin x$ is shown in Figure 7.16. From the graph, you can see that one solution is $x = 0$. Using the zoom and trace features of a graphing utility, you can approximate the positive solution to be $x \approx 1.8955$. Finally, by symmetry, you can approximate the negative solution to be $x \approx -1.8955$.

FIGURE 7.17

2.4 in.

0.75 in.

θ

EXAMPLE 13   Surface Area of a Honeycomb

The surface area of a honeycomb is given by the equation

$$ S = 6hs + \frac{3}{2}s^2\left(\frac{\sqrt{3} - \cos\theta}{\sin\theta}\right), \qquad 0 \le \theta \le 90°, $$

where $h = 2.4$ inches, $s = 0.75$ inches, and θ is the angle indicated in Figure 7.17.

A. What value of θ gives a surface area of 12 square inches?
B. What value of θ gives the minimum surface area?

SOLUTION

A. Let $h = 2.4$, $s = 0.75$, and $S = 12$.

$$ 10.8 + 0.84375\left(\frac{\sqrt{3} - \cos\theta}{\sin\theta}\right) = 12 $$

$$ 0.84375\left(\frac{\sqrt{3} - \cos\theta}{\sin\theta}\right) - 1.2 = 0 $$

The graph of

$$ y = 0.84375\left(\frac{\sqrt{3} - \cos\theta}{\sin\theta}\right) - 1.2 $$

is shown in Figure 7.18. Using the zoom and trace features, you can determine that $\theta \approx 59.9°$ and $\approx 49.9°$.

$$ y = 0.84375\left(\frac{\sqrt{3} - \cos\theta}{\sin\theta}\right) - 1.2 $$

0.05

0

90

−0.02

FIGURE 7.18

B. Graph the function

$$ S = 10.8 + 0.84375\left(\frac{\sqrt{3} - \cos\theta}{\sin\theta}\right), $$

as shown in Figure 7.19. You can zoom in on the minimum point on the graph, which occurs at $\theta \approx 54.7°$. By using calculus, it can be shown that

$$ \theta = \arccos\left(\frac{1}{\sqrt{3}}\right) \approx 54.7356 $$

is the exact minimum value.

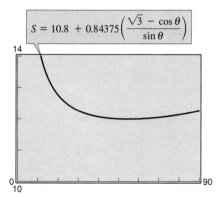

$$ S = 10.8 + 0.84375\left(\frac{\sqrt{3} - \cos\theta}{\sin\theta}\right) $$

14

0
10

90

FIGURE 7.19

DISCUSSION PROBLEM

EQUATIONS WITH NO SOLUTIONS

One of the following three equations has solutions and the other two don't. Which two equations do not have solutions?

(a) $\sin^2 x - 5 \sin x + 6 = 0$
(b) $\sin^2 x - 4 \sin x + 6 = 0$
(c) $\sin^2 x - 5 \sin x - 6 = 0$

Can you find conditions involving the constants b and c that will guarantee that the equation $\sin^2 x + b \sin x + c = 0$ has at least one solution?

WARM-UP

The following warm-up exercises involve skills that were covered in earlier sections. You will use these skills in the exercise set for this section.

In Exercises 1–6, find the values of θ in the interval $0 \le \theta < 2\pi$ that satisfy the equation.

1. $\cos \theta = -\dfrac{1}{2}$ **2.** $\sin \theta = \dfrac{\sqrt{3}}{2}$ **3.** $\cos \theta = \dfrac{\sqrt{2}}{2}$

4. $\sin \theta = -\dfrac{\sqrt{2}}{2}$ **5.** $\tan \theta = \sqrt{3}$ **6.** $\tan \theta = -1$

In Exercises 7–10, solve for x.

7. $\dfrac{x}{3} + \dfrac{x}{5} = 1$ **8.** $2x(x + 3) - 5(x + 3) = 0$

9. $2x^2 - 4x - 5 = 0$ **10.** $\dfrac{1}{x} = \dfrac{x}{2x + 3}$

SECTION 7.3 · EXERCISES

In Exercises 1–6, verify that the given values of x are solutions of the equation.

1. $2 \cos x - 1 = 0$

(a) $x = \dfrac{\pi}{3}$ (b) $x = \dfrac{5\pi}{3}$

2. $\csc x - 2 = 0$

(a) $x = \dfrac{\pi}{6}$ (b) $x = \dfrac{5\pi}{6}$

3. $3 \tan^2 2x - 1 = 0$

(a) $x = \dfrac{\pi}{12}$ (b) $x = \dfrac{5\pi}{12}$

4. $2 \cos^2 4x - 1 = 0$

(a) $x = \dfrac{\pi}{16}$ (b) $x = \dfrac{3\pi}{16}$

5. $2 \sin^2 x - \sin x - 1 = 0$

(a) $x = \dfrac{\pi}{2}$ (b) $x = \dfrac{7\pi}{6}$

6. $\sec^4 x - 4 \sec^2 x = 0$

(a) $x = \dfrac{2\pi}{3}$ (b) $x = \dfrac{5\pi}{3}$

In Exercises 7–20, solve the equation. Verify your result with a graphing utility.

7. $2 \cos x + 1 = 0$ **8.** $2 \sin x - 1 = 0$
9. $\sqrt{3} \csc x - 2 = 0$ **10.** $\tan x + 1 = 0$
11. $2 \sin^2 x = 1$ **12.** $\tan^2 x = 3$
13. $3 \sec^2 x - 4 = 0$ **14.** $\csc^2 x - 2 = 0$
15. $\tan x(\tan x - 1) = 0$ **16.** $\cos x(2 \cos x + 1) = 0$

17. $\sin x(\sin x + 1) = 0$ **18.** $4 \sin^2 x - 3 = 0$

19. $\sin^2 x = 3 \cos^2 x$

20. $(3 \tan^2 x - 1)(\tan^2 x - 3) = 0$

In Exercises 21–32, find all solutions of the equation in the interval $[0, 2\pi)$. Verify your results with a graphing utility.

21. $\sec x \csc x - 2 \csc x = 0$

22. $\sec^2 x - \sec x - 2 = 0$

23. $2 \sin^2 x + 3 \sin x + 1 = 0$

24. $3 \tan^3 x - \tan x = 0$

25. $2 \sec^2 x + \tan^2 x - 3 = 0$

26. $2 \sin^2 x = 2 + \cos x$

27. $2 \sin x + \csc x = 0$ **28.** $\csc x + \cot x = 1$

29. $\sin 2x = -\dfrac{\sqrt{3}}{2}$ **30.** $\tan 3x = 1$

31. $\cos \dfrac{x}{2} = \dfrac{\sqrt{2}}{2}$ **32.** $\sec 4x = 2$

In Exercises 33–36, solve the algebraic and trigonometric equations. Restrict the solutions of the trigonometric equations to the interval $[0, 2\pi)$.

33. $6y^2 - 13y + 6 = 0$
    $6 \cos^2 x - 13 \cos x + 6 = 0$

34. $y^2 + y - 20 = 0$
    $\sin^2 x + \sin x - 20 = 0$

35. $y^2 - 8y + 13 = 0$
    $\tan^2 x - 8 \tan x + 13 = 0$

36. $2y^2 + 6y - 1 = 0$
    $2 \cos^2 x + 6 \cos x - 1 = 0$

In Exercises 37–50, use a graphing utility to approximate all solutions of the equation in the interval $[0, 2\pi)$.

37. $2 \cos x - \sin x = 0$

38. $4 \sin^3 x - 2 \sin x - 1 = 0$

39. $\dfrac{1 + \sin x}{\cos x} + \dfrac{\cos x}{1 + \sin x} = 4$ **40.** $\dfrac{\cos x \cot x}{1 - \sin x} = 3$

41. $2 \sin x - x = 0$ **42.** $x \cos x - 1 = 0$

43. $\sec^2 x + 0.5 \tan x - 1 = 0$

44. $\csc^2 x + 0.5 \cot x - 5 = 0$

45. $2 \tan^2 x + 7 \tan x - 15 = 0$

46. $12 \cos^2 x + 5 \cos x - 3 = 0$

47. $12 \sin^2 x - 13 \sin x + 3 = 0$

48. $3 \tan^2 x + 4 \tan x - 4 = 0$

49. $\sin^2 x + 2 \sin x - 1 = 0$

50. $4 \cos^2 x - 4 \cos x - 1 = 0$

Extrema of a Function   In Exercises 51 and 52, (a) use a graphing utility to graph the function f and approximate the maximum and minimum points on the graph in the interval $[0, 2\pi]$. (b) Solve the given trigonometric equation and verify that its solutions are the x-coordinates of the maximum and minimum points of f.

Function	*Trigonometric Equation*
51. $f(x) = \sin x + \cos x$	$\cos x - \sin x = 0$
52. $f(x) = 2 \sin x + \cos 2x$	$2 \cos x - 4 \sin x \cos x = 0$

53. *Picard Iteration*   Use the following procedure to solve the equation $\cos x = x$. Begin by calculating $\cos 0.5$. Then take the cosine of your result. Repeat this procedure over and over until you observe that the result does not change. Describe another way to solve the same equation.

54. *How Many Solutions?*   Use a graphing utility to graph $y = \sin(1/x)$.

(a) How many solutions does the equation

$$\sin \frac{1}{x} = 0$$

have in the interval $[-1, 1]$? Describe one or more viewing rectangles that can be used to help support your conclusion.

(b) Does the equation $\sin(1/x) = 0$ have a greatest solution? If so, approximate the solution. If not, explain.

55. *Maximum Area*   The area of a rectangle inscribed in one arch of the graph of $y = \cos x$, as shown in the figure, is given by

$$A = 2x \cos x, \qquad -\frac{\pi}{2} < x < \frac{\pi}{2}.$$

Use a graphing utility to graph the area function, and approximate the area of the largest inscribed rectangle.

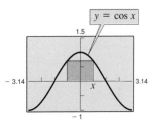

FIGURE FOR 55

56. *Sales*   The monthly sales (in thousands of units) of a seasonal product are approximated by

$$S = 74.50 + 43.75 \sin \frac{\pi t}{6},$$

where t is the time in months, with $t = 1$ corresponding to January (see figure). Determine the months when sales exceed 100,000 units.

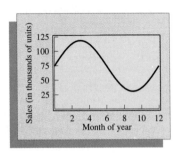

Sales (in thousands of units)

Month of year

FIGURE FOR 56

57. *Harmonic Motion*   A weight is oscillating on the end of a spring. The position of the weight relative to the point of equilibrium is given by

$$y = \tfrac{1}{4}(\cos 8t - 3 \sin 8t),$$

where y is the displacement in feet and t is the time in seconds (see figure). Find the times when the weight is at the point of equilibrium ($y = 0$) for $0 \le t \le 1$.

58. *Damped Harmonic Motion*   The displacement from equilibrium of a weight oscillating on the end of a spring is given by

$$y = 1.56e^{-0.22t} \cos 4.9t,$$

where y is the displacement in feet and t is the time in seconds (see figure). Use a graphing utility to graph the displacement function for $0 \le t \le 10$. Find the time beyond which the displacement does not exceed 1 inch from equilibrium.

59. *Projectile Motion*   A batted baseball leaves the bat at an angle of θ with the horizontal and an initial velocity of $v_0 = 100$ feet per second. The ball is caught by an outfielder 300 feet from home plate (see figure). Find θ if the range r of a projectile is given by

$$r = \tfrac{1}{32} v_0^2 \sin 2\theta.$$

60. *Projectile Motion*   A marksman intends to hit a target at a distance of 1000 yards with a gun that has a muzzle velocity of 1200 feet per second (see figure). Neglecting air resistance, determine the minimum elevation of the gun if the range is given by

$$r = \tfrac{1}{32} v_0^2 \sin 2\theta.$$

A number c is a **fixed point** of a function f if $f(c) = c$. For example, 2 is a fixed point of $f(x) = x^3 - x - 4$. Finding a fixed point of f is equivalent to finding a solution to the equation $f(x) = x$, or $f(x) - x = 0$.

In Exercises 61–64, find the smallest positive fixed point of the following functions.

61. $f(x) = \tan \dfrac{\pi x}{4}$

62. $f(x) = e^{-x}$

63. $f(x) = \dfrac{4x - x^2 + 2}{4}$

64. $f(x) = \dfrac{5x + 2 - x^3}{5}$

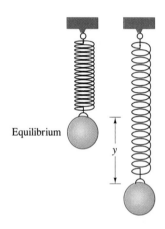

Equilibrium

y

FIGURE FOR 57 AND 58

θ

$r = 300$ ft

FIGURE FOR 59

θ

$r = 1000$ yd

FIGURE FOR 60

7.4   SUM AND DIFFERENCE FORMULAS

Introduction / Using Sum and Difference Formulas

Introduction

In this and the following section, you will study several trigonometric identities that are important in scientific applications. We begin with six sum and difference formulas that express trigonometric functions of $(u \pm v)$ as functions of u and v alone.

SUM AND DIFFERENCE FORMULAS

$$\sin(u + v) = \sin u \cos v + \cos u \sin v \qquad \sin(u - v) = \sin u \cos v - \cos u \sin v$$

$$\cos(u + v) = \cos u \cos v - \sin u \sin v \qquad \cos(u - v) = \cos u \cos v + \sin u \sin v$$

$$\tan(u + v) = \frac{\tan u + \tan v}{1 - \tan u \tan v} \qquad \tan(u - v) = \frac{\tan u - \tan v}{1 + \tan u \tan v}$$

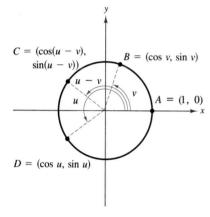

$C = (\cos(u - v),\ \sin(u - v))$

$B = (\cos v, \sin v)$

$A = (1, 0)$

$D = (\cos u, \sin u)$

FIGURE 7.20

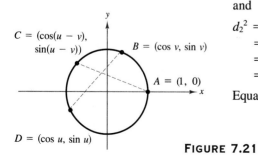

$C = (\cos(u - v),\ \sin(u - v))$

$B = (\cos v, \sin v)$

$A = (1, 0)$

$D = (\cos u, \sin u)$

FIGURE 7.21

PROOF

We prove only the formulas for $\cos(u \pm v)$. In Figure 7.20, let A be the point $(1, 0)$, and then use u and v to locate the points $B = (\cos v,\ \sin v)$, $C = (\cos(u - v),\ \sin(u - v))$, and $D = (\cos u,\ \sin u)$ on the unit circle. For convenience, assume that $0 < v < u < 2\pi$. From Figure 7.21, note that arcs AC and BD have the same length. Hence, *line segments* AC and BD are also equal in length. Let the length of $AC = d_1$, and the length of $BD = d_2$. Then $d_1 = d_2$, and $d_1{}^2 = d_2{}^2$. By the Distance Formula, we have

$$\begin{aligned}
d_1{}^2 &= [1 - \cos(u - v)]^2 + [0 - \sin(u - v)]^2 \\
&= 1 - 2\cos(u - v) + \cos^2(u - v) + \sin^2(u - v) \\
&= 2 - 2\cos(u - v)
\end{aligned}$$

and

$$\begin{aligned}
d_2{}^2 &= (\cos u - \cos v)^2 + (\sin u - \sin v)^2 \\
&= \cos^2 u - 2\cos u \cos v + \cos^2 v + \sin^2 u - 2\sin u \sin v + \sin^2 v \\
&= (\sin^2 u + \cos^2 u) + (\sin^2 v + \cos^2 v) - 2\cos u \cos v - 2\sin u \sin v \\
&= 2 - 2\cos u \cos v - 2\sin u \sin v.
\end{aligned}$$

Equating $d_1{}^2$ and $d_2{}^2$ yields

$$\begin{aligned}
2 - 2\cos(u - v) &= 2 - 2\cos u \cos v - 2\sin u \sin v \\
-2\cos(u - v) &= -2(\cos u \cos v + \sin u \sin v) \\
\cos(u - v) &= \cos u \cos v + \sin u \sin v.
\end{aligned}$$

REMARK Note that $\sin(u + v) \neq \sin u + \sin v$. Similar statements can be made for $\cos(u + v)$ and $\tan(u + v)$.

The formula for $\cos(u + v)$ can be established by considering $u + v = u - (-v)$ and using the formula just derived to obtain

$$\cos(u + v) = \cos[u - (-v)]$$
$$= \cos u \cos(-v) + \sin u \sin(-v) = \cos u \cos v - \sin u \sin v.$$

D I S C O V E R Y

(a) Use a graphing utility to graph $y = \cos(x + 2)$ and $y = \cos x + \cos 2$ in the same viewing rectangle. What can you conclude from the graphs? Is it true that $\cos(x + 2) = \cos x + \cos 2$?

(b) Use a graphing utility to graph $y = \sin(x + 4)$ and $y = \sin x + \sin 4$ in the same viewing rectangle. What can you conclude from the graphs? Is it true that $\sin(x + 4) = \sin x + \sin 4$?

Using Sum and Difference Formulas

EXAMPLE 1 Evaluating a Trigonometric Function

Find the exact value of $\cos 75°$.

SOLUTION

To find the *exact* value of $\cos 75°$, use the fact that $75° = 30° + 45°$. Consequently, the formula for $\cos(u + v)$ yields

$$\cos 75° = \cos(30° + 45°)$$
$$= \cos 30° \cos 45° - \sin 30° \sin 45°$$
$$= \frac{\sqrt{3}}{2}\left(\frac{\sqrt{2}}{2}\right) - \frac{1}{2}\left(\frac{\sqrt{2}}{2}\right) = \frac{\sqrt{6} - \sqrt{2}}{4}.$$

Check this with a calculator. You will find that $\cos 75° \approx 0.259 \approx (\sqrt{6} - \sqrt{2})/4$.

EXAMPLE 2 Evaluating a Trigonometric Function

Find the exact value of

$$\cos \frac{\pi}{12}.$$

SOLUTION

Using the fact that

$$\frac{\pi}{12} = \frac{\pi}{3} - \frac{\pi}{4},$$

together with the formula for $\cos(u - v)$, you obtain

$$\cos \frac{\pi}{12} = \cos\left(\frac{\pi}{3} - \frac{\pi}{4}\right)$$
$$= \cos \frac{\pi}{3} \cos \frac{\pi}{4} + \sin \frac{\pi}{3} \sin \frac{\pi}{4}$$
$$= \frac{1}{2}\left(\frac{\sqrt{2}}{2}\right) + \frac{\sqrt{3}}{2}\left(\frac{\sqrt{2}}{2}\right) = \frac{\sqrt{2} + \sqrt{6}}{4}.$$

EXAMPLE 3   Evaluating a Trigonometric Expression

Find the exact value of $\sin 42° \cos 12° - \cos 42° \sin 12°$.

SOLUTION

Recognizing that this expression fits the formula for $\sin(u - v)$, you can write

$$\sin 42° \cos 12° - \cos 42° \sin 12° = \sin(42° - 12°) = \sin 30° = \frac{1}{2}.$$

EXAMPLE 4   Evaluating a Trigonometric Expression

Find the exact value of

$$\frac{\tan 80° + \tan 55°}{1 - \tan 80° \tan 55°}.$$

SOLUTION

From the formula for $\tan(u + v)$, you have

$$\frac{\tan 80° + \tan 55°}{1 - \tan 80° \tan 55°} = \tan(80° + 55°) = \tan 135° = -\tan 45° = -1.$$

EXAMPLE 5   An Application of a Difference Formula

Find $\cos(u - v)$ given that

$$\cos u = -\frac{15}{17}, \quad \pi < u < \frac{3\pi}{2}, \quad \text{and} \quad \sin v = \frac{4}{5}, \quad 0 < v < \frac{\pi}{2}.$$

SOLUTION

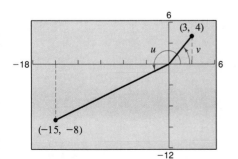

FIGURE 7.22

Using the given values for $\cos u$ and $\sin v$, you can sketch angles u and v, as shown in Figure 7.22. This implies that

$$\cos v = \frac{3}{5} \quad \text{and} \quad \sin u = -\frac{8}{17}.$$

Therefore,

$$\cos(u - v) = \cos u \cos v + \sin u \sin v$$

$$= \left(-\frac{15}{17}\right)\left(\frac{3}{5}\right) + \left(-\frac{8}{17}\right)\left(\frac{4}{5}\right) = -\frac{77}{85}.$$

EXAMPLE 6   Proving a Cofunction Identity

Use the formula for $\cos(u - v)$ to prove the cofunction identity

$$\cos\left(\frac{\pi}{2} - x\right) = \sin x.$$

SOLUTION

Using the difference formula $\cos(u - v) = \cos u \cos v + \sin u \sin v$ produces

$$\cos\left(\frac{\pi}{2} - x\right) = \cos \frac{\pi}{2} \cos x + \sin \frac{\pi}{2} \sin x$$
$$= (0) \cos x + (1) \sin x$$
$$= \sin x.$$

You should verify this identity by graphing

$$y = \cos\left(\frac{\pi}{2} - x\right)$$

and $y = \sin x$ on the same screen.

Sum and difference formulas can be used to derive **reduction formulas** involving expressions such as

$$\sin\left(\theta + \frac{n\pi}{2}\right) \quad \text{and} \quad \cos\left(\theta + \frac{n\pi}{2}\right),$$

where n is an integer.

EXAMPLE 7   Deriving Reduction Formulas

Simplify

$$\cos\left(\theta - \frac{3\pi}{2}\right).$$

SOLUTION

Using the formula $\cos(u - v) = \cos u \cos v + \sin u \sin v$ produces

$$\cos\left(\theta - \frac{3\pi}{2}\right) = \cos \theta \cos \frac{3\pi}{2} + \sin \theta \sin \frac{3\pi}{2}$$
$$= (\cos \theta)(0) + (\sin \theta)(-1)$$
$$= -\sin \theta.$$

EXAMPLE 8   Solving a Trigonometric Equation

Solve

$$\sin\left(x + \frac{\pi}{4}\right) + \sin\left(x - \frac{\pi}{4}\right) = -1$$

in the interval $[0, 2\pi)$.

SOLUTION

Using sum and difference formulas, you can rewrite the given equation as

$$\sin x \cos \frac{\pi}{4} + \cos x \sin \frac{\pi}{4} + \sin x \cos \frac{\pi}{4} - \cos x \sin \frac{\pi}{4} = -1$$

$$2 \sin x \cos \frac{\pi}{4} \stackrel{.}{=} -1$$

$$2(\sin x)\left(\frac{\sqrt{2}}{2}\right) = -1$$

$$\sin x = -\frac{1}{\sqrt{2}}$$

$$\sin x = -\frac{\sqrt{2}}{2}.$$

Therefore, the only solutions in the interval $[0, 2\pi)$ are $x = 5\pi/4$ and $x = 7\pi/4$. The graph of

$$y = 1 + \sin\left(x + \frac{\pi}{4}\right) + \sin\left(x - \frac{\pi}{4}\right),$$

shown in Figure 7.23, confirms these two solutions.

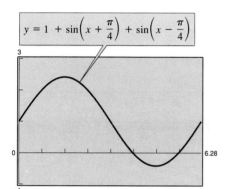

$$y = 1 + \sin\left(x + \frac{\pi}{4}\right) + \sin\left(x - \frac{\pi}{4}\right)$$

FIGURE 7.23

Example 9 shows how a sum formula can be used to rewrite a trigonometric expression in a form that is useful in calculus.

EXAMPLE 9   An Application from Calculus

Verify that

$$\frac{\sin(x + h) - \sin x}{h} = (\cos x)\left(\frac{\sin h}{h}\right) - (\sin x)\left(\frac{1 - \cos h}{h}\right),$$

where $h \neq 0$.

SOLUTION

$$\frac{\sin(x+h) - \sin x}{h} = \frac{\sin x \cos h + \cos x \sin h - \sin x}{h}$$

$$= \frac{\cos x \sin h - \sin x(1 - \cos h)}{h}$$

$$= (\cos x)\left(\frac{\sin h}{h}\right) - (\sin x)\left(\frac{1 - \cos h}{h}\right)$$

DISCUSSION PROBLEM

VERIFYING A SUM FORMULA

At the beginning of this section, we listed a proof of the formula for $\cos(u - v)$. Show how you can use this formula together with the identity

$$\sin x = \cos\left(\frac{\pi}{2} - x\right)$$

to prove the formula for $\sin(u + v)$. *Hint:* Start by writing

$$\sin(u + v) = \cos\left[\frac{\pi}{2} - (u + v)\right]$$

WARM-UP

The following warm-up exercises involve skills that were covered in earlier sections. You will use these skills in the exercise set for this section.

In Exercises 1–4, use the given information to find $\sin \theta$.

1. $\tan \theta = \frac{1}{3}$, θ in Quadrant I

2. $\cot \theta = \frac{3}{5}$, θ in Quadrant III

3. $\cos \theta = \frac{3}{4}$, θ in Quadrant IV

4. $\sec \theta = -3$, θ in Quadrant II

In Exercises 5 and 6, find all solutions in the interval $[0, 2\pi)$.

5. $\sin x = \frac{\sqrt{2}}{2}$

6. $\cos x = 0$

In Exercises 7–10, simplify the expression.

7. $\tan x \sec^2 x - \tan x$

8. $\dfrac{\cos x \csc x}{\tan x}$

9. $\dfrac{\cos x}{1 - \sin x} - \tan x$

10. $\dfrac{\cos^4 x - \sin^4 x}{\cos^2 x}$

SECTION 7.4 · EXERCISES

In Exercises 1–10, use the sum and difference identities to find the exact values of the sine, cosine, and tangent of the given angle.

1. $75° = 30° + 45°$

2. $15° = 45° - 30°$

3. $105° = 60° + 45°$

4. $165° = 135° + 30°$

5. $195° = 225° - 30°$

6. $255° = 300° - 45°$

7. $\dfrac{11\pi}{12} = \dfrac{3\pi}{4} + \dfrac{\pi}{6}$

8. $\dfrac{7\pi}{12} = \dfrac{\pi}{3} + \dfrac{\pi}{4}$

9. $\dfrac{17\pi}{12} = \dfrac{9\pi}{4} - \dfrac{5\pi}{6}$

10. $-\dfrac{\pi}{12} = \dfrac{\pi}{6} - \dfrac{\pi}{4}$

In Exercises 11–20, use the sum and difference identities to write the expression as the sine, cosine, or tangent of an angle.

11. $\cos 25° \cos 15° - \sin 25° \sin 15°$

12. $\sin 140° \cos 50° + \cos 140° \sin 50°$

13. $\sin 230° \cos 30° - \cos 230° \sin 30°$

14. $\cos 20° \cos 30° + \sin 20° \sin 30°$

15. $\dfrac{\tan 325° - \tan 86°}{1 + \tan 325° \tan 86°}$

16. $\dfrac{\tan 140° - \tan 60°}{1 + \tan 140° \tan 60°}$

17. $\sin 3 \cos 1.2 - \cos 3 \sin 1.2$

18. $\cos \dfrac{\pi}{7} \cos \dfrac{\pi}{5} - \sin \dfrac{\pi}{7} \sin \dfrac{\pi}{5}$

19. $\dfrac{\tan 2x + \tan x}{1 - \tan 2x \tan x}$

20. $\cos 3x \cos 2y + \sin 3x \sin 2y$

In Exercises 21–24, find the exact value of the trigonometric function given that

$$\sin u = \frac{5}{13}, \quad 0 < u < \frac{\pi}{2} \quad \text{and}$$

$$\cos v = -\frac{3}{5}, \quad \frac{\pi}{2} < v < \pi.$$

21. $\sin(u + v)$

22. $\cos(v - u)$

23. $\cos(u + v)$

24. $\sin(u - v)$

In Exercises 25–28, find the exact value of the trigonometric function given that

$$\sin u = \frac{7}{25}, \quad \frac{\pi}{2} < u < \pi \quad \text{and}$$

$$\cos v = \frac{4}{5}, \quad \frac{3\pi}{2} < v < 2\pi.$$

25. $\cos(u + v)$

26. $\sin(u + v)$

27. $\sin(v - u)$

28. $\cos(u - v)$

In Exercises 29–42, verify the identity.

29. $\sin\left(\dfrac{\pi}{2} + x\right) = \cos x$

30. $\sin(3\pi - x) = \sin x$

31. $\sin\left(\dfrac{\pi}{6} + x\right) = \dfrac{1}{2}(\cos x + \sqrt{3} \sin x)$

32. $\cos\left(\dfrac{5\pi}{4} - x\right) = -\dfrac{\sqrt{2}}{2}(\cos x + \sin x)$

33. $\cos(\pi - \theta) + \sin\left(\dfrac{\pi}{2} + \theta\right) = 0$

34. $\tan\left(\dfrac{\pi}{4} - \theta\right) = \dfrac{1 - \tan \theta}{1 + \tan \theta}$

35. $\cos(x + y) \cos(x - y) = \cos^2 x - \sin^2 y$

36. $\sin(x + y) \sin(x - y) = \sin^2 x - \sin^2 y$

37. $\sin(x + y) + \sin(x - y) = 2 \sin x \cos y$

38. $\cos(x + y) + \cos(x - y) = 2 \cos x \cos y$

39. $\cos(n\pi + \theta) = (-1)^n \cos \theta$, n is an integer

40. $\sin(n\pi + \theta) = (-1)^n \sin \theta$, n is an integer

41. $a \sin B\theta + b \cos B\theta = \sqrt{a^2 + b^2} \sin(B\theta + C)$, where $C = \arctan b/a$, $a > 0$

42. $a \sin B\theta + b \cos B\theta = \sqrt{a^2 + b^2} \cos(B\theta - C)$, where $C = \arctan a/b$, $b > 0$

In Exercises 43–46, use a graphing utility to verify the identity. (Graph both members of the equation and show that the graphs coincide.)

43. $\cos\left(\dfrac{3\pi}{2} - x\right) = -\sin x$

44. $\cos(\pi + x) = -\cos x$

45. $\sin\left(\dfrac{3\pi}{2} + \theta\right) + \sin(\pi - \theta) = \sin\theta - \cos\theta$

46. $\tan(\pi + \theta) = \tan\theta$

In Exercises 47–50, use the formulas given in Exercises 41 and 42 to write the trigonometric expression in the following forms. Use a graphing utility to verify your results.

(a) $\sqrt{a^2 + b^2}\ \sin(B\theta + C)$

(b) $\sqrt{a^2 + b^2}\ \cos(B\theta - C)$

47. $\sin\theta + \cos\theta$ **48.** $3\sin 2\theta + 4\cos 2\theta$

49. $12\sin 3\theta + 5\cos 3\theta$ **50.** $\sin 2\theta - \cos 2\theta$

In Exercises 51 and 52, use the formulas given in Exercises 41 and 42 to write the trigonometric expression in the form $a\sin B\theta + b\cos B\theta$. Use a graphing utility to verify your result.

51. $2\sin\left(\theta + \dfrac{\pi}{4}\right)$ **52.** $5\cos\left(\theta + \dfrac{3\pi}{4}\right)$

In Exercises 53 and 54, write the trigonometric expression as an algebraic expression.

53. $\sin(\arcsin x + \arccos x)$ **54.** $\sin(\arctan 2x - \arccos x)$

In Exercises 55–58, find all solutions of the equation in the interval $[0, 2\pi)$.

55. $\sin\left(x + \dfrac{\pi}{3}\right) + \sin\left(x - \dfrac{\pi}{3}\right) = 1$

56. $\sin\left(x + \dfrac{\pi}{6}\right) - \sin\left(x - \dfrac{\pi}{6}\right) = \dfrac{1}{2}$

57. $\cos\left(x + \dfrac{\pi}{4}\right) + \cos\left(x - \dfrac{\pi}{4}\right) = 1$

58. $\tan(x + \pi) - \cos\left(x + \dfrac{\pi}{2}\right) = 0$

In Exercises 59 and 60, use a graphing utility to approximate all solutions of the equation in the interval $[0, 2\pi)$.

59. $\cos\left(x + \dfrac{\pi}{4}\right) - \cos\left(x - \dfrac{\pi}{4}\right) = 1$

60. $\tan(x + \pi) + 2\sin(x + \pi) = 0$

61. *Standing Waves* The equation of a standing wave is obtained by adding the displacements of two waves traveling in opposite directions (see figure). Assume that each of the waves has amplitude A, period T, and wavelength λ. If the models for these waves are

$$y_1 = A\cos\left[2\pi\left(\dfrac{t}{T} - \dfrac{x}{\lambda}\right)\right] \quad \text{and} \quad y_2 = A\cos\left[2\pi\left(\dfrac{t}{T} + \dfrac{x}{\lambda}\right)\right],$$

show that

$$y_1 + y_2 = 2A\cos\dfrac{2\pi t}{T}\cos\dfrac{2\pi x}{\lambda}.$$

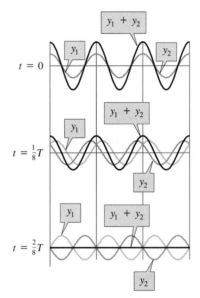

FIGURE FOR 61

62. *Harmonic Motion* A weight is attached to a spring suspended vertically from a ceiling. When a driving force is applied to the system, the weight moves vertically from its equilibrium position, and this motion is described by the model

$$y = \tfrac{1}{3}\sin 2t + \tfrac{1}{4}\cos 2t,$$

where y is the distance from equilibrium measured in feet and t is the time in seconds.

(a) Write the model in the form

$$y = \sqrt{a^2 + b^2}\ \sin(Bt + C).$$

    (See Exercise 41.)

(b) Use a graphing utility to graph the model.

(c) Find the amplitude of the oscillations of the weight.

(d) Find the frequency of the oscillations of the weight.

63. Verify the following identity used in calculus.

$$\frac{\cos(x + h) - \cos x}{h} = \cos x\left(\frac{\cos h - 1}{h}\right) - \sin x\left(\frac{\sin h}{h}\right)$$

64. Use the sum formulas for the sine and cosine to derive the formula

$$\tan(u + v) = \frac{\tan u + \tan v}{1 - \tan u \tan v}.$$

7.5 MULTIPLE-ANGLE AND PRODUCT-TO-SUM FORMULAS

Multiple-Angle Formulas / Power-Reducing Formulas / Half-Angle Formulas / Product-to-Sum Formulas

Multiple-Angle Formulas

In this section, you will study four other categories of trigonometric identities. The first involves functions of multiple angles such as $\sin ku$ and $\cos ku$. The second involves squares of trigonometric functions such as $\sin^2 u$. The third involves functions of half-angles such as $\sin u/2$, and the fourth involves products of trigonometric functions such as $\sin u \cos v$.

DISCOVERY

(a) Use a graphing utility to graph $y = \cos(2x)$ and $y = 2 \cos x$ in the same viewing rectangle. What can you conclude from the graphs? Is it true that $\cos(2x) = 2 \cos x$?

(b) Use a graphing utility to graph $y = \sin(4x)$ and $y = 4 \sin x$ in the same viewing rectangle. What can you conclude from the graphs? Is it true that $\sin(4x) = 4 \sin x$?

DOUBLE-ANGLE FORMULAS

$$\sin 2u = 2 \sin u \cos u$$
$$\cos 2u = \cos^2 u - \sin^2 u = 2 \cos^2 u - 1 = 1 - 2 \sin^2 u$$
$$\tan 2u = \frac{2 \tan u}{1 - \tan^2 u}$$

PROOF

To prove the first formula, let $v = u$ in the formula for $\sin(u + v)$, and obtain

$$\sin 2u = \sin(u + u)$$
$$= \sin u \cos u + \cos u \sin u$$
$$= 2 \sin u \cos u.$$

The other double-angle formulas can be proved in a similar way.

REMARK Note that $\sin 2u \neq 2 \sin u$. Similar statements can be made for $\cos 2u$ and $\tan 2u$.

EXAMPLE 1   Solving a Trigonometric Equation

Solve $2 \cos x + \sin 2x = 0$.

SOLUTION

The graph of $y = 2 \cos x + \sin 2x$, shown in Figure 7.24, suggests that there are two solutions in the interval $[0, 2\pi)$. To find these solutions analytically, begin by rewriting the equation so that it involves functions of x (rather than $2x$). Then factor and solve as usual.

$$2 \cos x + \sin 2x = 0 \qquad \textit{Original equation}$$
$$2 \cos x + 2 \sin x \cos x = 0 \qquad \textit{Double-angle formula}$$
$$2 \cos x(1 + \sin x) = 0 \qquad \textit{Factor}$$

$$\cos x = 0, \qquad 1 + \sin x = 0 \qquad \textit{Set factors to zero}$$

$$x = \frac{\pi}{2}, \frac{3\pi}{2} \qquad x = \frac{3\pi}{2} \qquad \textit{Solutions in } [0, 2\pi)$$

Therefore, the general solution is

$$x = \frac{\pi}{2} + 2n\pi \quad \text{and} \quad x = \frac{3\pi}{2} + 2n\pi,$$

where n is an integer.

FIGURE 7.24

EXAMPLE 2   Locating Relative Minimums and Maximums

Find the relative minimums and relative maximums of $y = 4 \cos^2 x - 2$ in the interval $[0, \pi]$.

SOLUTION

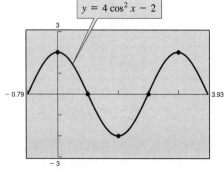

Using a double-angle identity, you can rewrite the given function as

$$y = 4 \cos^2 x - 2 = 2(2 \cos^2 x - 1) = 2 \cos 2x.$$

Using the techniques discussed in Section 6.4, you can recognize that the graph of this function has an amplitude of 2 and a period of π, as shown in Figure 7.25. The key points in the interval $[0, \pi]$ are as follows.

Maximum	Intercept	Minimum	Intercept	Maximum
$(0, 2)$	$\left(\dfrac{\pi}{4}, 0\right)$	$\left(\dfrac{\pi}{2}, -2\right)$	$\left(\dfrac{3\pi}{4}, 0\right)$	$(\pi, 2)$

FIGURE 7.25

EXAMPLE 3   **Evaluating Functions Involving Double Angles**

Use the fact that

$$\cos \theta = \frac{5}{13}, \qquad \frac{3\pi}{2} < \theta < 2\pi$$

to find $\sin 2\theta$, $\cos 2\theta$, and $\tan 2\theta$.

SOLUTION

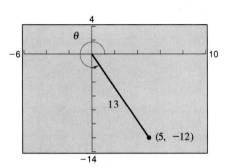

FIGURE 7.26

In Figure 7.26, you can see that $\sin \theta = y/r = -12/13$. Consequently, you can write the following.

$$\sin 2\theta = 2 \sin \theta \cos \theta = 2\left(\frac{-12}{13}\right)\left(\frac{5}{13}\right) = -\frac{120}{169}$$

$$\cos 2\theta = 2 \cos^2 \theta - 1 = 2\left(\frac{25}{169}\right) - 1 = -\frac{119}{169}$$

$$\tan 2\theta = \frac{\sin 2\theta}{\cos 2\theta} = \frac{120}{119}$$

The double-angle formulas are not restricted to angles 2θ and θ. Other *double* combinations such as 4θ and 2θ are also valid. Here are two examples.

$$\sin 4\theta = 2 \sin 2\theta \cos 2\theta \quad \text{and} \quad \cos 6\theta = \cos^2 3\theta - \sin^2 3\theta$$

EXAMPLE 4   **Deriving a Triple-Angle Formula**

Express $\sin 3x$ in terms of $\sin x$.

SOLUTION

Consider that $3x = 2x + x$ produces

$$\begin{aligned}
\sin 3x &= \sin(2x + x) \\
&= \sin 2x \cos x + \cos 2x \sin x \\
&= 2 \sin x \cos x \cos x + (1 - 2 \sin^2 x) \sin x \\
&= 2 \sin x \cos^2 x + \sin x - 2 \sin^3 x \\
&= 2 \sin x(1 - \sin^2 x) + \sin x - 2 \sin^3 x \\
&= 2 \sin x - 2 \sin^3 x + \sin x - 2 \sin^3 x \\
&= 3 \sin x - 4 \sin^3 x.
\end{aligned}$$

Try graphing $y = \sin 3x$ and $y = 3 \sin x - 4 \sin^3 x$ in the same viewing rectangle. Their graphs should coincide.

Power-Reducing Formulas

The double-angle formulas can be used to obtain the following **power-reducing formulas.**

POWER-REDUCING FORMULAS

$$\sin^2 u = \frac{1 - \cos 2u}{2} \qquad\qquad \cos^2 u = \frac{1 + \cos 2u}{2}$$

$$\tan^2 u = \frac{1 - \cos 2u}{1 + \cos 2u}$$

PROOF

The first two formulas can be verified by solving for $\sin^2 u$ and $\cos^2 u$, respectively, in the double-angle formulas

$$\cos 2u = 1 - 2 \sin^2 u \quad \text{and} \quad \cos 2u = 2 \cos^2 u - 1.$$

The third formula can be verified using the fact that

$$\tan^2 u = \frac{\sin^2 u}{\cos^2 u}.$$

Example 5 shows a typical power reduction that is used in calculus.

EXAMPLE 5   Reducing the Power of a Trigonometric Function

Rewrite $\sin^4 x$ as a sum involving first powers of the cosines of multiple angles.

SOLUTION

Note the repeated use of power-reducing formulas in the following procedure.

$$\sin^4 x = (\sin^2 x)^2 = \left(\frac{1 - \cos 2x}{2}\right)^2$$

$$= \frac{1}{4}(1 - 2\cos 2x + \cos^2 2x)$$

$$= \frac{1}{4}\left(1 - 2\cos 2x + \frac{1 + \cos 4x}{2}\right)$$

$$= \frac{1}{4} - \frac{1}{2}\cos 2x + \frac{1}{8} + \frac{1}{8}\cos 4x$$

$$= \frac{3}{8} - \frac{1}{2}\cos 2x + \frac{1}{8}\cos 4x$$

$$= \frac{1}{8}(3 - 4\cos 2x + \cos 4x)$$

Half-Angle Formulas

You can derive some useful alternative forms of the power-reducing formulas by replacing u with $u/2$. The results are **half-angle formulas.**

HALF-ANGLE FORMULAS

$$\sin\frac{u}{2} = \pm\sqrt{\frac{1 - \cos u}{2}}$$

$$\cos\frac{u}{2} = \pm\sqrt{\frac{1 + \cos u}{2}}$$

$$\tan\frac{u}{2} = \frac{1 - \cos u}{\sin u} = \frac{\sin u}{1 + \cos u}$$

The signs of $\sin u/2$ and $\cos u/2$ depend on the quadrant in which $u/2$ lies.

EXAMPLE 6   Using a Half-Angle Formula

Find the exact value of $\sin 105°$.

SOLUTION

Begin by noting that $105°$ is half of $210°$. Then, using the half-angle formula for $\sin(u/2)$ and the fact that $105°$ lies in Quadrant II, you have

$$\sin 105° = \sqrt{\frac{1 - \cos 210°}{2}}$$

$$= \sqrt{\frac{1 - (-\cos 30°)}{2}}$$

$$= \sqrt{\frac{1 + (\sqrt{3}/2)}{2}}$$

$$= \frac{\sqrt{2 + \sqrt{3}}}{2}.$$

Choose the positive square root because $\sin\theta$ is positive in Quadrant II. Use your calculator to evaluate $\sin 105°$ and $\sqrt{2 + \sqrt{3}}/2$ to see that both values are approximately 0.9659258.

EXAMPLE 7　Solving a Trigonometric Equation

Solve

$$2 - \sin^2 x = 2 \cos^2 \frac{x}{2}.$$

SOLUTION

The graph of $y = 2 - \sin^2 x - 2\cos^2(x/2)$, shown in Figure 7.27, suggests that there are three solutions in the interval $[0, 2\pi)$. To find these analytically, solve the given equation as follows.

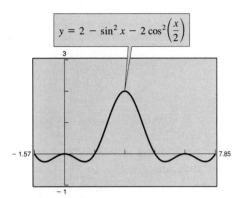

$$y = 2 - \sin^2 x - 2\cos^2\left(\frac{x}{2}\right)$$

FIGURE 7.27

$2 - \sin^2 x = 2 \cos^2 \dfrac{x}{2}$	*Original equation*
$2 - \sin^2 x = 2\left(\dfrac{1 + \cos x}{2}\right)$	*Half-angle formula*
$2 - \sin^2 x = 1 + \cos x$	*Simplify*
$2 - (1 - \cos^2 x) = 1 + \cos x$	*Pythagorean Identity*
$\cos^2 x - \cos x = 0$	*Simplify*
$\cos x(\cos x - 1) = 0$	*Factor*

By setting the factors $\cos x$ and $(\cos x - 1)$ equal to zero, you can find that the solutions in the interval $[0, 2\pi)$ are $x = \pi/2 \approx 1.57$, $x = 3\pi/2 \approx 4.71$, and $x = 0$. Therefore, the general solution is

$$x = 2n\pi, \quad x = \frac{\pi}{2} + 2n\pi, \quad \text{and} \quad x = \frac{3\pi}{2} + 2n\pi,$$

where n is an integer.

Product-to-Sum Formulas

Each of the following **product-to-sum formulas** is easily verified using the sum and difference formulas discussed in the preceding section.

PRODUCT-TO-SUM FORMULAS

$$\sin u \sin v = \frac{1}{2}[\cos(u - v) - \cos(u + v)]$$

$$\cos u \cos v = \frac{1}{2}[\cos(u - v) + \cos(u + v)]$$

$$\sin u \cos v = \frac{1}{2}[\sin(u + v) + \sin(u - v)]$$

$$\cos u \sin v = \frac{1}{2}[\sin(u + v) - \sin(u - v)]$$

EXAMPLE 8   Writing Products as Sums

Rewrite $\cos 5x \sin 4x$ as a sum or difference.

SOLUTION

$$\cos 5x \sin 4x = \frac{1}{2}[\sin(5x + 4x) - \sin(5x - 4x)] = \frac{1}{2}\sin 9x - \frac{1}{2}\sin x$$

Occasionally, it is useful to reverse the procedure and write a sum of trigonometric functions as a product. This can be accomplished with the following **sum-to-product formulas.**

SUM-TO-PRODUCT FORMULAS

$$\sin x + \sin y = 2 \sin\left(\frac{x + y}{2}\right) \cos\left(\frac{x - y}{2}\right)$$

$$\sin x - \sin y = 2 \cos\left(\frac{x + y}{2}\right) \sin\left(\frac{x - y}{2}\right)$$

$$\cos x + \cos y = 2 \cos\left(\frac{x + y}{2}\right) \cos\left(\frac{x - y}{2}\right)$$

$$\cos x - \cos y = -2 \sin\left(\frac{x + y}{2}\right) \sin\left(\frac{x - y}{2}\right)$$

EXAMPLE 9   Using a Sum-to-Product Formula

Find the exact value of $\cos 195° + \cos 105°$.

SOLUTION

Using the appropriate sum-to-product formula produces

$$\cos 195° + \cos 105° = 2 \cos\left(\frac{195° + 105°}{2}\right) \cos\left(\frac{195° - 105°}{2}\right)$$

$$= 2 \cos 150° \cos 45°$$

$$= 2\left(-\frac{\sqrt{3}}{2}\right)\left(\frac{\sqrt{2}}{2}\right)$$

$$= -\frac{\sqrt{6}}{2}.$$

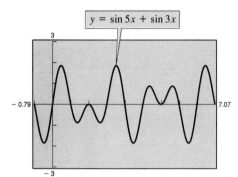

$y = \sin 5x + \sin 3x$

FIGURE 7.28

EXAMPLE 10   Solving a Trigonometric Equation

Solve $\sin 5x + \sin 3x = 0$.

SOLUTION

The graph of $y = \sin 5x + \sin 3x$, shown in Figure 7.28, suggests that there are eight solutions in the interval $[0, 2\pi)$. To find these analytically, proceed as follows.

$$\sin 5x + \sin 3x = 0 \qquad \textit{Original equation}$$

$$2 \sin\left(\frac{5x + 3x}{2}\right) \cos\left(\frac{5x - 3x}{2}\right) = 0 \qquad \textit{Sum-to-product formula}$$

$$2 \sin 4x \cos x = 0 \qquad \textit{Simplify}$$

By setting the factor $\sin 4x$ equal to zero, you find that the solutions in the interval $[0, 2\pi)$ are

$$x = 0, \quad \frac{\pi}{4}, \quad \frac{\pi}{2}, \quad \frac{3\pi}{4}, \quad \pi, \quad \frac{5\pi}{4}, \quad \frac{3\pi}{2}, \quad \frac{7\pi}{4}.$$

Moreover, the equation $\cos x = 0$ yields no additional solutions, and you can conclude the solutions are of the form

$$x = \frac{n\pi}{4},$$

where n is an integer.

EXAMPLE 11   Verifying a Trigonometric Identity

Verify the identity

$$\frac{\sin t + \sin 3t}{\cos t + \cos 3t} = \tan 2t.$$

SOLUTION

Using appropriate sum-to-product formulas, you obtain

$$\frac{\sin t + \sin 3t}{\cos t + \cos 3t} = \frac{2 \sin 2t \cos(-t)}{2 \cos 2t \cos(-t)} = \frac{\sin 2t}{\cos 2t} = \tan 2t.$$

DISCUSSION PROBLEM

....

DERIVING A TRIPLE-ANGLE FORMULA

In Example 4, you saw how to derive a formula for sin 3x. Show how you can derive a similar formula for cos 3x. That is, find a formula that expresses cos 3x in terms of cos x, and then verify your formula graphically.

WARM-UP

....

The following warm-up exercises involve skills that were covered in earlier sections. You will use these skills in the exercise set for this section.

In Exercises 1 and 2, factor the trigonometric expression.

1. $2 \sin x + \sin x \cos x$

2. $\cos^2 x - \cos x - 2$

In Exercises 3–6, find all solutions of the equation in the interval $[0, 2\pi)$.

3. $\sin 2x = 0$

4. $\cos 2x = 0$

5. $\cos \dfrac{x}{2} = 0$

6. $\sin \dfrac{x}{2} = 0$

In Exercises 7–10, simplify the expression.

7. $\dfrac{1 - \cos(\pi/4)}{2}$

8. $\dfrac{1 + \cos(\pi/3)}{2}$

9. $\dfrac{2 \sin 3x \cos x}{2 \cos 3x \cos x}$

10. $(1 - 2 \sin^2 x) \cos x - 2 \sin^2 x \cos x$

SECTION 7.5 · EXERCISES
....

In Exercises 1–10, use a graphing utility to graph the function and approximate its zeros in the interval $[0, 2\pi)$. If possible, find the exact values of the zeros algebraically.

1. $f(x) = \sin 2x - \sin x$

2. $f(x) = \sin 2x + \cos x$

3. $g(x) = 4 \sin x \cos x - 1$

4. $g(x) = \sin 2x \sin x - \cos x$

5. $h(x) = \cos 2x - \cos x$

6. $h(x) = \cos 2x + \sin x$

7. $y = \tan 2x - \cot x$

8. $y = \tan 2x - 2 \cos x$

9. $h(t) = \sin 4t + 2 \sin 2t$

10. $f(s) = (\sin 2s + \cos 2s)^2 - 1$

In Exercises 11–14, use a double-angle identity to rewrite the function. Use a graphing utility to graph both versions of the function and note that the graphs coincide. Identify the relative minimums and relative maximums over the interval $[0, 2\pi)$.

11. $f(x) = 6 \sin x \cos x$

12. $g(x) = 4 \sin x \cos x + 2$

13. $g(x) = 4 - 8 \sin^2 x$

14. $f(x) = (\cos x + \sin x)(\cos x - \sin x)$

In Exercises 15–20, find the exact values of sin 2u, cos 2u, and tan 2u by using the double-angle formulas.

15. $\sin u = \dfrac{3}{5}, \quad 0 < u < \dfrac{\pi}{2}$

16. $\cos u = -\dfrac{2}{3}, \quad \dfrac{\pi}{2} < u < \pi$

17. $\tan u = \dfrac{1}{2}, \quad \pi < u < \dfrac{3\pi}{2}$

18. $\cot u = -4, \quad \dfrac{3\pi}{2} < u < 2\pi$

19. $\sec u = -\dfrac{5}{2}, \quad \dfrac{\pi}{2} < u < \pi$

20. $\csc u = 3, \quad \dfrac{\pi}{2} < u < \pi$

In Exercises 21–26, use the power-reducing formulas to write the expression in terms of the first power of the cosine.

21. $\cos^4 x$ **22.** $\sin^4 x$

23. $\sin^2 x \cos^2 x$ **24.** $\cos^6 x$

25. $\sin^2 x \cos^4 x$ **26.** $\sin^4 x \cos^2 x$

In Exercises 27–32, use the half-angle formulas to determine the exact values of the sine, cosine, and tangent of the given angle.

27. $105°$ **28.** $165°$

29. $112° \, 30'$ **30.** $67° \, 30'$

31. $\dfrac{\pi}{8}$ **32.** $\dfrac{\pi}{12}$

In Exercises 33–38, find the exact values of $\sin(u/2)$, $\cos(u/2)$, and $\tan(u/2)$ by using the half-angle formulas.

33. $\sin u = \dfrac{5}{13}, \quad \dfrac{\pi}{2} < u < \pi$

34. $\cos u = \dfrac{3}{5}, \quad 0 < u < \dfrac{\pi}{2}$

35. $\tan u = -\dfrac{5}{8}, \quad \dfrac{3\pi}{2} < u < 2\pi$

36. $\cot u = 3, \quad \pi < u < \dfrac{3\pi}{2}$

37. $\csc u = -\dfrac{5}{3}, \quad \pi < u < \dfrac{3\pi}{2}$

38. $\sec u = -\dfrac{7}{2}, \quad \dfrac{\pi}{2} < u < \pi$

In Exercises 39–42, use the half-angle formulas to simplify the expression.

39. $\sqrt{\dfrac{1 - \cos 6x}{2}}$ **40.** $\sqrt{\dfrac{1 + \cos 4x}{2}}$

41. $-\sqrt{\dfrac{1 - \cos 8x}{1 + \cos 8x}}$ **42.** $-\sqrt{\dfrac{1 - \cos(x - 1)}{2}}$

In Exercises 43–46, use a graphing utility to graph the function and approximate its zeros in the interval $[0, 2\pi)$. If possible, find the exact values of the zeros algebraically.

43. $f(x) = \sin \dfrac{x}{2} + \cos x$

44. $h(x) = \sin \dfrac{x}{2} + \cos x - 1$

45. $h(x) = \cos \dfrac{x}{2} - \sin x$ **46.** $g(x) = \tan \dfrac{x}{2} - \sin x$

In Exercises 47–56, use the product-to-sum formulas to write the product as a sum.

47. $6 \sin \dfrac{\pi}{4} \cos \dfrac{\pi}{4}$ **48.** $4 \sin \dfrac{\pi}{3} \cos \dfrac{5\pi}{6}$

49. $\sin 5\theta \cos 3\theta$ **50.** $3 \sin 2\alpha \sin 3\alpha$

51. $5 \cos(-5\beta) \cos 3\beta$ **52.** $\cos 2\theta \cos 4\theta$

53. $\sin(x + y) \sin(x - y)$ **54.** $\sin(x + y) \cos(x - y)$

55. $\sin(\theta + \pi) \cos(\theta - \pi)$ **56.** $10 \cos 75° \cos 15°$

In Exercises 57–66, use the sum-to-product formulas to write the sum or difference as a product.

57. $\sin 60° + \sin 30°$ **58.** $\cos 120° + \cos 30°$

59. $\cos \dfrac{3\pi}{4} - \cos \dfrac{\pi}{4}$ **60.** $\sin 5\theta - \sin 3\theta$

61. $\cos 6x + \cos 2x$ **62.** $\sin x + \sin 5x$

63. $\sin(\alpha + \beta) - \sin(\alpha - \beta)$

64. $\cos\left(\theta + \dfrac{\pi}{2}\right) - \cos\left(\theta - \dfrac{\pi}{2}\right)$

65. $\cos(\phi + 2\pi) + \cos \phi$

66. $\sin\left(x + \dfrac{\pi}{2}\right) + \sin\left(x - \dfrac{\pi}{2}\right)$

In Exercises 67–70, use a graphing utility to graph the function and approximate its zeros in the interval $[0, 2\pi)$. If possible, find the exact values of the zeros algebraically.

67. $g(x) = \sin 6x + \sin 2x$

68. $h(x) = \cos 2x - \cos 6x$

69. $f(x) = \dfrac{\cos 2x}{\sin 3x - \sin x} - 1$

70. $f(x) = \sin^2 3x - \sin^2 x$

In Exercises 71–88, verify the identity. Use a graphing utility to confirm the identity.

71. $\csc 2\theta = \dfrac{\csc \theta}{2 \cos \theta}$

72. $\sec 2\theta = \dfrac{\sec^2 \theta}{2 - \sec^2 \theta}$

73. $\cos^2 2\alpha - \sin^2 2\alpha = \cos 4\alpha$

74. $\cos^4 x - \sin^4 x = \cos 2x$

75. $(\sin x + \cos x)^2 = 1 + \sin 2x$

76. $\sin \dfrac{\alpha}{3} \cos \dfrac{\alpha}{3} = \dfrac{1}{2} \sin \dfrac{2\alpha}{3}$

77. $\cos 3\beta = \cos^3 \beta - 3 \sin^2 \beta \cos \beta$

78. $\sin 4\beta = 4 \sin \beta \cos \beta (1 - \sin^2 \beta)$

79. $1 + \cos 10y = 2 \cos^2 5y$

80. $\dfrac{\cos 3\beta}{\cos \beta} = 1 - 4 \sin^2 \beta$

81. $\sec \dfrac{u}{2} = \pm \sqrt{\dfrac{2 \tan u}{\tan u + \sin u}}$

82. $\tan \dfrac{u}{2} = \csc u - \cot u$

83. $\dfrac{\cos 4x + \cos 2x}{\sin 4x + \sin 2x} = \cot 3x$

84. $\dfrac{\cos 3x - \cos x}{\sin 3x - \sin x} = -\tan x$

85. $\dfrac{\cos 4x - \cos 2x}{2 \sin 3x} = -\sin x$

86. $\dfrac{\sin x \pm \sin y}{\cos x + \cos y} = \tan \dfrac{x \pm y}{2}$

87. $\dfrac{\cos t + \cos 3t}{\sin 3t - \sin t} = \cot t$

88. $\sin\left(\dfrac{\pi}{6} + x\right) + \sin\left(\dfrac{\pi}{6} - x\right) = \cos x$

In Exercises 89 and 90, sketch the graph of the function by using the power-reducing formulas.

89. $f(x) = \sin^2 x$ **90.** $f(x) = \cos^2 x$

In Exercises 91 and 92, write the trigonometric expression as an algebraic expression.

91. $\sin(2 \arcsin x)$ **92.** $\cos(2 \arccos x)$

In Exercises 93 and 94, prove the product-to-sum formula.

93. $\cos u \sin v = \dfrac{1}{2}[\sin(u + v) - \sin(u - v)]$

94. $\cos u \cos v = \dfrac{1}{2}[\cos(u - v) + \cos(u + v)]$

95. *Area*   The lengths of the two equal sides of an isosceles triangle are 10 feet (see figure). The angle between the two sides is θ.
  (a) Express the area of the triangle as a function of $\theta/2$.
  (b) Express the area of the triangle as a function of θ and determine the value of θ so the area is maximum.

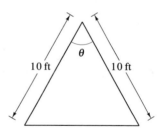

FIGURE FOR 95

96. *Projectile Motion*   The range of a projectile fired at an angle θ with the horizontal and with an initial velocity of v_0 feet per second is given by

$$r = \tfrac{1}{32} v_0^2 \sin 2\theta,$$

where r is measured in feet. Determine the expression for the range in terms of θ.

CHAPTER 7 · REVIEW EXERCISES

In Exercises 1–10, simplify the trigonometric expression.

1. $\dfrac{1}{\cot^2 x + 1}$

2. $\dfrac{\sin 2\alpha}{\cos^2 \alpha - \sin^2 \alpha}$

3. $\dfrac{\sin^2 \alpha - \cos^2 \alpha}{\sin^2 \alpha - \sin \alpha \cos \alpha}$

4. $\dfrac{\sin^3 \beta + \cos^3 \beta}{\sin \beta + \cos \beta}$

5. $\cos^2 \beta + \cos^2 \beta \tan^2 \beta$

6. $\dfrac{\sin \theta}{1 + \cos \theta} + \dfrac{1 + \cos \theta}{\sin \theta}$

7. $\tan^2 \theta (\csc^2 \theta - 1)$

8. $\dfrac{2 \tan(x + 1)}{1 - \tan^2(x + 1)}$

9. $1 - 4 \sin^2 x \cos^2 x$

10. $\sqrt{\dfrac{1 - \cos^2 x}{1 + \cos x}}$

In Exercises 11–30, verify the identity.

11. $\tan x(1 - \sin^2 x) = \frac{1}{2} \sin 2x$

12. $\cos x(\tan^2 x + 1) = \sec x$

13. $\sec^2 x \cot x - \cot x = \tan x$

14. $\sin^3 \theta + \sin \theta \cos^2 \theta = \sin \theta$

15. $\sin^5 x \cos^2 x = (\cos^2 x - 2 \cos^4 x + \cos^6 x) \sin x$

16. $\cos^3 x \sin^2 x = (\sin^2 x - \sin^4 x) \cos x$

17. $\sin 3\theta \sin \theta = \frac{1}{2}(\cos 2\theta - \cos 4\theta)$

18. $\sin 3x \cos 2x = \frac{1}{2}(\sin 5x + \sin x)$

19. $\sqrt{\dfrac{1 - \sin \theta}{1 + \sin \theta}} = \dfrac{1 - \sin \theta}{|\cos \theta|}$

20. $\sqrt{1 - \cos x} = \dfrac{|\sin x|}{\sqrt{1 + \cos x}}$

21. $\cos 3x = 4 \cos^3 x - 3 \cos x$

22. $\cos\left(x + \dfrac{\pi}{2}\right) = -\sin x$

23. $\cot\left(\dfrac{\pi}{2} - x\right) = \tan x$

24. $\sin(\pi - x) = \sin x$

25. $\dfrac{\sec x - 1}{\tan x} = \tan \dfrac{x}{2}$

26. $\dfrac{2 \cos 3x}{\sin 4x - \sin 2x} = \csc x$

27. $\dfrac{\cos 3x - \cos x}{\sin 3x - \sin x} = -\tan 2x$

28. $1 - \cos 2x = 2 \sin^2 x$

29. $2 \sin y \cos y \sec 2y = \tan 2y$

30. $\dfrac{\sin(\alpha + \beta)}{\cos \alpha \cos \beta} = \tan \alpha + \tan \beta$

In Exercises 31–36, use a graphing utility to verify the identity. (Graph each member of the equation, and note that the graphs coincide.)

31. $\sin\left(x - \dfrac{3\pi}{2}\right) = \cos x$

32. $\sin 4x = 8 \cos^3 x \sin x - 4 \cos x \sin x$

33. $\tan^2 x = \dfrac{1 - \cos 2x}{1 + \cos 2x}$

34. $\cos^2 5x - \cos^2 x = -\sin 4x \sin 6x$

35. $1 + \cos 2x + \cos 4x + \cos 6x = 4 \cos x \cos 2x \cos 3x$

36. $\sin 2x + \sin 4x - \sin 6x = 4 \sin x \sin 2x \sin 3x$

In Exercises 37–40, find the exact value of the trigonometric function by using the sum, difference, or half-angle formulas.

37. $\sin \dfrac{5\pi}{12} = \sin\left(\dfrac{2\pi}{3} - \dfrac{\pi}{4}\right)$

38. $\cos 285° = \cos(225° + 60°)$

39. $\cos(157° \, 30') = \cos \dfrac{315°}{2}$

40. $\sin \dfrac{3\pi}{8} = \sin\left[\dfrac{1}{2}\left(\dfrac{3\pi}{4}\right)\right]$

In Exercises 41–46, find the exact value of the trigonometric function given that $\sin u = \frac{3}{4}$, $\cos v = -\frac{5}{13}$, and u and v are in Quadrant II.

41. $\sin(u + v)$

42. $\tan(u + v)$

43. $\cos(u - v)$

44. $\sin 2v$

45. $\cos \dfrac{u}{2}$

46. $\tan 2v$

In Exercises 47–50, determine if the statement is true or false. If it is false, make the necessary correction.

47. If $\dfrac{\pi}{2} < \theta < \pi$, then $\cos \dfrac{\theta}{2} < 0$.

48. $\sin(x + y) = \sin x + \sin y$

49. $4 \sin(-x) \cos(-x) = -2 \sin 2x$

50. $4 \sin 45° \cos 15° = 1 + \sqrt{3}$

In Exercises 51–60, use a graphing utility to obtain a graph of the function and approximate its zeros in the interval $[0, 2\pi)$. If possible, find the exact values of the zeros algebraically.

51. $f(x) = \sin x - \tan x$

52. $f(x) = \csc x - 2 \cot x$

53. $g(x) = \sin 2x + \sqrt{2} \sin x$

54. $g(x) = \cos 4x - 7 \cos 2x - 8$

55. $h(x) = \cos^2 x + \sin x - 1$

56. $h(x) = \sin 4x - \sin 2x$

57. $y = \dfrac{1 + \sin x}{\cos x} + \dfrac{\cos x}{1 + \sin x} - 4$

58. $y = \cos x - \cos \dfrac{x}{2}$

59. $g(t) = \tan^3 t - \tan^2 t + 3 \tan t - 3$

60. $h(s) = \sin s + \sin 3s + \sin 5s$

In Exercises 61 and 62, write the trigonometric expression as a product.

61. $\cos 3\theta + \cos 2\theta$

62. $\sin\left(x + \dfrac{\pi}{4}\right) - \sin\left(x - \dfrac{\pi}{4}\right)$

In Exercises 63 and 64, write the trigonometric expression as a sum or difference.

63. $\sin 3\alpha \sin 2\alpha$

64. $\cos \dfrac{x}{2} \cos \dfrac{x}{4}$

In Exercises 65 and 66, write the trigonometric expression as an algebraic expression.

65. $\cos(2 \arccos 2x)$

66. $\sin(2 \arctan x)$

67. *Rate of Change*   The rate of change of the function $f(x) = 2\sqrt{\sin x}$ with respect to change in the variable x is given by the expression $\cos x / \sqrt{\sin x}$. Show that the expression for the rate of change can also be given by $\cot x \sqrt{\sin x}$.

68. *Projectile Motion*   A baseball leaves the hand of the first baseman at an angle of θ with the horizontal and an initial velocity of $v_0 = 80$ feet per second. The ball is caught by the second baseman 100 feet away. Find θ if the range r of a projectile is given by

$r = \frac{1}{32}v_0^2 \sin 2\theta.$

69. *Harmonic Motion*   A weight is attached to a spring suspended vertically from a ceiling. When a driving force is applied to the system, the weight moves vertically from its equilibrium position. This motion is described by the model.

$y = 1.5 \sin 8t - 0.5 \cos 8t,$

where y is the distance from equilibrium measured in feet and t is the time in seconds.

(a) Write the model in the form

$$y = \sqrt{a^2 + b^2} \sin(Bt + C).$$

(b) Use a graphing utility to obtain a graph of the model.

(c) Find the amplitude of the oscillations of the weight.

(d) Find the frequency of the oscillations of the weight.

70. *Volume*   A trough for feeding cattle is 16 feet long, and its cross sections are isosceles triangles with the two equal sides being 18 inches in length (see figure). The angle between the two equal sides is θ.

(a) Express the volume of the trough as a function of $\theta/2$.

(b) Express the volume of the trough as a function of θ and determine the value of θ so the volume is maximum.

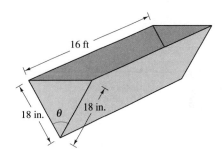

FIGURE FOR 70

ADDITIONAL TOPICS IN TRIGONOMETRY

8.1 LAW OF SINES

Law of Sines / The Ambiguous Case (SSA) / Applications / The Area of an Oblique Triangle

Law of Sines

In Chapter 6 you studied techniques for solving right triangles. In this section and the next, you will solve **oblique triangles**—triangles that have no right angles. As standard notation, we label the angles of a triangle as A, B, and C, and their opposite sides as a, b, and c, as shown in Figure 8.1.

To solve an oblique triangle, you need to know the measure of at least one side and any two other parts of the triangle—either two sides, two angles, or one angle and one side. This breaks down into four cases.

1. Two angles and any side (AAS or ASA).
2. Two sides and an angle opposite one of them (SSA).
3. Three sides (SSS).
4. Two sides and their included angle (SAS).

The first two cases can be solved using the **Law of Sines,** whereas the last two cases require the **Law of Cosines** (to be discussed in Section 8.2).

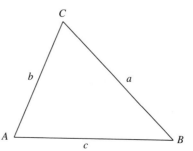

FIGURE 8.1

527

REMARK The Law of Sines can also be written in the reciprocal form

$$\frac{\sin A}{a} = \frac{\sin B}{b} = \frac{\sin C}{c}.$$

LAW OF SINES

If ABC is a triangle with sides a, b, and c, then

$$\frac{a}{\sin A} = \frac{b}{\sin B} = \frac{c}{\sin C}.$$

A is acute. A is obtuse.

Oblique Triangles

When using a calculator with the Law of Sines, remember to store all intermediate calculations. By not rounding until the final result, you minimize the round-off error.

EXAMPLE 1   Given Two Angles and One Side—AAS

Given a triangle with $C = 102.3°$, $B = 28.7°$, and $b = 27.4$ feet, as shown in Figure 8.2, find the remaining angle and sides.

SOLUTION

The third angle of the triangle is

$$A = 180° - B - C = 180° - 28.7° - 102.3° = 49.0°.$$

By the Law of Sines, you have

$$\frac{a}{\sin 49°} = \frac{b}{\sin 28.7°} = \frac{c}{\sin 102.3°}.$$

Because $b = 27.4$, you obtain

$$a = \frac{27.4}{\sin 28.7°}(\sin 49°) \approx 43.06 \text{ feet}$$

and

$$c = \frac{27.4}{\sin 28.7°}(\sin 102.3°) \approx 55.75 \text{ feet}.$$

Note that the ratio $27.4/\sin 28.7°$ occurs in both solutions, and you can save time by storing this result for repeated use.

FIGURE 8.2

When solving triangles, a careful sketch is useful as a quick test for the feasibility of an answer. Remember that the longest side lies opposite the largest angle, and the shortest side lies opposite the smallest angle of a triangle.

EXAMPLE 2   Given Two Angles and One Side—ASA

A pole tilts *toward* the sun at an 8° angle from vertical, and it casts a 22-foot shadow. The angle of elevation from the tip of the shadow to the top of the pole is 43°. How tall is the pole?

SOLUTION

In Figure 8.3, note that $A = 43°$, and $B = 90° + 8° = 98°$. Thus, the third angle is

$$C = 180° - A - B = 180° - 43° - 98° = 39°.$$

By the Law of Sines, you have

$$\frac{a}{\sin 43°} = \frac{c}{\sin 39°}.$$

Because $c = 22$ feet, the length of the pole is

$$a = \frac{22}{\sin 39°}(\sin 43°) \approx 23.84 \text{ feet}.$$

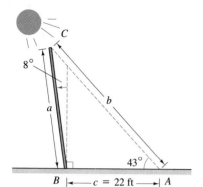

FIGURE 8.3

REMARK   For practice, try reworking Example 2 for a pole that tilts *away* from the sun under the same conditions.

The Ambiguous Case (SSA)

In Examples 1 and 2, you saw that two angles (whose sum is less than 180°) and one side determine a unique triangle. However, if two sides and one opposite angle are given, three possible situations can occur: (1) no such triangle exists, (2) one such triangle exists, or (3) two distinct triangles may satisfy the conditions. The possibilities in this *ambiguous* case (SSA) are summarized in the following table.

The Ambiguous Case (SSA) (given: *a*, *b*, and *A*)

	A Is Acute				A Is Obtuse	
Sketch $(h = b \sin A)$						
Necessary Condition	$a < h$	$a = h$	$a > b$	$h < a < b$	$a \leq b$	$a > b$
Triangles Possible	None	One	One	Two	None	One

To determine which of the possibilities holds for a given pair of sides and opposite angle, it helps to make a sketch.

EXAMPLE 3   Single-Solution Case—SSA

Given a triangle with $a = 22$ inches, $b = 12$ inches, and $A = 42°$, find the remaining side and angles.

SOLUTION

$b = 12$ in. C $a = 22$ in.

$42°$

A c B

One solution: $a > b$

FIGURE 8.4

Because A is acute and $a > b$, you know that B is also acute and there is only one triangle that satisfies the given conditions, as shown in Figure 8.4. Thus, by the Law of Sines, you have

$$\frac{22}{\sin 42°} = \frac{12}{\sin B},$$

which implies that

$$\sin B = 12\left(\frac{\sin 42°}{22}\right) \approx 0.3649803$$

$$B \approx 21.41°.$$

Now you can determine that $C \approx 180° - 42° - 21.41° = 116.59°$, and the remaining side is given by

$$\frac{c}{\sin 116.59°} = \frac{22}{\sin 42°}$$

$$c = \sin 116.59°\left(\frac{22}{\sin 42°}\right) \approx 29.40 \text{ inches.}$$

EXAMPLE 4   No-Solution Case—SSA

Show that there is no triangle that satisfies either of the following conditions.

A. $a = 15$, $b = 25$, $A = 85°$
B. $a = 15.2$, $b = 20$, $A = 110°$

SOLUTION

$a = 15$

$b = 25$

h

$85°$

A

No solution: $a < h$

FIGURE 8.5

A. Begin by making the sketch shown in Figure 8.5. From this figure it appears that no triangle is formed. You can verify this using the Law of Sines.

$$\frac{a}{\sin A} = \frac{b}{\sin B}$$

$$\frac{15}{\sin 85°} = \frac{25}{\sin B}$$

$$\sin B = 25\left(\frac{\sin 85°}{15}\right) \approx 1.660 > 1$$

This contradicts the fact that $|\sin B| \le 1$. Hence, no triangle can be formed having sides $a = 15$ and $b = 25$ and an angle of $A = 85°$.

B. Because A is obtuse and $a = 15.2$ is less than $b = 20$, you can conclude that there is *no solution*, as shown in Figure 8.6. Try using the Law of Sines to verify this.

■■■■■■■■■

$a = 15.2$

$b = 20$

$110°$

A

No solution: $a < b$ and $A > 90°$

FIGURE 8.6

EXAMPLE 5   Two-Solution Case—SSA
••••••••••••••••

Find two triangles for which $a = 12$ meters, $b = 31$ meters, and $A = 20.5°$.

SOLUTION

To begin, note that

$$h = b \sin A = 31(\sin 20.5°) \approx 10.86 \text{ meters.}$$

Hence, $h < a < b$, and you can conclude that there are two possible triangles. By the Law of Sines, you obtain

$$\frac{a}{\sin A} = \frac{b}{\sin B},$$

which implies that

$$\sin B = b\left(\frac{\sin A}{a}\right) = 31\left(\frac{\sin 20.5°}{12}\right) \approx 0.9047 \text{ meters.}$$

There are two angles $B_1 \approx 64.8°$ and $B_2 \approx 115.2°$ between $0°$ and $180°$ whose sine is 0.9047. For $B_1 \approx 64.8°$, you obtain

$$C \approx 180° - 20.5° - 64.8° = 94.7°$$

$$c = \frac{a}{\sin A}(\sin C) = \frac{12}{\sin 20.5°}(\sin 94.7°) \approx 34.15.$$

For $B_2 \approx 115.2°$, you obtain

$$C \approx 180° - 20.5° - 115.2° = 44.3°$$

$$c = \frac{a}{\sin A}(\sin C) = \frac{12}{\sin 20.5°}(\sin 44.3°) \approx 23.93 \text{ meters.}$$

The resulting triangles are shown in Figures 8.7 and 8.8.

■■■■■■■■■

$b = 31$ m $a = 12$ m

A $20.5°$ $64.8°$ B_1

FIGURE 8.7

$b = 31$ m $a = 12$ m

A $20.5°$ $115.2°$

B_2

FIGURE 8.8

FIGURE 8.9

FIGURE 8.10

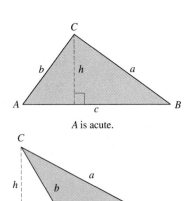

A is acute.

A is obtuse.

Oblique Triangles

FIGURE 8.11

Applications

EXAMPLE 6   An Application of the Law of Sines

The course for a boat race starts at point *A* and proceeds in the direction S 52° W to point *B*, then in the direction S 40° E to point *C*, and finally back to *A*, as shown in Figure 8.9. The point *C* lies 8 kilometers directly south of point *A*. Approximate the total distance of the race course.

SOLUTION

Because lines *BD* and *AC* are parallel, it follows that $\angle BCA = \angle DBC$. Consequently, triangle *ABC* has the measures shown in Figure 8.10. For angle *B*, you have

$$B = 180° - 52° - 40° = 88°.$$

Using the Law of Sines

$$\frac{a}{\sin 52°} = \frac{b}{\sin 88°} = \frac{c}{\sin 40°},$$

you can let $b = 8$ and obtain the following.

$$a = \frac{8}{\sin 88°}(\sin 52°) \approx 6.308$$

$$c = \frac{8}{\sin 88°}(\sin 40°) \approx 5.145$$

Finally, the total length of the course is approximately

$$\text{Length} \approx 8 + 6.308 + 5.145 = 19.453 \text{ kilometers.}$$

The Area of an Oblique Triangle

The procedure used to prove the Law of Sines leads to a simple formula for the area of an oblique triangle. Referring to Figure 8.11, note that each triangle has a height of

$$h = b \sin A.$$

Consequently, the area of each triangle is given by

$$\text{Area} = \frac{1}{2}(\text{base})(\text{height}) = \frac{1}{2}(c)(b \sin A) = \frac{1}{2}bc \sin A.$$

By similar arguments, you can develop the formula

$$\text{Area} = \frac{1}{2}ab \sin C = \frac{1}{2}ac \sin B.$$

AREA OF AN OBLIQUE TRIANGLE

The area of any triangle is given by one-half the product of the lengths of two sides times the sine of their included angle. That is,

$$\text{Area} = \frac{1}{2}bc \sin A = \frac{1}{2}ab \sin C = \frac{1}{2}ac \sin B.$$

EXAMPLE 7   Finding the Area of an Oblique Triangle

Find the area of a triangular lot having two sides of lengths 90 meters and 52 meters and an included angle of 102°.

SOLUTION

Consider $a = 90$ m, $b = 52$ m, and angle $C = 102°$, as shown in Figure 8.12. Then the area of the triangle is

$$\text{Area} = \frac{1}{2}ab \sin C = \frac{1}{2}(90)(52)(\sin 102°) \approx 2289 \text{ square meters.}$$

$b = 52$ m

$102°$

C $a = 90$ m

FIGURE 8.12

$$\frac{\sin 88°}{8 \text{ km}} = \frac{\sin 52°}{BC} \implies BC = 6.3$$

$$5.1$$

DISCUSSION PROBLEM

SOLVING RIGHT TRIANGLES

In this section, you have been using the Law of Sines to solve *oblique* triangles. Can the Law of Sines also be used to solve a right triangle? If so, write a short paragraph explaining how to use the Law of Sines to solve the following two triangles. Is there an easier way to solve these triangles?

(a) (AAS)   (b) (ASA)

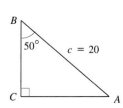

B

$50°$ $c = 20$

C A

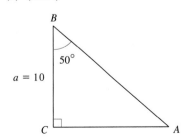

B

$50°$

$a = 10$

C A

WARM-UP
· · · · · · · · · · · · · · · ·

The following warm-up exercises involve skills that were covered in earlier sections. You will use these skills in the exercise set for this section.

In Exercises 1–6, solve the indicated *right* triangle. (In the right triangle, a and b are the lengths of the sides and c is the length of the hypotenuse.)

1. $a = 3$, $c = 6$ **2.** $a = 5$, $b = 5$ **3.** $b = 15$, $c = 17$

4. $A = 42°$, $a = 7.5$ **5.** $B = 10°$, $b = 4$ **6.** $B = 72° \ 15'$, $c = 150$

In Exercises 7 and 8, find the altitude of the triangle.

7.

8.

In Exercises 9 and 10, solve the equation for x.

9. $\dfrac{2}{\sin 30°} = \dfrac{9}{x}$ **10.** $\dfrac{100}{\sin 72°} = \dfrac{x}{\sin 60°}$

SECTION 8.1 · EXERCISES
· ·

In Exercises 1–16, use the given information to find the remaining sides and angles of the triangle labeled as shown in Figure 8.1.

1.

4.

5. $A = 36°$, $a = 8$, $b = 5$

6. $A = 60°$, $a = 9$, $c = 10$

7. $A = 150°$, $C = 20°$, $a = 200$

8. $A = 24.3°$, $C = 54.6°$, $c = 2.68$

2.

9. $A = 83° \ 20'$, $C = 54.6°$, $c = 18.1$

10. $A = 5° \ 40'$, $B = 8° \ 15'$, $b = 4.8$

11. $B = 15° \ 30'$, $a = 4.5$, $b = 6.8$

12. $C = 85° \ 20'$, $a = 35$, $c = 50$

13. $C = 145°$, $b = 4$, $c = 14$

14. $A = 100°$, $a = 125$, $c = 10$

3.

15. $A = 110° \ 15'$, $a = 48$, $b = 16$

16. $B = 2° \ 45'$, $b = 6.2$, $c = 5.8$

In Exercises 17–22, use the given information to find (if possible) the remaining sides and angles of the triangle. If two solutions exist, find both.

17. $A = 58°$, $a = 4.5$, $b = 12.8$
18. $A = 58°$, $a = 11.4$, $b = 12.8$
19. $A = 58°$, $a = 4.5$, $b = 5$
20. $A = 58°$, $a = 42.4$, $b = 50$
21. $A = 110°$, $a = 125$, $b = 200$
22. $A = 110°$, $a = 125$, $b = 100$

In Exercises 23 and 24, find a value for b such that the triangle has (a) one solution, (b) two solutions, and (c) no solution.

23. $A = 36°$, $a = 5$ **24.** $A = 60°$, $a = 10$

In Exercises 25–30, find the area of the triangle having the indicated sides and angles.

25. $C = 120°$, $a = 4$, $b = 6$
26. $B = 72° 30'$, $a = 105$, $c = 64$
27. $A = 43° 45'$, $b = 57$, $c = 85$
28. $A = 5° 15'$, $b = 4.5$, $c = 22$
29. $B = 130°$, $a = 62$, $c = 20$
30. $C = 84° 30'$, $a = 16$, $b = 20$

31. *Streetlight Design* Find the length d of the brace required to support the streetlight in the figure.

FIGURE FOR 31

32. *Height* Because of the prevailing winds, a tree grew so that it was leaning 6° from the vertical. At a point 100 feet away from the tree, the angle of elevation to the top of the tree is 22° 50' (see figure). Find the height h of the tree.

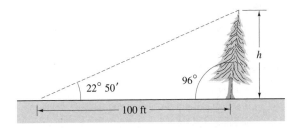

FIGURE FOR 32

33. *Bridge Design* A bridge is to be built across a small lake from B to C (see figure). The bearing from B to C is S 41° W. From a point A, 100 yards from B, the bearings to B and C are S 74° E and S 28° E, respectively. Find the distance from B to C.

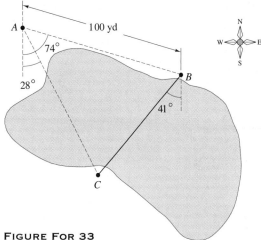

FIGURE FOR 33

34. *Railroad Track Design* The circular arc of a railroad curve has a chord of length 3000 feet, and a central angle of 40° (see figure). Find (a) the radius r of the circular arc and (b) the length s of the circular arc.

FIGURE FOR 34

35. *Altitude* The angles of elevation to an airplane from two points *A* and *B* on level ground are 51° and 68°, respectively. The points *A* and *B* are 6 miles apart, and the airplane is between these positions in the same vertical plane. Find the altitude of the airplane.

36. *Altitude* The angles of elevation to an airplane from two points *A* and *B* on level ground are 51° and 68°, respectively. The points *A* and *B* are 2.5 miles apart, and the airplane is east of both points in the same vertical plane. Find the altitude of the plane.

37. *Locating a Fire* Two fire towers *A* and *B* are 18.5 miles apart. The bearing from *A* to *B* is N 65° E. A fire is spotted by the ranger in each tower, and its bearings from *A* and *B* are N 28° E and N 16.5° W, respectively (see figure). Find the distance of the fire from each tower.

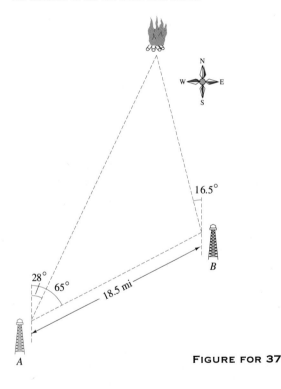

FIGURE FOR 37

38. *Distance* A boat is sailing due east parallel to the shoreline at a speed of 10 miles per hour. At a given time, the bearing to the lighthouse is S 72° E, and 15 minutes later the bearing is S 66° E (see figure). Find the distance from the boat to the shoreline if the lighthouse is at the shoreline.

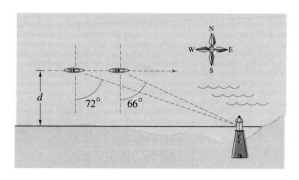

FIGURE FOR 38

39. *Distance* A family is traveling due west on a road that passes a famous landmark. At a given time, the bearing to the landmark is N 62° W, and after traveling 5 miles farther the bearing is N 38° W. What is the closest the family will come to the landmark while on the road?

40. *Engine Design* The connecting rod in a certain engine is 6 inches long, and the radius of the crankshaft is $1\frac{1}{2}$ inches (see figure). The spark plug fires at 5° before top dead center. How far is the piston from the top of its stroke at this time?

FIGURE FOR 40

41. *Verification of Testimony* The following information about a triangular parcel of land is given at a zoning board meeting: "One side is 450 feet long, and another is 120 feet long. The angle opposite the shorter side is 30°." Could this information be correct?

42. *Distance*   The angles of elevation to an airplane, θ and ϕ, are being continuously monitored at two observation points A and B, which are 2 miles apart (see figure). Write an equation giving the distance d between the plane and point B in terms of θ and ϕ.

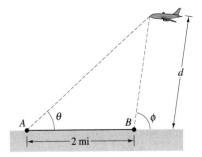

FIGURE FOR 42

8.2   LAW OF COSINES

Law of Cosines / Heron's Formula

Law of Cosines

Two cases remain in the list of conditions needed to solve an oblique triangle—SSS and SAS. The Law of Sines does not work in either of these cases. To see why, consider the three ratios given in the Law of Sines.

$$\frac{a}{\sin A} = \frac{b}{\sin B} = \frac{c}{\sin C}$$

To use the Law of Sines, you must know at least one side and its opposite angle. If you are given three sides (SSS), or two sides and their included angle (SAS), none of the above ratios would be complete. In such cases you must rely on the **Law of Cosines.**

LAW OF COSINES

If ABC is a triangle with sides a, b, and c, then the following equations are valid.

Standard Form

$$a^2 = b^2 + c^2 - 2bc \cos A$$

$$b^2 = a^2 + c^2 - 2ac \cos B$$

$$c^2 = a^2 + b^2 - 2ab \cos C$$

Alternative Form

$$\cos A = \frac{b^2 + c^2 - a^2}{2bc}$$

$$\cos B = \frac{a^2 + c^2 - b^2}{2ac}$$

$$\cos C = \frac{a^2 + b^2 - c^2}{2ab}$$

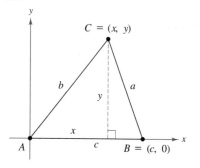

FIGURE 8.13

PROOF

We prove only the first equation for a triangle that has three acute angles, as shown in Figure 8.13. In the figure, note that vertex B has coordinates $(c, 0)$. Furthermore, C has coordinates (x, y), where $x = b \cos A$ and $y = b \sin A$. Because a is the distance from C to B, you have

$$a = \sqrt{(x - c)^2 + (y - 0)^2}$$
$$a^2 = (b \cos A - c)^2 + (b \sin A)^2$$
$$= b^2 \cos^2 A - 2bc \cos A + c^2 + b^2 \sin^2 A$$
$$= b^2(\sin^2 A + \cos^2 A) + c^2 - 2bc \cos A.$$

Using the identity $\sin^2 A + \cos^2 A = 1$ produces

$$a^2 = b^2 + c^2 - 2bc \cos A.$$

Similar arguments can be used to establish the other two equations.

Note that if $A = 90°$ in Figure 8.13, then $\cos A = 0$, and the first form of the Law of Cosines becomes the Pythagorean Theorem.

$$a^2 = b^2 + c^2$$

Thus, the Pythagorean Theorem is actually just a special case of the more general Law of Cosines.

EXAMPLE 1 Given Three Sides of a Triangle—SSS

Find the three angles of the triangle whose sides have lengths $a = 8$ feet, $b = 19$ feet, and $c = 14$ feet.

SOLUTION

It is a good idea first to find the angle opposite the longest side—side b in this case (see Figure 8.14). Using the Law of Cosines produces

$$\cos B = \frac{a^2 + c^2 - b^2}{2ac} = \frac{8^2 + 14^2 - 19^2}{2(8)(14)} \approx -0.45089.$$

Because $\cos B$ is negative, you know B is an *obtuse* angle given by $B \approx 116.80°$. At this point you could use the Law of Cosines to find $\cos A$ and $\cos C$. However, knowing that $B \approx 116.80°$, it is simpler to use the Law of Sines to obtain the following.

$$\frac{b}{\sin B} = \frac{a}{\sin A}$$

$$\sin A = a\left(\frac{\sin B}{b}\right) \approx 8\left(\frac{\sin 116.80°}{19}\right) \approx 0.37582$$

FIGURE 8.14

Because B is obtuse, you know that A must be acute, because a triangle can have, at most, one obtuse angle. Thus, $A \approx 22.08°$ and

$$C \approx 180° - 22.08° - 116.80° = 41.12°.$$

Do you see why it was wise to find the largest angle *first* in Example 1? Knowing the cosine of an angle, you can determine whether the angle is acute or obtuse. That is,

$$\cos \theta > 0 \quad \text{for} \quad 0° < \theta < 90° \qquad \textit{Acute}$$
$$\cos \theta < 0 \quad \text{for} \quad 90° < \theta < 180°. \qquad \textit{Obtuse}$$

So, in Example 1, once you found that B was obtuse, you could determine that A and C were both acute. If the largest angle is acute, then the remaining two angles will be acute also.

EXAMPLE 2   Given Two Sides and the Included Angle—SAS

The pitcher's mound on a softball field is 46 feet from home plate, and the distance between the bases is 60 feet, as shown in Figure 8.15. How far is the pitcher's mound from first base? (Note that the pitcher's mound is *not* halfway between home plate and second base.)

SOLUTION

From triangle HPF, you can see that $H = 45°$ (line HP bisects the right angle at H), $f = 46$, and $p = 60$. Using the Law of Cosines for this SAS case produces

$$\begin{aligned}
h^2 &= f^2 + p^2 - 2fp \cos H \\
&= 46^2 + 60^2 - 2(46)(60) \cos 45° \\
&\approx 1812.8.
\end{aligned}$$

Therefore, the approximate distance from the pitcher's mound to first base is

$$h \approx \sqrt{1812.8} \approx 42.58 \text{ feet.}$$

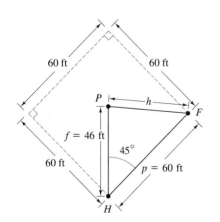

FIGURE 8.15

EXAMPLE 3   Given Two Sides and the Included Angle—SAS

A ship travels 60 miles due east, then adjusts its course 15° northward, as shown in Figure 8.16. After traveling 80 miles in that direction, how far is the ship from its point of departure?

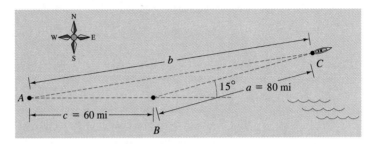

FIGURE 8.16

SOLUTION

You have $c = 60$, $B = 180° - 15° = 165°$, and $a = 80$. Consequently, by the Law of Cosines, you obtain

$$b^2 = a^2 + c^2 - 2ac \cos B$$
$$= 80^2 + 60^2 - 2(80)(60) \cos 165° \approx 19{,}273.$$

Therefore, the distance b is

$$b \approx \sqrt{19{,}273} \approx 138.8 \text{ miles.}$$

Heron's Formula

The following formula for the area of a triangle is credited to the Greek mathematician Heron (c. 100 B.C.).

HERON'S AREA FORMULA

Given any triangle with sides of lengths a, b, and c, the area of the triangle is

$$\text{Area} = \sqrt{s(s - a)(s - b)(s - c)},$$

where $s = (a + b + c)/2$ is one-half the perimeter of the triangle.

EXAMPLE 4   Using Heron's Area Formula

Find the area of the triangular region having sides of lengths $a = 47$ yards, $b = 58$ yards, and $c = 78.6$ yards.

SOLUTION

Because

$$s = \frac{1}{2}(a + b + c) = \frac{183.6}{2} = 91.8,$$

Heron's Formula yields

$$\begin{aligned} \text{Area} &= \sqrt{s(s - a)(s - b)(s - c)} \\ &= \sqrt{91.8(44.8)(33.8)(13.2)} \\ &\approx 1354.58 \text{ square yards.} \end{aligned}$$

DISCUSSION PROBLEM

THE AREA OF A TRIANGLE

We have now discussed three different formulas for the area of a triangle.

Standard formula: Area $= \frac{1}{2}bh$

Oblique triangle: Area $= \frac{1}{2}bc \sin A = \frac{1}{2}ab \sin C = \frac{1}{2}ac \sin B$

Heron's formula: Area $= \sqrt{s(s - a)(s - b)(s - c)}, \quad s = \frac{1}{2}(a + b + c)$

Use the most appropriate formula to find the area of each of the following triangles. Show your work and give your reason for choosing each formula.

(a)

(b)

(c)

WARM-UP

· · · · · · · · · · · · · · ·

The following warm-up exercises involve skills that were covered in earlier sections. You will use these skills in the exercise set for this section.

In Exercises 1 and 2, simplify the expression.

1. $\sqrt{(7-3)^2 + [1-(-5)]^2}$

2. $\sqrt{[-2-(-5)]^2 + (12-6)^2}$

In Exercises 3 and 4, find the distance between the two points.

3. $(4, -2), (8, 10)$

4. $(1, 3), (7, 12)$

In Exercises 5 and 6, find the area of the triangle.

5.

6.

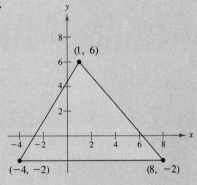

In Exercises 7–10, find (if possible) the remaining sides and angles of the triangle.

7. $A = 10°, \quad C = 100°, \quad b = 25$

8. $A = 20°, \quad C = 90°, \quad c = 100$

9. $B = 30°, \quad b = 6.5, \quad c = 15$

10. $A = 30°, \quad b = 6.5, \quad a = 10$

SECTION 8.2 · EXERCISES

· ·

In Exercises 1–14, use the Law of Cosines to solve the triangle.

1.

2.

3.

4.

5. $a = 9, \quad b = 12, \quad c = 15$

6. $a = 55, \quad b = 25, \quad c = 72$

7. $a = 75.4, \quad b = 52, \quad c = 52$

8. $a = 1.42, \quad b = 0.75, \quad c = 1.25$

9. $A = 120°, \quad b = 3, \quad c = 10$

10. $A = 55°, \quad b = 3, \quad c = 10$

11. $B = 8° 45', \quad a = 25, \quad c = 15$

12. $B = 75° 20', \quad a = 6.2, \quad c = 9.5$

13. $C = 125° 40', \quad a = 32, \quad b = 32$

14. $C = 15°, \quad a = 6.25, \quad b = 2.15$

In Exercises 15–20, complete the table by solving the parallelogram shown in the figure. (The lengths of the diagonals are c and d.)

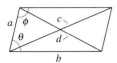

FIGURE FOR 15–20

	a	b	c	d	θ	ϕ
15.	4	6			30°	
16.	25	35				120°
17.	10	14	20			
18.	40	60		80		
19.	10		18	12		
20.		25	50	35		

In Exercises 21–26, use Heron's Formula to find the area of the triangle.

21. $a = 5, \quad b = 7, \quad c = 10$
22. $a = 2.5, \quad b = 10.2, \quad c = 9$
23. $a = 12, \quad b = 15, \quad c = 9$
24. $a = 75.4, \quad b = 52, \quad c = 52$
25. $a = 20, \quad b = 20, \quad c = 10$
26. $a = 4.25, \quad b = 1.55, \quad c = 3.00$

27. *Area*   The lengths of the sides of a triangular parcel of land are approximately 400 feet, 500 feet, and 700 feet. Approximate the area of the parcel.

28. *Area*   The lengths of two adjacent sides of a parallelogram are 4 yards and 6 yards. Find the area of the parallelogram if the angle between the two sides is 30°.

29. *Navigation*   A boat race is run along a triangular course marked by buoys A, B, and C. The race starts with the boats headed west. The other two sides of the course lie to the north of the first side, and their lengths are 3500 feet and 6500 feet (see figure). Find the bearings for the last two legs of the race.

FIGURE FOR 29

30. *Navigation*   A plane flies 675 miles from A to B with a bearing of N 75° E. Then it flies 540 miles from B to C with a bearing of N 32° E (see figure). Find the straight-line distance and bearing from C to A.

FIGURE FOR 30

31. *Distance*   Two ships leave a port at 9 A.M. One travels at a bearing of N 53° W at 12 miles per hour and the other at a bearing of S 67° W at 16 miles per hour. Approximately how far apart are they at noon that day?

32. *Distance*   A 100-foot vertical tower is to be erected on the side of a hill that makes an 8° angle with the horizontal (see figure). Find the length of each of the two guy wires that will be anchored 75 feet uphill and downhill from the base of the tower.

FIGURE FOR 32

33. *Surveying*   To approximate the length of a marsh, a surveyor walks 950 feet from point A to point B, then turns 80° and walks 800 feet to point C (see figure). Approximate the length $\overline{AC}$ of the marsh.

FIGURE FOR 33

34. *Surveying* A triangular parcel of land has 375 feet of frontage, and the other boundaries have lengths of 250 feet and 300 feet. What angles does the frontage make with the two other boundaries?

35. *Streetlight Design* Determine the angle θ in the design of the streetlight as shown in the figure.

FIGURE FOR 35

36. *Aircraft Tracking* In order to determine the distance between two aircraft, a tracking station continuously determines the distance to each aircraft and the angle α between them. Determine the distance a between the planes when $\alpha = 42°$, $b = 35$ miles, and $c = 20$ miles.

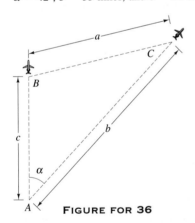

FIGURE FOR 36

37. *Engineering* If Q is the midpoint of the line segment $\overline{PR}$, find the lengths of the line segments $\overline{PQ}$, $\overline{QS}$, and $\overline{RS}$ on the truss rafter shown in the figure.

FIGURE FOR 37

38. *Paper Manufacturing* In a certain process with continuous paper, the paper passes across three rollers of radii 3 inches, 4 inches, and 6 inches (see figure). The centers of the 3-inch and 6-inch rollers are d inches apart, and the length of the arc in contact with the paper on the 4-inch roller is s inches. Complete the following table.

d (inches)	9	10	12	13	14	15	16
θ (degrees)							
s (inches)							

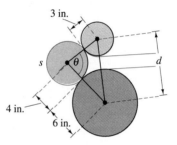

FIGURE FOR 38

39. *Navigation* On a certain map, Orlando is 7 inches due south of Niagara Falls, Denver is 10.75 inches from Orlando, and Denver is 9.25 inches from Niagara Falls (see figure).
(a) Find the bearing of Denver from Orlando.
(b) Find the bearing of Denver from Niagara Falls.

FIGURE FOR 39

40. *Navigation*   On a certain map, Minneapolis is 6.5 inches due west of Albany, Phoenix is 8.5 inches from Minneapolis, and Phoenix is 14.5 inches from Albany (see figure).
   (a) Find the bearing of Minneapolis from Phoenix.
   (b) Find the bearing of Albany from Phoenix.

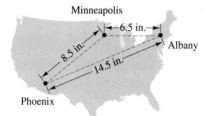

FIGURE FOR 40

41. *Baseball*   In a (square) baseball diamond with 90-foot sides, the pitcher's mound is 60 feet from home plate.
   (a) How far is it from the pitcher's mound to third base?
   (b) When a runner is halfway from second to third, how far is the runner from the pitcher's mound?

42. *Baseball*   The baseball player in center field is playing approximately 330 feet from the television camera that is behind home plate. A batter hits a fly ball that goes to the wall 420 feet from the camera (see figure). Approximate the number of feet that the center fielder had to run to make the catch if the camera turned 9° in following the play.

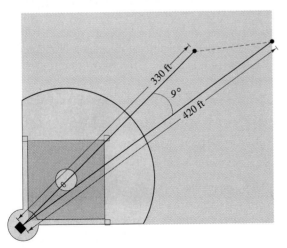

FIGURE FOR 42

43. *Awning Design*   A retractable awning lowers at an angle of 50° from the top of a patio door that is 7 feet high (see figure). Find the length x of the awning if no direct sunlight is to enter the door when the angle of elevation of the sun is greater than 65°.

44. *Circumscribed and Inscribed Circles*   Let R and r be the radii of the circumscribed and inscribed circles of a triangle ABC, respectively, and let $s = (a + b + c)/2$ (see figure). Prove the following.

   (a) $2R = \dfrac{a}{\sin A} = \dfrac{b}{\sin B} = \dfrac{c}{\sin C}$

   (b) $r = \sqrt{\dfrac{(s - a)(s - b)(s - c)}{s}}$

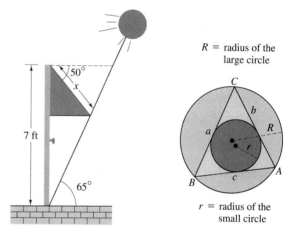

FIGURE FOR 43   FIGURE FOR 44

Circumscribed and Inscribed Circles   In Exercises 45 and 46, use the results of Exercise 44.

45. Given the triangle with $a = 25$, $b = 55$, and $c = 72$, find the areas of (a) the triangle, (b) the circumscribed circle, and (c) the inscribed circle.

46. Find the length of the largest circular track that can be built on a triangular piece of property whose sides measure 200 feet, 250 feet, and 325 feet.

47. Use the Law of Cosines to prove that
$$\frac{1}{2}bc(1 + \cos A) = \frac{a + b + c}{2} \cdot \frac{-a + b + c}{2}.$$

48. Use the Law of Cosines to prove that
$$\frac{1}{2}bc(1 - \cos A) = \frac{a - b + c}{2} \cdot \frac{a + b - c}{2}.$$

8.3 VECTORS IN THE PLANE

Vectors in the Plane / Component Form of a Vector / Vector Operations / Unit Vectors / Direction Angles / Applications of Vectors

Vectors in the Plane

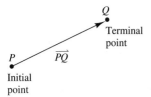

FIGURE 8.17

Many quantities in geometry and physics, such as area, time, and temperature, can be represented by a single real number. Other quantities, such as force and velocity, involve both *magnitude* and *direction* and cannot be completely characterized by a single real number. To represent such a quantity, we use a **directed line segment,** as shown in Figure 8.17. The directed line segment $\overrightarrow{PQ}$ has **initial point** P and **terminal point** Q, and we denote its **length** by $\|PQ\|$.

Two directed line segments that have the same length (or magnitude) and direction are called **equivalent.** For example, the directed line segments in Figure 8.18 are all equivalent. The set of all directed line segments that are equivalent to a given directed line segment $\overrightarrow{PQ}$ is a **vector v in the plane,** and we write $\mathbf{v} = \overrightarrow{PQ}$. Vectors are denoted by lower-case, boldface letters such as $\mathbf{u}$, $\mathbf{v}$, and $\mathbf{w}$.

FIGURE 8.18   Equivalent Directed Line Segments

EXAMPLE 1   Vector Representation by Directed Line Segments

The vector $\mathbf{u}$ is represented by the directed line segment from $P = (0, 0)$ to $Q = (3, 2)$, and the vector $\mathbf{v}$ is represented by the directed line segment from $R = (1, 2)$ to $S = (4, 4)$, as shown in Figure 8.19. Show that $\mathbf{u} = \mathbf{v}$.

SOLUTION

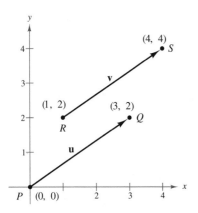

FIGURE 8.19

From the distance formula, you can see that $\overrightarrow{PQ}$ and $\overrightarrow{RS}$ have the *same length.*

$$\|\overrightarrow{PQ}\| = \sqrt{(3 - 0)^2 + (2 - 0)^2} = \sqrt{13}$$
$$\|\overrightarrow{RS}\| = \sqrt{(4 - 1)^2 + (4 - 2)^2} = \sqrt{13}$$

Moreover, both line segments have the *same direction* because they are both directed toward the upper right on lines having a slope of $\frac{2}{3}$. Thus, $\overrightarrow{PQ}$ and $\overrightarrow{RS}$ have the same length and direction, and you can conclude that $\mathbf{u} = \mathbf{v}$.

Component Form of a Vector

The directed line segment whose initial point is the origin is often the most convenient representative of a set of equivalent directed line segments. This representative of the vector **v** is in **standard position.**

A vector whose initial point is at the origin (0, 0) can be uniquely represented by the coordinates of its terminal point (v_1, v_2). We call this the **component form of a vector v** and write

$$\mathbf{v} = \langle v_1, v_2 \rangle.$$

The coordinates v_1 and v_2 are the **components** of **v**. If both the initial point and the terminal point lie at the origin, then **v** is the **zero vector** and is denoted by $\mathbf{0} = \langle 0, 0 \rangle$. To convert directed line segments to component form, use the following procedure.

COMPONENT FORM OF A VECTOR

The component form of the vector with initial point $P = (p_1, p_2)$ and terminal point $Q = (q_1, q_2)$ is

$$\overrightarrow{PQ} = \langle q_1 - p_1, q_2 - p_2 \rangle = \langle v_1, v_2 \rangle = \mathbf{v}.$$

The **length** (or magnitude) of **v** is given by

$$\|\mathbf{v}\| = \sqrt{(q_1 - p_1)^2 + (q_2 - p_2)^2} = \sqrt{v_1{}^2 + v_2{}^2}.$$

If $\|\mathbf{v}\| = 1$, then **v** is a **unit vector.** Moreover, $\|\mathbf{v}\| = 0$ if and only if **v** is the zero vector **0**.

Two vectors $\mathbf{u} = \langle u_1, u_2 \rangle$ and $\mathbf{v} = \langle v_1, v_2 \rangle$ are **equal** if and only if $u_1 = v_1$ and $u_2 = v_2$. For instance, in Example 1, the vector **u** from $P = (0, 0)$ to $Q = (3, 2)$ is

$$\mathbf{u} = \overrightarrow{PQ} = \langle 3 - 0, 2 - 0 \rangle = \langle 3, 2 \rangle,$$

and the vector **v** from $R = (1, 2)$ to $S = (4, 4)$ is

$$\mathbf{v} = \overrightarrow{RS} = \langle 4 - 1, 4 - 2 \rangle = \langle 3, 2 \rangle,$$

which shows that **u** and **v** are equal.

Component form of **v**:
$$\mathbf{v} = \langle -5, 12 \rangle$$

FIGURE 8.20

EXAMPLE 2 Finding the Component Form and Length of a Vector

Find the component form and length of the vector **v** that has initial point $(4, -7)$ and terminal point $(-1, 5)$.

SOLUTION

Let $P = (4, -7) = (p_1, p_2)$ and $Q = (-1, 5) = (q_1, q_2)$. The components of $\mathbf{v} = \langle v_1, v_2 \rangle$ are given by

$$v_1 = q_1 - p_1 = -1 - 4 = -5$$
$$v_2 = q_2 - p_2 = 5 - (-7) = 12.$$

Thus, $\mathbf{v} = \langle -5, 12 \rangle$ and the length of **v** is

$$\|\mathbf{v}\| = \sqrt{(-5)^2 + 12^2} = \sqrt{169} = 13,$$

as shown in Figure 8.20.

Vector Operations

The two basic vector operations are **scalar multiplication** and **vector addition**. (In this text, we use the term **scalar** to mean a real number.) Geometrically, the product of a vector **v** and a scalar k is the vector that is $|k|$ times as long as **v**. If k is positive, then $k\mathbf{v}$ has the same direction as **v**, and if k is negative, then $k\mathbf{v}$ has the opposite direction of **v**, as shown in Figure 8.21.

To add two vectors geometrically, position them (without changing length or direction) so that the initial point of one coincides with the terminal point of the other. The sum $\mathbf{u} + \mathbf{v}$ is formed by joining the initial point of the second vector **v** with the terminal point of the first vector **u**, as shown in Figure 8.22. Because the vector $\mathbf{u} + \mathbf{v}$ is the diagonal of a parallelogram having **u** and **v** as its adjacent sides, we call this the **parallelogram law** for vector addition.

Vector addition and scalar multiplication can also be defined using components of vectors.

FIGURE 8.21

FIGURE 8.22 To find $\mathbf{u} + \mathbf{v}$,

move the initial point of **v** to the terminal point of **u**.

Scalar Multiplication of **v**

DEFINITION OF VECTOR ADDITION AND SCALAR MULTIPLICATION

Let $\mathbf{u} = \langle u_1, u_2 \rangle$ and $\mathbf{v} = \langle v_1, v_2 \rangle$ be vectors and let k be a scalar (a real number). Then the **sum** of $\mathbf{u}$ and $\mathbf{v}$ is the vector

$$\mathbf{u} + \mathbf{v} = \langle u_1 + v_1, u_2 + v_2 \rangle, \qquad \textit{Sum}$$

and the **scalar multiple** of k times $\mathbf{u}$ is the vector

$$k\mathbf{u} = k\langle u_1, u_2 \rangle = \langle ku_1, ku_2 \rangle. \qquad \textit{Scalar multiple}$$

The **negative** of $\mathbf{v} = \langle v_1, v_2 \rangle$ is

$$-\mathbf{v} = (-1)\mathbf{v} = \langle -v_1, -v_2 \rangle, \qquad \textit{Negative}$$

and the **difference** of $\mathbf{u}$ and $\mathbf{v}$ is

$$\mathbf{u} - \mathbf{v} = \mathbf{u} + (-\mathbf{v}) = \langle u_1 - v_1, u_2 - v_2 \rangle. \quad \textit{Difference}$$

To represent $\mathbf{u} - \mathbf{v}$ graphically, we use directed line segments with the *same* initial points. The difference $\mathbf{u} - \mathbf{v}$ is the vector from the terminal point of $\mathbf{v}$ to the terminal point of $\mathbf{u}$, as shown in Figure 8.23.

Vector Subtraction

FIGURE 8.23

(a)

(b)

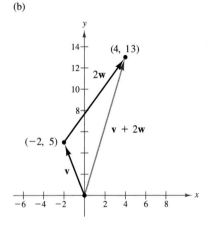

(c)

FIGURE 8.24

EXAMPLE 3 Vector Operations

Let $\mathbf{v} = \langle -2, 5 \rangle$ and $\mathbf{w} = \langle 3, 4 \rangle$, and find the following vectors.

A. $2\mathbf{v}$

B. $\mathbf{w} - \mathbf{v}$

C. $\mathbf{v} + 2\mathbf{w}$

SOLUTION

Sketches of the vectors are shown in Figure 8.24.

A. Because $\mathbf{v} = \langle -2, 5 \rangle$, you have

$$2\mathbf{v} = \langle 2(-2), 2(5) \rangle = \langle -4, 10 \rangle.$$

B. The difference of $\mathbf{w}$ and $\mathbf{v}$ is given by

$$\mathbf{w} - \mathbf{v} = \langle 3 - (-2), 4 - 5 \rangle = \langle 5, -1 \rangle.$$

C. Because $2\mathbf{w} = \langle 6, 8 \rangle$, it follows that

$$\begin{aligned} \mathbf{v} + 2\mathbf{w} &= \langle -2, 5 \rangle + \langle 6, 8 \rangle \\ &= \langle -2 + 6, 5 + 8 \rangle \\ &= \langle 4, 13 \rangle. \end{aligned}$$

Vector addition and scalar multiplication share many of the properties of ordinary arithmetic.

PROPERTIES OF VECTOR ADDITION AND SCALAR MULTIPLICATION

Let $\mathbf{u}, \mathbf{v},$ and $\mathbf{w}$ be vectors, and let c and d be scalars. Then the following properties are true.

1. $\mathbf{u} + \mathbf{v} = \mathbf{v} + \mathbf{u}$
2. $(\mathbf{u} + \mathbf{v}) + \mathbf{w} = \mathbf{u} + (\mathbf{v} + \mathbf{w})$
3. $\mathbf{u} + \mathbf{0} = \mathbf{u}$
4. $\mathbf{u} + (-\mathbf{u}) = \mathbf{0}$
5. $c(d\mathbf{u}) = (cd)\mathbf{u}$
6. $(c + d)\mathbf{u} = c\mathbf{u} + d\mathbf{u}$
7. $c(\mathbf{u} + \mathbf{v}) = c\mathbf{u} + c\mathbf{v}$
8. $1(\mathbf{u}) = \mathbf{u}, \ 0(\mathbf{u}) = \mathbf{0}$
9. $\|c\mathbf{v}\| = |c| \, \|\mathbf{v}\|$

Unit Vectors

In many applications of vectors, it is useful to find a unit vector that has the same direction as a given nonzero vector $\mathbf{v}$. To do this, divide $\mathbf{v}$ by its length to obtain

$$\mathbf{u} = \frac{\mathbf{v}}{\|\mathbf{v}\|} = \left(\frac{1}{\|\mathbf{v}\|}\right)\mathbf{v}. \qquad \textit{Unit vector}$$

Note that $\mathbf{u}$ is a scalar multiple of $\mathbf{v}$. The vector $\mathbf{u}$ has length 1 and the same direction as $\mathbf{v}$. We call $\mathbf{u}$ a **unit vector in the direction of v.**

EXAMPLE 4   Finding a Unit Vector

Find a unit vector in the direction of $\mathbf{v} = \langle -2, 5 \rangle$ and verify that the result has length 1.

SOLUTION

The unit vector in the direction of $\mathbf{v}$ is

$$\frac{\mathbf{v}}{\|\mathbf{v}\|} = \frac{\langle -2, 5 \rangle}{\sqrt{(-2)^2 + (5)^2}} = \frac{1}{\sqrt{29}}\langle -2, 5 \rangle = \left\langle \frac{-2}{\sqrt{29}}, \frac{5}{\sqrt{29}} \right\rangle.$$

This vector has length 1 because

$$\sqrt{\left(\frac{-2}{\sqrt{29}}\right)^2 + \left(\frac{5}{\sqrt{29}}\right)^2} = \sqrt{\frac{4}{29} + \frac{25}{29}} = \sqrt{\frac{29}{29}} = 1.$$

The unit vectors $\langle 1, 0 \rangle$ and $\langle 0, 1 \rangle$ are the **standard unit vectors** and are denoted by

$$\mathbf{i} = \langle 1, 0 \rangle \quad \text{and} \quad \mathbf{j} = \langle 0, 1 \rangle,$$

as shown in Figure 8.25. (Note that the lower-case letter $\mathbf{i}$ is written in boldface to distinguish it from the imaginary number $i = \sqrt{-1}$.) These vectors can be used to represent any vector $\mathbf{v} = \langle v_1, v_2 \rangle$ as follows.

$$\mathbf{v} = \langle v_1, v_2 \rangle = v_1\langle 1, 0 \rangle + v_2\langle 0, 1 \rangle = v_1\mathbf{i} + v_2\mathbf{j}$$

The scalars v_1 and v_2 are the **horizontal and vertical components of v,** respectively. The vector sum $v_1\mathbf{i} + v_2\mathbf{j}$ is a **linear combination** of the vectors $\mathbf{i}$ and $\mathbf{j}$. Any vector in the plane can be expressed as a linear combination of the standard unit vectors $\mathbf{i}$ and $\mathbf{j}$.

Standard Unit Vectors $\mathbf{i}$ and $\mathbf{j}$

FIGURE 8.25

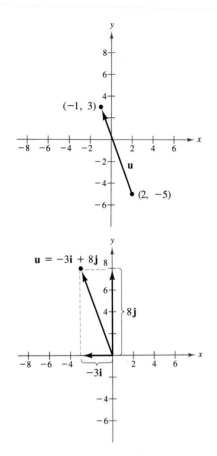

EXAMPLE 5   Representing a Vector as a Linear Combination of Unit Vectors

Let **u** be the vector with initial point $(2, -5)$ and terminal point $(-1, 3)$. Write **u** as a linear combination of the standard unit vectors **i** and **j**.

SOLUTION

$$\mathbf{u} = \langle -1 - 2, 3 - (-5) \rangle$$
$$= \langle -3, 8 \rangle$$
$$= -3\mathbf{i} + 8\mathbf{j}$$

This result is shown graphically in Figure 8.26.

EXAMPLE 6   Vector Operations

Let $\mathbf{u} = -3\mathbf{i} + 8\mathbf{j}$ and $\mathbf{v} = 2\mathbf{i} - \mathbf{j}$. Find $2\mathbf{u} - 3\mathbf{v}$.

SOLUTION

$$2\mathbf{u} - 3\mathbf{v} = 2(-3\mathbf{i} + 8\mathbf{j}) - 3(2\mathbf{i} - \mathbf{j})$$
$$= -6\mathbf{i} + 16\mathbf{j} - 6\mathbf{i} + 3\mathbf{j}$$
$$= -12\mathbf{i} + 19\mathbf{j}$$

FIGURE 8.26

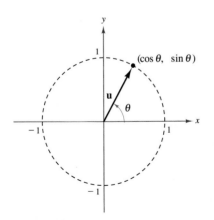

FIGURE 8.27

Direction Angles

If **u** is a *unit vector* such that θ is the angle (measured counterclockwise) from the positive x-axis to **u**, then the terminal point of **u** lies on the unit circle and you have

$$\mathbf{u} = \langle \cos \theta, \sin \theta \rangle = (\cos \theta)\mathbf{i} + (\sin \theta)\mathbf{j},$$

as shown in Figure 8.27. We call θ the **direction angle** of the vector **u**.

Suppose that **u** is a unit vector with direction angle θ. If **v** is any vector that makes an angle θ with the positive x-axis, then it has the same direction as **u** and you can write

$$\mathbf{v} = \|\mathbf{v}\| \langle \cos \theta, \sin \theta \rangle = \|\mathbf{v}\| (\cos \theta)\mathbf{i} + \|\mathbf{v}\| (\sin \theta)\mathbf{j}.$$

For instance, the vector **v** of length 3 making an angle of 30° with the positive
x-axis is given by

$$\mathbf{v} = 3(\cos 30°)\mathbf{i} + 3(\sin 30°)\mathbf{j} = \frac{3\sqrt{3}}{2}\mathbf{i} + \frac{3}{2}\mathbf{j},$$

where $\|\mathbf{v}\| = 3$.

Because $\mathbf{v} = a\mathbf{i} + b\mathbf{j} = \|\mathbf{v}\|(\cos \theta)\mathbf{i} + \|\mathbf{v}\|(\sin \theta)\mathbf{j}$, it follows that the
direction angle θ for **v** is determined from

$$\tan \theta = \frac{\sin \theta}{\cos \theta} = \frac{\|\mathbf{v}\| \sin \theta}{\|\mathbf{v}\| \cos \theta} = \frac{b}{a}.$$

FIGURE 8.28

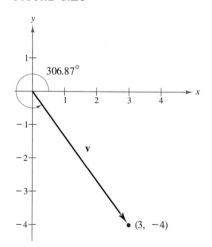

FIGURE 8.29

EXAMPLE 7   **Finding Direction Angles of Vectors**

Find the direction angles of the vectors.

A. $\mathbf{u} = 3\mathbf{i} + 3\mathbf{j}$
B. $\mathbf{v} = 3\mathbf{i} - 4\mathbf{j}$

SOLUTION

A. The direction angle is given by

$$\tan \theta = \frac{b}{a} = \frac{3}{3} = 1.$$

Therefore, $\theta = 45°$, as shown in Figure 8.28.

B. The direction angle is given by

$$\tan \theta = \frac{b}{a} = \frac{-4}{3}.$$

Moreover, because $\mathbf{v} = 3\mathbf{i} - 4\mathbf{j}$ lies in Quadrant IV, θ lies in Quadrant
IV and its reference angle is

$$\theta' = \left| \arctan\left(-\frac{4}{3}\right) \right| \approx |-53.13°| = 53.13°.$$

Therefore, $\theta \approx 360° - 53.13° = 306.87°$, as shown in Figure 8.29.

Applications of Vectors

Many applications of vectors involve the use of triangles and trigonometry in their solutions.

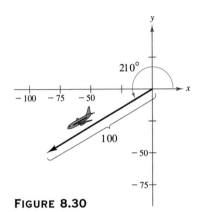

FIGURE 8.30

EXAMPLE 8   Finding Component Form, Given Magnitude and Direction

Find the component form of the vector that represents the velocity of an airplane descending at a speed of 100 miles per hour at an angle 30° below horizontal, as shown in Figure 8.30.

SOLUTION

The velocity vector $\mathbf{v}$ has a magnitude of 100 and a direction angle of $\theta = 210°$. Hence, the component form of $\mathbf{v}$ is

$$\mathbf{v} = \|\mathbf{v}\|(\cos\theta)\mathbf{i} + \|\mathbf{v}\|(\sin\theta)\mathbf{j}$$

$$= 100(\cos 210°)\mathbf{i} + 100(\sin 210°)\mathbf{j}$$

$$= 100\left(\frac{-\sqrt{3}}{2}\right)\mathbf{i} + 100\left(\frac{-1}{2}\right)\mathbf{j}$$

$$= -50\sqrt{3}\mathbf{i} - 50\mathbf{j}$$

$$= \langle -50\sqrt{3}, -50\rangle.$$

You should check to see that $\|\mathbf{v}\| = 100$.

EXAMPLE 9   An Application

A force of 600 pounds is required to pull a boat and trailer up a ramp inclined at 15° from horizontal. Find the combined weight of the boat and trailer. (Assume no friction is involved.)

SOLUTION

Based on Figure 8.31, you can make the following observations.

$\|\overrightarrow{BA}\|$ = force of gravity = combined weight of boat and trailer

$\|\overrightarrow{BC}\|$ = force against ramp

$\|\overrightarrow{AC}\|$ = force required to move boat up ramp = 600 pounds
(Note that AC is parallel to the ramp.)

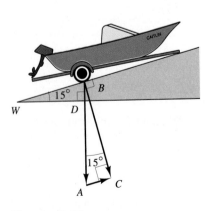

FIGURE 8.31

By construction, triangles *WBD* and *ABC* are similar. Hence, angle *ABC* is 15°. Therefore, in triangle *ABC* you have

$$\sin 15° = \frac{\|\overrightarrow{AC}\|}{\|\overrightarrow{BA}\|} = \frac{600}{\|\overrightarrow{BA}\|}$$

$$\|\overrightarrow{BA}\| = \frac{600}{\sin 15°} \approx 2318.$$

Consequently, the combined weight is approximately 2318 pounds.

EXAMPLE 10   An Application

An airplane is traveling at a fixed altitude with a negligible wind factor. The airplane is headed N 30° W at a speed of 500 miles per hour, as shown in Figure 8.32. As the airplane reaches a certain point, it encounters a wind with a velocity of 70 miles per hour in the direction N 45° E. What are the resultant speed and direction of the airplane?

SOLUTION

Using Figure 8.32, you can represent the velocity of the airplane by the vector

$$\mathbf{v}_1 = 500\langle\cos 120°, \sin 120°\rangle = \langle -250, 250\sqrt{3}\rangle$$

and the velocity of the wind by the vector

$$\mathbf{v}_2 = 70\langle\cos 45°, \sin 45°\rangle = \langle 35\sqrt{2}, 35\sqrt{2}\rangle.$$

Thus, the velocity of the airplane is given by the vector

$$\mathbf{v} = \mathbf{v}_1 + \mathbf{v}_2 = \langle -250 + 35\sqrt{2}, 250\sqrt{3} + 35\sqrt{2}\rangle \approx \langle -200.5, 482.5\rangle,$$

and the speed of the airplane is

$$\|\mathbf{v}\| = \sqrt{(-200.5)^2 + (482.5)^2} \approx 522.5 \text{ miles per hour.}$$

Finally, if θ is the direction angle of the flight path, you obtain

$$\tan \theta = \frac{482.5}{-200.5} \approx -2.4065,$$

which implies that

$$\theta \approx 180° + \arctan(-2.4065) \approx 180° - 67.4° = 112.6°.$$

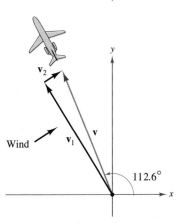

FIGURE 8.32

DISCUSSION PROBLEM

....

COMPARING VELOCITY AND SPEED

In everyday conversation, the terms "velocity" and "speed" are often used as synonyms. In mathematics and science, however, these terms are considered to be different. *Velocity* is a vector quantity that has both magnitude and direction, whereas *speed* is a single-dimension quantity that can be represented by nonnegative real numbers. Consider an object that has a velocity of **v** and a speed of s. How are these two quantities related to each other?

Which of the following statements is correct mathematically?

(a) While driving to work, I did not exceed a velocity of 55 miles per hour.

(b) While driving to work, I did not exceed a speed of 55 miles per hour.

WARM-UP

....

The following warm-up exercises involve skills that were covered in earlier sections. You will use these skills in the exercise set for this section.

In Exercises 1 and 2, find the distance between the points.

1. $(-2, 6), (5, -15)$ **2.** $(0, 0), (-3, -7)$

In Exercises 3 and 4, find an equation of the line through the two points.

3. $(3, 1), (-2, 4)$ **4.** $(-2, -3), (4, 5)$

In Exercises 5 and 6, find an angle θ $(0 \le \theta \le 360°)$ whose vertex is at the origin and whose terminal side passes through the given point.

5. $(-2, 5)$ **6.** $(4, -3)$

In Exercises 7–10, find the sine and cosine of the angle θ.

7. $\theta = 30°$ **8.** $\theta = 120°$

9. $\theta = 300°$ **10.** $\theta = 210°$

SECTION 8.3 · EXERCISES

In Exercises 1–6, use the figure to sketch a graph of the specified vector.

1. $-\mathbf{u}$ **2.** $3\mathbf{v}$

3. $\mathbf{u} + \mathbf{v}$ **4.** $\mathbf{u} + 2\mathbf{v}$

5. $\mathbf{u} - \mathbf{v}$ **6.** $\mathbf{v} - \frac{1}{2}\mathbf{u}$

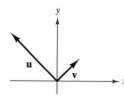

FIGURE FOR 1–6

In Exercises 7–16, find the component form and the magnitude of the vector $\mathbf{v}$.

7.

8.

9.

10.

11.

12.

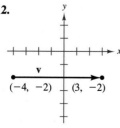

13. Initial point: $(-1, 5)$
Terminal point: $(15, 2)$

14. Initial point: $(1, 11)$
Terminal point: $(9, 3)$

15. Initial point: $(-3, -5)$
Terminal point: $(5, -1)$

16. Initial point: $(-3, 11)$
Terminal point: $(9, 40)$

In Exercises 17–26, find (a) $\mathbf{u} + \mathbf{v}$, (b) $\mathbf{u} - \mathbf{v}$, and (c) $2\mathbf{u} - 3\mathbf{v}$.

17. $\mathbf{u} = \langle 1, 2 \rangle$, $\mathbf{v} = \langle 3, 1 \rangle$

18. $\mathbf{u} = \langle 2, 3 \rangle$, $\mathbf{v} = \langle 4, 0 \rangle$

19. $\mathbf{u} = \langle -2, 3 \rangle$, $\mathbf{v} = \langle -2, 1 \rangle$

20. $\mathbf{u} = \langle 0, 1 \rangle$, $\mathbf{v} = \langle 0, -1 \rangle$

21. $\mathbf{u} = \langle 4, -2 \rangle$, $\mathbf{v} = \langle 0, 0 \rangle$

22. $\mathbf{u} = \langle 0, 0 \rangle$, $\mathbf{v} = \langle 2, 1 \rangle$

23. $\mathbf{u} = \mathbf{i} + \mathbf{j}$, $\mathbf{v} = 2\mathbf{i} - 3\mathbf{j}$

24. $\mathbf{u} = 2\mathbf{i} - \mathbf{j}$, $\mathbf{v} = -\mathbf{i} + \mathbf{j}$

25. $\mathbf{u} = 2\mathbf{i}$, $\mathbf{v} = \mathbf{j}$

26. $\mathbf{u} = 3\mathbf{j}$, $\mathbf{v} = 2\mathbf{i}$

In Exercises 27–30, find the magnitude and direction angle of the vector $\mathbf{v}$.

27. $\mathbf{v} = 5\langle \cos 30°, \sin 30° \rangle$

28. $\mathbf{v} = 8\langle \cos 135°, \sin 135° \rangle$

29. $\mathbf{v} = 6\mathbf{i} - 6\mathbf{j}$

30. $\mathbf{v} = -2\mathbf{i} + 5\mathbf{j}$

In Exercises 31–38, sketch $\mathbf{v}$ and find its component form. (Assume θ is measured counterclockwise from the x-axis to the vector.)

31. $\|\mathbf{v}\| = 3$, $\theta = 0°$

32. $\|\mathbf{v}\| = 1$, $\theta = 45°$

33. $\|\mathbf{v}\| = 1$, $\theta = 150°$

34. $\|\mathbf{v}\| = \frac{5}{2}$, $\theta = 45°$

35. $\|\mathbf{v}\| = 3\sqrt{2}$, $\theta = 150°$

36. $\|\mathbf{v}\| = 8$, $\theta = 90°$

37. $\|\mathbf{v}\| = 2$, $\mathbf{v}$ in the direction $\mathbf{i} + 3\mathbf{j}$

38. $\|\mathbf{v}\| = 3$, $\mathbf{v}$ in the direction $3\mathbf{i} + 4\mathbf{j}$

In Exercises 39–44, find the component form of $\mathbf{v}$ and sketch the specified vector operations geometrically, where

$$\mathbf{u} = 2\mathbf{i} - \mathbf{j} \quad \text{and} \quad \mathbf{w} = \mathbf{i} + 2\mathbf{j}.$$

39. $\mathbf{v} = \frac{3}{2}\mathbf{u}$ **40.** $\mathbf{v} = \mathbf{u} + \mathbf{w}$

41. $\mathbf{v} = \mathbf{u} + 2\mathbf{w}$ **42.** $\mathbf{v} = -\mathbf{u} + \mathbf{w}$

43. $\mathbf{v} = \frac{1}{2}(3\mathbf{u} + \mathbf{w})$ **44.** $\mathbf{v} = \mathbf{u} - 2\mathbf{w}$

In Exercises 45–48, find the component form of the sum of the vectors **u** and **v** with direction angles θ_u and θ_v respectively.

45. $\|\mathbf{u}\| = 5, \quad \theta_u = 0°$
$\|\mathbf{v}\| = 5, \quad \theta_v = 90°$

46. $\|\mathbf{u}\| = 2, \quad \theta_u = 30°$
$\|\mathbf{v}\| = 2, \quad \theta_v = 90°$

47. $\|\mathbf{u}\| = 20, \quad \theta_u = 45°$
$\|\mathbf{v}\| = 50, \quad \theta_v = 180°$

48. $\|\mathbf{u}\| = 35, \quad \theta_u = 25°$
$\|\mathbf{v}\| = 50, \quad \theta_v = 120°$

In Exercises 49–52, find a unit vector in the direction of the given vector.

49. $\mathbf{v} = 4\mathbf{i} - 3\mathbf{j}$

50. $\mathbf{v} = \mathbf{i} + \mathbf{j}$

51. $\mathbf{v} = 2\mathbf{j}$

52. $\mathbf{v} = \mathbf{i} - 2\mathbf{j}$

In Exercises 53–56, use the Law of Cosines to find the angle α between the given vectors. (Assume $0° \le \alpha \le 180°$.)

53. $\mathbf{v} = \mathbf{i} + \mathbf{j}, \quad \mathbf{w} = 2(\mathbf{i} - \mathbf{j})$

54. $\mathbf{v} = 3\mathbf{i} + \mathbf{j}, \quad \mathbf{w} = 2\mathbf{i} - \mathbf{j}$

55. $\mathbf{v} = \mathbf{i} + \mathbf{j}, \quad \mathbf{w} = 3\mathbf{i} - \mathbf{j}$

56. $\mathbf{v} = \mathbf{i} + 2\mathbf{j}, \quad \mathbf{w} = 2\mathbf{i} - \mathbf{j}$

In Exercises 57 and 58, find the angle between the forces, given the magnitude of their resultant (vector sum). (*Hint:* Write one force as a vector in the direction of the positive x-axis and the other as a vector at an angle θ with the positive x-axis.)

57. Force one: 45 pounds
Force two: 60 pounds
Resultant force: 90 pounds

58. Force one: 3000 pounds
Force two: 1000 pounds
Resultant force: 3750 pounds

59. *Resultant Force*   Forces with magnitudes of 35 pounds and 50 pounds act on a hook (see figure). The angle between the two forces is 30°. Find the direction and magnitude of the resultant (vector sum) of these two forces.

FIGURE FOR 59

60. *Resultant Force*   Forces with magnitudes of 500 pounds and 200 pounds act on a machine part at angles of 30° and −45°, respectively, with the x-axis (see figure). Find the direction and magnitude of the resultant (vector sum) of these forces.

FIGURE FOR 60

61. *Resultant Force*   Three forces with magnitudes of 75 pounds, 100 pounds, and 125 pounds act on an object at angles of 30°, 45°, and 120°, respectively, with the positive x-axis. Find the direction and magnitude of the resultant of these forces.

62. *Resultant Force*   Three forces with magnitudes of 70 pounds, 40 pounds, and 60 pounds act on an object at angles of −30°, 45°, and 135°, respectively, with the positive x-axis. Find the direction and magnitude of the resultant of these forces.

63. *Horizontal and Vertical Components of Velocity*   A ball is thrown with an initial velocity of 80 feet per second, at an angle of 50° with the horizontal (see figure). Find the vertical and horizontal components of the velocity.

FIGURE FOR 63

64. *Horizontal and Vertical Components of Velocity*   A gun with a muzzle velocity of 1200 feet per second is fired at an angle of 6° with the horizontal. Find the vertical and horizontal components of the velocity.

Cable Tension In Exercises 65 and 66, use the figure to determine the tension in each cable supporting the given load.

65.

66.

67. *Barge Towing* A loaded barge is being towed by two tugboats, and the magnitude of the resultant is 6000 pounds directed along the axis of the barge (see figure). Find the tension in the tow lines if they each make a 20° angle with the axis of the barge.

FIGURE FOR 67

68. *Shared Load* To carry a 100-pound cylindrical weight, two people lift on the ends of short ropes that are tied to an eyelet on the top center of the cylinder. Find the tension in the ropes if they each make a 30° angle with the vertical (see figure).

FIGURE FOR 68

69. *Navigation* An airplane is flying in the direction S 32° E, with an air speed of 540 miles per hour. Because of the wind, its ground speed and direction are 500 miles per hour and S 40° E, respectively (see figure). Find the direction and speed of the wind.

70. *Navigation* An airplane's velocity with respect to the air is 580 miles per hour, and it is headed N 58° W. The wind, at the altitude of the plane, is from the southwest and has a velocity of 60 miles per hour (see figure). What is the true direction of the plane, and what is its speed with respect to the ground?

FIGURE FOR 70

FIGURE FOR 69

71. *Work* A heavy implement is pulled 10 feet across a floor, using a force of 85 pounds. Find the work done if the direction of the force is 60° above the horizontal (see figure). (Use the formula for work, $W = FD$, where F is the component of the force in the direction of motion and D is the distance.)

FIGURE FOR 71

72. *Tether Ball* A tether ball weighing 1 pound is pulled outward from the pole by a horizontal force $\mathbf{u}$ until the rope makes a 30° angle with the pole (see figure). Determine the resulting tension in the rope and the magnitude of $\mathbf{u}$.

FIGURE FOR 72

73. *Technology*   Enter the following program in a graphing utility. (This program is for the TI-81; other versions are listed in the appendix.) Use $-6 \le x \le 6$ and $-2 \le y \le 6$, and enter $A = 5$, $B = 2$, $C = -4$, and $D = 3$. Explain what the program does.

```
:Disp "ENTER, (A, B)"          :Line (0, 0, A, B)
:Disp "ENTER, A"               :Line (0, 0, C, D)
:Input A                       :A+C→E
:Disp "ENTER, B"               :B+D→F
:Input B                       :Line (0, 0, E, F)
:Disp "ENTER, (C, D)"          :Line (A, B, E, F)
:Disp "ENTER, C"               :Line (C, D, E, F)
:Input C                       :Pause
:Disp "ENTER, D"               :ClrDraw
:Input D                       :End
```

8.4   TRIGONOMETRIC FORM OF A COMPLEX NUMBER

The Complex Plane   /   Trigonometric Form of a Complex Number   /
Multiplication and Division of Complex Numbers

The Complex Plane

In this section you will study the trigonometric form of a complex number. The convenience of this form will not be fully apparent until DeMoivre's Theorem is introduced in Section 8.5.

Just as real numbers can be represented by points on the real number line, you can represent a complex number

$$z = a + bi$$

as the point (a, b) in the **complex plane.** The horizontal axis is the **real axis** and the vertical axis is the **imaginary axis,** as shown in Figure 8.33.

The **absolute value** of the complex number $a + bi$ is defined to be the distance between the origin $(0, 0)$ and the point (a, b), as shown in Figure 8.34.

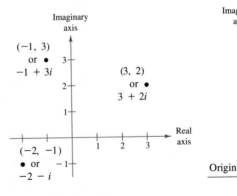

The Complex Plane

FIGURE 8.33

FIGURE 8.34

REMARK   Note that if the complex number $a + bi$ happens to be a real number (that is, if $b = 0$), then this definition agrees with that given for the absolute value of a real number.

$$|a + 0i| = \sqrt{a^2 + 0^2} = \sqrt{a^2} = |a|$$

DEFINITION OF THE ABSOLUTE VALUE OF A COMPLEX NUMBER

The **absolute value** of the complex number $z = a + bi$ is given by

$$|a + bi| = \sqrt{a^2 + b^2}.$$

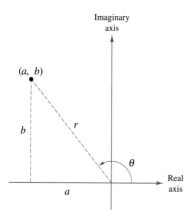

FIGURE 8.35

EXAMPLE 1   Finding the Absolute Value of a Complex Number

Plot the points corresponding to the following complex numbers and find the absolute value of each.

A. $z = -3i$ **B.** $z = -2 + 5i$

SOLUTION

The points are shown in Figure 8.35.

A. The complex number $z = 0 + (-3)i$ has an absolute value of

$$|z| = \sqrt{0^2 + (-3)^2} = \sqrt{9} = 3.$$

B. The complex number $z = -2 + 5i$ has an absolute value of

$$|z| = \sqrt{(-2)^2 + 5^2} = \sqrt{29}.$$

Complex Number: $a + bi$

FIGURE 8.36

Trigonometric Form of a Complex Number

In Section 3.5, you learned how to add, subtract, multiply, and divide complex numbers. To work effectively with *powers* and *roots* of complex numbers, it is helpful to write complex numbers in **trigonometric form.** In Figure 8.36, consider the nonzero complex number $a + bi$. By letting θ be the angle from the positive x-axis (measured counterclockwise) to the line segment connecting the origin and the point (a, b), you can write

$$a = r \cos \theta \quad \text{and} \quad b = r \sin \theta,$$

where $r = \sqrt{a^2 + b^2}$. Consequently, you have

$$a + bi = (r \cos \theta) + (r \sin \theta)i,$$

from which you obtain the following **trigonometric form of a complex number.**

REMARK The trigonometric form of a complex number is also called the **polar form.** Because there are infinitely many choices for θ, the trigonometric form of a complex number is not unique. Normally, we use θ values in the interval $0 \le \theta < 2\pi$, though on occasion we may use $\theta < 0$.

TRIGONOMETRIC FORM OF A COMPLEX NUMBER

Let $z = a + bi$ be a complex number. The **trigonometric form** of z is

$$z = r(\cos \theta + i \sin \theta),$$

where $a = r \cos \theta$, $b = r \sin \theta$, $r = \sqrt{a^2 + b^2}$, and $\tan \theta = b/a$. The number r is the **modulus** of z, and θ is an **argument** of z.

EXAMPLE 2   **Writing Complex Numbers in Trigonometric Form**

Write the complex numbers in trigonometric form.

A. $z = -2 - 2\sqrt{3}i$ **B.** $z = 6 + 2i$

Use radian measure for part (A) and degree measure for part (B).

SOLUTION

The graphs of the complex numbers are shown in Figure 8.37.

A. The absolute value of z is

$$r = |-2 - 2\sqrt{3}i| = \sqrt{(-2)^2 + (-2\sqrt{3})^2} = \sqrt{16} = 4,$$

and the angle θ is given by

$$\tan \theta = \frac{b}{a} = \frac{-2\sqrt{3}}{-2} = \sqrt{3}.$$

Because $\tan \pi/3 = \sqrt{3}$ and $z = -2 - 2\sqrt{3}i$ lies in Quadrant III, choose θ to be $\theta = \pi + \pi/3 = 4\pi/3$. Thus, the trigonometric form is

$$z = r(\cos \theta + i \sin \theta) = 4\left(\cos \frac{4\pi}{3} + i \sin \frac{4\pi}{3}\right).$$

B. Here you have $r = |6 + 2i| = 2\sqrt{10}$, with θ given by

$$\tan \theta = \frac{2}{6} = \frac{1}{3} \qquad \qquad \theta \text{ in Quadrant I}$$

$$\theta = \arctan \frac{1}{3} \approx 18.4°.$$

Therefore, the trigonometric form of z is

$$z = r(\cos \theta + i \sin \theta)$$

$$= 2\sqrt{10}\left[\cos\left(\arctan \frac{1}{3}\right) + i \sin\left(\arctan \frac{1}{3}\right)\right]$$

$$\approx 2\sqrt{10}(\cos 18.4° + i \sin 18.4°).$$

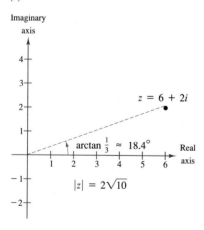

(a)

(b)

FIGURE 8.37

EXAMPLE 3   Writing a Complex Number in Standard Form

Write the complex number in standard form $a + bi$.

$$z = \sqrt{8}\left[\cos\left(-\frac{\pi}{3}\right) + i \sin\left(-\frac{\pi}{3}\right)\right]$$

SOLUTION

Because $\cos(-\pi/3) = 1/2$ and $\sin(-\pi/3) = -\sqrt{3}/2$, you can write

$$z = \sqrt{8}\left[\cos\left(-\frac{\pi}{3}\right) + i \sin\left(-\frac{\pi}{3}\right)\right]$$

$$= \sqrt{8}\left[\frac{1}{2} - \frac{\sqrt{3}}{2}i\right]$$

$$= 2\sqrt{2}\left[\frac{1}{2} - \frac{\sqrt{3}}{2}i\right]$$

$$= \sqrt{2} - \sqrt{6}i.$$

Multiplication and Division of Complex Numbers

The trigonometric form adapts nicely to multiplication and division of complex numbers. Suppose you are given two complex numbers

$$z_1 = r_1(\cos \theta_1 + i \sin \theta_1) \quad \text{and} \quad z_2 = r_2(\cos \theta_2 + i \sin \theta_2).$$

The product of z_1 and z_2 is

$$z_1 z_2 = r_1 r_2(\cos \theta_1 + i \sin \theta_1)(\cos \theta_2 + i \sin \theta_2)$$

$$= r_1 r_2[(\cos \theta_1 \cos \theta_2 - \sin \theta_1 \sin \theta_2)$$

$$+ i(\sin \theta_1 \cos \theta_2 + \cos \theta_1 \sin \theta_2)].$$

Using the sum and difference formulas for cosine and sine, you can rewrite this equation as

$$z_1 z_2 = r_1 r_2[\cos(\theta_1 + \theta_2) + i \sin(\theta_1 + \theta_2)].$$

This establishes the first part of the following rule.

PRODUCT AND QUOTIENT OF TWO COMPLEX NUMBERS

Let $z_1 = r_1(\cos \theta_1 + i \sin \theta_1)$ and $z_2 = r_2(\cos \theta_2 + i \sin \theta_2)$ be complex numbers.

$$z_1 z_2 = r_1 r_2[\cos(\theta_1 + \theta_2) + i \sin(\theta_1 + \theta_2)] \qquad \textit{Product}$$

$$\frac{z_1}{z_2} = \frac{r_1}{r_2}[\cos(\theta_1 - \theta_2) + i \sin(\theta_1 - \theta_2)], \quad z_2 \neq 0 \qquad \textit{Quotient}$$

Note that this rule says that to multiply two complex numbers, you multiply moduli and add arguments, whereas to divide two complex numbers you divide moduli and subtract arguments.

EXAMPLE 4 **Multiplying Complex Numbers in Trigonometric Form**

Find the product of the following complex numbers.

$$z_1 = 2\left(\cos\frac{2\pi}{3} + i\sin\frac{2\pi}{3}\right) \qquad z_2 = 8\left(\cos\frac{11\pi}{6} + i\sin\frac{11\pi}{6}\right)$$

Express your answer in standard form.

SOLUTION

$$z_1z_2 = 2\left(\cos\frac{2\pi}{3} + i\sin\frac{2\pi}{3}\right) \cdot 8\left(\cos\frac{11\pi}{6} + i\sin\frac{11\pi}{6}\right)$$

$$= 16\left[\cos\left(\frac{2\pi}{3} + \frac{11\pi}{6}\right) + i\sin\left(\frac{2\pi}{3} + \frac{11\pi}{6}\right)\right]$$

$$= 16\left(\cos\frac{5\pi}{2} + i\sin\frac{5\pi}{2}\right)$$

$$= 16\left(\cos\frac{\pi}{2} + i\sin\frac{\pi}{2}\right)$$

$$= 16[0 + i(1)] = 16i$$

Check this result by first converting to the standard forms $z_1 = -1 + \sqrt{3}i$ and $z_2 = 4\sqrt{3} - 4i$ and then multiplying algebraically, as in Section 3.5.

EXAMPLE 5 **Dividing Complex Numbers in Trigonometric Form**

Find z_1/z_2 for the two complex numbers

$$z_1 = 24(\cos 300° + i\sin 300°) \qquad z_2 = 8(\cos 75° + i\sin 75°).$$

Express your answer in standard form.

SOLUTION

$$\frac{z_1}{z_2} = \frac{24(\cos 300° + i \sin 300°)}{8(\cos 75° + i \sin 75°)}$$

$$= \frac{24}{8}[\cos(300° - 75°) + i \sin(300° - 75°)]$$

$$= 3[\cos 225° + i \sin 225°]$$

$$= 3\left[\left(-\frac{\sqrt{2}}{2}\right) + i\left(-\frac{\sqrt{2}}{2}\right)\right]$$

$$= -\frac{3\sqrt{2}}{2} - \frac{3\sqrt{2}}{2}i$$

DISCUSSION PROBLEM

····················

ADDITION OF TWO COMPLEX NUMBERS

In Section 8.3, we gave a graphical interpretation of addition of two vectors in the plane, called the parallelogram law for vector addition. A similar graphical interpretation can be given for addition of two complex numbers. Write a paragraph describing this interpretation, and illustrate your result with the complex numbers $z_1 = 1 + 2i$ and $z_2 = 3 + i$.

WARM-UP

··················

The following warm-up exercises involve skills that were covered in earlier sections. You will use these skills in the exercise set for this section.

In Exercises 1–4, write the complex number in standard form.

1. $-5 - \sqrt{-100}$ **2.** $7 + \sqrt{-54}$

3. $-4i + i^2$ **4.** $3i^3$

In Exercises 5–10, perform the indicated operations and write your result in standard form.

5. $(3 - 10i) - (-3 + 4i)$ **6.** $\left(2 + \sqrt{-50}\right) + \left(4 - \sqrt{2}i\right)$

7. $(4 - 2i)(-6 + i)$ **8.** $(3 - 2i)(3 + 2i)$

9. $\dfrac{1 + 4i}{1 - i}$ **10.** $\dfrac{3 - 5i}{2i}$

SECTION 8.4 · EXERCISES

In Exercises 1–6, represent the complex number graphically and find its absolute value.

1. $-5i$ **2.** -5

3. $-4 + 4i$ **4.** $5 - 12i$

5. $6 - 7i$ **6.** $-8 + 3i$

In Exercises 7–10, express the complex number in trigonometric form.

7.

8.

9.

10.

In Exercises 11–26, represent the complex number graphically, and find the trigonometric form of the number.

11. $3 - 3i$ **12.** $-2 - 2i$

13. $\sqrt{3} + i$ **14.** $-1 + \sqrt{3}i$

15. $-2\left(1 + \sqrt{3}i\right)$ **16.** $\frac{5}{2}\left(\sqrt{3} - i\right)$

17. $6i$ **18.** 4

19. $-7 + 4i$ **20.** $3 - i$

21. 7 **22.** $-2i$

23. $1 + 6i$ **24.** $2\sqrt{2} - i$

25. $-3 - i$ **26.** $1 + 3i$

In Exercises 27–36, represent the complex number graphically, and find the standard form of the number.

27. $2(\cos 150° + i \sin 150°)$

28. $5(\cos 135° + i \sin 135°)$

29. $\frac{3}{2}(\cos 300° + i \sin 300°)$

30. $\frac{3}{4}(\cos 315° + i \sin 315°)$

31. $3.75\left(\cos \dfrac{3\pi}{4} + i \sin \dfrac{3\pi}{4}\right)$

32. $8\left(\cos \dfrac{\pi}{12} + i \sin \dfrac{\pi}{12}\right)$

33. $4\left(\cos \dfrac{3\pi}{2} + i \sin \dfrac{3\pi}{2}\right)$

34. $7(\cos 0° + i \sin 0°)$

35. $3[\cos(18° \ 45') + i \sin(18° \ 45')]$

36. $6[\cos(230° \ 30') + i \sin (230° \ 30')]$

In Exercises 37–48, perform the indicated operation and leave the result in trigonometric form.

37. $\left[3\left(\cos \dfrac{\pi}{3} + i \sin \dfrac{\pi}{3}\right)\right]\left[4\left(\cos \dfrac{\pi}{6} + i \sin \dfrac{\pi}{6}\right)\right]$

38. $\left[\dfrac{3}{2}\left(\cos \dfrac{\pi}{2} + i \sin \dfrac{\pi}{2}\right)\right]\left[6\left(\cos \dfrac{\pi}{4} + i \sin \dfrac{\pi}{4}\right)\right]$

39. $[\frac{5}{3}(\cos 140° + i \sin 140°)][\frac{2}{3}(\cos 60° + i \sin 60°)]$

40. $[0.5(\cos 100° + i \sin 100°)][0.8(\cos 300° + i \sin 300°)]$

41. $[0.45(\cos 310° + i \sin 310°)][0.60(\cos 200° + i \sin 200°)]$

42. $(\cos 5° + i \sin 5°)(\cos 20° + i \sin 20°)$

43. $\dfrac{2(\cos 120° + i \sin 120°)}{4(\cos 40° + i \sin 40°)}$

44. $\dfrac{\cos 40° + i \sin 40°}{\cos 10° + i \sin 10°}$

45. $\dfrac{\cos(5\pi/3) + i \sin (5\pi/3)}{\cos \pi + i \sin \pi}$

46. $\dfrac{5(\cos 4.3 + i \sin 4.3)}{4(\cos 2.1 + i \sin 2.1)}$

47. $\dfrac{12(\cos 52° + i \sin 52°)}{3(\cos 110° + i \sin 110°)}$

48. $\dfrac{9(\cos 20° + i \sin 20°)}{5(\cos 75° + i \sin 75°)}$

In Exercises 49–54, (a) give the trigonometric form of the complex number, (b) perform the indicated operation using the trigonometric form, and (c) perform the indicated operation using the standard form and check your result with the answer to part (b).

49. $(2 + 2i)(1 - i)$ **50.** $(\sqrt{3} + i)(1 + i)$

51. $-2i(1 + i)$ **52.** $\dfrac{3 + 4i}{1 - \sqrt{3}i}$

53. $\dfrac{5}{2 + 3i}$ **54.** $\dfrac{4i}{-4 + 2i}$

55. Given two complex numbers $z_1 = r_1(\cos \theta_1 + i \sin \theta_1)$ and $z_2 = r_2(\cos \theta_2 + i \sin \theta_2)$, $z_2 \neq 0$, prove that

$$\frac{z_1}{z_2} = \frac{r_1}{r_2}[\cos(\theta_1 - \theta_2) + i \sin(\theta_1 - \theta_2)].$$

56. Show that the complex conjugate of $z = r(\cos \theta + i \sin \theta)$ is $\bar{z} = r[\cos(-\theta) + i \sin(-\theta)]$.

57. Use the trigonometric form of z and $\bar{z}$ in Exercise 56 to find (a) $z\bar{z}$ and (b) $z/\bar{z}$, $z \neq 0$.

58. Show that the negative of $z = r(\cos \theta + i \sin \theta)$ is $-z = r[\cos(\theta + \pi) + i \sin(\theta + \pi)]$.

In Exercises 59 and 60, sketch the graph of all complex numbers z satisfying the given condition.

59. $|z| = 2$ **60.** $\theta = \pi/6$

8.5 DeMoivre's Theorem and Nth Roots

Powers of Complex Numbers / Roots of Complex Numbers

Powers of Complex Numbers

In this section you will study procedures for finding powers and roots of complex numbers. To begin, consider the complex number (in trigonometric form) $z = r(\cos \theta + i \sin \theta)$. Repeated use of the multiplication rule from the previous section yields

$$z = r(\cos \theta + i \sin \theta)$$
$$z^2 = r(\cos \theta + i \sin \theta)r(\cos \theta + i \sin \theta)$$
$$= r^2(\cos 2\theta + i \sin 2\theta)$$
$$z^3 = z^2(z) = r^2(\cos 2\theta + i \sin 2\theta)r(\cos \theta + i \sin \theta)$$
$$= r^3(\cos 3\theta + i \sin 3\theta).$$

Similarly,

$$z^4 = r^4(\cos 4\theta + i \sin 4\theta)$$
$$z^5 = r^5(\cos 5\theta + i \sin 5\theta)$$
$$\vdots$$

This pattern leads to the following important theorem, which is named after the French mathematician Abraham DeMoivre (1667–1754).

DEMOIVRE'S THEOREM

If $z = r(\cos \theta + i \sin \theta)$ is a complex number and n is a positive integer, then

$$z^n = [r(\cos \theta + i \sin \theta)]^n = r^n(\cos n\theta + i \sin n\theta).$$

EXAMPLE 1 **Finding Powers of a Complex Number**

Use DeMoivre's Theorem to find $(-1 + \sqrt{3}i)^{12}$.

SOLUTION

First convert to trigonometric form.

$$-1 + \sqrt{3}i = 2\left(\cos \frac{2\pi}{3} + i \sin \frac{2\pi}{3}\right)$$

Then, by DeMoivre's Theorem, you have

$$(-1 + \sqrt{3}i)^{12} = \left[2\left(\cos \frac{2\pi}{3} + i \sin \frac{2\pi}{3}\right)\right]^{12}$$

$$= 2^{12}\left[\cos\left(12 \cdot \frac{2\pi}{3}\right) + i \sin\left(12 \cdot \frac{2\pi}{3}\right)\right]$$

$$= 4096(\cos 8\pi + i \sin 8\pi)$$

$$= 4096(1 + 0)$$

$$= 4096.$$

Are you surprised to see a real number as the answer?

Roots of Complex Numbers

Recall that a consequence of the Fundamental Theorem of Algebra is that a polynomial equation of degree n has n solutions in the complex number system. Hence, an equation such as $x^6 = 1$ has six solutions, which can be found by factoring and using the Quadratic Formula.

$$x^6 - 1 = (x^3 - 1)(x^3 + 1)$$
$$= (x - 1)(x^2 + x + 1)(x + 1)(x^2 - x + 1) = 0$$

Consequently, the solutions are

$$x = \pm 1, \quad x = \frac{-1 \pm \sqrt{3}i}{2}, \quad \text{and} \quad x = \frac{1 \pm \sqrt{3}i}{2}.$$

Each of these numbers is a *sixth root of* 1.

DEFINITION OF NTH ROOT OF A COMPLEX NUMBER

The complex number $u = a + bi$ is an **nth root** of the complex number z if

$$z = u^n = (a + bi)^n.$$

To find a formula for an nth root of a complex number, let u be an nth root of z, where

$$u = s(\cos \beta + i \sin \beta) \quad \text{and} \quad z = r(\cos \theta + i \sin \theta).$$

By DeMoivre's Theorem and the fact that $u^n = z$, you have

$$s^n(\cos n\beta + i \sin n\beta) = r(\cos \theta + i \sin \theta).$$

Now, taking the absolute value of both sides of this equation, it follows that $s^n = r$. Substituting back into the previous equation and dividing by r produces

$$\cos n\beta + i \sin n\beta = \cos \theta + i \sin \theta.$$

Thus, it follows that

$$\cos n\beta = \cos \theta \quad \text{and} \quad \sin n\beta = \sin \theta.$$

Because both sine and cosine have a period of 2π, these last two equations have solutions if and only if the angles differ by a multiple of 2π. Consequently, there must exist an integer k such that

$$n\beta = \theta + 2\pi k$$
$$\beta = \frac{\theta + 2\pi k}{n}.$$

By substituting this value for β into the trigonometric form of u, you obtain the result stated in the following theorem.

NTH ROOTS OF A COMPLEX NUMBER

REMARK Note that when k exceeds $n - 1$ the roots begin to repeat. For instance, if $k = n$, the angle

$$\frac{\theta + 2\pi n}{n} = \frac{\theta}{n} + 2\pi$$

is coterminal with θ/n, which is also obtained when $k = 0$.

For a positive integer n, the complex number $z = r(\cos \theta + i \sin \theta)$ has exactly n distinct nth roots given by

$$\sqrt[n]{r}\left(\cos \frac{\theta + 2\pi k}{n} + i \sin \frac{\theta + 2\pi k}{n}\right),$$

where $k = 0, 1, 2, \ldots, n - 1$.

FIGURE 8.38

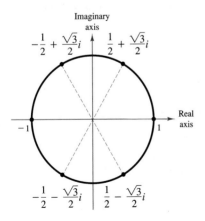

FIGURE 8.39

This formula for the nth roots of a complex number z has a nice geometric interpretation, as shown in Figure 8.38. Note that because the nth roots of z all have the same magnitude $\sqrt[n]{r}$, they all lie on a circle of radius $\sqrt[n]{r}$ with center at the origin. Furthermore, the n roots are equally spaced along the circle, because successive nth roots have arguments that differ by $2\pi/n$.

EXAMPLE 2   Finding nth Roots of a Real Number

Find all the sixth roots of 1.

SOLUTION

First, write 1 in the trigonometric form $1 = 1(\cos 0 + i \sin 0)$. Then, by the nth root formula, with $n = 6$ and $r = 1$, the roots have the form

$$\sqrt[6]{1}\left(\cos \frac{0 + 2\pi k}{6} + i \sin \frac{0 + 2\pi k}{6} \right),$$

or simply $\cos(\pi k/3) + i \sin(\pi k/3)$. Thus, for $k = 0, 1, 2, 3, 4, 5$, the sixth roots are as follows.

$$\cos 0 + i \sin 0 = 1$$

$$\cos \frac{\pi}{3} + i \sin \frac{\pi}{3} = \frac{1}{2} + \frac{\sqrt{3}}{2}i$$

$$\cos \frac{2\pi}{3} + i \sin \frac{2\pi}{3} = -\frac{1}{2} + \frac{\sqrt{3}}{2}i$$

$$\cos \pi + i \sin \pi = -1$$

$$\cos \frac{4\pi}{3} + i \sin \frac{4\pi}{3} = -\frac{1}{2} - \frac{\sqrt{3}}{2}i$$

$$\cos \frac{5\pi}{3} + i \sin \frac{5\pi}{3} = \frac{1}{2} - \frac{\sqrt{3}}{2}i$$

See Figure 8.39.

In Figure 8.39, notice that the roots obtained in Example 2 all have a magnitude of 1 and are equally spaced around this unit circle. Also, notice that the complex roots occur in conjugate pairs, as previously discussed in Section 3.6. We refer to the special case of the n distinct nth roots of 1 as the **nth roots of unity.**

EXAMPLE 3   Finding the *n*th Roots of a Complex Number

Find the three cube roots of $z = -2 + 2i$.

SOLUTION

Because z lies in the second quadrant, the trigonometric form of z is

$$z = -2 + 2i = \sqrt{8}(\cos 135° + i \sin 135°).$$

By our formula for *n*th roots, the cube roots have the form

$$\sqrt[6]{8}\left(\cos \frac{135° + 360°k}{3} + i \sin \frac{135° + 360°k}{3} \right).$$

Finally, for $k = 0, 1, 2$, you obtain the roots

$$\sqrt{2}(\cos 45° + i \sin 45°) = 1 + i$$
$$\sqrt{2}(\cos 165° + i \sin 165°) \approx -1.3660 + 0.3660i$$
$$\sqrt{2}(\cos 285° + i \sin 285°) \approx 0.3660 - 1.3660i.$$

REMARK   Note that the roots do *not* occur in conjugate pairs. Do you see why?

EXAMPLE 4   Finding the Roots of a Polynomial Equation

Solve $x^4 + 16 = 0$.

SOLUTION

The given equation can be written as

$$x^4 = -16 \quad \text{or} \quad x^4 = 16(\cos \pi + i \sin \pi),$$

which means that you can solve the equation by finding the four fourth roots of -16. Each of these roots has the form

$$\sqrt[4]{16}\left(\cos \frac{\pi + 2\pi k}{4} + i \sin \frac{\pi + 2\pi k}{4} \right).$$

Finally, using $k = 0, 1, 2, 3$, you obtain the roots

$$2\left(\cos \frac{\pi}{4} + i \sin \frac{\pi}{4} \right) = 2\left(\frac{\sqrt{2}}{2} + \frac{\sqrt{2}}{2}i \right) = \sqrt{2} + \sqrt{2}i$$
$$2\left(\cos \frac{3\pi}{4} + i \sin \frac{3\pi}{4} \right) = 2\left(-\frac{\sqrt{2}}{2} + \frac{\sqrt{2}}{2}i \right) = -\sqrt{2} + \sqrt{2}i$$
$$2\left(\cos \frac{5\pi}{4} + i \sin \frac{5\pi}{4} \right) = 2\left(-\frac{\sqrt{2}}{2} - \frac{\sqrt{2}}{2}i \right) = -\sqrt{2} - \sqrt{2}i$$
$$2\left(\cos \frac{7\pi}{4} + i \sin \frac{7\pi}{4} \right) = 2\left(\frac{\sqrt{2}}{2} - \frac{\sqrt{2}}{2}i \right) = \sqrt{2} - \sqrt{2}i.$$

DISCUSSION
PROBLEM
....

A FAMOUS
MATHEMATICAL
FORMULA

In this section you studied DeMoivre's Theorem, which gives a formula for raising a complex number to a positive integer power. Another famous formula that involves complex numbers and powers is called Euler's Formula, after the German mathematician Leonhard Euler (1707–1783). This formula states that

$$e^{a+bi} = e^a(\cos b + i \sin b).$$

Although the interpretation of this formula is beyond the scope of this text, we decided to include it because it gives rise to one of the most wonderful equations in mathematics.

$$e^{\pi i} + 1 = 0$$

This elegant equation relates the five most famous numbers in mathematics, 0, 1, π, e, and i, in a single equation. Show how Euler's Formula can be used to derive this equation.

WARM-UP
....

The following warm-up exercises involve skills that were covered in earlier sections. You will use these skills in the exercise set for this section.

In Exercises 1 and 2, simplify the expression.

1. $\sqrt[3]{54}$ **2.** $\sqrt[4]{16 + 48}$

In Exercises 3–6, write the complex number in trigonometric form.

3. $-5 + 5i$ **4.** $-3i$ **5.** -12 **6.** 12

In Exercises 7–10, perform the indicated operation. Leave the result in trigonometric form.

7. $\left(\cos \dfrac{\pi}{4} + i \sin \dfrac{\pi}{4}\right)\left(\cos \dfrac{\pi}{2} + i \sin \dfrac{\pi}{2}\right)$

8. $\left(\cos \dfrac{\pi}{12} + i \sin \dfrac{\pi}{12}\right)\left(\cos \dfrac{5\pi}{6} + i \sin \dfrac{5\pi}{6}\right)$

9. $\dfrac{6[\cos(2\pi/3) + i \sin(2\pi/3)]}{3[\cos(\pi/6) + i \sin(\pi/6)]}$

10. $\dfrac{2(\cos 55° + i \sin 55°)}{3(\cos 10° + i \sin 10°)}$

SECTION 8.5 · EXERCISES

In Exercises 1–12, use DeMoivre's Theorem to find the indicated powers of the complex number. Express the result in standard form.

1. $(1 + i)^5$ **2.** $(2 + 2i)^6$

3. $(-1 + i)^{10}$ **4.** $(1 - i)^{12}$

5. $2(\sqrt{3} + i)^7$ **6.** $4(1 - \sqrt{3}i)^3$

7. $[5(\cos 20° + i \sin 20°)]^3$

8. $[3(\cos 150° + i \sin 150°)]^4$

9. $\left(\cos \dfrac{5\pi}{4} + i \sin \dfrac{5\pi}{4}\right)^{10}$

10. $\left[2\left(\cos \dfrac{\pi}{2} + i \sin \dfrac{\pi}{2}\right)\right]^8$

11. $[5(\cos 3.2 + i \sin 3.2)]^4$

12. $(\cos 0 + i \sin 0)^{20}$

In Exercises 13–24, (a) use DeMoivre's Theorem to find the indicated roots of the complex number, (b) represent each of the roots graphically, and (c) express each of the roots in standard form.

13. Square roots of: $9(\cos 120° + i \sin 120°)$

14. Square roots of: $16(\cos 60° + i \sin 60°)$

15. Fourth roots of: $16\left(\cos \dfrac{4\pi}{3} + i \sin \dfrac{4\pi}{3}\right)$

16. Fifth roots of: $32\left(\cos \dfrac{5\pi}{6} + i \sin \dfrac{5\pi}{6}\right)$

17. Square roots of: $-25i$

18. Fourth roots of: $625i$

19. Cube roots of: $-\dfrac{125}{2}\left(1 + \sqrt{3}i\right)$

20. Cube roots of: $-8\sqrt{2}(1 - i)$

21. Cube roots of: 8

22. Fourth roots of: i

23. Fifth roots of: 1

24. Cube roots of: 1000

In Exercises 25–32, find all the solutions of the equation and represent the solutions on a unit circle.

25. $x^4 - i = 0$ **26.** $x^3 + 1 = 0$

27. $x^5 + 243 = 0$ **28.** $x^4 - 81 = 0$

29. $x^3 + 64i = 0$ **30.** $x^6 - 64i = 0$

31. $x^3 - (1 - i) = 0$ **32.** $x^4 + (1 + i) = 0$

CHAPTER 8 · REVIEW EXERCISES

In Exercises 1–16, solve the triangle (if possible). If two solutions exist, list both.

1. $a = 5$, $b = 8$, $c = 10$

2. $a = 6$, $b = 9$, $C = 45°$

3. $A = 12°$, $B = 58°$, $a = 5$

4. $B = 110°$, $C = 30°$, $c = 10.5$

5. $B = 110°$, $a = 4$, $c = 4$

6. $a = 80$, $b = 60$, $c = 100$

7. $A = 75°$, $a = 2.5$, $b = 16.5$

8. $A = 130°$, $a = 50$, $b = 30$

9. $B = 115°$, $a = 7$, $b = 14.5$

10. $C = 50°$, $a = 25$, $c = 22$

11. $A = 15°$, $a = 5$, $b = 10$

12. $B = 150°$, $a = 64$, $b = 10$

13. $B = 150°$, $a = 10$, $c = 20$

14. $a = 2.5$, $b = 15.0$, $c = 4.5$

15. $B = 25°$, $a = 6.2$, $b = 4$

16. $B = 90°$, $a = 5$, $c = 12$

In Exercises 17–20, find the area of the triangle.

17. $a = 4, b = 5, c = 7$ **18.** $a = 15, b = 8, c = 10$

19. $A = 27°, b = 5, c = 8$ **20.** $B = 80°, a = 4, c = 8$

21. *Height of a Tree*   Find the height of a tree that stands on a hillside of slope 32° (from the horizontal) if from a point 75 feet down the hill from the tree the angle of elevation to the top of the tree is 48° (see figure).

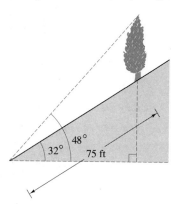

FIGURE FOR 21

22. *Surveying*   To approximate the length of a marsh, a surveyor walks 450 meters from point A to point B. Then the surveyor turns 65° and walks 325 meters to point C. Approximate the length AC of the marsh (see figure).

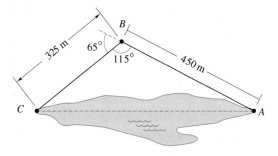

FIGURE FOR 22

23. *Height*   From a certain distance, the angle of elevation to the top of a building is 17°. At a point 50 meters closer to the building, the angle of elevation is 31°. Approximate the height of the building.

24. *River Width*   Determine the width of a river that flows due east, if a tree on the opposite bank has a bearing of N 22° 30′ E and, after walking 400 feet downstream, a surveyor finds the tree has a bearing of N 15° W.

25. *Navigation*   Two planes leave an airport at approximately the same time. One is flying at 425 miles per hour at a bearing of N 5° W, and the other is flying at 530 miles per hour at a bearing of N 67° E (see figure). How far apart are the planes after flying for 2 hours?

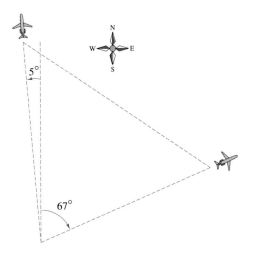

FIGURE FOR 25

26. *Geometry*   The lengths of the diagonals of a parallelogram are 10 feet and 16 feet. Find the lengths of the sides of the parallelogram if the diagonals intersect at an angle of 28°.

In Exercises 27–30, find the component form of the vector **v** satisfying the given conditions.

27. Initial point: (0, 10)   **28.** Initial point: (1, 5)
Terminal point: (7, 3)   Terminal point: (15, 9)

29. $\|\mathbf{v}\| = 8, \quad \theta = 120°$ **30.** $\|\mathbf{v}\| = \frac{1}{2}, \quad \theta = 225°$

In Exercises 31–34, find the component form of the specified vector and sketch its graph given that $\mathbf{u} = 6\mathbf{i} - 5\mathbf{j}$ and $\mathbf{v} = 10\mathbf{i} + 3\mathbf{j}$.

31. $\dfrac{1}{\|\mathbf{u}\|}\mathbf{u}$ **32.** $3\mathbf{v}$

33. $4\mathbf{u} - 5\mathbf{v}$ **34.** $\frac{1}{2}\mathbf{v}$

35. *Resultant Force* Find the direction and magnitude of the resultant of the three forces shown in the figure.

$\tan \beta = \frac{3}{4}$ $\tan \alpha = \frac{12}{5}$

FIGURE FOR 35

36. *Resultant Force* Forces with magnitudes of 85 pounds and 50 pounds act on a single point. Find the magnitude of the resultant if the angle between the forces is 15°.

37. *Rope Tension* A 100-pound weight is supported by two ropes, as shown in the figure. Find the tension in each rope.

FIGURE FOR 37

38. *Braking Force* A 500-pound motorcycle is headed up a hill inclined at 12°. What force is required to keep the motorcycle from rolling back down the hill when stopped at a red light?

39. *Navigation* An airplane has an air speed of 450 miles per hour at a bearing of N 30° E. If the wind velocity is 20 miles per hour from the west, find the ground speed and the direction of the plane.

40. *Angle Between Forces* Forces of 60 pounds and 100 pounds have a resultant force of 125 pounds. Find the angle between the two forces.

In Exercises 41–44, find the trigonometric form of the complex number.

41. $5 - 5i$

42. $-3\sqrt{3} + 3i$

43. $5 + 12i$

44. -7

In Exercises 45–48, write the complex number in standard form.

45. $100(\cos 240° + i \sin 240°)$

46. $24(\cos 330° + i \sin 330°)$

47. $13(\cos 0 + i \sin 0)$

48. $8\left(\cos \frac{5\pi}{6} + i \sin \frac{5\pi}{6}\right)$

In Exercises 49–52, (a) express the two complex numbers in trigonometric form, and (b) use the trigonometric form to find $z_1 z_2$ and z_1/z_2.

49. $z_1 = -5$, $z_2 = 5i$

50. $z_1 = 2\sqrt{3} - 2i$, $z_2 = -10i$

51. $z_1 = -3(1 + i)$, $z_2 = \left(\sqrt{3} + i\right)$

52. $z_1 = 5i$, $z_2 = 2(1 - i)$

In Exercises 53–56, use DeMoivre's Theorem to find the indicated power of the complex number. Express the result in standard form.

53. $\left[5\left(\cos \frac{\pi}{12} + i \sin \frac{\pi}{12}\right)\right]^4$

54. $\left[2\left(\cos \frac{4\pi}{15} + i \sin \frac{4\pi}{15}\right)\right]^5$

55. $(2 + 3i)^6$

56. $(1 - i)^8$

In Exercises 57–60, use DeMoivre's Theorem to find the roots of the complex number.

57. Sixth roots of: $-729i$

58. Fourth roots of: 256

59. Cube roots of: -1

60. Fourth roots of: $-1 + i$

In Exercises 61–64, find all solutions of the equation and represent the solutions on a unit circle.

61. $x^4 + 81 = 0$

62. $x^5 - 32 = 0$

63. $(x^3 - 1)(x^2 + 1) = 0$

64. $x^3 + 8i = 0$

CUMULATIVE TEST FOR CHAPTERS 6–8

Take this test as you would take a test in class. After you are done, check your work with the answers in the back of the book.

1. Express the angle $4\pi/9$ in degree measure and sketch the angle in standard position.

2. Express the angle $-120°$ in radian measure as a multiple of π and sketch the angle in standard position.

3. The terminal side of an angle θ in standard position passes through the point $(12, 5)$. Evaluate the six trigonometric functions of the angle.

4. If $\cos t = -\frac{2}{3}$ where $\pi/2 < t < \pi$, find $\sin t$ and $\tan t$.

5. Use a calculator to approximate $\sin(-1.25)$. Round your answer to four decimal places.

6. Use a calculator to approximate two values of θ ($0° \le \theta < 360°$) such that $\sec \theta = 2.125$. Round your answers to two decimal places.

7. Sketch the graph of each of the following functions through two periods.

   (a) $y = -3 \sin 2x$

   (b) $f(x) = 2 \cos\left(x - \frac{\pi}{4}\right)$

   (c) $g(x) = \tan\left(\frac{\pi x}{2}\right)$

   (d) $h(t) = \sec t$

8. Write a sentence describing the relationship between the graph of the functions $f(x) = \sin x$ and g.

   (a) $g(x) = 10 + \sin x$

   (b) $g(x) = \sin \frac{\pi x}{2}$

   (c) $g(x) = \sin\left(x + \frac{\pi}{4}\right)$

   (d) $g(x) = -\sin x$

9. Find a, b, and c so that the graph of $f(x) = a \sin(bx + c)$ matches the given figure.

10. Consider the function $f(x) = \sin 3x - 2 \cos x$.

    (a) Use a graphing utility to graph the function.

    (b) Determine the period of the function.

    (c) Approximate (accurate to one decimal place) the zero of the function in the interval $[0, 3]$.

    (d) Approximate (accurate to one decimal place) the maximum value of the function in the interval $[0, 3]$.

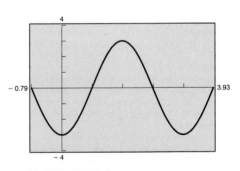

FIGURE FOR 9

11. Consider the function

$$f(t) = 2^{-t/2} \cos\left(\frac{\pi t}{2}\right)$$

where t is the time in seconds.

(a) Use a graphing utility to graph the function.

(b) Is the function periodic?

(c) Beyond what time t is the maximum value of the function less than 0.3?

12. Evaluate the expression *without* the aid of a calculator.

(a) $\arcsin(\frac{1}{2})$ (b) $\arctan \sqrt{3}$

13. Write an algebraic expression that is equivalent to $\sin(\arccos 2x)$.

14. From a point on the ground 600 feet from the foot of a cliff, the angle of elevation of the top of the cliff is $32° \, 30'$. How high is the cliff?

15. Add and simplify: $\dfrac{1 + \cos \beta}{\sin \beta} + \dfrac{\sin \beta}{1 + \cos \beta}$

16. Find all the solutions to the equation $2 \cos^2 x - \cos x = 0$ in the interval $[0, 2\pi)$.

17. Given $\sin x = \frac{2}{3}$, find the exact value of $\sin(2x)$ where x is a first quadrant angle.

18. Evaluate $\cos 105° = \cos(135° - 30°)$ *without* the aid of a calculator.

19. Find the remaining sides and angles of each triangle.

(a)

(b)

20. In a (square) baseball diamond with 90-foot sides, the pitcher's mound is 60 feet from home plate. How far is a runner from the pitcher's mound when the runner is halfway from third base to home?

21. Find the component form of $\mathbf{u} + \mathbf{v}$ if $\|\mathbf{u}\| = 3$, $\theta_{\mathbf{u}} = 30°$, $\|\mathbf{v}\| = 5$, and $\theta_{\mathbf{v}} = 120°$. (Assume the angles are measured counterclockwise from the x-axis to the vector.)

22. A projectile is fired with an initial velocity of 120 feet per second at an angle of $15°$ with the horizontal. Find the vertical and horizontal components of the velocity accurate to two decimal places.

23. Write the complex number $z = 2(1 - i)$ in trigonometric form and find z^3.

LINEAR MODELS AND SYSTEMS OF EQUATIONS

9.1 LINEAR MODELING AND SCATTER PLOTS

Introduction to Modeling / Direct Variation / Rates of Change / Scatter Plots

Introduction to Modeling

In developing a model to represent actual data, you strive for two (often conflicting) goals—accuracy and simplicity. That is, the model should be simple enough to be workable, yet accurate enough to produce meaningful results.

For instance, suppose you want to find a model that represents the population P of the United States from 1800 through 1890. The simplest model is a linear model of the form

$$P = at + b,$$

where $t = 0$ represents the year 1800, $t = 1$ represents 1810, and so on. By looking at Exercise 80 in Section 2.4, however, you can see that such a model would not be very accurate. In this case, you can obtain much more accuracy with the quadratic model

$$P = 0.6942t^2 + 6.183.$$

EXAMPLE 1   A Mathematical Model

The total amount of advertising expenses (in billions of dollars) in the United States from 1980 to 1989 is given in Table 9.1. (*Source:* McCann Erickson) A linear model that approximates these data is

$$y = 8.1377t + 53.029, \qquad 0 \le t \le 9,$$

where y represents the advertising expenses (in billions of dollars) and t represents the year, with $t = 0$ corresponding to 1980. Plot the actual data *and* the model on the same graph. How closely does the model represent the data?

TABLE 9.1

Year	1980	1981	1982	1983	1984	1985	1986	1987	1988	1989
Expenses	54.78	60.43	66.58	75.85	88.10	94.75	102.14	109.79	118.32	125.55

SOLUTION

The actual data are plotted in Figure 9.1, along with the graph of the model. From the figure, it appears that the model is a "good fit" for the actual data. You can see how well the model fits by comparing the actual values of y with the values of y given by the model, as shown in Table 9.2.

FIGURE 9.1

TABLE 9.2

t	0	1	2	3	4	5	6	7	8	9
Actual y	54.78	60.43	66.58	75.85	88.10	94.75	102.14	109.79	118.32	125.55
Model y	53.03	61.17	69.30	77.44	85.58	93.72	101.86	109.99	118.13	126.27

Direct Variation

There are two basic types of linear models. The more general model has a y-intercept that is nonzero: $y = mx + b$, $b \neq 0$. The simpler model has a y-intercept that is zero, $y = mx$. For this simpler model, we say that y **varies directly** as x, or that y is **proportional** to x.

DIRECT VARIATION

The following statements are equivalent.

1. y **varies directly** as x.
2. y is **directly proportional** to x.
3. $y = mx$ for some nonzero constant m.

The number m is the **constant of variation** or the **constant of proportionality.**

EXAMPLE 2   State Income Tax

In Pennsylvania, the state income tax is directly proportional to a person's *gross income.* Suppose you are working in Pennsylvania and your state income tax deduction was $31.50 for a gross monthly income of $1500. Find a model that gives the Pennsylvania state income tax in terms of gross income. Use this model to determine the tax for an income of $2200 per month.

SOLUTION

VERBAL MODEL   State income tax = Income tax rate · Gross income

LABELS

State income tax = y *(dollars)*

Income tax rate = m *(in decimal form)*

Gross income = x *(dollars)*

EQUATION

$y = mx$ *Direct variation model*

$31.50 = m(1500)$ *Substitute $y = 31.50$ and $x = 1500$*

$0.021 = m$ *Income tax rate*

Thus, the equation (or model) for state income tax in Pennsylvania is

$y = 0.021x$.

FIGURE 9.2

In other words, Pennsylvania has a state income tax rate of 2.1% of gross income. The graph of this equation is shown in Figure 9.2. If the gross monthly income is $2200, then the tax is $y = mx = 0.021(2200) = \$46.20$.

EXAMPLE 3   The English and Metric Systems

The speed of an automobile in miles per hour is directly proportional to the speed in kilometers per hour. Suppose you are traveling at a rate of 64 miles per hour, switch your speedometer reading to metric units, and notice that the speed is 103 kilometers per hour. Use this information to find a model that relates miles per hour to kilometers per hour.

SOLUTION

If you let y represent the speed in miles per hour and x represent the speed in kilometers per hour, then you know that y and x are related by the equation

$$y = mx.$$

To find the value of m, substitute the given values of $y = 64$ and $x = 103$, as follows.

$$y = mx \qquad \text{\textit{Direct variation model}}$$
$$64 = m(103) \qquad \text{\textit{Substitute }} y = 64 \text{ \textit{and} } x = 103$$
$$\frac{64}{103} = m$$
$$0.62136 \approx m \qquad \text{\textit{Conversion factor}}$$

Thus, the conversion factor from kilometers per hour to miles per hour is approximately 0.62136, and the model is

$$y = 0.62136x.$$

The graph for this equation is shown in Figure 9.3.

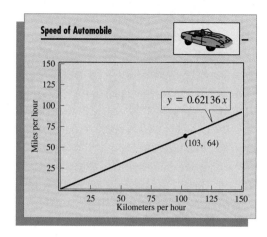

Speed of Automobile

$y = 0.621\,36\,x$

(103, 64)

Miles per hour

Kilometers per hour

FIGURE 9.3

Note from Example 3 that once you have found a model that converts speed in kilometers per hour to miles per hour, you can use the model to convert other speeds from the metric system to the English system, as shown in Table 9.3.

TABLE 9.3

Kilometers per hour	20.0	40.0	60.0	80.0	100.0	120.0
Miles per hour	12.4	24.9	37.3	49.7	62.1	74.6

Rates of Change

A second common type of linear model is one that involves a known rate of change. In the linear equation

$$y = mx + b,$$

you know that m represents the slope of the line. In real-life problems, the slope can be interpreted as the **rate of change** of y with respect to x. In applied problems, rates of change should always be listed in appropriate units of measure. This is demonstrated in Example 4.

EXAMPLE 4   Rates of Mountain Climbing

A mountain climber is climbing up a 500-foot cliff. By 1 P.M., the mountain climber has climbed 115 feet up the cliff. By 4 P. M., the climber has reached a height of 280 feet, as shown in Figure 9.4. Find the average climbing rate and use this rate to find the equation that relates the height of the climber to the time. Use the model to estimate the time when the climber will reach the top of the cliff.

500 ft

280 ft

115 ft

4:00 P.M.

1:00 P.M.

FIGURE 9.4

SOLUTION

Let y represent the height of the climber and let t represent the time. Then the two points that represent the climber's two positions are

$$(t_1, y_1) = (1, 115) \quad \text{and} \quad (t_2, y_2) = (4, 280).$$

Thus, the average climbing rate is

$$\text{Average climbing rate} = \frac{y_2 - y_1}{t_2 - t_1} = \frac{280 - 115}{4 - 1} = 55 \text{ feet per hour.}$$

Thus, an equation that relates the height of the climber to the time is

$$y - y_1 = m(t - t_1)$$ *Point-slope form*
$$y - 115 = 55(t - 1)$$ *Substitute $y_1 = 115$, $t_1 = 1$, and $m = 55$*
$$y = 55t + 60.$$ *Linear model*

To find the time when the climber reaches the top of the cliff, let $y = 500$ and solve for t to obtain

$$500 = 55t + 60$$
$$440 = 55t$$
$$8 = t.$$

Thus, continuing at the same rate, the climber will reach the top of the cliff by 8 P.M.

EXAMPLE 5   Population of Naples, Florida

Between 1980 and 1987, the population of the county of Naples, Florida increased at an average rate of approximately 6000 people per year. In 1980, the population was 86,000. (*Source:* Naples Chamber of Commerce) Find a model that gives the population of Naples in terms of the year, and use the model to estimate the population in 1990.

SOLUTION

Let y represent the population of Naples, and let t represent the year, with $t = 0$ corresponding to 1980. Letting $t = 0$ correspond to 1980 is convenient because you were given the population in 1980. Now, using the given rate of change, 6000 people per year, you obtain the following.

$$y = \quad mt + \quad b$$
$$y = 6000t + 86,000$$

Using this model, you can predict the 1990 ($t = 10$) population to be

$$1990 \text{ population} = 6000(10) + 86,000 = 146,000.$$

The graph of this model is shown in Figure 9.5. (In this particular example, the linear model is quite good—the actual population of Naples, Florida in 1990 was 145,000.)

FIGURE 9.5

Scatter Plots

The last type of linear modeling is a graphical approach that is commonly used in statistics. To find a model that approximates a set of actual data points, plot the points in a rectangular coordinate system. This collection of points is called a **scatter plot.** Once the points have been plotted, try to find the line that most closely represents the plotted points. (In this section, we will rely on a visual technique for fitting a line to a set of points. If you take a course in statistics, you will encounter *regression analysis* formulas that can fit a line to a set of points.)

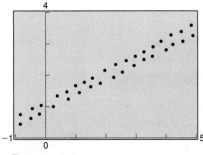

FIGURE 9.6

EXAMPLE 6   Fitting a Line to a Set of Points

The scatter plot in Figure 9.6 shows 35 different points in the plane. Find the equation of a line that approximately fits these points.

SOLUTION

From Figure 9.6 you can see that there is no line that *exactly* fits the given points. The points, however, do appear to follow a linear pattern. In Figure 9.7, notice that the line that appears to best describe the given points has about as many points above it as below it. From this figure, you can see that the "best-fitting line" has a y-intercept at about $(0, 1)$ and has a slope of about $\frac{1}{2}$. Thus, the equation of the line is

$$y = \frac{1}{2}x + 1.$$

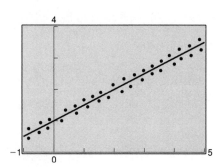

FIGURE 9.7

EXAMPLE 7   Prize Money at the Indianapolis 500

The total prize money (in millions of dollars) awarded at the Indianapolis 500 race from 1981 to 1989 is given in Table 9.4. (*Source:* Indianapolis Motor Speedway Hall of Fame) Construct a scatter plot that represents these points and find a linear model that approximates the given data.

TABLE 9.4

Year	1981	1982	1983	1984	1985	1986	1987	1988	1989
Prize	$1.61	$2.07	$2.41	$2.80	$3.27	$4.00	$4.49	$5.03	$5.72

Technology Note _____

Most graphing utilities have built-in statistical programs that can create scatter plots *and* find the equation of the line that best fits the data in the scatter plot. Use your graphing utility to plot the points given in Table 9.5: (1, 1.61), (2, 2.07), and so on. Then use the graphing utility's linear regression feature to find the best-fitting line. For this data, you should obtain $y = 0.511x + 0.932$. Can you justify that this line is a better fit of the data than the line obtained visually in Example 7?

SOLUTION

To begin, let y represent the prize money (in millions of dollars) and let t represent the year, with $t = 1$ corresponding to 1981. The scatter plot for the points is shown in Figure 9.8. From the scatter plot, draw a line that approximates the given data. Then, to find the equation of the line, approximate two points *on the line:* (1, 1.5) and (8, 5). The slope of this line is

$$m \approx \frac{y_2 - y_1}{t_2 - t_1} = \frac{5 - 1.5}{8 - 1} = 0.5.$$

FIGURE 9.8

Therefore, the equation of the line is

$$y - y_1 = m(t - t_1)$$
$$y - 1.5 = 0.5(t - 1)$$
$$y = 0.5t + 1.$$

To check your model, compare the actual y-values with the y-values given by the model, as shown in Table 9.5.

TABLE 9.5

t	1	2	3	4	5	6	7	8	9
Actual y	$1.61	$2.07	$2.41	$2.80	$3.27	$4.00	$4.49	$5.03	$5.72
Model y	$1.5	$2.0	$2.5	$3.0	$3.5	$4.0	$4.5	$5.0	$5.5

DISCUSSION PROBLEM

AN EXPERIMENT

Go to the library, or some other reference source, and find some data that you think describe a linear relationship. Plot the points and find the equation of a line that approximately represents the points.

WARM-UP

The following warm-up exercises involve skills that were covered in earlier sections. You will use these skills in the exercise set for this section.

In Exercises 1–4, sketch the graph of the line.

1. $y = 2x$ **2.** $y = \frac{1}{2}x$ **3.** $y = 2x + 1$ **4.** $y = \frac{1}{2}x + 1$

In Exercises 5 and 6, find an equation of the line that has the given slope and y-intercept.

5. Slope: 1, y-intercept: $(0, 2)$ **6.** Slope: $\frac{3}{2}$, y-intercept: $(0, 3)$

In Exercises 7–10, find an equation of the line that passes through the two points.

7. $(1, 3)$ and $(6, 8)$ **8.** $(0, 4)$ and $(7, 10)$
9. $(1, 5.2)$ and $(5, 4.7)$ **10.** $(2, 6.5)$ and $(8, 3.6)$

SECTION 9.1 · EXERCISES

1. *Employed Civilians*   The total number of employed civilians in the United States from 1982 to 1988 is given in the table. A linear model that approximates these data is

$$y = 93{,}836.8 + 2647.5t, \qquad 2 \le t \le 8,$$

where y represents the number of employed civilians (in thousands) and t represents the year, with $t = 0$ corresponding to 1980. Plot the actual data *and* the model on the same graph. How closely does the model represent the data? (*Source:* U.S. Bureau of Labor Statistics)

Year	1982	1983	1984	1985	1986	1987	1988
Actual number	99,526	100,834	105,005	107,150	109,597	112,440	114,968
Model number							

2. *Olympic Swimming*   The winning times in the women's 400-meter freestyle swimming event in the Olympics from 1948 to 1988 are given in the table. A linear model that approximates these data is

$$y = 5.5 - 0.033t,$$

where y represents the winning time in minutes and t represents the year, with $t = 0$ corresponding to 1940. Plot the actual data *and* the model on the same graph. How closely does the model represent the data? (*Source:* Olympic Committee)

Year	1948	1952	1956	1960	1964	1968
Actual time	5.30	5.20	4.91	4.84	4.72	4.53
Model time						

Year	1972	1976	1980	1984	1988
Actual time	4.32	4.16	4.15	4.12	4.06
Model time					

Direct Variation   In Exercises 3–8, assume that y is proportional to x. Use the given x-value and y-value to find a linear model that relates y and x.

	x-Value	y-Value
3.	$x = 5$	$y = 12$
4.	$x = 2$	$y = 14$
5.	$x = 10$	$y = 2050$
6.	$x = 6$	$y = 580$
7.	$x = 12$	$y = 1.75$
8.	$x = 15$	$y = 2.3$

9. *Simple Interest*   The simple interest that a person receives for an investment is directly proportional to the amount of the investment. Suppose that by investing $2500 in a certain bond issue, you obtained an interest payment of $187.50 at the end of 1 year. Find a model that gives the amount of interest I for this bond issue at the end of 1 year in terms of the amount invested P.

10. *Simple Interest*   The simple interest that a person receives for an investment is directly proportional to the amount of the investment. Suppose that by investing $5000 in a municipal bond, you obtained an interest payment of $337.50 at the end of 1 year. Find a model that gives the amount of interest I for this municipal bond at the end of 1 year in terms of the amount invested P.

11. *Property Tax*   The property tax in a certain city is based on the assessed value of the property. (The assessed value is often lower than the actual value of the property.) A house that has an assessed value of $50,000 has a property tax of $1840. Find a model that gives the amount of property tax y in terms of the assessed value x of the property. Use the model to find the property tax on a house that has an assessed value of $85,000.

12. *State Sales Tax*   The state sales tax in a certain state is based on retail price. An item that sells for $145.99 has a sales tax of $10.22. Find a model that gives the amount of sales tax y in terms of the retail price x. Use the model to find the sales tax on a purchase that has a retail price of $540.50.

13. *Centimeters and Inches*   Suppose you are using a yardstick that has both inches and centimeters. On the yardstick you notice that 13 inches is the same length as 33 centimeters. Use this information to find a model that relates centimeters to inches. Then use the model to complete the table.

Inches	5	10	20	25	30
Centimeters					

14. *Liters and Gallons*   Suppose you are buying gasoline and notice that 14 gallons of gasoline is the same as 53 liters. Use this information to find a linear model that relates gallons to liters. Use the model to complete the table.

Gallons	5	10	20	25	30
Liters					

Hooke's Law In Exercises 15–18, use Hooke's Law, which states that the distance a spring is stretched (or compressed) varies directly as the force on a spring.

15. A force of 50 pounds stretches a spring 5 inches.
  (a) How far will a force of 20 pounds stretch the spring?
  (b) What force is required to stretch the spring 1.5 inches?

Equilibrium

5 in.

50 lb

FIGURE FOR 15

16. A force of 50 pounds stretches a spring 3 inches.
  (a) How far will a force of 20 pounds stretch the spring?
  (b) What force is required to stretch the spring 1.5 inches?

17. The coiled spring of a toy supports the weight of a child. The spring compresses a distance of 1.9 inches under the weight of a 25-pound child. The toy will not work properly if its spring is compressed more than 3 inches. What is the weight of the heaviest child who should be allowed to use the toy?

18. An overhead garage door has two springs, one on each side of the door. A force of 15 pounds is required to stretch each spring 1 foot. Because of a pulley system, the springs stretch only one-half the distance the door travels. The door moves a total of 8 feet and the springs are at their natural length when the door is open. Find the combined lifting force applied to the door by the springs when the door is in the closed position.

8 ft

FIGURE FOR 18

In Exercises 19–22, you are given the dollar value of a product in 1990 *and* the rate at which the value of the item is expected to change during the next 5 years. Use this information to write a linear equation that gives the dollar value of the product in terms of the year. (Let $t = 0$ represent 1990.)

	1990 Value	*Rate*
19.	$20,500	$460 increase per year
20.	$745	$6.20 increase per year
21.	$1299	$289 decrease per year
22.	$12.49	$0.39 decrease per year

23. *Straight-Line Depreciation* A small business purchases a piece of equipment for $1200. After 5 years, the equipment will be outdated and have no value.
  (a) Write a linear equation giving the value V of the equipment during the 5 years it will be used.
  (b) Sketch the graph of the linear equation over the appropriate domain.
  (c) State the rate of change, and interpret its meaning in the context of the problem.

24. *Straight-Line Depreciation* A small business purchases a piece of equipment for $25,000. After 10 years the equipment will have to be replaced. Its salvage value at that time is expected to be $2000.
  (a) Write a linear equation giving the value V of the equipment during the 10 years it will be used.
  (b) Sketch the graph of the linear equation over the appropriate domain.
  (c) State the rate of change, and interpret its meaning in the context of the problem.

25. *Sales Price and List Price* A store is offering a 15% discount on all items in its inventory. Write a linear equation giving the sale price S for an item with a list price L.

26. *Sales Price and List Price* A store is offering a 25% discount on all summer shirts. Write a linear equation giving the sale price S for a summer shirt with a list price L.

27. *Hourly Wages* A manufacturer pays its assembly line workers $9.25 per hour. In addition, workers receive a piecework rate of $1.10 per unit produced. Write a linear equation for the hourly wages W in terms of the number of units x produced per hour.

28. *Sales Commission* A salesperson receives a monthly salary of $1200 plus a commission of 10% of sales. Write a linear equation for the salesperson's monthly wage W in terms of monthly sales S.

29. *Height of a Parachutist* After opening the parachute, the descent of a parachutist follows a linear model. At 2:08 P.M., the height of the parachutist is 7000 feet. At 2:10 P.M., the height is 4600 feet. Write a linear equation that gives the height of the parachutist in terms of the time t. (Let $t = 0$ represent 2:08 P.M., and let t be measured in seconds.) Use the equation to find the time when the parachutist will reach the ground.

30. *Distance Traveled by a Car* Suppose you are driving at a constant speed on a freeway. At 4:30 P.M., you drive by a sign that gives the distance to Montgomery, Alabama as 84 miles. At 4:59 P.M., you drive by another sign that says the distance to Montgomery is 56 miles. Write a linear equation that gives your distance from Montgomery in terms of the time t. (Let $t = 0$ represent 4:30 P.M., and let t be measured in minutes.) Use the equation to find the time when you will reach Montgomery.

31. *High School Enrollment* A high school had an enrollment of 1200 students in 1980. During the next 10 years, the enrollment increased by approximately 50 students per year. Write a linear equation giving the enrollment N in terms of the year t. (Let $t = 0$ correspond to the year 1980.) If this constant rate of growth continues, predict the enrollment in the year 2000.

32. *Cost of Renting* The monthly rent in a large office building is related to the size of the office that is rented. The monthly rent for an office that has 600 square feet of floor space is $750. Write a linear equation giving the monthly rent r in terms of the number of square feet of floor space x. Use the result to find the monthly rent for an office that has 1300 square feet of floor space.

In Exercises 33–36, state whether the data represented by the given scatter plot could be approximated by a linear model.

33. **34.**

35. **36.**

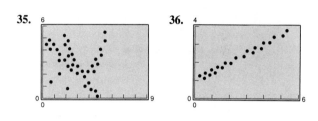

In Exercises 37–40, sketch the line that you think best approximates the data represented by the given scatter plot. Then find an equation of the line.

37. **38.**

39. **40.**

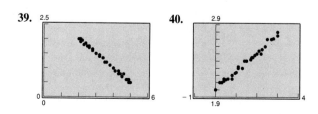

41. *Baseball Salaries*   The average annual salary of major league baseball players (in thousands of dollars) from 1979 to 1989 is shown in the accompanying scatter plot. (*Source:* Major League Baseball) Find the equation of the line that you think best fits these data. (Let *y* represent the average salary, and let *t* represent the year, with $t = 0$ corresponding to 1980.)

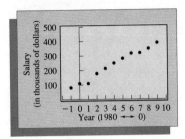

FIGURE FOR 41

42. *Discus Throw*   The lengths of the winning men's discus throws in the Olympics from 1900 to 1988 are shown in the accompanying scatter plot. (*Source:* Olympic Committee) Find the equation of the line that you think best fits these data. (Let *y* represent the length of the winning discus throw in feet, and let *t* represent the year, with $t = 0$ corresponding to 1900.)

FIGURE FOR 42

43. *Total Assets*   The total assets for Boatmen's Bancshares, Inc. from 1980 to 1989 (in millions of dollars) are shown in the accompanying scatter plot. Find the equation of the line that you think best fits these data. (Let *y* represent the total assets in millions of dollars, and let *t* represent the year, with $t = 0$ corresponding to 1980.) (*Source:* Standard OTC Stock Reports)

FIGURE FOR 43

44. *Book Value Per Share*   The book value per share for Universal Corporation from 1980 to 1989 (in dollars per share) is shown in the accompanying scatter plot. Find the equation of the line that you think best fits these data. (Let *y* represent the book value per share, and let *t* represent the year, with $t = 0$ corresponding to 1980.) (*Source:* Standard NYSE Stock Reports)

FIGURE FOR 44

9.2 SOLVING SYSTEMS OF EQUATIONS ALGEBRAICALLY AND GRAPHICALLY

The Method of Substitution / Graphical Approach to Finding Solutions / Applications

The Method of Substitution

Up to this point in the text, most problems have involved either a function of one variable or a single equation in two variables. However, many problems in science, business, and engineering involve two or more equations in two or more variables. To solve such problems, you need to find solutions of a **system of equations.** Here is an example of a system of two equations in x and y.

$$2x + y = 5 \qquad \text{\textit{Equation 1}}$$
$$3x - 2y = 4 \qquad \text{\textit{Equation 2}}$$

A **solution** of this system is an ordered pair that satisfies each equation in the system. When you find the set of all solutions, you are **solving the system of equations.** For instance, the ordered pair $(2, 1)$ is a solution of this system. To check this you can substitute 2 for x and 1 for y into *each* equation, as follows.

$$2(2) + 1 = 5 \qquad \text{\textit{Equation 1 checks}}$$
$$3(2) - 2(1) = 4 \qquad \text{\textit{Equation 2 checks}}$$

There are several different ways to solve systems of equations. In this chapter you will study the three most common techniques, beginning with the **method of substitution.** This method has five basic steps, which can be labeled *solve, substitute, solve, back-substitute,* and *check.*

EXAMPLE 1   Solving a System of Two Equations in Two Variables

Solve the system of equations.

$$x + y = 4 \qquad \text{\textit{Equation 1}}$$
$$x - y = 2 \qquad \text{\textit{Equation 2}}$$

SOLUTION

Solving for y in Equation 1 produces $y = 4 - x$. *Substituting* $(4 - x)$ for y in Equation 2 produces a single-variable equation that you can *solve* for x.

$$x - (4 - x) = 2 \qquad \text{\textit{Substitute for y}}$$
$$x - 4 + x = 2 \qquad \text{\textit{Single-variable equation}}$$
$$2x = 6$$
$$x = 3 \qquad \text{\textit{Solve for x}}$$

Finally, by *back-substituting* $x = 3$ into the equation $y = 4 - x$, you obtain $y = 1$. Thus, the solution is the ordered pair $(3, 1)$. Check this solution by substituting $x = 3$ and $y = 1$ into *both* equations in the original system.

DISCOVERY

Use a graphing utility to graph $y = -2x + 5$ and $y = 1.5x - 2$ on the same viewing rectangle. Then use the zoom feature to find the coordinates of the point of intersection of the two lines. Do you obtain the same coordinates as are obtained algebraically in the discussion at the right?

REMARK The term *back-substitution* implies that you work *backwards*. First you solve for one of the variables, and then you substitute that value *back* into one of the equations in the system to find the value of the other variable.

Because many steps are required to solve a system of equations, it is very easy to make errors in arithmetic. Thus, we *strongly* suggest that you always *check your solution by substituting it into each equation in the original system.*

METHOD OF SUBSTITUTION

To solve a system of two equations in two variables, use the following steps.

1. *Solve* one of the equations for one variable in terms of the other.
2. *Substitute* the expression found in Step 1 into the other equation to obtain an equation in one variable.
3. *Solve* the equation obtained in Step 2.
4. *Back-substitute* the solution in Step 3 into the expression obtained in Step 1 to find the value of the other variable.
5. *Check* the solution to see that it satisfies *each* of the original equations.

EXAMPLE 2 Solving a System by Substitution: One-Solution Case

A total of \$12,000 is invested in two funds paying 9% and 11% simple interest. If the yearly interest is \$1180, how much of the \$12,000 is invested at each rate?

SOLUTION

VERBAL MODEL

$$\begin{array}{ccc} \text{Investment in} & + & \text{Investment in} & = & \text{Total} \\ \text{9\% fund} & & \text{11\% fund} & & \text{investment} \end{array}$$

$$\text{9\% interest} + \text{11\% interest} = \text{Total interest}$$

LABELS

9% fund $= x$	*(dollars)*
11% fund $= y$	*(dollars)*
Total investment $= 12{,}000$	*(dollars)*
9% interest $= 0.09x$	*(dollars)*
11% interest $= 0.11y$	*(dollars)*
Total interest $= 1180$	*(dollars)*

SYSTEM

$$\begin{array}{ll} x + y = 12{,}000 & \text{\textit{Equation 1}} \\ 0.09x + 0.11y = 1{,}180 & \text{\textit{Equation 2}} \end{array}$$

To begin, it is convenient to multiply both sides of the second equation by 100 to obtain $9x + 11y = 118{,}000$. This step eliminates the need to work with decimals.

1. Solve for x in Equation 1.

$$x = 12{,}000 - y$$

2. Substitute this expression for x into the new Equation 2.

$$9(12{,}000 - y) + 11y = 118{,}000$$

3. Solve for y.

$$108{,}000 - 9y + 11y = 118{,}000$$
$$2y = 10{,}000$$
$$y = \$5000$$

4. Back-substitute the value $y = 5000$ to solve for x.

$$x = 12{,}000 - 5000 = \$7000$$

The solution is the ordered pair (7000, 5000). Check to see that $x = 7000$ and $y = 5000$ satisfy each of the original equations.

Note that the equations in Examples 1 and 2 are linear. That is, the variables x and y occurred to the first power only. The method of substitution can also be used to solve systems in which one or both of the equations are nonlinear.

EXAMPLE 3   Solving a System by Substitution: Two-Solution Case

Solve the system of equations.

$$x^2 - x - y = 1 \qquad\qquad \textit{Equation 1}$$
$$-x + y = -1 \qquad\qquad \textit{Equation 2}$$

SOLUTION

1. Solve for y in Equation 2.

$$y = x - 1$$

2. Substitute this expression for y into Equation 1.

$$x^2 - x - (x - 1) = 1$$

3. Solve for x.

$$x^2 - 2x + 1 = 1$$
$$x^2 - 2x = 0$$
$$x(x - 2) = 0$$
$$x = 0, \qquad x = 2$$

4. Back-substitute these values of x to solve for the corresponding values of y.

For $x = 0$: $y = 0 - 1 = -1$
For $x = 2$: $y = 2 - 1 = 1$

There are two solutions: $(0, -1)$ and $(2, 1)$. Check these solutions in the original system.

EXAMPLE 4   Solving a System by Substitution: No-Solution Case

Solve the system of equations.

$$-x + y = 4 \qquad \text{\emph{Equation 1}}$$
$$x^2 + y = 3 \qquad \text{\emph{Equation 2}}$$

SOLUTION

1. In this case, you can solve for y in Equation 1.

   $$y = x + 4$$

2. Substitute this expression for y into Equation 2.

   $$x^2 + (x + 4) = 3$$

3. Solve for x.

   $$x^2 + x + 4 = 3$$
   $$x^2 + x + 1 = 0$$
   $$x = \frac{-1 \pm \sqrt{1^2 - 4(1)(1)}}{2} \qquad \text{\emph{Quadratic Formula}}$$

Because the discriminant is negative, the equation $x^2 + x + 1 = 0$ has no (real) solution. Hence, this system has no (real) solution.

Graphical Approach to Finding Solutions

From Examples 2, 3, and 4, you can see that a system of two equations in two unknowns can have exactly one solution, more than one solution, or no solution. In practice, you can gain insight about the location and number of solutions of a system of equations by graphing each of the equations on the same coordinate plane. The solutions of the system correspond to the **points of intersection** of the graphs. For instance, in Figure 9.9(a) the two equations graph as two lines with a *single point* of intersection. The two equations in Example 3 graph as a parabola and a line with *two points* of intersection, as shown in Figure 9.9(b). Moreover, the two equations in Example 4 graph as a line and a parabola that happen to have *no points* of intersection, as shown in Figure 9.9(c).

Sometimes the graphical approach to solving a system of equations is easier than the method of substitution, and a graphing utility is especially helpful.

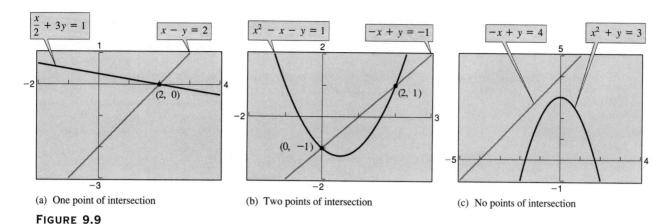

(a) One point of intersection

(b) Two points of intersection

(c) No points of intersection

FIGURE 9.9

REMARK   Example 5 shows the value of a graphical approach to solving systems of equations in two variables. Notice what would have happened if you had tried only the substitution method in Example 5. By substituting $y = \ln x$ into $x + y = 1$, you obtain $x + \ln x = 1$. It would be difficult to solve this equation for x using standard algebraic techniques.

EXAMPLE 5   **Solving a System of Equations**

Solve the system of equations.

$$y = \ln x \qquad\qquad \textit{Equation 1}$$
$$x + y = 1 \qquad\qquad \textit{Equation 2}$$

SOLUTION

The graph of each equation is shown in Figure 9.10. From this sketch it is clear that there is only one point of intersection. Also, it appears that $(1, 0)$ is the solution point, and you can confirm this by checking these coordinates in *both* equations.

CHECK: Let $x = 1$ and $y = 0$.

$$0 = \ln 1 \qquad\qquad \textit{Equation 1 checks}$$
$$1 + 0 = 1 \qquad\qquad \textit{Equation 2 checks}$$

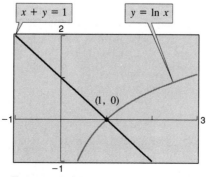

FIGURE 9.10

Applications

The total cost C of producing x units of a product typically has two components: the initial cost and the cost per unit. When enough units have been sold so that the total revenue R equals the total cost, the sales have reached the **break-even point.** The break-even point corresponds to the point of intersection of the cost and revenue curves.

EXAMPLE 6   An Application: Break-Even Analysis

A small business invests $10,000 in equipment to produce a product. Each unit of the product costs $0.65 to produce and is sold for $1.20. How many items must be sold before the business breaks even?

SOLUTION

The total cost of producing x units is

$$C = \overbrace{0.65x}^{\substack{\text{Cost per}\\ \text{unit}}} + \overbrace{10{,}000}^{\substack{\text{Initial}\\ \text{cost}}}, \qquad\qquad \textit{Equation 1}$$

and the revenue obtained by selling x units is

$$R = \overbrace{1.2x}^{\substack{\text{Price}\\ \text{per unit}}}. \qquad\qquad \textit{Equation 2}$$

Because the break-even point occurs when $R = C$, you have

$$1.2x = 0.65x + 10{,}000 \qquad \textit{Set R equal to C}$$
$$0.55x = 10{,}000$$
$$x = \frac{10{,}000}{0.55} \approx 18{,}182 \text{ units.}$$

Note in Figure 9.11 that sales less than the break-even point correspond to an overall loss, whereas sales greater than the break-even point correspond to a profit.

FIGURE 9.11

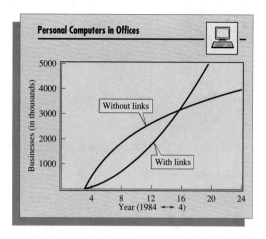

FIGURE 9.12

EXAMPLE 7   Computers in the Office

The number of business or government offices with personal computers (with and without communications links such as networks or modems) from 1984 to 1989 can be approximated by the models

$$y = -99.15 - 11.38t + 13.91t^2 \qquad \text{With communications links}$$
$$y = -2202.41 + 1934.45 \ln t, \qquad \text{Without communications links}$$

where y represents the number of businesses in thousands and t represents the year, with $t = 4$ corresponding to 1984. Sketch the graphs of these two models. In 1989 ($t = 9$), there were more offices without personal computer communications links than with personal computer communications links. According to the models, when will this change? (*Source:* Gartner Group, COMTEX database)

SOLUTION

The graphs of the two models are shown in Figure 9.12. According to the graphs, the number of offices with personal computer communications links will surpass the number without personal computer communications links in 1995 (when $t \approx 15.5$). Use the zoom and trace features of a graphing utility to verify this result.

DISCUSSION PROBLEM

POINTS OF INTERSECTION OF TWO GRAPHS

In this section, you learned that the graphs of two equations can intersect at zero, one, or more points. Use a graphing utility to graph the following systems. Which represents a system with no solution? Which represents a system with one solution? Which represents a system with two solutions?

(a) $x^2 + y^2 = 4$
$\quad\ \ x + y = 2$

(b) $x^2 + y^2 = 4$
$\quad\ \ x + y = \sqrt{8}$

(c) $x^2 + y^2 = 4$
$\quad\ \ x + y = 6$

Find three other systems of equations, one with no solution, one with one solution, and one with two solutions.

WARM-UP

The following warm-up exercises involve skills that were covered in earlier sections. You will use these skills in the exercise set for this section.

In Exercises 1–4, sketch the graph of the equation.

1. $y = -\frac{1}{3}x + 6$

2. $y = 2(x - 3)$

3. $x^2 + y^2 = 4$

4. $y = 5 - (x - 3)^2$

In Exercises 5–8, perform the indicated operations and simplify.

5. $(3x + 2y) - 2(x + y)$

6. $(-10u + 3v) + 5(2u - 8v)$

7. $x^2 + (x - 3)^2 + 6x$

8. $y^2 - (y + 1)^2 + 2y$

In Exercises 9 and 10, solve the equation.

9. $3x + (x - 5) = 15 + 4$

10. $y^2 + (y - 2)^2 = 2$

SECTION 9.2 · EXERCISES

In Exercises 1–10, solve the system graphically. Check your solution algebraically.

1. $2x + y = 4$
$\quad\ -x + y = 1$

2. $x -\ \ y = -5$
$\quad\ x + 2y =\ \ \ 4$

3. $x - y = -3$
$\quad x^2 - y = -1$

4. $3x - y = -2$
$\quad\ x^3 - y =\ \ \ 0$

5. $x + 3y = 15$
$x^2 + y^2 = 25$

6. $x \qquad - y = 0$
$x^3 - 5x + y = 0$

7. $\qquad x^2 - y = 0$
$x^2 - 4x + y = 0$

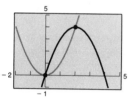

8. $y = \qquad - x^2 + 1$
$y = x^4 - 2x^2 + 1$

9. $x - 3y = -4$
$x^2 - y^3 = \quad 0$

10. $y = x^3 - 3x^2 + 3$
$y = \qquad - 2x + 3$

In Exercises 11–20, solve the system by the method of substitution.

11. $x - y = \quad 0$
$5x - 3y = 10$

12. $x + 2y = \quad 1$
$5x - 4y = -23$

13. $2x - y + 2 = 0$
$4x + y - 5 = 0$

14. $6x - 3y - 4 = 0$
$x + 2y - 4 = 0$

15. $30x - 40y - 33 = 0$
$10x + 20y - 21 = 0$

16. $1.5x + 0.8y = 2.3$
$0.3x - 0.2y = 0.1$

17. $\frac{1}{5}x + \frac{1}{2}y = \quad 8$
$x + \quad y = 20$

18. $\frac{1}{2}x + \frac{3}{4}y = 10$
$\frac{3}{2}x - \quad y = \quad 4$

19. $x - y = 0$
$2x + y = 0$

20. $x - 2y = \quad 0$
$3x - \quad y = \quad 0$

In Exercises 21–30, solve the system graphically or algebraically. Explain why you chose the method you used.

21. $y = 2x$
$y = x^2 + 1$

22. $x + y = 4$
$x^2 - y = 2$

23. $3x - 7y + 6 = 0$
$x^2 - y^2 = 4$

24. $x^2 + y^2 = 25$
$2x + \quad y = 10$

25. $y - e^{-x} = 1$
$y - \ln x = 3$

26. $y = \quad x^3 - 2x^2 + x - 1$
$y = -x^2 + 3x \qquad - 1$

27. $y = x^4 - 2x^2 + 1$
$y = 1 - \quad x^2$

28. $x^2 + y = 4$
$e^x - y = 0$

29. $\qquad xy - 1 = 0$
$2x - 4y + 7 = 0$

30. $x - 2y = 1$
$y = \sqrt{x - 1}$

In Exercises 31–42, use a graphing utility to find all points of intersection of the graphs of the pair of equations.

31. $x + \quad y \qquad = 4$
$x^2 + y^2 - 4x = 0$

32. $x - \quad y + 3 = 0$
$x^2 - 4x + 7 = y$

33. $2x - \quad y + \quad 3 = 0$
$x^2 + y^2 - 4x = 0$

34. $3x - 2y = 0$
$x^2 - y^2 = 4$

35. $\qquad x^2 + y^2 = 25$
$(x - 8)^2 + y^2 = 41$

36. $x^2 + y^2 = 8$
$y = x^2$

37. $\qquad y = e^x$
$x - y + 1 = 0$

38. $x + 2y = 8$
$y = \log_2 x$

39. $y = \sqrt{x}$
$y = x$

40. $x - \quad y = 3$
$x - y^2 = 1$

41. $x^2 + y^2 = 169$
$x^2 - 8y = 104$

42. $x^2 + y^2 = 4$
$2x^2 - \quad y = 2$

Break-Even Analysis In Exercises 43–46, find the sales necessary to break even ($R = C$) for the given cost C of x units, and the given revenue R obtained by selling x units. (Round to the nearest whole unit.)

43. $C = 8650x + 250,000, \quad R = 9950x$

44. $C = 5.5\sqrt{x} + 10,000, \quad R = 3.29x$

45. $C = 2.65x + 350,000, \quad R = 4.15x$

46. $C = 0.08x + 50,000, \quad R = 0.25x$

47. *Break-Even Point*   Suppose you are setting up a small business and have invested $16,000 to produce an item that will sell for $5.95. If each unit can be produced for $3.45, how many units must be sold to break even?

48. *Break-Even Point*   Suppose you are setting up a small business and have an initial investment of $5000. The unit cost of the product is $21.60, and the selling price is $34.10. How many units must be sold to break even?

49. *Investment Portfolio*   A total of $25,000 is invested in two funds paying 8% and 8.5% simple interest. If the yearly interest is $2060, how much of the $25,000 is invested at each rate?

50. *Investment Portfolio*   A total of $18,000 is invested in two funds paying 7.75% and 8.25% simple interest. If the yearly interest is $1455, how much of the $18,000 is invested at each rate?

51. *Choice of Two Jobs*   Suppose you are offered two different jobs selling dental supplies. One company offers a straight commission of 6% of sales. The other company offers a salary of $250 per week *plus* 3% of sales. How much would you have to sell in a week in order to make the straight commission offer better?

52. *Choice of Two Jobs*   Suppose you are offered two different jobs selling college textbooks. One company offers an annual salary of $20,000 *plus* a year-end bonus of 1% of your total sales. The other company offers a salary of $15,000 *plus* a year-end bonus of 2% of your total sales. How much would you have to sell in a year in order to make the second offer better?

53. *Log Volume*   You are offered two different rules for estimating the number of board feet in a log that is 16 feet long. One is the *Doyle Log Rule* and is modeled by
$$V = (D - 4)^2, \qquad 5 \le D \le 40,$$
and the other is the *Scribner Log Rule* and is modeled by
$$V = 0.79D^2 - 2D - 4, \qquad 5 \le D \le 40,$$
where D is the diameter of the log and V is its volume in board feet.
(a) Use a graphing utility to graph the log rules in the same viewing rectangle.
(b) For what diameter trees do the two scales agree?
(c) If you were selling large logs, which scale would you want to be used?

54. *Market Equilibrium*   The supply and demand curves for a business dealing with wheat are given by
Supply: $p = 1.45 + 0.00014x^2$
Demand: $p = (2.388 - 0.007x)^2$,
where p is the price in dollars per bushel and x is the quantity in bushels per day. Use a graphing utility to graph the supply and demand equations and find the market equilibrium. (The *market equilibrium* is the point of intersection of the graphs for $x > 0$.)

55. *Area*   What are the dimensions of a rectangular tract of land if its perimeter is 40 miles and its area is 96 square miles?

56. *Area*   What are the dimensions of an isoceles right triangle with a 2-inch hypotenuse and an area of 1 square inch?

57. Find an equation of a line whose graph intersects the graph of the parabola $y = x^2$ at (a) two points, (b) one point, and (c) no points. (There is more than one correct answer for each part of the exercise.)

58. Solve the system.
(a) $y = 2^x$
   $y = x^2$
(b) $y = 10^x$
   $y = x^{10}$

9.3   SYSTEMS OF LINEAR EQUATIONS IN TWO VARIABLES

The Method of Elimination / Graphical Interpretation of Solutions /
Applications

The Method of Elimination

In Section 9.2 you studied two methods of solving a system of equations (by substitution and by graphing). In this section, you will study a third method called the **method of elimination.** The key step in the method of elimination is to obtain, for one of the variables, coefficients that differ only in sign so that by *adding* the two equations this variable will be eliminated.

EXAMPLE 1   The Method of Elimination

Solve the system of linear equations.

$$3x + 2y = 4 \qquad \textit{Equation 1}$$
$$5x - 2y = 8 \qquad \textit{Equation 2}$$

SOLUTION

Begin by noting that the coefficients for y differ only in sign. By adding the two equations, you can eliminate y.

$$
\begin{aligned}
3x + 2y &= 4 \qquad && \textit{Equation 1}\\
5x - 2y &= 8 \qquad && \textit{Equation 2}\\
\hline
8x &= 12 \qquad && \textit{Add equations}
\end{aligned}
$$

Therefore, $x = \frac{3}{2}$. By back-substituting this value into the first equation, you can solve for y.

$$3x + 2y = 4 \qquad \textit{Equation 1}$$
$$3\left(\frac{3}{2}\right) + 2y = 4 \qquad \textit{Replace x by } \tfrac{3}{2}$$
$$2y = 4 - \frac{9}{2} = -\frac{1}{2} \qquad \textit{Solve for y}$$
$$y = -\frac{1}{4}$$

The solution is $\left(\frac{3}{2}, -\frac{1}{4}\right)$. You can check the solution *algebraically* by substituting in the original system, or *graphically*, as shown in Figure 9.13.

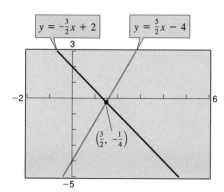

$y = -\frac{3}{2}x + 2$ $\qquad$ $y = \frac{5}{2}x - 4$

$\left(\frac{3}{2}, -\frac{1}{4}\right)$

FIGURE 9.13

Try using the method of substitution to solve the system given in Example 1. Which method do you think is easier? Many people find that the method of elimination is more efficient.

To obtain coefficients (for one of the variables) that differ only in sign, you often need to multiply one or both of the equations by a suitable constant.

EXAMPLE 2   The Method of Elimination

Solve the system of linear equations.

$$2x - 3y = -7 \qquad \qquad \textit{Equation 1}$$
$$3x + y = -5 \qquad \qquad \textit{Equation 2}$$

SOLUTION

For this system, you can obtain coefficients that differ only in sign by multiplying the second equation by 3.

$$
\begin{array}{rclll}
2x - 3y = -7 & \longrightarrow & 2x - 3y = & -7 & \textit{Equation 1} \\
3x + y = -5 & \longrightarrow & \underline{9x + 3y = -15} & & \textit{Multiply Equation 2 by 3} \\
& & 11x \quad\;\;\; = -22 & & \textit{Add equations}
\end{array}
$$

Thus, $x = -2$. By back-substituting this value of x into the first equation, you can solve for y.

$$
\begin{array}{lll}
2x - 3y = -7 & & \textit{Equation 1} \\
2(-2) - 3y = -7 & & \textit{Replace x by } -2 \\
-3y = -3 & & \textit{Add 4 to both sides} \\
y = 1 & & \textit{Solve for y}
\end{array}
$$

The solution is $(-2, 1)$. You can check the solution algebraically by substituting in the original system, or graphically, as shown in Figure 9.14.

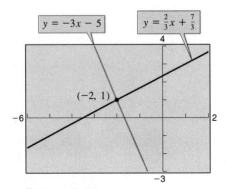

FIGURE 9.14

In Example 2, the two systems of linear equations

$$2x - 3y = -7 \quad \text{and} \quad 2x - 3y = -7$$
$$3x + y = -5 \qquad\qquad 9x + 3y = -15$$

are called **equivalent** because they have precisely the same solution set. The operations that can be performed on a system of linear equations to produce an equivalent system are (1) interchange two equations, (2) multiply an equation by a nonzero constant, and (3) add a multiple of an equation to another equation.

THE METHOD OF ELIMINATION

To use the **method of elimination** to solve a system of two linear equations in x and y, use the following steps.

1. Obtain coefficients for x (or y) that differ only in sign by multiplying all terms of one or both equations by suitably chosen nonzero constants.
2. Add the equations to eliminate one variable and solve the resulting equation.
3. Back-substitute the value obtained in Step 2 into either of the original equations and solve for the other variable.
4. Check your solution in both of the original equations.

EXAMPLE 3   The Method of Elimination

Solve the system of linear equations.

$$5x + 3y = 9 \qquad\qquad \textit{Equation 1}$$
$$2x - 4y = 14 \qquad\qquad \textit{Equation 2}$$

SOLUTION

You can obtain coefficients that differ only in sign by multiplying the first equation by 4 and multiplying the second equation by 3.

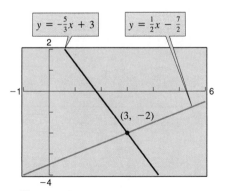

$$y = -\tfrac{5}{3}x + 3 \qquad y = \tfrac{1}{2}x - \tfrac{7}{2}$$

(3, −2)

FIGURE 9.15

$5x + 3y = 9$	$\longrightarrow$	$20x + 12y = 36$	*Multiply Equation 1 by 4*
$2x - 4y = 14$	$\longrightarrow$	$\underline{6x - 12y = 42}$	*Multiply Equation 2 by 3*
		$26x \qquad = 78$	*Add equations*

From this equation, you can see that $x = 3$. By back-substituting this value of x into the second equation, you can solve for y.

$$2x - 4y = 14 \qquad\qquad \textit{Equation 2}$$
$$2(3) - 4y = 14 \qquad\qquad \textit{Replace x by 3}$$
$$-4y = 8$$
$$y = -2 \qquad\qquad \textit{Solve for y}$$

The solution is $(3, -2)$. You can check the solution algebraically by substituting in the original system, or graphically, as shown in Figure 9.15.

Graphical Interpretation of Solutions

In Section 9.2, you saw that it is possible for a *general* system of equations to have exactly one solution, two or more solutions, or no solution. For a system of *linear* equations, this result can be strengthened. Specifically, if a system of linear equations has two different solutions, then it must have an infinite number of solutions! To see why this is true, consider the following graphical interpretations of a system of two linear equations in two variables. (Remember that the graph of a linear equation in two variables is a straight line.)

GRAPHICAL INTERPRETATION OF SOLUTIONS

For a system of two linear equations in two variables, the number of solutions is given by one of the following.

Number of Solutions	*Graphical Interpretation*
1. Exactly one solution	The two lines intersect at one point.
2. Infinitely many solutions	The two lines are identical.
3. No solution	The two lines are parallel.

These three possibilities are shown in Figure 9.16.

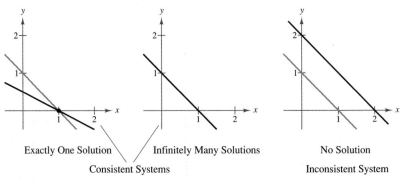

Exactly One Solution   Infinitely Many Solutions   No Solution

Consistent Systems   Inconsistent System

FIGURE 9.16

A system of linear equations is **consistent** if it has at least one solution, and it is **inconsistent** if it has no solution.

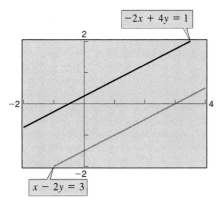

FIGURE 9.17

EXAMPLE 4   The Method of Elimination: No-Solution Case

Solve the system of linear equations.

$$x - 2y = 3 \qquad \text{\textit{Equation 1}}$$
$$-2x + 4y = 1 \qquad \text{\textit{Equation 2}}$$

SOLUTION

To obtain coefficients that differ only in sign, multiply the first equation by 2.

$$\begin{array}{lll} x - 2y = 3 & \longrightarrow & 2x - 4y = 6 \qquad \text{\textit{Multiply Equation 1 by 2}} \\ -2x + 4y = 1 & \longrightarrow & \underline{-2x + 4y = 1} \qquad \text{\textit{Equation 2}} \\ & & \qquad\quad 0 = 7 \qquad \text{\textit{False statement}} \end{array}$$

Because there are no values of x and y for which $0 = 7$, the system is inconsistent and has no solution. The lines corresponding to the two equations given in this system are shown in Figure 9.17. Note that the two lines are parallel, and therefore have no point of intersection. ·········

EXAMPLE 5   The Method of Elimination: Many-Solutions Case

Solve the following system of linear equations.

$$2x - y = 1 \qquad \text{\textit{Equation 1}}$$
$$4x - 2y = 2 \qquad \text{\textit{Equation 2}}$$

SOLUTION

To obtain coefficients that differ only in sign, multiply the second equation by $-\frac{1}{2}$.

$$\begin{array}{lll} 2x - y = 1 & \longrightarrow & 2x - y = 1 \qquad \text{\textit{Equation 1}} \\ 4x - 2y = 2 & \longrightarrow & \underline{-2x + y = -1} \qquad \text{\textit{Multiply Equation 2 by } }-\frac{1}{2} \\ & & \qquad\quad 0 = 0 \qquad \text{\textit{Add equations}} \end{array}$$

Because the two equations turn out to be equivalent (have the same solution set), the system has infinitely many solutions. The solution set consists of all points (x, y) lying on the line $2x - y = 1$, as shown in Figure 9.18. ·········

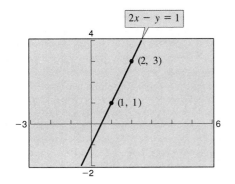

Infinite Number of Solutions

FIGURE 9.18

In Example 5, you could have reached the same conclusion by multiplying the first equation by 2 to obtain

$$4x - 2y = 2 \qquad \text{\textit{New Equation 1}}$$
$$4x - 2y = 2. \qquad \text{\textit{Equation 2}}$$

*Technology Note*_____

The general solution of the linear system

$$ax + by = c$$
$$dx + ey = f$$

is $x = (ce - bf)/(ae - db)$ and $y = (af - cd)/(ae - db)$. If $ae - db = 0$, then the system does not have a unique solution. A graphing utility program for solving such a system is given below. Try using this program to solve the system in Example 6.

```
Prgm1:SOLVE
:Disp "ENTER A,B,C,D,E,F"
:Input A
:Input B
:Input C
:Input D
:Input E
:Input F
:If AE-DB=0
:Goto 1
:(CE-BF)/(AE-DB)→X
:(AF-CD)/(AE-DB)→Y
:Disp X
:Disp Y
:Lbl 1
:End
```

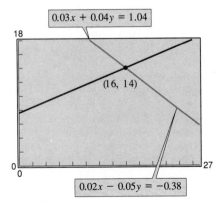

FIGURE 9.19

EXAMPLE 6   Solving a Linear System Having Decimal Coefficients

Solve the following system of linear equations.

$$0.02x - 0.05y = -0.38 \qquad \text{\textit{Equation 1}}$$
$$0.03x + 0.04y = 1.04 \qquad \text{\textit{Equation 2}}$$

SOLUTION

Because the coefficients in this system have two decimal places, begin by multiplying each equation by 100. (This produces an equivalent system in which the coefficients are all integers.)

$$2x - 5y = -38 \qquad \text{\textit{Revised Equation 1}}$$
$$3x + 4y = 104 \qquad \text{\textit{Revised Equation 2}}$$

Now, to obtain coefficients that differ only in sign, multiply the first equation by 3 and multiply the second equation by -2.

$$
\begin{array}{rcll}
2x - 5y = -38 & \longrightarrow & 6x - 15y = -114 & \text{\textit{Multiply Equation 1 by 3}} \\
3x + 4y = 104 & \longrightarrow & -6x - 8y = -208 & \text{\textit{Multiply Equation 2 by} } -2 \\
\hline
 & & -23y = -322 & \text{\textit{Add equations}}
\end{array}
$$

Thus, $y = \frac{-322}{-23} = 14$. Back-substituting this value into Equation 2 produces the following.

$$3x + 4y = 104 \qquad \text{\textit{Equation 2}}$$
$$3x + 4(14) = 104 \qquad \text{\textit{Replace y by} 14}$$
$$3x = 48$$
$$x = 16 \qquad \text{\textit{Solve for x}}$$

Therefore, the solution is (16, 14). Check this solution in each of the original equations in the system. You can also solve this system with a graphing utility by graphing the two lines

$$y = \frac{2}{5}x + \frac{38}{5}$$

$$y = -\frac{3}{4}x + 26$$

obtained by solving each equation for y. The intersection of the two lines, (16, 14), is the solution to the original system, as shown in Figure 9.19.

Applications

You have seen that systems of linear equations have many applications in science, business, health services, and government. The question that may come to mind is, How can I tell which application problems can be solved using a system of linear equations? The answer comes from the following considerations.

1. Does the problem involve more than one unknown quantity?
2. Are there two (or more) equations or conditions to be satisfied?

If one or both of these conditions occur, then the appropriate model for the problem may be a system of linear equations. Example 7 shows how to construct such a model.

EXAMPLE 7   An Application of a Linear System

An airplane flying into a headwind travels the 2000-mile flying distance between two cities in 4 hours and 24 minutes. On the return flight, the same distance is traveled in 4 hours. Find the ground speed of the plane and the speed of the wind, assuming that both remain constant.

SOLUTION

The two unknown quantities are the speeds of the wind and of the plane. If r_1 is the speed of the plane and r_2 is the speed of the wind, then

$$r_1 - r_2 = \text{speed of the plane } against \text{ the wind}$$
$$r_1 + r_2 = \text{speed of the plane } with \text{ the wind,}$$

as shown in Figure 9.20. Using the formula

$$\text{Distance} = (\text{rate})(\text{time})$$

for these two speeds, you can obtain the following equations.

$$2000 = (r_1 - r_2)\left(4 + \frac{24}{60}\right)$$

$$2000 = (r_1 + r_2)(4)$$

These two equations simplify as follows.

$$5000 = 11r_1 - 11r_2 \qquad \text{\textit{Equation 1}}$$
$$500 = r_1 + r_2 \qquad \text{\textit{Equation 2}}$$

By elimination, the solution is

$$r_1 = \frac{5250}{11} \approx 477.27 \text{ miles per hour}$$

$$r_2 = \frac{250}{11} \approx 22.73 \text{ miles per hour.}$$

Original flight

$r_1 - r_2$

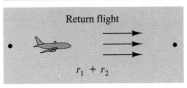

Return flight

$r_1 + r_2$

FIGURE 9.20

In a free market, the supply of and demand for many products are related to the price of the product. As the price of a product decreases, the demand (by *consumers*) increases whereas the supply (by *producers*) tends to decrease.

EXAMPLE 8   Finding the Point of Equilibrium

Suppose the demand and supply functions for a certain type of calculator are given by

$$p = 150 - 10x \qquad \textit{Demand equation}$$
$$p = 60 + 20x, \qquad \textit{Supply equation}$$

where p is the price in dollars and x represents the number of units (in millions). Find the **point of equilibrium** for this market by solving this system of equations. (The point of equilibrium is the price p and the number of units x that satisfy both the demand and supply equations.)

SOLUTION

For this system, you can use the method of substitution (because the two equations are given in a form in which p is written in terms of x). By substituting the value of p given in the second equation into the first equation, you obtain the following.

$$p = 150 - 10x \qquad \textit{First equation}$$
$$60 + 20x = 150 - 10x \qquad \textit{Replace p by } 60 + 20x$$
$$30x = 90 \qquad \textit{Add 10x and subtract 60}$$
$$x = 3 \qquad \textit{Divide both sides by 30}$$

Thus, the point of equilibrium occurs when the demand and supply are each 3 million units. (See Figure 9.21.) The price that corresponds to this x-value is obtained by back-substituting $x = 3$ into either of the original equations. For instance, back-substituting into the first equation produces

$$p = 150 - 10(3) = 150 - 30 = \$120.$$

Try back-substituting $x = 3$ into the second equation to see that you obtain the same price.

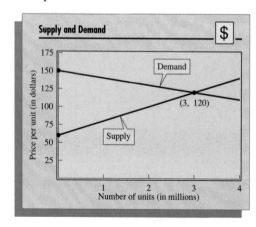

FIGURE 9.21

DISCUSSION
PROBLEM
. . . .

CREATING
CONSISTENT
AND
INCONSISTENT
SYSTEMS

Consider the following system of linear equations.

$$x - y = 4$$
$$-2x + 2y = k$$

(a) Find the value of k so that the system has an infinite number of solutions.
(b) Find one value of k so that the system has no solutions.
(c) Can the system have a unique solution? Why or why not?

WARM-UP
. . . .

The following warm-up exercises involve skills that were covered in earlier sections. You will use these skills in the exercise set for this section.

In Exercises 1 and 2, sketch the graph of the equation.

1. $2x + y = 4$ **2.** $5x - 2y = 3$

In Exercises 3 and 4, find an equation of the line passing through the two points.

3. $(-1, 3), (4, 8)$ **4.** $(2, 6), (5, 1)$

In Exercises 5 and 6, determine the slope of the line.

5. $3x + 6y = 4$ **6.** $7x - 4y = 10$

In Exercises 7–10, determine whether the lines represented by the pair of equations are parallel, perpendicular, or neither.

7. $2x - 3y = -10$
    $3x + 2y = 11$

8. $4x - 12y = 5$
    $-2x + 6y = 3$

9. $5x + y = 2$
    $3x + 2y = 1$

10. $x - 3y = 2$
    $6x + 2y = 4$

SECTION 9.3 · EXERCISES

In Exercises 1–10, solve the linear system by elimination. Label each line with the appropriate equation.

1. $2x + y = 4$
$x - y = 2$

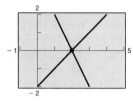

2. $x + 3y = 2$
$-x + 2y = 3$

3. $x - y = 0$
$3x - 2y = -1$

4. $2x - y = 2$
$4x + 3y = 24$

5. $x - y = 1$
$-2x + 2y = 5$

6. $3x + 2y = 2$
$6x + 4y = 14$

7. $3x - 2y = 6$
$-6x + 4y = -12$

8. $x - 2y = 5$
$6x + 2y = 7$

9. $9x - 3y = -1$
$3x + 6y = -5$

10. $5x + 3y = 18$
$2x - 7y = -1$

In Exercises 11–20, solve the system by elimination.

11. $x + 2y = 4$
$x - 2y = 1$

12. $3x - 5y = 2$
$2x + 5y = 13$

13. $2x + 3y = 18$
$5x - y = 11$

14. $x + 7y = 12$
$3x - 5y = 10$

15. $3x + 2y = 10$
$2x + 5y = 3$

16. $8r + 16s = 20$
$16r + 50s = 55$

17. $2u + v = 120$
$u + 2v = 120$

18. $5u + 6v = 24$
$3u + 5v = 18$

19. $6r - 5s = 3$
$10s - 12r = 5$

20. $1.8x + 1.2y = 4$
$9x + 6y = 3$

In Exercises 21–30, solve the system by elimination and verify the solution with a graphing utility.

21. $\dfrac{x}{4} + \dfrac{y}{6} = 1$
$x - y = 3$

22. $\dfrac{2}{3}x + \dfrac{1}{6}y = \dfrac{2}{3}$
$4x + y = 4$

23. $\dfrac{x + 3}{4} + \dfrac{y - 1}{3} = 1$
$2x - y = 12$

24. $\dfrac{x - 1}{2} + \dfrac{y + 2}{3} = 4$
$x - 2y = 5$

25. $2.5x - 3y = 1.5$
$10x - 12y = 6$

26. $0.02x - 0.05y = -0.19$
$0.03x + 0.04y = 0.52$

27. $0.05x - 0.03y = 0.21$
$0.07x + 0.02y = 0.16$

28. $0.2x - 0.5y = -27.8$
$0.3x + 0.4y = 68.7$

29. $4b + 3m = 3$
$3b + 11m = 13$

30. $3b + 3m = 7$
$3b + 5m = 3$

In Exercises 31 and 32, the graphs of the two equations appear to be parallel. Yet, when the system is solved algebraically, you will see that the system does have a solution. Find the solution and explain why it does not appear on the portion of the graph that is shown.

31. $200y - x = 200$
$199y - x = -198$

32. $25x - 24y = 0$
$13x - 12y = 120$

FIGURE FOR 31

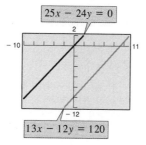

FIGURE FOR 32

33. *Airplane Speed*   An airplane flying into a headwind travels the 1800-mile flying distance between two cities in 3 hours and 36 minutes. On the return flight, the distance is traveled in 3 hours. Find the ground speed of the plane and the speed of the wind, assuming that both remain constant.

34. *Airplane Speed*   Two planes start from the same airport and fly in opposite directions. The second plane starts one-half hour after the first plane, but its speed is 50 miles per hour faster. Find the ground speed of each plane if 2 hours after the first plane starts the planes are 2000 miles apart.

35. *Acid Mixture*   Ten gallons of a 30% acid solution is obtained by mixing a 20% solution with a 50% solution. How much of each must be used?

36. *Fuel Mixture*   Five hundred gallons of 89 octane gasoline is obtained by mixing 87 octane gasoline with 92 octane gasoline. How much of each must be used?

37. *Investment Portfolio*   A total of $12,000 is invested in two corporate bonds that pay 10.5% and 12% simple interest. The annual interest is $1380. How much is invested in each bond?

38. *Investment Portfolio*   A total of $32,000 is invested in two municipal bonds that pay 5.75% and 6.25% simple interest. The annual interest is $1930. How much is invested in each bond?

39. *Ticket Sales*   Five hundred tickets were sold for a certain performance of a play. The tickets for adults and children sold for $7.50 and $4.00, respectively, and the total receipts for the performance were $3312.50. How many of each kind of ticket were sold?

40. *Shoe Sales*   Suppose you are the manager of a shoe store. On Saturday night you are going over the receipts of the previous week's sales. Two hundred and forty pairs of tennis shoes were sold. One style sold for $66.95 and the other sold for $84.95. The total receipts were $17,652. The cash register that was supposed to record the number of each type of shoe sold malfunctioned. Can you recover the information? If so, how many shoes of each type were sold?

Supply and Demand   In Exercises 41–46, use a graphing utility to graph the demand and supply equations and find the point of equilibrium.

Demand	*Supply*
41. $p = 50 - 0.5x$	$p = 0.125x$
42. $p = 60 - x$	$p = 10 + \frac{7}{3}x$
43. $p = 300 - x$	$p = 100 + x$
44. $p = 100 - 0.05x$	$p = 25 + 0.1x$
45. $p = 140 - 0.00002x$	$p = 80 + 0.00001x$
46. $p = 400 - 0.0002x$	$p = 225 + 0.0005x$

47. *Driving Distances*   In a trip of 300 miles, two people do the driving. One person drives three times as far as the other. Find the distance that each person drives.

48. *Truck Scheduling*   A contractor is hiring two trucking companies to haul 1600 tons of crushed stone for a highway construction project. The contracts state that one company is to haul four times as much as the other. Find the amount hauled by each.

Fitting a Line to Data   In Exercises 49–56, find the *least squares regression line*, $y = ax + b$, for the points

$(x_1, y_1), (x_2, y_2), \ldots, (x_n, y_n)$.

To find the line, solve the following system for a and b. Then use the linear regression feature of your graphing utility to confirm the result.

$$nb + \left(\sum_{i=1}^{n} x_i\right)a = \sum_{i=1}^{n} y_i$$

$$\left(\sum_{i=1}^{n} x_i\right)b + \left(\sum_{i=1}^{n} x_i^2\right)a = \sum_{i=1}^{n} x_i y_i$$

49. $5b + 10a = 20.2$
$\qquad 10b + 30a = 50.1$

50. $5b + 10a = 11.7$
$\qquad 10b + 30a = 25.6$

51. $7b + 21a = 35.1$
$\qquad 21b + 91a = 114.2$

52. $6b + 15a = 23.6$
$\qquad 15b + 55a = 48.8$

53. $(-2, 0), (0, 1), (2, 3)$

54. $(-3, 0), (-1, 1), (1, 1), (3, 2)$

55. $(0, 4), (1, 3), (1, 1), (2, 0)$

56. $(1, 0), (2, 0), (3, 0), (3, 1), (4, 1), (4, 2), (5, 2), (6, 2)$

57. *Demand Function*   A store manager wants to know the demand of a certain product as a function of the price. The daily sales for the different prices of the product are given in the following table.

Price (x)	$1.00	$1.25	$1.50
Demand (y)	450	375	330

Use the technique demonstrated in Exercises 49–56 to find the line that best fits the given data. Plot the points and graph the line. Then use the line to predict the demand when the price is $1.40.

58. *Yield*   A farmer used four test plots to determine the relationship between wheat yield in bushels per acre and the amount of fertilizer in hundreds of pounds per acre. The results are given in the following table.

Fertilizer (x)	1.0	1.5	2.0	2.5
Yield (y)	32	41	48	53

Use the technique demonstrated in Exercises 49–56 to find the line that best fits the given data. Plot the points and graph the line. Then use the line to estimate the yield for a fertilizer application of 160 pounds per acre.

In Exercises 59 and 60, find a system of linear equations having the given solution. (There is more than one correct answer.)

59. $(3, \frac{5}{2})$ **60.** $(8, -2)$

9.4 SYSTEMS OF LINEAR EQUATIONS IN MORE THAN TWO VARIABLES

Row-Echelon Form and Back-Substitution / Gaussian Elimination /
Graphical Interpretation of a Linear System in Three Variables /
Nonsquare Systems / Applications

Row-Echelon Form and Back-Substitution

The method of elimination can be applied to a system of linear equations in more than two variables. The goal is to rewrite the system in a form to which back-substitution can be applied. To see how this works, consider the following two systems of linear equations.

$$\begin{aligned} x - 2y + 3z &= 9 \\ -x + 3y \phantom{{}+ 3z} &= -4 \\ 2x - 5y + 5z &= 17 \end{aligned} \qquad \begin{aligned} x - 2y + 3z &= 9 \\ y + 3z &= 5 \\ z &= 2 \end{aligned}$$

Clearly, the system on the right is easier to solve. This system is in **row-echelon form,** which means that it follows a stair-step pattern and has leading coefficients of 1. To solve such a system, use back-substitution, working from the bottom equation to the top equation.

EXAMPLE 1 Using Back-Substitution to Solve a System in Row-Echelon Form

Solve the system of linear equations.

$$\begin{aligned} x - 2y + 3z &= 9 \qquad & \textit{Equation 1} \\ y + 3z &= 5 \qquad & \textit{Equation 2} \\ z &= 2 \qquad & \textit{Equation 3} \end{aligned}$$

SOLUTION

From Equation 3, you already know the value of z. To solve for y, substitute $z = 2$ into Equation 2 to obtain

$$\begin{aligned} y + 3(2) &= 5 \qquad & \textit{Substitute } z = 2 \\ y &= -1. \qquad & \textit{Solve for } y \end{aligned}$$

Finally, substitute $y = -1$ and $z = 2$ into Equation 1 to obtain

$$\begin{aligned} x - 2(-1) + 3(2) &= 9 \qquad & \textit{Substitute } y = -1, z = 2 \\ x &= 1. \qquad & \textit{Solve for } x \end{aligned}$$

The solution is $x = 1$, $y = -1$, and $z = 2$. Check this solution in the original system.

Gaussian Elimination

Two systems are **equivalent** if they have precisely the same solution set. To solve a system that is not in row-echelon form, change it to an *equivalent* system that is in row-echelon form by using the following operations. This process is called **Gaussian elimination,** after the German mathematician Carl Friedrich Gauss (1777–1855).

1. Interchange two equations.
2. Multiply one of the equations by a nonzero constant.
3. Add a multiple of one equation to another equation.

EXAMPLE 2   **Using Elimination to Solve a Linear System**

Solve the system of linear equations.

$$\begin{aligned} x - 2y + 3z &= 9 \\ -x + 3y \phantom{{}+3z} &= -4 \\ 2x - 5y + 5z &= 17 \end{aligned}$$

SOLUTION

Work from the upper left corner, saving the x in the upper left position and eliminate the other x's from the first column.

$$\begin{aligned} x - 2y + 3z &= 9 \\ y + 3z &= 5 \quad \longleftarrow \\ 2x - 5y + 5z &= 17 \end{aligned}$$

Adding the first equation to the second equation produces a new second equation.

$$\begin{aligned} x - 2y + 3z &= 9 \\ y + 3z &= 5 \\ -y - z &= -1 \quad \longleftarrow \end{aligned}$$

Adding -2 times the first equation to the third equation produces a new third equation.

Now that all but the first x have been eliminated from the first column, go to work on the second column. (You need to eliminate y from the third equation.)

$$\begin{aligned} x - 2y + 3z &= 9 \\ y + 3z &= 5 \\ 2z &= 4 \quad \longleftarrow \end{aligned}$$

Adding the second equation to the third equation produces a new third equation.

Finally, you need a coefficient of 1 for z in the third equation.

$$\begin{aligned} x - 2y + 3z &= 9 \\ y + 3z &= 5 \\ z &= 2 \quad \longleftarrow \end{aligned}$$

Multiplying the third equation by $\frac{1}{2}$ produces a new third equation.

This is the same system solved in Example 1. As in that example, you can conclude that the solution is $x = 1$, $y = -1$, and $z = 2$. The solution can also be written as the **ordered triple** $(1, -1, 2)$. Check this solution in the original system.

If, at some stage in the elimination process, you obtain an absurdity such as $0 = 7$, you can conclude that the original system is inconsistent.

EXAMPLE 3   An Inconsistent System

Solve the system of linear equations.

$$\begin{aligned} x - 3y + z &= 1 \\ 2x - y - 2z &= 2 \\ x + 2y - 3z &= -1 \end{aligned}$$

SOLUTION

$$\begin{aligned} x - 3y + z &= 1 \\ 5y - 4z &= 0 \quad \longleftarrow \\ x + 2y - 3z &= -1 \end{aligned}$$

Adding -2 times the first equation to the second equation produces a new second equation.

$$\begin{aligned} x - 3y + z &= 1 \\ 5y - 4z &= 0 \\ 5y - 4z &= -2 \quad \longleftarrow \end{aligned}$$

Adding -1 times the first equation to the third equation produces a new third equation.

$$\begin{aligned} x - 3y + z &= 1 \\ 5y - 4z &= 0 \\ 0 &= -2 \quad \longleftarrow \end{aligned}$$

Adding -1 times the second equation to the third equation produces a new third equation.

Because the third "equation" is absurd, you can conclude that the original system is inconsistent.

As with a system of linear equations in two variables, a system of linear equations in more than two variables must have (1) exactly one solution, (2) infinitely many solutions, or (3) no solution.

There is more than one way to describe the solutions of a system with infinitely many solutions. For example, consider a solution set that is described as

$$(a, a + 1, 2a), \quad \text{where } a \text{ is any real number.}$$

This means that each real number a produces a solution of the system. A few of the infinitely many possible solutions are found by letting $a = -1, 0, 1,$ and 2 to obtain $(-1, 0, -2)$, $(0, 1, 0)$, $(1, 2, 2)$, and $(2, 3, 4)$, respectively. Now consider the solutions represented by the ordered triple

$$(b - 1, b, 2b - 2), \quad \text{where } b \text{ is any real number.}$$

Here again, a few possible solutions are $(-1, 0, -2)$, $(0, 1, 0)$, $(1, 2, 2)$, and $(2, 3, 4)$, found by letting $b = 0$, 1, 2, and 3, respectively. Note that both descriptions result in the same collection of solutions. Thus, when comparing descriptions of an infinite solution set, keep in mind that the way you describe the set may be different from the way another person describes the set.

EXAMPLE 4   A System with Infinitely Many Solutions

Solve the system of linear equations.

$$
\begin{array}{rl}
x + y - 3z = -1 & \qquad \textit{Equation 1} \\
y - z = 0 & \qquad \textit{Equation 2} \\
-x + 2y \phantom{{}-z} = 1 & \qquad \textit{Equation 3}
\end{array}
$$

SOLUTION

Begin by rewriting the system in row-echelon form as follows.

$$
\begin{array}{rl}
x + y - 3z = -1 & \\
y - z = 0 & \\
3y - 3z = 0 & \longleftarrow
\end{array}
$$

Adding the first equation to the third equation produces a new third equation.

$$
\begin{array}{rl}
x + y - 3z = -1 & \\
y - z = 0 & \\
0 = 0 & \longleftarrow
\end{array}
$$

Adding -3 times the second equation to the third equation produces a new third equation.

This means that Equation 3 is *dependent* on Equations 1 and 2 in the sense that it gives no additional information about the variables. Thus, the original system is equivalent to the system

$$
\begin{array}{rl}
x + y - 3z = -1 & \\
y - z = 0. &
\end{array}
$$

In this last equation, solve for y in terms of z to obtain $y = z$. Back-substituting for y into the previous equation, you can find x in terms of z, as follows.

$$
\begin{array}{rl}
x + z - 3z = -1 & \\
x - 2z = -1 & \\
x = 2z - 1 &
\end{array}
$$

Finally, letting $z = a$, the solutions to the given system are all of the form

$$
x = 2a - 1, \qquad y = a, \qquad z = a,
$$

where a is a real number. Therefore, every ordered triple that is in the form $(2a - 1, a, a)$, where a is a real number, is a solution of the system.

Graphical Interpretation of a Linear System in Three Variables

Solutions of equations with three variables can be pictured with a **three-dimensional coordinate system.** To construct such a system, begin with the xy-coordinate plane in a horizontal position. Then draw the z-axis as a vertical line through the origin.

Every ordered triple (x, y, z) corresponds to a point in the three-dimensional coordinate system. For instance, the points corresponding to $(-2, 5, 4)$, $(2, -5, 3)$, $(1, 6, 0)$, and $(3, 3, -2)$ are shown in Figure 9.22.

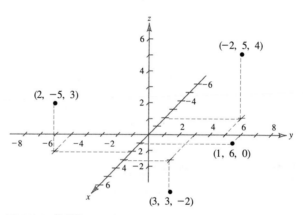

FIGURE 9.22

The **graph** of an equation in three variables consists of all points (x, y, z) that are solutions of the equation. The graph of a linear equation in three variables is a *plane*. Sketching graphs in a three-dimensional coordinate system is difficult because the sketch itself is only two-dimensional.

One technique for sketching a plane is to find the three points at which the plane intersects the axes. For instance, the plane given by

$$3x + 2y + 4z = 12$$

intersects the x-axis at the point $(4, 0, 0)$, the y-axis at the point $(0, 6, 0)$, and the z-axis at the point $(0, 0, 3)$.

By plotting these three points, connecting them with line segments, and shading the resulting triangular region, you can picture a portion of the graph, as shown in Figure 9.23.

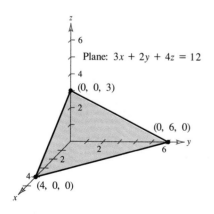

FIGURE 9.23

The graph of a system of three linear equations in three variables consists of *three* planes. When these planes intersect in a single point, the system has exactly one solution. When the three planes have no point in common, the system has no solution. When the three planes contain a common line, the system has infinitely many solutions. (See Figure 9.24.)

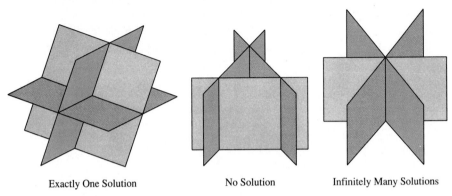

Exactly One Solution   No Solution   Infinitely Many Solutions

FIGURE 9.24

Nonsquare Systems

So far we have considered only **square** systems, for which the number of equations is equal to the number of variables. In a **nonsquare** system, the number of equations differs from the number of variables.

EXAMPLE 5   **A System with Fewer Equations than Variables**

Solve the system of linear equations.

$$
\begin{aligned}
x - 2y + z &= 2 && \textit{Equation 1}\\
2x - y - z &= 1 && \textit{Equation 2}
\end{aligned}
$$

SOLUTION

$$
\begin{aligned}
x - 2y + z &= 2\\
3y - 3z &= -3 \quad \longleftarrow
\end{aligned}
$$
Adding -2 times the first equation to the second equation produces a new second equation.

$$
\begin{aligned}
x - 2y + z &= 2\\
y - z &= -1 \quad \longleftarrow
\end{aligned}
$$
Multiplying the second equation by $\frac{1}{3}$ produces a new second equation.

Solving for y in terms of z, you obtain $y = z - 1$, and back-substitution into Equation 1 yields

$$
\begin{aligned}
x - 2(z - 1) + z &= 2\\
x - 2z + 2 + z &= 2\\
x &= z.
\end{aligned}
$$

Finally, by letting $z = a$, you obtain the solution

$$x = a, \qquad y = a - 1, \qquad \text{and} \qquad z = a$$

where a is a real number. Thus, every ordered triple of the form $(a, a - 1, a)$, where a is a real number, is a solution of the system.

Applications

Example 6 shows how to fit a parabola through three given points in the plane. This procedure can be generalized to fit an nth degree polynomial function to $n + 1$ points in the plane. The only restriction on the procedure is that (because you are trying to fit a *function* to the points) every point must have a distinct x-coordinate.

EXAMPLE 6   Curve-Fitting

Find a quadratic function

$$f(x) = ax^2 + bx + c$$

the graph of which passes through the points $(-1, 3)$, $(1, 1)$, and $(2, 6)$.

SOLUTION

Because the graph of f passes through the points $(-1, 3)$, $(1, 1)$, and $(2, 6)$, you can write the following equations.

$$f(-1) = a(-1)^2 + b(-1) + c = 3$$
$$f(1) = a(1)^2 + b(1) + c = 1$$
$$f(2) = a(2)^2 + b(2) + c = 6$$

This produces a system of linear equations in the variables a, b, and c.

$$\begin{aligned} a - b + c &= 3 \\ a + b + c &= 1 \\ 4a + 2b + c &= 6 \end{aligned}$$

Using the techniques of this section, you can find the solution of this system to be $a = 2$, $b = -1$, and $c = 0$. Thus, the equation of the parabola passing through the three given points is

$$f(x) = ax^2 + bx + c = 2x^2 - x,$$

as shown in Figure 9.25. You should check that the three given points satisfy this equation.

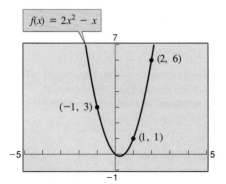

$f(x) = 2x^2 - x$

$(2, 6)$

$(-1, 3)$

$(1, 1)$

FIGURE 9.25

EXAMPLE 7   An Investment Portfolio

Suppose an investor has a portfolio totaling $450,000, and wishes to allocate this amount to the following types of investments: (1) certificates of deposit, (2) municipal bonds, (3) blue-chip stocks, and (4) growth or speculative stocks. The certificates of deposit pay 9% annually, and the municipal bonds pay 6% annually. Over a 5-year period, the investor expects the blue-chip stocks to return 10% annually, and expects the growth stocks to return 15% annually. The investor wants a combined annual return of 8%, and also wants to have only one-third of the portfolio invested in stocks. How much should be allocated to each type of investment?

SOLUTION

To solve this problem, let C, M, B, and G represent the amounts in the four types of investments. Because the total investment is $450,000, you can write

$$C + M + B + G = 450{,}000.$$

A second equation can be derived from the fact that the combined annual return should be 8%.

$$0.09C + 0.06M + 0.10B + 0.15G = 0.08(450{,}000)$$

Finally, because only one-third of the investment should be allocated to stocks, you can write

$$B + G = \frac{1}{3}(450{,}000).$$

These three equations make up the following system.

$$
\begin{aligned}
C + \quad M + \quad B + \quad G &= 450{,}000 \\
0.09C + 0.06M + 0.1B + 0.15G &= \quad 36{,}000 \\
B + \quad G &= 150{,}000
\end{aligned}
$$

Using elimination, you can find that the system has infinitely many solutions, which can be written as follows.

$$C = -\frac{5}{3}a + 100{,}000, \qquad M = \frac{5}{3}a + 200{,}000,$$

$$B = -a + 150{,}000, \qquad G = a$$

Thus, the investor has many different options. One possible solution is to choose $a = 30{,}000$, which yields the following portfolio.

1. Certificates of deposit: $50,000
2. Municipal bonds: $250,000
3. Blue-chip stocks: $120,000
4. Growth or speculative stocks: $30,000

EXAMPLE 8   Partial Fractions

Write the partial fraction decomposition for

$$\frac{3x + 4}{x^3 - 2x - 4}.$$

SOLUTION

Because $x^3 - 2x - 4 = (x - 2)(x^2 + 2x + 2)$, you can write

$$\frac{3x + 4}{x^3 - 2x - 4} = \frac{A}{x - 2} + \frac{Bx + C}{x^2 + 2x + 2}$$

$$3x + 4 = A(x^2 + 2x + 2) + (Bx + C)(x - 2)$$

$$3x + 4 = (A + B)x^2 + (2A - 2B + C)x + (2A - 2C)$$

By equating coefficients of like powers on opposite sides of the expanded equation, you obtain the following system of linear equations in A, B, and C.

$$
\begin{aligned}
A + B \quad\quad &= 0 \\
2A - 2B + C &= 3 \\
2A \quad\quad - 2C &= 4
\end{aligned}
$$

The solution of this system is $A = 1$, $B = -1$, and $C = -1$. Therefore, the partial fraction decomposition is

$$\frac{3x + 4}{x^3 - 2x - 4} = \frac{1}{x - 2} + \frac{-x - 1}{x^2 + 2x + 2} = \frac{1}{x - 2} - \frac{x + 1}{x^2 + 2x + 2}.$$

DISCUSSION PROBLEM

COMPUTER SOFTWARE

There are many computer software programs that will solve linear systems. Use your school's library, computer center, mathematics-learning center, or some other reference facility to find out about such a product. Write a short report about the capabilities of the software.

WARM-UP
....

The following warm-up exercises involve skills that were covered in earlier sections. You will use these skills in the exercise set for this section.

In Exercises 1–4, solve the system of linear equations.

1. $x + y = 25$
$\phantom{x + {}} y = 10$

2. $2x - 3y = 4$
$6x = -12$

3. $x + y = 32$
$x - y = 24$

4. $2r - s = 5$
$r + 2s = 10$

In Exercises 5–8, determine whether the ordered triple is a solution of the equation.

5. $5x - 3y + 4z = 2$
$(-1, -2, 1)$

6. $x - 2y + 12z = 9$
$(6, 3, 2)$

7. $2x - 5y + 3z = -9$
$(a - 2, a + 1, a)$

8. $-5x + y + z = 21$
$(a - 4, 4a + 1, a)$

In Exercises 9 and 10, solve for x in terms of a.

9. $x + 2y - 3z = 4$
$y = 1 - a, z = a$

10. $x - 3y + 5z = 4$
$y = 2a + 3, z = a$

SECTION 9.4 · EXERCISES
....

In Exercises 1–26, solve the system of linear equations.

1. $x + y + z = 6$
$2x - y + z = 3$
$3x - z = 0$

2. $x + y + z = 2$
$-x + 3y + 2z = 8$
$4x + y = 4$

3. $4x + y - 3z = 11$
$2x - 3y + 2z = 9$
$x + y + z = -3$

4. $2x + 2z = 2$
$5x + 3y = 4$
$\phantom{5x + {}} 3y - 4z = 4$

5. $\phantom{3x + {}} 6y + 4z = -12$
$3x + 3y = 9$
$2x - 3z = 10$

6. $2x + 4y + z = -4$
$2x - 4y + 6z = 13$
$4x - 2y + z = 6$

7. $3x - 2y + 4z = 1$
$x + y - 2z = 3$
$2x - 3y + 6z = 8$

8. $5x - 3y + 2z = 3$
$2x + 4y - z = 7$
$x - 11y + 4z = 3$

9. $3x + 3y + 5z = 1$
$3x + 5y + 9z = 0$
$5x + 9y + 17z = 0$

10. $2x + y + 3z = 1$
$2x + 6y + 8z = 3$
$6x + 8y + 18z = 5$

11. $x + 2y - 7z = -4$
$2x + y + z = 13$
$3x + 9y - 36z = -33$

12. $2x + y - 3z = 4$
$4x + 2z = 10$
$-2x + 3y - 13z = -8$

13. $x + 4z = 13$
$4x - 2y + z = 7$
$2x - 2y - 7z = -19$

14. $4x - y + 5z = 11$
$x + 2y - z = 5$
$5x - 8y + 13z = 7$

15. $x - 2y + 5z = 2$
$3x + 2y - z = -2$

16. $x - 3y + 2z = 18$
$5x - 13y + 12z = 80$

17. $2x - 3y + z = -2$
$-4x + 9y = 7$

18. $2x + 3y + 3z = 7$
$4x + 18y + 15z = 44$

19. $x + 3w = 4$
$\phantom{x + {}} 2y - z - w = 0$
$\phantom{x + {}} 3y - 2w = 1$
$2x - y + 4z = 5$

20. $x + y + z + w = 6$
$2x + 3y - w = 0$
$-3x + 4y + z + 2w = 4$
$x + 2y - z + w = 0$

21. $x + 4z = 1$
$x + y + 10z = 10$
$2x - y + 2z = -5$

22. $3x - 2y - 6z = -4$
$-3x + 2y + 6z = 1$
$x - y - 5z = -3$

23. $4x + 3y + 17z = 0$
$5x + 4y + 22z = 0$
$4x + 2y + 19z = 0$

24. $2x + 3y = 0$
$4x + 3y - z = 0$
$8x + 3y + 3z = 0$

25. $5x + 5y - z = 0$
$10x + 5y + 2z = 0$
$5x + 15y - 9z = 0$

26. $12x + 5y + z = 0$
$12x + 4y - z = 0$

In Exercises 27–30, find the equation of the parabola $y = ax^2 + bx + c$ that passes through the given points. Verify your result with a graphing utility.

27. $(0, -4), (1, 1), (2, 10)$ **28.** $(0, 5), (1, 6), (2, 5)$

29. $(1, 0), (2, -1), (3, 0)$ **30.** $(1, 2), (2, 1), (3, -4)$

In Exercises 31–34, find the equation of the circle

$$x^2 + y^2 + Dx + Ey + F = 0$$

that passes through the given points. Verify your result with a graphing utility.

31. $(0, 0), (2, -2), (4, 0)$ **32.** $(0, 0), (0, 6), (-3, 3)$

     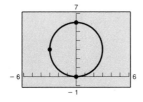

33. $(3, -1), (-2, 4), (6, 8)$ **34.** $(0, 0), (0, 2), (3, 0)$

Vertical Motion   In Exercises 35–38, find the position equation

$$s = \tfrac{1}{2}at^2 + v_0t + s_0$$

for an object that is moving vertically and is at the given positions at the specified times.

35. At $t = 1$ second, $s = 128$ feet
At $t = 2$ seconds, $s = 80$ feet
At $t = 3$ seconds, $s = 0$ feet

36. At $t = 1$ second, $s = 48$ feet
At $t = 2$ seconds, $s = 64$ feet
At $t = 3$ seconds, $s = 48$ feet

37. At $t = 1$ second, $s = 452$ feet
At $t = 3$ seconds, $s = 260$ feet
At $t = 4$ seconds, $s = 116$ feet

38. At $t = 2$ seconds, $s = 132$ feet
At $t = 3$ seconds, $s = 100$ feet
At $t = 4$ seconds, $s = 36$ feet

39. *Investments*   An inheritance of $16,000 was divided among three investments yielding a total of $990 in interest per year. The interest rates for the three investments were 5%, 6%, and 7%. Find the amount placed in each investment if the 5% and 6% investments were $3000 and $2000 less than the 7% investment, respectively.

40. *Investments*   Suppose you receive a total of $1520 a year in interest from three investments. The interest rates for the three investments are 5%, 7%, and 8%. The 5% investment is half of the 7% investment, and the 7% investment is $1500 less than the 8% investment. What is the amount of each investment?

41. *Borrowing*   A small corporation borrowed $775,000 to expand its product line. Some of the money was borrowed at 8%, some at 9%, and some at 10%. How much was borrowed at each rate if the annual interest was $67,500 and the amount borrowed at 8% was four times the amount borrowed at 10%?

42. *Borrowing*   A small corporation borrowed $800,000 to expand its product line. Some of the money was borrowed at 8%, some at 9%, and some at 10%. How much was borrowed at each rate if the annual interest was $67,000 and the amount borrowed at 8% was five times the amount borrowed at 10%?

Investment Portfolio   In Exercises 43 and 44, consider an investment with a portfolio totaling $500,000 that is to be allocated among the following types of investments: (1) certificates of deposit, (2) municipal bonds, (3) blue-chip stocks, and (4) growth or speculative stocks. How much should be allocated to each type of investment?

43. The certificates of deposit pay 10% annually, and the municipal bonds pay 8% annually. Over a 5-year period, the investor expects the blue-chip stocks to return 12% annually and the growth stocks to return 13% annually. The investor wants a combined annual return of 10% and also wants to have only one-fourth of the portfolio invested in stocks.

44. The certificates of deposit pay 9% annually, and the municipal bonds pay 5% annually. Over a 5-year period, the investor expects the blue-chip stocks to return 12% annually and the growth stocks to return 14% annually. The investor wants a combined annual return of 10% and also wants to have only one-fourth of the portfolio invested in stocks.

45. *Crop Spraying*   A mixture of 12 gallons of chemical A, 16 gallons of chemical B, and 26 gallons of chemical C is required to kill a certain destructive crop insect. Commercial spray X contains 1, 2, and 2 parts, respectively, of these chemicals. Commercial spray Y contains only chemical C. Commercial spray Z contains only chemicals A and B in equal amounts. How much of each type of commercial spray is needed to get the desired mixture?

46. *Chemistry*   A chemist needs 10 liters of a 25% acid solution. The solution is to be mixed from three solutions the concentrations of which are 10%, 20%, and 50%, respectively. How many liters of each solution should the chemist use to satisfy the following?
    (a) Use as little as possible of the 50% solution.
    (b) Use as much as possible of the 50% solution.
    (c) Use two liters of the 50% solution.

47. *Truck Scheduling*   A small company that manufactures products A and B has an order for 15 units of product A and 16 units of product B. The company has trucks of three different sizes that can haul the products, as shown in the table.

Truck	Product A	Product B
Large	6	3
Medium	4	4
Small	0	3

How many trucks of each size are needed to deliver the order? (Give *two* possible solutions.)

48. *Electrical Networks*   Applying Kirchhoff's Laws to the electrical network in the accompanying figure, the currents I_1, I_2, and I_3 must be the solution to the system

$$I_1 - I_2 + I_3 = 0$$
$$3I_1 + 2I_2 = 7$$
$$2I_2 + 4I_3 = 8,$$

where the current is measured in amperes. Find the currents.

FIGURE FOR 48

49. *Pulley System* A system of pulleys that are assumed to be frictionless and without mass are loaded with 128-pound and 32-pound weights (see figure). The tensions t_1 and t_2 in the ropes, and the acceleration a of the 32-pound weight, are found by solving the system

$$
\begin{aligned}
t_1 - 2t_2 &= 0 \\
t_1 \quad\;\; - 2a &= 128 \\
t_2 + \;\; a &= 32,
\end{aligned}
$$

where t_1 and t_2 are measured in pounds and a is in feet per second squared. Solve the system.

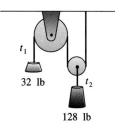

32 lb

t_1 t_2

128 lb

FIGURE FOR 49

50. *Pulley System* If the 32-pound weight is replaced by a 64-pound weight in the pulley system of Exercise 49, it is modeled by the following system of equations.

$$
\begin{aligned}
t_1 - 2t_2 &= 0 \\
t_1 \quad\;\; - 2a &= 128 \\
t_2 + 2a &= 64
\end{aligned}
$$

Solve the system and use your result for the acceleration to describe what (if anything) is happening in the system.

Partial Fractions In Exercises 51–54, write the partial fraction decomposition for the rational fraction (see Example 8).

51. $\dfrac{1}{x^3 - x} = \dfrac{A}{x} + \dfrac{B}{x - 1} + \dfrac{C}{x + 1}$

52. $\dfrac{3}{x^2 + x - 2} = \dfrac{A}{x - 1} + \dfrac{B}{x + 2}$

53. $\dfrac{x^2 - 3x - 3}{x(x - 2)(x + 3)} = \dfrac{A}{x} + \dfrac{B}{x - 2} + \dfrac{C}{x + 3}$

54. $\dfrac{12}{x(x - 2)(x + 3)} = \dfrac{A}{x} + \dfrac{B}{x - 2} + \dfrac{C}{x + 3}$

Fitting a Parabola In Exercises 55–58, find the least squares regression parabola $y = ax^2 + bx + c$ for the points $(x_1, y_1), (x_2, y_2), \ldots, (x_n, y_n)$.

To find the parabola, solve the following system of linear equations for a, b, and c.

$$
nc + \left(\sum_{i=1}^{n} x_i \right) b + \left(\sum_{i=1}^{n} x_i^2 \right) a = \sum_{i=1}^{n} y_i
$$

$$
\left(\sum_{i=1}^{n} x_i \right) c + \left(\sum_{i=1}^{n} x_i^2 \right) b + \left(\sum_{i=1}^{n} x_i^3 \right) a = \sum_{i=1}^{n} x_i y_i
$$

$$
\left(\sum_{i=1}^{n} x_i^2 \right) c + \left(\sum_{i=1}^{n} x_i^3 \right) b + \left(\sum_{i=1}^{n} x_i^4 \right) a = \sum_{i=1}^{n} x_i^2 y_i
$$

55.
$$
\begin{aligned}
4c \quad\; + 40a &= 19 \\
40b \quad\;\;\; &= -12 \\
40c \quad + 544a &= 160
\end{aligned}
$$

56.
$$
\begin{aligned}
5c \quad\; + 10a &= 8 \\
10b \quad\;\;\; &= 12 \\
10c \quad + 34a &= 22
\end{aligned}
$$

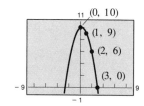

57.
$$
\begin{aligned}
4c + \;\;9b + \;\;29a &= 20 \\
9c + 29b + \;\;99a &= 70 \\
29c + 99b + 353a &= 254
\end{aligned}
$$

58.
$$
\begin{aligned}
4c + \;\;6b + 14a &= 25 \\
6c + 14b + 36a &= 21 \\
14c + 36b + 98a &= 33
\end{aligned}
$$

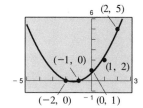

59. *Stopping Distances* In testing the new braking system on an automobile, the speed in miles per hour and the stopping distance in feet were recorded (see table).

Speed (x)	20	30	40	50	60
Stopping distance (y)	25	55	105	188	300

(a) Plot the data on the rectangular coordinate system.
(b) Fit a least squares regression parabola for the data and sketch the graph of the parabola on the coordinate system of part (a).

60. *Reproduction*   A wildlife management team studied the reproduction rates of deer in five tracts of a wildlife preserve. Each tract contained 5 acres. In each tract, the number of females and the percentage of females that had offspring the following year were counted. The results are given in the following table.

Number (x)	80	100	120	140	160
Percentage (y)	80	75	68	55	30

(a) Plot the data on the rectangular coordinate system.
(b) Fit the least squares regression parabola for the data and sketch the graph of the parabola on the coordinate system of part (a).

In Exercises 61 and 62, find a system of equations having the given solution. (There is more than one correct answer for each exercise.)

61. $(4, -1, 2)$ **62.** $\left(-\frac{3}{2}, 4, -7\right)$

9.5   MATRICES AND SYSTEMS OF LINEAR EQUATIONS

Matrices / Elementary Row Operations / Gaussian Elimination with Back-Substitution / Gauss-Jordan Elimination

Matrices

In this section you will study a streamlined technique for solving systems of linear equations. This technique involves the use of a rectangular array of real numbers called a **matrix.**

DEFINITION OF A MATRIX

If m and n are positive integers, then an $m \times n$ **matrix** (read "m by n") is a rectangular array

$$\begin{bmatrix} a_{11} & a_{12} & a_{13} & \cdots & a_{1n} \\ a_{21} & a_{22} & a_{23} & \cdots & a_{2n} \\ a_{31} & a_{32} & a_{33} & \cdots & a_{3n} \\ \vdots & \vdots & \vdots & & \vdots \\ a_{m1} & a_{m2} & a_{m3} & \cdots & a_{mn} \end{bmatrix} \left.\vphantom{\begin{matrix}a\\a\\a\\a\\a\end{matrix}}\right\} m \text{ rows}$$

$\underbrace{\qquad\qquad}_{n \text{ columns}}$

in which each **entry,** a_{ij}, of the matrix is a real number. An $m \times n$ matrix has m **rows** (horizontal lines) and n **columns** (vertical lines).

The entry in the ith row and jth column is denoted by the *double subscript* notation a_{ij}. We call i the **row subscript** because it gives the position in the horizontal lines, and j the **column subscript** because it gives the position in the vertical lines. A matrix having m rows and n columns is said to be of **order** $m \times n$. If $m = n$, the matrix is **square** of order n. For a square matrix, the entries $a_{11}, a_{22}, a_{33}, \ldots$ are the **main diagonal** entries.

EXAMPLE 1   Examples of Matrices

The following matrices have the indicated orders.

A. Order: 1×4

$$\begin{bmatrix} 1 & -3 & 0 & \frac{1}{2} \end{bmatrix}$$

B. Order: 2×2

$$\begin{bmatrix} 0 & 0 \\ 0 & 0 \end{bmatrix}$$

C. Order: 2×3

$$\begin{bmatrix} -1 & 0 & 5 \\ 2 & 1 & -4 \end{bmatrix}$$

D. Order: 3×2

$$\begin{bmatrix} 5 & 0 \\ 2 & -2 \\ -7 & 4 \end{bmatrix}$$

A matrix that has only one row is a **row matrix,** and a matrix that has only one column is a **column matrix.**

A matrix derived from a system of linear equations (each written in standard form with the constant term on the right) is called the **augmented matrix** of the system. Moreover, the matrix derived from the coefficients of the system (but which does not include the constant terms) is called the **coefficient matrix** of the system. Here is an example.

System	*Augmented Matrix*	*Coefficient Matrix*
$\begin{aligned} x - 4y + 3z &= 5 \\ -x + 3y - z &= -3 \\ 2x \qquad - 4z &= 6 \end{aligned}$	$\begin{bmatrix} 1 & -4 & 3 & \vdots & 5 \\ -1 & 3 & -1 & \vdots & -3 \\ 2 & 0 & -4 & \vdots & 6 \end{bmatrix}$	$\begin{bmatrix} 1 & -4 & 3 \\ -1 & 3 & -1 \\ 2 & 0 & -4 \end{bmatrix}$

When forming either the coefficient matrix or the augmented matrix of a system, you should begin by vertically aligning the variables in the equations and using 0's for the missing variables.

System	*Line Up Variables*	*Form Augmented Matrix*
$\begin{aligned} x + 3y &= 9 \\ -y + 4z &= -2 \\ x - 5z &= 0 \end{aligned}$	$\begin{aligned} x + 3y \qquad &= 9 \\ -y + 4z &= -2 \\ x \qquad - 5z &= 0 \end{aligned}$	$\begin{bmatrix} 1 & 3 & 0 & \vdots & 9 \\ 0 & -1 & 4 & \vdots & -2 \\ 1 & 0 & -5 & \vdots & 0 \end{bmatrix}$

Elementary Row Operations

In Section 9.4 you studied three operations that can be used on a system of linear equations to produce an equivalent system. In matrix terminology, these three operations correspond to **elementary row operations.** An elementary row operation on an augmented matrix of a given system of linear equations produces a new augmented matrix corresponding to a new (but equivalent) system of linear equations. Two matrices are **row-equivalent** if one can be obtained from the other by a sequence of elementary row operations.

ELEMENTARY ROW OPERATIONS

1. Interchange two rows.
2. Multiply a row by a nonzero constant.
3. Add a multiple of a row to another row.

Although elementary row operations are simple to perform, they involve a lot of arithmetic. Because it is easy to make a mistake, we suggest that you get in the habit of recording the elementary row operations performed in each step so that you can go back and check your work.

EXAMPLE 2   **Elementary Row Operations**

A. Interchange the first and second rows.

Original Matrix

$$\begin{bmatrix} 0 & 1 & 3 & 4 \\ -1 & 2 & 0 & 3 \\ 2 & -3 & 4 & 1 \end{bmatrix}$$

New Row-Equivalent Matrix

$$\begin{matrix} R_1 \\ R_2 \end{matrix} \begin{bmatrix} -1 & 2 & 0 & 3 \\ 0 & 1 & 3 & 4 \\ 2 & -3 & 4 & 1 \end{bmatrix}$$

B. Multiply the first row by $\frac{1}{2}$.

Original Matrix

$$\begin{bmatrix} 2 & -4 & 6 & -2 \\ 1 & 3 & -3 & 0 \\ 5 & -2 & 1 & 2 \end{bmatrix}$$

New Row-Equivalent Matrix

$$\frac{1}{2}R_1 \longrightarrow \begin{bmatrix} 1 & -2 & 3 & -1 \\ 1 & 3 & -3 & 0 \\ 5 & -2 & 1 & 2 \end{bmatrix}$$

C. Add -2 times the first row to the third row.

Original Matrix

$$\begin{bmatrix} 1 & 2 & -4 & 3 \\ 0 & 3 & -2 & -1 \\ 2 & 1 & 5 & -2 \end{bmatrix}$$

$-2R_1 + R_3 \longrightarrow$

New Row-Equivalent Matrix

$$\begin{bmatrix} 1 & 2 & -4 & 3 \\ 0 & 3 & -2 & -1 \\ 0 & -3 & 13 & -8 \end{bmatrix}$$

Note that we write the elementary row operation beside the row that has been changed.

In Section 9.4 you used Gaussian elimination with back-substitution to solve a system of linear equations. We now demonstrate the matrix version of Gaussian elimination. The two methods are essentially the same. The basic difference is that with matrices you do not need to keep writing the variables.

EXAMPLE 3   Using Elementary Row Operations to Solve a System

Technology Note

Most graphing utilities can perform elementary row operations on matrices. Read the user's manual for your graphing utility and duplicate the elementary row operations in the example at the right. (*Hint:* If your graphing utility *does not* store the matrices obtained in temporary results, we suggest that you do this after each elementary row operation.)

Linear System	*Associated Augmented Matrix*

$$\begin{aligned} x - 2y + 3z &= 9 \\ -x + 3y &= -4 \\ 2x - 5y + 5z &= 17 \end{aligned}$$

$$\left[\begin{array}{rrr|r} 1 & -2 & 3 & 9 \\ -1 & 3 & 0 & -4 \\ 2 & -5 & 5 & 17 \end{array} \right]$$

Add the first equation to the second equation.

Add the first row to the second row $(R_1 + R_2)$.

$$\begin{aligned} x - 2y + 3z &= 9 \\ y + 3z &= 5 \\ 2x - 5y + 5z &= 17 \end{aligned} \qquad R_1 + R_2 \longrightarrow$$

$$\left[\begin{array}{rrr|r} 1 & -2 & 3 & 9 \\ 0 & 1 & 3 & 5 \\ 2 & -5 & 5 & 17 \end{array} \right]$$

Add -2 times the first equation to the third equation.

Add -2 times the first row to the third row $(-2R_1 + R_3)$.

$$\begin{aligned} x - 2y + 3z &= 9 \\ y + 3z &= 5 \\ -y - z &= -1 \end{aligned} \qquad -2R_1 + R_3 \longrightarrow$$

$$\left[\begin{array}{rrr|r} 1 & -2 & 3 & 9 \\ 0 & 1 & 3 & 5 \\ 0 & -1 & -1 & -1 \end{array} \right]$$

Add the second equation to the third equation.

Add the second row to the third row $(R_2 + R_3)$.

$$\begin{aligned} x - 2y + 3z &= 9 \\ y + 3z &= 5 \\ 2z &= 4 \end{aligned} \qquad R_2 + R_3 \longrightarrow$$

$$\left[\begin{array}{rrr|r} 1 & -2 & 3 & 9 \\ 0 & 1 & 3 & 5 \\ 0 & 0 & 2 & 4 \end{array} \right]$$

Multiply the third equation by $\frac{1}{2}$.

Multiply the third row by $\frac{1}{2}$.

$$\begin{aligned} x - 2y + 3z &= 9 \\ y + 3z &= 5 \\ z &= 2 \end{aligned} \qquad \tfrac{1}{2}R_3 \longrightarrow$$

$$\left[\begin{array}{rrr|r} 1 & -2 & 3 & 9 \\ 0 & 1 & 3 & 5 \\ 0 & 0 & 1 & 2 \end{array} \right]$$

At this point, you can use back-substitution to find that the solution is $x = 1$, $y = -1$, and $z = 2$.

The last matrix in Example 3 is in **row-echelon form.** The term *echelon* refers to the stair-step pattern formed by the nonzero elements of the matrix. To be in this form, a matrix must have the following properties.

DEFINITION OF ROW-ECHELON FORM AND REDUCED ROW-ECHELON FORM

A matrix in **row-echelon form** has the following properties.

1. All rows consisting entirely of zeros occur at the bottom of the matrix.
2. For each row that does not consist entirely of zeros, the first nonzero entry is 1 (a **leading 1**).
3. For two successive (nonzero) rows, the leading 1 in the higher row is farther to the left than the leading 1 in the lower row.

A matrix in *row-echelon form* is in **reduced row-echelon form** if every column that has a leading 1 has zeros in every position above and below its leading 1.

EXAMPLE 4   **Row-Echelon Form**

The following matrices are in row-echelon form.

A. $\begin{bmatrix} 1 & 2 & -1 & 4 \\ 0 & 1 & 0 & 3 \\ 0 & 0 & 1 & -2 \end{bmatrix}$ **B.** $\begin{bmatrix} 0 & 1 & 0 & 5 \\ 0 & 0 & 1 & 3 \\ 0 & 0 & 0 & 0 \end{bmatrix}$

C. $\begin{bmatrix} 1 & -5 & 2 & -1 & 3 \\ 0 & 0 & 1 & 3 & -2 \\ 0 & 0 & 0 & 1 & 4 \\ 0 & 0 & 0 & 0 & 1 \end{bmatrix}$ **D.** $\begin{bmatrix} 1 & 0 & 0 & -1 \\ 0 & 1 & 0 & 2 \\ 0 & 0 & 1 & 3 \\ 0 & 0 & 0 & 0 \end{bmatrix}$

The matrices in (B) and (D) also happen to be in *reduced* row-echelon form. The following matrices are not in row-echelon form.

E. $\begin{bmatrix} 1 & 2 & -3 & 4 \\ 0 & 2 & 1 & -1 \\ 0 & 0 & 1 & -3 \end{bmatrix}$ **F.** $\begin{bmatrix} 1 & 2 & -1 & 2 \\ 0 & 0 & 0 & 0 \\ 0 & 1 & 2 & -4 \end{bmatrix}$

Every matrix is row-equivalent to a matrix in row-echelon form. For instance, in Example 4, you can change the matrix in part (E) to row-echelon form by multiplying its second row by $\frac{1}{2}$.

Gaussian Elimination with Back-Substitution

Guidelines for using Gaussian elimination with back-substitution to solve a system of linear equations are summarized as follows.

GAUSSIAN ELIMINATION WITH BACK-SUBSTITUTION

1. Write the augmented matrix of the system of linear equations.
2. Use elementary row operations to rewrite the augmented matrix in row-echelon form.
3. Write the system of linear equations corresponding to the matrix in row-echelon form, and use back-substitution to find the solution.

Gaussian elimination with back-substitution works well for solving systems of linear equations with a computer. For this algorithm, the order in which the elementary row operations are performed is important. We suggest operating from *left to right by columns,* using elementary row operations to obtain zeros in all entries directly below the leading 1's.

EXAMPLE 5   Gaussian Elimination with Back-Substitution

Solve the following system.

$$\begin{aligned} y + z - 2w &= -3 \\ x + 2y - z &= 2 \\ 2x + 4y + z - 3w &= -2 \\ x - 4y - 7z - w &= -19 \end{aligned}$$

SOLUTION

The augmented matrix for this system is

$$\begin{bmatrix} 0 & 1 & 1 & -2 & \vdots & -3 \\ 1 & 2 & -1 & 0 & \vdots & 2 \\ 2 & 4 & 1 & -3 & \vdots & -2 \\ 1 & -4 & -7 & -1 & \vdots & -19 \end{bmatrix}.$$

Begin by obtaining a leading 1 in the upper left corner by interchanging the first and second rows, and then proceed to obtain zeros elsewhere in the first column.

$$\begin{matrix} R_2 \\ R_1 \end{matrix} \begin{bmatrix} 1 & 2 & -1 & 0 & \vdots & 2 \\ 0 & 1 & 1 & -2 & \vdots & -3 \\ 2 & 4 & 1 & -3 & \vdots & -2 \\ 1 & -4 & -7 & -1 & \vdots & -19 \end{bmatrix} \qquad \begin{matrix} \textit{First column has leading 1} \\ \textit{in upper left corner} \end{matrix}$$

$$\begin{matrix} \\ \\ -2R_1 + R_3 \longrightarrow \\ -R_1 + R_4 \longrightarrow \end{matrix} \begin{bmatrix} 1 & 2 & -1 & 0 & \vdots & 2 \\ 0 & 1 & 1 & -2 & \vdots & -3 \\ 0 & 0 & 3 & -3 & \vdots & -6 \\ 0 & -6 & -6 & -1 & \vdots & -21 \end{bmatrix} \qquad \begin{matrix} \textit{First column has zeros} \\ \textit{below its leading 1} \end{matrix}$$

Now that the first column is already in the desired form, you can change the second, third, and fourth columns as follows.

$$6R_2 + R_4 \longrightarrow \begin{bmatrix} 1 & 2 & -1 & 0 & \vdots & 2 \\ 0 & 1 & 1 & -2 & \vdots & -3 \\ 0 & 0 & 3 & -3 & \vdots & -6 \\ 0 & 0 & 0 & -13 & \vdots & -39 \end{bmatrix}$$

Second column has zeros below its leading 1

$$\tfrac{1}{3}R_3 \longrightarrow \begin{bmatrix} 1 & 2 & -1 & 0 & \vdots & 2 \\ 0 & 1 & 1 & -2 & \vdots & -3 \\ 0 & 0 & 1 & -1 & \vdots & -2 \\ 0 & 0 & 0 & -13 & \vdots & -39 \end{bmatrix}$$

Third column has zeros below its leadng 1

$$-\tfrac{1}{13}R_4 \longrightarrow \begin{bmatrix} 1 & 2 & -1 & 0 & \vdots & 2 \\ 0 & 1 & 1 & -2 & \vdots & -3 \\ 0 & 0 & 1 & -1 & \vdots & -2 \\ 0 & 0 & 0 & 1 & \vdots & 3 \end{bmatrix}$$

Fourth column has a leading 1

The matrix is now in row-echelon form, and the corresponding system of linear equations is

$$\begin{aligned} x + 2y - z \quad\quad\quad &= \quad 2 \\ y + z - 2w &= -3 \\ z - \quad w &= -2 \\ w &= \quad 3. \end{aligned}$$

Using back-substitution, you can determine that the solution is $x = -1$, $y = 2$, $z = 1$, and $w = 3$. Check this solution in the original system.

■■■■■■■■■

When solving a system of linear equations, remember that it is possible for the system to have no solution. If, in the elimination process, you obtain a row with zeros except for the last entry, it is unnecessary to continue the elimination process. You can simply conclude that the system is inconsistent. For instance, applying Gaussian elimination to the system

$$\begin{aligned} x - \quad y + 2z &= 4 \\ x \quad\quad + \quad z &= 6 \\ 2x - 3y + 5z &= 4 \\ 3x + 2y - \quad z &= 1 \end{aligned}$$

produces

$$\begin{bmatrix} 1 & -1 & 2 & \vdots & 4 \\ 0 & 1 & -1 & \vdots & 2 \\ 0 & 0 & 0 & \vdots & -2 \\ 0 & 5 & -7 & \vdots & -11 \end{bmatrix}.$$

Note the the third row of this matrix consists of zeros except for the last entry. This means that the original system of linear equations is *inconsistent*.

Gauss-Jordan Elimination

With Gaussian elimination, elementary row operations are applied to a matrix to obtain a (row-equivalent) row-echelon form. A second method of elimination, called **Gauss-Jordan elimination,** after Carl Friedrich Gauss and Wilhelm Jordan (1842–1899), continues the reduction process until a *reduced* row-echelon form is obtained.

EXAMPLE 6   Gauss-Jordan Elimination

Use Gauss-Jordan elimination to solve the following system.

$$\begin{aligned} x - 2y + 3z &= 9 \\ -x + 3y &= -4 \\ 2x - 5y + 5z &= 17 \end{aligned}$$

SOLUTION

In Example 3, Gaussian elimination was used to obtain the following row-echelon form.

$$\begin{bmatrix} 1 & -2 & 3 & \vdots & 9 \\ 0 & 1 & 3 & \vdots & 5 \\ 0 & 0 & 1 & \vdots & 2 \end{bmatrix}$$

Now, rather than using back-substitution, apply elementary row operations until you obtain a matrix in reduced row-echelon form, as follows.

$$\begin{matrix} 2R_2 + R_1 \longrightarrow \end{matrix} \begin{bmatrix} 1 & 0 & 9 & \vdots & 19 \\ 0 & 1 & 3 & \vdots & 5 \\ 0 & 0 & 1 & \vdots & 2 \end{bmatrix}$$

Second column has zeros above its leading 1

$$\begin{matrix} -9R_3 + R_1 \longrightarrow \\ -3R_3 + R_2 \longrightarrow \end{matrix} \begin{bmatrix} 1 & 0 & 0 & \vdots & 1 \\ 0 & 1 & 0 & \vdots & -1 \\ 0 & 0 & 1 & \vdots & 2 \end{bmatrix}$$

Third column has zeros above its leading 1

Now, converting back to a system of linear equations, you can write

$$\begin{aligned} x &= 1 \\ y &= -1 \\ z &= 2. \end{aligned}$$

The beauty of Gauss-Jordan elimination is that, from the reduced row-echelon form, you can simply read the solution.

EXAMPLE 7 A System with an Infinite Number of Solutions

Solve the system of linear equations.

$$2x + 4y - 2z = 0$$
$$3x + 5y \quad\quad = 1$$

SOLUTION

Using Gauss-Jordan elimination, the augmented matrix reduces as follows.

$$\begin{bmatrix} 2 & 4 & -2 & \vdots & 0 \\ 3 & 5 & 0 & \vdots & 1 \end{bmatrix} \quad \tfrac{1}{2}R_1 \longrightarrow \begin{bmatrix} 1 & 2 & -1 & \vdots & 0 \\ 3 & 5 & 0 & \vdots & 1 \end{bmatrix}$$

$$-3R_1 + R_2 \longrightarrow \begin{bmatrix} 1 & 2 & -1 & \vdots & 0 \\ 0 & -1 & 3 & \vdots & 1 \end{bmatrix}$$

$$-R_2 \longrightarrow \begin{bmatrix} 1 & 2 & -1 & \vdots & 0 \\ 0 & 1 & -3 & \vdots & -1 \end{bmatrix}$$

$$-2R_2 + R_1 \longrightarrow \begin{bmatrix} 1 & 0 & 5 & \vdots & 2 \\ 0 & 1 & -3 & \vdots & -1 \end{bmatrix}$$

The corresponding system of equations is

$$x \quad\quad + 5z = \quad 2$$
$$y - 3z = -1.$$

Solving for x and y in terms of z, you have $x = -5z + 2$ and $y = 3z - 1$. Then, letting $z = a$, the solution set has the form

$$(-5a + 2, 3a - 1, a),$$

where a is a real number.

DISCUSSION PROBLEM

COMPARING GAUSSIAN ELIMINATION WITH GAUSS-JORDAN ELIMINATION

Solve the following system of linear equations in two ways: once with Gaussian elimination with back-substitution and once with Gauss-Jordan elimination. Then write a short paragraph describing the advantages of one method over the other.

$$3x - 2y + \quad z = -6$$
$$-x + \quad y - 2z = \quad 1$$
$$2x + 2y - 3z = -1$$

WARM-UP

The following warm-up exercises involve skills that were covered in earlier sections. You will use these skills in the exercise set for this section.

In Exercises 1–4, evaluate the given expression.

1. $2(-1) - 3(5) + 7(2)$ **2.** $-4(-3) + 6(7) + 8(-3)$

3. $11(\frac{1}{2}) - 7(-\frac{3}{2}) - 5(2)$ **4.** $\frac{2}{3}(\frac{1}{2}) + \frac{4}{3}(-\frac{1}{3})$

In Exercises 5 and 6, determine whether $x = 1$, $y = 3$, and $z = -1$ is a solution of the system of linear equations.

5. $\begin{aligned} 4x - 2y + 3z &= -5 \\ x + 3y - z &= 11 \\ -x + 2y &= 5 \end{aligned}$ **6.** $\begin{aligned} -x + 2y + z &= 4 \\ 2x - 3z &= 5 \\ 3x + 5y - 2z &= 21 \end{aligned}$

In Exercises 7–10, use back-substitution to solve the system of linear equations.

7. $\begin{aligned} 2x - 3y &= 4 \\ y &= 2 \end{aligned}$ **8.** $\begin{aligned} 5x + 4y &= 0 \\ y &= -3 \end{aligned}$

9. $\begin{aligned} x - 3y + z &= 0 \\ y - 3z &= 8 \\ z &= 2 \end{aligned}$ **10.** $\begin{aligned} 2x - 5y + 3z &= -2 \\ y - 4z &= 0 \\ z &= 1 \end{aligned}$

SECTION 9.5 · EXERCISES

In Exercises 1–6, determine the order of the matrix.

1. $\begin{bmatrix} 4 & -2 \\ 7 & 0 \\ 0 & 8 \end{bmatrix}$ **2.** $\begin{bmatrix} 5 & -3 & 8 & 7 \end{bmatrix}$

3. $\begin{bmatrix} -9 \\ 2 \\ 36 \\ 11 \\ 3 \end{bmatrix}$ **4.** $\begin{bmatrix} 11 & 0 & 8 & 5 & 5 \\ -3 & 7 & 15 & 0 & 10 \\ 0 & 6 & 3 & 3 & 9 \\ 12 & 4 & 16 & 9 & 0 \\ 1 & 1 & 6 & 7 & 8 \end{bmatrix}$

5. $\begin{bmatrix} 33 & 45 \\ -9 & 20 \end{bmatrix}$ **6.** $\begin{bmatrix} 4 \end{bmatrix}$

In Exercises 7–10, determine whether the matrix is in row-echelon form. If it is, determine if it is also in reduced row-echelon form.

7. $\begin{bmatrix} 1 & 0 & 0 & 0 \\ 0 & 1 & 1 & 5 \\ 0 & 0 & 0 & 0 \end{bmatrix}$ **8.** $\begin{bmatrix} 1 & 0 & 2 & 1 \\ 0 & 1 & -3 & 10 \\ 0 & 0 & 1 & 0 \end{bmatrix}$

9. $\begin{bmatrix} 2 & 0 & 4 & 0 \\ 0 & -1 & 3 & 6 \\ 0 & 0 & 1 & 5 \end{bmatrix}$ **10.** $\begin{bmatrix} 1 & 3 & 0 & 0 \\ 0 & 0 & 1 & 8 \\ 0 & 0 & 0 & 0 \end{bmatrix}$

In Exercises 11–14, fill in the blanks using elementary row operations to form a row-equivalent matrix.

11. $\begin{bmatrix} 1 & 4 & 3 \\ 2 & 10 & 5 \end{bmatrix}$
$\begin{bmatrix} 1 & 4 & 3 \\ 0 & \blacksquare & -1 \end{bmatrix}$

12. $\begin{bmatrix} 3 & 6 & 8 \\ 4 & -3 & 6 \end{bmatrix}$
$\begin{bmatrix} 1 & \blacksquare & \frac{8}{3} \\ 4 & -3 & 6 \end{bmatrix}$

13. $\begin{bmatrix} 1 & 1 & 4 & -1 \\ 3 & 8 & 10 & 3 \\ -2 & 1 & 12 & 6 \end{bmatrix}$
$\begin{bmatrix} 1 & 1 & 4 & -1 \\ 0 & 5 & \blacksquare & \blacksquare \\ 0 & 3 & \blacksquare & \blacksquare \end{bmatrix}$
$\begin{bmatrix} 1 & 1 & 4 & -1 \\ 0 & 1 & \blacksquare & \blacksquare \\ 0 & 3 & 20 & 4 \end{bmatrix}$

14. $\begin{bmatrix} 2 & 4 & 8 & 3 \\ 1 & -1 & -3 & 2 \\ 2 & 6 & 4 & 9 \end{bmatrix}$
$\begin{bmatrix} 1 & \blacksquare & \blacksquare & \blacksquare \\ 1 & -1 & -3 & 2 \\ 2 & 6 & 4 & 9 \end{bmatrix}$
$\begin{bmatrix} 1 & 2 & 4 & \frac{3}{2} \\ 0 & \blacksquare & -7 & \frac{1}{2} \\ 0 & 2 & \blacksquare & \blacksquare \end{bmatrix}$

15. Perform the indicated *sequence* of elementary row operations to write the matrix in reduced row-echelon form.
$\begin{bmatrix} 1 & 2 & 3 \\ 2 & -1 & -4 \\ 3 & 1 & -1 \end{bmatrix}$
(a) Add -2 times Row 1 to Row 2. (Only Row 2 should change.)
(b) Add -3 times Row 1 to Row 3. (Only Row 3 should change.)
(c) Add -1 times Row 2 to Row 3.
(d) Multiply Row 2 by $-\frac{1}{5}$.
(e) Add -2 times Row 2 to Row 1.

16. Perform the indicated *sequence* of elementary row operations to write the matrix in reduced row-echelon form.
$\begin{bmatrix} 7 & 1 \\ 0 & 2 \\ -3 & 4 \\ 4 & 1 \end{bmatrix}$
(a) Add Row 3 to Row 4. (Only Row 4 should change.)
(b) Interchange Rows 1 and 4. (Note that the first element in the matrix is now 1, and that it was obtained without introducing fractions.)
(c) Add 3 times Row 1 to Row 3.
(d) Add -7 times Row 1 to Row 4.
(e) Multiply Row 2 by $\frac{1}{2}$.
(f) Add the appropriate multiple of Row 2 to Rows 1, 3, and 4.

In Exercises 17–20, write the matrix in row-echelon form. Remember that the row-echelon form for a given matrix is not unique. (*Note:* For some exercises it may be advantageous to use the matrix capabilities of your graphing utility.)

17. $\begin{bmatrix} 1 & 1 & 0 & 5 \\ -2 & -1 & 2 & -10 \\ 3 & 6 & 7 & 14 \end{bmatrix}$

18. $\begin{bmatrix} 1 & 2 & -1 & 3 \\ 3 & 7 & -5 & 14 \\ -2 & -1 & -3 & 8 \end{bmatrix}$

19. $\begin{bmatrix} 1 & -1 & -1 & 1 \\ 5 & -4 & 1 & 8 \\ -6 & 8 & 18 & 0 \end{bmatrix}$

20. $\begin{bmatrix} 1 & -3 & 0 & -7 \\ -3 & 10 & 1 & 23 \\ 4 & -10 & 2 & -24 \end{bmatrix}$

In Exercises 21–24, write the matrix in *reduced* row-echelon form. (*Note:* For some exercises it may be advantageous to use the matrix capabilities of your graphing utility.)

21. $\begin{bmatrix} 3 & 3 & 3 \\ -1 & 0 & -4 \\ 2 & 4 & -2 \end{bmatrix}$

22. $\begin{bmatrix} 1 & 3 & 2 \\ 5 & 15 & 9 \\ 2 & 6 & 10 \end{bmatrix}$

23. $\begin{bmatrix} 1 & 2 & 3 & -5 \\ 1 & 2 & 4 & -9 \\ -2 & -4 & -4 & 3 \\ 4 & 8 & 11 & -14 \end{bmatrix}$

24. $\begin{bmatrix} 1 & -3 \\ -1 & 8 \\ 0 & 4 \\ -2 & 10 \end{bmatrix}$

In Exercises 25–28, write the system of linear equations represented by the augmented matrix.

25. $\begin{bmatrix} 4 & 3 & \vdots & 8 \\ 1 & -2 & \vdots & 3 \end{bmatrix}$

26. $\begin{bmatrix} 9 & -4 & \vdots & 0 \\ 6 & 1 & \vdots & -4 \end{bmatrix}$

27. $\begin{bmatrix} 1 & 0 & 2 & \vdots & -10 \\ 0 & 3 & -1 & \vdots & 5 \\ 4 & 2 & 0 & \vdots & 3 \end{bmatrix}$

28. $\begin{bmatrix} 5 & 8 & 2 & 0 & \vdots & -1 \\ -2 & 15 & 5 & 1 & \vdots & 9 \\ 1 & 6 & -7 & 0 & \vdots & -3 \end{bmatrix}$

In Exercises 29–32, write the system of linear equations represented by the augmented matrix. Then use back-substitution to find the solution. (Use variables x, y, and z.)

29. $\begin{bmatrix} 1 & -2 & \vdots & 4 \\ 0 & 1 & \vdots & -3 \end{bmatrix}$ **30.** $\begin{bmatrix} 1 & 5 & \vdots & 0 \\ 0 & 1 & \vdots & -1 \end{bmatrix}$

31. $\begin{bmatrix} 1 & -1 & 2 & \vdots & 4 \\ 0 & 1 & -1 & \vdots & 2 \\ 0 & 0 & 1 & \vdots & -2 \end{bmatrix}$ **32.** $\begin{bmatrix} 1 & 2 & -2 & \vdots & -1 \\ 0 & 1 & 1 & \vdots & 9 \\ 0 & 0 & 1 & \vdots & -3 \end{bmatrix}$

In Exercises 33–36, an augmented matrix that represents a system of linear equations (in variables x, y, and z) has been reduced using Gauss-Jordan elimination. Write the solution represented by the augmented matrix.

33. $\begin{bmatrix} 1 & 0 & \vdots & 7 \\ 0 & 1 & \vdots & -5 \end{bmatrix}$ **34.** $\begin{bmatrix} 1 & 0 & \vdots & -2 \\ 0 & 1 & \vdots & 4 \end{bmatrix}$

35. $\begin{bmatrix} 1 & 0 & 0 & \vdots & -4 \\ 0 & 1 & 0 & \vdots & -8 \\ 0 & 0 & 1 & \vdots & 2 \end{bmatrix}$ **36.** $\begin{bmatrix} 1 & 0 & 0 & \vdots & 3 \\ 0 & 1 & 0 & \vdots & -1 \\ 0 & 0 & 1 & \vdots & 0 \end{bmatrix}$

In Exercises 37–58, solve the system of equations. Use Gaussian elimination with back-substitution or Gauss-Jordan elimination. (*Note:* For some exercises it may be advantageous to use the matrix capabilities of your graphing utility.)

37. $x + 2y = 7$
$2x + y = 8$

38. $2x + 6y = 16$
$2x + 3y = 7$

39. $-3x + 5y = -22$
$3x + 4y = 4$
$4x - 8y = 32$

40. $x + 2y = 0$
$x + y = 6$
$3x - 2y = 8$

41. $8x - 4y = 7$
$5x + 2y = 1$

42. $2x - y = -0.1$
$3x + 2y = 1.6$

43. $-x + 2y = 1.5$
$2x - 4y = 3$

44. $x - 3y = 5$
$-2x + 6y = -10$

45. $x - 3z = -2$
$3x + y - 2z = 5$
$2x + 2y + z = 4$

46. $2x - y + 3z = 24$
$2y - z = 14$
$7x - 5y = 6$

47. $x + y - 5z = 3$
$x - 2z = 1$
$2x - y - z = 0$

48. $2x + 3z = 3$
$4x - 3y + 7z = 5$
$8x - 9y + 15z = 9$

49. $x + 2y + z = 8$
$3x + 7y + 6z = 26$

50. $4x + 12y - 7z - 20w = 22$
$3x + 9y - 5z - 28w = 30$

51. $3x + 3y + 12z = 6$
$x + y + 4z = 2$
$2x + 5y + 20z = 10$
$-x + 2y + 8z = 4$

52. $2x + 10y + 2z = 6$
$x + 5y + 2z = 6$
$x + 5y + z = 3$
$-3x - 15y - 3z = -9$

53. $2x + y - z + 2w = -6$
$3x + 4y + w = 1$
$x + 5y + 2z + 6w = -3$
$5x + 2y - z - w = 3$

54. $x + 2y + 2z + 4w = 11$
$3x + 6y + 5z + 12w = 30$

55. $x + 2y = 0$
$-x - y = 0$

56. $x + 2y = 0$
$2x + 4y = 0$

57. $x + y + z = 0$
$2x + 3y + z = 0$
$3x + 5y + z = 0$

58. $x + 2y + z + 3w = 0$
$x - y + w = 0$
$y - z + 2w = 0$

59. *Borrowing Money* A small corporation borrowed $1,500,000 to expand its product line. Some of the money was borrowed at 8%, some at 9%, and some at 12%. How much was borrowed at each rate if the annual interest was $133,000 and the amount borrowed at 8% was four times the amount borrowed at 12%?

60. *Borrowing Money* A small corporation borrowed $500,000 to expand its product line. Some of the money was borrowed at 9%, some at 10%, and some at 12%. How much was borrowed at each rate if the annual interest was $52,000 and the amount borrowed at 10% was $2\frac{1}{2}$ times the amount borrowed at 9%?

61. *Partial Fractions* Write the partial fraction decomposition for the rational expression

$$\frac{4x^2}{(x+1)^2(x-1)} = \frac{A}{x-1} + \frac{B}{x+1} + \frac{C}{(x+1)^2}.$$

62. *Electrical Network* The currents in a certain electrical network are given by the solution of the system

$I_1 - I_2 + I_3 = 0$
$2I_1 + 2I_2 = 7$
$2I_2 + 4I_3 = 8,$

where I_1, I_2, and I_3 are measured in amperes. Solve the system of equations.

In Exercises 63–66, find the specified equation that passes through the given points. Use a graphing utility to verify your result.

63. Parabola:

$y = ax^2 + bx + c$

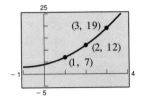

64. Parabola:

$y = ax^2 + bx + c$

65. Circle:

$x^2 + y^2 + Dx + Ey + F = 0$

66. Cubic polynomial:

$y = ax^3 + bx^2 + cx + d$

9.6   OPERATIONS WITH MATRICES
··

**Equality of Matrices / Matrix Addition and Scalar Multiplication /
Matrix Multiplication / Applications**

Equality of Matrices

In Section 9.5 you used matrices to solve systems of linear equations. Matrices, however, can do much more than that. There is a rich mathematical theory of matrices, and its applications are numerous. This section and the next introduce some fundamentals of matrix theory. It is standard mathematical convention to represent matrices in any of the following three ways.

1. A matrix can be denoted by an uppercase letter such as A, B, and C.
2. A matrix can be denoted by a representative element enclosed in brackets, such as $[a_{ij}]$, $[b_{ij}]$, and $[c_{ij}]$.
3. A matrix can be denoted by a rectangular array of numbers such as

$$A = [a_{ij}] = \begin{bmatrix} a_{11} & a_{12} & a_{13} & \cdots & a_{1n} \\ a_{21} & a_{22} & a_{23} & \cdots & a_{2n} \\ a_{31} & a_{32} & a_{33} & \cdots & a_{3n} \\ \vdots & \vdots & \vdots & & \vdots \\ a_{m1} & a_{m2} & a_{m3} & \cdots & a_{mn} \end{bmatrix}.$$

Two matrices are **equal** if their corresponding entries are equal.

DEFINITION OF EQUALITY OF MATRICES

Two matrices $A = [a_{ij}]$ and $B = [b_{ij}]$ are **equal** if they have the same order $(m \times n)$ and

$$a_{ij} = b_{ij}$$

for $1 \leq i \leq m$ and $1 \leq j \leq n$.

EXAMPLE 1   **Equality of Matrices**

Solve for a_{11}, a_{12}, a_{21}, and a_{22} in the following matrix equation.

$$\begin{bmatrix} a_{11} & a_{12} \\ a_{21} & a_{22} \end{bmatrix} = \begin{bmatrix} 2 & -1 \\ -3 & 0 \end{bmatrix}$$

SOLUTION

Because two matrices are equal only if corresponding entries are equal, we can conclude that

$$a_{11} = 2, \quad a_{12} = -1, \quad a_{21} = -3, \quad \text{and} \quad a_{22} = 0.$$

Matrix Addition and Scalar Multiplication

Add two matrices (of the same order) by adding their corresponding entries.

DEFINITION OF MATRIX ADDITION

If $A = [a_{ij}]$ and $B = [b_{ij}]$ are matrices of order $m \times n$, then their **sum** is the $m \times n$ matrix given by

$$A + B = [a_{ij} + b_{ij}].$$

The sum of two matrices of different orders is undefined.

EXAMPLE 2 Addition of Matrices

A. $\begin{bmatrix} -1 & 2 \\ 0 & 1 \end{bmatrix} + \begin{bmatrix} 1 & 3 \\ -1 & 2 \end{bmatrix} = \begin{bmatrix} -1+1 & 2+3 \\ 0-1 & 1+2 \end{bmatrix} = \begin{bmatrix} 0 & 5 \\ -1 & 3 \end{bmatrix}$

B. $\begin{bmatrix} 1 \\ -3 \\ -2 \end{bmatrix} + \begin{bmatrix} -1 \\ 3 \\ 2 \end{bmatrix} = \begin{bmatrix} 0 \\ 0 \\ 0 \end{bmatrix}$

C. The sum of

$$A = \begin{bmatrix} 2 & 1 & 0 \\ 4 & 0 & -1 \\ 3 & -2 & 2 \end{bmatrix} \quad \text{and} \quad B = \begin{bmatrix} 0 & 1 \\ -1 & 3 \\ 2 & 4 \end{bmatrix}$$

is undefined.

When working with matrices, you will usually refer to numbers as **scalars.** In this text, scalars will always be real numbers. You multiply a matrix A by a scalar c by multiplying each entry in A by c.

DEFINITION OF SCALAR MULTIPLICATION

If $A = [a_{ij}]$ is an $m \times n$ matrix and c is a scalar, then the **scalar multiple** of A by c is the $m \times n$ matrix given by

$$cA = [ca_{ij}].$$

Use $-A$ to represent the scalar product $(-1)A$. Moreover, if A and B are of the same order, then $A - B$ represents the sum of A and $(-1)B$. That is,

$$A - B = A + (-1)B. \qquad \textit{Subtraction of matrices}$$

EXAMPLE 3 Scalar Multiplication and Matrix Subtraction

For the matrices

$$A = \begin{bmatrix} 1 & 2 & 4 \\ -3 & 0 & -1 \\ 2 & 1 & 2 \end{bmatrix} \quad \text{and} \quad B = \begin{bmatrix} 2 & 0 & 0 \\ 1 & -4 & 3 \\ -1 & 3 & 2 \end{bmatrix},$$

find the following.

A. $3A$ **B.** $3A - B$

SOLUTION

A. $3A = 3\begin{bmatrix} 1 & 2 & 4 \\ -3 & 0 & -1 \\ 2 & 1 & 2 \end{bmatrix} = \begin{bmatrix} 3(1) & 3(2) & 3(4) \\ 3(-3) & 3(0) & 3(-1) \\ 3(2) & 3(1) & 3(2) \end{bmatrix} = \begin{bmatrix} 3 & 6 & 12 \\ -9 & 0 & -3 \\ 6 & 3 & 6 \end{bmatrix}$

B. $3A - B = \begin{bmatrix} 3 & 6 & 12 \\ -9 & 0 & -3 \\ 6 & 3 & 6 \end{bmatrix} - \begin{bmatrix} 2 & 0 & 0 \\ 1 & -4 & 3 \\ -1 & 3 & 2 \end{bmatrix} = \begin{bmatrix} 1 & 6 & 12 \\ -10 & 4 & -6 \\ 7 & 0 & 4 \end{bmatrix}$

It is often convenient to rewrite the scalar multiple cA by factoring c out of every entry in the matrix. For instance, in the following example, the scalar $\frac{1}{2}$ has been factored out of the matrix.

$$\begin{bmatrix} \frac{1}{2} & -\frac{3}{2} \\ \frac{5}{2} & \frac{1}{2} \end{bmatrix} = \frac{1}{2}\begin{bmatrix} 1 & -3 \\ 5 & 1 \end{bmatrix}$$

The properties of matrix addition and scalar multiplication are similar to those of addition and multiplication of real numbers, and we summarize them in the following list.

PROPERTIES OF MATRIX ADDITION AND SCALAR MULTIPLICATION

If A, B, and C are $m \times n$ matrices and c and d are scalars, then the following properties are true.

1. $A + B = B + A$ — *Commutative Property of Addition*
2. $A + (B + C) = (A + B) + C$ — *Associative Property of Addition*
3. $(cd)A = c(dA)$ — *Associative Property of Scalar Multiplication*
4. $1A = A$ — *Scalar Identity*
5. $c(A + B) = cA + cB$ — *Distributive Property*
6. $(c + d)A = cA + dA$ — *Distributive Property*

Note that the Associative Property of matrix addition allows you to write expressions such as $A + B + C$ without ambiguity because the same sum occurs no matter how the matrices are grouped. In other words, you obtain the same sum whether you group $A + B + C$ as $(A + B) + C$ or as $A + (B + C)$. This same reasoning applies to sums of four or more matrices.

One important property of addition of real numbers is that the number 0 is the additive identity. That is, $c + 0 = c$ for any real number c. For matrices, a similar property holds. That is, if A is an $m \times n$ matrix and O is the $m \times n$ **zero matrix** consisting entirely of zeros, then

$$A + O = A.$$

In other words, O is the **additive identity** for the set of all $m \times n$ matrices. For example, the following matrix is the additive identity for the set of all 2×3 matrices.

$$O = \begin{bmatrix} 0 & 0 & 0 \\ 0 & 0 & 0 \end{bmatrix} \qquad \textit{Zero 2 × 3 matrix}$$

Similarly, the additive identity for the set of all 3×4 matrices is

$$O = \begin{bmatrix} 0 & 0 & 0 & 0 \\ 0 & 0 & 0 & 0 \\ 0 & 0 & 0 & 0 \end{bmatrix}. \qquad \textit{Zero 3 × 4 matrix}$$

The algebra of real numbers and the algebra of matrices have many similarities. For example, compare the following solutions.

Real Numbers (Solve for x)	$m \times n$ Matrices (Solve for X)
$x + a = b$	$X + A = B$
$x + a + (-a) = b + (-a)$	$X + A + (-A) = B + (-A)$
$x + 0 = b - a$	$X + O = B - A$
$x = b - a$	$X = B - A$

The process of solving a matrix equation is demonstrated in Example 4.

EXAMPLE 4   Solving a Matrix Equation

Solve for X in the equation $3X + A = B$, where

$$A = \begin{bmatrix} 1 & -2 \\ 0 & 3 \end{bmatrix} \quad \text{and} \quad B = \begin{bmatrix} -3 & 4 \\ 2 & 1 \end{bmatrix}.$$

SOLUTION

Begin by solving the given equation for X to obtain

$$3X = B - A \quad \longrightarrow \quad X = \frac{1}{3}(B - A).$$

Now, using the given matrices A and B, you have

$$X = \frac{1}{3}\left(\begin{bmatrix} -3 & 4 \\ 2 & 1 \end{bmatrix} - \begin{bmatrix} 1 & -2 \\ 0 & 3 \end{bmatrix} \right) = \frac{1}{3}\begin{bmatrix} -4 & 6 \\ 2 & -2 \end{bmatrix} = \begin{bmatrix} -\frac{4}{3} & 2 \\ \frac{2}{3} & -\frac{2}{3} \end{bmatrix}.$$

Try using a graphing utility to solve this problem.

Matrix Multiplication

The third basic matrix operation is **matrix multiplication.** At first glance, the definition may seem unusual. You will see later, however, that this definition of the product of two matrices has many practical applications.

DEFINITION OF MATRIX MULTIPLICATION

If $A = [a_{ij}]$ is an $m \times n$ matrix and $B = [b_{ij}]$ is an $n \times p$ matrix, then the **product** AB is the $m \times p$ matrix

$$AB = [c_{ij}],$$

where $c_{ij} = a_{i1}b_{1j} + a_{i2}b_{2j} + a_{i3}b_{3j} + \cdots + a_{in}b_{nj}.$

This definition indicates a *row-by-column* multiplication, where the entry c_{ij} in the ith row and jth column of the product AB is obtained by multiplying the entries in the ith row of A by the corresponding entries in the jth column of B and then adding the results. The example that follows illustrates this process.

EXAMPLE 5 Finding the Product of Two Matrices

Technology Note

Most graphing utilities can perform matrix multiplication. Read the user's manual for your graphing utility and duplicate the matrix multiplication in Example 5. Then try multiplying two matrices A and B in which the number of columns of A is not equal to the number of rows of B. What error message does your graphing utility give?

Find the product AB where

$$A = \begin{bmatrix} -1 & 3 \\ 4 & -2 \\ 5 & 0 \end{bmatrix} \quad \text{and} \quad B = \begin{bmatrix} -3 & 2 \\ -4 & 1 \end{bmatrix}.$$

SOLUTION

First note that the product AB is defined because the number of columns of A is equal to the number of rows of B. Moreover, the product AB has order 3×2 and will take the form

$$\begin{bmatrix} -1 & 3 \\ 4 & -2 \\ 5 & 0 \end{bmatrix} \begin{bmatrix} -3 & 2 \\ -4 & 1 \end{bmatrix} = \begin{bmatrix} c_{11} & c_{12} \\ c_{21} & c_{22} \\ c_{31} & c_{32} \end{bmatrix}.$$

To find c_{11} (the entry in the first row and first column of the product), multiply corresponding entries in the first row of A and the first column of B. That is,

$$c_{11} = (-1)(-3) + (3)(-4) = -9$$

$$\begin{bmatrix} -1 & 3 \\ 4 & -2 \\ 5 & 0 \end{bmatrix} \begin{bmatrix} -3 & 2 \\ -4 & 1 \end{bmatrix} = \begin{bmatrix} -9 & c_{12} \\ c_{21} & c_{22} \\ c_{31} & c_{32} \end{bmatrix}.$$

Similarly, to find c_{12}, multiply corresponding entries in the first row of A and the second column of B to obtain

$$c_{12} = (-1)(2) + (3)(1) = 1$$

$$\begin{bmatrix} -1 & 3 \\ 4 & -2 \\ 5 & 0 \end{bmatrix} \begin{bmatrix} -3 & 2 \\ -4 & 1 \end{bmatrix} = \begin{bmatrix} -9 & 1 \\ c_{21} & c_{22} \\ c_{31} & c_{32} \end{bmatrix}.$$

Continuing this pattern produces the following results.

$$
\begin{aligned}
c_{21} &= (4)(-3) + (-2)(-4) = -4 \\
c_{22} &= (4)(2) + (-2)(1) = 6 \\
c_{31} &= (5)(-3) + (0)(-4) = -15 \\
c_{32} &= (5)(2) + (0)(1) = 10
\end{aligned}
$$

Thus, the product is

$$
AB = \begin{bmatrix} -1 & 3 \\ 4 & -2 \\ 5 & 0 \end{bmatrix} \begin{bmatrix} -3 & 2 \\ -4 & 1 \end{bmatrix}
$$

$$
= \begin{bmatrix} (-1)(-3) + (3)(-4) & (-1)(2) + (3)(1) \\ (4)(-3) + (-2)(-4) & (4)(2) + (-2)(1) \\ (5)(-3) + (0)(-4) & (5)(2) + (0)(1) \end{bmatrix}
$$

$$
= \begin{bmatrix} -9 & 1 \\ -4 & 6 \\ -15 & 10 \end{bmatrix}.
$$

Be sure you understand that for the product of two matrices to be defined, the number of columns of the first matrix must equal the number of rows of the second matrix. That is, the middle two indices must be the same and the outside two indices give the order of the product, as shown in the following diagram.

$$
\begin{array}{cccc}
A & B & = & AB \\
m \times n & n \times p & & m \times p
\end{array}
$$

↑ ⌊Equal⌋ ↑
⌊___Order of AB___⌋

The general pattern for matrix multiplication is as follows. To obtain the entry in the ith row and the jth column of the product AB, use the ith row of A and the jth column of B.

$$
\begin{bmatrix}
a_{11} & a_{12} & a_{13} & \cdots & a_{1n} \\
a_{21} & a_{22} & a_{23} & \cdots & a_{2n} \\
a_{31} & a_{32} & a_{33} & \cdots & a_{3n} \\
\cdot & \cdot & \cdot & & \cdot \\
a_{i1} & a_{i2} & a_{i3} & \cdots & a_{in} \\
\cdot & \cdot & \cdot & & \cdot \\
a_{m1} & a_{m2} & a_{m3} & \cdots & a_{mn}
\end{bmatrix}
\begin{bmatrix}
b_{11} & b_{12} & \cdots & b_{1j} & \cdots & b_{1p} \\
b_{21} & b_{22} & \cdots & b_{2j} & \cdots & b_{2p} \\
b_{31} & b_{32} & \cdots & b_{3j} & \cdots & b_{3p} \\
\cdot & \cdot & & \cdot & & \cdot \\
b_{n1} & b_{n2} & \cdots & b_{nj} & \cdots & b_{np}
\end{bmatrix}
=
\begin{bmatrix}
c_{11} & c_{12} & \cdots & c_{1j} & \cdots & c_{1p} \\
c_{21} & c_{22} & \cdots & c_{2j} & \cdots & c_{2p} \\
\cdot & \cdot & & \cdot & & \cdot \\
c_{i1} & c_{i2} & \cdots & c_{ij} & \cdots & c_{ip} \\
\cdot & \cdot & & \cdot & & \cdot \\
c_{m1} & c_{m2} & \cdots & c_{mj} & \cdots & c_{mp}
\end{bmatrix}
$$

$$a_{i1}b_{1j} + a_{i2}b_{2j} + a_{i3}b_{3j} + \cdots + a_{in}b_{nj} = c_{ij}$$

EXAMPLE 6   Matrix Multiplication

A. $\begin{bmatrix} 1 & 0 & 3 \\ 2 & -1 & -2 \end{bmatrix} \begin{bmatrix} -2 & 4 & 2 \\ 1 & 0 & 0 \\ -1 & 1 & -1 \end{bmatrix} = \begin{bmatrix} -5 & 7 & -1 \\ -3 & 6 & 6 \end{bmatrix}$

$\qquad\quad 2 \times 3 \qquad\qquad\quad 3 \times 3 \qquad\qquad\quad 2 \times 3$

REMARK In parts (B) and (C) of Example 6, note that the two products are different. Matrix multiplication is not, in general, commutative. That is, for most matrices, $AB \ne BA$.

B. $\begin{bmatrix} 1 & -2 & -3 \end{bmatrix} \begin{bmatrix} 2 \\ -1 \\ 1 \end{bmatrix} = \begin{bmatrix} 1 \end{bmatrix}$

$\qquad 1 \times 3 \qquad\quad 3 \times 1 \quad\; 1 \times 1$

C. $\begin{bmatrix} 2 \\ -1 \\ 1 \end{bmatrix} \begin{bmatrix} 1 & -2 & -3 \end{bmatrix} = \begin{bmatrix} 2 & -4 & -6 \\ -1 & 2 & 3 \\ 1 & -2 & -3 \end{bmatrix}$

$\quad\;\; 3 \times 1 \qquad 1 \times 3 \qquad\qquad 3 \times 3$

D. The product AB for

$$A = \begin{bmatrix} -2 & 1 \\ 1 & -3 \\ 1 & 4 \end{bmatrix} \quad \text{and} \quad B = \begin{bmatrix} -2 & 3 & 1 & 4 \\ 0 & 1 & -1 & 2 \\ 2 & -1 & 0 & 1 \end{bmatrix}$$

$\qquad\qquad\qquad\quad 3 \times 2 \qquad\qquad\qquad\quad 3 \times 4$

is not defined (nor is the product BA).

Use your graphing utility to verify these products.

PROPERTIES OF MATRIX MULTIPLICATION

If A, B, and C are matrices and c is a scalar, then the following properties are true.

1. $A(BC) = (AB)C$	*Associative Property of Multiplication*
2. $A(B + C) = AB + AC$	*Left Distributive Property*
3. $(A + B)C = AC + BC$	*Right Distributive Property*
4. $c(AB) = (cA)B = A(cB)$	

The $n \times n$ matrix that consists of 1's on its main diagonal and 0's elsewhere is the **identity matrix of order n** and is denoted by

$$I_n = \begin{bmatrix} 1 & 0 & 0 & \cdots & 0 \\ 0 & 1 & 0 & \cdots & 0 \\ 0 & 0 & 1 & \cdots & 0 \\ \vdots & \vdots & \vdots & & \vdots \\ 0 & 0 & 0 & \cdots & 1 \end{bmatrix}.$$ *Identity matrix*

Note that an identity matrix must be *square*. When the order is understood to be n, I_n is often denoted simply by I. If A is an $n \times n$ matrix, then the identity matrix has the properties

$$AI_n = A \quad \text{and} \quad I_n A = A.$$

For example,

$$\begin{bmatrix} 3 & -2 & 5 \\ 1 & 0 & 4 \\ -1 & 2 & -3 \end{bmatrix} \begin{bmatrix} 1 & 0 & 0 \\ 0 & 1 & 0 \\ 0 & 0 & 1 \end{bmatrix} = \begin{bmatrix} 3 & -2 & 5 \\ 1 & 0 & 4 \\ -1 & 2 & -3 \end{bmatrix}$$

and

$$\begin{bmatrix} 1 & 0 & 0 \\ 0 & 1 & 0 \\ 0 & 0 & 1 \end{bmatrix} \begin{bmatrix} 3 & -2 & 5 \\ 1 & 0 & 4 \\ -1 & 2 & -3 \end{bmatrix} = \begin{bmatrix} 3 & -2 & 5 \\ 1 & 0 & 4 \\ -1 & 2 & -3 \end{bmatrix}.$$

Applications

EXAMPLE 7   **An Application of Matrix Multiplication**

Two softball teams submit equipment lists to their sponsors.

	Women's Team	Men's Team
Bats	12	15
Balls	45	38
Gloves	15	17

Each bat costs $21, each ball costs $4, and each glove costs $30. Use matrices to find the total cost of equipment for each team.

SOLUTION

The equipment lists can be written in matrix form as

$$E = \begin{bmatrix} 12 & 15 \\ 45 & 38 \\ 15 & 17 \end{bmatrix},$$

and the cost per item can be written in matrix form as

$$C = \begin{bmatrix} 21 & 4 & 30 \end{bmatrix}.$$

The total cost of equipment for each team is given by the product

$$21(12) + 4(45) + 30(15) = 882 \quad \textit{(Women's team)}$$

$$CE = \begin{bmatrix} 21 & 4 & 30 \end{bmatrix} \begin{bmatrix} 12 & 15 \\ 45 & 38 \\ 15 & 17 \end{bmatrix} = \begin{bmatrix} 882 & 977 \end{bmatrix}.$$

$$21(15) + 4(38) + 30(17) = 977 \quad \textit{(Men's team)}$$

Thus, the total cost of equipment for the women's team is $882, and the total cost of equipment for the men's team is $977.

Another useful application of matrix multiplication is in representing a system of linear equations. Note how the system

$$a_{11}x_1 + a_{12}x_2 + a_{13}x_3 = b_1$$
$$a_{21}x_1 + a_{22}x_2 + a_{23}x_3 = b_2$$
$$a_{31}x_1 + a_{32}x_2 + a_{33}x_3 = b_3$$

can be written as the matrix equation $AX = B$, where A is the *coefficient matrix* of the system, and X and B are column matrices.

$$\underbrace{\begin{bmatrix} a_{11} & a_{12} & a_{13} \\ a_{21} & a_{22} & a_{23} \\ a_{31} & a_{32} & a_{33} \end{bmatrix}}_{A} \underbrace{\begin{bmatrix} x_1 \\ x_2 \\ x_3 \end{bmatrix}}_{X} = \underbrace{\begin{bmatrix} b_1 \\ b_2 \\ b_3 \end{bmatrix}}_{B}$$

EXAMPLE 8   Solving a System of Linear Equations

Solve the matrix equation $AX = B$ for X, where

Coefficient matrix   Constant matrix

$$A = \begin{bmatrix} 1 & -2 & 1 \\ 0 & 1 & 2 \\ 2 & 3 & -2 \end{bmatrix} \quad \text{and} \quad B = \begin{bmatrix} -4 \\ 4 \\ 2 \end{bmatrix}.$$

SOLUTION

As a system of linear equations, $AX = B$ is as follows.

$$\begin{aligned} x_1 - 2x_2 + x_3 &= -4 \\ x_2 + 2x_3 &= 4 \\ 2x_1 + 3x_2 - 2x_3 &= 2 \end{aligned}$$

Using Gauss-Jordan elimination on the augmented matrix of this system, you obtain

$$\begin{bmatrix} 1 & 0 & 0 & : & -1 \\ 0 & 1 & 0 & : & 2 \\ 0 & 0 & 1 & : & 1 \end{bmatrix}.$$

Thus, the solution of the system of linear equations is $x_1 = -1$, $x_2 = 2$, and $x_3 = 1$, and the solution of the matrix equation is

$$X = \begin{bmatrix} x_1 \\ x_2 \\ x_3 \end{bmatrix} = \begin{bmatrix} -1 \\ 2 \\ 1 \end{bmatrix}.$$

Use your graphing utility to verify that $AX = B$.

**DISCUSSION
PROBLEM**

**DIAGONAL
MATRICES**

A square matrix is called a **diagonal matrix** if each entry that is not on the main diagonal is zero. For instance,

$$A = \begin{bmatrix} -1 & 0 & 0 \\ 0 & 2 & 0 \\ 0 & 0 & 0 \end{bmatrix} \quad \text{and} \quad B = \begin{bmatrix} 2 & 0 & 0 & 0 \\ 0 & -1 & 0 & 0 \\ 0 & 0 & 3 & 0 \\ 0 & 0 & 0 & -2 \end{bmatrix}$$

are diagonal matrices. Write a paragraph describing a quick rule for multiplying a diagonal matrix by itself. Then illustrate your rule to find the matrices $A^2 = AA$ and $B^2 = BB$ for the given matrices A and B.

WARM-UP

The following warm-up exercises involve skills that were covered in earlier sections. You will use these skills in the exercise set for this section.

In Exercises 1 and 2, evaluate the expressions.

1. $-3(-\frac{5}{6}) + 10(-\frac{3}{4})4$ **2.** $-22(\frac{5}{2}) + 6(8)$

In Exercises 3 and 4, determine whether the matrices are in *reduced* row-echelon form.

3. $\begin{bmatrix} 0 & 1 & 0 & -5 \\ 1 & 0 & 3 & 2 \\ 0 & 0 & 1 & 0 \end{bmatrix}$ **4.** $\begin{bmatrix} 1 & 0 & 0 & 2 & 3 \\ 0 & 0 & 0 & 0 & 0 \\ 0 & 1 & 1 & 3 & 10 \end{bmatrix}$

In Exercises 5 and 6, write the augmented matrix for each system of linear equations.

5. $\begin{aligned} -5x + 10y &= 12 \\ 7x - 3y &= 0 \\ -x + 7y &= 25 \end{aligned}$ **6.** $\begin{aligned} 10x + 15y - 9z &= 42 \\ 6x - 5y &= 0 \end{aligned}$

In Exercises 7–10, solve the systems of linear equations represented by the augmented matrices.

7. $\begin{bmatrix} 1 & 0 & : & 0 \\ 0 & 1 & : & 2 \end{bmatrix}$ **8.** $\begin{bmatrix} 1 & 0 & -1 & : & 2 \\ 0 & 1 & 1 & : & 3 \end{bmatrix}$

9. $\begin{bmatrix} 1 & 2 & 1 & : & 0 \\ 0 & 0 & 1 & : & -1 \\ 0 & 0 & 0 & : & 0 \end{bmatrix}$ **10.** $\begin{bmatrix} 1 & -1 & 0 & : & 3 \\ 0 & 1 & -2 & : & 1 \\ 0 & 0 & 1 & : & -1 \end{bmatrix}$

SECTION 9.6 · EXERCISES

In Exercises 1–4, find x and y.

1. $\begin{bmatrix} x & -2 \\ 7 & y \end{bmatrix} = \begin{bmatrix} -4 & -2 \\ 7 & 22 \end{bmatrix}$ **2.** $\begin{bmatrix} -5 & x \\ y & 8 \end{bmatrix} = \begin{bmatrix} -5 & 13 \\ 12 & 8 \end{bmatrix}$

3. $\begin{bmatrix} 16 & 4 & 5 & 4 \\ -3 & 13 & 15 & 6 \\ 0 & 2 & 4 & 0 \end{bmatrix} = \begin{bmatrix} 16 & 4 & 2x+1 & 4 \\ -3 & 13 & 15 & 3x \\ 0 & 2 & 3y-5 & 0 \end{bmatrix}$

4. $\begin{bmatrix} x+2 & 8 & -3 \\ 1 & 2y & 2x \\ 7 & -2 & y+2 \end{bmatrix} = \begin{bmatrix} 2x+6 & 8 & -3 \\ 1 & 18 & -8 \\ 7 & -2 & 11 \end{bmatrix}$

In Exercises 5–10, find (a) $A + B$, (b) $A - B$, (c) $3A$, and (d) $3A - 2B$.

5. $A = \begin{bmatrix} 1 & -1 \\ 2 & -1 \end{bmatrix}$, $B = \begin{bmatrix} 2 & -1 \\ -1 & 8 \end{bmatrix}$

6. $A = \begin{bmatrix} 1 & 2 \\ 2 & 1 \end{bmatrix}$, $B = \begin{bmatrix} -3 & -2 \\ 4 & 2 \end{bmatrix}$

7. $A = \begin{bmatrix} 6 & -1 \\ 2 & 4 \\ -3 & 5 \end{bmatrix}$, $B = \begin{bmatrix} 1 & 4 \\ -1 & 5 \\ 1 & 10 \end{bmatrix}$

8. $A = \begin{bmatrix} 2 & 1 & 1 \\ -1 & -1 & 4 \end{bmatrix}$, $B = \begin{bmatrix} 2 & -3 & 4 \\ -3 & 1 & -2 \end{bmatrix}$

9. $A = \begin{bmatrix} 2 & 2 & -1 & 0 & 1 \\ 1 & 1 & -2 & 0 & -1 \end{bmatrix}$,

$B = \begin{bmatrix} 1 & 1 & -1 & 1 & 0 \\ -3 & 4 & 9 & -6 & -7 \end{bmatrix}$

10. $A = \begin{bmatrix} 3 \\ 2 \\ -1 \end{bmatrix}$, $B = \begin{bmatrix} -4 \\ 6 \\ 2 \end{bmatrix}$

In Exercises 11–16, find (a) AB, (b) BA, and, if possible, (c) A^2. (*Note:* $A^2 = AA$.)

11. $A = \begin{bmatrix} 1 & 2 \\ 4 & 2 \end{bmatrix}$, $\qquad B = \begin{bmatrix} 2 & -1 \\ -1 & 8 \end{bmatrix}$

12. $A = \begin{bmatrix} 2 & -1 \\ 1 & 4 \end{bmatrix}$, $\qquad B = \begin{bmatrix} 0 & 0 \\ 3 & -3 \end{bmatrix}$

13. $A = \begin{bmatrix} 3 & -1 \\ 1 & 3 \end{bmatrix}$, $\qquad B = \begin{bmatrix} 1 & -3 \\ 3 & 1 \end{bmatrix}$

14. $A = \begin{bmatrix} 1 & -1 \\ 1 & 1 \end{bmatrix}$, $\qquad B = \begin{bmatrix} 1 & 3 \\ -3 & 1 \end{bmatrix}$

15. $A = \begin{bmatrix} 1 & -1 & 7 \\ 2 & -1 & 8 \\ 3 & 1 & -1 \end{bmatrix}$, $\quad B = \begin{bmatrix} 1 & 1 & 2 \\ 2 & 1 & 1 \\ 1 & -3 & 2 \end{bmatrix}$

16. $A = \begin{bmatrix} 3 & 2 & 1 \end{bmatrix}$, $\qquad B = \begin{bmatrix} 2 \\ 3 \\ 0 \end{bmatrix}$

In Exercises 17–24, use a graphing utility to find AB, if possible.

17. $A = \begin{bmatrix} 2 & 1 \\ -3 & 4 \\ 1 & 6 \end{bmatrix}$, $\quad B = \begin{bmatrix} 0 & -1 & 0 \\ 4 & 0 & 2 \\ 8 & -1 & 7 \end{bmatrix}$

18. $A = \begin{bmatrix} 0 & -1 & 0 \\ 4 & 0 & 2 \\ 8 & -1 & 7 \end{bmatrix}$, $\quad B = \begin{bmatrix} 2 & 1 \\ -3 & 4 \\ 1 & 6 \end{bmatrix}$

19. $A = \begin{bmatrix} -1 & 3 \\ 4 & -5 \\ 0 & 2 \end{bmatrix}$, $\quad B = \begin{bmatrix} 1 & 2 \\ 0 & 7 \end{bmatrix}$

20. $A = \begin{bmatrix} 1 & 0 & 0 \\ 0 & 4 & 0 \\ 0 & 0 & -2 \end{bmatrix}$, $\quad B = \begin{bmatrix} 3 & 0 & 0 \\ 0 & -1 & 0 \\ 0 & 0 & 5 \end{bmatrix}$

21. $A = \begin{bmatrix} 5 & 0 & 0 \\ 0 & -8 & 0 \\ 0 & 0 & 7 \end{bmatrix}$, $\quad B = \begin{bmatrix} \frac{1}{5} & 0 & 0 \\ 0 & -\frac{1}{8} & 0 \\ 0 & 0 & \frac{1}{2} \end{bmatrix}$

22. $A = \begin{bmatrix} 0 & 0 & 5 \\ 0 & 0 & -3 \\ 0 & 0 & 4 \end{bmatrix}$, $\quad B = \begin{bmatrix} 6 & -11 & 4 \\ 8 & 16 & 4 \\ 0 & 0 & 0 \end{bmatrix}$

23. $A = \begin{bmatrix} 6 \\ -2 \\ 1 \\ 6 \end{bmatrix}$, $\qquad B = \begin{bmatrix} 10 & 12 \end{bmatrix}$

24. $A = \begin{bmatrix} 1 & 0 & 3 & -2 & 4 \\ 6 & 13 & 8 & -17 & 10 \end{bmatrix}$, $\quad B = \begin{bmatrix} 1 & 6 \\ 4 & 2 \end{bmatrix}$

In Exercises 25–28, solve for X given

$$A = \begin{bmatrix} -2 & -1 \\ 1 & 0 \\ 3 & -4 \end{bmatrix} \quad \text{and} \quad B = \begin{bmatrix} 0 & 3 \\ 2 & 0 \\ -4 & -1 \end{bmatrix}.$$

25. $X = 3A - 2B$ $\qquad$ **26.** $2X = 2A - B$

27. $2X + 3A = B$ $\qquad$ **28.** $2A + 4B = -2X$

In Exercises 29–32, find matrices A, X, and B such that the given system of linear equations can be written as the matrix equation $AX = B$. Solve the system of equations. Use a graphing utility to check your result.

29. $\quad -x + y = 4$
$\qquad -2x + y = 0$

30. $\quad 2x + 3y = 5$
$\qquad x + 4y = 10$

31. $\quad x - 2y + 3z = 9$
$\qquad -x + 3y - z = -6$
$\qquad 2x - 5y + 5z = 17$

32. $\quad x + y - 3z = -1$
$\qquad -x + 2y \quad = 1$
$\qquad -y + z = 0$

33. If a, b, and c are real numbers such that $c \neq 0$ and $ac = bc$, then $a = b$. However, if A, B, and C are matrices such that $AC = BC$, then A is *not* necessarily equal to B. Illustrate this using the following matrices.

$$A = \begin{bmatrix} 1 & 2 & 3 \\ 0 & 5 & 4 \\ 3 & -2 & 1 \end{bmatrix}, \quad B = \begin{bmatrix} 4 & -6 & 3 \\ 5 & 4 & 4 \\ -1 & 0 & 1 \end{bmatrix},$$

$$C = \begin{bmatrix} 0 & 0 & 0 \\ 0 & 0 & 0 \\ 4 & -2 & 3 \end{bmatrix}$$

34. If a and b are real numbers such that $ab = 0$, then $a = 0$ or $b = 0$. However, if A and B are matrices such that $AB = 0$, then it is *not* necessarily true that $A = 0$ or $B = 0$. Illustrate this using the following matrices.

$$A = \begin{bmatrix} 3 & 3 \\ 4 & 4 \end{bmatrix}, \quad B = \begin{bmatrix} 1 & -1 \\ -1 & 1 \end{bmatrix}$$

35. *Factory Production* A certain corporation has three factories, each of which manufactures two products. The number of units of product i produced at factory j in one day is represented by a_{ij} in the matrix

$$A = \begin{bmatrix} 60 & 40 & 20 \\ 30 & 90 & 60 \end{bmatrix}.$$

Find the production levels if production is increased by 20%. (*Hint:* Because an increase of 20% corresponds to 100% + 20%, multiply the given matrix by 1.2.)

36. *Factory Production*   A certain corporation has four factories, each of which manufactures two products. The number of units of product i produced at factory j in one day is represented by a_{ij} in the matrix

$$A = \begin{bmatrix} 100 & 90 & 70 & 30 \\ 40 & 20 & 60 & 60 \end{bmatrix}.$$

Find the production levels if production is increased by 10%. (*Hint:* Because an increase of 10% corresponds to 100% + 10%, multiply the given matrix by 1.1.)

37. *Crop Production*   A fruit grower raises two crops that are shipped to three outlets. The number of units of product i that are shipped to outlet j is represented by a_{ij} in the matrix

$$A = \begin{bmatrix} 100 & 75 & 75 \\ 125 & 150 & 100 \end{bmatrix}.$$

The profit per unit is represented by the matrix

$B = [\$3.75 \quad \$7.00]$.

Find the product BA, and state what each entry of the product represents.

38. *Total Revenue*   A manufacturer produces three different models of a given product that are shipped to two different warehouses. The number of units of model i that are shipped to warehouse j is represented by a_{ij} in the matrix

$$A = \begin{bmatrix} 5,000 & 4,000 \\ 6,000 & 10,000 \\ 8,000 & 5,000 \end{bmatrix}.$$

The price per unit is represented by the matrix

$B = [\$20.50 \quad \$26.50 \quad \$29.50]$.

Find the product BA, and state what each entry of the product represents.

39. *Inventory Levels*   A company sells five different models of computers through three retail outlets. The inventory of each model in the three outlets is given by the matrix S.

Model

$$S = \begin{matrix} & \begin{matrix} A & B & C & D & E \end{matrix} & \\ \begin{bmatrix} 3 & 2 & 2 & 3 & 0 \\ 0 & 2 & 3 & 4 & 3 \\ 4 & 2 & 1 & 3 & 2 \end{bmatrix} & \begin{matrix} 1 \\ 2 \\ 3 \end{matrix} & \text{Outlet} \end{matrix}$$

The wholesale and retail price for each model is given by the matrix T.

Price

$$T = \begin{matrix} & \overbrace{\begin{matrix} \text{Wholesale} & \text{Retail} \end{matrix}} & \\ \begin{bmatrix} \$840 & \$1100 \\ \$1200 & \$1350 \\ \$1450 & \$1650 \\ \$2650 & \$3000 \\ \$3050 & \$3200 \end{bmatrix} & \begin{matrix} A \\ B \\ C \\ D \\ E \end{matrix} & \text{Model} \end{matrix}$$

(a) What is the retail price of the inventory at Outlet 1?
(b) What is the wholesale price of the inventory at Outlet 3?
(c) Compute ST and interpret the result.

40. *Labor/Wage Requirements*   A company that manufactures boats has the following labor-hour and wage requirements.

Labor-hour Requirements (per boat)

	Department			
	Cutting	Assembly	Packaging	
$S =$	1.0 hour	0.5 hour	0.2 hour	Small
	1.6 hours	1.0 hour	0.2 hour	Medium
	2.5 hours	2.0 hours	0.4 hour	Large

Boat size

Wage Requirements (per hour)

	Plant		
	A	B	
$T =$	\$12	\$10	Cutting
	\$9	\$8	Assembly
	\$6	\$5	Packaging

Department

(a) What is the labor cost for a medium boat at Plant B?
(b) What is the labor cost for a large boat at Plant A?
(c) Compute ST and interpret the result.

41. *Voting Preference*   The matrix

From

$$P = \begin{matrix} & \begin{matrix} R & D & I \end{matrix} & \\ \begin{bmatrix} 0.6 & 0.1 & 0.1 \\ 0.2 & 0.7 & 0.1 \\ 0.2 & 0.2 & 0.8 \end{bmatrix} & \begin{matrix} R \\ D \\ I \end{matrix} & \text{To} \end{matrix}$$

is called a stochastic matrix. Each entry p_{ij} $(i \neq j)$ represents the proportion of the voting population that changes from party i to party j, and p_{ii} represents the proportion that remains loyal to the party from one election to the next. Use a graphing utility to find P^2. (This matrix gives the transition probabilities from the first election to the third.)

42. *Voting Preference*   Use a graphing utility to find P^3, P^4, P^5, P^6, P^7, and P^8 for the matrix given in Exercise 41. Can you detect a pattern as P is raised to higher and higher powers?

9.7   INVERSE MATRICES AND SYSTEMS OF LINEAR EQUATIONS

The Inverse of a Matrix   /   The Inverse of a 2 × 2 Matrix (Quick Method)   /   Systems of Linear Equations

The Inverse of a Matrix

This section further develops the algebra of matrices to include the solution of matrix equations involving matrix multiplication. To begin, consider the real number equation $ax = b$. To solve this equation for x, multiply both sides of the equation by a^{-1} (provided $a \neq 0$).

$$ax = b$$
$$(a^{-1}a)x = a^{-1}b$$
$$(1)x = a^{-1}b$$
$$x = a^{-1}b$$

The number a^{-1} is the *multiplicative inverse* of a because it has the property that $a^{-1}a = 1$. The definition of a multiplicative inverse of a matrix is similar.

DEFINITION OF AN INVERSE OF A MATRIX

Let A be a square matrix of order n. If there exists a matrix A^{-1} such that

$$AA^{-1} = I_n = A^{-1}A,$$

then A^{-1} is the **inverse** of A.

REMARK   The symbol A^{-1} is read "A inverse."

If a matrix A has an inverse, then A is **invertible** (or **nonsingular**); otherwise, A is **singular**. A nonsquare matrix cannot have an inverse. To see this, note that if A is of order $m \times n$ and B is of order $n \times m$ (where $m \neq n$), then the products AB and BA are of different orders and could therefore not be equal to each other. Not all square matrices possess inverses. If, however, a matrix does possess an inverse, then that inverse is unique.

EXAMPLE 1 The Inverse of a Matrix

Show that B is the inverse of A, where

$$A = \begin{bmatrix} -1 & 2 \\ -1 & 1 \end{bmatrix} \quad \text{and} \quad B = \begin{bmatrix} 1 & -2 \\ 1 & -1 \end{bmatrix}.$$

SOLUTION

Using the definition of an inverse matrix, you can show that B is the inverse of A by showing that $AB = I = BA$ as follows.

$$AB = \begin{bmatrix} -1 & 2 \\ -1 & 1 \end{bmatrix} \begin{bmatrix} 1 & -2 \\ 1 & -1 \end{bmatrix} = \begin{bmatrix} -1+2 & 2-2 \\ -1+1 & 2-1 \end{bmatrix} = \begin{bmatrix} 1 & 0 \\ 0 & 1 \end{bmatrix}$$

$$BA = \begin{bmatrix} 1 & -2 \\ 1 & -1 \end{bmatrix} \begin{bmatrix} -1 & 2 \\ -1 & 1 \end{bmatrix} = \begin{bmatrix} -1+2 & 2-2 \\ -1+1 & 2-1 \end{bmatrix} = \begin{bmatrix} 1 & 0 \\ 0 & 1 \end{bmatrix}$$

REMARK Recall that it is not always true that $AB = BA$, even if both products are defined. However, if A and B are both square matrices and $AB = I_n$, then it can be shown that $BA = I_n$. Hence, in Example 1, you only needed to check that $AB = I_2$.

The following example shows how to use a system of equations to find the inverse.

EXAMPLE 2 Finding the Inverse of a Matrix

Find the inverse of the matrix

$$A = \begin{bmatrix} 1 & 4 \\ -1 & -3 \end{bmatrix}.$$

SOLUTION

To find the inverse of A, try to solve the matrix equation $AX = I$ for X.

$$\overset{A}{\begin{bmatrix} 1 & 4 \\ -1 & -3 \end{bmatrix}} \overset{X}{\begin{bmatrix} x_{11} & x_{12} \\ x_{21} & x_{22} \end{bmatrix}} = \overset{I}{\begin{bmatrix} 1 & 0 \\ 0 & 1 \end{bmatrix}}$$

$$\begin{bmatrix} x_{11} + 4x_{21} & x_{12} + 4x_{22} \\ -x_{11} - 3x_{21} & -x_{12} - 3x_{22} \end{bmatrix} = \begin{bmatrix} 1 & 0 \\ 0 & 1 \end{bmatrix}$$

Equating corresponding entries, you obtain the following two systems of linear equations.

$$\begin{aligned} x_{11} + 4x_{21} &= 1 & x_{12} + 4x_{22} &= 0 \\ -x_{11} - 3x_{21} &= 0 & -x_{12} - 3x_{22} &= 1 \end{aligned}$$

From the first system you find that $x_{11} = -3$ and $x_{21} = 1$, and from the second system you find that $x_{12} = -4$ and $x_{22} = 1$. Therefore, the inverse of A is

$$X = A^{-1} = \begin{bmatrix} -3 & -4 \\ 1 & 1 \end{bmatrix}.$$

Try using matrix multiplication to check this result.

EXAMPLE 3   Finding the Inverse of a Matrix

Use a graphing utility to find the inverse of

$$A = \begin{bmatrix} 1 & -1 & 0 \\ 1 & 0 & -1 \\ 6 & -2 & -3 \end{bmatrix}.$$

SOLUTION

$$A^{-1} = \begin{bmatrix} -2 & -3 & 1 \\ -3 & -3 & 1 \\ -2 & -4 & 1 \end{bmatrix}$$

Try using matrix multiplication to confirm this result.

REMARK   The denominator $ad - bc$ is called the **determinant** of the 2×2 matrix A.

The Inverse of a 2 × 2 Matrix (Quick Method)

If A is a 2×2 matrix given by

$$A = \begin{bmatrix} a & b \\ c & d \end{bmatrix},$$

then A is invertible if and only if $ad - bc \neq 0$. Moreover, if $ad - bc \neq 0$, then the inverse is given by

$$A^{-1} = \frac{1}{ad - bc} \begin{bmatrix} d & -b \\ -c & a \end{bmatrix}.$$

Try verifying this inverse by multiplication.

Technology Note

Graphing utilities that can perform matrix operations usually have the capability of finding the **determinant** of a matrix. It can be shown that a square matrix has an inverse if and only if its determinant is not zero. Try using this result to decide which of the following have inverses.

$$A = \begin{bmatrix} 1 & 2 \\ 3 & 4 \end{bmatrix}, \qquad B = \begin{bmatrix} -1 & 2 \\ 4 & -8 \end{bmatrix}$$

EXAMPLE 4   Finding the Inverse of a 2 × 2 Matrix

If possible, find the inverses of the following matrices.

A. $A = \begin{bmatrix} 3 & -1 \\ -2 & 2 \end{bmatrix}$ **B.** $B = \begin{bmatrix} -1 & 3 \\ 2 & -6 \end{bmatrix}$

SOLUTION

A. For matrix A, we apply the formula for the inverse of a 2×2 matrix to obtain $ad - bc = (3)(2) - (-1)(-2) = 4$. Because this quantity is not zero, the inverse is formed by interchanging the entries on the main diagonal and changing the sign of the other two entries as follows.

$$A^{-1} = \frac{1}{4} \begin{bmatrix} 2 & 1 \\ 2 & 3 \end{bmatrix} = \begin{bmatrix} \frac{1}{2} & \frac{1}{4} \\ \frac{1}{2} & \frac{3}{4} \end{bmatrix}$$

B. For matrix B, we have $ad - bc = (-1)(-6) - (3)(2) = 0$, which means that B is not invertible.

Systems of Linear Equations

A system of linear equations can have exactly one solution, an infinite number of solutions, or no solution. If the coefficient matrix A of a *square* system (a system that has the same number of equations as variables) is invertible, the system has a unique solution, which is given as follows.

$$AX = B \qquad \text{\textit{Original equation}}$$
$$A^{-1}AX = A^{-1}B \qquad \text{\textit{Multiply both sides by } A^{-1} \text{ \textit{(on the left)}}}$$
$$X = A^{-1}B \qquad \text{\textit{Solution}}$$

A SYSTEM OF EQUATIONS WITH A UNIQUE SOLUTION

If A is an invertible matrix, then the system of linear equations represented by $AX = B$ has a unique solution given by

$$X = A^{-1}B.$$

EXAMPLE 5   Solving a System of Equations Using an Inverse

Use an inverse matrix to solve the following system.

$$2x + 3y + z = -1$$
$$3x + 3y + z = 1$$
$$2x + 4y + z = -2$$

SOLUTION

Begin by writing the linear system in matrix form.

$$\overset{A}{\begin{bmatrix} 2 & 3 & 1 \\ 3 & 3 & 1 \\ 2 & 4 & 1 \end{bmatrix}} \overset{X}{\begin{bmatrix} x \\ y \\ z \end{bmatrix}} = \overset{B}{\begin{bmatrix} -1 \\ 1 \\ -2 \end{bmatrix}}$$

To solve the system, enter A and B into your graphing utility and compute $A^{-1}B$.

$$X = A^{-1}B = \begin{bmatrix} 2 \\ -1 \\ -2 \end{bmatrix}$$

The solution is $x = 2$, $y = -1$, and $z = -2$.

DISCUSSION PROBLEM

....

THE FACTORIZATION PRINCIPLE

For *real numbers* the Factorization Principle states that if $ab = 0$, then either $a = 0$ or $b = 0$. It is possible, however, to find nonzero matrices whose product is zero. For instance,

$$\begin{bmatrix} 2 & -1 \\ -4 & 2 \end{bmatrix}\begin{bmatrix} 3 & -3 \\ 6 & -6 \end{bmatrix} = \begin{bmatrix} 0 & 0 \\ 0 & 0 \end{bmatrix}.$$

In order to obtain a factorization principle for matrices, we must restrict ourselves to a certain type of matrix. Complete the following factorization principle for matrices by determining which type of matrix will make the statement true. Then write a short paragraph that justifies your conclusion.

"Let A and B be square matrices, each of order $n \times n$. If either A or B are _____ and $AB = O$ where O is the $n \times n$ zero matrix, then $A = O$ or $B = O$."

WARM-UP

....

The following warm-up exercises involve skills that were covered in earlier sections. You will use these skills in the exercise set for this section.

In Exercises 1–8, perform the indicated matrix operation.

1. $4\begin{bmatrix} 1 & 6 \\ 0 & -4 \\ 12 & 2 \end{bmatrix}$

2. $\dfrac{1}{2}\begin{bmatrix} 11 & 10 & 48 \\ 1 & 0 & 16 \\ 0 & 2 & 8 \end{bmatrix}$

3. $\begin{bmatrix} 1 & -10 & 3 \\ 4 & 1 & 0 \end{bmatrix} - 2\begin{bmatrix} 3 & -4 & 8 \\ 0 & 7 & 1 \end{bmatrix}$

4. $\begin{bmatrix} 5 & 20 \\ -7 & 15 \end{bmatrix} - 3\begin{bmatrix} 6 & 3 \\ 4 & -2 \end{bmatrix}$

5. $\begin{bmatrix} 1 & -2 \\ -1 & 3 \end{bmatrix}\begin{bmatrix} 3 & 2 \\ 1 & 1 \end{bmatrix}$

6. $\begin{bmatrix} 1 & 0 \\ 0 & 1 \end{bmatrix}\begin{bmatrix} 6 & 5 \\ 3 & -2 \end{bmatrix}$

7. $\begin{bmatrix} 2 & 0 & 0 \\ 0 & -1 & 0 \\ 0 & 0 & 3 \end{bmatrix}\begin{bmatrix} \frac{1}{2} & 0 & 0 \\ 0 & -1 & 0 \\ 0 & 0 & \frac{1}{3} \end{bmatrix}$

8. $\begin{bmatrix} 1 & -1 & 0 \\ 1 & 0 & -1 \\ 6 & -2 & -3 \end{bmatrix}\begin{bmatrix} -2 & -3 & 1 \\ -3 & -3 & 1 \\ -2 & -4 & 1 \end{bmatrix}$

In Exercises 9 and 10, rewrite the matrices in reduced row-echelon form.

9. $\begin{bmatrix} 3 & -2 & 1 & 0 \\ 4 & -3 & 0 & 1 \end{bmatrix}$

10. $\begin{bmatrix} 1 & 1 & 2 & 1 & 0 & 0 \\ -1 & 0 & 3 & 0 & 1 & 0 \\ 1 & 2 & 8 & 0 & 0 & 1 \end{bmatrix}$

SECTION 9.7 · EXERCISES

In Exercises 1–8, show that B is the inverse of A.

1. $A = \begin{bmatrix} 2 & 1 \\ 5 & 3 \end{bmatrix}$, $B = \begin{bmatrix} 3 & -1 \\ -5 & 2 \end{bmatrix}$

2. $A = \begin{bmatrix} 1 & -1 \\ -1 & 2 \end{bmatrix}$, $B = \begin{bmatrix} 2 & 1 \\ 1 & 1 \end{bmatrix}$

3. $A = \begin{bmatrix} 1 & 2 \\ 3 & 4 \end{bmatrix}$, $B = \begin{bmatrix} -2 & 1 \\ \frac{3}{2} & -\frac{1}{2} \end{bmatrix}$

4. $A = \begin{bmatrix} 1 & -1 \\ 2 & 3 \end{bmatrix}$, $B = \begin{bmatrix} \frac{3}{5} & \frac{1}{5} \\ -\frac{2}{5} & \frac{1}{5} \end{bmatrix}$

5. $A = \begin{bmatrix} -2 & 2 & 3 \\ 1 & -1 & 0 \\ 0 & 1 & 4 \end{bmatrix}$, $B = \dfrac{1}{3}\begin{bmatrix} -4 & -5 & 3 \\ -4 & -8 & 3 \\ 1 & 2 & 0 \end{bmatrix}$

6. $A = \begin{bmatrix} 2 & -17 & 11 \\ -1 & 11 & -7 \\ 0 & 3 & -2 \end{bmatrix}$, $B = \begin{bmatrix} 1 & 1 & 2 \\ 2 & 4 & -3 \\ 3 & 6 & -5 \end{bmatrix}$

7. $A = \begin{bmatrix} 2 & 0 & 1 & 1 \\ 3 & 0 & 0 & 1 \\ -1 & 1 & -2 & 1 \\ 4 & -1 & 1 & 0 \end{bmatrix}$,

   $B = \begin{bmatrix} -1 & 2 & -1 & -1 \\ -4 & 9 & -5 & -6 \\ 0 & 1 & -1 & -1 \\ 3 & -5 & 3 & 3 \end{bmatrix}$

8. $A = \begin{bmatrix} -1 & 1 & 0 & -1 \\ 1 & -1 & 2 & 0 \\ -1 & 1 & 2 & 0 \\ 0 & -1 & 1 & 1 \end{bmatrix}$,

   $B = \dfrac{1}{3}\begin{bmatrix} -3 & 1 & 1 & -3 \\ -3 & -1 & 2 & -3 \\ 0 & 1 & 1 & 0 \\ -3 & -2 & 1 & 0 \end{bmatrix}$

In Exercises 9–20, find the inverse of the matrix (if it exists).

9. $\begin{bmatrix} 2 & 0 \\ 0 & 3 \end{bmatrix}$ 10. $\begin{bmatrix} 1 & 2 \\ 3 & 7 \end{bmatrix}$

11. $\begin{bmatrix} 1 & -2 \\ 2 & -3 \end{bmatrix}$ 12. $\begin{bmatrix} -7 & 33 \\ 4 & -19 \end{bmatrix}$

13. $\begin{bmatrix} -1 & 1 \\ -2 & 1 \end{bmatrix}$ 14. $\begin{bmatrix} 11 & 1 \\ -1 & 0 \end{bmatrix}$

15. $\begin{bmatrix} 2 & 4 \\ 4 & 8 \end{bmatrix}$ 16. $\begin{bmatrix} 2 & 3 \\ 1 & 4 \end{bmatrix}$

17. $\begin{bmatrix} 2 & 7 & 1 \\ -3 & -9 & 2 \end{bmatrix}$

18. $\begin{bmatrix} -2 & 5 \\ 6 & -15 \\ 0 & 1 \end{bmatrix}$

19. $\begin{bmatrix} 1 & 1 & 1 \\ 3 & 5 & 4 \\ 3 & 6 & 5 \end{bmatrix}$

20. $\begin{bmatrix} 1 & 2 & 2 \\ 3 & 7 & 9 \\ -1 & -4 & -7 \end{bmatrix}$

In Exercises 21–34, use a graphing utility to find the inverse of the matrix (if it exists).

21. $\begin{bmatrix} 1 & 2 & -1 \\ 3 & 7 & -10 \\ -5 & -7 & -15 \end{bmatrix}$

22. $\begin{bmatrix} 10 & 5 & -7 \\ -5 & 1 & 4 \\ 3 & 2 & -2 \end{bmatrix}$

23. $\begin{bmatrix} 1 & 1 & 2 \\ 3 & 1 & 0 \\ -2 & 0 & 3 \end{bmatrix}$

24. $\begin{bmatrix} 3 & 2 & 2 \\ 2 & 2 & 2 \\ -4 & 4 & 3 \end{bmatrix}$

25. $\begin{bmatrix} 0.1 & 0.2 & 0.3 \\ -0.3 & 0.2 & 0.2 \\ 0.5 & 0.4 & 0.4 \end{bmatrix}$

26. $\begin{bmatrix} 2 & 0 & 0 \\ 0 & 3 & 0 \\ 0 & 0 & 5 \end{bmatrix}$

27. $\begin{bmatrix} 1 & 0 & 0 \\ 3 & 4 & 0 \\ 2 & 5 & 5 \end{bmatrix}$

28. $\begin{bmatrix} 1 & 0 & 0 \\ 3 & 0 & 0 \\ 2 & 5 & 5 \end{bmatrix}$

29. $\begin{bmatrix} 1 & 0 & 3 & 0 \\ 0 & 2 & 0 & 4 \\ 1 & 0 & 3 & 0 \\ 0 & 2 & 0 & 4 \end{bmatrix}$

30. $\begin{bmatrix} -1 & 0 & 1 & 0 \\ 0 & 2 & 0 & -1 \\ 2 & 0 & -1 & 0 \\ 0 & -1 & 0 & 1 \end{bmatrix}$

31. $\begin{bmatrix} -8 & 0 & 0 & 0 \\ 0 & 1 & 0 & 0 \\ 0 & 0 & 4 & 0 \\ 0 & 0 & 0 & -5 \end{bmatrix}$

32. $\begin{bmatrix} 1 & 3 & -2 & 0 \\ 0 & 2 & 4 & 6 \\ 0 & 0 & -2 & 1 \\ 0 & 0 & 0 & 5 \end{bmatrix}$

33. $\begin{bmatrix} 1 & -2 & -1 & -2 \\ 3 & -5 & -2 & -3 \\ 2 & -5 & -2 & -5 \\ -1 & 4 & 4 & 11 \end{bmatrix}$

34. $\begin{bmatrix} 4 & 8 & -7 & 14 \\ 2 & 5 & -4 & 6 \\ 0 & 2 & 1 & -7 \\ 3 & 6 & -5 & 10 \end{bmatrix}$

In Exercises 35–46, use a graphing utility to solve (if possible) the system of linear equations.

35. $3x + 4y = -2$
$5x + 3y = 4$

36. $18x + 12y = 13$
$30x + 24y = 23$

37. $-0.4x + 0.8y = 1.6$
$2x - 4y = 5$

38. $13x - 6y = 17$
$26x - 12y = 8$

39. $3x + 6y = 5$
$6x + 14y = 11$

40. $3x + 2y = 1$
$2x + 10y = 6$

41. $4x - y + z = -5$
$2x + 2y + 3z = 10$
$5x - 2y + 6z = 1$

42. $4x - 2y + 3z = -2$
$2x + 2y + 5z = 16$
$8x - 5y - 2z = 4$

43. $5x - 3y + 2z = 2$
$2x + 2y - 3z = 3$
$x - 7y + 8z = -4$

44. $2x + 3y + 5z = 4$
$3x + 5y + 9z = 7$
$5x + 9y + 17z = 13$

45. $7x - 3y + 2w = 41$
$-2x + y - w = -13$
$4x + z - 2w = 12$
$-x + y - w = -8$

46. $2x + 5y + w = 11$
$x + 4y + 2z - 2w = -7$
$2x - 2y + 5z + w = 3$
$x - 3w = 1$

Circuit Analysis   In Exercises 51 and 52, consider the circuit in the figure. The currents I_1, I_2, and I_3 in amperes are given by the solution to the system of linear equations

$2I_1 + 4I_3 = E_1$
$I_2 + 4I_3 = E_2$
$I_1 + I_2 - I_3 = 0,$

where E_1 and E_2 are voltages. Find the unknown currents for the given voltages.

51. $E_1 = 14V$, $E_2 = 28V$ **52.** $E_1 = 10V$, $E_2 = 10V$

FIGURE FOR 51 AND 52

Bond Investments   In Exercises 47–50, consider a person who invests in AAA-rated bonds, A-rated bonds, and B-rated bonds. The average yield is 6.5% on AAA bonds, 7% on A bonds, and 9% on B bonds. Suppose the person invests twice as much in B bonds as in A bonds. A system of linear equations (where x, y, and z represent the amounts invested in AAA, A, and B bonds, respectively) is as follows.

$x + y + z = $ (total investment)
$0.065x + 0.07y + 0.09z = $ (annual return)
$2y - z = 0$

Find the amount invested in each type of bond, with the given total investment and annual return.

47. Total investment = $25,000
Annual return = $1900

48. Total investment = $45,000
Annual return = $3750

49. Total investment = $12,000
Annual return = $835

50. Total investment = $500,000
Annual return = $38,000

9.8   SYSTEMS OF INEQUALITIES

The Graph of an Inequality   /   Systems of Inequalities   /   Applications

The Graph of an Inequality

An ordered pair (a, b) is a **solution of an inequality** in x and y if the inequality is true when a and b are substituted for x and y, respectively. The **graph** of an inequality is the collection of all solutions of the inequality. To sketch the graph of an inequality such as $3x - 2y < 6$, begin by sketching the graph of the *corresponding equation* $3x - 2y = 6$. This graph is made with a dashed line for the strict inequalities $<$ and $>$ and a solid line for the inequalities $\leq$ and $\geq$. The graph of the equation will normally separate the plane into two or more regions. In each such region, one of the following must be true.

1. *All* points in the region are solutions of the inequality.
2. *No* points in the region are solutions of the inequality.

Thus, you can determine whether the points in an entire region satisfy the inequality by simply testing *one* point in the region.

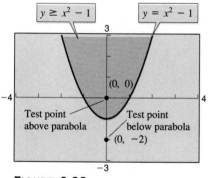

FIGURE 9.26

EXAMPLE 1   Graphing an Inequality

Sketch the graph of the inequality $y \geq x^2 - 1$.

SOLUTION

The graph of the corresponding *equation* $y = x^2 - 1$ is a parabola, as shown in Figure 9.26. By testing a point *above* the parabola $(0, 0)$ and a point *below* the parabola $(0, -2)$, you can see that the points that satisfy the inequality are those lying above (or on) the parabola.

The inequality given in Example 1 is a nonlinear inequality in two variables. This section, however, primarily discusses **linear inequalities** of the following forms.

$$ax + by < c \qquad ax + by \leq c$$
$$ax + by > c \qquad ax + by \geq c$$

The graph of each of these linear inequalities is a half-plane lying on one side of the line $ax + by = c$. The simplest linear inequalities are those corresponding to horizontal or vertical lines.

EXAMPLE 2   Graphing a Linear Inequality

Sketch the graphs of the following inequalities.

A. $x > -2$ **B.** $y \leq 3$

SOLUTION

A. The graph of the corresponding equation $x = -2$ is a vertical line. The points that satisfy the inequality $x > -2$ are those lying to the right of this line, as shown in Figure 9.27.

B. The graph of the corresponding equation $y = 3$ is a horizontal line. The points that satisfy the inequality $y \leq 3$ are those lying below (or on) this line, as shown in Figure 9.28.

FIGURE 9.27 $x > -2$ **FIGURE 9.28** $y \leq 3$

EXAMPLE 3   Graphing a Linear Inequality

Sketch the graph of $x - y < 2$.

SOLUTION

The graph of the corresponding equation $x - y = 2$ is a line, as shown in Figure 9.29. Because the origin $(0, 0)$ satisfies the inequality, the graph consists of the half-plane lying above the line. (Try checking a point below the line. Regardless of which point you choose, you will see that it does not satisfy the inequality.) For a linear inequality in two variables, you can sometimes simplify the graphing procedure by writing the inequality in *slope-intercept* form. For instance, by writing $x - y < 2$ in the form

$$y > x - 2,$$

you can see that the solution points lie *above* the line $x - y = 2$.

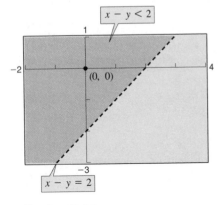

FIGURE 9.29

Systems of Inequalities

Many practical problems in business, science, and engineering involve systems of linear inequalities. Here are two examples of such systems.

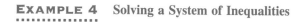

$$\begin{array}{ll} 2x - y \le 5 & x + y \le 12 \\ x + 2y > 2 & 3x - 4y \le 15 \\ & x \ge 0 \\ & y \ge 0 \end{array}$$

A **solution** of a system of inequalities in x and y is an ordered pair (x, y) that satisfies each inequality in the system. For instance, $(2, 4)$ is a solution of the system on the right because $x = 2$ and $y = 4$ satisfy each of the four inequalities in the system.

To graph a system of inequalities in two variables, first sketch the graph of each individual inequality (on the same coordinate system) and then find the region that is *common* to every graph in the system. For systems of linear inequalities, it is helpful to find the *vertices* of the solution region, as shown in the following example.

EXAMPLE 4   Solving a System of Inequalities

Sketch the graph (and label the vertices) of the solution set of the following system.

$$\begin{array}{l} x - y < 2 \\ x > -2 \\ y \le 3 \end{array}$$

SOLUTION

The graph of each inequality was sketched in Examples 2 and 3. The triangular region common to all three graphs can be found by superimposing the graphs on the same coordinate plane, as shown in Figure 9.30. To find the vertices of the region, solve the three systems of corresponding equations obtained by taking *pairs* of equations representing the boundaries of the individual regions.

Vertex A: $(-2, -4)$
Obtained by solving the system
$$\begin{array}{l} x - y = 2 \\ x = -2 \end{array}$$

Vertex B: $(5, 3)$
Obtained by solving the system
$$\begin{array}{l} x - y = 2 \\ y = 3 \end{array}$$

Vertex C: $(-2, 3)$
Obtained by solving the system
$$\begin{array}{l} x = -2 \\ y = 3 \end{array}$$

For the triangular region shown in Figure 9.30, each point of intersection of a pair of boundary lines corresponds to a vertex. With more complicated regions, two border lines can sometimes intersect at a point that is not a vertex, as shown in Figure 9.31. In order to keep track of which points of intersection are actually vertices of the region, make a careful sketch of the region and refer to your sketch as you find each point of intersection.

FIGURE 9.30

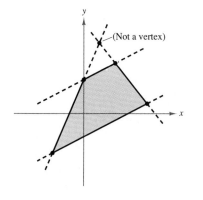

Boundary lines can intersect at a point that is not a vertex.

FIGURE 9.31

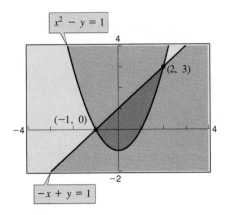

FIGURE 9.32

EXAMPLE 5   **Solving a System of Inequalities**
·············

Sketch the region represented by the system.

$$x^2 - y \leq 1$$
$$-x + y \leq 1$$

SOLUTION

As shown in Figure 9.32, the points that satisfy the inequality $x^2 - y \leq 1$ are the points lying above (or on) the parabola given by $x^2 - y = 1$. The points satisfying the inequality $-x + y \leq 1$ are the points lying on or below the line given by $-x + y = 1$. To find the points of intersection of the parabola and the line, solve the following system of corresponding equations.

$$x^2 - y = 1$$
$$-x + y = 1$$

Using the method of substitution, you can find the solutions to be $(-1, 0)$ and $(2, 3)$, as shown in Figure 9.32.   ·········

When solving a system of inequalities, you should be aware that the system might have no solution. For instance, the system

$$x + y > 3$$
$$x + y < -1$$

has no solution points, because the quantity $(x + y)$ cannot be both less than -1 and greater than 3, as shown in Figure 9.33.

Another possibility is that the solution set of a system of inequalities can be unbounded. For instance, the solution set of

$$x + y < 3$$
$$x + 2y > 3$$

forms an *infinite wedge,* as shown in Figure 9.34.

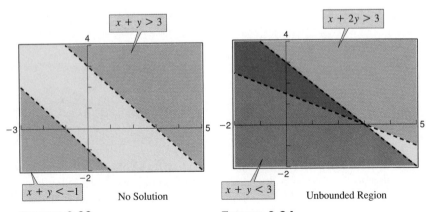

No Solution

Unbounded Region

FIGURE 9.33   **FIGURE 9.34**

Applications

EXAMPLE 6   An Application of a System of Inequalities
....

The liquid portion of a diet is to provide at least 300 calories, 36 units of vitamin A, and 90 units of vitamin C daily. A cup of dietary drink X provides 60 calories, 12 units of vitamin A, and 10 units of vitamin C. A cup of dietary drink Y provides 60 calories, 6 units of vitamin A, and 30 units of vitamin C. Set up a system of linear inequalities that describes the minimum daily requirements for calories and vitamins. Does a liquid diet of 2 units of X and 6 units of Y meet these requirements?

SOLUTION

Let x represent the number of cups of dietary drink X and let y represent the number of cups of dietary drink Y. Then, to meet the minimum daily requirements, the following inequalities must be satisfied.

$$\begin{aligned}
\text{\textit{For calories:}} \quad & 60x + 60y \geq 300 \\
\text{\textit{For vitamin A:}} \quad & 12x + 6y \geq 36 \\
\text{\textit{For vitamin C:}} \quad & 10x + 30y \geq 90 \\
& x \geq 0 \\
& y \geq 0
\end{aligned}$$

The last two inequalities are included because x and y cannot be negative. The graph of this system of inequalities is shown in Figure 9.35. Because the point (2, 6) lies inside the solution set of this system, the liquid diet meets the requirements.

FIGURE 9.35

Example 8 in Section 9.3 discussed the *point of equilibrium* for a demand and supply function. The next example discusses two related concepts that economists call **consumer surplus** and **producer surplus.** As shown in Figure 9.36, the consumer surplus is defined to be the area of the region that lies *below* the demand curve, *above* the horizontal line passing through the equilibrium point, and to the right of the *y*-axis. Similarly, the producer surplus is defined to be the area of the region that lies *above* the supply curve, *below* the horizontal line passing through the equilibrium point, and to the right of the *y*-axis. In general terms, consumer surplus is a measure of the amount of money that consumers would have been willing to pay *above what they actually paid.* Similarly, producer surplus is a measure of the amount of money that producers would have been willing to receive *below what they actually received.*

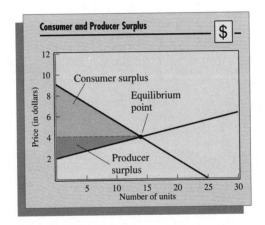

FIGURE 9.36

EXAMPLE 7 **Consumer and Producer Surplus**

Suppose that the demand and supply functions for a certain type of calculator are given by

$$p = 150 - 10x \qquad \text{\textit{Demand equation}}$$
$$p = 60 + 20x, \qquad \text{\textit{Supply equation}}$$

where *p* is the price in dollars and *x* represents the number of units (in millions). Find the consumer surplus and producer surplus for these two equations.

SOLUTION

To begin, find the point of equilibrium by solving the equation

$$60 + 20x = 150 - 10x.$$

In Example 8 of Section 9.3, the solution was found to be $x = 3$, which corresponded to an equilibrium price of $p = \$120$. Thus, the consumer surplus and producer surplus are the areas of the triangular regions given by the following sets of inequalities.

Consumer Surplus	*Producer Surplus*
$p \leq 150 - 10x$	$p \geq 60 + 20x$
$p \geq 120$	$p \leq 120$
$x \geq 0$	$x \geq 0$

Using Figure 9.37 and the formula for the area of a triangle, you can find that the consumer surplus is

$$\text{Consumer surplus} = \frac{1}{2}(\text{base})(\text{height}) = \frac{1}{2}(30)(3) = \$45 \text{ million}$$

and the producer surplus is

$$\text{Producer surplus} = \frac{1}{2}(\text{base})(\text{height}) = \frac{1}{2}(60)(3) = \$90 \text{ million}.$$

FIGURE 9.37

DISCUSSION PROBLEM

YOU BE THE INSTRUCTOR

Suppose you are tutoring a student in algebra and want to construct some practice problems for your student. Write a paragraph describing how you could write a system of linear inequalities that had a given region as its solution. Then apply your procedure to find two systems of linear inequalities that have the following regions as solutions.

(a) Region with $(0, 0)$, $(0, 2)$, $(3, 0)$, and $(2, 1)$ as vertices.
(b) Region with $(0, 0)$, $(0, 3)$, $(4, 0)$, and $(3, 2)$ as vertices.

   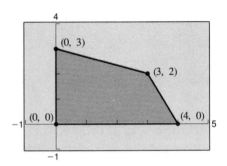

WARM-UP

The following warm-up exercises involve skills that were covered in earlier sections. You will use these skills in the exercise set for this section.

In Exercises 1–6, identify the graph of the equation.

1. $x + y = 3$ **2.** $4x - y = 8$

3. $y = x^2 - 4$ **4.** $y = -x^2 + 1$

5. $x^2 + y^2 = 9$ **6.** $\dfrac{x^2}{4} + \dfrac{y^2}{9} = 1$

In Exercises 7–10, solve the system of equations.

7. $\begin{aligned} x + 2y &= 3 \\ 4x - 7y &= -3 \end{aligned}$ **8.** $\begin{aligned} 2x - 3y &= 4 \\ x + 5y &= 2 \end{aligned}$

9. $\begin{aligned} x^2 + y &= 5 \\ 2x - 4y &= 0 \end{aligned}$ **10.** $\begin{aligned} x^2 + y^2 &= 13 \\ x + y &= 5 \end{aligned}$

SECTION 9.8 · EXERCISES

In Exercises 1–8, match the inequality with its graph. [The graphs are labeled (a), (b), (c), (d), (e), (f), (g), and (h).]

1. $x > 3$

2. $y \leq 2$

3. $2x + 3y \leq 6$

4. $2x - y \geq -2$

5. $x^2 + y^2 < 4$

6. $(x - 2)^2 + (y - 3)^2 > 4$

7. $xy > 2$

8. $y \leq 4 - x^2$

(a)

(b)

(c)

(d)

(e)

(f)

(g)

(h)

In Exercises 9-20, sketch the graph of the inequality.

9. $x \geq 2$

10. $x \leq 4$

11. $y \geq -1$

12. $y \leq 3$

13. $y < 2 - x$

14. $y > 2x - 4$

15. $2y - x \geq 4$

16. $5x + 3y \geq -15$

17. $(x + 1)^2 + (y - 2)^2 < 9$

18. $y^2 - x < 0$

19. $y \leq \dfrac{1}{1 + x^2}$

20. $y < \ln x$

In Exercises 21–40, sketch the graph of the solution of the system of inequalities and use a graphing utility to verify your result. (*Note:* If your graphing utility has *shading* capabilities, shade the region representing the solution.)

21. $x + y \leq 1$
  $-x + y \leq 1$
  $y \geq 0$

22. $3x + 2y < 6$
  $x \qquad > 0$
  $y > 0$

23. $x + y \leq 5$
  $x \qquad \geq 2$
  $y \geq 0$

24. $2x + y \geq 2$
  $x \qquad \leq 2$
  $y \leq 1$

25. $-3x + 2y < \ 6$
  $x + 4y > -2$
  $2x + \ y < \ 3$

26. $x - 7y > -36$
  $5x + 2y > \quad 5$
  $6x - 5y > \quad 6$

27. $2x + \ y > 2$
  $6x + 3y < 2$

28. $x - 2y < -6$
  $5x - 3y > -9$

29. $x \qquad \geq 1$
  $x - 2y \leq 3$
  $3x + 2y \geq 9$
  $x + \ y \leq 6$

30. $x - y^2 > 0$
  $x - y < 2$

31. $x^2 + y^2 \leq 9$
  $x^2 + y^2 \geq 1$

32. $x^2 + y^2 \leq 25$
  $4x - 3y \leq 0$

33. $x > y^2$
  $x < y + 2$

34. $x < 2y - y^2$
  $0 < \ x + y$

35. $y \leq \sqrt{3x} + 1$
  $y \geq x + 1$

36. $y < -x^2 + 2x + 3$
  $y > \ x^2 - 4x + 3$

37. $y < x^3 - 2x + 1$
  $y > -2x$
  $x \leq 1$

38. $y \geq x^4 - 2x^2 + 1$
  $y \leq 1 - x^2$

39. $x^2 y \geq 1$
  $0 < x \leq 4$
  $y \leq 4$

40. $y \leq e^{-x^2/2}$
  $y \geq 0$
  $-2 \leq x \leq 2$

In Exercises 41–46, derive a set of inequalities to describe the region.

41. Rectangular region with vertices at $(2, 1)$, $(5, 1)$, $(5, 7)$, and $(2, 7)$

42. Parallelogram region with vertices at $(0, 0)$, $(4, 0)$, $(1, 4)$, and $(5, 4)$

43. Triangular region with vertices at $(0, 0)$, $(5, 0)$, and $(2, 3)$

44. Triangular region with vertices at $(-1, 0)$, $(1, 0)$, and $(0, 1)$

45. Sector of a circle   **46.** Sector of a circle

FIGURE FOR 45

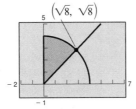

FIGURE FOR 46

47. *Furniture Production*   A furniture company can sell all the tables and chairs it produces. Each table requires 1 hour in the assembly center and $1\frac{1}{3}$ hours in the finishing center. Each chair requires $1\frac{1}{2}$ hours in the assembly center and $1\frac{1}{2}$ hours in the finishing center. The company's assembly center is available 12 hours per day, and its finishing center is available 15 hours per day. If x is the number of tables produced per day and y is the number of chairs produced per day, find a system of inequalities describing all possible production levels. Graph the system.

48. *Computer Inventory*   A store sells two models of a certain brand of computer. Because of the demand, it is necessary to stock twice as many units of model A as units of model B. The costs to the store for the two models are $800 and $1200, respectively. The management does not want more than $20,000 in computer inventory at any one time, and it wants at least four model A computers and two model B computers in inventory at all times. Devise a system of inequalities describing all possible inventory levels, and graph the system.

49. *Investment*   A person plans to invest $20,000 in two different interest-bearing accounts. Each account is to contain at least $5000. Moreover, one account should have at least twice the amount that is in the other account. Find a system of inequalities to describe the various amounts that can be deposited in each account, and graph the system.

50. *Concert Ticket Sales*   Two types of tickets are to be sold for a concert. One type costs $15 per ticket and the other type costs $25 per ticket. The promoter of the concert must sell at least 15,000 tickets, including 8000 of the $15 tickets and 4000 of the $25 tickets. Moreover, the gross receipts must total at least $275,000 in order for the concert to be held. Find a system of inequalities describing the different numbers of tickets that can be sold and graph the system.

51. *Diet Supplement*   A dietitian is asked to design a special diet supplement using two different foods. Each ounce of food X contains 20 units of calcium, 15 units of iron, and 10 units of vitamin B. Each ounce of food Y contains 10 units of calcium, 10 units of iron, and 20 units of vitamin B. The minimum daily requirements in the diet are 280 units of calcium, 160 units of iron, and 180 units of vitamin B. Find a system of inequalities describing the different amounts of food X and food Y that can be used in the diet, and graph the system.

52. *Diet Supplement*   A dietitian is asked to design a special diet supplement using two different foods. Each ounce of food X contains 20 units of calcium, 15 units of iron, and 10 units of vitamin B. Each ounce of food Y contains 10 units of calcium, 10 units of iron, and 20 units of vitamin B. The minimum daily requirements in the diet are 300 units of calcium, 150 units of iron, and 200 units of vitamin B. Find a system of inequalities describing the different amounts of food X and food Y that can be used in the diet, and graph the system.

Consumer and Producer Surplus   In Exercises 53–58, find the consumer surplus and producer surplus for the given pair of supply and demand equations.

Demand	Supply
53. $p = 50 - 0.5x$	$p = 0.125x$
54. $p = 60 - x$	$p = 10 + \frac{7}{3}x$
55. $p = 300 - x$	$p = 100 + x$
56. $p = 100 - 0.05x$	$p = 25 + 0.1x$
57. $p = 140 - 0.00002x$	$p = 80 + 0.00001x$
58. $p = 400 - 0.0002x$	$p = 225 + 0.0005x$

59. *Physical Fitness Facility*   An indoor running track is to be constructed with a space for body-building equipment inside the track (see figure). The inside of the track must be at least 125 meters long, and the body-building space must have an area of at least 500 square meters. Find a system of inequalities describing the various sizes of the track, and graph the system.

FIGURE FOR 59

CHAPTER 9 · REVIEW EXERCISES

In Exercises 1–6, solve the system by the method of substitution. Use a graphing utility to confirm your result.

1. $x + y = 2$
$x - y = 0$

2. $2x = 3(y - 1)$
$y = x$

3. $x^2 - y^2 = 9$
$x - y = 1$

4. $x^2 + y^2 = 169$
$3x + 2y = 39$

5. $y = 2x^2$
$y = x^4 - 2x^2$

6. $x = y + 3$
$x = y^2 + 1$

In Exercises 7–12, solve the system by elimination. Use a graphing utility to confirm your result.

7. $2x - y = 2$
$6x + 8y = 39$

8. $40x + 30y = 24$
$20x - 50y = -14$

9. $3x - 2y = 0$
$3x + 2(y + 5) = 10$

10. $7x + 12y = 63$
$2x + 3y = 15$

11. $1.25x - 2y = 3.5$
$5x - 8y = 14$

12. $1.5x + 2.5y = 8.5$
$6x + 10y = 24$

In Exercises 13–16, use a graphing utility to solve the system of equations.

13. $y^2 - 2y + x = 0$
$x + y = 0$

14. $y = 2x^2 - 4x + 1$
$y = x^2 - 4x + 3$

15. $y = 2(6 - x)$
$y = 2^{x-2}$

16. $y = \ln(x - 1) - 3$
$y = 4 - \frac{1}{2}x$

17. *Break-Even Point*   Suppose you are setting up a small business and have made an initial investment of $10,000. The unit cost of the product is $2.85 and the selling price is $4.95. How many units must you sell to break even? (Round your answer to the nearest whole unit.)

18. *Choice of Two Jobs*   You are offered two different jobs selling personal computers. One company offers an annual salary of $22,500 plus a year-end bonus of 1.5% of your total sales. The other company offers a salary of $20,000 plus a year-end bonus of 2% of your total sales. How much would you have to sell in order to make the second offer better?

19. *Acid Mixture*   One hundred gallons of a 60% acid solution are obtained by mixing a 75% solution with a 50% solution. How many gallons of each must be used to obtain the desired mixture?

20. *Cassette Tape Sales*   Suppose you are the manager of a music store. At the end of the week you are going over receipts for the previous week's sales. Six hundred and fifty cassette tapes were sold. One type of cassette sold for $9.95 and other sold for $14.95. The total cassette receipts were $7717.50. The cash register that was supposed to record the number of each type of cassette sold malfunctioned. Can you recover the information? If so, how many of each type of cassette were sold?

21. *Flying Speeds*   Two planes leave Pittsburgh and Philadelphia at the same time, each going to the other city. Because of the wind, one plane flies 25 miles per hour faster than the other. Find the ground speed of each plane if the cities are 275 miles apart and the planes pass one another (at different altitudes) after 40 minutes of flying time.

22. *Dimensions of a Rectangle*   The perimeter of a rectangle is 480 meters and its length is 150% of its width. Find the dimensions of the rectangle.

Supply and Demand   In Exercises 23 and 24, find the point of equilibrium for the pair of supply and demand equations.

Demand	Supply
23. $p = 37 - 0.0002x$	$p = 22 + 0.00001x$
24. $p = 120 - 0.0001x$	$p = 45 + 0.0002x$

In Exercises 25–30, solve the system of equations. (*Note:* For some exercises it may be advantageous to use the matrix capabilities of your graphing utility.)

25. $\begin{aligned} x + 2y + 6z &= 4 \\ -3x + 2y - z &= -4 \\ 4x + 2z &= 16 \end{aligned}$

26. $\begin{aligned} x + 3y - z &= 13 \\ 2x - 5z &= 23 \\ 4x - y - 2z &= 14 \end{aligned}$

27. $\begin{aligned} x - 2y + z &= -6 \\ 2x - 3y &= -7 \\ -x + 3y - 3z &= 11 \end{aligned}$

28. $\begin{aligned} 2x + 6z &= -9 \\ 3x - 2y + 11z &= -16 \\ 3x - y + 7z &= -11 \end{aligned}$

29. $\begin{aligned} 2x + 5y - 19z &= 34 \\ 3x + 8y - 31z &= 54 \end{aligned}$

30. $\begin{aligned} 2x + y + z + 2w &= -1 \\ 5x - 2y + z - 3w &= 0 \\ -x + 3y + 2z + 2w &= 1 \\ 3x + 2y + 3z - 5w &= 12 \end{aligned}$

In Exercises 31–34, use matrices and elementary row operations to solve the system of equations.

31. $\begin{aligned} -x + y + 2z &= 1 \\ 2x + 3y + z &= -2 \\ 5x + 4y + 2z &= 4 \end{aligned}$

32. $\begin{aligned} 2x + 3y + z &= 10 \\ 2x - 3y - 3z &= 22 \\ 4x - 2y + 3z &= -2 \end{aligned}$

33. $\begin{aligned} 2x + y + 2z &= 4 \\ 2x + 2y &= 5 \\ 2x - y + 6z &= 2 \end{aligned}$

34. $\begin{aligned} x + 2y + 6z &= 1 \\ 2x + 5y + 15z &= 4 \\ 3x + y + 3z &= -6 \end{aligned}$

In Exercises 35 and 36, find the equation of the parabola $y = ax^2 + bx + c$ that passes through the given points. Use a graphing utility to verify your result.

35. $(0, -6), (1, -3), (2, 4)$

FIGURE FOR 35

36. $(-5, 0), (1, -6), (2, 14)$

FIGURE FOR 36

In Exercises 37 and 38, find the equation of the circle

$$x^2 + y^2 + Dx + Ey + F = 0$$

that passes through the given points. Use a graphing utility to verify your result.

37. $(2, 2), (5, -1), (-1, -1)$

FIGURE FOR 37

38. $(4, 2), (1, 3), (-2, -6)$

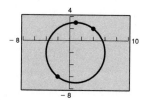

FIGURE FOR 38

39. *Crop Spraying* A mixture of 6 gallons of chemical A, 8 gallons of chemical B, and 13 gallons of chemical C is required to kill a certain destructive crop insect. Commercial spray X contains 1, 2, and 2 parts, respectively, of these chemicals. Commercial spray Y contains only chemical C. Commercial spray Z contains chemicals A, B, and C in equal amounts. How much of each type of commercial spray is needed to get the desired mixture?

40. *Investments* An inheritance of $20,000 was divided among three investments yielding $1780 in interest per year. The interest rates for the three investments were 7%, 9%, and 11%. Find the amount placed in each investment if the second and third were $3000 and $1000 less than the first, respectively.

41. *Fitting a Line to Data* Find the least squares regression line $y = ax + b$ for the points

$(x_1, y_1), (x_2, y_2), \ldots, (x_n, y_n)$.

To find the line, solve the following system of linear equations for a and b.

$5b + 10a = 17.8$

$10b + 30a = 45.7$

FIGURE FOR 41

42. *Fitting a Parabola to Data* Find the least squares regression parabola $y = ax^2 + bx + c$ for the points

$(x_1, y_1), (x_2, y_2), \ldots, (x_n, y_n)$.

To find the parabola, solve the following system of linear equations for a, b, and c.

$5c \quad + 10a = \quad 9.1$

$\quad 10b \quad = \quad 8.0$

$10c \quad + 34a = 19.8$

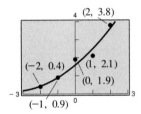

FIGURE FOR 42

In Exercises 43–50, perform the indicated matrix operations (if possible).

43. $\begin{bmatrix} 2 & 1 & 0 \\ 0 & 5 & -4 \end{bmatrix} - 3\begin{bmatrix} 5 & 3 & -6 \\ 0 & -2 & 5 \end{bmatrix}$

44. $-2\begin{bmatrix} 1 & 2 \\ 5 & -4 \\ 6 & 0 \end{bmatrix} + 8\begin{bmatrix} 7 & 1 \\ 1 & 2 \\ 1 & 4 \end{bmatrix}$

45. $\begin{bmatrix} 1 & 2 \\ 5 & -4 \\ 6 & 0 \end{bmatrix}\begin{bmatrix} 6 & -2 & 8 \\ 4 & 0 & 0 \end{bmatrix}$

46. $\begin{bmatrix} 1 & 5 & 6 \\ 2 & -4 & 0 \end{bmatrix}\begin{bmatrix} 6 & -2 & 8 \\ 4 & 0 & 0 \end{bmatrix}$

47. $\begin{bmatrix} 1 & 5 & 6 \\ 2 & -4 & 0 \end{bmatrix}\begin{bmatrix} 6 & 4 \\ -2 & 0 \\ 8 & 0 \end{bmatrix}$

48. $\begin{bmatrix} 4 \\ 6 \end{bmatrix}\begin{bmatrix} 6 & -2 \end{bmatrix}$

49. $\begin{bmatrix} 1 & 3 & 2 \\ 0 & 2 & -4 \\ 0 & 0 & 3 \end{bmatrix}\begin{bmatrix} 4 & -3 & 2 \\ 0 & 3 & -1 \\ 0 & 0 & 2 \end{bmatrix}$

50. $\begin{bmatrix} 2 & 1 \\ 6 & 0 \end{bmatrix}\left(\begin{bmatrix} 4 & 2 \\ -3 & 1 \end{bmatrix} + \begin{bmatrix} -2 & 4 \\ 0 & 4 \end{bmatrix}\right)$

In Exercises 51–54, find the inverse of the matrix (if it exists).

51. $\begin{bmatrix} 2 & 6 \\ 3 & -6 \end{bmatrix}$

52. $\begin{bmatrix} 3 & -10 \\ 4 & 2 \end{bmatrix}$

53. $\begin{bmatrix} 2 & 0 & 3 \\ -1 & 1 & 1 \\ 2 & -2 & 1 \end{bmatrix}$

54. $\begin{bmatrix} 1 & 4 & 6 \\ 2 & -3 & 1 \\ -1 & 18 & 16 \end{bmatrix}$

In Exercises 55–62, solve (if possible) the system of linear equations using the inverse of the coefficient matrix.

55. $x + 2y = -1$
$3x + 4y = -5$

56. $x + 3y = \quad 23$
$-6x + 2y = -18$

57. $-3x - 3y - 4z = \quad 2$
$\quad y + \quad z = -1$
$4x + 3y + 4z = -1$

58. $x - 3y - 2z = \quad 8$
$-2x + 7y + 3z = -19$
$x - \quad y - 3z = \quad 3$

59. $x + 3y + 2z = \quad 2$
$-2x - 5y - \quad z = \quad 10$
$2x + 4y \quad = -12$

60. $2x + 4y \quad = -12$
$3x + 4y - 2z = -14$
$-x + \quad y + 2z = \quad -6$

61. $2x + 3y - \quad 4z = \quad 1$
$x - \quad y + 2z = -4$
$3x + 7y - 10z = \quad 0$

62. $-x + \quad y + \quad z = \quad 6$
$4x - 3y + \quad z = 20$
$2x - \quad y + 3z = \quad 8$

63. *Mixture Problem*   A florist wants to arrange a dozen flowers consisting of two varieties—carnations and roses. Carnations cost $0.75 each and roses cost $1.50 each. How many of each should the florist use so the arrangement will cost $12.00?

64. *Break-Even Point*   A small business invests $25,000 in the equipment needed to produce a product. Each unit of the product costs $3.75 to produce and is sold for $5.25. How many items must be sold before the business breaks even?

In Exercises 65–72, sketch a graph of the solution set of the system of inequalities and use a graphing utility to verify your result. (*Note:* If your graphing utility has *shading* capabilities, then shade the region representing the solution.)

65. $\begin{aligned} x + 2y &\le 160 \\ 3x + y &\le 180 \\ x &\ge 0 \\ y &\ge 0 \end{aligned}$

66. $\begin{aligned} 2x + 3y &\le 24 \\ 2x + y &\le 16 \\ x &\ge 0 \\ y &\ge 0 \end{aligned}$

67. $\begin{aligned} 3x + 2y &\ge 24 \\ x + 2y &\ge 12 \\ 2 \le x &\le 15 \\ y &\le 15 \end{aligned}$

68. $\begin{aligned} 2x + y &\ge 16 \\ x + 3y &\ge 18 \\ 0 \le x &\le 25 \\ 0 \le y &\le 25 \end{aligned}$

69. $\begin{aligned} y &< x + 1 \\ y &> x^2 - 1 \end{aligned}$

70. $\begin{aligned} y &\le 6 - 2x - x^2 \\ y &\ge x + 6 \end{aligned}$

71. $\begin{aligned} 2x - 3y &\ge 0 \\ 2x - y &\le 8 \\ y &\ge 0 \end{aligned}$

72. $\begin{aligned} x^2 + y^2 &\le 9 \\ (x - 3)^2 + y^2 &\le 9 \end{aligned}$

In Exercises 73 and 74, derive a set of inequalities to describe the region.

73. Parallelogram with vertices at $(1, 5)$, $(3, 1)$, $(6, 10)$, $(8, 6)$

74. Triangle with vertices at $(1, 2)$, $(6, 7)$, $(8, 1)$

In Exercises 75 and 76, determine a system of inequalities that models the description and sketch a graph of the solution of the system.

75. *Fruit Distribution*   A Pennsylvania fruit grower has 1500 bushels of apples that are to be divided between markets in Harrisburg and Philadelphia. These two markets need at least 400 bushels and 600 bushels, respectively.

76. *Inventory Costs*   A warehouse operator has 24,000 square feet of floor space in which to store two products. Each unit of product I requires 20 square feet of floor space and costs $12 per day to store. Each unit of product II requires 30 square feet of floor space and costs $8 per day to store. The total storage cost per day cannot exceed $12,400.

In Exercises 77 and 78, find the consumer surplus and producer surplus for the pair of supply and demand equations.

Demand	Supply
77. $p = 160 - 0.0001x$	$p = 70 + 0.0002x$
78. $p = 130 - 0.0002x$	$p = 30 + 0.0003x$

CHAPTER 10

SEQUENCES, MATHEMATICAL INDUCTION, AND PROBABILITY

10.1 SEQUENCES AND SUMMATION NOTATION

Sequences / **Factorial Notation** / **Summation Notation** / **The Sum of an Infinite Sequence** / **Applications**

Sequences

A sequence is a *function* whose domain is the set of positive integers. Sequences are usually represented, however, by subscript notation, rather than the standard function notation. For instance, the terms of the sequence

$$f(1), f(2), f(3), f(4), \ldots, f(n), \ldots$$

are usually written as

$$a_1, a_2, a_3, a_4, \ldots, a_n, \ldots.$$

Note that subscripts make up the domain of the sequence, and they serve to identify the location of a term within the sequence. For instance, a_4 is the 4th term of the sequence and a_n is called the **nth term** of the sequence. The entire sequence is sometimes denoted by the short form $\{a_n\}$.

675

> **DEFINITION OF A SEQUENCE**
>
> An **infinite sequence** $\{a_n\}$ is a function whose domain is the set of positive integers. The function values
>
> $$a_1, a_2, a_3, a_4, \ldots, a_n, \ldots$$
>
> are called the **terms** of the sequence. If the domain of the function consists of the first n positive integers only, then the sequence is called a **finite sequence.**

On occasion it is convenient to begin subscripting a sequence with 0 instead of 1 so that the terms of the sequence become

$$a_0, a_1, a_2, a_3, a_4, \ldots, a_n, \ldots.$$

In such cases, a_n is still called the nth term of the sequence, even though it occupies the $(n + 1)$ position in the sequence.

EXAMPLE 1   Finding Terms in a Sequence

A. The first four terms of the sequence whose nth term is $a_n = 3n - 2$ are:

$$a_1 = 3(1) - 2 = 1$$
$$a_2 = 3(2) - 2 = 4$$
$$a_3 = 3(3) - 2 = 7$$
$$a_4 = 3(4) - 2 = 10.$$

B. The first four terms of the sequence whose nth term is $a_n = 3 + (-1)^n$ are:

$$a_1 = 3 + (-1)^1 = 3 - 1 = 2$$
$$a_2 = 3 + (-1)^2 = 3 + 1 = 4$$
$$a_3 = 3 + (-1)^3 = 3 - 1 = 2$$
$$a_4 = 3 + (-1)^4 = 3 + 1 = 4.$$

Technology Note

Try using your graphing utility to graph the sequences in Example 2. Try to duplicate the screens shown in the figure.

$X_{res} = 8$

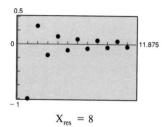

$X_{res} = 8$

EXAMPLE 2   Finding Terms in a Sequence

A. The first four terms of the sequence whose nth term is $a_n = \dfrac{2n}{1 + n}$ are:

$$a_1 = \frac{2(1)}{1 + 1} = \frac{2}{2} = 1$$

$$a_2 = \frac{2(2)}{1 + 2} = \frac{4}{3}$$

$$a_3 = \frac{2(3)}{1 + 3} = \frac{6}{4} = \frac{3}{2}$$

$$a_4 = \frac{2(4)}{1 + 4} = \frac{8}{5}.$$

B. The first four terms of the sequence whose nth term is $a_n = \dfrac{(-1)^n}{2n - 1}$ are:

$$a_1 = \frac{(-1)^1}{2(1) - 1} = \frac{-1}{2 - 1} = -1$$

$$a_2 = \frac{(-1)^2}{2(2) - 1} = \frac{1}{4 - 1} = \frac{1}{3}$$

$$a_3 = \frac{(-1)^3}{2(3) - 1} = \frac{-1}{6 - 1} = -\frac{1}{5}$$

$$a_4 = \frac{(-1)^4}{2(4) - 1} = \frac{1}{8 - 1} = \frac{1}{7}.$$

REMARK Try finding the first four terms of the sequence whose nth term is

$$a_n = \frac{(-1)^{n+1}}{2n - 1}.$$

How do they differ from the first four terms of the sequence in Example 2(B)?

It is important to realize that simply listing the first few terms is not sufficient to define a sequence—the nth term *must be given*. To see this, consider the following sequences, both of which have the same first three terms.

$$\frac{1}{2}, \frac{1}{4}, \frac{1}{8}, \frac{1}{16}, \ldots, \frac{1}{2^n}, \ldots$$

$$\frac{1}{2}, \frac{1}{4}, \frac{1}{8}, \frac{1}{15}, \ldots, \frac{6}{(n + 1)(n^2 - n + 6)}, \ldots$$

When given the first few terms of a sequence, you can, however, be asked to find the *apparent* nth term.

EXAMPLE 3   Finding the Apparent nth Term of a Sequence

Find the apparent nth term of each sequence.

A. 1, 3, 5, 7, . . .   **B.** 2, 5, 10, 17, . . .   **C.** $\dfrac{2}{1}, \dfrac{3}{2}, \dfrac{4}{3}, \dfrac{5}{4}, \ldots$

SOLUTION

A. n: 1   2   3   4   . . . n

           ↓   ↓   ↓   ↓   . . .   ↓

   Terms: 1   3   5   7   . . . a_n

Apparent pattern: Each term is 1 less than twice n, which implies that $a_n = 2n - 1$.

B. n: 1   2   3   4   . . . n

           ↓   ↓   ↓   ↓   . . .   ↓

   Terms: 2   5   10   17   . . . a_n

Apparent pattern: Each term is 1 more than the square of n, which implies that $a_n = n^2 + 1$.

C. n: 1   2   3   4   . . . n

           ↓   ↓   ↓   ↓   . . .   ↓

   Terms: $\dfrac{2}{1}$ $\dfrac{3}{2}$ $\dfrac{4}{3}$ $\dfrac{5}{4}$ . . . a_n

Apparent pattern: Each term has a denominator of n and a numerator that is 1 more than n, which implies that $a_n = (n + 1)/n$.

Factorial Notation

Some very important sequences in mathematics involve terms that are defined with special types of products called **factorials.**

DEFINITION OF FACTORIAL

If n is a positive integer, then n **factorial** is defined by

$$n! = 1 \cdot 2 \cdot 3 \cdot 4 \cdots (n - 1) \cdot n.$$

As a special case, zero factorial is defined to be $0! = 1$.

Technology Note_____

Most graphing utilities have the ability to compute $n!$. Learn how to use this feature of your graphing utility, and then use it to confirm the results given here. How large a value of $n!$ will your graphing utility allow you to compute?

Here are some values of $n!$ for the first several nonnegative integers.

$0! = 1$ $3! = 1 \cdot 2 \cdot 3 = 6$

$1! = 1$ $4! = 1 \cdot 2 \cdot 3 \cdot 4 = 24$

$2! = 1 \cdot 2 = 2$ $5! = 1 \cdot 2 \cdot 3 \cdot 4 \cdot 5 = 120$

The value of n does not have to be very large before the value of $n!$ becomes huge. For instance, $10! = 3,628,800$. Many calculators have a factorial key, denoted by $\boxed{\text{x!}}$.

Factorials follow the same conventions for order of operations as do exponents. For instance,

$$2n! = 2(n!) = 2(1 \cdot 2 \cdot 3 \cdot 4 \cdots n),$$

whereas $(2n)! = 1 \cdot 2 \cdot 3 \cdot 4 \cdots n \cdots (2n - 1)(2n).$

EXAMPLE 4   **Finding Terms of a Sequence Involving Factorials**

List the first five terms of the sequence whose nth term is $a_n = 2^n / n!$. Begin with $n = 0$.

SOLUTION

$$a_0 = \frac{2^0}{0!} = \frac{1}{1} = 1 \qquad a_3 = \frac{2^3}{3!} = \frac{8}{6} = \frac{4}{3}$$

$$a_1 = \frac{2^1}{1!} = \frac{2}{1} = 2 \qquad a_4 = \frac{2^4}{4!} = \frac{16}{24} = \frac{2}{3}$$

$$a_2 = \frac{2^2}{2!} = \frac{4}{2} = 2$$

When working with fractions involving factorials, you will often find that the fractions can be reduced. Here are two examples.

$$\frac{n!}{(n-1)!} = \frac{\cancel{1 \cdot 2 \cdot 3 \cdots (n-1)} \cdot n}{\cancel{1 \cdot 2 \cdot 3 \cdots (n-1)}} = n$$

$$\frac{8!}{2! \cdot 6!} = \frac{\cancel{1 \cdot 2 \cdot 3 \cdot 4 \cdot 5 \cdot 6} \cdot 7 \cdot 8}{1 \cdot 2 \cdot \cancel{1 \cdot 2 \cdot 3 \cdot 4 \cdot 5 \cdot 6}} = \frac{7 \cdot 8}{2} = 28$$

Summation Notation

There is a convenient notation for the sum of the terms of a finite sequence. It is called **summation notation** or **sigma notation** because it involves the use of the uppercase Greek letter sigma, written as Σ.

DEFINITION OF SUMMATION NOTATION

The sum of the first n terms of a sequence is represented by

$$\sum_{i=1}^{n} a_i = a_1 + a_2 + a_3 + a_4 + \cdots + a_n$$

where i is the **index of summation,** n is the **upper limit of summation,** and 1 is the **lower limit of summation.**

EXAMPLE 5   Summation Notation for Sums

REMARK In Example 5, note that the lower limit of a summation does not have to be 1. Also note that the index does not have to be the letter i. For instance, in part (B), the letter k is the index.

A. $\displaystyle\sum_{i=1}^{5} 3i = 3(1) + 3(2) + 3(3) + 3(4) + 3(5)$

$$= 3(1 + 2 + 3 + 4 + 5)$$
$$= 3(15) = 45$$

B. $\displaystyle\sum_{k=3}^{6} (1 + k^2) = (1 + 3^2) + (1 + 4^2) + (1 + 5^2) + (1 + 6^2)$

$$= 10 + 17 + 26 + 37 = 90$$

C. $\displaystyle\sum_{i=0}^{8} \frac{1}{i!} = \frac{1}{0!} + \frac{1}{1!} + \frac{1}{2!} + \frac{1}{3!} + \frac{1}{4!} + \frac{1}{5!} + \frac{1}{6!} + \frac{1}{7!} + \frac{1}{8!}$

$$= 1 + 1 + \frac{1}{2} + \frac{1}{6} + \frac{1}{24} + \frac{1}{120} + \frac{1}{720} + \frac{1}{5040} + \frac{1}{40,320}$$

$$\approx 2.71828$$

For this summation, note that the sum is very close to the irrational number $e \approx 2.718281828$. It can be shown that, as more terms of the sequence whose nth term is $1/n!$ are added, the sum becomes closer and closer to e.

PROPERTIES OF SUMS

1. $\displaystyle\sum_{i=1}^{n} ca_i = c \sum_{i=1}^{n} a_i$, c is any constant

2. $\displaystyle\sum_{i=1}^{n} (a_i + b_i) = \sum_{i=1}^{n} a_i + \sum_{i=1}^{n} b_i$

3. $\displaystyle\sum_{i=1}^{n} (a_i - b_i) = \sum_{i=1}^{n} a_i - \sum_{i=1}^{n} b_i$

Variations in the upper and lower limits of summation can produce quite different-looking summation notations for *the same sum.* For example, consider the following two sums.

$$\sum_{i=1}^{5} 3(2^i) = 3 \sum_{i=1}^{5} 2^i = 3(2^1 + 2^2 + 2^3 + 2^4 + 2^5)$$

$$\sum_{i=0}^{4} 3(2^{i+1}) = 3 \sum_{i=0}^{4} 2^{i+1} = 3(2^1 + 2^2 + 2^3 + 2^4 + 2^5)$$

The Sum of an Infinite Sequence

It is easy to see that the sum of the terms of any *finite* sequence must be a finite number. However, it may not be as easy to convince yourself that the sum of all the terms of an *infinite* sequence can also be a finite number. For instance, it can be shown that the sum of all of the terms of the sequence whose nth term is $1/2^n$ (with n beginning at 0) is

$$\sum_{n=0}^{\infty} \frac{1}{2^n} = 1 + \frac{1}{2} + \frac{1}{4} + \frac{1}{8} + \frac{1}{16} + \frac{1}{32} + \cdots = 2.$$

(See Figure 10.1.) This type of summation is called an **infinite series.**

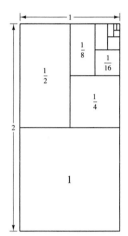

The total area is 2.

FIGURE 10.1

EXAMPLE 6   Finding the Sum of an Infinite Sequence

Find the sum of the infinite sequence.

$$\frac{3}{10^1}, \frac{3}{10^2}, \frac{3}{10^3}, \frac{3}{10^4}, \frac{3}{10^5}, \cdots$$

SOLUTION

$$\sum_{n=1}^{\infty} \frac{3}{10^n} = \frac{3}{10^1} + \frac{3}{10^2} + \frac{3}{10^3} + \frac{3}{10^4} + \frac{3}{10^5} + \cdots$$

$$= 0.3 + 0.03 + 0.003 + 0.0003 + 0.00003 + 0.000003 + \cdots$$

$$= 0.33333\ldots$$

$$= \frac{1}{3}$$

Applications

EXAMPLE 7   Population of the United States

From 1950 to 1989, the resident population of the United States can be approximated by the model

$$a_n = \sqrt{22{,}926 + 902.5n + 2.01n^2}, \qquad n = 0, 1, \ldots, 39,$$

where a_n is the population in millions and n represents the year, with $n = 0$ corresponding to 1950. (*Source:* U.S. Bureau of Census) Find the last five terms of this finite sequence.

SOLUTION

The last five terms of this finite sequence are as follows.

$$a_{35} = \sqrt{22{,}926 + 902.5(35) + 2.01(35^2)} \approx 238.7 \qquad \textit{1985 population}$$
$$a_{36} = \sqrt{22{,}926 + 902.5(36) + 2.01(36^2)} \approx 240.9 \qquad \textit{1986 population}$$
$$a_{37} = \sqrt{22{,}926 + 902.5(37) + 2.01(37^2)} \approx 243.0 \qquad \textit{1987 population}$$
$$a_{38} = \sqrt{22{,}926 + 902.5(38) + 2.01(38^2)} \approx 245.2 \qquad \textit{1988 population}$$
$$a_{39} = \sqrt{22{,}926 + 902.5(39) + 2.01(39^2)} \approx 247.3 \qquad \textit{1989 population}$$

The bar graph in Figure 10.2 graphically represents the population given by this sequence for the entire 40-year period from 1950 to 1989.

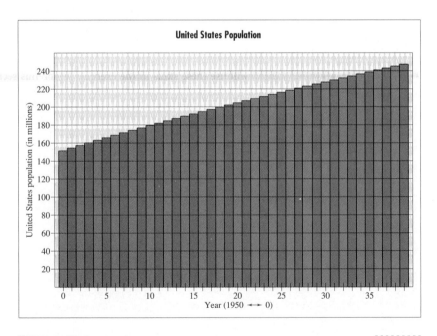

FIGURE 10.2

Consider the following sequence.

$$a_1 = 1$$

$$a_2 = 1 \cdot 3$$

$$a_3 = 1 \cdot 3 \cdot 5$$

$$a_4 = 1 \cdot 3 \cdot 5 \cdot 7$$

$$\vdots$$

$$a_n = 1 \cdot 3 \cdot 5 \cdots (2n - 1)$$

Is it true that the nth term of this sequence can be written as

$$a_n = \frac{(2n)!}{2^n n!}?$$

Write a paragraph that justifies your answer.

WARM-UP
....

The following warm-up exercises involve skills that were covered in earlier sections. You will use these skills in the exercise set for this section.

In Exercises 1 and 2, find the required value of the function.

1. $f(n) = \dfrac{2n}{n^2 + 1}$, $f(2)$ **2.** $f(n) = \dfrac{4}{3(n + 1)}$, $f(3)$

In Exercises 3–6, factor the expression.

3. $4n^2 - 1$ **4.** $4n^2 - 8n + 3$
5. $n^2 - 3n + 2$ **6.** $n^2 + 3n + 2$

In Exercises 7–10, perform the indicated operations and/or simplify.

7. $\left(\dfrac{2}{3}\right)\left(\dfrac{3}{4}\right)\left(\dfrac{4}{5}\right)\left(\dfrac{5}{6}\right)$ **8.** $\dfrac{2 \cdot 4 \cdot 6 \cdot 8}{2^4}$

9. $\dfrac{1}{2 \cdot 2} + \dfrac{1}{2 \cdot 3} + \dfrac{1}{2 \cdot 4}$ **10.** $\dfrac{1}{1 \cdot 2} + \dfrac{1}{2 \cdot 3} + \dfrac{1}{3 \cdot 4}$

SECTION 10.1 · EXERCISES

In Exercises 1–18, write the first five terms of the indicated sequence. (Assume n begins with 1.)

1. $a_n = 2n + 1$

2. $a_n = 4n - 3$

3. $a_n = 2^n$

4. $a_n = (\frac{1}{2})^n$

5. $a_n = (-2)^n$

6. $a_n = (-\frac{1}{2})^n$

7. $a_n = \dfrac{1 + (-1)^n}{n}$

8. $a_n = \dfrac{n}{n + 1}$

9. $a_n = 3 - \dfrac{1}{2^n}$

10. $a_n = \dfrac{3^n}{4^n}$

11. $a_n = \dfrac{1}{n^{3/2}}$

12. $a_n = \dfrac{3n^2 - n + 4}{2n^2 + 1}$

13. $a_n = \dfrac{3^n}{n!}$

14. $a_n = \dfrac{n!}{n}$

15. $a_n = \dfrac{(-1)^n}{n^2}$

16. $a_n = (-1)^n \left(\dfrac{n}{n + 1}\right)$

17. $a_1 = 3$ and $a_{k+1} = 2(a_k - 1)$

18. $a_1 = 4$ and $a_{k+1} = \left(\dfrac{k + 1}{2}\right) a_k$

In Exercises 19–24, simplify the ratio of factorials.

19. $\dfrac{4!}{6!}$

20. $\dfrac{25!}{23!}$

21. $\dfrac{(n + 1)!}{n!}$

22. $\dfrac{(n + 2)!}{n!}$

23. $\dfrac{(2n - 1)!}{(2n + 1)!}$

24. $\dfrac{(2n + 2)!}{(2n)!}$

In Exercises 25–36, write an expression for the *most apparent* nth term of the sequence. (Assume n begins with 1.)

25. $1, 4, 7, 10, 13, \ldots$

26. $3, 7, 11, 15, 19, \ldots$

27. $0, 3, 8, 15, 24, \ldots$

28. $1, \frac{1}{4}, \frac{1}{9}, \frac{1}{16}, \frac{1}{25}, \ldots$

29. $\frac{1}{2}, \frac{-1}{4}, \frac{1}{8}, \frac{-1}{16}, \ldots$

30. $\frac{1}{3}, \frac{2}{9}, \frac{4}{27}, \frac{8}{81}, \ldots$

31. $1 + \frac{1}{1}, 1 + \frac{1}{2}, 1 + \frac{1}{3}, 1 + \frac{1}{4}, 1 + \frac{1}{5}, \ldots$

32. $1 + \frac{1}{2}, 1 + \frac{3}{4}, 1 + \frac{7}{8}, 1 + \frac{15}{16}, 1 + \frac{31}{32}, \ldots$

33. $1, \frac{1}{2}, \frac{1}{6}, \frac{1}{24}, \frac{1}{120}, \ldots$

34. $2, -4, 6, -8, 10, \ldots$

35. $1, -1, 1, -1, 1, \ldots$

36. $1, 2, \dfrac{2^2}{2}, \dfrac{2^3}{6}, \dfrac{2^4}{24}, \dfrac{2^5}{120}, \ldots$

In Exercises 37–50, find the sum.

37. $\displaystyle\sum_{i=1}^{5} (2i + 1)$

38. $\displaystyle\sum_{i=1}^{6} (3i - 1)$

39. $\displaystyle\sum_{k=1}^{4} 10$

40. $\displaystyle\sum_{k=1}^{5} 6$

41. $\displaystyle\sum_{i=0}^{4} i^2$

42. $\displaystyle\sum_{i=0}^{5} 3i^2$

43. $\displaystyle\sum_{k=0}^{3} \dfrac{1}{k^2 + 1}$

44. $\displaystyle\sum_{j=3}^{5} \dfrac{1}{j}$

45. $\displaystyle\sum_{i=1}^{4} [(i - 1)^2 + (i + 1)^3]$

46. $\displaystyle\sum_{k=2}^{5} (k + 1)(k - 3)$

47. $\displaystyle\sum_{i=1}^{4} (9 + 2i)$

48. $\displaystyle\sum_{j=0}^{4} (-2)^j$

49. $\displaystyle\sum_{k=0}^{4} \dfrac{(-1)^k}{k + 1}$

50. $\displaystyle\sum_{k=0}^{4} \dfrac{(-1)^k}{k!}$

In Exercises 51–60, use sigma notation to write the given sum.

51. $\dfrac{1}{3(1)} + \dfrac{1}{3(2)} + \dfrac{1}{3(3)} + \cdots + \dfrac{1}{3(9)}$

52. $\dfrac{5}{1 + 1} + \dfrac{5}{1 + 2} + \dfrac{5}{1 + 3} + \cdots + \dfrac{5}{1 + 15}$

53. $[2(\frac{1}{8}) + 3] + [2(\frac{2}{8}) + 3] + \cdots + [2(\frac{8}{8}) + 3]$

54. $[1 - (\frac{1}{6})^2] + [1 - (\frac{2}{6})^2] + \cdots + [1 - (\frac{6}{6})^2]$

55. $3 - 9 + 27 - 81 + 243 - 729$

56. $1 - \frac{1}{2} + \frac{1}{4} - \frac{1}{8} + \cdots - \frac{1}{128}$

57. $\dfrac{1}{1^2} - \dfrac{1}{2^2} + \dfrac{1}{3^2} - \dfrac{1}{4^2} + \cdots - \dfrac{1}{20^2}$

58. $\dfrac{1}{1 \cdot 3} + \dfrac{1}{2 \cdot 4} + \dfrac{1}{3 \cdot 5} + \cdots + \dfrac{1}{10 \cdot 12}$

59. $\frac{1}{4} + \frac{3}{8} + \frac{7}{16} + \frac{15}{32} + \frac{31}{64}$

60. $\frac{1}{2} + \frac{2}{4} + \frac{6}{8} + \frac{24}{16} + \frac{120}{32} + \frac{720}{64}$

61. *Compound Interest* A deposit of \$5000 is made in an account that earns 8% interest compounded quarterly. The balance in the account after n quarters is given by

$$A_n = 5000\left(1 + \dfrac{0.08}{4}\right)^n, \qquad n = 1, 2, 3, \ldots.$$

(a) Compute the first eight terms of this sequence.

(b) Find the balance in this account after 10 years by computing the 40th term of the sequence.

62. *Compound Interest* A deposit of $100 is made *each* month in an account that earns 12% interest compounded monthly. The balance in the account after n months is given by

$$A_n = 100(101)[(1.01)^n - 1], \quad n = 1, 2, 3, \ldots.$$

(a) Compute the first six terms of this sequence.

(b) Find the balance after 5 years by computing the 60th term of the sequence.

(c) Find the balance after 20 years by computing the 240th term of the sequence.

63. *Hospital Costs* The average cost of a day in a hospital from 1980 to 1987 is given by the model

$$a_n = 242.67 + 42.67n, \quad n = 0, 1, 2, \ldots, 7,$$

where a_n is the average cost in dollars and n is the year, with $n = 0$ corresponding to 1980. (*Source:* American Hospital Association) Find the terms of this finite sequence and construct a bar graph that represents the sequence.

64. *Federal Debt* It took more than 200 years for the U.S. to accumulate a $1 trillion debt. Then it took just 8 years to get to $3 trillion. (*Source:* Treasury Department) The federal debt during the decade of the 1980s is approximated by the model

$$a_n = 0.1\sqrt{82 + 9n^2}, \quad n = 0, 1, 2, \ldots, 10,$$

where a_n is the debt in trillions and n is the year, with $n = 0$ corresponding to 1980. Find the terms of this finite sequence and construct a bar graph that represents the sequence.

65. *Corporate Dividends* The dividends declared per share of common stock of Ameritech Corporation for the years 1985 through 1990 are shown in the figure. (*Source:* Ameritech 1990 Annual Report) These dividends can be approximated by the model

$$a_n = 0.20n + 1.17, \quad n = 5, 6, 7, 8, 9, 10,$$

where a_n is the dividend in dollars and n is the year, with $n = 5$ corresponding to 1985. Approximate the sum of the dividends per share of common stock for the years 1985 through 1990 by evaluating

$$\sum_{n=5}^{10} (0.20n + 1.17).$$

Compare this sum with the result of adding the dividends as shown in the figure.

FIGURE FOR 65

66. *Total Revenue* From 1980 through 1989, the total annual sales for MCI Communications can be approximated by the model

$$a_n = 48.217n^2 + 228.1n + 311.28, \quad n = 0, 1, \ldots, 9,$$

where a_n is the annual sales (in millions of dollars) and n is the year, with $n = 0$ corresponding to 1980. (*Source:* MCI Communications) Find the total revenue from 1980 through 1989 by evaluating the sum

$$\sum_{n=0}^{9} (48.217n^2 + 228.1n + 311.28).$$

FIGURE FOR 66

In Exercises 67 and 68, use the following definition of the arithmetic mean $\bar{x}$ of a set of n measurements $x_1, x_2, \ldots, x_n$.

$$\bar{x} = \frac{1}{n} \sum_{i=1}^{n} x_i$$

67. Prove that $\displaystyle\sum_{i=1}^{n} (x_i - \bar{x}) = 0.$

68. Prove that $\displaystyle\sum_{i=1}^{n} (x_i - \bar{x})^2 = \sum_{i=1}^{n} x_i^2 - \frac{1}{n}\left(\sum_{i=1}^{n} x_i\right)^2.$

69. *Fibonacci Sequence*   In the study of the progeny of rabbits, Fibonacci (c. 1175–c.1250) encountered the now famous sequence bearing his name. The sequence is defined recursively by

$$a_{n+2} = a_n + a_{n+1} \quad \text{where} \quad a_1 = a_2 = 1.$$

(a) Write out the first 12 terms of the sequence.

(b) Write out the first 10 terms of the sequence defined by

$$b_n = \frac{a_{n+1}}{a_n}, \quad \text{for } n > 1.$$

(c) Using the definition of part (b), show that

$$b_n = 1 + \frac{1}{b_{n-1}}.$$

10.2 ARITHMETIC SEQUENCES

Arithmetic Sequences / The Sum of an Arithmetic Sequence /
Arithmetic Mean / Applications

Arithmetic Sequences

A sequence whose consecutive terms have a common difference is called an **arithmetic sequence.**

DEFINITION OF AN ARITHMETIC SEQUENCE

A sequence is **arithmetic** if the differences between consecutive terms are the same. Thus, the sequence

$$a_1, a_2, a_3, a_4, \ldots, a_n, \ldots$$

is arithmetic if there is a number d such that

$$a_2 - a_1 = d, \qquad a_3 - a_2 = d, \qquad a_4 - a_3 = d,$$

and so on. The number d is the **common difference** of the arithmetic sequence.

EXAMPLE 1 Examples of Arithmetic Sequences

A. The sequence whose nth term is $4n + 3$ is arithmetic. For this sequence, the common difference between consecutive terms is 4.

$$7, 11, 15, 19, \ldots, 4n + 3, \ldots$$

$$11 - 7 = 4$$

B. The sequence whose nth term is $7 - 5n$ is arithmetic. For this sequence, the common difference between consecutive terms is -5.

$$\underbrace{2, -3,}_{-3 - 2 = -5} -8, -13, \ldots, 7 - 5n, \ldots$$

C. The sequence whose nth term is $\frac{1}{4}(n + 3)$ is arithmetic. For this sequence, the common difference between consecutive terms is $\frac{1}{4}$.

$$\underbrace{1, \frac{5}{4},}_{\frac{5}{4} - 1 = \frac{1}{4}} \frac{3}{2}, \frac{7}{4}, \ldots, \frac{n + 3}{4}, \ldots$$

THE *N*TH TERM OF AN ARITHMETIC SEQUENCE

The nth term of an arithmetic sequence has the form

$$a_n = dn + c,$$

where d is the common difference between consecutive terms of the sequence and $c = a_1 - d$. An alternative form of the nth term of an arithmetic sequence is $a_n = a_1 + (n - 1)d$.

EXAMPLE 2   Finding the nth Term of an Arithmetic Sequence

Find a formula for the nth term of the arithmetic sequence whose common difference is 3 and whose first term is 2.

SOLUTION

Because the common difference is $d = 3$, you can write the following.

$$a_n = dn + c \qquad \textit{Formula for nth term}$$
$$a_n = 3n + c \qquad \textit{Substitute } d = 3$$

Using $a_1 = 2$, it follows that $2 = 3(1) + c$, which implies that $c = -1$. Thus, a formula for the nth term is

$$a_n = 3n - 1.$$

The sequence has the following form.

$$2, 5, 8, 11, 14, \ldots, 3n - 1, \ldots$$

EXAMPLE 3   Finding the nth Term of an Arithmetic Sequence

Find a formula for the nth term of the arithmetic sequence whose common difference is 5 and whose *second* term is 12. What is the 18th term of this sequence?

SOLUTION

Because the common difference is $d = 5$, you can write the following.

$$a_n = dn + c \qquad \qquad \textit{Formula for nth term}$$
$$a_n = 5n + c \qquad \qquad \textit{Substitute } d = 5$$

Using $a_2 = 12$, it follows that $12 = 5(2) + c$, which implies that $c = 2$. Thus, a formula for the nth term is

$$a_n = 5n + 2.$$

The sequence therefore has the form

$$7, 12, 17, 22, 27, \ldots, 5n + 2, \ldots,$$

and the 18th term of the sequence is $a_{18} = 5(18) + 2 = 92$.

If you know the nth term of an arithmetic sequence *and* you know the common difference of the sequence, then you can find the $(n + 1)$th term by using the following **recursion formula.**

$$a_{n+1} = a_n + d$$

With such a formula, you can find any term of an arithmetic sequence, *provided* you know the previous term. For example, if you know the first term, then you can find the second term. Then, knowing the second term, you can find the third term, and so on.

EXAMPLE 4   Using a Recursion Formula

Find the ninth term of the arithmetic sequence whose first two terms are 2 and 9.

SOLUTION

For this sequence you can find that $a_1 = 2$ and $a_2 = 9$ so that the common difference is $d = 9 - 2 = 7$. There are two ways to find the ninth term. One way is simply to write out the first nine terms (by repeatedly adding 7).

$$2, 9, 16, 23, 30, 37, 44, 51, 58$$

Another way to find the ninth term is first to find a formula for the nth term. Because the first term is 2, it follows that $c = a_1 - d = 2 - 7 = -5$. Therefore, a formula for the nth term of the sequence is $a_n = 7n - 5$, which implies that the ninth term is

$$a_9 = 7(9) - 5 = 58.$$

EXAMPLE 5 Finding the nth Term of an Arithmetic Sequence

The fourth term of an arithmetic sequence is 20, and the 13th term is 65. Write the first several terms of this sequence.

SOLUTION

To obtain the 13th term from the fourth term, you can add the common difference d to the fourth term nine times. That is

$$a_{13} = a_4 + 9d.$$

Because $a_4 = 20$ and $a_{13} = 65$, it follows that $65 = 20 + 9d$, which implies that $d = 5$. Now, from the formula for the nth term of an arithmetic sequence, you can write

$$a_n = dn + c$$
$$a_4 = 5(4) + c$$
$$20 = 20 + c$$
$$0 = c.$$

Thus, $a_n = dn = 5n$ and the first several terms of the sequence are as follows.

$$\begin{array}{ccccccccccccc} 1 & 2 & 3 & 4 & 5 & 6 & 7 & 8 & 9 & 10 & 11 & 12 & 13 \\ 5, & 10, & 15, & 20, & 25, & 30, & 35, & 40, & 45, & 50, & 55, & 60, & 65, & \ldots \end{array}$$

The Sum of an Arithmetic Sequence

The following result gives a formula for finding the *sum* of a finite arithmetic sequence.

THE SUM OF A FINITE ARITHMETIC SEQUENCE

The sum of a finite arithmetic sequence with n terms is

$$S = \frac{n}{2}(a_1 + a_n).$$

PROOF

Begin by generating the terms of the arithmetic sequence in two ways. In the first way, repeatedly add d to the first term to obtain

$$S = a_1 + a_2 + a_3 + \cdots + a_{n-2} + a_{n-1} + a_n$$

$$= a_1 + [a_1 + d] + [a_1 + 2d] + \cdots + [a_1 + (n - 1)d].$$

REMARK   Be sure you see that this formula only works for *arithmetic* sequences.

In the second way, repeatedly subtract d from the nth term to obtain

$$S = a_n + a_{n-1} + a_{n-2} + \cdots + a_3 + a_2 + a_1$$

$$= a_n + [a_n - d] + [a_n - 2d] + \cdots + [a_n - (n - 1)d].$$

If you add these two versions of S, the multiples of d subtract out and you obtain

$$2S = \overbrace{(a_1 + a_n) + (a_1 + a_n) + (a_1 + a_n) + \cdots + (a_1 + a_n)}^{n \text{ terms}}$$

$$= n(a_1 + a_n).$$

Thus, you have

$$S = \frac{n}{2}(a_1 + a_n).$$

EXAMPLE 6   Finding the Sum of an Arithmetic Sequence

Find the following sum.

$$1 + 3 + 5 + 7 + 9 + 11 + 13 + 15 + 17 + 19$$

SOLUTION

To begin, notice that the sequence is arithmetic (with a common difference of 2). Moreover, the sequence has 10 terms. Thus, the sum of the sequence is

$$S = 1 + 3 + 5 + 7 + 9 + 11 + 13 + 15 + 17 + 19$$
$$= \frac{n}{2}(a_1 + a_n)$$
$$= \frac{10}{2}(1 + 19)$$
$$= 5(20)$$
$$= 100.$$

EXAMPLE 7   Finding the Sum of an Arithmetic Sequence

Find the sum of the integers from 1 to 100.

SOLUTION

The integers from 1 to 100 form an arithmetic sequence

$$1, 2, 3, 4, 5, 6, \ldots, 99, 100$$

that has 100 terms. Thus, you can use the formula for the sum of an arithmetic sequence, as follows.

$$S = 1 + 2 + 3 + 4 + 5 + 6 + \cdots + 99 + 100$$
$$= \frac{n}{2}(a_1 + a_n)$$
$$= \frac{100}{2}(1 + 100)$$
$$= 50(101)$$
$$= 5050$$

EXAMPLE 8 Finding the Sum of an Arithmetic Sequence

Find the sum of the first 150 terms of the arithmetic sequence

$$5, 16, 27, 38, 49, \ldots.$$

SOLUTION

For this arithmetic sequence, you have $a_1 = 5$ and $d = 16 - 5 = 11$. Thus, $c = a_1 - d = 5 - 11 = -6$, and the nth term is

$$a_n = 11n - 6.$$

Therefore, $a_{150} = 11(150) - 6 = 1644$, and the sum of the first 150 terms is as follows.

$$S = \frac{n}{2}(a_1 + a_n)$$

$$= \frac{150}{2}(5 + 1644)$$

$$= 75(1649)$$

$$= 123{,}675$$

EXAMPLE 9 Finding the Sum of an Arithmetic Sequence

Verify the formula

$$S = 1 + 3 + 5 + \cdots + (2n - 1) = n^2.$$

SOLUTION

Using the formula for the sum of a finite arithmetic sequence, you can write the following.

$$S = 1 + 3 + 5 + \cdots + (2n - 1) \qquad a_n = 2n - 1$$

$$= \frac{n}{2}(a_1 + a_n)$$

$$= \frac{n}{2}[1 + (2n - 1)]$$

$$= \frac{n}{2}(2n)$$

$$= n^2$$

Arithmetic Mean

Recall that $(a + b)/2$ is the midpoint between the two numbers a and b on the real number line. As a result, the terms

$$a, \frac{a + b}{2}, b$$

have a common difference. The number $(a + b)/2$ is the **arithmetic mean** of the numbers a and b. You can generalize this concept by finding k numbers m_1, m_2, m_3, . . . , m_k between a and b such that the terms

$$a, m_1, m_2, m_3, \ldots, m_k, b$$

have a common difference. This process is referred to as **inserting k arithmetic means** between a and b.

EXAMPLE 10 Inserting Arithmetic Means Between Two Numbers

Insert three arithmetic means between 4 and 15.

SOLUTION

You need to find three numbers m_1, m_2, and m_3 such that the terms

$$4, m_1, m_2, m_3, 15$$

have a common difference. In this case you have $a_1 = 4$, $n = 5$, and $a_5 = 15$. Therefore, using the alternative form of a_n, you have

$$a_5 = 15 = a_1 + (n - 1)d = 4 + 4d.$$

Because $15 = 4 + 4d$, you find that $d = \frac{11}{4}$, and the three arithmetic means are as follows.

$$m_1 = a_1 + d = 4 + \frac{11}{4} = \frac{27}{4}$$

$$m_2 = m_1 + d = \frac{27}{4} + \frac{11}{4} = \frac{38}{4}$$

$$m_3 = m_2 + d = \frac{38}{4} + \frac{11}{4} = \frac{49}{4}$$

Applications

EXAMPLE 11   Seating Capacity

An auditorium has 20 rows of seats. There are 20 seats in the first row, 21 seats in the second row, 22 seats in the third row, and so on. (See Figure 10.3.) How many seats are there in all 20 rows?

FIGURE 10.3

SOLUTION

The number of seats in the rows forms an arithmetic sequence in which the common difference is $d = 1$. Because $c = a_1 - d = 20 - 1 = 19$, you can determine that the formula for the nth term in the sequence is $a_n = n + 19$. Therefore, the 20th term in the sequence is $a_{20} = 20 + 19 = 39$, and the total number of seats is

$$S = 20 + 21 + 22 + \cdots + 39$$

$$= \frac{n}{2}(a_1 + a_{20})$$

$$= \frac{20}{2}(20 + 39)$$

$$= 10(59)$$

$$= 590.$$

EXAMPLE 12   Total Sales

A small business sells $10,000 worth of products during its first year. The owner of the business has set a goal of increasing annual sales by $7500 each year for 9 years. Assuming that this goal is met, find the total sales during the first 10 years this business is in operation.

SOLUTION

The annual sales form an arithmetic sequence in which $a_1 = 10,000$ and $d = 7500$. Thus, $c = a_1 - d = 10,000 - 7500 = 2500$, and the nth term of the sequence is

$$a_n = 7500n + 2500.$$

This implies that the tenth term of the sequence is $a_{10} = 7500(10) + 2500 = 77,500$. Therefore, the total sales for the first 10 years is as follows.

$$S = \frac{n}{2}(a_1 + a_{10})$$

$$= \frac{10}{2}(10{,}000 + 77{,}500)$$

$$= 5(87{,}500)$$

$$= \$437{,}500$$

DISCUSSION PROBLEM

ARITHMETIC SEQUENCES

The first five terms of each of the indicated sequences are 1, 3, 5, 7, 9.

(a) $a_n = 2n - 1$ (b) $b_n = \sqrt{4n^2 - 4n + 1}$ (c) $c_n = \dfrac{2n^2 + n - 1}{n + 1}$

Does this fact *alone* mean that each sequence is arithmetic? Is each sequence arithmetic? Write a paragraph justifying your answer. Here is another sequence whose first five terms are 1, 3, 5, 7, 9. Is it arithmetic?

$$d_n = n^6 - 15n^5 + 85n^4 - 225n^3 + 274n^2 - 118n - 1$$

WARM-UP

The following warm-up exercises involve skills that were covered in earlier sections. You will use these skills in the exercise set for this section.

In Exercises 1 and 2, find the sum.

1. $\displaystyle\sum_{i=1}^{6} (2i - 1)$ **2.** $\displaystyle\sum_{i=1}^{10} (4i + 2)$

In Exercises 3 and 4, find the distance between the two real numbers.

3. $\frac{5}{2}, 8$ **4.** $\frac{4}{3}, \frac{14}{3}$

In Exercises 5 and 6, find the required value of the function.

5. $f(n) = 10 + (n - 1)4, \quad f(3)$ **6.** $f(n) = 1 + (n - 1)\frac{1}{3}, \quad f(10)$

In Exercises 7–10, evaluate the expression.

7. $\frac{11}{2}(1 + 25)$ **8.** $\frac{16}{2}(4 + 16)$

9. $\frac{20}{2}[2(5) + (12 - 1)3]$ **10.** $\frac{8}{2}[2(-3) + (15 - 1)5]$

SECTION 10.2 · EXERCISES

In Exercises 1–10 determine whether the sequence is arithmetic. If it is, find the common difference.

1. 4, 7, 10, 13, 16, . . .

2. 10, 8, 6, 4, 2, . . .

3. 1, 2, 4, 8, 16, . . .

4. 3, $\frac{5}{2}$, 2, $\frac{3}{2}$, 1, . . .

5. $\frac{9}{4}$, 2, $\frac{7}{4}$, $\frac{3}{2}$, $\frac{5}{4}$, . . .

6. −12, −8, −4, 0, 4, . . .

7. $\frac{1}{3}$, $\frac{2}{3}$, $\frac{4}{3}$, $\frac{8}{3}$, $\frac{16}{3}$, . . .

8. ln 1, ln 2, ln 3, ln 4, ln 5, . . .

9. 5.3, 5.7, 6.1, 6.5, 6.9, . . .

10. 1^2, 2^2, 3^2, 4^2, 5^2, . . .

In Exercises 11–18, write the first five terms of the specified sequence. Determine whether the sequence is arithmetic, and if it is, find the common difference.

11. $a_n = 5 + 3n$

12. $a_n = (2^n)n$

13. $a_n = \dfrac{1}{n+1}$

14. $a_n = 1 + (n-1)4$

15. $a_n = 100 - 3n$

16. $a_n = 2^{n-1}$

17. $a_n = 3 + \dfrac{(-1)^n 2}{n}$

18. $a_n = (-1)^n$

In Exercises 19–30, find a formula for a_n for the given arithmetic sequence.

19. $a_1 = 1$, $d = 3$

20. $a_1 = 15$, $d = 4$

21. $a_1 = 100$, $d = -8$

22. $a_1 = 0$, $d = -\frac{2}{3}$

23. $a_1 = x$, $d = 2x$

24. $a_1 = -y$, $d = 5y$

25. 4, $\frac{3}{2}$, −1, $-\frac{7}{2}$, . . .

26. 10, 5, 0, −5, −10, . . .

27. $a_1 = 5$, $a_4 = 15$

28. $a_1 = -4$, $a_5 = 16$

29. $a_3 = 94$, $a_6 = 85$

30. $a_5 = 190$, $a_{10} = 115$

In Exercises 31–40, write the first five terms of the arithmetic sequence.

31. $a_1 = 5$, $d = 6$

32. $a_1 = 5$, $d = -\frac{3}{4}$

33. $a_1 = -2.6$, $d = -0.4$

34. $a_1 = 16.5$, $d = 0.25$

35. $a_1 = \frac{3}{2}$, $a_{k+1} = a_k - \frac{1}{4}$

36. $a_1 = 6$, $a_{k+1} = a_k + 12$

37. $a_1 = 2$, $a_{12} = 46$

38. $a_4 = 16$, $a_{10} = 46$

39. $a_8 = 26$, $a_{12} = 42$

40. $a_3 = 19$, $a_{15} = -1.7$

In Exercises 41–48, find the sum of the first n terms of the arithmetic sequence.

41. 8, 20, 32, 44, . . . , $n = 10$

42. 2, 8, 14, 20, . . . , $n = 25$

43. −6, −2, 2, 6, . . . , $n = 50$

44. 0.5, 0.9, 1.3, 1.7, . . . , $n = 10$

45. 40, 37, 34, 31, . . . , $n = 10$

46. 1.50, 1.45, 1.40, 1.35, . . . , $n = 20$

47. $a_1 = 100$, $a_{25} = 220$, $n = 25$

48. $a_1 = 15$, $a_{100} = 307$, $n = 100$

In Exercises 49–60, find the indicated sum.

49. $\displaystyle\sum_{n=1}^{50} n$

50. $\displaystyle\sum_{n=1}^{100} 2n$

51. $\displaystyle\sum_{n=1}^{100} 5n$

52. $\displaystyle\sum_{n=51}^{100} 7n$

53. $\displaystyle\sum_{n=11}^{30} n - \sum_{n=1}^{10} n$

54. $\displaystyle\sum_{n=51}^{100} n - \sum_{n=1}^{50} n$

55. $\displaystyle\sum_{n=1}^{500} (n+3)$

56. $\displaystyle\sum_{n=1}^{250} (1000 - n)$

57. $\displaystyle\sum_{n=1}^{20} (2n+5)$

58. $\displaystyle\sum_{n=1}^{100} \frac{n+4}{2}$

59. $\displaystyle\sum_{n=0}^{50} (1000 - 5n)$

60. $\displaystyle\sum_{n=0}^{100} \frac{8 - 3n}{16}$

In Exercises 61–64, insert k arithmetic means between the given pair of numbers.

61. 5, 17, $k = 2$

62. 24, 56, $k = 3$

63. 3, 6, $k = 3$

64. 2, 5, $k = 4$

65. Find the sum of the first 100 odd integers.

66. Find the sum of the integers from -10 to 50.

67. *Job Offer*   A person accepts a position with a company and will receive a salary of $27,500 for the first year. The person is guaranteed a raise of $1500 per year for the first 5 years.
   (a) Determine the person's salary during the sixth year of employment.
   (b) Determine the person's total compensation from the company through 6 full years of employment.

68. *Job Offer*   A person accepts a position with a company and will receive a salary of $32,800 for the first year. The person is guaranteed a raise of $1750 per year for the first 5 years.
   (a) Determine the person's salary during the sixth year of employment.
   (b) Determine the person's total compensation from the company through 6 full years of employment.

69. *Seating Capacity*   Determine the seating capacity of an auditorium with 30 rows of seats if there are 20 seats in the first row, 24 seats in the second row, 28 seats in the third row, and so on.

70. *Seating Capacity*   Determine the seating capacity of an auditorium with 36 rows of seats if there are 15 seats in the first row, 18 seats in the second row, 21 seats in the third row, and so on.

71. *Brick Pattern*   A brick patio is in roughly the shape of a trapezoid (see figure). The patio has 20 rows of bricks. The first row has 14 bricks, and the 20th row has 33 bricks. How many bricks are in the patio?

FIGURE FOR 71

72. *Falling Object*   An object (with negligible air resistance) is dropped from a plane. During the first second of fall, the object falls 4.9 meters; during the next second, it falls 14.7 meters; during the third second, it falls 24.5 meters; during the fourth second, it falls 34.3 meters. If this arithmetic pattern continues, how many meters will the object have fallen in 10 seconds?

73. Prove that the sum of the first n positive integers,

$$S = 1 + 2 + 3 + \cdots + n,$$

is given by

$$S = \frac{n(n + 1)}{2}.$$

10.3 GEOMETRIC SEQUENCES

Geometric Sequences / The Sum of a Finite Geometric Sequence / Application

Geometric Sequences

In Section 10.2, you learned that a sequence whose consecutive terms have a common *difference* is an arithmetic sequence. In this section you will study another important type of sequence called a **geometric sequence.** Consecutive terms of a geometric sequence have a common *ratio,* as indicated in the following definition.

DEFINITION OF A GEOMETRIC SEQUENCE

A sequence is **geometric** if the ratios of consecutive terms are the same. Thus, the sequence

$$a_1, a_2, a_3, a_4, \ldots, a_n, \ldots$$

is geometric if there is a number r, $r \neq 0$, such that

$$\frac{a_2}{a_1} = r, \qquad \frac{a_3}{a_2} = r, \qquad \frac{a_4}{a_3} = r,$$

and so on. The number r is the **common ratio** of the geometric sequence.

EXAMPLE 1   **Examples of Geometric Sequences**

A. The sequence whose nth term is 2^n is geometric. For this sequence, the common ratio between consecutive terms is 2.

$$\underbrace{2, 4, 8, 16, \ldots, 2^n, \ldots}$$

$$\frac{4}{2} = 2$$

B. The sequence whose nth term is $4(3^n)$ is geometric. For this sequence, the common ratio between consecutive terms is 3.

$$\underbrace{12, 36, 108, 324, \ldots, 4(3^n), \ldots}$$

$$\frac{36}{12} = 3$$

c. The sequence whose nth term is $\left(-\frac{1}{3}\right)^n$ is geometric. For this sequence, the common ratio between consecutive terms is $-\frac{1}{3}$.

$$-\frac{1}{3}, \frac{1}{9}, -\frac{1}{27}, \frac{1}{81}, \ldots, \left(-\frac{1}{3}\right)^n, \ldots$$

$$\frac{1/9}{-1/3} = -\frac{1}{3}$$

In Example 1, notice that each of the geometric sequences has an nth term that is of the form ar^n, where the common ratio of the sequence is r.

REMARK If you know the nth term of a geometric sequence, the $(n + 1)$th term can be found by multiplying by r. That is,

$$a_{n+1} = ra_n.$$

THE NTH TERM OF A GEOMETRIC SEQUENCE

The nth term of a geometric sequence has the form

$$a_n = a_1 r^{n-1},$$

where r is the common ratio of consecutive terms of the sequence. Thus, every geometric sequence can be written in the following form.

$$a_1, \quad a_2, \quad a_3, \quad a_4, \quad a_5, \quad \ldots, \quad a_n, \quad \ldots$$

$$\downarrow \quad \downarrow \quad \downarrow \quad \downarrow \quad \downarrow \quad \ldots, \quad \downarrow \quad \ldots$$

$$a_1, \quad a_1 r, \quad a_1 r^2, \quad a_1 r^3 \quad a_1 r^4, \quad \ldots, \quad a_1 r^{n-1}$$

EXAMPLE 2   Finding the Terms of a Geometric Sequence

Write the first five terms of the geometric sequence whose first term is $a_1 = 3$ and whose common ratio is $r = 2$.

SOLUTION

Starting with 3, repeatedly multiply by 2 to obtain the following.

$$a_1 = 3$$
$$a_2 = 3(2^1) = 6$$
$$a_3 = 3(2^2) = 12$$
$$a_4 = 3(2^3) = 24$$
$$a_5 = 3(2^4) = 48$$

EXAMPLE 3   Finding a Term of a Geometric Sequence

Find the 12th term of the geometric sequence 5, 15, 45, ...

SOLUTION

The common ratio of this sequence is $r = \frac{15}{5} = 3$. Therefore, because the first term is $a_1 = 5$, you can determine the 12th term ($n = 12$) to be

$$a_{12} = a_1 r^{n-1} = 5(3)^{11} = 5(177,147) = 885,735.$$

EXAMPLE 4   Finding a Term of a Geometric Sequence

Find the 15th term of the geometric sequence whose first term is 20 and whose common ratio is 1.05.

SOLUTION

You can obtain the 15th term by multiplying the first term by r 14 times. Thus, because $a_1 = 20$ and $r = 1.05$, the 15th term ($n = 15$) is

$$a_{15} = a_1 r^{n-1} = 20(1.05)^{14} \approx 39.599.$$

EXAMPLE 5   Finding a Term of a Geometric Sequence

The 4th term of a geometric sequence is 125, and the 10th term is $\frac{125}{64}$. Find the 14th term.

SOLUTION

To obtain the 10th term from the 4th term, you can multiply the 4th term by r^6. That is, $a_{10} = a_4 r^6$. Because $a_{10} = \frac{125}{64}$ and $a_4 = 125$, you obtain the following.

$$\frac{125}{64} = 125r^6$$

$$\frac{1}{64} = r^6$$

$$\frac{1}{2} = r$$

Now, you can obtain the 14th term by multiplying the 10th term by r^4. That is,

$$a_{14} = a_{10}r^4 = \frac{125}{64}\left(\frac{1}{2}\right)^4 = \frac{125}{1024}.$$

The Sum of a Finite Geometric Sequence

THE SUM OF A FINITE GEOMETRIC SEQUENCE

The sum of the finite geometric sequence

$$a_1,\ a_1 r,\ a_1 r^2,\ a_1 r^3,\ a_1 r^4,\ \ldots,\ a_1 r^{n-1}$$

with common ratio $r \neq 1$ is given by

$$S = a_1 \left(\frac{1 - r^n}{1 - r} \right).$$

EXAMPLE 6   **Finding the Sum of a Finite Geometric Sequence**

$$\sum_{n=1}^{8} (0.3)^n = (0.3) + (0.3)^2 + (0.3)^3 + \cdots + (0.3)^8$$

$$= a_1 \left(\frac{1 - r^n}{1 - r} \right)$$

$$= (0.3) \left(\frac{1 - (0.3)^8}{1 - 0.3} \right)$$

$$\approx 0.429$$

When using the formula for the sum of a finite geometric sequence, be careful to check that the index begins at $i = 1$. If the index begins at $i = 0$, you must adjust the formula for the nth partial sum, as demonstrated in the following example.

EXAMPLE 7   **Finding the Sum of a Finite Geometric Sequence**

Find the sum

$$\sum_{i=0}^{10} 10 \left(-\frac{1}{2} \right)^i.$$

SOLUTION

By writing out a few terms you have

$$\sum_{i=0}^{10} 10 \left(-\frac{1}{2} \right)^i = 10 - 10 \left(\frac{1}{2} \right) + 10 \left(\frac{1}{2} \right)^2 - \cdots + 10 \left(\frac{1}{2} \right)^{10}.$$

You can see that the *first* term is $a_1 = 10$ and $r = -\frac{1}{2}$. Moreover, by starting with $i = 0$ and ending with $i = 10$, you are adding $n = 11$ terms, which means that the sum is

$$\sum_{i=0}^{10} 10 \left(-\frac{1}{2} \right)^i = a_1 \left(\frac{1 - r^n}{1 - r} \right) = 10 \left(\frac{1 - (-\frac{1}{2})^{11}}{1 - (-\frac{1}{2})} \right) \approx 6.670.$$

The formula for the sum of a *finite* geometric sequence can, depending on the value of r, be extended to find the sum of an *infinite* geometric sequence. Specifically, if the common ratio r has the property that $|r| < 1$, then it can be shown that r^n becomes arbitrarily close to zero as n increases without bound. Consequently,

$$S \to a_1 \left(\frac{1 - 0}{1 - r} \right) = \frac{a_1}{1 - r} \quad \text{as} \quad n \to \infty.$$

SUM OF AN INFINITE GEOMETRIC SEQUENCE

If $|r| < 1$, then the infinite geometric sequence

$$a_1, a_1 r, a_1 r^2, a_1 r^3, \dots, a_1 r^{n-1}, \dots$$

has the sum

$$S = \sum_{n=1}^{\infty} a_1 r^{n-1} = \frac{a_1}{1 - r}.$$

REMARK   The summation $a_1 + a_1 r + a_1 r^2 + a_1 r^3 + \cdots$ is called an **infinite geometric series.**

EXAMPLE 8   Finding the Sum of an Infinite Geometric Sequence

Find the sum of the following infinite geometric sequence.

$$4, 4(0.6), 4(0.6)^2, 4(0.6)^3, \dots, 4(0.6)^{n-1}, \dots$$

SOLUTION

Because $a_1 = 4$, $r = 0.6$, and $|r| < 1$, you have

$$S = \sum_{n=1}^{\infty} 4(0.6)^{n-1}$$

$$= \frac{a_1}{1 - r}$$

$$= \frac{4}{1 - (0.6)}$$

$$= 10.$$

Figure 10.4 shows the graph of

$$f(x) = \frac{4}{1 - 0.6} - \frac{4(0.6)^x}{1 - 0.6} = 10 - 10(0.6)^x,$$

which has a horizontal asymptote of $y = 10$.

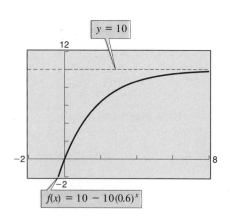

$y = 10$

$f(x) = 10 - 10(0.6)^x$

FIGURE 10.4

Application

EXAMPLE 9   An Application: Compound Interest

A deposit of $50 is made the first day of each month in a savings account that pays 12% compounded monthly. What is the balance at the end of 2 years?

SOLUTION

The formula for compound interest is

$$A = P\left(1 + \frac{r}{n}\right)^{tn},$$

where A is the balance of the account, P is the initial deposit, r is the annual percentage rate, n is the number of compoundings per year, and t is the time (in years). To find the balance in the account after 24 months, it is helpful to consider each of the 24 deposits separately. For example, the first deposit will gain interest for a full 24 months, and its balance will be

$$A_{24} = 50\left(1 + \frac{0.12}{12}\right)^{24} = 50(1.01)^{24}.$$

The second deposit will gain interest for 23 months, and its balance will be

$$A_{23} = 50\left(1 + \frac{0.12}{12}\right)^{23} = 50(1.01)^{23}.$$

The last (24th) deposit will gain interest for only 1 month, and its balance will be

REMARK This type of investment account is an *annuity*.

$$A_1 = 50\left(1 + \frac{0.12}{12}\right)^{1} = 50(1.01).$$

Finally, the total balance in the account will be the sum of the balances of the 24 deposits.

$$S = A_1 + A_2 + A_3 + \cdots + A_{23} + A_{24}$$
$$= 50(1.01) + 50(1.01)^2 + \cdots + 50(1.01)^{23} + 50(1.01)^{24}$$

Using the formula for the sum of a geometric sequence, with $A_1 = 50(1.01)$ and $r = 1.01$, you have

$$S = 50(1.01)\left(\frac{1 - (1.01)^{24}}{1 - 1.01}\right) = \$1362.16.$$

DISCUSSION PROBLEM

COMPARING TWO SEQUENCES

The first several terms of the sequences whose nth terms are $a_n = (0.99)^{n-1}$ and $b_n = 1 - (n - 1)(0.01)$ are almost the same.

(a) $a_1 = 1$
$a_2 = 0.99$
$a_3 = (0.99)^2 \approx 0.98$
$a_4 = (0.99)^3 \approx 0.97$
$a_5 = (0.99)^4 \approx 0.96$

(b) $b_1 = 1$
$b_2 = 1 - 0.01 = 0.99$
$b_3 = 1 - 2(0.01) = 0.98$
$b_4 = 1 - 3(0.01) = 0.97$
$b_5 = 1 - 4(0.01) = 0.96$

Yet the two sequences have very basic differences. Write a paragraph describing some of the differences between the two sequences.

WARM-UP

The following warm-up exercises involve skills that were covered in earlier sections. You will use these skills in the exercise set for this section.

In Exercises 1–4, evaluate the expression.

1. $\left(\frac{4}{5}\right)^3$ **2.** $\left(\frac{3}{4}\right)^2$

3. 2^{-4} **4.** $\dfrac{5}{3^4}$

In Exercises 5–10, simplify the expression.

5. $(2n)(3n^2)$ **6.** $n(3n)^3$

7. $\dfrac{4n^5}{n^2}$ **8.** $\dfrac{(2n)^3}{8n}$

9. $[2(3)^{-4}]^n$ **10.** $3(4^2)^{-n}$

SECTION 10.3 · EXERCISES

In Exercises 1–10, determine whether the sequence is geometric. If it is, find its common ratio.

1. 5, 15, 45, 135, . . .   **2.** 3, 12, 48, 192, . . .

3. 3, 12, 21, 30, . . .   **4.** 1, −2, 4, −8, . . .

5. $1, -\frac{1}{2}, \frac{1}{4}, -\frac{1}{8}, \ldots$ **6.** 5, 1, 0.2, 0.04, . . .

7. $\frac{1}{2}, \frac{2}{3}, \frac{3}{4}, \frac{4}{5}, \ldots$ **8.** $9, -6, 4, -\frac{8}{3}, \ldots$

9. $1, \frac{1}{2}, \frac{1}{3}, \frac{1}{4}, \ldots$ **10.** $\frac{1}{5}, \frac{2}{3}, \frac{3}{9}, \frac{4}{11}, \ldots$

In Exercises 11–20, write the first five terms of the geometric sequence.

11. $a_1 = 2, r = 3$ **12.** $a_1 = 6, r = 2$

13. $a_1 = 1, r = \frac{1}{2}$ **14.** $a_1 = 1, r = \frac{1}{3}$

15. $a_1 = 5, r = -\frac{1}{10}$ **16.** $a_1 = 6, r = -\frac{1}{4}$

17. $a_1 = 1, r = e$ **18.** $a_1 = 2, r = \sqrt{3}$

19. $a_1 = 3, r = \dfrac{x}{2}$ **20.** $a_1 = 5, r = 2x$

In Exercises 21–32, find the nth term of the geometric sequence.

21. $a_1 = 4$, $r = \frac{1}{2}$, $n = 10$

22. $a_1 = 5$, $r = \frac{3}{2}$, $n = 8$

23. $a_1 = 6$, $r = -\frac{1}{3}$, $n = 12$

24. $a_1 = 8$, $r = \sqrt{5}$, $n = 9$

25. $a_1 = 100$, $r = e^x$, $n = 9$

26. $a_1 = 1$, $r = -\dfrac{x}{3}$, $n = 7$

27. $a_1 = 500$, $r = 1.02$, $n = 40$

28. $a_1 = 1000$, $r = 1.005$, $n = 60$

29. $a_1 = 16$, $a_4 = \frac{27}{4}$, $n = 3$

30. $a_2 = 3$, $a_5 = \frac{3}{64}$, $n = 1$

31. $a_2 = -18$, $a_5 = \frac{2}{3}$, $n = 6$

32. $a_3 = \frac{16}{3}$, $a_5 = \frac{64}{27}$, $n = 7$

33. *Compound Interest*   A principal of $1000 is invested at 10% interest. Find the amount after 10 years if the interest is compounded (a) annually, (b) semiannually, (c) quarterly, (d) monthly, and (e) daily.

34. *Compound Interest*   A principal of $2500 is invested at 12% interest. Find the amount after 20 years if the interest is compounded (a) annually, (b) semiannually, (c) quarterly, (d) monthly, and (e) daily.

35. *Depreciation*   A company buys a machine for $135,000 that depreciates at the rate of 30% per year. (In other words, at the end of each year the depreciated value is 70% of what it was at the beginning of the year). Find the depreciated value of the machine after 5 full years.

36. *Population Growth*   A city of 250,000 people is growing at the rate of 1.3% per year. Estimate the population of the city 30 years from now.

In Exercises 37–46, find the indicated sum.

37. $\displaystyle\sum_{n=1}^{9} 2^{n-1}$

38. $\displaystyle\sum_{n=1}^{9} (-2)^{n-1}$

39. $\displaystyle\sum_{i=1}^{7} 64(-\tfrac{1}{2})^{i-1}$

40. $\displaystyle\sum_{i=1}^{6} 32(\tfrac{1}{4})^{i-1}$

41. $\displaystyle\sum_{i=1}^{10} 8(\tfrac{-1}{4})^{i-1}$

42. $\displaystyle\sum_{i=1}^{10} 5(\tfrac{-1}{3})^{i-1}$

43. $\displaystyle\sum_{n=0}^{20} 3(\tfrac{3}{2})^{n}$

44. $\displaystyle\sum_{n=0}^{15} 2(\tfrac{4}{3})^{n}$

45. $\displaystyle\sum_{n=0}^{5} 300(1.06)^{n}$

46. $\displaystyle\sum_{n=0}^{6} 500(1.04)^{n}$

47. *Annuities*   A deposit of $100 is made at the beginning of each month for 5 years in an account that pays 10%, compounded monthly. What is the balance A in the account at the end of 5 years?

$$A = 100\left(1 + \frac{0.10}{12}\right)^{1} + \cdots + 100\left(1 + \frac{0.10}{12}\right)^{60}$$

48. *Annuities*   A deposit of $50 is made at the beginning of each month for 5 years in an account that pays 12%, compounded monthly. What is the balance A in the account at the end of 5 years?

$$A = 50\left(1 + \frac{0.12}{12}\right)^{1} + \cdots + 50\left(1 + \frac{0.12}{12}\right)^{60}$$

49. *Annuities*   A deposit of P dollars is made at the beginning of each month in an account at an annual interest rate r, compounded monthly. The balance A after t years is

$$A = P\left(1 + \frac{r}{12}\right) + P\left(1 + \frac{r}{12}\right)^{2} + \cdots$$
$$+ P\left(1 + \frac{r}{12}\right)^{12t}.$$

Show that the balance is given by

$$A = P\left[\left(1 + \frac{r}{12}\right)^{12t} - 1\right]\left(1 + \frac{12}{r}\right).$$

50. *Annuities*   A deposit of P dollars is made at the beginning of each month in an account at an annual interest rate r, compounded continuously. The balance A after t years is

$$A = Pe^{r/12} + Pe^{2r/12} + \cdots + Pe^{12tr/12}.$$

Show that the balance is given by

$$A = \frac{Pe^{r/12}(e^{rt} - 1)}{e^{r/12} - 1}.$$

Annuities   In Exercises 51–54, consider making monthly deposits of P dollars into a savings account at an annual interest rate r. Use the results of Exercises 49 and 50 to find the balance A after t years if the interest is compounded (a) monthly and (b) continuously.

51. $P = \$50$, $r = 7\%$, $t = 20$ years

52. $P = \$75$, $r = 9\%$, $t = 25$ years

53. $P = \$100$, $r = 10\%$, $t = 40$ years

54. $P = \$20$, $r = 6\%$, $t = 50$ years

55. *Annuities*   Consider an initial deposit of P dollars into an account at an annual interest rate r, compounded monthly. At the end of each month a withdrawal of W dollars will occur and the account will be depleted in t years. The magnitude of the initial deposit is given by

$$P = W\left(1 + \frac{r}{12}\right)^{-1} + W\left(1 + \frac{r}{12}\right)^{-2} + \cdots$$
$$+ W\left(1 + \frac{r}{12}\right)^{-12t}.$$

Show that the initial deposit is given by

$$P = W\left(\frac{12}{r}\right)\left[1 - \left(1 + \frac{r}{12}\right)^{-12t}\right].$$

56. *Annuities*   Determine the amount that is required in an individual retirement account for an individual that retires at age 65 and wants an income from the account of $2000 per month for 20 years. Use the result of Exercise 55 and assume the account earns 9% compounded monthly.

57. *Profit*   The annual profit for the H. J. Heinz Company from 1980 through 1989 can be approximated by the model

$$a_n = 167.5e^{0.12n}, \qquad n = 0, 1, 2, \ldots, 9,$$

where a_n is the annual profit in millions of dollars and n represents the year, with $n = 0$ corresponding to 1980 (see figure). Use the formula for the sum of a geometric sequence to approximate the total profit earned during this 10-year period. (*Source:* H. J. Heinz Company)

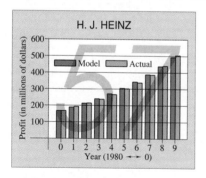

H. J. HEINZ

FIGURE FOR 57

58. *Would You Take This Job?*   Suppose you went to work at a company that pays $0.01 for the first day, $0.02 for the second day, $0.04 for the third day, and so on. If the daily wage keeps doubling, determine what your total income would be for working (a) 29 days, (b) 30 days, and (c) 31 days.

59. *Salary*   You accept a job with a salary of $30,000 for the first year. Suppose that during the next 39 years, you receive a 5% raise each year. What would be your total compensation over the 40-year period?

60. *Area*   The sides of a square are 16 inches in length. The square is divided into nine smaller squares and the center square is shaded (see figure). Each of the eight unshaded squares is then divided into nine smaller squares and the center square of each is shaded. If this process is repeated four more times, determine the area of the shaded region.

FIGURE FOR 60

In Exercises 61–70, find the sum of the infinite geometric series.

61. $\displaystyle\sum_{n=0}^{\infty} (\tfrac{1}{2})^n = 1 + \tfrac{1}{2} + \tfrac{1}{4} + \tfrac{1}{8} + \cdots$

62. $\displaystyle\sum_{n=0}^{\infty} 2(\tfrac{2}{3})^n = 2 + \tfrac{4}{3} + \tfrac{8}{9} + \tfrac{16}{27} + \cdots$

63. $\displaystyle\sum_{n=0}^{\infty} (-\tfrac{1}{2})^n = 1 - \tfrac{1}{2} + \tfrac{1}{4} - \tfrac{1}{8} + \cdots$

64. $\displaystyle\sum_{n=0}^{\infty} 2(-\tfrac{2}{3})^n = 2 - \tfrac{4}{3} + \tfrac{8}{9} - \tfrac{16}{27} + \cdots$

65. $\displaystyle\sum_{n=0}^{\infty} 4(\tfrac{1}{4})^n = 4 + 1 + \tfrac{1}{4} + \tfrac{1}{16} + \cdots$

66. $\displaystyle\sum_{n=0}^{\infty} (\tfrac{1}{10})^n = 1 + 0.1 + 0.01 + 0.001 + \cdots$

67. $8 + 6 + \tfrac{9}{2} + \tfrac{27}{8} + \cdots$

68. $3 - 1 + \tfrac{1}{3} - \tfrac{1}{9} + \cdots$

69. $4 - 2 + 1 - \tfrac{1}{2} + \cdots$

70. $2 + \sqrt{2} + 1 + \dfrac{1}{\sqrt{2}} + \cdots$

In Exercises 71 and 72, use a graphing utility to graph the function. Identify the horizontal asymptote of the graph and determine its relationship to the given series.

Function	*Series*
71. $f(x) = 6\left[\dfrac{1 - (0.5)^x}{1 - (0.5)}\right]$	$\displaystyle\sum_{n=0}^{\infty} 6\left(\tfrac{1}{2}\right)^n$
72. $f(x) = 2\left[\dfrac{1 - (0.8)^x}{1 - (0.8)}\right]$	$\displaystyle\sum_{n=0}^{\infty} 2\left(\tfrac{4}{5}\right)^n$

73. *Distance*   A ball is dropped from a height of 16 feet. Each time it drops h feet, it rebounds $0.81h$ feet. Find the total distance traveled by the ball.

74. *Time* The ball in Exercise 73 takes the following times for each fall.

$$s_1 = -16t^2 + 16, \qquad s_1 = 0 \text{ if } t = 1$$
$$s_2 = -16t^2 + 16(0.81), \qquad s_2 = 0 \text{ if } t = 0.9$$
$$s_3 = -16t^2 + 16(0.81)^2, \qquad s_3 = 0 \text{ if } t = (0.9)^2$$
$$s_4 = -16t^2 + 16(0.81)^3, \qquad s_4 = 0 \text{ if } t = (0.9)^3$$
$$\vdots \qquad\qquad\qquad \vdots$$
$$s_n = -16t^2 + 16(0.81)^{n-1}, \qquad s_n = 0 \text{ if } t = (0.9)^{n-1}$$

Beginning with s_2, the ball takes the same amount of time to bounce up as it does to fall, and thus the total time elapsed before it comes to rest is

$$t = 1 + 2 \sum_{n=1}^{\infty} (0.9)^n.$$

Find this total.

10.4 MATHEMATICAL INDUCTION
....

Mathematical Induction / Sums of Powers of Integers / Pattern Recognition / Finite Differences

Mathematical Induction

In this section you will study a form of mathematical proof, called the principle of **mathematical induction.** It is important that you clearly see the logical need for it, so let's take a closer took at a problem that was discussed earlier.

$$S_1 = 1 = 1^2$$
$$S_2 = 1 + 3 = 2^2$$
$$S_3 = 1 + 3 + 5 = 3^2$$
$$S_4 = 1 + 3 + 5 + 7 = 4^2$$
$$S_5 = 1 + 3 + 5 + 7 + 9 = 5^2$$

Judging from the pattern formed by these first five sums, it appears that the sum of the first n odd integers is

$$S_n = 1 + 3 + 5 + 7 + 9 + \cdots + (2n - 1) = n^2.$$

Although this particular formula is valid, it is important for you to see that recognizing a pattern and then simply *jumping to the conclusion* that the pattern must be true for all values of n is *not* a logically valid method of proof. There are many examples in which a pattern appears to be developing for small values of n and then at some point the pattern fails. One of the most famous cases of this was the conjecture by the French mathematician Pierre de Fermat (1601–1655), who speculated that all numbers of the form

$$F_n = 2^{2^n} + 1, \qquad n = 0, 1, 2, \ldots$$

are prime. For $n = 0, 1, 2, 3,$ and 4, the conjecture is true.

$$F_0 = 3, \ F_1 = 5, \ F_2 = 17, \ F_3 = 257, \ F_4 = 65{,}537$$

The size of the next Fermat number ($F_5 = 4{,}294{,}967{,}297$) is so great that it was difficult for Fermat to determine whether it was prime or not. However, another well-known mathematician, Leonhard Euler (1707–1783), later found the factorization

$$F_5 = 4{,}294{,}967{,}297 = 641(6{,}700{,}417),$$

which proved that F_5 is not prime, and therefore Fermat's conjecture was false.

Just because a rule, pattern, or formula seems to work for several values of n, you cannot simply decide that it is valid for all values of n without going through a *legitimate proof*.

THE PRINCIPLE OF MATHEMATICAL INDUCTION

REMARK   It is important to recognize that both parts of the Principle of Mathematical Induction are necessary.

Let P_n be a statement involving the positive integer n. If

1. P_1 is true, and
2. the truth of P_k implies the truth of P_{k+1}, for every positive integer k,

then P_n must be true for all positive integers n.

To apply the Principle of Mathematical Induction, you need to be able to determine the statement P_{k+1} for a given statement P_k.

EXAMPLE 1   A Preliminary Example

Determine the statement P_{k+1} for each of the following statements P_k.

A. P_k is the statement: $S_k = \dfrac{k^2(k+1)^2}{4}$.

B. P_k is the statement:

$$S_k = 1 + 5 + 9 + \cdots + [4(k-1) - 3] + (4k - 3).$$

C. P_k is the statement: $3^k \geq 2k + 1$.

SOLUTION

A. Substituting $k + 1$ for k, you obtain the statement P_{k+1}.

$$P_{k+1}: \quad S_{k+1} = \frac{(k+1)^2(k+1+1)^2}{4} \quad \text{\textit{Replace k by k + 1}}$$

$$= \frac{(k+1)^2(k+2)^2}{4} \quad \text{\textit{Simplify}}$$

B. In this case you have

$$P_{k+1}: \quad S_{k+1} = 1 + 5 + 9 + \cdots + (4[(k+1)-1]-3)$$
$$+ [4(k+1)-3]$$
$$= 1 + 5 + 9 + \cdots + (4k-3) + (4k+1).$$

C. Replacing k by $k+1$ in the statement $3^k \geq 2k+1$, you have

$$P_{k+1}: \quad 3^{k+1} \geq 2(k+1)+1$$
$$3^{k+1} \geq 2k+3.$$

EXAMPLE 2 Using Mathematical Induction

Use mathematical induction to prove the following formula.

$$S_n = 1 + 3 + 5 + 7 + \cdots + (2n-1) = n^2$$

SOLUTION

Mathematical induction consists of two distinct parts. First, you must show that the formula is true when $n = 1$.

REMARK When using mathematical induction to prove a *summation* formula (like the one in Example 2), it is helpful to think of S_{k+1} as $S_{k+1} = S_k + a_{k+1}$, where a_{k+1} is the $(k+1)$th term of the original sum.

1. When $n = 1$, the formula is valid, because

$$S_1 = 1 = 1^2.$$

The second part of mathematical induction has two steps. The first step is to assume that the formula is valid for *some* integer k. The second step is to use this assumption to prove that the formula is valid for the next integer, $k + 1$.

2. Assuming that the formula

$$S_k = 1 + 3 + 5 + 7 + \cdots + (2k-1) = k^2$$

is true, you must show that the formula $S_{k+1} = (k+1)^2$ is true.

$$S_{k+1} = 1 + 3 + 5 + 7 + \cdots + (2k-1) + [2(k+1)-1]$$
$$= [1 + 3 + 5 + 7 + \cdots + (2k-1)] + (2k+2-1)$$
$$= S_k + (2k+1)$$
$$= k^2 + 2k + 1 \qquad \textit{Because } S_k = k^2 \textit{ from above}$$
$$= (k+1)^2$$

Combining the results of parts (1) and (2), you can conclude by mathematical induction that the formula is valid for *all* positive integer values of n.

A well-known illustration used to explain why the principle of mathematical induction works is the unending line of dominoes shown in Figure 10.5. If the line actually contains infinitely many dominoes, then it is clear that you could not knock the entire line down by knocking down only *one domino* at a time. However, suppose it were true that each domino would knock down the next one as it fell. Then you could knock them all down simply by pushing the first one and starting a chain reaction. Mathematical induction works in the same way. If the truth of P_k implies the truth of P_{k+1} and if P_1 is true, then the chain reaction proceeds as follows:

P_1 implies P_2

P_2 implies P_3

P_3 implies P_4

and so on.

The first domino knocks over the second which knocks over
the third which knocks over the fourth and so on.

FIGURE 10.5

It occasionally happens that a statement involving natural numbers is not true for the first $k - 1$ positive integers but is true for all values of $n \geq k$. In these instances, you can use a slight variation of the principle of mathematical induction in which you verify P_k rather than P_1. This variation is called the **extended principle of mathematical induction.** To see the validity of this, note from Figure 10.5 that all but the first $k - 1$ dominoes can be knocked down by knocking over the kth domino. This suggests that you can prove a statement P_n to be true for $n \geq k$ by showing that P_k is true and that P_k implies P_{k+1}.

EXAMPLE 3   Using Mathematical Induction

Use mathematical induction to prove the following formula.

$$S_n = 1^2 + 2^2 + 3^2 + 4^2 + \cdots + n^2 = \frac{n(n + 1)(2n + 1)}{6}$$

SOLUTION

1. When $n = 1$, the formula is valid, because

$$S_1 = 1^2 = \frac{1(1 + 1)(2(1) + 1)}{6} = \frac{1(2)(3)}{6}.$$

2. Assuming that

$$S_k = 1^2 + 2^2 + 3^2 + 4^2 + \cdots + k^2 = \frac{k(k + 1)(2k + 1)}{6},$$

you must show that

$$S_{k+1} = \frac{(k + 1)(k + 2)(2k + 3)}{6}.$$

To do this, write the following.

$$
\begin{aligned}
S_{k+1} &= S_k + a_{k+1} \\
&= (1^2 + 2^2 + 3^2 + 4^2 + \cdots + k^2) + (k + 1)^2 \\
&= \frac{k(k + 1)(2k + 1)}{6} + (k + 1)^2 \qquad \textit{By assumption} \\
&= \frac{k(k + 1)(2k + 1) + 6(k + 1)^2}{6} \\
&= \frac{(k + 1)[k(2k + 1) + 6(k + 1)]}{6} \\
&= \frac{(k + 1)(2k^2 + 7k + 6)}{6} \\
&= \frac{(k + 1)(k + 2)(2k + 3)}{6}
\end{aligned}
$$

Combining the results of parts (1) and (2), you can conclude by mathematical induction that the formula is valid for *all n* ≥ 1.

Sums of Powers of Integers

The formula in Example 3 is one of a collection of useful summation formulas.

SUMS OF POWERS OF INTEGERS

1. $\displaystyle\sum_{i=1}^{n} i = 1 + 2 + 3 + 4 + \cdots + n = \frac{n(n+1)}{2}$.

2. $\displaystyle\sum_{i=1}^{n} i^2 = 1^2 + 2^2 + 3^2 + 4^2 + \cdots + n^2 = \frac{n(n+1)(2n+1)}{6}$

3. $\displaystyle\sum_{i=1}^{n} i^3 = 1^3 + 2^3 + 3^3 + 4^3 + \cdots + n^3 = \frac{n^2(n+1)^2}{4}$

4. $\displaystyle\sum_{i=1}^{n} i^4 = 1^4 + 2^4 + 3^4 + 4^4 + \cdots + n^4$

$$= \frac{n(n+1)(2n+1)(3n^2+3n-1)}{30}$$

5. $\displaystyle\sum_{i=1}^{n} i^5 = 1^5 + 2^5 + 3^5 + 4^5 + \cdots + n^5$

$$= \frac{n^2(n+1)^2(2n^2+2n-1)}{12}$$

EXAMPLE 4   Finding a Sum of Powers of Integers

Find the following sum.

$$1^3 + 2^3 + 3^3 + 4^3 + 5^3 + 6^3 + 7^3$$

SOLUTION

Using the formula for the sum of the cubes of the first n positive integers produces the following.

$$1^3 + 2^3 + 3^3 + 4^3 + 5^3 + 6^3 + 7^3 = \frac{7^2(7+1)^2}{4}$$

$$= \frac{49(64)}{4}$$

$$= 784$$

Check this sum by adding the numbers 1, 8, 27, 64, 125, 216, and 343.

Pattern Recognition

Although choosing a formula on the basis of a few observations does *not* guarantee the validity of the formula, pattern recognition *is* important. Once you have a pattern or formula that you think works, you can try using mathematical induction to prove your formula.

FINDING A FORMULA FOR THE *N*TH TERM OF A SEQUENCE

1. Calculate the first several terms of the sequence. (It is often a good idea to write the terms in both simplified and factored form.)
2. Try to find a recognizable pattern from these terms, and write down a formula for the *n*th term of the sequence. (This is your hypothesis. You might try computing one or two more terms in the sequence to test your hypothesis.)
3. Use mathematical induction to attempt to prove your hypothesis.

EXAMPLE 5   Finding a Formula for a Finite Sum

Find a formula for the following finite sum.

$$\frac{1}{1 \cdot 2} + \frac{1}{2 \cdot 3} + \frac{1}{3 \cdot 4} + \frac{1}{4 \cdot 5} + \cdots + \frac{1}{n(n+1)}$$

SOLUTION

Begin by writing out the sums of the first few terms.

$$S_1 = \frac{1}{1 \cdot 2} = \frac{1}{2} = \frac{1}{1+1}$$

$$S_2 = \frac{1}{1 \cdot 2} + \frac{1}{2 \cdot 3} = \frac{4}{6} = \frac{2}{3} = \frac{2}{2+1}$$

$$S_3 = \frac{1}{1 \cdot 2} + \frac{1}{2 \cdot 3} + \frac{1}{3 \cdot 4} = \frac{9}{12} = \frac{3}{4} = \frac{3}{3+1}$$

$$S_4 = \frac{1}{1 \cdot 2} + \frac{1}{2 \cdot 3} + \frac{1}{3 \cdot 4} + \frac{1}{4 \cdot 5} = \frac{48}{60} = \frac{4}{5} = \frac{4}{4+1}$$

Now, from this sequence of four sums, it appears that the formula for the *k*th sum is

$$S_k = \frac{1}{1 \cdot 2} + \frac{1}{2 \cdot 3} + \frac{1}{3 \cdot 4} + \frac{1}{4 \cdot 5} + \cdots + \frac{1}{k(k+1)} = \frac{k}{k+1}.$$

To prove the validity of this formula, use mathematical induction, as follows. Note that you have already verified the formula for $n = 1$, so you can begin by assuming that the formula is valid for $n = k$ and try to show that it is valid for $n = k + 1$.

$$S_{k+1} = \left[\frac{1}{1 \cdot 2} + \frac{1}{2 \cdot 3} + \frac{1}{3 \cdot 4} + \cdots + \frac{1}{k(k+1)} \right] + \frac{1}{(k+1)(k+2)}$$

$$= \frac{k}{k+1} + \frac{1}{(k+1)(k+2)} \qquad \textit{By assumption}$$

$$= \frac{k(k+2)+1}{(k+1)(k+2)}$$

$$= \frac{k^2+2k+1}{(k+1)(k+2)}$$

$$= \frac{(k+1)^2}{(k+1)(k+2)}$$

$$= \frac{k+1}{k+2}$$

Thus, the formula is valid.

EXAMPLE 6   Proving an Inequality by Mathematical Induction

Prove that $n < 2^n$ for all positive integers n.

SOLUTION

1. For $n = 1$, the formula is true, because

    $1 < 2^1$.

2. Assuming that

    $k < 2^k$,

    you need to show that $k + 1 < 2^{k+1}$. You have

    $$2^{k+1} = 2(2^k) > 2(k) = 2k. \qquad \textit{By assumption}$$

    Because $2k = k + k > k + 1$ for all $k > 1$, it follows that

    $$2^{k+1} > 2k > k + 1$$

    or

    $k + 1 < 2^{k+1}$.

Hence, $n < 2^n$ for all integers $n \geq 1$.

Finite Differences

The **first differences** of a sequence are found by subtracting consecutive terms. The **second differences** are found by subtracting consecutive first differences. The first and second differences of the sequence 3, 5, 8, 12, 17, 23, . . . , are as follows.

For this sequence, the second differences are all the same number. When this happens, the sequence has a quadratic model. (If the first differences are all the same number, then the sequence has a linear model. That is, it is arithmetic.)

EXAMPLE 7   Finding a Quadratic Model

Find a quadratic model for the sequence whose first three terms are 3, 5, and 8.

SOLUTION

You know the model has the form

$$f(n) = an^2 + bn + c.$$

By substituting 1, 2, and 3 for n, you can obtain a system of three linear equations in three variables.

$f(1) = a(1^2) + b(1) + c = 3$	*Substitute 1 for n*
$f(2) = a(2^2) + b(2) + c = 5$	*Substitute 2 for n*
$f(3) = a(3^2) + b(3) + c = 8$	*Substitute 3 for n*

You now have a system of three equations in a, b, and c.

$a + b + c = 3$	*Equation 1*
$4a + 2b + c = 5$	*Equation 2*
$9a + 3b + c = 8$	*Equation 3*

Using the techniques discussed in Chapter 9, you can find the solution to be $a = \frac{1}{2}$, $b = \frac{1}{2}$, and $c = 2$. Thus, a quadratic model is

$$f(n) = \frac{1}{2}n^2 + \frac{1}{2}n + 2.$$

Try checking the values of $f(1)$, $f(2)$, and $f(3)$.

Notice that we used the fact that the second diferences are all the same to conclude that the function in Example 7 *has* a quadratic model. To *find* the model, we used the first three values of the function to create a system of three linear equations.

DISCUSSION
PROBLEM
....
THE SUM OF
THE ANGLES
OF A REGULAR
POLYGON

A *regular n*-sided polygon is a polygon that has *n* equal sides and *n* equal angles. For instance, an equilateral triangle is a regular three-sided polygon. Each angle of an equilateral triangle measures 60° and the sum of all three angles is 180°. Similarly, the sum of the four angles of a regular four-sided polygon (a square) is 360°. From the following four regular polygons (see figure), find a formula for the sum of the angles of a regular *n*-sided polygon. Write a paragraph describing how you could *prove* that your formula is valid. Do you think that mathematical induction would be an appropriate technique to prove the validity of your formula?

(a) Equilateral   (b) Square   (c) Regular   (d) Regular
    Triangle   (360°)   Pentagon   Hexagon
    (180°)   (540°)   (720°)

WARM-UP
....

The following warm-up exercises involve skills that were covered in earlier sections. You will use these skills in the exercise set for this section.

In Exercises 1–4, find the required sum.

1. $\displaystyle\sum_{k=3}^{6} (2k - 3)$ **2.** $\displaystyle\sum_{j=1}^{5} (j^2 - j)$

3. $\displaystyle\sum_{k=2}^{5} \frac{1}{k}$ **4.** $\displaystyle\sum_{i=1}^{2} \left(1 + \frac{1}{i}\right)$

In Exercises 5–10, simplify the expression.

5. $\dfrac{2(k + 1) + 3}{5}$ **6.** $\dfrac{3(k + 1) - 2}{6}$

7. $2 \cdot 2^{2(k+1)}$ **8.** $\dfrac{3^{2k}}{3^{2(k+1)}}$

9. $\dfrac{k + 1}{k^2 + k}$ **10.** $\dfrac{\sqrt{32}}{\sqrt{50}}$

SECTION 10.4 · EXERCISES

In Exercises 1–4, find P_{k+1} for the given P_k.

1. $P_k = \dfrac{5}{k(k+1)}$

2. $P_k = \dfrac{1}{(k+1)(k+3)}$

3. $P_k = \dfrac{k^2(k+1)^2}{4}$

4. $P_k = \dfrac{k}{2}(3k-1)$

In Exercises 5–18, use mathematical induction to prove the given formula for every positive integer n.

5. $2 + 4 + 6 + 8 + \cdots + 2n = n(n+1)$

6. $3 + 7 + 11 + 15 + \cdots + (4n-1) = n(2n+1)$

7. $2 + 7 + 12 + 17 + \cdots + (5n-3) = \dfrac{n}{2}(5n-1)$

8. $1 + 4 + 7 + 10 + \cdots + (3n-2) = \dfrac{n}{2}(3n-1)$

9. $1 + 2 + 2^2 + 2^3 + \cdots + 2^{n-1} = 2^n - 1$

10. $2(1 + 3 + 3^2 + 3^3 + \cdots + 3^{n-1}) = 3^n - 1$

11. $1 + 2 + 3 + 4 + \cdots + n = \dfrac{n(n+1)}{2}$

12. $1^2 + 2^2 + 3^2 + 4^2 + \cdots + n^2 = \dfrac{n(n+1)(2n+1)}{6}$

13. $1^3 + 2^3 + 3^3 + 4^3 + \cdots + n^3 = \dfrac{n^2(n+1)^2}{4}$

14. $\left(1 + \dfrac{1}{1}\right)\left(1 + \dfrac{1}{2}\right)\left(1 + \dfrac{1}{3}\right)\cdots\left(1 + \dfrac{1}{n}\right) = n+1$

15. $\displaystyle\sum_{i=1}^{n} i^5 = \dfrac{n^2(n+1)^2(2n^2+2n-1)}{12}$

16. $\displaystyle\sum_{i=1}^{n} i^4 = \dfrac{n(n+1)(2n+1)(3n^2+3n-1)}{30}$

17. $\displaystyle\sum_{i=1}^{n} i(i+1) = \dfrac{n(n+1)(n+2)}{3}$

18. $\displaystyle\sum_{i=1}^{n} \dfrac{1}{(2i-1)(2i+1)} = \dfrac{n}{2n+1}$

In Exercises 19–28, find the indicated sum using the formulas for the sums of powers of integers.

19. $\displaystyle\sum_{n=1}^{20} n$

20. $\displaystyle\sum_{n=1}^{50} n$

21. $\displaystyle\sum_{n=1}^{6} n^2$

22. $\displaystyle\sum_{n=1}^{10} n^2$

23. $\displaystyle\sum_{n=1}^{5} n^3$

24. $\displaystyle\sum_{n=1}^{8} n^3$

25. $\displaystyle\sum_{n=1}^{6} n^4$

26. $\displaystyle\sum_{n=1}^{4} n^5$

27. $\displaystyle\sum_{n=1}^{6} (n^2 - n)$

28. $\displaystyle\sum_{n=1}^{10} (n^3 - n^2)$

In Exercises 29–34, find a formula for the sum of the first n terms of the sequence.

29. $3, 7, 11, 15, \ldots$

30. $25, 22, 19, 16, \ldots$

31. $1, \dfrac{9}{10}, \dfrac{81}{100}, \dfrac{729}{1000}, \ldots$

32. $3, -\dfrac{9}{2}, \dfrac{27}{4}, -\dfrac{81}{8}, \ldots$

33. $\dfrac{1}{4}, \dfrac{1}{12}, \dfrac{1}{24}, \dfrac{1}{40}, \ldots, \dfrac{1}{2n(n-1)}, \ldots$

34. $\dfrac{1}{2\cdot3}, \dfrac{1}{3\cdot4}, \dfrac{1}{4\cdot5}, \dfrac{1}{5\cdot6}, \ldots, \dfrac{1}{(n+1)(n+2)}, \ldots$

In Exercises 35–38, use mathematical induction to prove the given inequality for the indicated integer values of n.

35. $\left(\dfrac{4}{3}\right)^n > n, \quad n \geq 7$

36. $\dfrac{1}{\sqrt{1}} + \dfrac{1}{\sqrt{2}} + \dfrac{1}{\sqrt{3}} + \cdots + \dfrac{1}{\sqrt{n}} > \sqrt{n}, \quad n \geq 2$

37. $n! > 2^n, \quad n \geq 4$

38. $\left(\dfrac{x}{y}\right)^{n+1} < \left(\dfrac{x}{y}\right)^{n}, \quad$ if $n \geq 1$ and $0 < x < y$.

In Exercises 39–46, use mathematical induction to prove the given property for all positive integers n.

39. $(ab)^n = a^n b^n$

40. $\left(\dfrac{a}{b}\right)^n = \dfrac{a^n}{b^n}$

41. If $x_1 \neq 0$, $x_2 \neq 0, \ldots, x_n \neq 0$, then
$(x_1 x_2 x_3 \ldots x_n)^{-1} = x_1^{-1} x_2^{-1} x_3^{-1} \ldots x_n^{-1}$.

42. If $x_1 > 0$, $x_2 > 0, \ldots, x_n > 0$, then
$\ln (x_1 x_2 x_3 \ldots x_n) = \ln x_1 + \ln x_2 + \cdots + \ln x_n$.

43. Generalized Distributive Law:
$$x(y_1 + y_2 + \cdots + y_n) = xy_1 + xy_2 + \cdots + xy_n$$

44. $(a + bi)^n$ and $(a - bi)^n$ are complex conjugates for all $n \geq 1$.

45. A factor of $(n^3 + 3n^2 + 2n)$ is 3

46. A factor of $(2^{2n-1} + 3^{2n-1})$ is 5

In Exercises 47–50, write the first five terms of the sequence.

47. $a_0 = 1$
$a_n = a_{n-1} + 2$

48. $a_1 = 10$
$a_n = 4a_{n-1}$

49. $a_0 = 4$
$a_1 = 2$
$a_n = a_{n-1} - a_{n-2}$

50. $a_0 = 0$
$a_1 = 2$
$a_n = a_{n-1} + 2a_{n-2}$

In Exercises 51–60, write the first five terms of the sequence. Then calculate the first and second differences of the sequence. Does the sequence have a linear or quadratic model?

51. $f(1) = 0$
$a_n = a_{n-1} + 3$

52. $f(1) = 2$
$a_n = n - a_{n-1}$

53. $f(1) = 3$
$a_n = a_{n-1} - n$

54. $f(2) = -3$
$a_n = -2a_{n-1}$

55. $a_0 = 0$
$a_n = a_{n-1} + n$

56. $a_0 = 2$
$a_n = [a_{n-1}]^2$

57. $f(1) = 2$
$a_n = a_{n-1} + 2$

58. $f(1) = 0$
$a_n = a_{n-1} + 2n$

59. $a_0 = 1$
$a_n = a_{n-1} + n^2$

60. $a_0 = 0$
$a_n = a_{n-1} - 1$

In Exercises 61–64, find a quadratic model for the sequence with the indicated terms.

61. $a_0 = 3$, $a_1 = 3$, $a_4 = 15$

62. $a_0 = 7$, $a_1 = 6$, $a_3 = 10$

63. $a_0 = -3$, $a_2 = 1$, $a_4 = 9$

64. $a_0 = 3$, $a_2 = 0$, $a_6 = 36$

10.5 THE BINOMIAL THEOREM

Binomial Coefficients / Pascal's Triangle / Binomial Expansions

Binomial Coefficients

Recall that a **binomial** is a polynomial that has two terms. In this section, you will study a formula that gives a quick method of raising a binomial to a power. To begin, look at the expansion of $(x + y)^n$ for several values of n.

$$(x + y)^0 = 1$$
$$(x + y)^1 = x + y$$
$$(x + y)^2 = x^2 + 2xy + y^2$$
$$(x + y)^3 = x^3 + 3x^2y + 3xy^2 + y^3$$
$$(x + y)^4 = x^4 + 4x^3y + 6x^2y^2 + 4xy^3 + y^4$$
$$(x + y)^5 = x^5 + 5x^4y + 10x^3y^2 + 10x^2y^3 + 5xy^4 + y^5$$

There are several observations you can make about these expansions of $(x + y)^n$.

1. In each expansion, there are $n + 1$ terms.
2. In each expansion, x and y have symmetrical roles. The powers of x decrease by 1 in successive terms, whereas the powers of y increase by 1.
3. The sum of the powers of each term in a binomial expansion is n. For example, in the expansion of $(x + y)^5$, the sum of the powers of each term is 5, as follows.

$$\overset{4 + 1 = 5 \qquad 3 + 2 = 5}{(x + y)^5 = x^5 + 5\overbrace{x^4y^1} + 10\overbrace{x^3y^2} + 10x^2y^3 + 5xy^4 + y^5}$$

4. The first term is x^n, the last term is y^n, and each of these terms has a coefficient of 1.
5. The coefficients increase and then decrease in a symmetrical pattern. For $(x + y)^5$, the pattern is

$$1 \quad 5 \quad 10 \quad 10 \quad 5 \quad 1.$$

The most difficult part of a binomial expansion is finding the coefficients of the interior terms. To find these **binomial coefficients,** you can use a well-known theorem called the **Binomial Theorem.**

REMARK The symbol $\binom{n}{m}$ is often used in place of $_nC_m$ to denote binomial coefficients.

THE BINOMIAL THEOREM

In the expansion of $(x + y)^n$,

$$(x + y)^n = x^n + nx^{n-1}y + \cdots + {}_nC_mx^{n-m}y^m + \cdots + nxy^{n-1} + y^n,$$

the coefficient of $x^{n-m}y^m$ is given by

$$_nC_m = \frac{n!}{(n - m)!m!}.$$

Technology Note _____

Most graphing utilities have the ability to compute binomial coefficients. Learn how to use this feature of your graphing utility, and then use it to confirm the results given in Example 1.

EXAMPLE 1   **Finding Binomial Coefficients**

Find the following binomial coefficients.

A. $_8C_2$ **B.** $_{10}C_3$ **C.** $_7C_0$ **D.** $_6C_6$

SOLUTION

Note in parts (A) and (B) how the numerator is factored to cancel part of the denominator.

A. $_8C_2 = \dfrac{8!}{6!2!} = \dfrac{(8 \cdot 7) \cdot 6!}{6! \cdot 2!} = \dfrac{8 \cdot 7}{2 \cdot 1} = 28$

B. $_{10}C_3 = \dfrac{10!}{7!3!} = \dfrac{(10 \cdot 9 \cdot 8) \cdot 7!}{7! \cdot 3!} = \dfrac{10 \cdot 9 \cdot 8}{3 \cdot 2 \cdot 1} = 120$

C. $_7C_0 = \dfrac{7!}{7! \cdot 0!} = 1$

D. $_6C_6 = \dfrac{6!}{0! \cdot 6!} = 1$

Some calculators have a built-in binomial coefficient key. The TI-81 uses the nCr symbol in the math menu. Try verifying the above computations with your calculator.   ▬ ■■■■■■■

When $m \neq 0$ or $m \neq n$, as in parts (A) and (B) above, there is a simple pattern for evaluating binomial coefficients.

$$_8C_2 = \overset{\overset{\text{2 factors}}{\frown}}{\dfrac{8 \cdot 7}{\underset{\text{2 factorial}}{\underbrace{2 \cdot 1}}}} \quad \text{and} \quad _{10}C_3 = \overset{\overset{\text{3 factors}}{\frown}}{\dfrac{10 \cdot 9 \cdot 8}{\underset{\text{3 factorial}}{\underbrace{3 \cdot 2 \cdot 1}}}}$$

In general, you have the following.

$$_nC_m = \dfrac{\overset{\overset{m \text{ factors}}{\frown}}{n(n-1)(n-2)\cdots}}{m!}, \qquad 0 < m < n$$

EXAMPLE 2   Finding Binomial Coefficients

Find the following binomial coefficients.

A. $_7C_3$ **B.** $_7C_4$ **C.** $_{12}C_1$ **D.** $_{12}C_{11}$

SOLUTION

A. $_7C_3 = \dfrac{7 \cdot 6 \cdot 5}{3 \cdot 2 \cdot 1} = 35$

B. $_7C_4 = \dfrac{7 \cdot 6 \cdot 5 \cdot 4}{4 \cdot 3 \cdot 2 \cdot 1} = 35$

C. $_{12}C_1 = \dfrac{12}{1} = 12$

D. $_{12}C_{11} = \dfrac{12!}{1!11!} = \dfrac{(12) \cdot 11!}{1! \cdot 11!} = \dfrac{12}{1} = 12$ ▬ ■■■■■

It is not a coincidence that the results in parts (A) and (B), and similarly in parts (C) and (D), are the same. In general it is true that $_nC_m = {}_nC_{n-m}$. For instance,

$$_6C_0 = {}_6C_6 = 1, \quad _6C_1 = {}_6C_5 = 6, \quad \text{and} \quad _6C_2 = {}_6C_4 = 15.$$

This shows the symmetric property of binomial coefficients that was identified earlier. Notice how this property is used in Example 3.

EXAMPLE 3   Finding a Binomial Coefficient

Find the binomial coefficient $_{12}C_{10}$.

SOLUTION

Rather than calculating the binomial coefficient

$$_{12}C_{10} = \frac{12 \cdot 11 \cdot 10 \cdot 9 \cdot 8 \cdot 7 \cdot 6 \cdot 5 \cdot 4 \cdot 3}{10 \cdot 9 \cdot 8 \cdot 7 \cdot 6 \cdot 5 \cdot 4 \cdot 3 \cdot 2 \cdot 1},$$

you can use the fact that $_{12}C_{10} = {}_{12}C_2$ as follows.

$$_{12}C_{10} = {}_{12}C_2 = \frac{12 \cdot 11}{2 \cdot 1} = 66$$

Pascal's Triangle

There is a convenient way to remember the pattern for binomial coefficients. By arranging the coefficients in a triangular pattern, you obtain the following array, which is called **Pascal's Triangle.** This triangle is named after the famous French mathematician Blaise Pascal (1623–1662).

```
                        1
                     1     1
                  1     2     1
               1     3     3     1
            1     4     6     4     1
         1     5    10    10     5     1
      1     6    15    20    15     6     1
   1     7    21    35    35    21     7     1
```

The first and last numbers in each row of Pascal's Triangle is 1. Every other number in each row is formed by adding the two numbers immediately above the number. For example, the two numbers above 35 are 15 and 20.

15   20
  \ /
   35   15 + 20 = 35

Pascal noticed that numbers in this triangle are precisely the same numbers that are the coefficients of binomial expansions, as follows.

$$(x + y)^0 = 1$$
$$(x + y)^1 = 1x + 1y$$
$$(x + y)^2 = 1x^2 + 2xy + 1y^2$$
$$(x + y)^3 = 1x^3 + 3x^2y + 3xy^2 + 1y^3$$
$$(x + y)^4 = 1x^4 + 4x^3y + 6x^2y^2 + 4xy^3 + 1y^4$$
$$(x + y)^5 = 1x^5 + 5x^4y + 10x^3y^2 + 10x^2y^3 + 5xy^4 + 1y^5$$
$$(x + y)^6 = 1x^6 + 6x^5y + 15x^4y^2 + 20x^3y^3 + 15x^2y^4 + 6xy^5 + 1y^6$$
$$(x + y)^7 = 1x^7 + 7x^6y + 21x^5y^2 + 35x^4y^3 + 35x^3y^4 + 21x^2y^5 + 7xy^6 + 1y^7$$

Because the top row in Pascal's Triangle corresponds to the binomial expansion $(x + y)^0 = 1$, it is called the **zero row.** Similarly, the next row corresponds to the binomial expansion $(x + y)^1 = 1(x) + 1(y)$, and it is called the **first row.** In general, the ***n*th row** in Pascal's Triangle gives the coefficients of $(x + y)^n$.

EXAMPLE 4   Using Pascal's Triangle

Use Pascal's Triangle to find the following binomial coefficients.

$$_8C_0, \ _8C_1, \ _8C_2, \ _8C_3, \ _8C_4, \ _8C_5, \ _8C_6, \ _8C_7, \ _8C_8$$

SOLUTION

These nine binomial coefficients represent the eighth row of Pascal's Triangle. Thus, using the seventh row of the triangle, you can calculate the numbers in the eighth row, as follows

Binomial Expansions

EXAMPLE 5   Expanding a Binomial

Write the expansion of $(x + 1)^3$.

SOLUTION

The binomial coefficients from the third row of Pascal's Triangle are 1, 3, 3, 1. Therefore, the expansion is as follows.

$$(x + 1)^3 = (1)x^3 + (3)x^2(1) + (3)x(1^2) + (1)(1^3)$$
$$= x^3 + 3x^2 + 3x + 1$$

To expand binomials representing *differences,* rather than sums, you must alternate signs. Here are two examples.

$$(x - 1)^3 = x^3 - 3x^2 + 3x - 1$$
$$(x - 1)^4 = x^4 - 4x^3 + 6x^2 - 4x + 1$$

EXAMPLE 6   Expanding a Binomial

Write the expansion of $(x - 2)^3$.

SOLUTION

The binomial coefficients from the third row of Pascal's Triangle are 1, 3, 3, 1. Therefore, the expansion is as follows.

$$(x - 1)^3 = (1)x^3 - (3)x^2(2) + (3)x(2^2) - (1)(2^3)$$
$$= x^3 - 6x^2 + 12x - 8$$

EXAMPLE 7   Expanding a Binomial

Write the expansion for the following expression.

$$(x + 3)^4$$

SOLUTION

The binomial coefficients from the fourth row of Pascal's Triangle are 1, 4, 6, 4, 1. Therefore, the expansion is as follows.

$$(x + 3)^4 = (1)x^4 + (4)x^3(3) + (6)x^2(3^2) + (4)x(3^3) + (1)(3^4)$$
$$= x^4 + 12x^3 + 54x^2 + 108x + 81$$

EXAMPLE 8   Expanding a Binomial

Write the expansion of $(x - 2y)^4$.

SOLUTION

The binomial coefficients from the fourth row of Pascal's Triangle are 1, 4, 6, 4, 1. Therefore, the expansion is as follows.

$$(x - 2y)^4 = (1)x^4 - (4)x^3(2y) + (6)x^2(2y)^2 - (4)x(2y)^3 + (1)(2y)^4$$
$$= x^4 - 8x^3y + 24x^2y^2 - 32xy^3 + 16y^4$$

EXAMPLE 9   Finding a Specified Term in a Binomial Expansion

Find the sixth term in the expansion of $(3a + 2b)^{12}$.

SOLUTION

Using the Binomial Theorem, let $x = 3a$ and $y = 2b$ and note that in the *sixth* term the exponent of y is $m = 5$ and the exponent of x is $n - m = 12 - 5 = 7$. Consequently, the sixth term of the expansion is

$$_{12}C_5 x^7 y^5 = \frac{12 \cdot 11 \cdot 10 \cdot 9 \cdot 8}{5!}(3a)^7(2b)^5.$$

DISCUSSION PROBLEM

THE ROWS OF PASCAL'S TRIANGLE

By adding the terms in each of the rows of Pascal's Triangle, you obtain the following.

Row 0: $1 = 1$
Row 1: $1 + 1 = 2$
Row 2: $1 + 2 + 1 = 4$
Row 3: $1 + 3 + 3 + 1 = 8$
Row 4: $1 + 4 + 6 + 4 + 1 = 16$

Can you find a pattern for this sequence? Use this pattern to find the sum of the terms in the 10th row of Pascal's Triangle. Then check your answer by actually adding the terms of the 10th row.

WARM-UP

The following warm-up exercises involve skills that were covered in earlier sections. You will use these skills in the exercise set for this section.

In Exercises 1–6, perform the indicated operations and/or simplify.

1. $5x^2(x^3 + 3)$ **2.** $(x + 5)(x^2 - 3)$ **3.** $(x + 4)^2$
4. $(2x - 3)^2$ **5.** $x^2 y(3xy^{-2})$ **6.** $(-2z)^5$

In Exercises 7–10, evaluate the expression.

7. $5!$ **8.** $\dfrac{8!}{5!}$ **9.** $\dfrac{10!}{7!}$ **10.** $\dfrac{6!}{3!3!}$

SECTION 10.5 · EXERCISES

In Exercises 1–10, evaluate $_nC_m$. If your graphing utility has a binomial coefficient key (also called combinations function), use it to verify your answer.

1. $_5C_3$

2. $_8C_6$

3. $_{12}C_0$

4. $_{20}C_{20}$

5. $_{20}C_{15}$

6. $_{12}C_5$

7. $_{100}C_{98}$

8. $_{10}C_4$

9. $_{100}C_2$

10. $_{10}C_6$

In Exercises 11–30, use the Binomial Theorem to expand and simplify the expression.

11. $(x + 1)^4$

12. $(x + 1)^6$

13. $(a + 2)^3$

14. $(a + 3)^4$

15. $(y - 2)^4$

16. $(y - 2)^5$

17. $(x + y)^5$

18. $(x + y)^6$

19. $(r + 3s)^6$

20. $(x + 2y)^4$

21. $(x - y)^5$

22. $(2x - y)^5$

23. $(1 - 2x)^3$

24. $(5 - 3y)^3$

25. $(x^2 + 5)^4$

26. $(x^2 + y^2)^6$

27. $\left(\dfrac{1}{x} + y\right)^5$

28. $\left(\dfrac{1}{x} + 2y\right)^6$

29. $2(x - 3)^4 + 5(x - 3)^2$

30. $3(x + 1)^5 - 4(x + 1)^3$

In Exercises 31–36, use the Binomial Theorem to expand the complex number. Simplify your answer by recalling that $i^2 = -1$.

31. $(1 + i)^4$

32. $(2 - i)^5$

33. $(2 - 3i)^6$

34. $(5 + \sqrt{-9})^3$

35. $\left(\dfrac{-1}{2} + \dfrac{\sqrt{3}}{2}i\right)^3$

36. $(5 - \sqrt{3}i)^4$

In Exercises 37–40, expand the binomial using Pascal's Triangle to determine the coefficients.

37. $(2t - s)^5$

38. $(x + 2y)^5$

39. $(3 - 2z)^4$

40. $(3y + 2)^5$

In Exercises 41–48, find the coefficient a of the given term in the expansion of the binomial.

Binomial	Term
41. $(x + 3)^{12}$	ax^5
42. $(x^2 + 3)^{12}$	ax^8
43. $(x - 2y)^{10}$	ax^8y^2
44. $(4x - y)^{10}$	ax^2y^8
45. $(3x - 2y)^9$	ax^4y^5
46. $(2x - 3y)^8$	ax^6y^2
47. $(x^2 + 1)^{10}$	ax^8
48. $(z^2 - 1)^{12}$	az^6

Probability   In Exercises 49–52, consider n independent trials of an experiment where each trial has two possible outcomes called success and failure. The probability of a success on each trial is p and the probability of a failure is $q = 1 - p$. In this context the term

$$_nC_k p^k q^{n-k}$$

of the expansion of $(p + q)^n$ gives the probability of k successes in the n trials of the experiment. Expand the given binomial and find the required probability.

49. A fair coin is tossed seven times. Find the probability of obtaining four heads.

$$\left(\frac{1}{2} + \frac{1}{2}\right)^7$$

50. The probability of a baseball player getting a hit on any given time at bat is $\frac{1}{4}$. Find the probability that he gets three hits in his next 10 times at bat.

$$\left(\frac{1}{4} + \frac{3}{4}\right)^{10}$$

51. The probability of a salesman making a sale with any one customer is $\frac{1}{3}$. If the salesman makes eight contacts on a given day, find the probability that he makes four sales.

$$\left(\frac{1}{3} + \frac{2}{3}\right)^8$$

52. Find the probability that the salesman in Exercise 51 makes four sales in eight contacts if the probability of a sale with any one customer is $\frac{1}{2}$.

$$\left(\frac{1}{2} + \frac{1}{2}\right)^8$$

In Exercises 53–56, use the Binomial Theorem to approximate the given quantity accurate to three decimal places. For example, in Exercise 53 you have

$$(1.02)^8 = (1 + 0.02)^8 = 1 + 8(0.02) + 28(0.02)^2 + \cdots$$

53. $(1.02)^8$ **54.** $(2.005)^{10}$

55. $(2.99)^{12}$ **56.** $(1.98)^9$

In Exercises 57–60, use a graphing utility to graph f and g in the same viewing rectangle. What is the relationship between the two graphs? Use the Binomial Theorem to write the polynomial function g in standard form.

57. $f(x) = -x^2 + 3x + 2$
$g(x) = f(x - 2)$

58. $f(x) = 2x^2 - 4x + 1$
$g(x) = f(x + 3)$

59. $f(x) = x^3 - 4x$
$g(x) = f(x + 4)$

60. $f(x) = -x^4 + 4x^2 - 1$
$g(x) = f(x - 3)$

61. *Life Insurance*   The average amount of life insurance per household (by households that carry life insurance) from 1970 through 1988 can be approximated by the model

$$f(t) = 0.2187t^2 + 0.6715t + 26.67, \qquad 0 \le t \le 18.$$

In this model $f(t)$ represents the amount of life insurance (in thousands of dollars) and t represents the year, with $t = 0$ corresponding to 1970 (see figure). You want to adjust this model so that $t = 0$ corresponds to 1980 rather than 1970. To do this, you shift the graph of f 10 units *to the left* and obtain

$$g(t) = f(t + 10) = 0.2187(t + 10)^2 + 0.6715(t + 10) + 26.67.$$

Write this new polynomial function in standard form. (*Source:* American Council of Life Insurance)

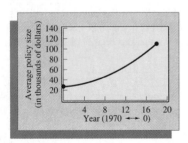

FIGURE FOR 61

62. *Health Maintenance Organizations*   The number of people enrolled in health maintenance organizations (HMOs) in the United States from 1976 through 1988 can be approximated by the model

$$f(t) = 215t^2 - 470t + 6700, \qquad 0 \le t \le 12.$$

In this model, $f(t)$ represents the number of people (in thousands) and t represents the year, with $t = 0$ corresponding to 1976 (see figure). You want to adjust this model so that $t = 0$ corresponds to 1980 rather than 1976. To do this, shift the graph of f four units *to the left* and obtain

$$g(t) = f(t + 4) = 215(t + 4)^2 - 470(t + 4) + 6700.$$

Write this new polynomial function in standard form. (*Source:* Group Health Insurance Association of America)

FIGURE FOR 62

In Exercises 63–66, prove the given property for all integers m and n where $0 \le m \le n$.

63. $_nC_m = \, _nC_{n-m}$

64. $_nC_0 - \, _nC_1 + \, _nC_2 - \cdots \pm \, _nC_n = 0$

65. $_{n+1}C_m = \, _nC_m + \, _nC_{m-1}$

66. $_{2n}C_n = (_nC_0)^2 + (_nC_1)^2 + (_nC_2)^2 + \cdots + (_nC_n)^2$

67. Prove that the sum of the numbers in the nth row of Pascal's Triangle is 2^n. (*Hint:* Consider $2^n = (1 + 1)^n$.)

68. Use a graphing utility to graph the following functions in the same viewing rectangle. Compare the graphs as you add terms. Which two functions have identical graphs and why?
(a) $f(x) = (1 - x)^3$
(b) $g(x) = 1 - 3x$
(c) $h(x) = 1 - 3x + 3x^2$
(d) $p(x) = 1 - 3x + 3x^2 - x^3$

10.6 COUNTING PRINCIPLES, PERMUTATIONS, COMBINATIONS

Simple Counting Problems / Counting Principles /
Permutations / Combinations

Simple Counting Problems

In the last two sections of this chapter, we give a brief introduction to some of the basic counting principles and their application to probability. In the next section, you will see that much of probability has to do with counting the number of ways an event can occur. Examples 1, 2, and 3 describe some simple counting problems.

EXAMPLE 1   A Random Number Generator

A random number generator (on a computer) selects an integer from 1 to 40. Find the number of ways the following events can occur.

A. An even integer is selected.

B. A number less than 10 is selected.

C. A prime number is selected.

SOLUTION

A. Since half of the numbers between 1 and 40 are even, this event can occur in 20 different ways.

B. The integers between 1 and 40 that are less than 10 are given in the following set.

$$\{1, 2, 3, 4, 5, 6, 7, 8, 9\}$$

Since this set has nine members, there are nine different ways this event can happen.

C. The prime numbers between 1 and 40 are given in the following set.

$$\{2, 3, 5, 7, 11, 13, 17, 19, 23, 29, 31, 37\}$$

Since this set has 12 members, there are 12 different ways this event can happen.

EXAMPLE 2 Selecting Pairs of Numbers at Random

Eight pieces of paper are numbered from 1 to 8 and placed in a box. One piece of paper is drawn from the box, its number is written down, and the piece of paper is replaced in the box. Then a second piece of paper is drawn from the box, and its number is written down. Finally, the two numbers are added together. How many different ways can a total of 12 be obtained?

SOLUTION

To solve this problem, you count the different ways that a total of 12 can be obtained using two numbers between 1 and 8.

First number + Second number = 12

After considering the various possibilities, you see that this equation can be solved in the following five ways.

First Number	Second Number
4	8
5	7
6	6
7	5
8	4

Thus, a total of 12 can be obtained in five different ways.

Solving counting problems can be tricky. Often, seemingly minor changes in the statement of a problem can affect the answer. For instance, compare the counting problem in the next example with that given in Example 2.

EXAMPLE 3 Selecting Pairs of Numbers at Random

Eight pieces of paper are numbered from 1 to 8 and placed in a box. Two pieces of paper are drawn from the box, the number on each piece of paper is written down, and the two are totaled. How many different ways can a total of 12 be obtained?

SOLUTION

To solve this problem, you count the different ways that a total of 12 can be obtained *using two different numbers* between 1 and 8.

First Number	Second Number
4	8
5	7
7	5
8	4

Thus, a total of 12 can be obtained in four different ways.

REMARK The difference between the counting problems in Examples 2 and 3 is that the random selection in Example 2 occurs **with replacement,** whereas the random selection in Example 3 occurs **without replacement,** which eliminates the possibility of choosing two 6's.

Counting Principles

In the first three examples, we looked at simple counting problems in which we can *list* each possible way that an event can occur. When it is possible, this is always the best way to solve a counting problem. However, some events can occur in so many different ways that it is not feasible to write out the entire list. In such cases, we must rely on formulas and counting principles. The most important of these is the **Fundamental Counting Principle.**

REMARK   The Fundamental Counting Principle can be extended to three or more events. For instance, the number of ways that three events E_1, E_2, and E_3 can occur is $m_1 \cdot m_2 \cdot m_3$.

FUNDAMENTAL COUNTING PRINCIPLE

Let E_1 and E_2 be two events. The first event E_1 can occur in m_1 different ways. After E_1 has occurred, E_2 can occur in m_2 different ways. The number of ways that the two events can occur is

$$m_1 \cdot m_2.$$

EXAMPLE 4   **Applying the Fundamental Counting Principle**

How many different pairs of letters from the English alphabet are possible? (Disregard the difference between uppercase and lowercase letters.)

SOLUTION

This experiment has two events. The first event is the choice of the first letter, and the second event is the choice of the second letter. Since the English alphabet contains 26 letters, it follows that each event can occur in 26 ways.

Two-letter "words"

26   26

Thus, using the Fundamental Counting Principle, it follows that the number of two-letter "words" is

$$26 \cdot 26 = 676.$$

EXAMPLE 5   Applying the Fundamental Counting Principle

Telephone numbers in the United States have ten digits. The first three are the *area code* and the next seven are the *local telephone number.* How many different telephone numbers are possible within each area code? (Note that a local telephone number cannot begin with 0 or 1.)

SOLUTION

Since the first digit cannot be 0 or 1, there are only eight choices for the first digit. For each of the other six digits, there are ten choices.

Thus, using the Fundamental Counting Principle, the number of local telephone numbers that are possible within each area code is

$$8 \cdot 10 \cdot 10 \cdot 10 \cdot 10 \cdot 10 \cdot 10 = 8{,}000{,}000.$$

Permutations

One important application of the Fundamental Counting Principle is in determining the number of ways that n elements can be arranged (in order). We call an ordering of n elements a **permutation** of the elements.

DEFINITION OF PERMUTATION

A **permutation** of n different elements is an ordering of the elements such that one element is first, one is second, one is third, and so on.

EXAMPLE 6   Listing Permutations

Write the different permutations of the letters A, B, and C.

SOLUTION

These three letters can be arranged in the following six different ways.

A, B, C,   B, A, C,   C, A, B
A, C, B,   B, C, A   C, B, A

Thus, you see that these three letters have six different permutations.

In Example 6, you were able to list the different permutations of three letters. However, you could also have used the Fundamental Counting Principle. To do this, you could reason that there are three choices for the first letter, two choices for the second, and only one choice for the third, as follows.

Permutations of three letters

$$3 \qquad 2 \qquad 1$$

Thus, the number of permutations of three letters is

$$3 \cdot 2 \cdot 1 = 3! = 6.$$

EXAMPLE 7 Finding the Number of Permutations of n Elements

How many different permutations are possible for the letters A, B, C, D, E, and F?

SOLUTION

There are too many different permutations to list, so you use the following reasoning.

1st position:	Any of the *six* letters.
2nd position:	Any of the remaining *five* letters.
3rd position:	Any of the remaining *four* letters.
4th position:	Any of the remaining *three* letters.
5th position:	Any of the remaining *two* letters.
6th position:	The *one* remaining letter.

Thus, the number of choices for the six positions is as follows.

Permutations of six letters

$$6 \qquad 5 \qquad 4 \qquad 3 \qquad 2 \qquad 1$$

Using the Fundamental Counting Principle, you find that the total number of permutations of the six letters is

$$6 \cdot 5 \cdot 4 \cdot 3 \cdot 2 \cdot 1 = 6! = 720.$$

The results obtained in Examples 6 and 7 can be generalized to conclude that the number of permutations of n different elements is $n!$.

NUMBER OF PERMUTATIONS OF N ELEMENTS

The number of permutations of n elements is given by

$$n \cdot (n - 1) \cdots 4 \cdot 3 \cdot 2 \cdot 1 = n!.$$

In other words, there are $n!$ different ways that n elements can be ordered.

EXAMPLE 8 Finding the Number of Permutations

Suppose that you are a supervisor for 11 different employees. One of your responsibilities is to perform an annual evaluation for each employee, and then rank the 11 different performances. (In other words, one employee must be ranked as having the best performance, one must be ranked second, and so on.) How many different rankings are possible?

SOLUTION

Since there are 11 different employees, you have 11 choices for first ranking. After choosing the first ranking, you can choose any of the remaining 10 for second ranking, and so on.

Rankings of 11 employees

| 11 | 10 | 9 | 8 | 7 | 6 | 5 | 4 | 3 | 2 | 1 |

Thus, the number of different rankings is

$$11! = 39,916,800.$$

Occasionally, you may be interested in ordering a *subset* of a collection of elements rather than the entire collection. For example, you might want to choose (and order) m elements out of a collection of n elements. Such an ordering is a **permutation of n elements taken m at a time.**

EXAMPLE 9 Permutations of n Elements Taken m at a Time

Eight horses are running in a race. In how many different ways can these horses come in first, second, and third? (Assume that there are no ties.)

SOLUTION

You have the following possibilities.

Win (1st position):   *Eight* choices
Place (2nd position): *Seven* choices
Show (3rd position):   *Six* choices

Using the Fundamental Counting Principle, multiply these three numbers together to obtain the following.

Different orders of horses

8   7   6

Thus, there are $8 \cdot 7 \cdot 6 = 336$ different orders.

The result of Example 9 can be generalized as follows.

PERMUTATIONS OF N ELEMENTS TAKEN M AT A TIME

The number of permutations of n elements taken m at a time is

$$_nP_m = \frac{n!}{(n - m)!} = n(n - 1)(n - 2) \cdots (n - m + 1).$$

Using this formula, you can rework Example 9 to find that the number of permutations of eight horses taken three at a time is

$$_8P_3 = \frac{8!}{(8 - 3)!} = \frac{8!}{5!} = \frac{8 \cdot 7 \cdot 6 \cdot 5!}{5!} = 8 \cdot 7 \cdot 6 = 336$$

which is the same answer you obtained in the solution of Example 9.

Remember that for permutations, order is important. Thus, if you are looking at the possible permutations of the letters A, B, C, and D taken three at a time, the permutations (A, B, D) and (B, A, D) would be different (since the *order* of the elements is different).

Suppose, however, that you are asked to find the possible permutations of the letters A, A, B, and C. The total number of permutations of the four letters would be $_4P_4 = 4!$. However, not all of these arrangements would be *distinguishable* because there are two A's in the list. To find the number of distinguishable permutations, you can use the following formula.

DISTINGUISHABLE PERMUTATIONS

Suppose a set of n objects has n_1 of one kind of object, n_2 of a second kind, n_3 of a third kind, and so on, with $n = n_1 + n_2 + n_3 + \cdots + n_k$. Then the number of **distinguishable permutations** of the n objects is

$$\frac{n!}{n_1! \cdot n_2! \cdot n_3! \cdots n_k!}.$$

EXAMPLE 10   **Distinguishable Permutations**

In how many distinguishable ways can the letters in BANANA be written?

SOLUTION

This word has six letters, of which three are A's, two are N's and one is a B. Thus, the number of distinguishable ways the letters can be written is

$$\frac{6!}{3! \cdot 2! \cdot 1!} = \frac{6 \cdot 5 \cdot 4 \cdot 3!}{3! \cdot 2!} = 60.$$

The 60 different "words" are as follows.

AAABNN	AAANBN	AAANNB	AABANN	AABNAN	AABNNA
AANABN	AANANB	AANBAN	AANBNA	AANNAB	AANNBA
ABAANN	ABANAN	ABANNA	ABNAAN	ABNANA	ABNNAA
ANAABN	ANAANB	ANABAN	ANABNA	ANANAB	ANANBA
ANBAAN	ANBANA	ANBNAA	ANNAAB	ANNABA	ANNBAA
BAAANN	BAANAN	BAANNA	BANAAN	BANANA	BANNAA
BNAAAN	BNAANA	BNANAA	BNNAAA	NAAABN	NAAANB
NAABAN	NAABNA	NAANAB	NAANBA	NABAAN	NABANA
NABNAA	NANAAB	NANABA	NANBAA	NBAAAN	NBAANA
NBANAA	NBNAAA	NNAAAB	NNAABA	NNABAA	NNBAAA

Combinations

When counting the numbers of possible permutations of a set of elements, *order* is important. As a final topic in this section, we look at a method of selecting subsets of a larger set in which order is *not important*. Such subsets are **combinations of *n* elements taken *m* at a time.** For instance, the combinations

$$\{A, B, C\} \quad \text{and} \quad \{B, A, C\}$$

are equivalent because both sets contain the same three elements, and the order in which the elements are listed is *not important*. Hence, we would count only one of the two sets. A common example of how a combination occurs is a card game in which the player is free to reorder the cards after they have been dealt.

EXAMPLE 11   **Combination of *n* Elements Taken *m* at a Time**

In how many different ways can three letters be chosen from the letters A, B, C, D, and E? (The order of the three letters is not important.)

SOLUTION

The following subsets represent the different combinations of three letters that can be chosen from five letters.

{A, B, C}   {A, B, D}
{A, B, E}   {A, C, D}
{A, C, E}   {A, D, E}
{B, C, D}   {B, C, E}
{B, D, E}   {C, D, E}

From this list, you conclude that there are ten different ways that three letters can be chosen from five letters.

The formula for the number of *combinations* of n elements taken m at a time is as follows.

COMBINATIONS OF *N* ELEMENTS TAKEN *M* AT A TIME

The number of combinations of n elements taken m at a time is

$$_nC_m = \frac{n!}{(n-m)!m!}.$$

Note that the formula for $_nC_m$ is the same as the one given for binomial coefficients. To see how this formula is used, solve the counting problem given in Example 11. In that problem, you must find the number of combinations of five elements taken three at a time. Thus, $n = 5$, $m = 3$, and the number of combinations is

$$_5C_3 = \frac{5!}{2!3!} = \frac{5 \cdot 4 \cdot 3}{3 \cdot 2 \cdot 1} = 10$$

which is the same answer you obtained in Example 11.

EXAMPLE 12 Combinations of n Elements Taken m at a Time

A standard poker hand consists of five cards dealt from a deck of 52. How many different poker hands are possible? (After the cards are dealt, the player may reorder them, and therefore order is not important.)

SOLUTION

Use the formula for the number of combinations of 52 elements taken five at a time, as follows.

$$_{52}C_5 = \frac{52!}{47!5!} = \frac{52 \cdot 51 \cdot 50 \cdot 49 \cdot 48}{5 \cdot 4 \cdot 3 \cdot 2 \cdot 1} = 2,598,960 \text{ different hands}$$

EXAMPLE 13   Combinations and the Fundamental
....   Counting Principle

The traveling squad for a college basketball team consists of two centers, five forwards, and four guards. In how many ways can the coach select a starting team of one center, two forwards, and two guards?

SOLUTION

The number of ways to select one center is

$$_2C_1 = \frac{2!}{1!(1!)} = 2.$$

The number of ways to select two forwards from among five is

$$_5C_2 = \frac{5!}{3!(2!)} = 10.$$

The number of ways to select two guards from among four is

$$_4C_2 = \frac{4!}{2!(2!)} = 6.$$

Therefore, the total number of ways to select a starting team is

$$_2C_1 \cdot {_5C_2} \cdot {_4C_2} = 2 \cdot 10 \cdot 6 = 120.$$

**DISCUSSION
PROBLEM**
....

**YOU BE THE
INSTRUCTOR**

Suppose you are teaching an algebra class and are writing a test for this chapter. Create two word problems that you think are appropriate for the test. One of the word problems should deal with permutations and the other should deal with combinations. (Assume that your students will have only five minutes to solve each problem.)

WARM-UP

The following warm-up exercises involve skills that were covered in earlier sections. You will use these skills in the exercise set for this section.

In Exercises 1–4, evaluate the expression.

1. $13 \cdot 8^2 \cdot 2^3$

2. $10^2 \cdot 9^3 \cdot 4$

3. $\dfrac{12!}{2!(7!)(3!)}$

4. $\dfrac{25!}{22!}$

In Exercises 5 and 6, find the binomial coefficient.

5. $_{12}C_7$

6. $_{25}C_{22}$

In Exercises 7–10, simplify the expression.

7. $\dfrac{n!}{(n-4)!}$

8. $\dfrac{(2n)!}{4(2n-3)!}$

9. $\dfrac{2 \cdot 4 \cdot 6 \cdot 8 \cdots (2n)}{2^n}$

10. $\dfrac{3 \cdot 6 \cdot 9 \cdot 12 \cdots (3n)}{3^n}$

SECTION 10.6 · EXERCISES

1. A bag contains 10 marbles numbered 1 through 10. A marble is selected, its number is recorded, and the marble is *replaced* in the bag. Then a second marble is drawn and its number recorded. Finally, the recorded numbers are added. How many different ways can a sum of 8 be obtained?

2. A bag contains 10 marbles numbered 1 through 10. Two marbles are selected and their numbers are recorded. Then the recorded numbers are added. How many different ways can a sum of 8 be obtained?

3. *Job Applicants*   A small college needs two additional faculty members: a chemist and a statistician. In how many ways can these positions be filled if there are three applicants for the chemistry position and four for the position in statistics?

4. *Computer Systems*   A customer in a computer store can choose one of three monitors, one of two keyboards, and one of four computers. If all the choices are compatible, how many different systems could be chosen?

5. *Toboggan Ride*   Four people are lining up for a ride on a toboggan, but only two of the four are willing to take the first position. With that constraint, in how many ways can the four people be seated on the toboggan?

6. *Course Schedule*   A college student is preparing a course schedule for the next semester. The student may select one of two mathematics courses, one of three science courses, and one of five courses from the social sciences and humanities. How many schedules are possible?

7. *License Plate Numbers*   In a certain state the automobile license places consist of two letters followed by a four-digit number. How many distinct license plate numbers can be formed?

8. *License Plate Numbers*   In a certain state the automobile license plates consist of two letters followed by a four-digit number. To avoid confusion between "O" and "zero" and "l" and "one," the letters "O" and "l" are not used. How many distinct license plate numbers can be formed?

9. *True-False Exam*   In how many ways can a six-question true-false exam be answered? (Assume that no questions are omitted.)

10. *Multiple Choice*   In how many ways can a 10-question multiple choice exam be answered if there are four choices of answers for each question? (Assume that no questions are omitted.)

11. *Three-Digit Numbers*   How many three-digit numbers can be formed under the following conditions?
    (a) The leading digit cannot be zero.
    (b) The leading digit cannot be zero and no repetition of digits is allowed.
    (c) The leading digit cannot be zero and the number must be a multiple of 5.
    (d) The number is at least 400.

12. *Four-Digit Numbers*   How many four-digit numbers can be formed under the following conditions?
    (a) The leading digit cannot be zero.
    (b) The leading digit cannot be zero and no repetition of digits is allowed.
    (c) The leading digit cannot be zero and the number must be less than 5000.
    (d) The leading digit cannot be zero and the number must be even.

13. *Combination Lock*   A combination lock will open when the right choice of three numbers (from 1 to 40, inclusive) is selected. How many different lock combinations are possible?

14. *Combination Lock*   A combination lock will open when the right choice of three numbers (from 1 to 50, inclusive) is selected. How many different lock combinations are possible?

15. *Concert Seats*   Three couples have reserved seats in a given row for a concert. In how many different ways can they be seated if
    (a) there are no seating restrictions?
    (b) the two members of each couple wish to sit together?

16. *Single File*   In how many orders can three girls and two boys walk through a doorway single-file if
    (a) there are no restrictions?
    (b) the boys go before the girls?
    (c) the girls go before the boys?

In Exercises 17–26, evaluate $_nP_m$.

17. $_4P_4$ 18. $_5P_5$
19. $_8P_3$ 20. $_{20}P_2$
21. $_{20}P_5$ 22. $_{100}P_1$
23. $_{100}P_2$ 24. $_{10}P_2$
25. $_5P_4$ 26. $_7P_4$

27. Write all the permutations of the letters A, B, C, and D.

28. Write all the permutations of the letters A, B, C, and D if the letters B and C must remain between the letters A and D.

29. *Posing for a Photograph*   In how many ways can five children line up in one row to have their picture taken?

30. *Riding in a Car*   In how many ways can six people sit in a six-passenger car?

31. *Choosing Officers*   From a pool of 12 candidates, the offices of president, vice-president, secretary, and treasurer will be filled. In how many different ways can the offices be filled, if each of the 12 candidates can hold any office?

32. *Assembly Line Production*   There are four processes involved in assembling a certain product, and these can be performed in any order. The management wants to test each order to determine which is the least time-consuming. How many different orders will have to be tested?

In Exercises 33–38, find the number of distinguishable permutations of the given group of letters.

33. A, A, G, E, E, E, M
34. B, B, B, T, T, T, T, T
35. A, A, Y, Y, Y, Y, X, X, X
36. K, K, M, M, M, L, L, N, N
37. A, L, G, E, B, R, A
38. M, I, S, S, I, S, S, I, P, P, I

39. Write all the possible selections of two letters that can be formed from the letters A, B, C, D, E, and F. (The order of the two letters is not important.)

40. Write all the possible selections of three letters that can be formed from the letters A, B, C, D, E, and F. (The order of the three letters is not important.)

41. *Forming an Experimental Group*   In order to conduct a certain experiment, four students are randomly selected from a class of 20. How many different groups of four students are possible?

42. *Test Questions*   A student may answer any 10 questions from a total of 12 questions on an exam. In how many different ways can the student select the questions?

43. *Lottery Choices*   There are 40 numbers in a particular state lottery. In how many ways can a player select six of the numbers? (The order of selection is not important.)

44. *Lottery Choices*   There are 50 numbers in a particular state lottery. In how many ways can a player select six of the numbers? (The order of selection is not important.)

45. *Number of Subsets*   How many subsets of four elements can be formed from a set of 100 elements?

46. *Number of Subsets*   How many subsets of five elements can be formed from a set of 80 elements?

47. *Forming a Committee*   A committee composed of three graduate students and two undergraduate students is to be selected from a group of eight graduates and five undergraduates. How many different committees can be formed?

48. *Defective Units*   A shipment of 12 microwave ovens contains three defective units. In how many ways can a vending company purchase four of these units and receive (a) all good units, (b) two good units, and (c) at least two good units?

49. *Job Applicants*   An employer interviews eight people for four openings in the company. Three of the eight people are women. If all eight are qualified, in how many ways could the employer fill the four positions if (a) the selection is random and (b) exactly two are women?

50. *Poker Hand*   Five cards are selected from an ordinary deck of 52 playing cards. In how many ways can you get a full house? (A full house consists of three of one kind and two of another. For example, A-A-A-5-5 and K-K-K-10-10 are full houses.)

51. *Forming a Committee*   Four people are to be selected at random from a group of four couples. In how many ways can this be done, given the following conditions?
(a) There are no restrictions.
(b) There is to be at least one couple in the group of four.
(c) The selection must include one member from each couple.

52. *Interpersonal Relationships*   The complexity of the interpersonal relationships increases dramatically as the size of a group increases. Determine the number of two-person relationships in a group of people of size (a) 3, (b) 8, (c) 12, and (d) 20.

In Exercises 53–56, find the number of diagonals of the given polygon. (A line segment connecting any two non-adjacent vertices is called a *diagonal* of the polygon.)

53. Pentagon   **54.** Hexagon

55. Octagon   **56.** Decagon (10 sides)

In Exercises 57 and 58, solve for n.

57. $14 \cdot {}_nP_3 = {}_{n+2}P_4$ **58.** ${}_nP_5 = 18\ {}_{n-2}P_4$

In Exercises 59–63, prove the identity.

59. ${}_nP_{n-1} = {}_nP_n$ **60.** ${}_nP_1 = {}_nC_1$

61. ${}_nC_{n-1} = {}_nC_1$ **62.** ${}_nC_n = {}_nC_0$

63. ${}_nC_m = \dfrac{{}_nP_m}{m!}$

10.7 PROBABILITY

Sample Spaces / The Probability of an Event / Mutually Exclusive
Events / Independent Events / The Complement of an Event

Sample Spaces

As a member of a complex society, you are used to living with varying
amounts of uncertainty. For example, you may be questioning the likelihood
of getting a good job after graduation, of winning a state lottery, of having an
accident on your next trip home, or of any of several other possibilities.

In assigning measurements to uncertainties in everyday life, we often use
ambiguous terminology, such as *fairly certain, probable,* or *highly unlikely.* In
mathematics, we attempt to remove this ambiguity by assigning a number to
the likelihood of the occurrence of an event. We call this measurement the
probability that the event will occur. For example, if we toss a fair coin, we
say that the probability that it will land heads up is one-half, or 50%.

In the study of probability, any happening whose result is uncertain is an
experiment. The various possible results of the experiment are **outcomes,** and
the collection of all possible outcomes of an experiment is the **sample space**
of the experiment. Finally, any subcollection of a sample space is an **event.** In
this section we will deal only with sample spaces in which each outcome is
equally likely, such as flipping a fair coin or tossing a fair die.

EXAMPLE 1   Finding the Sample Space

An experiment consists of tossing a six-sided die.

A. What is the sample space?
B. Describe the event corresponding to a number greater than 2 turning up.

SOLUTION

A. The sample space consists of six outcomes, which you represent by the
numbers 1 through 6. That is,

$$S = \{1, 2, 3, 4, 5, 6\}.$$

Note that each of the outcomes in the sample space is equally likely
(assuming the die is balanced).
B. The *event* corresponding to a number greater than 2 turning up is the
following subset of S.

$$A = \{3, 4, 5, 6\}$$

To describe sample spaces in such a way that each outcome is equally
likely, we must sometimes distinguish between various outcomes in ways that
appear artificial. The next example illustrates such a situation.

EXAMPLE 2   Finding the Sample Space

Find the sample spaces for the following.

A. One coin is tossed.
B. Two coins are tossed.
C. Three coins are tossed.

SOLUTION

A. Since the coin will land either heads up (denoted by H) or tails up (denoted by T), the sample space is

$$S = \{H, T\}.$$

B. Since either coin can land heads up or tails up, the possible outcomes are as follows.

HH = heads up on both coins
HT = heads up on first coin and tails up on second coin
TH = tails up on first coin and heads up on second coin
TT = tails up on both coins

Thus, the sample space is

$$S = \{HH, HT, TH, TT\}.$$

Note that you must distinguish between the two cases HT and TH, even though these two outcomes appear to be similar.

C. Following the notation of part (B), the sample space is

$$S = \{HHH, HHT, HTH, HTT, THH, THT, TTH, TTT\}.$$

The Probability of an Event

To calculate the probability of an event, you count the number of outcomes in the event and in the sample space. The *number of outcomes* in event E is denoted by $n(E)$, and the number of outcomes in the sample space S is denoted by $n(S)$.

THE PROBABILITY OF AN EVENT

If an event E has $n(E)$ equally likely outcomes and its sample space S has $n(S)$ equally likely outcomes, then the **probability** of event E is

$$P(E) = \frac{n(E)}{n(S)}.$$

Because the number of outcomes in an event must be less than or equal to the number of outcomes in the sample space, you can see that the probability of an event must be a number between 0 and 1. That is, for any event E, it must be true that $0 \leq P(E) \leq 1$.

PROPERTIES OF THE PROBABILITY OF AN EVENT

Let E be an event that is a subset of a finite sample space S.

1. $0 \leq P(E) \leq 1$
2. If $P(E) = 0$, then the event E *cannot occur*, and E is an **impossible event.**
3. If $P(E) = 1$, then the event E *must occur*, and E is a **certain event.**

EXAMPLE 3   Finding the Probability of an Event

Find the probability of the following events.

A. Two coins are tossed. What is the probability that both land heads up?

B. A card is drawn from a standard deck of playing cards. What is the probability that it is an ace?

SOLUTION

A. Following the procedure in Example 2(B), let

$$E = \{HH\} \quad \text{and} \quad S = \{HH, HT, TH, TT\}.$$

The probability of getting two heads is

$$P(E) = \frac{n(E)}{n(S)} = \frac{1}{4}.$$

B. Since there are 52 cards in a standard deck of playing cards and there are four aces (one in each suit), the probability of drawing an ace is

$$P(E) = \frac{n(E)}{n(S)} = \frac{4}{52} = \frac{1}{13}.$$

FIGURE 10.6

EXAMPLE 4   Finding the Probability of an Event

Two six-sided dice are tossed. What is the probability that the total of the two dice is 7? (See Figure 10.6.)

SOLUTION

Since there are six possible outcomes on each die, you use the Fundamental Counting Principle to conclude that there are

$$6 \cdot 6 = 36 \text{ different outcomes}$$

when two dice are tossed. To find the probability of rolling a total of 7, you must first count the number of ways this can occur.

	Total of 7					
First die	1	2	3	4	5	6
Second die	6	5	4	3	2	1

Thus, a total of 7 can be rolled in six ways, which means that the probability of rolling a 7 is

$$P(E) = \frac{n(E)}{n(S)} = \frac{6}{36} = \frac{1}{6}.$$

You could have written out each sample space in Examples 3 and 4 and simply counted the outcomes in the desired events. For larger sample spaces, however, you must make more use of the counting principles discussed in the previous section.

EXAMPLE 5   **Finding the Probability of an Event**

Twelve-sided dice can be constructed (in the shape of regular dodecahedrons) so that each of the numbers from 1 to 6 appears twice on each die, as shown in Figure 10.7. Prove that these dice can be used in any game requiring ordinary six-sided dice without changing the probability of different outcomes.

FIGURE 10.7

SOLUTION

For an ordinary six-sided die, each of the numbers 1, 2, 3, 4, 5, and 6 occurs only once, so the probability of any particular number coming up is

$$P(E) = \frac{n(E)}{n(S)} = \frac{1}{6}.$$

For one of the twelve-sided dice, each number occurs twice, so the probability of any particular number coming up is

$$P(E) = \frac{n(E)}{n(S)} = \frac{2}{12} = \frac{1}{6}.$$

Thus, the twelve-sided dice can be used in place of the six-sided dice without changing the probabilities.

EXAMPLE 6   The Probability of Winning a Lottery

A state lottery is set up so that each player chooses six different numbers from 1 to 40. If these six numbers match the six numbers drawn by the lottery commission, the player wins (or shares) the top prize. What is the probability of winning the top prize in this game?

SOLUTION

Since the order of the numbers is not important, use the formula for the number of combinations of 40 elements taken six at a time to determine the size of the sample space.

$$n(S) = {}_{40}C_6 = \frac{40 \cdot 39 \cdot 38 \cdot 37 \cdot 36 \cdot 35}{6 \cdot 5 \cdot 4 \cdot 3 \cdot 2 \cdot 1} = 3{,}838{,}380$$

If a person buys only one ticket, the probability of winning is

$$P(E) = \frac{n(E)}{n(S)} = \frac{1}{3{,}838{,}380}.$$

EXAMPLE 7   Random Selection

The total number of colleges and universities in the United States in 1987 is shown in Figure 10.8. (*Source:* U.S. National Center for Education Statistics) Suppose one institution is selected at random. What is the probability that the institution is in one of three southern regions?

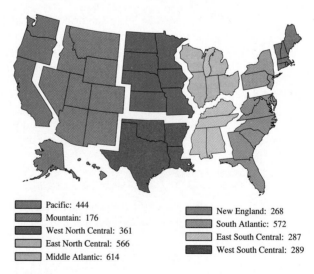

Pacific: 444
Mountain: 176
West North Central: 361
East North Central: 566
Middle Atlantic: 614

New England: 268
South Atlantic: 572
East South Central: 287
West South Central: 289

FIGURE 10.8

SOLUTION

Begin by finding the total number of colleges and universities.

$$\text{Total} = 268 + 614 + 566 + 361 + 572 + 287 + 289 + 176 + 444 = 3577$$

Since there are $572 + 287 + 289 = 1148$ colleges and universities in the three southern regions, the probability that the institution is from one of these regions is

$$P(E) = \frac{n(E)}{n(S)} = \frac{1148}{3577} \approx 0.321.$$

Mutually Exclusive Events

Two events A and B (from the same sample space) are **mutually exclusive** if A and B have no outcomes in common. In the terminology of sets, we say that the **intersection of A and B** is the empty set, which implies that

$$P(A \cap B) = 0.$$

For instance, if two dice are tossed, the event A of rolling a total of six and the event B of rolling a total of nine are mutually exclusive. To find the probability that one or the other of two mutually exclusive events will occur, *add* their individual probabilities.

PROBABILITY OF THE UNION OF TWO EVENTS

If A and B are events in the same sample space, then the probability of A or B occurring is given by

$$P(A \cup B) = P(A) + P(B) - P(A \cap B).$$

If A and B are mutually exclusive, then $P(A \cap B) = 0$ and it follows that

$$P(A \cup B) = P(A) + P(B).$$

EXAMPLE 8   Finding the Probability of the Union of Two Events

One card is selected from a standard deck of 52 playing cards. What is the probability that the card is either a heart or a face card?

SOLUTION

Since the deck has 13 hearts, the probability of selecting a heart (event A) is

$$P(A) = \frac{13}{52}.$$ *Selecting a heart*

Similarly, since the deck has 12 face cards, the probability of selecting a face card (event B) is

$$P(B) = \frac{12}{52}.$$ *Selecting a face card*

Now, because three of the cards are hearts and face cards (see Figure 10.9), it follows that

$$P(A \cap B) = \frac{3}{52}.$$

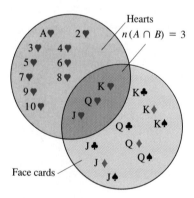

FIGURE 10.9

Finally, applying the formula for the probability of the union of two events, you conclude that the probability of selecting a heart or a face card is

$$P(A \cup B) = P(A) + P(B) - P(A \cap B)$$
$$= \frac{13}{52} + \frac{12}{52} - \frac{3}{52}$$
$$= \frac{22}{52} \approx 0.423.$$

Independent Events

Two events are **independent** if the occurrence of one has no effect on the occurrence of the other. To find the probability that two independent events will occur, *multiply* the probabilities of each. For instance, rolling a total of 12 with two-sided dice has no effect on the outcome for future rolls of the dice.

PROBABILITY OF INDEPENDENT EVENTS

If A and B are independent events, then the probability that both A and B will occur is

$$P(A \text{ and } B) = P(A) \cdot P(B).$$

EXAMPLE 9   Probability of Independent Events

A random number generator on a computer selects three integers from 1 to 20. What is the probability that all three numbers are less than or equal to 5?

SOLUTION

If the random number generator is truly random, then you can conclude that the selection of any given number will not affect the selection of the next number. This means that the three choices represent independent events. Furthermore, since the probability of selecting a number from 1 to 5 is

$$P(A) = \frac{5}{20} = \frac{1}{4}$$

you can conclude that the probability of selecting all three numbers less than or equal to 5 is

$$P(A) \cdot P(A) \cdot P(A) = \left(\frac{1}{4}\right)\left(\frac{1}{4}\right)\left(\frac{1}{4}\right) = \frac{1}{64}.$$

EXAMPLE 10   Probability of Independent Events

In 1988, 54.2% of the population of the United States were 30 years old or older. Suppose that in a survey, 10 people were chosen at random from the population. What is the probability that all 10 are 30 years old or older?

SOLUTION

Let A represent choosing a person who is 30 years old or older. Since the probability of choosing a person who is 30 years old or older is 0.542, you conclude that the probability that all 10 people are 30 years old or older is

$$P(A)^{10} = (0.542)^{10} \approx 0.0022.$$

The Complement of an Event

The **complement of an event** A is the collection of all outcomes in the sample space that are not in A. We denote the complement of event A by A'. Since $P(A \text{ or } A') = 1$ and since A and A' are mutually exclusive, we have $P(A) + P(A') = 1$. Therefore, the probability of A' is given by

$$P(A') = 1 - P(A).$$

For instance, if the probability of *winning* a certain game is

$$P(A) = \frac{1}{4}$$

then the probability of *losing* the game is

$$P(A') = 1 - \frac{1}{4} = \frac{3}{4}.$$

EXAMPLE 11   **Finding the Probability of the Complement of an Event**

A manufacturer has determined that a certain machine averages one faulty unit for every 1000 it produces. What is the probability that an order of 200 units will have one or more faulty units?

SOLUTION

To solve this problem as stated, you would need to find the probability of having exactly one faulty unit, exactly two faulty units, exactly three faulty units, and so on. However, using complements, you can simply find the probability that all units are perfect and then subtract this value from 1. Since the probability that any given unit is perfect is 999/1000, the probability that all 200 units are perfect is

$$P(A) = \left(\frac{999}{1000} \right)^{200} \approx 0.8186.$$

Therefore, the probability that at least one unit is faulty is

$$P(A') = 1 - P(A) \approx 0.1814.$$

DISCUSSION
PROBLEM

....

AN
EXPERIMENT
IN
PROBABILITY

In this section you have been finding probabilities from a *theoretical* point of view. Another way to find probabilities is from an *experimental* point of view. For instance, suppose you want to find the probability of obtaining a given total when two six-sided dice are tossed. The following BASIC program simulates the tossing of a pair of dice 5000 times.

```
 10 RANDOMIZE
 20 DIM TALLY(12)
 30 FOR I=1 TO 5000
 40 ROLLONE=INT(6*RND)+1
 50 ROLLTWO=INT(6*RND)+1
 60 DICETOTAL=ROLLONE+ROLLTWO
 70 TALLY(DICETOTAL)=TALLY(DICETOTAL)+1
 80 NEXT
 90 FOR I=2 TO 12
100 PRINT "TOTAL OF",I,"OCCURRED",TALLY(I),
    "TIMES"
110 NEXT
120 END
```

When you run this program, the printout is as follows.

```
TOTAL OF  2 OCCURRED 139 TIMES
TOTAL OF  3 OCCURRED 264 TIMES
TOTAL OF  4 OCCURRED 443 TIMES
TOTAL OF  5 OCCURRED 553 TIMES
TOTAL OF  6 OCCURRED 691 TIMES
TOTAL OF  7 OCCURRED 810 TIMES
TOTAL OF  8 OCCURRED 715 TIMES
TOTAL OF  9 OCCURRED 557 TIMES
TOTAL OF 10 OCCURRED 398 TIMES
TOTAL OF 11 OCCURRED 270 TIMES
TOTAL OF 12 OCCURRED 160 TIMES
```

In Example 4 you found that the theoretical probability of tossing a total of 7 on a pair of dice is $\frac{1}{6} \approx 0.167$. From this experiment, you find that the experimental probability of tossing a total of 7 on a pair of dice is $810/5000 \approx 0.162$. Try this experiment on a computer that has the BASIC language. By increasing the number of trials from 5000 to 10,000, does your experimental result get closer to the theoretical result?

WARM-UP

The following warm-up exercises involve skills that were covered in earlier sections. You will use these skills in the exercise set for this section.

In Exercises 1–8, evaluate the expression.

1. $\frac{1}{4} + \frac{5}{8} - \frac{5}{16}$

2. $\frac{4}{15} + \frac{3}{5} - \frac{1}{3}$

3. $\frac{5 \cdot 4}{5!}$

4. $\frac{5!22!}{27!}$

5. $\frac{4!8!}{12!}$

6. $\frac{9 \cdot 8 \cdot 7 \cdot 6 \cdot 5}{9!}$

7. $\frac{{}_5C_3}{{}_{10}C_3}$

8. $\frac{{}_{10}C_2 \cdot {}_{10}C_2}{{}_{20}C_4}$

In Exercises 9 and 10, evaluate the expression. (Round to three decimal places.)

9. $\left(\frac{99}{100}\right)^{100}$

10. $1 - \left(\frac{89}{100}\right)^{50}$

SECTION 10.7 · EXERCISES

In Exercises 1–6, determine the sample space for the given experiment.

1. A coin and a die are tossed.

2. A die is tossed twice and the sum of the points is recorded.

3. A taste tester has to rank three varieties of yogurt, A, B, and C, according to preference.

4. Two marbles are selected from a sack containing two red marbles, two blue marbles, and one black marble. The color of each marble is recorded.

5. Two county supervisors are selected from five supervisors, A, B, C, D, and E, to study a recycling plan.

6. A salesperson makes a presentation about a product in three homes per day. In each home there may be a sale (denote by S) or there may be no sale (denote by F).

Heads or Tails In Exercises 7–10, find the required probability in the experiment of tossing a coin three times. Use the sample space $S = \{HHH, HHT, HTH, HTT, THH, THT, TTH, TTT\}$.

7. The probability of getting exactly one tail.

8. The probability of getting a head on the first toss.

9. The probability of getting at least one head.

10. The probability of getting at least two heads.

Drawing a Card In Exercises 11–14, find the required probability in the experiment of selecting one card from a standard deck of 52 playing cards. (A face card is the J, Q, or K.)

11. The probability of getting a face card.

12. The probability of not getting a face card.

13. The probability of getting a black card that is not a face card.

14. The probability that the card will be a 6 or less.

Tossing a Die In Exercises 15–20, find the required probability in the experiment of tossing a six-sided die twice.

15. The probability that the sum is 4.

16. The probability that the sum is less than 11.

17. The probability that the sum is at least 7.

18. The probability that the total is 2, 3, or 12.

19. The probability that the sum is odd and no more than 7.

20. The probability that the sum is odd or a prime.

Drawing Marbles   In Exercises 21–24, find the required probability in the experiment of drawing two marbles (the first is *not* replaced before the second is drawn) from a bag containing one green, two yellow, and three red marbles.

21. The probability of drawing two red marbles.

22. The probability of drawing two yellow marbles.

23. The probability of drawing neither yellow marble.

24. The probability of drawing marbles of different colors.

In Exercises 25 and 26, you are given the probability that an event *will* happen. Find the probability that the event *will not* happen.

25. $p = 0.7$ **26.** $p = 0.36$

In Exercises 27 and 28, you are given the probability that an event *will not* happen. Find the probability that the event *will* happen.

27. $p = 0.15$ **28.** $p = 0.84$

29. *Alumni Association*   The alumni office of a college is sending a survey to selected members of the class of 1990. Of the 1254 people who graduated that year, 672 were women, 124 of whom went on to graduate school. Of the 582 male graduates, 198 went on to graduate school. If an alumni member is selected at random, what is the probability that the person is (a) female, (b) male, and (c) female and did not attend graduate school?

30. *Post High School Education*   In a high school graduating class of 72 students, 28 are on the honor roll. Of these 28, 18 are going on to college. Of the other 44 students, 12 are going on to college. If a student is selected at random from the class, what is the probability that the person chosen is (a) going to college, (b) not going to college, and (c) on the honor roll but not going to college?

31. *Winning an Election*   Taylor, Moore, and Jenkins are candidates for public office. It is estimated that Moore and Jenkins have about the same probability of winning, and Taylor is believed to be twice as likely to win as either of the others. Find the probability of each candidate winning the election.

32. *Winning an Election*   Three people have been nominated for president of a college class. From a small poll, it is estimated that the probability of the first candidate winning the election is 0.37, and the probability of the second candidate winning the election is 0.44. What is the probability that the third candidate will win?

33. *Preparing for a Test*   An instructor gives her class a list of 20 study problems, from which she will select 10 to be answered on an exam. If a given student knows how to solve 15 of the problems, find the probability that the student will be able to answer (a) all 10 questions on the exam, (b) exactly 8 questions on the exam, and (c) at least 9 questions on the exam.

34. *Preparing for a Test*   An instructor gives his class a list of eight study problems, from which he will select five to be answered on an exam. If a given student knows how to solve six of the problems, find the probability that the student will be able to answer (a) all five questions on the exam, (b) exactly four questions on the exam, and (c) at least four questions on the exam.

35. *Letter Mix-Up*   Four letters and envelopes are addressed to four different people. If the letters are randomly inserted into the envelopes, what is the probability that (a) exactly one will be inserted in the correct envelope and (b) at least one will be inserted in the correct envelope?

36. *Payroll Mix-Up*   Five paychecks and envelopes are addressed to five different people. If the paychecks are randomly inserted into the envelopes, what is the probability that (a) exactly one will be inserted in the correct envelope and (b) at least one will be inserted in the correct envelope?

37. *Game Show*   On a game show you are given five digits to arrange in the proper order to give the price of a car. If you are correct, you win the car. What is the probability of winning, given the following conditions?
(a) You guess the position of each digit.
(b) You know the first digit, but must guess the remaining four.

38. *Game Show*   On a game show you are given four digits to arrange in the proper order to give the price of a car. If you are correct, you win the car. What is the probability of winning, given the following conditions?
(a) You guess the position of each digit.
(b) You know the first digit, but must guess the remaining three.

39. *Drawing Cards from a Deck*   Two cards are selected at random from an ordinary deck of 52 playing cards. Find the probability that two aces are selected, given the following conditions.
(a) The cards are drawn in sequence, with the first card being replaced and the deck reshuffled prior to the second drawing.
(b) The two cards are drawn consecutively, without replacement.

40. *Poker Hand* Five cards are drawn from an ordinary deck of 52 playing cards. What is the probability of getting a full house?

41. *Defective Units* A shipment of 12 microwave ovens contains three defective units. A vending company has ordered four of these 12 units, and since each is identically packaged, the selection will be random. What is the probability that (a) all four units are good, (b) exactly two units are good, and (c) at least two units are good?

42. *Defective Units* A shipment of 20 compact disc players contains four defective units. A retail outlet has ordered five of these units. What is the probability that (a) all five players are good, (b) exactly four of the players are good, and (c) at least one of the players is defective?

43. *Random Number Generator* Two integers (between 1 and 30 inclusive) are chosen by a random number generator on a computer. What is the probability that (a) the numbers are both even, (b) one number is even and one is odd, (c) both numbers are less than 10, and (d) the same number is chosen twice?

44. *Random Number Generator* Two integers (between 1 and 40 inclusive) are chosen by a random number generator on a computer. What is the probability that (a) the numbers are both even, (b) one number is even and one is odd, (c) both numbers are no more than 30, and (d) the same number is chosen twice?

45. *Backup System* A space vehicle has an independent backup system for one of its communication networks. The probability that either system will function satisfactorily for the duration of a flight is 0.985. What is the probability that during a given flight (a) both systems function satisfactorily, (b) at least one system functions satisfactorily, and (c) both systems fail?

46. *Backup Vehicle* A fire company keeps two rescue vehicles to serve the community. Because of the demand on the company's time and the chance of mechanical failure, the probability that a specific vehicle is available when needed is 90%. If the availability of one vehicle is *independent* of the other, find the probability that (a) both vehicles are available at a given time, (b) neither vehicle is available at a given time, and (c) at least one vehicle is available at a given time.

47. *Making a Sale* A sales representative makes a sale at a rate of approximately one-fourth of all calls. If, on a given day, the representative contacts five potential clients, what is the probability that a sale will be made with (a) all five contacts, (b) none of the contacts, and (c) at least one contact?

48. *Making a Sale* A sales representative makes a sale at a rate of approximately one-third of all calls. If, on a given day, the representative contacts four potential clients, what is the probability that a sale will be made with (a) all four contacts, (b) none of the contacts, and (c) at least one contact?

49. *A Boy or a Girl?* Assume that the probability of the birth of a child of a particular sex is 50%. In a family with four children, what is the probability that (a) all the children are boys, (b) all the children are the same sex, and (c) there is at least one boy?

50. *A Boy or a Girl?* Assume that the probability of the birth of a child of a particular sex is 50%. In a family with six children, what is the probability that (a) all the children are girls, (b) all the children are the same sex, and (c) there is at least one girl?

51. *Is That Cash or Charge?* According to a survey by *USA Today,* the method used by Christmas shoppers to pay for gifts is as shown in the pie chart. Suppose two Christmas shoppers are chosen at random. What is the probability that both shoppers paid for their gifts only in cash?

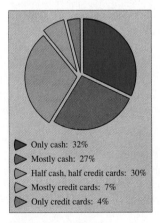

▶ Only cash: 32%
▶ Mostly cash: 27%
▶ Half cash, half credit cards: 30%
▶ Mostly credit cards: 7%
▶ Only credit cards: 4%

FIGURE FOR 51

52. *Flexible Work Hours*   In a survey by *Robert Hall International*, people were asked if they would prefer to work flexible hours—even if it meant slower career advancement—so they could spend more time with their family. The results of the survey are shown in the figure. Suppose three people from the survey were chosen at random. What is the probability that all three people would prefer flexible work hours?

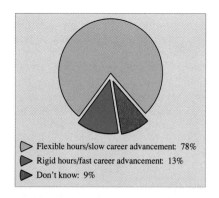

▷ Flexible hours/slow career advancement: 78%
▶ Rigid hours/fast career advancement: 13%
▶ Don't know: 9%

FIGURE FOR 52

CHAPTER 10 · REVIEW EXERCISES

In Exercises 1–4, use sigma notation to write the given sum.

1. $\dfrac{1}{2(1)} + \dfrac{1}{2(2)} + \dfrac{1}{2(3)} + \cdots + \dfrac{1}{2(20)}$

2. $2(1^2) + 2(2^2) + 2(3^2) + \cdots + 2(9^2)$

3. $\dfrac{1}{2} + \dfrac{2}{3} + \dfrac{3}{4} + \cdots + \dfrac{9}{10}$

4. $1 - \dfrac{1}{3} + \dfrac{1}{9} - \dfrac{1}{27} + \cdots$

In Exercises 5–18, find the sum.

5. $\displaystyle\sum_{i=1}^{6} 5$

6. $\displaystyle\sum_{k=2}^{5} 4k$

7. $\displaystyle\sum_{j=3}^{10} (2j - 3)$

8. $\displaystyle\sum_{j=1}^{8} (20 - 3j)$

9. $\displaystyle\sum_{i=0}^{6} 2^i$

10. $\displaystyle\sum_{i=0}^{4} 3^i$

11. $\displaystyle\sum_{i=0}^{\infty} \left(\dfrac{7}{8}\right)^i$

12. $\displaystyle\sum_{i=0}^{\infty} \left(\dfrac{1}{3}\right)^i$

13. $\displaystyle\sum_{k=0}^{\infty} 4\left(\dfrac{2}{3}\right)^k$

14. $\displaystyle\sum_{k=0}^{\infty} 1.3\left(\dfrac{1}{10}\right)^k$

15. $\displaystyle\sum_{k=1}^{11} \left(\dfrac{2}{3}k + 4\right)$

16. $\displaystyle\sum_{k=1}^{25} \left(\dfrac{3k + 1}{4}\right)$

17. $\displaystyle\sum_{n=0}^{10} (n^2 + 3)$

18. $\displaystyle\sum_{n=1}^{100} \left(\dfrac{1}{n} - \dfrac{1}{n + 1}\right)$

In Exercises 19–22, write the first five terms of the arithmetic sequence.

19. $a_1 = 3, d = 4$ **20.** $a_1 = 8, d = -2$

21. $a_4 = 10, a_{10} = 28$ **22.** $a_2 = 14, a_6 = 22$

In Exercises 23 and 24, write an expression for the nth term of the specified arithmetic sequence and find the sum of the first 20 terms of the sequence.

23. $a_1 = 100, d = -3$ **24.** $a_1 = 10, a_3 = 28$

25. Find the sum of the first 100 positive multiples of 5.

26. Find the sum of the integers from 20 to 80 (inclusive).

In Exercises 27–30, write the first five terms of the geometric sequence.

27. $a_1 = 4, r = -\frac{1}{4}$ **28.** $a_1 = 2, r = 2$

29. $a_1 = 9, a_3 = 4$ **30.** $a_1 = 2, a_3 = 12$

In Exercises 31 and 32, write an expression for the nth term of the specified geometric sequence and find the sum of the first 20 terms of the sequence.

31. $a_1 = 16, a_2 = -8$ **32.** $a_1 = 100, r = 1.05$

33. *Depreciation*   A company buys a machine for $120,000. During the next 5 years it will depreciate at the rate of 30% per year. (That is, at the end of each year the depreciated value will be 70% of what it was at the beginning of the year.)

(a) Find the formula for the nth term of a geometric sequence that gives the value of the machine t full years after it was purchased.

(b) Find the depreciated value of the machine at the end of 5 full years.

34. *Total Compensation*   Suppose you accept a job that pays a salary of $32,000 the first year and that you will receive a 5.5% raise each year for each of the next 39 years. What will your total salary be over the 40-year period?

35. *Compound Interest*   A deposit of $200 is made at the beginning of each month for 2 years into an account that pays 6%, compounded monthly. What is the balance in the account at the end of 2 years?

36. *Compound Interest*   A deposit of $100 is made at the beginning of each month for 10 years in an account that pays 6.5%, compounded monthly. What is the balance in the account at the end of 10 years?

In Exercises 37–40, use mathematical induction to prove the given formula for every positive integer n.

37. $1 + 4 + \cdots + (3n - 2) = \dfrac{n}{2}(3n - 1)$

38. $1 + \dfrac{3}{2} + 2 + \dfrac{5}{2} + \cdots + \dfrac{1}{2}(n + 1) = \dfrac{n}{4}(n + 3)$

39. $\displaystyle\sum_{i=0}^{n-1} ar^i = \dfrac{a(1 - r^n)}{1 - r}$

40. $\displaystyle\sum_{k=0}^{n-1} (a + kd) = \dfrac{n}{2}[2a + (n - 1)d]$

In Exercises 41–44, evaluate $_n C_m$. If your graphing utility has a binomial coefficient key (also called the combinations function), use it to verify your answer.

41. $_6 C_4$ **42.** $_{10} C_7$

43. $_{25} C_5$ **44.** $_{12} C_3$

In Exercises 45–50, use the Binomial Theorem to expand the binomial. Simplify your result. (Remember that $i = \sqrt{-1}$.)

45. $\left(\dfrac{x}{2} + y\right)^4$ **46.** $(a - 3b)^5$

47. $\left(\dfrac{2}{x} - 3x\right)^6$ **48.** $(3x + y^2)^7$

49. $(5 + 2i)^4$ **50.** $(4 - 5i)^3$

51. *Interpersonal Relationships*   The complexity of interpersonal relationships increases dramatically as the size of a group increases. Determine the number of different two-person relationships in a family of (a) 2, (b) 4, and (c) 6.

52. *Morse Code*   In Morse Code, all characters are transmitted using a sequence of dits and dahs. How many different characters can be formed by a sequence of three dits and dahs? (These can be repeated. For example, dit-dit-dit represents the letter s.)

53. *Amateur Radio*   A Novice Amateur Radio license consists of two letters, one digit, and then three more letters. How many different licenses can be issued if no restrictions are placed on the letters or digits?

54. *Connecting Points with Lines*   How many different straight-line segments are determined by (a) five non-collinear points and (b) ten noncollinear points?

55. *Matching Socks*   A man has five pairs of socks (no two pairs are the same color). If he randomly selects two socks from the drawer, what is the probability that he gets a matched pair?

56. *Bookshelf Order*   A child carries a five-volume set of books to a bookshelf. The child is not able to read, and hence cannot distinguish one volume from another. What is the probability that the books are shelved in the correct order?

57. *Roll of the Dice*   Are the chances of rolling a 3 with one die the same as the chances of rolling a total of 6 with two dice? If not, which has the higher probability?

58. *Roll of the Dice*   A die is rolled six times. What is the probability that each side will appear exactly once?

59. *Tossing a Coin*   Find the probability of obtaining at least one tail when a coin is tossed five times.

60. *Parental Independence*   In the *Marriott Seniors' Attitudes Survey,* senior citizens were asked if they would live with their children when they reached the point of not being able to live alone. The results are shown in the figure. Suppose three senior citizens who could not live alone are randomly selected. What is the probability that all three are not living with their children?

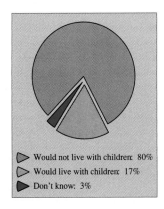

▷ Would not live with children: 80%
▷ Would live with children: 17%
▶ Don't know: 3%

FIGURE FOR 60

61. *Card Game*   Five cards are drawn from an ordinary deck of 52 playing cards. Find the probability of getting two pairs. (For example, the hand could be A-A-5-5-Q or 4-4-7-7-K.)

62. *Birthday Problem*
   (a) What is the probability that, in a group of 10 people, at least two have the same birthday? (Assume there are 365 different birthdays in a year.)
   (b) How large must the group be before the probability that two have the same birthday is at least 50%?

CHAPTER 11

PARAMETRIC EQUATIONS AND POLAR COORDINATES

11.1 PLANE CURVES AND PARAMETRIC EQUATIONS

Plane Curves / Sketching a Plane Curve / Eliminating the Parameter / Finding Parametric Equations for a Graph

Plane Curves

Up to this point, you have been representing a graph by a single equation involving the *two* variables x and y. In this section, you will study situations in which it is useful to introduce a *third* variable to represent a curve in the plane.

To see the usefulness of this procedure, consider the path followed by an object that is propelled into the air at an angle of 45°. If the initial velocity of the object is 48 feet per second, it can be shown that it follows the parabolic path given by

$$y = -\frac{x^2}{72} + x,$$ *Rectangular equation*

as shown in Figure 11.1. However, this equation does not tell the whole story. Although it does tell us *where* the object has been, it doesn't tell us *when* the object was at a given point (x, y) on the path. To determine this time, we introduce a third variable t, which we call a **parameter.** It is possible to write both x and y as functions of t to obtain the **parametric equations**

$$x = 24\sqrt{2}t \quad \text{and} \quad y = -16t^2 + 24\sqrt{2}t. \quad \text{\textit{Parametric equations}}$$

From this set of equations we can determine that at time $t = 0$, the object is at the point $(0, 0)$. Similarly, at time $t = 1$, the object is at the point $(24\sqrt{2}, 24\sqrt{2} - 16)$, and so on.

Rectangular equation:
$$y = -\frac{x^2}{72} + x$$

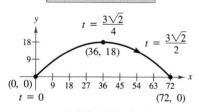

Parametric equations:
$$x = 24\sqrt{2}t$$
$$y = -16t^2 + 24\sqrt{2}t$$

Curvilinear Motion:
two variables for position
one variable for time

FIGURE 11.1

757

For this particular motion problem, x and y are continuous functions of t, and we call the resulting path a **plane curve.** (Recall that a *continuous function* is one whose graph can be traced without lifting the pencil from the paper.)

DEFINITION OF A PLANE CURVE

If f and g are continuous functions of t on an interval I, then the set of ordered pairs $(f(t), g(t))$ is a **plane curve** C. The equations $x = f(t)$ and $y = g(t)$ are **parametric equations** for C, and t is the **parameter.**

Sketching a Plane Curve

One way to sketch a curve represented by a pair of parametric equations is to plot points in the xy plane. Each set of coordinates (x, y) is determined from a value chosen for the parameter t. By plotting the resulting points in the order of *increasing* values of t, you trace the curve in a specific direction. This is called the **orientation** of the curve.

EXAMPLE 1   Sketching a Curve

Sketch the curve described by the parametric equations

$$x = t^2 - 4 \quad \text{and} \quad y = \frac{t}{2}, \qquad -2 \le t \le 3.$$

SOLUTION

Using values of t in the given interval, the parametric equations yield the points (x, y) shown in the table.

t	-2	-1	0	1	2	3
x	0	-3	-4	-3	0	5
y	-1	$-\frac{1}{2}$	0	$\frac{1}{2}$	1	$\frac{3}{2}$

By plotting these points in the order of increasing t, we obtain the curve shown in Figure 11.2. Note that the arrows on the curve indicate its orientation as t increases from -2 to 3.

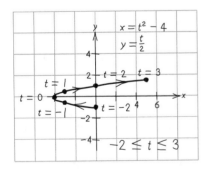

FIGURE 11.2

The graph shown in Figure 11.2 does not define y as a function of x. This points out one benefit of parametric equations—they can be used to represent graphs that are more general than graphs of functions.

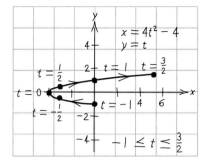

FIGURE 11.3

Two different sets of parametric equations can have the same graph. For example, the set of parametric equations

$$x = 4t^2 - 4 \quad \text{and} \quad y = t, \quad -1 \le t \le \frac{3}{2}$$

has the same graph as the set given in Example 1. However, by comparing the values of t in Figures 11.2 and 11.3, you can see that this second graph is traced out more *rapidly* (considering t as time) than the first graph. Thus, in applications, different parametric representations can be used to represent various *speeds* at which objects travel along a given path.

Another way to display a curve represented by a pair of parametric equations is to use a graphing utility. When you do this, be sure to set the graphing utility to parametric mode.

EXAMPLE 2 Using a Graphing Utility in Parametric Mode

Use a graphing utility to graph the curves represented by the parametric equations. For which curve is y a function of x?

A. $x = \cos^3 t$ **B.** $x = t$
       $y = \sin^3 t$ $y = t^3$

SOLUTION

Begin by setting the graphing utility to parametric *and* radian mode. When choosing a viewing rectangle, you must not only set minimum and maximum values of x and y, you must also set minimum and maximum values of t.

A. Enter the parametric equations for x and y. The curve is shown in Figure 11.4(a). From the graph, you can see that y is *not* a function of x.

B. Enter the parametric equations for x and y. The curve is shown in Figure 11.4(b). From the graph, you can see that y *is* a function of x.

Technology Note —————

When you use a graphing utility to graph the curve represented by a set of parametric equations, be sure to set the utility to parametric mode. If the parameter involves an angle, you must also set the angle measure to the proper mode (usually radians).

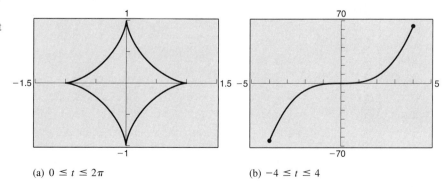

(a) $0 \le t \le 2\pi$ (b) $-4 \le t \le 4$

FIGURE 11.4

Eliminating the Parameter

Many curves that are represented by a set of parametric equations have graphs that can also be represented by a rectangular equation (in x and y). The process of finding the rectangular equation is called **eliminating the parameter.** Here is an example.

Parametric equations	$\rightarrow$	Solve for t in one equation	$\rightarrow$	Substitute into second equation	$\rightarrow$	Rectangular equation
$x = t^2 - 4$		$t = 2y$		$x = (2y)^2 - 4$		$x = 4y^2 - 4$
$y = \dfrac{t}{2}$						

After eliminating the parameter, you can recognize that the curve is a parabola with a horizontal axis and vertex at $(-4, 0)$.

Converting equations from parametric to rectangular form can change the ranges of x and y. In such cases, you should restrict x and y in the rectangular equation so that the graph of this equation matches the graph of the parametric equations.

Parametric equations:
$$x = \frac{1}{\sqrt{t+1}}, \quad y = \frac{t}{t+1}$$

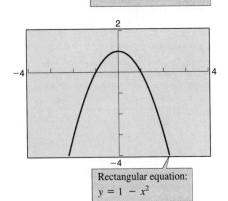

Rectangular equation:
$$y = 1 - x^2$$

FIGURE 11.5

EXAMPLE 3 **Adjusting the Domain after Eliminating the Parameter**

Identify the curve represented by the equations

$$x = \frac{1}{\sqrt{t+1}} \quad \text{and} \quad y = \frac{t}{t+1}.$$

SOLUTION

Solving for t in the equation for x produces

$$x = \frac{1}{\sqrt{t+1}} \quad \text{or} \quad x^2 = \frac{1}{t+1},$$

which implies that $t = (1 - x^2)/x^2$. Substituting into the equation for y, we obtain

$$y = \frac{t}{t+1} = \frac{(1 - x^2)/x^2}{[(1 - x^2)/x^2] + 1} = 1 - x^2.$$

From the rectangular equation, you can recognize the curve to be a parabola that opens downward and has its vertex at $(0, 1)$. The rectangular equation is defined for all values of x. From the parametric equation for x, however, you can see that the curve is defined only when $-1 < t$. Thus, you should restrict the domain of x to positive values, as shown in Figure 11.5. ﹅﹅﹅﹅﹅

It is not necessary for the parameter in a set of parametric equations to represent time. For instance, in the set of parametric equations in Example 4, *angle* is used as the parameter.

EXAMPLE 4   Using a Trigonometric Identity to Eliminate a Parameter

Identify the curve represented by

$$x = 3 \cos \theta \quad \text{and} \quad y = 4 \sin \theta, \qquad 0 \le \theta \le 2\pi.$$

SOLUTION

Begin by solving for $\cos \theta$ and $\sin \theta$ in the given equations.

$$\cos \theta = \frac{x}{3} \quad \text{and} \quad \sin \theta = \frac{y}{4} \qquad \textit{Solve for } \cos \theta \textit{ and } \sin \theta$$

You can use the identity $\cos^2 \theta + \sin^2 \theta = 1$ to form an equation involving only x and y.

$$\cos^2 \theta + \sin^2 \theta = 1 \qquad \textit{Trigonometric Identity}$$

$$\cos^2 \theta + \sin^2 \theta = \left(\frac{x}{3}\right)^2 + \left(\frac{y}{4}\right)^2 = 1 \qquad \textit{Substitute}$$

$$\frac{x^2}{9} + \frac{y^2}{16} = 1 \qquad \textit{Rectangular equation}$$

From the rectangular equation, you can see that the graph is an ellipse centered at $(0, 0)$, with vertices at $(0, 4)$ and $(0, -4)$, and minor axis of length $2b = 6$, as shown in Figure 11.6. Note that the ellipse is traced out *counterclockwise* as θ varies from 0 to 2π.

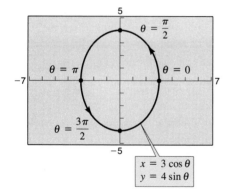

FIGURE 11.6

In Examples 3 and 4, it is important to realize that eliminating the parameter is primarily an aid to identifying the curve. If the parametric equations represent the path of a moving object, the graph alone is not sufficient to describe the object's motion. You still need the parametric equations to determine the *position, direction,* and *speed* at a given time.

Finding Parametric Equations for a Graph

How can we determine a set of parametric equations for a given graph or a given physical description? From the discussion following Example 1, we know that such a representation is not unique. This is further demonstrated in the following example, in which we find two different parametric representations for a graph.

EXAMPLE 5   **Finding Parametric Equations for a Given Graph**

Find a set of parametric equations to represent the graph of $y = 1 - x^2$, using the following parameters.

A. $t = x$ **B.** $t = 1 - x$

SOLUTION

A. Letting $t = x$, you obtain the parametric equations

$$x = t \quad \text{and} \quad y = 1 - x^2 = 1 - t^2.$$

B. Letting $t = 1 - x$, you obtain

$$x = 1 - t \quad \text{and} \quad y = 1 - (1 - t)^2 = 2t - t^2.$$

In Figure 11.7, note how the resulting curve is oriented by the increasing values of t. For part (A), the curve would have the opposite orientation.

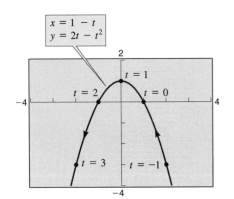

Graph of $y = 1 - x^2$

FIGURE 11.7

EXAMPLE 6   **Parametric Equations for a Cycloid**

Determine the **cycloid** traced out by a point P on the circumference of a circle of radius a as the circle rolls along a straight line in a plane.

SOLUTION

Use the parameter θ, where θ is the measure of the circle's rotation. Assume that the point $P = (x, y)$ begins at the origin. When $\theta = 0$, P is at the origin; when $\theta = \pi$, P is at a maximum point $(\pi a, 2a)$; and when $\theta = 2\pi$, P is back on the x-axis at $(2\pi a, 0)$. In Figure 11.8, you can see that $\angle APC = 180° - \theta$.

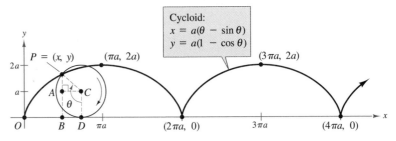

Cycloid:
$x = a(\theta - \sin\theta)$
$y = a(1 - \cos\theta)$

FIGURE 11.8

Hence, you have

$$\sin \theta = \sin(180° - \theta) = \sin(\angle APC) = \frac{AC}{a} = \frac{BD}{a}$$

$$\cos \theta = -\cos(180° - \theta) = -\cos(\angle APC) = \frac{AP}{-a},$$

which implies that $AP = -a \cos \theta$ and $BD = a \sin \theta$. Now, because the circle rolls along the x-axis, we know that $OD = \overset{\frown}{PD} = a\theta$. Furthermore, because $BA = DC = a$, we have

$$x = OD - BD = a\theta - a \sin \theta$$
$$y = BA + AP = a - a \cos \theta.$$

Therefore, the parametric equations are

$$x = a(\theta - \sin \theta) \quad \text{and} \quad y = a(1 - \cos \theta).$$

DISCUSSION PROBLEM

CHANGING THE ORIENTATION OF A CURVE

The **orientation** of a curve refers to the direction in which the curve is traced as the values of the parameter increase. For instance, as t increases, the circle given by

$$x = \cos t \quad \text{and} \quad y = \sin t$$

is traced out *counterclockwise*. Find a parametric representation for which the circle is traced out *clockwise*.

WARM-UP

The following warm-up exercises involve skills that were covered in earlier sections. You will use these skills in the exercise set for this section.

In Exercises 1–6, sketch the graph of the equation.

1. $y = -\frac{1}{4}x^2$ 2. $y = 4 - \frac{1}{4}(x - 2)^2$
3. $16x^2 + y^2 = 16$ 4. $-16x^2 + y^2 = 16$
5. $x + y = 4$ 6. $x^2 + y^2 = 16$

In Exercises 7–10, simplify the expression.

7. $10 \sin^2 \theta + 10 \cos^2 \theta$ 8. $5 \sec^2 \theta - 5$

9. $\sec^4 x - \tan^4 x$ 10. $\dfrac{\sin 2\theta}{4 \cos \theta}$

SECTION 11.1 · EXERCISES

In Exercises 1–20, sketch the curve represented by the parametric equations (indicate the direction of the curve). Use a graphing utility to confirm your result. Then eliminate the parameter and write a rectangular equation whose graph represents the curve.

1. $x = t$
$y = -2t$

2. $x = t$
$y = \frac{1}{2}t$

3. $x = 3t - 1$
$y = 2t + 1$

4. $x = 3 - 2t$
$y = 2 + 3t$

5. $x = \frac{1}{4}t$
$y = t^2$

6. $x = t$
$y = t^3$

7. $x = t + 1$
$y = t^2$

8. $x = \sqrt{t}$
$y = 1 - t$

9. $x = t^3$
$y = \dfrac{t}{2}$

10. $x = t - 1$
$y = \dfrac{t}{t - 1}$

11. $x = 3 \cos \theta$
$y = 3 \sin \theta$

12. $x = 4 \sin 2\theta$
$y = 2 \cos 2\theta$

13. $x = \cos \theta$
$y = 2 \sin^2 \theta$

14. $x = \sec \theta$
$y = \cos \theta$

15. $x = 4 + 2 \cos \theta$
$y = -1 + 4 \sin \theta$

16. $x = 4 \sec \theta$
$y = 3 \tan \theta$

17. $x = e^{-t}$
$y = e^{3t}$

18. $x = e^{2t}$
$y = e^{t}$

19. $x = t^3$
$y = 3 \ln t$

20. $x = \ln t$
$y = t^2$

In Exercises 21 and 22, describe how the curves differ from each other.

21. (a) $x = t$
$y = 2t + 1$

(b) $x = \cos \theta$
$y = 2 \cos \theta + 1$

(c) $x = e^{-t}$
$y = 2e^{-t} + 1$

(d) $x = e^{t}$
$y = 2e^{t} + 1$

22. (a) $x = t$
$y = t^2 - 1$

(b) $x = t^2$
$y = t^4 - 1$

(c) $x = \sin t$
$y = \sin^2 t - 1$

(d) $x = e^{t}$
$y = e^{2t} - 1$

In Exercises 23–26, eliminate the parameter and obtain the standard form of the rectangular equation.

23. Line through (x_1, y_1) and (x_2, y_2):
$x = x_1 + t(x_2 - x_1)$
$y = y_1 + t(y_2 - y_1)$

24. Circle:
$x = h + r \cos \theta$
$y = k + r \sin \theta$

25. Ellipse:
$x = h + a \cos \theta$
$y = k + b \sin \theta$

26. Hyperbola:
$x = h + a \sec \theta$
$y = k + b \tan \theta$

In Exercises 27–34, use the results of Exercises 23–26 to find a set of parametric equations for the line or conic.

27. Line: Passes through $(0, 0)$ and $(5, -2)$
28. Line: Passes through $(1, 4)$ and $(5, -2)$
29. Circle: Center: $(2, 1)$
    Radius: 4
30. Circle: Center: $(-3, 1)$
    Radius: 3
31. Ellipse: Vertices: $(\pm 5, 0)$
    Foci: $(\pm 4, 0)$
32. Ellipse: Vertices: $(4, 7)$, $(4, -3)$
    Foci: $(4, 5)$, $(4, -1)$
33. Hyperbola: Vertices: $(\pm 4, 0)$
    Foci: $(\pm 5, 0)$
34. Hyperbola: Vertices: $(0, \pm 1)$
    Foci: $(0, \pm 5)$

In Exercises 35 and 36, find two different sets of parametric equations for the rectangular equation.

35. $y = x^3$ **36.** $y = x^2$

In Exercises 37–42, use a graphing utility to graph the curve represented by the parametric equations.

37. Cycloid: $x = 2(\theta - \sin \theta)$
$$y = 2(1 - \cos \theta)$$

38. Cycloid: $x = \theta + \sin \theta$
$$y = 1 - \cos \theta$$

39. Prolate cycloid: $x = \theta - \frac{3}{2} \sin \theta$
$$y = 1 - \frac{3}{2} \cos \theta$$

40. Curtate cycloid: $x = 2\theta - \sin \theta$
$$y = 2 - \cos \theta$$

41. Witch of Agnesi: $x = 2 \cot \theta$
$$y = 2 \sin^2 \theta$$

42. Folium of Descartes: $x = \dfrac{3t}{1 + t^3}$
$$y = \dfrac{3t^2}{1 + t^3}$$

In Exercises 43–46, match the parametric equation with the correct graph and describe the viewing rectangle. [The graphs are labeled (a), (b), (c), and (d).]

43. Lissajous curve: $x = 4 \cos \theta$
$$y = 2 \sin 2\theta$$

44. Evolute of ellipse: $x = \cos^3 \theta$
$$y = 2 \sin^3 \theta$$

45. Involute of circle: $x = \cos \theta + \theta \sin \theta$
$$y = \sin \theta - \theta \cos \theta$$

46. Serpentine curve: $x = \cot \theta$
$$y = 4 \sin \theta \cos \theta$$

(a)

(b)

(c)

(d)

47. A wheel of radius a rolls along a straight line without slipping (see figure). Find the parametric equations for the curve generated by a point P that is b units from the center of the wheel. This curve is called a *curtate cycloid* when $b < a$.

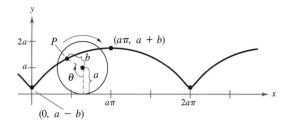

FIGURE FOR 47

48. A wheel of radius 1 rolls around the outside of a circle of radius 2 without slipping (see figure). Show that the parametric equations for the curve generated by a point on the rolling wheel are

$$x = 3 \cos \theta - \cos 3\theta \quad \text{and} \quad y = 3 \sin \theta - \sin 3\theta.$$

This curve is called an *epicycloid*.

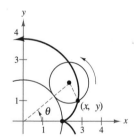

FIGURE FOR 48

11.2 POLAR COORDINATES
••
Introduction / Coordinate Conversion / Equation Conversion

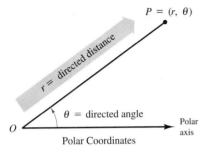

FIGURE 11.9

Introduction

To form the **polar coordinate system** in the plane, fix a point O, called the **pole** (or **origin**), and construct from O an initial ray called the **polar axis,** as shown in Figure 11.9. Each point P in the plane is assigned **polar coordinates** (r, θ) as follows.

1. $r =$ *directed distance* from O to P
2. $\theta =$ *directed angle*, counterclockwise from polar axis to segment $\overline{OP}$

   In the polar coordinate system, it is convenient to locate points with respect to a grid of concentric circles intersected by **radial lines** through the pole. This procedure is shown in Example 1.

EXAMPLE 1   Plotting Points in the Polar Coordinate System
••••••••••••••••

A. The point $(r, \theta) = (2, \pi/3)$ lies at the intersection of a circle of radius $r = 2$ and the terminal side of the angle $\theta = \pi/3$, as shown in Figure 11.10(a).
B. The point $(r, \theta) = (3, -\pi/6)$ lies in the fourth quadrant, 3 units from the pole. Note that negative angles are measured *clockwise,* as shown in Figure 11.10(b).
C. The point $(r, \theta) = (3, 11\pi/6)$ coincides with the point $(3, -\pi/6)$, as shown in Figure 11.10(c).

(a)

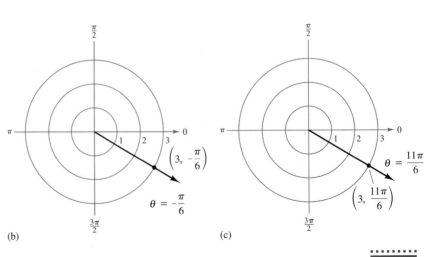

(b)   (c)

FIGURE 11.10

In rectangular coordinates, each point (x, y) has a unique representation. This is not true for polar coordinates. For instance, the coordinates (r, θ) and $(r, 2\pi + \theta)$ represent the same point. Another way to obtain multiple representations of a point is to use negative values of r. Because r is a *directed distance*, the coordinates (r, θ) and $(-r, \theta + \pi)$ represent the same point. In general, the point (r, θ) can be represented as

$$(r, \theta \pm 2n\pi) \quad \text{or} \quad (-r, \theta \pm (2n + 1)\pi),$$

where n is any integer. Moreover, the pole is represented by $(0, \theta)$, where θ is any angle.

EXAMPLE 2   Multiple Representation of Points

Plot the point $(3, -3\pi/4)$ and find three additional polar representations of this point, using $-2\pi < \theta < 2\pi$.

SOLUTION

The point is shown in Figure 11.11. Three other representations are as follows.

$$\left(3, \frac{-3\pi}{4} + 2\pi\right) = \left(3, \frac{5\pi}{4}\right) \qquad \text{\textit{Add} } 2\pi \text{ \textit{to} } \theta$$

$$\left(-3, \frac{-3\pi}{4} - \pi\right) = \left(-3, \frac{-7\pi}{4}\right) \qquad \begin{array}{l}\text{\textit{Replace} } r \text{ \textit{with} } -r; \\ \text{\textit{subtract} } \pi \text{ \textit{from} } \theta\end{array}$$

$$\left(-3, \frac{-3\pi}{4} + \pi\right) = \left(-3, \frac{\pi}{4}\right) \qquad \text{\textit{Replace} } r \text{ \textit{with} } -r; \text{ \textit{add} } \pi \text{ \textit{to} } \theta$$

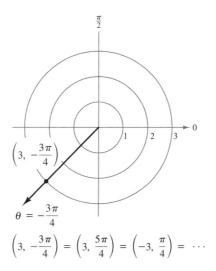

$$\left(3, -\frac{3\pi}{4}\right) = \left(3, \frac{5\pi}{4}\right) = \left(-3, \frac{\pi}{4}\right) = \cdots$$

FIGURE 11.11

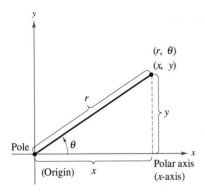

Relating Polar and Rectangular Coordinates

FIGURE 11.12

Coordinate Conversion

To establish the relationship between polar and rectangular coordinates, let the polar axis coincide with the positive x-axis and the pole with the origin, as shown in Figure 11.12. Because (x, y) lies on a circle of radius r, it follows that $r^2 = x^2 + y^2$. Moreover, for $r > 0$, the definitions of the trigonometric functions imply that

$$\tan \theta = \frac{y}{x}, \quad \cos \theta = \frac{x}{r}, \quad \text{and} \quad \sin \theta = \frac{y}{r}.$$

If $r < 0$, you can show that the same relationships hold. For example, consider the point (r, θ), where $r < 0$. Then, because $(-r, \theta + \pi)$ represents the same point and $-r > 0$, you have $-\sin \theta = \sin(\theta + \pi) = -y/r$, which implies that $\sin \theta = y/r$.

These relationships allow you to convert *coordinates* or *equations* from one system to the other, as indicated in the following rule.

COORDINATE CONVERSION

The polar coordinates (r, θ) are related to the rectangular coordinates (x, y) as follows.

$$x = r \cos \theta \quad \text{and} \quad \tan \theta = \frac{y}{x}$$

$$y = r \sin \theta \qquad\qquad r^2 = x^2 + y^2$$

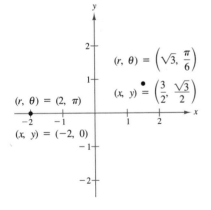

FIGURE 11.13

EXAMPLE 3   **Polar-to-Rectangular Conversion**

A. For the point $(r, \theta) = (2, \pi)$, you can write the following.

$$x = r \cos \theta = 2 \cos \pi = -2$$
$$y = r \sin \theta = 2 \sin \pi = 0$$

The rectangular coordinates are $(x, y) = (-2, 0)$, as shown in Figure 11.13.

B. For the point $(r, \theta) = (\sqrt{3}, \pi/6)$, you can write the following.

$$x = \sqrt{3} \cos \frac{\pi}{6} = \sqrt{3}\left(\frac{\sqrt{3}}{2}\right) = \frac{3}{2}$$

$$y = \sqrt{3} \sin \frac{\pi}{6} = \sqrt{3}\left(\frac{1}{2}\right) = \frac{\sqrt{3}}{2}$$

The rectangular coordinates are $(x, y) = (3/2, \sqrt{3}/2)$, as shown in Figure 11.13.

EXAMPLE 4   **Rectangular-to-Polar Conversion**

A. For the second quadrant point $(x, y) = (-1, 1)$, you can write

$$\tan \theta = \frac{y}{x} = -1 \quad \longrightarrow \quad \theta = \frac{3\pi}{4}.$$

Because θ lies in the same quadrant as (x, y), use positive r.

$$r = \sqrt{x^2 + y^2} = \sqrt{(-1)^2 + (1)^2} = \sqrt{2}$$

Thus, *one* set of polar coordinates is $(r, \theta) = (\sqrt{2}, 3\pi/4)$, as shown in Figure 11.14(a).

B. Because the point $(x, y) = (0, 2)$ lies on the positive y-axis, choose $\theta = \pi/2$ and $r = 2$. Thus, one set of polar coordinates is $(r, \theta) = (2, \pi/2)$, as shown in Figure 11.14(b).

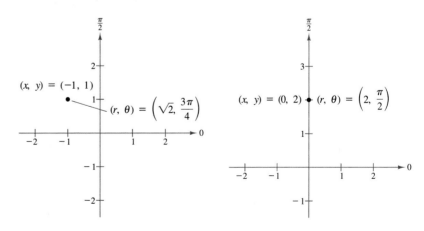

(a)   (b)

FIGURE 11.14

Equation Conversion

By comparing Examples 3 and 4, you can see that point conversion from the polar to the rectangular system is straightforward, whereas point conversion from the rectangular to the polar system is more involved. For equations, the opposite is true. To convert a rectangular equation to polar form, simply replace x by $r \cos \theta$ and y by $r \sin \theta$. For instance, the rectangular equation $y = x^2$ can be written in polar form as follows.

$$\underbrace{y = x^2}_{\substack{\text{Rectangular} \\ \text{equation}}} \longrightarrow \underbrace{r \sin \theta = (r \cos \theta)^2}_{\text{Polar equation}}$$

On the other hand, converting a polar equation to rectangular form can require considerable ingenuity.

EXAMPLE 5   Converting Polar Equations to Rectangular Form

Convert each polar equation to rectangular form. Then identify the graph.

A. $r = 2$ **B.** $\theta = \dfrac{\pi}{3}$ **C.** $r = \sec \theta$

SOLUTION

A. The graph of the polar equation $r = 2$ consists of all points that are 2 units from the pole. In other words, this graph is a circle centered at the origin and having a radius of 2, as shown in Figure 11.15(a). You can confirm this by converting to rectangular coordinates, using the relationship $r^2 = x^2 + y^2$.

$$\underbrace{r = 2}_{\text{Polar equation}} \longrightarrow r^2 = 2^2 \longrightarrow \underbrace{x^2 + y^2 = 2^2}_{\text{Rectangular equation}}$$

B. The graph of the polar equation $\theta = \pi/3$ consists of all points on the line that makes an angle of $\pi/3$ with the positive x-axis, as shown in Figure 11.15(b). To convert to rectangular form, you can make use of the relationship $\tan \theta = y/x$.

$$\underbrace{\theta = \frac{\pi}{3}}_{\text{Polar equation}} \longrightarrow \tan \theta = \sqrt{3} \longrightarrow \underbrace{y = \sqrt{3}x}_{\text{Rectangular equation}}$$

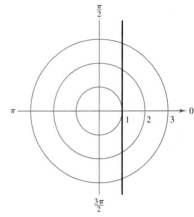

(a) Circle: $r = 2$

(b) Radial line: $\theta = \dfrac{\pi}{3}$

(c) Vertical line: $r = \sec \theta$

FIGURE 11.15

c. The graph of the polar equation $r = \sec \theta$ is not evident by simple inspection. You can convert to rectangular form by using the relationship $r \cos \theta = x$.

$$\underbrace{r = \sec \theta}_{\text{Polar equation}} \longrightarrow \quad r \cos \theta = 1 \longrightarrow \underbrace{x = 1}_{\text{Rectangular equation}}$$

Now, you can see that the graph is a vertical line, as shown in Figure 11.15(c).

Curve sketching by converting to rectangular form is not always convenient. In the next section, you will learn other techniques for sketching polar equations.

DISCUSSION PROBLEM

SIMPLIFYING A POLAR EQUATION

In the discussion before Example 5, we showed how to convert the rectangular equation $y = x^2$ to the polar equation

$$r \sin \theta = (r \cos \theta)^2.$$

Simplifying this equation by dividing both sides by r produces

$$\sin \theta = r \cos^2 \theta \quad \text{or} \quad r = \frac{\sin \theta}{\cos^2 \theta}.$$

By simplifying in this way, however, you risk the possibility of losing the pole $(0, \theta)$ as a solution point. For the equation shown above, division by r does not change the set of solution points, because the pole is a solution point of the simplified equation. Find a polar equation for which division by r *would* change the set of solution points.

WARM-UP

The following warm-up exercises involve skills that were covered in earlier sections. You will use these skills in the exercise set for this section.

In Exercises 1 and 2, find a positive angle coterminal with the given angle.

1. $\dfrac{11\pi}{4}$ **2.** $-\dfrac{5\pi}{6}$

In Exercises 3 and 4, find the sine and cosine of the angle in standard position with terminal side passing through the given point.

3. $(2, 1)$ **4.** $(4, -3)$

In Exercises 5 and 6, find the magnitude (in radians) of an angle in standard position with terminal side passing through the given point.

5. $(-4, 4)$ **6.** $(3, 2)$

In Exercises 7 and 8, evaluate the trigonometric function without the aid of a calculator.

7. $\sin\dfrac{4\pi}{3}$ **8.** $\cos\dfrac{3\pi}{4}$

In Exercises 9 and 10, use a calculator to evaluate the trigonometric function.

9. $\cos\dfrac{3\pi}{5}$ **10.** $\sin 1.34$

SECTION 11.2 · EXERCISES

In Exercises 1–10, plot the point given in polar coordinates and find the corresponding rectangular coordinates for the point.

1. $\left(4, \dfrac{3\pi}{6}\right)$ **2.** $\left(4, \dfrac{3\pi}{2}\right)$

3. $\left(-1, \dfrac{5\pi}{4}\right)$ **4.** $(0, -\pi)$

5. $\left(4, -\dfrac{\pi}{3}\right)$ **6.** $\left(-1, -\dfrac{3\pi}{4}\right)$

7. $\left(0, -\dfrac{7\pi}{6}\right)$ **8.** $\left(\dfrac{3}{2}, \dfrac{5\pi}{2}\right)$

9. $(\sqrt{2}, 2.36)$ **10.** $(-3, -1.57)$

In Exercises 11–20, the rectangular coordinates of a point are given. Plot the point and find *two* sets of polar coordinates for the point for $0 \le \theta < 2\pi$.

11. $(1, 1)$
12. $(0, -5)$
13. $(-6, 0)$
14. $(-3, -3)$
15. $(-3, 4)$
16. $(3, -1)$
17. $(-\sqrt{3}, -\sqrt{3})$
18. $(-2, 0)$
19. $(4, 6)$
20. $(5, 12)$

In Exercises 21–34, convert the rectangular equation to polar form.

21. $x^2 + y^2 = 9$

22. $x^2 + y^2 = a^2$

23. $x^2 + y^2 - 2ax = 0$

24. $x^2 + y^2 - 2ay = 0$

25. $y = 4$

26. $y = b$

27. $x = 10$

28. $x = a$

29. $3x - y + 2 = 0$

30. $4x + 7y - 2 = 0$

31. $xy = 4$

32. $y = x$

33. $(x^2 + y^2)^2 - 9(x^2 - y^2) = 0$

34. $y^2 - 8x - 16 = 0$

In Exercises 35–44, convert the polar equation to rectangular form.

35. $r = 4 \sin \theta$

36. $r = 4 \cos \theta$

37. $\theta = \dfrac{\pi}{6}$

38. $r = 4$

39. $r = 2 \csc \theta$

40. $r^2 = \sin 2\theta$

41. $r = 2 \sin 3\theta$

42. $r = \dfrac{1}{1 - \cos \theta}$

43. $r = \dfrac{6}{2 - 3 \sin \theta}$

44. $r = \dfrac{6}{2 \cos \theta - 3 \sin \theta}$

In Exercises 45–50, convert the polar equation to rectangular form and sketch its graph.

45. $r = 3$

46. $r = 8$

47. $\theta = \dfrac{\pi}{4}$

48. $\theta = \dfrac{5\pi}{6}$

49. $r = 3 \sec \theta$

50. $r = 2 \csc \theta$

51. Show that the distance between the points (r_1, θ_1), and (r_2, θ_2) is given by

$$\sqrt{r_1^2 + r_2^2 - 2r_1 r_2 \cos(\theta_1 - \theta_2)}.$$

52. Choose two points in the polar coordinate system. Use the formula given in Exercise 51 to find the distance between the two points. Then choose different polar coordinate representations of the same two points and apply the distance formula again. Discuss your result.

53. Convert the polar equation

$$r = 2(h \cos \theta + k \sin \theta)$$

to rectangular form and verify that it is the equation of a circle. Find the radius and the rectangular coordinates of the center of the circle.

54. Convert the polar equation $r = \cos \theta + 3 \sin \theta$ to rectangular form and identify the graph.

11.3 GRAPHS OF POLAR EQUATIONS

**Introduction / Using a Graphing Utility / Symmetry / Maximum
r-Values / Special Polar Graphs**

Introduction

In previous chapters, you spent a lot of time learning how to sketch graphs in rectangular coordinates. You began with the basic point-plotting method. Then you used sketching aids such as a graphing utility, symmetry, intercepts, asymptotes, periods, and shifts to further investigate the nature of the graph. In this section, you will approach curve sketching in the polar coordinate system in a similar way.

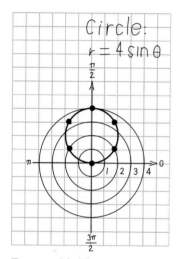

FIGURE 11.16

EXAMPLE 1 Graphing a Polar Equation by Point Plotting

Sketch the graph of the polar equation $r = 4 \sin \theta$.

SOLUTION

The sine function is periodic, so you can get a full range of r-values by considering values of θ in the interval $0 \le \theta \le 2\pi$, shown in the table.

θ	0	$\dfrac{\pi}{6}$	$\dfrac{\pi}{3}$	$\dfrac{\pi}{2}$	$\dfrac{2\pi}{3}$	$\dfrac{5\pi}{6}$	π	$\dfrac{7\pi}{6}$	$\dfrac{3\pi}{2}$	$\dfrac{11\pi}{6}$	2π
$4 \sin \theta$	0	2	$2\sqrt{3}$	4	$2\sqrt{3}$	2	0	-2	-4	-2	0

Plot these points as shown in Figure 11.16. In the figure, it appears that the graph is a circle of radius 2 whose center is at the point $(x, y) = (0, 2)$.

Using a Graphing Utility

Some graphing utilities have a polar-coordinate graphing mode. If your graphing utility *doesn't* have such a mode, but *does* have a parametric mode, you can use the following conversion to graph a polar equation.

POLAR EQUATIONS IN PARAMETRIC FORM

The graph of the polar equation $r = f(\theta)$ can be written in parametric form, using t as a parameter, as follows.

$$x = f(t) \cos t \quad \text{and} \quad y = f(t) \sin t$$

EXAMPLE 2   Graphing a Polar Equation with a Graphing Utility

Use a graphing utility to graph $r = 4 \sin \theta$.

SOLUTION

Begin by writing the equation in parametric form.

$$x = 4 \sin t \cos t$$
$$y = 4 \sin t \sin t$$

Set the graphing utility to parametric and radian mode. Use a viewing rectangle of $-6 \le x \le 6$ and $-4 \le y \le 4$, and let the parameter t vary from 0 to π. The graph is shown in Figure 11.17. In the figure, it appears that the graph is a circle, which reinforces the result obtained in Example 1.

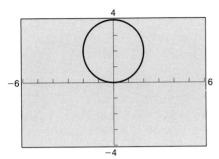

FIGURE 11.17

REMARK   You can confirm that the graph given in Examples 1 and 2 is a circle by rewriting the polar equation in rectangular form. If you do this, you will find that the rectangular equation is $x^2 + y^2 = 4y$. By completing the square, this equation can be written as $x^2 + (y - 2)^2 = 2^2$, which you know is the equation of a circle.

Symmetry

In Figure 11.17, the entire graph of the polar equation was traced as t increased from 0 to π. Try resetting your graphing utility so that t varies from 0 to 2π. Then, use the trace feature to follow the curve through increasing values of t, and you will see that the curve is traced out *twice*.

In Figure 11.17, you should also notice that the graph is *symmetric with respect to the line* $\theta = \pi/2$. Symmetry with respect to the line $\theta = \pi/2$ is one of three important types of symmetry to consider in polar curve-sketching. (See Figure 11.18.)

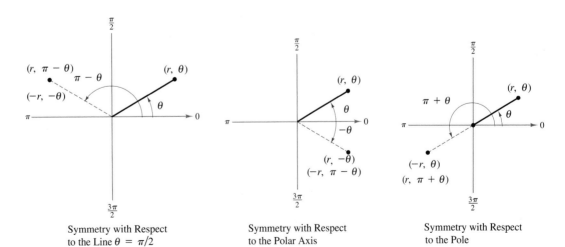

Symmetry with Respect
to the Line $\theta = \pi/2$

Symmetry with Respect
to the Polar Axis

Symmetry with Respect
to the Pole

FIGURE 11.18

TEST FOR SYMMETRY IN POLAR COORDINATES

The graph of a polar equation is symmetric with respect to the following if the given substitution yields an equivalent equation.

1. The line $\theta = \pi/2$: replace (r, θ) by $(r, \pi - \theta)$ or $(-r, -\theta)$.
2. The polar axis: replace (r, θ) by $(r, -\theta)$ or $(-r, \pi - \theta)$.
3. The pole: replace (r, θ) by $(r, \pi + \theta)$ or $(-r, \theta)$.

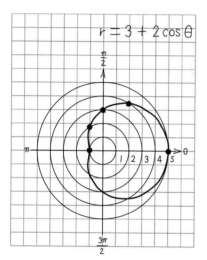

FIGURE 11.19

EXAMPLE 3   Finding Symmetry of the Graph of a Polar Equation

Sketch the graph of $r = 3 + 2 \cos \theta$, and discuss its symmetry.

SOLUTION

Replacing (r, θ) by $(r, -\theta)$ produces

$$r = 3 + 2 \cos(-\theta) = 3 + 2 \cos \theta.$$

Thus, you conclude that the curve is symmetric with respect to the polar axis. This conclusion can be confirmed by sketching the graph of the polar equation, as shown in Figure 11.19. A set of parametric equations for the graph is

$$x = (3 + 2 \cos t)(\cos t)$$
$$y = (3 + 2 \cos t)(\sin t).$$

By letting t vary from 0 to 2π, you can obtain the graph shown in Figure 11.19.

The three tests given for symmetry in polar coordinates are sufficient to guarantee symmetry, but they are not necessary. For instance, Figure 11.20 shows the graph of $r = \theta + 2\pi$ to be symmetric with respect to the line $\theta = \pi/2$. Yet the test fails to indicate symmetry because neither of the following replacements yields an equivalent equation.

Original Equation	Replacement	New Equation
$r = \theta + 2\pi$	(r, θ) by $(-r, -\theta)$	$-r = -\theta + 2\pi$
$r = \theta + 2\pi$	(r, θ) by $(r, \pi - \theta)$	$r = -\theta + 3\pi$

The equations discussed in Examples 1–3 are of the form

$$r = 4 \sin \theta = f(\sin \theta) \quad \text{and} \quad r = 3 + \cos \theta = g(\cos \theta).$$

The graph of the first equation is symmetric with respect to the line $\theta = \pi/2$, and the graph of the second equation is symmetric with respect to the polar axis. This observation can be generalized to yield the following *quick test for symmetry*.

Spiral of Archimedes:
$r = \theta + 2\pi, \ -4\pi \le \theta \le 0$

FIGURE 11.20

1. The graph of $r = f(\sin\theta)$ is symmetric with respect to the line $\theta = \pi/2$.
2. The graph of $r = g(\cos\theta)$ is symmetric with respect to the polar axis.

Maximum *r*-Values

The graph of a polar equation has a maximum *r*-value if there is a point on the graph that is farthest from the pole. For instance, in Example 1, the maximum value of r for $r = 4\sin\theta$ is 4. This value of r occurs when $\theta = \pi/2$.

EXAMPLE 4   **Finding a Maximum *r*-Value of a Polar Graph**

Find the maximum value of r for the graph of $r = 1 - 2\cos\theta$.

SOLUTION

Because the polar equation is of the form $r = 1 - 2\cos\theta = g(\cos\theta)$, you know that the graph is symmetric with respect to the polar axis. To sketch a graph of the equation, write it in parametric form.

$$x = (1 - 2\cos t)(\cos t)$$
$$y = (1 - 2\cos t)(\sin t)$$

Using a graphing utility and letting t vary from 0 to 2π, you can display the graph shown in Figure 11.21. Finally, using the trace feature of the graphing utility, you can conclude that the maximum value of r (the r-value of the point that is farthest from the pole) is 3. This value of r occurs when $t = \pi$ (or when $\theta = \pi$).

REMARK Note how the negative *r*-values determine the *inner loop* of the graph in Figure 11.21. This type of graph is called a **limaçon.**

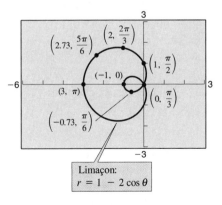

FIGURE 11.21

Some curves reach their maximum *r*-values at more than one point.

EXAMPLE 5 Finding a Maximum *r*-Value of a Polar Graph

Find the maximum *r*-value of the graph of $r = 2 \cos 3\theta$.

SOLUTION

Because $2 \cos 3\theta = 2 \cos(-3\theta)$, you can conclude that the graph is symmetric with respect to the polar axis. A set of parametric equations for the graph is given by

$$x = 2 \cos 3t \cos t$$
$$y = 2 \cos 3t \sin t.$$

REMARK The graph shown in Figure 11.22 is called a **rose curve,** and each of the loops on the graph is called a *petal* of the rose curve.

By letting *t* vary from 0 to π, you can use a graphing utility to display the graph shown in Figure 11.22. The maximum *r*-value for this graph is 2. This value occurs at *three* different points on the graph: $(r, \theta) = (2, 0)$, $(-2, \pi/3)$, and $(2, 2\pi/3)$.

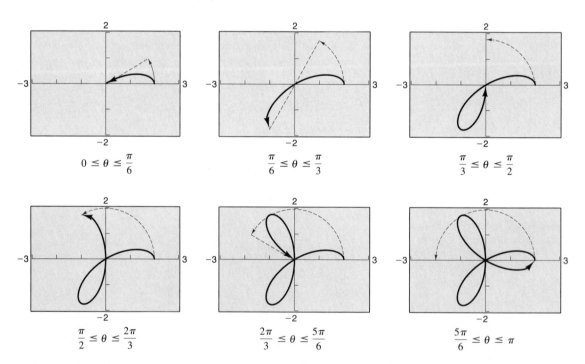

$$0 \leq \theta \leq \frac{\pi}{6} \qquad \frac{\pi}{6} \leq \theta \leq \frac{\pi}{3} \qquad \frac{\pi}{3} \leq \theta \leq \frac{\pi}{2}$$

$$\frac{\pi}{2} \leq \theta \leq \frac{2\pi}{3} \qquad \frac{2\pi}{3} \leq \theta \leq \frac{5\pi}{6} \qquad \frac{5\pi}{6} \leq \theta \leq \pi$$

FIGURE 11.22

Special Polar Graphs

Several important types of graphs have equations that are simpler in polar form than in rectangular form. For example, the circle $r = 4 \sin \theta$ in Example 1 has the more complicated rectangular equation $x^2 + (y - 2)^2 = 4$. The following list gives several other types of graphs that have simple polar equations.

Limaçons

$r = a \pm b \cos \theta$

$r = a \pm b \sin \theta$

$(0 < a, 0 < b)$

$\dfrac{a}{b} < 1$

Limaçon with
inner loop

$\dfrac{a}{b} = 1$

Cardioid
(heart-shaped)

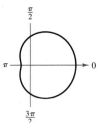

$1 < \dfrac{a}{b} < 2$

Dimpled
limaçon

$\dfrac{a}{b} \geq 2$

Convex
limaçon

Rose Curves

n petals if n is odd

$2n$ petals if n is even

$(n \geq 2)$

$r = a \cos n\theta$
Rose curve

$r = a \cos n\theta$
Rose curve

$r = a \sin n\theta$
Rose curve

$r = a \sin n\theta$
Rose curve

Circles and Lemniscates

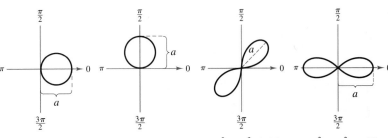

$r = a \cos \theta$
Circle

$r = a \sin \theta$
Circle

$r^2 = a^2 \sin 2\theta$
Lemniscate

$r^2 = a^2 \cos 2\theta$
Lemniscate

EXAMPLE 6   Sketching a Rose Curve

Sketch the graph of $r = 3 \cos 2\theta$.

SOLUTION

Begin with an analysis of the basic features of the graph.

Type of curve: Rose curve with $2n = 4$ petals

Symmetry: With respect to polar axis and the line $\theta = \dfrac{\pi}{2}$

Maximum value of r: $|r| = 3$ when $\theta = 0, \dfrac{\pi}{2}, \pi, \dfrac{3\pi}{2}$

Parametric equations: $x = 3 \cos 2t \cos t$

$y = 3 \cos 2t \sin t$

Using a graphing utility and letting t vary from 0 to 2π, you can graph the rose curve shown in Figure 11.23.

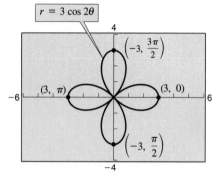

FIGURE 11.23

EXAMPLE 7   Sketching a Lemniscate

Sketch the graph of $r^2 = 9 \sin 2\theta$.

SOLUTION

Begin with an analysis of the basic features of the graph.

Type of curve: Lemniscate

Symmetry: With respect to the pole

Maximum value of r: $|r| = 3$ when $\theta = \dfrac{\pi}{4}$

Two sets of parametric equations: $x = 3\sqrt{\sin(2t)} \,(\cos t)$

$y = 3\sqrt{\sin(2t)} \,(\sin t)$

$x = -3\sqrt{\sin(2t)} \,(\cos t)$

$y = -3\sqrt{\sin(2t)} \,(\sin t)$

Using a graphing utility and letting t vary from 0 to $\pi/2$, you can graph the lemniscate shown in Figure 11.24.

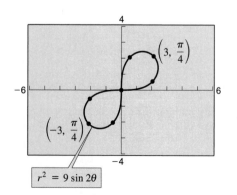

FIGURE 11.24

DISCUSSION PROBLEM

DIFFERENT TYPES OF LIMAÇONS

There are four different types of limaçons in the table showing special polar graphs. Explain the differences among the four types. Then classify each of the following as one of the special types and sketch its graph.

(a) $r = 3 + 3 \sin \theta$ (b) $r = 4 + 3 \sin \theta$
(c) $r = 2 + 3 \sin \theta$ (d) $r = 3 + \sin \theta$

WARM-UP

The following warm-up exercises involve skills that were covered in earlier sections. You will use these skills in the exercise set for this section.

In Exercises 1–4, determine the amplitude and period of the function.

1. $y = 5 \sin 4x$ **2.** $y = 3 \cos 2\pi x$

3. $y = -5 \cos \dfrac{5x}{2}$ **4.** $y = -\dfrac{1}{2} \sin \dfrac{x}{2}$

In Exercises 5–8, sketch the graph of the function through two periods.

5. $y = 2 \sin x$ **6.** $y = 3 \cos x$
7. $y = 4 \cos 2x$ **8.** $y = 2 \sin \pi x$

In Exercises 9 and 10, use the sum and difference identities to simplify the trigonometric expressions.

9. $\sin\left(x - \dfrac{\pi}{6}\right)$ **10.** $\sin\left(x + \dfrac{\pi}{4}\right)$

SECTION 11.3 · EXERCISES

In Exercises 1–6, test for symmetry with respect to $\theta = \pi/2$, the polar axis, and the pole.

In Exercises 7–10, find the maximum value of $|r|$.

1. $r = 10 + 6 \cos \theta$ **2.** $r = 16 \cos 3\theta$

3. $r = \dfrac{2}{1 + \sin \theta}$ **4.** $r = 6 \sin \theta$

5. $r = 4 \sec \theta \csc \theta$ **6.** $r^2 = 25 \sin 2\theta$

7. $r = 5 \cos 3\theta$
8. $r = -2 \cos \theta$
9. $r = 10(1 - \sin \theta)$
10. $r = 6 + 12 \cos \theta$

In Exercises 11–30, sketch the graph of the polar equation.

11. $r = 5$ **12.** $r = 2$

13. $\theta = \dfrac{\pi}{6}$ **14.** $\theta = -\dfrac{\pi}{4}$

15. $r = 3 \sin \theta$ **16.** $r = 3(1 - \cos \theta)$

17. $r = 4(1 + \sin \theta)$ **18.** $r = 3 - 2 \cos \theta$

19. $r = 4 + 3 \cos \theta$ **20.** $r = 2 + 4 \sin \theta$

21. $r = 3 - 4 \cos \theta$ **22.** $r = 2 \cos 3\theta$

23. $r = 3 \sin 2\theta$ **24.** $r = 2 \sec \theta$

25. $r = \dfrac{3}{\sin \theta - 2 \cos \theta}$ **26.** $r = \dfrac{6}{2 \sin \theta - 3 \cos \theta}$

27. $r^2 = 4 \cos 2\theta$ **28.** $r^2 = 4 \sin \theta$

29. $r = \dfrac{\theta}{2}$ **30.** $r = \theta$

In Exercises 31 and 32, convert the polar equation to rectangular form and show that the indicated line is an asymptote of the graph.

Polar Equation	Asymptote
31. $r = 2 - \sec \theta$	$x = -1$
32. $r = 2 + \csc \theta$	$y = 1$

33. The graph of $r = f(\theta)$ is rotated about the pole through an angle ϕ. Show that the equation for the rotated graph is $r = f(\theta - \phi)$.

34. Consider the graph of $r = f(\sin \theta)$.

(a) Show that if the graph is rotated counterclockwise $\pi/2$ radians about the pole, then the equation for the rotated graph is $r = f(-\cos \theta)$.

(b) Show that if the graph is rotated counterclockwise π radians about the pole, then the equation for the rotated graph is $r = f(-\sin \theta)$.

(c) Show that if the graph is rotated counterclockwise $3\pi/2$ radians about the pole, then the equation for the rotated graph is $r = f(\cos \theta)$.

In Exercises 35–38, use the results of Exercises 33 and 34.

35. Write an equation for the rose curve $r = 2 - \sin \theta$ after it has been rotated by the given amount.

(a) $\dfrac{\pi}{4}$ (b) $\dfrac{\pi}{2}$ (c) π (d) $\dfrac{3\pi}{2}$

36. Write an equation for the rose curve $r = 2 \sin 2\theta$ after it has been rotated by the given amount.

(a) $\dfrac{\pi}{6}$ (b) $\dfrac{\pi}{2}$ (c) $\dfrac{2\pi}{3}$ (d) π

37. Sketch the graph of each equation.

(a) $r = 1 - \sin \theta$ (b) $r = 1 - \sin\left(\theta - \dfrac{\pi}{4}\right)$

38. Sketch the graph of each equation.

(a) $r = 3 \sec \theta$ (b) $r = 3 \sec\left(\theta - \dfrac{\pi}{4}\right)$

(c) $r = 3 \sec\left(\theta + \dfrac{\pi}{3}\right)$ (d) $r = 3 \sec\left(\theta - \dfrac{\pi}{2}\right)$

11.4   POLAR EQUATIONS OF CONICS

Alternative Definition of Conics   /   Polar Equations of Conics   /   Applications

Alternative Definition of Conics

In Sections 4.4 and 4.5, you saw that the rectangular equations of ellipses and hyperbolas take simple forms when the origin lies at their *center*. There are, however, many important applications of conics in which it is more convenient to use one of the *foci* as the origin of the coordinate system. For example, the sun lies at the focus of the earth's orbit. Similarly, the light source of a parabolic reflector lies at its focus. In this section you will see that polar equations of conics take simple forms if one of the foci lies at the pole.

> **ALTERNATIVE DEFINITION OF CONIC**
>
> The locus of a point in the plane that moves so that its distance from a fixed point (focus) is in constant ratio to its distance from a fixed line (directrix) is a **conic.** The constant ratio is the **eccentricity** of the conic and is denoted by e. Moreover, the conic is an **ellipse** if $e < 1$, a **parabola** if $e = 1$, and a **hyperbola** if $e > 1$.

In Figure 11.25, note that for each type of conic, the pole corresponds to the fixed point (focus) given in the definition.

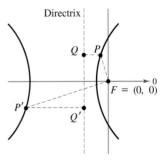

FIGURE 11.25

Polar Equations of Conics

PROOF

We give a proof for $r = ep/(1 + e \cos \theta)$ with $p > 0$. In Figure 11.26, consider a vertical directrix, p units to the right of the focus $F = (0, 0)$. If $P = (r, \theta)$ is a point on the graph of $r = ep/(1 + e \cos \theta)$, then the distance between P and the directrix is

$$PQ = |p - x| = |p - r \cos \theta|$$

$$= \left| p - \left(\frac{ep}{1 + e \cos \theta} \right) \cos \theta \right|$$

$$= \left| p \left(1 - \frac{e \cos \theta}{1 + e \cos \theta} \right) \right|$$

$$= \left| \frac{p}{1 + e \cos \theta} \right|$$

$$= \left| \frac{r}{e} \right|.$$

Because the distance between P and the pole is simply $PF = |r|$, the ratio of PF to PQ is

$$\frac{PF}{PQ} = \frac{|r|}{|r/e|} = |e| = e,$$

and, by definition, the graph of the equation must be a conic.

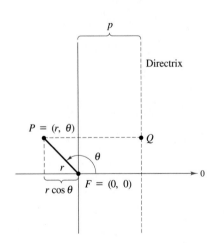

FIGURE 11.26

By completing the proofs of the other three cases, you can see that the equations

$$r = \frac{ep}{1 \pm e \cos \theta} \qquad \textit{Vertical directrix}$$

correspond to conics with vertical directrices and the equations

$$r = \frac{ep}{1 \pm e \sin \theta} \qquad \textit{Horizontal directrix}$$

correspond to conics with horizontal directrices. The converse is also true. That is, any conic with a focus at the pole and having a horizontal or vertical directrix can be represented by one of the given equations.

EXAMPLE 1   Determining a Conic from Its Equation

Identify the conic given by

$$r = \frac{15}{3 - 2 \cos \theta}$$

and sketch its graph.

SOLUTION

To determine the type of conic, rewrite the equation as

$$r = \frac{15}{3 - 2 \cos \theta} = \frac{5}{1 - (2/3) \cos \theta}.$$

From this form you can conclude that the graph is an ellipse with $e = \frac{2}{3}$. To graph the ellipse, use a graphing utility and the following parametric equations.

$$x = \frac{15 \cos t}{3 - 2 \cos t} \quad \text{and} \quad y = \frac{15 \sin t}{3 - 2 \cos t}$$

Letting t vary from 0 to 2π produces the graph shown in Figure 11.27. Notice that the graph has symmetry with respect to the polar axis.   ·········

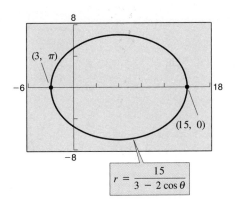

$$r = \frac{15}{3 - 2 \cos \theta}$$

FIGURE 11.27

For the ellipse in Figure 11.27, the major axis is horizontal and the vertices lie at $(15, 0)$ and $(3, \pi)$. Thus, the length of the *major* axis is $2a = 18$. To find the length of the *minor* axis, you can use the equations $e = c/a$ and $b^2 = a^2 - c^2$ to conclude that

$$b^2 = a^2 - c^2 = a^2 - (ea)^2 = a^2(1 - e^2). \qquad \textit{Ellipse}$$

Because $e = \frac{2}{3}$, it follows that $b^2 = 9^2[1 - (2/3)^2] = 45$, which implies that $b = \sqrt{45} = 3\sqrt{5}$. Thus, the length of the minor axis is $2b = 6\sqrt{5}$. A similar analysis for hyperbolas yields

$$b^2 = c^2 - a^2 = (ea)^2 - a^2 = a^2(e^2 - 1). \qquad \textit{Hyperbola}$$

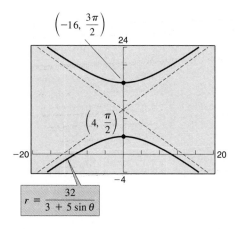

$$r = \frac{32}{3 + 5 \sin \theta}$$

FIGURE 11.28

EXAMPLE 2   Sketching a Conic from Its Polar Equation

Identify the conic given by

$$r = \frac{32}{3 + 5 \sin \theta}$$

and sketch its graph.

SOLUTION

To determine the type of conic, rewrite the equation as

$$r = \frac{32/3}{1 + (5/3) \sin \theta}.$$

Because $e = \frac{5}{3} > 1$, the graph is a hyperbola. The transverse axis of the hyperbola lies on the line $\theta = \pi/2$, and the vertices occur at $(4, \pi/2)$ and $(-16, 3\pi/2)$. Because the length of the transverse axis is 12, it follows that $a = 6$. To find b, you can write

$$b^2 = a^2(e^2 - 1) = 6^2\left[\left(\frac{5}{3}\right)^2 - 1\right] = 64.$$

Therefore, $b = 8$. Finally, use a and b to determine the asymptotes of the hyperbola and obtain the graph shown in Figure 11.28.

In the next example you are asked to find a polar equation for a specified conic. To do this, let p be the distance between the pole and the directrix. With this interpretation of p, we suggest the following guidelines for finding a polar equation for a conic.

1. Horizontal directrix above the pole: $r = \dfrac{ep}{1 + e \sin \theta}$

2. Horizontal directrix below the pole: $r = \dfrac{ep}{1 - e \sin \theta}$

3. Vertical directrix to the right of the pole: $r = \dfrac{ep}{1 + e \cos \theta}$

4. Vertical directrix to the left of the pole: $r = \dfrac{ep}{1 - e \cos \theta}$

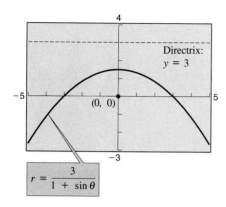

$$r = \frac{3}{1 + \sin \theta}$$

FIGURE 11.29

EXAMPLE 3 Finding the Polar Equation for a Conic
....

Find the polar equation for the parabola whose focus is the pole and whose directrix is the line $y = 3$.

SOLUTION

In Figure 11.29, you can see that the directrix is horizontal. Thus, you should choose an equation of the form

$$r = \frac{ep}{1 + e \sin \theta}.$$

Moreover, because the eccentricity of a parabola is $e = 1$ and the distance between the pole and the directrix is $p = 3$, you obtain

$$r = \frac{3}{1 + \sin \theta}.$$

Applications

Kepler's Laws (listed below), named after the German astronomer Johannes Kepler (1571–1630), can be used to describe the orbits of the planets about the sun.

1. Each planet moves in an elliptical orbit with the sun as a focus.
2. A ray from the sun to the planet sweeps out equal areas of the ellipse in equal times.
3. The square of the period is proportional* to the cube of the mean distance between the planet and the sun.

Although Kepler simply stated these laws on the basis of observation, they were later validated by Isaac Newton (1642–1727). In fact, Newton was able to show that each law can be deduced from a set of universal laws of motion and gravitation which govern the movement of all heavenly bodies, including comets and satellites. This is illustrated in the next example involving the comet named after the English mathematician and physicist Edmund Halley (1656–1742).

---

*Using Earth as a reference with a period of 1 year and a distance of 1 astronomical unit, the proportionality constant is 1. For example, because Mars has a mean distance to the sun of $d = 1.523$ AU, its period P is given by $d^3 = P^2$. Thus, the period for Mars is $P = 1.88$ years.

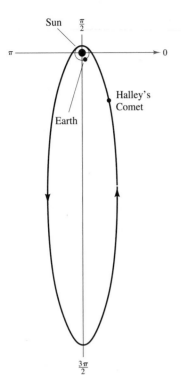

FIGURE 11.30

EXAMPLE 4   Halley's Comet

Halley's comet has an elliptical orbit with an eccentricity of $e \approx 0.97$. The length of the major axis of the orbit is approximately 36.18 astronomical units. (An astronomical unit is defined as the mean distance between the earth and the sun, 93 million miles.) Find a polar equation for the orbit. How close does Halley's comet come to the sun?

SOLUTION

Using a vertical axis, as shown in Figure 11.30, choose an equation of the form $r = ep/(1 + e \sin \theta)$. Because the vertices of the ellipse occur when $\theta = \pi/2$ and $\theta = 3\pi/2$, you can determine the length of the major axis to be the sum of the r-values of the vertices. That is,

$$2a = \frac{0.97p}{1 + 0.97} + \frac{0.97p}{1 - 0.97} \approx 32.83p \approx 36.18.$$

Thus, $p \approx 1.102$ and $ep \approx (0.97)(1.102) \approx 1.069$. Using this value in the equation, you have

$$r = \frac{1.069}{1 + 0.97 \sin \theta},$$

where r is measured in astronomical units. To find the closest point to the sun (the focus), you can write

$$c = ea \approx (0.97)(18.09) \approx 17.55.$$

Because c is the distance between the focus and the center, the closest point is

$$a - c \approx 18.09 - 17.55 \approx 0.54 \; AU \approx 50,000,000 \text{ miles.}$$

DISCUSSION PROBLEM

COMETS IN OUR SOLAR SYSTEM

Halley's comet is not the only spectacular comet that is periodically visible to viewers on earth. Use your school library to find information about another comet, and write a paragraph describing some of its characteristics.

WARM-UP

The following warm-up exercises involve skills that were covered in earlier sections. You will use these skills in the exercise set for this section.

In Exercises 1 and 2, plot the point given in polar coordinates and find the corresponding rectangular coordinates for the point.

1. $\left(-3, \dfrac{3\pi}{4}\right)$ **2.** $\left(4, -\dfrac{2\pi}{3}\right)$

In Exercises 3 and 4, plot the point given in rectangular coordinates and find two sets of polar coordinates for the point where $0 \le \theta < 2\pi$.

3. $(0, -3)$ **4.** $(-5, 12)$

In Exercises 5 and 6, convert the rectangular equation to polar form.

5. $x^2 + y^2 = 25$ **6.** $x^2 y = 4$

In Exercises 7 and 8, convert the polar equation to rectangular form.

7. $r \sin \theta = -4$ **8.** $r = 4 \cos \theta$

In Exercises 9 and 10, identify and sketch the graph of the polar equation.

9. $r = 1 - \sin \theta$ **10.** $r = 1 + 2 \cos \theta$

SECTION 11.4 · EXERCISES

In Exercises 1–6, match the polar equation with the correct graph. [The graphs are labeled (a), (b), (c), (d), (e), and (f).]

1. $r = \dfrac{6}{1 - \cos \theta}$ **2.** $r = \dfrac{2}{2 - \cos \theta}$

3. $r = \dfrac{3}{1 - 2 \sin \theta}$ **4.** $r = \dfrac{2}{1 + \sin \theta}$

5. $r = \dfrac{6}{2 - \sin \theta}$ **6.** $r = \dfrac{2}{2 + 3 \cos \theta}$

(c)

(d)

(a)

(b)

(e)

(f)

In Exercises 7–18, identify and sketch the graph of the polar equation. Use a graphing utility to confirm your sketch.

7. $r = \dfrac{2}{1 - \cos \theta}$

8. $r = \dfrac{4}{1 + \sin \theta}$

9. $r = \dfrac{5}{1 + \sin \theta}$

10. $r = \dfrac{6}{1 + \cos \theta}$

11. $r = \dfrac{2}{2 - \cos \theta}$

12. $r = \dfrac{3}{3 + \sin \theta}$

13. $r = \dfrac{4}{2 + \sin \theta}$

14. $r = \dfrac{6}{3 - 2 \cos \theta}$

15. $r = \dfrac{3}{2 + 4 \sin \theta}$

16. $r = \dfrac{5}{-1 + 2 \cos \theta}$

17. $r = \dfrac{3}{2 - 6 \cos \theta}$

18. $r = \dfrac{3}{2 + 6 \sin \theta}$

Conic	Vertex or Vertices
25. Parabola	$\left(1, -\dfrac{\pi}{2}\right)$
26. Parabola	$(4, 0)$
27. Parabola	$(5, \pi)$
28. Parabola	$\left(10, \dfrac{\pi}{2}\right)$
29. Ellipse	$(2, 0), (8, \pi)$
30. Ellipse	$\left(2, \dfrac{\pi}{2}\right), \left(4, \dfrac{3\pi}{2}\right)$
31. Ellipse	$(20, 0), (4, \pi)$
32. Hyperbola	$(2, 0), (10, 0)$
33. Hyperbola	$\left(1, \dfrac{3\pi}{2}\right), \left(9, \dfrac{3\pi}{2}\right)$
34. Hyperbola	$\left(4, \dfrac{\pi}{2}\right), \left(-1, \dfrac{3\pi}{2}\right)$

35. Show that the polar equation of the ellipse

$$\frac{x^2}{a^2} + \frac{y^2}{b^2} = 1 \quad \text{is} \quad r^2 = \frac{b^2}{1 - e^2 \cos^2 \theta}.$$

36. Show that the polar equation of the hyperbola

$$\frac{x^2}{a^2} - \frac{y^2}{b^2} = 1 \quad \text{is} \quad r^2 = \frac{-b^2}{1 - e^2 \cos^2 \theta}.$$

In Exercises 19–34, find a polar equation of the conic with its focus at the pole.

Conic	Eccentricity	Directrix
19. Parabola	$e = 1$	$x = -1$
20. Parabola	$e = 1$	$y = -2$
21. Ellipse	$e = \dfrac{1}{2}$	$y = 1$
22. Ellipse	$e = \dfrac{3}{4}$	$y = -2$
23. Hyperbola	$e = 2$	$x = 1$
24. Hyperbola	$e = \dfrac{3}{2}$	$x = -1$

In Exercises 37–42, use the results of Exercises 35 and 36 to write the polar form of the equation of the conic.

37. $\dfrac{x^2}{169} + \dfrac{y^2}{144} = 1$ **38.** $\dfrac{x^2}{25} + \dfrac{y^2}{16} = 1$

39. $\dfrac{x^2}{9} - \dfrac{y^2}{16} = 1$ **40.** $\dfrac{x^2}{36} - \dfrac{y^2}{4} = 1$

41. Hyperbola   One focus: $(5, 0)$

                Vertices: $(4, 0), (4, \pi)$

42. Ellipse   One focus: $(4, 0)$

                Vertices: $(5, 0), (5, \pi)$

In Exercises 43 and 44, sketch the graph of the rotated conic.

43. $r = \dfrac{2}{1 - \cos(\theta - \pi/4)}$ (See Exercise 7)

44. $r = \dfrac{4}{1 + \sin(\theta - \pi/3)}$ (See Exercise 8)

45. *Orbits of Planets*   The planets travel in elliptical orbits with the sun as a focus. Assume that the focus is at the pole, the major axis lies on the polar axis, and the length of the major axis is $2a$ (see figure). Show that the polar equation of the orbit is given by

$$r = \frac{(1 - e^2)a}{1 - e\cos\theta},$$

where e is the eccentricity.

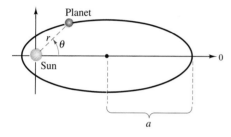

FIGURE FOR 45

46. *Orbits of Planets*   Use the result of Exercise 45 to show that the minimum distance (*perihelion distance*) from the sun to the planet is $r = a(1 - e)$ and the maximum distance (*aphelion distance*) is $r = a(1 + e)$.

Orbits of Planets   In Exercises 47 and 48, use the results of Exercises 45 and 46 to find the polar equation of the planet and the perihelion and aphelion distances.

47. Earth $a = 92.957 \times 10^6$ miles
      $e = 0.0167$

48. Pluto $a = 3.666 \times 10^9$ miles
      $e = 0.2481$

49. *Satellite Tracking*   A satellite in a 100-mile-high circular orbit around the earth has a velocity of approximately 17,500 miles per hour. If this velocity is multiplied by $\sqrt{2}$, then the satellite will have the minimum velocity necessary to escape the earth's gravity and it will follow a parabolic path with the center of the earth as the focus (see figure). Find a polar equation of the parabolic path of the satellite (assume the radius of the earth is 4000 miles).

FIGURE FOR 49

50. *Explorer 18*   On November 26, 1963, the United States launched Explorer 18. Its low and high points over the surface of the earth were 119 miles and 122,000 miles, respectively (see figure). The center of the earth is the focus of the orbit. Find the polar equation for the orbit and find the distance between the surface of the earth and the satellite when $\theta = 60°$.

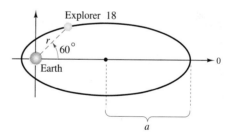

FIGURE FOR 50

CHAPTER 11 · REVIEW EXERCISES

In Exercises 1–12, sketch the curve represented by the parametric equations. Use a graphing utility to confirm your sketch. If possible, write the corresponding rectangular equation by eliminating the parameter.

1. $x = 2t$
  $y = 4t$

2. $x = t^2$
  $y = \sqrt{t}$

3. $x = 1 + 4t$
  $y = 2 - 3t$

4. $x = t + 4$
  $y = t^2$

5. $x = \dfrac{1}{t}$
  $y = t^2$

6. $x = \dfrac{1}{t}$
  $y = 2t + 3$

7. $x = 6 \cos \theta$
  $y = 6 \sin \theta$

8. $x = 3 + 3 \cos \theta$
  $y = 2 + 5 \sin \theta$

9. $x = \cos^3 \theta$
  $y = 4 \sin^3 \theta$

10. $x = \sec \theta$
  $y = \tan \theta$

11. $x = e^t$
  $y = e^{-t}$

12. $x = 2\theta - \sin \theta$
  $y = 2 - \cos \theta$

In Exercises 13–28, identify and sketch the graph of the polar equation. Use a graphing utility to confirm your sketch.

13. $r = 4$

14. $\theta = \dfrac{\pi}{12}$

15. $r = 4 \sin 2\theta$

16. $r = 2\theta$

17. $r = -2(1 + \cos \theta)$

18. $r = 3 - 4 \cos \theta$

19. $r = 4 - 3 \cos \theta$

20. $r = \cos 5\theta$

21. $r = -3 \cos 3\theta$

22. $r^2 = \cos 2\theta$

23. $r^2 = 4 \sin 2\theta$

24. $r = 3 \csc \theta$

25. $r = \dfrac{3}{\cos(\theta - \pi/4)}$

26. $r = \dfrac{4}{5 - 3 \cos \theta}$

27. $r = \dfrac{2}{1 - \sin \theta}$

28. $r = \dfrac{1}{1 + 2 \sin \theta}$

In Exercises 29–34, convert the polar equation to rectangular form.

29. $r = 3 \cos \theta$

30. $r = 4 \sec\left(\theta - \dfrac{\pi}{3}\right)$

31. $r = \dfrac{2}{1 + \sin \theta}$

32. $r = \dfrac{1}{2 - \cos \theta}$

33. $r^2 = \cos 2\theta$

34. $r = 10$

In Exercises 35 and 36, convert the rectangular equation to polar form.

35. $(x^2 + y^2)^2 = ax^2 y$

36. $x^2 + y^2 - 4x = 0$

In Exercises 37–42, find a polar equation for the line or conic.

37. Circle   Center: $\left(5, \dfrac{\pi}{2}\right)$
        Solution point: $(0, 0)$

38. Line   Solution point: $(0, 0)$
        Slope: $\sqrt{3}$

39. Parabola   Vertex: $(2, \pi)$
         Focus: $(0, 0)$

40. Parabola   Vertex: $\left(2, \dfrac{\pi}{2}\right)$
         Focus: $(0, 0)$

41. Ellipse   Vertices: $(5, 0), (1, \pi)$
         One focus: $(0, 0)$

42. Hyperbola   Vertices: $(1, 0), (7, 0)$
         One focus: $(0, 0)$

43. Find a parametric representation of the ellipse with center at $(-3, 4)$, major axis horizontal and 8 units in length, and minor axis 6 units in length.

44. Find a parametric representation of the hyperbola with vertices $(0, \pm 4)$ and foci at $(0, \pm 5)$.

45. Show that the Cartesian equation of a cycloid is

$$x = a \arccos \dfrac{a - y}{a} \pm \sqrt{2ay - y^2}.$$

46. The *involute of a circle* is described by the endpoint P of a string that is held taut as it is unwound from a spool (see figure). The spool does not rotate. Show that a parametric representation of the involute of a circle is given by

$$x = r(\cos \theta + \theta \sin \theta) \quad \text{and} \quad y = r(\sin \theta - \theta \cos \theta).$$

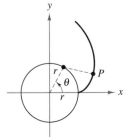

FIGURE FOR 46

47. Sketch the graph of the involute of a circle given by the parametric equations

$$x = 2(\cos \theta + \theta \sin \theta)$$
$$y = 2(\sin \theta - \theta \cos \theta).$$

CUMULATIVE TEST FOR CHAPTERS 9–11

Take this test as you would take a test in class. After you are done, check your work with the answers in the back of the book.

1. A college had an enrollment of 3250 students in 1990. During the next 3 years the enrollment increased by approximately 80 students per year. Write a linear equation giving the enrollment N in terms of the year t. (Let $t = 0$ correspond to the year 1990.) If this constant rate of growth continues, predict the enrollment in the year 2000.

2. The production (thousands of barrels daily) of crude oil and natural gas liquids by Exxon in the United States is given in the following table. (*Source:* 1991 Annual Report)

Year	1988	1989	1990	1991
Production	760	693	640	619

   Plot this data on a rectangular coordinate system and find an equation of a line that you think best approximates the data. (Let y represent the production and let t represent the year with $t = 0$ corresponding to 1988.)

3. Solve the system by the method of substitution.
$$y = 3 - x^2$$
$$2(y - 2) = x - 1$$

4. Use a graphing utility to solve the linear system graphically.
$$x + 3y = -1$$
$$2x + 4y = 0$$

5. Use Gauss-Jordan elimination to solve the linear system.
$$x + 3y - 2z = -7$$
$$-2x + y - z = -5$$
$$4x + y + z = 3$$

6. Find the value of a such that the system is inconsistent.
$$ax - 8y = 9$$
$$3x + 4y = 0$$

7. Find $2A - B$ given the following matrices.
$$A = \begin{bmatrix} 6 & -1 \\ 2 & 4 \\ -3 & 5 \end{bmatrix}, \quad B = \begin{bmatrix} 1 & 4 \\ -1 & 5 \\ 1 & 10 \end{bmatrix}$$

8. Find AB, if possible.

$$A = \begin{bmatrix} 4 & -3 \\ 2 & 1 \\ 5 & 0 \end{bmatrix}, \qquad B = \begin{bmatrix} 3 & -2 \\ 1 & -3 \end{bmatrix}$$

9. Find the inverse (if it exists) of the matrix.

$$A = \begin{bmatrix} 1 & 2 & -1 \\ 3 & 7 & -10 \\ -5 & -7 & -15 \end{bmatrix}$$

10. Sketch a graph of the solution of the system of inequalities.

$$3x + 4y \geq 16$$
$$3x - 4y \leq 8$$
$$y \leq 4$$

11. Find the sum of the first 20 terms of the arithmetic sequence.

$$8, 12, 16, 20, \ldots$$

12. Write the first five terms of the geometric sequence if $a_1 = 54$ and $r = -\frac{1}{3}$.

13. Use mathematical induction to prove the formula

$$3 + 7 + 11 + 15 + \cdots + (4n - 1) = n(2n + 1).$$

14. Use the Binomial Theorem to expand and simplify $(z - 3)^4$.

15. The equations for the demand and supply curves of a certain product are given by $p = 84 - \frac{1}{3}x$ and $p = \frac{1}{4}x$, respectively. Find the point of equilibrium.

16. Find constants D, E, and F so that the circle $x^2 + y^2 + Dx + Ey + F = 0$ passes through the points $(0, 0)$, $(0, 4)$, and $(3, -4)$.

17. You accept a job with a salary of \$32,000 for the first year. Suppose that during the next 9 years you receive a 5% raise each year. What would your total compensation be over the 10-year period?

18. Find a set of parametric equations of the line passing through the points $(2, -3)$ and $(6, 4)$. (The answer is not unique.)

19. Sketch the curve represented by the parametric equations $x = 3 + 3 \cos \theta$ and $y = 2 + 2 \sin \theta$. Write the corresponding rectangular equation by eliminating the parameter.

20. Convert the polar equation $r = 6 \cos \theta$ to rectangular form and sketch its graph.

21. Use a graphing utility to graph the polar equation $r = 2 \cos 2\theta \sec \theta$. Identify any asymptotes to the graph and write the equation of any asymptote in rectangular form.

22. Find a polar equation of the parabola with focus at the origin and vertex at $(1, \pi)$.

GRAPHING UTILITIES

Introduction

In Section 1.1, you studied the point-plotting method for sketching the graph of an equation. One of the disadvantages of the point-plotting method is that in order to get a good idea about the shape of a graph, you need to plot *many* points. With only a few points, you could badly misrepresent the graph. For instance, consider the equation

$$y = \frac{1}{30}x(39 - 10x^2 + x^4).$$

Suppose you plotted only five points: $(-3, -3)$, $(-1, -1)$, $(0, 0)$, $(1, 1)$, and $(3, 3)$, as shown in Figure A.1. From these five points, you might assume that the graph of the equation is a straight line. That, however, is not correct. By plotting several more points you can see that the actual graph is not straight at all! (See Figure A.2.)

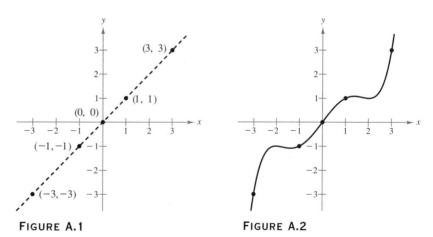

FIGURE A.1   FIGURE A.2

Thus, the point-plotting method leaves us with a dilemma. On the one hand, the method can be very inaccurate if only a few points are plotted. But, on the other hand, it is very time consuming to plot a dozen (or more) points.

Technology can help us solve this dilemma. Plotting several (even several hundred) points in a rectangular coordinate system is something that a graphing utility can do easily.

The point-plotting method is the method used by *all* graphing packages for computers and *all* graphing calculators. Each computer or calculator screen is made up of a grid of hundreds or thousands of small areas called **pixels.** Screens that have many pixels per inch are said to have a higher **resolution** than screens that don't have as many. For instance, the screen shown in Figure A.3(a) has a higher resolution than the screen shown in Figure A.3(b). Note that the "graph" of the line on the first screen looks more like a line than the "graph" on the second screen.

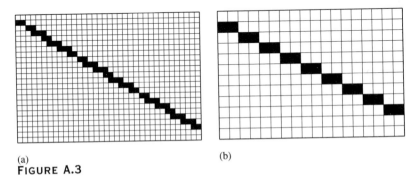

(a)   (b)

FIGURE A.3

Screens on most graphing calculators have 48 pixels per inch. Screens on computer monitors typically have between 32 and 100 pixels per inch.

EXAMPLE 1   Using Pixels to Sketch a Graph

Use the grid shown in Figure A.4 to sketch a graph of $y = \frac{1}{2}x^2$. Each pixel on the grid must be either on (shaded black) or off (unshaded).

SOLUTION

To shade the grid, we use the following rule. If a pixel contains a plotted point of the graph, then it will be "on"; otherwise, the pixel will be "off." Using this rule, the graph of the curve looks like that shown in Figure A.5.

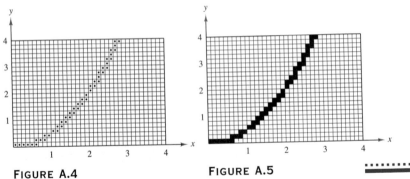

FIGURE A.4   **FIGURE A.5**

Basic Graphing

There are many different types of graphing utilities—graphing calculators and software packages for computers. The procedures used to draw a graph are similar with most of these utilities.

BASIC GRAPHING STEPS FOR A GRAPHING UTILITY

To draw the graph of an equation involving *x* and *y* with a graphing utility, use the following steps.

1. Rewrite the equation so that *y* is isolated on the left side of the equation.
2. Set the boundaries of the viewing rectangle by entering the minimum and maximum *x*-values and the minimum and maximum *y*-values.
3. Enter the equation in the form *y* = (expression involving *x*). Read the user's guide that accompanies your graphing utility to see how the equation should be entered.
4. Activate the graphing utility.

EXAMPLE 2   Sketching the Graph of an Equation

Sketch the graph of $2y + x^3 = 4x$.

SOLUTION

To begin, solve the given equation for *y* in terms of *x*.

$$2y + x^3 = 4x \qquad \text{\textit{Given equation}}$$
$$2y = -x^3 + 4x \qquad \text{\textit{Subtract } } x^3 \text{ \textit{ from both sides}}$$
$$y = -\frac{1}{2}x^3 + 2x \qquad \text{\textit{Divide both sides by 2}}$$

Set the viewing rectangle so that $-10 \le x \le 10$ and $-10 \le y \le 10$. (On some graphing utilities, this is the default setting.) Next, enter the equation into the graphing utility.

$$Y = -X \wedge 3/2 + 2 * X$$

Finally, activate the graphing utility. The display screen should look like that shown in Figure A.6.

FIGURE A.6

In Figure A.6, notice that the calculator screen does not label the tick marks on the *x*-axis or the *y*-axis. To see what the tick marks represent, check the values in the utility's "range."

FIGURE A.7

Range

Xmin = −10	*The minimum x-value is −10.*
Xmax = 10	*The maximum x-value is 10.*
Xscl = 1	*The x-scale is 1 unit per tick mark.*
Ymin = −10	*The minimum y-value is −10.*
Ymax = 10	*The maximum y-value is 10.*
Yscl = 1	*The y-scale is 1 unit per tick mark.*
Xres = 1	*The x-resolution is 1 plotted point per 1 pixel.*

These settings are summarized visually in Figure A.7.

EXAMPLE 3   Graphing an Equation Involving Absolute Value

Sketch the graph of $y = |x - 3|$.

SOLUTION

This equation is already written so that *y* is isolated on the left side of the equation, so you can enter the equation as follows.

$$Y = \text{abs}(X - 3)$$

After activating the graphing utility, its screen should look like the one shown in Figure A.8.

FIGURE A.8

Special Features

In order to be able to use your graphing calculator to its best advantage, you must be able to determine a proper viewing rectangle and use the zoom feature. The next two examples show how this is done.

EXAMPLE 4   Determining a Viewing Rectangle

Sketch the graph of $y = x^2 + 12$.

SOLUTION

Begin as usual by entering the equation.

$Y = X \wedge 2 + 12$

Activate the graphing utility. If you used a viewing rectangle in which $-10 \leq x \leq 10$ and $-10 \leq y \leq 10$, then no part of the graph will appear on the screen, as shown in Figure A.9(a). The reason for this is that the lowest point on the graph of $y = x^2 + 12$ occurs at the point (0, 12). With the viewing rectangle in Figure A.9(a), the largest y-value is 10. In other words, none of the graph is visible on a screen whose y-values range between -10 and 10.

To be able to see the graph, change Ymax $= 10$ to Ymax $= 30$, Yscl $= 1$ to Yscl $= 5$. Now activate the graphing utility and you will obtain the graph shown in Figure A.9(b). On this graph, note that each tick mark on the y-axis represents 5 units because you changed the y-scale to 5. Also note that the highest point on the y-axis is now 30 because you changed the maximum value of y to 30.

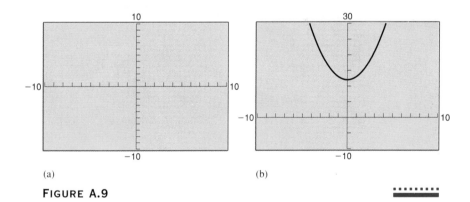

(a)   (b)

FIGURE A.9

EXAMPLE 5   Using the Zoom Feature

Sketch the graph of $y = x^3 - x^2 - x$. How many x-intercepts does this graph have?

SOLUTION

Begin by drawing the graph on a "standard" viewing rectangle as shown in Figure A.10(a). From the display screen, it is clear that the graph has at least one intercept (just to the left of $x = 2$), but it is difficult to determine whether

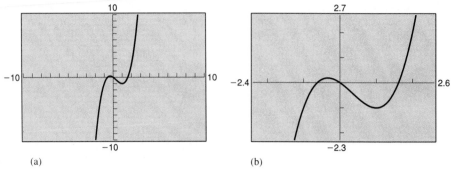

FIGURE A.10   (a)   (b)

the graph has other intercepts. To obtain a better view of the graph near $x = -1$, you can use the zoom feature of the graphing utility. The redrawn screen is shown in Figure A.10(b). From this screen you can tell that the graph has three x-intercepts whose x-coordinates are approximately -0.6, 0, and 1.6.

EXAMPLE 6   **Sketching More Than One Graph on the Same Screen**

Sketch the graphs of $y = -\sqrt{36 - x^2}$ and $y = \sqrt{36 - x^2}$ on the same screen.

SOLUTION

To begin, enter both equations in the graphing utility.

$$Y = \sqrt{(36 - X \wedge 2)}$$
$$Y = -\sqrt{(36 - X \wedge 2)}$$

Then, activate the graphing utility to obtain the graph shown in Figure A.11(a). Notice that the graph should be the upper and lower parts of the circle given by $x^2 + y^2 = 6^2$. The reason it doesn't look like a circle is that, with the standard settings, the tick marks on the x-axis are farther apart than the tick marks on the y-axis. To correct this, change the viewing rectangle so that $-15 \le x \le 15$. The redrawn screen is shown in Figure A.11(b). Notice that in this screen the graph appears to be more circular.

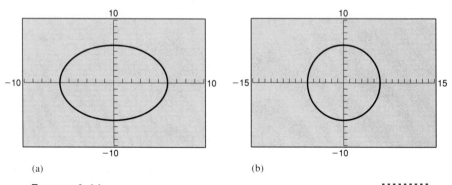

(a)   (b)

FIGURE A.11

DISCUSSION PROBLEM

....

A MISLEADING GRAPH

Sketch the graph of $y = x^2 - 12x$, using $-10 \le x \le 10$ and $-10 \le y \le 10$. The graph appears to be a straight line, as shown in the figure. However, this is misleading because the screen doesn't show an important portion of the graph. Can you find a range setting that reveals a better view of this graph?

WARM-UP

....

In Exercises 1–10, solve for y in terms of x.

1. $3x + y = 4$ **2.** $x - y = 0$

3. $2x + 3y = 2$ **4.** $4x - 5y = -2$

5. $3x + 4y - 5 = 0$ **6.** $-2x - 3y + 6 = 0$

7. $x^2 + y - 4 = 0$ **8.** $-2x^2 + 3y + 2 = 0$

9. $x^2 + y^2 = 4$ **10.** $x^2 - y^2 = 9$

APPENDIX A · EXERCISES

....

In Exercises 1–20, use a graphing utility to sketch the graph of the equation. Use a setting on each graph of $-10 \le x \le 10$ and $-10 \le y \le 10$.

```
RANGE
Xmin=-10
Xmax=10
Xscl=1
Ymin=-10
Ymax=10
Yscl=1
Xres=1
```

1. $y = x - 5$ **2.** $y = -x + 4$

3. $y = -\frac{1}{2}x + 3$ **4.** $y = \frac{2}{3}x + 1$

5. $2x - 3y = 4$ **6.** $x + 2y = 3$

7. $y = \frac{1}{2}x^2 - 1$ **8.** $y = -x^2 + 6$

9. $y = x^2 - 4x - 5$ **10.** $y = x^2 - 3x + 2$

11. $y = -x^2 + 2x + 1$ **12.** $y = -x^2 + 4x - 1$

13. $2y = x^2 + 2x - 3$ **14.** $3y = -x^2 - 4x + 5$

15. $y = |x + 5|$ **16.** $y = \frac{1}{2}|x - 6|$

17. $y = \sqrt{x^2 + 1}$ **18.** $y = 2\sqrt{x^2 + 2} - 4$

19. $y = \frac{1}{5}(-x^3 + 16x)$ **20.** $y = \frac{1}{8}(x^3 + 8x^2)$

In Exercises 21–30, use a graphing utility to match the equation with its graph. [The graphs are labeled (a), (b), (c), (d), (e), (f), (g), (h), (i), and (j).]

21. $y = x$ **22.** $y = -x$

23. $y = x^2$ **24.** $y = -x^2$

25. $y = x^3$ **26.** $y = -x^3$

27. $y = |x|$ **28.** $y = -|x|$

29. $y = \sqrt{x}$ **30.** $y = -\sqrt{x}$

(a)

(b)

(c)

(d)

(e)

(f)

(g)

(h)

(i)

(j)

In Exercises 31–34, use a graphing utility to sketch the graph of the equation. Use the indicated setting.

31. $y = -2x^2 + 12x + 14$ **32.** $y = -x^2 + 5x + 6$

RANGE		RANGE
Xmin=-5		Xmin=-8
Xmax=10		Xmax=4
Xscl=1		Xscl=1
Ymin=-5		Ymin=-5
Ymax=35		Ymax=15
Yscl=5		Yscl=5
Xres=1		Xres=1

33. $y = x^3 + 6x^2$ **34.** $y = -x^3 + 16x$

RANGE		RANGE
Xmin=-10		Xmin=-6
Xmax=5		Xmax=6
Xscl=1		Xscl=1
Ymin=-4		Ymin=-25
Ymax=36		Ymax=25
Yscl=3		Yscl=5
Xres=1		Xres=1

In Exercises 35–38, find a setting on a graphing utility so that the graph of the equation agrees with the graph shown.

35. $y = -x^2 - 4x + 20$ **36.** $y = x^2 + 12x - 8$

37. $y = -x^3 + x^2 + 2x$ **38.** $y = x^3 + 3x^2 - 2x$

In Exercises 39–42, use a graphing utility to find the number of x-intercepts of the equation.

39. $y = \frac{1}{8}(4x^2 - 32x + 65)$

40. $y = \frac{1}{4}(-4x^2 + 16x - 15)$

41. $y = 4x^3 - 20x^2 - 4x + 61$

42. $y = \frac{1}{4}(2x^3 + 6x^2 - 4x + 1)$

In Exercises 43–46, use a graphing utility to sketch the graphs of the equations on the same screen. Using a "square setting," what geometrical shape is bounded by the graphs?

43. $y = |x| - 4$
$y = -|x| + 4$

44. $y = x + |x| - 4$
$y = x - |x| + 4$

45. $y = -\sqrt{25 - x^2}$
$y = \sqrt{25 - x^2}$

46. $y = 6$
$y = -\sqrt{3}x - 4$
$y = \sqrt{3}x - 4$

Ever Been Married?   In Exercises 47–50, use the following models, which relate ages to the percentages of American males and females who have never been married.

$$y = \frac{0.36 - 0.0056x}{1 - 0.0817x + 0.00226x^2}, \quad \begin{array}{l}\text{Males} \\ 20 \le x \le 50\end{array}$$

$$y = \frac{100}{8.944 - 0.886x + 0.249x^2}, \quad \begin{array}{l}\text{Females} \\ 20 \le x \le 50\end{array}$$

In these models, y is the percent of the population (in decimal form) who have never been married and x is the age of the person. (*Source:* U.S. Bureau of the Census)

47. Use a graphing utility to sketch the graph of both equations giving the percentages of American males and females who have never been married. Use the following range settings.

```
RANGE
Xmin=20
Xmax=50
Xscl=5
Ymin=0
Ymax=1
Yscl=0.1
Xres=1
```

48. Write a short paragraph describing the relationship between the two graphs that were plotted in Exercise 47.

49. Suppose an American male is chosen at random from the population. If the person is 25 years old, what is the probability that he has never been married?

50. Suppose an American female is chosen at random from the population. If the person is 25 years old, what is the probability that she has never been married?

Earnings and Dividends   In Exercises 51–54, use the following model, which approximates the relationship between dividends per share and earnings per share for the Pall Corporation between 1982 and 1989.

$$y = -0.166 + 0.502x - 0.0953x^2, \quad 0.25 \le x \le 2$$

In this model, y is the dividends per share (in dollars) and x is the earnings per share (in dollars). (*Source:* Standard ASE Stock Reports)

51. Use a graphing utility to sketch the graph of the model that gives the dividend per share in terms of the earnings per share. Use the following range settings.

```
RANGE
Xmin=0
Xmax=2
Xscl=0.25
Ymin=0
Ymax=0.5
Yscl=0.1
Xres=1
```

52. According to the given model, what size dividend would the Pall Corporation pay if the earnings per share were $1.30?

53. Use a trace feature on your graphing utility to estimate the earnings per share that would produce a dividend per share of $0.25. The choices are labeled (a), (b), (c), and (d). (Find the y-value that is as close to 0.25 as possible. The x-value that is displayed will then be the approximate earnings per share that would produce a dividend per share of $0.25.)
(a) $1.00   (b) $1.03   (c) $1.06   (d) 1.09

54. The **Payout Ratio** for a stock is the ratio of the dividend per share to earnings per share. Use the model to find the payout ratio for an earnings per share of (a) $0.75, (b) 1.00, and (c) $1.25.

PROGRAMS

Programs for the TI-81 graphing calculator are given in several sections in the text. This appendix contains translations of these text programs for several other graphics calculators from Texas Instruments, Casio, and Sharp. Similar programs can be written for other brands and models of graphics calculators.

Enter a program in your calculator, then refer to the text discussion and apply the program as appropriate. Section references are provided to help you locate the text discussion of the programs and their use.

To illustrate the power and versatility of programmable calculators, a variety of types of programs are presented, including a simulation program (A Graph Reflecting Program), a tutorial program (A Program for Practice), and programs for solving an equation or system of equations.

Functions   (Section 1.3)

The program, found in the Technology Note, can be used to evaluate a function at a real value of x.

For a TI-81 program, see page 78.

Casio 6300 Program

EVALUATE:
Lbl 1:
"X="?→X:
"F(X)="◢Prog 0◢
Goto 1

To use this program, write the function as Prog 0.

Casio 7700 Program

EVALUATE
Lbl 1
"X="?→X
"F(X)=":f₁◢
Goto 1

To use this program, enter a function in f_1.

Sharp EL 9200, 9300 Program

```
Evaluate
-----------REAL
Goto top
Label eqtn
Y=f(X)
Return
Label top
Input X
Gosub equation
Print Y
Goto top
End
```

TI-85 Program

```
 PROGRAM:
:Lbl A
:Input "Enter x ",x
:Disp y1
:Goto A
```

To use this program, enter a function in $y1$.

Shifting, Reflecting, and Stretching Graphs   (Section 1.5)

The program, shown in Example 5, A Program for Practice, will sketch a graph of the function $y = R(x + H)^2 + V$ where $R = \pm 1$, H is an integer between -6 and 6, and V is an integer between -3 and 3. This program gives you practice working with reflections, horizontal shifts, and vertical shifts.

For a TI-81 program, see page 103.

Casio 6300 Program

```
R(X+H)²+V:
-6+Int (12Ran#)→H:
-3+Int (6Ran#)→V:
Ran#<.5⇒-1→R:1→R:
Range -9,9,1,-6,6,1:
Graph Y=R(X+H)²+V◢
"Y=R(X+H)²+V"◢
"R="◢R◢
"H="◢H◢
"V="◢V
```

Casio 7700 Program

```
R(X+H)²+V
-6+Int (12Ran#)→H
-3+Int (6Ran#)→V
Ran#<.5⇒-1→R:1→R
Range -9,9,1,-6,6,1
Graph Y=R(X+H)²+V◢
"Y=R(X+H)²+V"
"R=":R◢
"H=":H◢
"V=":V
```

Sharp EL 9200, 9300 Program

```
Parabola
-----------REAL
H=int (random*12)-6
V=int (random*6)-3
S=(random*2)-1
R=S/abs S
Range -9,9,1,-6,6,1
Graph R(X+H)²+V
Wait
Print "Y=R(X+H)²+V
Print R
Print H
Print V
End
```

Pressing Enter after the graph will display the coefficients.

TI-85 Program

```
PROGRAM:
:rand→H
:-6+int(12H)→H
:rand→V
:-3+int(6V)→V
:rand→R
:If R<.5
:-1→R
:If R>.49
:1→R
:y1=R(x+H)²+V
:-9→xMin
:9→xMax
:1→xScl
:-6→yMin
:6→yMax
:1→yScl
:DispG
:Pause
:Disp "Y=R(X+H)²+V"
:Disp "R=",R
:Disp "H=",H
:Disp "V=",V
```

Inverse Functions   (Section 1.7)

The program, shown in Example 5, A Graph Reflecting Program, graphs a function f *and* its reflection in the line $y = x$.

For a TI-81 program, see page 120.

Casio 6300 Program

```
REFLECTION:
"-A TO A"◢
"A="?→A:
Range -A,A,1,-2A÷3,2A÷3,1:
-A→B:
Lbl 1:
B→X:
Prog 0:
Ans→Y:
Plot B,Y:
B+A÷24→B:
B≤A⇒Goto 1:
-A→B:
Lbl 2:
B→X:
Prog 0:
Ans→Y:
Plot Y,B:
B+A÷24→B:
B≤A⇒Goto 2:Graph Y=X
```

To use this program, write the function as Prog 0 and set a viewing rectangle.

Casio 7700 Program

```
REFLECTION
"GRAPH -A TO A"
"A="?→A
Range -A,A,1,-2A÷3,2A÷3,1
Graph Y=f₁
-A→B
Lbl 1
B→X
Plot f₁,B
B+A÷32→B
B≤A⇒Goto 1:Graph Y=X
```

To use this program, enter the function in f_1 and set a viewing rectangle.

Sharp EL 9200, 9300 Program

```
Reflection
-----------REAL
Goto top
Label eqtn
Y=X^3+X+1
Return
Label rng
xmin=-10
xmax=10
xstp=(xmax-xmin)/10
ymin=2xmin/3
ymax=2xmax/3
ystp=xstp
Range xmin,xmax,xstp,ymin,ymax,ystp
Return
Label top
Gosub rng
Graph X
step=(xmax-xmin)/(94*2)
X=xmin
Label 1
Gosub eqtn
Plot X,Y
Plot Y,X
X=X+step
If X<=xmax Goto 1
End
```

TI-85 Program

```
PROGRAM:
:63xMin/127→yMin
:63xMax/127→yMax
:xScl→yScl
:y2=x
:DispG
:(xMax-xMin)/126→I
:xMin→x
:Lbl A
:PtOn(y1,x)
:x+I→x
:If x>xMax
:Stop
:Goto A
```

The Quadratic Formula   (Section 2.5)

The program, shown in a Technology Note, will display solutions to quadratic equations or the words "No Real Solution." To use the program, write the equation in standard form and then enter the values of a, b, and c.

For a TI-81 program, see page 174.

Casio 6300 Program

```
QUADRATICS:
"AX²+BX+C=0"◢
"A="?→A:
"B="?→B:
"C="?→C:
B²-4AC→D:
D<0⇒Goto 1:
"X="◢(-B+√D)÷2A ◢
"OR X="◢(-B-√D)÷2A:
Goto 2:
Lbl 1:
"NO REAL SOLUTION"
Lbl 2
```

Casio 7700 Program

```
QUADRATICS
"AX²+BX+C=0"
"A="?→A
"B="?→B
"C="?→C
B²-4AC→D
D<0⇒Goto 1
"X=":(-B+√D)÷2A ◢
"OR X=":(-B-√D)÷2A
Goto 2
Lbl 1
"NO REAL SOLUTION"
Lbl 2
```

Sharp EL 9200, 9300 Program

```
Quadratic
----------COMPLEX
Input A
Input B
Input C
D=B²-4AC
x1=(-B+√D)/(2A)
x2=(-B-√D)/(2A)
Print x1
Print x2
X=x1
Y=x2
End
```

This program is written in the program's complex mode, so both real and complex answers are given. The answers are also stored under variables X and Y so they can be used in the calculator mode.

TI-85 Program

```
PROGRAM:
:Input "ENTER A ",A
:Input "ENTER B ",B
:Input "ENTER C ",C
:B²-4*A*C→D
:Disp (-B+√D)/(2A)
:Disp (-B-√D)/(2A)
```

Solutions to quadratic equations are also available directly by using the TI-85 POLY function.

Other Types of Inequalities and Graphing Utilities (Section 2.8)

The program presented in the Discussion Problem, A Computer Experiment, evaluates an expression at several values. A visual display is printed indicating if the value is negative, zero, or positive.

Casio 6300 Program

```
SIGN:
"Left="?→A:
"Right="?→B:
Range A,B,1,-2,2,1:
(B-A)÷24→C:
Lbl 1:
A→X:
Prog 0:
Ans→Y:
Y=0⇒Plot A,0:Goto 2:
Goto 3:
Lbl 2:
Plot A,Y÷Abs Y:
Lbl 3:
A+C→A:
A≤B+1⇒Goto 1
```

To evaluate $x^2 - 9$, enter the expression as Prog 0. Then run the program. Press G↔T to view the graph.

Casio 7700 Program

```
SIGN
"GRAPH A TO B"
"A="?→A
"B="?→B
Range A,B,1,-2,2,1
(B-A)÷32→C
Lbl 1
A→X
f₁=0⇒Plot A,0:Goto 2
Goto 3
Lbl 2
Plot A,f₁÷Abs f₁
Lbl 3
A+C→A
A≤B+1⇒Goto 1
```

To evaluate $x^2 - 9$, enter the expression in f_1. Then run the program. Press G↔T to view the graph.

Angles and Their Measure   (Section 6.1)

The program, found in Discussion Problem, An Angle-Drawing Program, can be used to draw several different angles in either radian or degree mode.

For a TI-81 program, see page 396.

Casio 6300 Program

```
ANGLE:
"MODE:"◢
"0 = RADIAN"◢
"1 = DEGREE"?→M:
"ANGLE="?→T:
M=1⇒πT÷180→T:
Rad:
Range -1.5,1.5,1,-1,1,1:
T=0⇒Goto 2:
T÷Abs T→F:
0→N:
Lbl 1:
.25+.04N→R:
Plot Rcos (FN), Rsin (FN):
N+.2→N:
N≤AbsT⇒Goto 1:
Plot 0,0:
Plot cos T,sin T:
Line:
Lbl 2
```

Casio 7700 Program

```
ANGLE
"MODE:"
"0 FOR RADIAN"
"1 FOR DEGREE"
?→M
"ANGLE="?→T
M=1⇒πT÷180→T
Rad
Range -1.5,1.5,1,-1,1,1,0,T,.15
Graph r=.25+.04Abs θ
Plot 0,0
Plot cos T,sin T
Line
```

Press Mode Shift to change to polar mode when starting to write this program.

Sharp EL 9200, 9300 Program

```
Angle
------------REAL
m=sin⁻¹ 1/(π/2)
Input angle
Print " 0 for rad        1 for deg
Input d
If d=0 Goto 1
angle=angle*π/180
Label 1
Range -2.25,2.25,1.5,-1.5,1.5,1.5
s=angle/abs angle
loops=ipart (s*angle/(2π))+1
θ=0
ostep=angle/(30*loops)
r=1/loops
rstep=(1-r)/(30*loops)
xo=r
yo=0
n=0
Label top
r=r+rstep
θ=θ+ostep
x=r*cos (mθ)
y=r*sin (mθ)
Line xo,yo,x,y
xo=x
yo=y
n=n+1
If n<30*loops Goto top
Line 0,0,1.5x,1.5y
End
```

TI-85 Program

```
PROGRAM:
:Disp "ENTER MODE"
:Disp "0 RADIAN"
:Disp "1 DEGREE"
:Input M
:Input "ENTER ANGLE ",T
:If M==1
:πT/180→T
:Radian
:ClDrw
:FnOff
:Param
:-1.5→xMin
:1.5→xMax
:1→xScl
:-1→yMin
:1→yMax
:1→yScl
:0→tMin
:abs T→tMax
:.15→tStep
:cos T→A
:sin T→B
:xt1=(.25+.04t)cos t
:yt1=sign T*(.25+.04t)sin t
:DispG
:Line(0,0,A,B)
:Pause
:Func
```

Graphs of Sine and Cosine Functions   (Section 6.4)

The program, presented in the Discussion Problem, A Sine Show, simultaneously draws the unit circle and the corresponding points on the sine curve. After the circle and sine curve are drawn, you can connect points on the unit circle with their corresponding points on the sine curve by repeatedly pressing Enter.

For a TI-81 program, see page 433.

Casio 6300 Program

"SINESHOW"◢
Rad:
Range -2.25,π÷2,3,-1.19,
    1.19,1:
0→T:
Lbl 1:
Plot -1.25+cos T,sin T:
Plot T÷4,sin T:
T+.15→T:
T≤6.3⇒Goto 1:
Plot -1.25,-1.19
Plot -1.25,1.19:
Line:
0→N:
Lbl 2:
N+1→N:
Nπ÷6.5→T:
-1.25+cos T→A:
sin T→B:
T÷4→C:
Plot A,B:
Plot C,B:
Line◢
N<12⇒Goto 2

Casio 7700 Program

SINESHOW
Rad
Range -2.25,π÷2,3,-1.19,
    1.19,1,0,6.3,.15
Graph(X,Y)=(-1.25+cos T,sin
    T):Graph(X,Y)=(T÷4,sin T)
Plot -1.25,-1.19
Plot -1.25,1.19
Line
0→N
Lbl 1
N+1→N
Nπ÷6.5→T
-1.25+cos T→A
sin T→B
T÷4→C
Plot A,B
Plot C,B
Line◢
N<12⇒Goto 1

Press Mode Shift X to change to parametric mode when starting to write this program.

Sharp EL 9200, 9300 Program

```
SinShow
-----------REAL
m=sin⁻¹ 1/(π/2)
Range -2.25,π/2,3,-1.19,119,1
step=π/15
θ=0
xco=-0.25
xso-0
yo=0
Label 1
θ=θ+step
xc=cos (mθ)-1.25
xs=θ/4
y=sin (mθ)
Line xco,yo,xc,y
Line xso,yo,xs,y
xco=xc
xso=xs
yo=y
If θ<2π Goto 1
θ=0
Label 2
θ=θ+step
xc=cos (mθ)-1.25
xs=θ/4
y=sin (mθ)
Line xc,y,xs,y
If θ<2π Goto 2
End
```

TI-85 Program

```
 PROGRAM:
:Radian
:ClDrw:FnOff
:Param:SimulG
: -2.25→xMin
:π/2→xMax
:3→xScl
: -1.1→yMin
:1.1→yMax
:1→yScl
:0→tMin
:6.3→tMax
:.15→tStep
:xt1=-1.25+cos t
:yt1=sin t
:xt2=t/4
:yt2=sin t
:Line(-1.25,1.1,-1.25,1.1)
:DispG
:0→N
:Lbl A
:N+1→N
:N*π/6.5→T
: -1.25+cos T→A
:sin T→B
:T/4→C
:Line(A,B,C,B)
:Pause
:If N==12
:Goto B
:Goto A
:Lbl B
:Pause:Func:SeqG:Disp
```

Vectors in the Plane   (Section 8.3)

The program is presented in Exercise 73. You are asked to explain what the program does.

For TI-81 program, see page 560.

Casio 6300 Program	Casio 7700 Program
"ENTER (A,B)"◢	"ENTER (A,B)"
"A="?→A:	"A="?→A
"B="?→B:	"B="?→B
"ENTER (C,D)"◢	"ENTER (C,D)"
"C="?→C:	"C="?→C
"D="?→D:	"D="?→D
Range -6,6,1,-2,6,1:	Range -6,6,1,-2,6,1
Plot 0,0:	Plot 0,0
Plot A,B:	Plot A,B
Line:	Line
Plot 0,0:	Plot 0,0
Plot C,D:	Plot C,D
Line◢	Line◢
A+C→E:	A+C→E
B+D→F:	B+D→F
Plot 0,0:	Plot 0,0
Plot E,F:	Plot E,F
Line:	Line
Plot A,B:	Plot A,B
Plot E,F:	Plot E,F
Line:	Line
Plot C,D:	Plot C,D
Plot E,F:	Plot E,F
Line:	Line
Lbl 1	Lbl 1

Sharp EL 9200, 9300 Program

```
Input a
Input b
Input c
Input d
Range -6,6,1,-2,6,1
Line 0,0,a,b
Line 0,0,c,d
a=a+c
f=b+d
Line 0,0,e,f
Line a,b,e,f
Line c,d,e,f
End
```

TI-85 Program

```
PROGRAM:
:Disp "ENTER (A,B)"
:Input "ENTER A ",A
:Input "ENTER B ",B
:Disp "ENTER (C,D)"
:Input "ENTER C ",C
:Input "ENTER D ",D
:Line(0,0,A,B)
:Line(0,0,C,D)
:A+C→E
:B+D→F
:Line(0,0,E,F)
:Line(A,B,E,F)
:Line(C,D,E,F)
:Pause
:ClDrw:Disp
```

Systems of Linear Equations in Two Variables (Section 9.3)

The program, discussed in a Technology Note, will solve a system of two linear equations.

For a TI-81 program, see page 608.

Casio 6300 Program

```
SOLVE:
"A="?→A:
"B="?→B:
"C="?→C:
"D="?→D:
"E="?→E:
"F="?→F:
AE-DB=0⇒Goto 1:
"X="◢(CE-BF)÷(AE-DB)◢
"Y="◢(AF-CD)÷(AE-DB):
Goto 2:
Lbl 1:
"NO UNIQUE SOLUTION":
Lbl 2
```

Casio 7700 Program

```
SOLVE
"ENTER A,B,C,D,E,F"
"A="?→A
"B="?→B
"C="?→C
"D="?→D
"E="?→E
"F="?→F
AE-DB=0⇒Goto 1
"X=":(CE-BF)÷(AE-DB)◢
"Y=":(AF-CD)÷(AE-DB)
Goto 2
Lbl 1
"NO UNIQUE SOLUTION"
Lbl 2
```

Sharp EL 9200, 9300 Program

```
Solve
----------REAL
Input A
Input B
Input C
Input D
Input E
Input F
If A*E-D*B=0 Goto 1
X=(C*E-B*F)/(A*E-D*B)
Y=(A*F-C*D)/(A*E-D*B)
Print X
Print Y
End
Label 1
Print "No solution
End
```

Equations must be entered in the form: $Ax + By = C$; $Dx + Ey = F$. Uppercase letters are used so that the values can be accessed in the calculation mode of the calculator.

TI-85 Program

```
PROGRAM:
:Disp "ax+by=c"
:Input "Enter a ",A
:Input "Enter b ",B
:Input "Enter c ",C
:Disp "dx+ey=f"
:Input "Enter d ",D
:Input "Enter e ",E
:Input "Enter f ",F
:If A*E-D*B=0
:Goto A
:(C*E-B*F)/(A*E-D*B)→X
:(A*F-C*D)/(A*E-D*B)→Y
:Disp X
:Disp Y
:Lbl A
```

Sequences and Summation Notation   (Section 10.1)

The program, from a Discovery note, finds the sum of a finite sequence. For a TI-81 program, see page 682.

Casio 6300 Program

SUM:
"LOWER LIMIT"?→M:
"UPPER LIMIT"?→N:
0→S:
M→X:
Lbl 1:
Prog 0:
Ans+S→S:
X+1→X:
X≤N⇒Goto 1:
"SUM="◢S

To use this program, store the formula for the nth term as Prog 0.

Casio 7700 Program

SUM
"LOWER LIMIT"?→M
"UPPER LIMIT"?→N
0→S
M→X
Lbl 1
S+f_1→S
X+1→X
X≤N⇒Goto 1
"SUM=":S

To use this program, store the formula for the nth term in f_1.

Sharp EL 9200, 9300 Program

```
Sum
---------REAL
Goto 1
Label eqtn
y=√ (22926+902.5x+2.01x²
Return
Label 1
Print "Enter start
Input m
Print "Enter end
Input n
If n<m Goto 1
sum=0
x=m
Label 2
Gosub eqtn
sum=sum+y
x=x+1
If x<=n Goto 2
Print sum
End
```

To use this program, store the formula for the nth term into the subroutine 'eqtn' at the beginning of the program.

TI-85 Program

```
PROGRAM:
:Input "ENTER M ",M
:Input "ENTER N ",N
:0→S
:M→x
:Lbl A
:S+y1→S
:If x=N
:Goto B
:x+1→x
:Goto A
:Lbl B
:Disp S
```

To use this program, store the formula for the nth term as $y1$.

FRACTAL PROGRAMS

Fractal Gasket

```
:0→Xmin          :0→L                    :H+(B-H)/2→H
:100→Xmax        :PT-On(A,B)             :If T=2
:10→Xscl         :PT-On(C,D)             :G+(C-G)/2→G
:0→Ymin          :PT-On(E,F)             :If T=2
:100→Ymax        :Disp "START(X,Y)"      :H+(D-H)/2→H
:10→Yscl         :Input C                :If T=3
:0→A             :Input H                :G+(E-G)/2→G
:0→B             :Lbl 1                  :If T=3
:50→C            :L+1→L                  :H+(F-H)/2→H
:100→D           :Int(3Rand+1)→T         :PT-On(G,H)
:100→E           :If T=1                 :If L<1000
:0→F             :G+(A-G)/2→G            :Goto 1
:ClrDraw         :If T=1                 :End
```

Fractal Dragon

```
:0→Xmin          :Goto 3                 :.5→B
:10→Xmax         :Lbl 4                  :0→C
:1→Xscl          :AX+BY+C→R              :-.5→D
:0→Ymin          :DX+EY+F→S              :.5→E
:10→Ymax         :3.2R+2.5→U             :0→F
:1→Yscl          :4.25S+6.5→V            :Goto 4
:ClrDraw         :PT-On(U,V)             :Lbl 3
:0→X             :R→X                    :-.5→A
:0→Y             :S→Y                    :.5→B
:1→N             :N+1→N                  :2→C
:Lbl 1           :If N<=3000             :-.5→D
:Rand→P          :Goto 1                 :-.5→E
:If P<.5         :End                    :0→F
:Goto 2          :Lbl 2                  :Goto 4
:If P>.5         :.5→A                   :End
```

Fractal Fern

```
:0→Xmin              :-.0436→A            :.16→S
:50→Xmax             :-.0436→B            :0→A
:10→Xscl             :1→K                 :0→B
:0→Ymin              :If Z<.005           :0→K
:50→Ymax             :Goto 2              :Goto 5
:10→Yscl             :If Z<.1025          :Lbl 3
:ClrDraw             :Goto 3              :.3→R
:25→A                :If Z<.2             :.34→S
:25→B                :Goto 4              :.8552→A
:0→J                 :Lbl 5               :.8552→B
:Disp "START(X,Y)"   :RCcos A-SDsinB→E    :1.6→K
:Input C             :RCsinA+SDcosB+K→F   :Goto 5
:Input D             :E→C                 :Lbl 4
:Lbl 1               :F→D                 :.3→R
:8(A+D)-1→U          :J+1→J               :.37→S
:16(B+C)+20→V        :If J<10000          :2.0944→A
:PT-On(U,V)          :Goto 1              :-.8552→B
:Rand→Z              :End                 :.44→K
:.85→R               :Lbl 2               :Goto 5
:.85→S               :0→R                 :End
```

ANSWERS
Warm-Ups, Odd-Numbered Exercises, and Cumulative Tests

PREREQUISITES

Section 1 (page 7)

1. (a) 5, 1 **(b)** $-9, 5, 0, 1$ **(c)** $-9, -\frac{7}{2}, 5, \frac{2}{3}, 0, 1$ **(d)** $\sqrt{2}$

3. (a) $12, 1, \sqrt{4}$ **(b)** $12, -13, 1, \sqrt{4}$ **(c)** $12, -13, 1, \sqrt{4}, \frac{3}{2}$ **(d)** $\sqrt{6}$

5. (a) $\frac{6}{3}$ **(b)** $\frac{6}{3}$ **(c)** $-\frac{1}{3}, \frac{6}{3}, -7.5$ **(d)** $-\pi, \frac{1}{2}\sqrt{2}$

7. $\frac{3}{2} < 7$ **9.** $-4 > -8$

11. $\frac{5}{6} > \frac{2}{3}$

13. $-1 \le x \le 3$, bounded **15.** $10 < x$, unbounded

17. $(-\infty, 5]$ **19.** $(-\infty, 0)$

21. $[4, \infty)$ **23.** $(-2, 2)$

25. $[-1, 0)$

27. $(-\infty, 0)$ **29.** $(-\infty, 25]$

31. $[30, \infty)$ **33.** $[0.035, 0.06]$ **35.** -1 **37.** -9

39. 3.75 **41.** $|-3| > -|-3|$ **43.** $-5 = -|5|$

45. $-|-2| = -|2|$ **47.** $\frac{5}{2}$ **49.** 51 **51.** 14.99

53. $|x - 5| \le 3$ **55.** $|z - \frac{3}{2}| > 1$ **57.** $|y| \ge 6$

59. $\frac{127}{90}, \frac{584}{413}, \frac{7071}{5000}, \sqrt{2}, \frac{47}{33}$ **61.** 0.625 **63.** 0.123123 . . .

65. False. The reciprocal of 2 is $\frac{1}{2}$, which is not an integer.

67. True

Section 2 (page 16)

1. $7x, 4$ **3.** $x^2, -4x, 8$ **5.** $4x^3, x, -5$

7. (a) -10 **(b)** -6 **9. (a)** 14 **(b)** 2

11. (a) Division by 0 is undefined. **(b)** 0

13. Commutative (addition) **15.** Inverse (multiplication)

17. Distributive Property **19.** Identity (multiplication)

21. Associative and Commutative (multiplication) **23.** 0

25. Division by 0 is undefined. **27.** 2 **29.** 6

31. $\frac{1}{2}$ **33.** $\frac{3}{8}$ **35.** $\frac{3}{10}$ **37.** $\frac{1}{12}$ **39.** 48

41. -2.57 **43.** 1.56 **45.** 0.33 **47.** 1.11

49. 125 **51.** 729 **53.** 5184 **55.** $\frac{16}{3}$ **57.** -24

59. 5 **61.** $-125z^3$ **63.** $24y^{10}$ **65.** $3x^2$ **67.** $\frac{7}{x}$

69. $\frac{4}{3}(x + y)^2$ **71.** 1 **73.** $-2x^3$ **75.** $\frac{10}{x}$

77. 3^{3n} **79.** 5.75×10^7 **81.** 8.99×10^{-5}

83. 524,000,000 **85.** 0.00000000048

87. (a) 954.448 **(b)** 3.077×10^{10}

Section 3 (page 24)

1. $9^{1/2} = 3$ **3.** $\sqrt{196} = 14$ **5.** $(-216)^{1/3} = -6$

7. $\sqrt[3]{27^2} = 9$ **9.** $81^{3/4} = 27$ **11.** 3 **13.** 2

15. 6 **17.** 3 **19.** $\frac{1}{2}$ **21.** -125 **23.** 4 **25.** $\frac{1}{8}$

27. $\frac{27}{8}$ **29.** -4 **31.** $2\sqrt{2}$ **33.** 3×10^{-2}

35. $6|x|\sqrt{2x}$ **37.** $2x\sqrt[3]{2x^2}$ **39.** $\frac{5|x|\sqrt{3}}{y^2}$ **41.** $\frac{\sqrt{3}}{3}$

43. $4\sqrt[3]{4}$ **45.** $\frac{x(5 + \sqrt{3})}{11}$ **47.** $3(\sqrt{6} - \sqrt{5})$

49. $\frac{2}{\sqrt{2}}$ **51.** $\frac{2}{3(\sqrt{5} - \sqrt{3})}$ **53.** $-\frac{1}{2(\sqrt{7} + 3)}$

55. $3^{1/2} = \sqrt{3}$ **57.** $(x + 1)^{2/3} = \sqrt[3]{(x + 1)^2}$

59. $2\sqrt[4]{2}$ **61.** $\sqrt[8]{2x}$ **63.** $2\sqrt{x}$ **65.** $34\sqrt{2}$

67. $4\sqrt{y}$ **69.** $\frac{1}{x^3}$ **71.** $\frac{9y^{3/2}}{x^{2/3}}$ **73.** $\frac{3y^2}{4z^{4/3}}$ **75.** $x^{1/4}$

77. $c^{1/2}$ **79.** 7.550 **81.** 2.236 **83.** 9.137

85. $\sqrt{5} + \sqrt{3} > \sqrt{5 + 3}$ **87.** $5 > \sqrt{3^2 + 2^2}$

89. $\sqrt{3} \cdot \sqrt[4]{3} > \sqrt[8]{3}$ **91.** 1

Section 4 (*page 29*)

	Degree	Leading Coefficient
1.	2	2
3.	5	1
5.	5	4

7. Polynomial: $-3x^3 + 2x + 8$

9. Not a polynomial because of the operation of division.

11. Polynomial: $-y^4 + y^3 + y^2$ **13.** $-2x - 10$

15. $3x^3 - 2x + 2$ **17.** $8x^3 + 29x^2 + 11$

19. $12z + 8$ **21.** $3x^3 - 6x^2 + 3x$ **23.** $-15z^2 + 5z$

25. $30x^3 + 12x^2$ **27.** $x^2 + 7x + 12$

29. $6x^2 - 7x - 5$ **31.** $x^2 + 12x + 36$

33. $4x^2 - 20xy + 25y^2$

35. $x^2 + 2xy + y^2 - 6x - 6y + 9$ **37.** $x^2 - 100$

39. $x^2 - 4y^2$ **41.** $m^2 - n^2 - 6m + 9$ **43.** $4r^4 - 25$

45. $x^3 + 3x^2 + 3x + 1$ **47.** $8x^3 - 12x^2y + 6xy^2 - y^3$

49. $x - y$ **51.** $16x^6 - 24x^3 + 9$

53. $x^4 - x^3 + 5x^2 - 9x - 36$ **55.** $x^4 + x^2 + 1$

57. $2x^2 + 2x$ **59.** $x^3 + 4x^2 - 5x - 20$ **61.** $m + n$

Section 5 (*page 35*)

1. $3(x + 2)$ **3.** $2x(x^2 - 3)$ **5.** $(x - 1)(x + 5)$

7. $(x + 6)(x - 6)$ **9.** $(4y + 3)(4y - 3)$

11. $(x + 1)(x - 3)$ **13.** $(x - 2)^2$ **15.** $(2t + 1)^2$

17. $(5y - 1)^2$ **19.** $(x + 2)(x - 1)$

21. $(s - 3)(s - 2)$ **23.** $(y + 5)(y - 4)$

25. $(x - 20)(x - 10)$ **27.** $(3x - 2)(x - 1)$

29. $(3z + 1)(3z - 2)$ **31.** $(5x + 1)(x + 5)$

33. $(x - 2)(x^2 + 2x + 4)$ **35.** $(y + 4)(y^2 - 4y + 16)$

37. $(2t - 1)(4t^2 + 2t + 1)$ **39.** $(x - 1)(x^2 + 2)$

41. $(2x - 1)(x^2 - 3)$ **43.** $(3 + x)(2 - x^3)$

45. $(x + 2)(3x + 4)$ **47.** $(2x - 1)(3x + 2)$

49. $(3x - 1)(5x - 2)$

51.

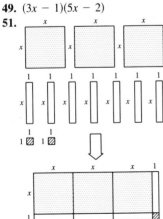

Section 6 (*page 41*)

1. All real numbers   **3.** All nonnegative real numbers

5. All real numbers x such that $x \neq 2$

7. All real numbers x such that $x \neq 0$ and $x \neq 4$

9. All real numbers x such that $x \geq -1$ **11.** $3x, x \neq 0$

13. $x - 2, x \neq 2$ **15.** $x + 2, x \neq -2$ **17.** $\dfrac{3x}{2}, x \neq 0$

19. $\dfrac{3y}{y + 1}, x \neq 0$ **21.** $-\dfrac{1}{2}, x \neq 5$ **23.** $\dfrac{x(x + 3)}{x - 2}, x \neq -2$

25. $\dfrac{y - 4}{y + 6}, y \neq 3$ **27.** $-(x^2 + 1), x \neq 2$ **29.** $z - 2$

31. $\dfrac{1}{5(x - 2)}, x \neq 1$ **33.** $\dfrac{r + 1}{r}, r \neq 1$

35. $\dfrac{2(y^2 + 2y + 4)}{y^2(y - 3)}, y \neq 2$ **37.** $\dfrac{3}{2}$

39. $x(x + 1), x \neq 0, -1$ **41.** $\dfrac{x + 5}{x - 1}$ **43.** $\dfrac{6x + 13}{x + 3}$

45. $-\dfrac{2}{x - 2}$ **47.** $\dfrac{x - 4}{(x + 2)(x - 2)(x - 1)}$

49. $\dfrac{2 - x}{x^2 + 1}, x \neq 0$ **51.** $\dfrac{2x^2 - 1}{(x^2 - 1)^{1/2}}$ **53.** $\dfrac{2(x - 3)}{(x - 2)^{4/3}}$

55. $\dfrac{1}{2}$ **57.** $\dfrac{1}{x}, x \neq -1$ **59.** $-\dfrac{2x + h}{x^2(x + h)^2}, h \neq 0$

53.

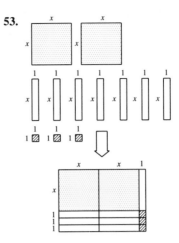

55. $x(x + 3)(x - 3)$ **57.** $x^2(x - 4)$ **59.** $(x - 1)^2$

61. $(1 - 2x)^2$ **63.** $2x(x + 1)(x - 2)$

65. $(9x + 1)(x + 1)$ **67.** $(3x + 1)(x^2 + 5)$

69. $x(x - 4)(x^2 + 1)$ **71.** $-x(x + 10)$

73. $(x + 1)^2(x - 1)^2$ **75.** $2(t - 2)(t^2 + 2t + 4)$

77. $(2x - 1)(6x - 1)$ **79.** $-(x + 1)(x - 3)(x + 9)$

61. $\dfrac{a + 2b}{(ab)^2}$ **63.** $\dfrac{2x - 1}{2x}$, $x > 0$ **65.** $-\dfrac{1}{t^2\sqrt{t^2 + 1}}$

67. $\dfrac{1}{\sqrt{x + 2} + \sqrt{x}}$

Section 7 (page 48)

1.   **3.**

5. 8   **7.** 5   **9.** $a = 4$, $b = 3$, $c = 5$
11. $a = 10$, $b = 3$, $c = \sqrt{109}$
13. (a)   **(b)** 10   **(c)** $(5, 4)$

15. (a)   **(b)** 17   **(c)** $\left(0, \frac{5}{2}\right)$

17. (a)   **(b)** $2\sqrt{10}$ **(c)** $(2, 3)$

19. (a)   **(b)** $\dfrac{\sqrt{82}}{3}$ **(c)** $\left(-1, \frac{7}{6}\right)$

21. (a)   **(b)** $\sqrt{110.97}$ **(c)** $(1.25, 3.6)$

23. (a)   **(b)** $6\sqrt{277}$ **(c)** $(6, -45)$

25. \$630,000   **27.** $\left(\sqrt{5}\right)^2 + \left(\sqrt{45}\right)^2 = \left(\sqrt{50}\right)^2$
29. All sides have a length of $\sqrt{5}$.   **31.** $x = 6, -4$
33. $y = \pm 15$ **35.** $3x - 2y - 1 = 0$
37. Quadrant IV   **39.** Quadrant I   **41.** Quadrant II
43. Quadrant III or IV   **45.** Quadrant I or III
47. Quadrant III
49.

The points are reflected through the y-axis.
51. $x^2 + y^2 = 9$ **53.** $(x - 2)^2 + (y + 1)^2 = 16$
55. $(x + 1)^2 + (y - 2)^2 = 5$
57. $(x - 3)^2 + (y - 4)^2 = 25$

CHAPTER 1

Section 1.1 (*page 59*)

WARM-UP   **1.** $14x - 42$ **2.** $-17s$ **3.** $-24y^7$

4. $\dfrac{2a}{3b^5}$ **5.** $5x^2\sqrt{6}$ **6.** $\dfrac{1}{2}$ **7.** $2x^2(x - 3)$

8. $2(t + 3)(t^2 + 3t - 2)$ **9.** $(3z + 10)(2z - 5)$

10. $(2s + 5)(2s - 5)$

1. (a) Yes   **(b)** Yes   **3. (a)** No   **(b)** Yes

5. (a) Yes   **(b)** Yes   **7.** 2   **9.** 4

11.

x	-4	-2	0	2	4
y	11	7	3	-1	-5
(x, y)	$(-4, 11)$	$(-2, 7)$	$(0, 3)$	$(2, -1)$	$(4, -5)$

13. c

```
Xmin=-2
Xmax=6
Xscl=1
Ymin=-1
Ymax=5
Yscl=1
```

14. f

```
Xmin=-4
Xmax=2
Xscl=1
Ymin=-2
Ymax=4
Yscl=1
```

15. d

```
Xmin=-3
Xmax=3
Xscl=1
Ymin=-1
Ymax=3
Yscl=1
```

16. a

```
Xmin=-1
Xmax=8
Xscl=1
Ymin=-1
Ymax=4
Yscl=1
```

17. e

```
Xmin=-2
Xmax=2
Xscl=1
Ymin=-2
Ymax=2
Yscl=1
```

18. b

```
Xmin=-4
Xmax=4
Xscl=1
Ymin=-3
Ymax=3
Yscl=1
```

19.

21.

23.

25.

27.

29.

31.

The graph intersects the x-axis twice.
The graph intersects the y-axis once.

33.

The graph intersects the x-axis three times.
The graph intersects the y-axis once.

35.

The graph intersects the x-axis twice.
The graph intersects the y-axis once.

37.

The graph intersects the x-axis once.
The graph intersects the y-axis once.

39.

The graph intersects the x-axis twice.
The graph intersects the y-axis once.

41.

The graph intersects the x-axis twice.
The graph intersects the y-axis once.

43.

The graph intersects the x-axis twice.
The graph intersects the y-axis once.

45. $y = \sqrt{64 - x^2}$, $y = -\sqrt{64 - x^2}$

47. $y = \sqrt{6(12 - x^2)}$, $y = -\sqrt{6(12 - x^2)}$

49.
```
Xmin=-1
Xmax=100
Xscl=5
Ymin=-1
Ymax=40
Yscl=2
```

51.
```
Xmin=-1
Xmax=20
Xscl=1
Ymin=-25
Ymax=150
Yscl=10
```

53.

The person would select the first viewing rectangle.

55. (a)

x	−1	0	1
y	−1	0	1

(b)

x	−1	$-\frac{3}{4}$	$-\frac{1}{2}$	$-\frac{1}{4}$	0	$\frac{1}{4}$	$\frac{1}{2}$	$\frac{3}{4}$	1
y	−1	−0.91	−0.79	−0.63	0	0.63	0.79	0.91	1

(c)

57.

(a) $y = 1.73$
(b) $x = -4$

59.

(a) $y = 2.47$
(b) $x = -1.65, 1$

61. (b)

63.

$16,890

65.

67. There are an unlimited number of correct answers, one of which is $a = 1$ and $b = -5$.

Section 1.2 (page 72)

WARM-UP   **1.** $-\frac{9}{2}$ **2.** $-\frac{13}{3}$ **3.** $-\frac{5}{4}$ **4.** $\frac{1}{2}$
5. $y = \frac{2}{3}x - \frac{5}{3}$ **6.** $y = -2x$ **7.** $y = 3x - 1$
8. $y = \frac{2}{3}x + 5$ **9.** $y = -2x + 7$ **10.** $y = x + 3$

1. $\frac{6}{5}$ **3.** 0   **5.** -3

7. $m = \frac{-3}{5}$ $m = 1$ **9.** $m = 2$

11. m is undefined.   **13.** $m = \frac{4}{3}$

15. $(0, 1), (3, 1), (-1, 1)$ **17.** $(6, -5), (7, -4), (8, -3)$
19. Perpendicular   **21.** Parallel   **23.** Collinear
25. $16{,}667$ ft ≈ 3.16 mi

27. $m = 5$; Intercept: $(0, 3)$

29. m is undefined. There is no y-intercept.

31. $3x + 5y - 10 = 0$ **33.** $x + 2y - 3 = 0$
35. $x + 8 = 0$ **37.** $3x - y - 2 = 0$
39. $8x + 6y - 47 = 0$
41. $x - 6 = 0$ **43.**

45.   **47.**

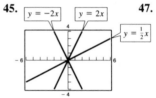

49.

a and b are the x- and y-intercepts of the graph of the line.
51. $3x + 2y - 6 = 0$
53. (a) $2x - y - 3 = 0$ **(b)** $x + 2y - 4 = 0$
55. (a) $y = 0$ **(b)** $x + 1 = 0$ **57.** $V = 125t + 2540$
59. $V = 2000t + 20{,}400$ **61.** b   **62.** c   **63.** a
64. d   **65.** $F = \frac{9}{5}C + 32$
67. (a) $S = 2200t + 28{,}500$ **(b)** \$39,500

69. (a) $V = -175t + 875$ **(b)**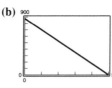
(c) \$525   **(d)** 3.86 yr

71. $W = 0.07S + 2500$
73. (a) $C = 16.75t + 36,500$ **(b)** $R = 37t$
(c) $t \approx 1802$ hr
75. The model approximates the daily cost y of producing x units of a product.

Section 1.3 (*page 84*)

WARM-UP   **1.** -73 **2.** 13   **3.** $2(x + 2)$
4. $-8(x - 2)$ **5.** $y = \frac{7}{5} - \frac{2}{5}x$ **6.** $y = \pm x$
7. $5xy\sqrt{2x}$ **8.** $3z\sqrt{2z^2 - 1}$ **9.** $\dfrac{x - y}{x + y}$
10. $\dfrac{x(x - 3)}{2}$

1. (a) Function
(b) Not a function because the element 1 in A is matched with two elements, -2 and 1, in B.
(c) Function
(d) Not a function because not all elements of A are matched with an element in B.
3. Not a function   **5.** Function   **7.** Function
9. Not a function
11. (a) $6 - 4(3) = -6$ **(b)** $6 - 4(-7) = 34$
(c) $6 - 4(t) = 6 - 4t$
(d) $6 - 4(c + 1) = 2(1 - 2c)$
13. (a) $\dfrac{1}{4 + 1} = \dfrac{1}{5}$ **(b)** $\dfrac{1}{0 + 1} = 1$ **(c)** $\dfrac{1}{4x + 1}$
(d) $\dfrac{1}{(x + h) + 1}$
15. (a) -1 **(b)** -9 **(c)** $2x - 5$ **(d)** $-\frac{5}{2}$
17. (a) 0   **(b)** 3   **(c)** $x^2 + 2x$ **(d)** -0.75
19. (a) 1   **(b)** -1 **(c)** 1   **(d)** $\dfrac{|x - 1|}{x - 1}$
21. (a) -1 **(b)** 2   **(c)** 4   **(d)** 6
23. All real numbers   **25.** $y \geq 10$
27. All real numbers except $t = 0$
29. All real numbers except $x = 0, -2$
31. $(-2, 4), (-1, 1), (0, 0), (1, 1), (2, 4)$
33. $(-2, 0), (-1, 1), (0, \sqrt{2}), (1, \sqrt{3}), (2, 2)$
35. (a) 1056.250   **(b)** 1470.084
37. (a) 0.118   **(b)** 21.277   **39.** $g(x) = cx^2, c = -2$

41. $r(x) = \dfrac{c}{x}, c = 32$ **43.** $2, h \neq 0$
45. $3xh + 3x^2 + h^2, h \neq 0$ **47.** $A = \dfrac{C^2}{4\pi}$
49. $A = \dfrac{x^2}{x - 1}, x > 1$
51. $V = 4x^2(27 - x), 0 < x < 27$
53. $h = \sqrt{d^2 - 2000^2}, 0 \leq d$
55. (a) $C = 12.30x + 98,000$ **(b)** $R = 17.98x$
(c) $P = 5.68x - 98,000$

Section 1.4 (*page 96*)

WARM-UP   **1.** 2   **2.** 0   **3.** $-\dfrac{3}{x}$ **4.** $x^2 + 3$
5. x-intercept: $(-\frac{12}{5}, 0)$
    y-intercept: $(0, 6)$
6. x-intercept: $(5, 0)$
    y-intercept: $(0, 3)$
7. All real numbers except $x = 4$
8. All real numbers except $x = 4, 5$ **9.** $t \leq \frac{5}{3}$
10. All real numbers

1.   **3.**
Domain: $[1, \infty)$ Domain: $(-\infty, -2], [2, \infty)$
Range: $[0, \infty)$ Range: $[0, \infty)$
5.   **7.** Function
```
Xmin=-3
Xmax=3
Xscl=1
Ymin=-1
Ymax=4
Yscl=1
```
Domain: $[-5, 5]$
Range: $[0, 5]$
9. Not a function   **11.** Function
```
Xmin=-1
Xmax=5
Xscl=1
Ymin=-3
Ymax=3
Yscl=1
```
```
Xmin=-5
Xmax=5
Xscl=1
Ymin=-4
Ymax=4
Yscl=1
```
13. b   **15.** a

17.

Increasing on $(-\infty, \infty)$

19.

Increasing on $(-\infty, 0)$, $(2, \infty)$
Decreasing on $(0, 2)$

21.

Increasing on $(-1, 0)$, $(1, \infty)$
Decreasing on $(-\infty, -1)$, $(0, 1)$

23.

Increasing on $(-2, \infty)$
Decreasing on $(-3, -2)$

25. Relative minimum: $(3, -9)$
27. Relative minimum: $(1, -7)$
    Relative maximum: $(-2, 20)$
29. Relative minimum: $(0.33, -0.38)$
31. **(b)**

(c) Maximum area:
625 sq ft, 25 ft × 25 ft

33.

350,000 units

35.

$f(x) = 3 - x$
$x \geq 0$

$f(x) = 2x + 3$
$x < 0$

37.

$f(x) = x^2 + 5$
$x \leq 1$

$f(x) = -x^2 + 4x + 3$
$x > 1$

39.

41. **(a)** $C = 0.65 + 0.42[\![t]\!]$
(b)

(c) Less than 13 minutes

43. **(a)** $(-5, 6)$ **(b)** $(-5, -6)$
45. **(a)** $\left(\frac{3}{2}, -2\right)$ **(b)** $\left(\frac{3}{2}, 2\right)$

47.

Even

49.

Neither even nor odd

51.

Odd

53.

Neither even nor odd

55.

Odd

57. Even

59. Odd
63. $(-\infty, 4]$

61. Neither even nor odd
65. $[-1, -1]$

67. $f(x) > 0$ for all x

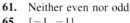

69. $h = (4x - x^2) - 3$

71. $h = 4x - 2x^2$ **73.** $L = (4 - y^2) - (y + 2)$

75.

Interval	Intake Pipe	Drain Pipe 1	Drain Pipe 2
[0, 5]	Open	Closed	Closed
[5, 10]	Open	Open	Closed
[10, 20]	Closed	Closed	Closed
[20, 30]	Closed	Closed	Open
[30, 40]	Open	Open	Open
[40, 45]	Open	Closed	Open
[45, 50]	Open	Open	Open
[50, 60]	Open	Open	Closed

Section 1.5 (page 106)

WARM-UP

1.

Domain: [−4, 4]
Range: [0, 4]

2.

Domain: (−∞, ∞)
Range: [0, ∞)

3.

Domain: (−∞, ∞)
Range: [−1, ∞)

4.

Domain: (−∞, ∞)
Range: (−∞, ∞)

5.

Domain: all real numbers
except x = 2 Range: {−1, 1}

6.

Domain: [2, ∞)
Range: [0, ∞)

7. Odd   **8.** Even   **9.** Even
10. Neither even nor odd

1.

3.

5.

7.
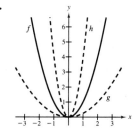

9. $g(x) = (x − 1)^2 + 1$
$h(x) = −(x − 2)^2 + 4$

11. $g(x) = (x − 3)^2 − 2$
$h(x) = −x^2 + 3$

13.

$g(x)$ is shifted two units to the left of $f(x)$.
$h(x)$ is a vertical shrink of $f(x)$.

15.

$g(x)$ is a vertical shrink of $f(x)$ and a reflection across
the x-axis.
$h(x)$ is a reflection across the y-axis.

17. $y = −(x^3 − 3x^2) + 1$
19. y is $f(x)$ shifted up two units.
21. y is $f(x)$ shifted right two units.
23. y is a vertical stretch of $f(x)$ by $\sqrt{2}$.
25. y is $f(x)$ shifted down one unit.
27. y is $f(x)$ shifted right one unit.
29. y is $f(x)$ reflected in the y-axis.

31.

33.

35.

37. A reflection in the x-axis followed by a vertical shift of
four units upward.
39. A horizontal shift of two units to the left and a vertical
shrink.
41. A horizontal stretch and a vertical shift of two units
upward.

43. (a)

(b) $P(x) = -2420 + 20x - 0.5x^2$
Vertical shift
(c) $P(x) = 80 + 0.2x - 0.00005x^2$
Horizontal stretch

45.

The three even functions are nonnegative. As the exponents increase, the graphs become flatter in the interval $(-1, 1)$.

47.

49.

51.

Section 1.6 *(page 114)*

WARM-UP   **1.** $\dfrac{1}{x(1 - x)}$ **2.** $-\dfrac{12}{(x + 3)(x - 3)}$

3. $\dfrac{3x - 2}{x(x - 2)}$ **4.** $\dfrac{4x - 5}{3(x - 5)}$ **5.** $\sqrt{\dfrac{x - 1}{x + 1}}$

6. $\dfrac{x + 1}{x(x + 2)}$ **7.** $5(x - 2)$ **8.** $\dfrac{x + 1}{(x - 2)(x + 3)}$

9. $\dfrac{1 + 5x}{3x - 1}$ **10.** $\dfrac{x + 4}{4x}$

1. (a) $2x$ **(b)** 2 **(c)** $x^2 - 1$ **(d)** $\dfrac{x + 1}{x - 1}, x \neq 1$

3. (a) $x^2 + 5 + \sqrt{1 - x}$ **(b)** $x^2 + 5 - \sqrt{1 - x}$
(c) $(x^2 + 5)\sqrt{1 - x}$ **(d)** $\dfrac{x^2 + 5}{\sqrt{1 - x}}, x < 1$

5. (a) $\dfrac{x + 1}{x^2}$ **(b)** $\dfrac{x - 1}{x^2}$ **(c)** $\dfrac{1}{x^3}$ **(d)** $x, x \neq 0$

7. 9 **9.** $4t^2 - 2t + 5$ **11.** 0 **13.** 26 **15.** $\frac{3}{5}$

17.

19.

21.

$0 \leq x \leq 2, f$
$x > 5, g$

23. $T = \frac{3}{4}x + \frac{1}{15}x^2$

25. (a) $(x - 1)^2$ **(b)** $x^2 - 1$ **(c)** x^4
27. (a) $20 - 3x$ **(b)** $-3x$ **(c)** $9x + 20$
29. (a) $\sqrt{x^2 + 4}$ **(b)** $x + 4$
31. (a) $x - \frac{8}{3}$ **(b)** $x - 8$
33. (a) $|x + 6|$ **(b)** $|x| + 6$ **35. (a)** 3 **(b)** 0
37. (a) 0 **(b)** 4 **39.** $f(x) = x^2, g(x) = 2x + 1$
41. $f(x) = \sqrt[3]{x}, g(x) = x^2 - 4$
43. $f(x) = \dfrac{1}{x}, g(x) = x + 2$
45. $f(x) = x^2 + 2x, g(x) = x + 4$
47. (a) $x \geq 0$ **(b)** All real numbers
(c) All real numbers
49. (a) All real numbers except $x = \pm 1$
(b) All real numbers
(c) All real numbers except $x = -2, 0$
51. (a) $(A \circ r)(t) = 0.36\pi t^2$
$A \circ r$ represents the area of the circle at time t.
(b)

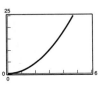

4.2 sec

53. (a) $(C \circ x)(t) = 3000t + 750$

$C \circ x$ represents the cost after t production hours.

(b)

4.75 hr

55. $R(x) = x - 1200$, $D(x) = 0.85x$

$(D \circ R)(x) = 0.85(x - 1200)$

$(D \circ R)(18{,}400) = \$14{,}620$

$(R \circ D)(x) = 0.85x - 1200$

$(R \circ D)(18{,}400) = \$14{,}440$

57. Odd

Section 1.7 (page 125)

WARM-UP   **1.** All real numbers   **2.** $[-1, \infty)$

3. All real numbers except $x = 0, 2$

4. All real numbers except $x = -\frac{5}{3}$ **5.** x **6.** x

7. x **8.** x **9.** $x = \dfrac{3}{2}y + 3$ **10.** $x = \dfrac{y^3}{2} + 2$

---

1. $f^{-1}(x) = \frac{1}{8}x$ **3.** $f^{-1}(x) = x - 10$

5. $f^{-1}(x) = x^3$

7. (a) $(f \circ g)(x) = f\left(\dfrac{x}{2}\right) = 2\left(\dfrac{x}{2}\right) = x$

$(g \circ f)(x) = g(2x) = \dfrac{2x}{2} = x$

(b)

9. (a) $(f \circ g)(x) = f\left(\dfrac{x-1}{5}\right) = \dfrac{5x + 1 - 1}{5} = x$

$(g \circ f)(x) = g(5x + 1) = 5\left(\dfrac{x-1}{5}\right) + 1 = x$

(b)

11. (a) $(f \circ g)(x) = f\left(\sqrt[3]{x}\right) = \left(\sqrt[3]{x}\right)^3 = x$

$(g \circ f)(x) = g(x^3) = \sqrt[3]{x^3} = x$

(b)

13. (a) $(f \circ g)(x) = f(x^2 + 4)$, $x \geq 0$

$= \sqrt{(x^2 + 4) - 4} = x$

$(g \circ f)(x) = g\left(\sqrt{x - 4}\right)$

$= \left(\sqrt{x - 4}\right)^2 + 4 = x$

(b)

15. (a) $(f \circ g)(x) = f\left(\sqrt{9 - x}\right)$, $x \leq 9$

$= 9 - \left(\sqrt{9 - x}\right)^2 = x$

$(g \circ f)(x) = g(9 - x^2)$

$= \sqrt{9 - (9 - x)^2} = x$

(b)

17. One-to-one   **19.** Not one-to-one

21. Not one-to-one   **23.** $f^{-1}(x) = \dfrac{x + 3}{2}$

25. $f^{-1}(x) = \sqrt[5]{x}$ **27.** $f^{-1}(x) = x^2$, $x \geq 0$

29. $f^{-1}(x) = \sqrt{4 - x^2}, 0 \le x \le 2$ **31.** $f^{-1}(x) = x^3 + 1$

5.

7.

33. Not one-to-one   **35.** $g^{-1}(x) = 8x$

37. $f^{-1}(x) = \sqrt{x} - 3, x \ge 0$ **39.** $h^{-1}(x) = \dfrac{1}{x}$

41. $f^{-1}(x) = \dfrac{x^2 - 3}{2}, x \ge 0$

9.

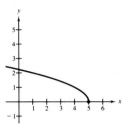

43. Not one-to-one   **45.** $f^{-1}(x) = -\sqrt{25 - x}$

47. $f^{-1}(x) = \sqrt{x} + 3, x \ge 0$ **49.** $f^{-1}(x) = x - 3, x \ge 0$

11.

The graph intersects the x-axis once.
The graph intersects the y-axis once.

51.

x	0	1	2	3	4
$f^{-1}(x)$	-2	0	1	2	4

13.

The graph intersects the x-axis three times.
The graph intersects the y-axis once.

53. 32   **55.** 600   **57.** $\dfrac{x + 1}{2}$ **59.** $\dfrac{x + 1}{2}$

61. (a) $y = \sqrt{\dfrac{x - 254.50}{0.03}}$

    y: percentage load, x: exhaust temperature

(b)

15.

The graph intersects the x-axis three times.
The graph intersects the y-axis once.

63. False   **65.** True

Chapter 1 Review Exercises (*page 126*)

1.

3.

17.

19.

The graph intersects the x-axis twice.
The graph intersects the y-axis once.

21. $t = \frac{7}{3}$ **23.** $t = 3$ **25.** $x = 0$
27. $5x - 12y + 2 = 0$ **29.** $2x - 7y + 2 = 0$
31. $3x - 2y - 10 = 0$ **33.** $2x + 3y - 6 = 0$

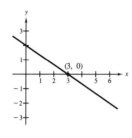

35. **(a)** $5x - 4y - 23 = 0$ **(b)** $4x + 5y - 2 = 0$
37. \$210,000
39. **(a)** 5   **(b)** 17   **(c)** $t^4 + 1$ **(d)** $-x^2 - 1$
41. **(a)** -14 **(b)** $-5x^2 - 30x - 39$ **(c)** -30
    (d) $-10x - 5t, t \neq 0$
43. **(a)**   **(b)**

(c)

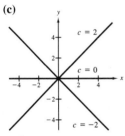

45. $[-5, 5]$ **47.** All real numbers except $s = 3$
49. All real numbers except $x = -2, 3$
51. **(a)** 16 ft/sec   **(b)** 1.5 sec   **(c)** -16 ft/sec
53. $A = x(12 - x), (0, 6]$ **55.** **(a)**

Constant: $(-\infty, -2), (2, \infty)$
Increasing: $(-2, 2)$
(b) Minimum: -4 on $(-\infty, -2)$
Maximum: 4 on $(2, \infty)$
(c) Odd

57. **(a)**

Increasing: $(-\infty, 0), (0, 3)$
Decreasing: $(3, \infty)$
(b) Maximum: $(3, 27)$ **(c)** Neither even nor odd
59. **(b)** $t = 4.92$ hr, $d = 64.02$ mi

61. **(a)** $f^{-1}(x) = 2x + 6$
(b)

(c) $f^{-1}(f(x)) = f^{-1}(\frac{1}{2}x - 3)$
$= 2(\frac{1}{2}x - 3) + 6 = x$
$f(f^{-1}(x)) = f(2x + 6)$
$= \frac{1}{2}(2x + 6) - 3 = x$
63. **(a)** $f^{-1}(x) = x^2 - 1, x \geq 0$
(b)

(c) $f^{-1}(f(x)) = f^{-1}(\sqrt{x + 1}), x \geq 0$
$= (\sqrt{x + 1})^2 - 1 = x$
$f(f^{-1}(x)) = f(x^2 - 1)$
$= \sqrt{(x^2 - 1) + 1} = x$
65. **(a)** $f^{-1}(x) = \sqrt{x + 5}, x \geq -5$
(b)

(c) $f^{-1}(f(x)) = f^{-1}(x^2 - 5), x \geq -5$
$= \sqrt{(x^2 - 5) + 5} = x$
$f(f^{-1}(x)) = f(\sqrt{x + 5}), x \geq 0$
$= (\sqrt{x + 5})^2 - 5 = x$

67. $x \geq 4, f^{-1}(x) = \sqrt{\dfrac{x}{2} + 4}$

69. $x \geq 2, f^{-1}(x) = \sqrt{x^2 + 4}, x \geq 0$

71. -7 **73.** 5   **75.** 23   **77.** 9

Chapter 2

Section 2.1 (*page 135*)

WARM-UP   **1.** $-3x - 10$ **2.** $5x - 12$ **3.** x

4. $x + 26$ **5.** $\dfrac{8x}{15}$ **6.** $\dfrac{3x}{4}$ **7.** $-\dfrac{1}{x(x + 1)}$

8. $\dfrac{5}{x}$ **9.** $\dfrac{7x - 8}{x(x - 2)}$ **10.** $-\dfrac{2}{x^2 - 1}$

---

1. Identity   **3.** Conditional   **5.** Identity
7. Identity   **9.** Conditional
11. (a) No   **(b)** No   **(c)** Yes   **(d)** No
13. (a) Yes   **(b)** Yes   **(c)** No   **(d)** No
15. (a) Yes   **(b)** No   **(c)** No   **(d)** No
17. (a) No   **(b)** No   **(c)** Yes   **(d)** Yes
19. 5   **21.** -4 **23.** 3   **25.** 9   **27.** -26
29. -4 **31.** $-\frac{6}{5}$ **33.** No solution   **35.** 10
37. 4   **39.** 3   **41.** 5   **43.** No solution   **45.** $\frac{11}{6}$
47. $\frac{5}{3}$ **49.** No solution   **51.** All real numbers
53. $\dfrac{1}{3 - a}, a \neq 3$ **55.** $\dfrac{1 + 4b}{2 + a}, a \neq -2$
57. $x \approx 138.889$ **59.** $x \approx 62.372$ **61.** $x \approx -2.386$
63. One equation of this form is $x + 4 = 3x$.   **65.** 10 in.
67. 61.2 in.

Section 2.2 (*page 145*)

WARM-UP   **1.** 14   **2.** 4   **3.** -3 **4.** 4   **5.** -2
6. 1   **7.** $\frac{2}{5}$ **8.** $\frac{10}{3}$ **9.** 6   **10.** $-\frac{11}{5}$

---

1. $n + (n + 1) = 2n + 1$ **3.** $50t$ **5.** $0.2x$
7. $6x$ **9.** $25x + 1200$ **11.** 262, 263   **13.** 37, 185
15. $-5, -4$ **17.** 13.5   **19.** 1192.5   **21.** 135%
23. 175
25. Income taxes: \$446 billion; Corporation taxes: \$103 billion; Social Security taxes: \$360 billion; Other: \$82 billion
27. \$22,316.98
29. January: \$71,590.00; February: \$85,908.00
31. 1700%   **33.** 860%   **35.** $15' \times 22\frac{1}{2}'$ **37.** 97
39. 3 hr   **41.** $\frac{1}{3}$ hr
43. (a) 3.8 hr, 3.2 hr   **(b)** 1.1 hr   **(c)** 25.6 mi
45. $66\frac{2}{3}$ mi/hr   **47.** 1.29 sec   **49.** 57.1 ft
51. 4.36 ft   **53.** \$10,000 at 11%, \$15,000 at $12\frac{1}{2}$%
55. First three quarters: 11.5%; Last quarter: 10%
57. 32.1 gal   **59.** 50 lb of each kind   **61.** 8064 units
63. 6 ft   **65.** $\dfrac{2A}{b}$ **67.** $\dfrac{I}{PT}$ **69.** $\dfrac{2A - ah}{h}$
71. $\dfrac{3V + \pi h^3}{3\pi h^2}$ **73.** $\dfrac{Fr^2}{\alpha m_1}$ **75.** $\dfrac{S - a}{S - L}$

Section 2.3 (*page 157*)

WARM-UP   **1.** $\frac{3}{2}$ **2.** -9 **3.** $\frac{40}{3}$ **4.** $\frac{250}{7}$ **5.** 2
6. -4 **7.**   **8.**

9.   **10.**

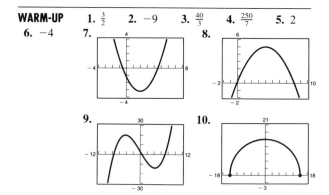

---

1. $(5, 0), (0, -5)$ **3.** $(-2, 0), (1, 0), (0, -2)$
5. $(0, 0), (-2, 0)$ **7.** $(1, 0), (0, \frac{1}{2})$
9.   **11.** $(-1.5, 0)$

13.   **15.** $13x - 89 = 0$

17. $\dfrac{2x}{3} + \dfrac{1}{x} - 10 = 0$

19. $\dfrac{3}{x+2} - \dfrac{4}{x-2} - 5 = 0$ **21.** $\dfrac{15}{4}$ **23.** 6

25. $-\dfrac{5}{8}$ **27.** 2.172, 7.828   **29.** -1.379

31. $\dfrac{1}{2}, -3, 3$ **33.** $-0.717, 2.107$ **35.** -1.333

37. $(1, 1)$ **39.** $(1.449, 1.898), (-3.449, -7.898)$

41. $(-2, 8), (1.333, 8)$ **43.** $(-1, 0), (2, 9)$

45. $(0, 0), (2, 8), (-2, 8)$

47. (a) 6.46   **(b)** 6.41, yes

49. (a) 1.00   **(b)** 1.01, yes

51. (a) $T = \dfrac{x}{63} + \dfrac{280 - x}{54}$ **53. (a)** $A = 0.33(55 - x) + x$

(b)

$0 < x < 280$

(c) 164.5 mi

55. $S = 8000 + \dfrac{1}{2}x$

(b)

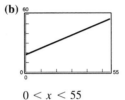

$0 < x < 55$

(c) 22.2 gal

57. $7600.00

(a) Decreases
(b) Increases

Section 2.4 (*page 168*)

WARM-UP   **1.** $\dfrac{\sqrt{14}}{10}$ **2.** $4\sqrt{2}$ **3.** 14   **4.** $\dfrac{\sqrt{10}}{4}$

5. $x(3x + 7)$ **6.** $(2x + 5)(2x - 5)$

7. $-(x - 7)(x - 15)$ **8.** $(x - 2)(x + 9)$

9. $(5x - 1)(2x + 3)$ **10.** $(6x - 1)(x - 12)$

1. $2x^2 + 5x - 3 = 0$ **3.** $x^2 - 6x + 7 = 0$

5. $3x^2 - 60x - 10 = 0$ **7.** $0, -\dfrac{1}{2}$ **9.** $4, -2$

11. -5 **13.** $3, -\dfrac{1}{2}$ **15.** $2, -6$ **17.** $-a$

19. ± 4 **21.** $\pm\sqrt{7} \approx \pm 2.65$ **23.** $\pm 2\sqrt{3} \approx \pm 3.46$

25. $12 + 3\sqrt{2} \approx 16.24, 12 - 3\sqrt{2} \approx 7.76$

27. $-2 + 2\sqrt{3} \approx 1.46, -2 - 2\sqrt{3} \approx -5.46$

29. 2   **31.** 0, 2   **33.** 4, -8

35. $-3 \pm \sqrt{7}$ **37.** $1 \pm \dfrac{\sqrt{6}}{3}$ **39.** $2 \pm 2\sqrt{3}$

41. $-1.111, 4.502$ **43.** $-35.805, 76.805$

45. $1 \pm \sqrt{2}$ **47.** $\pm\dfrac{3}{4}$ **49.** $\dfrac{3}{2}$ **51.** 6, -12

53. $5, -\dfrac{10}{3}$ **55.** 9, 3   **57.** $\dfrac{1}{2} \pm \sqrt{3}$ **59.** $\dfrac{3}{5} \pm \dfrac{\sqrt{2}}{2}$

61. $-1, -5$ **63.** $-\dfrac{1}{2}$ **65.** $\dfrac{1}{(x+1)^2 + 4}$

67. $\dfrac{1}{(x-2)^2 - 16}$ **69.** $\dfrac{1}{\sqrt{9 - (x-3)^2}}$

71. $34' \times 48'$ **73.** $\dfrac{\sqrt{1821}}{4} \approx 10.67$ sec

75. $\dfrac{5\sqrt{2}}{2} \approx 3.54$ cm   **77.** $1500\sqrt{2} \approx 2121.32$ ft

79. (a

(b) $x = 50,000, p = \$10$
(c) $x = 27,639, p = \$14.47$
$x = 72,361, p = \$5.53$

81. $0, -\dfrac{b}{a}$ **83.** $x^2 - 2x - 24 = 0$

Section 2.5 (*page 176*)

WARM-UP   **1.** $3\sqrt{17}$ **2.** $2\sqrt{3}$ **3.** $4\sqrt{6}$

4. $3\sqrt{73}$ **5.** 2, -1 **6.** $\dfrac{3}{2}, -3$ **7.** 5, -1

8. $\dfrac{1}{2}, -7$ **9.** 3, 2   **10.** 4, -1

1. One real solution   **3.** No real solutions

5. Two real solutions   **7.** $\dfrac{1}{2}, -1$ **9.** $\dfrac{1}{4}, -\dfrac{3}{4}$

11. $1 \pm \sqrt{3}$ **13.** $-7 \pm \sqrt{5}$ **15.** $-4 \pm 2\sqrt{5}$

17. $\dfrac{2}{3} \pm \dfrac{\sqrt{7}}{3}$ **19.** $-\dfrac{1}{3} \pm \dfrac{\sqrt{11}}{6}$ **21.** $-\dfrac{1}{2} \pm \sqrt{2}$

23. $\dfrac{2}{7}$ **25.** $-\dfrac{8}{5} \pm \dfrac{\sqrt{3}}{5}$ **27.** $6 \pm \sqrt{11}$

29. $0.976, -0.643$ **31.** $1.687, -0.488$ **33.** -11

35. $\pm\sqrt{10}$ **37.** $\dfrac{-3 \pm \sqrt{5}}{2}$ **39.** $-2, 4$ **41.** ± 2

43. 50, 50   **45.** 7, 8   **47.** 258 units   **49.** 653 units

51. 9 seats/row   **53.** 16   **55.** 6 in. $\times$ 6 in.

57. (a)

(b) 1990

59. 550 mi/hr, 600 mi/hr

61. $30\sqrt{6}$ ft ≈ 73.5 ft

63. (a)   **(c)** 439.1 mi

(b) 453.6 mi, 15.0 hr

Section 2.6 (page 188)

1. 3, −1, 0   **3.** −3, 0   **5.** 3, 1, −1
7. ±3, ±1   **9.** −$\frac{1}{5}$, −$\frac{1}{3}$ **11.** 1, −$\frac{125}{8}$ **13.** 50
15. −16   **17.** 0   **19.** 36   **21.** $\frac{101}{4}$ **23.** −59, 69
25. 1   **27.** 4, −5   **29.** $\dfrac{-3 \pm \sqrt{21}}{6}$ **31.** 1, −3
33. 3, −2   **35.** $\sqrt{3}$, −3   **37.** ±1   **39.** ±2
41. 0.25   **43.** 2, −5   **45.** 0, 4   **47.** 2, −1.50
49. −1   **51.** 10, −1   **53.** ±1.04   **55.** 16.76
57. 34   **59.** 400 mi/hr   **61.** 7%
63. (a)

(b) 211.6°   **(c)** 24.725 psi
65. 500 units
67. (b) 0 ≤ x ≤ 6
(c)

(d) 1.38 mi
69. $h = \dfrac{1}{\pi r}\sqrt{S^2 - \pi^2 r^4}$

Section 2.7 (page 197)

1. (a) Yes   **(b)** No   **(c)** Yes   **(d)** No
3. (a) Yes   **(b)** No   **(c)** No   **(d)** Yes
5. c   **6.** h   **7.** f   **8.** e   **9.** g   **10.** a
11. b   **12.** d
13. x < 3   **15.** x > −4

17. x ≥ 12   **19.** x < −$\frac{1}{2}$

21. −1 < x < 3   **23.** −$\frac{9}{2}$ < x < $\frac{15}{2}$

25. −$\frac{3}{4}$ < x < −$\frac{1}{4}$ **27.** −5 < x < 5

29. x < −6, x > 6   **31.** 16 ≤ x ≤ 24

33. x ≤ 16, x ≥ 24   **35.** 4 < x < 5

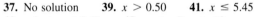

37. No solution   **39.** x > 0.50   **41.** x ≤ 5.45
43. −3 < x < 2.67   **45.** x ≤ −7, x ≥ 13
47. x ≤ −14.50, x ≥ −5.50   **49.** x ≤ 3   **51.** x ≤ $\frac{7}{2}$
53. |x| ≤ 2   **55.** |x − 9| ≥ 3   **57.** |x − 12| ≤ 10
59. |x + 3| > 5   **61.** More than 400 miles
63. r > 12.5%   **65.** x ≥ 36 units
67. (a) C = 1.45x + 150
(b) R = 2.95x
(c) P = 1.50x − 150
(d) 134 ≤ x ≤ 233

(e) 143 ≤ x ≤ 243
69. 1991   **71.** 106.864 ≤ area ≤ 109.464
73. 65.8 ≤ h ≤ 71.2

Section 2.8 (page 208)

WARM-UP 1. $y < -6$ 2. $z > -\frac{9}{2}$
3. $-3 \le x < 1$ 4. $x \le -5$ 5. $-3 < x$
6. $5 < x < 7$ 7. $-\frac{7}{2} \le x \le \frac{7}{2}$ 8. $x < 2, x > 4$
9. $x < -6, x > -2$ 10. $-2 \le x \le 6$

1. $[-3, 3]$ 3. $(-\infty, -5], [1, \infty)$ 5. $(-3, 2)$
7. $(-\infty, -1), (1, \infty)$ 9. $(-3, 1)$
11. $(-\infty, 0), (0, \frac{3}{2})$ 13. $[-2, 0], [2, \infty)$
15. $(-\infty, -1), (0, 1)$ 17. $(-\infty, -1), (4, \infty)$
19. $(5, 15)$ 21. $(-5, -\frac{3}{2}), (-1, \infty)$ 23. $(1, 2), (0, 1)$
25. $[-2, \infty)$ 27. $(-0.13, 25.13)$
29. $(-14, -2), (6, \infty)$ 31. $(-\infty, -2), (-1, 1), (3, \infty)$
33. $[-2, 2]$ 35. $(-\infty, 3], [4, \infty)$ 37. $[-4, 3]$
39. $(-3, 0], (3, \infty)$
41. (a) 10 sec (b) 4 sec $< t < 6$ sec
43. Between 13.8 meters and 36.2 meters
45. (a) $R = \dfrac{R_1 R_2}{R_1 + R_2}$ (b) $R = \dfrac{2R_1}{R_1 + 2}$
(c) $R_1 \ge 2$

47. 1994

Chapter 2 Review Exercises (page 209)

1. Identity
3. (a) No (b) Yes (c) Yes (d) No
5. 20 7. $\frac{1}{5}$ 9. $\frac{4}{3}, -\frac{1}{2}$ 11. $-4 \pm 3\sqrt{2}$
13. $6 \pm \sqrt{6}$ 15. 0, 1, 2 17. 2, 6 19. 5
21. $\dfrac{25}{4}$ 23. $-124, 126$ 25. $-4, \dfrac{-10 \pm \sqrt{95}}{5}$
27. $-5, 15$ 29. $-6.464, 0.464$ 31. 1.944
33. ± 0.707 35. 1, 3 37. $r = \sqrt{\dfrac{3V}{\pi h}}$
39. $p = \dfrac{k}{3\pi r^2 L}$ 41. $\left(-\dfrac{5}{3}, \infty\right)$ 43. $(-\infty, 3), (5, \infty)$
45. $(1, 3)$ 47. $(-\infty, 0], [3, \infty)$ 49. $(-\infty, 17.143)$
51. $(4, \infty)$ 53. $[5, \infty)$
55. September: \$325,000; October: \$364,000
57. 2.86 quarts 59. $1000\sqrt{2} \approx 1414.21$ ft
61. 4 farmers 63. 143,202 units 65. $x \ge 36$
67. $L \ge \dfrac{32}{\pi^2} \approx 3.24$ ft

CUMULATIVE TEST for Prerequisites, Chapters 1 and 2 (page 211)

1. $-\dfrac{437}{45}$ 2. $\dfrac{4x^3}{15y^5}$ 3. $2x^2|y|\sqrt{6y}$
4. $x^3 - x^2 - 5x + 6$ 5. $-x(x + 1)(6x - 1)$
6. $\dfrac{s - 1}{(s + 1)(s + 3)}$ 7. $\dfrac{1}{2(2x + 1)\sqrt{x}}$
8. (a) (b)

(c) (d)

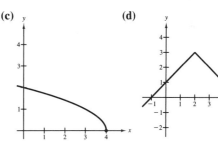

9. $C = 3$ 10. $(1, 11), (7, 7), (10, 5)$
11. $2x - y + 2 = 0$
12. (a) $\dfrac{3}{2}$ (b) Undefined (c) $\dfrac{t}{t - 1}$ (d) $\dfrac{s + 2}{s}$
13. $-\infty < x < 3, 0 < y$ 14. $A = \dfrac{\sqrt{3}}{4}s^2$
15. For some values of x, there is more than one corresponding value of y.
16. (a) Horizontal stretch by a factor of 2
(b) Vertical shrink by a factor of $\frac{1}{2}$
(c) Vertical translation of 2 units upward
(d) Horizontal translation of 2 units to the left
17. $(f \circ g)(x) = \sqrt{x^2 + 3}$ 18. $h^{-1}(x) = \frac{1}{5}(x + 2)$
19. (a) 7 (b) 5 (c) $\dfrac{-3 \pm \sqrt{3}}{3}$ (d) 6
20. 7.1 21. $-1 < x < 5$ 22. $-2 < x < 3$

23. \$8000 at 7.5%, \$4000 at 9% 24. 1.8 gal
25. $n = 9$

CHAPTER 3

Section 3.1 (*page 221*)

WARM-UP   **1.** $\frac{1}{2}, -6$ **2.** $-\frac{3}{5}, 3$ **3.** $\frac{3}{2}, -1$

4. -10 **5.** $3 \pm \sqrt{5}$ **6.** $-2 \pm \sqrt{3}$

7. $4 \pm \dfrac{\sqrt{14}}{2}$ **8.** $-5 \pm \dfrac{\sqrt{3}}{3}$ **9.** $-\dfrac{3}{2} \pm \dfrac{\sqrt{5}}{2}$

10. $-\dfrac{3}{2} \pm \dfrac{\sqrt{21}}{2}$

1. f   **2.** d

```
Xmin=-1
Xmax=6
Xscl=1
Ymin=-1
Ymax=5
Yscl=1
```

```
Xmin=-8
Xmax=1
Xscl=1
Ymin=-1
Ymax=6
Yscl=1
```

3. c   **4.** e

```
Xmin=-4
Xmax=4
Xscl=1
Ymin=-5
Ymax=2
Yscl=1
```

```
Xmin=-4
Xmax=4
Xscl=1
Ymin=-1
Ymax=6
Yscl=1
```

5. b   **6.** a

```
Xmin=-3
Xmax=5
Xscl=1
Ymin=-2
Ymax=5
Yscl=1
```

```
Xmin=-5
Xmax=1
Xscl=1
Ymin=-3
Ymax=3
Yscl=1
```

7.   **9.**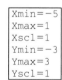

11. $f(x) = (x - 2)^2$ **13.** $f(x) = -(x + 2)^2 + 4$

15. $f(x) = -2(x + 3)^2 + 3$

17. Intercepts: $(\pm\sqrt{5}, 0), (0, -5)$
Vertex: $(0, -5)$

19. Intercepts: $(-5 \pm \sqrt{6}, 0), (0, 19)$
Vertex: $(-5, -6)$

21. Intercepts: $(4, 0), (0, 16)$
Vertex: $(4, 0)$

23. Intercepts: $(1 \pm \sqrt{6}, 0), (0, 5)$
Vertex: $(1, 6)$

25. Intercepts: $(0, 21)$
Vertex: $(\frac{1}{2}, 20)$

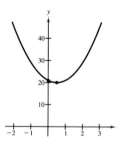

27. Intercepts: $(1, 0), (-3, 0), (0, 3)$
Vertex: $(-1, 4)$

29. Intercepts: $(3.29, 0), (4.71, 0), (0, 31)$
Vertex: $(4, -1)$

31. $f(x) = -\frac{1}{2}(x - 3)^2 + 4$ **33.** $f(x) = \frac{3}{4}(x - 5)^2 + 12$

35. $f(x) = x^2 - 2x - 3$, $g(x) = -x^2 + 2x + 3$
(The answer is not unique.)

37. $f(x) = x^2 - 10x$, $g(x) = -x^2 + 10x$
(The answer is not unique.)

39. $f(x) = 2x^2 + 7x + 3$, $g(x) = -2x^2 - 7x - 3$
(The answer is not unique.)

41. 55, 55

43. $A = x(50 - x)$, $0 < x < 50$

25 ft $\times$ 25 ft

45. 25 ft $\times$ 33$\frac{1}{3}$ ft   **47.** 4500 units

49. (a) No. The function is still increasing.
(b) 4024.5, 11.0

51. (a)

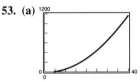

(b) 4 ft
(c) 16 ft
(d) $12 + 8\sqrt{3} \approx 25.86$ ft

53. (a)

(b) 166.7 board feet
(c) 26.6 in.

Section 3.2 (*page 233*)

WARM-UP   **1.** $(3x - 2)(4x + 5)$ **2.** $x(5x - 6)^2$
3. $z^2(12z + 5)(z + 1)$ **4.** $(y + 5)(y^2 - 5y + 25)$
5. $(x + 3)(x + 2)(x - 2)$ **6.** $(x + 2)(x^2 + 3)$
7. No real solution   **8.** $3 \pm \sqrt{5}$ **9.** $-\frac{1}{2} \pm \sqrt{3}$
10. ± 3

1. (a) $f(x)$ is the graph of y shifted right 2 units.
(b) $f(x)$ is the graph of y shifted down 2 units.
(c) $f(x)$ is the graph of y shifted right 2 units and down 2 units.
(d) $f(x)$ is the mirror image (with respect to the x-axis) of the graph of y with a vertical shrink of $\frac{1}{2}$.

3. e   **4.** c

```
Xmin=-3
Xmax=5
Xscl=1
Ymin=-1
Ymax=6
Yscl=1
```

```
Xmin=-2
Xmax=4
Xscl=1
Ymin=-2
Ymax=3
Yscl=1
```

5. b   **6.** f   **7.** a

```
Xmin=-5
Xmax=1
Xscl=1
Ymin=-12
Ymax=3
Yscl=3
```

```
Xmin=-3
Xmax=3
Xscl=1
Ymin=-6
Ymax=8
Yscl=2
```

```
Xmin=-3
Xmax=3
Xscl=1
Ymin=-3
Ymax=2
Yscl=1
```

8. g   **9.** d   **10.** h

```
Xmin=-4
Xmax=4
Xscl=1
Ymin=-2
Ymax=5
Yscl=1
```

```
Xmin=-3
Xmax=2
Xscl=1
Ymin=-2
Ymax=4
Yscl=1
```

```
Xmin=-3
Xmax=3
Xscl=1
Ymin=-4
Ymax=4
Yscl=1
```

11.   **13.**

15. Rises to the left. Rises to the right.
17. Falls to the left. Falls to the right.
19. Rises to the left. Falls to the right.   **21.** ± 5 **23.** 3
25. 1, -2 **27.** $2 \pm \sqrt{3}$ **29.** 2, 0   **31.** ± 1
33. $\pm\sqrt{5}$ **35.** No real zeros   **37.** $f(x) = x^2 - 10x$
39. $f(x) = x^2 + 4x - 12$ **41.** $f(x) = x^3 + 5x^2 + 6x$
43. $f(x) = x^4 - 4x^3 - 9x^2 + 36x$
45. $f(x) = x^2 - 2x - 2$

47.   **49.**

51.   **53.**

55.   **57.**

59.   **61.**

63. $[-1, 0]$, $[1, 2]$, $[2, 3]$ **65.** $[-2, -1]$, $[0, 1]$

67. (b) Domain: $0 < x < 6$ **69.**

(c)

Maximum when $x = 2$

(200, 320)

43. $\left(x - \sqrt{2}\right)\left[x^2 + \left(3 + \sqrt{2}\right)x + 3\sqrt{2}\right] - 8$, $f\left(\sqrt{2}\right) = -8$

45. (a) 1   **(b)** 4   **(c)** 4   **(d)** 1954

47. (a) 97   **(b)** $-\frac{5}{3}$ **(c)** 17   **(d)** -199

49. (a) 72   **(b)** 0   **(c)** 37.648   **(d)** 30

51. $2x^2 - x - 1$ **53.** $x^2 + 2x - 3$ **55.** $x^2 + 3x$

57. (a)

(b) and **(c)** 3290 rev/min

59. (a) $f(x) = (x - 2)x^2 + 5 = x^3 - 2x^2 + 5$

(b) $f(x) = (x + 3)(x^2 + 2) + 1 = x^3 + 3x^2 + 2x + 7$

Section 3.3 (*page 242*)

WARM-UP   **1.** $x^3 - x^2 + 2x + 3$

2. $2x^3 + 4x^2 - 6x - 4$ **3.** $x^4 - 2x^3 + 4x^2 - 2x - 7$

4. $2x^4 + 12x^3 - 3x^2 - 18x - 5$ **5.** $(x - 3)(x - 1)$

6. $2x(2x - 3)(x - 1)$ **7.** $x^3 - 7x^2 + 12x$

8. $x^2 + 5x - 6$ **9.** $x^3 + x^2 - 7x - 3$

10. $x^4 - 3x^3 - 5x^2 + 9x - 2$

1. $2x + 4$ **3.** $x^2 - 3x + 1$ **5.** $x^3 + 3x^2 - 1$

7. $7 - \dfrac{11}{x + 2}$ **9.** $3x + 5 - \dfrac{2x - 3}{2x^2 + 1}$

11. $x^2 + 2x + 4 + \dfrac{2x - 11}{x^2 - 2x + 3}$

13. $2x - \dfrac{17x - 5}{x^2 - 2x + 1}$ **15.** $3x^2 - 2x + 5$

17. $4x^2 - 9$ **19.** $-x^2 + 10x - 25$

21. $5x^2 + 14x + 56 + \dfrac{232}{x - 4}$

23. $10x^3 + 10x^2 + 60x + 360 + \dfrac{1360}{x - 6}$

25. $x^2 - 8x + 64$

27. $-3x^3 - 6x^2 - 12x - 24 - \dfrac{48}{x - 2}$

29. $-x^2 + 3x - 6 + \dfrac{11}{x + 1}$ **31.** $4x^2 + 14x - 30$

33. $(x - 2)(x + 3)(x - 1)$; Zeros: $x = 2$, $x = -3$, $x = 1$

35. $(2x - 1)(x - 5)(x - 2)$; Zeros: $x = \frac{1}{2}$, $x = 5$, $x = 2$

37. $\left(x + \sqrt{3}\right)\left(x - \sqrt{3}\right)(x + 2)$; Zeros: $x = -\sqrt{3}$, $x = \sqrt{3}$, $x = -2$

39. $(x - 1)\left(x - 1 - \sqrt{3}\right)\left(x - 1 + \sqrt{3}\right)$; Zeros: $x = 1$, $x = 1 + \sqrt{3}$, $x = 1 - \sqrt{3}$

41. $(x - 4)(x^2 + 3x - 2) + 3$, $f(4) = 3$

Section 3.4 (*page 255*)

WARM-UP   **1.** $f(x) = 3x^3 - 8x^2 - 5x + 6$

2. $f(x) = 4x^4 - 3x^3 - 16x^2 + 12x$

3. $x^4 - 3x^3 + 5 + \dfrac{3}{x + 3}$

4. $3x^3 + 15x^2 - 9 - \dfrac{2}{x + \frac{2}{3}}$ **5.** $\dfrac{1}{2}$, $-3 \pm \sqrt{5}$

6. 10, $-\frac{2}{3}$, $-\frac{3}{2}$ **7.** $-\frac{3}{4}$, $2 \pm \sqrt{2}$ **8.** $\frac{2}{5}$, $-\frac{7}{2}$, -2

9. $\pm\sqrt{2}$, ± 1 **10.** ± 2, $\pm\sqrt{3}$

1. One negative zero   **3.** No real zeros

5. One positive zero   **7.** One or three positive zeros

9. Two or no positive zeros   **11.** ± 1, ± 2, ± 4

13. ± 1, ± 3, $\pm\frac{1}{2}$, $\pm\frac{3}{2}$, $\pm\frac{1}{4}$, $\pm\frac{3}{4}$

15. (a) ± 1, ± 2, ± 4, ± 8, $\pm\frac{1}{2}$

(b)

(c) $-\frac{1}{2}$, 1, 2, 4

17. (a) ± 1, ± 3, $\pm\frac{1}{2}$, $\pm\frac{3}{2}$, $\pm\frac{1}{4}$, $\pm\frac{3}{4}$, $\pm\frac{1}{8}$, $\pm\frac{3}{8}$, $\pm\frac{1}{16}$, $\pm\frac{3}{16}$, $\pm\frac{1}{32}$, $\pm\frac{3}{32}$

(b)

(c) 1, $\frac{3}{4}$, $-\frac{1}{8}$

19. **(a)** ± 1, ± 2, ± 3, ± 6, ± 9, $\pm \frac{1}{2}$, $\pm \frac{3}{2}$, $\pm \frac{9}{2}$, $\pm \frac{1}{4}$, $\pm \frac{3}{4}$, $\pm \frac{9}{4}$, ± 18

(b)

(c) -2, $\dfrac{1}{8} \pm \dfrac{\sqrt{145}}{8}$

21. **(a)** Upper bound   **(b)** Lower bound   **(c)** Neither
23. **(a)** Neither   **(b)** Lower bound   **(c)** Upper bound
25. $1, 2, 3$ **27.** $1, -1, 4$ **29.** $-1, -10$ **31.** $1, 2$
33. $\frac{1}{2}, -1$ **35.** $1, -\frac{1}{2}$ **37.** $-\frac{3}{4}$ **39.** $\pm 1, \pm\sqrt{2}$
41. $0, -1, -3, 4$ **43.** $-2, 4, -\frac{1}{2}$ **45.** $\pm 2, \pm\frac{3}{2}$
47. $\pm 1, \frac{1}{4}$ **49.** d   **50.** a   **51.** b   **52.** c
53. $\frac{2}{3}$ rational, $\pm\sqrt{5}$ irrational
55. -7 rational, $2 \pm \sqrt{10}$ irrational
57. **(a)** ± 1 **59.** **(a)** $\pm 1, \pm 3$

(b)

(c) 0.68 **(c)** $-1.16, 1.45$
61. 3.77 in. $\times$ 7.77 in. $\times$ 0.614 in.   **63.** $384,356$
65. 4000 **67.** 0.53 **69.** 1.56

Section 3.5 (*page 268*)

WARM-UP   **1.** $2\sqrt{3}$ **2.** $10\sqrt{5}$ **3.** $\sqrt{5}$
4. $-6\sqrt{3}$ **5.** 12 **6.** 48 **7.** $\dfrac{\sqrt{3}}{3}$ **8.** $\sqrt{2}$
9. $-\dfrac{1}{2} \pm \dfrac{\sqrt{5}}{2}$ **10.** $-1 \pm \sqrt{2}$

1. $i, -1, -i, 1, i, -1, -i, 1, i, -1, -i, 1, i, -1, -i, 1$
3. $a = -10, b = 6$ **5.** $a = 6, b = 5$ **7.** $4 + 3i$
9. $2 - 3\sqrt{3}i$ **11.** $5\sqrt{3}i$ **13.** $-1 - 6i$ **15.** $-5i$
17. 8 **19.** $11 - i$ **21.** 4 **23.** $3 - 3\sqrt{2}i$
25. $\frac{1}{6} + \frac{7}{6}i$ **27.** $5 - 3i, 34$ **29.** $-2 + \sqrt{5}i, 9$
31. $-2\sqrt{3}$ **33.** -10 **35.** $5 + i$ **37.** $12 + 30i$
39. 24 **41.** $-9 + 40i$ **43.** -10 **45.** $\frac{16}{41} + \frac{20}{41}i$
47. $\frac{3}{5} + \frac{4}{5}i$ **49.** $-7 - 6i$ **51.** $-\frac{5}{4} - \frac{5}{4}i$
53. $\frac{35}{29} + \frac{595}{29}i$ **55.** $1 \pm i$ **57.** $-2 \pm \frac{1}{2}i$
59. $-\dfrac{3}{2}, -\dfrac{5}{2}$ **61.** $\dfrac{1}{8} \pm \dfrac{\sqrt{11}}{8}i$

63.

65.

67.

69. $0, 0, 0, 0, 0, 0$

71. $0.5i$, $-0.25 + 0.5i$, $-0.1875 + 0.25i$,
    $-0.0273 + 0.4063i$, $-0.1643 + 0.4778i$,
    $-0.2013 + 0.3430i$
73. $1, 2, 5, 26, 677, 458, 330$ **75.** $8, 8, 8$

Section 3.6 (*page 275*)

WARM-UP   **1.** $4 - \sqrt{29}i, 4 + \sqrt{29}i$
2. $-5 - 12i, -5 + 12i$ **3.** $-1 + 4\sqrt{2}i, -1 - 4\sqrt{2}i$
4. $6 + \frac{1}{2}i, 6 - \frac{1}{2}i$ **5.** $-13 + 9i$ **6.** $12 + 16i$
7. $26 + 22i$ **8.** 29 **9.** i **10.** $-9 + 46i$

1. $\pm 5i; (x + 5i)(x - 5i)$
3. $2 \pm \sqrt{3}; (x - 2 - \sqrt{3})(x - 2 + \sqrt{3})$
5. $\pm 3, \pm 3i; (x + 3)(x - 3)(x + 3i)(x - 3i)$
7. $1 \pm i; (z - 1 + i)(z - 1 - i)$
9. $-5, 4 \pm 3i; (t + 5)(t - 4 + 3i)(t - 4 - 3i)$
11. $-\frac{3}{4}, 1 \pm \frac{1}{2}i; (4x + 3)(2x - 2 + i)(2x - 2 - i)$
13. $-\frac{1}{5}, 1 \pm \sqrt{5}i;$
    $(5x + 1)(x - 1 + \sqrt{5}i)(x - 1 - \sqrt{5}i)$
15. $\pm i, \pm 3i; (x + i)(x - i)(x + 3i)(x - 3i)$
17. $2, \pm 2i; (x - 2)^2(x + 2i)(x - 2i)$
19. $-2, -\frac{1}{2}, \pm i; (x + 2)(2x + 1)(x + i)(x - i)$
21. $x^3 - x^2 + 25x - 25$ **23.** $x^3 - 10x^2 + 33x - 34$
25. $x^4 + 37x^2 + 36$ **27.** $x^4 + 8x^3 + 9x^2 - 10x + 100$
29. $16x^4 + 36x^3 + 16x^2 + x - 30$
31. **(a)** $(x^2 + 9)(x^2 - 3)$
    (b) $(x^2 + 9)(x + \sqrt{3})(x - \sqrt{3})$
    (c) $(x + 3i)(x - 3i)(x + \sqrt{3})(x - \sqrt{3})$

33. (a) $(x^2 - 2x - 2)(x^2 - 2x + 3)$

(b) $\left(x - 1 + \sqrt{3}\right)\left(x - 1 - \sqrt{3}\right)(x^2 - 2x + 3)$

(c) $\left(x - 1 + \sqrt{3}\right)\left(x - 1 - \sqrt{3}\right)\left(x - 1 + \sqrt{2}i\right)$
$\left(x - 1 - \sqrt{2}i\right)$

35. $\pm 5i, -\frac{3}{2}$ **37.** $\pm 2i, 1, -\frac{1}{2}$ **39.** $-3 \pm i, \frac{1}{4}$

41. $2, -3 \pm \sqrt{2}i$ **43.** $\frac{3}{4}, \frac{1}{2} \pm \frac{\sqrt{5}}{2}i$

45. No; setting $h = 64$ and solving the resulting equation yields imaginary roots.

47. $x^2 + b$

Chapter 3 Review Exercises (*page 276*)

1. Intercept: $(0, \frac{13}{4})$
Vertex: $(-\frac{3}{2}, 1)$

3. Intercepts: $\left(\dfrac{-5 \pm \sqrt{41}}{2}, 0\right), \left(0, -\dfrac{4}{3}\right)$

Vertex: $\left(-\dfrac{5}{2}, -\dfrac{41}{12}\right)$

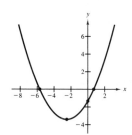

5. $f(x) = (x - 1)^2 - 4$ **7.** Minimum: -1

9. Maximum: 9   **11.** Maximum: 3

13. Minimum: $-\frac{41}{4}$ **15.** $(3, \frac{3}{2})$ **17.** 4500 units

19. $1029   **21.** Falls to the left. Falls to the right.

23. Rises to the left. Rises to the right.

25.

27.

29.

31.

33. $8x + 5 + \dfrac{2}{3x - 2}$ **35.** $x^2 - 2$

37. $x^2 - 3x + 2 - \dfrac{1}{x^2 + 2}$

39. $0.25x^3 - 3.5x^2 - 7x - 14 - \dfrac{28}{x - 2}$

41. $2x^2 - (3 - 4i)x + (1 - 2i)$

43. (a) No   **(b)** Yes   **(c)** Yes   **(d)** No

45. (a) No   **(b)** Yes   **(c)** Yes   **(d)** No

47. (a) 580   **(b)** 0   **49. (a)** -421 **(b)** 96

51. $-14 + 5i$ **53.** $40 + 65i$ **55.** $1 - 6i$

57. $f(x) = 6x^4 + 13x^3 + 7x^2 - x - 1$

59. $f(x) = 3x^4 - 14x^3 + 17x^2 - 42x + 24$

61. Two or no positive zeros. One negative zero.

63. $\pm 1, \pm 3, \pm 5, \pm 15, \pm \frac{1}{2}, \pm \frac{3}{2}, \pm \frac{5}{2}, \pm \frac{15}{2}, \pm \frac{1}{4}, \pm \frac{3}{4}, \pm \frac{5}{4},$
$\pm \frac{15}{4}$

65. $1, \frac{3}{4}$ **67.** $\frac{5}{6}, \pm 2i$ **69.** $-1, \frac{3}{2}, 3, \frac{2}{3}$

71. (a) ± 1 **73. (a)** $\pm 1, \pm 2, \pm 5, \pm 10$

(b)   **(b)**

(c) $-1.40, 0.47$ **(c)** 3.26

75. 11.30

CHAPTER 4

Section 4.1   (*page 287*)

WARM-UP   **1.** $(x - 5)(x + 2)$ **2.** $(x - 5)(x - 2)$
3. $x(x + 1)(x + 3)$ **4.** $(x^2 - 2)(x - 4)$

5.

6.

7.

8.

9. $x + 9 + \dfrac{42}{x - 4}$ **10.** $x + 1 + \dfrac{2}{x + 4}$

---

1. (a)

x	$f(x)$
1	-1
1.5	-2
1.9	-10
1.99	-100
1.999	-1000

x	$f(x)$
3	1
2.5	2
2.1	10
2.01	100
2.001	1000

x	$f(x)$
3	1
5	0.3333
10	0.1250
100	0.0102
1000	0.0010

(b) Vertical asymptote: $x = 2$; Horizontal asymptote:
$y = 0$
(c) Domain: all real numbers except $x = 2$

3. (a)

x	$f(x)$
1	3
1.5	9
1.9	57
1.99	597
1.999	5997

x	$f(x)$
3	9
2.5	15
2.1	63
2.01	603
2.001	6003

x	$f(x)$
3	9
5	5
10	3.75
100	3.0612
1000	3.0060

(b) Vertical asymptote: $x = 2$; Horizontal asymptote:
$y = 3$ as $x \to +\infty$ and $y = -3$ as $x \to -\infty$
(c) Domain: all real numbers except $x = 2$

5. (a)

x	$f(x)$
1	-1
1.5	-3.8571
1.9	-27.77
1.99	-297.75
1.999	-2997.75

x	$f(x)$
3	5.4
2.5	8.33
2.1	32.27
2.01	302.25
2.001	3002.25

x	$f(x)$
3	5.4
5	3.5714
10	3.1250
100	3.0012
1000	3.0000

(b) Vertical asymptote: $x = \pm 2$; Horizontal asymptote:
$y = 3$
(c) Domain: all real numbers except $x = \pm 2$

7. Domain: all $x \neq 0$
Vertical asymptote: $x = 0$
Horizontal asymptote: $y = 0$

9. Domain: all $x \neq 2$
Vertical asymptote: $x = 2$
Horizontal asymptote: $y = -1$

11. Domain: all $x \neq \pm 1$
Vertical asymptote: $x = \pm 1$
Slant asymptote: $y = x$

13. Domain: all reals
Horizontal asymptote: $y = 3$

15. f   **16.** e   **17.** a

```
Xmin=-5
Xmax=3
Xscl=1
Ymin=-3
Ymax=3
Yscl=1
```
```
Xmin=-1
Xmax=8
Xscl=1
Ymin=-3
Ymax=3
Yscl=1
```
```
Xmin=-3
Xmax=3
Xscl=1
Ymin=-1
Ymax=3
Yscl=1
```

18. b   **19.** c   **20.** d

```
Xmin=-3
Xmax=3
Xscl=1
Ymin=-5
Ymax=1
Yscl=1
```
```
Xmin=-2
Xmax=4
Xscl=1
Ymin=-1
Ymax=3
Yscl=1
```
```
Xmin=-4
Xmax=2
Xscl=1
Ymin=-3
Ymax=1
Yscl=1
```

21. (a) Domain of f: $(-\infty, -2)$, $(-2, \infty)$
Domain of g: $(-\infty, \infty)$
(b) No vertical asymptote

(c)

(d) Some viewing rectangles will show the difference in
domains. For instance, on the TI-81, use the standard
viewing rectangle.

23. (a) Domain of f: $(-\infty, 0), (0, 3), (3, \infty)$
Domain of g: $(-\infty, 0), (0, \infty)$
(b) $x = 0$
(c)

(d) Some viewing rectangles will show the difference in domains. For instance, on the TI-81, use the following range:

```
Xmin=-4.5
Xmax=5
Xscl=1
Ymin=-2
Ymax=2
Yscl=1
```

25. (a) $28\frac{1}{3}$ million **(b)** $170 million
  (c) $765 million **(d)** No
27. (a) 167, 250, 400 **(b)** 750
29. (a)

n	1	2	3	4	5	6	7	8	9	10
P	0.50	0.74	0.82	0.86	0.89	0.91	0.92	0.93	0.94	0.95

(b) 100%

Section 4.2 (*page 297*)

WARM-UP **1.** $(-3, 0), (0, 6)$ **2.** $(-3, 0), (0, \frac{12}{5})$
3. Odd **4.** Even
5. Domain: all real numbers $x \neq 8$
Vertical asymptote: $x = 8$
Horizontal asymptote: $y = 0$
6. Domain: all real numbers $x \neq -\frac{1}{4}$
Vertical asymptote: $x = -\frac{1}{4}$
Horizontal asymptote: $y = \frac{3}{4}$
7. Domain: all real numbers $x \neq \pm 3$
Vertical asymptotes: $x = \pm 3$
Horizontal asymptote: $y = 2$
8. Domain: all real numbers $x \neq 0$
Vertical asymptote: $x = 0$
Horizontal asymptote: $y = 4$
9. $2x + \dfrac{7}{2} + \dfrac{23}{2(2x - 1)}$ **10.** $x + \dfrac{1}{x^2}$

1.

3.

5.

7.

9.

11.

13.

15.

17.

19.

21.

23.

25.

27.

45.

47.

29.

31.

Domain:
all real numbers $x \neq 1$

Domain:
all real numbers $t \neq 0$

Range:
all real numbers $y \neq -1$

Range:
all real numbers $y \neq 3$

49.

51.

The fraction is not
reduced to lowest terms.

33.

35.

Domain:
all real numbers

Domain:
all real numbers $x \neq 0$

Range: $0 < y \leq 4$

Range: $-\infty < y < \infty$

53.

Relative minimum: $(-2, -1)$
Relative maximum: $(0, 3)$

55. (b) $0 \leq x \leq 240$

(c)

Increases at a slower
rate approaching 75%

57. (b) $x > 2$

(c)

5.87 in. $\times$ 11.75 in.

59.

40 units

37.

39.

61. (a) $C = 0$. As time passes, the body will remove all of
the chemical from the bloodstream.

(b)

4.5 hr

41.

43.

Section 4.3 (page 306)

WARM-UP **1.** $\dfrac{5x + 2}{x(x + 1)}$ **2.** $\dfrac{2(4x + 3)}{x(x + 2)}$

3. $\dfrac{11x - 1}{(x - 2)(2x - 1)}$ **4.** $-\dfrac{3x + 1}{(x + 5)(x + 12)}$

5. $\dfrac{x^2 - 3x - 5}{(x - 3)^3}$ **6.** $-\dfrac{5x + 6}{(x + 2)^2}$ **7.** $-\dfrac{x + 9}{x(x^2 + 3)}$

8. $\dfrac{4x^2 + 5x + 31}{(x + 1)(x^2 + 5)}$ **9.** $\dfrac{x(3x + 1)}{(x^2 + 1)^2}$ **10.** $\dfrac{x^3 + x^2 + 1}{(x^2 + x + 1)^2}$

---

1. $\dfrac{1}{2}\left(\dfrac{1}{x - 1} - \dfrac{1}{x + 1}\right)$ **3.** $\dfrac{1}{x} - \dfrac{1}{x + 1}$

5. $\dfrac{1}{x} - \dfrac{2}{2x + 1}$ **7.** $\dfrac{1}{x - 1} - \dfrac{1}{x + 2}$

9. $\dfrac{3}{2x - 1} - \dfrac{2}{x + 1}$ **11.** $-\dfrac{3}{x} - \dfrac{1}{x + 2} + \dfrac{5}{x - 2}$

13. $\dfrac{3}{x} - \dfrac{1}{x^2} + \dfrac{1}{x + 1}$ **15.** $\dfrac{2}{x} - \dfrac{1}{x^2} - \dfrac{2}{x + 1}$

17. $\dfrac{3}{x - 3} + \dfrac{9}{(x - 3)^2}$ **19.** $-\dfrac{1}{x} + \dfrac{2x}{x^2 + 1}$

21. $\dfrac{1}{3(x^2 + 2)} - \dfrac{1}{6(x + 2)} + \dfrac{1}{6(x - 2)}$

23. $\dfrac{1}{8(2x + 1)} + \dfrac{1}{8(2x - 1)} - \dfrac{x}{2(4x^2 + 1)}$

25. $\dfrac{1}{x^2 + 2} + \dfrac{x}{(x^2 + 2)^2}$ **27.** $\dfrac{1}{x + 1} + \dfrac{2}{x^2 - 2x + 3}$

29. $2x + \dfrac{1}{2}\left(\dfrac{3}{x - 4} - \dfrac{1}{x + 2}\right)$

31. $x + 3 + \dfrac{6}{x - 1} + \dfrac{4}{(x - 1)^2} + \dfrac{1}{(x - 1)^3}$

33. $\dfrac{1}{2a}\left(\dfrac{1}{a + x} + \dfrac{1}{a - x}\right)$ **35.** $\dfrac{1}{a}\left(\dfrac{1}{x} + \dfrac{1}{a - x}\right)$

Section 4.4 (page 317)

WARM-UP **1.** $9x^2 + 16y^2 = 144$ **2.** $x^2 + 4y^2 = 32$
3. $16x^2 - y^2 = 4$ **4.** $243x^2 + 4y^2 = 9$
5. $c = 2\sqrt{2}$ **6.** $c = \sqrt{13}$ **7.** $c = 2\sqrt{3}$
8. $c = \sqrt{5}$ **9.** $d = 4$ **10.** $d = 2$

---

1. a

```
Xmin=-7
Xmax=7
Xscl=1
Ymin=-2
Ymax=8
Yscl=1
```

2. c

```
Xmin=-7
Xmax=7
Xscl=1
Ymin=-8
Ymax=2
Yscl=1
```

3. d

```
Xmin=-2
Xmax=9
Xscl=1
Ymin=-4
Ymax=4
Yscl=1
```

4. h

```
Xmin=-9
Xmax=2
Xscl=1
Ymin=-4
Ymax=4
Yscl=1
```

5. g

```
Xmin=-4
Xmax=4
Xscl=1
Ymin=-3
Ymax=3
Yscl=1
```

6. f

```
Xmin=-3
Xmax=3
Xscl=1
Ymin=-2
Ymax=2
Yscl=1
```

7. e

```
Xmin=-4
Xmax=4
Xscl=1
Ymin=-3
Ymax=3
Yscl=1
```

8. b

```
Xmin=-4
Xmax=4
Xscl=1
Ymin=-3
Ymax=3
Yscl=1
```

9. Vertex: $(0, 0)$
Focus: $\left(0, \frac{1}{16}\right)$

11. Vertex: $(0, 0)$
Focus: $\left(-\frac{3}{2}, 0\right)$

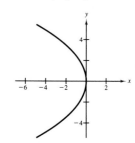

13. Vertex: $(0, 0)$
Focus: $(0, -2)$

15.

17. $x^2 = -6y$ **19.** $y^2 = -8x$ **21.** $x^2 = 4y$

23. $x^2 = -8y$ **25.** $y^2 = 9x$ **27.** $x^2 = 12y$

29. Center: $(0, 0)$ **31.** Center: $(0, 0)$
Vertices: $(\pm 5, 0)$ Vertices: $(0, \pm 5)$

33. Center: $(0, 0)$ **35.**
Vertices: $(\pm 3, 0)$

37. $\dfrac{x^2}{1} + \dfrac{y^2}{4} = 1$ **39.** $\dfrac{x^2}{25} + \dfrac{y^2}{21} = 1$

41. $\dfrac{x^2}{36} + \dfrac{y^2}{11} = 1$ **43.** $\dfrac{21x^2}{400} + \dfrac{y^2}{25} = 1$

45. $\left(\pm \tfrac{3}{2}, 0\right)$, 5 ft   **47.**

49.   **51.**

53. Center: $(0, 0)$ **55.** Center: $(0, 0)$
Vertices: $(\pm 1, 0)$ Vertices: $(0, \pm 1)$

     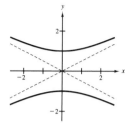

57. Center: $(0, 0)$ **59.**
Vertices: $(0, \pm 5)$

     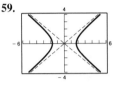

61. $\dfrac{y^2}{4} - \dfrac{x^2}{12} = 1$ **63.** $\dfrac{x^2}{1} - \dfrac{y^2}{9} = 1$

65. $\dfrac{17y^2}{1024} - \dfrac{17x^2}{64} = 1$ **67.** $\dfrac{y^2}{9} - \dfrac{4x^2}{9} = 1$

69. $x \approx 110.3$ mi   **71.** Proof

73. The shape continuously changes from an ellipse with a vertical major axis of length 8 and minor axis of length 2 to a circle with a diameter of 8 and then to an ellipse with a horizontal major axis of length 16 and minor axis of length 8.

Section 4.5   (*page 326*)

WARM-UP   **1.** Hyperbola   **2.** Ellipse   **3.** Parabola
4. Hyperbola   **5.** Ellipse   **6.** Circle
7. Hyperbola   **8.** Parabola   **9.** Parabola
10. Ellipse

1. Vertex: $(1, -2)$
Focus: $(1, -4)$
Directrix: $y = 0$

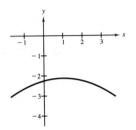

3. Vertex: $\left(5, -\frac{1}{2}\right)$
Focus: $\left(\frac{11}{2}, -\frac{1}{2}\right)$
Directrix: $x = \frac{9}{2}$

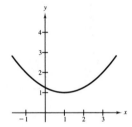

25. Center: $(1, 5)$
Vertices: $(1, 5 \pm 5)$
Foci: $(1, 5 \pm 4)$

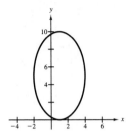

27. Center: $(-2, 3)$
Vertices: $(-2, 3 \pm 3)$
Foci: $\left(-2, 3 \pm \sqrt{5}\right)$

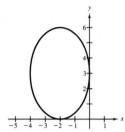

5. Vertex: $(1, 1)$
Focus: $(1, 2)$
Directrix: $y = 0$

7. Vertex: $(-2, -3)$
Focus: $(-4, -3)$
Directrix: $x = 0$

29. Center: $(1, -1)$
Vertices: $\left(1 \pm \frac{5}{4}, -1\right)$
Foci: $\left(1 \pm \frac{3}{4}, -1\right)$

31. Center: $\left(\frac{1}{2}, -1\right)$
Vertices: $\left(\frac{1}{2} \pm \sqrt{5}, -1\right)$
Foci: $\left(\frac{1}{2} \pm \sqrt{2}, -1\right)$

9. Vertex: $(-2, 1)$
Focus: $\left(-2, -\frac{1}{2}\right)$
Directrix: $y = \frac{5}{2}$

11. Vertex: $\left(\frac{1}{4}, -\frac{1}{2}\right)$
Focus: $\left(0, -\frac{1}{2}\right)$
Directrix: $x = \frac{1}{2}$

33. $\dfrac{(x - 2)^2}{4} + \dfrac{(y - 2)^2}{1} = 1$ **35.** $\dfrac{x^2}{48} + \dfrac{(y - 4)^2}{64} = 1$

37. $\dfrac{(x - 3)^2}{9} + \dfrac{(y - 5)^2}{16} = 1$ **39.** $\dfrac{x^2}{16} + \dfrac{(y - 4)^2}{12} = 1$

41. $\dfrac{x^2}{25} + \dfrac{y^2}{16} = 1$

43. Perihelion: 2,756,832,000; Aphelion: 4,575,168,000

45. $e \approx 0.052$

47. Center: $(1, -2)$
Vertices: $(1 \pm 2, -2)$
Foci: $\left(1 \pm \sqrt{5}, -2\right)$

13. $(y - 2)^2 = -8(x - 3)$ **15.** $x^2 = 8(y - 4)$
17. $(y - 2)^2 = 8x$ **19.** $x^2 = -(y - 4)$
21. (a) $17,500\sqrt{2}$ mi/hr   **(b)** $x^2 = -16,400(y - 4100)$
23. (a)

(b) Maximum height: 7.1 ft
Range: 15.7 ft

49. Center: $(2, -6)$
Vertices: $(2, -6 \pm 1)$
Foci: $\left(2, -6 \pm \sqrt{2}\right)$

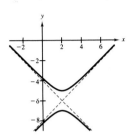

51. Center: $(2, -3)$
Vertices: $(2 \pm 1, -3)$
Foci: $\left(2 \pm \sqrt{10}, -3\right)$

53. Degenerate hyperbola
Lines: $y + 3 = \pm\frac{1}{3}(x + 1)$

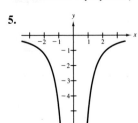

55. Center: $(1, -3)$
Vertices: $\left(1, -3 \pm \sqrt{2}\right)$
Foci: $\left(1, -3 \pm 2\sqrt{5}\right)$

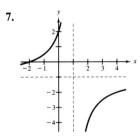

57. $\dfrac{(x-4)^2}{4} - \dfrac{y^2}{12} = 1$

59. $\dfrac{(y-5)^2}{16} - \dfrac{(x-4)^2}{9} = 1$

61. $\dfrac{y^2}{9} - \dfrac{4(x-2)^2}{9} = 1$

63. $\dfrac{(x-3)^2}{9} - \dfrac{(y-2)^2}{4} = 1$

65. Circle

67. Hyperbola

69. Ellipse

71. Parabola

Chapter 4 Review Exercises   (*page 329*)

1. Domain: all reals such that $x \neq -3$
Vertical asymptote: $x = -3$
Horizontal asymptote: $y = 0$

3. Domain: all reals such that $x \neq \pm 2$
Vertical asymptote: $x = 2$, $x = -2$
Horizontal asymptote: $y = 1$

5.

7.

9.

11.

13.

15.

17.

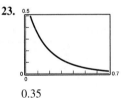

19. As x increases, the cost approaches the horizontal asymptote, $\overline{C} = 0.5$.

21. (a) $176 million
(b) $528 million
(c) $1584 million
(d) Not possible, C approaches infinity

23.

0.35

25. $\dfrac{3}{x+2} - \dfrac{4}{x+4}$

27. $1 - \dfrac{25}{8(x+5)} + \dfrac{9}{8(x-3)}$

29. $\dfrac{1}{2}\left(\dfrac{3}{x-1} - \dfrac{x-3}{x^2+1}\right)$

31. $\dfrac{3x}{x^2+1} + \dfrac{x}{(x^2+1)^2}$

33. Parabola

35. Parabola

37. Degenerate circle

•(1, 2)

39. Ellipse

41. Ellipse

43. Hyperbola

45. Hyperbola

$$y = 5x + \sqrt{24x^2 - 1}$$
$$y = 5x - \sqrt{24x^2 - 1}$$

47. $(x - 4)^2 = -8(y - 2)$

49. $(y - 2)^2 = -4x$

51. $\dfrac{(x - 2)^2}{25} + \dfrac{y^2}{21} = 1$

53. $\dfrac{2x^2}{9} + \dfrac{y^2}{36} = 1$

55. $\dfrac{y^2}{1} - \dfrac{x^2}{8} = 1$

57. $\dfrac{5(x - 4)^2}{16} - \dfrac{5y^2}{64} = 1$

59. $(0, 50)$

CHAPTER 5

Section 5.1   (*page 341*)

WARM-UP   **1.** 5^x **2.** 3^{2x} **3.** 4^{3x} **4.** 10^x
5. 4^{2x} **6.** 4^{10x} **7.** $(\frac{3}{2})^x$ **8.** 4^{3x}
9. 2^{-x} **10.** 2^x

1. 946.852   **3.** 747.258   **5.** 0.006   **7.** 673.639
9. 0.472

11. g

```
Xmin=-3
Xmax=3
Xscl=1
Ymin=-1
Ymax=3
Yscl=1
```

12. e

```
Xmin=-3
Xmax=3
Xscl=1
Ymin=-5
Ymax=1
Yscl=1
```

13. b

```
Xmin=-3
Xmax=3
Xscl=1
Ymin=-1
Ymax=3
Yscl=1
```

14. h

```
Xmin=-3
Xmax=3
Xscl=1
Ymin=-5
Ymax=1
Yscl=1
```

15. d

```
Xmin=-3
Xmax=3
Xscl=1
Ymin=-5
Ymax=1
Yscl=1
```

16. a

```
Xmin=-3
Xmax=3
Xscl=1
Ymin=0
Ymax=4
Yscl=1
```

17. f

```
Xmin=-1
Xmax=5
Xscl=1
Ymin=-5
Ymax=1
Yscl=1
```

18. c

```
Xmin=-2
Xmax=4
Xscl=1
Ymin=-1
Ymax=3
Yscl=1
```

19.

$y = 4^x$

$y = 3^x$

$x < 0$

21.

23.

25.

27.

29.

31.

33.

35.

37.

39. (a)

(b)

Increasing: $(0, 2)$
Decreasing: $(-\infty, 0)$, $(2, \infty)$
Relative minimum: $(0, 0)$
Relative maximum: $(2, 0.54)$

Increasing: $(-\infty, 1.44)$
Decreasing: $(1.44, \infty)$
Relative maximum:
$(1.44, 4.25)$

41.

n	1	2	4
A	\$7764.62	\$8017.84	\$8155.09

n	12	365	Continuous compounding
A	\$8250.97	\$8298.66	\$8300.29

43.

n	1	2	4
A	\$24,115.73	\$25,714.29	\$26,602.23

n	12	365	Continuous compounding
A	\$27,231.38	\$27,547.07	\$27,557.94

45.

t	1	10	20
P	\$91,393.12	\$40,656.97	\$16,529.89

t	30	40	50
P	\$6720.55	\$2732.37	\$1110.90

47.

t	1	10	20
P	\$90,521.24	\$36,940.70	\$13,646.15

t	30	40	50
P	\$5040.98	\$1862.17	\$687.90

49. \$222,822.57
51. (a) \$472.70
   (b) \$298.29; The graph of p is a decreasing function with domain $(0, 1725)$ and range $(0, 499.50)$.
53. (a) 100
   (b) 300
   (c) 900
55. (a) 25 units
   (b) 16.30 units
   (c)

57. (a)
   (b) 80%
   (c) 1550

59.
   \$11,250

Section 5.2   (*page 350*)

(*page 350*)

WARM-UP   **1.** 3   **2.** 0   **3.** -1 **4.** 1   **5.** 7.389
6. 0.368   **7.** Graph is shifted 2 units to the left.
8. Graph is reflected about the x-axis.
9. Graph is shifted down 1 unit.
10. Graph is reflected about the y-axis.

---

1. 4   **3.** $\frac{1}{2}$ **5.** 0   **7.** -2 **9.** 3
11. 2   **13.** $\log_5 125 = 3$ **15.** $\log_{81} 3 = \frac{1}{4}$
17. $\log_6 \frac{1}{36} = -2$ **19.** $\ln 20.0855 \approx 3$ **21.** 2.538
23. -0.319 **25.** 2.913

27.

29.

31. d   **32.** e   **33.** a

```
Xmin=-1
Xmax=4
Xscl=1
Ymin=-1
Ymax=3
Yscl=1
```

```
Xmin=-1
Xmax=4
Xscl=1
Ymin=-2
Ymax=2
Yscl=1
```

```
Xmin=-3
Xmax=3
Xscl=1
Ymin=-2
Ymax=2
Yscl=1
```

34. c

```
Xmin=-1
Xmax=4
Xscl=1
Ymin=-2
Ymax=2
Yscl=1
```

35. f

```
Xmin=-3
Xmax=2
Xscl=1
Ymin=-2
Ymax=2
Yscl=1
```

36. b

```
Xmin=-4
Xmax=1
Xscl=1
Ymin=-2
Ymax=2
Yscl=1
```

37. Domain: $(0, \infty)$
Vertical asymptote: $x = 0$
Intercept: $(1, 0)$

39. Domain: $(-2, \infty)$
Vertical asymptote: $x = -2$
Intercepts: $(-1, 0), (0, -\log_3 2)$

41. Domain: $(2, \infty)$
Vertical asymptote: $x = 2$
Intercept: $(3, 0)$

43. Increasing: $(2, \infty)$
Decreasing: $(0, 2)$
Relative minimum: $(2, 1.693)$

(2, 1.693)

45. (a

$\sqrt[3]{x}$ is increasing more
rapidly than $\ln x$.

(b)

$\sqrt[4]{x}$ is increasing more
rapidly than $\ln x$.

47. (a) 80   **(b)** 68.1   **(c)** 62.3

49.

r	0.005	0.010	0.015	0.020	0.025	0.030
t	138.6 yr	69.3 yr	46.2 yr	34.7 yr	27.7 yr	23.1 yr

51.

17.66 ft^3/min

53. 20 yr

55. \$280,178.40

57. 21,357 ft·lb

59. (a)

x	1	5	10	10^2	10^4	10^6
$f(x)$	0	0.322	0.230	0.046	0.00092	0.0000138

(b) 0

Section 5.3   (*page 359*)

WARM-UP   **1.** 2   **2.** -5 **3.** -2 **4.** -3

5. e^5 **6.** $\dfrac{1}{e}$ **7.** e^6 **8.** 1   **9.** x^{-2}

10. $x^{1/2}$

1. $\dfrac{\log_{10} 5}{\log_{10} 3}$ **3.** $\dfrac{\log_{10} x}{\log_{10} 2}$ **5.** $\dfrac{\ln 5}{\ln 3}$ **7.** $\dfrac{\ln x}{\ln 2}$

9. 1.771   **11.** -2.000 **13.** -0.417 **15.** 2.633

17. $\log_{10} 5 + \log_{10} x$ **19.** $\log_{10} 5 - \log_{10} x$

21. $4 \log_8 x$ **23.** $\frac{1}{2} \ln z$ **25.** $\ln x + \ln y + \ln z$

27. $\frac{1}{2} \ln(a - 1)$

29. $\ln z + 2 \ln(z - 1)$ **31.** $\frac{1}{3} \ln x - \frac{1}{3} \ln y$

33. $4 \ln x + \frac{1}{2} \ln y - 5 \ln z$

35. $2 \log_b x - 2 \log_b y - 3 \log_b z$ **37.** $\ln 2x$

39. $\log_4 \dfrac{z}{y}$ **41.** $\log_2(x + 4)^2$ **43.** $\log_3 \sqrt[3]{5x}$

45. $\ln \dfrac{x}{(x + 1)^3}$ **47.** $\log_3 \dfrac{x - 2}{x + 2}$

49. $\ln \dfrac{x}{(x^2 - 4)^2}$ **51.** $\ln \sqrt[3]{\dfrac{x(x + 3)^2}{x^2 - 1}}$

53. $\ln \dfrac{\sqrt[3]{y(y + 4)^2}}{y - 1}$ **55.** $\ln \dfrac{9}{\sqrt{x^2 + 1}}$ **57.** 0.9208

59. 1.8957   **61.** -0.1781 **63.** 0.9136   **65.** 2.0365

67. 2   **69.** 2.4   **71.** 4.5   **73.** $\frac{3}{2}$

75. $\frac{1}{2} + \frac{1}{2} \log_7 10$ **77.** $-3 - \log_5 2$ **79.** $6 + \ln 5$

81. $\beta = 10(\log_{10} I + 16)$, 60 db

83.

f and h have the same graphs.

Section 5.4 *(page 368)*

WARM-UP   **1.** $\dfrac{\ln 3}{\ln 2}$ **2.** $1 + \dfrac{2}{\ln 4}$ **3.** $\dfrac{e}{2}$ **4.** $2e$

5. $2 \pm i$ **6.** $\frac{1}{2}, 1$ **7.** $2x$ **8.** $3x$ **9.** $2x$
10. $-x^2$

1. 2   **3.** -2 **5.** 3   **7.** 64   **9.** $\frac{1}{10}$ **11.** x^2
13. $5x + 2$ **15.** x^2 **17.** $\ln 10 \approx 2.303$ **19.** 0
21. $\dfrac{\ln 12}{3} \approx 0.828$ **23.** $\ln \dfrac{5}{3} \approx 0.511$ **25.** $\ln 5 \approx 1.609$
27. $2 \ln 75 \approx 8.6350$ **29.** $\log_{10} 42 \approx 1.623$
31. $\dfrac{\ln 80}{2 \ln 3} \approx 1.994$ **33.** 2
35. $\dfrac{\ln 2}{12 \ln(1 + 0.10/12)} \approx 6.960$
37. 3.847   **39.** 12.207
41. 0.059   **43.** 21.330   **45.** $e^{-3} \approx 0.050$
47. $\dfrac{e^{2.4}}{2} \approx 5.512$ **49.** $e^2 - 2 \approx 5.389$
51. $1 + \sqrt{1 + e} \approx 2.928$ **53.** 103
55. $\dfrac{-1 + \sqrt{17}}{2} \approx 1.562$ **57.** 4   **59.** No solution
61. 33.115   **63.** 14.369   **65.** 8.2 yr   **67.** 12.9 yr
69. (a) 1426 units   **(b)** 1498 units
71. (a)

(b) $V = 6.7$
The asymptote represents the limiting yield per acre.
(c) 29.33 yr
73. (a)

(b) $y = 0, y = 100$
(c) Males: 69.71 in.; Females: 64.51 in.

Section 5.5 *(page 378)*

WARM-UP
1.

2.

3.

4.

5.

6.

7. $\dfrac{1}{2} \ln \dfrac{7}{3} \approx 0.424$ **8.** $\dfrac{\ln(0.001)}{-0.2} \approx 34.539$
9. $\dfrac{1}{5} e^{7/2} \approx 6.623$ **10.** $\dfrac{1}{2} e^2 \approx 3.695$

Initial Investment	Annual % Rate	Effective Yield	Time to Double	Amount After 10 Years
1. $1000	12%	12.75%	5.78 yr	$3320.12
3. $750	8.94%	9.35%	$7\frac{3}{4}$ yr	$1833.67
5. $500	9.5%	9.97%	7.30 yr	$1292.85
7. $6392.79	11%	11.63%	6.30 yr	$19,205.00
9. $5000	8%	8.33%	8.66 yr	$11,127.70

11. $112,087.09
13. (a) 6.642 yr   **(b)** 6.330 yr   **(c)** 6.302 yr
(d) 6.301 yr

15.

r	2%	4%	6%	8%	10%	12%
t	54.93	27.47	18.31	13.73	10.99	9.16

17.

Continuous compounding at 7% grows faster.

Isotope	Half-life (Years)	Initial Quantity	Amount After 1000 Years	Amount After 10,000 Years
19. ^{226}Ra	1620	10 g	6.52 g	0.14 g
21. ^{14}C	5730	6.70 g	5.95 g	2 g
23. ^{230}Pu	24,360	2.16 g	2.1 g	1.63 g

25. $\frac{1}{4}\ln 10 \approx 0.5756$ **27.** $\frac{1}{4}\ln\frac{1}{4} \approx -0.3466$

29. 105,300, 2013   **31.** $k = 0.0137$, 3288

33. $y = 4.22e^{0.0430t}$, 9.97 million   **35.** 3.15 hr

37. 95.8%   **39.** $9281

41. **(a)** $S(t) = 100(1 - e^{-0.1625t})$ **(b)** 55,625

43.

64.5 in.

45. **(a)**

$p = 10,000$. This represents the carrying capacity of the lake for this species of fish.

(b) 1252 fish   **(c)** 7.8 months

47. **(a)** $S = 10(1 - e^{-0.0575x})$ **(b)** 3314

49. **(a)** 7.91   **(b)** 7.68

51. **(a)** 20   **(b)** 70   **(c)** 95   **(d)** 120

53. 95%   **55.** 4.64   **57.** 1.58×10^{-6} moles per liter

59. 10^7

61. **(a)**   **(b)** Interest payments, 27.7 yr

63. 7:30 A.M.

Chapter 5 Review Exercises   (*page 382*)

1. d

```
Xmin=-4
Xmax=3
Xscl=1
Ymin=-1
Ymax=4
Yscl=1
```

2. f

```
Xmin=-3
Xmax=4
Xscl=1
Ymin=-1
Ymax=4
Yscl=1
```

3. a

```
Xmin=-4
Xmax=4
Xscl=1
Ymin=-5
Ymax=1
Yscl=1
```

4. b

```
Xmin=-4
Xmax=4
Xscl=1
Ymin=0
Ymax=6
Yscl=1
```

5. c

```
Xmin=-3
Xmax=6
Xscl=1
Ymin=-3
Ymax=3
Yscl=1
```

6. e

```
Xmin=-1
Xmax=7
Xscl=1
Ymin=-4
Ymax=3
Yscl=1
```

7.

9.

11.

13.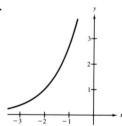

15.

n	1	2	4
A	$9499.28	$9738.91	$9867.22

n	12	365	Continuous compounding
A	$9956.20	$10,000.27	$10,001.78

17.

t	1	10	20
P	\$184,623.27	\$89,865.79	\$40,379.30

t	30	40	50
P	\$18,143.59	\$8152.44	\$3663.13

19. \$1,069,047.14   **21.** 229.2 units per milliliter

23.

Speed	50	55	60	65	70
Miles per gallon	28	26.4	24.8	23.4	22.0

25.   **27.**

29.   **31.** $\log_4 64 = 3$

33. 3   **35.** -2 **37.** 7   **39.** 0
41. 1.585   **43.** 2.132   **45.** $1 + 2\log_5 x$
47. $\log_{10} 5 + \frac{1}{2}\log_{10} y - 2\log_{10} x$
49. $\ln(x^2 + 1) + \ln(x - 1)$
51. $\log_2 5x$ **53.** $\ln \dfrac{\sqrt{|2x - 1|}}{(x + 1)^2}$ **55.** $\ln \dfrac{3\sqrt[3]{4 - x^2}}{x}$
57. False   **59.** False   **61.** 1.6542   **63.** 0.2823
65. 27.16 mi   **67.** $\ln 12 \approx 2.485$
69. $-\dfrac{\ln 44}{5} \approx -0.757$ **71.** $\ln 2 \approx 0.693,\ \ln 5 \approx 1.609$
73. $\frac{1}{3}e^{8.2} \approx 1213.650$ **75.** $3e^2 \approx 22.167$
77. $y = 2e^{0.1014t}$ **79.** $y = 4e^{-0.4159t}$
81. (a) 1151 units   (b) 1325 units
83. (a) 8.94%   (b) \$1834.37   (c) 9.36%
85. $10^{-3.5}$

CUMULATIVE TEST for Chapters 3–5   (*page 385*)

1. Vertex: $\left(\frac{3}{2}, 2\right)$ **2.** $f(x) = -\frac{1}{4}x^2 + 6$

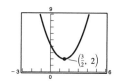

3. Upward to the left
Downward to the right
4. $f(x) = 2x^3 + 3x^2 - 18x + 8$
5.

6. $3x - 2 - \dfrac{3x - 2}{2x^2 + 1}$ **7.** $3x^2 + 6x + 7 + \dfrac{18}{x - 2}$
8. $23 + 2i$ **9.** $\frac{3}{2}, 2 \pm 3i$ **10.** $-\frac{4}{3}, \frac{3}{2}, 4$
11. 2.4
12. (a)   (b)

(c) 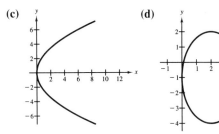   (d)

13. $\dfrac{(y - 2)^2}{4/5} - \dfrac{x^2}{16/5} = 1$

14. (a)

(b)

15. 3   **16.** $\ln\left(\dfrac{x^2}{\sqrt{x+5}}\right)$ **17. (a)** 1.24   **(b)** 12.80

18. $2000   **19.** $16,302.05

CHAPTER 6

Section 6.1 (*page 397*)

WARM-UP   **1.** 45   **2.** 70   **3.** $\dfrac{\pi}{6}$ **4.** $\dfrac{\pi}{3}$ **5.** $\dfrac{\pi}{4}$

6. $\dfrac{4\pi}{3}$ **7.** $\dfrac{\pi}{9}$ **8.** $\dfrac{11\pi}{6}$ **9.** 45   **10.** 45

---

1. (a) Quadrant II   **3. (a)** Quadrant III
   (b) Quadrant IV   **(b)** Quadrant I
5. (a) Quadrant I   **7. (a)** Quadrant IV
   (b) Quadrant III   **(b)** Quadrant II
9. (a) Quadrant III
   (b) Quadrant II

11. (a)   **(b)**

13. (a)   **(b)**

15. (a)   **(b)**

17. (a) 396°, −324°   **19. (a)** 660°, −60°
   (b) 315°, −405°   **(b)** 20°, −340°
21. (a) $\dfrac{19\pi}{9}$, $-\dfrac{17\pi}{9}$ **23. (a)** $\dfrac{7\pi}{4}$, $-\dfrac{\pi}{4}$

   (b) $\dfrac{10\pi}{3}$, $-\dfrac{2\pi}{3}$ **(b)** $\dfrac{28\pi}{15}$, $-\dfrac{32\pi}{15}$

25. (a) Complement: 72°; Supplement: 162°
   (b) Complement: none; Supplement: 65°
27. (a) Complement: $\dfrac{\pi}{6}$; Supplement: $\dfrac{2\pi}{3}$

   (b) Complement: none; Supplement: $\dfrac{\pi}{4}$

29. (a) $\dfrac{\pi}{6}$ **31. (a)** $-\dfrac{\pi}{9}$

   (b) $\dfrac{5\pi}{6}$ **(b)** $-\dfrac{4\pi}{3}$

33. (a) 270°   **35. (a)** 420°
   (b) 210°   **(b)** −66°
37. 2.007   **39.** −3.776   **41.** 9.285   **43.** −0.014
45. 25.714°   **47.** 337.5°   **49.** −756°
51. −114.592°
53. (a) 54.75°   **55. (a)** 85.308°
   (b) −128.5°   **(b)** 330.007°
57. (a) 240° 36′   **59. (a)** 143° 14′ 22″
   (b) −145° 48′   **(b)** −205° 7′ 8″
61. $\frac{4}{15}$ rad   **63.** 1.724 rad   **65.** 15π in. ≈ 47.12 in.
67. 12 m   **69.** 591.72 mi   **71.** 1141 mi   **73.** 4.655°
75. $\frac{1}{4}$ rad ≈ 14.32°
77. (a) 560.2 rev/min   **79. (a)** 80π rad/sec
   (b) 3520 rad/min   **(b)** 78.54 ft/sec

Section 6.2 (*page 408*)

WARM-UP   **1.** $2\sqrt{5}$ **2.** $3\sqrt{10}$ **3.** 10
4. $3\sqrt{2}$ **5.** 1.24   **6.** 317.55   **7.** 63.13
8. 133.57   **9.** 2,785,714.29   **10.** 28.80

---

1. $\sin\theta = \dfrac{1}{2}$

$\cos\theta = \dfrac{\sqrt{3}}{2}$

$\tan\theta = \dfrac{\sqrt{3}}{3}$

$\csc\theta = 2$

$\sec\theta = \dfrac{2\sqrt{3}}{3}$

$\cot\theta = \sqrt{3}$

3. $\sin\theta = \dfrac{3}{5}$

$\cos\theta = \dfrac{4}{5}$

$\tan\theta = \dfrac{3}{4}$

$\csc\theta = \dfrac{5}{3}$

$\sec\theta = \dfrac{5}{4}$

$\cot\theta = \dfrac{4}{3}$

5. $\sin\theta = \dfrac{\sqrt{161}}{15}$

$\cos\theta = \dfrac{8}{15}$

$\tan\theta = \dfrac{\sqrt{161}}{8}$

$\csc\theta = \dfrac{15\sqrt{161}}{161}$

$\sec\theta = \dfrac{15}{8}$

$\cot\theta = \dfrac{8\sqrt{161}}{161}$

7. $\sin\theta = \dfrac{15}{17}$

$\cos\theta = \dfrac{8}{17}$

$\tan\theta = \dfrac{15}{8}$

$\csc\theta = \dfrac{17}{15}$

$\sec\theta = \dfrac{17}{8}$

$\cot\theta = \dfrac{8}{15}$

9. $\cos\theta = \dfrac{\sqrt{5}}{3}$

$\tan\theta = \dfrac{2\sqrt{5}}{5}$

$\csc\theta = \dfrac{3}{2}$

$\sec\theta = \dfrac{3\sqrt{5}}{5}$

$\cot\theta = \dfrac{\sqrt{5}}{2}$

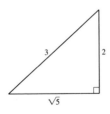

11. $\sin\theta = \dfrac{\sqrt{3}}{2}$

$\cos\theta = \dfrac{1}{2}$

$\tan\theta = \sqrt{3}$

$\csc\theta = \dfrac{2\sqrt{3}}{3}$

$\cot\theta = \dfrac{\sqrt{3}}{3}$

13. $\sin\theta = \dfrac{3\sqrt{10}}{10}$

$\cos\theta = \dfrac{\sqrt{10}}{10}$

$\csc\theta = \dfrac{\sqrt{10}}{3}$

$\sec\theta = \sqrt{10}$

$\cot\theta = \dfrac{1}{3}$

15. $\sin\theta = \dfrac{2\sqrt{13}}{13}$

$\cos\theta = \dfrac{3\sqrt{13}}{13}$

$\tan\theta = \dfrac{2}{3}$

$\csc\theta = \dfrac{\sqrt{13}}{2}$

$\sec\theta = \dfrac{\sqrt{13}}{3}$

17. **(a)** $\sqrt{3}$
(b) $\dfrac{1}{2}$
(c) $\dfrac{\sqrt{3}}{2}$
(d) $\dfrac{\sqrt{3}}{3}$

19. **(a)** $\dfrac{1}{3}$
(b) $\dfrac{2\sqrt{2}}{3}$
(c) $\dfrac{\sqrt{2}}{4}$
(d) 3

21. **(a)** $\dfrac{1}{2}$
(b) 1

23. **(a)** 1
(b) $\dfrac{\sqrt{2}}{2}$

25. **(a)** 0.1736
(b) 0.1736

27. **(a)** 0.2815
(b) 3.5523

29. **(a)** 1.3499
(b) 1.3432

31. **(a)** 5.0273
(b) 0.1989

33. (a) 1.1884   **35.** (a) $30° = \dfrac{\pi}{6}$

   (b) 1.1884   (b) $30° = \dfrac{\pi}{6}$

37. (a) $60° = \dfrac{\pi}{3}$ **39.** (a) $60° = \dfrac{\pi}{3}$

   (b) $45° = \dfrac{\pi}{4}$ (b) $45° = \dfrac{\pi}{4}$

41. (a) $55° \approx 0.96$ **43.** (a) $50° \approx 0.873$
   (b) $89° \approx 1.55$ (b) $25° \approx 0.436$
45. 57.74   **47.** 14.43   **49.** 15.56
51. 9.19   **53.** 15 ft   **55.** 19.32 ft   **57.** 2145.10 ft
59. $(x_1, y_1) = \left(10\sqrt{3}, 10\right),\ (x_2, y_2) = \left(10, 10\sqrt{3}\right)$
61. $\sin 25° \approx 0.42,\ \cos 25° \approx 0.91,\ \tan 25° \approx 0.47,$
   $\csc 25° \approx 2.37,\ \sec 25° \approx 1.10,\ \cot 25° \approx 2.14$
63. True, $\csc x = \dfrac{1}{\sin x}$ **65.** False, $\dfrac{\sqrt{2}}{2} + \dfrac{\sqrt{2}}{2} \neq 1$
67. False, $1.7321 \neq \sin 2°$

Section 6.3 (*page 422*)

WARM-UP   **1.** $\sin 30° = \dfrac{1}{2}$ **2.** $\tan 45° = 1$

3. $\cos \dfrac{\pi}{4} = \dfrac{\sqrt{2}}{2}$ **4.** $\cot \dfrac{\pi}{3} = \dfrac{\sqrt{3}}{3}$

5. $\sec \dfrac{\pi}{6} = \dfrac{2\sqrt{3}}{3}$ **6.** $\csc \dfrac{\pi}{4} = \sqrt{2}$

7. $\sin \theta = \dfrac{3\sqrt{13}}{13}$ **8.** $\sin \theta = \dfrac{\sqrt{5}}{3}$

   $\cos \theta = \dfrac{2\sqrt{13}}{13}$ $\tan \theta = \dfrac{\sqrt{5}}{2}$

   $\csc \theta = \dfrac{\sqrt{13}}{3}$ $\csc \theta = \dfrac{3\sqrt{5}}{5}$

   $\sec \theta = \dfrac{\sqrt{13}}{2}$ $\sec \theta = \dfrac{3}{2}$

   $\cot \theta = \dfrac{2}{3}$ $\cot \theta = \dfrac{2\sqrt{5}}{5}$

9. $\cos \theta = \dfrac{2\sqrt{6}}{5}$ **10.** $\sin \theta = \dfrac{2\sqrt{2}}{3}$

   $\tan \theta = \dfrac{\sqrt{6}}{12}$ $\cos \theta = \dfrac{1}{3}$

   $\csc \theta = 5$ $\tan \theta = 2\sqrt{2}$

   $\sec \theta = \dfrac{5\sqrt{6}}{12}$ $\csc \theta = \dfrac{3\sqrt{2}}{4}$

   $\cot \theta = 2\sqrt{6}$ $\cot \theta = \dfrac{\sqrt{2}}{4}$

1. (a) $\sin \theta = \dfrac{4}{5}$ (b) $\sin \theta = -\dfrac{15}{17}$
   $\cos \theta = \dfrac{3}{5}$ $\cos \theta = \dfrac{8}{17}$
   $\tan \theta = \dfrac{4}{3}$ $\tan \theta = -\dfrac{15}{8}$
   $\csc \theta = \dfrac{5}{4}$ $\csc \theta = -\dfrac{17}{15}$
   $\sec \theta = \dfrac{5}{3}$ $\sec \theta = \dfrac{17}{8}$
   $\cot \theta = \dfrac{3}{4}$ $\cot \theta = -\dfrac{8}{15}$

3. (a) $\sin \theta = \dfrac{1}{2}$ (b) $\sin \theta = -\dfrac{\sqrt{2}}{2}$

   $\cos \theta = -\dfrac{\sqrt{3}}{2}$ $\cos \theta = -\dfrac{\sqrt{2}}{2}$

   $\tan \theta = -\dfrac{\sqrt{3}}{3}$ $\tan \theta = 1$

   $\csc \theta = 2$ $\csc \theta = -\sqrt{2}$

   $\sec \theta = -\dfrac{2\sqrt{3}}{3}$ $\sec \theta = -\sqrt{2}$

   $\cot \theta = -\sqrt{3}$ $\cot \theta = 1$

5. (a) $\sin \theta = \dfrac{24}{25}$ (b) $\sin \theta = -\dfrac{24}{25}$
   $\cos \theta = \dfrac{7}{25}$ $\cos \theta = \dfrac{7}{25}$
   $\tan \theta = \dfrac{24}{7}$ $\tan \theta = -\dfrac{24}{7}$
   $\csc \theta = \dfrac{25}{24}$ $\csc \theta = -\dfrac{25}{24}$
   $\sec \theta = \dfrac{25}{7}$ $\sec \theta = \dfrac{25}{7}$
   $\cot \theta = \dfrac{7}{24}$ $\cot \theta = -\dfrac{7}{24}$

7. (a) $\sin \theta = \dfrac{5\sqrt{29}}{29}$ (b) $\sin \theta = -\dfrac{5\sqrt{34}}{34}$

   $\cos \theta = -\dfrac{2\sqrt{29}}{29}$ $\cos \theta = \dfrac{3\sqrt{34}}{34}$

   $\tan \theta = -\dfrac{5}{2}$ $\tan \theta = -\dfrac{5}{3}$

   $\csc \theta = \dfrac{\sqrt{29}}{5}$ $\csc \theta = -\dfrac{\sqrt{34}}{5}$

   $\sec \theta = -\dfrac{\sqrt{29}}{2}$ $\sec \theta = \dfrac{\sqrt{34}}{3}$

   $\cot \theta = -\dfrac{2}{5}$ $\cot \theta = -\dfrac{3}{5}$

9. (a) Quadrant III   **11.** (a) Quadrant II
   (b) Quadrant II   (b) Quadrant IV
13. $\sin \theta = \dfrac{3}{5}$ **15.** $\sin \theta = -\dfrac{15}{17}$
   $\cos \theta = -\dfrac{4}{5}$ $\cos \theta = \dfrac{8}{17}$
   $\tan \theta = -\dfrac{3}{4}$ $\tan \theta = -\dfrac{15}{8}$
   $\csc \theta = \dfrac{5}{3}$ $\csc \theta = -\dfrac{17}{15}$
   $\sec \theta = -\dfrac{5}{4}$ $\sec \theta = \dfrac{17}{8}$
   $\cot \theta = -\dfrac{4}{3}$ $\cot \theta = -\dfrac{8}{15}$

17. $\sin \theta = \dfrac{\sqrt{3}}{2}$

$\cos \theta = -\dfrac{1}{2}$

$\tan \theta = -\sqrt{3}$

$\csc \theta = \dfrac{2\sqrt{3}}{3}$

$\sec \theta = -2$

$\cot \theta = -\dfrac{\sqrt{3}}{3}$

21. $\sin \theta = -\dfrac{2\sqrt{5}}{5}$

$\cos \theta = -\dfrac{\sqrt{5}}{5}$

$\tan \theta = 2$

$\csc \theta = \dfrac{-\sqrt{5}}{2}$

$\sec \theta = -\sqrt{5}$

$\cot \theta = \dfrac{1}{2}$

19. $\sin \theta = 0$

$\cos \theta = -1$

$\tan \theta = 0$

$\csc \theta$ is undefined.

$\sec \theta = -1$

$\cot \theta$ is undefined.

23. **(a)** $\theta' = 23°$ **(b)** $\theta' = 53°$

25. **(a)** $\theta' = 65°$ **(b)** $\theta' = 72°$

    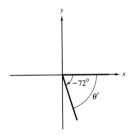

27. **(a)** $\theta' = \dfrac{\pi}{3}$ **(b)** $\theta' = \dfrac{\pi}{6}$

    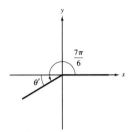

29. **(a)** $\theta' = 3.5 - \pi$ **(b)** $\theta' = 2\pi - 5.8$

    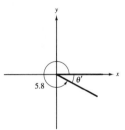

31. **(a)** $\sin(225°) = -\dfrac{\sqrt{2}}{2}$ **(b)** $\sin(-225°) = \dfrac{\sqrt{2}}{2}$

$\cos(225°) = -\dfrac{\sqrt{2}}{2}$ $\cos(-225°) = -\dfrac{\sqrt{2}}{2}$

$\tan(225°) = 1$ $\tan(-225°) = -1$

33. **(a)** $\sin(750°) = \dfrac{1}{2}$ **(b)** $\sin(510°) = \dfrac{1}{2}$

$\cos(750°) = \dfrac{\sqrt{3}}{2}$ $\cos(510°) = -\dfrac{\sqrt{3}}{2}$

$\tan(750°) = \dfrac{\sqrt{3}}{3}$ $\tan(510°) = -\dfrac{\sqrt{3}}{3}$

35. **(a)** $\sin \dfrac{4\pi}{3} = -\dfrac{\sqrt{3}}{2}$ **(b)** $\sin \dfrac{2\pi}{3} = \dfrac{\sqrt{3}}{2}$

$\cos \dfrac{4\pi}{3} = -\dfrac{1}{2}$ $\cos \dfrac{2\pi}{3} = -\dfrac{1}{2}$

$\tan \dfrac{4\pi}{3} = \sqrt{3}$ $\tan \dfrac{2\pi}{3} = -\sqrt{3}$

37. **(a)** $\sin\left(-\dfrac{\pi}{6}\right) = -\dfrac{1}{2}$ **(b)** $\sin \dfrac{5\pi}{6} = \dfrac{1}{2}$

$\cos\left(-\dfrac{\pi}{6}\right) = \dfrac{\sqrt{3}}{2}$ $\cos \dfrac{5\pi}{6} = -\dfrac{\sqrt{3}}{2}$

$\tan\left(-\dfrac{\pi}{6}\right) = -\dfrac{\sqrt{3}}{3}$ $\tan \dfrac{5\pi}{6} = -\dfrac{\sqrt{3}}{3}$

39. (a) $\sin \dfrac{11\pi}{4} = \dfrac{\sqrt{2}}{2}$ **(b)** $\sin\left(-\dfrac{13\pi}{6}\right) = -\dfrac{1}{2}$

$\cos \dfrac{11\pi}{4} = -\dfrac{\sqrt{2}}{2}$ $\cos\left(-\dfrac{13\pi}{6}\right) = \dfrac{\sqrt{3}}{2}$

$\tan \dfrac{11\pi}{4} = -1$ $\tan\left(-\dfrac{13\pi}{6}\right) = -\dfrac{\sqrt{3}}{3}$

41. (a) 0.1736 **43. (a)** -0.3420
   (b) 5.7588   **(b)** -0.3420
45. (a) 1.7321 **47. (a)** 0.3640
   (b) 1.7321   **(b)** 0.3640
49. (a) $30° = \dfrac{\pi}{6},\ 150° = \dfrac{5\pi}{6}$

   (b) $210° = \dfrac{7\pi}{6},\ 330° = \dfrac{11\pi}{6}$

51. (a) $60° = \dfrac{\pi}{3},\ 120° = \dfrac{2\pi}{3}$

   (b) $135° = \dfrac{3\pi}{4},\ 315° = \dfrac{7\pi}{4}$

53. (a) $45° = \dfrac{\pi}{4},\ 225° = \dfrac{5\pi}{4}$ **55. (a)** 54.99°, 125.01°

   (b) $150° = \dfrac{5\pi}{6},\ 330° = \dfrac{11\pi}{6}$ **(b)** 195.00°, 345.00°

57. (a) 0.175, 6.109 **59. (a)** 0.873, 4.014
   (b) 2.201, 4.083   **(b)** 1.693, 4.835

61. $\dfrac{4}{5}$ **63.** $-\dfrac{\sqrt{13}}{2}$ **65.** $\dfrac{8}{5}$

67. (a) 25.2° F **69. (a)** 0.25 ft
   (b) 65.1° F   **(b)** 0.0177 ft
   (c) 50.8° F   **(c)** -0.2475 ft
71. (a) 10 mi
   (b) 5 mi
   (c) 5.77 mi

Section 6.4 (page 434)

WARM-UP **1.** 6π **2.** $\dfrac{1}{2}$ **3.** $\dfrac{\pi}{6}$ **4.** $\dfrac{7\pi}{6}$ **5.** -2

6. $-\dfrac{4}{3}$ **7.** 1 **8.** 0 **9.** 1 **10.** 0

1. Period: π **3.** Period: 4π
   Amplitude: 2   Amplitude: $\dfrac{3}{2}$

```
Xmin: 0
Xmax: 3π
Xscale: π/2
Ymin: −3
Ymax: 3
Yscale: 1
```

```
Xmin: 0
Xmax: 4π
Xscale: π
Ymin: −2
Ymax: 2
Yscale: 1
```

5. Period: 2
   Amplitude: $\dfrac{1}{2}$

```
Xmin: 0
Xmax: 6
Xscale: 1
Ymin: −2
Ymax: 2
Yscale: 0.5
```

7. Period: $\pi/5$; Amplitude: 3 **9.** Period: $\dfrac{1}{2}$; Amplitude: 3
11. *Shift* the graph of f π units to the right to obtain the graph of g. **13.** *Reflect* the graph of f about the x-axis to obtain the graph of g. **15.** *Shift* the graph of f 2 units up to obtain the graph of g.

17.   **19.**

21.   **23.**

25.   **27.**

29.   **31.**

33.   **35.**

37.

39.

41.

43.

45.

47.

49.

51.

53.

55. $-\dfrac{5\pi}{6}, -\dfrac{\pi}{6}, \dfrac{7\pi}{6}, \dfrac{11\pi}{6}$ **57.** $-\dfrac{7\pi}{4}, -\dfrac{\pi}{4}, \dfrac{\pi}{4}, \dfrac{7\pi}{4}$

59. $f(x) = 2 \cos x + 2$ **61.** $y = 2 \sin 4x$

63. $y = \cos\left(2x + \dfrac{\pi}{2}\right)$

65.

$(-1.480, 0.455), (0.672, 3.914)$

67. (a) 6
(b) 10 cycles/min
(c)

69. (a) $\frac{1}{440}$
(b) 440
(c)

71.

Maximum sales: June
Minimum sales: December

73. $g(x) = 2f(x)$ **75.** $g(x) = f(x - \pi)$

Section 6.5   (*page 443*)

WARM-UP   **1.** 0   **2.** $\dfrac{\sqrt{2}}{2}$ **3.** 1

4. 0   **5.** 0   **6.** 0

7.

8.

9.

10.

1. c

Xmin: $-\dfrac{\pi}{2}$
Xmax: $\dfrac{3\pi}{2}$
Xscale: $\dfrac{\pi}{4}$
Ymin: -3
Ymax: 3
Yscale: 1

2. g

Xmin: $-\dfrac{\pi}{3}$
Xmax: π
Xscale: $\dfrac{\pi}{6}$
Ymin: -2
Ymax: 2
Yscale: 1

3. e

```
Xmin: -2π
Xmax: 2π
Xscale: π/2
Ymin: -3
Ymax: 3
Yscale: 1
```

4. a

```
Xmin: -π
Xmax: 5π
Xscale: π
Ymin: -5
Ymax: 5
Yscale: 1
```

5. d

```
Xmin: -1
Xmax: 4
Xscale: 1
Ymin: -2
Ymax: 2
Yscale: 1
```

6. h

```
Xmin: -1
Xmax: 3
Xscale: 0.5
Ymin: -2
Ymax: 2
Yscale: 1
```

7. b

```
Xmin: -π
Xmax: 2π
Xscale: π/2
Ymin: -3
Ymax: 3
Yscale: 1
```

8. f

```
Xmin: -0.5
Xmax: 2
Xscale: 0.25
Ymin: -4
Ymax: 4
Yscale: 1
```

9.

11.

13.

15.

17.

19.

21.

23.

25.

27.

29.

31.

33.

35.

37.

39.

41. $-\dfrac{7\pi}{4}, -\dfrac{3\pi}{4}, \dfrac{\pi}{4}, \dfrac{5\pi}{4}$ **43.** $-\dfrac{4\pi}{3}, -\dfrac{2\pi}{3}, \dfrac{2\pi}{3}, \dfrac{4\pi}{3}$

45. Even

47. (a)

49. $d = 6 \cot x$

(b) $(0.524, 2.618)$

(c) As x approaches π, f approaches 0 and g increases without bound. g is the reciprocal of f.

Section 6.6   (*page 449*)

WARM-UP

1. $f(x) = -1 : \dfrac{3\pi}{2}$

$f(x) = 0 : 0, \pi, 2\pi$

$f(x) = 1 : \dfrac{\pi}{2}$

2. $f(x) = -1 : \pi$

$f(x) = 0 : \dfrac{\pi}{2}, \dfrac{3\pi}{2}$

$f(x) = 1 : 0, 2\pi$

3. $f(x) = -1 : \dfrac{3\pi}{4}, \dfrac{7\pi}{4}$

$f(x) = 0 : 0, \dfrac{\pi}{2}, \pi, \dfrac{3\pi}{2}, 2\pi$

$f(x) = 1 : \dfrac{\pi}{4}, \dfrac{5\pi}{4}$

4. $f(x) = -1 : 2\pi$

$f(x) = 0 : \pi$

$f(x) = 1 : 0$

11.

Period: 4π
Relative maxima: $(0, 0)$, $(6.2831, 2)$
Relative minima: $(2.636, -1.125)$, $(9.930, -1.125)$

5.

6.

7.

8.

13.

15.

9. $0, \dfrac{\sqrt{3}\pi}{12}, \dfrac{\sqrt{2}\pi}{8}, \dfrac{\pi}{6}, 0$

10. $0, \dfrac{3 + \pi}{6}, \dfrac{2\sqrt{2} + \pi}{4}, \dfrac{3\sqrt{3} + 2\pi}{6}, \dfrac{\pi + 2}{2}$

17.

19.

1.

3.

21.

23.

25.

The functional values approach 0 as x increases without bound.

5.

7.

Period: 2π
Relative maximum: $(0.785, 1.414)$
Relative minimum: $(3.927, -1.414)$

27.

The functional values approach 0 as x increases without bound.

29.

9.

Period: 2π
Relative maximum: $(1.047, 2.598)$
Relative minimum: $(5.236, -2.598)$

The functional values approach 0 as x approaches 0.

31.

The functional values approach 0 as x approaches 0.

33.

y increases without bound.

35.

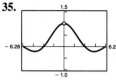

$g(x)$ approaches the value of 1.

37.

$f(x)$ oscillates between -1 and 1.

39.

$f = g$

41.

$f = g$

43.

45.

47.

49.

We can explain the cycles of this predator-prey population by noting the cause and effect pattern.

51.

Section 6.7 *(page 451)*

1. $\dfrac{\pi}{6}$ **3.** $\dfrac{\pi}{3}$ **5.** $\dfrac{\pi}{6}$ **7.** $\dfrac{5\pi}{6}$ **9.** $-\dfrac{\pi}{3}$ **11.** $\dfrac{2\pi}{3}$

13. $\dfrac{\pi}{3}$ **15.** 0   **17.** 1.29   **19.** -0.85 **21.** -1.11

23. 0.32   **25.** 1.99   **27.** 0.74   **29.**

31. 0.3   **33.** -0.1 **35.** 0

37. $\dfrac{3}{5}$ **39.** $\dfrac{\sqrt{5}}{5}$ **41.** $\dfrac{12}{13}$

43. $\dfrac{\sqrt{34}}{5}$

45. $y = \pm 1$ **47.** $\dfrac{1}{x}$

49. $\sqrt{1 - 4x^2}$ **51.** $\sqrt{1 - x^2}$ **53.** $\dfrac{\sqrt{9 - x^2}}{x}$

55. $\dfrac{\sqrt{2}}{\sqrt{2 - x^2}}$ **57.** $\dfrac{9}{\sqrt{x^2 + 81}}$ **59.** $\dfrac{|x - 1|}{\sqrt{x^2 - 2x + 10}}$

61.

63.

65. $f(t) = 3\sqrt{2}\,\sin\!\left(2t + \dfrac{\pi}{4}\right)$

67. (a)

(b) 2.236 ft
(c) $\beta = 0$; As the distance from the picture increases without bound, the angle β approaches 0.

69. (a) 14.5°
  (b) 30.0°

71. $y = \text{arccot } x$ if and only if $\cot y = x$, where $0 < y < \pi$.

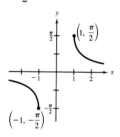

73. $y = \text{arccsc } x$ if and only if $\csc y = x$, where
$-\dfrac{\pi}{2} \le y < 0$ or $0 < y \le \dfrac{\pi}{2}$.

Section 6.8 (*page 470*)

WARM-UP   **1.** 8.45   **2.** 78.99   **3.** 1.06   **4.** 1.24
5. 4.88   **6.** 34.14   **7.** 4, π **8.** $\frac{1}{2}$, 2   **9.** 3, $\frac{2}{3}$
10. 0.2, 8π

1. $a \approx 3.64$ **3.** $a \approx 8.26$
  $c \approx 10.64$ $c \approx 25.38$
  $B = 70°$ $A = 19°$
5. $a \approx 91.34$ **7.** $c \approx 11.66$
  $b \approx 420.70$ $A \approx 30.96°$
  $B = 77° \, 45'$ $B \approx 59.04°$
9. $a \approx 49.48$
  $A \approx 72.08°$
  $B \approx 17.92°$
11. 2.56 in.   **13.** 121.2 ft   **15.** 15.4 ft   **17.** 56.3°
19. 12.68°   **21.** 5099 ft   **23.** 19.9 ft
25. 508 miles north; 650 miles east   **27.** N 56.3° W
29. (a) N 58° E   (b) 68.8 yd   **31.** 1657 ft
33. 17,054 ft $\approx$ 3.23 mi   **35.** 29.389 in.
37. $y = \sqrt{3}r$ **39.** $a \approx 7$, $c \approx 12.2$
41. (a) 4   **43.** (a) $\frac{1}{16}$
  (b) 4   (b) 60
  (c) $\frac{1}{16}$ (c) $\frac{1}{120}$
45. $\omega = 528\pi$

Chapter 6 Review Exercises (*page 474*)

1. $\dfrac{3\pi}{4}$, $-\dfrac{5\pi}{4}$ **3.** 250°, $-470°$

5. 135.28°   **7.** 5.38°   **9.** 135° 16′ 12″   **11.** $-85°$ 9′
13. 128.57°   **15.** $-200.54°$ **17.** 8.3776

19. -0.5890 **21.** 72°   **23.** $\dfrac{\pi}{5}$

25. $\sin \theta = \dfrac{4}{5}$ **27.** $\sin \theta = \dfrac{2\sqrt{53}}{53}$

  $\cos \theta = \dfrac{3}{5}$ $\cos \theta = -\dfrac{7\sqrt{53}}{53}$

  $\tan \theta = \dfrac{4}{3}$ $\tan \theta = -\dfrac{2}{7}$

  $\csc \theta = \dfrac{5}{4}$ $\csc \theta = \dfrac{\sqrt{53}}{2}$

  $\sec \theta = \dfrac{5}{3}$ $\sec \theta = -\dfrac{\sqrt{53}}{7}$

  $\cot \theta = \dfrac{3}{4}$ $\cot \theta = -\dfrac{7}{2}$

29. $\sin \theta = -\dfrac{3\sqrt{13}}{13}$ **31.** $\sin \theta = -\dfrac{\sqrt{11}}{6}$

  $\cos \theta = -\dfrac{2\sqrt{13}}{13}$ $\cos \theta = \dfrac{5}{6}$

  $\tan \theta = \dfrac{3}{2}$ $\tan \theta = -\dfrac{\sqrt{11}}{5}$

  $\csc \theta = -\dfrac{\sqrt{13}}{3}$ $\csc \theta = -\dfrac{6\sqrt{11}}{11}$

  $\sec \theta = -\dfrac{\sqrt{13}}{2}$ $\cot \theta = -\dfrac{5\sqrt{11}}{11}$

  $\cot \theta = \dfrac{2}{3}$

33. $\cos \theta = -\dfrac{\sqrt{55}}{8}$

$\tan \theta = -\dfrac{3\sqrt{55}}{55}$

$\csc \theta = \dfrac{8}{3}$

$\sec \theta = -\dfrac{8\sqrt{55}}{55}$

$\cot \theta = -\dfrac{\sqrt{55}}{3}$

35. $\sqrt{3}$ **37.** $-\dfrac{\sqrt{3}}{2}$ **39.** $-\dfrac{\sqrt{2}}{2}$

41. 0.65   **43.** 3.24   **45.** $135° = \dfrac{3\pi}{4}, 225° = \dfrac{5\pi}{4}$

47. $210° = \dfrac{7\pi}{6}, 330° = \dfrac{11\pi}{6}$

49. $57° \approx 0.9948, 123° \approx 2.1467$

51. $165° \approx 2.8798, 195° \approx 3.4034$

53. $\dfrac{\sqrt{-x^2 + 2x}}{-x^2 + 2x}$ **55.** $\dfrac{2\sqrt{4 - 2x^2}}{4 - x^2}$

57.   **59.**

61.   **63.**

65.   **67.**

69.   **71.**

73.   **75.**

77.   **79.**

81.

Periodic
Relative maximum: (1.571, 2.718)
Relative minimum: (4.712, 0.368)

83.

Periodic
Relative maxima: (0.615, 0.770), (2.526, 0.770), (4.712, 0)
Relative minima: (1.571, 0), (3.757, −0.770),
(5.668, −0.770)

85. 7.66 m   **87.** 1.33 mi   **89.** 268.8 ft

91. (a)   **(b)**

(c) $\sin x = x - \dfrac{x^3}{3!} + \dfrac{x^5}{5!} - \dfrac{x^7}{7!} + \dfrac{x^9}{9!}$

$\cos x = 1 - \dfrac{x^2}{2!} + \dfrac{x^4}{4!} - \dfrac{x^6}{6!} + \dfrac{x^8}{8!}$

The accuracy increases with additional terms.

CHAPTER 7

Section 7.1 (*page 484*)

WARM-UP

1. $\sin\theta = \dfrac{3\sqrt{13}}{13}$

$\cos\theta = \dfrac{2\sqrt{13}}{13}$

$\csc\theta = \dfrac{\sqrt{13}}{3}$

$\sec\theta = \dfrac{\sqrt{13}}{2}$

$\cot\theta = \dfrac{2}{3}$

2. $\sin\theta = \dfrac{2\sqrt{2}}{3}$

$\cos\theta = \dfrac{1}{3}$

$\tan\theta = 2\sqrt{2}$

$\csc\theta = \dfrac{3\sqrt{2}}{4}$

$\cot\theta = \dfrac{\sqrt{2}}{4}$

3. $\sin\theta = -\dfrac{3\sqrt{58}}{58}$

$\cos\theta = \dfrac{7\sqrt{58}}{58}$

$\tan\theta = -\dfrac{3}{7}$

$\csc\theta = -\dfrac{\sqrt{58}}{3}$

$\sec\theta = \dfrac{\sqrt{58}}{7}$

$\cot\theta = -\dfrac{7}{3}$

4. $\sin\theta = \dfrac{\sqrt{5}}{5}$

$\cos\theta = -\dfrac{2\sqrt{5}}{5}$

$\tan\theta = -\dfrac{1}{2}$

$\csc\theta = \sqrt{5}$

$\sec\theta = -\dfrac{\sqrt{5}}{2}$

$\cot\theta = -2$

5. $\dfrac{1}{2}$ **6.** $\dfrac{5}{4}$ **7.** $\dfrac{\sqrt{73}}{8}$ **8.** $\dfrac{2}{3}$ **9.** $\dfrac{x^2+x+16}{4(x+1)}$

10. $\dfrac{8x-2}{1-x^2}$

1. $\tan x = \dfrac{\sqrt{3}}{3}$

$\csc x = 2$

$\sec x = \dfrac{2\sqrt{3}}{3}$

$\cot x = \sqrt{3}$

3. $\cos\theta = \dfrac{\sqrt{2}}{2}$

$\tan\theta = -1$

$\csc\theta = -\sqrt{2}$

$\cot\theta = -1$

5. $\sin x = \dfrac{2}{3}$

$\cos x = -\dfrac{\sqrt{5}}{3}$

$\csc x = \dfrac{3}{2}$

$\sec x = -\dfrac{3\sqrt{5}}{5}$

$\cot x = -\dfrac{\sqrt{5}}{2}$

7. $\sin\theta = -\dfrac{2\sqrt{5}}{5}$

$\cos\theta = -\dfrac{\sqrt{5}}{5}$

$\csc\theta = -\dfrac{\sqrt{5}}{2}$

$\sec\theta = -\sqrt{5}$

$\cot\theta = \dfrac{1}{2}$

9. $\cos\theta = 0$; $\tan\theta$ is undefined. $\csc\theta = -1$; $\sec\theta$ is undefined.

11. d **12.** e **13.** a **14.** f **15.** b **16.** c **17.** b **18.** c **19.** e **20.** a **21.** f **22.** d

23. $\sec\phi$ **25.** $\sin\beta$ **27.** $\cos x$ **29.** 1

31. $-\tan x$ **33.** $\tan x$ **35.** $1+\sin y$ **37.** $\sin^2 x$

39. $\sin^2 x\tan^2 x$ **41.** $\sec^4 x$ **43.** $\sin^2 x - \cos^2 x$

45. $1 + 2\sin x\cos x$ **47.** $\tan^2 x$ **49.** $2\csc^2 x$

51. $2\sec x$ **53.** $1+\cos y$ **55.** $3(\sec x + \tan x)$

57. Identity **59.** Not an identity

61. (a) $0 \le x \le \dfrac{\pi}{2}$, $\dfrac{3\pi}{2} \le x \le 2\pi$ (b) $\dfrac{\pi}{2} \le x \le \dfrac{3\pi}{2}$

63. $5\cos\theta$ **65.** $3\tan\theta$ **67.** $5\sec\theta$ **69.** $\cos\theta$

71. $27\sec^3\theta$ **73.** $0 \le \theta < \dfrac{\pi}{2}$, $\dfrac{3\pi}{2} < \theta \le 2\pi$

75. $\ln|\cot\theta|$ **77.** False, $\dfrac{\sin k\theta}{\cos k\theta} = \tan k\theta$ **79.** True

81. (a) $\csc^2 132° - \cot^2 132° \approx 1.8107 - 0.8107 = 1$

  (b) $\csc^2\dfrac{2\pi}{7} - \cot^2\dfrac{2\pi}{7} \approx 1.6360 - 0.6360 = 1$

83. (a) $\cos(90° - 80°) = \sin 80° \approx 0.9848$

  (b) $\cos\left(\dfrac{\pi}{2} - 0.8\right) = \sin 0.8 \approx 0.7174$

85. $\cos\theta = \pm\sqrt{1-\sin^2\theta}$

$\tan\theta = \pm\dfrac{\sin\theta}{\sqrt{1-\sin^2\theta}}$

$\csc\theta = \dfrac{1}{\sin\theta}$

$\sec\theta = \pm\dfrac{1}{\sqrt{1-\sin^2\theta}}$

$\cot\theta = \pm\dfrac{\sqrt{1-\sin^2\theta}}{\sin\theta}$

Section 7.2 (*page 491*)

WARM-UP

1. (a) $x^2(1-y^2)$ **2.** (a) $x^2(1+y^2)$

  (b) $\sin^4 x$ (b) 1

3. (a) $(x^2+1)(x^2-1)$

  (b) $\sec^2 x(\tan^2 x - 1)$

4. (a) $(z+1)(z^2-z+1)$

  (b) $(\tan x + 1)(\tan^2 x - \tan x + 1)$

5. (a) $(x-1)(x^2+1)$ **6.** (a) $(x^2-1)^2$

  (b) $(\cot x - 1)\csc^2 x$ (b) $\cos^4 x$

7. (a) $\dfrac{y^2-x^2}{x}$ **8.** (a) $\dfrac{x^2-1}{x^2}$

  (b) $\tan x$ (b) $\sin^2 x$

9. (a) $\dfrac{y^2 + (1 + z)^2}{y(1 + z)}$ **10. (a)** $\dfrac{y(1 + y) - z^2}{z(1 + y)}$

(b) $2 \csc x$ **(b)** $\dfrac{\tan x - 1}{\sec x(1 + \tan x)}$

Exercises 1–50 are proofs.

51. $\sin \theta = \pm\sqrt{1 - \cos^2 \theta}$; $\dfrac{7\pi}{4}$

53. $\sqrt{\tan^2 x} = |\tan x|$; $\dfrac{3\pi}{4}$ **55.** $\mu = \tan \theta$

Section 7.3 (page 502)

WARM-UP

1. $\dfrac{2\pi}{3}, \dfrac{4\pi}{3}$ **2.** $\dfrac{\pi}{3}, \dfrac{2\pi}{3}$ **3.** $\dfrac{\pi}{4}, \dfrac{7\pi}{4}$ **4.** $\dfrac{7\pi}{4}, \dfrac{5\pi}{4}$

5. $\dfrac{\pi}{3}, \dfrac{4\pi}{3}$ **6.** $\dfrac{3\pi}{4}, \dfrac{7\pi}{4}$ **7.** $\dfrac{15}{8}$ **8.** $-3, \dfrac{5}{2}$

9. $\dfrac{2 \pm \sqrt{14}}{2}$ **10.** $-1, 3$

Exercises 1–6 are proofs.

7. $\dfrac{2\pi}{3} + 2n\pi, \dfrac{4\pi}{3} + 2n\pi$ **9.** $\dfrac{\pi}{3} + 2n\pi, \dfrac{2\pi}{3} + 2n\pi$

11. $\dfrac{\pi}{4} + \dfrac{n\pi}{2}$ **13.** $\dfrac{\pi}{6} + n\pi, \dfrac{5\pi}{6} + n\pi$ **15.** $n\pi, \dfrac{\pi}{4} + n\pi$

17. $n\pi, \dfrac{3\pi}{2} + 2n\pi$ **19.** $\dfrac{\pi}{3} + n\pi, \dfrac{2\pi}{3} + n\pi$

21. $\dfrac{\pi}{3}, \dfrac{5\pi}{3}$ **23.** $\dfrac{7\pi}{6}, \dfrac{3\pi}{2}, \dfrac{11\pi}{6}$ **25.** $\dfrac{\pi}{6}, \dfrac{5\pi}{6}, \dfrac{7\pi}{6}, \dfrac{11\pi}{6}$

27. No solution   **29.** $\dfrac{2\pi}{3}, \dfrac{5\pi}{6}, \dfrac{5\pi}{3}, \dfrac{11\pi}{6}$

31. $\dfrac{\pi}{2}$ **33.** $\dfrac{2}{3}, \dfrac{3}{2}$; 0.8411, 5.4421

35. $4 \pm \sqrt{3}$; 1.1555, 1.3981, 4.2971, 4.5397

37. 1.107, 4.249   **39.** 1.0472, 5.2360

41. 0, 1.895   **43.** 0, 2.678, 3.142, 5.820, 6.283

45. 0.9828, 1.7682, 4.1244, 4.9098

47. 0.3398, 0.8481, 2.2935, 2.8018   **49.** 0.4271, 2.7145

51.

53. 0.7391, approximate the zeros of $f(x) = \cos x - x$.

Maximum: (0.785, 1.414)
Minimum: (3.927, −1.414)

55.

1.122 square units

57. 0.04, 0.43, 0.83   **59.** 37°, 53°   **61.** 1   **63.** $\sqrt{2}$

Section 7.4 (page 511)

WARM-UP

1. $\dfrac{\sqrt{10}}{10}$ **2.** $\dfrac{-5\sqrt{34}}{34}$ **3.** $-\dfrac{\sqrt{7}}{4}$ **4.** $\dfrac{2\sqrt{2}}{3}$

5. $\dfrac{\pi}{4}, \dfrac{3\pi}{4}$ **6.** $\dfrac{\pi}{2}, \dfrac{3\pi}{2}$ **7.** $\tan^3 x$ **8.** $\cot^2 x$

9. $\sec x$ **10.** $1 - \tan^2 x$

1. $\sin 75° = \dfrac{\sqrt{2}}{4}\left(1 + \sqrt{3}\right)$

$\cos 75° = \dfrac{\sqrt{2}}{4}\left(\sqrt{3} - 1\right)$

$\tan 75° = \sqrt{3} + 2$

3. $\sin 105° = \dfrac{\sqrt{2}}{4}\left(\sqrt{3} + 1\right)$

$\cos 105° = \dfrac{\sqrt{2}}{4}\left(1 - \sqrt{3}\right)$

$\tan 105° = -2 - \sqrt{3}$

5. $\sin 195° = \dfrac{\sqrt{2}}{4}\left(1 - \sqrt{3}\right)$

$\cos 195° = -\dfrac{\sqrt{2}}{4}\left(\sqrt{3} + 1\right)$

$\tan 195° = 2 - \sqrt{3}$

7. $\sin \dfrac{11\pi}{12} = \dfrac{\sqrt{2}}{4}\left(\sqrt{3} - 1\right)$

$\cos \dfrac{11\pi}{12} = -\dfrac{\sqrt{2}}{4}\left(\sqrt{3} + 1\right)$

$\tan \dfrac{11\pi}{12} = -2 + \sqrt{3}$

9. $\sin \dfrac{17\pi}{12} = -\dfrac{\sqrt{2}}{4}\left(\sqrt{3} + 1\right)$ **11.** $\cos 40°$

$\cos \dfrac{17\pi}{12} = \dfrac{\sqrt{2}}{4}\left(1 - \sqrt{3}\right)$

$\tan \dfrac{17\pi}{12} = 2 + \sqrt{3}$

13. $\sin 200°$ **15.** $\tan 239°$ **17.** $\sin 1.8$ **19.** $\tan 3x$

21. $\frac{33}{65}$ **23.** $-\frac{56}{65}$ **25.** $-\frac{3}{5}$ **27.** $\frac{44}{125}$

Exercises 29–46 are proofs.

47. (a) $\sqrt{2}\,\sin\left(\theta + \dfrac{\pi}{4}\right)$ **49.** (a) $13\,\sin(3\theta + 0.3948)$

(b) $\sqrt{2}\,\cos\left(\theta - \dfrac{\pi}{4}\right)$ (b) $13\,\cos(3\theta - 1.1760)$

51. $\sqrt{2}\,\sin\theta + \sqrt{2}\,\cos\theta$ **53.** 1

55. $\dfrac{\pi}{2}$ **57.** $\dfrac{\pi}{4},\dfrac{7\pi}{4}$ **59.** 3.927, 5.498

Section 7.5   (page 521)

WARM-UP   **1.** $\sin x(2 + \cos x)$

2. $(\cos x - 2)(\cos x + 1)$ **3.** $0, \dfrac{\pi}{2}, \pi, \dfrac{3\pi}{2}$

4. $\dfrac{\pi}{4}, \dfrac{3\pi}{4}, \dfrac{5\pi}{4}, \dfrac{7\pi}{4}$ **5.** π **6.** 0   **7.** $\dfrac{2 - \sqrt{2}}{4}$

8. $\dfrac{3}{4}$ **9.** $\tan 3x$ **10.** $\cos x(1 - 4\sin^2 x)$

1.

$0, \dfrac{\pi}{3}, \pi, \dfrac{5\pi}{3}$

3.

$\dfrac{\pi}{12}, \dfrac{5\pi}{12}, \dfrac{13\pi}{12}, \dfrac{17\pi}{12}$

5.

$0, \dfrac{2\pi}{3}, \dfrac{4\pi}{3}$

7.

$\dfrac{\pi}{2}, \dfrac{\pi}{6}, \dfrac{5\pi}{6}, \dfrac{7\pi}{6}, \dfrac{3\pi}{2}, \dfrac{11\pi}{6}$

9.

$0, \dfrac{\pi}{2}, \pi, \dfrac{3\pi}{2}$

11. $f(x) = 3\sin 2x$

Relative maxima: (0.785, 3), (3.927, 3)
Relative minima: (2.356, −3), (5.498, −3)

13. $g(x) = 4\cos 2x$

Relative maxima: (0, 4), (3.142, 4)
Relative minima: (1.571, −4), (4.712, −4)

15. $\sin 2u = \dfrac{24}{25}$

$\cos 2u = \dfrac{7}{25}$

$\tan 2u = \dfrac{24}{7}$

17. $\sin 2u = \dfrac{4}{5}$ **19.** $\sin 2u = -\dfrac{4\sqrt{21}}{25}$

$\cos 2u = \dfrac{3}{5}$ $\cos 2u = -\dfrac{17}{25}$

$\tan 2u = \dfrac{4}{3}$ $\tan 2u = \dfrac{4\sqrt{21}}{17}$

21. $\frac{1}{8}(3 + 4\cos 2x + \cos 4x)$ **23.** $\frac{1}{8}(1 - \cos 4x)$

25. $\frac{1}{16}(1 + \cos 2x)(1 - \cos 4x)$

27. $\sin 105° = \frac{1}{2}\sqrt{2 + \sqrt{3}}$

$\cos 105° = -\frac{1}{2}\sqrt{2 - \sqrt{3}}$

$\tan 105° = -2 - \sqrt{3}$

29. $\sin 112° 30' = \frac{1}{2}\sqrt{2 + \sqrt{2}}$

$\cos 112° 30' = -\frac{1}{2}\sqrt{2 - \sqrt{2}}$

$\tan 112° 30' = -1 - \sqrt{2}$

31. $\sin\dfrac{\pi}{8} = \dfrac{1}{2}\sqrt{2 - \sqrt{2}}$ **33.** $\sin\dfrac{u}{2} = \dfrac{5\sqrt{26}}{26}$

$\cos\dfrac{\pi}{8} = \dfrac{1}{2}\sqrt{2 + \sqrt{2}}$ $\cos\dfrac{u}{2} = \dfrac{\sqrt{26}}{26}$

$\tan\dfrac{\pi}{8} = \sqrt{2} - 1$ $\tan\dfrac{u}{2} = 5$

35. $\sin\dfrac{u}{2} = \sqrt{\dfrac{89 - 8\sqrt{89}}{178}}$ **37.** $\sin\dfrac{u}{2} = \dfrac{3\sqrt{10}}{10}$

$\cos\dfrac{u}{2} = -\sqrt{\dfrac{89 + 8\sqrt{89}}{178}}$ $\cos\dfrac{u}{2} = -\dfrac{\sqrt{10}}{10}$

$\tan\dfrac{u}{2} = \dfrac{8 - \sqrt{89}}{5}$ $\tan\dfrac{u}{2} = -3$

39. $|\sin 3x|$ **41.** $-|\tan 4x|$

43. π **45.** $\dfrac{\pi}{3}, \pi, \dfrac{5\pi}{3}$

47. $3\left(\sin\dfrac{\pi}{2} + \sin 0\right)$ **49.** $\dfrac{1}{2}(\sin 8\theta + \sin 2\theta)$

51. $\dfrac{5}{2}(\cos 8\beta + \cos 2\beta)$ **53.** $\dfrac{1}{2}(\cos 2y - \cos 2x)$

55. $\dfrac{1}{2}(\sin 2\theta + \sin 2\pi)$ **57.** $2 \sin 45° \cos 15°$

59. $-2 \sin\dfrac{\pi}{2} \sin\dfrac{\pi}{4}$ **61.** $2 \cos 4x \cos 2x$

63. $2 \cos \alpha \sin \beta$ **65.** $2 \cos(\phi + \pi) \cos \pi$

67. $0, \dfrac{\pi}{4}, \dfrac{\pi}{2}, \dfrac{3\pi}{4}, \pi, \dfrac{5\pi}{4}, \dfrac{3\pi}{2}, \dfrac{7\pi}{4}$ **69.** $\dfrac{\pi}{6}, \dfrac{5\pi}{6}$

Exercises 71–87 are proofs.

89.

91. $2x\sqrt{1 - x^2}$ **93.** Proof

95. **(a)** $A = 100 \sin\dfrac{\theta}{2} \cos\dfrac{\theta}{2}$

(b) $A = 50 \sin \theta$; The area is maximum when $\theta = \dfrac{\pi}{2}$.

Chapter 7 Review Exercises   (*page 524*)

1. $\sin^2 x$ **3.** $1 + \cot \alpha$ **5.** 1   **7.** 1
9. $\cos^2 2x$

Exercises 11–35 are proofs.

37. $\dfrac{\sqrt{2}}{4}\left(\sqrt{3} + 1\right)$ **39.** $-\dfrac{1}{2}\sqrt{2 + \sqrt{2}}$

41. $-\dfrac{3}{52}\left(5 + 4\sqrt{7}\right)$ **43.** $\dfrac{1}{52}\left(36 + 5\sqrt{7}\right)$

45. $\dfrac{1}{4}\sqrt{2\left(4 - \sqrt{7}\right)}$

47. False; If $\dfrac{\pi}{2} < \theta < \pi$, then $\cos\dfrac{\theta}{2} > 0$.   **49.** True

51. $0, \pi$

53. $0, \dfrac{3\pi}{4}, \pi, \dfrac{5\pi}{4}$

55. $0, \dfrac{\pi}{2}, \pi$

57. $\dfrac{\pi}{3}, \dfrac{5\pi}{3}$

59. $\dfrac{\pi}{4}, \dfrac{5\pi}{4}$

61. $2 \cos\dfrac{5\theta}{2} \cos\dfrac{\theta}{2}$

63. $\dfrac{1}{2}(\cos \alpha - \cos 5\alpha)$ **65.** $8x^2 - 1$ **67.** Proof

69. **(a)** $y = \dfrac{1}{2}\sqrt{10} \sin(8t - \arctan\dfrac{1}{3})$

(b)

(c) $\dfrac{1}{2}\sqrt{10}$

(d) $\dfrac{4}{\pi}$

CHAPTER 8

Section 8.1   (*page 534*)

WARM-UP   **1.** $b = 3\sqrt{3}, A = 30°, B = 60°$
2. $c = 5\sqrt{2}, A = 45°, B = 45°$
3. $a = 8, A \approx 28.07°, B \approx 61.93°$
4. $b \approx 8.33, c \approx 11.21, B = 48°$
5. $a \approx 22.69, c \approx 23.04, A = 80°$
6. $a \approx 45.73, b \approx 142.86, A = 17° 45'$
7. 8.48   **8.** 12.94   **9.** 2.25   **10.** 91.06

1. $C = 105°$, $b \approx 14.14$, $c \approx 19.32$
3. $C = 110°$, $b \approx 22.44$, $c \approx 24.35$
5. $B \approx 21.55°$, $C \approx 122.45°$, $c \approx 11.49$
7. $B = 10°$, $b \approx 69.46$, $c \approx 136.81$
9. $B = 42° 4'$, $a \approx 22.05$, $b \approx 14.88$
11. $A \approx 10° 11'$, $C \approx 154° 19'$, $c \approx 11.03$
13. $A \approx 25.57°$, $B \approx 9.43°$, $a \approx 10.5$
15. $B \approx 18° 13'$, $C \approx 51° 32'$, $c \approx 40.06$
17. No solution
19. Two solutions; $B \approx 70.4°$, $C \approx 51.6°$, $c \approx 4.16$; $B \approx 109.6°$, $C \approx 12.4°$, $c \approx 1.14$
21. No solution
23. (a) $b \leq 5$, $b = \dfrac{5}{\sin 36°}$

(b) $5 < b < \dfrac{5}{\sin 36°}$

(c) $b > \dfrac{5}{\sin 36°}$

25. 10.4   27. 1675.2   29. 474.9   31. 6 ft
33. 77 yd   35. 5 mi   37. 26.1 mi, 15.9 mi
39. 4.55 mi   41. No solution

Section 8.2 (page 542)

WARM-UP   1. $2\sqrt{13}$ 2. $3\sqrt{5}$ 3. $4\sqrt{10}$
4. $3\sqrt{13}$ 5. 20   6. 48
7. $a \approx 4.62$, $c \approx 26.20$, $B = 70°$
8. $a \approx 34.20$, $b \approx 93.97$, $B = 70°$ 9. No solution
10. $a \approx 15.09$, $B \approx 18.97°$, $C \approx 131.03°$

1. $A \approx 27.7°$, $B \approx 40.5°$, $C \approx 111.8°$
3. $B \approx 23.8°$, $C \approx 126.2°$, $a \approx 12.4$
5. $A \approx 36.9°$, $B \approx 53.1°$, $C \approx 90°$
7. $A \approx 92.9°$, $B \approx 43.55°$, $C \approx 43.55°$
9. $a \approx 11.79$, $B \approx 12.7°$, $C \approx 47.3°$
11. $A \approx 158° 36'$, $C \approx 12° 38'$, $b \approx 10.4$
13. $A = 27° 10'$, $B = 27° 10'$, $c \approx 56.9$

	a	b	c	d	θ	ϕ
15.	4	6	9.67	3.23	30°	150°
17.	10	14	20	13.86	68.2°	111.8°
19.	10	11.57	18	12	67.1°	112.9°

21. 16.25   23. 54   25. 96.82   27. 97,979.6 ft²
29. N 52° 37' E, S 64° 40' E   31. 43.3 mi
33. 1344 ft   35. 114.95°
37. $\overline{PQ} \approx 9.4$ ft, $\overline{QS} \approx 5.0$ ft, $\overline{RS} \approx 12.8$ ft
39. (a) N 58.3° W   41. (a) 63.7 ft
(b) S 81.6° W   (b) 47.6 ft
43. 3.26 ft

45. (a) 570.60
(b) 5910.68
(c) 177.09
47. Proof

Section 8.3 (page 557)

WARM-UP   1. $7\sqrt{10}$ 2. $\sqrt{58}$
3. $3x + 5y - 14 = 0$ 4. $4x - 3y - 1 = 0$
5. 111.8°   6. 323.1°   7. $\dfrac{1}{2}, \dfrac{\sqrt{3}}{2}$ 8. $\dfrac{\sqrt{3}}{2}, -\dfrac{1}{2}$
9. $-\dfrac{\sqrt{3}}{2}, \dfrac{1}{2}$ 10. $-\dfrac{1}{2}, -\dfrac{\sqrt{3}}{2}$

1.   3.

5.

7. $\mathbf{v} = \langle 3, 4 \rangle$, $\|\mathbf{v}\| = 5$ 9. $\mathbf{v} = \langle -3, 2 \rangle$, $\|\mathbf{v}\| = \sqrt{13}$
11. $\mathbf{v} = \langle 0, 5 \rangle$, $\|\mathbf{v}\| = 5$
13. $\mathbf{v} = \langle 16, -3 \rangle$, $\|\mathbf{v}\| = \sqrt{265}$
15. $\mathbf{v} = \langle 8, 4 \rangle$, $\|\mathbf{v}\| = 4\sqrt{5}$
17. (a) $\langle 4, 3 \rangle$ 19. (a) $\langle -4, 4 \rangle$
(b) $\langle -2, 1 \rangle$ (b) $\langle 0, 2 \rangle$
(c) $\langle -7, 1 \rangle$ (c) $\langle 2, 3 \rangle$
21. (a) $\langle 4, -2 \rangle$ 23. (a) $3\mathbf{i} - 2\mathbf{j}$
(b) $\langle 4, -2 \rangle$ (b) $-\mathbf{i} + 4\mathbf{j}$
(c) $\langle 8, -4 \rangle$ (c) $-4\mathbf{i} + 11\mathbf{j}$
25. (a) $2\mathbf{i} + \mathbf{j}$ 27. $\|\mathbf{v}\| = 5$, $\theta = 30°$
(b) $2\mathbf{i} - \mathbf{j}$
(c) $4\mathbf{i} - 3\mathbf{j}$
29. $\|\mathbf{v}\| = 6\sqrt{2}$, $\theta = 315°$

31. $\mathbf{v} = \langle 3, 0 \rangle$

33. $\mathbf{v} = \left\langle -\dfrac{\sqrt{3}}{2}, \dfrac{1}{2} \right\rangle$

35. $\mathbf{v} = \left\langle -\dfrac{3\sqrt{6}}{2}, \dfrac{3\sqrt{2}}{2} \right\rangle$

37. $\mathbf{v} = \left\langle \dfrac{\sqrt{10}}{5}, \dfrac{3\sqrt{10}}{5} \right\rangle$

39. $\mathbf{v} = \left\langle 3, -\dfrac{3}{2} \right\rangle$

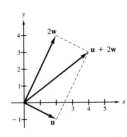

41. $\mathbf{v} = \langle 4, 3 \rangle$

43. $\mathbf{v} = \left\langle \dfrac{7}{2}, -\dfrac{1}{2} \right\rangle$

45. $\langle 5, 5 \rangle$ **47.** $\langle (10\sqrt{2} - 50), 10\sqrt{2} \rangle$ **49.** $\dfrac{4}{5}\mathbf{i} - \dfrac{3}{5}\mathbf{j}$
51. $\mathbf{j}$ **53.** 90°   **55.** 63.4°   **57.** 62.7°
59. 12.3°, 82.2 lb   **61.** 71.3°, 228.5 lb

63. Horizontal component: 80 cos 50° ≈ 51.42 ft/sec;
     Vertical component: 80 sin 50° ≈ 61.28 ft/sec
65. $T_{AC} \approx 879.4$ lb, $T_{BC} \approx 652.7$ lb
67. 3192.5 lb   **69.** N 25.2° E, 82.8 mph   **71.** 425 ft-lb

Section 8.4   (*page 566*)

WARM-UP   **1.** $-5 - 10i$ **2.** $7 + 3\sqrt{6}i$
3. $-1 - 4i$ **4.** $-3i$ **5.** $6 - 14i$
6. $6 + 4\sqrt{2}i$ **7.** $-22 + 16i$ **8.** 13
9. $-\dfrac{3}{2} + \dfrac{5}{2}i$ **10.** $-\dfrac{5}{2} - \dfrac{3}{2}i$

1. 5

3. $4\sqrt{2}$

5. $\sqrt{85}$

7. $4\left(\cos \dfrac{\pi}{2} + i \sin \dfrac{\pi}{2} \right)$

9. $3\sqrt{2}\left(\cos \dfrac{5\pi}{4} + i \sin \dfrac{5\pi}{4} \right)$

11. $3\sqrt{2}\left(\cos \dfrac{7\pi}{4} + i \sin \dfrac{7\pi}{4} \right)$ **13.** $2\left(\cos \dfrac{\pi}{6} + i \sin \dfrac{\pi}{6} \right)$

15. $4\left(\cos \dfrac{4\pi}{3} + i \sin \dfrac{4\pi}{3}\right)$

17. $6\left(\cos \dfrac{\pi}{2} + i \sin \dfrac{\pi}{2}\right)$

31. $\dfrac{-15\sqrt{2}}{8} + \dfrac{15\sqrt{2}}{8}i$

33. $-4i$

19. $\sqrt{65}(\cos 2.62 + i \sin 2.62)$

21. $7(\cos 0 + i \sin 0)$

35. $2.8408 + 0.9643i$

37. $12\left(\cos \dfrac{\pi}{2} + i \sin \dfrac{\pi}{2}\right)$

39. $\dfrac{10}{9}(\cos 200° + i \sin 200°)$

41. $0.27(\cos 150° + i \sin 150°)$

43. $\dfrac{1}{2}(\cos 80° + i \sin 80°)$

45. $\cos \dfrac{2\pi}{3} + i \sin \dfrac{2\pi}{3}$

47. $4[\cos(-58°) + i \sin(-58°)]$

23. $\sqrt{37}(\cos 1.41 + i \sin 1.41)$

25. $\sqrt{10}(\cos 3.46 + i \sin 3.46)$

49. (a) $2\sqrt{2}(\cos 45° + i \sin 45°)$,
$\sqrt{2}[\cos(-45°) + i \sin(-45°)]$
(b) $4(\cos 0° + i \sin 0°) = 4$
(c) 4

51. (a) $2[\cos(-90°) + i \sin(-90°)]$,
$\sqrt{2}(\cos 45° + i \sin 45°)$
(b) $2\sqrt{2}[\cos(-45°) + i \sin(-45°)] = 2 - 2i$
(c) $-2i - 2i^2 = -2i + 2 = 2 - 2i$

53. (a) $5(\cos 0° + i \sin 0°)$, $\sqrt{13}(\cos 56.31° + i \sin 56.31°)$
(b) $\dfrac{5}{\sqrt{13}}[\cos(-56.31°) + i \sin(-56.31°)]$
$\approx 0.7692 - 1.154i$
(c) $\dfrac{10}{13} - \dfrac{15}{13}i \approx 0.7692 - 1.154i$

57. (a) r^2
(b) $\cos 2\theta + i \sin 2\theta$

27. $-\sqrt{3} + i$

29. $\dfrac{3}{4} - \dfrac{3\sqrt{3}}{4}i$

59.

Section 8.5   (*page 573*)

WARM-UP   **1.** $3\sqrt[3]{2}$ **2.** $2\sqrt{2}$
3. $5\sqrt{2}(\cos 135° + i \sin 135°)$
4. $3(\cos 270° + i \sin 270°)$
5. $12(\cos 180° + i \sin 180°)$ **6.** $12(\cos 0° + i \sin 0°)$
7. $\cos \dfrac{3\pi}{4} + i \sin \dfrac{3\pi}{4}$ **8.** $\cos \dfrac{11\pi}{12} + i \sin \dfrac{11\pi}{12}$
9. $2\left(\cos \dfrac{\pi}{2} + i \sin \dfrac{\pi}{2}\right)$ **10.** $\dfrac{2}{3}(\cos 45° + i \sin 45°)$

---

1. $-4 - 4i$ **3.** $-32i$ **5.** $-128\sqrt{3} - 128i$
7. $\dfrac{125}{2} + \dfrac{125\sqrt{3}}{2}i$ **9.** i **11.** $608.02 + 144.69i$
13. (a) $3(\cos 60° + i \sin 60°)$
  $3(\cos 240° + i \sin 240°)$
(b)

(c) $\dfrac{3}{2} + \dfrac{3\sqrt{3}}{2}i, \ -\dfrac{3}{2} - \dfrac{3\sqrt{3}}{2}i$

15. (a) $2\left(\cos \dfrac{\pi}{3} + i \sin \dfrac{\pi}{3}\right)$
  $2\left(\cos \dfrac{5\pi}{6} + i \sin \dfrac{5\pi}{6}\right)$
  $2\left(\cos \dfrac{4\pi}{3} + i \sin \dfrac{4\pi}{3}\right)$
  $2\left(\cos \dfrac{11\pi}{6} + i \sin \dfrac{11\pi}{6}\right)$

(b)

(c) $1 + \sqrt{3}i, \ -\sqrt{3} + i, \ -1 - \sqrt{3}i, \ \sqrt{3} - i$

17. (a) $5\left(\cos \dfrac{3\pi}{4} + i \sin \dfrac{3\pi}{4}\right)$
  $5\left(\cos \dfrac{7\pi}{4} + i \sin \dfrac{7\pi}{4}\right)$

(b)

(c) $-\dfrac{5\sqrt{2}}{2} + \dfrac{5\sqrt{2}}{2}i, \ \dfrac{5\sqrt{2}}{2} - \dfrac{5\sqrt{2}}{2}i$

19. (a) $5\left(\cos \dfrac{4\pi}{9} + i \sin \dfrac{4\pi}{9}\right)$
  $5\left(\cos \dfrac{10\pi}{9} + i \sin \dfrac{10\pi}{9}\right)$
  $5\left(\cos \dfrac{16\pi}{9} + i \sin \dfrac{16\pi}{9}\right)$

(b)

(c) $0.8682 + 4.924i, \ -4.698 - 1.710i, \ 3.830 - 3.214i$
21. (a) $2(\cos 0 + i \sin 0)$
  $2\left(\cos \dfrac{2\pi}{3} + i \sin \dfrac{2\pi}{3}\right)$
  $2\left(\cos \dfrac{4\pi}{3} + i \sin \dfrac{4\pi}{3}\right)$

(b)

(c) $2, \ -1 + \sqrt{3}i, \ -1 - \sqrt{3}i$

23. (a) $\cos 0 + i \sin 0$

$\cos \dfrac{2\pi}{5} + i \sin \dfrac{2\pi}{5}$

$\cos \dfrac{4\pi}{5} + i \sin \dfrac{4\pi}{5}$

$\cos \dfrac{6\pi}{5} + i \sin \dfrac{6\pi}{5}$

$\cos \dfrac{8\pi}{5} + i \sin \dfrac{8\pi}{5}$

(b)

25. $\cos \dfrac{\pi}{8} + i \sin \dfrac{\pi}{8}$

$\cos \dfrac{5\pi}{8} + i \sin \dfrac{5\pi}{8}$

$\cos \dfrac{9\pi}{8} + i \sin \dfrac{9\pi}{8}$

$\cos \dfrac{13\pi}{8} + i \sin \dfrac{13\pi}{8}$

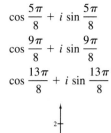

(c) $1,\ 0.3090 + 0.9511i,\ -0.8090 + 0.5878i,$
$-0.8090 - 0.5878i,\ 0.3090 - 0.9511i$

27. $3\left(\cos \dfrac{\pi}{5} + i \sin \dfrac{\pi}{5}\right)$

$3\left(\cos \dfrac{3\pi}{5} + i \sin \dfrac{3\pi}{5}\right)$

$3(\cos \pi + i \sin \pi)$

$3\left(\cos \dfrac{7\pi}{5} + i \sin \dfrac{7\pi}{5}\right)$

$3\left(\cos \dfrac{9\pi}{5} + i \sin \dfrac{9\pi}{5}\right)$

29. $4\left(\cos \dfrac{\pi}{2} + i \sin \dfrac{\pi}{2}\right)$

$4\left(\cos \dfrac{7\pi}{6} + i \sin \dfrac{7\pi}{6}\right)$

$4\left(\cos \dfrac{11\pi}{6} + i \sin \dfrac{11\pi}{6}\right)$

31. $\sqrt[6]{2}(\cos 105° + i \sin 105°)$

$\sqrt[6]{2}(\cos 225° + i \sin 225°)$

$\sqrt[6]{2}(\cos 345° + i \sin 345°)$

Chapter 8 Review Exercises (*page 573*)

1. $A \approx 29.7°,\ B \approx 52.4°,\ C \approx 97.9°$
3. $C = 110°,\ b \approx 20.4,\ c \approx 22.6$
5. $A = 35°,\ C = 35°,\ b \approx 6.6$ **7.** No solution
9. $A \approx 25.9°,\ C \approx 39.1°,\ c \approx 10.1$
11. $B \approx 31.2°,\ C \approx 133.8°,\ c \approx 13.9$
    $B \approx 148.8°,\ C \approx 16.2°,\ c \approx 5.39$
13. $A \approx 9.9°,\ C \approx 20.1°,\ b \approx 29.1$
15. $A \approx 40.9°,\ C \approx 114.1°,\ c \approx 8.6$
    $A \approx 139.1°,\ C \approx 15.9°,\ c \approx 2.6$
17. 9.798   **19.** 9.08   **21.** 31 ft   **23.** 31.1 m
25. 1135 mi   **27.** $\langle 7, -7 \rangle$ **29.** $\left\langle -4, 4\sqrt{3} \right\rangle$
31. $\left\langle \dfrac{6}{\sqrt{61}}, -\dfrac{5}{\sqrt{61}} \right\rangle$ **33.** $\langle -26, -35 \rangle$

35. $92.3°,\ 117.0$ **37.** 100 lb
39. 460.3 mph, N 32.2° E
41. $5\sqrt{2}(\cos 315° + i \sin 315°)$
43. $13(\cos 67.38° + i \sin 67.38°)$
45. $-50 - 50\sqrt{3}i$ **47.** 13
49. (a) $z_1 = 5(\cos \pi + i \sin \pi)$

$z_2 = 5\left(\cos \dfrac{\pi}{2} + i \sin \dfrac{\pi}{2}\right)$

(b) $z_1 z_2 = 25\left(\cos \dfrac{3\pi}{2} + i \sin \dfrac{3\pi}{2}\right)$

$\dfrac{z_1}{z_2} = \cos \dfrac{\pi}{2} + i \sin \dfrac{\pi}{2}$

51. (a) $z_1 = 3\sqrt{2}\left(\cos \dfrac{5\pi}{4} + i \sin \dfrac{5\pi}{4}\right)$

$z_2 = 2\left(\cos \dfrac{\pi}{6} + i \sin \dfrac{\pi}{6}\right)$

(b) $z_1 z_2 = 6\sqrt{2}\left(\cos \dfrac{17\pi}{12} + i \sin \dfrac{17\pi}{12}\right)$

$\dfrac{z_1}{z_2} = \dfrac{3\sqrt{2}}{2}\left(\cos \dfrac{13\pi}{12} + i \sin \dfrac{13\pi}{12}\right)$

53. $\dfrac{625}{2} + \dfrac{625\sqrt{3}}{2}i$ **55.** $2035 - 828i$

57. $3\left(\cos \dfrac{\pi}{4} + i \sin \dfrac{\pi}{4}\right)$

$3\left(\cos \dfrac{7\pi}{12} + i \sin \dfrac{7\pi}{12}\right)$

$3\left(\cos \dfrac{11\pi}{12} + i \sin \dfrac{11\pi}{12}\right)$

$3\left(\cos \dfrac{5\pi}{4} + i \sin \dfrac{5\pi}{4}\right)$

$3\left(\cos \dfrac{19\pi}{12} + i \sin \dfrac{19\pi}{12}\right)$

$3\left(\cos \dfrac{23\pi}{12} + i \sin \dfrac{23\pi}{12}\right)$

59. $\cos \dfrac{\pi}{3} + i \sin \dfrac{\pi}{3} = \dfrac{1}{2} + \dfrac{\sqrt{3}}{2}i$

$\cos \pi + i \sin \pi = -1$

$\cos \dfrac{5\pi}{3} + i \sin \dfrac{5\pi}{3} = \dfrac{1}{2} - \dfrac{\sqrt{3}}{2}i$

61. $3\left(\cos \dfrac{\pi}{4} + i \sin \dfrac{\pi}{4}\right) = \dfrac{3\sqrt{2}}{2} + \dfrac{3\sqrt{2}}{2}i$

$3\left(\cos \dfrac{3\pi}{4} + i \sin \dfrac{3\pi}{4}\right) = -\dfrac{3\sqrt{2}}{2} + \dfrac{3\sqrt{2}}{2}i$

$3\left(\cos \dfrac{5\pi}{4} + i \sin \dfrac{5\pi}{4}\right) = -\dfrac{3\sqrt{2}}{2} - \dfrac{3\sqrt{2}}{2}i$

$3\left(\cos \dfrac{7\pi}{4} + i \sin \dfrac{7\pi}{4}\right) = \dfrac{3\sqrt{2}}{2} - \dfrac{3\sqrt{2}}{2}i$

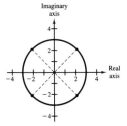

63. $\cos 0 + i \sin 0 = 1$

$\cos \dfrac{\pi}{2} + i \sin \dfrac{\pi}{2} = i$

$\cos \dfrac{2\pi}{3} + i \sin \dfrac{2\pi}{3} = -\dfrac{1}{2} + \dfrac{\sqrt{3}}{2}i$

$\cos \dfrac{4\pi}{3} + i \sin \dfrac{4\pi}{3} = -\dfrac{1}{2} - \dfrac{\sqrt{3}}{2}i$

$\cos \dfrac{3\pi}{2} + i \sin \dfrac{3\pi}{2} = -i$

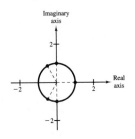

CUMULATIVE TEST for Chapters 6–8   (page 576)

1. 80°

2. $-\dfrac{2\pi}{3}$

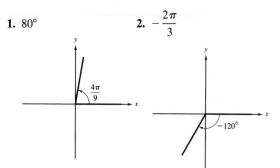

3. $\sin \theta = \dfrac{5}{13}$ $\csc \theta = \dfrac{13}{5}$

$\cos \theta = \dfrac{12}{13}$ $\sec \theta = \dfrac{13}{12}$

$\tan \theta = \dfrac{5}{12}$ $\cot \theta = \dfrac{12}{5}$

4. $\sin t = \dfrac{\sqrt{5}}{3}$, $\tan t = -\dfrac{\sqrt{5}}{2}$

5. -0.9490 **6.** $61.93°$, $298.07°$

7. (a)   **(b)**

(c)   **(d)**

8. (a) The graph of g is 10 units above the graph of f.
(b) The period of f is 2π and the period of g is 4.
(c) The graph of g is $\pi/4$ units to the left of the graph of f.
(d) The graph of g is a reflection in the x-axis of the graph of f.

9. $y = 3 \sin\left(2x - \dfrac{\pi}{2}\right)$ **10. (a)**

(b) 2π
(c) $x \approx 1.9$
(d) $f(2.7) \approx 2.8$

11. (a)

(b) No

(c) $t \approx 0.75$

12. (a) $\dfrac{\pi}{6}$ **(b)** $\dfrac{\pi}{3}$ **13.** $\sqrt{1 - 4x^2}$

14. 382 ft   **15.** $2 \csc \beta$

16. $\dfrac{\pi}{3}, \dfrac{\pi}{2}, \dfrac{3\pi}{2}, \dfrac{5\pi}{3}$ **17.** $\dfrac{4\sqrt{5}}{9}$ **18.** $\dfrac{\sqrt{2}}{4}\left(1 - \sqrt{3}\right)$

19. (a) $c \approx 57.57$, $B \approx 22.69°$, $C \approx 112.31°$

(b) $a \approx 9.91$, $B \approx 23.79°$, $C \approx 126.21°$

20. 42.5 ft

21. $\left(\dfrac{3\sqrt{3} - 5}{2}\right)i + \left(\dfrac{3 + 5\sqrt{3}}{2}\right)j \approx 0.10i + 5.83j$

22. Horizontal component: 115.91 ft/sec
Vertical component: 31.06 ft/sec

23. $z = 2\sqrt{2}(\cos 315° + i \sin 315°)$

$z^3 = 16\sqrt{2}(\cos 225° + i \sin 225°) = -16 - 16i$

CHAPTER 9

Section 9.1   (*page 588*)

WARM-UP

1.

2.

3.

4.

5. $y = x + 2$ **6.** $y = \frac{3}{2}x + 3$ **7.** $y = x + 2$

8. $y = \frac{6}{7}x + 4$ **9.** $y = -0.125x + 5.325$

10. $y = -\frac{29}{60}x + \frac{112}{15}$

1.

Year	1982	1983	1984	1985
Model number	99,132	101,779	104,427	107,074

Year	1986	1987	1988
Model number	109,722	112,369	115,017

3. $y = \frac{12}{5}x$ **5.** $y = 205x$ **7.** $y = \frac{7}{48}x$

9. $I = 0.075P$ **11.** $y = 0.0368x$, \$3128

13. $C = \frac{33}{13}I$

Inches	5	10	20	25	30
Centimeters	12.7	25.4	50.8	63.5	76.2

15. (a) 2 in.   **(b)** 15 lb   **17.** 39.47 lb

19. $y = 20,500 + 460t$ **21.** $y = 1299 - 289t$

23. (a) $V = 1200 - 240t$

(b)

(c) -240; This represents the annual depreciation.

25. $S = 0.85L$ **27.** $W = 9.25 + 1.10x$

29. $h = 7000 - 20t$, 2:14 P.M.

31. $N = 1200 + 50t$, 2200   **33.** Linear

35. Not linear   **37.**

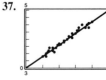

$y = 0.4x + 3$

39.

$y = -0.5x + 3$

41. $y = 31.5t + 110$

43. $y = 1.6t - 0.5$

Section 9.2   (*page 600*)

WARM-UP

1.

2.

3.

4.

5. x **6.** $-37v$ **7.** $2x^2 + 9$ **8.** -1
9. $x = 6$ **10.** $y = 1$

1. $(1, 2)$ **3.** $(-1, 2), (2, 5)$ **5.** $(0, 5), (3, 4)$
7. $(0, 0), (2, 4)$ **9.** $(-1, 1), (8, 4)$ **11.** $(5, 5)$
13. $\left(\frac{1}{2}, 3\right)$ **15.** $(1.5, 0.3)$ **17.** $\left(\frac{20}{3}, \frac{40}{3}\right)$ **19.** $(0, 0)$
21. $(1, 2)$ **23.** $\left(\frac{29}{10}, \frac{21}{10}\right), (-2, 0)$ **25.** $(0.28, 1.75)$
27. $(-1, 0), (0, 1), (1, 0)$ **29.** $\left(\frac{1}{2}, 2\right), \left(-4, -\frac{1}{4}\right)$

31.

33.

$(2, 2), (4, 0)$ No points of intersection

35.

$(3, \pm 4)$

37.

$(0, 1)$

39.

$(0, 0), (1, 1)$

41.

$(0, -13), (\pm 12, 5)$

43. 193 units   **45.** 233,334 units   **47.** 6400 units
49. \$13,000 at 8%, \$12,000 at 8.5%   **51.** \$8333.33
53. **(a)**

(b) 24.7 in.   **(c)** Doyle Rule   **55.** 8 mi $\times$ 12 mi
57. **(a)** $y = 2x$ **(b)** $y = 0$ **(c)** $y = x - 2$

Section 9.3   (*page 612*)

WARM-UP

1.

2.

3. $x - y + 4 = 0$ **4.** $5x + 3y - 28 = 0$ **5.** $-\frac{1}{2}$
6. $\frac{7}{4}$ **7.** Perpendicular   **8.** Parallel
9. Neither parallel nor perpendicular   **10.** Perpendicular

1. $(2, 0)$ **3.** $(-1, -1)$ **5.** Inconsistent
7. $(2a, 3a - 3)$ **9.** $\left(-\frac{1}{3}, -\frac{2}{3}\right)$ **11.** $\left(\frac{5}{2}, \frac{3}{4}\right)$

13. $(3, 4)$ **15.** $(4, -1)$ **17.** $(40, 40)$
19. Inconsistent   **21.** $\left(\frac{18}{5}, \frac{3}{5}\right)$ **23.** $(5, -2)$
25. $\left(a, \frac{5}{6}a - \frac{1}{2}\right)$ **27.** $\left(\frac{90}{31}, -\frac{67}{31}\right)$ **29.** $\left(-\frac{6}{35}, \frac{43}{35}\right)$
31. $(79{,}400, 398)$; The scale is incorrect for seeing the point of intersection.
33. 550 mph, 50 mph
35. $\frac{20}{3}$ gal of 20% solution, $\frac{10}{3}$ gal of 50% solution
37. $4000 at 10.5%, $8000 at 12%
39. 375 adults, 125 children

41.
(80, 10)

43.
(100, 200)

45.
(2,000,000, 100)

47. 75 mi, 225 mi

49. $y = 0.97x + 2.10$
53. $y = \frac{3}{4}x + \frac{4}{3}$
57.
$y = -240x + 685$
349 units

51. $y = 0.318x + 4.061$
55. $y = -2x + 4$
59. $\begin{aligned} x + 2y &= 8 \\ x + 4y &= 13 \end{aligned}$

Section 9.4 (page 624)

WARM-UP   **1.** $(15, 10)$ **2.** $\left(-2, -\frac{8}{3}\right)$ **3.** $(28, 4)$
4. $(4, 3)$ **5.** Not a solution   **6.** Not a solution
7. Solution   **8.** Solution   **9.** $5a + 2$
10. $a + 13$

1. $(1, 2, 3)$ **3.** $(2, -3, -2)$ **5.** $(5, -2, 0)$
7. Inconsistent   **9.** $\left(1, -\frac{3}{2}, \frac{1}{2}\right)$
11. $(-3a + 10, 5a - 7, a)$ **13.** $\left(13 - 4a, \frac{45}{2} - \frac{15}{2}a, a\right)$

15. $(-a, 2a - 1, a)$ **17.** $\left(\frac{1}{2} - \frac{3}{2}a, 1 - \frac{2}{3}a, a\right)$
19. $(1, 1, 1, 1)$ **21.** Inconsistent   **23.** $(0, 0, 0)$
25. $\left(-\frac{3}{5}a, \frac{4}{5}a, a\right)$ **27.** $y = 2x^2 + 3x - 4$
29. $y = x^2 - 4x + 3$ **31.** $x^2 + y^2 - 4x = 0$
33. $x^2 + y^2 - 6x - 8y = 0$
35. $a = -32$, $v_0 = 0$, $s_0 = 144$
37. $a = -32$, $v_0 = -32$, $s_0 = 500$
39. $4000 at 5%, $5000 at 6%, $7000 at 7%
41. $300,000 at 8%, $400,000 at 9%, $75,000 at 10%
43. $250{,}000 - \frac{1}{2}s$ in certificates of deposit, $125{,}000 + \frac{1}{2}s$ in municipal bonds, $125{,}000 - s$ in blue-chip stocks, s in growth stocks
45. 20 gal of spray X, 18 gal of spray Y, 16 gal of spray Z
47. 4 medium *or* 2 large, 1 medium 2 small
49. $t_1 = 96$ lb, $t_2 = 48$ lb, $a = -16$ ft/sec^2
51. $\dfrac{1}{2}\left(-\dfrac{2}{x} + \dfrac{1}{x - 1} + \dfrac{1}{x + 1}\right)$
53. $\dfrac{1}{2}\left(\dfrac{1}{x} - \dfrac{1}{x - 2} + \dfrac{2}{x + 3}\right)$
55. $y = -\frac{5}{24}x^2 - \frac{3}{10}x + \frac{41}{6}$ **57.** $y = x^2 - x$
59. (a)
(b) $y = 0.141x^2 - 4.427x + 58.400$
61. $\begin{aligned} 2x + 3y + z &= 7 \\ x - 2y + 4z &= 14 \\ x - 2y + 2z &= 10 \end{aligned}$

Section 9.5 (page 637)

WARM-UP   **1.** -3 **2.** 30   **3.** 6   **4.** $-\frac{1}{9}$
5. Solution   **6.** Not a solution   **7.** $(5, 2)$
8. $\left(\frac{12}{5}, -3\right)$ **9.** $(40, 14, 2)$ **10.** $\left(\frac{15}{2}, 4, 1\right)$

1. 3×2 **3.** 5×1 **5.** 2×2
7. Reduced row-echelon form
9. Not in row-echelon form
11. $\begin{bmatrix} 1 & 4 & 3 \\ 0 & 2 & -1 \end{bmatrix}$

13. $\begin{bmatrix} 1 & 1 & 4 & -1 \\ 0 & 5 & -2 & 6 \\ 0 & 3 & 20 & 4 \end{bmatrix}$, $\begin{bmatrix} 1 & 1 & 4 & -1 \\ 0 & 1 & -\frac{2}{5} & \frac{6}{5} \\ 0 & 3 & 20 & 4 \end{bmatrix}$

15. (a) $\begin{bmatrix} 1 & 2 & 3 \\ 0 & -5 & -10 \\ 3 & 1 & -1 \end{bmatrix}$ **(b)** $\begin{bmatrix} 1 & 2 & 3 \\ 0 & -5 & -10 \\ 0 & -5 & -10 \end{bmatrix}$

(c) $\begin{bmatrix} 1 & 2 & 3 \\ 0 & -5 & -10 \\ 0 & 0 & 0 \end{bmatrix}$ **(d)** $\begin{bmatrix} 1 & 2 & 3 \\ 0 & 1 & 2 \\ 0 & 0 & 0 \end{bmatrix}$

(e) $\begin{bmatrix} 1 & 0 & -1 \\ 0 & 1 & 2 \\ 0 & 0 & 0 \end{bmatrix}$

17. $\begin{bmatrix} 1 & 1 & 0 & 5 \\ 0 & 1 & 2 & 0 \\ 0 & 0 & 1 & -1 \end{bmatrix}$ **19.** $\begin{bmatrix} 1 & -1 & -1 & 1 \\ 0 & 1 & 6 & 3 \\ 0 & 0 & 0 & 0 \end{bmatrix}$

21. $\begin{bmatrix} 1 & 0 & 0 \\ 0 & 1 & 0 \\ 0 & 0 & 1 \end{bmatrix}$ **23.** $\begin{bmatrix} 1 & 2 & 0 & 0 \\ 0 & 0 & 1 & 0 \\ 0 & 0 & 0 & 1 \\ 0 & 0 & 0 & 0 \end{bmatrix}$

25. $4x + 3y = 8$
$\quad\ \ x - 2y = 3$

27. $x \qquad\ \ + 2z = -10$
$\qquad 3y - z = \quad 5$
$\quad 4x + 2y \qquad = \quad 3$

29. $x - 2y = \quad 4$
$\qquad\quad y = -3$
$(-2, -3)$

31. $x - y + 2z = \quad 4$
$\qquad\ y - z = \quad 2$
$\qquad\qquad z = -2$
$(8, 0, -2)$

33. $(7, -5)$ **35.** $(-4, -8, 2)$ **37.** $(3, 2)$
39. $(4, -2)$ **41.** $\left(\frac{1}{2}, -\frac{3}{4}\right)$ **43.** Inconsistent
45. $(4, -3, 2)$ **47.** $(2a + 1, 3a + 2, a)$
49. $(5a + 4, -3a + 2, a)$ **51.** $(0, 2 - 4a, a)$
53. $(1, 0, 4, -2)$ **55.** $(0, 0)$ **57.** $(-2a, a, a)$
59. \$800,000 at 8%, \$500,000 at 9%, \$200,000 at 12%

61. $\dfrac{1}{x - 1} + \dfrac{3}{x + 1} - \dfrac{2}{(x + 1)^2}$ **63.** $y = x^2 + 2x + 4$
65. $x^2 + y^2 - 5x - 3y + 6 = 0$

Section 9.6   (page 651)

WARM-UP   **1.** -27.5 **2.** -7
3. Not in reduced row-echelon form
4. Not in reduced row-echelon form
5. $\begin{bmatrix} -5 & 10 & : & 12 \\ 7 & -3 & : & 0 \\ -1 & 7 & : & 25 \end{bmatrix}$

6. $\begin{bmatrix} 10 & 15 & -9 & : & 42 \\ 6 & -5 & 0 & : & 0 \end{bmatrix}$
7. $(0, 2)$ **8.** $(2 + a, 3 - a, a)$
9. $(1 - 2a, a, -1)$ **10.** $(2, -1, -1)$

1. $x = -4, y = 22$ **3.** $x = 2, y = 3$
5. (a) $\begin{bmatrix} 3 & -2 \\ 1 & 7 \end{bmatrix}$ **(b)** $\begin{bmatrix} -1 & 0 \\ 3 & -9 \end{bmatrix}$ **(c)** $\begin{bmatrix} 3 & -3 \\ 6 & -3 \end{bmatrix}$
(d) $\begin{bmatrix} -1 & -1 \\ 8 & -19 \end{bmatrix}$

7. (a) $\begin{bmatrix} 7 & 3 \\ 1 & 9 \\ -2 & 15 \end{bmatrix}$ **(b)** $\begin{bmatrix} 5 & -5 \\ 3 & -1 \\ -4 & -5 \end{bmatrix}$
(c) $\begin{bmatrix} 18 & -3 \\ 6 & 12 \\ -9 & 15 \end{bmatrix}$ **(d)** $\begin{bmatrix} 16 & -11 \\ 8 & 2 \\ -11 & -5 \end{bmatrix}$

9. (a) $\begin{bmatrix} 3 & 3 & -2 & 1 & 1 \\ -2 & 5 & 7 & -6 & -8 \end{bmatrix}$
(b) $\begin{bmatrix} 1 & 1 & 0 & -1 & 1 \\ 4 & -3 & -11 & 6 & 6 \end{bmatrix}$
(c) $\begin{bmatrix} 6 & 6 & -3 & 0 & 3 \\ 3 & 3 & -6 & 0 & -3 \end{bmatrix}$
(d) $\begin{bmatrix} 4 & 4 & -1 & -2 & 3 \\ 9 & -5 & -24 & 12 & 11 \end{bmatrix}$

11. (a) $\begin{bmatrix} 0 & 15 \\ 6 & 12 \end{bmatrix}$ **(b)** $\begin{bmatrix} -2 & 2 \\ 31 & 14 \end{bmatrix}$ **(c)** $\begin{bmatrix} 9 & 6 \\ 12 & 12 \end{bmatrix}$

13. (a) $\begin{bmatrix} 0 & -10 \\ 10 & 0 \end{bmatrix}$ **(b)** $\begin{bmatrix} 0 & -10 \\ 10 & 0 \end{bmatrix}$ **(c)** $\begin{bmatrix} 8 & -6 \\ 6 & 8 \end{bmatrix}$

15. (a) $\begin{bmatrix} 6 & -21 & 15 \\ 8 & -23 & 19 \\ 4 & 7 & 5 \end{bmatrix}$ **(b)** $\begin{bmatrix} 9 & 0 & 13 \\ 7 & -2 & 21 \\ 1 & 4 & -19 \end{bmatrix}$

(c) $\begin{bmatrix} 20 & 7 & -8 \\ 24 & 7 & -2 \\ 2 & -5 & 30 \end{bmatrix}$

17. Not possible

19. $\begin{bmatrix} -1 & 19 \\ 4 & -27 \\ 0 & 14 \end{bmatrix}$ **21.** $\begin{bmatrix} 1 & 0 & 0 \\ 0 & 1 & 0 \\ 0 & 0 & \frac{7}{2} \end{bmatrix}$

23. $\begin{bmatrix} 60 & 72 \\ -20 & -24 \\ 10 & 12 \\ 60 & 72 \end{bmatrix}$ **25.** $\begin{bmatrix} -6 & -9 \\ -1 & 0 \\ 17 & -10 \end{bmatrix}$

27. $\begin{bmatrix} 3 & 3 \\ -\frac{1}{2} & 0 \\ -\frac{13}{2} & \frac{11}{2} \end{bmatrix}$

29. $A = \begin{bmatrix} -1 & 1 \\ -2 & 1 \end{bmatrix}$, $X = \begin{bmatrix} x \\ y \end{bmatrix}$, $B = \begin{bmatrix} 4 \\ 0 \end{bmatrix}$, $x = 4$, $y = 8$

31. $A = \begin{bmatrix} 1 & -2 & 3 \\ -1 & 3 & -1 \\ 2 & -5 & 5 \end{bmatrix}$, $X = \begin{bmatrix} x \\ y \\ z \end{bmatrix}$, $B = \begin{bmatrix} 9 \\ -6 \\ 17 \end{bmatrix}$,

$x = 1$, $y = -1$, $z = 2$

33. $AC = BC = \begin{bmatrix} 12 & -6 & 9 \\ 16 & -8 & 12 \\ 4 & -2 & 3 \end{bmatrix}$ **35.** $\begin{bmatrix} 72 & 48 & 24 \\ 36 & 108 & 72 \end{bmatrix}$

37. $AB = [\$1250 \quad \$1331.25 \quad \$981.25]$; The entries represent the profit from the two products at each of the three outlets.

39. (a) $18,300   **(b)** $21,260

(c) $\begin{bmatrix} \$15,770 & \$18,300 \\ \$26,500 & \$29,250 \\ \$21,260 & \$24,150 \end{bmatrix}$

The entries are the wholesale and retail price of the inventory at each outlet.

41. $\begin{bmatrix} 0.40 & 0.15 & 0.15 \\ 0.28 & 0.53 & 0.17 \\ 0.32 & 0.32 & 0.68 \end{bmatrix}$

Section 9.7 (page 659)

WARM-UP   **1.** $\begin{bmatrix} 4 & 24 \\ 0 & -16 \\ 48 & 8 \end{bmatrix}$ **2.** $\begin{bmatrix} \frac{11}{2} & 5 & 24 \\ \frac{1}{2} & 0 & 8 \\ 0 & 1 & 4 \end{bmatrix}$

3. $\begin{bmatrix} -5 & -2 & -13 \\ 4 & -13 & -2 \end{bmatrix}$ **4.** $\begin{bmatrix} -13 & 11 \\ -19 & 21 \end{bmatrix}$

5. $\begin{bmatrix} 1 & 0 \\ 0 & 1 \end{bmatrix}$ **6.** $\begin{bmatrix} 6 & 5 \\ 3 & -2 \end{bmatrix}$ **7.** $\begin{bmatrix} 1 & 0 & 0 \\ 0 & 1 & 0 \\ 0 & 0 & 1 \end{bmatrix}$

8. $\begin{bmatrix} 1 & 0 & 0 \\ 0 & 1 & 0 \\ 0 & 0 & 1 \end{bmatrix}$ **9.** $\begin{bmatrix} 1 & 0 & 3 & -2 \\ 0 & 1 & 4 & -3 \end{bmatrix}$

10. $\begin{bmatrix} 1 & 0 & 0 & -6 & -4 & 3 \\ 0 & 1 & 0 & 11 & 6 & -5 \\ 0 & 0 & 1 & -2 & -1 & 1 \end{bmatrix}$

Exercises 1–8 are proofs.

9. $\begin{bmatrix} \frac{1}{2} & 0 \\ 0 & \frac{1}{3} \end{bmatrix}$ **11.** $\begin{bmatrix} -3 & 2 \\ -2 & 1 \end{bmatrix}$ **13.** $\begin{bmatrix} 1 & -1 \\ 2 & -1 \end{bmatrix}$

15. Does not exist   **17.** Does not exist

19. $\begin{bmatrix} 1 & 1 & -1 \\ -3 & 2 & -1 \\ 3 & -3 & 2 \end{bmatrix}$ **21.** $\begin{bmatrix} -175 & 37 & -13 \\ 95 & -20 & 7 \\ 14 & -3 & 1 \end{bmatrix}$

23. $\frac{1}{2}\begin{bmatrix} -3 & 3 & 2 \\ 9 & -7 & -6 \\ -2 & 2 & 2 \end{bmatrix}$ **25.** $\frac{5}{11}\begin{bmatrix} 0 & -4 & 2 \\ -22 & 11 & 11 \\ 22 & -6 & -8 \end{bmatrix}$

27. $\begin{bmatrix} 1 & 0 & 0 \\ -0.75 & 0.25 & 0 \\ 0.35 & -0.25 & 0.2 \end{bmatrix}$ **29.** Does not exist

31. $\begin{bmatrix} -\frac{1}{8} & 0 & 0 & 0 \\ 0 & 1 & 0 & 0 \\ 0 & 0 & \frac{1}{4} & 0 \\ 0 & 0 & 0 & -\frac{1}{5} \end{bmatrix}$ **33.** $\begin{bmatrix} -24 & 7 & 1 & -2 \\ -10 & 3 & 0 & -1 \\ -29 & 7 & 3 & -2 \\ 12 & -3 & -1 & 1 \end{bmatrix}$

35. $(2, -2)$ **37.** Inconsistent   **39.** $\left(\frac{2}{3}, \frac{1}{2}\right)$

41. $(-1, 3, 2)$ **43.** $\left(\frac{5}{16}a + \frac{13}{16}, \frac{19}{16}a + \frac{11}{16}, a\right)$

45. $(5, 0, -2, 3)$

47. $10,000 in AAA rated bonds, $5000 in A rated bonds, $10,000 in B rated bonds

49. $9000 in AAA rated bonds, $1000 in A rated bonds, $2000 in B rated bonds

51. $I_1 = -3$ amps, $I_2 = 8$ amps, $I_3 = 5$ amps

Section 9.8 (page 669)

WARM-UP   **1.** Line   **2.** Line   **3.** Parabola
4. Parabola   **5.** Circle   **6.** Ellipse   **7.** $(1, 1)$
8. $(2, 0)$ **9.** $(2, 1)$, $\left(-\frac{5}{2}, -\frac{5}{4}\right)$ **10.** $(2, 3)$, $(3, 2)$

1. f   **2.** h   **3.** e   **4.** c   **5.** a   **6.** g
7. b   **8.** d

9.   **11.**

13.

15.

33.

35.

17.

19.

37.

39.

21.

23.

41. $2 \leq x \leq 5$
$1 \leq y \leq 7$

43. $y \leq \frac{3}{2}x$
$y \leq -x + 5$
$y \geq 0$

45. $x^2 + y^2 \leq 16$
$x \geq 0$
$y \geq 0$

47. $x + \frac{3}{2}y \leq 12$
$\frac{4}{3}x + \frac{3}{2}y \leq 15$
$x \geq 0$
$y \geq 0$

25.

27.

49. $x + y \leq 20{,}000$
$y \geq 2x$
$x \geq 5{,}000$
$y \geq 5{,}000$

29.

31.

51. $20x + 10y \geq 280$
$15x + 10y \geq 160$
$10x + 20y \geq 180$
$x \geq 0$
$y \geq 0$

53. Consumer surplus: 1600; Producer surplus: 400
55. Consumer surplus: 5000; Producer surplus: 5000
57. Consumer surplus: 40,000,000; Producer surplus: 20,000,000

59.
$$xy \geq 500$$
$$2x + \pi y \geq 125$$
$$x \geq 0$$
$$y \geq 0$$

Chapter 9 Review Exercises (*page 671*)

1. $(1, 1)$ **3.** $(5, 4)$ **5.** $(0, 0), (2, 8), (-2, 8)$

7. $\left(\frac{5}{2}, 3\right)$ **9.** $(0, 0)$ **11.** $\left(\frac{14}{5} + \frac{8}{5}a, a\right)$

13.

$(0, 0), (-3, 3)$

15.

$(4, 4)$

17. 4762 units

19. 40 gal of the 75% solution, 60 gal of the 50% solution

21. Pittsburgh to Philadelphia: 218.75 mi/hr; Philadelphia to Pittsburgh: 193.75 mi/hr

23. $\left(\frac{500,000}{7}, \frac{159}{7}\right)$ **25.** $(4.8, 4.4, -1.6)$

27. $(3a + 4, 2a + 5, a)$ **29.** $(-3a + 2, 5a + 6, a)$

31. $(2, -3, 3)$ **33.** $\left(-2a + \frac{3}{2}, 2a + 1, a\right)$

35. $y = 2x^2 + x - 6$

37. $x^2 + y^2 - 4x + 2y - 4 = 0$

39. 10 gal of spray X, 5 gal of spray Y, 12 gal of spray Z

41. $y = 1.01x + 1.54$ **43.** $\begin{bmatrix} -13 & -8 & 18 \\ 0 & 11 & -19 \end{bmatrix}$

45. $\begin{bmatrix} 14 & -2 & 8 \\ 14 & -10 & 40 \\ 36 & -12 & 48 \end{bmatrix}$ **47.** $\begin{bmatrix} 44 & 4 \\ 20 & 8 \end{bmatrix}$

49. $\begin{bmatrix} 4 & 6 & 3 \\ 0 & 6 & -10 \\ 0 & 0 & 6 \end{bmatrix}$ **51.** $\begin{bmatrix} \frac{1}{5} & \frac{1}{5} \\ \frac{1}{10} & -\frac{1}{15} \end{bmatrix}$

53. $\begin{bmatrix} \frac{1}{2} & -1 & -\frac{1}{2} \\ \frac{1}{2} & -\frac{2}{3} & -\frac{5}{6} \\ 0 & \frac{2}{3} & \frac{1}{3} \end{bmatrix}$ **55.** $(-3, 1)$ **57.** $(1, 1, -2)$

59. $(2, -4, 6)$ **61.** Inconsistent

63. 8 carnations, 4 roses

65.

67.

69.

71.

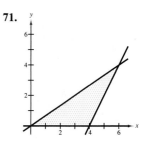

73.
$$-x + y \leq 4$$
$$2x + y \leq 22$$
$$-x + y \geq -2$$
$$-2x + y \geq 7$$

75.
$$x + y \leq 1500$$
$$x \geq 400$$
$$y \geq 600$$

77. Consumer surplus: 4,500,000; Producer surplus: 9,000,000

CHAPTER 10

Section 10.1 (*page 684*)

WARM-UP   **1.** $\frac{4}{5}$ **2.** $\frac{1}{3}$ **3.** $(2n + 1)(2n - 1)$

4. $(2n - 1)(2n - 3)$ **5.** $(n - 1)(n - 2)$

6. $(n + 1)(n + 2)$ **7.** $\frac{1}{3}$ **8.** 24   **9.** $\frac{13}{24}$

10. $\frac{3}{4}$

1. 3, 5, 7, 9, 11   **3.** 2, 4, 8, 16, 32

5. $-2, 4, -8, 16, -32$ **7.** $0, 1, 0, \frac{1}{2}, 0$

9. $\frac{5}{2}, \frac{11}{4}, \frac{23}{8}, \frac{47}{16}, \frac{95}{32}$ **11.** $1, \frac{1}{2^{3/2}}, \frac{1}{3^{3/2}}, \frac{1}{4^{3/2}}, \frac{1}{5^{3/2}}$

13. $3, \frac{9}{2}, \frac{9}{2}, \frac{27}{8}, \frac{81}{40}$ **15.** $-1, \frac{1}{4}, -\frac{1}{9}, \frac{1}{16}, -\frac{1}{25}$

17. $3, 4, 6, 10, 18$ **19.** $\frac{1}{30}$ **21.** $n + 1$

23. $\dfrac{1}{2n(2n + 1)}$ **25.** $a_n = 3n - 2$ **27.** $a_n = n^2 - 1$

29. $a_n = \dfrac{(-1)^{n+1}}{2^n}$ **31.** $a_n = 1 + \dfrac{1}{n}$ **33.** $a_n = \dfrac{1}{n!}$

35. $a_n = (-1)^{n+1}$ **37.** 35 **39.** 40 **41.** 30

43. $\dfrac{9}{5}$ **45.** 238 **47.** 56 **49.** $\dfrac{47}{60}$ **51.** $\sum\limits_{i=1}^{9} \dfrac{1}{3i}$

53. $\sum\limits_{i=1}^{8} \left[2\left(\dfrac{i}{8}\right) + 3 \right]$ **55.** $\sum\limits_{i=1}^{6} (-1)^{i+1} 3^i$

57. $\sum\limits_{i=1}^{20} \dfrac{(-1)^{i+1}}{i^2}$ **59.** $\sum\limits_{i=1}^{5} \dfrac{2^i - 1}{2^{i+1}}$

61. (a) $A_1 = \$5100.00$, $A_2 = \$5202.00$, $A_3 = \$5306.04$, $A_4 = \$5412.16$, $A_5 = \$5520.40$, $A_6 = \$5630.81$, $A_7 = \$5743.43$, $A_8 = \$5858.30$
(b) $\$11,040.20$

63. (a) $a_0 = 242.67$, $a_1 = 285.34$, $a_2 = 328.01$, $a_3 = 370.68$, $a_4 = 413.35$, $a_5 = 456.02$, $a_6 = 498.69$, $a_7 = 541.36$

(b)

65. 16.02
67. Proof
69. (a) $1, 1, 2, 3, 5, 8, 13, 21, 34, 55, 89, 144$
(b) $2, \frac{3}{2}, \frac{5}{3}, \frac{8}{5}, \frac{13}{8}, \frac{21}{13}, \frac{34}{21}, \frac{55}{34}, \frac{89}{55}, \frac{144}{89}$

Section 10.2   (page 696)

WARM-UP   **1.** 36 **2.** 240 **3.** $\frac{11}{2}$ **4.** $\frac{10}{3}$ **5.** 18
6. 4 **7.** 143 **8.** 160 **9.** 430 **10.** 256

1. Arithmetic sequence, $d = 3$
3. Not an arithmetic sequence
5. Arithmetic sequence, $d = -\frac{1}{4}$
7. Not an arithmetic sequence
9. Arithmetic sequence, $d = 0.4$
11. $8, 11, 14, 17, 20$; Arithmetic sequence, $d = 3$
13. $\frac{1}{2}, \frac{1}{3}, \frac{1}{4}, \frac{1}{5}, \frac{1}{6}$; Not an arithmetic sequence

15. $97, 94, 91, 88, 85$; Arithmetic sequence, $d = -3$
17. $1, 4, \frac{7}{3}, \frac{7}{2}, \frac{13}{5}$; Not an arithmetic sequence
19. $a_n = 1 + (n - 1)3$ **21.** $a_n = 100 + (n - 1)(-8)$
23. $a_n = x + (n - 1)(2x)$ **25.** $a_n = 4 + (n - 1)\left(-\frac{5}{2}\right)$
27. $a_n = 5 + (n - 1)\left(\frac{10}{3}\right)$ **29.** $a_n = 100 + (n - 1)(-3)$
31. $5, 11, 17, 23, 29, \ldots$
33. $-2.6, -3.0, -3.4, -3.8, -4.2, \ldots$
35. $\frac{3}{2}, \frac{5}{4}, 1, \frac{3}{4}, \frac{1}{2}, \ldots$ **37.** $2, 6, 10, 14, 18, \ldots$
39. $-2, 2, 6, 10, 14, \ldots$ **41.** 620 **43.** 4600
45. 265 **47.** 4000 **49.** 1275 **51.** $25,250$
53. 355 **55.** $126,750$ **57.** 520 **59.** $44,625$
61. $9, 13$ **63.** $\frac{15}{4}, \frac{9}{2}, \frac{21}{4}$ **65.** $10,000$
67. (a) $\$35,000$ (b) $\$187,500$ **69.** 2340
71. 470 bricks

Section 10.3   (page 704)

WARM-UP   **1.** $\frac{64}{125}$ **2.** $\frac{9}{16}$ **3.** $\frac{1}{16}$ **4.** $\frac{5}{81}$

5. $6n^3$ **6.** $27n^4$ **7.** $4n^3$ **8.** n^2 **9.** $\dfrac{2^n}{81^n}$

10. $\dfrac{3}{16^n}$

1. Geometric sequence, $r = 3$
3. Not a geometric sequence
5. Geometric sequence, $r = -\frac{1}{2}$
7. Not a geometric sequence
9. Not a geometric sequence   **11.** $2, 6, 18, 54, 162, \ldots$
13. $1, \frac{1}{2}, \frac{1}{4}, \frac{1}{8}, \frac{1}{16}, \ldots$ **15.** $5, -\frac{1}{2}, \frac{1}{20}, -\frac{1}{200}, \frac{1}{2000}, \ldots$
17. $1, e, e^2, e^3, e^4$ **19.** $3, \dfrac{3x}{2}, \dfrac{3x^2}{4}, \dfrac{3x^3}{8}, \dfrac{3x^4}{16}, \ldots$
21. $\left(\dfrac{1}{2}\right)^7$ **23.** $-\dfrac{2}{3^{10}}$ **25.** $100e^{8x}$ **27.** $500(1.02)^{39}$
29. 9 **31.** $-\frac{2}{9}$
33. (a) $\$2593.74$ (b) $\$2653.30$ (c) $\$2685.06$
(d) $\$2707.04$ (e) $\$2717.91$
35. $\$22,689.45$ **37.** 511 **39.** 43 **41.** 6.4
43. $29,921.31$ **45.** 2092.60 **47.** $\$7808.24$
49. Proof   **51.** (a) $\$26,198.27$ (b) $\$26,263.88$
53. (a) $\$637,678.02$ (b) $\$645,861.43$
57. $\$3048.1$ million   **59.** $\$3,623,993.23$ **61.** 2
63. $\frac{2}{3}$ **65.** $\frac{16}{3}$ **67.** 32 **69.** $\frac{8}{3}$
71.

The horizontal asymptote of the graph of f is the sum of the series.

73. 152.42 ft

Section 10.4 (*page 717*)

WARM-UP   **1.** 24   **2.** 40   **3.** $\frac{77}{60}$ **4.** $\frac{7}{2}$

5. $\frac{2k+5}{5}$ **6.** $\frac{3k+1}{6}$ **7.** $8 \cdot 2^{2k} = 2^{2k+3}$ **8.** $\frac{1}{9}$

9. $\frac{1}{k}$ **10.** $\frac{4}{5}$

1. $\dfrac{5}{(k+1)(k+2)}$ **3.** $\dfrac{(k+1)^2(k+2)^2}{4}$

Exercises 5–17 are proofs.

19. 210   **21.** 91   **23.** 225   **25.** 2275   **27.** 70

29. $n(2n+1)$ **31.** $10[1-(0.9)^n]$ **33.** $\dfrac{n}{2(n+1)}$

Exercises 35–45 are proofs.

47. 1, 3, 5, 7, 9   **49.** 4, 2, −2, −4, −2

51. 0 3 6 9 12
    3 3 3 3
      0 0 0
Linear

53. 3 1 −2 −6 −11
    −2 −3 −4 −5
     −1 −1 −1
Quadratic

55. 0 1 3 6 10
    1 2 3 4
     1 1 1
Quadratic

57. 2 4 6 8 10
    2 2 2 2
     0 0 0
Linear

59. 1 2 6 15 31
    1 4 9 16
     3 5 7
Neither linear nor quadratic

61. $f(n) = n^2 - n + 3$ **63.** $f(n) = \frac{1}{2}n^2 + n - 3$

Section 10.5 (*page 725*)

WARM-UP   **1.** $5x^5 + 15x^2$ **2.** $x^3 + 5x^2 - 3x - 15$

3. $x^2 + 8x + 16$ **4.** $4x^2 - 12x + 9$ **5.** $\dfrac{3x^3}{y}$

6. $-32z^5$ **7.** 120   **8.** 336   **9.** 720   **10.** 20

1. 10   **3.** 1   **5.** 15,504   **7.** 4950   **9.** 4950

11. $x^4 + 4x^3 + 6x^2 + 4x + 1$

13. $a^3 + 6a^2 + 12a + 8$

15. $y^4 - 8y^3 + 24y^2 - 32y + 16$

17. $x^5 + 5x^4y + 10x^3y^2 + 10x^2y^3 + 5xy^4 + y^5$

19. $r^6 + 18r^5s + 135r^4s^2 + 540r^3s^3 + 1215r^2s^4 + 1458rs^5 + 729s^6$

21. $x^5 - 5x^4y + 10x^3y^2 - 10x^2y^3 + 5xy^4 - y^5$

23. $1 - 6x + 12x^2 - 8x^3$

25. $x^8 + 20x^6 + 150x^4 + 500x^2 + 625$

27. $\dfrac{1}{x^5} + \dfrac{5y}{x^4} + \dfrac{10y^2}{x^3} + \dfrac{10y^3}{x^2} + \dfrac{5y^4}{x} + y^5$

29. $2x^4 - 24x^3 + 113x^2 - 246x + 207$ **31.** −4

33. $2035 + 828i$ **35.** 1

37. $32t^5 - 80t^4s + 80t^3s^2 - 40t^2s^3 + 10ts^4 - s^5$

39. $81 - 216z + 216z^2 - 96z^3 + 16z^4$ **41.** 1,732,104

43. 180   **45.** −326,592   **47.** 210   **49.** $\frac{35}{128} \approx 0.273$

51. $\frac{1120}{6561} \approx 0.171$ **53.** 1.172   **55.** 510,568.785

57.

Shift 2 units to the right.
$g(x) = -x^2 + 7x - 8$

59.

Shift 4 units to the left.
$g(x) = x^3 + 12x^2 + 44x + 48$

61. $g(t) = 0.2187t^2 + 5.0455t + 55.255$

Section 10.6 (*page 737*)

WARM-UP   **1.** 6656   **2.** 291,600   **3.** 7960

4. 13,800   **5.** 792   **6.** 2300

7. $n(n-1)(n-2)(n-3)$ **8.** $n(n-1)(2n-1)$

9. $n!$ **10.** $n!$

1. 7   **3.** 12   **5.** 12   **7.** 6,760,000   **9.** 64

11. (a) 900   **(b)** 648   **(c)** 180   **(d)** 600

13. 64,000   **15. (a)** 720   **(b)** 48   **17.** 24

19. 336   **21.** 1,860,480   **23.** 9900   **25.** 120

27. ABCD, ABDC, ACBD, ACDB, ADBC, ADCB, BACD, BADC, CABD, CADB, DABC, DACB, BCAD, BDAC, CBAD, CDAB, DBAC, DCAB, BCDA, BDCA, CBDA, CDBA, DBCA, DCBA

29. 120   **31.** 11,880   **33.** 420   **35.** 1260

37. 2520

39. AB, AC, AD, AE, AF, BC, BD, BE, BF, CD, CE, CF, DE, DF, EF

41. 4845   **43.** 3,838,380   **45.** 3,921,225   **47.** 560

49. (a) 70   **(b)** 30   **51. (a)** 70   **(b)** 54   **(c)** 16

53. 5   **55.** 20   **57.** $n = 5$ or $n = 6$

Section 10.7 (*page 750*)

1. {(h, 1), (h, 2), (h, 3), (h, 4), (h, 5), (h, 6), (t, 1), (t, 2), (t, 3), (t, 4), (t, 5), (t, 6)}
3. {ABC, ACB, BAC, BCA, CAB, CBA}
5. {AB, AC, AD, AE, BC, BD, BE, CD, CE, DE}
7. $\frac{3}{8}$ **9.** $\frac{7}{8}$ **11.** $\frac{3}{13}$ **13.** $\frac{5}{13}$ **15.** $\frac{1}{12}$ **17.** $\frac{7}{12}$
19. $\frac{1}{3}$ **21.** $\frac{1}{5}$ **23.** $\frac{2}{5}$ **25.** 0.3   **27.** 0.85
29. (a) $\frac{112}{209}$ **(b)** $\frac{97}{209}$ **(c)** $\frac{274}{627}$
31. $P(\{\text{Taylor wins}\}) = 0.50$, $P(\{\text{Moore wins}\}) = P(\{\text{Jenkins wins}\}) = 0.25$
33. (a) $\frac{21}{1292} \approx 0.016$ **(b)** $\frac{225}{646} \approx 0.348$ **(c)** $\frac{49}{323} \approx 0.152$
35. (a) $\frac{1}{3}$ **(b)** $\frac{5}{8}$ **37. (a)** $\frac{1}{120}$ **(b)** $\frac{1}{24}$
39. (a) $\frac{1}{169}$ **(b)** $\frac{1}{221}$ **41. (a)** $\frac{14}{55}$ **(b)** $\frac{12}{55}$ **(c)** $\frac{54}{55}$
43. (a) $\frac{1}{4}$ **(b)** $\frac{1}{2}$ **(c)** $\frac{9}{100}$ **(d)** $\frac{1}{30}$
45. (a) 0.9702   **(b)** 0.9998   **(c)** 0.0002
47. (a) $\frac{1}{1024}$ **(b)** $\frac{243}{1024}$ **(c)** $\frac{781}{1024}$
49. (a) $\frac{1}{16}$ **(b)** $\frac{1}{8}$ **(c)** $\frac{15}{16}$ **51.** 0.1024

Chapter 10 Review Exercises (*page 753*)

1. $\sum_{k=1}^{20} \frac{1}{2k}$ **3.** $\sum_{k=1}^{9} \frac{k}{k+1}$ **5.** 30   **7.** 80
9. 127   **11.** 8   **13.** 12   **15.** 88   **17.** 418
19. 3, 7, 11, 15, 19   **21.** 1, 4, 7, 10, 13
23. $a_n = 100 + (n-1)(-3)$, 1430   **25.** 25,250
27. $4, -1, \frac{1}{4}, -\frac{1}{16}, \frac{1}{64}$
29. $9, 6, 4, \frac{8}{3}, \frac{16}{9}$ or $9, -6, 4, -\frac{8}{3}, \frac{16}{9}$
31. $a_n = 16\left(-\frac{1}{2}\right)^{n-1}$, 10.67
33. (a) $a_t = 120,000(0.7)^t$ **(b)** \$20,168.50
35. \$5111.82
Exercises 37 and 39 are proofs.
41. 15   **43.** 53,130
45. $\frac{x^4}{16} + \frac{x^3 y}{2} + \frac{3x^2 y^2}{2} + 2xy^3 + y^4$
47. $\frac{64}{x^6} + \frac{576}{x^4} + \frac{2160}{x^2} - 4320 + 4860x^2 - 2916x^4 + 729x^6$
49. $41 + 840i$ **51. (a)** 1   **(b)** 6   **(c)** 15
53. 118,813,760   **55.** $\frac{1}{9}$
57. $P(\{3\}) = \frac{1}{6}$
$P(\{(1, 5), (5, 1), (2, 4), (4, 2), (3, 3)\}) = \frac{5}{36}$
59. $\frac{31}{32}$ **61.** $\frac{123,552}{2,598,960} \approx 0.0475$

CHAPTER 11

Section 11.1 (*page 764*)

WARM-UP

1.   **2.**

3.   **4.**

5.   **6.**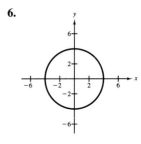

7. 10   **8.** $5 \tan^2 \theta$
9. $\sec^2 x + \tan^2 x$ **10.** $\frac{1}{2} \sin \theta$

1.

$y = -2x$

3.

$2x - 3y + 5 = 0$

5.

$y = 16x^2$

7.

$y = (x - 1)^2$

9.

$y = \frac{1}{2}\sqrt[3]{x}$

11.

$x^2 + y^2 = 9$

13.

$y = 2 - 2x^2, \; -1 \le x \le 1$

15.

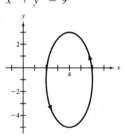

$\dfrac{(x - 4)^2}{4} + \dfrac{(y + 1)^2}{16} = 1$

17.

$\sqrt[3]{y} = \dfrac{1}{x}, \; y = \dfrac{1}{x^3}, \; x > 0, \; y > 0$

19.

$y = \ln x$

21. Each curve represents a portion of the line $y = 2x + 1$.

Domain	Orientation
(a) $-\infty < x < \infty$	Up
(b) $-1 \le x \le 1$	Oscillates
(c) $0 < x < \infty$	Down
(d) $0 < x < \infty$	Up

23. $y - y_1 = \dfrac{y_2 - y_1}{x_2 - x_1}(x - x_1)$

25. $\dfrac{(x - h)^2}{a^2} + \dfrac{(y - k)^2}{b^2} = 1$

27. $x = 5t$
$y = -2t$
Solution not unique

29. $x = 2 + 4\cos\theta$
$y = 1 + 4\sin\theta$
Solution not unique

31. $x = 5\cos\theta$
$y = 3\sin\theta$
Solution not unique

33. $x = 4\sec\theta$
$y = 3\tan\theta$
Solution not unique

35. *Examples*

$x = t, \; y = t^3$
$x = \sqrt[3]{t}, \; y = t$
$x = \tan t, \; y = \tan^3 t$

37.

39.

41.

43. b

45. d

47. $x = a\theta - b\sin\theta$ and
$y = a - b\cos\theta$.

Section 11.2 (*page 772*)

WARM-UP

1. $\dfrac{3\pi}{4}$ **2.** $\dfrac{7\pi}{6}$ **3.** $\sin\theta = \dfrac{\sqrt{5}}{5}$, $\cos\theta = \dfrac{2\sqrt{5}}{5}$

4. $\sin\theta = -\dfrac{3}{5}$, $\cos\theta = \dfrac{4}{5}$ **5.** $\dfrac{3\pi}{4}$ **6.** 0.5880

7. $-\dfrac{\sqrt{3}}{2}$ **8.** $-\dfrac{\sqrt{2}}{2}$ **9.** -0.3090 **10.** 0.9735

1.

(0, 4)

3.

$$\left(\frac{\sqrt{2}}{2}, \frac{\sqrt{2}}{2}\right)$$

17.

$$\left(\sqrt{6}, \frac{5\pi}{4}\right), \left(-\sqrt{6}, \frac{\pi}{4}\right)$$

19.

$$\left(2\sqrt{13}, 0.983\right), \left(-2\sqrt{13}, 4.124\right)$$

21. $r = 3$ **23.** $r = 2a \cos \theta$ **25.** $r = 4 \csc \theta$

27. $r = 10 \sec \theta$ **29.** $r = \dfrac{-2}{3 \cos \theta - \sin \theta}$

31. $r^2 = 4 \sec \theta \csc \theta = 8 \csc 2\theta$

33. $r^2 = 9 \cos 2\theta$ **35.** $x^2 + y^2 - 4y = 0$

37. $\sqrt{3}x - 3y = 0$ **39.** $y = 2$

41. $(x^2 + y^2)^2 = 6x^2y - 2y^3$

43. $4x^2 - 5y^2 - 36y - 36 = 0$

45. $x^2 + y^2 = 9$ **47.** $x - y = 0$

5.

$$\left(2, -2\sqrt{3}\right)$$

7.

(0, 0)

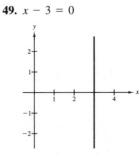

49. $x - 3 = 0$ **51.** Proof

53. $(x - h)^2 + (y - k)^2 = h^2 + k^2$
Center: (h, k)
Radius: $\sqrt{h^2 + k^2}$

9.

(−1.004, 0.996)

11.

$$\left(\sqrt{2}, \frac{\pi}{4}\right), \left(-\sqrt{2}, \frac{5\pi}{4}\right)$$

13.

(6, π), (−6, 0)

15.

(5, 2.214), (−5, 5.356)

Section 11.3   *(page 781)*

WARM-UP   **1.** Amplitude: 5; Period: $\pi/2$

2. Amplitude: 3; Period: 1

3. Amplitude: 5; Period: $\frac{4}{5}$ **4.** Amplitude: $\frac{1}{2}$; Period: 4π

5.

6.

7.

8.

9. $\dfrac{1}{2}\left(\sqrt{3}\,\sin x - \cos x\right)$ **10.** $\dfrac{\sqrt{2}}{2}(\cos x + \sin x)$

1. Polar axis   **3.** $\theta = \dfrac{\pi}{2}$ **5.** $\theta = \dfrac{\pi}{2}$, polar axis, pole

7. Maximum: $|r| = 5$ when $\theta = 0, \dfrac{\pi}{3}, \dfrac{2\pi}{3}$

9. Maximum: $|r| = 20$ when $\theta = \dfrac{3\pi}{2}$

Zero: $r = 0$ when $\theta = \dfrac{\pi}{2}$

11.

13.

15.

17.

19.

21.

23.

25.

27.

29.

31. $y = \pm \left|\dfrac{x}{x+1}\right| \sqrt{3 - 2x - x^2}$ **33.** Proof

35. (a) $r = 2 - \dfrac{\sqrt{2}}{2}(\sin\theta - \cos\theta)$

(b) $r = 2 + \cos\theta$
(c) $r = 2 + \sin\theta$
(d) $r = 2 - \cos\theta$

37. (a)   (b)

Section 11.4   (page 789)

WARM-UP

1. $\left(\dfrac{3\sqrt{2}}{2}, -\dfrac{3\sqrt{2}}{2}\right)$ **2.** $\left(-2, -2\sqrt{3}\right)$

3. $\left(3, \dfrac{3\pi}{2}\right), \left(-3, \dfrac{\pi}{2}\right)$ **4.** $(13, 1.9656), (-13, 5.1072)$

5. $r = 5$ **6.** $r^3 = 4 \sec^2 \theta \csc \theta$
7. $y = -4$ **8.** $x^2 + y^2 - 4x = 0$
9.   **10.**

---

1. c   **3.** a   **5.** b
7.   **9.**

11.   **13.**

15.   **17.**

19. $r = \dfrac{1}{1 - \cos \theta}$ **21.** $r = \dfrac{1}{2 + \sin \theta}$

23. $r = \dfrac{2}{1 + 2 \cos \theta}$ **25.** $r = \dfrac{2}{1 - \sin \theta}$

27. $r = \dfrac{10}{1 - \cos \theta}$ **29.** $r = \dfrac{16}{5 + 3 \cos \theta}$

31. $r = \dfrac{20}{3 - 2 \cos \theta}$ **33.** $r = \dfrac{9}{4 - 5 \sin \theta}$

35. Proof   **37.** $r^2 = \dfrac{24{,}336}{169 - 25 \cos^2 \theta}$

39. $r^2 = \dfrac{144}{25 \cos^2 \theta - 9}$ **41.** $r^2 = \dfrac{144}{25 \cos^2 \theta - 16}$

43.   **45.** Proof

47. $r = \dfrac{9.2931 \times 10^7}{1 - 0.0167 \cos \theta}$, 9.1405×10^7, 9.4509×10^7

49. $r = \dfrac{8200}{1 + \sin \theta}$

Chapter 11 Review Exercises (*page 792*)

1. $2x - y = 0$

3. $3x + 4y - 11 = 0$

5. $y = \dfrac{1}{x^2}$

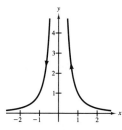

7. $x^2 + y^2 = 36$

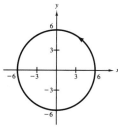

9. $x^{2/3} + \left(\dfrac{y}{4}\right)^{2/3} = 1$

11. $xy = 1, \; x > 0, \; y > 0$

13. Circle

15. Rose curve

17. Cardioid

19. Limaçon

21. Rose curve

23. Lemniscate

25. Line

27. Parabola

29. $x^2 + y^2 - 3x = 0$ **31.** $x^2 + 4y - 4 = 0$

33. $(x^2 + y^2)^2 - x^2 + y^2 = 0$ **35.** $r = a \cos^2 \theta \sin \theta$

37. $r = 10 \sin \theta$ **39.** $r = \dfrac{4}{1 - \cos \theta}$

41. $r = \dfrac{5}{3 - 2 \cos \theta}$

43. $x = -3 + 4 \cos \theta, \; y = 4 + 3 \sin \theta$

45. Proof

47.

CUMULATIVE TEST for Chapters 9–11 (*page 793*)

1. $n = 3250 + 80t, 4050$ **2.** $y = 750 - 48t$

3. $(1, 2), (-\frac{3}{2}, \frac{3}{4})$ **4.** $(2, -1)$ **5.** $(1, -2, 1)$
6. $a = -6$

7. $\begin{bmatrix} 11 & -6 \\ 5 & 3 \\ -7 & 0 \end{bmatrix}$ **8.** $\begin{bmatrix} 9 & 1 \\ 7 & -7 \\ 15 & -10 \end{bmatrix}$

9. $\begin{bmatrix} -175 & 37 & -13 \\ 95 & -20 & 7 \\ 14 & -3 & 1 \end{bmatrix}$

10.

11. 920   **12.** $54, -18, 6, -1, \frac{2}{3}$ **13.** Proof
14. $z^4 - 12z^3 + 54z^2 - 108z + 81$
15. $x = 144, p = \$36$
16. $x^2 + y^2 - \frac{41}{3}x - 4y = 0$ **17.** \$402,493
18. $x = 2 + 4t, y = -3 + 7t$

19. $\dfrac{(x-3)^2}{9} + \dfrac{(y-2)^2}{4} = 1$ **20.** $x^2 + y^2 - 6x = 0$

21. Vertical asymptote: $x = -2$ **22.** $r = \dfrac{2}{1 - \cos\theta}$

APPENDIX A   (*page A7*)

WARM-UP   **1.** $y = 4 - 3x$ **2.** $y = x$
3. $y = \frac{2}{3}(1 - x)$ **4.** $y = \frac{2}{5}(2x + 1)$
5. $y = \frac{1}{4}(5 - 3x)$ **6.** $y = \frac{2}{3}(-x + 3)$
7. $y = 4 - x^2$ **8.** $y = \frac{2}{3}(x^2 - 1)$
9. $y = \pm\sqrt{4 - x^2}$ **10.** $y = \pm\sqrt{x^2 - 9}$

1.   **3.**
5.   **7.**
9.   **11.**
13.   **15.**
17.   **19.**

21. (d)   **23.** (a)   **25.** (i)   **27.** (j)   **29.** (e)

31.

33.

47.

49. 0.59

35.
```
Xmin = -10
Xmax = 10
Xscl = 1
Ymin = -12
Ymax = 30
Yscl = 6
Xres = 1
```

37.
```
Xmin = -10
Xmax = 10
Xscl = 1
Ymin = -10
Ymax = 10
Yscl = 1
Xres = 1
```

51.

53. (b)

39. No intercepts   **41.** Three x-intercepts

43. Square   **45.** Circle

INDEX OF APPLICATIONS

Geometric Applications

Area of a corral, 222
Brick pattern, 697
Dimensions of a box, 257
Dimensions of a container, 81
Dimensions of a corral, 177
Dimensions of a field, 208
Dimensions of a rectangle, 61, 128, 298
Dimensions of a triangular sign, 169
Size of a postal service package, 257
Surface area of a honeycomb, 501
Volume of a box, 86, 178, 234
Volume of a package to be mailed, 86
Volume of a water trough, 525

Interest Rate Applications

Annual percentage rate, 371
Annuities, 705, 706
Bond investment, 660
Comparing investment returns, 148, 378
Compound interest, 189, 208, 210, 337, 342, 369, 378, 384, 684, 754
Doubling time for an investment, 370
Effective yield, 371
Investment mixture, 148, 594, 625, 670, 672
Investment portfolio, 602, 613, 622, 626
Investment time, 352
Simple interest, 142, 198, 589
Trust fund growth, 342, 382

Miscellaneous Applications

Air traffic control, 116
Alumni association, 751
Amateur radio, 754
Amount of print on a page, 295
Angle between a path and a river, 406
Angle of depression, 410
Angle of elevation to the bottom of a smokestack, 463
Automobile aerodynamics, 107, 223
Backup system for a space vehicle, 752

Backup vehicle for a fire company, 752
Baseball, 545
Bookshelf order, 754
Boy or girl?, 752
Coin toss, 738
Combination lock, 738
Computer systems, 599, 737
Concert seats, 738
Course grade, 147
Course schedule, 737
Cutting across the lawn, 166
Diet supplement, 665, 670
Difference in latitudes, 398, 399
Docking a boat, 460
Drawing cards from a deck, 750, 751
Forming a committee, 739
Forming an experimental group, 738
Game show, 751
Height of a flagpole, 148
Height of a juice can, 144
Height of a kite, 169
Instrumentation, 399
Interpersonal relationships, 739, 754
Lawn mowing, 177
Letter mix-up, 751
License plate numbers, 737
Location of a fire, 473, 536
Log volume, 602
LORAN, 319
Lottery choices, 738
Marble draw, 737, 751
Matching socks, 754
Maximum angle of elevation for a ladder, 463
Morse Code, 754
Number of board feet in a log, 223
Number of possible poker hands, 735
Number of possible telephone numbers, 730
Page design, 298
Pairs of letters in the alphabet, 729
Parachutist height, 591
Payroll mix-up, 751
Photography, 460
Piano tuning, 436
Poker hand, 739, 752
Population of Naples, Florida, 585
Posing for a photograph, 738
Preparing for a test, 751

Prize money at the Indianapolis 500, 586
Random number generator, 752
Satellite antenna, 317
Seating capacity, 694, 697
Seating capacity of a classroom, 177
Seizure of illegal drugs, 329
Softball equipment costs, 649
Sound intensity, 353, 360, 384
Snow removal, 383
Speed in kilometers, 582
Starting team, 736
Streetlight height, 410
Swimming pool depth, 464
Test questions, 736, 737
Throwing a rock on the moon, 175
Toboggan ride, 737
Tossing a die, 742, 743, 750
True-false exam, 737
Typing speed, 384
Ventilation rates, 352
Verification of testimony, 536
Waiting times, 382
Winning an election, 751
Winning the lottery, 744
Wheat yield, 614

Time and Distance Applications

Accuracy of measurement, 199
Aircraft tracking, 544
Airplane speed, 210, 613
Airspeed, 189
Altitude of an airplane, 536
Angle of elevation, 406
Angular speed, 399
Average speed of a truck, 179
Baseball diamond, 190
Circular saw speed, 399
Climb rate, 384
Course for a boat race, 532
Discus throw, 592
Distance between cities, 398, 476
Distance between the pitcher's mound and first base, 534
Distance between ships, 473, 543
Distance to shoreline, 536
Distance from a boat to the dock, 179
Driving distances, 613
Falling object, 697

U.S. Demographics Applications

INDEX

Formulas from Geometry

Triangle

$$h = a \sin \theta$$

$$\text{Area} = \frac{1}{2}bh$$

Law of Cosines:

$$c^2 = a^2 + b^2 - 2ab \cos \theta$$

Right Triangle

Pythagorean Theorem:

$$c^2 = a^2 + b^2$$

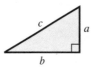

Equilateral Triangle

$$h = \frac{\sqrt{3}s}{2}$$

$$\text{Area} = \frac{\sqrt{3}s^2}{4}$$

Parallelogram

$$\text{Area} = bh$$

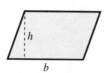

Trapezoid

$$\text{Area} = \frac{h}{2}(a + b)$$

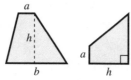

Circle

$$\text{Area} = \pi r^2$$

$$\text{Circumference} = 2\pi r$$

Sector of Circle

$$\text{Area} = \frac{\theta r^2}{2}$$

$$s = r\theta$$

(θ in radians)

Circular Ring

(p = average radius, w = width of ring)

$$\text{Area} = \pi(R^2 - r^2)$$
$$= 2\pi pw$$

Ellipse

$$\text{Area} = \pi ab$$

$$\text{Circumference} \approx 2\pi \sqrt{\frac{a^2 + b^2}{2}}$$

Cone

(A = area of base)

$$\text{Volume} = \frac{Ah}{3}$$

Right Circular Cone

$$\text{Volume} = \frac{\pi r^2 h}{3}$$

$$\text{Lateral Surface Area} = \pi r\sqrt{r^2 + h^2}$$

Frustrum of Right Circular Cone

$$\text{Volume} = \frac{\pi(r^2 + rR + R^2)h}{3}$$

$$\text{Lateral Surface Area} = \pi s(R + r)$$

Right Circular Cylinder

$$\text{Volume} = \pi r^2 h$$
$$\text{Lateral Surface Area} = 2\pi rh$$

Sphere

$$\text{Volume} = \frac{4}{3}\pi r^3$$

$$\text{Surface Area} = 4\pi r^2$$